IFIP Advances in Information and Communication Technology

630

Editor-in-Chief

Kai Rannenberg, Goethe University Frankfurt, Germany

Editorial Board Members

IFIP – The International Federation for Information Processing

IFIP was founded in 1960 under the auspices of UNESCO, following the first World Computer Congress held in Paris the previous year. A federation for societies working in information processing, IFIP's aim is two-fold: to support information processing in the countries of its members and to encourage technology transfer to developing nations. As its mission statement clearly states:

IFIP is the global non-profit federation of societies of ICT professionals that aims at achieving a worldwide professional and socially responsible development and application of information and communication technologies.

IFIP is a non-profit-making organization, run almost solely by 2500 volunteers. It operates through a number of technical committees and working groups, which organize events and publications. IFIP's events range from large international open conferences to working conferences and local seminars.

The flagship event is the IFIP World Computer Congress, at which both invited and contributed papers are presented. Contributed papers are rigorously refereed and the rejection rate is high.

As with the Congress, participation in the open conferences is open to all and papers may be invited or submitted. Again, submitted papers are stringently refereed.

The working conferences are structured differently. They are usually run by a working group and attendance is generally smaller and occasionally by invitation only. Their purpose is to create an atmosphere conducive to innovation and development. Refereeing is also rigorous and papers are subjected to extensive group discussion.

Publications arising from IFIP events vary. The papers presented at the IFIP World Computer Congress and at open conferences are published as conference proceedings, while the results of the working conferences are often published as collections of selected and edited papers.

IFIP distinguishes three types of institutional membership: Country Representative Members, Members at Large, and Associate Members. The type of organization that can apply for membership is a wide variety and includes national or international societies of individual computer scientists/ICT professionals, associations or federations of such societies, government institutions/government related organizations, national or international research institutes or consortia, universities, academies of sciences, companies, national or international associations or federations of companies.

More information about this series at http://www.springer.com/series/6102

Alexandre Dolgui · Alain Bernard ·
David Lemoine · Gregor von Cieminski ·
David Romero (Eds.)

Advances in Production Management Systems

Artificial Intelligence for Sustainable and Resilient Production Systems

IFIP WG 5.7 International Conference, APMS 2021
Nantes, France, September 5–9, 2021
Proceedings, Part I

 Springer

Editors
Alexandre Dolgui (iD)
IMT Atlantique
Nantes, France

David Lemoine (iD)
IMT Atlantique
Nantes, France

David Romero (iD)
Tecnológico de Monterrey
Mexico City, Mexico

Alain Bernard (iD)
Centrale Nantes
Nantes, France

Gregor von Cieminski (iD)
ZF Friedrichshafen AG
Friedrichshafen, Germany

ISSN 1868-4238   ISSN 1868-422X (electronic)
IFIP Advances in Information and Communication Technology
ISBN 978-3-030-85876-6   ISBN 978-3-030-85874-2 (eBook)
https://doi.org/10.1007/978-3-030-85874-2

This Springer imprint is published by the registered company Springer Nature Switzerland AG
The registered company address is: Gewerbestrasse 11, 6330 Cham, Switzerland

Preface

The scientific and industrial relevance of the development of sustainable and resilient production systems lies in ensuring future-proof manufacturing and service systems, including their supply chains and logistics networks. "Sustainability" and "Resilience" are essential requirements for competitive manufacturing and service provisioning now and in the future. Industry 4.0 technologies, such as artificial intelligence; decision aid models; additive and hybrid manufacturing; augmented, virtual, and mixed reality; industrial, collaborative, mobile, and software robots; advanced simulations and digital twins; and smart sensors and intelligent industrial networks, are key enablers for building new digital and smart capabilities in emerging cyber-physical production systems in support of more efficient and effective operations planning and control. These allow manufacturers and service providers to explore more sustainable and resilient business and operating models. By making innovative use of the aforementioned technologies and their enabled capabilities, they can pursue the triple bottom line of economic, environmental, and social sustainability. Furthermore, industrial companies will be able to withstand and quickly recover from disruptions that pose threats to their operational continuity. This is in the face of disrupted, complex, turbulent, and uncertain business environments, like the one triggered by the COVID-19 pandemic, or environmental pressures calling for decoupling economic growth from resource use and emissions.

The International Conference on Advances in Production Management Systems 2021 (APMS 2021) in Nantes, France, brought together leading international experts on manufacturing, service, supply, and logistics systems from academia, industry, and government to discuss pressing issues and research opportunities mostly in smart manufacturing and cyber-physical production systems; service systems design, engineering, and management; digital lean operations management; and resilient supply chain management in the Industry 4.0 era, with particular focus on artificial intelligence-enabled solutions.

Under the influence of the COVID-19 pandemic, the event was organised as online conference sessions. A large international panel of experts (497 from 50 countries) reviewed all the submissions (with an average of 3.2 reviews per paper) and selected the best 377 papers (70% of the submitted contributions) to be included in these international conference proceedings. The topics of interest at APMS 2021 included artificial intelligence techniques, decision aid, and new and renewed paradigms for sustainable and resilient production systems at four-wall factory and value chain levels, comprising their associated models, frameworks, methods, tools, and technologies for smart and sustainable manufacturing and service systems, as well as resilient digital supply chains. As usual for the APMS conference, the Program Committee was particularly attentive to the cutting-edge problems in production management and the quality of the papers, especially with regard to the applicability of the contributions to industry and services.

The APMS 2021 conference proceedings are organized into five volumes covering a large spectre of research concerning the global topic of the conference: "Artificial Intelligence for Sustainable and Resilient Production Systems".

The conference was supported by the International Federation of Information Processing (IFIP), which is celebrating its 60th Anniversary, and was co-organized by the IFIP Working Group 5.7 on Advances in Production Management Systems, IMT Atlantique (Campus Nantes) as well as the Centrale Nantes, University of Nantes, Rennes Business School, and Audecia Business School. It was also supported by three leading journals in the discipline: Production Planning & Control (PPC), the International Journal of Production Research (IJPR), and the International Journal of Product Lifecycle Management (IJPLM).

Special attention has been given to the International Journal of Production Research on the occasion of its 60th Anniversary. Since its foundation in 1961, IJPR has become one of the flagship journals of our profession. It was the first international journal to bring together papers on all aspects of production research: product/process engineering, production system design and management, operations management, and logistics. Many exceptional scientific results have been published in the journal.

We would like to thank all contributing authors for their high-quality work and for their willingness to share their research findings with the APMS community. We are also grateful to the members of the IFIP Working Group 5.7, the Program Committee, and the Scientific Committee, along with the Special Sessions organizers for their support in the organization of the conference program. Concerning the number of papers, special thanks must be given to the local colleagues who managed the reviewing process as well as the preparation of the conference program and proceedings, particularly Hicham Haddou Benderbal and Maria-Isabel Estrepo-Ruiz from IMT Atlantique.

September 2021

Alexandre Dolgui
Alain Bernard
David Lemoine
Gregor von Cieminski
David Romero

Organization

Conference Chair

Alexandre Dolgui   IMT Atlantique, Nantes, France

Conference Co-chair

Gregor von Cieminski   ZF Friedrichshafen, Germany

Conference Honorary Co-chairs

Dimitris Kiritsis   EPFL, Switzerland
Kathryn E. Stecke   University of Texas at Dallas, USA

Program Chair

Alain Bernard   Centrale Nantes, France

Program Co-chair

David Romero   Tecnológico de Monterrey, Mexico

Program Committee

Alain Bernard   Centrale Nantes, France
Gregor von Cieminski   ZF Friedrichshafen, Germany
Alexandre Dolgui   IMT Atlantique, Nantes, France
Dimitris Kiritsis   EPFL, Switzerland
David Romero   Tecnológico de Monterrey, Mexico
Kathryn E. Stecke   University of Texas at Dallas, USA

International Advisory Committee

Farhad Ameri   Texas State University, USA
Ugljesa Marjanovic   University of Novi Sad, Serbia
Ilkyeong Moon   Seoul National University, South Korea
Bojan Lalic   University of Novi Sad, Serbia
Hermann Lödding   Hamburg University of Technology, Germany

Organizing Committee Chair

David Lemoine   IMT Atlantique, Nantes, France

Organizing Committee Co-chair

Hichem Haddou Benderbal   IMT Atlantique, Nantes, France

Doctoral Workshop Chairs

Abdelkrim-Ramzi   IMT Atlantique, Nantes, France
  Yelles-Chaouche
Seyyed-Ehsan   IMT Atlantique, Nantes, France
  Hashemi-Petroodi

Award Committee Chairs

Nadjib Brahimi   Rennes School of Business, France
Ramzi Hammami   Rennes School of Business, France

Organizing Committee

Romain Billot   IMT Atlantique, Brest, France
Nadjib Brahimi   Rennes School of Business, France
Olivier Cardin   University of Nantes, France
Catherine Da Cunha   Centrale Nantes, France
Alexandre Dolgui   IMT Atlantique, Nantes, France
Giannakis Mihalis   Audencia, Nantes, France
Evgeny Gurevsky   University of Nantes, France
Hichem Haddou Benderbal   IMT Atlantique, Nantes, France
Ramzi Hammami   Rennes School of Business, France
Oncu Hazir   Rennes School of Business, France
Seyyed-Ehsan   IMT Atlantique, Nantes, France
  Hashemi-Petroodi
David Lemoine   IMT Atlantique, Nantes, France
Nasser Mebarki   University of Nantes, France
Patrick Meyer   IMT Atlantique, Brest, France
Merhdad Mohammadi   IMT Atlantique, Brest, France
Dominique Morel   IMT Atlantique, Nantes, France
Maroua Nouiri   University of Nantes, France
Maria-Isabel Restrepo-Ruiz   IMT Atlantique, Nantes, France
Naly Rakoto   IMT Atlantique, Nantes, France
Ilhem Slama   IMT Atlantique, Nantes, France
Simon Thevenin   IMT Atlantique, Nantes, France
Abdelkrim-Ramzi   IMT Atlantique, Nantes, France
  Yelles-Chaouche

Scientific Committee

Erry Yulian Triblas Adesta	International Islamic University Malaysia, Malaysia
El-Houssaine Aghezzaf	Ghent University, Belgium
Erlend Alfnes	Norwegian University of Science and Technology, Norway
Hamid Allaoui	Université d'Artois, France
Thecle Alix	IUT Bordeaux Montesquieu, France
Farhad Ameri	Texas State University, USA
Bjørn Andersen	Norwegian University of Science and Technology, Norway
Eiji Arai	Osaka University, Japan
Jannicke Baalsrud Hauge	KTH Royal Institute of Technology, Sweden/BIBA, Germany
Zied Babai	Kedge Business School, France
Natalia Bakhtadze	Russian Academy of Sciences, Russia
Pierre Baptiste	Polytechnique de Montréal, Canada
Olga Battaïa	Kedge Business School, France
Farouk Belkadi	Centrale Nantes, France
Lyes Benyoucef	Aix-Marseille University, France
Bopaya Bidanda	University of Pittsburgh, USA
Frédérique Biennier	INSA Lyon, France
Jean-Charles Billaut	Université de Tours, France
Umit S. Bititci	Heriot-Watt University, UK
Magali Bosch-Mauchand	Université de Technologie de Compiègne, France
Xavier Boucher	Mines St Etienne, France
Abdelaziz Bouras	Qatar University, Qatar
Jim Browne	University College Dublin, Ireland
Luis Camarinha-Matos	Universidade Nova de Lisboa, Portugal
Olivier Cardin	University of Nantes, France
Sergio Cavalieri	University of Bergamo, Italy
Stephen Childe	Plymouth University, UK
Hyunbo Cho	Pohang University of Science and Technology, South Korea
Chengbin Chu	ESIEE Paris, France
Feng Chu	Paris-Saclay University, France
Byung Do Chung	Yonsei University, South Korea
Gregor von Cieminski	ZF Friedrichshafen, Germany
Catherine Da Cunha	Centrale Nantes, France
Yves Dallery	CentraleSupélec, France
Xavier Delorme	Mines St Etienne, France
Frédéric Demoly	Université de Technologie de Belfort-Montbéliard, France
Mélanie Despeisse	Chalmers University of Technology, Sweden
Alexandre Dolgui	IMT Atlantique, Nantes, France
Slavko Dolinšek	University of Ljubljana, Slovenia

Thomas R. Kurfess	Georgia Institute of Technology, USA
Andrew Kusiak	University of Iowa, USA
Bojan Lalić	University of Novi Sad, Serbia
Samir Lamouri	ENSAM Paris, France
Lenka Landryova	Technical University of Ostrava, Czech Republic
Alexander Lazarev	Russian Academy of Sciences, Moscow, Russia
Jan-Peter Lechner	First Global Liaison, Germany
Gyu M. Lee	Pusan National University, South Korea
Kangbok Lee	Pohang University of Science and Technology, South Korea
Genrikh Levin	National Academy of Sciences, Belarus
Jingshan Li	University of Wisconsin-Madison, USA
Ming K. Lim	Chongqing University, China
Hermann Lödding	Hamburg University of Technology, Germany
Pierre Lopez	LAAS-CNRS, France
Marco Macchi	Politecnico di Milano, Italy
Ugljesa Marjanovic	University of Novi Sad, Serbia
Muthu Mathirajan	Indian Institute of Science, India
Gökan May	University of North Florida, USA
Khaled Medini	Mines St Etienne, France
Jörn Mehnen	University of Strathclyde, UK
Vidosav D. Majstorovich	University of Belgrade, Serbia
Semyon M. Meerkov	University of Michigan, USA
Joao Gilberto Mendes dos Reis	UNIP Paulista University, Brazil
Hajime Mizuyama	Aoyama Gakuin University, Japan
Ilkyeong Moon	Seoul National University, South Korea
Eiji Morinaga	Osaka Prefecture University, Japan
Dimitris Mourtzis	University of Patras, Greece
Irenilza de Alencar Naas	UNIP Paulista University, Brazil
Masaru Nakano	Keio University, Japan
Torbjörn Netland	ETH Zürich, Switzerland
Gilles Neubert	EMLYON Business School, Saint-Etienne, France
Izabela Nielsen	Aalborg University, Denmark
Tomomi Nonaka	Ritsumeikan University, Japan
Jinwoo Park	Seoul National University, South Korea
François Pérès	INP-Toulouse, ENIT, France
Fredrik Persson	Linköping Institute of Technology, Sweden
Giuditta Pezzotta	University of Bergamo, Italy
Selwyn Piramuthu	University of Florida, USA
Alberto Portioli Staudacher	Politecnico di Milano, Italy
Daryl Powell	Norwegian University of Science and Technology, Norway
Vittaldas V. Prabhu	Pennsylvania State University, USA
Jean-Marie Proth	Inria, France
Ricardo José Rabelo	Federal University of Santa Catarina, Brazil

Rahul Rai	University at Buffalo, USA
Mario Rapaccini	Florence University, Italy
Nidhal Rezg	University of Lorraine, France
Ralph Riedel	Westsächsische Hochschule Zwickau, Germany
Irene Roda	Politecnico di Milano, Italy
Asbjörn Rolstadås	Norwegian University of Science and Technology, Norway
David Romero	Tecnológico de Monterrey, Mexico
Christoph Roser	Karlsruhe University of Applied Sciences, Germany
André Rossi	Université Paris-Dauphine, France
Martin Rudberg	Linköping University, Sweden
Thomas E. Ruppli	University of Basel, Switzerland
Krzysztof Santarek	Warsaw University of Technology, Poland
Subhash Sarin	VirginiaTech, USA
Suresh P. Sethi	The University of Texas at Dallas, USA
Fabio Sgarbossa	Norwegian University of Science and Technology, Norway
John P. Shewchuk	Virginia Polytechnic Institute and State University, USA
Dan L. Shunk	Arizona State University, USA
Ali Siadat	Arts et Métiers ParisTech, France
Riitta Smeds	Aalto University, Finland
Boris Sokolov	Russian Academy of Sciences, Russia
Vijay Srinivasan	National Institute of Standards and Technology, USA
Johan Stahre	Chalmers University of Technology, Sweden
Kathryn E. Stecke	The University of Texas at Dallas, USA
Kenn Steger-Jensen	Aalborg University, Denmark
Volker Stich	RWTH Aachen University, Germany
Richard Lee Storch	University of Washington, USA
Jan Ola Strandhagen	Norwegian University of Science and Technology, Norway
Stanislaw Strzelczak	Warsaw University of Technology, Poland
Nick Szirbik	University of Groningen, The Netherlands
Marco Taisch	Politecnico di Milano, Italy
Lixin Tang	Northeastern University, China
Kari Tanskanen	Aalto University School of Science, Finland
Ilias Tatsiopoulos	National Technical University of Athens, Greece
Sergio Terzi	Politecnico di Milano, Italy
Klaus-Dieter Thoben	Universität Bremen, Germany
Manoj Tiwari	Indian Institute of Technology, India
Matthias Thüre	Jinan University, China
Jacques H. Trienekens	Wageningen University, The Netherlands
Mario Tucci	Universitá degli Studi di Firenze, Italy
Shigeki Umeda	Musashi University, Japan
Bruno Vallespir	University of Bordeaux, France
François Vernadat	University of Lorraine, France

Agostino Villa	Politecnico di Torino, Italy
Lihui Wang	KTH Royal Institute of Technology, Sweden
Sabine Waschull	University of Groningen, The Netherlands
Hans-Hermann Wiendahl	University of Stuttgart, Germany
Frank Werner	University of Magdeburg, Germany
Shaun West	Lucerne University of Applied Sciences and Arts, Switzerland
Joakim Wikner	Jönköping University, Sweden
Hans Wortmann	University of Groningen, The Netherlands
Desheng Dash Wu	University of Chinese Academy of Sciences, China
Thorsten Wuest	West Virginia University, USA
Farouk Yalaoui	University of Technology of Troyes, France
Noureddine Zerhouni	Université Bourgogne Franche-Comte, France

List of Reviewers

Abbou Rosa
Abdeljaouad Mohamed Amine
Absi Nabil
Acerbi Federica
Aghelinejad Mohsen
Aghezzaf El-Houssaine
Agrawal Rajeev
Agrawal Tarun Kumar
Alexopoulos Kosmas
Alix Thecle
Alkhudary Rami
Altekin F. Tevhide
Alves Anabela
Ameri Farhad
Andersen Ann-Louise
Andersen Bjorn
Anderson Marc
Anderson Matthew
Anholon Rosley
Antosz Katarzyna
Apostolou Dimitris
Arica Emrah
Arlinghaus Julia Christine
Aubry Alexis
Baalsrud Hauge Jannicke
Badulescu Yvonne Gabrielle
Bakhtadze Natalia
Barbosa Christiane Lima
Barni Andrea

Batocchio Antonio
Battaïa Olga
Battini Daria
Behrens Larissa
Ben-Ammar Oussama
Benatia Mohamed Amin
Bentaha M.-Lounes
Benyoucef Lyes
Beraldi Santos Alexandre
Bergmann Ulf
Bernus Peter
Berrah Lamia-Amel
Bertnum Aili Biriita
Bertoni Marco
Bettayeb Belgacem
Bevilacqua Maurizio
Biennier Frédérique
Bititci Umit Sezer
Bocanet Vlad
Bosch-Mauchand Magali
Boucher Xavier
Bourguignon Saulo Cabral
Bousdekis Alexandros
Brahimi Nadjib
Bresler Maggie
Brunoe Thomas Ditlev
Brusset Xavier
Burow Kay
Calado Robisom Damasceno

Calarge Felipe
Camarinha-Matos Luis Manuel
Cameron David
Cannas Violetta Giada
Cao Yifan
Castro Eduardo Lorenzo
Cattaruzza Diego
Cerqueus Audrey
Chang Tai-Woo
Chaves Sandra Maria do Amaral
Chavez Zuhara
Chen Jinwei
Cheng Yongxi
Chiacchio Ferdinando
Chiari da Silva Ethel Cristina
Childe Steve
Cho Hyunbo
Choi SangSu
Chou Shuo-Yan
Christensen Flemming Max Møller
Chung Byung Do
Ciarapica Filippo Emanuele
Cimini Chiara
Clivillé Vincent
Cohen Yuval
Converso Giuseppe
Cosenza Harvey
Costa Helder Gomes
Da Cunha Catherine
Daaboul Joanna
Dahane Mohammed
Dakic Dusanka
Das Dyutimoy Nirupam
Das Jyotirmoy Nirupam
Das Sayan
Davari Morteza
De Arruda Ignacio Paulo Sergio de
De Campos Renato
De Oliveira Costa Neto Pedro Luiz
Delorme Xavier
Deroussi Laurent
Despeisse Mélanie
Di Nardo Mario
Di Pasquale Valentina
Dillinger Fabian
Djedidi Oussama

Dolgui Alexandre
Dolinsek Slavko
Dou Runliang
Drei Samuel Martins
Dreyer Heidi
Dreyfus Paul-Arthur
Dubey Rameshwar
Dümmel Johannes
Eloranta Eero
Emmanouilidis Christos
Ermolova Maria
Eslami Yasamin
Fast-Berglund Åsa
Faveto Alberto
Federico Adrodegari
Feng Xuehao
Finco Serena
Flores-García Erik
Fontaine Pirmin
Fosso Wamba Samuel
Franciosi Chiara
Frank Jana
Franke Susanne
Freitag Mike
Frick Jan
Fruggiero Fabio
Fu Wenhan
Fujii Nobutada
Gahan Padmabati
Gaiardelli Paolo
Gallo Mosè
Ganesan Viswanath Kumar
Gaponov Igor
Gayialis Sotiris P.
Gebennini Elisa
Ghadge Abhijeet
Ghrairi Zied
Gianessi Paolo
Giret Boggino Adriana
Gloeckner Robert
Gogineni Sonika
Gola Arkadiusz
Goodarzian Fariba
Gosling Jon
Gouyon David
Grabot Bernard

Grangeon Nathalie
Grassi Andrea
Grenzfurtner Wolfgang
Guerpinar Tan
Guillaume Romain
Guimarães Neto Abelino Reis
Guizzi Guido
Gupta Sumit
Gurevsky Evgeny
Habibi Muhammad Khoirul Khakim
Haddou Benderbal Hichem
Halse Lise Lillebrygfjeld
Hammami Ramzi
Hani Yasmina
Hashemi-Petroodi S. Ehsan
Havzi Sara
Hazir Oncu
Hedayatinia Pooya
Hemmati Ahmad
Henchoz El Kadiri Soumaya
Heuss Lisa
Hibino Hironori
Himmiche Sara
Hnaien Faicel
Hofer Gernot
Holst Lennard Phillip
Hovelaque Vincent
Hrnjica Bahrudin
Huber Walter
Husniah Hennie
Hvolby Hans-Henrik
Hwang Gyusun
Irohara Takashi
Islam Md Hasibul
Iung Benoit
Ivanov Dmitry
Jacomino Mireille
Jagdev Harinder
Jahn Niklas
Jain Geetika
Jain Vipul
Jasiulewicz-Kaczmarek Małgorzata
Jebali Aida
Jelisic Elena
Jeong Yongkuk
Johansen John

Jones Al
Jun Chi-Hyuck
Jun Hong-Bae
Jun Sungbum
Juned Mohd
Jünge Gabriele
Kaasinen Eija
Kaihara Toshiya
Kalaboukas Kostas
Kang Yong-Shin
Karampatzakis Dimitris
Kayikci Yasanur
Kedad-Sidhoum Safia
Keepers Makenzie
Keivanpour Samira
Keshari Anupam
Kim Byung-In
Kim Duck Young
Kim Hwa-Joong
Kim Hyun-Jung
Kinra Aseem
Kiritsis Dimitris
Kitjacharoenchai Patchara
Kjeldgaard Stefan
Kjersem Kristina
Klimchik Alexandr
Klymenko Olena
Kollberg Thomassen Maria
Kolyubin Sergey
Koomsap Pisut
Kramer Kathrin
Kulvatunyou Boonserm (Serm)
Kumar Ramesh
Kurata Takeshi
Kvadsheim Nina Pereira
Lahaye Sébastien
Lalic Danijela
Lamouri Samir
Lamy Damien
Landryova Lenka
Lechner Jan-Peter
Lee Dong-Ho
Lee Eunji
Lee Kangbok
Lee Kyungsik
Lee Minchul

Lee Seokcheon
Lee Seokgi
Lee Young Hoon
Lehuédé Fabien
Leiber Daria
Lemoine David
Li Haijiao
Li Yuanfu
Lim Dae-Eun
Lim Ming
Lima Adalberto da
Lima Nilsa
Lin Chen-ju
Linares Jean-marc
Linnartz Maria
Listl Franz Georg
Liu Ming
Liu Xin
Liu Zhongzheng
Lödding Hermann
Lodgaard Eirin
Loger Benoit
Lorenz Rafael
Lu Jinzhi
Lu Xingwei
Lu Xuefei
Lucas Flavien
Lüftenegger Egon
Luo Dan
Ma Junhai
Macchi Marco
Machado Brunno Abner
Maier Janine Tatjana
Maihami Reza
Makboul Salma
Makris Sotiris
Malaguti Roney Camargo
Mandal Jasashwi
Mandel Alexander
Manier Hervé
Manier Marie-Ange
Marangé Pascale
Marchesano Maria Grazia
Marek Svenja
Marjanovic Ugljesa
Marmolejo Jose Antonio

Marques Melissa
Marrazzini Leonardo
Masone Adriano
Massonnet Guillaume
Matsuda Michiko
Maxwell Duncan William
Mazzuto Giovanni
Medić Nenad
Medini Khaled
Mehnen Jorn
Mendes dos Reis João Gilberto
Mentzas Gregoris
Metaxa Ifigeneia
Min Li Li
Minner Stefan
Mishra Ashutosh
Mitra Rony
Mizuyama Hajime
Mogale Dnyaneshwar
Mohammadi Mehrdad
Mollo Neto Mario
Montini Elias
Montoya-Torres Jairo R.
Moon Ilkyeong
Moraes Thais De Castro
Morinaga Eiji
Moser Benedikt
Moshref-Javadi Mohammad
Mourtzis Dimitris
Mundt Christopher
Muši Denis
Nääs Irenilza De Alencar
Naim Mohamed
Nakade Koichi
Nakano Masaru
Napoleone Alessia
Nayak Ashutosh
Neroni Mattia
Netland Torbjørn
Neubert Gilles
Nguyen Du Huu
Nguyen Duc-Canh
Nguyen Thi Hien
Nielsen Izabela
Nielsen Kjeld
Nishi Tatsushi

Nogueira Sara
Noh Sang Do
Nonaka Tomomi
Noran Ovidiu
Norre Sylvie
Ortmeier Frank
Ouazene Yassine
Ouzrout Yacine
Özcan Uğur
Paes Graciele Oroski
Pagnoncelli Bernardo
Panigrahi Sibarama
Panigrahi Swayam Sampurna
Papakostas Nikolaos
Papcun Peter
Pashkevich Anatol
Pattnaik Monalisha
Pels Henk Jan
Pérès François
Persson Fredrik
Pezzotta Giuditta
Phan Dinh Anh
Piétrac Laurent
Pinto Sergio Crespo Coelho da
Pirola Fabiana
Pissardini Paulo Eduardo
Polenghi Adalberto
Popolo Valentina
Portioli Staudacher Alberto
Powell Daryl
Prabhu Vittaldas
Psarommatis Foivos
Rabelo Ricardo
Rakic Slavko
Rapaccini Mario
Reis Milena Estanislau Diniz Dos
Resanovic Daniel
Rey David
Riedel Ralph
Rikalović Aleksandar
Rinaldi Marta
Roda Irene
Rodriguez Aguilar Roman
Romagnoli Giovanni
Romeo Bandinelli
Romero David

Roser Christoph
Rossit Daniel Alejandro
Rudberg Martin
Sabitov Rustem
Sachs Anna-Lena
Sahoo Rosalin
Sala Roberto
Santarek Kszysztof
Satolo Eduardo Guilherme
Satyro Walter
Savin Sergei
Schneider Daniel
Semolić Brane
Shafiq Muhammad
Sharma Rohit
Shin Jong-Ho
Shukla Mayank
Shunk Dan
Siadat Ali
Silva Cristovao
Singgih Ivan Kristianto
Singh Sube
Slama Ilhem
Smaglichenko Alexander
Smeds Riitta Johanna
Soares Paula Metzker
Softic Selver
Sokolov Boris V.
Soleilhac Gauthier
Song Byung Duk
Song Xiaoxiao
Souier Mehdi
Sørensen Daniel Grud Hellerup
Spagnol Gabriela
Srinivasan Vijay
Stavrou Vasileios P.
Steger-Jensen Kenn
Stich Volker
Stipp Marluci Andrade Conceição
Stoll Oliver
Strandhagen Jan Ola
Suh Eun Suk
Suleykin Alexander
Suzanne Elodie
Szirbik Nick B.
Taghvaeipour Afshin

Taisch Marco
Tanimizu Yoshitaka
Tanizaki Takashi
Tasić Nemanja
Tebaldi Letizia
Telles Renato
Thevenin Simon
Thoben Klaus-Dieter
Thurer Matthias
Tiedemann Fredrik
Tisi Massimo
Torres Luis Fernando
Tortorella Guilherme Luz
Troyanovsky Vladimir
Turcin Ioan
Turki Sadok
Ulrich Marco
Unip Solimar
Valdiviezo Viera Luis Enrique
Vallespir Bruno
Vasic Stana
Vaz Paulo
Vespoli Silvestro
Vicente da Silva Ivonaldo
Villeneuve Eric
Viviani Jean-Laurent
Vještica Marko
Vo Thi Le Hoa
Voisin Alexandre
von Cieminski Gregor
Von Stietencron Moritz
Wagner Sarah
Wang Congke
Wang Hongfeng
Wang Yin

Wang Yingli
Wang Yuling
Wang Zhaojie
Wang Zhixin
Wellsandt Stefan
West Shaun
Wiendahl Hans-Hermann
Wiesner Stefan Alexander
Wikner Joakim
Wiktorsson Magnus
Wimmer Manuel
Woo Young-Bin
Wortmann Andreas
Wortmann Johan Casper
Wuest Thorsten
Xu Tiantong
Yadegari Ehsan
Yalaoui Alice
Yang Danqin
Yang Guoqing
Yang Jie
Yang Zhaorui
Yelles Chaouche Abdelkrim Ramzi
Zaeh Michael Friedrich
Zaikin Oleg
Zambetti Michela
Zeba Gordana
Zhang Guoqing
Zhang Ruiyou
Zheng Feifeng
Zheng Xiaochen
Zoitl Alois
Zolotová Iveta
Zouggar Anne

Contents – Part I

Intelligent Systems for Manufacturing Planning and Control in the Industry 4.0

Learning and Robust Decision Support Systems
for Agile Manufacturing environments

Low-Code and Model-Driven Engineering for Production System

Meta-Heuristics and Optimization Techniques for Energy-Oriented Manufacturing Systems

Metaheuristics for Production Systems

**Modern Analytics and New AI-Based Smart Techniques
for Replenishment and Production Planning Under Uncertainty**

System Identification for Manufacturing Control Applications

The Future of Lean Thinking and Practice

Artificial Intelligence Based Optimization Techniques for Demand-Driven Manufacturing

Goods and Activities Tracking Through Supply Chain Network Using Machine Learning Models

Lahcen Tamym[1]($\boxtimes$), Ahmed Nait Sidi Moh[2], Lyes Benyoucef[3],
and Moulay Driss El Ouadghiri[1]

[1] Moulay Ismail University, IA Laboratory, Meknes, Maroc
l.tamym@edu.umi.ac.ma, d.elouadghiri@umi.ac.ma
[2] Picardie Jules Verne University, IT Laboratory (LTI), Saint Quentin, France
ahmed.nait@u-picardie.fr
[3] Aix-Marseille University, University of Toulon, CNRS, LIS, Marseille, France
lyes.benyoucef@lis-lab.fr

Abstract. End-consumers satisfaction with the higher efficiency and reliability of the products and services provided by the enterprises is a highly important factor in their competitiveness. However, providing efficient tracking and tracing of shipped products enhance customer loyalty and the enterprise image. Satisfied customers are one of the enterprise's greatest assets. In doing so, we are mainly interested in detection of fraudulent transactions and late delivery of orders, as well as tracking commodities and related supply chain costs over different countries. Two datasetes are used for model training and validation: DataCo Supply Chain Dataset and SCMS Delivery History Dataset. A case study is worked out, and the finding results are compared to some related works in the literature. The obtained results show the added value of our proposed models.

Keywords: Artificial intelligence · Goods tracking · Machine learning · Supply chain network

1 Context and Motivations

Managing and predicting the future performances of supply chain network (SCN) operations are the most challenging tasks facing many enterprises in today's business. It is the primary reason to leverage more relevant modeling approaches. Artificial intelligence (AI) and machine learning (ML) are the two tools that we will use in this study. Moreover, tracking every SCN activity from procurement of raw materials to final product delivery to end-customers remains an essential process for networked enterprises. Hence, predictive analytics enable real-time monitoring of shipment and predicting delays and risks related to the goods flow on roads, plants, warehouses, distribution centers, etc. Furthermore, this leads

A. Dolgui et al. (Eds.): APMS 2021, IFIP AICT 630, pp. 3–12, 2021.
https://doi.org/10.1007/978-3-030-85874-2_1

researchers and professionals to ask this question: What are more relevant tools for SCN management?. Accordingly, enterprises start to pay more attention to machine learning models and what they can do to improve their SCNs. Also, one asks how this powerful technology can address the operation problems linked to their network's activities. In this research work, we are interested in studying ML algorithms for tracking and monitoring goods flow through SCNs. The reason behind this interest is that end-consumer satisfaction with a higher quality of products and services are the main decisive elements within enterprises [1]. Our objective is to develop flexible, scalable, robust, and data-driven models for goods tracking within large-scale and dynamic SCNs. Often, these networks are exposed to various levels of uncertainty [2] which complicate their management and future predictions. The developed models are based on two datasets: DataCo Supply Chain Dataset and SCMS Delivery History Dataset. A case study is worked out, and developed models are analyzed and discussed. Findings results are compared to some developed research works in the literature and show that the proposed models in this work are promising.

The remainder of the paper is organized as follows: Sect. 2 reviews the importance of ML in SCN Tracking. The adopted research methodology is addressed in Sect. 3. Section 4 illustrates two case studies and discusses finding results. Finally, Sect. 5 concludes the paper and gives some challenges and future work outlines.

2   Literature Review

Modern and international (global) networked enterprises generate vast amounts of complex data. ML can analyze and process these data and use the extracted information to enhance network management. Many applications based on ML to support this kind of network have been developed in the literature. Learning modelling to generate goods tracking solutions for networked enterprises is a critical process. Besides, ML improves the robustness of solutions.

2.1   SCN Management

SCN management involves integrating networked enterprises' activities such as suppliers, manufacturers, distributors, third-party service providers, customers, etc. This integration needs coordination, collaboration, and enduring alliances between all entities of the network. It leads to the enhancement of the visibility of management processes involved in SCN activities such as: sourcing, procurement, demand forecasting, materials requisition, order processing and fulfillment, transportation services, invoicing and payment processing, and goods flow tracking through the network [3]. Finding the right strategy to track and manage each stage of the network is challenging for these linked enterprises. The management of SCN provides, with more efficiency, the opportunity for the distribution of goods across the network [4]. Hence, this helps to achieve a high degree of satisfaction with requirements at a minimum cost [5]. Moreover, goods and activities tracking improves customer service level, optimizes the production cycle, reduces warehouse inventory, improves enterprise productivity and profitability, controls the production process, etc. [6].

2.2   Goods Tracking Within a SCN

Quickly developing information technologies, optimization algorithms, internet of things (IoT), AI methods optimize logistic processes across networked enterprises. Relevant solutions offered by these technologies combined with Big-Data (BD) analytics (e.g., GPS vehicle tracking data, information of customers and their locations, changing the information on traffic volume on route sections, organization/enterprise specific historical data, etc.) are required [7]. Furthermore, the efficiency of goods distribution and services through SCNs is improved by machine learning algorithms based on the flow of input data [8]. Using GPS technology coupled with radio frequency identification (RFID) traces offers a complementary source of data used to identify logistics facilities in urban areas using density-based clustering [9]. Also, this will enable efficient tracking and tracing of trucks on the roads or locomotives on rails or ships in oceans. Using these location technologies, tracing delivery status for customers often involves many parties to check the conditions and status of the cargo during shipments [3]. In addition, it helps to eliminate customers' doubts by answering their frequent queries, such as, "Has my cargo arrived?", "When is my cargo arrived?", and "How is the current state of my cargo?". Therefore, enterprises are investing considerable amounts of money in providing tracking services to their customers. Table 1 summarises some goods and activities tracking applications through SCN in the literature.

Table 1. Goods and activities tracking applications

Tracking applications	Models, methods, and platforms	References
Determining the position of the trains and their expected time of arrival at destination. As well as, recording the evolution of critical parameters inside the cars during transportation	GRailChem: Identification of Software Specifications through Quality Function Deployment	[10]
Collaborative platform based on advanced technologies for positioning, identification, communication, tracking and data sharing about logistic flows within supply chains.	IoT, Cloud computing, GPS/GPRS and RFID	[11]
Decision-making agents in a blood supply chain network via Machine Learning in order to solve large-scale optimization problems	ANN, CART, RF, k-NN	[12]
Predicting fraudulent transactions, and mitigating future dangers within smart supply chains	Random Forest, Rpart	[13]

3   Research Methodology

In this study, we aim to use machine learning models to track goods and activities through a SCN. Figure 1 shows the global framework of ML applications in SCNs tracking. This framework is composed of five major components: *1)* SCNs data sources in which each single SC provides its data in different formats. *2)* Data preprocessing in which the data are being processed and prepared as input of ML models. *3)* Use of ML models. *4)* Predictive analytics. *5)* The outputs of predictive analytics which are goods and activities tracking along with the network.

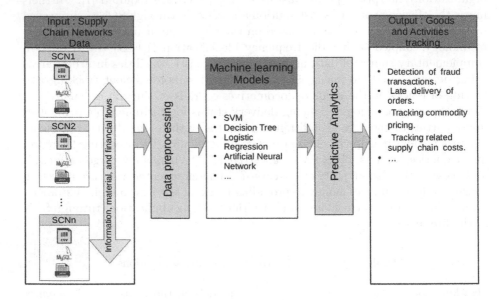

Fig. 1. Global framework of ML applications in SCN tracking

We adopt the case study methodology to validate our approach. In doing so, we conduct our research on two real datasets described below in Sect. 4.1. The best model based on their performance in the simulation study is selected to be used in practice. In the following, we briefly review the background of the candidate ML models before their implementation for the case studies.

3.1   Artificial Neural Network (ANN)

ANN is a general function approximator, which learns the relationship between independent and dependent variables after performing a learning process from training data [12]. In addition, due to its nonlinear characteristics, ANN performs well when modeling complex data patterns with nonlinear functions. ANNs are composed of processing units called neurons. According to their architecture, and how neurons interact in the network and their structure, they can generally be divided into three classifications: multilayer feedforward network, recurrent network and mesh network [14].

3.2 Support Vector Machine (SVM)

SVM is a set of related supervised learning methods for classification and regression and belongs to the family of generalized linear classifiers. In other words, SVM is a classification and regression prediction tool that uses machine learning theory to maximize prediction accuracy while automatically avoiding overfitting the data. In addition, SVMs are systems that use a hypothesis space of linear functions in a high-dimensional feature space and are trained using a learning algorithm from optimization theory, which implements learning bias from statistical learning theory.

3.3 Decision Tree (DT)

DT is a supervised learning technique that can be used for both classification and regression problems. It is a tree-structured classifier, where internal nodes represent the features of a dataset, branches represent the decision rules, and each leaf node represents the outcome. It is a graphical representation for getting all the possible solutions to a problem/decision based on given conditions. It is called a decision tree because similar to a tree, it starts with the root node, which expands on different branches and constructs a tree-like structure. In order to build a tree, we use the CART algorithm, which stands for Classification and Regression Tree algorithm.

3.4 Logistic Regression (LR)

Logistic regression or logit model is a binomial regression model. As for all binomial regression models, it aims to model a simple mathematical model and possible with numerous real observations. In other words, to associate to a vector of random variables $(x_1, \ldots, x_K)$ a binomial random variable generically noted y. Logistic regression is a special case of the generalized linear model.

4 Goods Tracking: Case Studies

In order to show how ML technology offers many solutions to any SC's enterprise, we conducted our research work on two datasets, "SCMS Delivery History" and "DataCo Supply Chain" by leveraging different ML models and evaluating the performance of each model by the accuracy of prediction.

4.1   Used Datasets

SCMS Delivery History Dataset [15]. This dataset provides transportation modes and pricing data of health commodities in the supply chain. It identified antiretroviral (ARV) and HIV laboratories shipped to supporting countries. Also, it provides the commodity pricing and related supply chain costs necessary to move the commodity to the countries for use. After analyzing these data, we came out by the flowing statistics; the top country for pack price is Nigeria - 25,620.72, top Shipping Mode: Air, the Max Air Shipment Mode is: 1000, top Manufacturing Site: Aurobindo Unit III, India - 3172, top Air Manufacturing Site: Aurobindo Unit III, India - 1694. Further analysis of this dataset is given in Fig. 2.

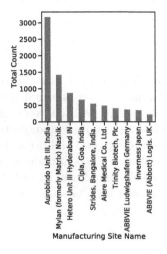 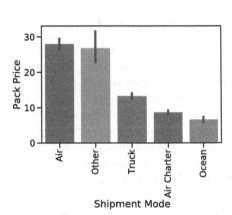

Fig. 2.   (1) Top 10 manufacturing sites (left). (2) Shipment mode per pack price (right)

DataCo Supply Chain Dataset [16] which is used by the enterprise DataCo Global for the analysis, and consists of roughly 180k transactions from supply chains for 3 years. It's a dataset of Supply Chain, which allows the use of Machine Learning Algorithms. These data offer areas of important registered activities such as, provisioning, production, sales, commercial distribution. In this dataset, we are interested in detection of fraud transactions and late delivery of orders.

On the one hand, finding which payment method is used to conduct frauds can be useful to prevent fraud from happening in the future. Figure 3 shows which payment method is preferred the most by people in different regions. While, Fig. 4 indicates which region and what product is being suspected to the fraud the most.

On the other hand, when products are not delivered on time to customers, this will be a source of doubts and decreases in satisfaction. Consequently, this

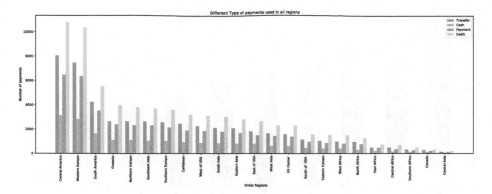

Fig. 3. Different preferred payment methods in different regions

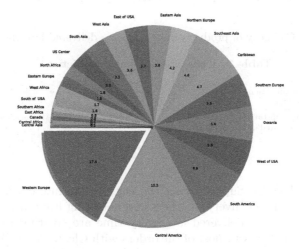

Fig. 4. Different regions that are suspected to the fraud the most

leads to trust loss. Thus, solving the late delivery problem is vital to any supply chain enterprise within the SCN. From the performed analysis, Fig. 5 shows what category of products are being delivered late the most.

4.2 Results

This section details the experimental results obtained from comparing popular ML classifiers and measuring their performances in terms of accuracy. The goal is to find out which ML model performs better on both datasets described above. For SCMS Delivery History Dataset, we are interested in transportation mode prediction based on the scheduled delivery date, delivered to customer date, cargo weight, and freight cost, etc. In doing so, we studied and examined diffident ML models such as ANN, SVM, DT and LR. Hence, the obtained results exposed in Table 2 show that we were able to reach a significant accuracy of

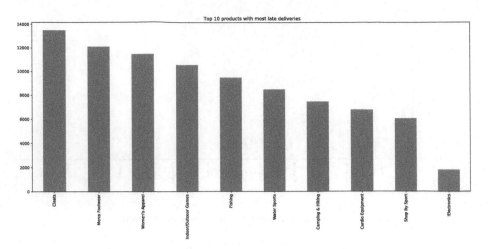

Fig. 5. Category of products that are being delivered late the most

Table 2. Transportation mode prediction.

Dataset	Classification problem	Classes	Samples	Accuracy			
SCMS delivery history	Transportation mode prediction	Air, Truck, Air charter, Ocean, Other	10324	ANN	SVM	Decision tree	Logistic regression
				0.89	0.833	0.80	–

prediction. For DataCo Supply Chain Dataset, we are interested in two classification problems: late delivery of orders and detecting fraudulent transactions. All the orders that are delivered late every time are creating risks to the SC enterprises. In this dataset, most of the orders with Cleats, Men's Footwear, and Women's Apparel category products are causing late delivery, as well as these products, are suspected to fraud the most. Indeed, for predicting late delivery risk and detecting fraud, we applied the same ML models for the first dataset. The accuracy of each model are mentioned in Table 3. The finding results are compared to the obtained results in [13], Table 4. Indeed, we can see that the proposed models for fraud detection are outperformed the results found in [13].

Table 3. Late delivery of orders and detecting fraudulent transactions.

Dataset	Classification problem	Classes	Samples	Accuracy			
DataCo Supply Chain				ANN	SVM	Decision Tree	Logistic regression
	Late delivery risk	0, 1	180519	0.9778	0.988	**0.993**	0.9884
	Frauds detection	0, 1	180519	0.98	0.9775	**0.9907**	0.978

Table 4. Detecting fraudulent transactions [13].

DataCo supply chain	Classification problem	Random forest	Rpart
	Frauds detection	0.8155	0.761

After leveraging different ML models on both datasets, we have obtained the best results in prediction. These will allow networked enterprises to be able to track different activities and goods through the network, as well as, solving many problems that will occur in the future. It enables us to build a robust network and remain competitive in the global market.

5   Conclusion

In this research work, we showed interest in applying machine learning models in supply chain networks. Tracking every SC activity and goods through the network, from procurement of raw materials to final product delivery to end customers, remains an essential process for networked enterprises. Hence, machine learning predictive analytics enable real-time monitoring of shipment and predicting delays and risks related to the goods flows and related activities. We selected the four most well-known machine learning models to examine our research work. These models can be trained to be used in day-to-day operational decision-making through SCNs.

Consequently, the use of machine learning for this kind of tracking will arise many challenges such as data privacy, understanding of data related to SCN, which is a complex part of this application due to missing data and the scarcity of data. In addition, in the case of a real-time application, it required performing tools and sophisticated techniques.

Finally, as future work, we expect to apply deep learning models for enhancing the solutions offered by tracking in SCN, especially for real-time tracking. Moreover, studying a real-life scenario of SCN will be one of our primary concerns in the near future.

References

1. America, S.: Track/trace solutions for the logistics supply chain. https://www.supplychainmarket.com/doc/tracktrace-solutions-for-the-logistics-0001. Accessed 07 June 2021
2. Biller, B., Yi, J.: Optimizing supply chain robustness through simulation and machine learning. https://www.sas.com/content/dam/SAS/support/en/sas-global-forum-proceedings/2020/4535-2020.pdf. Accessed 07 June 2021
3. He, W., Tan, E., Lee, E., Li, T.: A solution for integrated track and trace in supply chain based on RFID and GPS, pp. 1–6 (2009). https://doi.org/10.1109/ETFA.2009.5347146

4. Kadadevaramath, R.S., Chen, J.C., Latha Shankar, B., Rameshkumar, K.: Application of particle swarm intelligence algorithms in supply chain network architecture optimization. Expert Syst. Appl. **39**(11), 10160–10176 (2012). https://doi.org/10.1016/j.eswa.2012.02.116
5. Boiko, A., Shendryk, V., Boiko, O.: Information systems for supply chain management: uncertainties, risks and cyber security. Procedia Comput. Sci. **149**, 65–70 (2019). https://doi.org/10.1016/j.procs.2019.01.108
6. McKinsey, C.: Next generation supply chain: Supply chain 2020 (2020). Accessed 10 June 2020
7. Tamym, L., Benyoucef, L., Nait Sidi Moh, A., El Ouadghiri, M.D.: A big data based architecture for collaborative networks: Supply chains mixed-network. Comput. Commun. 175, 102–111 (2021). https://doi.org/10.1016/j.comcom.2021.05.008
8. Tarapata, Z., Nowicki, T., Antkiewicz, R., Dudzinski, J., Janik, K.: Data-driven machine learning system for optimization of processes supporting the distribution of goods and services a case study. Procedia Manuf. **44**, 60–67 (2020). https://doi.org/10.1016/j.promfg.2020.02.205
9. Trent, N.M., Joubert, J.W., Gidofalvi, G., Kordnejad, B.: A matching algorithm to study the evolution of logistics facilities extracted from GPS traces. Transp. Res. Procedia **46**, 237–244 (2020). https://doi.org/10.1016/j.trpro.2020.03.186
10. Vlad, R.C., Benyoucef, L., Vlad, S.: Identification of software specifications through quality function deployment. In: 2006 IEEE International Conference on Automation, Quality and Testing, Robotics, vol. 2, pp. 74–79 (2006). https://doi.org/10.1109/AQTR.2006.254603
11. Gnimpieba, Z.D.R., Nait-Sidi-Moh, A., Durand, D., Fortin, J.: Using internet of things technologies for a collaborative supply chain: application to tracking of pallets and containers. Procedia Comput. Sci. **56**, 550–557 (2015). https://doi.org/10.1016/j.procs.2015.07.251
12. Abbasi, B., Babaei, T., Hosseinifard, Z., Smith-Miles, K., Dehghani, M.: Predicting solutions of large-scale optimization problems via machine learning: a case study in blood supply chain management. Comput. Oper. Res. **119**, 104941 (2020). https://doi.org/10.1016/j.cor.2020.104941
13. Constante-Nicolalde, F.-V., Guerra-Terán, P., Pérez-Medina, J.-L.: Fraud prediction in smart supply chains using machine learning techniques. In: Botto-Tobar, M., Zambrano Vizuete, M., Torres-Carrión, P., Montes León, S., Pizarro Vásquez, G., Durakovic, B. (eds.) ICAT 2019. CCIS, vol. 1194, pp. 145–159. Springer, Cham (2020). https://doi.org/10.1007/978-3-030-42520-3_12
14. Zhang, Z.: Multivariate Time Series Analysis in Climate and Environmental Research (2018). https://doi.org/10.1007/978-3-319-67340-0
15. Ardeshana, D.: Supply chain shipment pricing data. https://www.kaggle.com/divyeshardeshana/supply-chain-shipment-pricing-data. Accessed 07 June 2021
16. Constante, F., Silva, F., Pereira, A.: Dataco smart supply chain for big data analytics data. https://data.mendeley.com/datasets/8gx2fvg2k6/5. Accessed 07 June 2021

Long Term Demand Forecasting System for Demand Driven Manufacturing

Sleiman Rita[⊠], Tran Kim-Phuc, and Thomassey Sébastien

Laboratoire de Génie et Matériaux Textiles, Univ. Lille, ENSAIT, GEMTEX,
59000 Lille, France
rita.sleiman@ensait.fr

Abstract. Demand-Driven Manufacturing (DDM) is the solution that most companies are heading to in our days. Although this strategy consists of producing goods based on what consumers demand, companies should also rely on accurate forecasting systems to prepare their production chain for such an operation by supplying enough raw material, increasing production capacity to fit the desired demand, etc.... However, due to the fact that most companies have been relying on massive production, most sales forecasting systems usually used rely on sales data of previous years that, not only contain the actual demand, but takes into consideration the marketing strategy effects like massive promotions. Hence, the resulting forecasts do not mainly reflect consumers' demand. For this reason, a switch to demand forecasting, instead of sales forecasting, is essential to ensure a good transition to DDM. This paper proposes an artificial intelligence based demand forecasting system that aims to determine "potential sales", mainly reflecting consumers' demand, by correcting historical sales data from external variables' effects. A comparison with other sales forecasting models is performed and validated on real data of a French fashion retailer. Results show that the proposed system is both robust and accurate, and it outperforms all the other models in terms of forecasting errors.

Keywords: Demand Driven Manufacturing · Sales forecasting · Demand forecasting · Historical sales correction

1 Introduction

For many years, the market of consumer goods relies on overconsumption with mass production and aggressive marketing campaigns. This approach requires the companies to focus on low cost production with off-shore sourcing and involves both high volume purchases and long lead time [1].

Due to the needs for more personalized products and environmental awareness of the consumers, this strategy reaches its limits in many industrial and commercial sectors [2]. Consequently, many companies move toward a Demand Driven Manufacturing (DDM) strategy [3]. DDM strategy aims to produce goods based on consumers' demand instead of sales or target forecasts [4]. According to Gartner, nearly 90% of production

© IFIP International Federation for Information Processing 2021
Published by Springer Nature Switzerland AG 2021
A. Dolgui et al. (Eds.): APMS 2021, IFIP AICT 630, pp. 13–20, 2021.
https://doi.org/10.1007/978-3-030-85874-2_2

industries which are not demand-driven, are planning to be [5]. This is mainly because of the benefits a DDM approach could offer, such as increasing profitability, reducing wastefulness, and most importantly improving customers' satisfaction.

Even though a DDM strategy relies on flexible and reactive production and supply chain, companies still require accurate forecasting systems to anticipate their raw material supplies, production capacity, … and meet the consumer expectations in terms of lead time. However, current sales forecasting techniques do not reflect exactly consumer's demand since they rely on historical data including the constant discounts or commercial offers. Moreover, in a DDM approach, only goods that are going to be sold are produced, which implies the application of a totally different marketing strategy. Hence, in order to ensure a successful transition to the DDM strategy, companies should switch from a sales forecasting system to a demand forecasting system.

Recently, Artificial Intelligence AI techniques have presented great improvements in many fields and especially in forecasting [6, 7]. In fact, with the AI techniques and the heterogeneous data sources available nowadays, new forecasting systems can be developed to determine consumer demand by modeling the impact of the different exogenous variables on sales.

This paper proposes a demand forecasting system that aims to correct historical sales, using AI techniques, by removing the influences caused by external factors, such as promotions, before moving to the prediction process. In fact, by modeling the impact of the previous discount strategy, historical sales could be corrected, presenting then potential sales that mainly reflect consumers' demand. This results in an accurate and robust forecasting model which can be an additional tool to help companies better react to the rapidly changing market, and meet the demand of materials, warehouses, etc… for the production process.

The following parts will be structured as follows. A brief literature review about existing sales forecasting systems is presented in Sect. 2. Section 3 describes the proposed methodology in detail. Results and discussion are presented in Sect. 4. The conclusion is presented in the last section.

2   Literature Review

Retail companies, based on a mass production strategy, generally rely also on sales forecasting systems in order to optimize their production and supply chain. Hence, sales forecasting has been always studied by researchers in the literature, which presents a wide variety of sales forecasting systems, adapted to different contexts [8–10].

The most commonly used methods for sales forecasting are statistical time series analysis tools that primarily seek to identify trends and seasonality. Among the existing statistical methods, "Auto-Regressive Integrated Moving Average" ARIMA and "Seasonal Auto-Regressive Integrated Moving Average" SARIMA are widely used for sales forecasting [11]. Similarly, SARIMAX is an extension of SARIMA when explanatory variables are available. Moreover, deep learning has recently shown promising results in nonlinear sequence learning problems. Notably, Recurrent Neural Network (RNN) and Long Short Term Memory (LSTM) networks are popular deep learning techniques and have outperformed popular machine learning methods for time series forecasting [12]. RNN and LSTM networks, unlike other neural networks, have the property of retaining information over time.

The methods already mentioned are likely to be adequate to learn seasonality in a time series. However, in the context of sales forecasting, there are many exogenous variables that can influence the predictions. Thus, several hybrid methods that can take advantage of both time series analysis and explanatory variables are proposed in the literature [11]. Punia et al. [13] proposed a new forecasting method that combines LSTM, to model the time aspect of the input series, and Random Forest (RF), to predict the impact of explanatory variables not detected by LSTM. The obtained results showed that their method outperformed other methods, ARIMAX, LSTM and RF. Another more interpretable working methodology is to correct the sales history by removing the impact of explanatory variables before making the prediction of the time series, as proposed by Thomassey et al. [14].

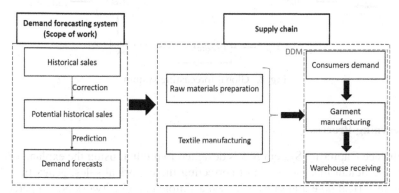

Fig. 1. Demand forecasting based DDM approach

3 Methodology

The main goal of this paper is to build a demand forecasting based DDM approach as illustrated in Fig. 1. Using the demand forecasts, production managers can better manage the supply chain by anticipating the required raw materials and adapting their production capacity to meet actual consumers' demand.

The approach adopted in this paper was inspired by the forecasting system proposed in [14] in which a fuzzy logic system is optimized to predict the influences of the explanatory variables on sales. The work done in this paper uses a similar approach for correcting historical sales (year $\in [1, \dots, n]$) by removing the influence of external variables before predicting sales for year $n + 1$. The following parts describes in details the proposed methodology as well as the learning process.

3.1 Global Forecasting System

The proposed forecasting system, presented in Fig. 2, is composed of three main stages:

- The influences of explanatory variables are removed from historical sales data using the Influence Capturing System *ICS*,
- The resulting historical potential sales are used to make predictions for next year's potential sales,
- The final sales predictions are obtained by adding the influences of explanatory variables corresponding to the next year to the previous predictions using ICS^{-1}.

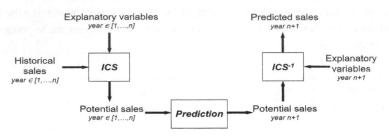

Fig. 2. Global forecasting system

3.2 Learning Process

The Influence Capturing System *ICS* is designed to predict, using the explanatory variables, a coefficient that has a role of correcting the historical sales, generating then a series of historical potential sales. We used a simple neural network NN (a perceptron) to predict these correction coefficients, based on the assumption that a NN can learn to generate efficient and sophisticated rules for prediction.

Thereafter, for predicting the potential sales of the next year, we applied the seasonality average, which is one of the simplest time series forecasting methods. We selected this basic model in order to check the ability of the model in the optimization of the correction coefficients, without having additional parameters to adjust, which increases the complexity in the overall learning process.

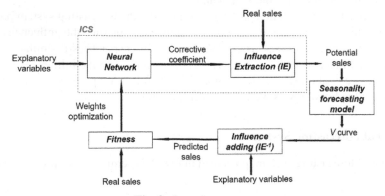

Fig. 3. Learning process

Figure 3 above presents the learning process of the proposed system in detail. In fact, the NN must be optimized in order to predict the most reliable and efficient correction coefficients. To do so, we used a genetic algorithm GA where each chromosome is formed by real genes representing the weights of the neural network. The learning loop is composed of the following important steps:

- Using the explanatory variables as inputs, the NN predicts the corresponding correction coefficient (cc), which is considered to be a multiplicative coefficient that quantifies the impact of exogenous variables on sales,
- The Influence Extraction function *IE* calculates the potential sales as input to the prediction model,
- The V-curve is the predicted life curve obtained from the potential sales (without influences of the explanatory variables),
- The influences of the explanatory variables are re-added to the obtained V-curve, using IE^{-1}, to perform the final prediction,
- The GA's fitness function is calculated from the sales thus predicted and the actual sales by calculating the root mean square error RMSE:

$$fitness = 1/RMSE \tag{1}$$

- The GA sets new weights for the neural network to increase the value of the fitness function,
- The optimal parameters of the neural network that allows the determination of the optimal life curve V* (corrected historical sales) are obtained when the maximum number of iteration of the GA is reached.

Once the optimal *ICS* model is obtained, the final forecast is calculated by adding the influence of the explanatory variables of the future season (the 52 weeks to be predicted), to the optimal life curve V*.

4   Results and Discussion

4.1   Data Used

The proposed forecasting system was applied to real world data of a French fashion retailer. It was tested to perform a one year sales prediction (52 weeks) of a T-shirt's family of products. We used three years of historical sales data (2016, 2017, 2018) for the learning process, and one year, 2019, for testing.

In order to test the ability of the proposed system to capture the influence of the explanatory variables on the sales, those variables have to be wisely selected and must be the most significant ones. Therefore, since obtaining the influence of promotions on sales was important to our industry partners, the explanatory variables chosen were:

- The average percentage of discount per family of products,
- The type of commercial operation OP applied (no OP, winter/summer sales of long duration, or 10-days winter/summer sales of short duration),

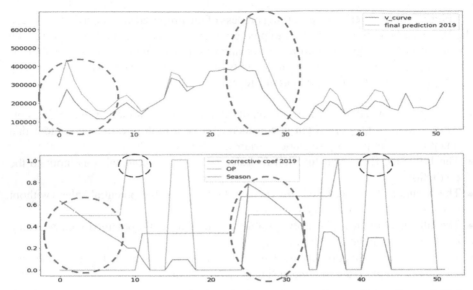

Fig. 4. Corrected sales (v-curve) and final prediction (top), correction coefficient (bottom) (Color figure online)

- The season (fall, winter, spring, summer),
- The remaining duration of the sale period (100% at the beginning of the sale and 0% at the end) to locate at which phase of the sales period we are.

4.2 Prediction Results

Figure 4 shows, for the year 2019, the optimal V-curve representing the prediction without the influence of exogenous variables, the predicted sales after reinjection of these influences, the corresponding predicted corrective coefficients for each week, as well as a visualization of some of the explanatory variables used. The results obtained demonstrate the effectiveness of the proposed method as well as the ability of the neural network, combined with GA, to model the influences of the explanatory variables. It is clear from Fig. 4 that during winter/summer sales (shown in red dashed circles), the influence of the explanatory variables is more visible than in normal weeks. The correction coefficient is at its highest at the beginning of the winter/summer sales, and decreases continuously throughout the promotions period: we can clearly see in the predictions for the year 2019 that the peak in weeks 26 and 27 is caused by the beginning of the summer sales (corrective coefficient, in this case, is equal to 90%). This correction is of less importance during 10-days sales (shown in black dashed circles), which is logical since during this type of operation, promotions are not applied on the entire collection which explains the lower peaks in those periods.

We evaluated our proposed methodology by comparing it to three other forecasting methods in terms of Root Mean Squared Error (RMSE), Mean Absolute Error (MAE) and Mean Absolute Percentage Error (MAPE). We used for comparison two of the classical time series forecasting methods, SARIMA and SARIMAX. In addition, we

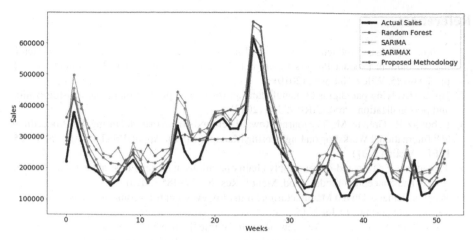

Fig. 5. 2019 sales predictions for the different methods

Table 1. Results on 2019 test data.

	RMSE	MAE	MAPE
SARIMA	67970	56109	31.01
SARIMAX	73133	62710	34.57
RANDOM FOREST	63451	55825	31.97
PROPOSED METH.	**56135**	**43908**	**23.89**

applied the Random Forest, a popular machine learning algorithm, to our forecasting problem by adding the week number as an additional input to the other explanatory variables used. Results shown in the following table (Table 1) show that the proposed methodology yielded better results when applied to 2019 test data, by having the lower forecasting errors for the three of the metrics used. Figure 5 shows a comparison of the prediction results obtained by the different methods mentioned above.

5   Conclusion

This paper presents a demand forecasting system that is able to correct historical sales by eliminating the effect of marketing strategies such as promotions. The proposed system plays a vital role for companies when shifting to DDM strategy. It helps them optimizing the supply chain by adapting their resources to the demand. It was shown that it is able to perform well compared to other existing sales forecasting systems due to the fact that it relies on potential sales to perform the predictions. This system can be improved with the help of experts in fields like marketing, fashion, ... in order to add additional features to the learning process for obtaining potential sales that better reflect consumers' demand.

References

1. Koren, Y.: Mass Production and Lean Manufacturing Book: The Global Manufacturing Revolution: Product-Process-Business Integration and Reconfigurable Systems, vol. 4, pp. 103–125. Wiley, Hoboken (2010)
2. Hu, S.: Evolving paradigms of manufacturing: from mass production to mass customization and personalization. Proc. CIRP **7**, 3–8 (2013)
3. Lebovitz, R., Graban, M.: The journey toward demand driven manufacturing. In: Proceedings 2nd International Workshop on Engineering Management for Applied Technology, pp. 29–35. IEEE, Austin (2001)
4. Tiedemann, F.: Demand-driven supply chain operations management strategies – a literature review and conceptual model. Prod. Manuf. Res. **8**, 427–485 (2020)
5. What is Demand-Driven Manufacturing? https://www.synchrono.com/resources/demand-driven-manufacturing/. 14 Jul 2015
6. Raza, M.Q., Khosravi, A.: A review on artificial intelligence based load demand forecasting techniques for smart grid and buildings. Renew. Sustain. Energy Rev. **50**, 1352–1372 (2015)
7. Thomassey, S., Zeng, X.: Introduction: Artificial Intelligence for Fashion Industry in the Big Data Era. In: Thomassey, S., Zeng, X. (eds.) Artificial Intelligence for Fashion Industry in the Big Data Era. SSFB, pp. 1–6. Springer, Singapore (2018). https://doi.org/10.1007/978-981-13-0080-6_1
8. Choi , T.-M., Hui, P., Liu, N., Ng, S.-F., Yu, Y.: Fast fashion sales forecasting with limited data and time. Decision Support Syst. **59** (2013)
9. Chang, P.-C., Liu, C.-H., Wang, Y.-W.: A hybrid model by clustering and evolving fuzzy rules for sales decision supports in printed circuit board industry. Decis. Support Syst. **42**, 1254–1269 (2006)
10. Chen, I.-F., Lu, C.-J.: Sales forecasting by combining clustering and machine-learning techniques for computer retailing. Neural Comput. Appl. **28**(9), 2633–2647 (2016). https://doi.org/10.1007/s00521-016-2215-x
11. Liu, N., Ren, S., Choi, T., Hui C., Ng, S.: Sales forecasting for fashion retailing service industry: a review. Math. Probl. Eng. 1–9 (2013)
12. Fischer, T., Krauss, C.: Deep learning with long short-term memory networks for financial market predictions. Eur. J. Oper. Res. **270**, 654–669 (2018)
13. Punia, S., Nikolopoulos, K., Singh, S.P., Jitendra, K., Litsiou, K.: Deep learning with long short-term memory networks and random forests for demand forecasting in multi-channel retail. Int. J. Prod. Res. **58**, 4964–4979 (2020)
14. Thomassey, S., Happiette, M., Castelain, J.M.: A short and mean-term automatic forecasting system—application to textile logistics. Eur. J. Oper. Res. **161**, 275–284 (2005)

FBD_Bmodel Digital Platform: A Web-Based Application for Demand Driven Fashion Supply Chain

Sébastien Thomassey$^{(\boxtimes)}$ ⓘ and Xianyi Zeng ⓘ

Laboratoire de Génie et Matériaux Textiles, Univ. Lille, ENSAIT, GEMTEX,
59000 Lille, France
sebastien.thomassey@ensait.fr

Abstract. The new consumption behaviors and environmental awareness are pushing the textile apparel industry to profound transformations. Co-design and production on demand are two success factors for this paradigm shift but require efficient and practical tools for companies. In this context, the European H2020 FBD_BModel project provides to practitioner a suitable digital platform. More specifically for the supply chain management, efficient and well-known algorithms are implemented in an user-friendly web-based application composed of two modules. The first module aims at selecting suppliers with multi criteria decision making techniques. This is particularly important to deal with a huge variety of products and a large number of small factories with their own features. The second modules proposed a genetic algorithm-based optimization for order scheduling and supplier allocation. In a demand driven strategy, this task is crucial to reach the requirements in terms of cost and lead time. This paper provides a brief description of the methods implemented in the web-based application. A numerical example, based on real data of the industrial partners of the FBD_Bmodel project, shows the results obtained with the proposed solution.

Keywords: Web-based application · Multi criteria supplier selection · On-demand production planning

1 Introduction

1.1 FDB_Bmodel Project

The textile and clothing industry is an important part of the European economy, but over recent years a large amount of production capacity has shifted to countries with lower wage costs. Nowadays this strategy reaches its limits for many reasons: complex quality management, long and uncertain lead time, and more importantly the consumer's expectations in terms of personalization and, ethic and environmental awareness. In this context, the textile industry has to switch into new business models more consumer focused and demand driven to enhance its competitiveness. For this purpose, an interactive cloud-based digital design and supply chain platform has been developed in the

© IFIP International Federation for Information Processing 2021
Published by Springer Nature Switzerland AG 2021
A. Dolgui et al. (Eds.): APMS 2021, IFIP AICT 630, pp. 21–30, 2021.
https://doi.org/10.1007/978-3-030-85874-2_3

European H2020 FBD_BModel project (www.fbd-bmodel.eu). This project aims to propose a new digital technology platform to connect different parts of the textile-apparel supply chain, from fibre, yarn and fabric producers to garment manufacturers, for the development of a new consumer-based business model in the big data era. The platform is composed of two main modules: a co-design module and a demand driven supply chain module. The co-design module enables the consumer to be directly involved in the design process from a set of recommendations, taking account of fitting, hand feel, and wear comfort. The second module, presented in this paper, focuses on optimized allocation of production orders designed in the first module. The supply chain module addresses the issue of small series production on demand which is a very challenging problem for the traditional textile-apparel industry.

To be more specific, small textile manufacturers already exist in Europe, but they are usually isolated from each other, and thus, the proposed FBD_BModel digital enables different actors in the supply chain to collaborate, from fibre and yarn producers, fabric and garment manufacturers, to designers and production planners. A web-based application (http://scpms.ensait.fr/) to support managers' decisions for supplier selection and dynamic planning of production orders by graphical simulations is proposed.

The remainder of the paper focuses on the methods used in the demand driven supply chain module of the FBD_Bmodel platform. A brief literature review about small series on demand production is presented in Sect. 2. Section 3 describes the proposed methodology in detail. Results obtained with the web-based application are presented in Sect. 4. The conclusion is presented in the last section.

2 Literature Review

There exists an extensive literature on supply chain management strategies in traditional fashion industry. However, there is a significant dearth of literature on the study of supply chain management strategies for small-series on demand (make to order) production in fashion industry. This can be mainly due to the fact that small-series fashion is an emerging fashion paradigm. In order to propose suitable solutions for companies, it is crucial to determine what are the major challenges that small-series fashion paradigm generates given the extent of personalization expected by the customers from small-series fashion products and the required level of strategic responsiveness, coordination, and flexibility of all the actors in small-series supply chain, mainly suppliers and retailers.

2.1 Small Series on Demand Production in Industries

A systematic literature review is conducted using Scopus database between 2000 and 2020 to collect existing literature on supply chain management in small-series (make-to-order) in industries (not only fashion industry). This approach aims to investigate the different SCM problems. In total, 59 articles have been selected and classified into the main supply chain topics as illustrated in Fig. 1.

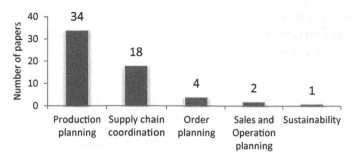

Fig. 1. Article distribution as per the main supply chain topics.

2.2 Small Series on Demand Production in Fashion Industry

Following the same systematic literature review approach, the existing literature on the studies on supply chain management in small-series (make-to-order) in fashion industry is collected. This search only yielded to four articles which cover the main two topics given in the Fig. 1: production planning [1, 2] and supply chain coordination [3, 4]. In [1], an optimal decision support system for risk management for Made To Order fashion retailers is proposed. The system provides significant insights into how manage the replenishment and develop quick response strategies while negotiating with the suppliers. In [2], an overall cost optimization with genetic algorithm is developed for packaging and distribution of multi sizes fashion products in a Made to Order framework. A multi agent simulation is presented in [3] to demonstrate the advantage of a collaborative cloud-based platform in achieving sustainability in demand driven supply chain. In [4], the authors investigate what are the main factors for successful collaboration in fashion supply chain and how it can drive MTO fashion companies to make optimal decisions.

Based on this literature study, it emerges that the key aspects of small-series fashion SCM are related to production planning and supply chain co-ordination. For this reason, the FBD_Bmodel project provides to fashion companies a digital platform to enhance collaboration between the many small manufacturers and an easy to use production planning to dynamically allocate orders to the most suitable manufacturers.

Considering the large variety of considered products and the large number of potential suppliers, the production planning is composed of two steps:

1- A multi criteria supplier selection system enables the definition of a set of suitable suppliers according to their abilities to fulfill the requirements given to produce one type of garments.
2- A production planning system then dynamically allocates the orders to the selected suppliers according to their production capacity and expected delivery dates.

Considering the current financial and technical states of the existing small fashion manufacturing units in Europe, we do not establish a full computerized production planning system at this stage but propose to first optimize their supply chain management so that production activities of different producers can be more efficiently organized. The Fig. 2 gives an overview of the FBD_Bmodel digital platform and the demand driven production planning module.

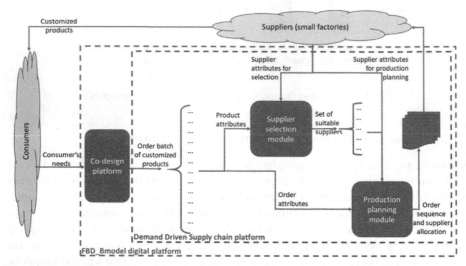

Fig. 2. FBD_Bmodel platform and demand driven production planning module.

3   Methodology

3.1   Multi Criteria Decision Making for Supplier Selection

In the context of small-series apparel production, one of the key objectives is to identify the most important criteria, both quantitative and qualitative, from the point of view of sourcing managers.

Thus, the first stage of the proposed web-based application enables the managers to define their own criteria according their business and expectations. An Analytic Hierarchy Process (AHP) [5] is implemented to weight the relative importance of supplier selection criteria. AHP is one of the most widely applied methods for solving multi criteria decision problems. Its popularity is mainly due to its ability to compare relative performance of actions or alternatives with pairwise comparison. It is also relevant to our scenario in which accurate data on different suppliers are usually missing due to their confidentiality, and experience-based expert evaluations constitute the main information source in the supply chain management. For an easier use, the web-based application relies on the Saaty's linguistic scale for the pairwise comparison as illustrated in Fig. 3.

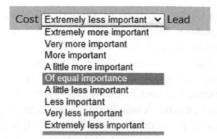

Fig. 3. Pairwise comparison between the criteria "cost" and "lead time" with the Saaty's scale in the web-based application

Based on the criteria evaluation by AHP, a TOPSIS method is applied to evaluate supplier's performances corresponding to each criterion. In the proposed application, the manager evaluates each potential supplier with the Likert linguistic scale (Fig. 4). Finally, the top n suppliers are selected for the production planning.

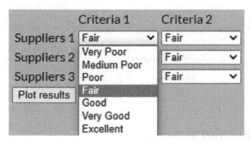

Fig. 4. Supplier evaluation for each considered criterion with the Likert scale in the web-based application

3.2 Production Planning

For the small-series fashion production, it is crucial to allocate customer orders in a real time to the best garment suppliers to reach the business objectives, especially in terms of costs and lead time. In the proposed cloud-based digital platform, information required for the production planning and supplier allocation are available including order attributes, such as product technical features, quantities, expected delivery time, and supplier attributes such as available production capacity, production/delivery cost and time. However, to utilize this information for the decision making related to identifying suitable garment suppliers that contribute to the order fulfilment is often a complex optimization problem.

Considering that suppliers selected by the selection module reach all the requirements (capability, quality, logistic services, packaging,…) for the production of the considered products, the production planning module only focuses on the main operational criteria: cost and lead time.

Thus, to define the optimization problem, three decision variables are considered: delivery date, cost and penalty, where penalty corresponds to extra costs due to late delivery. The objective function is defined as the minimum of the total cost to produce and deliver a given batch of orders considering the expected delivery date of the customers. The balance between cost and lead time can be set up by the manager with a penalty rate according to his operational and business objectives. A high rate improves the number of orders delivered on time. A small rate generates more cost focused solutions. The optimization process is performed with a Genetic Algorithm (GA). The use of genetic algorithms to optimize production schedules has been widely demonstrated in the literature [6]. Although GAs do not ensure to find the best optimum solution, they provide satisfactory results in a reasonable time for our operational problem. The chromosomes, encoding potential solutions, represent a sequence of the orders of the considered batch as illustrated in Table 1. Then, each order is assigned to the supplier given the minimum total cost (production, delivery, penalty for late costs), considering the workload generated by the order already allocated. Thus, this algorithm is able to find the best balance between the cheapest production and delivery costs and the available capacity to ensure a delivery on time.

Table 1. A chromosome encoding the order sequence of batch of size n

Gene number	1	2	...	n
Order ID	i	j	...	k

4 Implementation and Results

This section presents an example of the implementation of the proposed methodology with the web-based application developed in the framework of the European H2020 FBD_Bmodel (http://scpms.ensait.fr/). This simulation relies on real data provided by the industrial partners of the project.

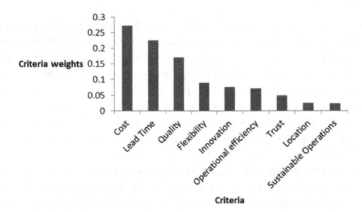

Fig. 5. AHP ranking of supplier selection criteria

4.1 Supplier Selection

The first step consists of weighting the criteria from pairwise comparison performed by the manager with the online application. The Fig. 5 presents the results obtained with the AHP process on the 9 criteria defined by the manager.

At this stage, it can be stated that some criteria can be considered as insignificant and deleted. For instance, in the Fig. 5, the manager could choose to select only the three first criteria (cost, lead time, quality).

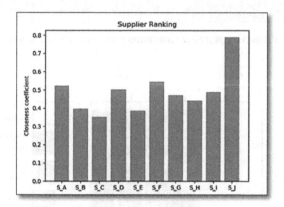

Fig. 6. Supplier ranking by TOPSIS method

From these weights, a TOPSIS method is applied to rank the potential suppliers. The Fig. 6 shows the results obtained on a database of 10 suppliers. From this result, the manager selects the set of suppliers which are suitable for the production to reach the expected requirements. In this numerical example, the manager has selected 5 suppliers (threshold score of 0.49).

4.2 Production Planning

For the production planning, the web-based application takes into account the operational attributes of the suppliers: production and delivery costs and times, and real time available production capacity. In this example, a daily batch composed of 30 orders is considered. During the simulation, additional batches can be added periodically or manually. In this case, the optimization process proposes a re-allocation of remaining orders to provide a new optimum solution. The results are displayed in the web-based application through a numerical table (Fig. 7), a step by step simulation (Fig. 8) and KPI graphs (Fig. 9).

The analysis of the Fig. 9 highlights that the overall profit stops growing from week 30. This means that some orders are delivered late and involves penalty. This simulation can help managers to take the suitable decision in a such situation (reject order, communicate with customers,...).

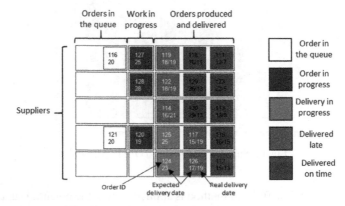

| Supplier ID | Orders in the queue | Work in progress | Orders produced and delivered | | | | KPI | |

Suppliers data, current time = 33

Id	Next orders	Current orders	Orders done	Time	Profit	%Late	Mean late
11	134; 131; 132; 144; 155	133	125; 122; 115	88	150.0	33.33%	1.33
12	154; 151; 145; 152; 153	135	114; 112	78	140.0	50.0%	3.0
13	141; 143	142	124; 123; 113	80	-140.0	66.67%	6.33
14	None	None	121; 111	32	370.0	0.0%	0.0
15	None	None	None	0	0.0	0.0%	0.0
Mean					520.0	40.0%	2.9
All the commands are displayed.							
A new file will be asked in 7.							

Fig. 7. Production planning simulation presented in a numerical table

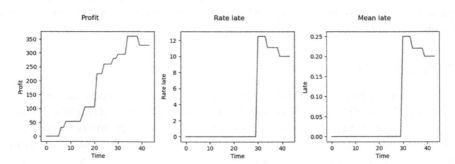

Fig. 8. Graphical step by step simulation tool

Fig. 9. KPI plots during the step by step simulation

4.3   Result Comparison

In order to evaluate the benefit of the proposed methodology, two simulations are performed using the same orders and suppliers. The first simulation, called "MaxProfit", deals with the flow of orders one by one (no batch of orders) and allocates the order to the supplier which ensures the maximum of profit. The second simulation, called "Min-Delay", is similar but the order allocation is based on the reduction of delay. Thus, these two simulations propose a single criterion optimization of a flow of orders, whereas our proposed model provides a multi-criteria optimization of a batch of orders.

Table 2. Result comparison between the proposed model and single criterion models

	MaxProfit	MinDelay	Proposed model
Profit (sum)	1866	−108	325
Delay (sum)	5038	0	7

The Table 2 shows that the proposed model provides the best balance between the profit and the delay. From a practical point of view, our model also emerges as the only reasonable solution to enable a production on demand. Profit based strategy produces interesting short-term benefits. However, the huge delay will certainly lead to a customer dissatisfaction and long-term losses. The delay-based strategy enables the production of all the order on time, but it generates production and shipment costs higher than sales revenues.

5   Conclusion

Face to the new consumption behaviors and environmental awareness, the fashion industry has to change its outdated business model. The personalization of products and the production on demand are the two key success factors to support this change proposed by the European H2020 FBD_Bmodel project. The digital platform developed in the framework of this project provides to companies the required tools to switch into a demand driven strategy. In this new context, the main issues for supply chain are the coordination between actors and the production planning. The proposed web-based application offers a cloud-based service to coordinate the supply chain with a real time-sharing data. The supplier selection and production planning tools enable the managers to easily implement multi criteria and optimization methods to reach the requirements of their business. The platform is already operational and will be still developed in the framework if the Fashion Big Data Foundation (www.fbd-bmodel.eu/fashion-big-data-foundation/) which aims at exploiting FBD_BModel project results.

References

1. Choi, T.-M.: Impacts of retailer's risk averse behaviors on quick response fashion supply chain systems. Ann. Oper. Res. **268**(1–2), 239–257 (2018)
2. Wong, W.K., Leung, S.Y.S.: Carton box optimization problem of VMI-based apparel supply chain. In: ICMIT 2006 Proceedings - 2006 IEEE International Conference on Management of Innovation and Technology, pp. 911–15, IEEE, Singapore (2006)

3. Ma, K., Wang, L., Chen, Y.: A collaborative cloud service platform for realizing sustainable make-to-order apparel supply chain. Sustainability **10**(1) (2017)
4. de Leeuw, S., Fransoo, J.: Drivers of close supply chain collaboration: one size fits all? Int. J. Oper. Prod. Manag. **29**(7), 720–739 (2009)
5. Saaty, T.L.: A scaling method for priorities in hierarchical structures. J. Math. Psychol. **15**(3), 234–281 (1977)
6. Sadegheih, A.: Scheduling problem using genetic algorithm, simulated annealing and the effects of parameter values on GA performance. Appl. Math. Model. **30**(2), 147–154 (2006)

Data-Driven Approach for Credit Card Fraud Detection with Autoencoder and One-Class Classification Techniques

Abdoul-Fatao Ouedraogo[1], Cédric Heuchenne[2], Quoc-Thông Nguyen[3(✉)], and Hien Tran[1]

[1] Institute of Artificial Intelligence and Data Science, Dong A University, Da Nang, Vietnam
[2] HEC Management School, University of Liège, 4000 Liège, Belgium
[3] Université de Lille, ENSAIT, GEMTEX, 59000 Lille, France
quoc-thong.nguyen@ensait.fr

Abstract. With the development of e-commerce, payment by credit card has become an essential means for the purchases of goods and services online. Especially, the Manufacturing Sector faces a high risk of fraud online payment. Its high turnover is the reason making this sector is lucrative with fraud. This gave rise to fraudulent activity on the accounts of private users, banks, and other services. For this reason, in recent years, many studies have been carried out using machine learning techniques to detect and block fraudulent transactions. This article aims to present a new approach based on real-time data combining two methods for the detection of credit card fraud. We first use the variational autoencoder(VAE) to obtain representations of normal transactions, and then we train a support vector data description (SVDD) model with these representations. The advantage of the representation learned automatically by the variational autoencoder is that it makes the data smoother, which makes it possible to increase the detection performance of one-class classification methods. The performance evaluation of the proposed model is done on real data from European credit cardholders. Our experiments show that our approach has obtained good results with a very high fraud detection rate.

Keywords: Anomalies detection · Outliers · Autoencoder · Variational autoencoder · One class classification · Credit card fraud

1 Introduction

In recent years with the development of e-commerce, we observe an increase in the volumes of electronic transactions leading to an increase in credit card fraud. Since then,fraud detection has become a topic that reaches out to all industries, such as financial industries, banks, government agencies and insurance, etc. Sectors that often process a large of the transaction, for example, the

© IFIP International Federation for Information Processing 2021
Published by Springer Nature Switzerland AG 2021
A. Dolgui et al. (Eds.): APMS 2021, IFIP AICT 630, pp. 31–38, 2021.
https://doi.org/10.1007/978-3-030-85874-2_4

Manufacturing industry, have been a victim of fraud easily. Especially, in the era when the relation between finance and manufacturing is concrete [6,17]. Despite the efforts of struggling organizations, millions of dollars are wasted each year due to fraud. For that, many techniques [5] have been developed in recent years for cybersecurity and reducing fraudulent transactions [13,19]. Using developed data mining tools such as machine learning through algorithms such as support vector machine, random forest, neural networks, impending models can be produced to detect these fraudulent transactions. These anticipation models can help focus resources in the most efficient way to recover or recover losses due to fraud. Although these methods overcome the deficiency of knowledge acquisition in traditional rule-based expert systems. They still have some deficiencies, especially these methods are based on the idea of supervised learning, which needs a balanced dataset of both normal transactions and fraudulent transactions. So these methods do not work well in case of fraud detection since fraudulent transactions are much fewer than normal transactions.

Therefore, we propose a new approach for credit card fraud detection using a variational autoencoder and one-class classification techniques. In contrast with traditional classification methods which are focused on classifying samples of two or more classes, one-class classification methods try on to learn a model on samples of one class and distinguish them from samples of the other classes. In our work, we focus on distinguishing fraudulent transactions from normal transactions, but we use, normal transactions to train our model to distinguish the other class (fraudulent transactions).

The rest of the paper is structured as follows. Section 2 presents the related work, Sect. 3 explains our approach with Variational Autoencoder (VAE) and SVDD. Then the Sect. 4 presents the implementation and results analysis. Finally, the conclusion is given in Sect. 5.

2 Related Works

With the development of e-commerce, the credit card has become an essential payment method for online purchases of goods and services, and since then fraudsters have taken advantage of it to carry out unhealthy activities and steal users money. Due to these problems, several researches on the detection of the credit card fraud have been conducted in order to reduce losses. Many techniques for detecting credit card fraud have been presented in recent years [5]. In [16], the authors presented a new approach for automatic detection of frauds in credit card transactions based on non-linear signal processing and it can be applied to several datasets using parameters derived from key performance indicators of business. Bahnsen et al. [2] proposed a cost the sensitive method based on Bayes minimum risk to represent realistically the monetary gains and losses due to fraud detection.

Hegazy et al. [11] developed Frequent Pattern based on customer's previous transaction activity as Legal or Fraud transactions introducing using Rough Set and Decision Tree Technique clustering algorithm in Enhanced Fraud Miner algorithm which attained good improvement in finding the false alarm rate when compared to other models. Dai et al. [7] proposed a method that combined the supervised and unsupervised approach by fusing various models to train and record the spending behavior for each cardholder based on their previous transactions and for every new transaction the fraud score is computed from the fraud pattern. A hybrid and adaptive method is presented by Batani [3] to detect fraud using cardholder's financial status, social status, and OTP by assigning weights using Artificial Neural Networks to produce cardholder's social status and Hidden Markov Model to extract financial profile from bank database.

Awoyemi et al. [1] compared Naïve Bayes, K-nearest neighbor, and Logistic regression models and concluded that K-NN performs well. Tran et al. [18] proposed two real-time data-driven approaches, one-class support vector machine (OCSVM) and T2 control chart which attained good accuracy and low false positives. Dal Pozzolo et al. [9] compared Random Forests (RF) with Neural Network (NN) and Support Vector Machine (SVM) where the Random Forests performed well as expected and suggested the accuracy can be improved by increasing the training data size. Carneiro et al. [4] applied 10-fold cross-validation to Random Forests, SVM, and Logistic regression and tested with balanced and unbalanced data then concluded that Random Forests attained the best performance.

Fu, Cheng, and Tu [10] captured the essential characteristics of frauds by using a model based on the convolutional neural network (CNN). Jurgovsky et al. [12] proposed LSTM (Long Short Term Memory) to aggregate the previous purchase pattern of the cardholder and to improve the accuracy of the incoming transaction, compared sequence learner LSTM and static learner (Random Forest) where LSTM is prone to overfitting even with few nodes, hence suggested increasing the size of data. In [15], 10-layer deep Variational Auto-Encoder (VAE) was applied and compared with Decision Tree, SVM, and Ensemble Classifier (AdaBoost algorithm) where AdaBoost achieved high Precision and recall for VAE. Pumsirirat and Yan [14] proposed Auto-Encoder and Restricted Boltzmann and confirmed supervised learning is appropriate for the historical transaction in credit card fraud detection.

3   Proposed Approach Description

In this Section, we propose our solution which is an approach combining the variational autoencoder(VAE) and the support vector data description(SVDD). Initially, the model will be trained on the VAE through which we will obtain residuals, which will then be used to train our SVDD model. The Fig. 1 shows the structure of our proposed approach.

3.1   Description of Variational Autoencoder

A variational autoencoder is an autoencoder whose encoding distribution is regularized during training to avoid over-fitting and to ensure that the latent space

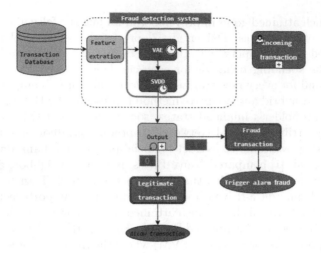

Fig. 1. Approach to the proposed solution

has good properties allowing us to generate new data. Statistically, the variational autoencoder is a technique based on Bayesian learning. Unlike a traditional autoencoder, the VAE represents the input as a probability distribution with a mean and standard deviation rather than a set of numbers. We then sample from the latent distribution and get some numbers. We feed those numbers through decoding. We retrieve an example that looks like something from the original dataset, except that it was newly created by the model. The model is structured as follows: Firstly, the input is encoded as a distribution over the latent space. Secondly, a point in latent space is sampled from this distribution. In the third step, the sampled point is decoded and the reconstruction error can be calculated. finally, the reconstruction error is downgraded via the network. The structure of original VAE is shown in Fig. 2.

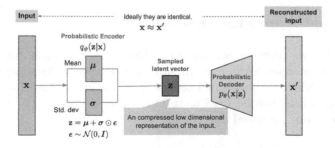

Fig. 2. Illustration of variationnel autoencoder.

3.2   Support Vector Data Description

Support vector data description (SVDD) is a technique related to One-class SVM [20]. Instead of finding a maximum margin hyperplane in feature space that best separates the mapped data from the origin as One-class SVM, the object of SVDD is to find the smallest hypersphere with center $\mathbf{c}$ and radius R that covers the normal instances in the training data-set. The SVDD is a useful method for outlier detection and has been applied to a variety of applications. Denote $\mathbf{x}_i \in \mathbb{R}^n, i = 1 \dots, N$ as a set of training data. The SVDD is equivalent to solving the following *primal optimization*:

$$\begin{array}{c} \underset{R, \mathbf{a}, \xi}{\text{Minimize }} R^2 + C \sum_{k=i}^{N} \xi_i \\[2mm] \text{subject to } (x_i - a)^T (x_i - a) \le R^2 + \xi_i \; \forall \xi_i \ge 0 \end{array} \tag{1}$$

the parameter $C > 0$ is used to control the influence of the slack variables ξ_i. After the optimization problem is solved, a hyper-spherical model is characterized by the center $\mathbf{a}$ and the radius R. By incorporating the constraint into (1), the optimization problem is solved using Lagrange's method:

$$L(R, a, \alpha, \xi_i) = R^2 + C \sum_i \xi_i - \sum_i \alpha \{R^2 + \xi_i - (x_i^2 - 2ax_i + a^2)\} - \sum_i \gamma_i \xi_i \tag{2}$$

With the Lagrange multiplier $\alpha_i \ge 0$ and $\gamma_i \ge 0$. By setting the partial derivatives to 0, new constraints are obtained:

$$\sum_i \alpha_i,$$

$$a = \frac{\sum_i \alpha_i x_i}{\sum_i \alpha_i} = \sum_i \alpha_i x_i, \tag{3}$$

$$C - \alpha_i - \gamma_i = 0 \forall i$$

We can remove the variable γ_i from equation (3) since $\alpha_i \ge 0$, then let us use the constraints $0 \le \alpha_i \le C, \forall_i$. By rewriting (2) and replacing in (3) we have:

$$L = \sum_i \alpha_i < x_i, x_i > - \sum_{i,j} \alpha_i \alpha_j < x_i, x_j > \tag{4}$$

with constraints $0 \le \alpha_i \le C, \sum_i \alpha_i = 1$.

To determine if a z test point is in the sphere, the distance to the center of the sphere must be calculated. A test object z is accepted when the distance is less than the radius, that is, when $(z - a)^T (z - a) \le R^2$. Expressing the center of the sphere in terms of support vectors, we accept the objects when:

$$< z, z > -2 \sum_i \alpha_i < z, x_i > + \sum_{i,j} \alpha_i \alpha_j < x_i, x_j > \le R^2. \tag{5}$$

Using kernel functions leads to a better compact representation of the training data. The SVDD formation with kernel functions leads to the flexible data description. The Gaussian kernel function used in this paper is defined as

$$K(x_i, x_j) = \exp(-||x_i - x_j||_2^2/s^2), \tag{6}$$

where s is Gaussian bandwidth parameter.

4 Implementation and Results

4.1 Dataset

Our data comes from online e-commerce transactions of European credit cards provided in [8]. Data sets contain credit card transactions over a two-day collection period in September 2013 by European cardholders. There is a total of 284315 transactions without fraudulent transactions and 492 fraudulent transactions. The dataset contains numerical variables which are the result of a principal component analysis (PCA).

In the first part of the application of the variational autoencoder for the extraction of the characteristics we used 70% of the normal data for the training and 30% of the normal + the 492 of the fraudulent data for the test. In the second part of the application of SVDD we were forced to decrease the data due to a memory problem of our machine to facilitate the process of reading the data. For this, we have created 20 training sets each containing 10,000 data belonging to the normal data and 3000 for the test set. We then evaluate the model on each training data and then calculate the average.

4.2 Performance Analysis

In binary classification, a machine learning model can make two types of errors when testing. It can either falsely predict sample data from the positive class as negative or sample data from the negative class as positive. The metric evaluation in the case of an unbalanced dataset requires taking into account the true positive rate and the false positive rate. The metrics we used for evaluation are: The AUC(Area Under Curve-Receiver) score, Recall, Precision and F1_score.

4.3 Results and Interpretation

We compare our VAE + SVDD approach with AE + SVDD. We used the AUC and F1 measurement ratio to judge the accuracy of the method. We trained our SVDD model using the Gaussian bandwidth **s** parameter. We used the values from the following set: s = [0.001, 0.04, 0.1, 0.5]. The table 1 shows the results of the two approaches with different values of the Gaussian kernel **s** parameter. We notice an increase in the number of **supports vectors** as we increase the value of **s** and the noticeable change in performance of the VAE + SVDD and AE + SVDD algorithms. For each value of **s** given we notice that the performance of the model in terms of the F1 score of VAE + SVDD is superior to AE + SVDD. We can say that this is due to the fact that in the VAE the data is smoother than the classic autoencoder (AE).

Table 1. Comparison of accuracy (in %) with different value of s.

s	Method	nSVs	Precision	Recall	F1	AUC
0.001	VAE+SVDD	8	99.96	97.07	93.07	87.74
	AE+SVDD	10	99	86.68	92.85	86.80
0.04	VAE+SVDD	81	99.36	96.69	97.93	95.68
	AE+SVDD	130	98.52	96.78	97.21	95.10
0.1	VAE+SVDD	118	98.80	96.75	97.77	95.71
	AE+SVDD	310	96.29	97.33	96.81	95.60
0.5	VAE+SVDD	739	91.34	97.15	94.16	94.84
	AE+SVDD	2813	64.14	98.94	80	96.56

5   Conclusion

In this paper, we proposed a new approach for real time data-driven fraud detection using variational autoencoder and support vector data description. Thirst the model is trained with the variational autoencoder to learn the representation of normal transaction and then we this representation to train our SVDD. The advantage of this technique is that the representation learns by the VAE permit increasing the performance of the SVDD. The overall results in terms of value AUC, precision, F1 show good accuracy for our model. In the future, we will try to tune the value of the kernel bandwidth parameter s, since that the performance of the SVDD depends on this parameter.

References

1. Awoyemi, J.O., Adetunmbi, A.O., Oluwadare, S.A.: Credit card fraud detection using machine learning techniques: a comparative analysis. In: 2017 International Conference on Computing Networking and Informatics (ICCNI), pp. 1–9. IEEE (2017)
2. Bahnsen, A.C., Stojanovic, A., Aouada, D., Ottersten, B.: Cost sensitive credit card fraud detection using bayes minimum risk. In: 2013 12th International Conference on Machine Learning and Applications, vol. 1, pp. 333–338. IEEE (2013)
3. Batani, J.: An adaptive and real-time fraud detection algorithm in online transactions. Int. J. Comput. Sci. Bus. Inf. **17**(2), 1–12 (2017)
4. Carneiro, N., Figueira, G., Costa, M.: A data mining based system for credit-card fraud detection in e-tail. Decis. Support Syst. **95**, 91–101 (2017)
5. Chaudhary, K., Yadav, J., Mallick, B.: A review of fraud detection techniques: credit card. Int. J. Comput. Appl. **45**(1), 39–44 (2012)
6. Cheng, Y., Wu, D.D., Olson, D.L., Dolgui, A.: Financing the newsvendor with preferential credit: bank vs. manufacturer. Int. J. Prod. Res. **59**(14), 4228–4247 (2021). https://doi.org/10.1080/00207543.2020.1759839
7. Dai, Y., Yan, J., Tang, X., Zhao, H., Guo, M.: Online credit card fraud detection: a hybrid framework with big data technologies. In: 2016 IEEE Trustcom/BigDataSE/ISPA, pp. 1644–1651. IEEE (2016)

8. Dal Pozzolo, A., Boracchi, G., Caelen, O., Alippi, C., Bontempi, G.: Credit card fraud detection and concept-drift adaptation with delayed supervised information. In: 2015 international joint conference on Neural networks (IJCNN), pp. 1–8. IEEE (2015)

9. Dal Pozzolo, A., Caelen, O., Le Borgne, Y.A., Waterschoot, S., Bontempi, G.: Learned lessons in credit card fraud detection from a practitioner perspective. Expert Syst. Appl. **41**(10), 4915–4928 (2014)

10. Fu, K., Cheng, D., Tu, Y., Zhang, L.: Credit card fraud detection using convolutional neural networks. In: Hirose, A., Ozawa, S., Doya, K., Ikeda, K., Lee, M., Liu, D. (eds.) ICONIP 2016. LNCS, vol. 9949, pp. 483–490. Springer, Cham (2016). https://doi.org/10.1007/978-3-319-46675-0_53

11. Hegazy, M., Madian, A., Ragaie, M.: Enhanced fraud miner: credit card fraud detection using clustering data mining techniques. Egypt. Comput. Sci. J. (ISSN: 1110–2586) **40**(03), 72–81 (2016)

12. Jurgovsky, J., et al.: Sequence classification for credit-card fraud detection. Expert Syst. Appl. **100**, 234–245 (2018)

13. Nguyen, Q.T., Tran, K.P., Castagliola, P., Huong, T.T., Nguyen, M.K., Lardjane, S.: Nested one-class support vector machines for network intrusion detection. In: 2018 IEEE Seventh International Conference on Communications and Electronics (ICCE), pp. 7–12. IEEE (2018)

14. Pumsirirat, A., Yan, L.: Credit card fraud detection using deep learning based on auto-encoder and restricted boltzmann machine. Int. J. Adv. Comput. Sci. Appl. **9**(1), 18–25 (2018)

15. Raza, M., Qayyum, U.: Classical and deep learning classifiers for anomaly detection. In: 2019 16th International Bhurban Conference on Applied Sciences and Technology (IBCAST), pp. 614–618. IEEE (2019)

16. Salazar, A., Safont, G., Soriano, A., Vergara, L.: Automatic credit card fraud detection based on non-linear signal processing. In: 2012 IEEE International Carnahan Conference on Security Technology (ICCST), pp. 207–212. IEEE (2012)

17. Tran, P.H., Rakitzis, A., Nguyen, H., Nguyen, Q.T., Tran, H., Tran, K.P., Heuchenne, C.: New methods for anomaly detection: Run rules multivariate coefficient of variation control charts. In: 2020 International Conference on Advanced Technologies for Communications (ATC), pp. 40–44. IEEE (2020)

18. Tran, P.H., Tran, K.P., Huong, T.T., Heuchenne, C., HienTran, P., Le, T.M.H.: Real time data-driven approaches for credit card fraud detection. In: Proceedings of the 2018 International Conference on E-Business and Applications, pp. 6–9 (2018)

19. Truong, T.H., Ta, P.B., Nguyen, Q.T., Du Nguyen, H., Tran, K.P.: A data-driven approach for network intrusion detection and monitoring based on kernel null space. In: Duong, T.Q., Vo, N.-S., Nguyen, L.K., Vien, Q.-T., Nguyen, V.-D. (eds.) INISCOM 2019. LNICST, vol. 293, pp. 130–140. Springer, Cham (2019). https://doi.org/10.1007/978-3-030-30149-1_11

20. Vapnik, V.: The Nature of Statistical Learning Theory. Springer, New York (1995) https://doi.org/10.1007/978-1-4757-3264-1

A Model for a Multi-level Disassembly System Under Random Disassembly Lead Times

Ilhem Slama[1]([⊠]), Oussama Ben-Ammar[2][iD], and Alexandre Dolgui[1][iD]

[1] IMT Atlantique, LS2N-CNRS, La Chantrerie, 4 rue Alfred Kastler, B.P. 20722, 44307 Nantes, France
{ilhem.slama,alexandre.dolgui}@imt-atlantique.fr
[2] Department of Manufacturing Sciences and Logistics, Mines Saint-Etienne, University Clermont Auvergne, CNRS, UMR 6158 LIMOS CMP, Gardanne, France
oussama.ben-ammar@emse.fr

Abstract. This paper deals with the problem of planned disassembly lead time calculation in a Reverse Material Requirement Planning (RMRP) environment under uncertainty. A multi-level disassembly system with one type of end-of-life product and several types of components at each level is considered for the first time in the disassembly planning problem under uncertainty. The paper presents a mathematical model with corresponding proofs. The objective of the proposed model is to minimise the total expected cost which is composed of holding and backlogging costs. Some advantages of the proposed model and perspectives of this research are discussed.

Keywords: Reverse supply chain · Disassemble-to-order · Stochastic lead times

1 Introduction and Related Publications

With accumulated environmental pressure on industrial activities, the reverse flow has become indispensable. The remanufacturing process is a crucial step in the reverse logistics network, and it concerns all tasks associated with the collection, disassembly, refurbishing, repair, recycling, disposal, etc. of end-of-life (EoL) products [1]. In the scientific literature, the disassembly process has recently received a lot of attention due to its importance in the recovery of products. It allows the selective separation of parts in order to recover materials, isolate hazardous substances and separate reusable items [2].

The current paper proposes to model the disassembly planning problem, which is one of the main problems associated with product recovery. The motivations for initiating tactical disassembly planning are very varied and multiple. On a large scale, optimal planning of disassembly operations is necessary to efficiently process a large volume of products to be upgraded. It also aims to

A. Dolgui et al. (Eds.): APMS 2021, IFIP AICT 630, pp. 39–47, 2021.
https://doi.org/10.1007/978-3-030-85874-2_5

organise a succession of operations over time in order to meet the demands for components on predefined delivery dates.

Making decisions in an uncertain environment is a difficult task for many industrial sectors. In fact, some parameters are often considered deterministic, when in reality they are inherently uncertain. There are many sources of uncertainty related to demand and the quantity and quality of parts that can disrupt the disassembly process. For example, a machine failure can interrupt the disassembly process and subsequently, component disassembly times become longer than expected. Consequently, these uncertainties disrupt the level of stock, and thus, create disruption and unnecessary storage. Several methods have been developed in the literature to take into account the effect of uncertainty in the disassembly planning problem. Without trying to do an exhaustive review of the literature, we discuss the previous works on disassembly planning problem under uncertainty. For a more exhaustive literature review, readers can refer to [3,4].

The models proposed in the literature can be classified as a single or multi-period planning problem, two or multi echelon bill of materials (BOM) (see Table 1). Also, they can be divided into four different categories depending on the type of uncertainty: (1) demand (see [5,6]), (2) disassembly yield (see for example the works of [7–9]), (3) yield and demand [10] and (4) disassembly lead time (DLT). The latter is defined as the time difference between placing a disassembly order and receiving the disassembled item at each level of the BOM.

For different reasons (machine breakdowns, absenteeism, quality problems, etc.), the disassembly lead times are often stochastic. To minimise the effects of these random factors, companies can implement safety lead times (or safety stock), but theses stocks are very expensive. On the other hand, if there are not enough stocks, we can observe stockout and the corresponding backlog cost. So, the main goal is to minimise the total cost which is composed of holding and backlog costs.

As far as can be determined from the literature, for the uncertainty of timing, the number of publications that study disassembly systems is very modest compared to those that deal with assembly systems [17,18]. In the paper of [12], only the uncertainty of DLT of the EoL product is studied. The case of multi-period, single product type and two-level disassembly system is investigated. The disassemble capacity is supposed infinite. The Scenario-based stochastic Linear Programming model (S-LP) is developed. The proposed approach is used to determine the optimal EoL products to be disassembled in order to minimise the Average Total Cost (ATC) over the planning horizon. In the work of [11], the authors developed a mathematical model to found the optimal plan of disassembly/assembly system under breakdowns machine and stochastic lead times. A heuristic is developed to determine the optimal ordered date of the EoL product as well as the optimum release dates of new external components. Later, [14] proposed a generalisation of the discrete Newsboy formulae to find the optimal release date when the time of disassembling the EoL product is random variable. The case of one-period, single product type and two-level disassembly system is treated. In the same year, [13] extend the work of [14] by considering the

Table 1. Summary of relevant literature under uncertainly

Authors	Resolution	Uncertainty				
		Yield	Demand	DLT	#Periods	#Levels
[5]	MILP, Lagrangian heuristics		✓		m	2
[6]	MILP, Lagrangian heuristics		✓		m	2
[7]	Lagrangian heuristics	✓			1	2
[8]	Heuristics	✓			1	2
[9]	Fuzzy goal programming	✓			1	2
[10]	MILP, Outer-approximation	✓	✓		m	2
[11]	Analytical model, Heuristic			✓	1	2
[12]	S-LP			✓	m	2
[13]	Analytical model, Newsboy formulae			✓	1	2
[14]	Analytical model, Newsboy formulae			✓	1	2
[15]	2S-MILP, SAA			✓	m	2
[16]	2S-MILP, GA			✓	m	2
Current Paper	Analytical model			✓	**1**	**m**

m: multi-

uncertainty of disassembly lead times of each component. In the same context, [15] extend the work proposed by [12] by considering the time limit of disassembly capacity in each period of the planning horizon. The problem is formulated as a two-stage stochastic Mixed Integer Linear Programming (2S-MILP) model. The Sample Average Approximation (SAA) approach is developed in order to minimise the ATC. Recently, [16] addressed a multi-period disassembly lot-sizing problem. The case of single product type and two-level disassembly system is studied. The problem is formulated as 2S-MILP model through all possible scenarios. To solve large scale problems, the authors proposed a basic genetic algorithm (GA).

As presented above, all the previous works under uncertainty of DLT are confined to the two-level disassembly system. Solving the studied problem with a multi-level BOM is more complex because of dependencies between the different sub-assemblies and components at each level. For this reason, this paper extends the work of [14] and [13] by considering a multi-level disassembly system to study a one-period planning for the disassemble-to-order (DTO) problem. A mathematical model is developed to calculate the total expected costs composed of the component backlog and holding costs.

The rest of this paper is organised as follows. Section 2 describes the problem. Section 3 presents the stochastic model of the multi-level disassembly to-order problem. Section 4 presents the conclusions with avenues for future studies.

2   Problem Description

We consider the problem with the multi-level disassembly system (with several types of components at each level) as shown in Fig. 1. The non-leaf item i (can be root or sub-assembly $(i \in \mathcal{A}^1)$) represents the item to disassemble. It has more than one child and a child element denotes non-root item (can be part or sub-assembly) that has only one parent. Customers have a fixed demand for all disassembled leaf item $(i \in \mathcal{A}^0)$. Theses demands must be delivered with certain delivery day.

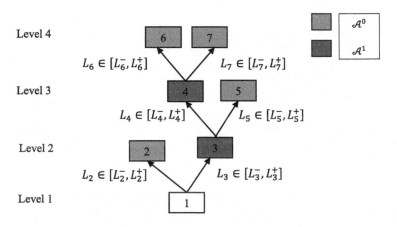

Fig. 1. A multi-level disassembly system.

Once the disassembly process is started, the items recovery process provides no information about the state of components until the end of the disassembly process. Then, each item can be received after a stochastic disassembly lead time where the items undergo several renovation processes (such as repair and cleaning). The DLT of each item L_i is a random discrete variable with a known probability distribution and bounded over known intervals $(L_i \in [L_i^-, L_i^+])$. Here, we supposed that the probability is not identically distributed, that's to say, the DLT for each item don't following the same probability distribution.

The assumptions of the studied problem can be summarised as follows:

1. The one-period planning for the DTO environment and a single demand for each type of component is considered;
2. At each level, all parent items must proceed to disassembly once they are ready;

3. If the date of obtaining an item from its parent is less than its scheduled disassembly start date, this item will be kept until the scheduled release time, which incurs a holding cost;
4. If, at a certain level in the BOM, a component is not received as expected, a backlog cost is incurred.

3   Problem Formulation

The aim of this research is to develop a mathematical model for multi-level disassembly systems under a fixed part's demand and uncertainty of parts disassembly lead times.

Let $i = 1$ be the index of the EoL product, n the index of the last disassembled item and the following three sets: (i) $\mathcal{A}$ the set of all elements $i = 1, \ldots, n$, (ii) $\mathcal{A}^0$ the set of all obtained items that we can not disassemble and to be delivered to clients and (iii) $\mathcal{A}^1$ the set of all obtained items that we can disassemble. Therefore $\mathcal{A} = \{1\} \cup \mathcal{A}^0 \cup \mathcal{A}^1$ Here, we have only demands for items i from the last level. i.e. $i \in \mathcal{A}^0$. The notation used in the paper are presented in Table 2.

Table 2. Model notation and definition

Parameters	
i	Index of items, $i = 1, \ldots, n$
$p(i)$	Index of the parent of item i, $\forall i \in \mathcal{A}^0 \cup \mathcal{A}^1$
T_i	Delivery date for item i, $\forall i \in \mathcal{A}^0$
h_i	Unit inventory holding cost for item i, $\forall i \in \mathcal{A}^0 \cup \mathcal{A}^1$
b_i	Unit backlogging cost for item i, $\forall i \in \mathcal{A}^0 \cup \mathcal{A}^1$
L_i	Actual disassembly lead time of item i, $\forall i \in \mathcal{A}^0 \cup \mathcal{A}^1$
Variables	
X_i	**Decision variable**: Planned date of availability of item i, $\forall i \in \mathcal{A}^1$
Functions	
$\mathbb{E}[\![.]\!]$	Excepted value
$\mathbb{F}_i[\![.]\!]$	Distribution function of the random variable L_i, $\forall i \in \mathcal{A}^0 \cup \mathcal{A}^1$
T_i^+	$max(M_i; T_i)$, $\forall i \in \mathcal{A}^0$
T_i^-	$min(M_i; T_i)$, $\forall i \in \mathcal{A}^0$

The total cost is equal to the sum of backlogging and inventory holding costs for all components.

Proposition 1. *For the system described in the previous section, the total cost, noted by* $TC(X, \mathcal{L})$*, is as follows:*

$$TC(X, \mathcal{L}) = \sum_{i \in \mathcal{A}^0} (b_i + h_i) \times max(T_i; M_i) + \sum_{i \in \mathcal{A}^1} (b_i + h_i) \times max(X_i; M_i)$$
$$- \sum_{i \in \mathcal{A}^0} b_i T_i - \sum_{i \in \mathcal{A}^1} b_i X_i - \sum_{i \in \mathcal{A}^0 \cup \mathcal{A}^1} h_i M_i \tag{1}$$

Proof. In this prof, several costs will be detailed. Let M_i be the actual availability date of item i; $M_i = X_1 + L_i \; \forall i \in \mathcal{A}^1$ and $p(i) = 1$. We first calculate $C_{h1}(X, L)$ the inventory holding cost of components disassembled from EoL product ($\forall i \in \mathcal{A}^1$, $p(i) = 1$):

$$C_{h1}(X, L) = \sum_{\substack{i \in \mathcal{A}^1 \\ p(i)=1}} h_i(X_i - min(X_i; M_i)) \tag{2}$$

Let M_i be the actual availability date of item i; $M_i = max(X_{p(i)}; M_{p(i)}) + L_i$ $\forall i \in \mathcal{A}^1$ and $p(i) > 1$. Then, we can calculate $C_h(X, L)$ the inventory holding cost of components disassembled from items:

$$C_h(X, L) = \sum_{\substack{i \in \mathcal{A}^1 \\ p(i)>1}} h_i(X_i - min(X_i; M_i)) \tag{3}$$

Let M_i be the actual availability date of item i; $M_i = max(T_i; M_{p(i)}) + L_i$ $\forall i \in \mathcal{A}^0$. We calculate $C_{h0}(X, L)$ the inventory holding cost of items that we have to deliver to clients:

$$C_{h0}(X, L) = \sum_{i \in \mathcal{A}^0} h_i(T_i - min(T_i; M_i)) \tag{4}$$

From Expressions (2)–(4), we can deduce the total holding cost:

$$C_H(X, L) = \sum_{i \in \mathcal{A}^0} h_i(T_i - min(T_i; M_i)) + \sum_{i \in \mathcal{A}^1} h_i(X_i - min(X_i; M_i)) \tag{5}$$

By the same way, we can easily deduce the total backlogging cost:

$$C_B(X, L) = \sum_{i \in \mathcal{A}^0} b_i(max(T_i; M_i) - T_i) + \sum_{i \in \mathcal{A}^1} b_i(max(X_i; M_i) - X_i) \tag{6}$$

Finally, the total cost can be formulated from Expressions (5)–(6).

Proposition 2. *The mathematical expectation of the total cost is given by the following expression:*

$$\mathbb{E}[C(X, L)] = \sum_{i \in \mathcal{A}^0} (b_i + h_i) \times \sum_{s \geq T_i} (1 - \mathcal{F}_i(s)) + \sum_{i \in \mathcal{A}^1} (b_i + h_i) \times \sum_{s \geq X_i} (1 - \mathcal{F}_i(s))$$

$$+ \sum_{i \in \mathcal{A}^0} h_i T_i - \sum_{i \in \mathcal{A}_{\setminus 1}} h_i (\mathbb{E}[L_i] + \sum_{s \geq X_{p(i)}} (1 - \mathcal{F}_{p(i)}(s)))$$

$$+ \sum_{i \in \mathcal{A}^1} h_i X_i - \sum_{i \in \mathcal{A}_{\setminus 1}} h_i X_{p(i)}$$

where:

$$\mathcal{F}_i(s) = \begin{cases} 1 & \text{if } i = 1 \\ \mathbb{F}_i(-X_{p(i)} + s) & \text{if } p(i) = 1 \\ \mathbb{F}_i(-X_{p(i)} + s) \displaystyle\sum_{\substack{v_i + w_i = s \\ v_i + w_i \in \mathbb{N}}} \mathbb{P}[L_i = v_i] \times \mathcal{F}_{p(i)}(w_i) & \text{otherwise} \end{cases}$$

Proof. First, we formulate $\mathbb{E}[M_i]$, $\mathbb{E}[max(X_i; M_i)]$ and $\mathbb{E}[max(T_i; M_i)]$. For all $i \in \mathcal{A}$ and $p(i) = 1$, M_i is the actual availability date of item i; $M_i = X_1 + L_i$. So $\mathbb{E}[M_i] = \mathbb{E}[L_i] + X_1$. For all $i \in \mathcal{A}^1$ and $p(p(i)) = 1$, M_i is the actual availability date of item i. So M_i is equal to $max(X_{p(i)}; M_{p(i)}) + L_i$ and:

$$\mathbb{E}[M_i] = \mathbb{E}[L_i] + \sum_{s \geq 0}(1 - \mathbb{P}[X_{p(i)} \leq s]\mathbb{P}[M_{p(i)} \leq s])$$

Moreover, knowing that $Pr[X_{p(i)} \leq s] = 0 \; \forall s \in [0, X_{p(i)}[$ and $Pr[X_{p(i)} \leq s] = 1 \; \forall s \geq X_{p(i)}$, then:

$$\mathbb{E}[M_i] = \mathbb{E}[L_i] + X_{p(i)} + \sum_{s \geq X_{p(i)}}(1 - \mathbb{P}[M_{p(i)} \leq s])$$

Knowing that $M_{p(i)} = X_1 + L_{p(i)}$, so:

$$\mathbb{E}[M_i] = \mathbb{E}[L_i] + X_{p(i)} + \sum_{s \geq X_{p(i)}}(1 - \mathbb{F}_{p(i)}(-X_1 + s)) \tag{7}$$

For all $i \in \mathcal{A}$ and $p(p(p(i)))) = 1$, M_i is the actual availability date of item i. So M_i is equal to $max(X_{p(i)}; M_{p(i)}) + L_i$ and:

$$\mathbb{E}[M_i] = \mathbb{E}[L_i] + X_{p(i)}$$

$$+ \sum_{s \geq X_{p(i)}}(1 - \mathbb{F}_{p(i)}(-X_{p(p(i))} + s)) \sum_{\substack{o_1 + o_2 = s \\ o_1 + o_2 \in \mathbb{N}}}(\mathbb{P}[L_{p(i)} = o_1]\mathbb{P}[M_{p(p(i))} \leq o_2)])$$

By using the recursive function, we can easily formulate $\mathbb{E}[M_i]$, $\mathbb{E}[max(X_i; M_i)]$ and $\mathbb{E}[max(T_i; M_i)]$ as follows:

$$\mathbb{E}[M_i] = \mathbb{E}[L_i] + X_{p(i)} + \sum_{s \geq X_{p(i)}}(1 - \mathcal{F}_{p(i)}(s)) \tag{8}$$

$$\mathbb{E}[max(X_i; M_i)] = X_i + \sum_{s \geq X_i}(1 - \mathcal{F}_i(s)) \tag{9}$$

$$\mathbb{E}[max(T_i; M_i)] = T_i + \sum_{s \geq T_i}(1 - \mathcal{F}_i(s)) \tag{10}$$

Then, the expression of the expected total cost can be deduced.

4   Conclusion and Perspectives

In this preliminary work, we model a multi-level disassembly problem in a DTO environment. We consider a one type of EoL product and several types of components at each level. The disassembly lead times at each level are discrete independent random variables, and the items demand at the finished level is fixed. The disassembly of the components is carried out as soon as their parents are available. The demand of the leaf items should be satisfied on predefined delivery dates. Otherwise a backlogging cost is incurred. If a given component is available before the delivery date, we stored it until this period. The developed mathematical model calculates the expected value of the sum of backlogging and inventory costs.

The expected total cost is not linear. In the future, we will develop an optimisation approach to optimise the release dates for the non-leaf items. Research into solving this problem is in progress. The developed approach is based on genetic algorithm developed for assembly systems under uncertainty of lead times [19].

References

1. Kim, D.H., Doh, H.H., Lee, D.H.: Multi-period disassembly levelling and lot-sizing for multiple product types with parts commonality. Proc. Inst. Mech. Eng. Part B: J. Eng. Manuf. **232**(5), 867–878 (2018)
2. Slama, I., Ben-Ammar, O., Dolgui, A., Masmoudi, F.: New mixed integer approach to solve a multi-level capacitated disassembly lot-sizing problem with defective items and backlogging. J. Manuf. Syst. **56**, 50–57 (2020)
3. Slama, I., Ben-Ammar, O., Masmoudi, F., Dolgui, A.: Disassembly scheduling problem: literature review and future research directions. IFAC-PapersOnLine **52**(13), 601–606 (2019)
4. Kim, H.J., Lee, D.H., Xirouchakis, P.: Disassembly scheduling: literature review and future research directions. Int. J. Prod. Res. **45**(18–19), 4465–4484 (2007)
5. Kim, H.J., Xirouchakis, P.: Capacitated disassembly scheduling with random demand. Int. J. Prod. Res. **48**(23), 7177–7194 (2010)
6. Fang, C., Liu, X., Pardalos, P.M., Long, J., Pei, J., Zuo, C.: A stochastic production planning problem in hybrid manufacturing and remanufacturing systems with resource capacity planning. J. Global Optim. **68**(4), 851–878 (2017). https://doi.org/10.1007/s10898-017-0500-6
7. Inderfurth, K., Vogelgesang, S., Langella, I.M.: How yield process misspecification affects the solution of disassemble-to-order problems. Int. J. Prod. Econ. **169**, 56–67 (2015)
8. Inderfurth, K., Langella, I.M.: Heuristics for solving disassemble-to-order problems with stochastic yields. OR Spectrum **28**(1), 73–99 (2006)
9. Kongar, E., Gupta, S.M.: Disassembly to order system under uncertainty. Omega **34**(6), 550–561 (2006)
10. Liu, K., Zhang, Z.H.: Capacitated disassembly scheduling under stochastic yield and demand. Eur. J. Oper. Res. **269**(1), 244–257 (2018)
11. Guiras, Z., Turki, S., Rezg, N., Dolgui, A.: Optimization of two-level disassembly/remanufacturing/assembly system with an integrated maintenance strategy. Appl. Sci. **8**(5), 666 (2018)
12. Slama, I., Ben-Ammar, O., Masmoudi, F., Dolgui, A.: Scenario-based stochastic linear programming model for multi-period disassembly lot-sizing problems under random lead time. IFAC-PapersOnLine **52**(13), 595–600 (2019)
13. Slama, I., Ben-Ammar, O., Dolgui, A., Masmoudi, F.: Newsboy problem with two-level disassembly system and stochastic lead time. ROADEF (2020)

14. Slama, I., Ben-Ammar, O., Dolgui, A., Masmoudi, F.: A newsboy formulae to optimize planned lead times for two-level disassembly systems. IFAC-PapersOnLine **53**(2), 10816–10821 (2020)
15. Slama, I., Ben-Ammar, O., Dolgui, A., Masmoudi, F.: A stochastic model for a two-level disassembly lot-sizing problem under random lead time. In: Lalic, B., Majstorovic, V., Marjanovic, U., von Cieminski, G., Romero, D. (eds.) APMS 2020. IAICT, vol. 591, pp. 275–283. Springer, Cham (2020). https://doi.org/10.1007/978-3-030-57993-7_32
16. Slama, I., Ben-Ammar, O., Dolgui, A., Masmoudi, F.: Approches d'optimisation pour un problème de planification de désassemblage sous incertitude des délais de désassemblage. Génie industriel et productique **3**(1) (2020)
17. Ben-Ammar, O., Castagliola, P., Dolgui, A., Hnaien, F.: A hybrid genetic algorithm for a multilevel assembly replenishment planning problem with stochastic lead times. Comput. Ind. Eng.**149**, 106794 (2020)
18. Slama, I., Ben-Ammar, O., Dolgui, A., Masmoudi, F.: Genetic algorithm and Monte Carlo simulation for a stochastic capacitated disassembly lot-sizing problem under random lead times. Comput. Ind. Eng., 107468 (2021)
19. Ben-Ammar, O., Dolgui, A.: Optimal order release dates for two-level assembly systems with stochastic lead times at each level. Int. J. Prod. Res. **56**(12), 4226–4242 (2018)

Hybrid Approaches for Production Planning and Scheduling

Scheduling of Parallel 3D-Printing Machines with Incompatible Job Families: A Matheuristic Algorithm

Mohammad Rohaninejad[1]([⊠]) [ID], Zdeněk Hanzálek[1] [ID],
and Reza Tavakkoli-Moghaddam[2] [ID]

[1] Industrial Informatics Department, Czech Institute of Informatics Robotics
and Cybernetics, Czech Technical University in Prague, Prague, Czech Republic
{Mohammad.Rohani.Nezhad,Zdenek.Hanzalek}@cvut.cz
[2] School of Industrial Engineering, College of Engineering, University of Tehran,
Tehran, Iran
Tavakoli@ut.ac.ir

Abstract. Additive manufacturing (AM) is a promising technology for the rapid prototyping and production of highly customized products. The scheduling of AM machines has an essential role in increasing profitability and has recently received a great deal of attention. This paper investigates the scheduling of batch processing of parallel 3d-printing machines to minimize the total weighted tardiness. Accordingly, a mathematical model is proposed to formulate the problem considering the sequence-dependent setup time and incompatible job families, where jobs of different families are processed with different materials and desired quality. Due to the high complexity of the problem, an efficient matheuristic algorithm is presented based on the hybridization of a genetic algorithm and a local search method based on mixed integer programming (MIP). Computational results show that the proposed approach is efficient and promising to solve the problem.

Keywords: Additive manufacturing · Batch processing · Scheduling · Matheuristic

1 Introduction and Literature Review

Additive manufacturing (AM) that also called 3D-printing is a remarkable technology in the context of industry 4.0, which is rapidly developing smart manufacturing systems. various 3D-printing machine types are developed and applied in prototyping, production, and biomedicine [1]. In terms of industrial production, manufacturing companies are employing 3D-printing technology for facilitating the fabrication of highly customized, and lighter weight products. Powder-based, liquid-based, and solid or wire extrusion techniques are the main processing technologies applied in 3D-printing machines [2] that produce parts by depositing material layer upon layer according to a predesigned computer pattern.

© IFIP International Federation for Information Processing 2021
Published by Springer Nature Switzerland AG 2021
A. Dolgui et al. (Eds.): APMS 2021, IFIP AICT 630, pp. 51–61, 2021.
https://doi.org/10.1007/978-3-030-85874-2_6

This research focuses on the scheduling of a special kind of powder-based 3D-printing machine known as Selective Laser Melting (SLM) machine. We consider several independent machines working in parallel. In the SLM machine, the laser beam hits the metal powder and welds its particles together. Then, a new layer of metal powder is added and this process continues until the final product is reached. In the current study, the scheduling of parallel SLM machines consists of batching a variety of parts with incompatible job families and then determining the allocation and sequencing of the formed batches in such a way that the total cost of tardiness is minimized ($\mathbf{P_m}|batch, incompatible| \sum w_j T_j$).

According to the shift of AM from making the prototype to real parts production, the production planning and scheduling in AM systems has changed to a crucial problem. Special characteristics of AM environments, such as the wide variety of orders, high production cost, high purchasing cost of AM machines in industrial dimension, and dependence on the orientation of parts in machines, etc. have made the scheduling of AM more complex than the other scheduling problems. Li et al. [3] proposed a mathematical model and two different heuristics to solve the problem. Dvorak et al. [4] presented the scheduling of 3D-printing machines in a job shop while minimizing makespan and satisfying deadlines. Li et al. [5] proposed an approach to make decisions simultaneously on the acceptance and scheduling in AM production. Zhou et al. [6] and Mai et al. [7] studied the scheduling of distributed AM in cloud manufacturing [8]. Regarding to SLM machines, Li et al. [3] proposed two heuristic procedures named 'best-fit' and 'adapted best-fit' to minimize the production cost per volume of material on nonidentical SLM machines. Griffiths et al. [9] studied part orientation and 2D bin packing in the SLM machine to minimize the production cost.

There are few studies on parallel batch processing machine scheduling in AM. Zhang et al. [10] have developed an improved evolutionary algorithm for ($\mathbf{P_m}|batch|C_{max}$) in SLA (Stereo Lithography Appearance) 3D printing machines. They have combined a genetic algorithm with a heuristic placement strategy to take into account the allocation and placement of parts integrally. Kucukkoc [11] has addressed scheduling problem of Single, parallel identical and parallel non-identical AM machines to minimize the makespan. He developed an MILP model that can easily be adopted by AM firms. Our study extended Kucukkoc [11] research. In his research, there was only one type of material and desired quality, and the objective function was the makespan. In contrast, we considered parts with different material types and desired quality, sequence-dependent setup times, and total weighted tardiness as the objective function. Hence, a new mathematical model is presented and due to the high complexity of the problem, a novel matheuristic algorithm based on the combination of Genetic algorithm and an efficient MIP-based local search is developed. Regarding to the computational results, it is clear that the proposed algorithm is an effective step forward to solve the proposed problem.

The rest of this paper proceeds as follows. Section 2 illustrates the problem description and presents the corresponding mixed integer linear programming (MILP) model. In Sect. 3, the proposed matheuristic algorithm is described.

Section 4 presents the computational results and evaluation of the proposed method. Finally, Sect. 5 concludes the paper and presents some directions for future research.

2 Problem Description

This section describes the investigated 3D-printing scheduling problem, its assumptions, and the mathematical model. There is a set of parts ($i \in I$) with specific properties that must be produced on a set of parallel SLM machines ($m \in M$), while machines have different area of build platform (CA_m) and height of build platform (CH_m). The characteristics of the parts include material type ($Mt_i \in K$), area (ap_i), height (hp_i), volume (vp_i), desired quality ($Qu_i \in Q$), as well as the due date (dd_i) and tardiness penalty per time unit (tc_i). There is a set of batches ($b \in B$), and the parts with different families (different material types or different desired quality) cannot be assigned to the same batch. The processing speed of the machine depends on the material type and the desired quality of its allocated batch, and the processing time of each batch depends on the total volume and the maximum height of its assigned parts. In other words, the total volume of parts affects the total time required to melt the metal powder and the maximum height of assigned parts affects the number of times to add a new layer of metal powder. After processing each batch, the cleaning and setting of machines should be performed for starting the next batch, while the time required for the new setup depends on the material type of the previous batch. Other parameters and variables and the corresponding mathematical model (Model 1) are as follows.

Parameters

vt_m^{kq} Time for melting material k with quality q on machine m per volume unit

ht_m^k Time required for powder layering of material type k on machine m

σ_m^{0k} Setup time to start the first batch with material type k on machine m

$\sigma_m^{kk'}$ Setup time required to start the batch with material type k on machine m when the material type of the previous batch on the machine was k'

G Big positive number

Variables

x_{ibm} 1 if part i is processed in batch b by machine m; 0, otherwise

y_{mb}^{kq} 1 if material k is employed for batch b on machine m to produce the parts with quality q; 0, otherwise

p_{mb} Processing time of batch b on machine m

tr_i Tardiness of part i

C_{mb} Completion time of batch b on machine m

c_i Completion time of part i

$$Min \sum_{i \in I} tc_i \cdot tr_i \qquad \forall i \tag{1}$$

$$s.t. \sum_{m \in M} \sum_{b \in B} x_{ibm} = 1 \qquad \forall i \tag{2}$$

$$\sum_{i \in I} ap_i \cdot x_{ibm} \leq CA_m \qquad \forall m, \forall b \tag{3}$$

$$hp_i \cdot x_{ibm} \leq CH_m \qquad \forall i, \forall m, \forall b \tag{4}$$

$$y_{mb}^{kq} \cdot G \geq \sum_{\substack{i \in I \,|\, Mt_i = k \\ \& \, Qu_i = q}} x_{ibm} \qquad \forall m, \forall k, \forall q, \forall b \tag{5}$$

$$\sum_{k \in K} \sum_{q \in Q} y_{mb}^{kq} \leq 1 \qquad \forall m, \forall b \tag{6}$$

$$y_{mb}^{kq} \leq \sum_{\substack{i \in I \,|\, Mt_i = k \\ \& \, Qu_i = q}} x_{ibm} \qquad \forall m, \forall k, \forall q, \forall b \tag{7}$$

$$\sum_{\substack{i' \in I \\ |\, Mt_{i'} = k \\ \& \, Qu_{i'} = q}} x_{i'bm} \leq G \cdot (1 - x_{ibm}) \quad \forall i, \forall m, \forall k, \forall q, \forall b \,|\, (Mt_i \neq k \text{ or } Qu_i \neq q) \tag{8}$$

$$p_{mb} \geq vt_m^{kq} \sum_{i \in I} vp_i \cdot x_{ibm} + ht_m^k \cdot \max_{i \in I} \{hp_i \cdot x_{ibm}\} - G \cdot (1 - y_{mb}^{kq}) \quad \forall m, \forall k, \forall q, \forall b \tag{9}$$

$$\sum_{i \in I} x_{ib+1m} \leq G \cdot \sum_{i \in I} x_{ibm} \qquad \forall m, \forall b \leq B - 1 \tag{10}$$

$$C_{m1} \geq p_{m1} + \sigma_m^{0k} - G \cdot (1 - \sum_{q \in Q} y_{m1}^{kq}) \qquad \forall m, \forall k, b = 1 \tag{11}$$

$$C_{mb} \geq C_{mb-1} + p_{mb} + \sigma_m^{k'k} + G \cdot (\sum_{q \in Q} y_{mb-1}^{k'q} + \sum_{q \in Q} y_{mb}^{kq} - 2) \qquad \forall m, \forall k, k', b \neq 1 \tag{12}$$

$$c_i \geq C_{mb} - G \cdot (1 - x_{ibm}) \qquad \forall i, \forall m, \forall b \tag{13}$$

$$tr_i \geq c_i - dd_i \qquad \forall i \tag{14}$$

$$x_{ibm}, y_{mb}^{kq} \in \{0, 1\}; \ C_{mb}, c_i, tr_i, p_{mb} \geq 0 \qquad \forall i, \forall m, \forall k, \forall q, \forall b \tag{15}$$

The relation (1) indicates the objective function of the problem, which is the minimization of the total tardiness cost. Constraint (2) ensures that each part is assigned to one batch. The capacities of SLM machines in terms of area and height of building platform is observed by constraints (3) and (4). Constraints (2)–(7) determine the material type and quality of each formed batch. Constraint (8) prevents the assignment of parts with different material and desired quality to the same batch. The production time of each batch based on the total material volume and the maximum height of its assigned parts is determined by constraint (9). This constraint can be linearized by using variable $\gamma_{m,b}$ instead of $\max_{i \in I}\{hp_i \cdot x_{ibm}\}$ while $\gamma_{m,b} \geq (hp_i \cdot x_{ibm})$ for all i, m and b. Constraint (10) ensures that the parts cannot be assigned to a specific batch while its previous batch is not formed. This constraint, along with constraints (11) and (12) are necessary to determine the completion time of the batches. The tardiness of each part is computed by constraints (13) and (14). Finally, Constraint (15) specifies the ranges for the variables of Model 1.

3   Solution Procedure

In this section, a hybrid algorithm called GA-MLS-α% is proposed based on a hybridization of the genetic algorithm (GA) and a local search based on mixed-integer programming (MIP-based local search). In this hybrid algorithm, the GA is used to optimize the sub-problems related to determining the sequence of parts, and allocation of parts to the machine. Then the assignment of parts to the batches is performed by an effective heuristic named batching heuristic. Finally, the MIP-based local search is implemented on the α% of the best solutions in the current population to exchange the batch of parts respecting their sequence. This process continues until the termination condition is met. This procedure is terminated by reaching one of the cases i) a given number of iterations or ii) a computational time limit. Figure 1 illustrates the procedure of the proposed algorithm.

Fig. 1. Schematic pattern of proposed Mathcuristic algorithm

3.1   Solution Representation and Initial Population

The utilized solution representation consists of a matrix S with two rows and $|I|$ columns. In the S matrix, the elements of the first row indicate the set of parts $(i \in I)$ while their arrangement delineates the relative execution sequence of parts. The components in the second row determine the assigned machines to their corresponding part in the first row. Figure 2 shows a solution for a problem with 10 parts and 2 machines. In this figure, the columns with the same color show parts that have the same material type and desired quality (same family). For generating the initial population different rules are applied. Sequence of parts is obtained by three rules using: i) random generation ii) shortest processing time (SPT) first and iii) earliest due date (EDD) first. Moreover, the assignment of machines to parts is obtained i) randomly and by ii) earliest time of machine availability (ETA) rule [12].

Parts	8	6	5	2	10	1	3	7	9	4
Machines	2	1	1	2	1	2	1	2	1	1

Fig. 2. Solution representation for a problem with 10 parts and 2 machines

3.2   Crossover and Mutation Operators

The crossover and mutation operators are performed in the same way that proposed by Rohaninejad et al. [13] In the crossover operator, first, ρ $(1 \leq \rho < I)$ parts are randomly selected. Then, all selected parts are transferred to the first offspring in the same sequence and position related to the first parent. The assigned machines for these parts are selected from the second parent. Next, the remaining parts are transferred to the offspring respecting their sequence in the second parent, and their assigned machines are determined according to the first parent. A reverse procedure of the first offspring is used for the second offspring. In the mutation operator, first, 50% of the parts are selected randomly, and their sequence and assigned machines are determined randomly as well. The remained parts are copied to the mutated individual according to their order of placement and machine assignment in the previous individual.

3.3 Batching Heuristic Method

This section presents an effective heuristic for the assignment of parts to batches. As shown in Fig. 2, the proposed solution representation lacks any information regarding this decision variable. This pattern of solution representation contributes to a faster search in the solution space and provides feasible solutions in any condition in combination with the proposed batching heuristic. In this method, the parts are assigned to an opened batch as much as possible with maximum observance of their sequence. Algorithm 1 shows the pseudo code of the proposed batching heuristic method.

Algorithm 1: Batching (assignment of parts to the batches) heuristic

---

Result: The corresponding schedule of solution representation
input : The solution representation matrix (S); $nb = 0$; MC=[ ]; MK=[ ]; RC=[ ]
for $\rho = 1$ *to* $|I|$ **do**
    $i = S[1, \rho]$ and $m = S[2, \rho]$ and $k = Mt_i$
    if $\nexists$ *batch* $b \leq nb$ *while* $MC[b] = m$ *and* $MK[b] = k$ *and* $RC[b] \geq ap_i$ **then**
        Open new batch $(b = nb + 1)$ and $b \leftarrow i$
        $MC[b] = m$; $MK[b] = k$; $RC[b] = CA_m - ap_i$
        $nb = nb + 1$
    else
        Find the smallest b which $MC[b]=m$ and $MK[b]=k$ and $RC[b] \geq ap_i$ **then**
        $b \leftarrow i$ and $RC[b] = RC[b] - ap_i$

3.4 MIP-Based Local Search

In each iteration of the solution algorithm, an MIP-based local search is performed on the $\alpha\%$ of the best solutions in the current population. The MIP-based local search explores the neighborhood of the original solution. According to this local search, the batching decision variables will be optimized again by a new MIP model (Model 2) with respect to the sequence of parts and their assigned machines corresponding to the original solution. The proposed local search steps in each iteration of the GA are as follows respectively.

- Create set $\mathbb{E}$ including $\alpha\%$ of the best solutions in the current population.

- Set the model 2 for each solution in $\mathbb{E}$.
- Solve model 2 for each solution in $\mathbb{E}$ and determine the batching variables again.

In Model 2, the objective function (1) and constraints (4), (6), (11), (12), (14), and (15) are repeated without any change. Constraints (3), (2), (7), (8), (9), (10) and (13) just needs to be written for every combination of m and i that $\omega[m, i] > 0$. The constraint (2) is replaced by constraint (16) and the constraints (17) and (18) must be added in Model 2. Constraint (17) ensures that the order of the parts with the same material and quality is according to their order on the original solution. Constraint (18) guarantees that the parts can be processed before a part with a lower sequence number just to fill the remaining capacity of the previous batches.

$\varphi[m]$ Number of parts that assigned to the machine m

$\omega[m, i]$ Sequence number of part i in solution representation if m is assigned to i; 0, otherwise

$$\sum_{b \in B \mid b \leq \varphi[m]} x_{ibm} = 1 \qquad \forall i, \forall m \mid \omega[m, i] > 0 \tag{16}$$

$$\sum_{b'=1 \mid b' \leq \varphi[m] \,\&\, b' > b} x_{ib'm} \leq G.(1 - x_{i'bm})$$
$$\forall i, \forall i', \forall m, \forall b \mid \omega[m, i] > 0 \,\&\, \omega[m, i'] > 0 \,\&\, \omega[m, i] < \omega[m, i'] \tag{17}$$
$$\&\, Mt_i = Mt_{i'} \,\&\, Qu_i = Qu_{i'}$$

$$\sum_{\substack{i' \in I \\ \mid \omega[m, i'] > 0 \\ \omega[m, i'] > \omega[m, i] \\ \&\, Mt_{i'} \neq Mt_i \\ \&\, Qu_{i'} \neq Qu_i}} x_{i'bm} \leq G.(1 - x_{ib'm}) + G. \sum_{\substack{i' \in I \\ \mid \omega[m, i'] > 0 \\ \omega[m, i'] < \omega[m, i]}} x_{i'bm} \tag{18}$$

$$\forall i, \forall m, \forall b \leq \varphi[m], \forall b' \leq \varphi[m] \mid b < b' \,\&\, \omega[m, i] > 0$$

4   Computational Results

In this section, 10 random instances are solved to evaluate the validation of Model 1 and efficiency of the proposed algorithm. The instances are labeled with $(I - M - F)$, which represent the number of parts, machines, and job families, respectively. The proposed algorithm with different $\alpha\%$ (GA_MLS_$\alpha\%$) is compared with two different metaheuristic algorithms that named GA_BH and GA_ATC and the mathematical formulation (Model 1). The GA_BH algorithm is developed based on combination of proposed genetic algorithm and batching heuristic. The GA_ATC is a custom version of the genetic algorithm that presented by Balasubramanian et al. [14]. They proposed a GA-based algorithm for $(\mathbf{P_m}|batch, incompatible| \sum w_j T_j)$ while first assigns jobs to machines using a GA, then forms batches on each machine and sequences them by a dispatching rule called Apparent Tardiness Cost (ATC). In this study the GA algorithms and mathematical models (Models 1 and 2) are coded by Python. Also, we have used the CPLEX solver for solving the mathematical models. For each algorithm, we have set the run-time limit to 1800 s. In Table 1, a detailed results of proposed algorithms are given. In order to analyze the results of the table, first the RPD% criteria is calculated for each algorithm. The RPD% specifies the Relative Percentage Deviation from mean of the objective functions that obtained by each algorithm. Accordingly, an efficient algorithm has a lower value of RPD%. Based on this criteria, it can be found that the GA_MLS_10% is the best algorithm with the average of RPD% equal to −6.6%. The average of RPD% for all instances are equal to −3.3%, −2.9%, 3.6%, 2.9% and 6.4% for GA_MLS_5%, GA_MLS_15%, GA_BH, GA_ATC and CPLEX, respectively.

Figure 3 shows the computational time of different proposed algorithms. According to this figure, the GA_MLS_α% algorithms are defensibly able to solve medium-size problems in a reasonable time.

Table 1. Compare performance of the proposed algorithms

Instances	CPLEX		GA-BH		GA-ATC		GA-MLS-5%		GA-MLS-10%		GA-MLS-15%	
	Best Obj	Time (s)	Best Obj	Time (s)	Best Obj	Time (s)	Best Obj	Time (s)	Best Obj	Time (s)	Best Obj	Time (s)
8-2-2	839	50	839	6	885	8	839	11	839	18	839	26
10-2-2	504	127	732	9	732	11	732	17	504	32	504	44
12-2-4	1805	>1800	1688	12	1956	15	1688	35	1688	72	1688	106
15-3-4	2994	>1800	2712	16.6	2740	22	2728	57	2642	102	2606	152
20-2-6	4779	>1800	4627	18	5074	34	4472	149	4472	330	4413	492
25-3-6	10683	>1800	10472	23	11027	55	10521	285	9860	498	10412	729
30-3-6	8840	>1800	8316	26	8532	86	8467	401	8320	784	8145	1144
35-3-6	7768	>1800	7477	28	6430	164	5925	722	5860	1365	5925	>1800
40-3-6	15318	>1800	10548	36	12919	123	9155	1640	10441	>1800	12370	>1800
45-4-6	13664	>1800	11203	56	10036	238	9712	>1800	10285	>1800	12421	>1800
Average	**6689**	**>1457**	**6098**	**23**	**5795**	**76**	**5423**	**>512**	**5491**	**>680**	**5932**	**>810**

The box plot in Fig. 4 is employed and depicted based on RPD% criteria of GA_BH, GA_ATC and GA_MLS_10% as the best of GA_MLS_α% algorithms. According to Fig. 4 the GA_MLS_10% has significantly better performance so that 3/4 of its RPD values are at least smaller than 3/4 of the RPD values related to other methods.

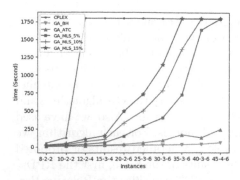

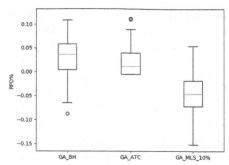

Fig. 3. Comparing computational time

Fig. 4. Comparing the RPD% (Box plot)

5   Conclusion

This research addresses a scheduling problem in an AM environment with unrelated SLM machines and incompatible job families. A new mathematical model is presented and due to the high complexity of the problem, an efficient matheuristic method based on the combination of genetic algorithm and a MIP-based local search was developed. Computational results showed the efficiency of the proposed matheuristic method especially for medium-sized problems.

Combination of scheduling and bin packing of parts in 3D-printing machines can be an interesting topic for further research. Besides, studying the given problem with stochastic parameters (e.g., setup time, demand, and available time of machines) brings the problem closer to more realistic conditions.

Acknowledgements. The research has been supported by the Ministry of Education, Youth and Sports within the dedicated program ERC CZ under the project POSTMAN with reference LL1902.

References

1. Berman, B.: 3D printing: the new industrial revolution. Bus. Horiz. **55**(2), 155–162 (2012)
2. Rajaguru, K., Karthikeyan, T., Vijayan, V.: Additive manufacturing-State of art. Mater. Today Proc. **21**, 628–633 (2020)
3. Li, Q., Kucukkoc, I., Zhang, D.Z.: Production planning in additive manufacturing and 3D printing. Comput. Oper. Res. **83**, 157–172 (2017)
4. Dvorak, F., Micali, M., Mathieug, M.: Planning and scheduling in additive manufacturing. Inteligencia Artif. **21**(62), 40–52 (2018)
5. Li, Q., Zhang, D., Wang, S., Kucukkoc, I.: A dynamic order acceptance and scheduling approach for additive manufacturing on-demand production. Int. J. Adv. Manuf. Technol. **105**(9), 3711–3729 (2019). https://doi.org/10.1007/s00170-019-03796-x

6. Zhou, L., Zhang, L., Laili, Y., Zhao, C., Xiao, Y.: Multi-task scheduling of distributed 3D printing services in cloud manufacturing. Int. J. Adv. Manuf. Technol. **9**, 3003–3017 (2018). https://doi.org/10.1007/s00170-017-1543-z
7. Mai, J., Zhang, L., Tao, F., Ren, L.: Customized production based on distributed 3D printing services in cloud manufacturing. Int. J. Adv. Manuf. Technol. **9**, 71–83 (2015). https://doi.org/10.1007/s00170-015-7871-y
8. Vahedi-Nouri, B., Tavakkoli-Moghaddam, R., Rohaninejad, M.: A multi-objective scheduling model for a cloud manufacturing system with pricing, equity, and order rejection. IFAC-PapersOnLine **52**(13), 2177–2182 (2019)
9. Griffiths, V., Scanlan, J.P., Eres, M.H., Martinez-Sykora, A., Chinchapatnam, P.: Cost-driven build orientation and bin packing of parts in Selective Laser Melting (SLM). Eur. J. Oper. Res. **273**(1), 334–352 (2019)
10. Zhang, J., Yao, X., Li, Y.: Improved evolutionary algorithm for parallel batch processing machine scheduling in additive manufacturing. Int. J. Prod. Res. **58**(8), 2263–2282 (2020)
11. Kucukkoc, I.: MILP models to minimise makespan in additive manufacturing machine scheduling problems. Comput. Oper. Res. **105**, 58–67 (2019)
12. Rohaninejad, M., Sahraeian, R., Nouri, B.V.: Multi-objective optimization of integrated lot-sizing and scheduling problem in flexible job shops. RAIRO-Oper. Res. **50**(3), 587–609 (2016)
13. Rohaninejad, M., Kheirkhah, A., Fattahi, P., Vahedi-Nouri, B.: A hybrid multi-objective genetic algorithm based on the ELECTRE method for a capacitated flexible job shop scheduling problem. Int. J. Adv. Manuf. Technol. **9**, 51–66 (2014). https://doi.org/10.1007/s00170-014-6415-1
14. Balasubramanian, H., Mönch, L., Fowler, J., Pfund, M.: Genetic algorithm based scheduling of parallel batch machines with incompatible job families to minimize total weighted tardiness. Int. J. Prod. Res. **42**(8), 1621–1638 (2004)

An Iterated Greedy Matheuristic for Scheduling in Steelmaking-Continuous Casting Process

Juntaek Hong[iD], Kwansoo Lee, Kangbok Lee[(✉)][iD], and Kyungduk Moon[iD]

Pohang University of Science and Technology, Pohang, South Korea
kblee@postech.ac.kr

Abstract. The steelmaking-continuous casting (SCC) is a bottleneck process in the steel production. Due to elevated product variety and environmental restrictions on the steelmaking industry, efficient operation of the SCC has become more crucial. This paper considers an SCC scheduling problem to minimize the weighted sum of total waiting time, total earliness, and total tardiness while satisfying the maximum waiting time and the continuous casting constraints. We propose a generic mixed integer linear programming (MILP) model that can express various SCC scheduling requirements. Using the MILP model, we develop an iterated greedy matheuristic inspired by the iterated greedy method. An initial SCC schedule is constructed by solving small MILP models one after another. Then, it is improved by solving a series of small MILP models representing the destruction and construction of the prior schedule. Through a numerical experiment, we show that the proposed algorithm can obtain efficient solutions in a short time and outperforms an NSGA-II algorithm for most test cases of practical size.

Keywords: SCC scheduling · MILP · Iterated greedy · Matheuristic

1 Introduction

Due to a compelling pressure on environmental sustainability, strict regulations have been applied to steel companies on expanding their production capacity. In addition, customers require a variety of products that are produced with different processes. This calls for better operations and scheduling capabilities to fully utilize the running equipment. Steel production involves three main phases called ironmaking, steelmaking-continuous casting (SCC), and rolling [6]. Among these three phases, the SCC is a bottleneck process and thus its scheduling has a significant impact on productivity.

The SCC process consists of three consecutive stages: steelmaking, refining, and continuous casting. During the SCC process, molten iron is processed as a batch called a *charge*, which has a target chemical composition. The *steelmaking* stage is to produce molten steel from molten iron by removing impurities and

© IFIP International Federation for Information Processing 2021
Published by Springer Nature Switzerland AG 2021
A. Dolgui et al. (Eds.): APMS 2021, IFIP AICT 630, pp. 62–72, 2021.
https://doi.org/10.1007/978-3-030-85874-2_7

adding particular substances. Through *refining* stages, the chemical composition of a charge is further adjusted to a target value. A steel company may have different types of refining stages according to applied technologies such as CS, LF, RH, and CASOB [3]. These refining stages often have an order that a charge is processed through; however, a charge may skip certain refining stages according to its associated final product. The *continuous casting* stage is to make a solid and flat cuboid called a *slab* from multiple charges. To produce slabs, charges must be continuously poured into a machine one by one without idle time. A sequence of charges to be cast continuously in a casting machine is called a *cast*.

The main challenge in SCC scheduling comes from continuous casting and strict waiting time constraints between stages. By continuous casting restrictions, charges in a cast must arrive at the continuous casting stage in a timely manner. This makes the SCC scheduling difficult since all of the previous stages for those charges need to be finished within a very short time range. Moreover, the temperature of a charge needs to be maintained during waiting time between two processes. If the temperature drops, the charge must be reheated with additional cost and the charge may have serious quality issues. To prevent this, the waiting time between two consecutive stages for each charge has a maximum limit. These two constraints are essential in the SCC scheduling; however, it is difficult to achieve them at the same time. Some recent studies have used artificial bee colony algorithm [7], non-dominated sorting genetic algorithm-II (NSGA-II) [5], and Lagrangian relaxation [1] to solve SCC scheduling problems. We refer to [4] as the summary for previous studies.

In this paper, we propose a generic mixed integer linear programming (MILP) model that can handle most of the practical requirements found in the literature such as stage skipping and unrelated speed of machines. We present our model and its assumptions in Sect. 2. In Sect. 3, we develop an algorithm consisting of initial solution heuristic and improving heuristic using our MILP model. Our algorithm employs small MILP subproblems to express hard constraints, which is the key difference from the previous (meta)heuristics. Our numerical experiment in Sect. 4 shows that the MILP-based algorithm outperforms an NSGA-II for most test instances.

2   Problem Description

We consider the steelmaking stage (SM), multiple refining stages in an order (e.g., RF1, ..., RF3), and the continuous casting stage (CC). Each stage has unrelated parallel machines; in other words, the processing time of a charge at a stage depends on the machine to which the charge is assigned. The transportation time between two stages depends on the pair of machines that a charge is processed by. A cast has a sequence of charges that must be continuously processed without idle time at the CC stage. We model this condition as a large penalty for the idle time in the objective. We call this the *cast break penalty*, which must be minimized to be 0 through optimization. At the last stage, the first charge of a cast needs a setup time of a given duration.

A charge has its own given route for visiting stages such that (i) the route follows a stage sequence, (ii) SM is the first stage, (iii) CC is the last stage, and (iv) some refining stages can be skipped. The waiting time of a charge between two consecutive stages in its route has a maximum limit. Each charge has a due date at the CC stage. If processing of a charge at the CC stage is completed earlier or later than its due date, earliness penalty or tardiness penalty is incurred proportional to the time difference. The objective is to minimize the weighted sum of penalties for cast break, the total waiting time of charges, the total earliness, and the total tardiness. We use the following notations to develop our MILP model.

Parameters

Ω The set of all charges, $\Omega = \{1, 2, ..., n\}$ where n is the number of charges

K The set of all casts, $K = \{1, 2, ..., m\}$ where m is the number of casts

Ω_k The sequence of charges in cast k, $\Omega_k := \{\Omega_k[1], \Omega_k[2], ..., \Omega_k[n_k]\}$ where n_k is the number of charges in cast k ($\forall k \in K$)

$\hat{\Omega}_k$ The set of pairs of two consecutive charges in cast k,
$\hat{\Omega}_k := \{(\Omega_k[s], \Omega_k[s+1]) : s \in \{1, 2, ..., n_k - 1\}\}$ ($\forall k \in K$)

J The sequence of all stages, $J = \{1, 2, ..., l\}$ where l is the last stage for CC

J_i The sequence of stages in charge i's route, $J_i := \{J_i[1], J_i[2], ..., J_i[l_i]\}$ ($\forall i \in \Omega$) where l_i is the number of stages in charge i's route ($\forall i \in \Omega$); $J_i[1] = 1, J_i[l_i] = l$

$\hat{J}_i$ The set of pairs of two consecutive stages in the route of charge i,
$\hat{J}_i := \{(J_i[w], J_i[w+1]) : w \in \{1, 2, ..., l_i - 1\}\}$ ($\forall i \in \Omega$)

H_j The set of machines at stage j ($\forall j \in J$)

p_{ijh} The processing time of charge i at stage j on machine h ($\forall i \in \Omega, j \in J_i, h \in H_j$)

$t_{h,h'}$ The transportation time from machine h to h' ($\forall h, h' \in \bigcup_{j \in J} H_j$)

r_{ij} The earliest release time of charge i at stage j given as
$r_{i1} := 0$ and $r_{ij'} := r_{ij} + \min_{h \in H_j, h' \in H_{j'}}\{p_{ijh} + t_{h,h'}\}$ for $\forall i \in \Omega, (j, j') \in \hat{J}_i$

S_{kh} The setup time of cast k on machine h at the last stage ($\forall k \in K, h \in H_l$)

d_i The due date of charge i at the last stage ($\forall i \in \Omega$)

τ The maximum waiting time

E_1-E_4 Coefficients of penalty for (cast break/waiting time/earliness/tardiness)

Q A sufficiently large number

Decision Variables (Domain)

X_{irj} 1 if charge i precedes charge r on the same machine at stage j, 0 otherwise ($X_{irj} \in \{0, 1\}$ for $\forall i, r \in \Omega, i \neq r, j \in J_i \cap J_r$)

Y_{ijh} 1 if charge i at stage j is assigned to machine h, 0 otherwise ($Y_{ijh} \in \{0, 1\}$ for $\forall i \in \Omega, j \in J_i, h \in H_j$)

C_{ij} The completion time of charge i at stage j ($C_{ij} \geq 0$ for $\forall i \in \Omega, j \in J_i$)

u_{ih} The idle time between two consecutive charges i and i' in a cast
on machine h at the last stage ($u_{ih} \geq 0$ for $\forall k \in K, (i, i') \in \hat{\Omega}_k, h \in H_l$)
W_{ij} The waiting time of charge i between consecutive stages j and j' in its
route
($W_{ij} \geq 0$ for $\forall i \in \Omega, (j, j') \in \hat{J}_i$)
α_i The earliness of charge i ($\alpha_i \geq 0$ for $\forall i \in \Omega$)
β_i The tardiness of charge i ($\beta_i \geq 0$ for $\forall i \in \Omega$)

The Master MILP

Minimize

$$E_1 \cdot \sum_{k=1}^{m} \sum_{s=1}^{n_k-1} \sum_{h \in H_l} u_{\Omega_k[s],h} + E_2 \cdot \sum_{i=1}^{n} \sum_{w=1}^{l_i-1} W_{i,J_i[w]} + E_3 \cdot \sum_{i=1}^{n} \alpha_i + E_4 \cdot \sum_{i=1}^{n} \beta_i \quad (1)$$

subject to

$$\sum_{h \in H_j} Y_{ijh} = 1 \qquad \forall i \in \Omega, j \in J_i \qquad (2)$$

$$X_{irj} + X_{rij} \geq Y_{ijh} + Y_{rjh} - 1 \qquad \forall i, r \in \Omega, i \neq r, j \in J_i \cap J_r, h \in H_j \qquad (3)$$

$$X_{irj} + X_{rij} \leq 1 - (Y_{ijh} - Y_{rjh}) \qquad \forall i, r \in \Omega, i \neq r, j \in J_i \cap J_r, h \in H_j \qquad (4)$$

$$Y_{ilh} = Y_{rlh} \qquad \forall k \in K, (i, r) \in \hat{\Omega}_k, h \in H_l \qquad (5)$$

$$X_{irl} = 1 \qquad \forall k \in K, (i, r) \in \hat{\Omega}_k \qquad (6)$$

$$C_{ij} \geq r_{ij} + p_{ijh} \cdot Y_{ijh} \qquad \forall i \in \Omega, j \in J_i, h \in H_j \qquad (7)$$

$$C_{rj} - C_{ij} \geq p_{rjh} - Q(2 - Y_{ijh} - Y_{rjh} + X_{rij}) \qquad (8)$$
$$\forall i, r \in \Omega, i \neq r, j \in J_i \cap J_r, h \in H_j$$

$$C_{rl} - C_{il} \geq (p_{rlh} + S_{kl}) - Q(2 - Y_{ilh} - Y_{rlh} + X_{ril}) \qquad (9)$$
$$\forall k, q \in K, k \neq q, h \in H_l, (i, r) = (\Omega_q[n_q], \Omega_k[1])$$

$$C_{ij'} - (C_{ij} + W_{ij}) \geq (t_{h,h'} + p_{ij'h'}) - Q(2 - Y_{ijh} - Y_{ij'h'}) \qquad (10)$$
$$\forall i \in \Omega, (j, j') \in \hat{J}_i, h \in H_j, h' \in H_{j'}$$

$$C_{ij'} - (C_{ij} + W_{ij}) \leq (t_{h,h'} + p_{ij'h'}) + Q(2 - Y_{ijh} - Y_{ij'h'}) \qquad (11)$$
$$\forall i \in \Omega, (j, j') \in \hat{J}_i, h \in H_j, h' \in H_{j'}$$

$$u_{ih} - (C_{rl} - C_{il} - p_{rlh}) \geq -Q(1 - Y_{rlh}) \qquad (12)$$
$$\forall k \in K, (i, r) \in \hat{\Omega}_k, h \in H_l$$

$$\beta_i - \alpha_i = C_{il} - d_i \qquad \forall i \in \Omega \qquad (13)$$

$$W_{ij} \leq \tau \qquad \forall i \in \Omega, j \in J_i \qquad (14)$$

The objective function (1) is to minimize the total weighted penalty. Each term denotes the penalty for cast break, the total waiting time, the earliness, and the tardiness, respectively. Constraints (2) ensure that a charge is assigned to exactly one machine at each stage in its route. Constraints (3) and (4) restrict either of two charges precedes the other if and only if they are assigned to the same machine in each stage. Constraints (5) imply that the charges in a cast must be assigned to the same machine at the last stage, and constraints (6) restrict their precedence to conform with the given sequence. Constraints (7) mean that a charge can be processed only after its release time at a stage. Constraints (8) restrict a charge to be processed only after its preceding charges at the same machine are processed. Constraints (9) mean that the first charge of a cast needs a setup time after completing the last charge of preceding casts. Constraints (10) and (11) imply that the difference of the completion times at two consecutive stages is the sum of waiting time, transportation time, and the processing time at the later stage. Constraints (12) define the idle time between two consecutive charges in a cast at the last stage. Note that the equality holds if the idle time is minimized to be zero. Constraints (13) are from the definition of the earliness and the tardiness of a charge. Constraints (14) provide a limit on the maximum waiting time between two consecutive stages. The domain of each variable is presented together with its definition.

3 Solution Methodology

We develop the iterated greedy matheuristic for SCC process scheduling following the framework by [8]. We sequentially add cast after cast to construct an initial schedule considering the earliness and tardiness function of each cast. We propose two heuristics using destruction and construction (DC) of a part of a schedule to improve the objective value. We call them DC-cast and DC-charge according to the destruction method. Construction is done by solving an MILP where most of binary variables remain fixed. After applying DC-cast and DC-charge heuristics, the resulting solution is passed to an MILP solver to improve their objective value until a given time limit is reached.

3.1 Finding an Initial Schedule

Let MILP(K') be the MILP model in Sect. 2 with restricted set of casts $K' \subseteq K$ (e.g., MILP(K) denotes the master MILP). We first find the 'desired starting time' of each cast $(:=t_k^*)$, which is the starting time of the first charge of cast k in the optimal solution of MILP($\{k\}$) for $k \in K$. We reindex K following the ascending order of t_k^*. An initial solution is generated by sequentially assigning binary variables for all of the charges in cast k in K. Let $\Lambda(k)$ and $\tilde{\Lambda}(k)$ denote the sets of binary variables and their fixed values in MILP($\{1, \ldots, k\}$), respectively. We can find an initial schedule according to the following procedure.

Initial Heuristic $(:=$IH$)$

1) Solve MILP($\{1\}$) and determine $\tilde{\Lambda}(1)$ from $\Lambda(1)$ part of an optimal solution.
2) For $k = 2$ to m
   Solve MILP($\{1, \ldots, k\}$) subject to $\Lambda(k-1) = \tilde{\Lambda}(k-1)$

Determine $\tilde{\Lambda}(k)$ from $\Lambda(k)$ part of an optimal solution.

Figure 1 shows an example with three casts with three charges in each cast. Since an MILP in the loop has a small number of binary variables, an initial schedule can be obtained in a short time.

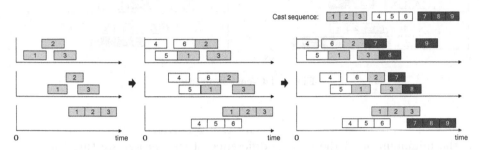

Fig. 1. The initial heuristic

3.2 Improving a Schedule: Destruction and Construction

Given a feasible schedule, we destruct some charges from the schedule and re-insert them to construct possibly a better schedule, and we call it destruction and construction (DC) heuristic. In a mathematical model perspective, if all binary variables are fixed, then all continuous variables can be easily (in a very short time) determined by solving the resulting linear programming model. Thus, we assume a given schedule implies that all binary variables have their fixed values. Then, destruction of charges implies that we relax the corresponding binary variables (sequencing variables X and assignment variables Y) and all continuous variables, but keep the remaining binary variables at their values. Since the resulting MILP after destruction has a small number of binary variables, it can be solved in a short time.

DC-Cast (:=DA)
Suppose a feasible solution of the MILP model is given. The DC-cast heuristic destructs all of the charges in a cast from the given solution and re-optimize their machine assignments and relative position to the other charges. It iterates for casts in K following the increasing order of starting times of first charges in the given schedule. Figure 2 shows an example where the cast containing charges 4–6 is selected.

DC-Charge (:=DH)
The DC-charge heuristic maintains a time window of the given length D for each stage. The algorithm destructs all charges of which the starting times have an overlap with the time windows, and constructs a new schedule by inserting the destructed charges. Then, the time windows are shifted forth by Δ and the procedure is continued until the end of the schedule is reached. Since the starting time of a charge is delayed over stages, we apply the lag of starting times to the

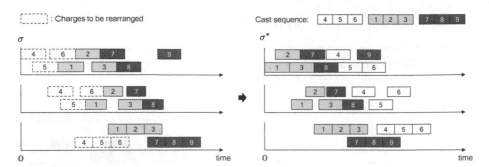

Fig. 2. DC-cast heuristic

windows for two consecutive stages ($:=\delta$). Using a given schedule, δ is computed as the minimum of (i) the average difference of the earliest starting times for the first and the last stages, and (ii) the average difference of latest completion times for the first and the last stages. Figure 3 shows an example where charges 1, 4, 5, and 6 are selected.

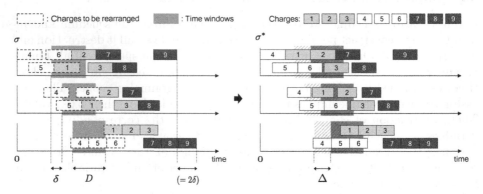

Fig. 3. DC-charge heuristic

3.3 Iterated Greedy Matheuristic

We put the proposed components together in an algorithm which we refer to as the Iterated Greedy Matheuristic (IGM). IGM begins with IH to obtain an initial schedule. Then, we improve the solution by DC heuristic consisting of R^{DA} runs of DA followed by R^{DH} runs of DH. If the objective value is not improved during a run of DA or DH, we stop the successive run and proceed to the next component. The DC heuristic (consisting multiple runs of DA and DH) is repeated R^{DC} times. After obtaining a feasible solution with our heuristics, we feed it into an MILP solver as an incumbent solution to improve it using the master MILP until a given time limit is reached; we call this procedure the

MILP Improvement (MI). In short, IGM can be summarized as the following sequence of algorithms:

$$\text{IH} \to (\text{DA} \times R^{\text{DA}} \text{ times} \to \text{DH} \times R^{\text{DH}} \text{ times}) \times R^{\text{DC}} \text{ times} \to \text{MI}.$$

4   Numerical Results

To demonstrate the performance of the proposed algorithm, we generated problem instances according to realistic production environment.

- Machine environment: SCC process consists of five stages and twelve machines, where the numbers of machines in SM, RF1, RF2, RF3, and CC stage are 4, 2, 2, 2, and 4, respectively.
- Casts: A cast contains three to nine charges. We create casts of random number of charges until the total number of charges is between 30 and 36. Therefore, each problem instance consists of four to twelve casts.
- Charges: The first and last stages are mandatory for all charges, but the three refining stages in the middle are not; a charge has a probability of two-thirds in skipping each refining stage. A processing time (in minutes) of a charge in each machine is generated from uniform distribution; $U(45, 55)$ for the SM stage, $U(30, 40)$ for the RF1, RF2, and RF3 stages, and $U(35, 45)$ for the CC stage.
- Restrictions: Transportation time between all machines $(t_{h,h'})$ are set to be 10 min, and the maximum waiting time (τ) is 30 min. The setup times of casts on all machines at the last stage (S_{kh}) are set to be 30 min.
- Objective coefficients: Penalty for earliness and tardiness is 1, and penalty for the waiting time is 1.5. Since minimizing the cast break has the top priority among objectives, we set cast break penalty coefficient as 100,000.

We set $(D, \Delta, R^{\text{DC}}, R^{\text{DA}}, R^{\text{DH}}) = (90, 90, 2, 3, 1)$ as the control parameters for IGM. We provide the time limit of 60 s to each run of DA and DH. The total time limit for IGM is set as 600 s.

Since our problem is more general than problems discussed in the literature, we compared the proposed solution method with an algorithm based on NSGA-II by [2]. We use a pair of lists as a chromosome representation. The first list represents sequence of casts in each CC machines, and the second represents charges ordered by their completion times in the CC stage. We follow the framework by [2] and genetic operations (crossover and mutation) by [5]. Note that, although it takes negligible time for genetic operations, simple dispatching rules often generate infeasible solutions due to hard constraints. Thus, we also devised a decoding method of solving a linear programming problem to get a feasible solution. We consider another competitor which solves the master MILP model in Sect. 2 (:=MILP). The total time limit for MILP and NSGA-II is set as 1200 s, and the population size of NSGA-II is set as 200. All algorithms are implemented by Gurobi version 9.0.3 using Python 3.8.

In order to evaluate the performance of an algorithm, we define the optimality gap as $(Z - LB)/LB$ where Z is the objective function value found by

Table 1. Comparison of three algorithms

No.	Objective			LB			Optimality gap		
	IGM	MILP	NSGA-II	IGM	MILP	Best	IGM	MILP	NSGA-II
0	4456.0	4591.0	4543.0	4375.0	4375.0	4375.0	1.85%	4.94%	3.84%
1	5350.0	5954.5	5617.0	5209.0	5218.0	5218.0	2.53%	14.11%	7.65%
2	5227.5	6192.5	5653.0	5080.0	5080.0	5080.0	2.90%	21.90%	11.28%
3	4064.5	4583.0	4301.0	3702.0	3707.0	3707.0	9.64%	23.63%	16.02%
4	3929.5	4387.5	4133.0	3865.0	3851.0	3865.0	1.67%	13.52%	6.93%
5	6395.5	6641.0	6527.0	6091.0	5895.2	6091.0	5.00%	9.03%	7.16%
6	4648.5	5466.0	5078.0	4462.0	4433.0	4462.0	4.18%	22.50%	13.81%
7	5671.0	7750.0	5985.5	5321.0	5333.0	5333.0	6.34%	45.32%	12.24%
8	4703.5	5760.0	4995.5	4436.0	4429.0	4436.0	6.03%	29.85%	12.61%
9	5647.0	7572.0	5850.0	5364.0	5088.0	5364.0	5.28%	41.16%	9.06%
10	6500.5	10553.0	7134.0	5955.0	5778.7	5955.0	9.16%	77.21%	19.80%
11	5669.0	6673.5	6075.5	5349.0	5349.0	5349.0	5.98%	24.76%	13.58%
12	5616.5	6830.0	5868.0	5070.0	4863.4	5070.0	10.78%	34.71%	15.74%
13	5493.5	6597.5	5653.0	5363.0	5353.9	5363.0	2.43%	23.02%	5.41%
14	4472.0	5265.5	4719.5	4329.0	4334.0	4334.0	3.18%	21.49%	8.89%
15	4457.5	4895.0	4833.0	4304.0	4305.0	4305.0	3.54%	13.70%	12.26%
16	4007.5	4496.0	4208.5	3758.0	3765.0	3765.0	6.44%	19.42%	11.78%
17	5597.5	5615.0	5627.0	5509.0	5518.0	5518.0	1.44%	1.76%	1.98%
18	4766.5	6722.0	4946.0	4638.0	4649.0	4649.0	2.53%	44.59%	6.39%
19	4634.0	4965.5	4661.0	4536.0	4536.0	4536.0	2.16%	9.47%	2.76%
20	4668.0	5125.0	4813.0	4466.0	4064.2	4466.0	4.52%	14.76%	7.77%
21	5722.0	6609.5	6132.0	5554.0	5554.0	5554.0	3.02%	19.00%	10.41%
22	4573.5	4976.0	4611.0	4059.0	3929.2	4059.0	12.68%	22.59%	13.60%
23	4406.0	4866.5	4432.0	3799.0	3802.0	3802.0	15.89%	28.00%	16.57%
24	5812.0	8509.0	6230.5	5503.0	5511.0	5511.0	5.46%	54.40%	13.06%
25	4621.0	5143.0	4773.0	4528.0	4534.0	4534.0	1.92%	13.43%	5.27%
26	4577.0	4841.5	4651.0	4513.0	4513.0	4513.0	1.42%	7.28%	3.06%
27	4960.5	6591.5	5230.5	4873.0	4797.1	4873.0	1.80%	35.27%	7.34%
28	4914.0	6310.5	5126.0	4539.0	4502.3	4539.0	8.26%	39.03%	12.93%
29	5462.0	6389.0	5707.0	5254.0	5219.3	5254.0	3.96%	21.60%	8.62%
Average							5.07%	25.05%	9.93%

the algorithm and *LB* is the best known lower bound from IGM and MILP. The result of the experiment on 30 randomly generated problem instances is summarized in Table 1. All best solutions by both methods have no cast break.

Table 2. IGM average performance

Comp.	Gap (%)	Improv (%p)	Elapsed time (s)	Comp time (s)
IH	9.15	-	28.2	28.2
DA	6.94	2.20	75.3	47.0
DH	5.62	1.32	175.7	100.4
DA	5.51	0.11	197.8	22.1
DH	5.25	0.26	277.6	79.8
MI	5.07	0.18	600.5	323.0

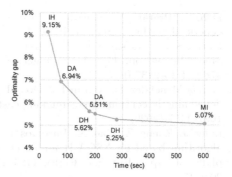

Fig. 4. IGM average performance.

The average optimality gap is 5.07% for IGM, 25.05% for MILP, and 9.93% for NSGA-II. Although only a half amount of time is given, IGM shows better and stable performance; it obtained the best solution in each of all problem instances.

In order to see the performance of each component of IGM, we calculated the average optimality gap of the solution for each of the six components of IGM for 30 practical size instances. The average time for each component is calculated as well. We summarize the average values in Table 2 and visualize them in Fig. 4. As expected, the improvement percentage decreases over time. From the average performance, the user may choose the total running time of the algorithm. Even when only a short computation time is given, IGM yields better solutions than other algorithms; on average, the initial solution of IGM is already better than the final solution of NSGA-II. Moreover, practitioners have the advantage of spending more time on computing since the difference of 0.1% matters in the cost-intensive steel industry.

5   Conclusion

In this paper, we proposed a generic MILP that can handle various features in the SCC scheduling. We also proposed the iterated greedy matheuristic that can find a feasible solution satisfying hard constraints concerning the maximum waiting time and continuous casting. By the numerical results, we showed that our algorithm is able to obtain better solutions than an NSGA-II algorithm with most test instances in less running time. Since our model can encompass most of the essential features found in the literature, it has much potential to be applied for difficult scheduling problems in practice such as rescheduling and controllable processing time.

References

1. Cui, H., Luo, X., Wang, Y.: Scheduling of steelmaking-continuous casting process using deflected surrogate Lagrangian relaxation approach and DC algorithm. Comput. Ind. Eng. **140**, 106271 (2020)

2. Deb, K., Pratap, A., Agarwal, S., Meyarivan, T.: A fast and elitist multiobjective genetic algorithm: NSGA-II. IEEE Trans. Evol. Comput. **6**(2), 182–197 (2002)
3. Dutta, S.K., Chokshi, Y.B.: Secondary steelmaking. In: Basic Concepts of Iron and Steel Making, pp. 497–536. Springer, Singapore (2020). https://doi.org/10.1007/978-981-15-2437-0_17
4. García-Menéndez, D., Morán-Palacios, H., Ortega-Fernández, F., Díaz-Piloñeta, M.: Scheduling in continuous steelmaking casting: a systematic review. ISIJ Int. **60**(6), 1097–1107 (2020)
5. Long, J., Zheng, Z., Gao, X., Pardalos, P.M.: A hybrid multi-objective evolutionary algorithm based on NSGA-II for practical scheduling with release times in steel plants. J. Oper. Res. Soc. **67**(9), 1184–1199 (2016). https://doi.org/10.1057/jors.2016.17
6. Missbauer, H., Hauber, W., Stadler, W.: A scheduling system for the steelmaking-continuous casting process. A case study from the steel-making industry. Int. J. Prod. Res. **47**(15), 4147–4172 (2009)
7. Pan, Q.K.: An effective co-evolutionary artificial bee colony algorithm for steelmaking-continuous casting scheduling. Eur. J. Oper. Res. **250**(3), 702–714 (2016)
8. Ruiz, R., Stützle, T.: A simple and effective iterated greedy algorithm for the permutation flowshop scheduling problem. Eur. J. Oper. Res. **177**(3), 2033–2049 (2007)

Hybridization of Mixed-Integer Linear Program and Discrete Event Systems for Robust Scheduling on Parallel Machines

A. Aubry[1]([✉]), P. Marangé[1], D. Lemoine[2], S. Himmiche[1], and S. Norre[3]

[1] Université de Lorraine, CNRS, CRAN, 54000 Nancy, France
{alexis.aubry,pascale.marange,sara.himmiche}@univ-lorraine.fr
[2] IMT-Atlantique, LS2N UMR 6004, Nantes, France
david.lemoine@imt-atlantique.fr
[3] Clermont Auvergne University, LIMOS UMR 6158, Clermont-Ferrand, France
sylvie.norre@uca.fr

Abstract. This paper proposes an approach for robust scheduling on parallel machines. This approach is based on a combination of robust mathematical and discrete event systems models which are iteratively called in order to converge towards a schedule with the required robustness level defined by the decision maker. Experimentations on a small instance (10 jobs and 2 unrelated machines) and a more complex one (30 jobs and 6 uniform machines) show that this approach permits to converge quickly to a robust schedule even if the probability distribution associated to the uncertainties are not symmetrical. The approach achieves a better rate of convergence than those of the literature's methods.

Keywords: Robust scheduling · Robust mixed integer programming model · Discrete event systems · Parallel machines

1 Introduction

Scheduling under uncertainties is still a present concern in Operation Research and Decision Aiding. Many researchers are interested in determining a robust schedule which is rather insensitive to the data uncertainties and which is able to absorb the perturbations without unreasonably degrading its performances. However, the concept of robustness is differently defined according to the domains. An approach for robust optimization has been proposed by [1], based on a Robust Mixed Integer Programming Model. In order to obtain the robustness level wanted by the decision maker, a vector Ω, which corresponds to the maximum allowed deviation of input parameters, has to be fixed. This vector can be interpreted as a robustness coefficient. The authors have shown

© IFIP International Federation for Information Processing 2021
Published by Springer Nature Switzerland AG 2021
A. Dolgui et al. (Eds.): APMS 2021, IFIP AICT 630, pp. 73–80, 2021.
https://doi.org/10.1007/978-3-030-85874-2_8

that if the uncertainties on parameters are independent and symmetrically distributed, the vector Ω can be analytically computed. But, such an hypothesis is not often verified in real scheduling problems. In [2], a methodology for iteratively and numerically tuning Ω has been proposed thanks to a combination of a robust mathematical programming and Discrete Event Systems models when the probability distribution associated to the uncertainties are not symmetrical. This generic method has been applied on a scheduling problem with parallel machines and the results show that this approach is a good mean for tuning the Ω parameters. However, the mechanism for updating coefficients Ω from one iteration to another was simple and naive. Moreover, it did not take into account the characteristics of the current schedule solution (in particular the load of the machines). As a result, the convergence of the method toward a solution with the required robustness level was relatively slow. Our contribution in this paper is to propose a new mechanism for updating robustness coefficients Ω to increase the rate of convergence of our method in case of scheduling problem on parallel machines. The problem is thus denoted as $RK||C_{max}$ which consists in minimizing the makespan (C_{max}) on K parallel machines.

The paper is built as follows. The first section presents the robust mixed integer programming model for scheduling on parallel machines. The second section presents the methodology and details the mechanism for updating the robustness coefficients Ω. The third section discusses the results on two instances: a simple instance composed of 10 jobs and 2 unrelated machines and a more complex one composed of 30 jobs and 6 uniform machines. Finally, the last section deals with the conclusion and the perspectives.

2   Robust Formulation of $RK||C_{max}$

The main assumptions for $RK||C_{max}$ are the following:

- all jobs are available at time 0,
- the K machines are always available (no breakdown etc.),
- processing times for the jobs are independent,
- a machine cannot process more than one job at any time and preemption is not allowed.

Parameters and decision variables of the model are summarized in Table 1.

Table 1. Notations of the model

N:	Number of jobs which have to be scheduled
K:	Number of parallel machines
t_{jk}:	Processing time for job j on the machine k, $\forall (j,k) \in \{1,\ldots,N\} \times \{1,\ldots,K\}$
x_{jk}:	$\begin{cases} 1 & \text{if } j \text{ is executed on machine } k \\ 0 & \text{otherwise} \end{cases}$, $\forall (j,k) \in \{1,\ldots,N\} \times \{1,\ldots,K\}$
C_{max}:	is the makespan value

Since processing times are uncertain, we assume that

$$\forall (j,k) \in \{1,\ldots,N\} \times \{1,\ldots,K\}, \ t_{jk} \in \left[t_{jk}^{\min}, t_{jk}^{\max}\right]$$

Following the methodology of [1], uncertain processing times are modelled as

$$t_{jk} = \bar{t}_{jk} + \zeta_{jk}\hat{t}_{jk}$$

where

- $\bar{t}_{jk} = \frac{t_{jk}^{\max}+t_{jk}^{\min}}{2}$ and $\hat{t}_{jk} = \frac{t_{jk}^{\max}-t_{jk}^{\min}}{2}$
- ζ_{jk} is a random variable which takes its values in $[-1,1]$

Thus, the robust model can be formulated as follows:

Minimize C_{max} (1)

s.t.

$$\sum_{k=1}^{K} x_{jk} = 1 \quad \forall j \in \{1,\ldots,N\} \tag{2}$$

$$\sum_{j=1}^{N} \bar{t}_{jk}x_{jk} + \max_{\sum_{j=1}^{N}|\zeta_{jk}| \leq \Omega_k} \left(\sum_{j=1}^{N} \hat{t}_{jk}\zeta_{jk}x_{jk}\right) \leq C_{max} \quad \forall k \in \{1,\ldots,K\} \tag{3}$$

$$x_{jk} \in \{0,1\} \quad \forall(j,k) \in \{1,\ldots,N\} \times \{1,\ldots,K\} \tag{4}$$

where $\Omega = (\Omega_k)_{k\in\{1,\ldots,K\}}$ constrains the maximum deviation of processing times allowed on each machine k. It can be interpreted as a robustness coefficient: the larger Ω_k is, the more conservative is the constraint (3). We denote as X^Ω an optimal schedule provided by the robust model with the input Ω and as $C_{\max}(X^\Omega)$, the associated optimal makespan.

Let $\tilde{C}_{\max}(X^\Omega)$ be defined as the random variable associated to the makespan, when X^Ω is executed in the workshop (with the uncertain values t_{jk}). It is possible to define a robustness indicator as the probability that $\tilde{C}_{\max}(X^\Omega)$ is lower than $C_{\max}(X^\Omega)$. More formally, this indicator is given by the Eq. (5):

$$\Gamma(C_{\max}(X^\Omega)) = \mathbb{P}\left[\tilde{C}_{\max}(X^\Omega) \leq C_{\max}(X^\Omega)\right] \tag{5}$$

Our goal is to find Ω to guarantee that the scheduling X^Ω reaches a certain level of robustness Γ^{ref}. As [1] have shown that in case of each ζ_{jk} is symmetrically distributed in $[-1,1]$, determining such Ω can be done analytically. Next section provides a methodology which allows to reach this goal in a general case.

3   Our Methodology

In this section, we denote as X_k^Ω the schedule extracted from X^Ω by considering only the set of jobs processed on machine k, $k \in \{1,\ldots,K\}$.

Basically, our methodology is based on the following observations:

1. In a workshop of parallel machines, machines are independent meaning that

$$\Gamma(C_{\max}(X^{\Omega})) = \prod_{k=1}^{K} \Gamma(C_{\max}(X_k^{\Omega}))$$

2. if $\Gamma(C_{\max}(X^{\Omega})) < \Gamma^{ref}$ then there exists at least one $k \in \{1, \ldots, K\}$ such that $\Gamma(C_{\max}(X_k^{\Omega})) < \sqrt[K]{\Gamma^{ref}}$ which is equivalent to

$$\mathbb{P}\left[\tilde{C}_{\max}(X_k^{\Omega}) \leq C_{\max}(X_k^{\Omega})\right] < \sqrt[K]{\Gamma^{ref}}$$

Thus, for such a k, we estimate a value $\tilde{d}(X_k^{\Omega}) > C_{\max}(X_k^{\Omega})$ for which the following constraint is satisfied.

$$\mathbb{P}\left[\tilde{C}_{\max}(X_k^{\Omega}) \leq \tilde{d}(X_k^{\Omega})\right] = \sqrt[K]{\Gamma^{ref}} \tag{6}$$

Therefore, to obtain this robustness score for the scheduling X_k^{Ω}, we have to compute a new robustness coefficient Ω_k^{new} in order to satisfy the constraint (7).

$$\max_{\sum_{j \in X_k^{\Omega}} |\zeta_{jk}| \leq \Omega_k^{new}} \left(\sum_{j \in X_k^{\Omega}} \hat{t}_{jk}\zeta_{jk}\right) = \tilde{d}(X_k^{\Omega}) - \sum_{j \in X_k^{\Omega}} \bar{t}_{jk} \tag{7}$$

This constraint is derived from (3) in which we allow the deviation of uncertainties constrained by Ω_k^{new} until we reach $\tilde{d}(X_k^{\Omega})$.

As we want to be the less conservative as possible (that means, in our case, that Ω_k^{new} should be as small as possible), the following proposition can be stated:

Proposition 1. *Solving Eq. (7) is equivalent to solve the following continuous Knapsack problem:*

$$Minimize\ \Omega_k^{new} = \sum_{j \in X_k^{\Omega}} \zeta_{jk} \tag{8}$$

s.t.

$$\sum_{j \in X_k^{\Omega}} \hat{t}_{jk}\zeta_{jk} = \tilde{d}(X_k^{\Omega}) - \sum_{j \in X_k^{\Omega}} \bar{t}_{jk} \tag{9}$$

$$\zeta_{jk} \in [0, 1] \quad \forall j \in X_k^{\Omega} \tag{10}$$

As the continuous Knapsack problem is known to be polynomial and can be easily solved by a greedy algorithm, we can use such algorithm to find the value of Ω_k^{new} that satisfies (7).

A similar reasoning can be applied if $\Gamma(C_{\max}(X^{\Omega})) > \Gamma^{ref}$ and leads to the same result.

Based on the previous proposition, our methodology can be summarized into 4 steps:

Step 1: For $\Omega = (\Omega_k)_{k \in \{1,\ldots,K\}}$, an optimization module based on a linear solver provides X^Ω an optimal schedule according to the robust model presented in the previous section [1].

Step 2: Thanks to Discrete Event Systems models and tools, $\Gamma(C_{\max}(X^\Omega))$ is then evaluated. If $\Gamma(C_{\max}(X^\Omega)) \in [\Gamma^{ref} - \epsilon, \Gamma^{ref} + \epsilon]$ then the process stops and X^Ω is the required schedule solution, else the third step is engaged. ϵ is a parameter that helps to fix the required level of accuracy.

Step 3: For each $k \in \{1, \cdots, K\}$, the value of $\tilde{d}(X_k^\Omega)$ that satisfies constraint (6) is then determined thanks to another Discrete Event Systems module. Ω is then updated in the Step 4.

Step 4: Thanks to Eq. (7), $\forall k \in \{1, \cdots, K\}$, Ω_k^{new} is then computed using the Proposition 1 and we loop back to Step 1 with $\Omega = (\Omega_k^{new})_{k \in \{1,\ldots,K\}}$.

Steps 2 and 3 use models and tools from discrete event systems (DES) [3]. Discrete event systems (DES) allow to model the behavior of a system by considering its possible states and the possible events (allowing the evolution from one state to another). The event is an instantaneous occurrence of an action or a phenomenon in the system environment. The evolution on the event occurrence can be deterministic when the behavior is known with certainty or stochastic when the behavior is uncertain and the evolution can lead to different states. The works of [4–6] have shown that DES are particularly relevant for scheduling evaluation due to their ability to model the behavior of industrial systems and perturbations. Indeed, DES allow to represent many dynamic features such as the communication between the elements of the workshop (jobs, resources), the time and the probabilistic behavior of perturbations. Many stochastic discrete event system languages allow to model these characteristics: Stochastic Petri Nets [7], Stochastic automata [8], Stochastic Automata Networks [9].

The method for evaluating the impact of a set of perturbations on a given schedule uses the approach proposed by [4]. The approach models the characteristics of the workshop (operations, resources), and the probability distribution associated to the perturbation by a discretization of this one and allows the evaluation of different elements: the robustness indicator $\Gamma(C_{\max}(X^\Omega))$ as in step 2, the minimal duration $\tilde{d}(X_k^\Omega)$ as in step 3, ...

4 Case Studies

4.1 A Simple Instance

In this first application, 10 jobs are considered. These jobs can be executed on two unrelated parallel machines (the problem is $R2||C_{max}$). Γ^{ref} is fixed to 90% and ϵ is fixed to 1% such that $\Gamma(C_{\max}(X^\Omega))$ has to be in $[89\%, 91\%]$ for concluding to the acceptability of the solution X^Ω. We applied the two approaches defined (from [2] and the presented one) by starting with $\Omega = [0,0]$ (meaning that no uncertainty is considered).

The Table 2 summarizes the results by giving the extremal iterations of the combined approach presented in [2]. Two solutions are explored during the different iterations. The solution $X1$ allocates the first machine to jobs 1, 4, 6, 7, 8 and the second machine to jobs 2, 3, 5, 9, 10. The solution $X2$ allocates the first machine to jobs 1, 4, 6, 7, 8, 10 and the second machine to jobs 2, 3, 5, 9.

Table 2. Obtained iterations for $R2||C_{max}$ with the approach from [2]

Iteration i	Ω	Solution		Ω^{new}
		X^{Ω}	$C_{max}\left(X^{\Omega}\right)$	
0	[0, 0]	X_1	12	[0.10, 0.18]
$\vdots$	$\vdots$	$\vdots$	$\vdots$	$\vdots$
10	[0.53, 0.66]	X_1	13.98	$\emptyset$

Table 3. Obtained iterations for the problem $R2||C_{max}$ with our approach

Iteration i	Input Ω	Step 1		Step 2	Step 3	Step 4
		X^{Ω}	$C_{max}\left(X^{\Omega}\right)$	$\Gamma\left(C_{max}\left(X^{\Omega}\right)\right)$	$\left[\tilde{d}\left(X_k^{\Omega}\right)\right]_{k\in\{1,2\}}$	Ω^{new}
0	[0, 0]	X_1	12	0.65	[13, 14]	[0.50, 0.66]
1	[0.50, 0.66]	X_1	14	0.90	$\emptyset$	$\emptyset$

We can conclude that the improved approach finds the right solution in the first iteration (as $\Gamma\left(C_{max}\left(X^{\Omega}\right)\right) = 90\%$, it is not necessary to update Ω and to run a new iteration). Thus, the improved method decreases drastically the number of necessary iterations for converging to a comparable solution.

4.2 A More Complex Instance

We consider 30 jobs which can be executed on 6 uniform machines (the problems is $Q6||C_{max}$). The machines are such that the first machine is the fastest and the sixth is the slowest. Γ^{ref} is fixed to 90% and ϵ is fixed to 1%.

We applied the two approaches by starting with $\Omega = [0,0,0,0,0,0]$.

The Fig. 1 presents the evolution of the average value of Ω and $\Gamma(C_{max}\left(X_k^{\Omega}\right))$ according to the iteration when applying the two approaches. First, it can be observed that even after 10 iterations, the targeted performance Γ^{ref} is not reached when applying the approach of [2] and $\Gamma\left(C_{max}\left(X_k^{\Omega}\right)\right)$ remains low. Moreover, Ω increases very slowly when applying the approach of [2] in comparison with our approach. We can postulate that a lot of iterations is still necessary for reaching the target when applying the approach of [2].

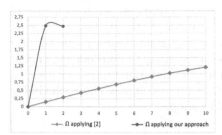

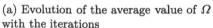

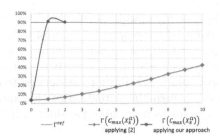

(a) Evolution of the average value of Ω with the iterations

(b) Evolution of $\Gamma(C_{\max}\left(X_k^\Omega\right))$ with the iterations

Fig. 1. Comparison of the results when applying the two approaches

Table 4. Obtained iterations for the problem $Q6||C_{\max}$ with our approach

Iteration i	Input Ω	Step 1		Step 2	Step 3	Step 4
		X^Ω	$C_{\max}\left(X^\Omega\right)$	$\Gamma\left(C_{\max}\left(X^\Omega\right)\right)$	$\left[\tilde{d}\left(X_k^\Omega\right)\right]_{k\in\{1,2\}}$	Ω^{new}
0	[0, 0, 0, 0, 0, 0]	X_0	926	3.6%	[968, 969, 974, 971, 976, 979]	[2.67, 2.80, 2.50, 2.50, 2.23, 2.18]
1	[2.67, 2.80, 2.50, 2.50, 2.23, 2.18]	X_1	973	91.1%	[972, 970, 971, 973, 973, 976]	[2.67, 2.67, 2.39, 2.50, 2.26, 2.32]
2	[2.67, 2.67, 2.39, 2.50, 2.26, 2.32]	X_2	972.72	90.3%	$\emptyset$	$\emptyset$

The Table 4 detailed the iterations when applying our improved approach. After the first iteration, the obtained value of $\Gamma\left(C_{\max}\left(X^\Omega\right)\right)$ is lightly too high such that a second iteration for adjusting the values of Ω is necessary. The second iteration allows to reach the targeted performance. If we accept to degrade the optimal deterministic makespan ($C_{\max} = 926$ with the solution X_0) of only 5%, then it is possible to guarantee this makespan despite the uncertainties with a probability of 90% giving a good compromise between optimality (C_{max}) and robustness (Γ). This confirms globally the results obtained with the simple instance: the improved approach permits to converge faster to a robust solution.

5   Conclusion and Perspectives

We have proposed an approach combining robust mathematical programming and Discrete Event Systems models for the building of a robust scheduling on parallel machines. This allows to reach the level of robustness desired by the decision-maker by finely assessing the degree of robustness of the solutions provided by the optimization module, regardless of the probability distributions that follow the uncertainties on the model input data. The probability distribution associated to the uncertainties are supposed independent but not necessarily symmetrical. Experiments on two instances show that our approach permits to converge quickly to a robust schedule and improves the rate of convergence of literature's methods. Several perspectives to this work can be considered. First, at short term, a more specific distribution of levels of robustness can be considered, taking into account, for example, the configuration of the production system, the criticality of certain machines (for instance, requiring greater robustness for bottleneck machines, ...). It would also be interesting to consider dependent probability distributions associated to the uncertainties. Long term perspectives will concern the extension of this approach to more complex shop scheduling problems as flow shop, job shop or hybrid flow shop.

References

1. Bertsimas, D., Sim, M.: The price of robustness. Oper. Res. **2**(1), 35–53 (2004)
2. Marangé, P., et al.: Coupling robust optimization and model-checking techniques for robust scheduling in the context of *Industry 4.0*. In: Sokolov, B., Ivanov, D., Dolgui, A. (eds.) Scheduling in Industry 4.0 and Cloud Manufacturing. ISORMS, vol. 289, pp. 103–124. Springer, Cham (2020). https://doi.org/10.1007/978-3-030-43177-8_6
3. Cassandras, C.G., Lafortune, S.: Introduction to Discrete Event Systems, 3rd edn. Springer, Cham (2021)
4. Himmiche, S., Aubry, A., Marangé, P., Pétin, J.-F., Duflot, M.: Using statistical-model-checking-based simulation for evaluating the robustness of a production schedule. In: 7th Workshop on Service Orientation in Holonic and Multi-Agent Manufacturing, SOHOMA 2017, Nantes, France, October 2017 (2017)
5. Lefebvre, D., Mejia, G.: Robust scheduling in uncertain environment with Petri nets and beam search. IFAC-PapersOnLine **51**(11), 1077–1082 (2018)
6. Cherif, G., Leclercq, E., Lefebvre, D.: Scheduling problems for a class of hybrid FMS using T-TPN and beam search. J. Control Autom. Electr. Syst. **32**(3), 591–604 (2021). https://doi.org/10.1007/s40313-021-00700-5
7. Chiola, G., Marsan, M.A., Balbo, G., Conte, G.: Generalized stochastic Petri nets: a definition at the net level and its implications. IEEE Trans. Softw. Eng. **19**(2), 89–107 (1993)
8. Alur, R., Dill, D.L.: A theory of timed automata. Theoret. Comput. Sci. **126**(2), 183–235 (1994)
9. Plateau, B., Atif, K.: Stochastic automata network of modeling parallel systems. IEEE Trans. Softw. Eng. **17**(10), 1093–1108 (1991)

An Unrelated Parallel Machines Rescheduling Problem: An Industrial Case Study

Alice Berthier[✉], Alice Yalaoui, Hicham Chehade, Farouk Yalaoui,
Lionel Amodeo, and Christian Bouillot

Computer Laboratory and Digital Society (LIST3N), UTT, Université de Technologie
de Troyes, 12 rue Marie Curie, CS42060, 10004 Troyes Cedex, France
alice.berthier@utt.fr

Abstract. This study tackles an unrelated parallel machines rescheduling problem. Sequence and machine dependent setup times and limited resources are taken into consideration. The study focuses on the objective of proposing an efficient and stable rescheduling solution. The resolution approach is explained and illustrated. Different indicators to optimize the rescheduling planning are tested and results are analyzed. The problem is inspired from a concrete case of textile industry.

Keywords: Rescheduling · Unrelated parallel machines · Genetic algorithm

1 Introduction

The purpose of this paper is to propose a method to adapt the production scheduling when disruption occurs. The stake is to have a limited impact on the workshop organization and the productivity performances.

The workshop considered in this study is composed of unrelated parallel machines with machine and sequence dependent setup times. Two types of limited resources are considered: number of operators available that limits the number of parallel machines able to run at the same time and number of adjusters that limits the number of setup. Each adjuster can do only one setup at a time. The objective is to reschedule a known number of jobs after a disruption.

An initial production planning is provided by a scheduling algorithm already implemented with c_{max} minimization. However, perfect production conditions are very unrealistic, disruptions can occur and the initial planning may no longer be up to date. The different disruptions that can occur in this problem are:

- Arrival of a new job
- Deletion of a job
- Machine breakdown

A. Dolgui et al. (Eds.): APMS 2021, IFIP AICT 630, pp. 81–91, 2021.
https://doi.org/10.1007/978-3-030-85874-2_9

– Lack of human resources (operator or adjuster)

The rescheduling objective is to find the best possible planning to finish all the jobs as soon as possible by keeping stability in the planning initially provided and integrating work in progress information. This is why this study is focused on the objective of maximizing performance ($min\ c_{max}$) while maintaining stability.

This problem stems from a real case encountered in textile industry, facing the industry 4.0 revolution. The development of online-business requires more and more flexibility and reactivity, specially with the COVID 19 crisis context as e-business have greatly increased (+100% in 2020). The adaptation needed is reflected in the entire process of the clothing manufacturing industry from the knitting of the fabric to the assembling stage.

The rest of the study is organized as follows. Section 2 gives a literature review on this kind of problem. Section 3 provides contribution of this study with the exposition of resolution method. The next section gives results obtained. A conclusion end up the study in Sect. 5.

2   State of the Art

In the literature, only two works tackle problems on the same type of system studied in this paper. Work of Berthier et al. [4] deals with a dynamic layout problem in the same industrial environment. The importance of flexibility in such workshop may be encountered at a tactical level. In [5], the authors propose a complete study of the scheduling problem (MILP and AG) to deal with c_{max} minimization in such systems.

In fact, often, real-world scheduling problems are dynamic systems and they need to respond to exogenous events [6]. Different rescheduling approaches are proposed in the literature.

The first one is to use a standard scheduling method with the new data after disruption. This can rich high quality solution on the performance objective. However, solution stability is not guarantee [10]. On real life production, getting a totally different schedule is very unfavorable to a good workshop organization and management.

The second one is to use a proactive scheduling. This is generated by inserting idle time between the pre-scheduling activities, enabling the disruptions to be smoothed out through the system in order to maintain the schedule quality [1]. Stochastic approaches are an other way to do it [13].

The last one is reactive scheduling, commonly referred to as rescheduling. It is a procedure to modify the existing schedule during processing to adapt to changes in a production or operational environment. Kim [8] recently studies a rescheduling problem of unrelated parallel machines with job-dependent setup times under forecasted machine breakdown.

To briefly review some authors that tackle similar problems in literature: [16] consider an hybrid flowshop with random disturbance and develop and implement a heuristic on an expert system software. In [11] incoming workflows to be executed on a large-scale distributed system are modeled as directed graphs, where tasks may fail their computations. Heuristics for the problem have been implemented in a specific application simulator. In [14] a steel making continuous caster process is considered with uncertain tasks and a Lagrangian Decomposition method is developed to solve it. [17] consider a flexible job shop with partial and total rescheduling to deal with rush orders, job cancellations and machine breakdowns. Finally, [3] tackles a dynamic job shop with new orders, rush orders, order cancellations, due date changes and machine breakdowns. Rescheduling is event driven and it is carried out considering different criteria in lexicographic order.

On a majority of studies, contrary to scheduling problems, the complexity comes from the combination of two conflicting objectives. Rescheduling problems are taken into consideration: performance and stability measurements. Multiple indicators in the literature are proposed. The definition and use of appropriate performance metrics or quality indicators is crucial. Currently, there are many proposed metrics [7] that can be classified into unary, which assign each non-dominated set a number that reflects a certain quality aspect, and binary, which assign a number to a pair of Pareto approximations. However, each industry has its own characteristics that involves specific indicators. For example, stability can be evaluate by the number of jobs processed on different machines in the original and new schedules [2]. Other approaches defined stability in terms of deviation of job starting times between the original and revised schedules and the difference of job sequences [9,12].

3 Resolution Method

The contribution of this study is to explore multiple evaluation metrics of the rescheduling solution. First, instances are randomly generated and schedule with the genetic algorithm developed by Berthier et al. [5]. This algorithm is based on makespan minimization. The entire production has to be finished as soon as possible without any priority under the time horizon. Then, disturbances are generated. The new problem is to reschedule with two conflicting objectives: keep a good performance but also guarantee stability. The flowchart of the resolution approach is given in Fig. 1.

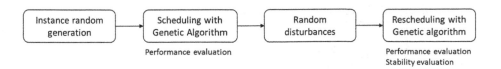

Fig. 1. Flowchart of the resolution approach

The stability in rescheduling is more complex to evaluate than c_{max} evaluation. This study focuses on the measurement of the number of machine assignment differences between the initial scheduling and the rescheduling planning for each job. To illustrate this, an example is given in the following. This example does not take human resources limitation into consideration. Table 1 gives the processing time p_{mi} of each machine $m = (1...M)$ for each job $i = (1...N)$ per unite and the quantity of each job is given in the last row of the table. Table 2 gives the setup times between jobs $i = (0...N)$ and $j = (1...N)$ on machine 1, 2 and 3. Figure 2 shows the result of the example instance scheduling. The c_{max} value reached is 29. Now, supposing that M2 becomes unavailable from time 7 to time 37. If jobs 4 and 5 are shifted after the disruption, the c_{max} value is increasing up to 54 but stability measurement is equal to 0: no job is machine changed (Fig. 3). But if machine job assignment is change as in Fig. 4, the stability indicator is degraded to 2. However, the performance measure c_{max} is improve to 42.

This stability indicator is explored in different combinations and analyzed in order to get the most pertinent and efficient rescheduling planning to the company. These indicator can be compared to a limit parameter. If the limit is crossed, the objective function is penalized. This allows a tolerance and plays up on the performance objective.

Table 1. Processing times p_{mi}

p_{mi}	1	2	3	4	5	6
M1	6	3	5	4	7	5
M2	4	4	9	3	5	4
M3	5	2	7	4	6	6
Quantity	3	5	2	4	2	3

Table 2. Setup times s_{mij}

s_{1ij}	1 2 3 4 5 6	s_{2ij}	1 2 3 4 5 6	s_{3ij}	1 2 3 4 5 6
0	1 3 2 2 4 1	0	3 4 2 1 3 3	0	1 2 3 4 5 2
1	0 1 2 4 3 1	1	0 2 3 3 4 4	1	0 3 5 1 1 3
2	1 0 4 4 1 4	2	2 0 1 1 4 2	2	4 0 3 1 1 1
3	2 4 0 3 3 3	3	4 3 0 4 3 4	3	2 1 0 2 2 1
4	3 2 4 0 1 2	4	4 4 2 0 1 1	4	1 2 3 0 2 2
5	4 4 3 3 0 4	5	1 2 4 3 0 4	5	1 1 1 2 0 1
6	4 1 1 2 1 0	6	2 3 2 3 2 0	6	1 2 2 1 3 0

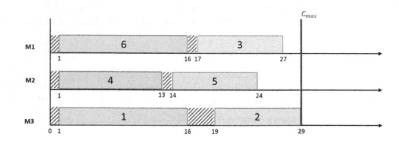

Fig. 2. Initial scheduling of the example

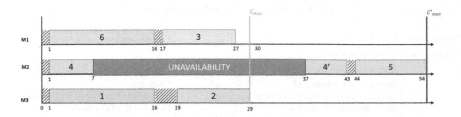

Fig. 3. Rescheduling example after machine unavailability with stability equal to 0

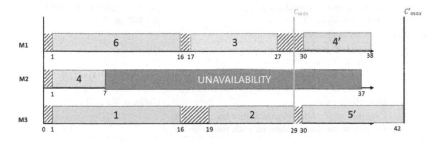

Fig. 4. Rescheduling example after machine unavailability with stability equal to 2

3.1 Instances Generator

In order to have several instances of characteristics close to the real data, an instance generator has been developed. Instances can be used to analyze the different indicators under different parameter conditions on the rescheduling tool.

The random generation is established as follows with different probability laws on each step. The generation is divided into two main parts:

– Generation of initial instances that will be scheduled using the scheduling genetic algorithm of the previous study with this industrial partner
– Generation of disturbances on this solution

Table 3 details the different step to generate an instance inspired from [15]. Each instance is generated with the probability law indicated in Table 3. The data generated are the number of jobs to schedule, machine eligibility for each job, processing times and setup times. This instance is scheduled with these initial data. After that, one disturbance for this instance is generated randomly among the four disturbance types. The rescheduling process used in this study is event-driven. Each time a disturbance occurs, rescheduling is triggered. Only one disturbance is generated for each instance. After disturbance, the new availability of each resource has to be calculated. In the example of Fig. 3, when disturbance occurs at time 7, M1 (resp. M3) is unavailable until time 16 (resp. time 16) to finish job 6 (resp. 1). Taking into consideration M1 and M3 availability and the unavailability of M2, the instance is rescheduled.

Table 3. Instances random generator

Step number	Detail	Probability law
Instances to scheduling operation		
1	Number of jobs to schedule	Uniform [50;350]
2	For each job, number of machines eligible (max 5 machines) and machines affectation	Discrete $P(1) = 0.4$; $P(2) = 0.3$; $P(3) = 0.15$; $P(4) = 0.1$; $P(5) = 0.05$
3	For each job on each machine eligible, the processing time	Uniform [450;2500]
4	For each job on each machine eligible, the setup time $a * \min(p_{mi}, p_{mj})$ where $a = U(A; B)$	Uniform [A;B] = [0.01;0.1]; [0.05;0.1]; [0.1;0.2]; [0.1;0.2] or [0.2;0.5]
Disturbed instances to rescheduling operation		
5	The kind of disturbance (4 types) 1. Arrival of new job; 2. Deletion of a job; 3. Machine breakdown; 4. Lack of human resources	Discrete $P(1) = 1/4$; $P(2) = 1/4$ $P(3) = 1/4$; $P(4) = 1/4$
6	Disturbance date	Uniform $[0; c_{max}]$
7	Calculation of resources availability to determine the minimum starting date on each resource	

3.2   Objective Functions

The resolution method is based on the same genetic algorithm (GA) used in [5]. The solution representation uses in this GA is given in Fig. 5. The representation chosen is an array table with two rows and as many columns as scheduled jobs. In the first row, each job is assigned once and the order will be the sequencing decoding order. The machine assigned for each job is indicated in the second row. To initialize the population of solution, as in numerous papers, a randomized initialization is used.

Job	6 4 3 5 1 2
Machine	1 2 3 2 2 3

Fig. 5. Solution chromosome example

Only the objective function is changed. Different objective functions have been studied in this paper. The first goal of planning rescheduling is to keep the efficiency of the solution, which corresponds to the optimization of the makespan value (c_{max}). This is still the main objective, as performance is more important than stability for the industrial partner. Thus, the first objective function studied is only to minimize the value of c_{max}. The other objective functions are composed of two elements to optimize: the c_{max} and a metric to guarantee as much as possible the stability between the initial planning and the rescheduling one. The indicator of stability chosen is the number of assignment job/machine differences.

A penalty cost is used for stability, to allow a tolerance threshold. A fixed number of disturbance over the total number of jobs can be tolerated. When changes occur right after the rescheduling date, it can disturb the organization already in place: setups are made, workers already have information about what they have to do next. However, when changes occur at the end of the horizon, the schedule can change. So it is not really disturbing. Finally, seven objective functions are compared, each one is linear combination:

1. Minimization of c_{max}
2. Minimization of c_{max} and assignment differences
3. Minimization of c_{max} and penalty if assignment differences are up to 10% of jobs
4. Minimization of c_{max} and penalty if assignment differences are up to 30% of jobs
5. Minimization of c_{max} and penalty if assignment differences are up to 50% of jobs
6. Minimization of c_{max} and penalty if assignment differences occur less than 24 h after rescheduling date
7. Minimization of c_{max} and penalty if assignment differences occur less than 48 h after rescheduling date

4   Results

60 instances with different disturbances have been generated. The average size of instances is 189 jobs to schedule initially. For each instance, all the objective functions have been applied and compared. After disturbance, 111 jobs in average has to be reschedule. The disturbance date is generated in average at 26% of the c_{max} value of the initial schedule optimization. Instances have been grouped, related to the type of disturbance. For each group, results are the average of the solution evaluation. Table 4 shows for each group of instances, the performance objective c_{max} reached when it is the single objective function. Stability value of the solution is the reference to evaluate the other objective functions (Sect. 3.2). This value is calculated as follow: for each job i, if the initial machine assignment is different than after rescheduling, $a_i = 1$, else $a_i = 0$. The value in Table 4 is: $\sum_{i=1}^{N} a_i$. For performance and stability, standard deviation are given. Depending on the disruption and instance data, performance and stability may be affected in different ways. Distribution of performance (c_{max}) are given by box plots (Fig. 6). The performance value distribution change from one group to another. Averages and minimum are still very closed but maximum and quartiles diverge.

In Table 5, the results with the application of the six other objective functions are given as deviation compared to the references. It can be observed that the efficiency objective is not very degraded compared to when it is the only

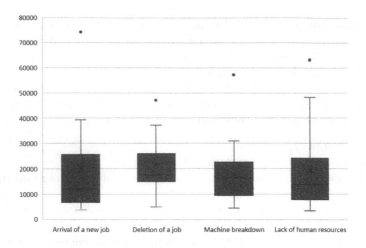

Fig. 6. Performance value distribution for each type of disturbance

one optimize. However, the stability is considerably increased by up to 97% when job/machine assignment differences are taken into consideration. As previously, for each job i, if the initial machine assignment is different than after rescheduling with the specific objective function, $b_i = 1$, else $b_i = 0$. The stability value in Table 5 is calculated by: $(\sum_{i=1}^{N} b_i - \sum_{i=1}^{N} a_i)/\sum_{i=1}^{N} a_i$. If the stability value is 0%, it means that the number of job assignment changes is the same than rescheduling optimization when stability are not considered. For instance, for group Arrival of a new job, if in Table 5, stability value reaches -100%, it means that 40 jobs has no assignment changes compared to initial scheduling planning. When the value is superior to 0%, it means that more machine assignment changes are generated than in the reference rescheduling solution. It happens when assignment changes penalized only beyond a large percentage of jobs (Table 5, Arrival of a new job, objective function 4 and 5).

Table 4. Results reference on optimization of c_{max} for the different disturbances

Objective function	Instance size	1	
Disturbance	Initial number of jobs	Performance	Stability
Arrival of a new job	183 ± 101	$23\ 129 \pm 22\ 068$	40 ± 27
Deletion of a job	204 ± 57	$21\ 492 \pm 11\ 212$	23 ± 26
Machine breakdown	181 ± 87	$21\ 607 \pm 17\ 964$	43 ± 40
Lack of human resources	188 ± 59	$18\ 966 \pm 11\ 188$	27 ± 27
Total	189 ± 72	$20\ 786 \pm 14\ 626$	32 ± 31

Table 5. Efficiency and stability results with the different objective function for the different disturbances

Objective function	2		3	
Disturbance	Performance	Stability	Performance	Stability
Arrival of a new job	5% ± 9	−96% ± 6	8% ± 13	−67% ± 33
Deletion of a job	5% ± 9	−100% ± 1	1% ± 3	−67% ± 40
Machine breakdown	8% ± 14	−98% ± 4	0% ± 6	−59% ± 47
Lack of human resources	6% ± 13	−96% ± 10	1% ± 6	−54% ± 60
Total	6% ± 12	−97% ± 7	2% ± 7	−60% ± 49
Objective function	4		5	
Disturbance	Performance	Stability	Performance	Stability
Arrival of a new job	3% ± 7	13% ± 39	2% ± 5	13% ± 85
Deletion of a job	0% ± 7	−56% ± 47	0% ± 6	−56% ± 47
Machine breakdown	0% ± 6	−40% ± 49	0% ± 4	−56% ± 52
Lack of human resources	1% ± 5	−18% ± 55	1% ± 4	−21% ± 60
Total	1% ± 6	−27% ± 49	1% ± 5	−29% ± 63
Objective function	6		7	
Disturbance	Performance	Stability	Performance	Stability
Arrival of a new job	4% ± 15	−58% ± 47	5% ± 13	−61% ± 48
Deletion of a job	−2% ± 5	−65% ± 42	−1% ± 7	−62% ± 45
Machine breakdown	−2% ± 6	−57% ± 49	2% ± 6	−68% ± 40
Lack of human resources	1% ± 6	−70% ± 40	1% ± 5	−67% ± 55
Total	0% ± 8	−64% ± 43	1% ± 8	−65% ± 48

5 Conclusion

The originality of the problem studied in this paper is the specific application to the textile industry. New evaluation methods of stability in rescheduling problem have been tested in order to offer the industrial partner an efficient solution. The continuity of this study is to allow to the company to reschedule the workshop production every time an unpredictable disruption occurs. The method has to be tested on real instances. It is the next step of this study with the industrial partner. Generated several disruptions on same instances is an other perspective. It is a very important prerequisite to have an agile and reactive production plan. It is also a first step on the road to the 4.0 factory transformation. Different evaluation functions have been tested and evaluated thanks to a random instance generator. With random generated data similar to real material, the company will be able to choose the evaluation scenario most appropriate to rescheduling, knowing the impact on both efficiency and stability. To future perspective, the Pareto front can be determine in order to let the industrial choose the solution between a set of solutions that is the most pertinent.

Acknowledgment. This research was supported by ANRT (Association National Recherche Technologie). These acknowledgements also go to our industrial partner. Their participation allows us to work on research topics applied to the current industrial context.

References

1. Arnaout, J.P.: Rescheduling of parallel machines with stochastic processing and setup times. J. Manufact. Syst. **33**(3), 376–384 (2014)
2. Azizoglu, M., Alagöz, O.: Parallel-machine rescheduling with machine disruptions. IIE Trans. **37**(12), 1113–1118 (2005)
3. Baykasoğlu, A., Karaslan, F.S.: Solving comprehensive dynamic job shop scheduling problem by using a grasp-based approach. Int. J. Prod. Res. **55**(11), 3308–3325 (2017)
4. Berthier, A., Yalaoui, A., Chehade, H., Yalaoui, F., Amodeo, L., Coquelet, G.: Machines group and load balancing: an industrial case. IFAC-PapersOnLine **52**(13), 415–420 (2019)
5. Berthier, A., Yalaoui, A., Chehade, H., Yalaoui, F., Amodeo, L., Bouillot, C.: Unrelated parallel machines scheduling with dependent setup times in textile industry. In: CIE (submitted) (2021)
6. Framinan, J.M., Ruiz, R.: Architecture of manufacturing scheduling systems: literature review and an integrated proposal. Eur. J. Oper. Res. **205**(2), 237–246 (2010)
7. Jiang, S., Ong, Y.S., Zhang, J., Feng, L.: Consistencies and contradictions of performance metrics in multiobjective optimization. IEEE Trans. Cybern. **44**(12), 2391–2404 (2014)
8. Kim, Y.-I., Kim, H.-J.: Rescheduling of unrelated parallel machines with job-dependent setup times under forecasted machine breakdown. Int. J. Prod. Res., 1–23 (2020). https://doi.org/10.1080/00207543.2020.1775910
9. Liu, Z., Lu, L., Qi, X.: Cost allocation in rescheduling with machine unavailable period. Eur. J. Oper. Res. **266**(1), 16–28 (2018)
10. Mohan, J., Lanka, K., Rao, A.N.: A review of dynamic job shop scheduling techniques. Procedia Manufact. **30**, 34–39 (2019)
11. Olteanu, A., Pop, F., Dobre, C., Cristea, V.: A dynamic rescheduling algorithm for resource management in large scale dependable distributed systems. Comput. Math. Appl. **63**(9), 1409–1423 (2012)
12. Pfeiffer, A., Kádár, B., Monostori, L.: Stability-oriented evaluation of hybrid rescheduling methods in a job-shop with machine breakdowns. In: Proceedings of the 39th CIRP ISMS, pp. 173–178 (2006)
13. Ruszczyński, A., Shapiro, A.: Stochastic programming models. Handb. Oper. Res. Manage. Sci. **10**, 1–64 (2003)
14. Sun, L., Luan, F., Pian, J.: An effective approach for the scheduling of refining process with uncertain iterations in steel-making and continuous casting process. IFAC-PapersOnLine **48**(3), 1966–1972 (2015)
15. Yalaoui, F., Chu, C.: An efficient heuristic approach for parallel machine scheduling with job splitting and sequence-dependent setup times. IIE Trans. **35**(2), 183–190 (2003)

16. Yin, J., Li, T., Chen, B., Wang, B.: Dynamic rescheduling expert system for hybrid flow shop with random disturbance. Procedia Eng. **15**, 3921–3925 (2011)
17. Zhang, S., Wong, T.N.: Flexible job-shop scheduling/rescheduling in dynamic environment: a hybrid MAS/ACO approach. Int. J. Prod. Res. **55**(11), 3173–3196 (2017)

Tactical Planning and Predictive Maintenance: Towards an Integrated Model Based on ε-reliability

David Lemoine[1,2]($\boxtimes$) and Bruno Castanier[3,4]

[1] IMT Atlantique, Nantes, France
david.lemoine@imt-atlantique.fr
[2] LS2N, CNRS UMR 6004, Nantes, France
[3] Angers University, Angers, France
bruno.castanier@univ-angers.fr
[4] LARIS, CNRS EA7315, Angers, France

Abstract. Elaborating some Master Scheduling Programs to maximize the customer product demands in respect to the different logistics costs and optimizing maintenance policies are classically addressed independently by two scientific communities whose interests may in some cases diverge. The objective of this paper is to build, based on recent contributions from the field of maintenance optimization, an integrated optimization approach for tactical production plans and maintenance decisions. This goal of integrating as much information as possible into more holistic approaches and more relevant decisions is clearly one of the challenges that can be found in the precepts of the "Industry of the Future". In this paper, we propose, through a modeling of the effects of the degradation of the production system on its production efficiency, to show a benefit of the simultaneous consideration of both concerns. Feasibility criteria are also proposed to ensure the robustness of given tactical plans against the hazards of degradation and failure of the production system.

Keywords: Tactical planning · Predictive maintenance · Faisability criterion · Stochastic simulation-based approach

1 Introduction

Tactical Production Planing problems are often modelled by so-called "Lot-Sizing" models which are based on an estimated capacity of the production system. This leads to plans that are at best sub-optimised, at worst unfeasible, and many studies have attempted to refine this estimate by taking into account operational constraints, in particular by integrating scheduling constraints [1]. Nevertheless, few researches take into account the impact of the ageing of this system and the loss of capacity caused by maintenance operations, whether preventive or curative. Moreover, when maintenance is considered, it is only seen as

© IFIP International Federation for Information Processing 2021
Published by Springer Nature Switzerland AG 2021
A. Dolgui et al. (Eds.): APMS 2021, IFIP AICT 630, pp. 92–101, 2021.
https://doi.org/10.1007/978-3-030-85874-2_10

a capacity-consuming activity (when maintenance models are based exclusively on lifetime laws, block or age-based policies can be used to define periodicity constraints that facilitate capacity reservation [2]). Planning maintenance therefore amounts to determining the best compromise between minimising disruption to production and guaranteeing reliable performance at the lowest cost. But, if we consider that ageing performance can vary according to the use and the operations carried out, it is possible to differentiate degradation behaviours according to the items whose production is planned. Thus, we see an interdependence between the two types of planning: maintenance decisions are made according to the planned production as planned production is a function of the maintenance decisions. Thus, just like the production planning process, maintenance planning is also a performance lever for the production system and it makes sense to consider them into an integrated process.

In the search for performance and the associated instrumentation of production tools, conditional type approaches for which the maintenance decision is defined according to a health state estimated with the information collected on the system [3], are based on state indicators (typically the performance level of the system) or prognosis indicators such as the Residual Lifetime (RUL). These indicators allow to define optimality structures for maintenance decision policies. The use of the Residual Lifetime clearly serves as a basis for predictive maintenance whose importance is growing in the context of Industry 4.0. That is why, from [4], we propose a new methodology based on this indicator (more precisely on a reliability threshold estimated over a production period instead of a limit degradation level).

2 Problem Modeling

In order to provide feasible production plans, tactical production planning requires a good estimate of production capacities. However, these estimates may vary throughout the planning horizon, especially due to degradation of production resources that may lead to decreases in machine efficiency but also to a range of breakdowns. Thus, in a first part we give a general lot sizing model with finite capacities which allows to obtain different production plans (end items as well as components). It is known to be the classical model which extends material requirements planning (MRP) concept by taking into account production capacities [5]. Then we will detail in a second part the way we model the loss of performance related to the degradation of machines.

2.1 The Tactical Planning Model

The dynamic multi-level capacitated lot-sizing problem (MLCLSP) was introduced in [6]. Here, we detail the formulation given by [7]. Parameters and decision variables of the model are summarized in Table 1.

Table 1. Notations of the MLCLSP

Index sets	
$\mathcal{N}$	: Set of items, $\mathcal{N} = \{1, \cdots, N\}$
$\mathcal{T}$	: Set of periods, $\mathcal{T} = \{1, \cdots, T\}$
$\mathcal{S}_i$	: Set of direct successors of item i in the Bill Of Material (BOM)
Parameters	
a_{ij}	: Quantity of item i directly required to produce one unit of item j
C_t	: Available capacity of production system at period t
$D_{i,t}$	: External demand of item i at period t
h_i	: Unitary holding cost of item i per unit and period
s_i	: Setup cost of item i
p_i	: Production time per unit of item i
b_i	: Setup time of item i
l_i	: Planned lead time for item i
Variables	
$X_{i,t}$	: Binary setup variable of item i at period t
$Q_{i,t}$	: Production quantity of item i at period t
$I_{i,t}$	: Inventory of item i at the end of period t

Thus, we can write the model as follows:

$$\text{Minimize} \sum_{t \in \mathcal{T}} \sum_{i \in \mathcal{N}} (s_i X_{i,t} + h_i I_{i,t}) \tag{1}$$

s.t.

$$I_{i,t} = I_{i,t-1} + Q_{i,t-l_i} - \sum_{j \in \mathcal{S}_i} a_{ij} Q_{j,t} - D_{i,t} \quad \forall (i,t) \in \mathcal{N} \times \mathcal{T} \tag{2}$$

$$\sum_{i \in \mathcal{N}} (p_i Q_{i,t} + b_i X_{i,t}) \leq C_t \quad \forall (k,t) \in \mathcal{K} \times \mathcal{T} \tag{3}$$

$$Q_{i,t} \leq C_t X_{i,t} \quad \forall (i,t) \in \mathcal{N} \times \mathcal{T} \tag{4}$$

$$Q_{i,t}, I_{i,t} \geq 0 \quad \forall (i,t) \in \mathcal{N} \times \mathcal{T} \tag{5}$$

$$X_{i,t} \in \{0,1\} \quad \forall (i,t) \in \mathcal{N} \times \mathcal{T} \tag{6}$$

(1) is the logistic costs we seek to minimize. (2) is the inventory balance constraint and (3) is the capacity constraint concerning production and setup time. (4) ensures that production of item i takes place at period t, only if the resource is setup for this item. (5) and (6) are positivity and integrity constraints.

In such a model, it can be seen that p_i, the capacity consumed to produce one item i, is independent of the performance level of production system. The aim of the next section is to explain the way we use to tackle fill this gap.

2.2 Modeling of the Performance Degradation for Production System

Here, we consider that the production system degrades as it is used: this degradation results in a loss of real capacity by increasing operating times. We denote x_τ the effective performance rate at workload level τ since the last preventive maintenance, which we assume to be measurable for all τ. We also assume that the degradation of this rate is a continuous, workload-dependent, increasing stochastic process and that its expectation is a function of the load induced by the manufactured product (its unit processing time).

More formally, we note $\{X_\tau, \tau > 0\}$ the stochastic process modeling the evolution of the degradation of the performance rate of the production system where τ represents the workload already processed by the production system. We assume that at the new state (X_0) the rate is equal to 1 and that the process is strictly decreasing until 0 (state in which the machine is so degraded that it is not able to produce anymore). We suppose that on an interval $[\tau, \tau + \Delta\tau]$, the loss of performance is modeled by a random variable which follows a Gamma distribution $\Gamma(\alpha\Delta\tau, \beta)$ where α and β were previously estimated. This modelling in the form of a homogeneous gamma process is classical in maintenance [8]. However, as the operating times are particularly low with respect to the planning horizon, we assume in our modeling that the performance rate is constant during the manufacturing of a product unit and that its evolution only occurs at the end of the production of this unit.

As previously mentioned, we also take into account the increase in the duration of the operating times as a function of the level of the performance rate of the system. More precisely, if x_τ represents the performance rate of the production system at the load level τ, we note $p_i(x_\tau)$ the unit production capacity of an item i associated with this rate and we will thus have, for a non-maintained system, $p_i(x_\tau)$ the production capacity of an item i associated with this rate:

- $x_{\tau+p_i(x_\tau)} < x_\tau$,
- $p_i\left(x_{\tau+p_i(x_\tau)}\right) \geq p_i(x_\tau)$.

We also take into account the failures (breakdowns) of the production system, failures that we always assume to be cataleptic and requiring corrective maintenance (that takes C_{Corr} units of capacity) to get the system back on line. We assume that these failures are distributed according to a failure rate $\lambda(x)$ which depends on the performance rate of the system. Moreover, we assume that this rate decreases in x. Thus, the lower the performance rate of the system, the higher the probability of failures. Since we have made the assumption that the performance rate is constant during the manufacturing of an item, it will be the same for the failure rate and if the manufacturing of an item i starts at workload level τ, then the expected number of failures during its manufacturing will be $\lambda(x_\tau) p_i(x_\tau)$.

Figure 1 illustrates the modeling of the performance rate for a given production period, considering the system as new at the beginning of the period. It can

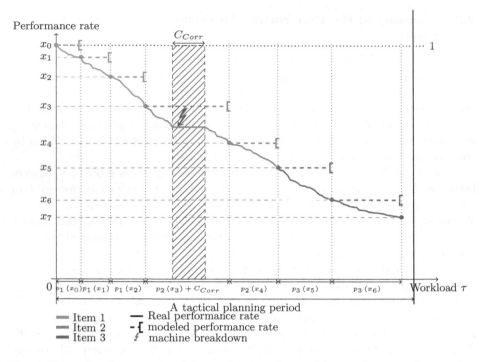

Fig. 1. Example of a scenario of the realization of a production plan according to the evolution of the performance degradation

be seen from this model that the integration of the system degradation implies taking into account the sequencing of the production lots.

2.3   The Performance Indicator: The ε-Reliability

In this section, we define a feasibility indicator that ensures the robustness of the production plan with a certain level of probability ε. Based on the ε-feasible indicator provided by [4], we recall the concept of ε-feasibility for one period and we define the ε-reliability indicator on which we base our proposal.

Definition 1 (ε-feasible Period). *A period $t \in [1, T]$ is said to be ε-feasible if and only if the probability of not exceeding the production capacity (taking into account all the capacity consumption, including maintenance) is greater than or equal to ε.*

Using this indicator, [4] qualify a production plan as ε-feasible if all its periods are $\sqrt[T]{\varepsilon}$-feasible. This definition allows them to develop an algorithmic solution based on the simulation of the entire production plan. However, the obligation to have an identical probability of success at each period induces a rigidity that we propose to remove thanks to the ε-reliability.

Definition 2 (ε-reliable production plan). *A production plan is called ε-reliable if and only if each production period $t \in [1, T]$ is ε_t-feasible and $\prod_{t=1}^{T} \varepsilon_t \geq \varepsilon$.*

Indeed, by using such a definition, we allow more flexibility on the distribution of the robustness over the periods of the planning horizon while ensuring the same overall level of robustness of the production plan.

3   Our Approach

Conditional maintenance approaches allow maintenance to be organised as best as possible, essentially on the basis of the degradation state of the system itself. A predictive strategy can be seen as conditional maintenance for which the decision variable is usually a residual life. This residual lifetime is characterised by a conditional reliability that is a function of this same state. In [4], authors studied a conditional scheme for which the decision threshold was optimised to guarantee the best compromise between performance rate and available capacity. The maintenance decision can then be made at any time during production, regardless of organisational constraints. Here, we propose to develop a predictive maintenance policy allowing a restoration of the production system according to its state of performance while taking into account the customer's requests translated in the tactical plan. We will consider that this maintenance can be done at most once per period and can be carried out either at the beginning or at the end of the production period, thus joining a number of operational practices.

Our maintenance policy is based on the ε-reliability indicator. Therefore, at the beginning of each period t, this allows us to adjust its ε_t-feasibility according to the previous periods according to the allocation principle defined below.

Definition 3 (Feasibility allocation). *For each period $t \in [1, T]$, we define*

$$\varepsilon_t = \sqrt[T-(t-1)]{\varepsilon} \prod_{j=1}^{t} FR_j (x_{j-1}) \qquad (7)$$

where $FR_j (x_j)$ is the probability of achieving the production plan at period j knowing the performance level x_{j-1} of the production system at the end of manufacturing in precedent period.

Thus, we propose to define a predictive maintenance strategy based on the estimation of the ability of the system to achieve its production plan at each period. The maintenance decision is no longer defined on the basis of lifetime or calendar parameters but is a function of the current state of the system estimated after the production of each item. Even if its implementation in an operational context is more difficult than traditional approaches, these predictive approaches, which are similar to conditional maintenance under certain assumption, offer real potential for improving performance, particularly in economic point of view [9].

Then, our methodology can be summarized into five iterative steps:

Step 1: The datas are readen and the lot-sizing model is initialized with the estimated production capacities C_t for each period t. The effective performance rate for the production system at the beginning is x_0.

Step 2: Thanks to the lot-sizing model, an optimal production plan is elaborated (by using, for instance, a mixed integer linear program or an optimization method), $t \leftarrow 1$.

Step 3: 1. ε_t is computed thanks to the feasibility-allocation formula (7)
2. The production plan is simulated at period t according to the performance rate x_{t-1} (the performance rate at the beginning of period t). The probability of achieving the production plan at period t $FR_t(x_{t-1})$ is then computed.
3. if $FR_t(x_{t-1}) \geq \varepsilon_t$ then go to Step 4 else
   * if there is no preventive maintenance at the beginning of period t, schedule one: $x_{t-1} = 1$. Go back to 2.
   * if there is a preventive maintenance at the beginning of period t, C_t is the decreased and the lot-sizing model is updated. Got to Step 2.

Step 4: x_t is computed as the median of all observed performance rates at the end of period t thank to the simulation model. $t \leftarrow t + 1$. Go to Step 5

Step 5: If $t = T + 1$ then Stop (a feasible plan has been elaborated) else go to Step 3.

At each period t, in the simulation process two kinds of maintenance are considered:

– If a failure occurs, minimal corrective maintenance (with no effect on the performance rate of the production system) is performed (in this case a capacity consumption corresponding to the maintenance time) and a corrective maintenance cost is added.
– If a preventive maintenance occurs, then a capacity consumption corresponding to the maintenance preventive is taken into account and a preventive maintenance cost is added.

Figure 2 sketches our methodology.

4   A Software Tool

To improve the applicability of our approach in an industrial context or at least to get their feeling, the algorithm is directly implemented in a computer program with an ergonomic and user-friendly interface. The final results are numerically and graphically presented.

This interface is divided into four modules:

1. a data management module for loading, saving or importing data from an external database;
2. a tactical planning process module for building and optimising the mathematical model based on instances using, for instance, the Cplex solver;

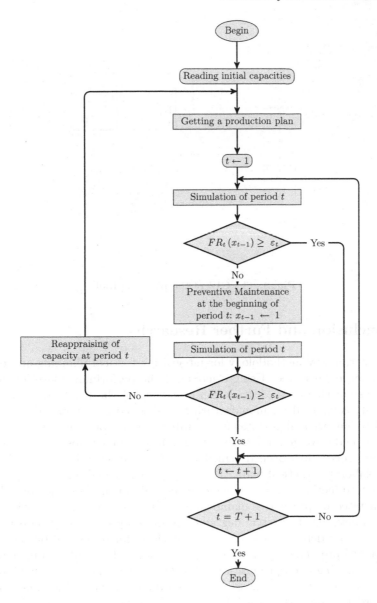

Fig. 2. Optimization scheme for the considered predictive maintenance policy

3. a simulation module for estimating the feasibility of production plans;
4. a graphical interface for the specification of the problem with all the parameters (capacities, costs, degradation, etc.), the presentation of the intermediate results obtained during the optimisation procedure and the final solution through different graphs presenting the associated indicators (Fig. 3).

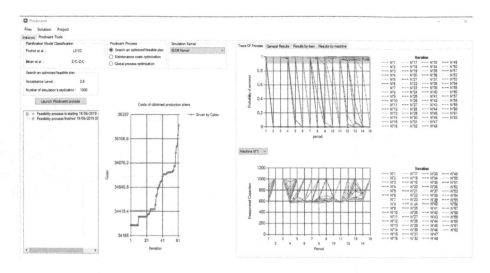

Fig. 3. The GUI of the planning tool

5   Conclusion and Further Research

In this paper, a new methodology for integrating tactical planning and maintenance has been presented. Using a model of the performance level of the production system thanks to degradation or ageing of the production system on the capacity consumed for manufacturing, and based on a new indicator called ε-reliability, an original maintenance strategy, based on considerations developed in a predictive maintenance context, has been proposed. A Feasibility-Allocation process has been designed in order to ensure a certain robustness level for elaborated tactical plans. Thus, our model extends classical approaches combining production and maintenance essentially focused on the unavailability times generated by preventive maintenance, with a stronger contribution on the interaction between the system degradation and its productivity. This has been integrated into a demonstration software platform for industrial purposes.

The model presented opens up many areas of development for future work in both the modelling and optimisation fields. One of the first points that would be interesting to address is the possibility of modulating the maintenance decision rules in order to offer the possibility of an optimised positioning of preventive maintenance according to opportunities linked, for example, to changes in series time or others. As we pointed out that scheduling has an impact on the performance level of the production system, integrating sequencing decision on the manufacturing of each production lot could be an interesting area of improvement. Another perspective of research could be to develop a model for which the preventive maintenance decision is not restricted to a total recovery of performance but to define the effectiveness of the operation to be implemented according to the capacities not consumed by the production plans, the effectiveness being able to be correlated with an effective maintenance time. On the field of optimisation and more precisely on the criteria to be taken into account, even if the feasibility partially captures the volatility of the global planning problem, it could be interesting to extend the average maintenance criteria.

References

1. Dauzère-Péres, S., Lasserre, J.B.: Integration of lotsizing and scheduling decisions in a job-shop. Eur. J. Oper. Res. **75**(2), 413–426 (1994)
2. Pandey, D., Kulkarny, M.S., Vrat, P.: A methodology for joint optimization for maintenance planning, process quality and production scheduling. Comput. Ind. Eng. **61**(4), 1098–1106 (2011)
3. Jafari, L., Makis, V.: Joint optimal lot sizing and preventive maintenance policy for a production facility subject to condition monitoring. Int. J. Prod. Econ. **169**(C), 156–168 (2015)
4. Castanier, B., Lemoine, D.: A preliminary integrated model for optimizing tactical production planning and condition-based maintenance. In: Industrial Engineering and Systems Management - IESM 2011, Metz, France, pp. 998–1007 (2011)
5. Comelli, M., Gourgand, M., Lemoine, D.: A review of tactical planning models. J. Syst. Sci. Syst. Eng. **17**(2), 204–229 (2006)
6. Billington, P.J., McClain, J.O., Thomas, L.J.: Mathematical programming approaches to capacity-constrained MRP systems: review. Formulation Probl. Reduction Manag. Sci. **29**(10), 1126–1141 (1983)
7. Buschkühl, L., Sahling, F., Helber, S., Tempelmeier, H.: Dynamic capacitated lotsizing problems: a classification and review of solution approaches. OR Spect. **32**, 231–261 (2010). https://doi.org/10.1007/s00291-008-0150-7
8. Van Noortwijk, J.M.: A survey of the application of gamma processes in maintenance. Reliab. Eng. Syst. Saf. **94**, 2–21 (2009)
9. Castanier, B., Bérenguer, C., Grall, A.: A sequential condition-based repair/replacement policy with non periodic inspections for a system subject to continuous wear. Appl. Stoch. Model. Bus. Ind. **19**, 327–347 (2003)

Intelligent Systems for Manufacturing Planning and Control in the Industry 4.0

Comparison Between Product and Process Oriented Zero-Defect Manufacturing (ZDM) Approaches

Foivos Psarommatis[✉] and Dimitris Kiritsis

École Polytechnique Fédérale de Lausanne, ICT for Sustainable Manufacturing, EPFL
SCI-STI-DK, Lausanne, Switzerland
`foivos.psarommatis@epfl.ch`

Abstract. Contemporary manufacturing companies pay a lot of attention to product quality as this aspect affects directly their competitiveness, productivity and the reputation of the company. Traditional quality improvement methods such as Six Sigma, Lean etc. seems unable to cope with the market's quality standards. Contemporary technological advancements allowed the successful implementation of Zero Defect Manufacturing (ZDM) which is replacing traditional quality improvement methods. According to a recent review article ZDM can be implemented in two ways the product oriented and the process oriented approach, but there is no clear understanding of the advantages and disadvantages of each approach. The current research proposes a methodology for quantifying the performance of each approach. To accomplish that a set of ZDM parameters is defined to describe the problem and the proposed methodology is applied on a specific industrial use case in order to enumerate the ZDM parameters. The results from the application of the proposed methodology will assist manufacturers and researchers to select the most suitable approach to their specific case in order to achieve sustainable manufacturing. The results showed that the performance of either product or process oriented approach is heavily depending on the input parameters and use case.

Keywords: Zero Defect Manufacturing · ZDM · Product oriented · Process oriented · Quality management

1 Introduction and State of the Art

Contemporary manufacturing companies pay a lot of attention to product quality as this aspect affects directly their competitiveness, productivity and the reputation of the company [1]. Low quality products may have numerus negative implications for a manufacturing company such as direct economic losses or increasing of the negative environmental impact of the production system. At the same time there can be also indirect economic losses due to customer dissatisfaction, which can have severe impact to the profitability of a manufacturing company [2, 3]. Therefore, manufacturers must implement at least one Continues Improvement (CI) method, such as Lean manufacturing,

© IFIP International Federation for Information Processing 2021
Published by Springer Nature Switzerland AG 2021
A. Dolgui et al. (Eds.): APMS 2021, IFIP AICT 630, pp. 105–112, 2021.
https://doi.org/10.1007/978-3-030-85874-2_11

Six Sigma etc. in order to ensure that the produced products are of high quality and the performance of the production at acceptable levels [4]. Traditional CI methods are widely used in the manufacturing domain but because of their design are struggling to cope with the current needs of the market [5]. In a recent literature review paper the characteristics of the traditional quality improvement methods were analyzed and their enabling factors and barriers were identified ending to the conclusion that there is a need for new quality improvement methods that can reach higher levels of sustainability [6].

Contemporary technological advancements allowed the successful implementation of an approach called Zero Defect Manufacturing (ZDM) [7, 8]. The implementation of ZDM can offer to manufacturers possibilities that previous CI methods were unable to provide [8] and at the same time improve the performance of a system. ZDM is implemented using four individual strategies named "detect", "predict", "repair" and "prevent" as described by Psarommatis et al. [8]. Those strategies and their connections between them can be seen in Fig. 1. A key feature of ZDM is the fact that for every quality oriented event whether it is detection or prediction a mitigation action must be performed. Doing that it can be assured that at the end of the production there are only acceptable parts and no defected products will end to the customers.

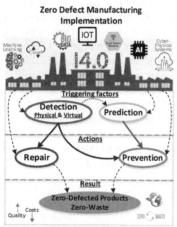

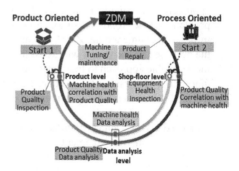

Fig. 1. ZDM implementation strategies [8]   **Fig. 2.** ZDM product and process approaches [8]

ZDM utilizes many of the tools and methods that traditional quality improvement methods are using, but the biggest difference is the addition of the "prediction" approach and therefore it is able to offer more efficient prevention actions, serving the objective "do things right the first time". Because of the uncertainty that manufacturing systems have defects are an unavoidable phenomenon, ZDM utilizes the predictive techniques to aim for the best solution but it also utilizes corrective and preventive techniques to act in case of a defect. Using all three techniques corrective, preventive and predictive can significantly increase the level of efficiency and sustainability, something that manufacturing companies are keen to achieve [9].

ZDM approach can be implemented on both the product and process level, something that is not the case for traditional quality improvement methods which are implemented only on the process level [6, 10]. Figure 2 illustrates the product and process approach that ZDM can implement [8]. The difference is the starting point of the implementation of the ZDM. On the one hand product ZDM starts from the investigation and analysis of the quality of the product and in case of abnormalities are identified, then the process/machine is investigated. On the other hand, the process ZDM starts from the investigation and analysis of the health of a machine and, by extend, the process and, again, if abnormalities are observed the quality of the produced product is investigated. In both approaches the same steps are followed but in different order. The result from both approaches is the same, which is achieving ZDM. What is important is that for the successful implementation of ZDM data from both the product and process levels must be taken [11] regardless the ZDM approach. Early studies in ZDM presented high quality solutions utilizing data from both the product and process level without differentiating them [12]. In fact many studies have been performed using one of the two ZDM approaches with significant results [13, 14], but without maximizing their results from selecting the most effective ZDM approach for their use case.

Contemporary manufacturing companies are mainly focusing on the number of products they produce, acquiring new customers, increasing distribution networks, and preparing for next season without considering the severity of the cost of poor product quality [15]. This cost includes both internal and external costs, from the direct costs arising from a defective product to the disruption of the consumer relationships and company's reputation [16]. Poor quality costs can be classified to the following categories: rework costs, freight costs, chargebacks, product returns and loss of sales [17, 18]. According to the American Society for Quality (ASQ) companies lacking effective quality management often have a cost of poor quality equal to 20% of sales or more [19].

To the authors' best knowledge all the studies implementing ZDM are selecting an approach without evidence of its superiority than the other ZDM approach. In literature there is no study that identifies the key parameters that defines the two ZDM approaches and study their performance. This has as a result researchers and manufacturers to select either approach according to their experience. Furthermore, the identification and the definition of the two ZDM approaches was introduced in 2020 by Psarommatis et al. [6, 8], therefore it is logical that there are no studies on this topic. The last decade many studies have been performed towards a product oriented approaches [20–23]. Therefore, the current paper aims to provide a methodology for comparing of the two ZDM approaches and define the parameters that should drive the decision for selecting either product or process oriented ZDM implementation.

2   Proposed Methodology

In the current chapter the proposed methodology for the generic quantification of the performance of product and process oriented ZDM will be presented. The goal was to create a lean method easy to use to support manufacturers and researchers on selecting the proper approach depending on their specific case for harvesting as much as possible from ZDM implementation. The first step for establishing the proposed method was to define the two approaches and identify the key parameters that are involved.

Table 1 presents the key parameters identified for the formalization of the two ZDM approaches. Manufacturers implementing quality improvement methods because their systems are characterized by a certain defect rate (DR) which must be reduced. The defect rate has direct link with the losses that are arising due to poor quality (PQLR). The PQLR is also linked with the corresponding profit margin that manufacturers set to their products. In the product oriented (PRD) ZDM all the products are inspected therefore the cost of inspection is a key factor on this approach. Furthermore, if defects are detected then they must be repaired to meet the specification. The inspection process has a specific accuracy, meaning that some defects might pass undetected according to that accuracy. When defects are detected the process data are analyzed to identify the cause of the defect and correct it. The analysis of the process data has a cost which needs to be included (MDAC).

Table 1. Defined problem parameters

Parameter name	Notation	Parameter description
Defect Rate	DR	- Is a percentage that shows how many defects are estimated that will occur
Profit	PRF	- Is a percentage illustrating the profit margin that a manufacturer sets compared to the products production cost
Poor Quality Ratio	PQLR	- It is a percentage showing the potential losses due to poor quality compared to the total sales. In this factor the following aspects are included: freight costs, chargebacks, product returns and loss of sales
Inspection Cost	PIC	- It is a percentage showing how much it costs the inspection per unit of product compared to the unit cost
Machine Data Analysis Cost	MDAC	- It is a percentage showing how much it costs the data analysis per unit of product compared to the unit cost
Machine Data Correlation Accuracy	MDA	- It is a percentage showing the probability of the accuracy of the system that correlates machine data with product defects
Inspection Accuracy	IA	- It is a percentage showing the probability of being accurate the inspection equipment and accurately detect a product defect
Rework Cost	RC	- It is a percentage showing the cost that is required for reworking a part compared to the unit cost

On the other hand, the processes oriented (PRS) ZDM as stated by Fig. 2 analyses all the process data for all the products being produced, which implies a Machine Data Analytics Cost, MDAC. If abnormalities are detected to the process data, inspection is performed to the related parts. If the inspection results to a detection of a defect, this defect must be repaired. As in the product-oriented approach the PQLR is also present on the process oriented approach.

To make the proposed method as generic as possible and independent of use case all the defined parameters presented in Table 1 are in percentages and the cost-oriented values are related to the unit cost, which is set to be 1. Equations 1–8 are used to calculate the performance of each approach. More specifically, the performance of each approach is given by Eq. 8, which contains only the terms that are different in both cases and all the terms that are included to both cases, such as maintenance are not studied. The outcome of Eq. 8 is measured in money units and represents the cost that each approach is adding to the total production cost. Therefore, the best performed approach is the one with the lowest adding cost.

$$Salles = unitCost * lifeVolume * (1 + PRF) \tag{1}$$

$$TheoreticalDefects(ThD) = DR * lifeVolume \tag{2}$$

$$UndetectedDefects(UnD) = \begin{cases} ThD - lifeVolume * DR * IA &, PRD \\ ThD - ThD * MDA * IA &, PRS \end{cases} \tag{3}$$

$$PoorQualityLosses(PQL) = \frac{UnD * PQLR * Salles}{ThD} \tag{4}$$

$$ICtotal = \begin{cases} ThD * IA * PIC &, PRD \\ ThD * MDA * IA * PIC &, PRS \end{cases} \tag{5}$$

$$MDACtotal = \begin{cases} ThD * IA * MDAC &, PRD \\ ThD * MDA * MDAC &, PRS \end{cases} \tag{6}$$

$$RCtotal = \begin{cases} ThD * IA * RC &, PRD \\ ThD * MDA * IA * RC &, PRS \end{cases} \tag{7}$$

$$\boldsymbol{Perf = ICtotal + MDACtotal + PQL + RCtotal} \tag{8}$$

3 Visualization of PRD and PRS ZDM Approaches

Using the methodology presented in Sect. 2 and using specific enumerated values of the parameters defined in Table 1 the performance of PRD and PRS are visualized for a specific industrial use case in the semi-conductor domain. Initial trials showed that the parameters named PIC and MDAC (Table 1) have the highest influence to the final result. Therefore, those values were selected to take multiple values keeping the rest constant. More specifically parameters DR, PRF, PQLR, MDA, IA, and RC have taken the actual value that it is been used in the real industrial use case while the values for the PIC and MDAC were taken a value from a range using as limits some extreme values. To visualize and compare the two approaches the relative difference between PRD and PRS approaches were used, slightly modified (Eq. 9). The modification is that in the numerator the difference between the $Perf_{PRD}$ and $Perf_{PRS}$ is calculated without converting it to the absolute value. This means that when the relative difference is positive the PRD approach is better and when it is negative the PRS is better.

$$relDif = 100\% * \frac{Perf_{PRD} - Perf_{PRS}}{\frac{Perf_{PRD} + Perf_{PRS}}{2}} \tag{9}$$

Figure 3 illustrates the visualization of the quantification of the performance of PRD and PRS approaches. On the x-axis is the parameter PIC which takes values between [0.01,0.36] and each plot has six lines representing MDAC. The results show that for low PIC and high MDAC values the PRD approach is better where as for the opposite situation high PIC and low MDAC the PRS is better. The two top plots of Fig. 3 have PQLR 0.05 which is low compared to the literature and the two bottom plots have PQLR 0.3. Those values were selected as extreme values in order to visualize the effect of PQLR parameter. The effect that PQLR has to the solution is that the higher it is the plots are moving upwards and at the same time the slope of the curves is decreased. The life volume does not have any influence on the final result. Furthermore, the rest of the parameters PRF, MDA, IA and RC have less effect but always at the same direction. Depending on their values they intensify or lessen the performance of each approach.

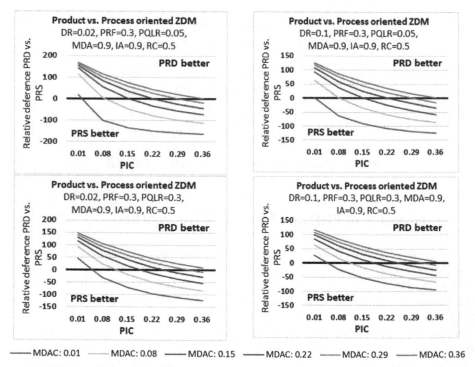

Fig. 3. Product and process oriented ZDM comparison for the current use case

4 Conclusions and Future Work

This paper proposed a method for quantifying the selection of product and process oriented ZDM approaches. The proposed method was based on identifying the differences between the two approaches and quantify only those. To this extend eight parameters were defined based on which the quantification of the performance of each ZDM approach was performed. From those eight parameters the inspection cost (PIC) and the machine data analysis cost (MDAC) were the parameters that affect the selection the most. The results from the performed analysis revealed that the selection of product or process oriented ZDM approach is heavily depending on the application and the selections that manufacturers will perform in term of equipment. Therefore, as conclusion from the analysis someone can keep that both approaches can be efficient but depending on the selections one of them will produce better results than the other one. Therefore, the practicality of the proposed approach is that researchers and manufactures could use the proposed methodology to compare both ZDM prior to the implementation of a ZDM application in order to select the most efficient and sustainable way to implement ZDM. The selection of the proper ZDM approach will ensure that no resources are wasted and at the same time increase the sustainability of the system which is crucial step to accomplish. Future research will focus on the enhancement of the proposed approach for identifying in more details the parameters that are involved in the problem.

Acknowledgments. The presented work was partially supported by the projects Eur3ka and QU4LITY, EU H2020 projects under grant agreements No 101016175 and No 825030 accordingly. The paper reflects the authors' views and the Commission is not responsible for any use that may be made of the information it contains.

References

1. Colledani, M., Coupek, D., Verl, A., Aichele, J., Yemane, A.: Design and evaluation of in-line product repair strategies for defect reduction in the production of electric drives. Proc. CIRP **21**, 159–164 (2014). https://doi.org/10.1016/j.procir.2014.03.186
2. Jun, J., Chang, T.-W., Jun, S.: Quality prediction and yield improvement in process manufacturing based on data analytics. Processes **8**(9), 1068 (2020). https://doi.org/10.3390/pr8091068
3. Psarommatis, F., Zheng, X., Kiritsis, D.: A two-layer criteria evaluation approach for rescheduling efficiently semi-automated assembly lines with high number of rush orders. Proc. CIRP **97**, 172–177 (2021). https://doi.org/10.1016/j.procir.2020.05.221
4. Özcan, A.M., Akdoğan, A., Durakbasa, N.M.: Improvements in manufacturing processes by measurement and evaluation studies according to the quality management system standard in automotive industry. In: Durakbasa, N.M., Gençyılmaz, M.G. (eds.) ISPR 2020. LNME, pp. 483–492. Springer, Cham (2021). https://doi.org/10.1007/978-3-030-62784-3_41
5. Eleftheriadis, R.J., Myklebust, O.: A guideline of quality steps towards zero defect manufacturing in industry. In: 2016 International Conference on Industrial Engineering and Operations Management, pp. 332–340 (2016)
6. Psarommatis, F., Prouvost, S., May, G., Kiritsis, D.: Product quality improvement policies in industry 4. 0: characteristics, enabling factors, barriers, and evolution toward zero defect manufacturing. Front. Comput. Sci. **2**(August), 1–15 (2020). https://doi.org/10.3389/fcomp.2020.00026

7. Mourtzis, D., Vlachou, E., Milas, N.: Industrial big data as a result of IoT adoption in manufacturing. Proc. CIRP **55**, 290–295 (2016). https://doi.org/10.1016/J.PROCIR.2016.07.038

8. Psarommatis, F., May, G., Dreyfus, P.-A., Kiritsis, D.: Zero defect manufacturing: state-of-the-art review, shortcomings and future directions in research. Int. J. Prod. Res. **7543**, 1–17 (2020). https://doi.org/10.1080/00207543.2019.1605228

9. Krishna, L.S.R., Srikanth, P.J.: Evaluation of environmental impact of additive and subtractive manufacturing processes for sustainable manufacturing. Mater. Today Proc. (2021). https://doi.org/10.1016/j.matpr.2020.12.060

10. Psarommatis, F., Kiritsis, D.: A scheduling tool for achieving zero defect manufacturing (ZDM): a conceptual framework. In: Moon, I., Lee, G.M., Park, J., Kiritsis, D., von Cieminski, G. (eds.) APMS 2018. IAICT, vol. 536, pp. 271–278. Springer, Cham (2018). https://doi.org/10.1007/978-3-319-99707-0_34

11. Myklebust, O.: Zero defect manufacturing: a product and plant oriented lifecycle approach. Proc. CIRP **12**, 246–251 (2013). https://doi.org/10.1016/j.procir.2013.09.043

12. Eleftheriadis, R.J., Myklebust, O.: A guideline of quality steps towards zero defect manufacturing in industry. In: Proceedings of the International Conference on Industrial Engineering and Operations Management, pp. 332–340 (2016)

13. Eger, F., Reiff, C., Brantl, B., Colledani, M., Verl, A.: Correlation analysis methods in multi-stage production systems for reaching zero-defect manufacturing. Proc. CIRP **72**, 635–640 (2018). https://doi.org/10.1016/j.procir.2018.03.163

14. Sousa, J., Ferreira, J., Lopes, C., Sarraipa, J., Silva, J.: Enhancing the steel tube manufacturing process with a zero defects approach. In: ASME International Mechanical Engineering Congress and Exposition, Proceedings (IMECE), vol. 2B-2020, February 2020. https://doi.org/10.1115/IMECE2020-24678

15. Cheah, S.J., Amirul, A.S., Taib, F.: Tracking hidden quality costs in a manufacturing company: an action research. Int. J. Qual. Reliab. Manag. **28**(4), 405–425 (2011). https://doi.org/10.1108/02656711111121816

16. Tannock, J., Saelem, S.: Manufacturing disruption costs due to quality loss. Int. J. Qual. Reliab. Manag. **24**(3), 263–278 (2007). https://doi.org/10.1108/02656710710730861

17. Taidi, R.: Cost of poor quality : quality management in lean manufacturing and the effectiveness of the ' Zero defects ' goal " 1," Sci. Coop. Int. J. Financ. Business, Econ. Mark. Inf. Syst. **1**(1), 61–70 (2015)

18. Faciane, M.: Reducing the costs of poor quality: a manufacturing case study. Walden Diss. Dr. Stud., Jan. 2018. https://scholarworks.waldenu.edu/dissertations/5329. Accessed 01 Mar 2021

19. "What is Cost of Quality (COQ)? I ASQ." https://asq.org/quality-resources/cost-of-quality. Accessed 02 Mar 2021

20. Myklebust, O.: Zero defect manufacturing: a product and plant oriented lifecycle approach. Proc. CIRP **12**, 246–251 (2013). https://doi.org/10.1016/j.procir.2013.09.043

21. Hoang, X.L., Hildebrandt, C., Fay, A.: Product-oriented description of manufacturing resource skills. IFAC-PapersOnLine **51**(11), 90–95 (2018). https://doi.org/10.1016/j.ifacol.2018.08.240

22. Zheng, X., Psarommatis, F., Petrali, P., Turrin, C., Lu, J., Kiritsis, D.: A quality-oriented digital twin modelling method for manufacturing processes based on a multi-agent architecture. Proc. Manuf. **51**, 309–315 (2020). https://doi.org/10.1016/j.promfg.2020.10.044

23. Psarommatis, F., Kiritsis, D.: Identification of the inspection specifications for achieving zero defect manufacturing. In: Ameri, F., Stecke, K.E., von Cieminski, G., Kiritsis, D. (eds.) APMS 2019. IAICT, vol. 566, pp. 267–273. Springer, Cham (2019). https://doi.org/10.1007/978-3-030-30000-5_34

Industry 4.0: An Indian Perspective

Anbesh Jamwal[1] , Rajeev Agrawal[1(✉)], Monica Sharma[1,2], and Saurabh Pratap[3]

[1] Department of Mechanical Engineering, Malaviya National Institute of Technology,
Jaipur, India
ragrawal.mech@mnit.ac.in
[2] Department of Management Studies, Malaviya National Institute of Technology, Jaipur, India
[3] Department of Mechanical Engineering, Indian Institute of Technology-BHU, Varanasi, India

Abstract. Industry 4.0 technologies have changed the manufacturing trends in global industries. Industries are adopting Industry 4.0 business models to complete mass customized demands and to compete with global industries. Industry 4.0 can be considered as the current trend of data exchange in manufacturing processes and automation. In India, Industry 4.0 is in its initial stages where the terms digitalization and Industry 4.0 are more widely accepted than fourth industrial revolution. The research work on Industry 4.0 is still limited in India. However, the Government of India has launched some policies and initiatives related to Industry 4.0 and its technologies. The main aim of this paper (1) to provide the more depth insight about the Industry 4.0 and similar terms. (2) to suggest the policies related to India for the transition to Industry 4.0. Indian industries should consider the Industry 4.0 practices seriously as they are shifting their business models from traditional to Industry 4.0 business models. Some issues related to Industry 4.0 implementation like cyber security, machine-to-machine interaction, reliability and stability of CPS should be considered in a better way. In this paper we have discussed about the different initiative by Government of India related for Industry 4.0 technologies. There is need to work on (1) Initiatives related to high investments and technological developments in SMEs and MSMEs industry sectors (2) Identification of infrastructure facilities required for Industry 4.0 and current readiness score of industries. (3) Initiatives related to awareness about Industry 4.0 benefits for industries as well as society.

Keywords: Industry 4.0 · Fourth industrial revolution · Policies · Challenges · Sustainability · India

1 Introduction

The fourth industrial revolution is also known as Industry 4.0 which is current trend of data exchange and automation in industries [1]. In past few years, Industry 4.0 is emerged as an emerging area of interest for both academics and industries. "Smart manufacturing" is known as the central element for Industry 4.0 which considers the integration of manufacturing activities within the industry, includes supply chain activities and product life cycle [2]. The Industry 4.0 relies on the data gathering from manufacturing activities

© IFIP International Federation for Information Processing 2021
Published by Springer Nature Switzerland AG 2021
A. Dolgui et al. (Eds.): APMS 2021, IFIP AICT 630, pp. 113–123, 2021.
https://doi.org/10.1007/978-3-030-85874-2_12

within industry, intelligent decision making based on data analytics and provide useful information for further actions [3]. The main key enabling technologies for Industry 4.0 are CPS, machine learning, BDA, deep learning, blockchain technology, Internet of things (IoT) and cloud computing [4]. In Industry 4.0 "smart factory" can be referred to transition from traditional automation to fully flexible and connected manufacturing systems in which data from manufacturing activities can be used to learn and adapt the dynamic changes in market [5]. In the smart factories the term "Cyber physical systems" can be referred to monitor the physical activities and processes in the industry, make decentralized and intelligent decisions, create a virtual space of physical entities. The term "IoT" can be referred to CPS which can cooperate and communicate with humans as well as each other in real time with the help of internet services [6]. Global industries are now adopting Industry 4.0 practices to meet global standards and maintain market reputation [4, 7]. The concept of Industry 4.0 is widely accepted in both developing and developed nations [2]. However, few countries have achieved sustainability in Industry 4.0 practices while some are still struggling with the roadmap developments for Industry 4.0 [8]. India can be considered as a major manufacturing hub which manufacture in which automobile sector is main. Indian industries are now focusing on the implementation of Industry 4.0 technologies and practices [9, 10]. However, the term "fourth industrial revolution" is more familiar and appealing than "Industry 4.0" in most of countries and it has different level of acceptance [11]. It is true that we are in the initial phases of fourth industrial revolution where basic requirement is automation and digitalization of industries [12]. Advanced technologies like artificial intelligence, machine learning, deep learning and blockchain technology can be acts as an enabler for the transition of industries from Industry 3.0 to fourth industrial revolution. The terms "Fourth industrial revolution" and "Industry 4.0" are the same or there is any difference between these terms? Can we use these two terms interchangeably? In the present study we have used the "Industry 4.0" as the representative term to investigate whether these two terms are similar or there is any difference between these terms? What are the different policies for Industry 4.0 in India? These all questions have been addressed in this study. In the next section of paper, we have discussed different Industry 4.0 technologies, various challenges and enablers, design principles and value drivers for the better understanding of Industry 4.0 concept. In the last section of paper, we have discussed various policy and implications related issues for Indian industries.

2   Industry 4.0

2.1   Definition and Concept in Literature

The term "Industry 4.0" was firstly coined at the Hannover fair, Germany in 2011 which has gained attention from practitioners, policymakers, politicians, government officials and researchers all over the world [1]. Basically, Industry 4.0 is driven by main disruptions are: IoT, additive manufacturing, BDA, machine learning, artificial intelligence, blockchain technology which are providing the digital solutions to the manufacturing organizations [4]. Industry 4.0 is characterized by the mass customization of products within highly flexible and reconfigurable manufacturing systems [7].

In this context there is need for digitalize and redesign traditional manufacturing/ production systems for the transition of Industry 4.0 from Industry 3.0. Also, the concept of Industry 4.0 is linked with the other emerging concepts e.g., circular economy, bioeconomy, green economy. Besides this, Industry 4.0 promises for shorter delivery time, higher quality products, more automated and efficient manufacturing systems, profitable and smart products and agility in production systems to handle volatile market demands [13]. These above characteristics and key enabling technologies are not the reason for "4.0". However, it is true that this is major fourth upheaval in the manufacturing sector after the lean production systems revolution (1960s), flexible manufacturing systems (1980s), reconfigurable manufacturing systems (1990s), Automation and agent-based manufacturing (2000s). Most of digital technologies associated with Industry 4.0 have been developed few years ago and some of them are still not ready for use up to scale in most of developing nations. Few studies reported that these technologies are reliable and cost effective for some specific industrial applications in manufacturing sector [14, 15]. Table 1 shows the different key enabling technologies of Industry 4.0.

Table 1. Different Industry 4.0 technologies with their description and benefits to industries

Key enabling technology	Description	Benefits to industries
Digital Twin	Digital twins are real time virtual representation of processes or physical entities in a system. These are virtual model of a product, process or service	Reliability improvement, productivity, reduce market reputation and product availability risks
Big data analytics	Big data analytics helps to extract to useful information from large volume of data	Improved operational efficiency and customer satisfaction
Blockchain Technology	Blockchain technology is a decentralized and distributor ledger which records the provenance of digital asset	Reduced costs, better transparency, enhanced security
Cloud computing	Cloud computing is delivery of computing services which includes: storage, servers, software, analytics and database	Increased collaboration, quality control, cost savings
Internet of things	Internet of things defined as networking of physical objects embedded with sensors or software's	Cost reduction, mobility and agility
Artificial intelligence	It is the simulation of human intelligence processes by machines	Reduction in human errors, faster decisions

(continued)

Table 1. (*continued*)

Key enabling technology	Description	Benefits to industries
Machine learning & Deep learning	Machine learning is a approach for data analysis which automate analytical model development. Deep learning is the class of machine learning approaches uses multiple layers for data extraction	Optimization, conditional monitoring, predictive maintenance, simulation and modeling
Additive manufacturing	Additive manufacturing is 3D printing process focus on layer-by-layer manufacturing for lighter and stronger parts	Cost reduction, mass customization, waste reduction
Flexible and Reconfigurable manufacturing	Flexible manufacturing systems can easily adapt the changes in quantity and type of manufacturing. Reconfigurable manufacturing systems helps to adapt the dynamic changes in market	Cost reduction, quality improvement, customer satisfaction
AR and VR technologies	AR and VR technologies helps to bridge gap between physical and virtual world	Risk reduction, training

Manufacturing in Industry 4.0 means machines are intelligent enough to operate themselves and adapt the dynamic changes in market [16]. Machines in Industry 4.0 considered as an independent entity which focus on data collection, analysis and intelligent decision making [17]. The concept of self-optimization, self-customization and self-cognition have made this possible through which manufacturers can communicate with the computers also. Smart factory can be considered as one of key feature in Industry 4.0 [18]. The term "Smart Factory" in Industry 4.0 describes highly connected and digitalized environment where the equipment and machines are able to improve the process with the help of self-optimization and automation [19].

2.2   Value Drivers, Design Principles and Challenges in Industry 4.0

Industry 4.0 is one of the emerging concepts in the developing nations and delivering values to industries and manufactures. To experience the benefits of Industry 4.0 in developing nations there is need to consider both the role and opportunities of Industry 4.0 in industries [4, 9, 10]. In Industry 4.0 large amount of data is generated from manufacturing processes and activities which needs to processed and refined with the advanced analytical tools. For this purpose, machine learning and deep learning tools are the suitable approaches [14, 15]. Considering the current manufacturing scenario, it

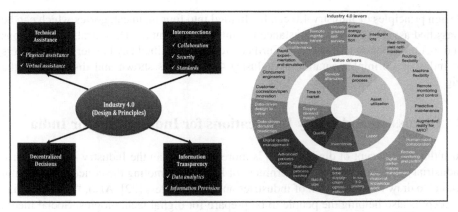

Fig. 1. Industry 4.0 design and principles, value drivers (Adapted from: [20])

is important to focus on tool wear rate, predictive maintenance and machine degradation issues. Which type of data can be useful for the future reference and use? Which technology will give the most return in the investment and which technologies are not suitable for industry?

To answer such type of the questions a digital compass can be used presented in the Fig. 1 which consists of eight main drivers of Industry 4.0 with 26 levers. Further, the

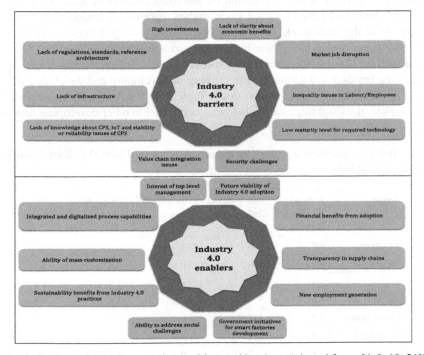

Fig. 2. Industry 4.0 implementation enablers and barriers (Adapted from: [4, 9, 10, 21])

design principles of Industry 4.0 can be divided into four main categories which can be classified as: (1) Technical Assistance (2) Interconnection (3) Decentralized decisions and, (4) Information transparency. Further, we have identified key barriers and enablers to Industry 4.0 implementation to Industry 4.0 which is shown and discussed in the Fig. 2.

3   Discussion and Policy Implications for Industry 4.0 for India

In India, the concept of digitalization is more popular than the Industry 4.0 and fourth industrial revolution because Government of India is promoting the concept of "Digital India" to draw more attention of industries and stakeholders [22]. Also, "Digital India" concept is also helping the people to be prepare for digital technologies. Social media and other media platforms are also promoting the concept of Industry 4.0 and related technologies for the adoption of new industry practices [23]. MNCs are now investing more for Industry 4.0 in the India due to cheap labour and government policies related to Industry 4.0 [9, 10]. However, some of the researchers are also very concerned with the Industry 4.0 research trend in India since the Industry 4.0 and related technologies has not been clearly defined. Now the various industries are adopting the Industry 4.0 practices in India [24, 25].

Several studies reported that the developing nations like India still lacks in positive attitude, management support, skilled labour and infrastructure for Industry 4.0 pratices adoption [9, 10]. There is need to rethink on the social, economic and environmental aspects of Industry 4.0 [26]. However, some studies reported the consideration of these three aspects in the framework development for Industry 4.0 practices for India [4, 9, 10, 27]. But these studies have some limitations and applicability in case of SMEs and MSMEs sectors. These points should be considered for the Indian industries to the shift to- wards the Industry 4.0 adoption. The ranking of developing and developed nations working for the Industry 4.0 is shown in the Table 2. In the results it can be seen that India is ranked at 91 and this ranking is low as compared to other developing nations.

Table 2. Global competitiveness ranking for Industry 4.0 (Adapted from The Global information Technology Report [12])

Rank	Nation	Network Readiness Index	Environment Index	Readiness Index	Usage Index	Impact Sub-Index
1	Singapore	6.0	6.0	6.1	6.0	6.1
2	Finland	6.0	5.6	6.6	5.8	5.8
3	Sweden	5.8	5.3	6.3	5.9	5.8
4	Norway	5.8	5.5	6.4	5.8	5.6
5	United States	5.8	5.3	6.4	5.8	5.8
6	Netherlands	5.8	5.5	5.9	5.9	6.0
91	India	3.8	3.7	4.4	3.3	3.6

European countries are more focused towards the Industry 4.0 practices. However, some studies have reported the consideration of sustainability aspects in Industry 4.0 practices in these countries [2, 8]. The developed nations have higher adoption level for Industry 4.0 practices because of infrastructure and technological advancements as an enabler and this acts as barrier for developing nations like India [4]. The main requirement for Industry 4.0 practice is shop floor digitalization and automation which is still missing in most of SMEs of developing nations [12]. These nations need to rethink and revisit their manufacturing systems in order to implement the Industry 4.0 practices effectively. In the European countries main participants for Industry 4.0 roadmap developments are universities, research institutes, central government and stakeholder's support. This example of the developed nations can provide the guideline for roadmap development for Industry 4.0 for India. It is true that Industry 4.0 implementation barriers, polices and drivers are highly dependent on the geographical region but the theories for Industry 4.0 are same all over the globe. In the Table 3 we have discussed the plans and initiative by Government of India for Industry 4.0 technologies.

Table 3. Initiatives by Government of India related to Industry 4.0 technologies

Ministry	Initiative
Ministry of HRD	ICTs, National Digital Library, Shodhganga, Virtual Lab project
Ministry of Heavy Industries	Smart advanced manufacturing and rapid transformation hub (SAMRATH)
Department of Science and Technology	National mission on interdisciplinary Cyber physical systems
Ministry of Electronics and IT	Digital India for digitalization
NITI Aayog	National strategy on Artificial intelligence
NITI Aayog	Blockchain: The India Strategy
Ministry of Agriculture	RFID and Blockchain in Animal Husbandry and Dairying
Ministry of Electronics and Information Technology	National Strategy for additive manufacturing
Ministry of Electronics and IT	National cloud initiative of MeghRaj
Ministry of Electronics and IT	Cyber Swachhta Kendra
Department of Science and Technology	Cognitive science research initiative
Department of Science and Technology	Big data initiative

As we have found that some of the initiatives are not clearly elaborated and defined and some of initiatives are still in their initial stages which requires coordination between the industries, stakeholders and ministries for respective initiatives. Indian government is quite aware about the digitalization concept and role of digitalization for the development of Industry 4.0 practices but still some of the initiatives are at initial stages and requires high level of effort for successful implementation. The following policies are suggested for the implementation of Industry 4.0 practices effectively in the India:

(1) The policies and strategies by the Government of India should be refined for the Industry 4.0 implementation and more elaborated towards the sustainability in manufacturing systems. In depth analysis of policies by Government of India for Industry 4.0 shows that industries and concerned stakeholders are recognizing the unfavorable conditions for social and economic aspects. (2) Initiatives related to high investments and technological developments in SMEs and MSMEs industry sectors. (3) Identification of infrastructure facilities required for Industry 4.0 and current readiness score of industries. (4) Initiatives related to awareness about Industry 4.0 benefits for industries as well as society. (5) There is need of concrete workplans which can help for the shift towards social and economic systems in Industry 4.0. (6) There is need of collaboration of local governments, SMEs, MNEs, MSMEs sector, universities and re- search institutes for Industry 4.0 awareness and establishment of required infrastructure. (7) There is need of sustainable scheduling and process plans to maximize the efficiency of operating systems. (8) There is need to minimize the polarization which may be occur due to the job loss or job change due to implementation of Industry 4.0 (9) To prepare and respond new workforce with required skills for Industry 4.0 and formulation of plans, roadmaps for effective implementation of Industry 4.0 practices in India. (10) A collaborative platform for everyone where the effectiveness of policies and coordination among the different sectors can be ensured.

4 Summary and Conclusion

The main objectives of this paper are: (1) Detailed analysis and understanding of various technologies about the Industry 4.0 (2) Policies recommendation for Indian industries for the transition to Industry 4.0. Indian industries are now adopting the digital technologies in their industries. The term "Digitalization" and "Industry 4.0" is more acceptable in India than "fourth industrial revolution" because these terms look more familiar with the different cases and scenarios in India. It is true that we are in the initial stages of fourth industrial revolution which builds on digitalization and automation in manufacturing. However, the initiatives from Indian government are now addressing these challenges and technologies in a better way through the various programs. Industries from India needs to consider Industry 4.0 as a serious issue because in India the manufacturing sector is largely dependent on SMEs which are still following the traditional approaches. Some major issues like Machine-to-machine interaction, blockchain, high computation power, cyber security and reliability and stability of CPS should be taken care in a better way for the implementation of Industry 4.0. We have discussed the different initiative of Government of India and policies recommendation in the third section of study. In India, SMEs plays a significant role in development of the economy, the innovations in MNEs is also largely dependent on the SMEs. There is need to coordination between the SMEs in order to implement the Industry 4.0. Thus, it can be stated that digitalization of shop floor and automation is the main requirement for the implementation of Industry 4.0 in SMEs in India.

Like every research we have some limitation in this study. This study doesn't provide the validate empirical findings to support the policies implications as very few studies have been conducted on Industry 4.0 and most of them are not validated because in India Industry 4.0 is in initial stages. The policies recommended are based on the initiatives, developed nations and literature available. However, we have followed the reports and research findings presented in different seminars and awareness programs. Second, the difference between the synonyms of Industry 4.0 is provided but rationale is not well grounded. The reason behind this, mostly authors have used and using these terms interchangeably. The reliable statistics of actual progress about the Industry 4.0 implementation is not provided because most of the reports on the actual progress are not validated or empirically proven. This research can be extended in the different directions for Indian industries. In the future the impact of Industry 4.0 on the business, economic, social and environmental perspective can be investigated for SMEs or MSMEs. Inter country comparison can be also done for the Industry 4.0 practices in future. However, some studies have shown these cases but these studies having some limitations and limited applicability. This will help to find out the common driver and feature of Industry 4.0 for each nation because the theories related to the Industry 4.0 are same across the globe.

References

1. Kim, J.H.: A review of cyber-physical system research relevant to the emerging IT trends: industry 4.0, IoT, big data, and cloud computing. J. Ind. Integr. Manage. **2**, 1750011 (2017)
2. Machado, C.G., Winroth, M.P., Ribeiro da Silva, E.H.D.: Sustainable manufacturing in Industry 4.0: an emerging research agenda. Int. J. Prod. Res. **58**, 1462–1484 (2020). https://doi.org/10.1080/00207543.2019.1652777
3. Alcácer, V., Cruz-Machado, V.: Scanning the industry 4.0: a literature review on technologies for manufacturing systems. Eng. Sci. Technol. Int. J. **22**, 899–919 (2019). https://doi.org/10.1016/j.jestch.2019.01.006
4. Raj, A., Dwivedi, G., Sharma, A., Lopes de Sousa Jabbour, A.B., Rajak, S.: Barriers to the adoption of industry 4.0 technologies in the manufacturing sector: an inter-country comparative perspective. Int. J. Prod. Econ. **224**, 107546–107546 (2020). https://doi.org/10.1016/j.ijpe.2019.107546
5. Chen, G., Wang, P., Feng, B., Li, Y., Liu, D.: The framework design of smart factory in discrete manufacturing industry based on cyber-physical system. Int. J. Comput. Integr. Manuf. **33**, 79–101 (2020). https://doi.org/10.1080/0951192X.2019.1699254
6. Latorre-Biel, J.-I., Faulín, J., Juan, A.A., Jiménez-Macías, E.: Petri net model of a smart factory in the frame of industry 4.0. IFAC-PapersOnLine **51**, 266–271 (2018). https://doi.org/10.1016/j.ifacol.2018.03.046
7. Lopes de Sousa Jabbour, A.B., Jabbour, C.J.C., Godinho Filho, M., Roubaud, D.: Industry 4.0 and the circular economy: a proposed research agenda and original roadmap for sustainable operations. Ann. Oper. Res. **270**(1–2), 273–286 (2018). https://doi.org/10.1007/s10479-018-2772-8
8. de Sousa Jabbour, A.B.L., Jabbour, C.J.C., Foropon, C., Filho, M.G.: When titans meet – Can industry 4.0 revolutionise the environmentally-sustainable manufacturing wave? The role of critical success factors. Technol. Forecast. Soc. Change **132**, 18–25 (2018). https://doi.org/10.1016/j.techfore.2018.01.017
9. Yadav, G., Kumar, A., Luthra, S., Garza-Reyes, J.A., Kumar, V., Batista, L.: A framework to achieve sustainability in manufacturing organisations of developing economies using industry 4.0 technologies' enablers. Comput. Ind. **122** (2020). https://doi.org/10.1016/j.compind.2020.103280

10. Jamwal, A., Agrawal, R., Sharma, M., Kumar, V., Kumar, S.: Developing a sustainability framework for industry 4.0. Proc. CIRP. **98**, 430–435 (2021)
11. Sung, T.K.: Industry 4.0: a Korea perspective. Technol. Forecast. Soc. Change **132**, 40–45 (2018)
12. Mittal, S., Khan, M.A., Romero, D., Wuest, T.: A critical review of smart manufacturing & Industry 4.0 maturity models: Implications for small and medium-sized enterprises (SMEs). J. Manuf. Syst. **49**, 194–214 (2018).
13. Akdil, K.Y., Ustundag, A., Cevikcan, E.: Maturity and readiness model for industry 4.0 strategy. In: Industry 4.0: Managing The Digital Transformation. SSAM, pp. 61–94. Springer, Cham (2018). https://doi.org/10.1007/978-3-319-57870-5_4
14. Bajic, B., Cosic, I., Lazarevic, M., Sremcev, N., Rikalovic, A.: Machine learning techniques for smart manufacturing: applications and challenges in industry 4.0. department of industrial engineering and management Novi Sad, Serbia, vol. 29 (2018)
15. Jamwal, A., Agrawal, R., Sharma, M., Kumar, A., Kumar, V., Garza-Reyes, J.A.A.: Machine learning applications for sustainable manufacturing: a bibliometric-based review for future research. J. Enterprise Inf. Manage. (2021). https://doi.org/10.1108/JEIM-09-2020-0361. ahead-of-print
16. Adenuga, O.T., Mpofu, K., Ramatsetse, B.I.: Exploring energy efficiency prediction method for Industry 4.0: A reconfigurable vibrating screen case study. In: Vosniakos G.-C., M.A., Pellicciari M.,. Benardos P. (ed.) Procedia Manufacturing, pp. 243–250. Elsevier B.V. (2020). https://doi.org/10.1016/j.promfg.2020.10.035
17. Brozzi, R., Forti, D., Rauch, E., Matt, D.T.: The advantages of industry 4.0 applications for sustainability: results from a sample of manufacturing companies. Sustainability (Switzerland) **12**, (2020). https://doi.org/10.3390/su12093647
18. Felstead, M.: Cyber-physical production systems in industry 4.0: Smart factory performance, innovation-driven manufacturing process innovation, and sustainable supply chain networks. Econ. Manage. Financ. Markets **14**, 37–43 (2019). https://doi.org/10.22381/EMFM14420195
19. Osterrieder, P., Budde, L., Friedli, T.: The smart factory as a key construct of industry 4.0: a systematic literature review. Int. J. Prod. Econ. **221**, 107476–107476 (2020). https://doi.org/10.1016/j.ijpe.2019.08.011
20. Baur, C., Wee, D.: Manufacturing's Next Act. McKinsey & Company, vol. 6 (2015)
21. Krishnan, S., Gupta, S., Kaliyan, M., Kumar, V., Garza-Reyes, J.A.: Assessing the key enablers for Industry 4.0 adoption using MICMAC analysis: a case study. Int. J. Product. Perform. Manage. (2021)
22. Safar, L., Sopko, J., Dancakova, D., Woschank, M.: Industry 4.0-awareness in South India. Sustainability (Switzerland) **12**, 3207–3207 (2020). https://doi.org/10.3390/SU12083207
23. Dutta, G., Kumar, R., Sindhwani, R., Singh, R.K.: Digital transformation priorities of India's discrete manufacturing SMEs – a conceptual study in perspective of Industry 4.0. Competitiv. Rev. 289–314 (2020). https://doi.org/10.1108/CR-03-2019-0031
24. Talib, S., Sharma, A., Gupta, S., Gaurav, G., Pathak, V., Shukla, R.K.: Analysis of Influential enablers for sustainable smart manufacturing in Indian manufacturing industries using TOPSIS approach. In: Phanden, R.K., Mathiyazhagan, K., Kumar, R., Paulo Da-vim, J. (eds.) Advances in Industrial and Production Engineering, pp. 621-628. Springer, Singapore (2021)
25. Aggarwal, A., Gupta, S., Ojha, M.K.: Evaluation of key challenges to industry 4.0 in Indian context: a DEMATEL approach. In: Shanker, K., Shankar, R., Sindhwani, R. (eds.) Advances in Industrial and Production Engineering. LNME, pp. 387–396. Springer, Singapore (2019). https://doi.org/10.1007/978-981-13-6412-9_37

26. Jamwal, A., Agrawal, R., Sharma, M., Kumar, V.: Review on multi-criteria decision analysis in sustainable manufacturing decision making Int. J. Sustain. Eng. (2020). https://doi.org/10.1080/19397038.2020.1866708

27. Kamble, S.S., Gunasekaran, A., Ghadge, A., Raut, R.: A performance measurement system for industry 4.0 enabled smart manufacturing system in SMMEs- a review and empirical investigation. Int. J. Prod. Econ. **229** (2020)

Opportunities of Blockchain Traceability Data for Environmental Impact Assessment in a Context of Sustainable Production

Vincent Carrières[1,2]([✉]), Andrée-Anne Lemieux[3], and Robert Pellerin[1]

[1] Ecole Polytechnique de Montréal, 2500, Chemin de Polytechnique, Montréal H3T1J4, Canada
vincent.carrieres@polymtl.ca
[2] Arts et Métiers, 151 Boulevard de l'Hospital, 75013 Paris, France
[3] Institut Français de la Mode, 34 quai d'Austerlitz, 75013 Paris, France

Abstract. Supply chains face various challenges for collecting reliable, transparent, and up-to-date data due to their increased complexity and globalization. This threatens their sustainability and limits the efficiency of environmental impact assessment of products with Life Cycle Assessment (LCA) methodology. This paper explores the opportunities, limitations, and research paths for assessing products' environmental impact using blockchain-based traceability data based on a systematic literature review. Results showed that blockchains are mainly used for product traceability and could be further used for the environmental impact assessment of products. A first architecture model and integration framework was proposed in the literature for the integration of blockchain-based LCA systems. However, the maturity of blockchain and supply chain organization are the prevalent barriers to implementing these systems. Further research is essential to shape these first results with strong opportunities identified.

Keywords: Blockchain · Traceability · LCA · Environmental impact · Sustainability · Literature review

1 Introduction

In recent years, sustainable production became a priority of industrial companies, guided by the Sustainable Development Goals (SDGs) of the United Nations that materialize 17 goals to achieve by 2030 [1]. The quest for environmental sustainability is mainly focused on reducing industrial emissions that have a persistent impact on the environment, such as global warming or ozone depletion, and ensuring the use of renewable resources [2]. Therefore, there is a strong need to access tools that can measure the environmental impact of industrial activities [3].

Life Cycle Assessment, one of the most widely used methods for assessing the environmental impact of a product during its whole life cycle [2], largely contributed to the acceleration of an environmentally sustainable production [4]. This methodological framework is divided in four main steps: goal and scope definition, Life Cycle Inventory

© IFIP International Federation for Information Processing 2021
Published by Springer Nature Switzerland AG 2021
A. Dolgui et al. (Eds.): APMS 2021, IFIP AICT 630, pp. 124–133, 2021.
https://doi.org/10.1007/978-3-030-85874-2_13

(LCI), Life Cycle Impact Assessment (LCIA) and interpretation of results. LCA studies can be used by industrial practitioners to identify the environmental "hotspots" of their production and to make decisions on the supply chain organization and product design [4] or to communicate the product's environmental impact to consumers [3].

However, although they can contribute up to 90% of a company's environmental impact [5], sustainable supply chains are hard to operationalize due to their increasing complexity and globalization [6], with difficulty ensuring traceability, transparency [7], accountability, and managing risks [8, 9]. The lack of knowledge of the suppliers' practices limits the environmental impact measurement and management [5]. Moreover, they heavily rely on centralized information systems with risks of single-point failure [7, 8] and the lack of information sharing across supply chains is not adapted to their dynamic nature [10]. These challenges faced by sustainable supply chains considerably affect LCA results' efficiency [3] with difficulty collecting available and reliable data [2]. Up to 70 to 80% of the time and resources for a LCA project is allocated to data gathering [1]. Data quality and integrity problems affect the reliability of the LCA results [2, 3]. Moreover, the temporal evolution of the environmental impact of industrial activities is significant [11] and requires conducting dynamic LCAs with up-to-date data [1].

To tackle those challenges, blockchain technology has been presented in recent scientific literature as a robust solution for establishing an efficient decentralized traceability system [12] by recording reliable, accountable, and up-to-date data across supply chains. In this context, the number of successful blockchain-based traceability platform case studies grew exponentially [13]. Despite the evident possibilities that blockchain traceability platforms offer to improve LCA conduction, there is an extensive research gap in the domain, with very little prior research done to evaluate the opportunities and the limits of combining these technologies [3]. The objective of this paper is to cover the range of opportunities of blockchain for sustainable supply chains and environmental impact assessment, and to identify the barriers to its adoption in the industry based on a literature review. The following research questions (RQs) will be addressed:

RQ1: What are the benefits of blockchain technology for supply chains and how is it used for product traceability?

RQ2: How can blockchain-based traceability platforms help create sustainable supply chains and conduct environmental impact assessment of products?

RQ3: What are the current limitations and barriers to the implementation of blockchain-based systems in the industry?

The remaining of this article is organized as follows. First, the research methodology used to conduct the systematic literature review and the analysis framework will be described in Sect. 2. Section 3 will cover the articles' main propositions, organized following the previously defined analysis framework. Finally, a general conclusion and a discussion about the future research perspectives will be presented in Sect. 4.

2   Research Methodology

This paper proposes a systematic literature review about the potential use of blockchain traceability data for assessing the environmental impact of products. The research methodology was carried out in four steps. First, a general query was realized on Google

Scholar using the keywords 'blockchain', 'traceability' and 'sustainability'. A total of 8770 articles were identified in the process. A preliminary analysis of these results permitted to refine the list of relevant keywords. The definition of inclusion and exclusion criteria of this systematic literature review was then based and adapted on two existing frameworks, classifying Multi-Criteria Decision Methods (MCDM) [31] and Machine Learning (ML) Algorithms [32] for sustainable manufacturing (SM). These frameworks describe three phases meant to cover all the aspects of MDCM and ML Algorithms in SM. The first phase of classification is to consider the aspects of sustainable manufacturing that are covered among environmental, social and economic aspects. In this study, only the environmental aspect of sustainability will be explored. The main barriers and enablers of SM regarding the environment will be included while the aspects of influencing factors, manufacturing strategies and performance indicators of SM will be excluded from this study. A technology assessment specific to blockchain and its benefits for SM will also be included in this phase. The second phase is to consider which techniques and models are covered in the review [31]. In the scope of our study, we only include blockchain traceability and LCA models. The use of ML algorithms, MCDM or all other technical or methodological enablers for SM are excluded from this review. Finally, the third phase of classification establishes which benefits of sustainability aspects can be included in a literature review [31, 32]. In this study, all environmental benefits will be discussed, including greenhouse gases (GHG) emissions, waste reduction, water footprint, and product quality.

After defining the inclusion and exclusion criteria of this study, a query was built for Scopus and Web of Science databases around the concepts of blockchain, traceability and sustainability: ABS (blockchain) AND ABS (traceability OR tracking OR trace OR assessment) AND ABS (sustainab* OR lca OR "life cycle assessment" OR footprint OR "environmental impact").We then proceeded to two sortings. First, only articles published in scientific journals, conference papers, and conference reviews in English were considered. The subjects of health, immunology, veterinary, biochemistry, and dietetics were also excluded being too distant from our scope. This brought the results to 64 documents on Scopus and 58 on Web of Science. All remaining documents from both databases were downloaded and duplicates were removed. In the second sorting, articles were read, which led to the exclusion of papers following the inclusion and exclusion criteria defined in the previous paragraph. Also, articles discussing financial or energy trading applications were removed because they were not focused on the traceability of physical industrial products. Following this second sorting, 29 articles relevant to the scope of our study were analysed.

The presentation of our results is organized to address the three research questions formulated in the introduction. RQ1 will be tackled in Sect. 3.1 with a presentation of blockchain technology and its benefits in an industrial context. Section 3.2 then focuses on the specific use of blockchain for the traceability of supply chains. To address RQ2, Sect. 3.3 will draw the opportunities of blockchain traceability for ensuring the sustainability of supply chains. Section 3.4 will review the proposed frameworks and implementations of blockchain-based impact assessment models. Finally, Sect. 3.5 will present the limitations and adoption barriers to the implementation of blockchain traceability in sustainable supply chains and give insight to RQ3.

3 Results

3.1 Presentation of Blockchain and Its Benefits

The blockchain is a shared and distributed ledger composed of a series of data blocks, linked in a chain using cryptographic methods [14, 15]. This ledger acts as a decentralized database that records, in a secure and immutable way, every transaction that has been executed in the network [7]. Multiple copies of the ledger are shared with all the peers of the network, each node possessing a full copy of the blockchain updated in real time [16, 17]. Each data block includes at least the transaction data, the hash of the block, a timestamp, and the hash of the previous block [13]. Any attempt to corrupt a block's data would therefore create a cryptographic link disruption with the following blocks values [14]. Consensus algorithms are used to establish trust. Before being recorded, each transaction is verified against the ledger's current state, ensuring that all peers of the network agree on the network's current state [14, 18]. Smart contracts also set rules for processing the transactions without the need for a third-party intermediary [15].

The main benefit of blockchain is that it is virtually impossible to alter because all network peers keep all transaction data [16]. It ensures, at the same time, the immutability, integrity, anonymity, and persistence of the data recorded in it [5]. The decentralization of the network also allows easier access to data for all blockchain users [8] and the safeguards permit to enforce trust between users [14].

3.2 Use of Blockchain for Product Traceability and Certification

Supply chain traceability is a frequently discussed solution to sustainable supply chain issues [14]. In the last few years, blockchain-based traceability platforms have been successfully implemented in various sectors covering the fashion industry [14, 19], the mining sector [6, 19], the pharmaceutical industry [6], and most of all the agri-food industry [18, 20–22]. Indeed, blockchain technology's inherent characteristics such as auditability, immutability, and transparency are valuable assets for product traceability in these industries [23]. Firstly, blockchain-based traceability is valuable for sharing information and providing a technology-based trust among stakeholders, like in its application in the organic cotton supply chain [14]. Secondly, the digitalization of supply chains using blockchain technology is also developing in cobalt mining and pharmaceutical industries to increase operational efficiency [6].

However, the main applications of blockchain-based traceability systems can be seen in the agri-food industry to trace food quality [19] and build more agile supply chains. These systems considerably reduce the product's origin identification time and facilitate eventual recall [22], with authentic data recorded from sourcing to sales stages [20]. Therefore, blockchain traceability is suitable for the origin or quality certification of food products [23]. It also has several benefits for supply chains, such as improvement of collaboration and reduced economic loss or product waste [17]. Blockchain-based traceability platforms can also be coupled with IoT or RFID technologies that oversee data collection along the supply chain and allow full digitalization [21, 22]. Blockchain-based traceability can also be used for communicating transparent information to the consumer about the origin of a final product [18, 21].

3.3 Opportunities of Blockchain for Sustainable Supply Chains

The huge potential of blockchain traceability that led industrial companies to use it for ensuring the quality, provenance, or safety of products can also be used to ensure the environmental sustainability of supply chains [17]. For example, a blockchain-based traceability infrastructure can monitor and trace flawed products accurately, decreasing the need to rework and recall [24] and therefore reducing resource consumption, generated waste, and GHG emissions [7, 17]. Blockchain platforms can also act as a monitoring system for the sustainable sourcing of raw materials [19] to avoid overexploitation and rational use of natural resources [10] by ensuring the provenance of data along the supply chain. They could also monitor and certify an ethical and sustainable production [25] by delivering transaction certificates proving the origin and quality of products, ensure that sustainable standards are being implemented across the supply chain [1]. Also, they could help businesses in managing the environmental sustainability performance of their activity [3] by providing robust indicators based on accurately corrected data and simplify sustainability reporting by making all necessary data immediately available and traceable. They could even help waste information management as part of a circular economy [26] and trace dangerous products and chemicals [17].

However, the foremost discussed opportunity of blockchain traceability for an environmentally sustainable supply chain is its ability to track the level of CO_2 emissions [27, 28] and the water consumption of a product during its entire life cycle [10]. The benefits and opportunities of blockchain traceability platforms for LCA data collection will be further explored in the next section.

3.4 Review of Blockchain-Based Impact Assessment Methods

Blockchain traceability systems could help overcome the complexity of conducting an LCA by facilitating the process of data collection [2]. Blockchain would considerably help data acquisition, give an objective insight into the functional unit and enable the accounting of all possible inputs of complex supply chains [3]. Moreover, it would allow a more fine-grained and relevant impact assessment based on actual production data and real-time data [1]. Blockchain-based LCA would also be beneficial at the design stage for eco-conception.

With all these opportunities in mind, a framework for implementing a blockchain-based LCA and a system architecture were developed [3]. It consists of a blockchain traceability platform that collects additional environmental-related data (electricity consumption, waste emission…) in traceability transactions and integrates them in the LCA calculation. It is a multilayer system with data collection with IoT, a recording of data with blockchain, an impact calculation with LCA, and visualization of impact with big data analytics [3]. Therefore, blockchain serves as a bridge between data collection and big data analytics. Combining IoT, big data analytics and blockchain is an efficient way to considerably reduce the cost and time of conducting an LCA [2]. It can also be integrated with ERP systems for even more efficient data collection [1]. Blockchain-based LCA systems could therefore automate the calculation of the environmental impact, save time and resources, and build consumer trust with the possibility to communicate real-time impact of products [3].

3.5 Adoption Barriers to Blockchain Traceability for Impact Assessment

Although blockchain-based impact assessment methods seem incredibly promising, they still face limitations due to blockchain's adoption barriers in supply chains. These implementation barriers are divided into four categories detailed in the table below [29].

Table 1. Classification of blockchain-based LCA adoption barriers

Types of adoption barriers	Challenges	Description	Articles
Technological	Scalability	Difficulty of blockchain to deal with a growing number of transactions	3, 7, 16, 22, 29, 30
	Throughput and latency	Difficulty to deal with the large number of simultaneous transaction of a SC	22
	Negative perception	Blockchain technology can be associated to cryptocurrencies, malicious activities and high-energy consumption	3, 7, 29
	Immutability	Recorded errors stay indefinitely on the blockchain	3, 7, 20, 29, 30
	Interoperability	Can be difficult to operate with other systems	16, 20, 26
Organizational	Cost for setup and maintenance	Especially the cost of data collection and the cost of the infrastructure in itself	1, 3, 7, 20, 22, 29
	Lack of managerial commitment	It might be due to a lack of knowledge of blockchain abilities	2, 7, 29
	Lack of expertise	Lack of technical expertise and knowledge about blockchain	7, 20, 22, 29
	Lack of tools for blockchain implementation	No standards or appropriate methods, tool or metrics avaialable	7, 29
	Resistance to change	Hesitation and opposition to altering and replacing already existing systems	7, 20, 29
SC Inter-Organizational	Opposition to data sharing by stakholders	Stakeholders might be skeptical or opposed to sharing their sustainability data with others	1, 7, 20, 29

(continued)

Table 1. (*continued*)

Types of adoption barriers	Challenges	Description	Articles
	Problem of collaboration	Lack of communication and collaboration because of diverging objectives along the SC	7, 20, 29
	Cultural differences	Different organizational culture can hinder the adoption of blockchain	7, 29
External environment	Lack of governmental regulation	The absence of regulation can slowdown the adoption of blockchain	7, 20, 29
	Lack of external stakeholders' implication	NGOs and communities do not support blockchain technology	7, 29

The most significant barriers identified are the technological and supply chain environment barriers [2, 29]. Measuring the confidence level of data recorded on the blockchain is another issue [16, 20].

4 Discussion

There is undoubtedly a consensus in the literature that blockchain technology is booming and is prioritized for the digital traceability of industrial goods because of its inherent qualities. Many articles discuss case studies of successful blockchain-based traceability platforms in various industrial sectors and the general opportunities of blockchain-based systems for ensuring transparency, trust, and traceability in complex supply chains. However, the subject of using these blockchain-based systems for sustainability is still very limited in the literature. This approach seems very new, as the few papers on this subject were all published in 2020 or 2021. Although these articles are scarce, they all agree that blockchain's benefits for supply chain traceability can serve for monitoring sustainability and that blockchain-based traceability could encapsulate data about the environmental emissions and the use of resources of industrial activities.

To go further, the link between the concept of blockchain technology and the concept of LCA is still largely unexplored, with only three existing articles. Moreover, this research path remains very conceptual, constituting a large research gap between the theory and the field ability to implement a functional and robust system on a large scale. Only one paper proposed an implementation framework and system architecture, while the others only listed the benefits of blockchain-based LCA. With these three articles, blockchain-based LCA systems' technical feasibility was demonstrated, and the benefits and adoption barriers were clearly identified.

Future scopes of research are numerous. First of all, although a first framework and architecture of a blockchain-based LCA system was developed, it clearly lacks a methodology to implement the system. Future research focusing on an implementation process identifying the stakeholders, their roles and relations, the deliverables of the project and addressing the problematics identified in Sect. 3.5 would be an important contribution. Another research opportunity would be to develop a Proof of Concept of a blockchain-based LCA system in an industrial supply chain to prove that it is applicable and integrable and to provide feedback from a case company before full-scale implementation. Based on an already blockchain-traced supply chain, the traceability data model's extension to include data related to the environmental impact, and the integration of the traceability platform with an LCA calculation software and big data analytics represent also interesting opportunities. The possibility of integrating an interface to this system for the final consumer to have access to an up-to-date environmental impact of a product based on real production data via QR code, for example, could add value as well. Finally, another scope of study could be a literature review covering the benefits of blockchain for the two other pillars of sustainability: social and economic.

5 Conclusion

In conclusion, this article's contribution was to shed light upon the opportunities, limitations, and possible research paths on the use of blockchain traceability platforms for the environmental impact assessment of products by exploring the existing literature. The originality of this paper is to focus specifically on blockchain-based LCA concerning all the above-mentioned aspects of their conceptualization and implementation. New paths of research have also been unveiled in the discussion section. The implication of this literature review is therefore to help the future development of blockchain-based LCA systems by practitioners and researchers by proposing an overview of the current state of research on this topic and by synthetizing all knowledge related to the benefits and difficulties of their implementation.This was done facing the already proven benefits of blockchain traceability for supply chains in general with the current limits of sustainable supply chains and impact assessment methods. This literature review however faces a few limitations. First of all, blockchain-based LCA models are not discussed in the scope of this study and are only briefly presented in Sect. 3.4. This study therefore remains a theoric contribution to the subject and does not propose any system implementation. Also, although a systematic literature review methodology was applied, we acknowledge that this paper is not a full picture of the blockchain-based LCA subject as it considers only peer-reviewed journal papers, conference papers and reviews. Blockchain-based LCA pilot projects in the industry are for example not covered. A future scope of research could be a literature review overcoming these limitations.

References

1. Teh, D., Khan, T., Corbitt, B., Ong, C.E.: Sustainability strategy and blockchain-enabled life cycle assessment: a focus on materials industry. Environ. Syst. Decis. **40**(4), 605–622 (2020). https://doi.org/10.1007/s10669-020-09761-4
2. Farooque, M., Jain, V., Zhang, A., Li, Z.: Fuzzy DEMATEL analysis of barriers to blockchain-based life cycle assessment in China. Comput. Ind. Eng. **147**, 106684 (2020). https://doi.org/10.1016/j.cie.2020.106684

3. Zhang, A., Zhong, R.Y., Farooque, M., Kang, K., Venkatesh, V.G.: Blockchain-based life cycle assessment: an implementation framework and system architecture. Resour. Conserv. Recycl. **152**, 104512 (2020). https://doi.org/10.1016/j.resconrec.2019.104512

4. Hauschild, M., Jeswiet, J., Alting, L.: From life cycle assessment to sustainable production: status and perspectives. CIRP Ann. **54**, 1–21 (2005). https://doi.org/10.1016/s0007-8506(07)60017-1

5. Wang, M., Wang, B., Abareshi, A.: Blockchain technology and its role in enhancing supply chain integration capability and reducing carbon emission: a conceptual framework. Sustainability. **12**, 10550 (2020). https://doi.org/10.3390/su122410550

6. Hastig, G.M., Sodhi, M.S.: Blockchain for supply chain traceability: business requirements and critical success factors. Prod. Oper. Manag. **29**, 935–954 (2020). https://doi.org/10.1111/poms.13147

7. Saberi, S., Kouhizadeh, M., Sarkis, J., Shen, L.: Blockchain technology and its relationships to sustainable supply chain management. Int. J. Prod. Res. **57**, 2117–2135 (2018). https://doi.org/10.1080/00207543.2018.1533261

8. Mukherjee, A.A., Singh, R.K., Mishra, R., Bag, S.: Application of blockchain technology for sustainability development in agricultural supply chain: justification framework. Oper. Manag. Res. **1**, 16 (2021). https://doi.org/10.1007/s12063-021-00180-5

9. Katsikouli, P., Wilde, A.S., Dragoni, N., Høgh-Jensen, H.: On the benefits and challenges of blockchains for managing food supply chains. J. Sci. Food Agric. (2020). https://doi.org/10.1002/jsfa.10883

10. Park, A., Li, H.: The effect of blockchain technology on supply chain sustainability performances. Sustainability. **13**, 1726 (2021). https://doi.org/10.3390/su13041726

11. Pigné, Y., et al.: A tool to operationalize dynamic LCA, including time differentiation on the complete background database. Int. J. Life Cycle Assess. **25**(2), 267–279 (2019). https://doi.org/10.1007/s11367-019-01696-6

12. Sunny, J., Undralla, N., Madhusudanan Pillai, V.: Supply chain transparency through blockchain-based traceability: an overview with demonstration. Comput. Ind. Eng. **150**, 106895 (2020). https://doi.org/10.1016/j.cie.2020.106895

13. Demestichas, K., Peppes, N., Alexakis, T., Adamopoulou, E.: Blockchain in agriculture traceability systems: a review. Appl. Sci. **10**, 4113 (2020). https://doi.org/10.3390/app10124113

14. Agrawal, T.K., Kumar, V., Pal, R., Wang, L., Chen, Y.: Blockchain-based framework for supply chain traceability: a case example of textile and clothing industry. Comput. Ind. Eng. **154**, 107130 (2021). https://doi.org/10.1016/j.cie.2021.107130

15. Lim, M.K., Li, Y., Wang, C., Tseng, M.-L.: A literature review of blockchain technology applications in supply chains: a comprehensive analysis of themes, methodologies and industries. Comput. Ind. Eng. **154**, 107133 (2021). https://doi.org/10.1016/j.cie.2021.107133

16. Köhler, S., Pizzol, M.: Technology assessment of blockchain-based technologies in the food supply chain. J. Clean. Prod. **269**, 122193 (2020). https://doi.org/10.1016/j.jclepro.2020.122193

17. Mahyuni, L.P., Adrian, R., Darma, G.S., Krisnawijaya, N.N.K., Dewi, I.G.A.A.P., Permana, G.P.L.: Mapping the potentials of blockchain in improving supply chain performance. Cogent Bus. Manage. **7**, 1788329 (2020). https://doi.org/10.1080/23311975.2020.1788329

18. Feng, H., Wang, X., Duan, Y., Zhang, J., Zhang, X.: Applying blockchain technology to improve agri-food traceability: a review of development methods, benefits and challenges. J. Clean. Prod. **260**, 121031 (2020). https://doi.org/10.1016/j.jclepro.2020.121031

19. Rosado da Cruz, A., Cruz, E.: Blockchain-based traceability platforms as a tool for sustainability. In: Proceedings of the 22nd International Conference on Enterprise Information Systems. SCITEPRESS - Science and Technology Publications (2020)

20. Kamble, S.S., Gunasekaran, A., Sharma, R.: Modeling the blockchain enabled traceability in agriculture supply chain. Int. J. Inf. Manage. **52**, 101967 (2020). https://doi.org/10.1016/j.ijinfomgt.2019.05.023

21. Alonso, R.S., Sittón-Candanedo, I., García, Ó., Prieto, J., Rodríguez-González, S.: An intelligent Edge-IoT platform for monitoring livestock and crops in a dairy farming scenario. Ad Hoc Netw. **98**, 102047 (2020). https://doi.org/10.1016/j.adhoc.2019.102047

22. Zhao, G., et al.: Blockchain technology in agri-food value chain management: a synthesis of applications, challenges and future research directions. Comput. Ind. **109**, 83–99 (2019). https://doi.org/10.1016/j.compind.2019.04.002

23. Karamachoski, J., Marina, N., Taskov, P.: Blockchain-based application for certification management. Teh. glas. (Online) **14**, 488–492 (2020). https://doi.org/10.31803/tg-20200811113729

24. Shoaib, M., Lim, M.K., Wang, C.: An integrated framework to prioritize blockchain-based supply chain success factors. IMDS. **120**, 2103–2131 (2020). https://doi.org/10.1108/imds-04-2020-0194

25. Saurabh, S., Dey, K.: Blockchain technology adoption, architecture, and sustainable agri-food supply chains. J. Clean. Prod. **284**, 124731 (2021). https://doi.org/10.1016/j.jclepro.2020.124731

26. Paliwal, V., Chandra, S., Sharma, S.: Blockchain technology for sustainable supply chain management: a systematic literature review and a classification framework. Sustainability. **12**, 7638 (2020). https://doi.org/10.3390/su12187638

27. Rosado da Cruz, A., Santos, F., Mendes, P., Cruz, E.: Blockchain-based traceability of carbon footprint: a solidity smart contract for ethereum. In: Proceedings of the 22nd International Conference on Enterprise Information Systems. SCITEPRESS - Science and Technology Publications (2020)

28. Shakhbulatov, D., Arora, A., Dong, Z., Rojas-Cessa, R.: Blockchain implementation for analysis of carbon footprint across food supply chain. In: 2019 IEEE International Conference on Blockchain (Blockchain). IEEE (2019)

29. Kouhizadeh, M., Saberi, S., Sarkis, J.: Blockchain technology and the sustainable supply chain: theoretically exploring adoption barriers. Int. J. Prod. Econ. **231**, 107831 (2021). https://doi.org/10.1016/j.ijpe.2020.107831

30. Bakarich, K.M., Castonguay, J. "Jack", O'Brien, P.E.: The Use of Blockchains to Enhance Sustainability Reporting and Assurance*. Account Perspect. 19, 389–412 (2020). https://doi.org/10.1111/1911-3838.12241

31. Jamwal, A., Agrawal, R., Sharma, M., Kumar, V.: Review on multi-criteria decision analysis in sustainable manufacturing decision making. Int. J. Sustainable Eng., 1–24 (2020). https://doi.org/10.1080/19397038.2020.1866708

32. Jamwal, A., Agrawal, R., Sharma, M., Kumar, A., Kumar, V., Garza-Reyes, J.A.A.: Machine learning applications for sustainable manufacturing: a bibliometric-based review for future research. JEIM. ahead-of-print (2021). https://doi.org/10.1108/jeim-09-2020-0361

Demand Forecasting for an Automotive Company with Neural Network and Ensemble Classifiers Approaches

Eleonora Bottani$^{(\boxtimes)}$ ⓘ, Monica Mordonini$^{(\boxtimes)}$ ⓘ, Beatrice Franchi$^{(\boxtimes)}$ ⓘ, and Mattia Pellegrino$^{(\boxtimes)}$ ⓘ

Department of Engineering and Architecture, University of Parma, Viale delle Scienze 181/A, 43124 Parma, Italy

{eleonora.bottani,monica.mordonini,beatrice.franchi, mattia.pellegrino}@unipr.it

Abstract. This work proposes the development and testing of three machine learning technique for demand forecasting in the automotive industry: Artificial Neural Network (ANN) and two types of Ensemble Learning models, i.e. AdaBoost and Gradient Boost. These models demonstrate the great potential that machine learning has over traditional demand forecasting methods. These three models will be compared to each other on the basis of the coefficient of determination R^2 and it will be shown which model has the greatest accuracy.

Keywords: Demand forecasting · Automotive · ANN · AdaBoost · Gradient Boost

1 Introduction

In economics terms, "demand" describes the consumers' desire and willingness to pay a price for receiving specific goods or services and can be interpreted as the amount of desire expressed by the buyers. Accurate demand forecasting allows the company's managers to improve their market performance, increasing profit and delineating internal policies and procedures on a sound basis. To this end, various tools have been proposed in the last decades for dealing with sales forecasting and making the process more accurate. These tools range from the traditional time series/statistical forecasting methods (e.g., exponential smoothing, moving average, ARIMA, or multivariate regressions) to the more recent applications of artificial intelligence (AI), including, among others, artificial neural networks, fuzzy logic or genetic algorithms [1]. As a matter of fact, research activities intended to develop more effective business forecasting techniques have recently evoked the usage of tools from the computational AI area. Machine learning (ML), as a branch of AI, is currently one of the most popular tools applied to demand forecasting. ML describes a suite of approaches able to provide systems with the ability to automatically improve their performance by learning from experience without being

A. Dolgui et al. (Eds.): APMS 2021, IFIP AICT 630, pp. 134–142, 2021.
https://doi.org/10.1007/978-3-030-85874-2_14

explicitly programmed. The present work proposes the comparison of various ML tools applied for the purpose of demand forecasting in the particular context of the automotive industry. In particular, the following ML approaches will be discussed in this paper: an Artificial Neural Network (ANN) implementation and two types of Ensemble Learning, i.e. AdaBoost and Gradient Boost.

For an exhaustive review of the relevant literature on the use of ANN in demand forecasting, see [2], who have proposed an ANN implementation in the automotive context with the purpose of forecasting the demand of finished products. In the automotive field there are very few studies focusing on the issue of demand forecasting. To the best of the authors' knowledge, besides [2], the studies expressively focusing on this topic have been by [3] and [4]. In all studies, ANNs have been implemented as the demand forecasting tool. For literature review on AdaBoost used as an efficient predictor see [5], who demonstrated that AdaBoost is an appropriate model to evaluate the financial risk of Korean construction companies. For studies regarding the usage of the Gradient Boost algorithm in the context of sales forecasting, the reader is referred to [6]. In that work, Gradient Boost has shown good accuracy in forecasting and future B2B sales prediction.

Because the studies applying ANNs, AdaBoost and Gradient Boost approaches in the automotive field are very limited, this specific sector was chosen as the implementation context for this study. Besides this aspect, it is critical for an automotive company to forecast the future demands for finished products or spare parts, and it is also essential for optimizing supply chain operations and reducing costs [4].

The remainder of the paper is organized as follows. Section 2 details the methodological approach followed for carrying out the research. Section 3 shows the implementation of the chosen approaches and the corresponding outcomes, together with the comparison with the ANN approach previously applied. The relating results are discussed in Sect. 4. Conclusions, implications and future research directions are finally delineated in Sect. 5.

2   Background Modelling

2.1   Framework

The approach proposed by [2] consists of several steps, which represent a useful guideline for building new methods to analyze a demand forecasting problem. The steps are reported in Fig. 1.

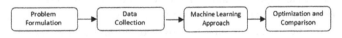

Fig. 1. Methodology logic tree.

1. *Problem Formulation:* The proposed context concerns the demand forecasting problem in an automotive company, called Company A for the sake of confidentiality.
2. *Data collection:* Company A provided us with a dataset for working about the context's task (see Sect. 2.2 for a detailed description of the dataset).

3. *ML approach:* We built a new neural network to work with our dataset, and we implemented other two algorithms to work with: AdaBoost and Gradient Boost.
4. *Optimization and comparison:* We compared the estimates obtained the used methods.

2.2 Dataset Description

The dataset contains three-monthly data from 2013 to 2018 (670 observations overall). Each row in the dataset represents a different part of the car: nose, front spoiler, machine structure, arms, brake discs, upright and bearings. Some components can be "right" or "left", "upper" or "lower" and, consequently, the final number of components analysed is eighteen. Seven key variables are to be taken into account as inputs:

1. Components' category, items number that can be grouped into a main class;
2. Championship to which sales data are related, since different championships correspond to different climatic conditions and cultural factors, which may affect accidents or spare parts demand;
3. Number of cars competing in each championship;
4. Number of races in each championship;
5. Ageing, simply attributable as YES or NO depending on the component;
6. Car life cycle, i.e. first year of life, interim period and last year of life;
7. Trimester, i.e. July–September, October–December, January–March, etc.

The following variables will be used to predict sales: number of cars; number of races; ageing.

2.3 Machine Learning Techniques

Neural Network. The ANN created in this study is a feed-forward neural network. As it can be seen in Fig. 2(a), a feed-forward NN consists of an input layer of neurons, an arbitrary number of hidden layers, and an output layer. Each neuron of a certain layer is connected to each neuron of the next layer. Figure 2(b) shows one single neuron, which receives inputs (i_n signals weighted by weights w_n) from each neuron of the previous layer. Additionally, it receives a so-called bias input i_{bias} with weight w_{bias}. The transfer function $f\left(\sum\right)$ of a neuron translates the sum of all the weighted inputs into an output signal, which serves as input for all the neurons of the following layer [7].

The most used method to train a neural network is to present a set of samples (training set) as input to the network. The answer provided by the network for each example is compared to the desired answer; the difference (error) between the two is then evaluated and based on its value, the weights are adjusted. This process is repeated across the entire training set until the network outputs return an error lower than a predetermined threshold.

Boosting. The ensemble learning is a way to combine different basic classifiers to derive a new one, more complex and more efficient. Moreover, these basic classifiers can be different in terms of hyper-parameters, representation and training set. The boosting

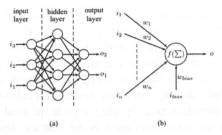

(a)   (b)

Fig. 2. (a) Structure of a feed-forward neural network. (b) Model of a single neuron.

algorithm belongs to this particular category and includes the AdaBoost and the Gradient boost techniques.

AdaBoost. Adaptive Boosting (AdaBoost, [8]) was the first boosting algorithm developed for classification and regression. It fits a sequence of weak learners on different weighted training data. The algorithm starts by predicting the original data set and giving equal weight to each observation. If the prediction is incorrect, using the first learner, the algorithm will give a higher weight to the observation. This procedure is iterated until the model reaches a predefined (threshold) value of accuracy. However, decision stumps are used with AdaBoost. They split the samples into two subsets based on the value of one generic feature. Each stump sets a feature and a threshold, and then splits the data into two new groups on each threshold side. Figure 3 provides an example of the classic AdaBoost working.

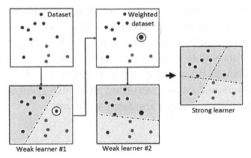

Fig. 3. Example of implementation of an AdaBoost classifier on a dataset with two features and two classes. Weak learner #1 improves on the mistake made by Weak learner #2.

AdaBoost has many advantages and disadvantages. It is typically easy to use because it does not need complex parameters' tuning procedures; similarly, it shows low sensitivity to the overfitting phenomenon. It is able to learn from a little set of features and add, in an incremental way, new information on which to work about. However, AdaBoost is quite sensitive to data having noises or abnormal values and, typically, it works with binary data, which can make it hard to adapt the algorithm to a categorical classification.

Gradient Boosting. This algorithm proposes a predictive model in the form of a combined set of weak predictive models, typically decision trees. After its original formulation, explicit regression gradient boosting algorithms were developed by [9, 10]. Gradient boosting trains many models in a sequential way. Each new model gradually minimizes the whole system loss function, using the Gradient descent method, i.e. a first-order iterative optimization algorithm for finding a local minimum of a differentiable function. The criterion is to take repeated steps in the gradient opposite direction of the function at its current point, because it is the steepest descent (see Fig. 4). The learning procedure fits new models to provide a better accuracy of the response variable. The aim is to construct new base learners which can be correlated with the loss function negative gradient.

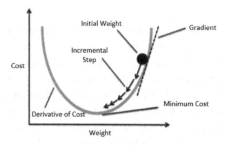

Fig. 4. Gradient descent on a series.

Gradient Boost too has some characteristics that makes it optimal for the targeted implementation. It often provides predictive accuracy that cannot be beat, it is very flexible, it can optimally deal with different loss functions and provide some hyperparameter tuning that make the function fit very flexible. Unlike AdaBoost, it works with both categorical and binary data without difficulties. Moreover, it can handle missing data. Nevertheless, Gradient Boost always tries to minimize all errors, which can bring to overemphasize outliers and cause overfitting. It is also computationally expensive, and its high flexibility requires many parameters to be set.

3 Case Study

3.1 Context

The company in which this study has been carried out (referred to as Company A for the sake of confidentiality) is based in the North of Italy and operates in the production of racing cars, by assembling components which can be either supplied or made in-house. Typically, cars are directly sold to teams participating to worldwide championships, while for components, the market is wider since also other companies or privates can be reached.

3.2 Neural Network Implementation

A feed-forward neural network was used in this work. The procedure used for the training process was iterated 1000 times and it is as follows: first of all, the input data were taken from the training dataset, adjusted based on their weights, and retrieved *via* a method that computes the output. After, the back-propagated error rate is computed as the difference between the predicted output of the neuron and the expected output of the training dataset. Finally, some minor weight adjustments are made using the error weighted derivative formula.

3.3 AdaBoost Implementation

The implementation of this algorithm follows the steps listed below:

1. Normalization of each entry in the dataset;
2. Grouping of the data into the "train" and "test" sets;
3. Definition of the AdaBoost regressor;
4. Tuning of the hyper-parameters of a grid search. A grid search defines a search space as a grid of hyper-parameter values and evaluate every position in the grid. Hyper-parameters specification taken into account in this work include decision trees dimension and learning rate values.
5. Score computation and analysis.

3.4 Gradient Boost Implementation

For the targeted implementation, Gradient Boost had been chosen in the light of its optimal accuracy. The implementation of Gradient Boost follows the same steps listed for AdaBoost in the previous subsection.

4 Results

For an evaluation of the three different models implemented (ANN, AdaBoost and Gradient Boost algorithms) it is paramount to determine their goodness and accuracy. To do this, the coefficient of determination R^2 and RMSE were computed. R^2 index was because, for the purpose of our study, it is important that the algorithm is able to predict the real numerical data (i.e. to forecast the sales data). Indeed, R^2 is a statistical index that aims at evaluating whether the regression model can actually be used to make reliable predictions. R^2 is calculated as the ratio between the model deviance (σ^2_{model}) and the total deviance (σ^2) (Formula 1). R^2 measures the accuracy of the models implemented, in terms of its ability to fit the data. A value close to 1 means that there is an almost perfect correlation between the model and the data; on the contrary, a value close to 0 indicates absence of correlation between them, meaning that the adaptation of the mean is equivalent to the model created. Therefore, the more R2 approaches 1, the greater the goodness of the model.

The root mean square error, on the other hand, show the difference between predicted values and those observed in the model (Formula 2).

$$(1)\ R^2 = \frac{\sigma^2_{model}}{\sigma^2} = \frac{\Sigma(\hat{y}_i-\bar{y})^2}{\Sigma(y_i-\bar{y})^2} \qquad (2)\ \sqrt{\frac{1}{n}\Sigma_{i=1}^n (f_i - o_i)^2}$$

Formula 1. Computation of R^2 **Formula 2**. Computation of Root Mean Squared Error

Where n is the number of samples, f are the predicted values and o are the empirical observed data. Therefore, the more RMSE approaches 0, the greater the goodness of the model. Moreover, the algorithms were validated using a k-fold cross validation. K-fold cross validation consists in splitting a dataset in K sections, where each fold is used as a testing set at some point.

The general procedure is as follows:

1. Shuffle the dataset randomly;
2. Split the dataset into k groups;
3. For each unique group:
    1. Take the group as a hold out or test data set;
    2. Take the remaining groups as a training data set;
    3. Fit a model on the training set and evaluate it on the test set;
    4. Retain the evaluation score and discard the model;
4. Summarize the skill of the model using the sample of model evaluation scores.

Table 1 shows the R2 and RMSE values for the models implemented in our study:

Table 1. R^2 and RMSE values for each model implemented.

	Neural network	AdaBoost	Gradient boost
R^2	−0.10	0.37	0.27
RMSE	0.14	0.07	0.06

As can be seen, the best combination of R^2 and RMSE values (respectively equal to 0.37 and 0.07) is observed for the AdaBoost algorithm. Taking into account the relatively small sample of observations, the value denotes an excellent result. For Gradient Boost, R^2 scores 0.27 and RMSE scores 0.06. These values are way lower than AdaBoost, it is because AdaBoost works very well with weak learners and its exponential loss function fits well with the proposed model and generally it works better than Gradient Boost with small datasets. Nonetheless, in the light of the small size of the dataset, they could still be considered as acceptable. Finally, the ANN shows a negative R^2 (−0.10); this result clearly denotes the inability of the neural network model to fit to the data. Negative values of R^2 can be observed if the predictions that are compared with the correspondent results were not obtained from a procedure adhering model using such data. Once again, the possible reason is to be searched in the narrowness of the series used, which prevents the correct adaptation of the ANN to the specific problem. In addition, Fig. 5 shows the predictions made by the previously described algorithms. The blue curve represents the real sales values, the red one instead is the prediction. The x-axis reflects the number of samples analyzed, while the y-axis reports the sales value.

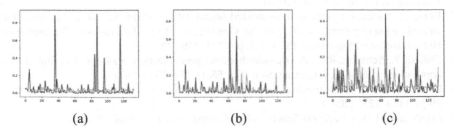

(a)   (b)   (c)

Fig. 5. Algorithms' predictions. (a) Neural network, (b) AdaBoost, (c) Gradient boost

5 Conclusions

The aim of this study was the implementation of three ML models for demand forecasting of eighteen car components for an automotive company located in the North of Italy, i.e. Neural Network, AdaBoost and Gradient Boost. The model that provides greater prediction accuracy turned out to be the AdaBoost algorithm, with an R^2 of 0,37 and a RMSE of 0,07 respectively. This means that AdaBoost algorithm fits well the categorization model proposed in this work and it is the best configuration among the three. Further insights can be considered. To have sales forecast data yet more accurate and precise, it would be interesting to repeat the study with larger datasets, consisting of thousands of rows. Furthermore, it could be interesting to repeat the study using a different time span (e.g. annual), as well as to study the demand forecasting for a greater number of car components. As a suitable future research direction, this study could be replicated in fields other than the automotive one, to take into account the presence of different components and to test its validity in various contexts.

References

1. Salais, T., Saucedo, J., Rodriguez Aguilar, R., Vela-Haro, J.: Demand prediction using a soft-computing approach: a case study of automotive industry. Appl. Sci. **10**(3), 829 (2020)
2. Bottani, E., Tebaldi, L., Pindari, S.: Demand forecasting in an automotive company: an artificial neural network approach. In: Affenzeller, M., et al. (eds.) The 31st European Modeling & Simulation Symposium, vol. 1, pp. 162–167 (2019)
3. Shahrabi, J., Mousavi, S.S., Heydar, M.: Supply chain demand forecasting: a comparison of machine learning techniques and traditional methods. J. Appl. Sci. **9**(3), 521–527 (2009)
4. González Vergas, C.A., Cortés, M.E.: Automobile spare-parts forecasting: a comparative study of time series methods. Int. J. Automot. Mech. Eng. **14**(1), 3898–3912 (2017)
5. Heo, J., Yang, J.: AdaBoost based bankruptcy forecasting of Korean construction companies. Appl. Soft Comput. **24**, 494–499 (2014)

6. Wisesa, O., Adriansyah, A., Osamah, I., Khalaf, O.: Prediction analysis sales for corporate services telecommunications company using gradient boost algorithm. In: Adriansyah, A. (ed.) 2nd International Conference on Broadband Communications, Wireless Sensors and Powering, vol. 1, pp. 101–106 (2020)
7. Blum, C., Socha, K.: Training feed-forward neural networks with ant colony optimization: an application to pattern classification. In: Gomide, F. (ed.) 5th International Conference on Hybrid Intelligent Systems, IEEE, vol. 1, pp. 233–238 (2005)
8. Freund, Y., Schapire, R.E.: A Decision-theoretic generalization of on-line learning and an application to boosting. J. Comput. Syst. Sci. **55**(1), 119–139 (1997)
9. Friedman, J.H.: Greedy function approximation: a gradient boosting machine. Ann. Stat. **29**(5), 1189–1232 (2001)
10. Friedman, J.H.: Stochastic gradient boosting. Comput. Stat. Data Anal. **38**(4), 367–378 (2002)

A Deep Learning Algorithm for the Throughput Estimation of a CONWIP Line

Silvestro Vespoli$^{(\boxtimes)}$, Andrea Grassi, Guido Guizzi, and Valentina Popolo

University of Naples Federico II, 80125 Napoli, NA, Italy
{silvestro.vespoli,andrea.grassi,guido.guizzi,
valentina.popolo}@unina.it

Abstract. The ability to meet increasingly personalized market demand in a short period of time and at a low cost can be regarded as a fundamental principle for industrialized countries' competitive revival. The aim of Industry 4.0 is to resolve the long-standing conflict between the individuality of on-demand output and the savings realized through economies of scale. Significant progress has been established in the field of Industry 4.0 technologies, but there is still an open gap in the literature regarding methodologies for efficiently manage the available productive resources of a manufacturing system. The CONtrolled Work-In-Progress (CONWIP) production logic, proposed by Spearman et al., allows controlling the Work-In-Progress (WIP) in a production system while monitoring the throughput. However, an affordable estimation tool is still required to deal with the increased variability that enters the current production system. Taking advantage of recent advances in the field of machine learning, this paper contributes to the development of a performance estimation tool for a production line using a deep learning neural network. The results demonstrated that the proposed estimation tool can outperform the current best-known mathematical model by estimating the throughput of a CONWIP Flow-Shop production line with a given variability and WIP value set into the system.

Keywords: Industry 4.0 · Industrial production system · CONWIP Flow-Shop · Throughput estimation · Deep learning

1 Introduction

The continuous transformation of the competitive manufacturing landscape, new challenges spanning innovation, efficiency, expense, and time-to-market all reflect opportunities that a modern company cannot afford to miss. The ability to meet increasingly personalized market demand in a short period of time and at a low cost can be regarded as a fundamental principle for industrialized countries' competitive revival against emerging countries with lower technological development but lower social and labor costs [3]. In this context, it is important to develop the ability to efficiently distribute available resources, as well as the ability to rethink and revolutionize the methods and controlling approaches of production processes in order to react appropriately to new market challenges [5].

© IFIP International Federation for Information Processing 2021
Published by Springer Nature Switzerland AG 2021
A. Dolgui et al. (Eds.): APMS 2021, IFIP AICT 630, pp. 143–151, 2021.
https://doi.org/10.1007/978-3-030-85874-2_15

The effect of a production paradigm based on increased product customization and shorter time-to-market was significant enough to justify the born of a new industrial paradigm: the Fourth Industrial Revolution (or Industry 4.0). While previous industrial revolutions were marked primarily by major technological developments, this one pursues logistical/management goals, which are related to the new need for product customization and the consequent versatility needed by a manufacturing plant [1, 12, 15]. Hence, the aim of Industry 4.0 is to resolve the long-standing conflict between the individuality of on-demand output and the savings realized through economies of scale [6, 7]. Significant progress has been established in the field of Industry 4.0 technologies, but to the best of the author's knowledge, there is still an open gap in the literature regarding methodologies for efficiently using the data flow generated by Industry 4.0 Cyber-Physical Systems (CPSs) [14, 18].

Industry 4.0 is intended to enable the transition from a traditional manufacturing model (Mass Production) to a customization-oriented one (Mass Customization). This transformation, however, must be accompanied by a change in the logic of the Manufacturing Planning and Control (MPC) structure. In fact, the main problem in a Mass Customization business scenario is the variability that enters the system as a result of consumer customization requests. And the issue is that, for the time being, this variability can only be dealt with by a traditional MPC scheme, such as Manufacturing Resource Planning (MRP-II, in the following MRP), which act on the manufacturing system with a "push" logic controlling the throughput and monitor the Work-In-Progress (WIP).

In the scientific literature, several control strategies suggesting autonomous and independent control principles have been proposed. Among these, Dolgui et al. pioneered a new research area based on the application of classical Control Theory to scheduling and inventory control systems [4, 9–11, 16]. Sokolov et al. in [16], in particular, investigated the advantages and limitations of various control approaches and algorithms for the optimal solution of short-term scheduling of a manufacturing system. However, these control strategies requires important change into the production system while the manufacturing firms are still in search of more simple solution, able to controls the WIP level, while monitoring the throughput of the system. One of these solution may be offered from the CONtrolled Work-In-Progress (CONWIP) logic, proposed by Spearman et al. [17] in the 1990. They demonstrated that pull systems are more effective than push systems and that pull systems need less WIP to achieve the same value of throughput.

The issue is that, in order to implement a CONWIP production system, the amount of WIP to be allowed in the production system must be defined. The selection of the correct WIP numbers to be admitted is critical for the manufacturing system's performance. In fact, different values of WIP determine different values of the production system's throughput and crossing time. A high level of WIP, in particular, ensures a higher value of throughput at the expense of a higher value of the time required for a job to cross the production system. Low levels of WIP, on the other hand, ensure that jobs have a better crossing time at the expense of the manufacturing system's throughput. As a result, given the current manufacturing paradigm, it is critical to have a production system that allows for dynamically changing the amount of WIP, depending on the required throughput from the market or from the other production line, while keeping the time to cross the production system as short as possible.

In this sense, the aim of this paper is to contribute to the development of a production line performance estimation tool, able to take into account the variability of the processing time that enters the production system and the number of WIP values set. To this extent, a deep learning algorithmic approach for the throughput estimation of a CONWIP Flow Shop production line is proposed. Then, its performance has been assessed against the last-known mathematical model of CONWIP production systems proposed by Spearman et al. in [8] and compared with the results obtained from a simulation model. The remainder of the paper is structured as follow: Sect. 2 introduces the Problem Statement of the paper; Sect. 3 introduces the proposed approach, focusing on both the simulation method for generating data and the proposed deep learning algorithm; Sect. 4 discusses the results, comparing them to the best-known mathematical model; and Sect. 5 concludes the paper.

2 Problem Statement

Suppose to have a FlowShop CONWIP line with 5 machines where the processing times are generated by a fixed average gamma distribution Fig. 1. The choice of the gamma distribution is motivated by the desire to introduce controllable variability into the production line. It is, in fact, a continuous probability distribution that includes, among other things, the exponential distributions, and it is used in literature to simulate situations that are far from the *memoryless* characteristic of the exponential distribution. Without loss of generality, we considered different productive scenario in which the average processing time is fixed to 10 min and the variability that enters in the system is controlled by a change in the *alpha* value of the above-mentioned gamma distribution.

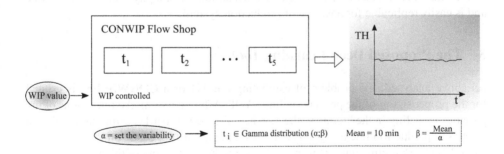

Fig. 1. The considered CONWIP Flow-Shop production line

As said above, in a CONWIP line, the THroughput (TH) is an observable performance parameter that can be controlled by directly acting on the system's authorized WIP level. Spearman et al. in [8, 17] investigated the dynamics of a CONWIP system and developed mathematical models that described its behavior as a function of controlled variables and boundary conditions. They focused on the behavior of the best possible condition (no variability and balanced line, with the same performing times at all stations) and the worst possible condition. These scenarios are interesting because they represent the best and worst possible performance that a CONWIP production system may show. Furthermore, the researchers assessed the behavior of the same system in a practical case (i.e., the practical worst case, or PWC) in which the performing times of jobs at the stations are exponentially distributed, preserving the balanced line condition in terms of average processing times. Hence, the mathematical relationships that link TH and Cyclet Time (CT) to the WIP introduced in the system are known in these cases.

However, their mathematical model is based on the strong assumption of an exponential processing time distribution case, that is not of great help when the variability is different from the exponential case. To this extent, Hopp and Spearman in [8] have then proposed an iterative model based on average value considerations, taking the advantage of the Mean Value Analysis, able to correctly estimate the TH of a CONWIP line with different level of variability, selecting as input for the model the value of WIP admitted in production and the quadratic coefficient of variation of the processing time distribution. However, as already showed by [2] their estimation suffers from an approximation error when forced to work with variability far from the exponential ones, due to the fact that the model's assumptions are not properly verified in these cases.

Therefore, the goal of this paper is to use a machine learning algorithm, based on Deep Learning Neural Network architecture to estimate the Throughput of the production line based on the same input considered by Hopp and Spearman in their last work (i.e., the WIP to be admitted in production and the quadratic coefficient of variation of the processing time distribution). The proposed model's limitations must be found in the requirement for a consistent amount of data that is wide and complete, as well as the fact that the trained model is specific to the considered production system architecture. The proposed method, on the other hand, has the advantage of having a data-driven model architecture that can be trained with data from a simulator or a physical production line and is easily replicable for any type of production system.

3 The Proposed Deep Learning Tool

As above analysed, the problem of estimating the TH of a CONWIP line is critical for the proper sizing of the production line's WIP. After analyzing the limitations of the previous modeling in the literature, the goal here is to develop a TH estimation tool for a CONWIP production line using a machine learning algorithm based on Deep Learning Neural Network architecture. However, in order to begin training of this kind of model, a large amount of data must be collected. To that end, a simulation model using the Discrete-Event and Agent-Based techniques with the help of the Anylogic simulation software has been created.

The model's Main agent is depicted in the Fig. 2. As can be seen, the simulation tool is very simple, consisting of five different services blocks (that simulate the processing machines) and other blocks presented for statistical purposes. To collect all the data required, the model was run for different values of variability (i.e., varying the α value of the processing time distribution at step of 0.1 for value between 0.5 and 3) and of

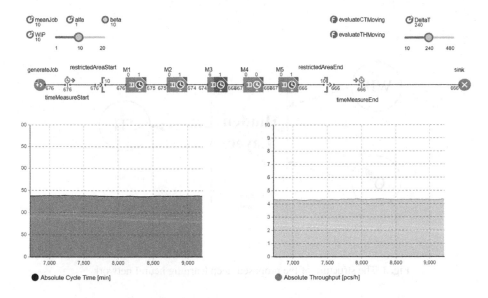

Fig. 2. The main agent of the simulation tool

WIP (i.e. varying it between 1 and 20), for a simulation time of 4 years (in order to be sure that the steady state is reached), replicated 40 times for each combination of parameter. Then, the TH and CT of the production line were collected and saved in an Excel spreadsheet after each simulation run.

Once the experimental data-set has been acquired, we proceeded to build the deep learning neural network for the estimation of the TH. These networks are structured of multiple layers of neurons: we have a first layer known as the input layer, which in our case will be made up of two inputs, the WIP of the production line and the quadratic coefficient of variation within the line; different hidden layers with variable number of neurons, which are responsible for numerical interpolation; a final layer that represents the output of the network (i.e. the TH in the considered case) Fig. 3.

Once the network's architecture in terms of input and output has been established, the network's hyper-parameters, such as the number of neurons inside the hidden layer, activation functions of the neurons, loss function, and so on, must be determined. Unfortunately, there is no objective method for selecting these parameters [13]. For this reason, the network has been scaled with a "Trial and Error" approach and the results shown in the following paragraph.

4   The Deep Learning Algorithm - Experimental and Validation Scenario

The model was developed on Google Colaboratory using the Tensor Flow Keras library. The dataset used for model training was made up of 20800 data points extracted from the simulator and divided into three sections: training (75%), validation (20%), and test (5%).

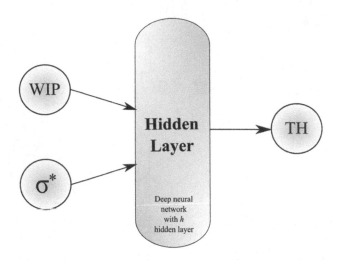

Fig. 3. The structure of the proposed deep learning neural network

As previously stated, several experiments has been carried out in order to find the best combination of hyper-parameters through a trial and error procedure. To ensure an effective comparison of the results, we fixed the seed so that we could see how the model responds to changes in hyper-parameters. After experimenting with different configurations, we concluded that the best results were obtained with a neural network composed of the following layers: an input layer that accepts the WIP values in the production system as well as the quadratic coefficient of variation; a hidden normalization layer; two dense hidden layers of 12 neurons each with *elu* as activation function; an output layer formed by a single neuron.

It should be noted that, prior to arriving at this network configuration, several experiments, which were omitted for space reasons has been carried out, which involved reduced neural network structures (single hidden layer, different number of neurons, different combination of activation function, etc.). For the loss function, we preferred the use of the classic Mean Squared Error (MSE), adopting the ADAM optimizer with a learning rate of 0.01. Also in this case, experiments with different learning rate has been carried out and this value resulted as the ones that performed with good value of MSE also in the Test phase. Regarding the epoch number, we experienced the best performances to a value around 20 epochs for the proposed structure. The results of the deep learning neural network model are shown in the Fig. 4.

Finally, in order to assess the performances of the proposed model, fixed the variability of the system (i.e., α), we compared the predicted values of the TH to the average values obtained from the simulation and to the values obtained from the iterative Spearman's model [8]. As illustrated in Fig. 5 in which the scenario with $\alpha = 3$ is drawn, the proposed neural network model is capable of forecasting the TH of the productive line with high accuracy (i.e., with a MSE value in the order of 10^{-2}) whereas the Hopp and Spearman's iterative models deviate consistently as the value of the WIP in the line increases. To summarize, the Hopp and Spearman iterative model is extremely

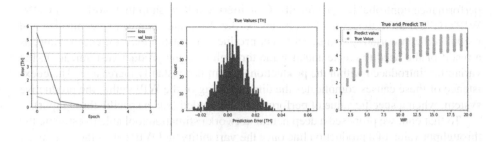

Fig. 4. Results of the deep learning neural network model.

precise for values of variability close to the exponential (i.e. alpha equal to 1), but it begins to earn systemic errors when the variability that enters the system deviates from this hypothesis. Instead, the proposed model proved to be accurate even when different levels of variability were introduced into the system.

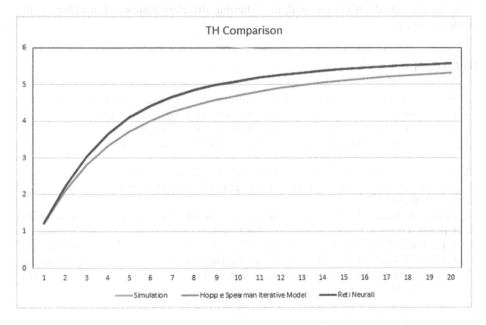

Fig. 5. Comparison of the proposed deep learning neural network model with the iterative *Spearman et al.* [8] model and the data from the simulation tool in a scenario with $\alpha = 3$.

5   Conclusion

In today's production scenario, where time to market has a significant added value, even when compared to simple productivity, it is critical for production lines to have performance controllable dynamically. Considering a flow-shop that works in a CON-WIP configuration, this control knob may be the WIP value that can be controlled and modulated appropriately to meet different production constraints. At the same time, as a result of the need to create added value through extreme product customization, the variability introduced within the production system is constantly increasing. The coexistence of these causes complicates the dimensioning of the WIP within the productive system, when a specific value of performances is needed (e.g. a specific throughput).

To that end, we proposed a deep neural network estimation tool able to estimate the throughput value of a production line once the variability and WIP enters the system are known. The current work demonstrated that this tool can make very accurate predictions of production performance, allowing a much finer sizing of WIP than was previously possible even in scenarios with non-exponential variability. The current model's limitation is that it was tested on an a-priori known production line model with a fixed average processing time and number of machines. However, the same methodology here proposed may be applied with a larger dataset that will allow a greater generalisation of the problem. The authors hope that future research will focus on extending this work's reasoning to more general neural network architectures that can take into account different average production times and, in particular, different number of machines in the production line.

References

1. Beier, G., Ullrich, A., Niehoff, S., Reißig, M., Habich, M.: Industry 4.0: how it is defined from a sociotechnical perspective and how much sustainability it includes - a literature review. J. Clean. Prod. **259** (2020). https://doi.org/10.1016/j.jclepro.2020.120856
2. Buzacott, J.A., Shanthikumar, J.G.: Stochastic Models of Manufacturing Systems, 1st edn. Prentice Hall, Hoboken (1993)
3. Culot, G., Nassimbeni, G., Orzes, G., Sartor, M.: Behind the definition of Industry 4.0: analysis and open questions. Int. J. Prod. Econ. **226**, 107617 (2020). https://doi.org/10.1016/j.ijpe.2020.107617
4. Dolgui, A., Ivanov, D., Sethi, S.P., Sokolov, B.: Scheduling in production, supply chain and Industry 4.0 systems by optimal control: fundamentals, state-of-the-art and applications. Int. J. Prod. Res. **57**(2), 411–432 (2019). https://doi.org/10.1080/00207543.2018.1442948
5. Fogliatto, F.S., Da Silveira, G.J., Borenstein, D.: The mass customization decade: an updated review of the literature. Int. J. Prod. Econ. **138**(1), 14–25 (2012). https://doi.org/10.1016/j.ijpe.2012.03.002
6. Grassi, A., Guizzi, G., Santillo, L.C., Vespoli, S.: The manufacturing planning and control system: a journey towards the new perspectives in industry 4.0 architectures. In: Scheduling in Industry 4.0 and Cloud Manufacturing, pp. 193–216. Springer, Cham (2020)
7. Hermann, M.; Pentek, T.: Design principles for industrie 4.0 scenarios: a literature review, vol. 1, no. 1, p. 15 (2015). https://doi.org/10.1109/HICSS.2016.488
8. Hopp, W.J., Spearman, M.L.: Factory Physics, 3rd edn. Waveland Press Inc, Long Grove, Illinois (2011)
9. Ivanov, D., Dolgui, A., Sokolov, B.: Scheduling of recovery actions in the supply chain with resilience analysis considerations. Int. J. Prod. Res. **56**(19), 6473–6490 (2018). https://doi.org/10.1080/00207543.2017.1401747

10. Ivanov, D., Dolgui, A., Sokolov, B., Werner, F., Ivanova, M.: A dynamic model and an algorithm for short-term supply chain scheduling in the smart factory industry 4.0. Int. J. Prod. Res. **54**(2), 386–402 (2016). https://doi.org/10.1080/00207543.2014.999958

11. Ivanov, D., Sethi, S., Dolgui, A., Sokolov, B.: A survey on control theory applications to operational systems, supply chain management, and Industry 4.0. Ann. Rev. Control **46**, 134–147 (2018). https://doi.org/10.1016/j.arcontrol.2018.10.014

12. Oztemel, E., Gursev, S.: Literature review of Industry 4.0 and related technologies. J. Intell. Manuf. **31**(1), 127–182 (2018). https://doi.org/10.1007/s10845-018-1433-8

13. Patterson, J., Gibson, A.: Deep Learning: A Practitioner's Approach, 1st edn. O'Reilly, Sebastopol (2017)

14. Riedl, M., Zipper, H., Meier, M., Diedrich, C.: Cyber-physical systems alter automation architectures. Annu. Rev. Control. **38**(1), 123–133 (2014). https://doi.org/10.1016/j.arcontrol.2014.03.012

15. Shan, S., Wen, X., Wei, Y., Wang, Z., Chen, Y.: Intelligent manufacturing in industry 4.0: a case study of Sany heavy industry. Syst. Res. Behav. Sci. **37**(4), 679–690 (2020). https://doi.org/10.1002/sres.2709

16. Sokolov, B., Dolgui, A., Ivanov, D.: Optimal control algorithms and their analysis for short-term scheduling in manufacturing systems. Algorithms **11**(5) (2018). https://doi.org/10.3390/a11050057

17. Spearman, M.L., Woodruff, D.L., Hopp, W.J.: CONWIP: a pull alternative to Kanban. Int. J. Prod. Res. **28**(5), 879–894 (1990). https://doi.org/10.1080/00207549008942761

18. Vespoli, S., Grassi, A., Guizzi, G., Santillo, L.C.: Evaluating the advantages of a novel decentralised scheduling approach in the Industry 4.0 and cloud manufacturing era. IFAC-PapersOnLine **52**, 2170–2176 (2019). https://doi.org/10.1016/j.ifacol.2019.11.527

Dynamic Scheduling in a Flow Shop Using Deep Reinforcement Learning

Maria Grazia Marchesano$^{(\boxtimes)}$, Guido Guizzi, Liberatina Carmela Santillo, and Silvestro Vespoli

University of Naples Federico II, 80125 Napoli, NA, Italy
{mariagrazia.marchesano,guido.guizzi,santillo,
silvestro.vespoli}@unina.it

Abstract. Machine Learning (ML) techniques and algorithms, which are emerging technologies in Industry 4.0, present new possibilities for complex scheduling methods. Since different rules can be applied to different circumstances, it can be difficult for the decision-maker to choose the right rule at any given time. The purpose of the paper is to build an "intelligent" tool that adapts its choices in response to changes in the state of the production line. A Deep Q-Network (DQN), a typical Deep Reinforcement Learning (DRL) method, is proposed for creating a self-optimizing scheduling policy. The system has a set of known dispatching rules for each machine's queue, from which the best one is dynamically chosen, according to the system state. The novelty of the paper is how the reward function, state, and action space are modelled. A series of experiments were conducted to determine the best DQN network size and the most influential hyperparameters for training.

Keywords: Reinforcement learning · DQN · Scheduling · Flow shop

1 Introduction

The Industry 4.0 and emerging technologies offer new possibilities for dynamic scheduling strategies using Machine Learning (ML) techniques and algorithms [19]. This brings with it a number of significant new challenges and planning opportunities. Since different rules can be applied to different situations, it can be difficult for the decision-maker to select the best rule at any given time. Moreover, dispatch rules are limited to their local information horizons, so, there is no rule that exceeds others by different goals, scenarios and conditions of the system [15]. Many approaches have been taken in the literature to address the problem of scheduling and production optimal control, and [3] presents a very comprehensive literature review. In the literature [7] suggests that real-time knowledge of the production system can lead to significant improvements in dynamic scheduling performance. Even a decentralized scheduling approach can bring benefits to the performances of a production line [4]. To overcome problems

© IFIP International Federation for Information Processing 2021
Published by Springer Nature Switzerland AG 2021
A. Dolgui et al. (Eds.): APMS 2021, IFIP AICT 630, pp. 152–160, 2021.
https://doi.org/10.1007/978-3-030-85874-2_16

that might occur when dealing with problems in which there is no complete knowledge of the system dynamics the methods and the algorithms of the ML, the deep learning (DL) [8] and reinforcement learning (RL) [9] can be exploited. In [10] convolutional and generative adversarial neural networks are employed in manufacturing and in dynamic scheduling, also Heger in [5] proposes a ML method that adjusts the parameters of the dispatching rule based on the system state. The method of Deep Reinforcement Learning (DRL) is the proper way to produce a self optimization scheduling policy, so that the accurate simulation and high performance data provided by a simulation tool can be used. DRL has recently been studied and used in the manufacturing systems because its characteristics allow it to address decision-making problems that can be difficult in today's complex and changing manufacturing systems environment [21]. A RL-based task-assigning strategy to enable multi-project scheduling in the Cloud Manufacturing perspective is addressed in [2]. The aim of the present paper is to create an "intelligent" tool that updates its choices in response to changes in the production line's situation. It can have a potential practical use because the data from the production line can be sent to a controller as inputs, and a decision can be made in the event of a disruption or a sudden change in the line. In [11] there is a similar approach to the one here proposed, but their goals are different (minimize the makespan), and even the design of the RL model, as in their case is implemented with Petri Net. In [12] there is the implementation of the RL using DQN combined with edge computing framework, for the scheduling of a job shop. Otherwise the approach proposed here is validated with a flow shop and a series of experiments is carried out to evaluate the best hyperparameters and network structure to be used by the DQN to achieve the best performance values. Besides the manner in which state, reward function, and action space are modelled is what distinguishes this approach from other presented in literature.

2 Problem Formulation

In this section we will discuss about the problem of scheduling in a flow shop with DRL as the paper focuses on the construction of an DRL-supported method that employs the DQN to choose the best rule for scheduling jobs on machines of a flow shop production line. Reinforcement Learning (RL) is a mathematical formalization of a problem involving decision-making. Since it focuses on goal-directed learning from feedback, RL is distinct from other Machine Learning approaches. Instead of being told what actions to take, the learning agent must find out for itself which actions result in the greatest reward, by putting them to the test by "trial and error". The learning agent refers to the entity that acts and learns from the environment (simulation model) through observations, performs specific actions, and receives a reward. The virtual environment is the world in which the learner works. The observation is state-related: the learning agent receives knowledge about the current state of the system. Every piece of information contained in a system is almost impossible to know, therefore only a selected subset of real information is provided for the learning agent in the form of an observation. Deep Reinforcement Learning (DRL) is a method of Reinforcement Learning that employs Deep Neural Networks (DNN) to approximate the value function and the representation of the state and the action space. The issue is that dispatching rules are not always the best ones; depending on the configuration of the problem and the conditions, one rule may be superior to another. In the literature the decision making problem related to the best dispatching option to choose in a flow shop has been assessed by [14]. The authors consider as a point of strength not to require training but only the optimization of the network's weights to achieve good performances. Otherwise, we investigate how develop the network of a suitable dimension with certain values of hyperparameters to accomplish this task. Simulation has been extensively used to investigate the performance of dispatching rules. Aside from some general and common findings, one widely accepted conclusion is that on a global scale, no dispatching rule is superior to the others. Certain ones, such as shortest processing time (SPT), perform well on some performance measures, such as mean flow time (the amount of time jobs spend in the system), but poorly on others, such as maximum job lateness. As a result, their performance is highly dependent on the studied system's configuration, operating conditions, and the performance criterion used to test the rules. As a result, decision-makers can have difficulty determining which dispatching rules are best suited to their problem. Simulation samples are used as training sets in the learning approaches that have been proposed. These sets provide examples of dispatching rule choices that have resulted in good or poor results, allowing an automated system to learn. The production line simulated is based on the work of Hoop and Sperman. The authors in [6] investigated the behavior of a CONWIP production line under various conditions. The scenarios depict the best and worst possible performance of a CONWIP production line, respectively. They studied the action of a production line in a real-world scenario (the Practical Worst Case, PWC) in which the processing times of job are exponentially distributed through the workstations, in a balanced line (the average working time is the same for each phase of work). Since system entities do not respond autonomously to environmental changes in a CONWIP [1] we propose a system/model that dynamically identifies, with the use of DQN, the best rule to use for job processing according to the system condition.

3   The Proposed Method

In recent years, a new algorithm known as deep Q-network (DQN) has been designed; it combines a classic RL algorithm known as Q-Learning with a deep neural network (DNN). Mnih in [13] proposed this algorithm. DQN is an RL tool and an extension of the Q-learning approach in which a deep neural network replaces the state-action tables. The DQN's learning of the value function is affected by weight changes based on the loss function: $L_t = (E[r + \gamma \, max_a \, Q(s_{(t+1)}, a_t)] - Q(s_t, a_t))^2$ in which $E[r + max_a \, Q(s_{(t+1)}, a_t)]$ represents the optimum predicted reward associated with the transition to the state $s_{(t+1)}$; r is the reward associated with the action a_t and the state s_t; is the discount factor used to balance immediate and potential reward; and $Q(s_t, a_t)$ is the network's approximate value. Back-propagation is used in the network to propagate the errors calculated by the loss function, which fits the principle of gradient descent. The policy's behaviour is determined by a ε -greedy approach to strike a balance between exploring new states and manipulating existing good policies. Regarding the method proposed, the reward function is formulated in accordance with the work of Hoop and Sperman, so the function will be linked to the throughput (TH) of the line. The function have its intersection with the x-axis, representing the TH_{mobile} of the line, at the TH relative to the PWC, TH_{PWC}; it is asymptotic to zero, because the TH is a quantity that cannot take negative values; and it has its maximum in the TH relative to the best case scenario. The TH corresponding to the best case is compensated with the highest reward, and values greater than this are evenly and equally weighted.

$$reward = \begin{cases} \dfrac{\log(\frac{w_0+W-1}{W}\frac{1}{r_b} TH_{mobile})}{\log((\frac{w_0+W-1}{W})^{\frac{1}{score_{max}}})}, & if \quad TH_{mobile} \in [0; r_b] \\ score_{max}, & if \quad TH_{mobile} \in [r_b; \infty] \end{cases} \tag{1}$$

In (1), TH_{mobile} is the throughput calculated in a time window of 240 min, w_0 is the critical WIP of the production line, W is the amount of the WIP set constant in our CONWIP flow shop and r_b is the rate of the workstation that has the highest long-term utilization that is the TH in the best case (Hopp and Sperman in [6]). The $score_{max}$ in the (1) is the max reward that the system can achieve and in this work we chose to set it at 100 in order to balance the penalization and/or rewarding and the generalization of the learning. Shi et al. in [20] looked into the issue of how to model the state in an RL approach. The aim of [20] is to schedule tasks in the production line avoiding conflicts. In this paper, we have modelled the state that takes into account the jobs' characteristics as well as the line's current parameter. The vector of observations ($S_1, ..., S_{20}$ in

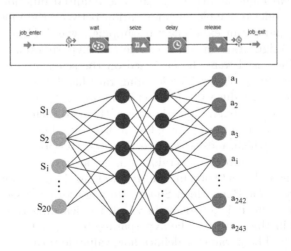

Fig. 1. The representation of the approach proposed

Fig. 1) that the DQN algorithm uses as input for training consists of the number of jobs in the queue, the sum of the processing times in the queue on each machine, the standard deviation of the processing times in the queue, and the predicted utilization on each machine. The learning agent selects the rule to use for each machine and schedules jobs for this delta T based on the chosen rule for an interval of time equal to the raw time of the line. The space of possible actions that the system can execute is linked to the scheduling rule chosen; each machine can choose between three different rules. The first rule is First In First Out (FIFO). The second is SPT, which schedules jobs with the shortest processing times. The third is longest processing time LPT. Each action represents a possible combination of rules for the five machines, e.g. [SPT, SPT, FIFO, LPT]. The number of potential choices would be 3^5, that is 243, using three rules for each of the five machines (see Fig. 1).

4 Experimental Approach

The most important aspect of this work is the development of a system, which allows us to dynamically select the processing rule for each machine and the evaluation of the DQN network's characteristics. We used Anylogic, a multi-method simulation software, and a framework called Reinforcement Learning for Java (rl4j), which is built into the DeepLearning4J library. The model is a flow shop made up of 5 workstations/machines that is simulated using Anylogic's discrete event simulation (DES) tool. At the beginning of the simulation an initial number of jobs are injected in the line, as the production system is a CONWIP, this number will be kept constant in the system. The jobs that are processed in the system are modeled as agents using a simple state-chart (queue-working-final state), and their processing times are determined by an exponential distribution with a mean of 10 min, which has a high degree of variability and is more reflective of a real manufacturing system. The required functions are added to the simulation model to enable communication between the model and the RL system. In this paper, an experimental campaign was built to determine the best network configuration in terms of size and hyperparameters. The hyperparameter's values used were chosen based on the scientific literature and the characteristics of our problem. The learning rate has been set to 0,001, which is an acceptable value since a high coefficient (e.g., 1) causes parameters to leap, while a small one (e.g., 0.00001) causes them to inch along steadily [18]. Regularization is a technique for avoiding overfitting. The "L2" regularization algorithm is used, which adds a term to the objective function that decreases squared weights. L2 improves generalization, smoothes model output as input moves, and assists the network in ignoring weights it does not need [18]. As in [16], RMSProp (for Root Mean Square Propagation) is used as a gradient-ascent algorithm, and it is a process in which the learning rate is adapted for each parameter in the network. The hyperparameter γ, that is the discount factor, is set to 0.99. The parameter defines how valuable future rewards are. This aids in demonstrating the convergence of specific algorithms. We also compare the performance using Adam (a more recently developed updating technique) as in [17], it derives learning rates from estimates of first and second moments of the gradients. We have investigated 8 training experiments: 2 different size of the network (1 hidden layer-150 nodes and 2 hidden layers-300 nodes); 2 values of the L2 regularization (0-0.001); and 2 types of updating technique RMSProp and Adam. The L2 regularization is what makes the learning process more general, allowing the learning agent to complete its task without overfitting. Since we want to see how the structure affects the results, we aggregate the data and look at the pattern of the performance parameters, in terms of rule chosen, when changing the number of layers and the values of hyperparameter. The learning agent frequently chooses the SPT (see Fig. 2), rule for which we have performance of high TH almost equal to the TH of the best case studied by Hopp and Sperman in [6], since the reward function is modeled in optics of maximization of the TH. Discussing the results, we can say that when the process of learning is more generic (L2 = 0.001), the policy resulting learns to achieve a good combination of throughput (TH) and cycle time due to the choice of the SPT rule which is known to be one of the better rule to solve the scheduling problem when maximise the TH. Instead, when the regularization is set to 0, the system returns a policy that chooses even the other two rules (FIFO and LPT). Overall, we can say that since we have set the goal of maximize the TH, the proposed tool has learnt how to schedule a good combination of DR. Considering the performance linked to the dimension of DNN, since the number of time the SPT rule is chosen by the learning agent is greater in the case the DNN is smaller (1 hidden layer and 150 nodes), we can say that we can also have smaller training time. Discussing the learning process it converges in the 100 epochs considered. It is true in most of the setting in terms of mean reward, as it increase over time until it reaches a maximum (Fig. 3).

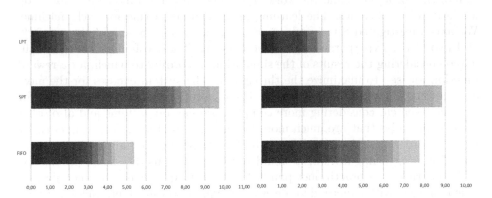

Fig. 2. Frequency of the DR choice. On the left, 1 Hidden Layer 150 nodes. On the right, 2 Hidden Layers 300 nodes.

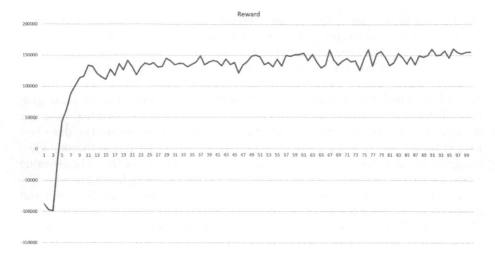

Fig. 3. The average reward per epoch (1 Hidden Layer 150 nodes, l2=0, Adam).

5   Conclusion

In this paper we presented an intelligent system consisting of machines and a learning agent developed with DQN that have decision-making autonomy and intelligence to learn about rapidly changing environments. What is new about the approach proposed is how the state, the action space and the reward are formulated. We modeled the state by taking into account the characteristics of the jobs in the queues of the working station. The action space is the rule chosen by each machine and the reward function is modelled considering the maximization of the throughput and the work of [6]. The simulation model is a flow shop made up of 5 machines. The learning agent chooses a rule for each machine. We have investigated 8 training experiments changing the size of the network, and two of the hyperparameters of the training. The method proposed is validated considering the results of the simulation, according to which, for a reward function focused to maximize the throughput, the system chooses for the most of time the SPT rule in any scenario. These results can put the foundation for a wider research, considering more complex production systems and also other dispatching rules that are much more feasible in a real manufacturing environment. In order to make the proposed tool more generic and applicable in every manufacturing configuration, it would be possible to modify some parameters and scenarios. In a practitioner point of view, this approach will generally provide managers with a method for decision-making to optimize production system control in highly complex and dynamic environments.

Acknowledgement. The authors would like Tecnologica S.r.l. for granting the research.

References

1. Bendul, J.C., Blunck, H.: The design space of production planning and control for industry 4.0. Computers in Industry 105, 260–272 (2019). https://doi.org/10.1016/j.compind.2018.10.010
2. Chen, S., Fang, S., Tang, R.: A reinforcement learning based approach for multi-projects scheduling in cloud manufacturing. Int. J. Prod Res. 57(10), 3080–3098 (2019). https://doi.org/10.1080/00207543.2018.1535205
3. Dolgui, A., Ivanov, D., Sethi, S.P., Sokolov, B.: Scheduling in production, supply chain and Industry 4.0 systems by optimal control: fundamentals, state-of-the-art and applications. Int. J. Prod. Res. 57(2), 411–432 (2019). https://doi.org/10.1080/00207543.2018.1442948
4. Grassi, A., Guizzi, G., Santillo, L.C., Vespoli, S.: Assessing the performances of a novel decentralised scheduling approach in Industry 4.0 and cloud manufacturing contexts. Int. J. Prod. Res. 1–20 (2020). https://doi.org/10.1080/00207543.2020.1799105
5. Heger, J., Branke, J., Hildebrandt, T., Scholz-Reiter, B.: Dynamic adjustment of dispatching rule parameters in flow shops with sequence-dependent set-up times. Int. J. Prod. Res. 54(22), 6812–6824 (2016). https://doi.org/10.1080/00207543.2016.1178406
6. Hopp, W.J., Spearman, M.L.: Factory Physics: foundation of manufacturing management. Irwin/McGraw-Hill, second edition edn. (2001)
7. Ivanov, D., Sokolov, B., Chen, W., Dolgui, A., Werner, F., Potryasaev, S.: A control approach to scheduling flexibly configurable jobs with dynamic structural-logical constraints. IISE Trans. 53(1), 21–38 (2021). https://doi.org/10.1080/24725854.2020.1739787
8. Kim, H., Lim, D.E., Lee, S.: Deep learning-based dynamic scheduling for semiconductor manufacturing with high uncertainty of automated material handling system capability. IEEE Trans. Semicond. Manuf. 33(1), 13–22 (2020). https://doi.org/10.1109/TSM.2020.2965293
9. Kim, Y.G., Lee, S., Son, J., Bae, H., Chung, B.D.: Multi-agent system and reinforcement learning approach for distributed intelligence in a flexible smart manufacturing system. J. Manuf. Syst. 57(August 2019), 440–450 (2020). https://doi.org/10.1016/j.jmsy.2020.11.004
10. Kusiak, A.: Convolutional and generative adversarial neural networks in manufacturing. Int. J. Prod. Res. 58(5), 1594–1604 (2020). https://doi.org/10.1080/00207543.2019.1662133
11. Lee, J.H., Kim, H.J., Lee, J.H.: Reinforcement learning for robotic flow shop scheduling with processing time variations variations. Int. J. Prod. Res. 1–23 (2021). https://doi.org/10.1080/00207543.2021.1887533
12. Lin, C.C., Deng, D.J., Chih, Y.L., Chiu, H.T.: Smart manufacturing scheduling with edge computing using multiclass deep Q network. IEEE Trans. Industr. Inf. 15(7), 4276–4284 (2019). https://doi.org/10.1109/TII.2019.2908210
13. Mnih, V., et al.: Human-level control through deep reinforcement learning. Nature 518(7540), 529–533 (2015). https://doi.org/10.1038/nature14236
14. Mouelhi-Chibani, W., Pierreval, H.: Training a neural network to select dispatching rules in real time. Comput. Industr. Eng. 58(2), 249–256 (2010). https://doi.org/10.1016/j.cie.2009.03.008
15. Oukil, A., El-Bouri, A.: Ranking dispatching rules in multi-objective dynamic flow shop scheduling: a multi-faceted perspective. Int. J. Prod. Res. 59(2), 388–411 (2021). https://doi.org/10.1080/00207543.2019.1696487

16. Park, I.B., Huh, J., Kim, J., Park, J.: A reinforcement learning approach to robust scheduling of semiconductor manufacturing facilities. IEEE Trans. Autom. Sci. Eng. **17**(3), 1420–1431 (2020). https://doi.org/10.1109/TASE.2019.2956762
17. Park, J., Chun, J., Kim, S.H., Kim, Y., Park, J.: Learning to schedule job-shop problems: representation and policy learning using graph neural network and reinforcement learning. Int. J. Prod. Res. 1–18 (2021). https://doi.org/10.1080/00207543.2020.1870013
18. Patterson, J., Gibson, A.: Deep Learning: A Practitioner's Approach. 1st edit edn, O'Reilly, Sebastopol (2017)
19. Priore, P., Ponte, B., Puente, J., Gómez, A.: Learning-based scheduling of flexible manufacturing systems using ensemble methods. Comput. Industr. Eng. **126**(September), 282–291 (2018). https://doi.org/10.1016/j.cie.2018.09.034
20. Shi, D., Fan, W., Xiao, Y., Lin, T., Xing, C.: Intelligent scheduling of discrete automated production line via deep reinforcement learning. Int. J. Prod. Res. **58**(11), 3362–3380 (2020). https://doi.org/10.1080/00207543.2020.1717008
21. Xia, K., et al.: A digital twin to train deep reinforcement learning agent for smart manufacturing plants: Environment, interfaces and intelligence. J. Manuf. Syst. 1–21 (2020). https://doi.org/10.1016/j.jmsy.2020.06.012

A Text Understandability Approach
for Improving Reliability-Centered Maintenance
in Manufacturing Enterprises

Theresa Madreiter[1,2](✉) ⓘ, Linus Kohl[1,2] ⓘ, and Fazel Ansari[1,2] ⓘ

[1] Research Group of Smart and Knowledge-Based Maintenance, TU Wien, Vienna, Austria
{theresa.madreiter,linus.kohl,fazel.ansari}@tuwien.ac.at
[2] Fraunhofer Austria Research GmbH, Vienna, Austria

Abstract. Textual data majorly reflects objective and subjective human specific knowledge. Focusing on big data in industrial and operation management, the value of textual data is oftentimes undermined. Optimal use of data reinforces the integrative modeling and analysis of RAM (Reliability, Availability, Maintainability). Data-driven reliability engineering and maintenance management, gains benefit from textual data, especially for identifying unknown failure modes and causes, and solving problems. The scientific challenge is how to effectively discover knowledge from text data and convert it into automated processes for inferential reasoning, predicting and prescribing. This paper outlines how the reliability-centered maintenance in production systems can be improved by explicating and discovering human-specific knowledge from maintenance reports and related textual documents. Hence, a theoretical model for text understanding is proposed, which is demonstrated as a proof-of-concept demonstrator using real world manufacturing datasets. The text understanding model is represented by a three-dimensional matrix comprising three indexes, i.e. text readability, word associations within texts as well as sentiment. The implementation of the model as a software prototype involves using text mining techniques and machine learning algorithms. This paper emphasizes on the importance of knowledge extraction from text in the context of industrial maintenance, by demonstrating how an increased value of text understandability of maintenance reports correlates to an early stage detection of failure, the reduction of human failures and leads to an immense improvement of explication of human knowledge.

Keywords: Reliability · Maintenance · Human failure · Text mining · Industry 4.0

1 Introduction: Unexhausted Potentials of Unstructured Data in Reliability Engineering and Maintenance

A high failure rate in an industrial system ultimately leads to high instability and low-efficiency in production, high operation costs, and poor process quality [1]. Failure rate

A. Dolgui et al. (Eds.): APMS 2021, IFIP AICT 630, pp. 161–170, 2021.
https://doi.org/10.1007/978-3-030-85874-2_17

is, therefore, a key indicator for evaluating a successful maintenance management strategy in reliability-centered manufacturing. In the era of Industry 4.0, success in terms of reliability engineering and maintenance management i) requires the reinforcement of data-driven strategies focusing on reliability, availability and maintainability (RAM), and thus ii) demands knowledge-based maintenance (KBM) strategies encompassing both predictive and prescriptive maintenance approaches [2]. KBM employs artificial intelligence (AI) for integrative analysis, modeling, predicting and reducing the likelihood of failures and thus increasing reliability and availability in production systems. Gaining benefits from multi-channel, multi-structured data sources, is thereby essential for thriving data-driven reliability engineering and KBM. Plausible implementation of data-driven reliability engineering and KBM across manufacturing enterprises, however, confront the following challenges, namely: i) inappropriate and inefficient use of multiple data sources, ii) suboptimal use of multi-structured data, iii) multimodality of data i.e. missing semantic correlation of information, iv) multiple and overlapping reliability-centered and maintenance strategy approaches, v) multidimensionality of maintenance organizations including actors and backend/frontend teams, processes and IT-systems, and vi) lack of benchmarked use-cases and economically as well as technically evaluated KBM approaches in industrial applications.

With the integration of IoT-based and embedded sensory systems in Cyber Physical Production Systems (CPPS) [3] as well as constantly evolving AI technologies, new possibilities for industrial application of data-driven reliability engineering and KBM strategies arise. However, in the literature of production and operation management, data-driven reliability engineering and KBM are mostly understood as umbrella terms referring to Condition based Maintenance (CbM) and Predictive Maintenance (PdM), i.e. applying statistical- and machine learning (ML) on structured data in order to optimize RAM [2]. Often the value of unstructured data, in particular text, is undermined or totally ignored [2]. This is mainly due to its unstructured data format, thus requiring preprocessing for converting text into machine-readable formats. Additionally, maintenance reports (e.g. log books, shift books, failure reports, repair protocols, etc.) are often characterized by informal language, incomplete sentences, incorrect syntax and technical terminologies, making knowledge extraction even more challenging. Therefore, standard text mining (TM) approaches are not sufficient for this type of text. In real-world manufacturing systems, however, the primary data type found in industrial databases is textual data, majorly reflecting objective and subjective human specific knowledge [4]. When pursing data-driven reliability engineering and KBM approaches focusing strictly on structured data, the potential of a large portion of relevant information is remained unexhausted. This reflects the fundamental problem of industrial maintenance in today's production systems, that relevant, up-to-date, and comprehensive knowledge is missing, which avoids achieving informed decisions [2]. In other words, informed decision-making should be based on multiple data sources and multimodal data, including structured and unstructured formats. In addition, optimal use of multiple data sources and multi-structured data may reinforce the integrative modeling and analysis of RAM indicators. Data-driven reliability engineering and KBM, therefore, may gain benefit from textual data, especially for identifying unknown failure modes and causes as well as improving troubleshooting processes for solving (non-routine/routine) problems and therefore lowering the human failure rate. The scientific challenge is how to effectively discover knowledge from text data and convert it into automated processes for inferential reasoning and predicting the moment of failure, and ultimately prescribing appropriate handling measures timely. In order to exploit the full potential of text and therefore, overcome the quality obstacles of maintenance reports, text understandability should be achieved, i.e. going beyond standard TM approaches (cf. Sect. 2).

Considering the discussion above the following research question emerges, "How can text understandability (TU) in industrial maintenance contribute to an increased reliability and thus, a lowered failure rate?" The objective of this paper is, therefore, to i) propose a concept for TU in the context of industrial maintenance, focusing on creation of an objective function representing multidimensional TU and ii) provide a proof-of-concept software prototype for demonstrating plausible industrial application of the aforementioned concept.

The rest of the paper is structured as follows: Section 2 provides a literature review on the necessity of TU in maintenance. Section 3 introduces the concept of TU, its industrial proof-of-concept implementation and expected industrial impact. Finally, Sect. 4 concludes the discussion and identifies the pathways for future research.

2 State-of-the-Art and -Practice: Why Does Text Understandability in Maintenance Matter?

Knowledge extraction and discovery from text is used to discover hidden patterns and valuable information using AI algorithms [4]. Where knowledge discovery focuses on identifying and understanding valid, novel and useful patterns in data [5], TM applies this approach to machine supported analysis of text. TM involves information retrieval and extraction technique as well as natural language processing (NLP) combined with algorithms from machine learning and statistics to process and analyze unstructured data sources [6]. This enables (semi-)automated identification of relevant words in those texts using Named Entity Recognition (NER) and Part-of-Speech (POS) Tagging. Linking these words to quantitative information (e.g. costs, production quantities) can further enhance text understanding and therefore lead to increased knowledge gain [7]. These matched entities can then be used in subsequent steps to enrich databases and ML models further [8]. A typical TM pipeline for extracting relevant knowledge from one or more data sources includes the following steps: i) extracting the text from documents or web pages [9], ii) preprocessing and iii) extracting domain-specific information using advanced techniques like NER [8]. This entity relation extraction allows linking entities labelled by domain-specific tags and the information related to them.

However, a major challenge for the extraction of knowledge from maintenance reports is their unique form, often not meeting standard text quality measures in terms of syntax and semantics. Maintenance reports often feature informal language, special characters, individual abbreviations, domain (company) specific expressions and incomplete sentences [7, 10, 11]. Additionally, maintenance reports are often multilingual featuring English as well as non-English expressions and thus the quality of reports often depends on the qualification and competence level of maintenance operators [7]. Effective knowledge extraction requires handcrafted solutions for measuring associations, and the structured representation of domain-specific context [11]. In order to overcome the limitations of current approaches, the human (expert) ability to understand text should be reproduced by algorithms. Therefore, the knowledge extraction from maintenance reports requires text understandability methods, rather than a standard TM pipeline.

Despite foreseeable advantages of text understandability, the body of literature in maintenance mainly reflects knowledge extraction and discovery from textual data, using TM. The majority of the state-of-the-art approaches restrictively aims to extract specific information from text rather than fostering TU. Notable examples are summarized in Table 1, which consider textual maintenance data in various industries, trying to extract specific information, e.g. the time of failure or frequent occurring incidents.

Table 1. Research considering TM in maintenance

Key statement	Extracted information	Industry
Increased accuracy of failure times for reliability using TM [12]	Time of failure	Energy industry Food industry
Detection of causalities and comprehension of incident progress patterns using NLP [13]	Flows of events of accidents	Space industry
Extraction of information about component failure patterns using TM, which enables the identification of frequent warning and failure incidences [14]	Components causing frequent warnings/failures	Facility management
Frequent incidents detection in building sectors based on characteristics using text analytics [15]	Frequent incidents	Facility management

In order to fully comprehend textual data in maintenance and exploit the comprised knowledge, a close to human-like TU model for the analysis of textual documents should be established. According to psycholinguistics, the human's TU is a complex and dynamic process, that takes place on various levels, including a syntactic and a semantic level [16]. In order to comprehend text, humans build and access a complex inner dictionary, storing syntactic and semantic information as well as generated inference, by linking previously gained knowledge with information from recent events [17, 18]. As a first approach a compositional framework for text understanding has been introduced by Ansari [7], focusing on text analysis in industrial maintenance.

3   Text Understandability in Maintenance: Conception and Industrial Proof-of-Concept Implementation

3.1   Text Understandability as an Objective Function

TU is defined as an objective function representing the multidimensionality of automated text comprehension, where multiple dimensions and related criteria identified mainly from language; syntax, semantics, and context as well as target objective function (e.g. cost, quality, time, productivity, etc.) contribute to a holistic modeling of TU. In this paper, the multidimensionality of TU is limited to three dimensions i) text readability, ii) extracting hidden sentiments and iii) existing associations, where each dimension increases the comprehension of text. Thereby, text readability, assures the interpretability of textual data, sentiment analysis reveals an author's opinion towards a certain topic or event, and association measurement extracts associable terms and expressions to enable further inference generation through linking newly extracted information with previously stored knowledge. TU can, therefore, be visualized as vector in a n-dimensional space, representing the relations between its features. Figure 1 depicts the n-dimensionality while the proposed objective function is limited to three dimensions.

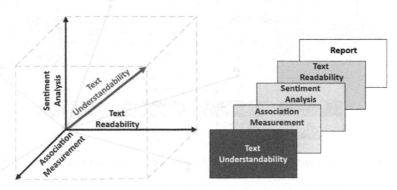

Fig. 1. Representation of a 3-D objective function for TU [19]

3.2   Procedural Model for Realizing Text Understandability

Based on the aforementioned concept, a procedural model for the realization of TU in the use case of industrial maintenance has been designed, as illustrated in Fig. 2. The concept is based on a standard maintenance process, where after the repair of failure, a maintenance report is written. Given an input maintenance report, the text readability is evaluated, since the extraction of relevant information requires the fulfillment of at least some basic readability criteria. However, readability standards applied to textual data depend on the information that needs to be extracted from text. Notably, generic quantitative measurements for text readability to evaluate the text readability from a human's perspective (e.g. Flesch-Kincaid Grade Level Formula) assess text readability based on very limited factors (i.e. number of words and syllables) [20]. Therefore, the text readability proposed in this paper enhances and adapts existing approaches for the evaluation of human text readability [21] and additionally incorporates indicators for machine readability (i.e. unusual punctuations or spelling mistakes), that prevent the usage of automatic syntax parsers [21, 22]. In particular, text readability is evaluated through i) text length, ii) detectable language, iii) usage of special characters as well as iv) correct spelling, enabling the exclusion of uninterpretable reports, and thus a higher accuracy of recommended reports.

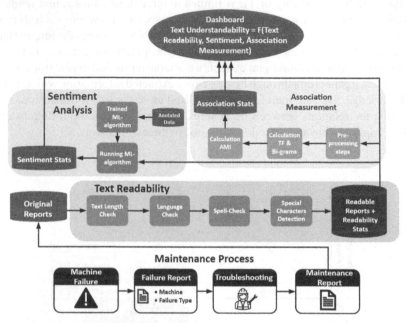

Fig. 2. Procedural model for TU in the use case of industrial maintenance [19]

Further, psycholinguistics suggest that humans achieve text comprehension and further inference generation through linking newly extracted information with previously stored knowledge. On this bases, association measurement takes place within reports to identify associative features (i.e. machine, operator, etc.). For each single report and the selected feature, comparing to all reports belonging to the selected feature, the most associable expressions and bigrams are being extracted using term-frequency (TF) and bigram-frequency (BF). The applied approach is based on term frequency – inverse document frequency (TF-IDF), a method successfully applied in the field of law to measure similarities among legal documents [23]. Due to the short texts and the initial removal of stop words, TF and BF are used due to achieving better results than TF-IDF. Within a report, the context dependent associability of used words and bigrams to a specific feature, is reflected by an Association Measurement Index (AMI) calculated based on TF and BF.

Sentiment analysis is frequently used in social media to gain insights on how users feel about certain topics [24]. However, the application of sentiment analysis is not limited to social media and can also be applied to technical documents. Applying sentiment analysis on maintenance reports reveals the opinion of maintenance employees towards certain maintenance actions and provides further information especially in terms of very short reports [7]. Due to the short text length of maintenance reports and their similarity to short social media posts, the proposed approach employs supervised ML algorithms, which are often effectively applied to determine the sentiment of tweets [24]. Certain classifiers such as Support Vector Machine (SVM), Logistic regression (LR) and Bernoulli naïve bayes (BNB) have been trained on pre-annotated test datasets. Due to achieving the highest accuracy (BNB: 78.1%, SVM: 75.0%, LR: 72.3%) on a pre-annotated test dataset, the BNB classifier is used to determine the sentiment for each processed maintenance report.

In a last step the TU is calculated based on text readability, the AMI as well as the assessed sentiment. Then the TU, as well as the extracted understandability features, are displayed in a dashboard for each report.

3.3 Development of Proof-of-Concept (PoC): TU-MARS Software

Based on the proposed procedural model, a software demonstrator for "Text Understandability by Measuring Associations, Readability and Sentiment (TU-MARS)" has been implemented. TU-MARS analyzes maintenance reports from the semiconductor industry in the format of unstructured free texts, written by maintenance operators after the fix of an incident. The to-be analyzed reports are characterized by their i) short text length, ii) incorrect syntax and iii) often-missing semantics due to being quickly written in case of incident correction. Additionally, metadata such as the affected machine and the classified down event are provided. TU-MARS analyzes previously written maintenance reports and displays its TU measures as well as its multidimensional TU aspects, including text readability statistics, the sentiment and associable terms and bigrams in a dashboard, for a chosen equipment and an occurred down event (see Fig. 3).

3.4 Potential Impact of TU in Industrial Maintenance

Through determining the TU of maintenance reports, knowledge from text can be included in informed decision-making processes, positively affecting industrial maintenance decisions and planning measures. A maintenance process usually starts with the occurrence of an incident on a specific machine and the classification of the failure by a machine operator. TU-MARS is able to identify highly interpretable and relevant previously written reports that have led to successful troubleshooting in the past, based on TU. For a specific machine and the occurred down event, maintenance operators are provided with the most fitting maintenance reports, based on their TU. Considering the displayed TU-measures in Fig. 3, the selected recommended report shows a TU of 85.69% due to the high interpretability (text readability: 83.33%), high relevancy (AMI: 73.75%) as well as a successful outcome (sentiment: pos) of the report. Based on the displayed associable maintenance actions and the domain specific knowledge of the maintenance technician, efficient maintenance operations for the current failure event

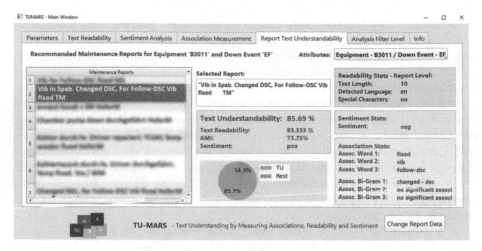

Fig. 3. TU-MARS dashboard for TU [19]

can be derived and adopted. The proposed solution is based on the same dataset used by Ansari et al. [25], where the authors were able to increase the uptime by 6.7% and the mean failure detection time by 97.3%, based on word recommendations for a classified failure event, and recommending the best-fitting maintenance operator. TU-MARS does not only provide word recommendations, but also previously written reports featuring a high interpretability, that lead to successful maintenance operations in the past and are highly associable to the current failure. Therefore, it can be expected, the mean failure detection time will increase by at least additional 10%, while also lowering the human failure rate up to 15%, by providing guidance during the maintenance operation. Thereby, each TU dimension contributes valuable information, enabling an increase of knowledge exploitation and potentially leading to a reduced equipment downtime, lowered human failure rate and earlier failure detection (cf. Fig. 4).

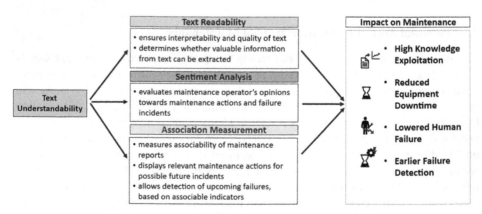

Fig. 4. Impact of TU on industrial maintenance

4 Conclusion and Future Research Agenda

This paper introduces a transferable and scalable concept and PoC for TU, demonstrating the potential of AI-enhanced text analytics in industrial maintenance. Compared to already existing approaches, TU offers a novel approach of knowledge extraction from text, by enabling multilevel text comprehension. TU-MARS displays beneficial maintenance reports and relevant technical terms, specifically for affected machines and occurred incidents, which the maintenance technician has to repair. The proposed concept is capable of reducing the human failure rate and time to failure detection, thus achieving an increased reliability, by effectively using hidden knowledge stored in maintenance reports. It ultimately enhances informed decision making in maintenance and production planning. Although, the proposed concept addresses the opportunities provided by TU in maintenance, the proposed approach needs to be further developed and verified dealing with the following industry-oriented and scientific challenges:

- *Exploring economic significance of text analytics in maintenance*, so that information from textual data are incorporated in production and maintenance planning and knowledge loss is prevented,
- *Establishing context specificity for text analytics in technical environments*, since standard TM solutions are not suitable to handle context-specific terminologies or abbreviations, and
- *Implementation of feedback loops*, so that the analytical results can be validated by domain experts in order to increase the value of proposed results of TU-MARS.

Finally, yet importantly, TU-MARS will be further developed by introducing further syntax-, semantic-, language- and context-specific dimensions focusing, but not limited to, industrial maintenance.

References

1. Zhang, D., Zhang, Y., Yu, M., Chen, Y.: Reliability evaluation and component importance measure for manufacturing systems based on failure losses. J. Intell. Manuf. **28**(8), 1859–1869 (2015). https://doi.org/10.1007/s10845-015-1073-1
2. Ansari, F., Glawar, R., Nemeth, T.: PriMa: a prescriptive maintenance model for cyber-physical production systems. Int. J. Comput. Integr. Manuf. (2019). https://doi.org/10.1080/0951192X.2019.1571236
3. Ansari, F., Hold, P., Sihn, W.: Human-Centered Cyber Physical Production System: How Does Industry 4.0 Impact on Decision-Making Tasks? IEEE, Piscataway, NJ (2018)
4. Gandomi, A., Haider, M.: Beyond the hype: big data concepts, methods, and analytics. Int. J. Inf. Manage. (2015). https://doi.org/10.1016/j.ijinfo-mgt.2014.10.007
5. Hotho, A., Nürnberger, A., Paass, G.: A brief survey of text mining. LDV Forum **20**, 19–62 (2005)
6. Geierhos, M., Bäumer, F.S.: Text mining. https://www.enzyklopaedie-der-wirtschaftsinformatik.de/lexikon/technologien-methoden/text-mining (2020). Accessed 12 June 2021
7. Ansari, F.: Cost-based text understanding to improve maintenance knowledge intelligence in manufacturing enterprises. Comput. Ind. Eng. (2020). https://doi.org/10.1016/j.cie.2020.106319

8. Sumithra, M.K., Sridhar, R.: Information retrieval in financial documents. In: Singh, P.K., Noor, A., Kolekar, M.H., Tanwar, S., Bhatnagar, R.K., Khanna, S. (eds.) Evolving Technologies for Computing, Communication and Smart World. LNEE, vol. 694, pp. 265–274. Springer, Singapore (2021). https://doi.org/10.1007/978-981-15-7804-5_20

9. Ansari, F., Fathi, M., Chala, S.A.: Towards implementing context-aware dynamic text field for web-based data collection. IJHFE (2016). https://doi.org/10.1504/IJHFE.2016.10003149

10. Strack, B., Lenart, M., Frank, J., Kramer, N.: Ontology for maintenance of onshore wind turbines. Forsch. Ingenieurwes. **85**(2), 265–272 (2021). https://doi.org/10.1007/s10010-021-00466-x

11. Alfeo, A.L., Cimino, M.G.C.A., Vaglini, G.: Technological troubleshooting based on sentence embedding with deep transformers. J. Intell. Manuf. **32**(6), 1699–1710 (2021). https://doi.org/10.1007/s10845-021-01797-w

12. Arif-Uz-Zaman, K., Cholette, M.E., Ma, L., Karim, A.: Extracting failure time data from industrial maintenance records using text mining. Adv. Eng. Inform. (2017). https://doi.org/10.1016/j.aei.2016.11.004

13. Nakata, T.: Text-mining on incident reports to find knowledge on industrial safety. In: 2017 Annual Reliability and Maintainability Symposium (RAMS), IEEE, pp. 1–5 (2017)

14. Gunay, H.B., Shen, W., Yang, C.: Text-mining building maintenance work orders for component fault frequency. Build. Res. Inf. (2019). https://doi.org/10.1080/09613218.2018.1459004

15. Bortolini, R., Forcada, N.: Analysis of building maintenance requests using a text mining approach: building services evaluation. Build. Res. Inf. (2020). https://doi.org/10.1080/09613218.2019.1609291

16. Osterhout, L., Kim, A., Kuperberg, G.: The Neurobiology of Sentence Comprehension. In: The Cambridge Handbook of Psycholinguistics, pp. 365–389. Cambridge University Press, Cambridge (2008)

17. Aitchison, J.: Words in the Mind. An Introduction to the Mental Lexicon, 4th edn. Wiley-Blackwell, Chichester, West Sussex, Malden, MA (2012)

18. Graesser, A., Britton, B.: Five metaphors for text understanding. In: Models of Understanding Text, pp. 341–351. (1996)

19. Madreiter, T.: Design and development of a prototype of a text understanding tool for maintenance 4.0 by measuring associations, readability and sentiment (TUMARS). Master Thesis, Vienna University of Technology (2020)

20. Kincaid, J.P., Fishburne, R., Jr., Rogers, R., Chissom, B.: Derivation of New Readability Formulas (Automated Readability Index, Fog Count and Flesch Reading Ease Formula) for Navy Enlisted Personnel. Institute for Simulation and Training (1975)

21. Collins-Thompson, K.: Recent advances in automatic readability assessment and text simplification. ITL (2014). https://doi.org/10.1075/itl.165.2.01col

22. Kiefer, C.: Assessing the Quality of Unstructured Data: An Initial Overview. LDWA (2016)

23. Mandal, A., Chaki, R., Saha, S., Ghosh, K., Pal, A., Ghosh, S.: Measuring similarity among legal court case documents. In: Proceedings of the 10th Annual ACM India Compute Conference (2017). https://doi.org/10.1145/3140107.3140119

24. Poornima, A., Priya, K.S.: A comparative sentiment analysis of sentence embedding using machine learning techniques. In: 2020 6th International Conference on Advanced Computing and Communication Systems (ICACCS), IEEE, pp. 493–496 (2020)

25. Ansari, F., Kohl, L., Giner, J., Meier, H.: Text mining for AI enhanced failure detection and availability optimization in production systems. CIRP Ann. (2021). https://doi.org/10.1016/j.cirp.2021.04.045

Manufacturing Strategy Dimensions as I4.0 Performance Antecedents in Developing Economies

Amit Kumar Gupta and Narain Gupta[✉]

Management Development Institute Gurgaon, Gurugram, India
naraingupta@mdi.ac.in

Abstract. The challenge with technology implementation in today's world is the industrial workforce's acceptance, awareness, and cost implications. This also requires old systems to be obsolete and complete staff training on the new system change. This research aimed to understand the readiness, acceptance, and implementation of the concept of I4.0 and performance in the Indian industrial sector for achieving a business edge. In addition, the paper strives to analyze the impact of dimensions of manufacturing strategy (i.e., cost, delivery, flexibility, and quality) on I4.0 performance. The conceptual framework was developed under the lenses of dynamic capability theory [1–3].

The survey method was used to collect the perception data from middle to above middle executives. To test the hypotheses, CB-SEM measurement and path models were developed using the IBM- AMOS 25. A random sampling using an in-person survey and an online sample collection method was used to obtain the sample data. A total of 232 valid sample data were eventually analyzed out of the total collected 273 datasets to check the reliability of our hypothesis. The results showed that quality and the delivery performance had a strong positive relationship with industry 4.0 supplier performance (i4.0SP) while cost and flexibility performance failed to improve i4.0SP significantly. Academically this research contributes to the literature of industry 4.0 and dynamic capability theory. The findings of this research give clear directions to the manufacturing organizations of the developing nations to focus their efforts towards inbound logistics to improve the i4.0SP.

Keywords: Industry 4.0 supplier performance · Cost · Quality · Flexibility · Delivery · Manufacturing strategies

1 Introduction

Developments in advanced technology have led the manufacturing strategies to be data-driven and based on the internet. The "fourth Industrial Revolution", commonly known as Industry 4.0, aims to shape industrial efficiency and productivity [4]. Manufacturing strategy reflects the development of competency by the firm to gain a competitive advantage and enables it to achieve the desired manufacturing structure, infrastructure,

© IFIP International Federation for Information Processing 2021
Published by Springer Nature Switzerland AG 2021
A. Dolgui et al. (Eds.): APMS 2021, IFIP AICT 630, pp. 171–179, 2021.
https://doi.org/10.1007/978-3-030-85874-2_18

and a set of specific capabilities. Manufacturing strategy is evaluated through multi-competitive performance criteria. The most important criterion is cost, delivery, flexibility, and quality performance [3, 5]. Supplier performance can be measured using three basic parameters, i.e., price, quality, and production cost. The cost includes Total Cost of Operations (TCO), which constitutes baseline cost, delivery, storage, security, internal movement, machine processing, disposal, and final delivery. The concept of the Internet of Things (IoT), Cloud computing, Cyber-Physical systems (CPS) is few such facilitators [6]. The overarching theme of this study is to evaluate the role, acceptance, implementation with respect to manufacturing strategies and industry 4.0 supplier performance (i4.0SP). One of the prime objectives of industry 4.0 is to achieve a significant level of operational effectiveness and automatization in the manufacturing industry while working with multiple suppliers at a given point in time. Operations process effectiveness, supplier and customer relationships lead to competitive advantage for the organizations. Industry 4.0 has contributed to full digital integration end-to-end [7]. With these arguments, we pose our first research question as follows. *Which performance dimensions of the organizations drive the performance in developing nations?*

In both developing nations, firms today pose great challenges from production, customization, shortened lifecycle, and competitors' entry into their zone. In the context of MSME [8–10], the supply chain and environment are reported as important enablers to sustainability in Industry 4.0. The cumulative analysis of the various studies shows limited work on the implementation of industry 4.0 in the Indian domain. The key factors identified [11] towards the smooth acceptance of industry 4.0 were top management support and government policies. Most of the studies have taken an Industry-specific view versus a company sector analysis. It is important to identify the focused performance dimension as a strategy of the firms in developing nations in order to drive the i4.0SP. With these contexts and background, we propose our second research question as follows. *What focused supplier strategies can be developed by the manufacturing organizations of the developing nations to reap i4.0SP?*

A sampling in the manufacturing companies in developing nations, taking the view of vendor managers, suppliers, and customers, provides a new perspective of the emerging technology and its needs. We aim to analyze the manufacturing strategies and i4.0SP in the Indian Automobile sector in the current study. The automobile sector in India covers the major share in the manufacturing industries in India [11, 12].

2 Literature Review

2.1 Cost Performance (CP) and i4.0SP (ISP)

The effect of Industry 4.0 improving cost performance is overtly focused on (1) mechanization, water power, steam system; (2) mass production, assembly line and electricity line; (3) computers and automation; (4) Cyber-Physical Systems (CPS) respectively. The cost performance has also been witnessed in the case of cloud computing [13] and various other technologies [6]. Cloud computing and cognitive computing within the umbrella of the Internet of things. An environment where machinery and equipment are aligned and work together to improve processes, in turn saving the cost of production and manufacturing. Thus, multilayered IoT systems help industries in reaching a balanced state of flexibility and efficiency to optimally reduce cost and increase the possibility of customization. In the above company's example, the energy consumption was optimized by the application to be reduced by 10%. Improved efficiency at lower cost with higher revenue and increased innovation are the byproducts of Industry 4.0.

H1. *The cost performance positively influences i4.0SP.*

2.2 Delivery Performance (DP) and I4.0SP

The lead time of major raw materials to be turned to finished goods can be greatly improved by adopting the Industry 4.0 phenomenon. Industry 4.0 is about connectivity; it is an opportunity to radically change how the industry responds to the needs of society. Internet of Things (IoT), Radiofrequency identification (RFID) or wireless reader communication are ways to differentiate, assess, and track the objects and orders during the manufacturing process. It also is a seamless way of chronologically tagging the part (s) in a product cycle. RFID readers allow users to distinguish, monitor and track objects automatically with RFID tagging [2, 14, 15]. Hence, a smart, interconnected pervasive environment is the foundation of Industry 4.0 while managing the delivery performance by enhancing speed, reliability and improved production cycle. Major industries using this phenomenon are warehouse, healthcare, textile, consumer goods etc. [16]. The delivery flexibility and speed directly influence the profitability and market share of the manufacturing firms [17]. With these arguments, we present our next hypothesis:

H2. *The delivery performance positively influences i4.0SP.*

2.3 Flexibility Performance (FLP) and i4.0SP

There are two types of flexibility: machine flexibility and routing flexibility. The fourth industrial revolution brings along intelligence in the system to enhance and improve the physical product's data. The mere possibility of reacting to change in manufacturing processes and adapting to any new developmental process within as less time is what we call flexibility in the system. Industry 4.0 flexibility performance can be measured through the readiness of the system to predict, process and prevent order management and failure in the process.

The focus on supply chain orientation, supply chain integration grounded in industry 4.0 shows a positive influence on the supply chain performance [18]. Business process management (BPM) a framework of Industry 4.0 provides flexibility. BPM analysis measures, models, automates, optimizes, and improves manufacturing processes. Machine-to-machine two-part communication is one of the applications. The opportunity to make production 30% faster and 25% cheaper is the goal of the systems approach.

H3. *The flexibility performance positively influences i4.0SP.*

2.4 Quality Performance (QP) and i4.0SP

Quality and process are the drivers of improvement of Industry 4.0 [19]. Integration of new technologies plays a crucial role in enhancing the performance of Industry 4.0

[20]. [21] argued that better industrial performance can be achieved through the adoption of Industry 4.0. Quality is the key parameter for manufacturing process-related requirements [22]. [23–25] elaborated that quality leads to product performance which further avoids production deficiencies and finally results in customer satisfaction. The study by [26–28] found that quality provides holistic product and service characteristics that include engineering, manufacturing, marketing, and maintenance to meet customer expectations. [29] epitomized the eight different dimensions of quality: Aesthetics; Perceived quality; Performance, Conformance; Features; Serviceability; Reliability, Durability. With these arguments, we present our next hypothesis:

H4. *The quality performance positively influences i4.0SP.*

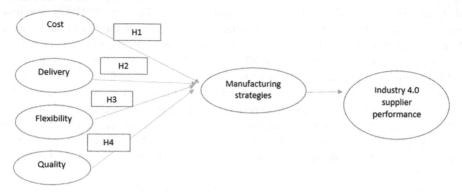

Fig. 1. Proposed theoretical model

3 Methodology

This current study based on the proposed theoretical model (Fig. 2) intends to examine the i4.0SP and its drivers in terms of different operations performance competitive dimensions. The perception data were collected from the middle to top executives in a developing nation from predominantly textile, automobile, machinery, and consumer goods firm (s). The study has been operationalized in India, which is one of the fastest developing economies of the world in recent times.

3.1 Research Instruments/Questionnaire

The scale and questionnaire are attached in the appendix. For measuring cost performance, the scale items are adopted from the study by [30, 31]. [32, 33] measurement scales adopted for delivery performance. For flexibility performance, we adopted scale items from the study by [34–36]. [33, 37, 38] are used to adopt scale for quality performance. Finally, for measuring i4.0SP, the scale items were adopted from the study by [39, 40]. The i4.0SP and manufacturing strategies items were measured using perception scales with 1 and 7 as the ranges of responses.

3.2 Sample Size and Data Collection

The target respondents were the Managers (Assistant Manager, Deputy Manager, senior managers), store in charge, operations head within the seller management, supply chain, commercials, backend operations, or sales representatives majorly. A total of 5 constructs with 28 manifests required us to collect 5x (i.e. 140 samples) the number of sample data as per [41]. Consequently, we collected 273 datasets which were higher than the required range. A final number of complete and filtered responses are 232, which was imported in SPSS. After the removal of outliers, the data set reduced to 225 responses.

4 Analysis and Findings

The measures were tested for its reliability and validity. The convergent and discriminant validity were ensured.

4.1 Scale Reliability, Measurement Model and Validity Test

The alpha values for the constructs were above the required thresholds.

Constructs were also found valid (Table 1) as average variance extracted (AVE) and composite reliability (CR) values were greater than 0.5 and 0.7 respectively i.e., convergent validity [42] and the AVE values were greater than maximum shared squared variance (MSV) of each construct i.e., discriminant validity [43]. Fit indices of the model for the estimation of the validity were $\chi 2/df = 1.562$; SRMR $= 0.029$; GFI $= 0.86$; CFI $= 0.974$; TLI $= 0.97$; RMSEA $= 0.049$; PCLOSE $= 0.545$. These indices suggested that the model is a good fit [44].

Table 1. Validity measures

Details	Alpha	CR	AVE	MSV	MaxR(H)	QP	CP	DP	FLP	ISP
QP	0.943	0.943	0.769	0.686	0.949	0.877				
CP	0.889	0.886	0.665	0.587	0.967	0.766	0.815			
DP	0.950	0.950	0.792	0.587	0.980	0.766	0.739	0.890		
FLP	0.950	0.950	0.791	0.686	0.986	0.828	0.742	0.702	0.890	
ISP	0.958	0.957	0.737	0.593	0.989	0.770	0.721	0.718	0.713	0.859

4.2 Structure Equation Model: (Hypothesis Testing)

The conceptual model was subjected to structural equation modeling using the Most likelihood estimation (MLE) method [45] using the AMOS tool. Figure 2 represents the structural equation model, and the hypothesis outcome is summarized in Table 2.

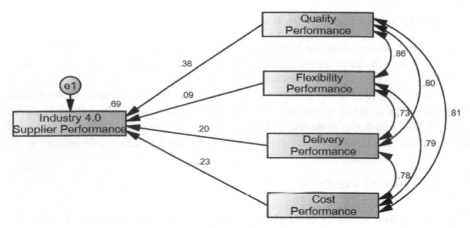

Fig. 2. Structure equation model

Table 2. Hypothesis results

Hypothesis	Beta	S.E	C.R	p val	Outcome
H1. Cost performance positively influences i4.0SP	0.228	0.074	3.265	0.001	Accepted
H2. Delivery performance positively influences i4.0SP	0.201	0.063	3.064	0.002	Accepted
H3. Flexibility performance positively influences i4.0SP	0.089	0.075	1.183	0.237	Rejected
H4. Quality performance positively influences i4.0SP	0.379	0.085	4.466	***	Accepted

5   Results

The study focused on evaluating the effect of dimension of manufacturing strategy (i.e. flexibility, cost, delivery and quality) on i4.0SP. We have observed the model to be significant at 5% confidence interval level. The observations from the structural equation modeling are as follows:

The hypothesis H1 gets accepted basis analysis (Beta = 0.228, p = 0.001). This shows that there was a positive effect of cost on i4.0SP. The hypothesis H2 states true basis analysis (Beta = 0.201, p = 0.002). The third hypothesis states the i4.0SP improves when flexibility performance goes up gets rejected based on analysis values (Beta = 0.089, t = 1.092, p = 0.237). The fourth hypothesis states that the i4.0SP Improves when quality performance goes up. gets accepted basis received values (Beta = 0.379, p = 0.000). Table 2 shows all the results.

The delivery and quality were the two major performance dimensions observed significant and important for manufacturing organizations in developing nations besides the cost performance. Further to this, the quality is observed as the focused strategy for the manufacturing organizations in developing nations followed by the delivery dimension. Cost efficiency has always been vital to the price sensitive consumer markets. Most of the flexibility aspects are part of operational goals in the firm, and they demand trust-building, relationship withholding with long-term vendors who are supplying raw materials, so a systematic change will need all the personnel issues that might arise from such revolution.

This theoretical research contribution adds to the dynamic capability view [46], where the focus on quality and delivery becomes the dynamic capabilities of the manufacturing organizations for an improved sense and response. The findings of this research have explicit business relevance. The practicing managers gain insights that the quality delivery consciousness is now significantly improving among the consumers of the developing nations. The digitalization, social media, and technology have made consumers more aware. A focus on quality and delivery from suppliers may intern results in improved customer performance and dynamic delivery capability [17, 46].

No research is free of limitations. The findings of this research are also limited to the country where the research was operationalized. In order to develop robust findings, the study needs replication in various other developing nations. The focus of the study was mainly the manufacturing sector; therefore, the findings may further be only applied to a limited arena. The study can be extended to the services sector, especially because the services sector is growing exponentially in developing nations.

References

1. Yadavalli, V.S., Darbari, J.D., Bhayana, N., Jha, P.C., Agarwal, V.: An integrated optimization model for selection of sustainable suppliers based on customers' expectations. Oper. Res. Perspect. (2019). https://doi.org/10.1016/j.orp.2019.100113
2. Alyahya, S., Wang, Q., Bennett, N.: Application and integration of an RFID-enabled warehousing management system – a feasibility study. J. Ind. Inf. Integr. (2016). https://doi.org/10.1016/j.jii.2016.08.001
3. Amoako-Gyampah, K., Acquaah, M.: Manufacturing strategy, competitive strategy and firm performance: An empirical study in a developing economy environment. Int. J. Prod. Econ. (2008). https://doi.org/10.1016/j.ijpe.2007.02.030
4. Aggarwal, A., Gupta, S., Ojha, M.K.: Evaluation of Key challenges to industry 4.0 in Indian context: A DEMATEL approach. In: Advances in Industrial and Production Engineering. Lecture Notes in Mechanical Engineering (2019). https://doi.org/10.1007/978-981-13-6412-9_37
5. Dangayach, G.S., Deshmukh, S.G.: Manufacturing strategy Literature review and some issues. Int. J. Oper. Prod. Manag. (2001). https://doi.org/10.1108/01443570110393414
6. Mitra, T., Kapoor, R., Gupta, N.: Time to Recognize Digital Disruption (DT): adoption of DT in digital Supply Chain (US Companies). Acad. Manag. Proc. (2020). https://doi.org/10.5465/ambpp.2020.19003abstract
7. Bag, S.: Supplier management and sustainable innovation in supply networks: an empirical study. Glob. Bus. Rev. (2018). https://doi.org/10.1177/0972150918760051
8. Jamwal, A., Agrawal, R., Sharma, M., Kumar, V., Kumar, S.: Developing a sustainability framework for Industry 4.0. In: Procedia CIRP (2021)
9. Gupta, A.K., Gupta, N.: Environment practices mediating the environmental compliance and firm performance: an institutional theory perspective from emerging economies. Glob. J. Flex. Syst. Manag. 22(3), 157–178 (2021). https://doi.org/10.1007/s40171-021-00266-w

10. Gupta, A.K., Gupta, N.: Effect of corporate environmental sustainability on dimensions of firm performance – Towards sustainable development: Evidence from India. J. Clean. Prod. 253, 119948 (2020). Doi:https://doi.org/10.1016/J.JCLEPRO.2019.119948

11. Krishnan, S., Gupta, S., Kaliyan, M., Kumar, V., Garza-Reyes, J.A.: Assessing the key enablers for Industry 4.0 adoption using MICMAC analysis: a case study. Int. J. Product. Perform. Manag. (2021). https://doi.org/10.1108/IJPPM-02-2020-0053

12. Yadav, G., Kumar, A., Luthra, S., Garza-Reyes, J.A., Kumar, V., Batista, L.: A framework to achieve sustainability in manufacturing organisations of developing economies using industry 4.0 technologies' enablers. Comput. Ind. (2020). https://doi.org/10.1016/j.compind.2020.103280

13. Khan, H., Jiong, Y.: Cloud computing effect on enterprises in terms of cost. Int. J. Comput. Trends Technol. (2019). https://doi.org/10.14445/22312803/ijctt-v67i5p103

14. Wang, N., Liang, H., Ge, S., Xue, Y., Ma, J.: Enablers and inhibitors of cloud computing assimilation: an empirical study. Internet Res. (2019). https://doi.org/10.1108/INTR-03-2018-0126

15. Hu, Y.-J.: Exploring the relationship between perceived risk and customer involvement, brand equity and customer loyalty as mediators. Int. J. Organ. Innov. (2012)

16. Kazan, H., Özer, G., Çetin, A.T.: The effect of manufacturing strategies on financial performance. Meas. Bus. Excell. (2006). https://doi.org/10.1108/13683040610652186

17. Sardana, D., Terziovski, M., Gupta, N.: The impact of strategic alignment and responsiveness to market on manufacturing firm's performance. Int. J. Prod. Econ. (2016). https://doi.org/10.1016/j.ijpe.2016.04.018

18. Dhaigude, A.S., Kapoor, R., Gupta, N., Padhi, S.S.: Linking supply chain integration to supply chain orientation and performance – a knowledge integration perspective from Indian manufacturing industries. J. Knowl. Manag. (2021). https://doi.org/10.1108/JKM-01-2020-0064

19. Dubey, R., Gunasekaran, A., Childe, S.J., Blome, C., Papadopoulos, T.: Big data and predictive analytics and manufacturing performance: integrating institutional theory, resource-based view and big data culture. Br. J. Manag. (2019). https://doi.org/10.1111/1467-8551.12355

20. Xu, L., Da, Xu, E.L., Li, L.: Industry 4.0: state of the art and future trends. Int. J. Prod. Res. (2018). https://doi.org/10.1080/00207543.2018.1444806

21. Dalenogare, L.S., Benitez, G.B., Ayala, N.F., Frank, A.G.: The expected contribution of Industry 4.0 technologies for industrial performance. Int. J. Prod. Econ. (2018). https://doi.org/10.1016/j.ijpe.2018.08.019

22. Garvin, D.A.: Competing on the eight dimensions of quality. IEEE Eng. Manag. Rev. (1996)

23. DeFeo, J.: The Juran Trilogy: Quality Planning

24. Juran, J.M.: Juran on planning for quality. New York Free Press (1988)

25. Juran, J.: Juran on quality by design: the new steps for planning quality into goods and services (1992)

26. Chiarini, A., et al.: Japanese total quality control, TQM, Deming's system of profound knowledge, BPR, Lean and Six Sigma. TQM Mag. (2006)

27. Chiarini, A.: Japanese total quality control, TQM, deming's system of profound knowledge, BPR, lean and six sigma: comparison and discussion. Int. J. Lean Six Sigma. (2011). https://doi.org/10.1108/20401461111189425

28. Dahlgaard, J.J., Reyes, L., Chen, C.K., Dahlgaard-Park, S.M.: Evolution and future of total quality management: management control and organisational learning. Total Qual. Manag. Bus. Excell. (2019). https://doi.org/10.1080/14783363.2019.1665776

29. Garvin, D.A.: Competing on the eight dimensions of quality harvard business review competing on the eight dimensions of quality. Harv. Bus. Rev. (1987)

30. Esfahbodi, A., Zhang, Y., Watson, G.: Sustainable supply chain management in emerging economies: Trade-offs between environmental and cost performance. Int. J. Prod. Econ. (2016). https://doi.org/10.1016/j.ijpe.2016.02.013
31. Nowak, L.I., Washburn, J.H.: Antecedents to client satisfaction in business services. J. Serv. Mark. (1998). https://doi.org/10.1108/08876049810242713
32. Morash, E.A.: Supply chain strategies, capabilities, and performance. Transp. J. (2001)
33. Salam, M.A.: Analyzing manufacturing strategies and Industry 4.0 supplier performance relationships from a resource-based perspective. Benchmarking (2019). https://doi.org/10.1108/BIJ-12-2018-0428
34. Kurien, G.P., Qureshi, M.N.: Analysis and measurement of supply chain flexibility. Int. J. Logist. Syst. Manag. (2015). https://doi.org/10.1504/IJLSM.2015.069078
35. Fantazy, K.A., Kumar, V., Kumar, U.: An empirical study of the relationships among strategy, flexibility, and performance in the supply chain context. Supply Chain Manag. (2009). https://doi.org/10.1108/13598540910954520
36. Kumar, V., Fantazy, K.A., Kumar, U., Boyle, T.A.: Implementation and management framework for supply chain flexibility. J. Enterp. Inf. Manag. (2006). https://doi.org/10.1108/17410390610658487
37. Lo, V.H.Y., Yeung, A.: Managing quality effectively in supply chain: a preliminary study. Supply Chain Manag. (2006). https://doi.org/10.1108/13598540610662103
38. Seth, N., Deshmukh, S.G., Vrat, P.: A framework for measurement of quality of service in supply chains. Supply Chain Manag. (2006). https://doi.org/10.1108/13598540610642501
39. Nwankwo, S., Obidigbo, B., Ekwulugo, F.: Allying for quality excellence: scope for expert systems in supplier quality management. Int. J. Qual. Reliab. Manag. (2002). https://doi.org/10.1108/02656710210413516
40. Walsh, G., Dinnie, K., Wiedmann, K.P.: How do corporate reputation and customer satisfaction impact customer defection? a study of private energy customers in Germany. J. Serv. Mark. (2006). https://doi.org/10.1108/08876040610691301
41. Hair, J.F., Black, W.C., Babin, B.J., Anderson, R.E.: Multivariate Data Analysis (2010)
42. Hair, J.F., Sarstedt, M., Hopkins, L., Kuppelwieser, V.G.: Partial least squares structural equation modeling (PLS-SEM): an emerging tool in business research (2014)
43. Fornell, C., Larcker, D.: Evaluating structural equation models with unobservable variables and measurement error. J. Mark. Res. (1981). https://doi.org/10.2307/3151312
44. Hair, J.F., Black, W.C., Babin, B.J., Anderson, R.E.: Multivariate Data Analysis Seventh Edition (2014)
45. Ping, R.A.: A parsimonious estimating technique for interaction and quadratic latent variables. J. Mark. Res. (1995). https://doi.org/10.2307/3151985
46. Gupta, A.K., Gupta, N.: Innovation and culture as a dynamic capability for firm performance: a study from emerging markets. Glob. J. Flex. Syst. Manag. 20(4), 323–336 (2019). https://doi.org/10.1007/s40171-019-00218-5

Exploring Interdependency Effects of Production Orders as Central Impact Factors of Logistics Performance in Manufacturing Systems

Victor Vican[1]([✉]) [iD] and Julia Arlinghaus[2] [iD]

[1] Jacobs University gGmbH, Campus Ring 1, 28759 Bremen, Germany
[2] Fraunhofer-Institut Für Fabrikbetrieb Und -Automatisierung IFF, Sandtorstraße 22, 39106 Magdeburg, Germany
Julia.Arlinghaus@iff.fraunhofer.de

Abstract. Production planning relies on accurate predictions of logistics performance indicators for production orders. Unforeseen interdependencies operational among production orders, such as unplanned prioritisation, may lead to compounding delay effects, which may negatively affect logistics performance. In this contribution, we present a general framework as well as new interdisciplinary methods for understanding production order interdependencies. We deliver first evidence of such effects in real manufacturing systems, which may lead to performance improvements when predicting logistics performance. Based on the results of this contribution, first insights into the drivers of such effects are derived.

Keywords: Interdependency effects · Prediction · Logistics performance

1 Introduction and Background

Predicting accurate order throughput times and due dates is a core process for manufacturers [1, 2]. Conventional production planning systems in practice rely on forward/backward scheduling methods for the critical path of work orders, often using inaccurate master data. Uncertainties (e.g. quality defects, unplanned prioritization, sequence deviations, etc.) that occur during operations contribute to the inaccuracy of master data. This in turn negatively impacts the predictability of logistics performance for work orders, as those uncertainties cause unforeseeable order delays which can propagate through a production system - in other words, orders seem to influence each other over time and different machines [3–5]. Previous research has shown that some commonalities amongst order characteristics (e.g. production steps, overlap in the bill of materials, etc.) but also process parameters can be used to forecast the lateness of production orders [6]. This leads us to the main assumption of this research: so-called *interdependency effects* of orders within a certain temporal and local neighbourhood (orders for instance being processed in the same week/day and on the same and/or neighbour machines) impact

© IFIP International Federation for Information Processing 2021
Published by Springer Nature Switzerland AG 2021
A. Dolgui et al. (Eds.): APMS 2021, IFIP AICT 630, pp. 180–187, 2021.
https://doi.org/10.1007/978-3-030-85874-2_19

logistics performance in terms of due date reliability or lead time (detailed definition see Bendul et al. [7]). In the context of this research a temporal neighbourhood of orders refers to the difference in timestamps of different (jobs or) orders on particular machines; spatial neighbourhood does not refer to physical separation but rather to the common machines or workstations defined in the workplan of two or more orders. An intelligent production planning system should take into account such interdependencies in order to improve the validity of the production plan, thus improving logistics performance indicators such as average order lateness.

In a previous study, we were able to show how interdependency effects and their effect on logistics performance can be measured in manufacturing systems with a novel measurement approach based on *Granular Matter Theory* [7]. Aforementioned study shows simulative results of particularly complex discrete, job shop manufacturing environments in which – due to factors such as a highly interconnected network of machines, highly fluctuating processing times and varying work plans due to the complexity of end products – interdependencies are expected to be of significant importance. In this research, we thus aim to validate results obtained from the measurement approach for interdependencies these simulation models and prove similar effects in a real job shop production system.

The remainder of the article is structured as follows: in Sect. 2 we review relevant literature in production research and related fields and derive a research gap. In Sect. 3 we introduce the research method used to investigate interdependency effects. In Sect. 4 we present and discuss the results of the analysis. This contribution is concluded in Sect. 5.

2   State of the Art

Interdependencies in Production Systems and the Effect on Logistics Performance: In production research, there are various studies investigating effects among production orders with varying definitions and modelling approaches. Song et al. [8] investigated propagating delays among operations on subsequent machines along the work plan of components for one final product. Koh [9] simulated propagation delays between production operations for unique end products. Backus et al. [10] use a predictive model to determine order cycle times by incorporating features of production orders in close temporal proximity as predictors. Azadeh and Ziaeifar [11] predicted manufacturing lead times based characteristics of orders in the same processing sequence. Windt and Hütt [6] identify relevant drivers of order lateness in manufacturing systems and suggest that order characteristics can be used as predictors for lateness. In summary of the aforementioned studies, some of the relevant order characteristics include product types, length of work plans, job priorities, the depth and width of the Bill-of-Material, the number of processing steps, lot sizes and lot times, employee- and machine-based setup times, while logistics KPIs studied include due date deviations, order and job and throughput times. These studies suggest a relation between orders processed with similar workplans on the same machines within the same time and their delay.

Interdependency Effects in Related Disciplines - Granular Matter Theory: Interdependency effects have been studied in different research disciplines. In Physics,

Granular Matter Theory was developed to model physical interactions of granular solid particles, such as sand grains. Granular matter shows specific characteristics, different from solid or liquid matters, whereby self-organized flows emerge as a result from microscopic particle-particle and particle-wall interactions. Macroscopic models, utilizing numerical particle simulations and quantitative experiments are applied to predict the self-organized flows leading to phenomena, such as convective motion causing mixing and segregation. Figure 1 left schematically shows such a granular matter system of a large number of discrete particles in a funnel, which interact through short-distance mechanical contact within a defined system boundary. Elements with similar characteristics (highlighted in different shades of grey) "unmix" and segregate. These theoretical ideas have already been transferred to *other* research fields successfully: most notably in traffic research for example, interdependencies between cars on road were used to predict flow speeds [11]. In contrast, interdependencies are conceptually missing from one of the most established models in production research, namely Wiendahl's funnel model Fig. 1 right), even though it closely resembles granular matter systems. In said model, inflow, outflow and characteristics of production orders have been used to explain fundamental production logistics cause-and-effect-relationships. Thus, when considering the flow of materials or production orders, interdependency effects resemble those mixing and segregation effects typically found in granular matter systems.

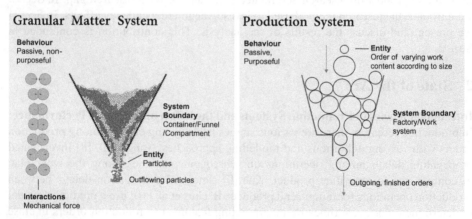

Fig. 1. A granular matter system (left, based on Pöschel and Schwager [12]) can be used as a proxy for a holistic framework for interdependencies in production systems (right, based on Wiendahl [13]).

Research Gap: The previous sections have highlighted studies, in which different kinds of interdependency effects have implicitly been analysed in production networks. The research gap can be summarized in the following points:

- None of the reviewed approaches from manufacturing research present a general definition of interdependency effects,
- There are only informal hypotheses or a framework regarding the effect on logistics performance.

This leads to the central hypothesis of this research: *Granular Matter Theory can be applied to production systems by modelling interdependencies among the production orders in order to predict system performance, in form of productivity, lead time or due date reliability.*

3 Materials and Methods

Application of Enrichment Analysis to Production Data: Observing interdependencies and resulting system behaviour between particles in granular matter systems can be achieved via direct observation in cheap and easy to replicate experimental settings. Observing interdependencies amongst production orders, however, requires physical access to multiple production companies as well as a highly intensive and long data collection phase. Basing observations on production feedback data instead circumvents a tedious data collection process, as such data contains both spatial and temporal information as well as data on many different production order characteristics for long periods of time. From the set of order characteristics, only some may be responsible for causing an interdependency. Since we hypothesize, that interdependencies are linked to differences in order lateness among different (groups of) production orders, it can be expected that only orders in a spatiotemporal neighbourhood are characterized by different patterns of order delay. Hence, a data analytic method to find interdependencies in production data needs to a) discover groups of similar data, b) assess those groups' distribution of relative lateness (i.e. the net difference between planned and actual processing time), c) show that by deleting only orders in spatiotemporal neighbourhoods, the distribution of lateness changes.

Windt and Hütt [6] presented the so-called Enrichment Analysis (EA), which closely matches those requirements. The method was adapted by Bendul et al. [7] and consists of the following steps: a) cluster feedback data based on order characteristics into $k = 2,3,4...50$ clusters, b) compute μ enrichment via z-score of the distribution of discretized order delay in clusters, c) identify and delete orders in spatiotemporal proximity, d) repeat measurement and observe statistical difference. With respect to the method initially proposed by Windt and Hütt [6], steps c) and d) were introduced by Bendul et al. [7] and represent an extension to the method, rooted in the ideas of granular matter theory. This modified EA relies on defining case-specific spatiotemporal neighbourhoods within which orders might interact. We set these parameters to the average operation throughput times (TPT) and the average number of common subsequences among all workplans.

Data Description: We collected 1 calendar year of data from a job shop manufacturer anonymised as *Company B* and selected relevant order parameters as suggested by literature: BOM depth & width, set up times (operation and employee-based), lot times and sizes, transport times, setup times, location in process sequence, and number of process steps. Relative lateness was calculated for all operations as the net total difference between planned and actual processing time. A preliminary analysis of value distributions has shown some outlier values exceeding ±100 for operation setup times, employee-based setup times, transport times, planned operation times, throughput times and lateness.

Table 1. Description of *Company B* data set

# Orders	# Operations	*Order* TPT (days) CV[a] Plan	*Order* TPT (days) CV[a] Act.	*Operation* TPT (days) CV[a] Plan	*Operation* TPT (days) CV[a] Act.	Avg. workplan length (# machines)
18,294	100,313	1.00	1.24	1.25	3.27	5.48

[a]Coefficient of Variation

Those orders were deleted. Furthermore, negative values of -100 for all parameters except lateness were deleted. Data was centred and scaled before applying an unweighted k-means++ algorithm. As Table 1 shows, after pre-processing there are 18,294 orders with 100,313 operations used in the analysis, leading to an average of 5,48 operations for each order and the stated average throughput times (and variation).

Setting an appropriate neighbourhood size within which orders might interact should follow some general assumptions: 1) Set temporal neighbourhood size to at least the average operation, (alternatively order) throughput time – a preliminary analysis of the operation and order throughput times is required, 2) set spatial neighbourhood size to the average number of common subsequences among all workplans – again, a preliminary iterative analysis can be used on a case by case basis. We set a time horizon for the temporal search space to three, seven, and fourteen calendar days and a temporal search space to one, two, and three machines. Since the exact temporal neighbourhood at which the strongest interdependency signal is observed cannot be determined prior to executing the algorithm, these values provide approximations to narrow down the expected range of observation.

4   Results and Discussion

Interpreting the Results: The EA yields Fig. 2, where each graph shows the k-number of clusters production data was clustered into on the x-axis. The y-axis shows the average enrichment of lateness in the respective configuration. Each series denotes a temporal neighbourhood within which orders were deleted. Additionally, the red series shows the mean enrichment for clusters of production data, where no orders were deleted, thus serving as the baseline. Each individual of the three graphs used a different spatial neighbourhood of 1–3 machines top to bottom. Observing a difference in the peak enrichment from the baseline to any scenario where data in spatiotemporal neighbourhoods (i.e. where orders share the same machines on their workplans with operations scheduled during the respective time window) were deleted implies the presence of interdependencies.

Are There Interdependencies Between Production Orders in Real Data? The most distinct separation from the baseline curve can be observed at a temporal neighbourhood of *three days* and spatial neighbourhood of *three common machines* (green, bottom). This roughly corresponds to the average operation TPT of 3.46 days and about half the mean workplan length. Increasing the temporal search space up to fourteen days yields no meaningful clustering configuration greater than $k = 2$ and hence no interdependency effects, comparable to a scenario where production orders and their lateness were shuffled randomly. The results of the analysis suggest that production orders interdepend in certain, case-dependent spatiotemporal neighbourhoods. Furthermore, these results affirm previous insights from studies in simulated job shops with comparable results by Bendul et al. [7].

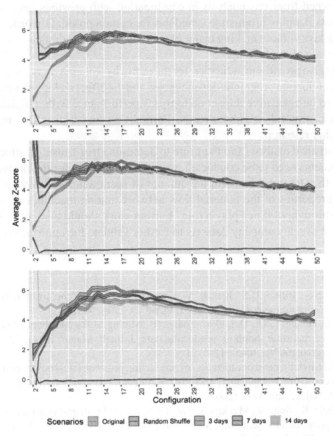

Fig. 2. Results of the enrichment analysis for *Company B* indicate interdependency effects between production orders for a spatiotemporal neighbourhood of three days and three common machines

5   Conclusion and Outlook

The analysis presented in this contribution has shown that the novel data analytical approach can be applied for discovering interdependencies in real production data. We were able to show how different search spaces affect the emergence of interdependencies and validate previous simulation results. The results of the analysis primarily indicated that orders which share similar machines on their workplans and are scheduled for similar times show an increased potential for mutual increases in relative lateness (i.e. total deviation from planned to actual processing times). As is common practice, increases in total processing times for orders are often compensated by increasing the master data used in production planning without further analysis. While the root of these interdependencies are complex and subject to further analyses from additional operational data, immediate lessons learned from this analysis in combination with previous research confirms that avoiding overlapping production schedules for certain production orders may avoid unnecessary delays without making major changes to workplans or increasing the master data used in production planning.

The results also provide an indication for the gap in hypotheses regarding the relationship between production order interdependencies and the effect on logistics performance: there appears to be a negative impact on logistics performance with a higher overlap of orders in spatiotemporal neighbourhoods. Formalising and testing this hypothesis is subject of further research.

EA is a statistical analysis and therefore to determine true causal relationships, simulation experiments need to be conducted, specifically also test for the impact of certain factors: Does the strength vary with the amount of spatiotemporal overlap? What role do structural properties of the material flow network among machines play? Does the variability in throughput times play a role? Further work should also include analysing a broader range of real company datasets to further validate the approach presented.

References

1. Nudurupati, S.S., Bititci, U.S., Kumar, V., Chan, F.T.S.: State of the art literature review on performance measurement. Comput. Ind. Eng. **60**(2), 279–290 (2011)
2. Zhong, R.Y., Huang, G.Q., Dai, Q.Y., Zhang, T.: Mining SOTs and dispatching rules from RFID-enabled real-time shopfloor production data. J. Intell. Manuf. **25**(4), 825–843 (2012). https://doi.org/10.1007/s10845-012-0721-y
3. Helbing, D.: Modeling and optimization of production processes: lessons from traffic dynamics. In: Radons, G., Neugebauer, R. (eds.) Nonlinear Dynamics of Production Systems, pp. 85–105. Wiley, New York (2004)
4. Van der Weele, K., Spit, W., Mekkes, T., van der Meer, D.: From granular flux model to traffic flow description. In: Hoogendoorn, S.P., Luding, S., Bovy, P.H.L., Schreckenberg, M., Wolf, D.E. (eds.) Traffic and Granular Flow'03, pp. 569–577. Springer, Berlin Heidelberg (2005). https://doi.org/10.1007/3-540-28091-X_58
5. Koh, S.C.L.: MRP-controlled batch-manufacturing environment under uncertainty. J. Oper. Res. Soc. **55**(3), 219–232. http://www.palgrave-journals.com/jors/journal/v55/n3/full/2601710a.html. Accessed 24 March 2015
6. Windt, K., Hütt, M.-T.: Exploring due date reliability in production systems using data mining methods adapted from gene expression analysis. CIRP Ann. Manuf. Technol. **60**(1), 473–476 (2011)
7. Bendul, J., Vican, V., Hütt, M.-T.: An improved production planning approach under the consideration of production order interdependencies. In: Borangiu, T., Trentesaux, D., Leitão, P., Giret Boggino, A., Botti, V. (eds.) SOHOMA 2019. SCI, vol. 853, pp. 232–243. Springer, Cham (2020). https://doi.org/10.1007/978-3-030-27477-1_18

8. Song, D., Hicks, C., Earl, C.F.: Setting planned job release times in stochastic assembly systems with resource constraints. Int. J. Prod. Res. **39**(6), 1289–1301 (2001). http://oro.open.ac.uk/7409/
9. Backus, P., Janakiram, M., Mowzoon, S., Runger, G.C., Bhargava, A.: Mining approach factory cycle-time prediction with a data-mining approach. IEEE Trans. Semicond. Manuf. **19**(2), 252–258 (2006)
10. Azadeh, A., Ziaeifar, A.: An inteligent algorithm for optimum forecasting of manfuacturing lead times in fuzzy and crisp environments. Int. J. Logist. Syst. Manage. **16**(2), 186–210 (2013)
11. Chowdhury, D., Santen, L., Schadschneider, A.: Statistical physics of vehicular traffic and some related systems. Phys. Rep. Rev. Sect. Phys. Lett. [Internet] **329**(February 2008), 199–329 (2000). http://linkinghub.elsevier.com/retrieve/pii/S0370157399001179
12. Pöschel, T., Schwager, T.: Computational Granular Dynamics - Models and Algorithms, p. 324. Springer, Berlin Heidelberg New York (2004). https://doi.org/10.1007/3-540-27720-X
13. Wiendahl, H.-P.: Load-Oriented Manufacturing Control [Internet]. Carl Hanser Verlag, München (1987). http://www.springer.com/gp/book/9783642633430. Accessed 4 Dec 2015

Design of a Li-Fi Transceiver for Distributed Factory Planning Applications

Vasu Dev Mukku[1]([⊠])(iD), Sebastian Lang[1,2](iD), Tobias Reggelin[1](iD), and Paul Reichardt[1](iD)

[1] Otto von Guericke University Magdeburg, Universitätsplatz 2, 39106 Magdeburg, Germany
vasu.mukku@ovgu.de
[2] Fraunhofer Institute for Factory Operation and Automation IFF, Sandtorstraße 22, 39106 Magdeburg, Germany

Abstract. Light-Fidelity (Li-Fi) is a wireless communication technology, which uses light as the medium of communication. In this paper, we discuss Li-Fi as a communication strategy for building dynamic factory layouts. Advantages of Li-Fi are the low energy consumption, the straightforward implementation, the cost-efficient maintenance and the easy identification of factory layouts. This paper focuses on designing a customized Li-Fi transceiver, which provides point-to-point and full-duplex communication within an Industry 4.0 learning factory. Furthermore, we propose a conceptual model for the adaption of Li-Fi communication in distributed factory planning applications. Finally, we describe the prototypical implementation of the proposed conceptual model. The primary scientific contribution of this paper is to present the reliability of a custom-designed four-way Li-Fi transceiver inside an industry 4.0 learning laboratory.

Keywords: Li-Fi (Light-Fidelity) transceivers · Industry 4.0 learning laboratory · Full-duplex communication · Dynamic factory layouts · Factory planning applications

1 Introduction

In recent times, the majority of production processes takes place in static factory layouts. However, the usage of modular structures to quickly change factory layouts promises a significant improvement in terms of flexibility compared to static factory layouts.

Wireless communication technology is one of the critical factors for designing modular and distributed structures inside a factory. On the other hand, radio

© IFIP International Federation for Information Processing 2021
Published by Springer Nature Switzerland AG 2021
A. Dolgui et al. (Eds.): APMS 2021, IFIP AICT 630, pp. 188–197, 2021.
https://doi.org/10.1007/978-3-030-85874-2_20

frequency (RF) technology is mostly used for setting up modular factory structures among many existing communication technologies. Nevertheless, RF has several limitations, including interference, high latency, spectrum deficiency and factory layout identification.

Currently, we are developing an Industry 4.0 Learning Laboratory to demonstrate the state of the art concepts and technological advances. In addition, one of the considered research fields is to build stand-alone factory modules with wireless communication capabilities.

Our previous work illustrates the importance of Li-Fi communication and proposes a concept for an industry 4.0 learning laboratory [14]. The authors propose the application of Light-Fidelity (Li-Fi) due to its benefits such as high bandwidth, speed, immune to interference from electromagnetic sources and Line of Sight (LOS) communication. The main goal of this paper is to implement a Li-Fi communication protocol and design a Li-Fi transceiver for the distributed factory modules. Meanwhile, we need to address the following research questions:

1. What is the need for a Li-Fi transceiver to build stand-alone factory modules?
2. How to adapt the Li-Fi communication protocol for building dynamic factory layouts in the industry 4.0 learning laboratory?
3. What is the reliability of Li-Fi communication in an industry 4.0 learning laboratory?

Furthermore, the research questions are addressed by integrating the four-way Li-Fi transceivers into the stand-alone laboratory modules. In particular, the paper describes the software implementation of a Li-Fi protocol, the hardware design of a Li-Fi transceiver, and investigating the protocol's reliability.

The structure of this paper is organized into five sections. Section 2 summarizes the related work in Li-Fi communication and our concept for an Industry 4.0 learning laboratory. Section 3 illustrates the software and hardware implementation of Li-Fi communication. Section 4 presents our experiments and results. Section 5 is dedicated to the conclusions and outlook.

2 Related Work

This section describes our work on an Industry 4.0 learning laboratory and presents the results of a literature study on Li-Fi communication.

2.1 Industry 4.0 Learning Laboratory

Our Industry 4.0 learning laboratory is an updated version from an older model factory with a static layout to educate the students in analyzing and planning production and logistics processes [6]. Further research was carried out regarding modulizing the factory, extending the flexibility to design and implement dynamic system structures. Hofmann et al. implemented a factory system structure in a virtual commissioning tool before its physical implementation [6]. Lang et al. introduced modular plug-and-play conveying systems for distributed factory structures. Currently, each factory module in the laboratory is equipped with an RFID reader-writer, controlled by an Arduino-Mega 2560 single-board micro-controller with RS 485 communication [10]. Later on, the research extends towards stand-alone modules with the integration of Li-Fi communication.

2.2   Literature Study on Li-Fi Communication

Li-Fi is a high speed bi-directional, fully connected, visible-light wireless communication system and is complementary to Wi-Fi, which uses radiofrequency for communication. A speed up to 10 Gbps can be obtained using Li-Fi, which is 250 times more than that of a super-fast broadband [8]. The visible light spectrum and the IR spectrum are unregulated and provide 780 THz of bandwidth. The visible light spectrum ranges from 380 to 780 nm in wavelength [4]. In IEEE 802.15.7 standards, there is a definition of a physical and MAC layer for short-range wireless communication using visible light as the communication medium [16]. Li-Fi's two main benefits are the high data transmission rate and the high level of data transmission security [7]. In Li-Fi, the receivers must be positioned in specific locations like the transmitters can have a line of sight. Kim et al. [9] propose a scheme for device management and data transport in IoT networks using Visible Light Communication (VLC). The authors use the unidirectional transmission to send the location-based VLC data. From the VLC receiver, the data is forwarded to aggregation agents and a central server in the network. Mariappan et al. [11] proposed a concept of "Internet of Light" (IoL) and Integrating IoT agent on IoL gateway to create a heterogeneity gateway for IoT devices. Recently, Zhang et al. [17] introduced an indoor positioning system based on VLC, with asynchronous transmitters. Chowdhury et al. present an overview of industrial communications using VLC technologies such as device-to-device (D2D), machine- to-machine (M2M), chip-to-chip, device/machine-to-user, user-to-device/machine [3]. Schmid et al. [15] propose the concept of Light Emitting Diode (LED) as a photodetector to receive optical messages using the same LED that is used for transmission, which reduces the complexity of the device. The achievable data rates in Li-Fi are in the ascending order of phosphorous coated LED, red, green and blue (RGB) LEDs, Gallium Nitride (GaN) micro LEDs and laser-based lighting [4].

2.3   Conceptual Model

Figure 1 illustrates the conceptual model with various laboratory modules. Each block in the figure represents a stand-alone module equipped with the Li-Fi transceiver. The conceptual model considers a master-slave architecture. Initially, we test the working of Li-Fi transceivers with the layout as shown in Fig. 1.

The RFID reader detects the destination information from slave one and forwards it to the master node. The master node processes the information, communicates with slave one and forwards the information through different

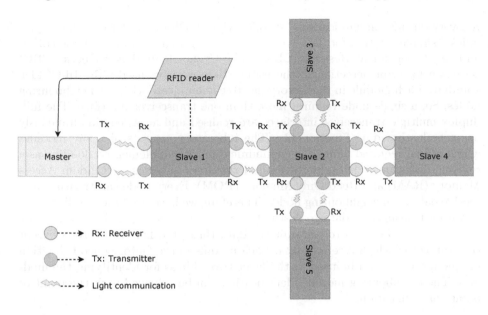

Fig. 1. Conceptual model

slaves to the destination. Once the product reaches the destination, then the slave sends an acknowledgement to the master node.

3 Implementation

3.1 Software Implementation of Li-Fi Protocol

We choose RIOT-OS for developing the Li-Fi protocol and control logic of various laboratory modules. In addition, RIOT-OS provides a variety of functions for implementing the Li-Fi protocol. The operating system provides the multi-threading functionality for designing the four-way transceivers for each factory module [1,2,5,12]. During the implementation of the protocol, we used the frame format as shown in Fig. 2 is derived from the High-Level Data Link Control (HDLC) protocol as discussed [13]. Manchester encoding technique used for clock

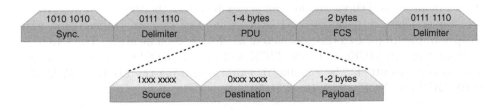

Fig. 2. Frame format of Li-Fi communication protocol

recovery during communication. On–off keying (OOK) modulation scheme provides a simple solution for data transmission using Light-emitting Diode (LED) and Light Dependent Resistor (LDR). The Cyclic Redundancy Check (CRC) is chosen for error detection in the frame. Here we have used CRC-16-CCITT standard. Each module in the factory has to communicate with the neighbouring nodes. So, a single node requires more than one transceiver interface. The full-duplex multiple transceiver interfaces are realised and accessed simultaneously using multi-threading functionality. The laboratory consists of many modules which indeed required multi-hop communication. We implemented flooding as a routing algorithm which requires limited resources in terms of Random Access Memory (RAM) and Read Only Memory (ROM). Every node can transmit and receive data from neighbouring nodes. Therefore, we have used the flooding algorithm for transmitting data to destination with intermediate nodes. Every node which receives data can re-transmit the data through other transceivers except the transceiver which received data. Each module in the factory encoded with a unique device ID can be used as the layer two address for identifying the modules. The neighbouring module identification can be achieved with the point to point communication.

Li-Fi Transceiver Functions

The functions shown in Fig. 3 are used to design the Li-Fi transceiver. The main transmission and reception functions are defined in the "LiFi class". The public function send_data() initiates the transmission. The private functions such as send_sync(), send_delimiter(), send_byte() are responsible for creating the frame of data for transmission. The encoding is carried by man_one() and man_zero(). The public function receive() is responsible for the reception of data. The private functions such as get_classifier(), sync_clock() and get_delimiter() are used for identifying incoming data. The get_bit() function is used for decoding the Manchester data. The basic idea is to implement multiple transceivers with full-duplex communication because each factory module has to send and receive data simultaneously. The decision nodes in the factory planning laboratory have four neighbouring nodes, and each node has to access all the neighbouring nodes. Each node requires four Li-Fi transceiver interfaces to access the neighbouring nodes simultaneously. The multi-threading functionality allows creating multiple and concurrent threads for transceivers. Each transceiver is assigned two threads, one for transmission and another one for reception. All threads access the same shared memory, and these threads can access based on the thread priority. Each transceiver interface performs concurrent execution of data transmission and reception. Figure 4 shows the parameters used for communication. The CLOCK cycle contains 10 TICKs and each TICK of 3 ms. In one CLOCK cycle, one bit of data is transmitted. The classifier is calibrated using the MINIMUM HIGH LOW DIFFERENCE, which is set to 50.

```
class LiFi {
// private functions
 private:
 //transmitter functions
        void man_one();//<-- sending manchester one
        void man_zero();//<--sending macherster zero
        uint8_t send_byte(uint8_t b, uint8_t ones_in_a_row);//<-- sending one uint8_t of data
        void send_sync();
        void send_delimiter(void);
 //receiver functions
        int get_classifier();
        int get_level();
        int sync_clock();
        int get_delimeter();
        int get_bit();
        int get_byte(uint8_t *dest);|
        int receive_frame(uint8_t *buf, uint8_t buf_size);
 //public functions
 public:
  //transmitter fuctions
        LiFi(int sPin, adc_t rPin);
        void send_data(const uint8_t *data, uint8_t data_len);
 //receiver functions
        int receive(uint8_t *buf, uint8_t buf_size);
};
```

Fig. 3. Pseudo code of Li-Fi transceiver

```
#define TICK 3//<-- number of milli seconds per tick (--> use for delay())
#define CLOCK_HALF 5 // <-- number of ticks per half clock
#define CLOCK (2 * CLOCK_HALF) // <-- number of ticks per clock (1 data bit)
#define GET_CLASSIFIER_TICKS (TICK * CLOCK * 3)
#define MINIMUM_HIGH_LOW_DIFFERENCE 50 // <-- used in get_classifier()
```

Fig. 4. Li-Fi communication protocol parameters

3.2   Hardware Design of Li-Fi Transceiver

We used Arduino-Mega 2560 as a development board because it is an inexpensive and powerful tool to interface with the sensors and supports different development platforms. The Arduino-Mega 2560 uses a 16 MHz crystal oscillator for the controller clock. The Arduino has analog and digital General Purpose Input and Output (GPIO) pins and an inbuilt Analog to Digital Converter (ADC). Universal Serial Bus (USB) interface used to program the Arduino board. The components required to build a Li-Fi transceiver are Arduino controller, LED as a transmitter, LDR as a receiver, two 270 Ω resistors. Figure 5 shows the circuit schematic of a four-way Li-Fi transceiver.

4   Experiments and Results

This section describes the experiments conducted to identify maximum communication distance and the protocol's reliability with various parameters of the protocol. With the verified parameters of the protocol, integration of Li-Fi communication in Industry 4.0 learning laboratory is tested with the prototype.

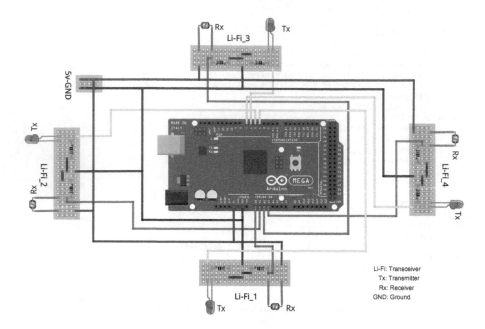

Fig. 5. Four-way Li-Fi transceiver

4.1   Maximum Communication Distance

This experiment aims to find the maximum communication distance and identify a suitable transceiver pair with different color transmitting LED and LDR as the receiver. After a series of iterations with different color LEDs as transmitters, the obtained maximum communication distances are as illustrated in Table 1.

Table 1. Maximum communication distance with different color LEDs and TICK sizes

Color of LED	With 3 ms TICK	With 4 ms TICK
YELLOW	3 cm	13 cm
RED	6 cm	17 cm
GREEN	4.4 cm	23 cm
BLUE	8 cm	30 cm
WHITE	30 cm	68 cm

4.2   Reliability of Li-Fi Communication

This experiment aims to find the reliability of Li-Fi communication between two modules, based on different communication distances, payloads and with 3 ms TICK size. The protocol's reliability is verified with a white LED as a transmitter and LDR as a receiver. The data frame shown in Fig. 2 is transmitted 100 times with different payloads and verified how many times the data is successfully received. The communication distance is varied from 5 cm to 20 cm. Table 2 illustrates the reliability of the Li-Fi communication.

Table 2. Reliability with different communication distances with 3 ms TICK size

Payload	5 cm	10 cm	15 cm	20 cm
1 B	99%	97%	96%	96%
2 B	99%	98%	96%	96%
3 B	98%	96%	95%	94%
4 B	97%	96%	95%	93%
5 B	97%	95%	93%	91%

4.3   Integration of Li-Fi Communication in an Industry 4.0 Learning Laboratory

The main objective of this experiment is to test the Li-Fi transceiver in the Industry 4.0 Learning Laboratory and finding the reliability of multi-hop communication. Figure 6 shows the layout of the Industry 4.0 learning laboratory

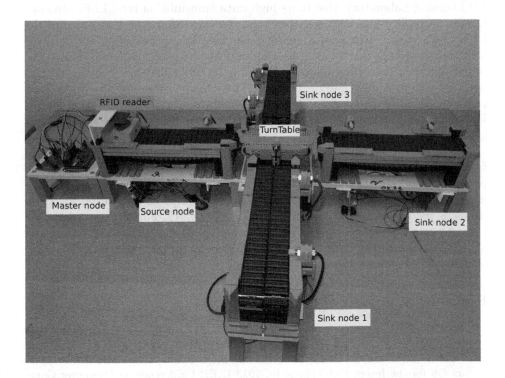

Fig. 6. Prototype of industry 4.0 learning laboratory with Li-Fi communication

with Li-Fi transceivers and stand-alone factory resources. The hardware required for this experimental setup of the prototype is factory modules equipped with Arduino-Mega 2560, RFID reader, tags, Li-Fi transceiver modules, relay modules, 9-V batteries for the power source. This experimental setup creates a distributed structure with the turntable as a decision node and Master node with the RFID reader and source and three sink nodes. Reliability of multi-hop Li-Fi communication with 3 ms TICK achieved as 95% on three hops.

5   Conclusion and Future Work

In this paper, we demonstrated the implementation of the four-way Li-Fi transceiver and communication protocol. Based on the experimental results discussed in the above section, the Li-Fi communication protocol was evaluated. The maximum communication distance achieved with 3 ms TICK is 30 cm with a white LED as a transmitter and LDR as a receiver. Furthermore, the Li-Fi transceiver provides 99% reliability in terms of communication with single hop and 95% with three-hops concerning the optimal parameters of the Li-Fi protocol. As we are developing dynamic layouts in the laboratory, the four-way transceiver on each factory module can serve the purpose of dynamic factory planning application.

To summarized, Li-Fi is a suitable communication method for the Industry 4.0 Learning Laboratory. Due to its high data transmission rate, Li-Fi can contribute to applications with real-time requirements. Moreover, the design of the Li-Fi transceiver is inexpensive, and the hardware implementation and setup is straightforward. In this paper, the communication speed achieved is less compared to the actual speed of Li-Fi, which is in terms of Gbps. The speed can be increased with high-speed processors. For example, the Arduino-Mega 2560 provides an ADC clock with 9.6154 kHz, which impacts communication speed. However, the communication speed is sufficient for the Industry 4.0 Learning Laboratory.

As of now, the Li-Fi has been successfully integrated into our Industry 4.0 Learning Laboratory. For further research, one can explore various areas of the proposed field. For instance, the routing algorithm can be improved by implementing dynamic routing techniques and can increase communication speed by choosing a controller which provides a high ADC clock. Furthermore, the error correction and re-transmission of data can improve the efficiency and robustness of the communication. Each transceiver interface performs concurrent execution of data transmission and reception.

References

1. Baccelli, E., et al.: RIOT: an open source operating system for low-end embedded devices in the IoT. IEEE Internet Things J. 5(6), 4428–4440 (2018)
2. Baccelli, E., Hahm, O., Güneş, M., Wahlisch, M., Schmidt, T.C.: RIOT OS: towards an OS for the Internet of Things. In: 2013 IEEE Conference on Computer Communications Workshops (INFOCOM WKSHPS), pp. 79–80. IEEE (2013)

3. Chowdhury, M.Z., Hossan, M.T., Islam, A., Jang, Y.M.: A comparative survey of optical wireless technologies: architectures and applications. IEEE Access **6**, 9819–9840 (2018)
4. Haas, H.: LiFi is a paradigm-shifting 5G technology. Rev. Phys. **3**, 26–31 (2018)
5. Hahm, O., Baccelli, E., Petersen, H., Tsiftes, N.: Operating systems for low-end devices in the internet of things: a survey. IEEE Internet Things J. **3**(5), 720–734 (2015)
6. Hofmann, W., Langer, S., Lang, S., Reggelin, T.: Integrating virtual commissioning based on high level emulation into logistics education. Procedia Eng. **178**, 24–32 (2017)
7. Isik, M.F., Yartasi, B., Haboglu, M.R.: Applicability of Li-Fi technology for industrial automation systems. Int. J. Electron. Electr. Eng. **5**(1), 21–25 (2017)
8. Khan, L.U.: Visible light communication: applications, architecture, standardization and research challenges. Digital Commun. Netw. **3**(2), 78–88 (2017)
9. Kim, C.M., Koh, S.J.: Device management and data transport in IoT networks based on visible light communication. Sensors **18**(8), 2741 (2018)
10. Lang, S., Reggelin, T., Jobran, M., Hofmann, W.: Towards a modular, decentralized and digital industry 4.0 learning factory. In: 2018 Sixth International Conference on Enterprise Systems (ES), pp. 123–128. IEEE (2018)
11. Mariappan, V., Jung, S., Lee, S., Cha, J.: IoL field gateway: an integrated IoT agent using networked smart LED lighting controller. Inf. Commun. Mag. **34**(2), 12–19 (2017)
12. Milinković, A., Milinković, S., Lazić, L.: Choosing the right RTOS for IoT platform. Infoteh-Jahorina **14**, 504–509 (2015)
13. Mishra, N.K.: Xilinx HDLC bit stuffed algorithm for insertion and deletion and checking 32bit CRC for 16 bit address. http://citeseerx.ist.psu.edu/viewdoc/summary?doi=10.1.1.300.4842
14. Mukku, V.D., Lang, S., Reggelin, T.: Integration of LiFi technology in an industry 4.0 learning factory. Procedia Manuf. **31**, 232–238 (2019)
15. Schmid, S., Corbellini, G., Mangold, S., Gross, T.R.: An LED-to-LED visible light communication system with software-based synchronization. In: 2012 IEEE Globecom Workshops, pp. 1264–1268. IEEE (2012)
16. Standard, I.: IEEE approved draft standard for short-range wireless optical communication using visible light. IEEE P802.15.7/D8, April 2011, pp. 1–306, February 2011. https://doi.org/10.1109/IEEESTD.2011.5764866
17. Zhang, W., Chowdhury, M.S., Kavehrad, M.: Asynchronous indoor positioning system based on visible light communications. Opt. Eng. **53**(4), 045105 (2014)

Metamodeling of Deteriorating Reusable Articles in a Closed Loop Supply Chain

Eoin Glennane and John Geraghty[✉]

Advanced Processing Technology Research Center (APT), School of Mechanical
and Manufacturing Engineering, Dublin City University, Dublin 9, Ireland
eoin.glennane2@mail.dcu.ie, john.geraghty@dcu.ie

Abstract. In this paper a closed loop supply chain for a reusable, deteriorating tool is presented. The tool is used in a manufacturing process on an item in a linear supply chain. A model is created for the linear item supply chain and the tools closed loop supply chain to analyse the interactions between them and various input parameters so that output responses of the system can be modelled. Three approaches are taken to model the system, a brute force factorial design, a modified version of a Latin hypercube space filling design, and a fast flexible space filling design. It is found that all three methods can describe responses that require only a few inputs well but cannot accurately predict more complex responses without all the relevant factors. Space filling designs should be used if more factors are needed as they minimise the total amount of simulations needed to produce an accurate model.

Keywords: Reusable articles · Deteriorating article · Closed loop supply chain · ExtendSim · Space filling design · Metamodeling

1 Introduction

Improving efficiency of supply chains, implementing reverse supply chains and remanufacturing are all topics of research that are becoming more important as the world's resources become scarcer. The desire for companies to embrace this movement has been driven by environmental, social, and financial motivations as more research proves the efficacy of implementing such systems (Mastos et al. 2019).

This paper presents supply chain that produces two items, one high and one low quality, using the same deteriorating tool. The company running the supply chain wants to know how well it is running. To do this a simulated version of the item processing supply chain as well as the tool supply chain is created. The company currently orders new tools to replenish the supply of tools for each line as they are needed but random ordering times can be costly, and less dependable when trying to meet production targets. Instead, an ordering policy for purchasing new tools according to a schedule should be created that aims to meet production targets at a high percentage of the time. To create an ordering policy that will meet its targets and can be adjusted according to multiple input factors is the ultimate goal for the company.

A. Dolgui et al. (Eds.): APMS 2021, IFIP AICT 630, pp. 198–207, 2021.
https://doi.org/10.1007/978-3-030-85874-2_21

ExtendSim, a program for modelling discrete event, continuous, agent based, discrete rate and mixed mode processes, was used to create and run the simulations. All simulations were conducted on a desktop computer with 32 gb of RAM, an ASUS Strix GTX 970 Graphics Card, and an Intel Core i5-9600K CPU @ 3.7 GHz. Design-Expert, a statistical software package was used to design the experimental scenarios. Microsoft Excel, JMP (another statistical software analysis package) and Design Expert were used to analyse the results of the simulations. In the final iteration of the model, each simulation took 5–7 s to complete and over eight thousand simulations were conducted for a total computational time of roughly 13.3 h. On a higher specification CPU this time may be reduced.

2 Objectives

The main objective of the paper is to analyse and compare multiple metamodeling methods applied to a Closed Loop Supply Chain (CLSC) that included a reusable article. A sufficiently accurate metamodel of a CLSC could aid in the decision-making process and allow a company to predict the outcome of choosing certain production parameters or the effect of setting certain ordering policies without having to simulate each individual scenario which could number in the 1000's or 10,000s and could take hours or days to run for more complex supply chains.

The objective of the metamodeling methods is to minimise the number of simulations needed to produce an accurate metamodel. As a system becomes more complex, the computational time needed to complete a single run increases exponentially hence the need to minimise the total number of simulations. Within each metamodel, the goal is to minimise and maximise certain responses such as the time an item spent queueing or the time between new tool orders, respectively.

3 Literature Review

Closed Loop Supply Chains are a key component of this study. While the items being processed by the model are not in a closed loop, the tools used to process the items can be classed as a reusable product (Carrasco-Gallego et al. 2012) and also a deteriorating product (Moubed et al. 2021) inside a closed loop supply chain. Singh and Saxena (2013) explored a mathematical approach to a very similar problem in which remanufacturing of a pair of deteriorating items of two different qualities was integrated into a closed loop supply chain. This paper takes a simulation-based approach.

Metamodeling has become an important tool for operational efficiency in many different types of industries, from design of vegetative filter strips (Lauvernet and Helbert 2020) to satellite visibility prediction (Wang et al. 2019) and more. With the goal of simulating how a complex system reacts to inputs accurately and quickly, metamodeling, if conducted correctly, can output a simple model of a system and remove the need to conduct further simulations. The Latin Hypercube design has been shown to work with this type of model, one that includes random demand while minimising system outages (Chen et al. 2019). Factorial designs are useful and quick at examining models with multiple independent variables (Haerling (Adamson) and Prion 2020) however the total amount of simulations can increase significantly as a model becomes more complex.

4   Model Development

With the goal of examining how a reusable article interacts with a supply chain, model development began in ExtendSim with the linear, forward supply chains for the items. The model changed many times throughout the course of model development as more about the interactions between certain aspects of the model were understood. The mechanisms by which the tool returned to the supply chain for use changed multiple times over the course of the model development but always kept to a similar pattern.

The tool would be kept in a queue until an item entered the queue. The tool and item would leave the queue together, the item would be processed while the tool waited in another queue for the item to finish processing. Once the item was finished being processed it was again, released from the second queue with the tool, at which point the item would exit the supply chain, having been processed, while the tool was redirected to be artificially deteriorated. Depending on the numerical value for the tool's quality post degradation, the tool would then be sent back to its original queue to wait for another item or be sent to an identical queue to be used in a lower quality production line or discarded entirely.

The model went through three major iterations, being finalised once all the factors chosen could be input from a database into the system correctly and the responses of the system were calculated and input into a database correctly. The final HQ Item supply chain is shown in Fig. 1.

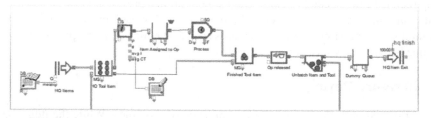

Fig. 1. Finalised item supply chain

Item creation was a factor that seemed to have the most effect on the responses in the system and was one of the hardest areas to balance so that all factors and responses could be measured adequately. Process Time for the Machine was set to a lognormal distribution with a mean of 1 and a standard deviation of 0.1 while the distribution for the "Create" Block was an exponential distribution that was varied over the simulations between a mean of 1.1 and 1.25. The Lognormal distribution has been shown to model activity time (Trietsch et al. 2012) in real scenarios while the Exponential distribution has been shown to model interarrival times in processes such as the one in this model (Helbing et al. 2006) in industry settings. One of these responses is measured by the "Information Block" directly after the "Queue Matching" block labelled "HQ Tool Item" in Fig. 1.

The number of tools currently in the system was tracked using a "sensor" block as seen in Fig. 2. With the sensor block located just after tool creation, it can track how

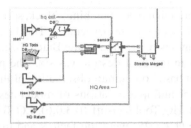

Fig. 2. Tool creation and return

many items have entered the supply chain, while the "hq exit" variable tracks the number of tools that have left this specific supply chain. When the number tracked by the sensor incremented below the limit set by the user or by the scenario criteria, a signal would be sent to purchase new tools for the system.

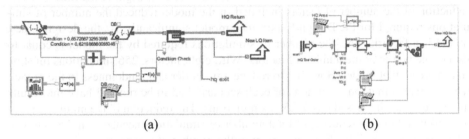

(a)   (b)

Fig. 3. (a) Tool degradation and (b) New tool creation

When each tool is detached from a processed item, it goes through the degradation and return process as shown in Fig. 3(a). The "Get" and "Set" blocks, accompanied by math and equation blocks, simulate the degradation of the tool by incrementing the condition variable of each individual tool that passes through by a certain amount. Once a tool is degraded, its new condition variable is checked, and the tool is either returned to its original pool of tools or sent to the low quality production line. For example, if a slightly used tool entered the "Get" block with a value of 0.62 and was degraded by 0.05 to a value of 0.57, and the cut-off point for high quality tools was 0.6, then the tool would be sent on the downward path to be used in the lower quality production chain. One of the criteria that was chosen as an important variable was the cut-off point at which a tool was demoted to another supply line or discarded altogether.

Creating new tools for the system is the area that took the greatest number of iterations to complete fully before it behaved in a way that could be analysed correctly and easily, the final iteration of which is seen in Fig. 3(b). Whenever the sensor block's reading for "number of items currently in the area" goes below a threshold as set by the user/scenario, a signal is sent to send new tools into the supply chain to be used. Using another sensor block, an information block and an "Unbatching" block, the system, when it senses this signal, it opens the gate for a single tool to be allowed through. These single tools passed through the information block which measures the average amount of time between each of the orders, then passes through the "Unbatching" block, splitting the tool into multiple tools according to a variable set by the user/scenario. This factor of the number of tools the individual tool is split into is referred to as the Batch Size.

The number of factors in the final design was six. The names and limits of each of the factors were decided based on human observation of the model, considering the response of the system over multiple iterations of model design. Initial Tools (4,15), Low Inventory Limit (0,4), HQ Tool Cut-off (0.3,0.6), LQ Tool Cut-off (0,0.2), Batch Size (1,6), and Item Mean (1.1,1.25) were the factors and limits chosen. The number of responses for the system was four and included Time between Orders (for tools) and Item Queue Time for each of the two supply lines.

5 Metamodeling

With the limits for the factors chosen and the responses ready to calculate, the meta-modeling could begin. Two iterations of metamodeling occurred, with the result of the first iteration being a reduction in the number of factors from eight to the final six. The reduction of the number of factors included in the model reduced the number of simulations required for the Design Expert metamodel significantly. As the design expert model is a factorial one, the number of simulations required by the model is equal to two to the power of the number of factors. With eight factors, 256 simulations must be run to create that model. However, to reduce any outlier and randomness in the model, it was decided that ten repetitions of each scenario had to be run and have the results averaged which increased this to 2560 simulations. The reduction of the number of factors from eight to six reduced the total number of simulations needed from 2560 to just 640, a reduction of 75%. This adjustment of the number of factors also influenced both JMP space filling metamodel designs. Both space filling designs had the total number of simulations required lowered from 800 to 600, a reduction of 25%.

The first metamodel created in JMP was a Latin hypercube-based design. This type of design has been shown to produce accurate metamodels and assist in the decision making process when multiple variables and responses are taken into account (Ben Ali et al. 2018). One problem that was encountered in this path was that the Latin Hypercube generator in JMP only allowed continuous values for each of its factors. While testing this data in ExtendSim, many problems occurred with duplication of items and tools when a factor such as batch size had a non-integer value attached, so changes to the Latin Hypercube Model had to be made. Each of the factors that required only integer values had its generated results rounded to the nearest integer, simulating that the data was categorical. Three Categorical factors (Initial Tools, Low Inventory Limit and Batch Size) and three Continuous factors (HQ Tool Cut-off, LQ Tool Cut-off and Item Mean) were included in the experimental design.

While this may have compromised the integrity of the metamodeling method, the other option was to not use the method altogether. This modified approach did not contain any of the duplication errors and the results produced were error free in initial testing. This method is mentioned from here on as the Rounded Latin Hypercube (RLHC) method. The Fast Flexible Filling Design (FFFD) in JMP allowed for categorical data alongside continuous data so no cleaning of the input factors for the simulations was required. This was chosen alongside RLHC for comparison.

6 Simulation Setup

Databases were created in ExtendSim so that any number or combination of runs could be setup to simulate back-to-back. The amount of runs that ExtendSim conducted was always equal to the number of rows in the factors database so once the run button was pressed, ExtendSim ran all the simulations required. The data recorded in each run was written into another database for the responses of the system at the end of each run. This data was exported to excel where each of the ten duplicate runs were averaged. The averaged results could then be exported back into Design Expert and JMP as needed and analysis of the results was conducted.

7 Results

The aim of using the metamodels is to create an accurate model of the system while minimising the amount of computation needed to make it accurate. As each of the three methods needed roughly the same amount of simulation time (600–640 runs each) to complete their models in the final iteration, they all perform the same in this aspect. The way in which they must be compared is then by the accuracy of their models for each of the responses. Comparison of the R^2 values for each of the models for each of the responses was conducted and tabulated in Table 1. An R^2 value above 0.90 is deemed to be accurate and can be classified as successfully emulating the simulation, provided it is not disqualified in the validation stage.

The Design Expert metamodel, would be expected to achieve very accurate results when predicting all four values in the simulations, whereas the FFFD or RLHC would not be expected to predict LQ Time between Orders or LQ Item Queue Time very well in comparison to the other two criteria. This is the case as can be seen in Table 1, however, the DE model, while producing a high R^2 value for two of the criteria, does not predict an accurate value for the scenario (highlighted in red).

Table 1. Predicted vs simulated results

	Sim Results	FFFD Predicted		RLHC Predicted		DE Predicted	
	Results	R^2	Sim	R^2	Sim	R^2	Sim
HQ TBO	28.84	0.921	29.09	0.934	28.86	0.995	29.7
LQ TBO	201.7	0.453	116.99	0.580	294.97	0.962	43.5
HQ IQT	0.95	0.921	1.18	0.934	1.18	0.908	1.71
LQ IQT	0.41	0.453	0.52	0.580	0.48	0.887	0.43

Validation of the models was conducted by taking a random model scenario and running it ten times to get an average result and comparing each of the model's predictions to the averaged result of the simulation. The ten simulations were run with the following factors: Initial Tools = 10, Low inventory Limit = 2, HQ Tool Cut-off = 0.45, LQ Tool

Cut-off $= 0$, Batch Size $= 4$, Item Mean $= 1.175$. In Design Expert, the confirmation tab allows the user to input numbers for each factor and will output the expected responses. In JMP, a profiler was constructed using a partial least squared regression method for both JMP models that allowed the user to input values for the factors and receive estimated responses.

8 Discussion

Modelling the HQ time between orders seemed to be the one area that all three models successfully completed, all yielding R^2 values greater than 0.9 as well as all having accurate (<5% error) estimations in comparison to the averaged simulation results. The other three responses were not as close in estimation except for the Design Expert model in predicting the low quality queue time response. This estimation only yielding an error of 3.6% in comparison to the simulations while the RLHC and FFFD responded with errors of 15.4% and 25.6% respectively.

Estimating the low quality time between orders was the worst predicted response for all models with the best model (FFFD) yielding a value 42% lower than the simulated value while the RLHC and Design Expert Model estimated $+46\%$ and -78% of the simulated value. Even though the Design Expert model had an R^2 value that indicates that is has produced an accurate model, the predicted value is very far off the simulated result. The same phenomenon occurred with the design expert model for predicting the high quality item queue time with an R^2 value of 0.9081 yet the estimate is 79.7% greater than the simulated value. The RLHC and FFFD both yielded values ~24% greater than the measured value for high quality item queue time.

The models producing good results for "HQ time between orders" in comparison to the other three responses may be due to the number of variables that influence the results. For example, the high quality item line only takes item inputs from one area and new tool inputs from one area, whereas the low quality line takes item inputs from one area but takes new tool inputs from two areas, one being controlled by an ordering policy while the other is semi-random inputs of tools from the high quality line. Figure 4(a) illustrates this type of occurrence in the lower quality line as a group of tools all get demoted to the lower line in a small time frame, resulting in a huge number of LQ tools and a large time frame for the LQ tools to diminish again. This type of influx into the low quality line is something that none of the models consider. If another factor were added to the models that represented this behaviour in the system, there could be increase accuracy in the three models' predictions.

The RLHC model for the low quality responses was poor. With an R^2 value of 0.5797 for both LQ responses, some important factor is clearly missing. While some factors such as initial tools, low inventory limit and batch size had little to no effect on each response, factors such as mean items and HQ/LQ tool cut-off had a significant impact.

There are a few areas of the model that could be looked at to address this issue, the first being the rate at which tools leave the high quality area and enter the low quality area. The linear rate of addition of tools to the LQ tool supply, as seen in Fig. 4(b), could be an example of a factor that could be incorporated into the model specifically for the low-quality responses. The same theory could be applied to the FFFD model.

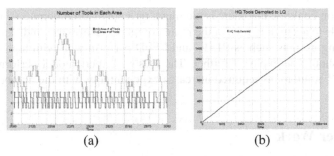

Fig. 4. (a) Tool tracking mid-simulation and (b) Linear rate of demotion of HQ tools

Randomness in the ExtendSim simulation may also be a contributing factor to the lack of accuracy of the metamodels. Item generation, Item process time, and the rate of tool degradation were all influenced by random numbers while also being three areas of the model with a huge influence on results. While only the mean item generation was included as a factor in each of the models, adding these three areas of randomness as factors to the models could produce more accurate results in the metamodeling process.

Equations to calculate each of the responses for each of the metamodeling methods based on the input factors provided were created. Table 2 contains the "HQ Time between Orders" equations for each of the metamodel types.

Table 2. HQ time between orders equations

Multiplier			Factor
DE	RLHC	FFFD	
−0.082	−8.13	−13.69	Intercept
0.03	22.34	24.86	*Mean items +
4.54	7.16	7.41	*Batch size +
0.089	−38.79	−37.46	*HQ tool cut-off +
0	−0.036	0.051	*Initial tools +
0	−0.045	0.14	*Low inventory limit
−10.17	0	0	*HQ tool cut-off *batch size +
6.35	0	0	*Batch size *Mean items

9 Conclusions

All three models, Design Expert, RLHC, and FFFD, accurately predict the response with the least amount of input: High Quality Time between Orders. However, the more complex responses of the system are not accurately captured in any of the three models. One of the reasons for this may be the lack of relevant factors analysed by the simulation.

Another reason could be that there is too much unaccounted randomness in the system for the models to accurately predict the more complex performance indicators. The use of space filling designs such as RLHC and FFFD perform well with high numbers of factors and should be explored further. The Design Expert model performs well but the number of simulations required increases exponentially with the number of factors present.

10   Further Work

Only two types of space filling designs for metamodel creation were explored in this paper, a modified version of the Latin Hypercube and JMP's Fast Flexible Filing Design. Both methods are one-shot, non-sequential designs so sequential methods (Crombecq et al. 2011) may be able to create accurate models with even lower numbers of simulations required.

References

1. Ben Ali, M., D'Amours, S., Gaudreault, J., Carle, M.A.: Configuration and evaluation of an integrated demand management process using a space-filling design and Kriging metamodeling. Oper. Res. Perspect. **5**, 45–58 (2018). https://doi.org/10.1016/j.orp.2018.01.002
2. Carrasco-Gallego, R., Ponce-Cueto, E., Dekker, R.: Closed-loop supply chains of reusable articles: a typology grounded on case studies. Int. J. Prod. Res. **50**(19), 5582–5596 (2012). https://doi.org/10.1080/00207543.2011.649861
3. Chen, Q., et al.: Supply adequacy assessment of the gas pipeline system based on the Latin hypercube sampling method under random demand. J. Nat. Gas Sci. Eng. **71**(July), 102965 (2019). https://doi.org/10.1016/j.jngse.2019.102965
4. Crombecq, K., Laermans, E., Dhaene, T.: Efficient space-filling and non-collapsing sequential design strategies for simulation-based modeling. Eur. J. Oper. Res. **214**(3), 683–696 (2011). https://doi.org/10.1016/j.ejor.2011.05.032
5. Haerling (Adamson), K., Prion, S.: Two-by-two factorial design. Clin. Simul. Nurs. **49**, 90–91 (2020). https://doi.org/10.1016/j.ecns.2020.06.004
6. Helbing, D., Treiber, M., Kesting, A.: Understanding interarrival and interdeparture time statistics from interactions in queuing systems. Phys. A **363**(1), 62–72 (2006). https://doi.org/10.1016/j.physa.2006.01.048
7. Lauvernet, C., Helbert, C.: Metamodeling methods that incorporate qualitative variables for improved design of vegetative filter strips. Reliab. Eng. Syst. Saf. **204**(February 2019), 107083 (2020). https://doi.org/10.1016/j.ress.2020.107083
8. Mastos, T.D., et al.: Introducing an application of an industry 4.0 solution for circular supply chain management. Sci. Total Environ. 135907 (2019). https://doi.org/10.1016/j.jclepro.2021.126886
9. Moubed, M., Boroumandzad, Y., Nadizadeh, A.: A dynamic model for deteriorating products in a closed-loop supply chain. Simul. Model. Pract. Theory **108**, 102269 (2021). https://doi.org/10.1016/j.simpat.2021.102269
10. Singh, S.R., Saxena, N.: A closed loop supply chain system with flexible manufacturing and reverse logistics operation under shortages for deteriorating items. Procedia Technol. **10**, 330–339 (2013). https://doi.org/10.1016/j.protcy.2013.12.368

11. Trietsch, D., Mazmanyan, L., Gevorgyan, L., Baker, K.R.: Modeling activity times by the Parkinson distribution with a lognormal core: theory and validation. Eur. J. Oper. Res. **216**(2), 386–396 (2012). https://doi.org/10.1016/j.ejor.2011.07.054
12. Wang, X., Han, C., Yang, P., Sun, X.: Onboard satellite visibility prediction using metamodeling based framework. Aerosp. Sci. Technol. **94**, 105377 (2019). https://doi.org/10.1016/j.ast.2019.105377

Risk Assessment and Mitigation for Industry 4.0: Implementation of a Digital Risk Quick Check

Julia C. Arlinghaus(✉) and Falko Bendik(✉)

Otto-von-Guericke Universität Magdeburg, Universitätsplatz 2, 39106 Magdeburg, Germany
{julia.arlinghaus,falko.bendik}@ovgu.de

Abstract. While academics and professionals overwhelmingly agree that current advances in manufacturing present tremendous capabilities to advance manufacturing processes, their view and awareness of the related risk management varies widely. We have developed a method of classifying digital technologies, assessing risk factors and assigning situation-specific mitigation strategies to a variety of digital manufacturing applications. It is based on the analyses of over 350 digital manufacturing projects and over 40 in-depth interviews with academic and industry experts.

A classification of digital technologies and risk factors including fields of application serves as the basis for the web-based assessment and mitigation tool designed to evaluate digitalization projects in all areas of manufacturing and logistics as well as in all phases of development.

Keywords: Digital manufacturing · Risk management · Cybersecurity · Digitalization

1 Introduction

Academics and professionals overwhelmingly agree that current advances in Industry 4.0 and manufacturing present tremendous capabilities. Risks associated with the implementation of digitalization technologies in all areas of production processes and logistics have largely been neglected or confined to so-called cyber risks. The corporate risks related to digitalization technologies harbor several positive and negative implications. Improved product traceability comes at the cost of greater technology dependence and vulnerability to technical failures. While visibility and integration on the business model level may improve inventory and service levels and permit segmentation and individualization of supply chain strategies, they can simultaneously increase complexity, jeopardize data ownership, and create new avenues for cyberattacks (see Fig. 1) [1]. Digitalization can generate risk factors that include vulnerability to technical malfunctions, data tampering, safety and security, health and motivation hazards, dependence on limited resources, coordination complexity, and potential additional costs after implementation [2, 3].

© IFIP International Federation for Information Processing 2021
Published by Springer Nature Switzerland AG 2021
A. Dolgui et al. (Eds.): APMS 2021, IFIP AICT 630, pp. 208–217, 2021.
https://doi.org/10.1007/978-3-030-85874-2_22

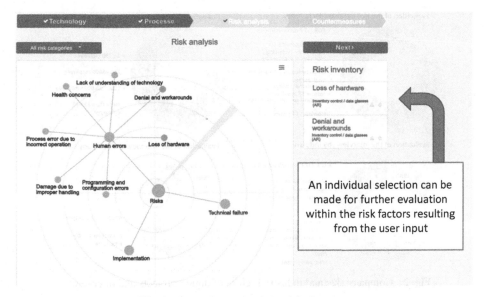

Fig. 1. Examples technology risk situations

Based on a set of 361 digital projects and 42 in-depth interviews with experts, we develop a method for assessing risks factors for and assigning situation-specific mitigation strategies to a set of assorted digital manufacturing applications. A classification of risk factors and fields of application serves as the basis for the web-based assessment and mitigation tool designed to prepare and evaluate digitalization projects in all areas of manufacturing and logistics. The web-based tool has value for stakeholders, ranging from small and medium-sized manufacturers, technology vendors and academics. It rapidly delivers a free and reliable overview of risks for specific combinations of technologies and processes along with the relevant mitigation strategies. Figure 2 provides an overview of company size and industry sectors compiled for the digital projects and interviews conducted with experts.

The remainder of this article is structured as follows: In Sect. 2, we provide a survey of the theoretical background of digitalization in Industry 4.0 manufacturing applications and related digital risk management in order to identify the research gap. In Sect. 3, we present the methodological approach applied. In Sect. 4, we examine the study's main findings in a technology classification, a risk classification, and different risk types paired with mitigation strategies. In Sect. 5, we present the structure and some screenshots of the method's implementation as a web-based tool and discuss some interesting facts we discerned.

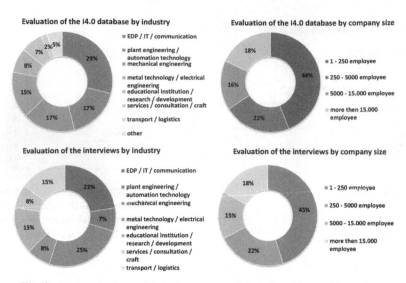

Fig. 2. Company size and industry sectors of digital projects and interviews

2 Theoretical Background

2.1 Risk Management in Industry 4.0

In the past decade, Industry 4.0 has become synonymous with innovative products, services and business models that increase efficiency, sustainability, robustness and flexibility [4]. Risk management covering more than cyber risk has emerged in research only recently in the last few years. Two risk types in smart factories arising from technical failures, specifically errors and attacks get distinguished by [5]. Errors include human, technical and organizational failures as well as force majeure. Attacks comprise targeted or untargeted malicious threats (e.g., hacking or phishing). [6] similarly identify organizational and human factors as main issues in operational risk assessments. Different risk factors and their relation to the benefits of underlying digitalization projects were mapped in [7]. Furthermore, [8] developed a risk framework for Industry 4.0 that addresses the triple bottom line of sustainability. Moreover, [1] show the impact of the ripple effect on digitalization and Industry 4.0. While they focus on the opportunities of certain digitalization applications for manufacturing and logistics, the authors identify concomitant challenges and risk factors generated by them. Big data analytics related to technology risks have been explored in several studies of manufacturing and logistics, such as [3] and [2]. Knowledge about the risks in the digital technology landscape is scant, though. On the one hand, the current literature on digital technologies tends to overemphasize the positive impacts and transformational capabilities of digital technologies, while underestimating the potential risks connected with their implementation [9]. On the other hand, the literature on manufacturing and logistics risk management provides numerous models and frameworks for types and sources of risks as well as mitigation strategies. Recent studies, e.g. [10] on the use of big data in customer research and manufacturing and [3] on big data for demand planning and return management, [6] focus heavily on big data technologies and emphasize identifying potential applications for such technologies in supply chain operations.

2.2 Research Gap

Systematic empirical evidence of risk factors associated with the implementation of Industry 4.0 technologies is absent in the current literature. Academics and professionals both need to understand risk systematically in order to be able to mitigate and minimize it in operations management [8, 11]. Whereas businesses are quite aware of the benefits and capabilities of digital projects, the literature still treats specific technologies, related risk and potential mitigation strategies separately. Current studies largely stress potential risks associated with the final concept of Industry 4.0 but do not provide specific insight into different risk types that typically arise in different fields of application. Moreover, tools with which critical information can be assessed in an easily structured manner are lacking in industrial practice.

3 Methodology

The methodology adopted follows a five-step research approach (see Fig. 3).

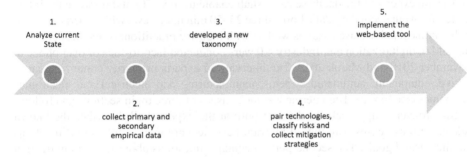

Fig. 3. Five-step research approach

First, current studies were analyzed systematically to develop a thorough under-standing of the current literature on Industry 4.0, digitalization technologies and risk management. The current studies provided an introduction to risk factors and uncertainties inherent to Industry 4.0 technologies. In a second step, extensive primary and secondary empirical data were collected from 361 Industry 4.0 applications for digital manufacturing in Germany drawn from the "Plattform Industrie 4.0"[1] [12], and 42 in-depth interviews conducted with experts. In the third step, we developed a new taxonomy of relevant digitalization technologies and risk factors in the manufacturing environment

---

[1] Created and managed by the German Federal Ministry for Economic Affairs and Energy in collaboration with the Federal Ministry of Education and Research.

based on the case analyses and interviews (see Fig. 4). In step 4, we paired the technology and risk classifications with fields of application and mitigation strategies and devised a three-step method that guides users from processes and potential technology applications to mitigation strategies for all areas of manufacturing and logistics. The final step was the implementation as a web-based tool.

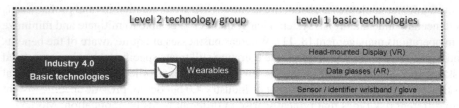

Fig. 4. Technology taxonomy example

The "Plattform Industrie 4.0" is intended as a transfer/share of know-how and best practices of Industry 4.0 project implementations. It contains structured information on developmental stages of digitalization projects, examples of products/applications, regions and company sizes. Additionally it provides unstructured information on applied technologies, envisioned benefits; lessons learned and adopted project approaches. Interviews with experts in the database cases shall enable us to verify and improve the information from our secondary data. Forty-three 25–50 min interviews with experts involved in the online database use cases as well as with industry practitioners and academics in the field of digitalization and Industry 4.0 were conducted face-to-face or over phone in November 2018 and March 2019. The interviewed experts primarily come from automotive, equipment, automated systems manufacturing and electrical and electronics companies (see Fig. 2). The interview guide consists of three main sections and follows a semi-structured approach: In the first portion the expert shall describes the known Industry 4.0 use cases, naming all relevant basic technologies, application/ functions and the desired goals. The second portion contains questions about risk and mitigation strategies. Interviews with experts in the database cases shall verify and improve the information of our secondary data and shall give an additional perspective of the impact of specific technologies on the risk situation.

4 Findings

4.1 Industry 4.0 Technology Risks

The use case and interview data analyzed reveal several key risk factors for Industry 4.0 technologies, specifically workplace risks and industry-specific and company-specific risks. These risk types are drawn from established risk management frameworks, e.g., [13, 14]. Since legal risks in the workplace frequently arise during the implementation phase and primarily involve aspects of workplace law, data privacy and data protection, many experts see a need in the operation phase to address cyber risks in previously unaffected areas. Direct and indirect dependences and a lack of flexibility can pose serious industry-specific threats to companies. Various solutions require vendor-specific hardware, software and expertise. Users who integrate vendors' Industry 4.0 solutions in their systems do not have full control of their own product's reliability and are dependent on vendors when they need to repair, replace or upgrade their Industry 4.0 components. Our data reveals several important company-specific issues related to human adoption, errors and attacks. Humans come into play as a risk source during the operation phase, albeit to a lesser extent than during the implementation phase. Figure 5 presents an overview of all workplace, industry-specific and company-specific risks factors emerging from the data.

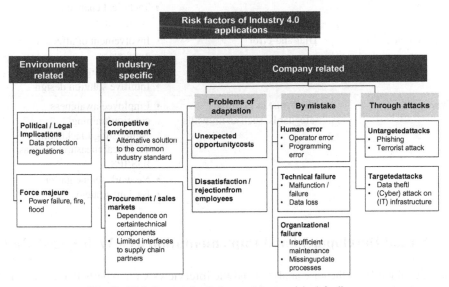

Fig. 5. Risk factors for Industry 4.0 - empirical findings

4.2 Risk Priorities, Recent Approaches and Mitigation Strategies: Empirical Findings

Specific risks of Industry 4.0 implementation and operation phases of were identified based on the empirical findings. Table 1 presents several interesting examples emerging from the data as well as the related risk priorities, risk management approaches and potential mitigation strategies.

Table 1. Overview of risk management approaches and mitigation strategies

Risk priority	Recent risk management approaches	Potential mitigation strategies
Lack of technological expertise	• Rejecting projects, maintaining the status quo	• Screening of vendor markets • Use of outside consulting services
Legal risk	• Consulting with the employee council as part of introduction	• Inclusion of the employee council • Revision of employment contracts • Technical changes, certification
Employee adoption	• Trial-and-error	• Involvement of affected employees • Skills training • Intuitive solution design
Cyber risk	• Blind trust in existing safeguards, such as firewalls	• Employee awareness creation/training, whitelisting/blacklisting • Technical measures such as IDS/IPS • Network segmentation • Backup strategy

5 Method Development and Implementation as a Web-Based Tool

We ascertained from the case analyses and the interviews with experts that the method ought to build on the idea that the situation-specific risk (mapping the risks and potential mitigation strategies) is contingent on two major impact factors: (1) the technology applied and (2) the process/operation. We therefore decided to make a combination of process and technology the main input for users. First, users can provide input related to the specific technology. A higher-order classification of available technologies was developed based on a combination of data and typologies in the literature, e.g., [15, 16], in order to be able to cover a wide range of technologies and assess the specific risks. This step made it possible to develop a two-level typology of Industry 4.0 technologies. The rationale behind this classification is to ensure that practitioners can provide input based on simple, established technologies (level 1) while ascertaining the risk profile for technologies (level 2). The implicit assumption is that one group of technologies (e.g., wearables) will present identical types of risks in specific industrial contexts. Users of the tool provide input on both the technology and the target process for which the technology is or will be used. The output consists of situation-specific risk factors and potential mitigation strategies (see Fig. 6 for input and output information).

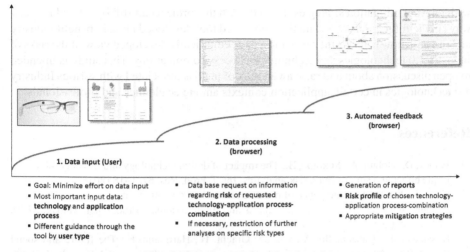

- Goal: Minimize effort on data input
- Most important input data: **technology** and **application process**
- Different guidance through the tool by **user type**

- Data base request on information regarding **risk** of requested technology-application process-combination
- If necessary, restriction of further analyses on specific risk types

- Generation of **reports**
- **Risk profile** of chosen technology-application process-combination
- Appropriate **mitigation strategies**

Fig. 6. How the web-based tool works

6   Discussion and Conclusion

This study presents key findings and maps risk factors associated with Industry 4.0 applications in manufacturing and logistics. An extensive literature review and the secondary and primary data collected deliver several key insights into the main risk factors in the phases of technology implementation and operation. These technologies may also pose additional risks to digitalization projects, however, namely, inflexibility, increased latency of the existing production system, increased complexity, difficult integration in current IT systems, and a lack of adequate knowledge and skills among key staff. Based on the empirical findings and current literature, we developed a web-based tool that maps and assesses risk factors related to Industry 4.0 applications. The proposed approach is rooted in the assumption that both the technology and the specific process determine the risk factors. The tool uses the individual application context and the technology as input and delivers potential risk factors together with possible mitigation strategies to the user. The new risk factor typology that emerges from the data reveals that several risk factors pose serious threats to digital projects, e.g., human factors, cyberattacks, legal issues, and dependences. This research study produced a valuable method for assessing risk factors related to Industry 4.0 applications quickly and accurately. It is intended to provide practitioners free and reliable input to assess risks and develop mitigation strategies. The tool has two novel features: its focus on "technology-process" combinations since the risks associated with certain digital technologies may arise from the characteristics of specific processes and the abstract technology classification that correlates certain risks with a given group of technologies (e.g., wearables) rather than a single specific technology. The higher-order technology classification for assessing and mitigating risks enables the tool to cover a wider range of commercially available technologies. The web-based tool is valuable to stakeholders from small and medium-sized manufacturers, technology vendors and academics because it quickly provides a free and reliable overview of the risks of specific technology-process combinations along with relevant mitigation strategies. Even though this project can still be refined in many ways in the future, this study and the web-based tool developed already benefit industry and research now because they provide a new, empirically developed view of the risks of Industry 4.0 technologies and technology-process combinations. This study is intended to open discussion about and raise awareness of the risk associated with various Industry 4.0 technologies in certain application contexts among academics and professionals.

References

1. Ivanov, D., Dolgui, A., Sokolov, B.: The impact of digital technology and Industry 4.0 on the ripple effect and supply chain risk analytics. Int. J. Prod. Res. **57**, 1–18 (2018)
2. Guha, S., Kumar, S.: Emergence of big data research in operations management information systems, and healthcare: past contributions and future roadmap. Prod. Oper. Manag. **27**(9), 1724–1735 (2017)
3. Rossmann, B., Canzaniello, A., von der Gracht, H., Hartmann, E.: The future and social impact of big data analytics in supply chain management: results from a delphi study. Technol. Forecast. Soc. Change **130**, 135–149 (2017)
4. McKinsey Digital 2015 - Industry 4.0 How to navigate digitization of the manufacturing sector. https://www.mckinsey.com/~/media/McKinsey/Business%20Functions/Operat ions/Our%20Insights/Industry%2040%20How%20to%20navigate%20digitization%20of% 20the%20manufacturing%20sector/Industry-40-How-to-navigate-digitization-of-the-man ufacturing-sector.ashx. Accessed 05 Apr 2021
5. Hertel, M.: Risiken der Industrie 4.0 – Eine Strukturierung von Bedrohungsszenarien der Smart Factory. HMD Praxis der Wirtschaftsinformatik **52**(5), 724–738 (2015). https://doi.org/10.1365/s40702-015-0161-1
6. Brocal, F., González, C., Komljenovic, D., Katina, P., Sebastián, M.: Emerging risk management in Industry 4.0: an approach to improve organizational and human performance in the complex systems. Complexity **2**, 1–13 (2019)
7. Zimmermann, M., Rosca, E., Antons, O., Bendul, J.C.: Supply chain risks in times of Industry 4.0: insights from German cases. In: 9th IFAC Conference on Manufacturing Modelling, Management and Control, Berlin (2019)
8. Birkel, H., Veile, J., Müller, J., Hartmann, E., Voigt, K.-I.: Development of a risk framework for Industry 4.0 in the context of sustainability for established manufacturers. Sustainability **11**(2), 384 (2019)
9. Flyverbom, M., Deibert, R., Matten, D.: The governance of digital technology, big data, and the internet: new roles and responsibilities for business. Bus. Soc. **58**(1), 3–19 (2019)
10. Kuo, Y., Kusiak, A.: From data to big data in production research: the past and future trends. Int. J. Prod. Res. **26**(1), 1–26 (2018)
11. Tupa, J., Simota, J., Steiner, F.: Aspects of risk management implementation for Industry 4.0. Procedia Manuf. **11**, 1223–1230 (2017)
12. Plattform Industrie 4.0, Bundesministerium für Wirtschaft und Energie. https://www.pla ttform-i40.de/PI40/Navigation/Karte/SiteGlobals/Forms/Formulare/karte-anwendungsbeisp iele-formular.html. Accessed 05 Apr 2021
13. Chopra, S., Sodhi, M.: Managing risk to avoid supply-chain breakdown. MIT Sloan Manag. Rev. **46**(1), 53–61 (2004)

14. Rao, S., Goldsby, T.: Supply chain risks: a review and typology. Int. J. Logist. Manag. **20**(1), 97–123 (2009)
15. Xu, L.D., Xu, E.L., Li, L.: Industry 4.0: state of the art and future trends. Int. J. Prod. Res. **56**(8), 2941–2962 (2018)
16. Oztemel, E., Gursev, S.: Literature review of Industry 4.0 and related technologies. J. Intell. Manuf. **31**(1), 127–182 (2018). https://doi.org/10.1007/s10845-018-1433-8

Digital Twin Framework for Machine Learning-Enabled Integrated Production and Logistics Processes

Noel P. Greis[1]([⊠]) [iD], Monica L. Nogueira[1] [iD], and Wolfgang Rohde[2] [iD]

[1] North Carolina State University, Raleigh, NC 27695, USA
npgreis@ncsu.edu
[2] Siemens Corporation, Charlotte, NC 28273, USA

Abstract. This paper offers an integrated framework bridging production and logistics processes that employs a machine learning-enabled digital twin to ensure adaptive production scheduling and resilient supply chain operations. The digital-twin based architecture will enable manufacturers to proactively manage supply chain risk in an increasingly complex and dynamic environment. This integrated framework enables "sense-and-respond" capabilities, i.e. the ability to sense potential supplier and production risks that affect ultimate delivery to the customer, to update anticipated customer delivery dates, and recommend mitigating steps that minimize any anticipated disruption. In its core functionality this framework senses disruptions at a supplier facility that cascade down the upstream supply chain and employs the predictive capabilities of its machine learning-based engine to trigger and support adaptive changes to the manufacturer's MES system. Any changes to the production schedule that cannot be accommodated in a revised schedule are propagated across the downstream supply chain alerting end customers to any changes.

Keywords: Production scheduling · Supplier risk · Digital twin · Machine learning

1 Introduction

In manufacturing companies today, MES and SCM information systems often work independently without any built-in feedback between systems. The information originating in either of these systems, even if potentially affecting the other, is typically not transparent across systems and latency issues can be a problem. The resultant information silos, then, may not use the most current information for decision-making. As a result, once the factory floor learns about any supply chain or supplier disruption, it is often too late to be accommodated systematically and seamlessly and can require manual rescheduling of planned production tasks. Bridging MES and SCM systems for disruption management and mitigation requires two-way information flows in order to achieve efficient utilization of resources and improved downstream deliveries.

© IFIP International Federation for Information Processing 2021
Published by Springer Nature Switzerland AG 2021
A. Dolgui et al. (Eds.): APMS 2021, IFIP AICT 630, pp. 218–227, 2021.
https://doi.org/10.1007/978-3-030-85874-2_23

With sense-and-respond capabilities, a manufacturer is better able to manage unexpected delays and disruptive events and avoid the latencies in response that drive inefficiencies. The approach described herein responds to the need for a concrete and practical approach that links production control to logistics risk due to supplier issues, transport delays, and other unexpected disruptions on the manufacturer's own factory floor. First, this framework integrates the flows of information about anticipated disruptions across the supplier and production processes bridging the siloes that separate them today. With this data as input, the model leverages the digital twin construct to create a virtual model of the production system that drives a machine learning engine to predict order completion and customer delivery dates. By implementing machine learning within a digital twin framework, it is possible to continuously update the model with real-time data instead of relying on offline adjustments to the production schedule or expert knowledge. Finally, the approach is practical in that it does not require sharing of confidential or proprietary data by supply chain partners, requiring only internal process data at the manufacturer, historical supplier performance data, contracted supplier delivery dates and actual, scheduled shipment arrival dates at the end customer.

2 Related Research

2.1 Disruption Management

Recent research has focused on data-driven tools that enable manufacturers to proactively manage supply chain disruptions to better manage risk and achieve resiliency [1–3]. The overarching goal of many of these efforts is to develop tools that sense impending supply chain risks and respond with agility—or what is referred to as "sense-and-respond" capability. Data-driven methods have been tasked with disruption and attendant risk management in a range of applications related to the framework described herein including procurement and supplier sourcing, transportation and logistics, and shop-floor production control—applications where sufficient data is typically available for model training and validation. With respect to scheduling of production systems that rely on the synchronized arrival of many parts and components, delays can be accommodated up to a break-down point beyond which the schedule fails and service targets are not met. Melançon et al. [4] developed a system that uses machine learning to send alerts when conditions on the supply chain such as combinations of events or small deviations lead to service failures. The system anticipates conditions and raises alerts in time for planners to take corrective action, but not so early that the issues would naturally be taken care of in the next production plan. With respect to supplier risk, Cavalcante et al. [5] combine simulation and machine learning to select suppliers and evaluate on-time delivery as an indicator of supplier reliability. Estimating transport delays of materials is critical to production scheduling for optimized operations. Birkel et al. [6] provide an overview of the challenges of applying predictive analytics in transport logistics. Ouedraogo et al. [7] address transport risk for multi-modal container transport, while Van der Spoel et al. [8] address a gap in the literature concerning arrival vs. travel/journey time prediction for overland trucking. Viellechner and Spinler [9] compare machine learning methods for predicting delays in ocean container shipments. Servos et al. [10] compare the performance of different machine learning methods in predicting disruptions and delay in the multimodal transport of containers.

2.2 Digital Twin

The digital twin is a virtual version of physical products, assets, processes and systems constructed for the purpose of "testing" in the virtual world prior to implanting in the real-world. One can think of the digital twin as an information mirroring concept that is able to "reflect" the behavior and real-time state of a physical object with sufficient accuracy that the manufacturing processes and production operations can be analyzed, predicted and optimized. Enabled by real-time data capture and sharing in an IIoT environment, dynamic changes can be communicated quickly between the physical and virtual worlds. One of the most researched applications of the digital twin has been modeling the product lifecycle (PLM) to capture all stages of product realization to create a comprehensive reference model to enable better product design and engineering, manufacturing and, ultimately, service [11, 12]. Fewer, but a growing number, of research has focused on production control and management—the application of relevance here. Janesch et al. [13] combine a model-based digital twin and a data-driven digital twin with machine learning to explore the life cycle of manufacturing systems. Leng et al. [14] developed a digital twin-driven approach for rapid reconfiguration of automated manufacturing systems. Other applications have addressed the generation of designs for an automated flow shop manufacturing system [15] and digital twin-based production lines [16]. Min et al. [17] provide a machine-learning enabled digital twin-based framework for production optimization in the petrochemical industry.

2.3 Machine Learning for Production Control

The explosion of data-collection on the factory floor offers new opportunities to make intelligent data-driven decisions for production control. An assessment of the state-of-the-art of machine learning in production planning and control is provided by Cadavid et al. [18] and Weichert et al. [19]. Meiners et al. [20] offer an approach that implements machine learning to analyze data generated along the process chain for complex patterns that can inform improvements. Related to the framework proposed herein, and given its importance in meeting customer delivery requirements, prediction of lead times has received attention. Employing a digital twin of the processes, with online connection to the manufacturing execution system (MES) for frequent retraining of the models to keep the prediction model up to date, Gyulai et al. [21] compare analytical and machine learning models for a flow-shop environment. Mezzogori et al. [22] employ statistical and neural network techniques to predict lead times in a 6-machine job shop. Using the current workload and the expected lead time of entry jobs, the authors use artificial neural networks (ANNs) to predict reliable delivering dates. Cycle time prediction, another key indicator of delivery reliability, has also been addressed. Predicting cycle times can be challenging because process flows may include hundreds of process steps, routings through the factory, and possible equipment failures. Can et al. [23] apply genetic programming, an artificial intelligence (AI) technique, to develop predictive models of process cycle times based on system status information gathered in real-time from manufacturing execution systems.

3 Machine Learning-Enabled Digital Twin Framework

This paper develops a machine learning-enabled digital twin framework for production control and disruption management. As supply chains become leaner and more unforgiving of disruption, AI-enabled tools are being called upon to not only anticipate disruptive events but also to monitor and recognize disruptions in real time, to understand the supply chain's vulnerability to disruption, to determine the impact of any delays on production, and to recommend mitigating actions. The proposed framework addresses key sources of potential disruption that affect the execution of customer order and its delivery to the end customer. As shown in Fig. 1 below, production supply chain disruptions due to the supplier can include delays in inbound material arrival, production down time, and transport delays to the manufacturer and end customer. The supplier, manufacturer and end customer share order quantities and contracted delivery dates through their information systems, but do not formally share information related to delays that may impact downstream operations. The challenge for manufacturers is to exploit information currently available to them to reduce delays and improve resiliency.

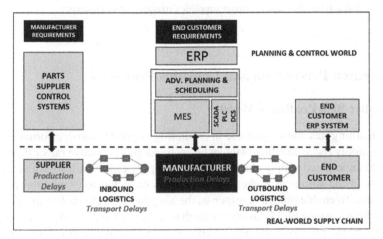

Fig. 1. Typical supply chain for a manufacturer with an upstream supplier and downstream customer with siloed information systems and potential disruptions.

The *Machine Learning-Enabled Digital Twin Framework*, comprised of three modules, is illustrated conceptually in Fig. 2 below. The *Supplier Risk Prediction Module* uses historical data of supplier performance to reveal patterns of delays, either events in the supplier's factory or logistics delays in shipping to the manufacturer. Machine learning models in the *Digital Twin Learning Engine* use the updated supplier arrival dates to predict updates to the production schedule and any changes in planned order completion dates. Expected order completion dates are then input to a *Customer Transit*

Module that optimizes the best route from a cost/time perspective for shipment of the order to the end customer given the expected disruption and associated delay.

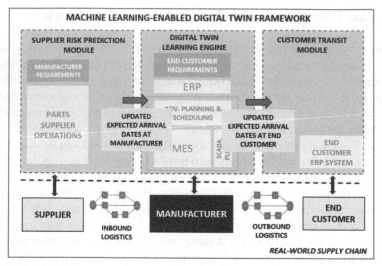

Fig. 2. *Machine Learning-Enabled Digital Twin Framework* predicts and adjusts for production and logistics disruptions that cascade from supplier through to end customer.

4   Integrated Production and Logistics Processes

4.1   Supplier Risk Prediction Model

Machine learning has shown promise in predicting supplier (non-)performance and in managing supply risks, enabling manufacturers to adopt a proactive rather than reactive response to anticipated supply chain disruption. Supply risk manifests when the actual arrival date of the shipment at the manufacturer is expected to exceed the contracted delivery date. To enable proactive response, the *Supplier Risk Prediction Module* implements machine learning to (1) classify orders that are of high and low risk of experiencing delays beyond the promised arrival date and/or (2) predict the arrival date of that shipment based on the supplier's previous experience with orders of similar characteristics. The machine learning model is trained using several years of historical data downloaded from the manufacturer's (or supplier's) ERP and other available databases, supplemented by simulated data as necessary, to provide a best prediction of the actual arrival date. Training input data include parameters such as *Supplier Name, Shipment ID, Shipment Volume, Shipment Description, Shipment Type, Order Date, Receive-By Date, Planned Ship Date, Contracted Arrival Date, Shipment Origin/Destination,* and *Carrier/Mode.* Once trained, the fitted Supplier Risk Prediction Module provides the manufacturer with the predicted arrival date which can be compared against the contracted date to provide a measure of supplier risk. The output of the *Supplier Risk Prediction Module*, i.e. predicted arrival date at the manufacturer (regression) or a days-late indicator (classification), is then passed to the *Digital Twin Learning Engine*.

The proposed *Supplier Risk Prediction Model* is developed for a supplier who must coordinate the arrival of materials and sub-components to meet delivery commitments to the OEM. Supplier delays can range from frequent short-term delays of 12–48 h to longer-term delays that may extend weeks. Supplier delays can affect 25% of deliveries to a customer depending on industry. In these cases, patterns of delivery delays specific to suppliers, or to types of products, or to products of specific materials can provide critical information for production scheduling. For this effort, we restrict our attention to historical delivery information, and information derived from it, to give insights into these patterns. If a particular supplier is habitually late with a certain type of order, the machine learning model can predict the length of the delay (c.f. 12 h or 2 days) based on previous supplier behavior.

A number of machine learning methods will be explored including random forest, support vector machines, k-nearest neighbors and ANNs, or logistic regression for binary target outputs. In previous work, random forest has shown to be a good method for handling data imbalances when there are fewer delayed orders than on-time orders. Delivery delays are often further amplified by exogenous events that can be difficult to predict and assess such as possibility of transport strikes or seasonal severe weather. While this model does not address these rare disruptive events, such factors could be included in the model by creating an input parameter that captures the overall environmental risk as determined by the supply chain manager. In other work, the authors have explored extracting disruption event data via APIs or by web scraping and other methods using selected sources such as *NOAA's National Weather Service (NWS) Public Alerts* and the *Global Database of Events, Language, and Tone* that provides worldwide coverage and retrieval of geopolitical and business-related disruption information.

4.2 Digital Twin Learning Engine

Unexpected events are known risks in manufacturing. Typical disruptions are a) machine failure, b) urgent job arrival, c) job cancellation, d) due date changes, e) change in job priority, and f) shortage of materials. The latter event (f) also can be caused by a delay in the arrival of material. Typically, the manufacturer receives an alert with the new adjusted date of expected material availability. This event will trigger a rescheduling process for the manufacturing in the factory. Manufacturers currently have two policies for rescheduling. Updates can be made manually by a supervisor/operator, typically experienced, who can decide on corrective actions for the factory floor. The new schedule will be edited into the production plan and executed. This procedure can be applied if the overall production plan for the factory is not too complex and timing restrictions not too tight. Depending on the complexity of the production process, tightness of time-dependencies between orders, and production delays associated with switching between orders, manual correction of the schedule is not always feasible. In this case the factory floor schedule needs to be recalculated in consideration of all factory floor activities. In general, manual adjustments tend to have less severe consequences for completion times and fewer ripple effects for other orders on the same factory floor. However, the quality and reliability of manual rescheduling depends on the quality of prediction of the supervisor/operator.

Using estimated shipment arrival dates from the *Supplier Risk Prediction Module*, the *Digital Twin Learning Engine* systematically produces updated order completion dates and recommends mitigating changes to the production schedule at the OEM that minimize delays. The *Digital Twin Learning Engine* is comprised of two parts, the *Digital Twin* and the *Sense-and-Respond Machine Learning Model*. The *Digital Twin* mirrors real-world operations on the shop floor to include data from Enterprise Resource Planning systems (ERP) that manage orders received from the customer, Advanced Planning and Scheduling (APS) systems that create a master schedule for received orders, and Manufacturing Execution Systems (MES) that manage the execution of real-time, physical processes to fulfill customer orders by contracted delivery dates. The *Sense-and-Respond Machine Learning Model* learns the dynamic patterns of the production environment from historical ERP, APS and MES data. When a supplier delay or disruption is anticipated, the model predicts the impact of the disruption on the contracted order completion date and recommends a revised production schedule and order completion dates for affected and other orders. The model will recommend mitigating machine-task assignments to the MES. If no mitigating scheduling changes can be made, the model adjusts the date of expected production completion and alerts customers. The model can prioritize customer orders, as appropriate. Other strategies such as overtime production can also be considered. As shown in Fig. 3 below, the machine learning-enabled digital twin framework includes:

1) The "physical" factory to include all the physical assets such as machines and production equipment, robots, etc. needed to fulfill customer orders;
2) The "digital" factory to include the *Digital Twin* and *Sense-and-Respond Learning Model* and other data needed to determine delivery requirements; and
3) The mapping between the physical and digital worlds for real-time data exchange.

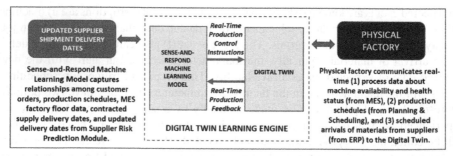

Fig. 3. The *Digital Twin Learning Engine* learns patterns of production on the factory floor.

The *Digital Twin Learning Engine* allows real-time updating of the MES and other systems based on predicted changes in arrivals of critical parts to the OEM rather than resorting to off-line adjustments to production control. The *Digital Twin* offers a continuous, interactive and real-time dialogue between the virtual and physical models of the factory floor. The *Digital Twin* is connected to relevant production systems such as MES, APS and ERP, receiving both current production schedules and timestamped snapshots of machine status and order information and assignments. Updated delivery dates from the *Supplier Risk Prediction Model*, plus real-time machine status updates and current production schedules, are input to the *Sense-and-Respond Machine Learning Model* which recommends adjustments in the production schedule, c.f. timing and sequencing of orders on specific machines. Training of the *Sense-and-Respond Machine Learning Model* can be accomplished using a number of machine learning algorithms such as support vector machines, AdaBoost optimizers, random forest or ANN. Model outputs are passed to the Digital Twin for verification and validation, and then returned to the "real" MES system for production schedule updating.

Communications between the *Sense-and-Respond Machine Learning Model* and the *Digital Twin* is achieved by information exchange using a shared database and several dedicated, automated services. The *Digital Twin* pulls data from (and pushes data to) a database that it shares with the other manufacturing management systems, e.g. ERP, MES, SCADA, etc., and which is also being continuously updated with predicted supplier delivery information flowing from the *Supplier Risk Prediction Model*. Auxiliary services prepare this information for consumption by the *Sense-and-Respond Learning Model*. The model then produces, as output, revised production schedules and machine assignments (or other pre-determined types of outcomes that the model has been trained to produce). Model outputs are consumed by another auxiliary service/software application that will store the result(s) in the shared database and can also transform the outputs into visualizations for human consumption and display on pre-programmed dashboards. The arrival of a new prediction into the shared database will trigger another service that will retrieve this information and feed it back to the *Digital Twin* to launch a new simulation to evaluate and validate that the recommended revised production schedule can respond to the delay(s) adequately and as intended. Once validated, this information is then updated in the manufacturing management systems for execution of the revised schedule on the factory floor.

4.3 Customer Transit Module

Updated estimates of order completion dates are passed to the *Customer Transit Module*. As noted earlier predicting shipment transit times and associated risks of disruption is a difficult problem, dependent on factors such as transport mode, routing, time of year/week/day, and external factors, most importantly weather and traffic. In this framework, the *Customer Transit Module* receives an estimated order completion date from the *Digital Twin Learning Engine* and projects an adjusted arrival date at the end customer. In this way, disruptions along the supply chain from supplier to manufacturing through delivery to the end customer are cascaded and incorporated into projected delivery date. Predicted transit times are modeled on a route-by-route basis, using historical data to estimate the transit time for future shipments using machine learning or optimization. Thus, the module consists of an ensemble of classifiers/models for different modes that are trained and tested using historical shipment data. The estimated transit time produced by the module and the baseline transit time established by the shipment planner are compared to determine any further delays. Depending on transport mode and geographic location, the predicted transit times can be adjusted for weather and traffic events obtained from public data sources such as weather stations, social media and news aggregators.

5 Conclusions

In this paper we respond to a gap in both practice and research by proposing a machine learning-enabled digital twin framework that bridges the gap between production process and logistics processes for the purpose of reducing supply chain risk due to disruptions in either the logistics or production environments at the supplier and manufacturer. Machine learning models provide updated estimates of expected delivery dates at each stage of the supply chain which can be applied in a digital twin simulated environment and folded into the manufacturer's MES system with recommended possible actions to mitigate those delays. Revised delivery dates can then be passed to the end customer in a seamless flow.

References

1. Baryannis, G., Validi, S., Dani, S., Antoniou, G.: Supply chain risk management and artificial intelligence: state of the art and future research directions. Int. J. Prod. Res. **57**(7), 2179–2202 (2019). https://doi.org/10.1080/00207543.2018.1530476
2. Ivanov, D., Dolgui, A.: A digital supply chain twin for managing disruption risks and resiliencies in the era of Industry 4.0. Prod. Plan. Control **32**(9), 775–788 (2021). https://doi.org/10.1080/09537287.2020.1768450
3. Ivanov, D., Dolgui, A.: Low-Certainty-Need (LCN) supply chains: a new perspective in managing disruption risks and resilience. Int. J. Prod. Res. **57**(15–16), 5119–5136 (2019). https://doi.org/10.1080/00207543.2018.1521025
4. Melançon, G.G., Grangier, P., Prescott-Gagnon, E., Sabourin, E., Rousseau, L.-M.: A machine learning-based system for predicting service level failures in supply chains. INFORMS J. Appl. Anal. **51**(3), 200–212 (2021). https://doi.org/10.1287/inte.2020.1055
5. Cavalcante, I., Frazzon, E., Forcellini, F., Ivanov, D.: A supervised machine learning approach to data-driven simulation of resilient supplier selection in digital manufacturing. Int. J. Inf. Manag. **49**, 86–97 (2019). https://doi.org/10.1016/j.ijinfomgt.2019.03.004
6. Birkel, H., Kopyto, M., Lutz, C.: Challenges of applying predictive analytics in transport logistics. In: Laumer, S., Quesenberry, J.L., Joseph, D., Maier, C., Beimborn, D., Srivastava, S.C. (eds.) Proceedings of the 2020 on Computers and People Research Conference (SIGMIS-CPR 2020), pp. 144–151. ACM, New York (2020). https://doi.org/10.1145/3378539.3393864
7. Ouedraogo, C.A., Namakiaraghi, S., Rosemont, C., Montarnal, A., Lauras, M., Gourc, D.: Traceability and risk management in multi-modal container transport: a small - scale review of methods and technologies. In: Benadada, Y., Mhada, F.-Z. (eds.) 5th International Conference on Logistics Operations Management (GOL), pp. 1–7. IEEE, Piscataway (2020). https://doi.org/10.1109/GOL49479.2020.9314760
8. van der Spoel, S., Amrit, C., van Hillegersberg, J.: Predictive analytics for truck arrival time estimation: a field study at a European distribution centre. Int. J. Prod. Res. **55**(17), 5062–5078 (2020). https://doi.org/10.1080/00207543.2015.1064183

9. Viellechner, A., Spinler, S.: Novel data analytics meets conventional container shipping: predicting delays by comparing various machine learning algorithms. In: Bui, T.X. (ed.) Proceedings of the 53rd Hawaii International Conference on System Sciences (HICSS), pp. 1278–1287. ScholarSpace (2020). https://doi.org/10.24251/HICSS.2020.158

10. Servos, N., Liu, X., Teucke, M., Freitag, M.: Travel time prediction in a multimodal freight transport relation using machine learning algorithms. Logistics 4(1), 1 (2020). https://doi.org/10.3390/logistics4010001

11. Schleich, B., Anwer, N., Mathieu, L., Wartzack, S.: Shaping the digital twin for design and production engineering. CIRP Ann. 66(1), 141–144 (2017). https://doi.org/10.1016/j.cirp.2017.04.040

12. Tao, F., Qi, Q., Liu, A., Kusiak, A.: Data-driven smart manufacturing. J. Manuf. Syst. 48(Part C), 157–169 (2018). https://doi.org/10.1016/j.jmsy.2018.01.006

13. Jaensch, F., Csiszar, A., Scheifele, S., Verl, A.: Digital twins of manufacturing systems as a base for machine learning. In: Verl, A., Xu, W. (eds.) 25th International Conference on Mechatronics and Machine Vision in Practice (M2VIP), pp. 1–6. IEEE, Piscataway (2018). https://doi.org/10.1109/M2VIP.2018.8600844

14. Leng, J., et al.: Digital twin-driven rapid reconfiguration of the automated manufacturing system via an open architecture model. Robot. Comput. Integr. Manuf. 63, 101895 (2020). https://doi.org/10.1016/j.rcim.2019.101895

15. Liu, Q., Zhang, H., Leng, J., Chen, X.: Digital twin-driven rapid individualised designing of automated flow-shop manufacturing system. Int. J. Prod. Res. 57(12), 3903–3919 (2019). https://doi.org/10.1080/00207543.2018.1471243

16. Vachálek, J., Bartalský, L., Rovný, O., Šišmišová, D., Morháč, M., Lokšík, M.: The digital twin of an industrial production line within the Industry 4.0 concept. In: Fikar, M., Kvasnica, M. (eds.) 2017 21st International Conference on Process Control (PC), pp. 258–262. IEEE, Piscataway (2017). https://doi.org/10.1109/PC.2017.7976223

17. Min, Q., Lu, Y., Liu, Z., Su, C., Wang, B.: Machine learning based digital twin framework for production optimization in petrochemical industry. Int. J. Inf. Manag. 49, 502–519 (2019). https://doi.org/10.1016/j.ijinfomgt.2019.05.020

18. Usuga Cadavid, J.P., Lamouri, S., Grabot, B., Pellerin, R., Fortin, A.: Machine learning applied in production planning and control: a state-of-the-art in the era of industry 4.0. J. Intell. Manuf. 31(6), 1531–1558 (2020). https://doi.org/10.1007/s10845-019-01531-7

19. Weichert, D., Link, P., Stoll, A., Rüping, S., Ihlenfeldt, S., Wrobel, S.: A review of machine learning for the optimization of production processes. Int. J. Adv. Manuf. Technol. 104(5–8), 1889–1902 (2019). https://doi.org/10.1007/s00170-019-03988-5

20. Meiners, M., Mayr, A., Thomsen, M., Franke, J.: Application of machine learning for product batch oriented control of production processes. Procedia CIRP 93, 431–436 (2020). https://doi.org/10.1016/j.procir.2020.04.006

21. Gyulai, D., Pfeiffer, A., Nick, G., Gallina, V., Sihn, W., Monostori, L.: Lead time prediction in a flow-shop environment with analytical and machine learning approaches. IFAC-PapersOnLine 51(11), 1029–1034 (2018). https://doi.org/10.1016/j.ifacol.2018.08.472

22. Mezzogori, D., Romagnoli, G., Zammori, F.: Deep learning and WLC: how to set realistic delivery dates in high variety manufacturing systems. IFAC-PapersOnLine 52(13), 2092–2097 (2019). https://doi.org/10.1016/j.ifacol.2019.11.514

23. Can, B., Heavey, C.: A demonstration of machine learning for explicit functions for cycle time prediction using MES data. In: Roeder, T.M., Frazier, P.I., Szechtman, R., Zhou, E. (eds.) 2016 Winter Simulation Conference (WSC), pp. 2500–2511. IEEE, Piscataway (2016). https://doi.org/10.1109/WSC.2016.7822289

A Smart Contracts and Tokenization Enabled Permissioned Blockchain Framework for the Food Supply Chain

Akshay Patidar[1] , Monica Sharma[1,2](✉) , Rajeev Agrawal[2] ,
and Kuldip Singh Sangwan[3]

[1] Department of Management Studies, Malaviya National Institute of Technology,
J.L.N. Marg, Jaipur 302017, Rajasthan, India
msharma.dms@mnit.ac.in
[2] Department of Mechanical Engineering, Malaviya National Institute of Technology,
J.L.N. Marg, Jaipur 302017, Rajasthan, India
[3] Department of Mechanical Engineering, Birla Institute of Technology and Science Pilani,
Vidya Vihar, Pilani 333031, Rajasthan, India

Abstract. The food supply chain is gaining a lot of attention these days. Due to the relativity of the food supply chain with human health directly, focusing on its problems and issues has become the need of the hour. Several issues like food safety, food contamination, and adulteration, food losses are some of the issues. Among these issues, food losses are critically important as they affect sustainable development as well. Among the several critical causes of this food loss problem, handling losses are most important and are very less studied. Handling losses are important as the causes of these losses are controllable and can be easily mitigated with the help of science and technology. This research is an effort in the defined direction. With the help of technology like blockchain and its capabilities, the authors in this study developed a framework for the food supply chain that if implemented can help in reducing handling losses.

Keywords: Food supply chain · Traceability · Blockchain · Smart contracts · Tokenization

1 Introduction

Food loss or Food waste is the biggest problem these days. There are several causes of food losses. These food losses can be categorized into harvesting loss due to mechanization, production practices, moisture, season and temperature, etc., storage losses due to deterioration, shrinkage, spoilage, moisture and time, etc., processing losses due to shrinkage, poor handling, packaging failures, transportation, etc., packaging losses due to packaging failures and transportation, etc., distribution and sales losses due to supersizing, poor inventory, dented cans, and temperature, etc., and consumption losses at customer end due to leftovers, impulsive buying, bulk purchases, and functions or

© IFIP International Federation for Information Processing 2021
Published by Springer Nature Switzerland AG 2021
A. Dolgui et al. (Eds.): APMS 2021, IFIP AICT 630, pp. 228–235, 2021.
https://doi.org/10.1007/978-3-030-85874-2_24

parties, etc. [1]. If sets of all the causes of the losses are created and the intersection point of maximum causes are determined, only some of the factors will be revealed as responsible for losses. Among these two issues are pretty evident i.e., transportation issue and handling issue. But as these issues are indirectly connected to other issues as well so there is a strong need to develop a solution that can mitigate this cause of food losses and have a significant impact on other causes for reducing food losses as well.

This improper handling is evident at various stages of the food supply chain. From the beginning i.e., procurement to distribution including storage at collection center or warehouse or depo or retail store, and during transportation, at all steps, there are some food losses due to human negligence or due to lack of automation [2]. Considering this problem, there is a strong need to cater to this condition and use technology like blockchain technology which has the power of transparency, trust, and most importantly immutability. Further smart contract also helps an organization to maintain the standards within limits.

This study focuses on the same problem and discusses a framework to reduce the effect of this problem. The paper is constructed as follows: Sect. 2 discusses the related works done in this area and proposed work, Sect. 3 focuses on the description of the proposed framework followed by Sect. 4 discussing academic, managerial, and future research implication related to the framework. The Paper concludes with the last section followed by the references.

2 Related Work

The smart food supply chain relies on the applicability of several advanced techniques such as IoT, Big Data, Cloud and Fog Computing, Artificial Intelligence (AI), and the most related one i.e., blockchain [3]. Blockchain has the power of creating transparency, trust by providing immutable records in a distributed ledger [4]. Due to its functionality, blockchain proves to be the most secure platform for creating supply chain visibility.

Blockchain powers the digitalization and also helps in improving the tracking and tracing capability of the food supply chain which not only enhances the provenance but also creates trust among the stakeholders. Blockchain enhances the information transactional and automational characteristics that also help in enhancing the predictive analytical capability of the stakeholders in the food supply chain [5]. This technology after getting information like temperature, humidity, production images, and other related variables, stores the information in a distributive ledger. Figure 1 shows the blockchain and its relevance with smart contracts.

The use of smart contracts and tokenization adds to the efficiency of the system. Smart contracts are simply a programmed or automated agreement which triggers an action, whenever a defined variable measure beyond limits [6]. These smart contracts normally trigger a penalty or reward mechanism. To maintain this penalty and reward, there must be some digital currency or cryptocurrency. Creating this digital or cryptocurrency is known as the tokenization concept. This tokenization depends on the nature of the blockchain and the algorithm used for the consensus mechanism. Literature discusses permissioned or private and public blockchain. Classic case of blockchain i.e., bitcoin is an example of public blockchain where token was in the form of bitcoin [7]. A private or permissioned

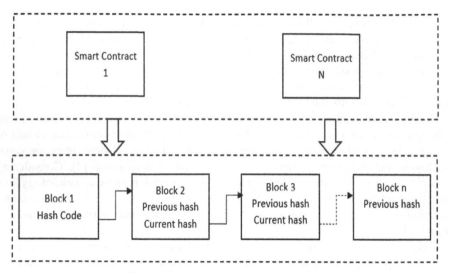

Fig. 1. Smart contract and the blockchain

blockchain is mostly used by a closed user group where people can transact among themselves. The consensus mechanism in the public blockchain is very complicated and hence reduces the transaction speed due to a large number of stakeholders involvement whereas a private blockchain has a limited number of stakeholders involved that increases the efficiency and speed of the transactions. For the consensus mechanism of transaction, there are several algorithms like proof of work and proof of stake. The selection of these algorithms also helps in the overall performance of the blockchain. Since all the data is stored at all the nodes, it increases the space and time requirements. Therefore, proof of stake is preferred over the proof of work as it requires lesser space and time.

Many authors have reported the use case of blockchain in the food supply chain. Agri-blockIoT is a fully decentralized blockchain-based traceability solution for the agri-food supply chain but lacks the safety and security aspect of the food product which is highly required for perishable products [8]. Using smart contracts is also evident in the literature as a study focused on information asymmetry and using long short-term memory a deep learning network developed a credit evaluation system for farmers which enhances reliability and authenticity of information among the traders, this study lacked the product safety variables [9]. Another study focused on Chinese markets and tried to solved food safety issues by addressing the food traceability problem. This study again lacked the smart contract and tokenized approach [10]. Another study focused on RFID tags and blockchain technology to enhance the agri-food supply chain traceability in China. The study provided the building process of this system [11] but the study lacked the penalties mechanism which acts as a reinforcement technique for the betterment [12]. A study focused over-application of blockchain and other necessary conditions and discussed the boundary conditions along with standardization and data governance related to information sharing [13]. Another study focused on RFID-based information architecture where a proof of object authentication protocol is used which is analogous to the proof of work protocol. Also, the author conducted a detailed security analysis to test the vulnerability from cyber-attacks [14]. Another author in his study discussed blockchain-based agri-food supply chain and authored it as a complete solution where authors focused on the need for a reliable system and recorded transaction to the blockchain which uploads the data to interplanetary file storage system (IPFS). Also, the study includes smart contracts for security and vulnerability analysis but unfortunately, it lacked the provenance aspects of the food products.

Therefore, after reviewing the related work in the literature, the author here proposes a study providing a framework that focuses on smart contract and tokenization enabled permissioned blockchain-based smart food supply chain fulfilling all research gaps evident in our review for the related work.

3 Proposed Framework

The given framework is a conceptual framework of a permissioned blockchain where consent for every transaction will be given by the manager as a consensus mechanism. Framework consists of farmers or producers termed as 'F', collection centers for collection purposes from F, storage centers to be used as the hub for distribution to stores termed as 'S'.

3.1 Smart Contract and Tokenization Enabled Blockchain-Based Smart Food Supply Chain System

Blockchain technology is a distributed ledger technology that records the transactions among various nodes. Hence here transactions are done among the stakeholders, who are acting as a node, and a self-developed cryptocurrency called tokens is used for circulation in the supply chain.

Smart contracts are programmed contracts with defined limits of variables, if at any point of the supply chain, the variable value goes beyond the limit; it will trigger the penalty to be imposed on the concerned stakeholder of the supply chain. This penalty will be compensated by paying the additional tokens. Hence here a proof of stake algorithm will be used, it will record the transactions in the blocks. It also makes the system more efficient and robust as it will help in reducing the time and space complexity of the system.

3.2 Framework Description

In the framework shown in Fig. 2, Blue (solid) arrows represent the flow of goods, green (dotted) arrow represents the flow of cryptocurrency or tokens and red (dashed) arrow represents the point of smart contracts. Location, Temperature, etc. are the variable that can be monitored and act as triggering variables for smart contracts.

As per the budgetary calculation, Supply Chain Manager will send or allot cryptocurrency or tokens to the stores for purchasing purposes and physical currency to the collection centers for payments to the seller. The physical currency will be issued against the cryptocurrency or tokens, centers will return to the manager. Farmers or sellers will

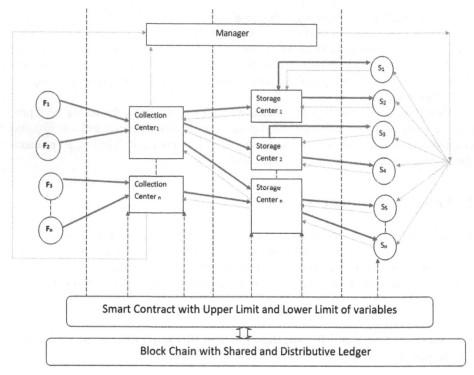

Fig. 2. Smart contract enabled permissioned blockchain framework (Color figure online)

approach defined centers to sell their perishable produce with defined standards. Designated centers will collect the product, monitors the variables either using IOT devices or some other devices and pay farmers or producers accordingly with the permission of the manager. This transaction along with the variables will be noted in the distributed ledger of the supply chain which is with every stakeholder of the supply chain. Store-based on their demand forecasts will place the order to the storage center and will initiate the transaction. The storage center based on order will complete the transaction by receiving cryptocurrency and releasing the goods. Here Variables will be again monitored before loading and unloading by the logistics partner. The storage center when required will place the order to center and initiate the transaction. Center on receiving the order will send the goods and receive the cryptocurrency. The same process of measuring variables using devices will be done here also. This transaction along with measured variables will be entered into the distributive ledger. Throughout this process, there will be active smart contracts that will get triggered only by getting a variable value beyond limits.

This framework will help to resolve the issue of.

1. Demand and supply uncertainty by providing the industry capability to improve the accuracy of forecasting employing enhanced visibility.

2. Food losses due to improper handling by enabling industries to monitor handling data during product movement and also because of the use of smart contracts that triggers whenever the decided variable crosses the limits.
3. Customer dissatisfaction because of lack of provenance enabling them to track and trace the variables like location, temperature setting, etc.
4. Lack of Supply chain Visibility by storing all the transactional data to the blockchain platform in the form of blocks.
5. Transparency, Trust, and data immutability are developed in the system as the data is stored in the blocks as per the transactions and this data can only be tampered with by the authority of the blockchain platform i.e., the manager.
6. Inventory losses as this framework supports implementation of Fist Expired First Out and accordingly pricing can be used.

4 Implications

4.1 Managerial and Academic

With the completion of one cycle of product and currency flow, it will ensure the following things:

1. It can help in spoilage as it records the variable data of products related to perishability measures and hence FIFO policy (first in first out policy) can be implemented.
2. The product is moving safely
3. As perishability is a matter of concern, variables are monitored seriously.
4. All the transactions (Distributive ledger) can also be shared with customers to increase responsiveness.
5. Implementation of smart contracts enabled penalty can act as reinforcement to stakeholders and will reduce the losses because of improper handling.
6. Once losses will be reduced, customer satisfaction will increase.
7. Improved efficiency and responsiveness.
8. Overall waste will be reduced and social, environmental, and economic performance will be enhanced.
9. The information sharing is done using this framework; therefore, uncertainty can be handled and in case of excess demand, it can be fulfilled with the center having greater availability.
10. This framework can provide traceability of the goods, transparency in the supply chain, and trust among the stakeholders.

4.2 Future Research

1. The proposed framework can be used by the supermarket retail industry and Dairy industry as these two industries follow such kind of supply chain model but without blockchain and IoT devices. With little modifications, it can be applied to the healthcare industry for medicine supplies especially vaccines too.

2. Optimization of the above framework can also be done to determine the total cost, minimized waste quantity, and other related sustainability parameters.
3. Other measuring parameters like response time, moisture content, elapsed duration after first received can be used as triggers for smart contracts.

5 Conclusion

To the best of the authors knowledge, this is the first framework based on tokenization mechanism and smart contract enabled permissioned blockchain for the food supply chain. Tracking and tracing is one of the important aspects of the food supply chain. Most of the studies are focusing on this aspect of the food supply chain but perishability and causes of perishability are rarely considered. This study considered perishability, causes of perishability along with some reinforcement measures to mitigate the causes of food waste by using a smart contract-based penalty mechanism. The conceptual framework represented in the study considers almost all aspects of blockchain to enhance the efficiency and responsiveness of the food supply chain. Implementing this framework will help in reducing food wastes but will ensure the handling of the food products. This can help an origination in getting a competitive advantage and can help their customers to track and trace the product, not in terms of geographical locations but also handling conditions quantitatively.

References

1. Gardas, B.B., Raut, R.D., Narkhede, B.: Evaluating critical causal factors for post-harvest losses (PHL) in the fruit and vegetables supply chain in India using the DEMATEL approach. J. Clean. Prod. **199**, 47–61 (2018)
2. Kopec, D., Kabir, M.H., Reinharth, D., Rothschild, O., Castiglione, J.A.: Human errors in medical practice: systematic classification and reduction with automated information systems. J. Med. Syst. **27**(4), 297–313 (2003). https://doi.org/10.1023/A:1023796918654
3. Lin, J., Shen, Z., Zhang, A., Chai, Y.: Blockchain and IoT based food traceability for smart agriculture. In: Proceedings of the 3rd International Conference on Crowd Science and Engineering, pp. 1–6 (2018)
4. Pearson, S., et al.: Are distributed ledger technologies the panacea for food traceability? Glob. Food Secur. **20**, 145–149 (2019)
5. Patidar, A., Sharma, M., Agrawal, R.: Prioritizing drivers to creating traceability in the food supply chain. Procedia CIRP **98**, 690–695 (2021)
6. Wall, E., Malm, G.: Using blockchain technology and smart contracts to create a distributed securities depository (2016)
7. Guegan, D.: Public blockchain versus private blockchain (2017)
8. Caro, M.P., Ali, M.S., Vecchio, M., Giaffreda, R.: Blockchain-based traceability in agri-food supply chain management: a practical implementation. In: 2018 IoT Vertical and Topical Summit on Agriculture-Tuscany (IOT Tuscany), pp. 1–4. IEEE (2018)
9. Mao, D., Wang, F., Hao, Z., Li, H.: Credit evaluation system based on blockchain for multiple stakeholders in the food supply chain. Int. J. Environ. Res. Public Health **15**(8), 1627 (2018)
10. Tse, D., Zhang, B., Yang, Y., Cheng, C., Mu, H.: Blockchain application in food supply information security. In: 2017 IEEE International Conference on Industrial Engineering and Engineering Management (IEEM), pp. 1357–1361. IEEE (2017)

11. Tian, F.: An agri-food supply chain traceability system for China based on RFID & blockchain technology. In: 2016 13th International Conference on Service Systems and Service Management (ICSSSM), pp. 1–6. IEEE (2016)
12. Maag, J.W.: Rewarded by punishment: reflections on the disuse of positive reinforcement in schools. Except. Child. **67**(2), 173–186 (2001)
13. Behnke, K., Janssen, M.F.: Boundary conditions for traceability in food supply chains using blockchain technology. Int. J. Inf. Manag. **52**, 101969 (2020)
14. Mondal, S., Wijewardena, K.P., Karuppuswami, S., Kriti, N., Kumar, D., Chahal, P.: Blockchain inspired RFID-based information architecture for food supply chain. IEEE Internet Things J. **6**(3), 5803–5813 (2019)

Learning and Robust Decision Support Systems for Agile Manufacturing environments

Due Date-Related Order Prioritization
for Scheduling with Decision Support
in Dynamic Environments

Michael Bojko(✉), Susanne Franke, Luigi Pelliccia, and Ralph Riedel

Department of Factory Planning and Intra Logistics, Chemnitz University of Technology,
Chemnitz, Germany
{michael.bojko,susanne.franke}@mb.tu-chemnitz.de

Abstract. With the recent and ongoing pursuits to introduce digitalization to corporate shop floors, decision support systems (DSS) for improved task distribution also gain importance. These systems aim to achieve higher effectiveness, efficiency as well as satisfaction of factory staff. However, the necessary implementations and standards for the successful introduction of DSS are not yet available for every given production environment. In this paper, an approach developed by the Department of Factory Planning and Intra Logistics to introduce decision support in dynamic production environments is presented. The concept allows workers to easily identify orders and tasks of high priority in a complex and highly dynamic environment, to meet the assigned due dates, and to increase customer satisfaction. The proposed concept considers priority-relevant parameters, derives priorities for incoming and pending orders dynamically in real-time, and allows to feed the priority values into a DSS for scheduling orders and their related tasks. The concept can be implemented as a standalone module to production environments as well as being integrated into existing scheduling systems.

Keywords: Smart factory · Prioritization · Scheduling · Decision support

1 Introduction

Modern solutions for Human-Machine Interaction (HMI) for cyber-physical systems (CPS) can provide a high degree of adaptability to skills, competencies and preferences of individual workers. At the same time, they help to cope with the challenges of a highly customized production. Among other objectives, companies aim to increase the flexibility of factory staff deployment, shorten lead times for (new) products, and provide context-based decision support. In pursuit of these goals, the development of adaptive solutions for HMI, which improve workflows, is required, and for this purpose, Decision Support Systems (DSS) are increasingly applied and utilized in factories. DSS applied to production environments as CPS are able to take various parameters into account to improve e.g. task distribution, worker wellbeing as well as work satisfaction. Additionally, DSS can be part of workers' training, allowing them to be knowledgeable in operating smart factories [1, 2].

© IFIP International Federation for Information Processing 2021
Published by Springer Nature Switzerland AG 2021
A. Dolgui et al. (Eds.): APMS 2021, IFIP AICT 630, pp. 239–248, 2021.
https://doi.org/10.1007/978-3-030-85874-2_25

One area of DSS application in production workshops focusses on planning, monitoring, and improving order execution as well as on improving equipment utilization (cf. OEE). Especially in branches with increasing or yet highly individualized products planning and execution of orders in an optimized manner represents a complex, multi-criterial task mainly carried out by experienced employees. Besides defining a sequence for order execution based on work plans and assigning resources, such as workers and equipment, it is also required to determine the priority of each task in order to define the optimized sequencing of multiple orders during sequence planning [3, 4]. In industrial environments, several rules and parameters are applied to derive a task priority based on e.g. customer requirements as well as local or global optimization goals [3, 5–7]. E.g. the sequencing rule earliest operation due-date was thoroughly investigated in [8, 9]. In the latter paper, a model for evaluating and improving schedule compliance is presented. The influence of rush orders on the production plan is the focus of [10] and is evaluated by modelling throughput times. A decision support for order acceptance based on calculated possible delivery dates is presented in [11].

A study conducted at the Factory2Fit pilot sites [12] showed the negative impact of dissatisfied customers on work satisfaction. This negative influence results from e.g. (allegedly) missed or unclear deadlines. To increase work satisfaction, a DSS can be utilized to reduce the amount of unfavorably scheduled orders, thereby also minimizing manual re-scheduling expenses as well as creating transparency for the workers and customers in order to create awareness for the situation and to reduce negative impacts on work satisfaction [13]. Corporate in-house departments and external customers requesting services from the production are both treated equally as customers since their satisfaction is identified as important. To achieve high customer satisfaction, punctuality is considered crucial [11, 14]. Due to the high number of tasks in a production department, the varying lead times of orders, and sometimes lack of forecast, in many production workshops the employees need to estimate each task's priority solely based on experience. To reduce the impact caused by the complex priority assessment in large numbers and to increase customer satisfaction by enhanced transparency, a due-date-related prioritization is proposed.

2 Concept of the Due Date-Related Order Prioritization

2.1 Use Cases for the Due Date-Related Order Prioritization

The use cases for developing the concept for dynamic due date-related prioritization have been defined by the industrial partners of Factory2Fit [12, 15]. Therefore, the processes of the departments hosting the pilot use cases, the process-related parameters, and the related procedures, as well as the existing systems were investigated. One use case was hosted by a metrology lab processing a wide range of products to ensure the quality of processes and products on-site, the other one by an assembly department for heating, ventilation, and air conditioning (HVAC) units [12].

The processes of the pilot use cases as well as the process-related parameters and procedures were investigated and resulted in the Factory2Fit DSS and its incorporated functionalities, whereas the dynamic, due date-related prioritization represents one of these functionalities. The parameters identified for the prioritization of orders and tasks in the highly dynamic and complex environment of a metrology lab and for the more extensive and detailed operations in an assembly department as well as their meaning and application are applied in the DSS to derive the priorities for incoming and pending orders. In the following sections, the respective meanings, the necessity of mapping the variables, and its effect on the order priority are explained. Even though the concept initially has been developed as a part of the Factory2Fit DSS, it can be applied and implemented as a standalone module as well as part of other DSS and factory systems.

2.2 Initial Integration of Order and Task-Relevant Data

For calculating a dynamic, due date-related priority P_j for each pending or incoming order j, the required remaining processing time p_j to execute all tasks p_{jk} needs to be determined. The value of p_j can be derived from the remaining processing times of the remaining tasks p_{jk} assigned to the order by the work plan as in (1). We assume that the total amount of orders and tasks are m and n, respectively, and that the respective statements hold for all $j = 1, \ldots, m$ and $k = 1, \ldots, n$.

$$p_j = \sum_{k=1}^{n} p_{jk}, p_{jk} > 0 \quad \forall\, j = 1, \ldots, m \tag{1}$$

As stated above, punctuality is crucial to keep customers satisfied and thus to reduce the negative impact of dissatisfied customers on workers. Therefore, the due time (relative) or due date (absolute) d_j of an order j is a core element of the prioritization. For defining d_j of an order j, either a maximum order lead time to process all tasks of order j (Option 1) or a fixed due date where all tasks of order j have to be completed (Option 2) can be applied. In many production workshops, orders arrive without forecast, and all tasks p_{jk} related to a pending order j have to be processed within a maximum allowed order lead time l_j (Option 1). In some branches, however, orders are assigned a fixed due date d_j, and all tasks p_{jk} of order j need to be finalized when this specified date is reached (Option 2). Hence, both options need to be addressed by the proposed concept. For Option 1 the received time/date (abs.) r_j of order j, as well as the maximum order lead time l_j of order j, are required as input for (2) to calculate the due time/date d_j of order j.

$$d_j = r_j + l_j, r_j, l_j > 0 \quad \forall\, j = 1, \ldots, m \tag{2}$$

For Option 2 the received time (rel.) or received date (abs.) r_j of order j, as well as the fixed due time (rel.) or fixed due date (abs.) d_j of order j, are needed as input parameters to calculate the maximum allowed order lead time l_j of order j as in (3).

$$l_j = d_j - r_j, d_j > r_j > 0 \quad \forall\, j = 1, \ldots, m \tag{3}$$

To ensure customers are kept satisfied and unfavorable scheduling is minimized, all incoming and pending tasks p_{jk} need to be processed in time. Due to the high variety of processing times, especially novice workers need to be supported in identifying the latest start time s_j of an order j to ensure the due date d_j is met. Based on the information available and the introduced parameters, the latest start time (rel.) or latest start date (abs.) can be calculated based on the backward scheduling approach [16] as in (4).

$$s_j = r_j + l_j - \sum_{k=1}^{n} p_{jk} = r_j + l_j - p_j = d_j - p_j \quad \forall j = 1, \ldots, m \qquad (4)$$

In industrial environments, multiple influences can affect the planned processing times. To reduce the risk of missed due dates due to e.g. equipment downtimes and the expenses due to e.g. defining handling processes in the work plans, a buffer can be applied to the remaining processing time p_j via the parameter v_1. The parameter v_1 is set once during the setup and allows to add a buffer by increasing the processing time by a percentage of it, resulting in an adjusted remaining processing time $p_j{}^*$ as in (5).

$$p_j^* = \sum_{k=1}^{n} p_{jk} + \left(\sum_{k=1}^{n} p_{jk} \right) \bullet v_1 = p_j + \left(p_j \bullet v_1 \right) = p_j \bullet (1 + v_1) \quad \forall j = 1, \ldots, m \qquad (5)$$

Here, it is assumed that $v_1 \geq 0$. Equivalent to the determination of the latest start time (rel.) or latest start date (abs.) s_j using the remaining processing time p_j of order j to meet the due time (rel.) or due date (abs.) d_j an adjusted latest start time (rel.) or adjusted latest start date (abs.) $s_j{}^*$ can be determined by (6) using the adjusted remaining processing time $p_j{}^*$. If a pending order j has not been started when passing the adjusted latest start date $s_j{}^*$, the assigned due date d_j cannot be met with the assigned work plan.

$$s_j^* = r_j + l_j - \left(p_j \bullet (1 + v_1) \right) = d_j - p_j^* \quad \forall j = 1, \ldots, m \qquad (6)$$

To signal reaching the adjusted latest start date $s_j{}^*$ of an order j to the workers and supervisors by means of the priority P_j assigned to the order j, the dynamic, due date-related prioritization is designed such that the priority $P_j(t)$ intersects the x-axis for $t = s_j{}^*$. Subsequently, the value of priority $P_j(t)$ for order j at $t = s_j{}^*$ equals zero.

2.3 Types of Orders and Their Influence on Priority

During the definition phase, three relevant types of order priorities have been determined based on widely applied practices and procedures in production workshops:

1. Standard priority type, assigned to e.g. standard customer orders.
2. Increased priority type, assigned to e.g. replacement deliveries or urgent orders.
3. Reduced priority type, assigned to e.g. dispensable or optional inhouse orders.

These types of priority also need to be utilized when deriving the priority P_j for order j. To represent the types, the parameters a, b and c are introduced, with a, b and c assigning the priority of standard, increased and reduced priority type order, respectively. Additionally, they represent the initial priorities P_j for the types when an order is scheduled at r_j. For the dynamic, due date-related prioritization, a decreasing value of P_j indicates a higher priority of order j. Therefore, the relation is defined as $0 \leq b < a < c$.

The parameters allow adjusting the relation and difference of the three order types according to the specific requirements at a factory. Due to every order j having assigned only one specific order priority type, it is necessary to distinguish between the three existing order types during the calculation of the priority P_j for order j, and thus the binary parameters v_{2j} and v_{3j} are included in the prioritization concept (see Table 1).

Table 1. Case distinction for order priority types for order j

Standard Priority Order (a)	$v_{2j} = 0, v_{3j} = 0$
Increased Priority Order (b)	$v_{2j} = 1, v_{3j} = 0$
Reduced Priority Order (c)	$v_{2j} = 0, v_{3j} = 1$

2.4 Deriving the Priority and Adjusted Priority of an Order

Based on the categories for deriving the priority in order to optimize the identified KPIs for production environments, the individual priority values for the orders can be derived dynamically. While for the standard priority order type the priority decreases linearly over time, the priority value for an increased priority order or a reduced priority order changes the gradient at point $(s_j*, P_j(s_j*)) = (s_j*, 0)$. Since the functions are piecewise linear and continuous, these points with changing gradients correspond to the kinks.

The parameters utilized for deriving the priority $P_j(t)$ are shown in (7).

$$P_j(t) = \begin{cases} \left(\left(-\frac{\left(a-\left(v_{2j}\bullet(a-b)\right)+\left(v_{3j}\bullet(c-a)\right)\right)}{\left|l_j-\left(p_j\bullet\left(1+v_{1j}\right)\right)\right|}\bullet(t-r_j)\right)+\left(a-\left(v_{2j}\bullet(a-b)\right)+\left(v_{3j}\bullet(c-a)\right)\right)\right), r_j \leq t < s_j^* \\ \left(\left(-\frac{\left(a+\left(v_{2j}\bullet(a-b)\right)-\left(v_{3j}\bullet(c-a)\right)\right)}{\left|l_j-\left(p_j\bullet\left(1+v_{1j}\right)\right)\right|}\bullet(t-r_j)\right)+\left(a+\left(v_{2j}\bullet(a-b)\right)-\left(v_{3j}\bullet(c-a)\right)\right)\right), t \geq s_j^* \end{cases} \tag{7}$$

During the pilot definition and use case analysis, some non-standard influences on a small number of orders have been identified. To reduce complexity, these rare events are not represented specifically in the dynamic, due date-related prioritization concept. Nevertheless, the proposed concept provides an option for manual intervention and to alter the priority $P_j(t)$ of an order j has been integrated, resulting in an adjusted dynamic, due date-related priority $P_j*(t)$. To implement the manual intervention in case of non-standard conditions, the parameter v_{4j} is introduced as in (8) to allow altering the priority by a specific offset and to modify the priority $P_j(t)$ by the value of v_{4j} for $t \in [r_j, e_j)$ with e_j depicting the actual completion time (rel.) or date (abs.) of order j. The upper boundary e_j arises from completed orders where calculating priorities becomes obsolet. The decision was made to not allow a manual reduction of the priority P_j (i.e. increasing the calculated value of P_j) due to the restriction that all due dates of all orders and tasks should be met. If an order's priority needs to be reduced, the supervisor should negotiate an elongated maximum allowed order lead time l_j or a postponed due date d_j with the customer instead and thus achieving a reduced order priority.

$$P_j^*(t) = P_j(t) - v_{4j}, v_{4j} \geq 0 \quad \forall j = 1, \ldots, m \tag{8}$$

The adjusted priority P_j* can be calculated dynamically by a DSS for each incoming and pending order and subsequently be displayed to the workers as well as be used for scheduling the orders. The adjusted priority P_j* for each order is calculated for the first time when an order is forwarded to the DSS for scheduling and is subsequently updated based on defined time intervals as well as on defined events, such as completion of a task or arrival of a new order. The adjusted priority P_j* calculated by the DSS is also directly influenced by the strategy for documenting the actual task processing progress.

When the actual progress is only documented after the completion of a task, the adjusted priority P_j^* will be calculated as if the order has not been started until the completion is documented. The adjusted priority P_j^* is then recalculated according to the updated adjusted remaining processing time p_j^* as in (5) of all remaining tasks p_{jk} of order j. Whereas in case of documenting the actual progress of order processing continuously or incrementally, the adjusted priority P_j^* of order j is also updated continuously or incrementally, and thus will retain a positive value in case the order is processed in a correct manner to meet its due date d_j.

2.5 Investigation of the Parameters

We will now evaluate the parameters of the concept given in (8) and propose methods on how to define the respective values. We start with buffer v_1, which is applied to the process time as depicted in (5). Since the exact determination of process times often is hard to be ensured in practice, v_1 is introduced to ensure that production plans can be met even when uncertainties, such as assigning employees having differing levels of competence, machine failure, or inaccurate process time data, occur. Initially the value of v_1 as a fixed percentage of process time can be based on the employees' experience. Depending on the company-specific circumstances, the intial buffer usually is set between 10 and 20%. It can be refined incrementally by analysing data on actual process times. It should be the goal to describe the distribution of these values, allowing to make statements on how planned process times deviate from actual ones, make precise predictions which process times can be expected in future and, hence, how v_1 should be optimized to match the intended outcome. This improves the transparency of the production processes and supports the employees in the decision-making process. The required steps are described in the following.

First, the probability distributions for the process times have to be defined. Therefore, besides measured times (e.g. utilizing REFA), process times based on Methods-Time Measurement (MTM) [17] can be used. However, this only reflects worker-related influences and not machinery-related occurrences, which have to be considered as well. The process time, as well as e.g. the Mean Time To Repair (MTTR) of a machine, can be modelled by an exponential or lognormal distribution, see e.g. [18]. After suitable probability distributions are chosen, the parameters which define the shape of the distributions have to be set. There exist several methods for estimating parameters, e.g. the Bayesian estimator or the maximum likelihood method [19]. If there is no information available on the distribution that might reflect the process time or the standard distributions do not fit the data well, parameter-free methods like Kaplan-Meier- or Nelson-Aalen estimator [20] can be utilized. The distribution of the actual process times can also be calculated by a non-parametric kernel density estimation. While this method is more precise than the other ones mentioned, it requires a comprehensive database.

In order to validate that the particular choice of distribution and the estimated parameters fit the data (i.e. the process times), distribution tests like Kolmogorov-Smirnov or χ^2 goodness-of-fit test can be applied. Note that in (5), the same percentage value is applied to all remaining process times p_j. As an additional improvement, order-specific parameters v_{1j} can be introduced, thereby allowing a more precise adjustment of the buffer values and, hence, reducing the deviation from the planned and actual time. It should be mentioned however that this requires a thorough knowledge about the individual process times for all processes.

Next, we investigate the classification of orders according to their priority a, b and c. To cope with high numbers of pending orders and tasks in factories as well as with the complexity of identifying orders and tasks with high priority, production planners already utilize manifold procedures for prioritization in their current practices. These classification procedures are often based either on customer classification (e.g. a-class customer/n-class customer or OEM/Tier-n), product classification (e.g. a-class product/n-class product based on profit margin) or on experience and management decisions. The classification categories and procedures applied are often derived and optimized over a long period of time, represent the corporate knowledge and are well accepted within the organization. Therefore, they give valuable input for the decision support provided by the proposed concept. When introducing the proposed concept in an organization clear rules for assigning a priority type to an order j need to be defined initially. These rules can either be defined e.g. by comprehensive lists of customers, products and/or constraints assigned to each priority type, or they can be derived from order data being available for each order j to be processed, such as quantity of ordered products, height of penalties or service level agreement with the respective customer.

While v_1 as well as the order priority type are set before scheduling, v_{4j} allows a dynamic, manual adjustment of the order priority. The specific choice of v_{4j} has a direct impact on the extend of the intervention (note: the higher the priority of an order j, the lower the value of $P_j(t)$): In order to increase the priority, v_{4j} decreases $P_j(t)$ to $P_j*(t)$. We suggest that one of the following two options is applied: The range of v_{4j} can be limited based on the priority type of the respective order as suggested in (9). Subsequently, orders of lower priority allow a wider range for v_{4j}, and vice versa.

$$v_{4j} \in \begin{cases} [0, a] & \text{if order j belongs to category a} \\ [0, b] & \text{if order j belongs to category b} \\ [0, c] & \text{if order j belongs to category c} \end{cases} \quad (9)$$

Alternatively, the range of v_{4j} also can be determined utilizing the current absolute priority as dynamic upper boundary $[0, |P_j(t)|]$ for v_{4j}. Further, setting v_{4j} can be limited depending on the role of the employee inducing the shift: employees on a higher level may have more power on the intensity of the priority change. This can be realized by including positive factors in the computation of the upper boundaries, respectively.

2.6 Example Application for the Due Date-Related Order Prioritization

For an example application we assume that an order $j = 1$ with the sequential tasks 1.1 ($p_{11} = 10$), 1.2 ($p_{12} = 20$) and 1.3 ($p_{13} = 10$) has to be prioritized with received time $r_1 = 0$ and due time $d_1 = 70$. The parameters for order 1 are set to $v_1 = 10\%$ and $v_{41} = 0$ and the values for the priority types are a = 0,5, b = 0,25 and c = 0,75.

The diagram shown in Fig. 1 visualizes the priority $P_1*(t)$ for order 1 over time and shows the influence of the remaining processing time $p_j(t)$ on the tasks to be fulfilled. Hereby, the coloured lines represent the values for reduced (light), standard (medium) and increased priority (dark), respectively: the lower the value $P_1*(t)$, the higher the priority. The respective latest start time s_1 of the order is calculated as in (4) and also visualized for the three tasks.

In the upper part of Fig. 1, the processing time $p_j(t)$ is updated only on completion of the respective task, the value of $P_j^*(t)$ then shows a significant rise since it is only evaluated for a discrete number of values for $p(t)$ in this scenario (see (7)). The lower part shows a real-time (online) update of p_j. The actual processing of the tasks 1.1, 1.2 and 1.3 is represented by the coloured boxes.

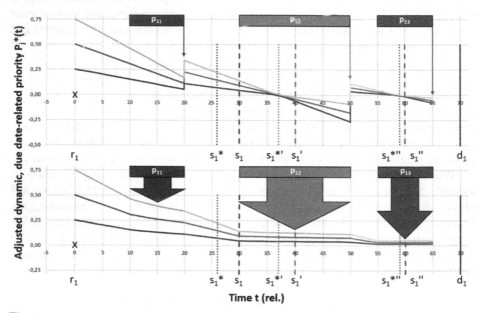

Fig. 1. Visualization of $P_j^*(t)$ in case of event-discrete (above) and real-time (below) update of the remaining processing time p_j for order 1 with tasks 1.1, 1.2 and 1.3 as standard, increased and reduced priority type order (Color figure online)

3 Discussion and Conclusion

The proposed approach is provided to be incorporated in a DSS for scheduling and is designed to determine the adjusted dynamic, due date-related priority as input for the DSS. For e.g. online optimization in a real environment the DSS incorporating the proposed approach will provide the processing times for the tasks to be prioritized. These processing times can either be defined by methods such as MTM or REFA and are applicable for almost any worker or can depend on the skills of the designated or assigned worker/worker class. However, this must be implemented in the DSS utilizing the proposed approach. The approach can be applied in both cases and will calculate the adjusted dynamic, due date-related priority $Pj^*(t)$ based on the data provided by the DSS. In case of early completion of tasks or orders, e.g. due to execution by a more skilled worker, the DSS should trigger a rescheduling and reprioritization on completion.

In case of the integrating the proposed approach in an offline simulation environment, the processing times for tasks need to be defined as described before, yet the workers executing the tasks can e.g. be defined as personas holding a specific set of skills. This results in actual processing times of the specific persona for specific tasks, or the actual processing times within the simulation environment can be derived by applying probability distributions based on the processing times of the workplans.

Regarding the priority classification of the orders into the categories a,b and c, a further specification in the sense of creating an order of the orders/jobs within the categories will be part of our future research. Based on our experience, the usage of three categories reflects the practical expectations and implementation very well. However, production planners usually have deeper knowledge about certain orders and a tendency towards individual priorities. This is already partly addressed by the parameter v_{4j} (which allows an intervention and a dynamic adjustment of the priority), it can however be modeled using the original "before-hand" classification. The introduction of additional discrete parameters or the modification of the discrete values v_{2j} and v_{3j} to continuous ones requires a thorough investigation of the properties of the resulting model.

The current concept focuses on time-based order prioritization and does not include a financial evaluation of orders. Therefore, a cost term introducing contribution margins of orders could be introduced. This can e.g. be realized by including a penalty term in (8). Further research has to be conducted on how to model the penalty to reflect different types of financial prioritization in companies and workshops. Additionally, the properties of this term, its parameters, and the resulting concept have to be investigated.

An alternative to extend the model to a financial point of view leads to a third open research question: the embedding of the model into an optimization problem and its subsequent solution process. For example, it is possible to model the financial evaluation as a separate objective function, which is optimized for the set of feasible schedules. The specific function(s) have to be defined before the resulting program and its properties can be investigated in order to apply suitable algorithms.

References

1. Ruppert, T., Jaskó, S., Holczinger, T., Abonyi, J.: Enabling technologies for Operator 4.0: a survey. Appl. Sci. **8**, 1650 (2018)
2. Romero, D., Bernus, P., Noran, O., Stahre, J., Fast-Berglund, Å.: The Operator 4.0: human cyber-physical systems & adaptive automation towards human-automation symbiosis work systems. In: Nääs, I., et al. (eds.) APMS 2016. IAICT, vol. 488, pp. 677–686. Springer, Cham (2016). https://doi.org/10.1007/978-3-319-51133-7_80
3. Hannah, S.D., Neal, A.: On-the-fly scheduling as a manifestation of partial-order planning and dynamic task values. Hum. Factors **56**, 1093–1112 (2014)
4. Lödding, H.: Handbook of Manufacturing Control. Springer, Heidelberg (2013). https://doi.org/10.1007/978-3-642-24458-2
5. Chen, X., Bojko, M., Riedel, R., Apostolakis, K.C., Zarpalas, D., Daras, P.: Human-centred adaptation and task distribution utilizing levels of automation. IFAC-PapersOnLine **51**, 54–59 (2018)
6. Werner, F., Burtseva, L., Sotskov, Y. (eds.): Algorithms for Scheduling Problems. MDPI, Basel (2018)

7. Kopanos, G.M.: Solving Large-Scale Production Scheduling and Planning in the Process Industries. Springer, Cham (2019). https://doi.org/10.1007/978-3-030-01183-3
8. Piontek, A., Lödding, H.: Determining the potential to improve schedule compliance. Procedia CIRP **63**, 477–482 (2017)
9. Lödding, H., Piontek, A.: The surprising effectiveness of earliest operation due-date sequencing. Prod. Plann. Control **28**(5), 459–471 (2017)
10. Trzyna, D., Kuyumcu, A., Lödding, H.: Throughput time characteristics of rush orders and their impact on standard orders. Procedia CIRP **3**, 311–316 (2012)
11. Mundt, C., Lödding, H.: Order acceptance and scheduling with a throughput diagram. In: Lalic, B., Majstorovic, V., Marjanovic, U., von Cieminski, G., Romero, D. (eds.) APMS 2020. IAICT, vol. 591, pp. 351–359. Springer, Cham (2020). https://doi.org/10.1007/978-3-030-57993-7_40
12. Kaasinen, E., et al.: Empowering and engaging industrial workers with Operator 4.0 solutions. Comput. Ind. Eng. **139**, 10567 (2019)
13. Tsourma, M., Zikos, S., Drosou, A., Tzovaras, D.: Online task distribution simulation in smart factories. In: 2018 2nd International Symposium on Small-Scale Intelligent Manufacturing Systems (SIMS), Cavan, 16 April 2018–18 April 2018, pp. 1–6. IEEE (2018)
14. Künzel, H.: Erfolgsfaktor Kundenzufriedenheit: Handbuch für Strategie und Umsetzung, 2nd edn. Springer, Berlin (2012). https://doi.org/10.1007/978-3-642-32552-6
15. humAn CEntred Factories (ACE) Cluster (ed.): Human-centered factories from theory to industrial practice. Lessons learned and recommendations (2019)
16. Project management - Project network techniques; Descriptions and concepts (DIN 69900) (2009)
17. Maynard, H.B., Stegemerten, G.J., Schwab, J.L.: Methods-time measurement (1948)
18. Holický, M.: Introduction to Probability and Statistics for Engineers. Springer, Heidelberg (2013). https://doi.org/10.1007/978-3-642-38300-7
19. Barbu, A., Zhu, S.-C.: Monte Carlo Methods, 1st edn. Springer, Singapore (2020). https://doi.org/10.1007/978-981-13-2971-5
20. Colosimo, E., Ferreira, F., Oliveira, M., Sousa, C.: Empirical comparisons between Kaplan-Meier and Nelson-Aalen survival function estimators. J. Stat. Comput. Simul. **72**, 299–308 (2002)

Knowledge Graphs in Digital Twins for AI in Production

Pieter Lietaert$^{(\boxtimes)}$ (iD), Bart Meyers (iD), Johan Van Noten (iD), Joren Sips, and Klaas Gadeyne (iD)

Flanders Make, Gaston Geenslaan 8, 3100 Heverlee, Belgium
`pieter.lietaert@flandersmake.be`

Abstract. AI is increasingly penetrating the production industry. Today, however, AI is still used in a limited way in a production environment, often focusing on a single production step and using out-of-the-box AI algorithms. AI models that use information spanning a complete production line and even larger parts of the product lifecycle could add significant value for production companies. In this paper, we suggest a digital twin architecture to support the complete AI lifecycle (discovering correlations, learning, deploying and validating), based on a knowledge graph that centralizes all information. We show how this digital twin could ease information access to different heterogenous data sources and pose opportunities for a wider application of AI in production industry. We illustrate this approach using a simplified industrial example of a compressor housing production, leading to preliminary results that show how a data scientist can efficiently access, through the knowledge graph, all necessary data for the creation of an AI model.

Keywords: Digital twin · Knowledge graph · Data architecture · AI in production

1 Introduction

With the production (=manufacturing and assembly) industry moving towards Industry 4.0, a large amount of information is recorded and collected by smart and interconnected Cyber-Physical Production Systems (CPPS). This information could and should be leveraged to learn from the past and from similar cases using Artificial Intelligence (AI) systems, where we use the definition of AI in [1] in this paper. AI systems can support or automate decisions, such as: intelligently pick product samples for quality inspection, optimize product and production performance, reduce the number of required iterations for tuning the machine settings in case of a production line changeover, to increase the sustainability of the product, etc. The enormous potential of AI in production has been valued by Accenture as 3,7 trillion USD by 2035 [2]. A Gartner study indicates that the AI transformation in production has started, as AI implementations grew by 37% during 2018, and by 270% over the last four years [3].

Today, production companies typically use AI only by employing out-of-the-box algorithms, in a singled-out production step, such as image recognition for quality control

© IFIP International Federation for Information Processing 2021
Published by Springer Nature Switzerland AG 2021
A. Dolgui et al. (Eds.): APMS 2021, IFIP AICT 630, pp. 249–257, 2021.
https://doi.org/10.1007/978-3-030-85874-2_26

(defect detection). Such AI algorithms are typically black-box, as those also commonly used in other domains, by companies like GAFA (Google, Apple, Facebook and Amazon). These algorithms require large amounts of data for training and validation, acquired by measuring targeted values relevant to the production step under consideration.

A largely unsolved challenge, however, is how AI algorithms can use information over multiple production steps, possibly even the entire product lifecycle, from design to product use. This challenge becomes even more apparent when considering the trend towards high mix, low volume (HMLV) production, with smaller series and more operator involvement for better flexibility. In this setting, the amount of data gathered for one variant is typically limited and too diverse to apply out-of-the-box AI algorithms. In addition, AI systems are only considered trustworthy [4] in the context of production if it is possible to explain to operators why a certain suggestion is made, demanding a more transparent AI approach.

One particular challenge that a data scientist faces when creating reliable and transparent models in this context, is the ability to access all required and relevant information (and preferentially not more) over the complete lifecycle of AI design, i.e. while finding correlations, learning, deployment, execution and validation. Information spanning larger parts of the product lifecycle typically requires access to multiple, heterogeneous data sources, including relational and non-relational (fi. time-series) databases, simulations, web APIs, user manuals, etc. The case of HMLV production further intensifies the need for gathering data from diverse sources, since model reliability can drastically be improved by supplementing the limited amount of measurement data with additional information, such as domain expert knowledge, operator experience and physics models. Currently, searching for the correct information in a typical industrial context causes prohibitively expensive overhead to the data scientist who is trying to find new correlations and models that could add a lot of value to the company. We will also investigate these challenges in the ICT-38–2020 ASSISTANT project.

In this paper, we consider this information access problem and suggest a data architecture centered around a digital twin that is based on a domain-wide knowledge graph. In Sect. 2 we describe this approach, illustrating it with an example of compressor housing manufacturing. In Sect. 3, we describe some experiments, illustrating the type of techniques that would enable easy data access in a knowledge graph centered architecture. In the final section we summarize our findings and present the next steps to take for its realization.

2   Approach

In an industrial context, a data scientist needs to (1) gather data over a vast set of heterogeneous data sources and (2) gather knowledge about the many production processes that exist in the company. In order to support this data scientist, we suggest the use of a digital twin built around a formal knowledge graph. Here, we use the term digital twin to indicate the central part of the data architecture in the production company, storing and providing access to all offline and online data. A knowledge graph, as the name suggests, organizes the information in a graph-like, and thus interlinked way. It has been made famous by initiatives, like, for example, DBpedia [5] and Google Knowledge Graph

[6]. In an industrial context, the knowledge graph can be used to capture and formalize the available, domain-wide meta-data, to formalize implicit expert knowledge and to provide the central access point to retrieve information. With regards to legacy data storage and scalability, typically, the knowledge graph should not contain large amounts of actual data, such as time series individuals. Instead, it should reference access to this data and therefore rely on meta-data.

The knowledge graph serves three main goals:

1. create a common vocabulary across the multiple disciplines in production,
2. facilitate knowledge search, capture and creation, i.e. identification of domain concepts and (new) relations among these concepts, and,
3. facilitate data search, i.e. connecting the domain concepts to the set of heterogeneous data sources.

The first goal will enable involved parties throughout the company to better find and understand data available to them and to more easily access the data they need. There has been research on how to describe production domain knowledge in a formal way [7–12]. However, many of the schemes lack expressiveness in certain areas, like ways to describe operator knowledge, or lack the ability to directly include known physics relations, models or constraints. Furthermore, although there are examples towards integrating formalized schemes in industrial applications, see e.g. [13, 14], there does not seem to be widespread adaptation yet.

The second goal involves creating knowledge from that data. This is not restricted to linking raw data, i.e. the knowledge graph should allow to link domain concepts and data sources themselves, e.g. linking types, algorithms, models and simulations. With the proper tools, different users can add new concepts and links to the knowledge graph, increasing knowledge within the company over time. There are a number of technologies available to realize linked data in the knowledge graph. For example, the World Wide Web Consortium (W3C) introduced the Resource Description Framework (RDF) [17] in 1996 as a way to describe linked data. Later it added reasoning rules, like for example expressed in the Web Ontology Language (OWL), that allow to find new links more easily in an algorithmic way. Another one is metamodeling [20], which allows the precise description of the types, relationships and constraints for a domain.

When using a knowledge graph, the third goal, i.e. data access, can be facilitated through semantic queries, see e.g. [15, 16, 21, 22]. The semantic query ensures that users can ask for exactly the data they need, rather than collecting data from different data sources and combining (joining) data manually. Furthermore, the user does not have to be concerned with the actual data sources that are being queried, if the central knowledge graph enables a performant connection between the contained concepts and the actual data sources. Data federation through a central, semantic query point is already possible using integrated software like the Ontotext platform [18], Timbr [19] and many others. However, it seems that this type of software has not penetrated many production company workflows yet.

This leads us to suggest the generic, high-level, digital twin centered architecture that can be seen in Fig. 1. Here, we take typical data architecture practice in industry, and add the idea of a knowledge graph based digital twin, creating an architecture that can support the data scientists in all phases of AI model creation. On the input side on the left, different devices are connected to a gateway, that either sends the data to storage, or can be directly queried in the case of online applications, like dashboarding and streaming analytics. In case of storage, in the offline zone on top, the incoming machine data is typically consolidated together with data coming from other company sources such as order processing or Manufacturing Execution Systems (MES). Next, a curated data zone should be created, with cleaned data. Moreover, it combines data from different sources throughout the product lifecycle, such as simulation data, type info, or operator knowledge. Next, different stakeholders such as business users and data scientists can use the digital twin to discover existing and add new information and knowledge (dashed arrows) and, finally, access data through queries facilitated - ideally automatically generated - by the digital twin (full arrow between knowledge graph and offline query). Similarly, for people using online applications, the digital twin serves as a reference to the concepts that are important to the application and facilitates online querying of the data provided by the gateway. Note that this architecture can also serve as a starting point for integration of existing data federation tools in the production company.

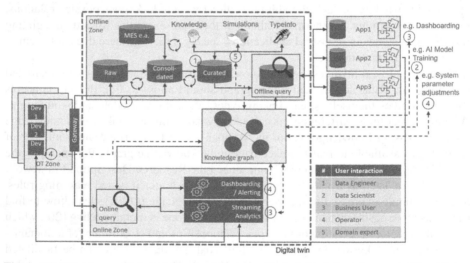

Fig. 1. High-level overview example of architecture with digital twin based on central knowledge graph.

The knowledge graph centered architecture should enable the three goals mentioned before. To illustrate this, consider the following example of a compressor housing that undergoes a series of CNC-controlled machining operations. This example is a very simplified version of one of the industrial partners in the ICT-38–2020 ASSISTANT project. In Fig. 2, a number of relevant concepts relating to this part of the production process have been expressed in a high-level, abstract view of a knowledge graph (in blue).

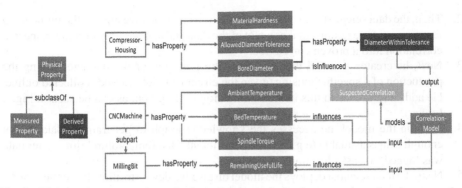

Fig. 2. High-level, abstract view of a knowledge graph for the compressor housing example. (Color figure online)

Notice how the overview on the left contains the concepts of a measured physical property and derived physical property. This allows different stakeholders throughout the company to relate their interpretation of physical quantities, like material hardness and temperature, to concepts in the knowledge graph, easing the interpretation of data on these quantities from different sources, like measurements or physics models. Furthermore, concepts like 'suspected correlation' in the knowledge graph allow to express relations that are based on operator experience, rather than using pure data.

In order to see how the knowledge graph can be used to create new knowledge, we can apply it to the data scientist's workflow for creating an AI model. We can subdivide this workflow in 7 steps, depicted in Fig. 3.

Identify potential correlation	Analyze correlation	Create model	Train model	Deploy model	Execute model	Validate model
• Input from manufacturing expert	• Plot, calculate coefficient	• Regression, simulation, … • Python, R, Simulink, …	• Additional experiments • Smaller data amounts • Databricks, etc.	• On cluster, edge, … • Compile	• Predict, edge, … • Make decision based on prediction	• Compare model output with test data

Fig. 3. Overview of the seven steps a data scientist can take to create an AI model.

Assume the accuracy of the housing's rotor bore diameter is one of the main influencers of the efficiency of the compressor. A data scientist is tasked to create a model that predicts, during production, whether the diameter will be in tolerance, and he takes the following steps.

1. First, he asks a domain expert, who is familiar with the production process, for influencing factors of the bore diameter. The domain expert, based on his experience of the production process, adds a 'SuspectedCorrelation' to the knowledge graph, which relates different production properties as factors influencing the bore diameter, see Fig. 2 (yellow).

2. Then, the data scientist consults this correlation concept, investigates the influencing factors, and, for example, makes a plot of the data and can possibly turn the suspected correlation into a proven correlation.
3. Next, he creates a model that computes the precision of the diameter during the production of a specific housing, given the circumstantial evidence collected online. He adds a reference to this model to the knowledge graph, as can be seen in Fig. 2 (green).
4. To train the model, he accesses the knowledge graph to get training data. If not enough data is available (e.g. find out if sufficient 'BedTemperature' time series data was logged), he asks for more experiments.
5. Next, the data scientist deploys the model on an edge device to allow live computation of the diameter. He adds meta-data of this deployment, e.g. on which device it is running, to the knowledge graph (for example as a property of the model). Since the model is referenced like this, it is easy to find and access by other stakeholders in the future, e.g. a control engineer who wants to use the model in a smart controller.
6. He also introduces a 'DiameterWithinTolerance' property, see Fig. 2 (red), as the output of the model. When actual computations are made by the model, the property references this new data in the knowledge graph. He connects this property to the concept of the bore diameter, so that it can easily be found in the future when investigating the bore diameter.
7. Finally, the data scientist validates the model based on input from an operator. He can use the knowledge graph to quickly find the measurements from the operator, needed for validation.

Of course, the knowledge graph should be able to link the concepts in the graph to the correct data. This is also apparent in the above described 7-step process. For example, in step 2, to be able to plot the data, and in step 4, to be able to train the data, the data scientist should be able to easily access the individual data elements that where linked as influencing factors of the diameter, such as time series temperature data, measured diameters, or tool information on remaining life. Furthermore, once the model is trained and deployed, other people, also later in time, should be able to find such models in the knowledge graph, run them on new input data and get the output data values. Note that the knowledge graph centered architecture is not only suited for AI model creation, but also provides the basis for, more generally, access to all knowledge gathered and contained in the company.

In the next section, we illustrate how interaction with the knowledge graph could look like, using semantic querying with two different techniques.

3 Querying Examples

In this section, we present two different implementations for data access through a digital twin based on the knowledge graph in Fig. 2: (1) a knowledge graph represented using the W3C RDF triples format accessed through SPARQL queries to retrieve the data from a relational database, or, (2) a meta-model style knowledge graph accessed through GraphQL queries, where a GraphQL schema and implementation provides access to the data stored in the knowledge graph.

Presume the data scientist wants to investigate all influencing factors of the bore diameter, in the "offline zone", as in step 2 in the previous section. In Fig. 4, on the left, you can see a SPARQL query that would result in actual data values for all of the influencing factors and the bore diameter. The SPARQL query allows an intuitive way of accessing related data. In this example, all compressor housings are linked to the bed temperature of the CNC machine they were milled on, to the remaining life of the milling bit that was used and to the bore diameter value that resulted from the milling process. We can use Ontop [21] to perform this SPARQL query over data stored in a relational database. This avoids the user having to get familiar with the technical database schema and, rather, allows users to ask questions over a knowledge graph storing concepts like 'CompressorHousing', 'CNCMachine', connected by properties such as 'milledBy'.

On the right, an equivalent query in GraphQL is shown. In the GraphQL case, data is also accessed through intuitive connections expressed in the GraphQL schema, such as an asset of type 'CompressorHousing' having properties like serial number and operations. Technical data access, e.g. using queries directly to the relational database storing the data, is again avoided by translating the GraphQL query through, in this case, a custom API.

Both examples show data access through a central knowledge graph, using two different technologies, avoiding the requirement of an often complex, technical understanding of where and how the data is stored and instead employing intuitive concepts contained in the knowledge graph to get the required data.

```
SELECT ?housing ?bedTemperatureValue
       ?usefulLifeValue ?boreDiameterValue
WHERE {
  ?housing a :CompressorHousing;
           :milledBy ?cncMachine;
           :hasProperty ?boreDiameter;
  ?cncMachine a :CNCMachine;
              :hasProperty ?bedtemperature;
              :subpart ?millingbit.
  ?millingbit a :MillingBit;
              :hasProperty ?usefulLife.
  ?bedtemperature a :MeasuredValue;
                  :hasValue ?bedTemperatureValue.
  ?usefulLife a :MeasuredProperty;
              :hasValue ?usefulLifeValue.
  ?boreDiameter a :BoreDiameter;
                :hasValue ?BoreDiameterValue.
}
```

```
query {
  asset(type: "CompressorHousing") {
    serialNumber
    indicator(name: "BoreDiameter")
    operation(name: "Milling") {
      indicator(name: "bedTemperature")
      indicator(name: "usefulLife")
    }
  }
}
```

Fig. 4. Examples of two different queries on the knowledge graph in Fig. 2.

4 Conclusion

We identify access of data and knowledge as a main bottleneck for manufacturing companies to apply AI solutions. To address this, we investigated the use of a knowledge graph that can be queried, and an architecture to apply the knowledge graph in a manufacturing context. We illustrated how the knowledge graph can support the data scientist in accessing information from heterogeneous data sources, including expert knowledge, throughout the complete AI lifecycle. A small query example showed how this can be applied in practice and how the knowledge graph facilitates efficient data access for the data scientist.

Three challenges remain before being able to apply this approach successfully in a production context.

First, the domain concepts in the knowledge graph should have the proper expressiveness in order to properly add less tangible information, such as operator experience, correlations, models and uncertainty.

Second, although the information access through querying was illustrated with two examples, we are still in the process of validating, together with production companies, which approach is best suited in the context of querying information from the knowledge graph based digital twin for AI.

Finally, the data architecture that was presented, showed data querying of the offline and online data sources as separate steps. It is not clear yet what the best practices are to link the information in the knowledge graph to the data sources. We will investigate these challenges in the ICT-38–2020 ASSISTANT project.

Acknowledgments. This research was supported by Flanders Make, the strategic research center for the manufacturing industry. This paper was partially funded by the DTDesign ICON (Flanders Innovation & Entrepreneurship FM/ICON :: HBC.2019.0079) project. We would also like to acknowledge the European Commission for funding through the ASSISTANT project, grant number 101000165.

References

1. A definition of Artificial Intelligence: main capabilities and scientific disciplines. https://digital-strategy.ec.europa.eu/en/library/definition-artificial-intelligence-main-capabilities-and-scientific-disciplines. Accessed 18 June 2021
2. Manufacturing the future. https://www.accenture.com/_acnmedia/pdf-74/accenture-pov-manufacturing-digital-final.pdf. Accessed 10 Mar 2021
3. Gartner Survey of More Than 3,000 CIOs Reveals That Enterprises Are Entering the Third Era of IT. https://www.gartner.com/en/newsroom/press-releases/2018-10-16-gartner-survey-of-more-than-3000-cios-reveals-that-enterprises-are-entering-the-third-era-of-it. Accessed 10 Mar 2021
4. Ethics guidelines for trustworthy AI. https://ec.europa.eu/digital-single-market/en/news/ethics-guidelines-trustworthy-ai. Accessed 10 Mar 2021
5. DBpedia. https://wiki.dbpedia.org/. Accessed 10 Mar 2021
6. Introducing the knowledge graph: things not strings. https://blog.google/products/search/introducing-knowledge-graph-things-not/. Accessed 10 Mar 2021
7. Gayathri, R., Uma, V.: Ontology based knowledge representation technique, domain modeling languages and planners for robotic path planning: a survey. ICT Express **4**(2), 69–74 (2018)
8. Sampath Kumar, V., et al.: Ontologies for Industry 4.0. Knowl. Eng. Rev. **34**(17), 1–14 (2019)
9. Kourtis, G., Kavakli, E., Sakellariou, R.: A rule-based approach founded on description logics for Industry 4.0 smart factories. IEEE Trans. Ind. Inform. **15**(9), 4888–4899 (2019)
10. Giustozzi, F., Saunier, J., Zanni-Merk, C.: Context modeling for Industry 4.0: an ontology based approach. Procedia Comput. Sci. **126**, 675–684 (2018)

11. Cao, Q., Giustozzi, F., Zanni-Merk, C., De Bertrand de Beuvron, F., Reich, C.: Smart condition monitoring for Industry 4.0 manufacturing processes: an ontology-based approach. Cybern. Syst. **50**, 1–15 (2019)
12. Heng, Z., Utpal, R., Yung-Tsun, T.L.: Enriching analytics models with domain knowledge for smart manufacturing data analysis. Int. J. Prod. Res. **58**(20), 6399–6415 (2020)
13. Kalaycı, E.G., et al.: Semantic integration of bosch manufacturing data using virtual knowledge graphs. In: Pan, J.Z., et al. (eds.) ISWC 2020. LNCS, vol. 12507, pp. 464–481. Springer, Cham (2020). https://doi.org/10.1007/978-3-030-62466-8_29
14. Kharlamov, E., et al.: Ontology based data access in statoil. J. Web Semant. **44**, 3–36 (2017)
15. Kharlamov, E., et al.: Optique: towards OBDA systems for industry. In: Cimiano, P., Fernández, M., Lopez, V., Schlobach, S., Völker, J. (eds.) ESWC 2013. LNCS, vol. 7955, pp. 125–140. Springer, Heidelberg (2013). https://doi.org/10.1007/978-3-642-41242-4_11
16. Grangel-Gonzalez, I., Halilaj, L., Coskun, G., Auer, S., Collarana, D., Hoffmeister, M.: Towards a semantic administrative shell for Industry 4.0 components. In: Proceedings - 2016 IEEE 10th International Conference on Semantic Computing, ICSC 2016, pp. 230–237 (2016)
17. RDF. https://www.w3.org/RDF/. Accessed 10 Mar 2021
18. Ontotext platform. https://www.ontotext.com/products/ontotext-platform/. Accessed 10 Mar 2021
19. Timbr. http://timbr.ai/platform/. Accessed 10 Mar 2021
20. Thomas, K.: Matters of (meta-)modeling. Softw. Syst. Model. **5**(4), 369–385 (2006). https://doi.org/10.1007/s10270-006-0017-9
21. Calvanese, D., et al.: Ontop: answering SPARQL queries over relational databases. Semant. Web **8**(3), 471–487 (2017)
22. Sequeda, J., Miranker, D.: Ultrawrap: SPARQL execution on relational data. J. Web Semant. **22**, 19–39 (2013)

Smart Short Term Capacity Planning: A Reinforcement Learning Approach

Manuel Schneckenreither[ID], Sebastian Windmueller, and Stefan Haeussler[(✉)][ID]

Department of Information Systems, Production and Logistics,
University of Innsbruck, Innsbruck, Austria
`stefan.haeussler@uibk.ac.at`

Abstract. Capacity planning is an important production control function that significantly influences firm performance. Especially, in the short term, we face a dynamically changing system which calls for an adaptive capacity planning system that reacts based on the current state of the shop floor. Thus, this paper analyzes the performance of a reinforcement learning (RL) algorithm for overtime planning for a make-to-order job shop. We compare the performance of the RL algorithm to mechanisms that set overtime-hours statically or randomly over time. Performance is measured in total costs which consist of overtime, holding and backorder costs. The results show that our tested benchmarks can be outperformed by the RL algorithm, where the major savings were achieved due to less needed overtime.

Keywords: Reinforcement learning · Capacity planning · Simulation

1 Introduction

Capacity planning is an important production control function that significantly influences firm performance. It is often divided into long, mid and short term capacity planning [1,14,27]. Long-term capacity planning focuses on yearly resource requirements for manufacturing including plant locations and capacities, planning with suppliers and establishing new technologies or processes. In the medium-term the focus is on monthly or quarterly resource requirements, such as the amount of workforce, raw materials and inventories. In the short term, capacity planning is made on a daily or weekly basis. The task is to match resources, work centers and jobs based on the specific job's requirements [1], where one of the main issues is to balance overtime, holding and backorder costs. This paper focuses on short term capacity planning for a make-to-order manufacturer. Due to the short term nature, we are facing a dynamically changing system with e.g., machine failures, delays and other factors interrupting the manufacturing process. Thus, it would be beneficial to have an adaptive planning system that plans capacities based on the current state of the shop floor. This paper addresses this problem by proposing a smart short term capacity planning

© IFIP International Federation for Information Processing 2021
Published by Springer Nature Switzerland AG 2021
A. Dolgui et al. (Eds.): APMS 2021, IFIP AICT 630, pp. 258–266, 2021.
https://doi.org/10.1007/978-3-030-85874-2_27

approach using Machine Learning. More precisely, we test the performance of a reinforcement learning algorithm in comparison to some static approaches with regard to holding, backorder and overtime costs.

2   Literature Review

This literature review is divided into two parts: First, we review the literature on short term capacity planing and second we review the literature on applications of reinforcement learning algorithms in short term production planning and control problems.

There are quite some research papers that use overtime as a way to overcome the problem of high lateness costs, where most authors use heuristics and mathematical programming. Yang et al. [28] look into a single machine shop floor environment that is purely deterministic. Their proposed priority algorithm, for balancing the use of overtime and regular time, showed close to optimal solutions, however is limited by the low shop floor complexity and the deterministic environment. A similar environment is considered by Jaramillo and Erkoc [7], where a finite set of jobs runs in a single machine job shop. Their proposed heuristic managed to beat a mathematical model in CPU-time and cost performance. Ornek and Cengiz [15] employ multiple stacked linear programming models to design a dynamic production planning system that controls lot sizes, alternative job routing and overtime decisions which results in a capacity feasible material plan for a job shop environment. Yuan et al. [29] develop a production planning model that determines planned lead times and production lot sizes to minimize inventory and overtime costs in a job shop production system. Finally, Chen et al. [1] propose a model for make-to-order companies which allows for selecting only the most profitable orders while maintaining delivery date adherence. They suggest using overtime and outsourcing for short term capacity planning, although back-ordering is not allowed in their mixed-integer programming model. They highlight the viability of their approach to small problems sizes, but state that more efficient algorithms are needed to tackle the capacity planning issue on an industrial scale.

Machine learning can be divided into the categories of supervised learning, unsupervised learning and reinforcement learning [25]. In supervised learning the algorithms are presented with input-output tuples and seek to find a function that best describes this data, where best is defined as the least squared error. In unsupervised learning the algorithms are given data without output labels. They use the structure of the data to cluster it or learn latent variables in Bayesian models. Finally, in reinforcement learning (RL) the input/output pairs are actually never presented to the algorithm, but a function rewards the outcome of previously (by an agent) chosen actions. Thus, it models the human learning capabilities by trial-and-error as the agent usually starts without prior knowledge [19,25]. There are numerous highly-sophisticated algorithms available [6,12,13,24]. With regard to RL techniques applied to short term production planning problems, several papers were published. To the best of our knowledge there are only two studies that use RL techniques for order release planning. Paternina-Arboleda and Das [16] use an R-learning approach called 'SMART' (developed in [2]) to release orders in a single product, serial flow line. They compare its performance to conventional order release policies (e.g., Kanban and CONWIP) and show that the RL algorithm yields less inventory and is more agile, meaning that it can react more quickly to the dynamic production environment. Schneckenreither and Haeussler [21] use several different value iteration RL algorithms (Q and R-learning) to make periodic order release decisions for a flow shop production system. They show that their approach outperforms static order release mechanisms by yielding lower costs, lateness and standard deviation of lateness.

With regard to dynamic scheduling, there is a growing increase in the use of RL algorithms where most papers focus on value iteration algorithms. Paternina-Arboleda and Das [17] use a relaxed SMART algorithm (R-learning) for a three product, stochastic lot scheduling problem. They show that their approach is computationally feasible and is able to reduce the inventory while keeping the backorders at low levels. Wang and Usher [26] use Q-learning for a job routing problem in a 10 machines job shop and show that the RL algorithm performs equally or better than the benchmark heuristics. An interesting extension is presented by Qu et al. [18] who show that Q-learning can be applied to consider scheduling together with optimal assignment of multi-skilled workers. Furthermore, some papers apply deep Q-learning to scheduling problems where the early works of Zhang and Dietterich [30,31] apply RL for payload scheduling of NASA space shuttles. They find that RL outperforms an approach that combines heuristics and simulated annealing by yielding a lower makespan. Finally, [3,9,10] apply a policy iteration algorithm for scheduling in a job shop where the former two consider eight machines and three production stages. Their RL algorithm outperforms their benchmark: a two stage decision rule that prioritizes orders with regard to their waiting time and then selects the machine with the least workload. In [3] the RL algorithm is tested to a number of scheduling benchmark problems from the OR library ranging from 5 resources and 10 jobs to 15 resources and 30 jobs and modify them by including stochasticity. They show that for deterministic and stochastic scenarios the RL algorithm outperforms scheduling rules such as FIFO and SPT. However, to the best of the authors' knowledge there is no application of RL to short term capacity planning problems.

3   Job Shop Model and Short Term Capacity Planning Models

We use a hypothetical job shop in a rolling horizon environment similar to the study of [22] (see Fig. 1). We consider a make-to-order restricted job shop, where all arriving orders are collected in an order pool. The orders are processed at the work centers M1, M2 and M3 (each containing a queue and a machine), and the final products are stored in the finished goods inventory (FGI) until their due

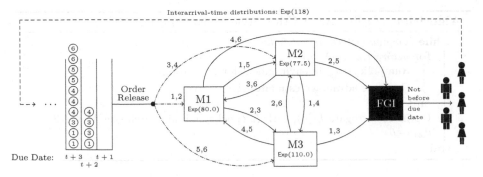

Fig. 1. Job shop simulation model with routing, processing time distributions and demand interarrival time distributions [22].

date. There are three machines and six different product types and all machines can process each product type and each machine can only process one job at a time. We expect the incoming orders to be uniformly distributed among the product types. The routing of each product type is given by the edge names, where the number corresponds to the product type. Therefore, each job has to go once through every machine before it is completed, but the routing differs between the six product types and there are no return visits. Thus, each job has to pass three production steps before it is finished (see Fig. 1). A period is set to 16 h (that is 960 min) and at the beginning of each working day, jobs get released to the shop floor following a backward infinite loading (BIL) logic which releases orders based on static lead time (3 periods) which is subtracted from the due date. The system employs a first-come-first-serve rule for the scheduling of jobs. Once a job has been finished, it gets moved to the finished goods inventory where it waits to be shipped at its designated due date. If the job is finished before its due date, it has to wait until the due date is reached and then gets shipped (early shipping is prohibited). If the job is finished after its designated due date, it gets shipped right away.

The processing times are exponentially distributed and are given under the corresponding node labels of the machines in Fig. 1. The interarrival times of orders arriving at the system are exponentially distributed with a mean of 118 min. Orders that arrive to the system are assigned a due date which indicates the time at which the order has to be shipped. The due date slack is always ten periods. The interarrival times were set to yield an utilization of 95% at the bottleneck work center (M3) if no overtime is considered. The simulation model was implemented using Python 3.8.

Using Overtime. Overtime is modelled as a decrease in processing time [11], which we only apply to the bottleneck machine M3. As one period or work day has 16 h, an overtime of 12.5% refers to an additional 2, 25% refers to an additional 4 and an overtime of 50% refers to an additional 8 h of available capacity.

Algorithm 1: PPO, Actor-Critic Style (Adapted from [24])

---

while *stopping criteria is not fulfilled* **do**

> **for** *actor=1,2,...,N* **do**
>> Run policy $\pi_{\theta_{old}}$ in environment for T timesteps
>>
>> Compute advantage estimates $\hat{A}_1, \ldots, \hat{A}_T$
>
> **end**
>
> Optimise surrogate $L_t(\theta)$, with K epochs and minibatch size $M \leqslant NT$
>
> $\theta_{old} \leftarrow \theta$

end

Costs. The cost parameters are set by assuming an increase in value from WIP holding (WIP_C: \$1 per order and period) to the final goods inventory (FGI) holding costs (FGI_C: \$4 per order and period). The backorder costs are set very high (BO_C: \$16 per order and period) due to the MTO environment. If overtime was used during a period, a base cost of \$8 multiplied with the amount of extra hours is incurred to pay the additional hours that workers had to put in. Overtime costs (OT_C) are the only costs that are incurred globally as a flat-rate cost, instead of a cost per individual job.

Short Term Capacity Planing. The challenge of the problem at hand is to find an optimal balance of the costs incurred through the production, i.e. WIP_C, FGI_C, and BO_C, and the costs accumulated due to overtime OT_C. Therefore, short term capacity planning is a complex timing problem due to the cost structure, the non-linearity of the system and its' periodicity. In this paper we test three different short term capacity planing approaches: (i) three different static benchmarks which either plan with no overtime at all (no_OT) or fix the number of overtime-hours to 2, 4 or 8 (OT_2, OT_4 and OT_8 respectively). (ii) two random mechanisms which randomly choose between either zero, two and four ($OT\_Ran\_0\_2\_4$) or zero, four and eight overtime-hours ($OT\_Ran\_0\_4\_8$) and (iii) one reinforcement learning algorithm. For the later we use the Proximal Policy Optimization (PPO) algorithm of [24], which is an actor-critic policy gradient method that learns from its interaction with the environment. The policy (actor) and state-action function (critic) are represented by an artificial neural network (ANN) while parallel agents gather multiple consecutive experiences of the environment before each update, similar to n-step Q-Learning [12]. Algorithm 1 presents the PPO algorithm. There are N actors that compute the advantage estimates on the old policy $\pi_{\theta_{old}}$. Therefore, PPO maintains a state value function $V(s, a)$ and a policy function $\pi_\theta(s, a)$. The former evaluates each state-action pair (s, a) by a scalar value by means of the returned reward in the steps after visiting this state action pair, while the later describes the probability to choose the given action a in state s. Using the state value evaluation of T consecutively visited states an advantage is calculated that forms the basis of the policy function update: $\hat{A}_t = -V(s_t, a_t) + \sum_{i=0}^{T-1} \gamma^i r_{t+i} + \gamma^T V(s_{t+T}, a_{t+T})$, where r_t is the returned reward at time step t and $0 < \gamma < 1$ the discount factor.

In particular the advantage estimates for each time step of the agents, computed with the returned rewards and state values, form the surrogate loss. In the most intuitive way this is $L_t(\theta) = r_t(\theta)\hat{A}_t$ with the probability ratio $r_t(\theta) = \frac{\pi_\theta(a_t|s_t)}{\pi_{\theta_{old}}(a_t|s_t)}$. Hence, it is a simple form of trust region policy optimisation [23]. Therefore, the more stochastic the policy function in regard to the last policy $\pi_{\theta_{old}}$ the smaller the probability ratio $r_t(\theta)$, as well as the better the value function describes the actual expected discounted future reward the smaller the advantages $\hat{A}_t$ and therefore the surrogate loss, i.e. updates to the policy. We set the discount factor $\gamma = 0.99$ throughout the paper and furthermore use clipping with $\epsilon = 0.2$, for the updates to prevent diverging policies. The loss is back-propagated through the artificial neural network by the Adam optimiser with default parameterisation [8]. We use this algorithm with 2048 experiences between each update with minibatch size 64 and 10 learning epochs on each policy improvement. Overall the policy is trained for 1 million periods.

4 Results

The length of each simulation run was 8000 periods including a warm-up period of 1000 periods and each scenario was run for 30 replications. Table 1 shows the results of the evaluations. The first column denotes the tested short term capacity planning approaches, namely (i) the static approaches are either denoted as OT_k where k represents the set number of overtime-hours or No_OT which plans no overtime at all, (ii) the random overtime approaches $OT\_Ran\_0\_2\_4$ and $OT\_Ran\_0\_4\_8$ which randomly decide whether overtime will be planned or not and (iii) the used RL algorithm denoted as either $PPO\_0\_2\_4$ or $PPO\_0\_4\_8$ depending on the set of valid actions the agent can execute. Column two to six depict the cost-based performance measures in Dollars: the Total Costs, the costs for held finished goods inventory (FGI_C), backorder costs (BO_C), costs for overtime-hours (OT_C) and WIP inventory holding costs (WIP_C). Finally, the last column shows the service level denoted as SL (%) reached in percent which is defined as the percentage of orders that were finished before their due date. The mean of the performance measures are compared and tested using a Wilcoxon signed-rank test at a significance level of $p = 0.05$. All values in Table 1 marked with an asterisk are not significantly different from the best performing model.

One can see that the two RL algorithms ($PPO\_0\_2\_4$ and $PPO\_0\_4\_8$) perform best regarding total costs. The best performing RL algorithm ($PPO\_0\_4\_8$) yields only 80.54% and 80.25% of total costs in comparison to the best static (OT_2) and random approach ($OT\_Ran\_0\_2\_4$) respectively. This is mainly due to the savings in overtime costs where the best RL algorithm yields less than a third of the other two approaches. Furthermore, it is noteworthy that the WIP costs of the RL algorithms are rather high, only the WIP_C of No_OT are higher. This shows that the RL algorithms seems to find a good balance between highly utilized machines while maintaining good due date adherence.

Table 1. Costs and service levels of the tested short term capacity planning models, sorted by total costs

Model	Total cost	FGI_C	BO_C	OT_C	WIP_C	SL (%)
$PPO\_0\_4\_8$	411,234	259,577	66,896	34,450	50,312	93%
$PPO\_0\_2\_4$	417,765*	264,294*	66,369*	37,874*	49,228*	93%*
OT_2	510,609	300,218	57,585	112,000	40,806	94%*
$OT\_Ran\_0\_2\_4$	512,461	297,130	61,735	111,810	41,785	93%*
No_OT	587,826	173,770	312,342	0	101,715	66%
$OT\_Ran\_0\_4\_8$	614,014	340,668	19,972	224,183	29,190	98%
OT_4	614,832	347,913	15,572	224,000	27,347	98%
OT_8	853,620	384,561	3,261	448,000	17,798	100%

*not significant different

5   Conclusion

Short term capacity planning can have a huge impact on the company performance. For this operative task a dynamic model is needed to react to the dynamic production system. Therefore, this paper analyzes the potential of smart short term capacity planning models, more precisely we test a reinforcement learning (RL) model on this task. We use a simulation of a three-stage make-to-order job-shop and compare its performance to simple benchmark heuristics. Performance is measured by total costs consisting of holding, backorder and overtime costs and the service level which is defined as the percentage of orders finished before its' due date. The results show that the RL algorithm yields the lowest total costs which is mainly due to savings regarding overtime costs.

The main limitations of our study are threefold: (i) the results and findings are only limited to simulated case, (ii) while a promising RL algorithm was tested, there are others that might be even better suited for this task, e.g., [20] presents a very promising RL algorithm for capacity planning and (iii) our experimental design should be extended: First, by testing different demand and processing time distributions and second by comparing the performance of a RL algorithm to state-of-the-art approaches using optimization models such as [15] or [1]. Third, including more sophisticated order release models [4,5,22] to test the interrelation with order release planning is an interesting direction for future research.

References

1. Chen, C.S., Mestry, S., Damodaran, P., Wang, C.: The capacity planning problem in make-to-order enterprises. Math. Comput. Model. **50**(9–10), 1461–1473 (2009)
2. Das, T.K., Gosavi, A., Mahadevan, S., Marchalleck, N.: Solving semi-Markov decision problems using average reward reinforcement learning. Manag. Sci. **45**(4), 560–574 (1999)
3. Gabel, T., Riedmiller, M.: Distributed policy search reinforcement learning for job-shop scheduling tasks. Int. J. Prod. Res. **50**(1), 41–61 (2012)

4. Haeussler, S., Netzer, P.: Comparison between rule-and optimization-based workload control concepts: a simulation optimization approach. Int. J. Prod. Res. **58**(12), 3724–3743 (2020)
5. Haeussler, S., Schneckenreither, M., Gerhold, C.: Adaptive order release planning with dynamic lead times. IFAC-PapersOnLine **52**(13), 1890–1895 (2019)
6. Hessel, M., et al.: Rainbow: combining improvements in deep reinforcement learning. In: Proceedings of the AAAI Conference on Artificial Intelligence, vol. 32 (2018)
7. Jaramillo, F., Erkoc, M.: Minimizing total weighted tardiness and overtime costs for single machine preemptive scheduling. Comput. Ind. Eng. **107**, 109–119 (2017)
8. Kingma, D.P., Ba, J.: Adam: a method for stochastic optimization. arXiv preprint arXiv:1412.6980 (2014)
9. Kuhnle, A., Röhrig, N., Lanza, G.: Autonomous order dispatching in the semiconductor industry using reinforcement learning. Procedia CIRP **79**, 391–396 (2019). https://doi.org/10.1016/j.procir.2019.02.101. 12th CIRP Conference on Intelligent Computation in Manufacturing Engineering, 18-20 July 2018, Gulf of Naples, Italy
10. Kuhnle, A., Schäfer, L., Stricker, N., Lanza, G.: Design, implementation and evaluation of reinforcement learning for an adaptive order dispatching in job shop manufacturing systems. Procedia CIRP **81**, 234–239 (2019)
11. Land, M.J., Stevenson, M., Thürer, M., Gaalman, G.J.: Job shop control: in search of the key to delivery improvements. Int. J. Prod. Econ. **168**, 257–266 (2015)
12. Mnih, V., et al.: Asynchronous methods for deep reinforcement learning. In: International Conference on Machine Learning, pp. 1928–1937. PMLR (2016)
13. Mnih, V., et al.: Human-level control through deep reinforcement learning. Nature **518**(7540), 529–533 (2015)
14. Olhager, J., Rudberg, M., Wikner, J.: Long-term capacity management: linking the perspectives from manufacturing strategy and sales and operations planning. Int. J. Prod. Econ. **69**(2), 215–225 (2001)
15. Ornek, A., Cengiz, O.: Capacitated lot sizing with alternative routings and overtime decisions. Int. J. Prod. Res. **44**(24), 5363–5389 (2006)
16. Paternina-Arboleda, C.D., Das, T.K.: Intelligent dynamic control policies for serial production lines. IIE Trans. **33**(1), 65–77 (2001)
17. Paternina-Arboleda, C.D., Das, T.K.: A multi-agent reinforcement learning approach to obtaining dynamic control policies for stochastic lot scheduling problem. Simul. Model. Pract. Theory **13**(5), 389–406 (2005)
18. Qu, S., Wang, J., Govil, S., Leckie, J.O.: Optimized adaptive scheduling of a manufacturing process system with multi-skill workforce and multiple machine types: an ontology-based, multi-agent reinforcement learning approach. Procedia CIRP **57**, 55–60 (2016)
19. Russell, S., Norvig, P.: Artificial Intelligence: A Modern Approach. Prentice Hall, Upper Saddle River (2002)
20. Schneckenreither, M.: Average reward adjusted discounted reinforcement learning: near-blackwell-optimal policies for real-world applications. arXiv preprint arXiv:2004.00857 (2020)
21. Schneckenreither, M., Haeussler, S.: Reinforcement learning methods for operations research applications: the order release problem. In: Nicosia, G., Pardalos, P., Giuffrida, G., Umeton, R., Sciacca, V. (eds.) LOD 2018. LNCS, vol. 11331, pp. 545–559. Springer, Cham (2019). https://doi.org/10.1007/978-3-030-13709-0_46
22. Schneckenreither, M., Haeussler, S., Gerhold, C.: Order release planning with predictive lead times: a machine learning approach. Int. J. Prod. Res. **59**(11), 3285–3303 (2021)

23. Schulman, J., Levine, S., Abbeel, P., Jordan, M., Moritz, P.: Trust region policy optimization. In: International Conference on Machine Learning, pp. 1889–1897. PMLR (2015)
24. Schulman, J., Wolski, F., Dhariwal, P., Radford, A., Klimov, O.: Proximal policy optimization algorithms. arXiv preprint arXiv:1707.06347 (2017)
25. Sutton, R.S., Barto, A.G., et al.: Introduction to Reinforcement Learning, vol. 135. MIT Press, Cambridge (1998)
26. Wang, Y.C., Usher, J.M.: A reinforcement learning approach for developing routing policies in multi-agent production scheduling. Int. J. Adv. Manuf. Technol. **33**(3–4), 323–333 (2007)
27. Wortman, J., Euwe, M., Taal, M., Wiers, V.: A review of capacity planning techniques within standard software packages. Prod. Plan. Control **7**(2), 117–128 (1996)
28. Yang, B., Geunes, J., O'Brien, W.J.: A heuristic approach for minimizing weighted tardiness and overtime costs in single resource scheduling. Comput. Oper. Res. **31**(8), 1273–1301 (2004)
29. Yuan, R., Graves, S.C.: Setting optimal production lot sizes and planned lead times in a job shop. Int. J. Prod. Res. **54**(20), 6105–6120 (2016)
30. Zhang, W., Dietterich, T.G.: A reinforcement learning approach to job-shop scheduling. IJCAI **95**, 1114–1120 (1995)
31. Zhang, W., Dietterich, T.G.: High-performance job-shop scheduling with a time-delay TD (λ) network. In: Advances in Neural Information Processing Systems, pp. 1024–1030 (1996)

Reactive Scheduling by Intelligent DSS

Yumin He[1(✉)], Yaohu Lin[1], Hongbo Liu[2], and Mengpeng Guo[3]

[1] Beihang University, Beijing 100191, People's Republic of China
heyumin@buaa.edu.cn
[2] Avic Chengdu Civil Aircraft Co., Ltd., Sichuan 610000, People's Republic of China
[3] Beijing Shuguang Aviation Electric Co., Ltd., Beijing 101300, People's Republic of China

Abstract. Agile manufacturing is in practice by many companies. In agile manufacturing environments, it is important for companies to make quick response to the changes in the environments. This paper proposes an intelligent decision support system (DSS) for reactive scheduling to handle disturbances in agile manufacturing environments. The intelligent decision support system integrates a knowledge-based system for intelligent and multiple criteria decision-making. The intelligent DSS includes three basic modules, the database module, the model base module, and the interface module. The framework of the intelligent DSS is presented. The objective-oriented data model, the knowledge-based rules, and rule induction are designed. The reactive scheduling algorithm is developed. Radio frequency identification and knowledge acquisition tools are applied by the intelligent DSS. The intelligent DSS can be implemented by applying contemporary information technology and can provide an approach to make reactive production scheduling decisions quickly to handle disturbances for manufacturing firms to obtain competitive advantage and agility.

Keywords: Reactive scheduling · Multi-criteria decision making · Decision support system · Inductive learning · Knowledge-based System · Agile manufacturing

1 Introduction

Agile manufacturing provides a new way for new challenges and wants companies to react quickly to customer demands and market changes [1]. In manufacturing and supply chain environments, disturbances may occur, such as a machine failure, job priority changes, unavailable materials, and so forth [2, 3]. Therefore, companies have to react quickly to environment changes to obtain competitive advantage and agility.

This paper considers a production scheduling problem with disturbances in agile manufacturing environments. The shop floor contains multiple resources to produce orders. The suitability and availability of the resources are not guaranteed. Disturbances occur in the shop floor and reactive scheduling is applied. An intelligent DSS is proposed. The approach applies the technology of database and knowledge base.

© IFIP International Federation for Information Processing 2021
Published by Springer Nature Switzerland AG 2021
A. Dolgui et al. (Eds.): APMS 2021, IFIP AICT 630, pp. 267–274, 2021.
https://doi.org/10.1007/978-3-030-85874-2_28

Researchers have studied reactive scheduling. For example, Du and Chiou [2] proposed a reactive scheduling architecture based on objective-oriented database technology. They applied version management of an object-oriented database, demonstrated the different types strategies for reactive scheduling, and considered two types of unexpected events.

Sauer [4] studied vertical data integration that used data from a shop floor. The vertical data integration was made for scheduling decisions on higher levels so as to support reactive scheduling in supply chains.

Paprocka and Skołud [3] proposed a hybrid multi-objective immune algorithm for predictive and reactive scheduling. Their approach applied heuristics to minimize the impact of disrupted operations on scheduling. Their approach considered and predicted time of failure and used maintenance work into a schedule.

2   Intelligent DSS for Reactive Scheduling

Agile manufacturing is in practice by many companies. Information technology is suggested for agile manufacturing practices to obtain competitive advantage and agility [5].

The decision support system (DSS) is part of information technology/information system and mainly contains a database management system, a model base system, and a user interface system [6]. An decision support system can support decision-making in many situations such as production planning, inventory control, and so forth [6].

The knowledge-based system (KBS) has been employed in computer-based decision-making. Two primary approaches utilizing KBSs are the use of KBSs directly as a type of DSSs and the integration of KBSs with conventional DSSs [7].

In this paper, an intelligent decision support system is proposed for reactive scheduling in agile manufacturing environments. The intelligent DSS integrates a knowledge-based system to make intelligent decisions. Customers and the shop floor are in the Internet environments. The intelligent DSS includes mainly three modules, the database module, the model base module, and the interface module.

The architecture of the intelligent DSS is illustrated in Fig. 1. RFID technology is the significant advance in managing dynamic systems, which contains the components of tags attached to the objects to be identified [8]. Tools in the DSS includes knowledge acquisition tools, RFID tag identification tools, FRID information processing tools, and other tools. Services include web servers, DNS servers, ONS servers, database servers, and other servers.

3   Components in Intelligent DSS

3.1   Object-Oriented Data Model

Object-oriented database technology has been applied in reactive scheduling [2]. An object-oriented data model is developed for the database model of the intelligent DSS. Figure 2 shows the object-oriented data model. In the figure, primary and foreign keys of an entity are expressed by underlines and stars, respectively. A crow's foot is used to express one to many relationships. Optional and mandatory relationships are expressed by circles and bars, respectively [9].

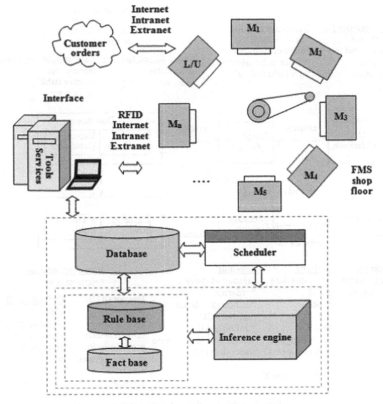

Fig. 1. Architecture of the intelligent DSS.

3.2 Reactive Rules

The rule base, fact base, and inference engine are designed for the model management module. Researchers have considered disturbances in shop floor such as machine breakdowns, lack of materials, and so forth [2, 3]. The disturbances considered are newly added machines, machine breakdowns, and rushed orders. Knowledge-based rules are developed to handle disturbances.

The production scheduling problem is a multiple criteria decision-making (MCDM) problem. A additive utility function is applied [10]. Notation used to describe the rules is listed in Table 1. The rules developed in the rule base include the following.

Rule 1. If $m = \{no\} \rightarrow s = \{no\}$;

Rule 2. If $t_n \geq 4$ and $m = \{new\} \rightarrow s = \{new\}$;

Rule 3. If $f_o \geq 90\%$ and $m = \{new\} \rightarrow s = \{new\}$;

Rule 4. If $t_n \geq 4 \rightarrow s = \{no\}$;

Rule 5. If $f_o \geq 90\% \rightarrow s = \{no\}$;

Rule 6. If $t_n < 4$ and $f_o < 90\% \rightarrow s = \{new\}$;

Rule 7. If $d = \{added\} \rightarrow r = \{1\}$;

Rule 8. If $d = \{broken\} \rightarrow r = \{0\}$;

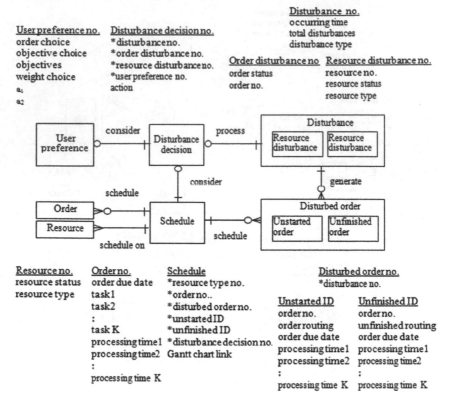

User preference no.
order choice
objective choice
objectives
weight choice
a_1
a_2

Disturbance decision no.
*disturbance no.
*order disturbance no.
*resource disturbance no.
*user preference no.
action

Disturbance no.
occurring time
total disturbances
disturbance type

Order disturbance no.
order status
order no.

Resource disturbance no.
resource no.
resource status
resource type

Resource no.
resource status
resource type

Order no.
order due date
task 1
task 2
:
task K
processing time 1
processing time 2
:
processing time K

Schedule
*resource type no.
*order no..
*disturbed order no.
*unstarted ID
*unfinished ID
*disturbance decision no.
Gantt chart link

Disturbed order no.
*disturbance no.

Unstarted ID
order no.
order routing
order due date
processing time 1
processing time 2
:
processing time K

Unfinished ID
order no.
unfinished routing
order due date
processing time 1
processing time 2
:
processing time K

Fig. 2. Object-oriented data model.

Rule 9. If $d = \{rushed\} \rightarrow o = \{1\}$;
Rule 10. If $c = \{user\} \rightarrow$ obtain a_1 and a_2 from a user;
Rule 11. If $a_1 \neq 0$ and $a_2 \neq 0 \rightarrow U = a_1 u_1(x_1) + a_2 u_2(x_2)$;
Rule 12. If $a_1 \neq 0$ and $a_2 = 0 \rightarrow U = a_1 u_1(x_1)$;
Rule 13. If $a_1 = 0$ and $a_2 \neq 0 \rightarrow U = a_2 u_2(x_2)$.

The system status and manager can be one parameter in the set of 'no' and 'new'. The 'no' means not to change the current schedule. The 'new' means to change the current schedule to a new schedule. For example, if $f_o \geq 90\%$ and $m = \{new\}$ in Rule 3. The rule gives the status of the shop floor with the total orders finished are larger than 90% and the manager decides to change to a new schedule. This rule results in the formulation of a new schedule by the system when the status occurs. When a disturbance occurs, the status of the shop floor is monitored and checked. The DSS can apply the rules to result in appropriate decisions.

3.3 Rule Induction

Rule induction is conducted in handling disturbances in the inference engine. Inductive learning ability is designed. The mechanism of rule induction is illustrated in Fig. 3. First,

Table 1. Notation for rules.

Symbol	Description
d	Disturbance type, $d \in \{added, broken, rushed\}$
tn	Total disturbances
fo	Total orders finished
s	System status, $s \in \{no, new\}$
m	Manage $r, m \in \{no, new\}$
o	Order, $o \in \{0, 1\}$
r	Resource, $r \in \{0, 1\}$
c	Weight choice, $c \in \{user, system\}$
U	Additive utility function
$u_1(x_1)$	Utility function 1
$u_2(x_2)$	Utility function 2
$a1$	Weight for $u_1(x_1)$
$a2$	Weight for $u_2(x_2)$

the fact base and the rule base are formed. The next step is the reasoning recurrence of resolving facts to obtain sub-facts, matching facts to obtain candidate rules, and matching rules to obtain candidate facts. If there are disturbances in the shop floor, the fact base is automatically updated. After the reasoning recurrence is accomplished, the rule base is automatically updated.

4   Reactive Scheduling Algorithm

The production scheduling problem is an MCDM problem. The additive utility function is applied to the problem as stated before. The objective of the problem is described in the following. Symbols used are provided in Table 1.

$$\text{Min} \quad U = a_1 u_1(x_1) + a_2 u_2(x_2)$$
$$0 \le a_1 \le 1, 0 \le a_2 \le 1, a_1 + a_2 = 1. \tag{1}$$

The reactive scheduling algorithm is developed. Resources are used to perform a group of tasks which belong to manufacturing orders having their processing routings, processing times, and due dates. Symbols used in the algorithm are described in Table 2. The pseudo code of the algorithm is presented in the following.

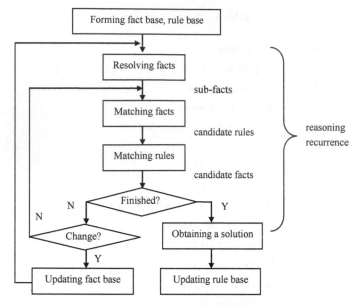

Fig. 3. Mechanism of rule induction.

Table 2. Symbol for algorithm.

Symbol	Description
i'	Resource type
I'	Total resource types
k	Operation
K	Total operations
j	Order
i	Resource
$\varnothing$	Empty set
tm	Temporary storage
tr	Temporary storage

Reactive Scheduling Algorithm

$i' \leftarrow 1$;
$k \leftarrow 1$;
while $k < K$ do
$t_m \leftarrow$ orders of operation k;
   while $i' < I$ do
   $t_r \leftarrow$ orders $\in t_m$ and to be assigned to resource type i';
      while $t_r \neq \emptyset$ do
      $j \leftarrow$ orders $\in t_r$ and having minimal U by Equation (1);
      $i \leftarrow$ resource having the same type of i' and having the earliest
      available time;
      assign j to i;
      remove j from t_r;
      remove j from t_m;
      end
   $i' = i' + 1$;
   end
$k = k + 1$;
end

The algorithm is to make new schedules immediately and continuously according to current situations of the shop floor. The information such as disturbance occurring times and other relevant data can be obtained through a monitoring system. The DSS processes these information and other information to analyze the status of the shop floor. The monitoring system can utilize information technology such as RFID that is the significant advance in managing dynamic systems as described before.

In the intelligent DSS, the algorithm, the knowledge-based rules, the inference engine work together to make intelligent decisions for handling disturbances. The reactive rules are applied by the DSS to make decisions on if a new schedule needs to be developed or not. The rules are updated after disturbances occur. Once the DSS makes a decision of formulating a new schedule, this reactive algorithm is applied to make a new schedule.

5 Conclusion

This paper proposes an intelligent DSS for reactive scheduling to handle disturbances in agile manufacturing environments. The proposed approach applies information technology, which is different from many traditional production scheduling approaches. The objective-oriented data model, the knowledge-based rules, and the rule induction mechanism are designed. The reactive scheduling algorithm is developed.

In agile manufacturing environments, it is important for manufacturing firms to react quickly in the changing environments for agility. The intelligent DSS can be implemented by applying contemporary information technology. It could provide an approach for reactive scheduling to handle disturbances for manufacturing firms to obtain competitive advantage and agility.

Acknowledgment. The authors would like to thank the session chair and the referees for the efforts and valuable comments.

References

1. Singh, P.L., et al.: Evaluation of common barriers to the combined lean-green-agile manufacturing system by two-way assessment method. In: Shanker, K., et al. (eds.) Advances in Industrial and Production Engineering, LNME, pp. 653–672 (2019)
2. Du, T.C., Chiou, R.J.: Applying version management of object-oriented database technology in reactive scheduling. Int. J. Prod. Res. **38**, 1183–1200 (2000)
3. Paprocka, I., Skołud, B.: A hybrid multi-objective immune algorithm for predictive and reactive scheduling. J. Sched. **20**(2), 165–182 (2017). https://doi.org/10.1007/s10951-016-0494-9
4. Sauer, J.: Vertical data integration for reactive scheduling. Künstl Intell. **24**, 123–129 (2010)
5. Rao, J.J., Kumar, V.: Technology adoption in the SME sector for promoting agile manufacturing practices. In: Satapathy, S.C., Bhateja, V., Das, S. (eds.) Smart Intelligent Computing and Applications. SIST, vol. 105, pp. 659–665. Springer, Singapore (2019). https://doi.org/10.1007/978-981-13-1927-3_69
6. Vargas, A., Boza, A., Patel, S., Patel, D., Cuenca, L., Ortiz, A.: Inter-enterprise architecture as a tool to empower decision-making in hierarchical collaborative production planning. Data Knowl. Eng. **105**, 5–22 (2016)
7. Ho, T.B.: Rule induction in constructing knowledge-based decision support. In: Decision Support Systems for Sustainable Development, a Source Book of Methods and Applications, International Development Research Center and Kluwer Academic Publishers, pp. 263–270 (2000)
8. Dolgui, A., Proth, J.-M.: Special section on radio frequency identification. IEEE Trans. Ind. Inf. **8**, 688 (2012)
9. Simsion, G.C.: Data Modeling Essentials, Analysis, Design, and Innovation, the Coriolis Groups (2001)
10. Ballestero, E., Romero, C.: Multiple Criteria Decision Making and Its Applications to Economic Problems, Kluwer Academic Publishers (1998)

Worker in the Loop: A Framework for Enabling Human-Robot Collaborative Assembly

Eleni Tzavara, Panagiotis Angelakis, George Veloudis, Christos Gkournelos⬤,
and Sotiris Makris(✉)⬤

Laboratory for Manufacturing Systems and Automation (LMS), Department of Mechanical
Engineering and Aeronautics, University of Patras, 26504 Patras, Greece
makris@lms.mech.upatras.gr

Abstract. Industry has taken a big leap forward by placing a human in the center of interest by turning the working areas into a collaborative environment between operators and robots. In this environment, human behavior is a major uncertainty factor that can affect operator's safety and execution status. Furthermore, the creation of a digital twin including the whole workstation area, the operators and the procedures that take part in there, is a way to design and integrate collaborative systems using a virtual space. This paper aims to overview the current state of the technological trends in human detection, human task monitoring and digital twin integration. Also, the design of the upcoming solution of a case study from the automotive industry will be represented.

Keywords: Human-robot collaboration · Human task monitoring · Digital twin · Robot behavior

1 Introduction

In the existing assembly systems, the ability to offer more variants per model and introduce new models faster is limited by the current technologies and equipment of mass production processes, which are incapable of supporting product diversity [1]. One of the most promising approaches over the last years is to increase the sensitivity of the production system to internal and external changes. Several paradigms such as flexible [2], reconfigurable [3], lean [4], holonic [5], self organizing [6] assembly systems have been realized in the last decades to meet these requirements.

In the last years, hybrid production systems [7], that combines flexibility and reconfigurability, enabling the collaboration between humans and robots is gaining increasing interest by the research community and the industrial world [8]. The desired result from creating human-robot collaborative environments is to utilize in their full extent the skills of human operators such ass intelligence and cognitive capabilities supporting them through robot's strength and dexterity. The main concept is that in a shared workplace, several tasks are assigned to operators and robots following a production order. Those tasks' instructions must be followed strictly. There are numerous issues though,

© IFIP International Federation for Information Processing 2021
Published by Springer Nature Switzerland AG 2021
A. Dolgui et al. (Eds.): APMS 2021, IFIP AICT 630, pp. 275–283, 2021.
https://doi.org/10.1007/978-3-030-85874-2_29

that need to be addressed to create a completely human-friendly working environment in the manufacture [9].

The major factor that is mainly unpredictable in such a collaborative environment, is human behavior, which can cause changes or issues in both production execution and safety. To ensure the prevention of issues in the production line, human detection, and task prevision are crucial. Last decades there is extended research on human modeling and monitoring [10]. In terms of monitoring the execution of human tasks, Andrianakos et al. [11] proposed a solution for monitoring the execution of human tasks. This solution is based on object detection and hand detection using in parallel machine learning techniques. Another way to achieve human modeling was proposed by M. Urgo et al. [12] combining a human pose estimation with a statistical model for operator's task identification. In [13] researchers suggested a solution based on the Dynamic Time Wrapping (DTW) algorithm, which is based on the measurement of similarity between two temporal sequences. Similar approach, we can see in [14]. In this work a product assembly task has been modeled as a sequence of human motions and the human motion prediction problem is solved by Hidden Markov Model (HMM).

In parallel with human task monitoring, robot behavior may need to be adapted to its current state. Considering many cases in which something can change the predefined robots' trajectory, it is clear that the adaptation is crucial for both human safety and task execution [15]. This need for adaptation leads to the creation of a virtual representation of the system that can monitor the behavior of the involved resources [16]. The use of the Digital Twin (DT) concept has gained a lot of attention given the advantages that it may offer towards more autonomous and intelligent systems [17]. This technology has promising results and seems to be compulsory component in smart manufacturing systems [18].

As previously stated, the current level of technology allows for a rather advanced model of Human Robot Collaboration (HRC). Different ways of human detection and task monitoring have been developed in recent years, which in conjunction with Digital Twins could lead to a flexible, reconfigurable, and safe production system. This paper presents a framework that includes the design of the abovementioned components for enabling the synergy between humans and robots in flexible manufacturing systems. The desirable solution will be deployed in an assembly use case from the automotive industry. The paper is organized as follows: Sect. 2 describes the main approach and the design of the framework; in Sect. 3, the way that the whole framework will be implemented is analyzed; Sect. 4 presents the automotive case study in which this work will be deployed and finally Sect. 5 reports the conclusion and the future work.

2   Approach

Following the aforementioned challenges in the creation of a collaborative and at the same time safe workplace, a framework will be presented in the current work that aims to include the workers in the control loop of the production with robots. Figure 1 presents the conceptual architecture of the proposed framework. The whole procedure is represented as a loop that starts and ends with the human worker.

The two modules that extract information from the worker are the Human Body Detection (HBD) and Human Task Prediction (HTP). These are capturing the data from different types of sensors, such as 3D vision sensors 2D laser scanners and wearable IMUs. The output data from those two modules alongside with the robot state, become inputs in the DT module which is responsible for informing Assembly Execution Controller and also Human side interfaces. More specifically, Human side interfaces are informed from the DT about human's and robot's current task and give feedback to the human. The loop ends when the operator is notified about errors in the assembly, execution status of the whole procedure, and warnings regarding human safety.

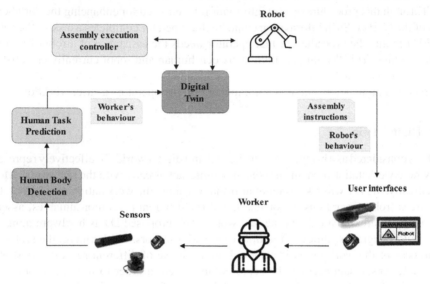

Fig. 1. Worker in the loop of Human-Robot collaborative assembly

2.1 Human Body Detection

The detection of human existence is a mandatory component in a H-R collaborative assembly system for ensuring the safety of the operator. Aiming beyond the standard means of safety detection that causes emergency stops on robots when the worker is near, advanced information is needed alongside with direct interface with robot trajectory execution. Robot follows a predefined trajectory in order to execute its task. By detecting the accurate position of the operator, it must be ready to adjust the trajectory to avoid the operator and ensure human's safety. Beyond safety of operator, replan of robot's trajectory can lead to a more efficient production, since the stoppage time of emergency is eliminated. HBD provides more detailed information regarding the human body posture and position on the workspace. 2D and 3D data are fused for providing the position of the whole human body.

2.2 Human Task Prediction

In the actual assembly line, operators and robots follow a predefined order of tasks. While the tasks that are executed by robots can be monitored, human processes cannot be fully tracked. Operators have several degrees of freedom which means that the way a task is executed, defers from person to person. In addition to this, an operator can make additional moves such as touch his head or adjust his uniform. This is a deviation from the predefined order of actions which should not be considered an error. This component aims to predict human intention and task status taking into consideration the different ways a task can be executed and also the minor deviations that may occur during execution. In order to be able to deal with the uncertainties and the noise in the measurements HTP module consists of probabilistic models.

Through this procedure, useful information is retrieved for enhancing the collaboration of the worker. Such information could be that operator completes a task so the robot could continue the procedure or that operator needs the assistance of a robot for completing a task. This "communication" between human and robot currently established through buttons that directly informs the system about the worker's status. HTP provides indirect communication, and it is not imposing on the operators a strict workflow.

2.3 Digital Twin

A DT is considered as a bridge between the real and digital world. To effectively represent the whole workstation area this module must interact directly with the real world. More specifically, the DT will take as input information about the workstation area layout, the resources (robot operations, robot state), and the different parts (consumables, assembly parts, fixtures) that exist in the real world. The proposed DT is hardware agnostic and could integrate seamlessly multiple robots and sensors. Furthermore, the real-time awareness of the workstation is achieved with the use of different sensors. As shown in Fig. 1, sensor data needs to be captured and fitted in order to provide information for keeping up to date with the digital models. Apart from retrieving data, DT provides feedback to the operators through User Interfaces. The operator is informed about the execution status, robot's tasks, warnings, and errors that may occur in the assembly.

3 Implementation

As described in Sect. 2, the whole framework consists of three modules that need to be implemented, HBD, HTP, and DT. The implementation is based on ROS [19] principles. Each of the included modules is implemented as ROS nodes which exchange information by using the ROS interfaces (topics, services, actions). The initial setup of the collaborative workplace consists of a stationary 3D camera placed in front of the operator, to have good visual coverage of the human, and four IMU sensors attached on the operator's hands.

HBD requires the use of a 3D data in order to detect the operator's position. Skeleton tracking is a complicated aspect that is solved with the use of OpenPose [20] which is a real-time software that detects multi-person human body-parts key points such as hands, legs, core, and head which are provided in a quite accurate approach. Since OpenPose provides only 2D detection, the use of an algorithm that synchronizes these body parts with a Point Cloud (PCL) is used to extract the 3D location of these points Fig. 2 presents

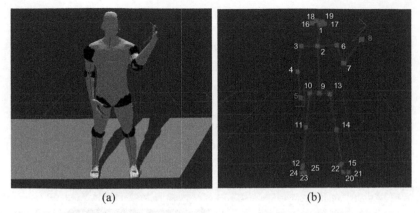

(a)   (b)

Fig. 2. a) Pointcloud data combined with skeleton information b) detected skeleton points.

the extracted result first using only the OpenPose and then the combination of OpenPose with Pointcloud.

The HBD provides information about 25 human body key points. Focusing on tasks that are performed with hands the HTP module extracts the positions of human wrists from points 5 (right hand) and 8 (left hand). Additionally, the operator is equipped with two IMUs on his wrists. These sensors smooth the detected body parts coming from the HBD and most usefully augment these parts' 3D position with orientation information in the form of quaternions.

The HTP module apart from the data that is captured from the human, uses semantic information from the workplace. The workstation is divided into several schematic areas which are labelled according to heuristic knowledge on use case. Examples of such areas could be "kitting" areas, "assembly table" "machines' fixtures" etc. The combination of the abovementioned extracted information is fed into a probabilistic Hidden Markov Model (HMM) that achieves human task monitoring. The use of this model requires state modelling. An example of this modelling for a "Pick-n-Place" task presented in Table 1.

In Fig. 3 it is provided to the left the simulation environment of observation "O1" and its DT on the right. Simulation environment is built in GAZEBO physics simulation [21]. By combining the output data from HBD, HTD, and the robot state, DT is responsible for informing operator about the current state of the assembly. More specific ROS services and actions are sent to the operator as actions or goals in order to inform him about the assigned task or warnings. DT also provides interfaces for robot integration and connection with external software that will monitor the production system. These will be detailed described on future publications.

Table 1. Observation table of HMM for a Pick-n-Place task

Observation	Description
s	Initial state
O1	Grab cylinder
O2	Pick cylinder
O3	Place cylinder
t	End of "pick and place"

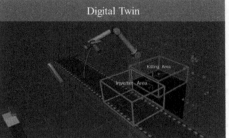

Fig. 3. DT representation alongside with the simulation environment

4   Automotive Case Study

The proposed framework will be implemented in an automotive mechanical plant at the production line of the electric motors. This use case is focusing on the assembly of the inverter with the e-motor. The e-motors are transferred in the specific workstation on a conveyor and inverters are stored on a kitting area inside the workstation. The inverter needs to be placed on the e-motor and screwed with eight screws. A robot and an operator is allocated on this workstation for carrying the assembly tasks. The main goal of this implementation is seamless human-robot collaborate, the dynamic allocation of tasks to each resource for maximizing the production efficiency always ensuring the operator's safety.

For the initial testing of our developments a simple pick and place scenario has been deployed. This scenario includes a block with twelve holes that travels on the conveyor and a kitting area with cylinders that should be placed inside the holes. Both human worker and robot is suitable to pick and place these cylinders. Robot is aware of the execution progress of the operator's task and the human existence. By monitoring the status execution of the human tasks, the robot will be informed about the failure or the completion and it will proceed to its task.

In case the operator misses a task, robot will be informed, and it will execute the task instead of interrupting the whole process. From the other side operator is aware of robot's status and could intervene in case of a failure. The information about next task will be extracted from the DT. To test the whole design described above, an initial scenario has been deployed in GAZEBO simulation as shown the Fig. 4.

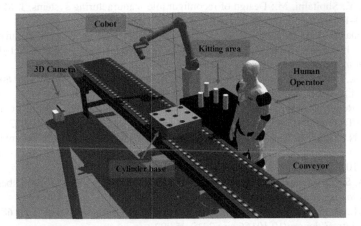

Fig. 4. Automotive case study workstation simulation

5   Conclusion

The latest trends in manufacturing, pose the need to create more human friendly assembly by embracing the Human-Robot collaboration. Reorganization of tasks can lead to a more efficient assembly basically because of the elimination of stoppage time in case of errors. The development and the continuous research on this topic can lead to a more efficient and autonomous assembly. It is also important to mention that those developments can affect the line performance. Driven by this need, an initial description of framework that will improve the H-R collaboration was presented in the previous sections. By the development of this framework, the issues that may occur can be detected and resolved in real time, to prevent adjustment and reschedule of the production plan or the process.

As future plans, we intend to create a testbed in the laboratory for the actual implementation of the design that was described above. Numerous of tests will be executed in order to validate the whole use case on the testbed and also on the actual factory premises.

Acknowledgements. This work has been partially funded by the EC research project "ASSISTANT – Learning and robust decision Support systems for agile manufacturing environments" (Grant Agreement: 101000165) (www.assistant-project.eu).

References

1. Chryssolouris, G.: Manufacturing Systems: Theory and Practice. Springer New York, New York, NY (2006). https://doi.org/10.1007/0-387-28431-1

2. Chryssolouris, G., Georgoulias, K., Michalos, G.: Production systems flexibility: theory and practice. In: IFAC Proceedings Volumes (IFAC-PapersOnline), pp. 15–21. IFAC Secretariat (2012). https://doi.org/10.3182/20120523-3-RO-2023.00442

3. Koren, Y., Shpitalni, M.: Design of reconfigurable manufacturing systems. J. Manuf. Syst. **29**, 130–141 (2010). https://doi.org/10.1016/J.JMSY.2011.01.001

4. Houshmand, M., Jamshidnezhad, B.: An extended model of design process of lean production systems by means of process variables. Robot. Comput. Integr. Manuf. **22**, 1–16 (2006). https://doi.org/10.1016/j.rcim.2005.01.004

5. Giret, A., Botti, V.: Engineering holonic manufacturing systems. Comput. Ind. **60**, 428–440 (2009). https://doi.org/10.1016/j.compind.2009.02.007

6. Scholz-Reiter, B., Freitag, M.: Autonomous processes in assembly systems. CIRP Ann. - Manuf. Technol. **56**, 712–729 (2007). https://doi.org/10.1016/j.cirp.2007.10.002

7. Kousi, N., Michalos, G., Aivaliotis, S., Makris, S.: An outlook on future assembly systems introducing robotic mobile dual arm workers. Procedia CIRP. **72**, 33–38 (2018). https://doi.org/10.1016/j.procir.2018.03.130

8. Makris, S.: Cooperating Robots for Flexible Manufacturing. Springer, Heidelberg (2021). https://doi.org/10.1007/978-3-030-51591-1

9. Wang, L., et al.: Symbiotic human-robot collaborative assembly. CIRP Ann. **68**, 701–726 (2019). https://doi.org/10.1016/j.cirp.2019.05.002

10. Tsarouchi, P., Michalos, G., Makris, S., Athanasatos, T., Dimoulas, K., Chryssolouris, G.: On a human–robot workplace design and task allocation system. Int. J. Comput. Integr. Manuf. **30**, 1272–1279 (2017). https://doi.org/10.1080/0951192X.2017.1307524

11. Andrianakos, G., Dimitropoulos, N., Michalos, G., Makris, S.: An approach for monitoring the execution of human based assembly operations using machine learning. In: Procedia CIRP, pp. 198–203. Elsevier B.V. (2020). https://doi.org/10.1016/j.procir.2020.01.040.

12. Urgo, M., Tarabini, M., Tolio, T.: A human modelling and monitoring approach to support the execution of manufacturing operations. CIRP Ann. **68**, 5–8 (2019). https://doi.org/10.1016/j.cirp.2019.04.052

13. Maderna, R., Lanfredini, P., Zanchettin, A.M., Rocco, P.: Real-time monitoring of human task advancement. IEEE Int. Conf. Intell. Robot. Syst. 433–440 (2019). https://doi.org/10.1109/IROS40897.2019.8967933.

14. Liu, H., Wang, L.: Human motion prediction for human-robot collaboration. J. Manuf. Syst. **44**, 287–294 (2017). https://doi.org/10.1016/j.jmsy.2017.04.009

15. Sankar, S., Tsai, C.Y.: Ros-based human detection and tracking from a wireless controlled mobile robot using kinect. Appl. Syst. Innov. **2**, 1–12 (2019). https://doi.org/10.3390/asi2010005

16. Váncza, J., Monostori, L.: Cyber-physical manufacturing in the light of professor Kanji Ueda's Legacy. In: Procedia CIRP. pp. 631–638. Elsevier B.V. (2017). https://doi.org/10.1016/j.procir.2017.04.059

17. Kousi, N., Gkournelos, C., Aivaliotis, S., Giannoulis, C., Michalos, G., Makris, S.: Digital twin for adaptation of robots' behavior in flexible robotic assembly lines. Procedia Manuf. **28**, 121–126 (2019). https://doi.org/10.1016/J.PROMFG.2018.12.020

18. Alexopoulos, K., Nikolakis, N., Chryssolouris, G.: Digital twin-driven supervised machine learning for the development of artificial intelligence applications in manufacturing. Int. J. Comput. Integr. Manuf. **33**, 429–439 (2020). https://doi.org/10.1080/0951192X.2020.1747642

19. Quigley, M., et al.: ROS: an open-source robot operating system. In: International Conference on Robotics and Automation (2009)

20. Cao, Z., Hidalgo, G., Simon, T., Wei, S.E., Sheikh, Y.: OpenPose: realtime multi-person 2D pose estimation using part affinity fields. IEEE Trans. Pattern Anal. Mach. Intell. **43**, 172–186 (2021). https://doi.org/10.1109/TPAMI.2019.2929257
21. Gazebo Robot Simulation. http://gazebosim.org/.. Accessed 14 Jul 2021

Decision Support on the Shop Floor Using Digital Twins

Architecture and Functional Components for Simulation-Based Assistance

Franz Georg Listl[1,2]([✉]), Jan Fischer[2], Roland Rosen[2], Annelie Sohr[2], Jan C. Wehrstedt[2], and Michael Weyrich[1]

[1] Institute of Automation and Software Engineering, University of Stuttgart, Stuttgart, Germany
[2] Technology Department, Siemens AG, Munich, Germany
{franz.listl,jan.fischer,roland.rosen,annelie.sohr,
janchristoph.wehrstedt}@siemens.com

Abstract. Increased flexibility and improved resilience in production and manufacturing processes are goals that are becoming more and more important in the context of Industry 4.0 and from the experience of the Covid-19 pandemic. At the same time, efficient operation of production must be guaranteed to achieve economic as well as ecological objectives. Intelligent assistance systems follow the idea to support stakeholders of production systems in their decisions and can thus be useful applications for helping to master the various challenges and to meet these goals. In this paper, we describe functional components of these decision support systems: data provision and data extraction, knowledge base, simulation models, model execution and analytics, and application and user interaction. We show the underlying technologies and illustrate why these assistant systems are valuable for several stakeholders.

Keywords: Decision support · Digital Twin · Shop floor management · Simulation

1 Introduction

The optimal operation of automated production systems in the process and manufacturing industry is an ongoing challenge. With the continuous advancements of Industry 4.0, there are more and more opportunities for a more customized and flexible manufacturing of products. Simultaneously, this leads to ever smaller batch sizes and more diverse products with shorter order times and more significant changes in order quantity. In addition to considering quality, time, and cost targets against this backdrop, the flexibility and resilience of the manufacturing processes on the shop floor are therefore inevitably becoming more relevant. Accordingly, the challenges get much more complex with the possibilities of Industry 4.0 and must be solved. Some of these challenges on the shop floor include:

© IFIP International Federation for Information Processing 2021
Published by Springer Nature Switzerland AG 2021
A. Dolgui et al. (Eds.): APMS 2021, IFIP AICT 630, pp. 284–292, 2021.
https://doi.org/10.1007/978-3-030-85874-2_30

- Virtual sensor: Analyze the behavior and monitor states where no sensor is available.
- Forecasting: Predict future behavior, detect undesirable trends, and prevent them.
- Optimizing of the plant operation: Apply optimization methods to improve plant performance.
- Replay of situations: Analyze situations reversely based on recorded values, e.g., for root cause analysis.
- Offline reconfiguration planning based on the current plant state evaluation for reduced downtime.

In this context, our vision of a Digital Twin can solve such problems and covers the entire lifecycle of production systems and products. However, since such solutions have not yet been sufficiently researched and therefore represent future work, in this paper, we focus on the path to our vision and identify essential functional components for decision support on the shop floor.

2 The Vision of Digital Twin in Production

While so far data-based approaches and artificial intelligence (AI) methods dominate in operation phase, simulation is currently primarily used in design and engineering. A simulation model represents the planned real system and calculates its properties or validates its behavior. With the advancement of simulation technology and the available computing power, these simulation models become more detailed and cover more aspects of the system under development. They thus represent a Digital Twin of the planned system, which leads to an extended understanding of the term Digital Twin [1]. The vision of the Digital Twin refers to a virtual representation and a description of a component, product, system, infrastructure, or process by a set of well-aligned, descriptive, and executable models. It is a semantically linked collection of all relevant digital artifacts, including design and engineering data, operational data, and behavioral descriptions. It exists and evolves along the whole life cycle. Digital Twins integrate the currently available and commonly required information and knowledge and is synchronized with the real twin if it exists.

With the understanding of the seamless reuse of simulation models over all phases of system development and their use for virtual commissioning, simulation models will be applied more and more in the operation and service phases in the future [2]. The combined use of rigorous models from simulation - mainly physics-based models in the manufacturing domain - and AI methods that process operational data will facilitate new, more powerful applications. The decision support for the shop floor and its architecture concept shown in this paper are a step towards this ambitious goal.

3 Related Work

The term Digital Twin has been used for several years now. It is still understood very differently, depending on the perspective and its application, but it is always considered a technological approach with potential, as can be seen in [3–5]. One explanation for the different definitions lies in the large variety of physical elements that the Digital Twin can be linked to. It represents the current status of the real system and can be e.g. used for diagnoses [6] but also in applications to improve the performance of manufacturing systems [7]. Hence, different architectures and frameworks for the implementation of Digital Twins and Digital Twin based applications exist. [8] indicates a Digital Twin to consist of three main building blocks: the physical space, the information processing layer, and the virtual space. The information processing contains essential points with data storage, data processing, and data mapping. In [9], a Digital Twin architecture for a manufacturing cell is presented that consists of six layers. These layers are the physical devices, the local controllers, the local data repositories, the IOT gateway, cloud-based information repositories, and emulation and simulation. OPC UA is used as the communication standard over almost all components. In general, these two works only deal to a small extent with the applications and the functionality and logic that makes the implementation of the application possible, but rather deal with the infrastructure required to implement a Digital Twin. Our work starts at this point and focuses on the functionality and components needed to create applications, more precisely decision support systems, based on the Digital Twin.

[10] presents a survey on decision support systems in manufacturing. The authors discuss simulation-based decision support systems in manufacturing as well as approaches integrating simulation and AI methods. On that basis, a theoretical framework for decision support system development, mainly consisting of a simulation model, a database, an AI component, and a user interface, is presented. [11] discusses digital twin-based machine learning applications in more detail, presenting a framework for implementing them in general. The framework consists of a layer-based architecture for Cyber Physical Systems and Digital Twin, where the Digital Twin mainly serves the purpose of providing data for machine learning algorithms. These works have identified critical components and already address the challenge of linking artificial intelligence methodologies with the model-based approaches of a decision support system. Nevertheless, the approaches miss technologies for integrating production data from heterogeneous sources in knowledge-based models, as well as the flexibility in task completion through hybrid methodologies of AI and simulation. We see the classification in the overall system, including the knowledge representation as improvement to the pure mapping between physical data and virtual operation.

4 Functional Components for Simulation-Based Assistance

4.1 Overview

Decision Support Systems (DSS), in general, are interactive computer-based systems, which utilize data, models, knowledge, and communication technologies to support people who are required to solve complex problems [10, 12]. In our understanding, a decision support system for the shop floor specifies this definition. It bears the integration and connection of heterogeneous production data, simulation models, and AI models, as well as the utilization of reusable and flexible components to address the growing challenges. In this work, we have identified these functional components to build upon to implement decision support systems: data provision and data extraction, knowledge base, simulation models, model execution and analytics, and applications and user interaction.

Figure 1 gives an overview of the building blocks and shows a high-level architecture of the Digital Twin that arises from these. In the following paragraphs, we want to discuss these building blocks' functionalities, how they interact and highlight their requirements.

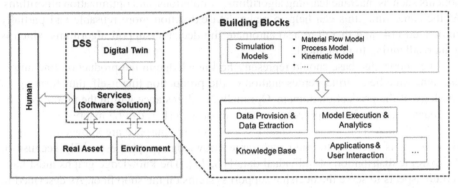

Fig. 1. Building blocks of decision support for the shop floor. (extended from [1])

4.2 Data Provision and Data Extraction from Heterogeneous IT-Systems

For Industry 4.0 technologies, usually a large amount of data is permanently collected by various sensors, connected machines, systems, and digital models. Due to the evolutionary development of most factories – i.e., new machines and new technologies are permanently integrated into the legacy systems or existing structures of the production system – the data landscape in production systems is very heterogeneous and comes from very different sources, such as MES, ERP, SCADA, machine data and is provided in different structured and unstructured formats e.g., XML, JSON, CSV.

Decision support systems need this data to provide the user with analytical components to make decisions in different situations. However, to feed these analytical components at all, this data must first be extracted from the mentioned systems. For this purpose, already several data-extraction, data-mining [13] and data-cleansing techniques and tools exist that need to be adapted to the production system domain [14, 15]. Nevertheless, data connectors for the different data sources have to be implemented. This is usually a tool or system-specific, or even factory-specific task and often has to be set up and configured anew in each project. To reduce the factory-specific configuration effort, two things need to be simplified:

1. Connectors to existing big data providers in factories such as ERP, MES, etc., based on data communication standards such as OPC-UA or REST, need to be set up.
2. Mapping between the often proprietary data models of existing IT systems and standardized data models needs to be simplified (auto mappers, style sheets, appropriate UI support, data analytics…).

4.3 Knowledge Base – Data Integration in Semantic Models

It is desirable to relate the just mentioned data and the respective data generators to create a knowledge base, the second building block, to enable and empower analytical components such as machine learning algorithms, simulations, and optimization algorithms. At the same time, this can help to make data extraction more reusable and partially automated [14] and therefore also automate the decision-support algorithms which is quite challenging to implement.

The knowledge base should represent the knowledge in the production line and at the same time be a virtual representation of the production line itself, thus forming an ontology of the production domain. Optimally, each instance within the production, be it a machine, a product, a process, a material, or a worker, can be mapped and related to each other. A more recent technology used for this purpose are knowledge graphs. However, it is not easy to build such large knowledge graphs, especially because of the extreme distribution of individual data [16, 17]. The knowledge graphs must have certain aspects to serve the decision support systems on the shop floor. As described in [18], the use of different layers and applications in decision support requires reusable, standardized, flexible, and extensible means for data exchange between them. This is an essential prerequisite for ensuring that decision support solutions do not have to be rebuilt entirely for each factory but that certain parts can be reused across projects - i.e., following a library or framework approach. In addition, the knowledge graphs must provide structures for two core aspects in particular:

1. Simulation knowledge, which leads to the linkage of simulation components and by that enables the automatic model generation of simulation models.
2. Production knowledge, which brings a deeper understanding of the data and the connections between them.

4.4 Multi-level Simulation Models

As described above, a knowledge base gives meaning to the data and allows the data to be connected to AI and simulation models. The simulation models, our third functional component, form the basis for the analytic algorithms and represent the current state of production at different levels. That means that depending on the task for decision support, there are different modeling options and levels of details used, e.g., within one production unit or for the entire production stage. In the context of factory simulation, the two main simulation types are material flow simulation and 3D kinematic simulation. In material flow simulation, the logistics inside a production system are modeled e.g., to analyze the dimensioning of the factory and the planning of the production with respect to efficiency, utilization, and in-time delivery, also considering failure situations. 3D-kinematic simulation is used to analyze the interaction within the production cell between machines, like robots, humans, and the product. It is mainly used during the detailed design and commissioning phase [19]. Regardless of the type of simulation, the setup of these models usually requires a huge effort for both the data acquisition as well as the model generation itself [20].

4.5   Model Execution and Analytics for Monitoring, Planning and Scheduling

To deliver value to different stakeholders on the shop floor, the models described above need to be executed, and further analytics need to be added. Besides simulation and optimization, AI is increasingly coming to the fore. The target is to give decision support in a descriptive, predictive, and prescriptive manner.

Descriptive Analytics. Data from the current or a previous situation are fed into the simulation model, which is then executed. The simulated plant behavior is further analyzed or evaluated with respect to relevant Key Performance Indicators (KPI), e.g., machine utilization, lead times, blockages, bottlenecks, in-time delivery.

Predictive Analytics. Data for upcoming production scenarios are fed into the simulation model, which is then executed. Different alternatives for operational decisions, e.g., production order sequencing and worker assignments, should be examined with respect to the KPIs mentioned above. A systematic experiment management can make use of machine learning approaches reinforcing the most relevant and promising decision alternatives. Uncertainties and risks should be taken into account by also executing particular stochastic deviation and failure scenarios.

Prescriptive Analytics. To evaluate upcoming decisions in a systematic way to end up with the best decisions is part of the field of optimization. Production planning and scheduling tasks often lead to NP-hard optimization problems [21]. Therefore, analytical solvers are applicable only in small-size scenarios. For larger problems, meta-heuristics like genetic algorithms, ant algorithms, or neighborhood search are often used instead [22]. It may be a promising approach using machine learning to acquire fast but realistic surrogate models. Any decisions based on heuristics or abstract surrogate models should be further validated by a detailed simulation to end up with a feasible solution (Fig. 2).

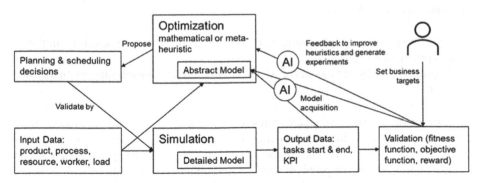

Fig. 2. Hybrid approach for production planning and scheduling

To summarize, the described analytics all require access to field data to synchronize the simulation models with the current situation in the physical world. Hybrid approaches of analytical and data-driven methods can help to manage complexity, but of course, require a lot of data and face challenges in adapting to scenarios not foreseen by previous data.

4.6   User-Specific Application and Interaction

In our last building block, the data calculated by the analytical components is prepared and provided to the various stakeholders. The data must be prepared differently depending on the current situation of the stakeholders in the production. For example, in the case of short-term machine failures, a machine operator needs quick solutions that are understandable. Virtual voice assistants and mobile devices are ideally suited for this purpose. The implementation of the assistant on a personal mobile device answers individual questions and problems so that each person is optimally supported in his or her own work processes. By contrast, planners of larger production sections, for example, may need more information about the problem at hand and the associated solution. For these stakeholders with in-depth technical knowledge, a desktop application with many details to browse through and interact with may be the more appropriate application. Therefore, a solution for the application layer should provide certain flexibility and choices for different representations and information of the data coming from the analytical part within the respective application to serve the different stakeholders depending on their task at hand, their level of knowledge and their authorization.

5   Conclusion

This paper has presented the idea of an operator assistance system for manufacturing and process industries and its main components, namely the data provision and data extraction, the knowledge base, multi-level simulation models, model execution and analytics, and application and user interaction. The functionality of each component and the connection points between them were outlined. Furthermore, the connection to our vision of the Digital Twin as a tool for decision support of the future was shown, where our future work will be dedicated to the implementation. From a scientific point of view, two topics are in the foreground:

1. The conception and implementation of an integrated knowledge base for simulation and production knowledge.
2. Approaches for hybrid models of AI and simulation for decision support on the shop floor.

Furthermore, we will investigate on how to implement more natural interaction mechanisms between production stakeholders and decision support systems. The evaluation of this concept and the individual components within the decision support system is performed using a scheduling problem within a manufacturing environment. The specific tasks concern the validation and optimization of manufacturing schedules, as well as support for make or buy decisions regarding individual parts.

References

1. Rosen, R., Fischer, J., Boschert, S.: Next generation digital twin: an ecosystem for mechatronic systems? IFAC-PapersOnLine **52**(15), 265–270 (2019). https://doi.org/10.1016/j.ifacol.2019.11.685

2. Rosen, R., et al.: Die rolle der simulation im kontext des digitalen zwillings. In: ATP Magazine, no. 04, (2021)
3. Negri, E., Fumagalli, L., Macchi, M.: A review of the roles of digital twin in CPS-based production systems. Procedia Manuf. **11**, 939–948 (2017). https://doi.org/10.1016/j.promfg. 2017.07.198
4. Tao, F., Cheng, J., Qi, Q., Zhang, M., Zhang, H., Sui, F.: Digital twin-driven product design, manufacturing and service with big data. Int. J. Adv. Manuf. Technol. **94**(9–12), 3563–3576 (2017). https://doi.org/10.1007/s00170-017-0233-1
5. Schleich, B., Anwer, N., Mathieu, L., Wartzack, S.: Shaping the digital twin for design and production engineering. CIRP Ann. **66**(1), 141–144 (2017). https://doi.org/10.1016/j.cirp. 2017.04.040
6. Boschert S., Heinrich C., Rosen R.: Next Generation Digital Twin (2018)
7. Overton, J., Brigham, J.: The digital twin: data-driven simulations innovate the manufacturing process. DXC Technology, Whitepaper (2017). https://assets1.dxc.technology/analytics/dow nloads/DXC-Analytics-Digital-Twin.pdf
8. Zheng, Y., Yang, S., Cheng, H.: An application framework of digital twin and its case study. J. Ambient. Intell. Humaniz. Comput. **10**(3), 1141–1153 (2018). https://doi.org/10.1007/s12 652-018-0911-3
9. Redelinghuys, A., Basson, A., Kruger, K.: A six-layer digital twin architecture for a manufacturing cell. In: Borangiu, T., Trentesaux, D., Thomas, A., Cavalieri, S. (eds.) SOHOMA 2018. SCI, vol. 803, pp. 412–423. Springer, Cham (2019). https://doi.org/10.1007/978-3-030-03003-2_32
10. Kasie, F.M., Bright, G., Walker, A.: Decision support systems in manufacturing: a survey and future trends. J. Modell. Manage. **12**(3), 432–454 (2017). https://doi.org/10.1108/JM2-02-2016-0015
11. Alexopoulos, K., Nikolakis, N., Chryssolouris, G.: Digital twin-driven supervised machine learning for the development of artificial intelligence applications in manufacturing. Int. J. Comput. Integr. Manuf. **33**(5), 429–439 (2020). https://doi.org/10.1080/0951192X.2020.174 7642
12. Power, D.J.: Decision Support Systems: Concepts and Resources For Managers. Quorum Books, Westport, Conn (2002)
13. Cheng, Y., Chen, K., Sun, H., Zhang, Y., Tao, F.: Data and knowledge mining with big data towards smart production. J. Ind. Inf. Integr. **9**, 1–13 (2018). https://doi.org/10.1016/j.jii.2017. 08.001
14. Nath, R.P.D., Romero, O., Pedersen, T.B., Hose, K.: High-level ETL for Semantic Data Warehouses (2020). arXiv: http://arxiv.org/abs/2006.07180. Accessed 26 Mar 2021
15. Skoutas, D., Simitsis, A.: Designing ETL processes using semantic web technologies. In: Proceedings of the 9th ACM international workshop on Data warehousing and OLAP - DOLAP 2006, Arlington, Virginia, USA, p. 67, (2006). doi: https://doi.org/10.1145/1183512.1183526
16. Hogan, A., et al.: Knowledge Graphs (2020). arXiv: http://arxiv.org/abs/2003.02320. Accessed 22 Mar 2021
17. He, Q., Chen, B.-C., Agarwal, D.: Building the LinkedIn knowledge graph. LinkedIn Blog (2016). https://engineering.linkedin.com/blog/2016/10/building-the-linkedin-knowle dge-graph. Accessed 26 Mar 2021
18. List, F.G., Fischer, J., Beyer, D., Weyrich, M.: Knowledge representation in modeling and simulation: a survey for the production and logistic domain. In: 2020 25th IEEE International Conference on Emerging Technologies and Factory Automation (ETFA), Vienna, Austria, pp. 1051–1056 (2020). https://doi.org/10.1109/ETFA46521.2020.9211994
19. Smirnov, D., Schenk, T., Wehrstedt, J.C.: Hierarchical simulation of production systems. In: 2018 IEEE 14th International Conference on Automation Science and Engineering (CASE), Munich, pp. 875–880 (2018). https://doi.org/10.1109/COASE.2018.8560436

20. Rosen, R., Beyer, D., Fischer, J., Klein, W., Malik, V., Wehrstedt, J.C.: Flexiblere Produktion durch digitale Zwillinge in der Automatisierungstechnik – Methode zur automatischen Generierung digitaler Zwillinge für eine Brownfield-Produktion. In: Automation 2020: Shaping Automation for our Future, pp. 1039–1054. VDI Verlag (2020). https://doi.org/10.51202/9783181023754-1039
21. Pinedo, M.: Scheduling: Theory, Algorithms, and Systems, 5th edn. Springer, Cham Heidelberg New York Dordrecht London (2016)
22. Thevenin, S., Zufferey, N.: Learning variable neighborhood search for a scheduling problem with time windows and rejections. Discrete. Appl. Math. **261**, 344–353 (2019). https://doi.org/10.1016/j.dam.2018.03.019

A Taxonomy for Resistance Concepts
in Manufacturing Networks

Ferdinand Deitermann[(✉)] and Thomas Friedli

University of St. Gallen, 9008 St. Gallen, Switzerland
ferdinand.deitermann@unisg.ch

Abstract. Manufacturing networks - global production networks and international manufacturing networks - are exposed to an increase in uncertainty, which can cause disturbances. To cope with these disturbances, scholars presented different concepts, such as robustness, resilience, responsiveness, flexibility, changeability, adaptability, and agility. However, these terms are not clearly and concisely defined and lack a common understanding. With this study, we intend to address this issue and contribute to a better understanding and differentiation. We develop a taxonomy with descriptive dimensions and characteristics for the different resistance concepts for manufacturing networks, which will provide a tool to better understand the differences and commonalities between them. It is a vital first step that creates a common ground for further investigations. Practitioners can use the taxonomy to build a sound understanding and improve their manufacturing network.

Keywords: Manufacturing network resilience · Robustness · Taxonomy

1 Introduction

Globalization has significantly changed the economic landscape for manufacturing companies over the last decades [1]. Increasing competition and opportunities led companies to create greater value by exploiting advantages, such as lower cost resources or access to new markets [2]. In consequence, companies of any size now operate as global production networks (GPNs) [1], which can be considered "one of the most critical forms of organization in the manufacturing sector" [1]. Intra-firm GPNs even account for one third of the global trade [1].

However, the growth of manufacturing networks (MNs) due to the challenge to create greater value increases their complexity and susceptibility to risk [3]. Such risks result from the current competitive and rapidly changing environment. Scholars in the field of operations management (OM) and supply chain management (SCM) called for, proposed, and investigated different concepts to deal with these uncertainties [4–6]. These concepts are, among others, the following: resilience, robustness, responsiveness, flexibility, agility, changeability, and adaptability.

However, they are often used interchangeable and not clearly distinguishable [5, 7]. Nevertheless, for research progress in any field, the establishment of a clear definition

© IFIP International Federation for Information Processing 2021
Published by Springer Nature Switzerland AG 2021
A. Dolgui et al. (Eds.): APMS 2021, IFIP AICT 630, pp. 293–302, 2021.
https://doi.org/10.1007/978-3-030-85874-2_31

is a necessary first step [5]. Some authors already enhanced the understanding of some concepts by developing clearer and more distinguishable definitions. Nevertheless, to the best of our knowledge, there is yet no comprehensive approach, i.e. a taxonomy, to classify a larger number of the respective terms based on their constituent factors.

Taxonomies support researchers and practitioners in comprehending and analyzing complex issues by providing a structure and organization of a knowledge base for a certain research field [8, 9]. Therefore, we hypothesize that a taxonomy for resistance concepts for MNs will help to clarify and distinguish different concepts. The research question for this study is therefore as follows:

RQ: *What are key dimensions and characteristics of concepts that describe a form of resistance in manufacturing networks?*

We answer this research question by following the well-used and structured method from [9]. The development of a taxonomy intends to identify common characteristics of resistance concepts and make them distinguishable. Hence, the paper is organized as follows: After the introduction, we discuss the related literature on MNs and different concepts that describe a form of resistance in MNs. Second, we introduce our research methodology. Third, we present the final taxonomy. Lastly, we discuss the theoretical and practical implications of this paper, as well as its limitations and possible future research.

2   Research Background

The MN theory originates from the OM field [10]. Historically, researchers categorize MNs as internal networks that are wholly owned by a single company. A MN can be defined as "a factory network with matrix connections, where each node (i.e. factory) affects the other nodes and cannot be managed in isolation" [10]. Due to the takeoff of globalization in the 1980s and 1990s, companies established more factories internationally and research on this topic increased [10]. Different subdomains emerged under the umbrella of MN research, i.e. GPNs and international manufacturing networks (IMNs). All nodes within an IMN are owned by a single company, whereas a GPN includes nodes owned by other companies.

Although such networks are beneficial in some areas, they increase the susceptibility to risks [3]. Risks are ever present in daily operations of companies worldwide [11] and can have different appearances: A distinction can be made between internal (e.g. machine failure) and external risks (e.g. environmental disaster). Additionally, change events can have the manifestation as disastrous, disruptive, or small. Hereinafter, we use the neutral term *change events* to describe any type of risks.

To cope with such change events, scholars introduced different terms and concepts [4–6]. These concepts are, among others, the following: resilience, robustness, responsiveness, flexibility, agility, changeability, and adaptability. However, the concepts to characterize a form of resistance are not defined in a clear and concise way, which is also well-acknowledged. This problem does not only exist in the specific field of MN, but in OM and SCM as well (e.g. see [4, 5]).

An example of a vague definition can be found for robustness: "robustness describes the stability against varying conditions" [7, 12]. It is often associated with a stable performance despite the impacts of change events [7, 12–14]. Some scholars classify robustness as a concept very close to resilience [7]. Conflicting views on both concepts exist. [7] categorize resilience and agility as robustness characteristics. In contrast, [15] state that resilience has robustness properties. Some scholars argue that resilience is the ability to resist even greater change events than robustness.

Additional controversies can be found for the terms flexibility and responsiveness. [16] defines flexibility as part of responsiveness, whereas [17] categorizes responsiveness as part of flexibility. While flexibility is a mature concept, responsiveness is still lagging a clear conceptualization [4]. Based on a literature review, [4] conceptualizes flexibility as the "ability of a system to change status within an existing configuration." Accordingly, [4] defines responsiveness as the "propensity for purposeful and timely behavior change in the presence of stimulating stimuli."

Another example of such a controversy is the subsumption of flexibility as part of agility (see [17–19]), whereas [20] categorizes agility as part of flexibility. [4] defines agility as the "ability of the system to rapidly reconfigure." Furthermore, agility is seen by [1] as a concept on network level to establish changeability.

Changeability as a concept is often referred to as "actions to adjust flexibility limits" [21]. The concept incorporates flexibility and rapidity and can be categorized as "a part of adaptability" [22]. According to [22] and [16] adaptability describes the ability of a system to change due to change events.

So far, scholars limited their research to the detailed definition of one concept (e.g. see [4]) or the distinction between a small number of specific concepts (e.g. see [5]).

3 Research Approach

3.1 Taxonomy Development Process

We have adopted the approach developed by [9] for the development of our taxonomy. The method provides a rigor process and has been used in high-ranking journal articles and conference proceedings [8]. It consists of three stages: first, meta-characteristics and ending conditions are defined. Meta-characteristics depend on the purpose of the taxonomy. Objective and subjective ending conditions are provided by [9]. During the second stage, dimensions and characteristics of the taxonomy are developed: empirical-to-conceptual (E2C) and conceptual-to-empirical (C2E). During the E2C approach the researcher identifies subsets of objects and common characteristics. The C2E approach guides the researcher to develop dimensions and characteristics based on their own notions. The last stage compares the taxonomy to the ending conditions.

3.2 Taxonomy Development

Meta-characteristic: Our contribution aims to provide a sound basis for future research and discussion by enabling the classification of a resistance concept based on its constituent factors. The meta-characteristics are "key-characteristics of concepts for MNs to withstand internal and external change events."

Ending Conditions: For our taxonomy, we use the objective and subjective ending conditions from [9], as they provide a sound approach to evaluate the taxonomy.

First Iteration (E2C): To get a comprehensive overview of the concepts to describe resistance in MNs, we conducted an exhaustive systematic literature review. Literature reviews provide a vital and qualified mean [23] to summarize and progress the current state of knowledge in a certain field [24]. We chose the methodology from [25] because of its recipe alike process, which covers all important phases of a literature review.

To ensure a certain quality, the results were limited to peer-reviewed articles in scientific journals or conference proceedings [24]. The search was conducted using the three major databases Emerald, EBSCOhost and Science Direct and yielded 1369 results. After the removal of duplicates and the screening of titles and abstracts for relevance, the number of articles was reduced to 64. A forward and backward search identified 46 articles. 28 relevant articles remained after a full text analysis.

First, we clustered the articles according to their contributions to different concepts (see Table 1). For the taxonomy development, we initially focused on the six concepts that were mentioned most often: flexibility, robustness, changeability, resilience, agility, and responsiveness. At this point we were able to identify a pattern: The definitions and descriptions often follow a systems perspective. They describe a form of input – a change event – which is mitigated by some form of capabilities of the network, in order to reach a desired system state. This is in consensus with the findings of [38]. We thus defined the meta-dimensions as *input, capabilities,* and *output/objectives.*

Second Iteration (E2C): We used a coding book (MS Excel) to extract and evaluate the information in more detail. We identified the constituent factors *severity of change, anticipation of change, pace of reaction, range of reaction* and *system state.*

Third Iteration (C2E): The extensive knowledge and experience of the researchers led to the development of the categories *area of reaction* and *measurement level.*

Fourth Iteration (E2C): We applied definitions from related research areas, i.e. OM and SCM, since not all ending conditions were fulfilled after the third iteration. This step was necessary due to two factors: 1) The literature on different concepts is rather scarce and different understandings are not sufficiently discussed. 2) Concepts and definitions are discussed in more detail in OM and SCM (e.g. flexibility [5]). The OM area is suited for this application as it can be considered superordinate to MN research. Depending on the understanding of MNs (i.e. intra-firm networks or inter-firm networks), SCM can be considered a part of those [10]. We used review articles to ensure the rigorousness of the results.

Fifth Iteration (E2C): Adding new dimensions in the fourth iteration required a fifth iteration [9]. We tested the taxonomy, using all existing definitions and description of concepts and found no dimensions or characteristics to add.

Ending Conditions: After the fifth iteration, the taxonomy fulfilled all ending conditions proposed by [9]: 1) All articles from the literature review and additions from OM and SCM literature have been examined. 2) We did not split or merge objects in the last iteration. 3) Each characteristic of each dimension was classified with at least one object. 4) We did not add any new dimensions or characteristics in the last iteration. 5) Neither did we merge or split dimensions or characteristics. 6) There are no dimension duplications and each dimension is unique. 7) Similar, no characteristic duplications exist within

Table 1. Contributions of scholars to different terms and concepts

	Flexibility	Robustness	Changeability	Resilience	Agility	Responsiveness	Adaptability	Reliability	Stability	Resistance
Papers	[1, 6, 7, 15, 17, 18, 20, 26–30]	[1, 7, 12–15, 20, 31–33]	[1, 7, 18, 19, 21, 22, 28, 34]	[1, 3, 7, 11, 15, 35]	[7, 17, 28, 36, 37]	[1, 15, 16, 26]	[1]	[15]	-	-

one dimension. 8) Each combination of characteristics is unique; however, the various definitions may be broadly similar. 9) The taxonomy includes no unnecessary dimensions or characteristics and the number of dimensions falls into the proposed number of nine. 10) The existing dimensions and characteristics allow to differentiate every object. 11) It is comprehensive because all objects can be classified (see also iteration five). 12) The taxonomy can easily be extended by adding new dimensions or characteristics. 13) The taxonomy provides valuable and non-redundant information for the characterization of resistance concepts in MNs.

4   A Taxonomy to Describe Concepts for MN Resistance

The taxonomy consists of three meta-dimensions, eight dimensions with twenty-three characteristics (see Table 2). The column on the far-right provides additional information on whether a characteristic of a dimension is exclusive (E) or non-exclusive (N). We opted for a morphological box to visualize the taxonomy. This allows us to illustrate the set of relationships contained in a complex problem in an intuitive way.

4.1   Meta-dimension: Input

The first meta-dimension, *input*, considers the dimensions and characteristics of change events, which influence the MN. We identified the two dimensions *severity of change* and *anticipation of change* as constituent features.

The dimension *severity of change* describes possible impacts of an internal or external event that a MN must be able to withstand. [1] describe that robustness has to mitigate "disruptive internal and external changes." [7] characterize resilience as the ability of a system to "tolerate disturbances." They establish a dependency between the nature of change events and the appropriate mitigation actions. [3] describe resilience as the "speed of reaction to disruptions." Hence, resilience is the ability to react to high severity events, which is indicated by the term "disruptions." The *severity of change* is characterized for agility as well. [7] state that "agility enables for adoption to bigger disturbances." Flexibility, however, is seen as the ability to deal with small changes [18]. Based on those definitions and descriptions, we derived the characteristics of *low, medium,* and *high*. The characteristics are non-exclusive, as a concept can be constructed to handle different severities.

The dimension *anticipation of change* refers to a second category of characteristics to describe change events. It differentiates between *foreseeable* and *unforeseeable* change events, which is based on the following definitions: [1] and [35] describe resilience as a concept reacting to unforeseeable events. Similar, [6] (flexibility), [19] (changeability), [22] (changeability) and [17] (agility) use this dimension to describe change events. [16] characterizes a responsive system as able to react to "predictable and unpredictable changes." Therefore, we termed the dimension non-exclusive. Although there are different categorizations to characterize change events (see [3] and [7]), the chosen dimension is in conformance with all analyzed definitions.

Table 2. Taxonomy for manufacturing network resistance concepts visualized as a morphological box

Meta-dimension	Dimension	Characteristics				E/N
Input	Severity of change	Low		Medium	High	N
	Anticipation of change	Foreseeable		Unforeseeable		N
Capabilities	Pace of reaction	Rapid		Purposeful		E
	Range of reaction	Persist		Adapt	Transform	E
	Level of reaction	Micro		Meso	Macro	N
	Area of reaction	Strategy		Configuration	Coordination	N
Output/ Objective	System state	Stability/ Equilibrium	Bounce-back	New optimum	Not applicable	N
	Measurement level	Operational		Tactical	Strategic	N

4.2 Meta-dimension: Capabilities

The second meta-dimension, *capabilities*, contains five dimensions. It describes how, to what degree, and where the MN reacts to change events.

The first dimension, *pace of reaction*, indicates the speed at which a certain concept reacts to the impact of change events. A majority of the concepts are characterized as rapid or fast (i.e. [3, 7] – resilience, [15] – responsiveness, [17, 29] – flexibility, [22] – changeability, [7, 17] – agility). [16] adds that a responsive system should make a "balanced response." As a result, we differentiate between the characteristics *rapid* and *purposeful*. *Rapid* expresses the absolute need for a quick reaction of the system. On the contrary, *purposeful* expresses the need for a system to react in an acceptable time period to reach its objectives. The dimension is exclusive.

The dimension *range of reaction* describes to what extent the capabilities of the system can be altered in case of change events. The capabilities can *persist*, describing a reaction without significantly changing the capabilities. [28] describe agility as a concept that functions "without changing the network structure itself." However, the capabilities can also *adapt*, which describes the readjustment of capabilities within predefined limits. See for example the definitions from [18] and [22], where flexibility corridors and enablers of change can be adapted. Transform refers to the adjustment of capabilities without predefined limits. [28], for example, state that "transformability is the tactical ability to adapt, i.e. the ability of an entire factory structure (physical, organizational, etc.) to switch to another product family." The dimension is exclusive.

The *level of reaction* refers to the production level where a reaction of the system's capabilities will occur. Flexibility can for example occur on the "*micro* level (single resources of a system) or *macro* level (whole system)" [30]. Related to MNs, the characteristics ranging from micro to macro level can be put into comparison with the range from workstation level to network level perspective. For a more precise classification, we added a *meso* level, describing e.g. flexibility on plant level [27, 29]. Since reactions can occur on several levels, the dimension is non-exclusive.

The dimension *area of reaction* allows to classify the reaction into an area of a MN. We grouped the areas following [2]: *strategy, configuration, coordination*. A classification into one or more areas can be found in the works of several authors, such as [1, 7, 16, 26, 29, 36]. [1], for example, locate the adaptation of capabilities into the configuration area, whereas [7] locate it to the entire network; however, with a focus on coordination. Hence, the dimension is non-exclusive.

4.3 Meta-dimension: Output/Objective

The third meta-dimension is *output/objective*. It allows for the characterization of the output from a reaction of the capabilities to change events.

The outcome, which results from the application of a certain concept is described by the dimension *system state*. Some authors detailed a post-disruption system state in their definitions, i.e. [1, 5, 7, 11, 12, 15, 18]. According to [7, 12] robustness describes "the stability against different varying conditions." [1] however, applied the stability paradigm to resilience. [7] understands resilience more extensively and names three system states depending on the severity of the change event: stable performance, fast regain of the initial performance, and adaptation of a new optimal state. This leads to the characteristics *stability/equilibrium, bounce-back*, and *new optimum*. Several authors did not specify an outcome or used a vague description, such as [39] ("achieve its goals in the presence of disturbances") or [15] ("dampen the effects of demand changes"). Although we advise to define a system state, we included the characteristic *not applicable* to account for definitions without one. The dimension is non-exclusive, following [7].

The *measurement level* classifies the aggregation level of the KPIs, where the achievement ratio of the concept is measured. We developed the following characteristics: *operational* [28], *tactical* [17], and *strategic* [7, 13, 17, 28, 32, 33]. An example for strategic KPIs are the site roles, which determine the level of robustness [32, 33]. Flexibility can be measured on all levels. The dimension is thus non-exclusive.

5 Conclusion

We developed a taxonomy for MN resistance concepts, following the method from [9]. It consists of eight dimensions and twenty-three characteristics. Our work allows for a deeper and more transparent understanding of individual concepts, hence **contributing to scientific progress in the field of MNs**. It enables to clearly differentiate between various concepts. The results of this research can be the basis for the development of sound methods and processes for the increase of resistance in MNs. **Managerial contributions** of this study are the usage as an instrument to analyze and describe concepts. It can support practitioners by facilitating a better understanding and differentiation as a basis for the shift towards more resistance in MNs.

The **limitations** of our research are the number of publications in the field of MNs. To account for this deficiency, we included publications from OM and SCM. The data collection itself is open to interpretation, meaning that other researchers might derive other dimensions and characteristics depending on personal preferences. Furthermore, our taxonomy is a time-bound snapshot that needs to be updated to remain relevant. This is important due to the evolving nature of research on resistance in MNs.

Future research avenues are the development of archetypical patterns for different terms to establish a sound and distinguishable understanding. Second, dimensions and characteristics to describe solutions that might dissolve or prevent a performance decrease due to a change event could be added.

References

1. Lanza, G., et al.: Global production networks: design and operation. CIRP Ann. **68**(2), 823–841 (2019)
2. Friedli, T., Mundt, A., Thomas, S.: Strategic Management of Global Manufacturing Networks. Springer, Berlin, Heidelberg (2014)
3. Niknejad, A., Petrovic, D.: Analysis of impact of uncertainty in global production networks' parameters. Comput. Ind. Eng. **111**, 228–238 (2017)
4. Holweg, M.: The three dimensions of responsiveness. Int. J. Oper. Prod. Manage. **25**(7), 603–622 (2005)
5. Bernardes, E., Hanna, M.D.: A theoretical review of flexibility, agility and responsiveness in the operations management literature. Int. J. Oper. Prod. Manage. **29**(1), 30–53 (2009)
6. Fredriksson, A., Wänström, C.: Manufacturing and supply chain flexibility – towards a tool to analyse production network coordination at operational level. Strat. Outsour. Int. J. **7**(2), 173–194 (2014)
7. Stricker, N., Lanza, G.: The concept of robustness in production systems and its correlation to disturbances. Procedia CIRP **19**, 87–92 (2014)
8. Gelhaar, J., Groß, T., Otto, B.: A taxonomy for data ecosystems. In: Proceedings of the 54th Hawaii International Conference on System Sciences (2021)
9. Nickerson, R.C., Varshney, U., Muntermann, J.: A method for taxonomy development and its application in information systems. Eur. J. Inf. Syst. **22**(3), 336–359 (2013)
10. Rudberg, M., Olhager, J.: Manufacturing networks and supply chains: an operations strategy perspective. Omega **31**(1), 29–39 (2003)
11. Palmer, C., Urwin, E.N., Niknejad, A., Petrovic, D., Popplewell, K., Young, R.I.M.: An ontology supported risk assessment approach for the intelligent configuration of supply networks. J. Intell. Manuf. **29**(5), 1005–1030 (2016). https://doi.org/10.1007/s10845-016-1252-8
12. Stricker, N., Pfeiffer, A., Moser, E., Kádár, B., Lanza, G., Monostori, L.: Supporting multi-level and robust production planning and execution. CIRP Ann. **64**(1), 415–418 (2015)
13. Treber, S., Breig, R., Kentner, M., Häfner, B., Lanza, G.: Information exchange in global production networks: increasing transparency by simulation, statistical experiments and selection of digitalization activities. Procedia CIRP **84**, 225–230 (2019)
14. van Grunsven, L., Hutchinson, F.E.: The evolution of the electronics industry in Johor (Malaysia): Strategic coupling, adaptiveness, adaptation, and the role of agency. Geoforum **74**, 74–87 (2016)
15. Kristianto, Y., Gunasekaran, A., Helo, P.: Building the "Triple R" in global manufacturing. Int. J. Prod. Econ. **183**, 607–619 (2017)
16. Saad, S.M., Gindy, N.N.Z.: Future shape of the responsive manufacturing enterprise. Benchmark. Int. J. **14**(1), 140–152 (2007)

17. Lin, B.-W.: Original equipment manufacturers (OEM) manufacturing strategy for network innovation agility: the case of Taiwanese manufacturing networks. Int. J. Prod. Res. **42**(5), 943–957 (2004)
18. Lanza, G., Moser, R.: Strategic planning of global changeable production networks. Procedia CIRP **3**, 257–262 (2012)
19. Weber, J., Stäbler, M., Thielen, S., Paetzold, K.: Modularity as key enabler for scalability of final assembly units in the automotive sector. Procedia CIRP **57**, 224–228 (2016)
20. Johansson, P.E.C., Delin, F., Jansson, S., Moestam, L., Fast-Berglund, Å.: Global truck production – the importance of having a robust manufacturing preparation process. Procedia CIRP **57**, 631–636 (2016)
21. Buergin, J., et al.: Robust assignment of customer orders with uncertain configurations in a production network for aircraft manufacturing. Int. J. Prod. Res. **57**(3), 749–763 (2019)
22. Moser, E., Huss, A.K., Liebrecht, C., Lanza, G.: A portfolio theory approach to identify risk-efficient enablers of change in global production networks. Procedia CIRP **63**, 768–773 (2017)
23. Baker, M.J.: Writing a literature review. Mark. Rev. **1**(2), 219–247 (2000)
24. Rowley, J., Slack, F.: Conducting a literature review. Manage. Res. News. **27**(6), 31–39 (2004)
25. vom Brocke, J., Simons, A., Niehaves, B., Riemer, K., Plattfaut, R., Cleven, A.: Reconstructing the giant: on the importance of Rigour in documenting the literature search process. In: ECIS 2009 Proceedings (161), (2009)
26. Andersen, T.J.: Multinational risk and performance outcomes: effects of knowledge intensity and industry context. Int. Bus. Rev. **21**(2), 239–252 (2012)
27. Szwejczewski, M., Sweeney, M.T., Cousens, A.: The strategic management of manufacturing networks. J. Manuf. Technol. Manage. **27**(1), 124–149 (2016)
28. Mikusz, M., Heber, D., Katzfuß, C., Monauni, M., Tauterat, T.: Changeable manufacturing on the network level. Procedia CIRP **41**, 27–32 (2016)
29. Mair, A.: Honda's global flexifactory network. Int. J. Oper. Prod. Manage. **14**(3), 6–23 (1994)
30. de Toni, A., Tonchia, S.: Manufacturing flexibility: a literature review. Int. J. Prod. Res. **36**(6), 1587–1617 (1998)
31. Nigro, G.L., La Diega, S.N., Perrone, G., Renna, P.: Coordination policies to support decision making in distributed production planning. Robot. Comput. Integr. Manuf. **19**(6), 521–531 (2003)
32. Paulo Fusco, J., Spring, M.: Flexibility versus robust networks: the case of the Brazilian automotive sector. Integr. Manuf. Syst. **14**(1), 26–35 (2003)
33. Ferdows, K.: Making the Most of Foreign Factories. Harvard Business Review, (1997)
34. Wiendahl, H.-P., et al.: Changeable manufacturing - classification, design and operation. CIRP Ann. **56**(2), 783–809 (2007)
35. Mella, P.: The ghost in the production machine: the laws of production networks. Kybernetes **48**(6), 1301–1329 (2019)
36. Jin, B.: Achieving an optimal global versus domestic sourcing balance under demand uncertainty. Int. J. Oper. Prod. Manage. **24**(12), 1292–1305 (2004)
37. Chatha, K.A., Butt, I.: Themes of study in manufacturing strategy literature. Int. J. Oper. Prod. Manage. **35**(4), 604–698 (2015)
38. Ebrahim, Z., Ahmad, N.A., Muhamad, M.R.: Understanding responsiveness in manufacturing operations. In: International Symposium on Research in Innovation and Sustainability 2014 (ISoRIS 2014), Malacca, Malaysia (2014)
39. Matson, J.B., McFarlane, D.C.: Assessing the responsiveness of existing production operations. Int. J. Oper. Prod. Manage. **19**(8), 765–784 (1999)

Real-Time Machine Learning Automation Applied to Failure Prediction in Automakers Supplier Manufacturing System

Arthur Beltrame Canciglierie[1,2]([✉]), Tainá da Rocha[1,2], Anderson L. Szejka[1], Leandro dos Santos Coelho[1,3], and Osiris Canciglieri Junior[1]

[1] Industrial and Systems Engineering Graduate Program (PPGEPS), Pontifical Catholic University of Parana (PUCPR), Curitiba, Brazil
`arthur.canciglieri2@br.bosch.com`, {`anderson.szejka,`
`osiris.canciglieri`}`@pucpr.br`
[2] Robert Bosch, Ind. Plant - Curitiba, Curitiba, Brazil
[3] Department of Electrical Engineering (PPGEE), Federal University of Parana (UFPR), Polytechnic Center, Curitiba, Brazil

Abstract. The Industry 4.0 smart factories allow both optimization and integration of internal processes, utilizing the predictability of failure elements/components in a manufacturing process to prevent reprovals at the end of the process for quality control. The Supervised Machine Learning (ML) methods could be useful to detect anomalies and gain even more value throughout the entire supply chain. The ML approaches face barriers since it demands a changing in the production plant mindset to a more digital production and in the organization's structure for a more advanced data security. The paper aims to propose a smart inconsistency and fail prediction system for manufacturing systems of an automakers supplier assembly process based on the applications of ML techniques. The data provided for the training showed significant deviations and non-linearity allied to only 5 attributes as input variables, which is considered a small number of features for similar problems in the literature. The trained model was then applied to the assembly line with unobserved data of new products, with its result compared with similar previous productions. The results of the tests showed that the proposed stacking model lessens the possibility of rework in the next stages of assembly and creates a more precise process control for the supervisor. The implementation's results pointed out the potential of the stacking model proposed to be a useful tool in the context of Industry 4.0 since the reductions mean greater availability of production time and lower costs with quality control.

Keywords: Industry 4.0 · Machine learning · Quality control · Failure prediction · Smart manufacturing · Automaker supplier

1 Introduction

Nowadays, the increased use of traceability and connectivity technologies by the automotive industry and its suppliers has made it possible to collect and study manufacturing

A. Dolgui et al. (Eds.): APMS 2021, IFIP AICT 630, pp. 303–310, 2021.
https://doi.org/10.1007/978-3-030-85874-2_32

data focusing on process control and its optimization. There is a collective need from global industries to digitize products and processes in the context of the fourth industrial revolution, thus guaranteeing product quality and digital excellence [1]. The heart of Industry 4.0 is the rise of smart factories, which includes smart networking between industry units, processes, and operations. It focuses on flexibility and interoperability of processes, integrating the customer's and supplier's information and requirements with the adoption of new business models [2].

requirements with the adoption of new business models [2].

Implementing the new paradigm of Industry 4.0 follows three characteristics: i) The horizontal integration across the entire value network; ii) End-to-end engineering across the entire product lifecycle management, and iii) Vertical integration and networked manufacturing systems [3]. The vertical integration and networked manufacturing systems allow both optimization and integration of internal processes, which leads to a higher understanding of the whole manufacturing process and quality control of the product features.

For quality control, the predictability of failure elements/components in a manufacturing process can help prevent reprovals at the end of the process, and thus ensuring higher quality for the end-user. In this way, AI techniques come to assist the process of failure prediction to make the whole process more robust and less subjective. It integrates technologies/machinery, workers, and information, creating an agile and responsive process, and process control systems [4, 5].

The paper aims to propose a smart inconsistency and fail prediction system for manufacturing systems based on the applications of ML techniques. The validation of the system is in a real environment of assembly of parts for the automotive sector to carry out the control quality, generating a powerful tool for the production line' supervisors.

2 Related Works

Over recent years, industries and research centers have made significant efforts and progress into implementing smart manufacturing and smart industries techniques in the Industry 4.0 era. According to [6–9], in the last decade, the manufacturing industries are having more demand for customized products without losing quality and production indicator and remaining competitive. The companies need to analyze and remodel their processes in this new context of production.

Industries experience a complex manufacturing environment based on multicriteria decisions, and the forecast for manufacturing processes influence the quality and efficiency indicators significantly [10, 11]. Machine Learning core technologies work well with the complexes problems generated inside de industry and can be applied to reduce fixed costs, rework indicators, and improve key production indicators and speed [12].

The use of artificial intelligence and machine learning in the quality control of companies is becoming increasingly frequent. In the production floor, one of the most challenging problem for quality and process control is the product measurement variability in processes like assembly and machining and can occur in industries such as the automotive, since it can be influenced by various factors [13, 14]. According to [15], Machine Learning applications can help Lean Manufacturing lines to have more quality and efficiency, especially in the automotive supplier industry, where the connectivity from machines and production lines data is vital for efficient production. The application of machine learning models can be facilitated by a smart manufacturing environment since they refer to the new paradigm of production where manufacturing machines are fully connected, monitored, and controlled via smart systems, improving productivity, sustainability and reducing costs [16–18].

Finally, adapting machine learning concepts to a domain of knowledge within a real industrial process can present several challenges. One of the challenges is that ML applications cannot impact machine cycle times, and often must be optimized to not significantly impact process times. In addition, the processing power of machines on the production line is generally limited to the production processes themselves, requiring the design of shared processing in the cloud to achieve robust ML model training and satisfactory results [19]. Therefore, the quality control in real time in automotive supplier processes by ML models are still very limited to the complexity and training time required by the chosen models, being often simplified to obtain results that do not negatively impact other production indicators.

3   Problem Statement

This case study was carried out between two workstations located in an assembly line of an Automaker's Supplier Plant, and all names of variables and parts were adapted due to the Company's data security policies. The assembly process focused in this paper is shown in Fig. 1.

In this assembly process, the first station (Fig. 1 - station "A") receives two cylindrical parts (Fig. 1 - Detail "C1" and "C2") from previous machining processes and measures the internal height of the first part (Fig. 1 – dimension "X") and the external height from the second part ("Y" of Fig. 1). With these both measures, it calculates a compensational washer (Fig. 1 - Detail "W") using a Setup variable from the configuration of the product, and an Operator adjusts to adequate the manufacturing assembly into product requirements. The Setup Variable comes from customers' requirements, and the Operators adjustment is a readjustment to deal with deviations and inaccuracies, whether they are from previous machining processes or for general deviations from the assembly line.

From this, the assembled part is processed by operations "B" and "C" and performs a quality check at station "D". In this station (Fig. 1 - Station "D"), a remeasurement process, more accurate, checks whether the product complies with the specifications and whether the assembly at station "A" was correct (Fig. 1 - Detail "Q") and generates the Target Value in this study.

All variables are collected through sensors, which generate a text file at stations "A" (input) and "D" (target) containing all the information collected by the machines of each part. Every new part that passes through the stations then generates a text file being identified by a unique code of the part and that contains its variables which is transferred to a backup server to carry out quality and traceability analyses.

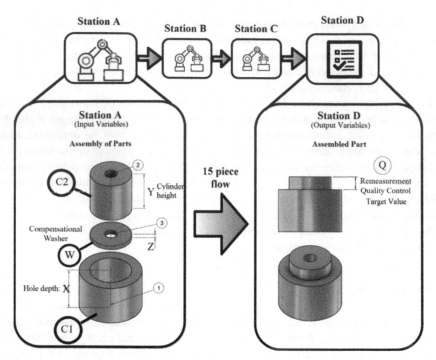

Fig. 1. Diagram of the automaker's supplier assembly process.

4   Conceptual Proposal

The proposed solution is to use a machine learning architecture for quality control that reads the text file generated by the machine before being sent to the backup server, since the creation of this file is instantaneous and presents all the available variables, and then makes prediction and an automatic adjustment at station "A" piece-by-piece based in historic production data. For the training of the ML models and analysis of variable behavior, it was used the historical data stored on the backup server of the production line, in which there is the text files with the individual data of all the parts that were processed in the last 3 years. This process can be seen in Fig. 2.

Five ML models were chosen for the architecture: i) *K*-Nearest Neighbor (*KNN*), ii) Random Forest (*RF*), iii) Gradient Boosting Machine (*GBM*), iv) Light GBM and v) XGBOOST. These ML models are classified into 3 groups of learning: association, interaction, and ensemble learning. These ML methods were chosen for their effectiveness in other similar case studies in the literature [20, 21] and for their simplified implementation on an assembly line since they are white-box methods, and it is possible to understand the importance of the variables.

The research focus is on the application of a machine learning model architecture and on overcoming the challenges faced in real-time implementation on a production line, where there are several factors to be considered. Therefore, models already used widely in the literature and with easy access to programming libraries were chosen, since this research does not propose a comparison of performance between individual models, being used a range of different algorithms for better overall performance. Finally, several algorithms like those proposed were discarded due to the difficulty of implementing them on computers within the production line, where access to information and programming libraries is restricted by secrecy and security.

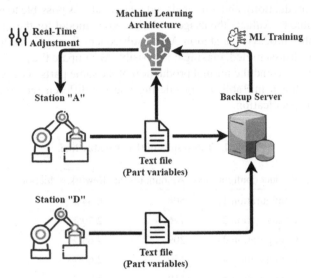

Fig. 2. Data flow diagram

After choosing the models to be used, a Staking structure of the machine learning models was designed, where KNN, RF, GBM and light GBM would be used as primary estimators since they present different types of learning methods between themselves and can gain knowledge in a different and optimized way, and XGBOOST as a meta-estimator. The XGBOOST model was chosen as a meta-estimator for its performance in similar benchmarks problems [22, 23] and the full use of available hardware.

The models were trained using the six variables (variable "X", "Y", "Z", "Setup variable", "Operator Adjustment" and "Remeasurement-Target Value"), mentioned in Fig. 1. All estimators were trained with historical production data of 120.000 product database and the grid-search of the hyperparameter was done for the tuning and optimization of each single model.

5   Results

The conceptual proposal provided the necessary knowledge for the functional test on the assembly line. The models used hyperparameters with the best result of the grid-search, and all attributes for better accuracy. The functional test was carried out on the assembly line during regular operation, indicating the adjustment of the washer in real-time by the created stacking model.

Moreover, to test the flexibility and robustness of the proposed model, tests were carried out on 10 different configurations of products with 7400 test parts supplied to different customers. Each consumer company requires different product configurations, such as different levels of quality, product requirements and geometries with different characteristics.

The rework indicators collected at station D were compared using the machine learning architecture proposed with productions of the same configuration of product without its use (normal production), and thus analyzed whether it was possible to reduce rework. It was not possible to evaluate the usage of the proposed model for the same parts since after the assembly processes at station A and subsequent B and C, the assembled part can no longer be disassembled, making it impossible to compare the production with the proposed architecture and the normal production of the same parts. The results obtained in the tests are shown in Table 1, considering that the different configurations mean distinct product specification.

Table 1. Test results of the assembly line.

Product configuration	Amount tested	Rework reduction
Configuration 1	508	0.54%
Configuration 2	726	2.79%
Configuration 3	209	4.65%
Configuration 4	150	2.60%
Configuration 5	719	5.28%
Configuration 6	258	6.03%
Configuration 7	96	8.57%
Configuration 8	584	-2.12%
Configuration 9	2139	1.20%
Configuration 10	1992	1.90%
Total	**7381**	**3.14%**

Table 1 shows that the use of the proposed staking model had a positive result in reducing rework in 9 configurations of products, and only 1 had a negative outcome. The only negative result was motivated by the developed architecture not being able to adapt to configuration 8 and thus accurately predict new parts in real time, in addition to reasons of temperature variation and dirt that can influence the system outcome.

In general, there was a 3.14% reduction in rework that represents a direct decrease in quality control costs and a more stable assembly line. Thus, the tests indicate that the proposed stacking model lessens the possibility of rework and creates a more precise process control for the supervisor.

6   Conclusion

In this article, we proposed and analyzed the process and results of implementing a machine learning stacking model on an automotive parts assembly line. The data provided for the training showed significant deviations and non-linearity allied to only 5 attributes as input variables, which is considered a small number of features for similar problems in the literature. An extensive grid search was performed with cross-validation to obtain the best hyperparameters for the problem and training the proposed model with a dataset of 2 months of production data.

The trained model was then applied to the assembly line with unobserved data and new products, and its result compared with similar previous productions. Around 7400 parts were tested, obtaining an average rework reduction of 3.14%.

The proposed model is highly robust and can be used in several similar problems, in which an adjustment is made, and a quality control is carried out based on this adjustment. The idea is that the quality control should measure the target value of all parts, and thus create machine learning models to understand the relationship between the input variables (until the part is adjusted) and the quality control variable. The proposed model was tested for mechanical adjustments made with washers, but it is possible to be used for mechanical adjustments of different types, and thus be used in almost any assembly process in the automotive industry as well as various processes.

The next steps for this research are to increase the robustness of the proposed model and increase its accuracy with different and newer machine learning models. Besides that, the proposed model must be tested on production and assembly lines of different products with other characteristics to test its flexibility and robustness with different problems.

References

1. Lu, Y., Chao, L., Wang, K.I.K., Huang, H., Xu, X.: Digital twin-driven smart manufacturing: connotation, reference model, applications and research issues. Robot. Comput. Integr. Manuf. **29**, 101837 (2020)
2. Kamble, S.S., Gunasekaran, A., Sharma, R.: Analysis of the driving and dependence power of barriers to adopt industry 4.0 in Indian manufacturing industry. Comput. Indus. **101**, 10719 (2018)
3. Peres, R.S., Rocha, A.D., Leitao, P., Barata, J.: IDARTS–Towards intelligent data analysis and real-time supervision for industry 4.0. Comput. Ind. **101**, 138–146 (2018)
4. Raj, A., Dwivedi, G., Sharma, A., de Sousa Jabbour, A.B., Rajak, S.: Barriers to the adoption of industry 4.0 technologies in the manufacturing sector: an inter-country comparative perspective. Int. J. Prod. Econ. **224**, 107546 (2020)
5. Szejka, A.L., Canciglieri Jr., O., Loures, E.R., Panetto, H., Aubry, A.: Requirements interoperability method to support integrated product development. In: 45th Computers and Industrial Engineering, vol. 147, pp. 1–8. Metz (2015)
6. Bauters, K., Cottyn, J., Claeys, D., Slembrouck, M., Veelaert, P., Van Landeghem, H.: Automated work cycle classification and performance measurement for manual workstations. Robot. Comput. Integr. Manuf. **51**, 139–157 (2018)
7. Tvenge, N., Martinsen, K.: Integration of digital learning in industry 4.0. Procedia Manuf. **23**, 261–266 (2018)

8. Gattullo, M., Scurati, G.W., Fiorentino, M., Uva, A.E., Ferrise, F., Bordegoni, M.: Towards augmented reality manuals for industry 4.0: a methodology. Robot. Comput. Integr. Manuf. **56**, 276–286 (2019)

9. Adamczyk, B.S., Szejka, A.L., Canciglieri, O.: Knowledge-based expert system to support the semantic interoperability in smart manufacturing. Comput. Ind. **115**, 103161 (2020). https://doi.org/10.1016/j.compind.2019.103161

10. Lingitz, L., et al.: Lead time prediction using machine learning algorithms: a case study by a semiconductor manufacturer. Procedia CIRP **72**, 1051–1056 (2018)

11. Sharp, M., Ak, R., Hedberg, T., Jr.: A survey of the advancing use and development of machine learning in smart manufacturing. J. Manuf. Syst. **48**, 170–179 (2018)

12. Murphy, R., Newell, A., Hargaden, V., Papakostas, N.: Machine learning technologies for order flowtime estimation in manufacturing systems. Procedia CIRP **81**, 701–706 (2019)

13. Weichert, D., Link, P., Stoll, A., Rüping, S., Ihlenfeldt, S., Wrobel, S.: A review of machine learning for the optimisation of production processes. Int. J. Adv. Manuf. Technol. **104**(5–8), 1889–1902 (2019)

14. Carvalho, T.P., Soares, F.A., Vita, R., Francisco, R.D.P., Basto, J.P., Alcalá, S.G.: A systematic literature review of machine learning methods applied to predictive maintenance. Comput. Indus. Eng. **137**, 1060424 (2019)

15. Şenkayas, H., Gürsoy, Ö.: Industry 4.0 Applications and Digitalization of Lean Production Lines. The Annals of the University of Oradea, p.124 (2018)

16. Wang, J., Ma, Y., Zhang, L., Gao, R.X., Wu, D.: Deep learning for smart manufacturing: methods and applications. J. Manuf. Syst. **48**, 144–156 (2018)

17. Scurati, G.W., Gattullo, M., Fiorentino, M., Ferrise, F., Bordegoni, M., Uva, A.E.: Converting maintenance actions into standard symbols for Augmented Reality applications in Industry 4.0. Comput. Indus. **98**, 68–79 (2018). https://doi.org/10.1016/j.compind.2018.02.001

18. O'Donovan, P., Gallagher, C., Leahy, K., O'Sullivan, D.T.: A comparison of fog and cloud computing cyber-physical interfaces for Industry 4.0 real-time embedded machine learning engineering applications. Comput. Ind. **110**, 12–35 (2019)

19. Oh, Y., Busogi, M., Ransikarbum, K., Shin, D., Kwon, D., Kim, N.: Real-time quality monitoring and control system using an integrated cost-effective support vector machine. J. Mech. Sci. Technol. **33**(12), 6009–6020 (2019)

20. Peres, R.S., Barata, J., Leitao, P., Garcia, G.: Multistage quality control using machine learning in the automotive industry. IEEE Access **7**, 79908–79916 (2019)

21. Jia, Y., et al.: GNSS-R soil moisture retrieval based on a XGboost machine learning aided method: Performance and validation. Remote Sensing **11**(14), 1655 (2019)

22. Park, S., Moon, J., Jung, S., Rho, S., Baik, S.W., Hwang, E.: A two-stage industrial load forecasting scheme for day-ahead combined cooling, heating and power scheduling. Energies **13**(2), 443 (2020)

23. Gao, K., Chen, H., Zhang, X., Ren, X., Chen, J., Chen, X.: A novel material removal prediction method based on acoustic sensing and ensemble XGBoost learning algorithm for robotic belt grinding of Inconel 718. Int. J. Adv. Manuf. Technol. **105**(1–4), 217–232 (2019). https://doi.org/10.1007/s00170-019-04170-7

Resilient Project Scheduling Using Artificial Intelligence: A Conceptual Framework

Sarra Dahmani[1]📷, Oussama Ben-Ammar[2](✉)📷, and Aïda Jebali[1]📷

[1] SKEMA Business School, Université Côte d'Azur, Paris, France
{sarra.dahmani,aida.jebali}@skema.edu
[2] Department of Manufacturing Sciences and Logistics, Mines Saint-Etienne,
University Clermont Auvergne, CNRS, UMR 6158 LIMOS CMP, Gardanne, France
oussama.ben-ammar@emse.fr

Abstract. This paper explores the role that Artificial Intelligence (AI) can play in building resilient project schedules. Based on a literature review and brainstorming sessions, we introduce a conceptual framework that details how AI-enabled predictive and prescriptive analytics can be leveraged to improve project schedule resilience. The latter specifies the potential of AI to make use of historical and real-time data to better contain the effect of disruptions on project schedules.

Keywords: Project schedule · Artificial intelligence · Uncertainty · Resilience

1 Introduction

Project management with its various knowledge areas according to the Project Management Body of Knowledge (PMBoK) represents a growing subject in different disciplines in research. Attending effectiveness in managing project and especially in building schedules remains a challenge [1]. Change is part of a project process. Living with change, and having the ability to adapt project schedules quickly to disruptive unforeseen events is part of project management capabilities. This has been treated in literature under resilience for project management. Project risk management and dealing with uncertainties in project schedules has represented an important field in engineering oriented project management literature. Recent trends in literature defend the fact that facilitating change is more effective than attempting to prevent it [2]. For a project organization, building the ability to respond to unpredictable events is more important than trusting the ability to plan for disaster. In the same time, we witness the relevant diffusion of industry 4.0 driven technologies in organizations, through integrating information and communication technologies within organizations [3]. These technologies enable autonomous and dynamic processes through the

© IFIP International Federation for Information Processing 2021
Published by Springer Nature Switzerland AG 2021
A. Dolgui et al. (Eds.): APMS 2021, IFIP AICT 630, pp. 311–320, 2021.
https://doi.org/10.1007/978-3-030-85874-2_33

joint deployment of big data and Artificial Intelligence (AI). Similarly, historical data stemming from past projects and real-time data on current projects can be extracted to fuel AI models and timely derive scheduling decisions. In particular, such models will be used to intelligently anticipate and quickly respond to different disruptions.

Existing research has tended to focus on optimizing project scheduling problems for a proactive strategy. This raises many questions about whether AI and available data should be used to build resilient project schedules through both proactive and reactive strategies. In this preliminary work, we follow an exploratory approach to understand how AI techniques can be leveraged to bring resilience to project schedules. First, we conducted a literature review in order to identify the existent knowledge related to our research question. Based on a critical analysis of the literature, we conducted three brainstorming sessions over which we develop a conceptual framework that indicates how AI can be used in this field.

The paper is decomposed into seven sections. Sections 2 and 3 give a brief overview of existing literature on uncertainty and resilience in project management, and especially project scheduling. Section 4 investigates the existing AI techniques and analytics. Section 5 presents the notable works on AI in project scheduling. In Sect. 6, we expose the proposed conceptual framework for resilient project scheduling. Finally, Sect. 7 provides directions for future research at the confluence of resilience, project scheduling and AI.

2   Project Scheduling Under Uncertainty

Uncertainties in projects can be triggered by internal or external factors. The internal factors are those directly related to the project and can be organizational, related to the project's scope, or available resources. External factors are rather related to the market, technology, sociopolitical, environmental, and logistics [4].

A growing body of literature has investigated project scheduling problem under uncertainty of activity duration, resource usage and availability [4]. In the recent literature reviews presented in [4,5], one can see that project scheduling problems are classified into the following main categories: *"Basic Project Scheduling Problem (PSP), Resource-Constrained Project Scheduling Problem (RCPSP), Resource-Constrained Project Scheduling Problem with multiple objectives (Multi-Objective RCPSP), Multi-Mode Resource-Constrained Project Scheduling Problem (MRCPSP), Time/Cost Trade-off Problem (TCTP) and Resource - Constrained Multiple Project Scheduling Problem (RCMPSP)"*. To overcome uncertainty, proactive and reactive strategies are widely adopted. For more details on the specific features of these problem categories, the related modeling approaches and solution procedures, readers can refer to [4,5].

3   Resilience

To understand resilience, it's important to differentiate it from other notions and concepts that are closely related to it as reliability, robustness and agility. For this purpose, some of the notable definitions of these concepts are presented in Table 1. For more definitions, the interested readers can refer to [6–9]. In this research, we consider that resilience brings the broadest sens of dealing with disruptions whether they are internal or external to the system. As such, its attainment relies on flexibility, robustness, reliability and agility. An in-depth analysis of the literature in order to identify a common definition of resilience allows us to identify three interrelated notions: system, disturbance and equilibrium [10–13].

Table 1. Definition of some resilience related notions

Notion	Definition
Agility	*"an iterative approach to delivering a project throughout its life cycle, based on the maximization of simplicity and quality and with flexibility focusing on the continual readiness to embrace change."* [2]
Robustness	*"the ability of a system or product to perform its intended function, with the presence of noise factors, in a consistent manner."* [14]
Reliability	*"a key performance indicator of any industrial production system, is the probability that a system will be able to perform its function without failing for a specific time period under certain operating conditions."* [15]
Resilience	*"the capacity of social, economic and environmental systems to cope with a hazardous event or trend or disturbance, responding or reorganizing in ways that maintain their essential function, identity and structure while also maintaining the capacity for adaptation, learning and transformation."* [16]

Resilience represents the capacity of the system to find an equilibrium after undergoing a disruption. The resilience can be measured through specific indicators in terms of: time needed to regain the equilibrium for the system, amount or cost of damages caused by the disturbances, and it could be the magnitude of disturbance that can be absorbed before the system changes its structure by changing the variables and processes that control behavior [10].

Despite the progress of literature, project resilience in particular remains a concept for which in-depth bibliographical references remain limited [11]. Based on an empirical study on major infrastructure projects, this concept was first introduced in [12] and defined as: *"(i) the project system's ability to restore capacity and continuously adapt to changes and (ii) to fulfill its objectives in order to continue to function at its fullest possible extent, in spite of threatening critical events.*" In [13], project resilience is defined as the capacity of the project system to be aware of its surroundings and vulnerabilities, and to adapt in order to recover from disruptive events and achieve its objectives. According to [17], resilience in project can be defined through four criteria: (i) have enough free slacks, (ii) free slacks are distributed evenly in the schedule, (iii) have enough interval between the finish time of an activity and the start time(s) of its successor(s); and (iv) intervals are distributed evenly in the schedule. In this vein, Yeganeh and Zegordi [14] incorporate resiliency criteria based on activity float in building project schedule under uncertainty.

4   AI Techniques and Analytics

Different definitions of AI can be found in the literature. In [18], the authors define AI as a system's ability to accurately interpret external data, learn from the data, and use what it learns to complete specific goals and tasks.

Table 2. Summary of papers using AI in project scheduling.

Ref.	PM proc. group	Uncertain parameter(s)	Type of analytics	AI techniques
[19]	P	Duration	Prescriptive	RL
[20]	P/E/M&C	Effort	Prescriptive	QL
		Arrival of tasks		
		Employee availability		
[21]	P	Tasks' dates	Prescriptive	GA, Parallel Schedule
		Duration		Generation Schemes
[22]	P/E	Uncertainty at early	Prescriptive	Mining approach
		planning stages		Case-based reasoning
[23]	P	Duration	Predictive	ANN
[24]	P	Duration	Predictive	Nearest Neighbour
[25]	M&C	Duration	Predictive	SVM
[26]	P	Effort and duration	Predictive	ML
[27]	P/M&C	Duration	Predictive	ANN
[28]	P	Product development projects	Predictive	ANN, Fuzzy neural system
[29]	E/C	Projects delay risk	Predictive	ML

In the sequel of the availability of massive amounts of data generated by the Internet and the breakthrough advancement in computing over the last years, the popularity of AI has soared. The main techniques of AI are pattern recognition (PR), machine learning (ML), deep learning (DL), and reinforcement learning (RL), where many of them are related. Among the methods and algorithms that are used in these techniques, one can list artificial neural networks (ANN), support vector machines (SVM), Q-learning (QL), decision trees, fuzzy logic, evolutionary algorithms such as Genetic Algorithm (GA) and so on. Let us briefly introduce the above-mentioned AI techniques. For more details about these AI techniques, we refer the readers to [30–32] and related works.

Analytics can be defined as the use of data stemming from different sources and quantitative analysis to gain insights and drive informed decisions. As such, it is clear that advances in AI techniques will take analytics one step forward by improving its capabilities. Analytics includes three main stages characterized by different levels of difficulty, value, and intelligence [33]: (i) descriptive analytics, answering the questions "What has happened?", "Why did it happen?", but also "What is happening now?" (mainly in a streaming context); (ii) predictive analytics, answering the questions "What will happen?" and "Why will it happen?" in the future, and (ii) prescriptive analytics, answering the questions "What should I do?" and "Why should I do it?". However, as noted in [34], prescriptive analytics, which is aimed at making quicker, better, and optimized data-driven decisions, is still less mature than descriptive and predictive analytics, and as such, it is increasingly attracting the attention of researchers. AI techniques are particularly prominent in advancing predictive and prescriptive analytics.

5   AI in Project Management and Scheduling

Very recently, some surveys have been conducted in order to investigate the use of AI in project management [35–38]. The initial applications were mainly concerned with project information, project tasks, critical path method, and program evaluation and review technique where noticeably most of them are related to project scheduling [39]. For instance, in [39] the authors stated that AI could be used to analyze large datasets to find patterns, trends, and problems that need attention, based on knowledge from previous projects. AI techniques could also be leveraged to monitor how the project is going and make changes to future activities if needed. As such, AI can be particularly useful in project scheduling, costing and risk management and can be deployed in both project planning and control, which is in harmony with the findings of the recent surveys presented in [37,38]. Furthermore, AI can be used to assess the strengths of employees and leverage that to improve projects and support management and also to assist in the day-to-day tracking of projects to identify anomalies and outliers. Robotic Process Automation (RPA) is another prevalent application of AI in projects [40]. RPA can indeed be deployed to help project managers in their day-to-day work by freeing them from repetitive, high-volume tasks, like merging data from different systems to generate reports and project documents.

Table 2 reports some of the most relevant papers that use AI techniques and methods in project scheduling under uncertainty. Following the PMBoK, the second column of the table (PM proc. group) indicates for each paper the involved project management process group, namely planning (P), Executing (E), Monitoring and Controlling (M&C). The third, fourth and fifth columns provide for each paper (Ref.) the considered type of uncertainty, analytics and AI techniques, respectively. AI techniques are used either to develop project schedules and hence support decision making [19–22] or to predict more accurately the inputs of project scheduling, such as activity duration [23], or some project performances such as the project duration and cost [24–28] or delay risks [29]. Most of the works that include AI-enabled prescriptive analytics are using AI techniques along with optimization techniques to develop "better" project schedules. It is worth noting here that some meta-heuristics such as GA and modeling techniques such fuzzy logic, are often considered as AI techniques. For purpose of illustration, only [21] has been cited here. Markedly, the works devoted to the construction of project scheduling under uncertainty combining ML, DL and RL with optimization techniques are rather scant, even though the latter are often aimed at incorporating uncertainty. Only a few papers try to develop a resilient project schedule [14,17] but they do not use AI techniques. Using these techniques to build a resilient project schedule is hence very promising.

6   Conceptual Framework

Given the importance of adopting systemic approach in building resilient project schedule, the proposed conceptual framework (see Fig. 1) is based on three fundamental process groups in project management: Planning - Executing and Monitoring & Controlling. In the following, we detail the conceptual framework from the general vision of how AI can be useful to project scheduling according to project process groups; to the specific aspects focused on how available data can allow this.

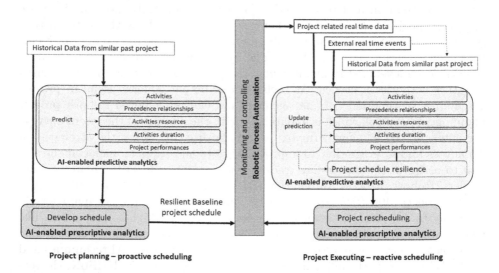

Fig. 1. Framework for building AI-enabled resilient project scheduling

First, in planning, we call for a proactive approach to build a resilient baseline schedule. During execution, the project schedule will be updated following a reactive scheduling approach whenever recommended by available data and predictions. Monitoring and controlling will ensure the continual transmission of available data related to the project progress. Relying on academic and professional referential literature, we select five fundamental elements of project scheduling: (1) activities, (2) precedence relationships, (3) resources, (4) activity durations, and (5) project performances (see Fig. 1). AI-enabled analytics can play an important role in predicting these elements at the planning and then during project execution. For example, artificial neural network, fuzzy neural system, support vector machine or genetic algorithm combined with K-nearest neighbor can be used to predict the real duration of a project or to tackle the uncertainties at different levels of planning [37].

Concerning data, we distinguish three main categories: (i) Historical data from past similar projects, this represents what comes from the knowledge system existing in the company allowing gathering data from all previous project experiences; (ii) external real time events allowing to consider in real time the events that may impact significantly the project schedule, this can be also understood as disruptions; (iii) and the project related real time data that includes all data coming from monitoring and controlling and from other sources that would impact the project schedule system.

We consider the importance of including resilience criteria since the development of the baseline project schedule. This resilience is based on historical data and emphasizes the learning from previous projects using AI techniques. During execution, resilience pertains to the ability of the scheduling system to react and adapt quickly to disruptions. From this perspective, the prediction of project schedule resilience will indicate in a timely manner if rescheduling is needed. Obviously, this depends on the ability of the current schedule to absorb disruptions, i.e. its robustness. The involved decisions in proactive and reactive scheduling will be facilitated by AI-enabled prescriptive analytics.

7   Discussion and Conclusions

Markedly, the application of AI to project scheduling relies on the availability of large historical datasets and project information. AI-enabled predictive and prescriptive analytics can be jointly used in this case to generate more accurate predictions and support decisions related to scheduling.

We built upon the gap identified in literature related to the scarcity of works studying resilience in project schedules. We define a conceptual framework to emphasize the value AI techniques can contribute to build better resilient project schedules. This represents a first step in a large exploratory approach we aim to create in the field.

This preliminary work will lay the ground for a more ambitious research that aims at the development and the adoption of intelligent project scheduling tools combining AI and optimization techniques. These tools should help project managers in building resilient schedules through better anticipation of disruptions and rapid adaptation. Our methodology will consider the importance of bridging the gap between project management community and AI and Operations Research specialists.

References

1. Fernandes, G., Ward, S., Araújo, M.: Improving and embedding project management practice in organisations–a qualitative study. Int. J. Project Manage. **33**(5), 1052–1067 (2015)
2. Fowler, M., Highsmith, J., et al.: The agile manifesto. Softw. Dev. **9**(8), 28–35 (2001)
3. Fatorachian, H., Kazemi, H.: A critical investigation of industry 4.0 in manufacturing: theoretical operationalisation framework. Prod. Plann. Control **29**(8), 633–644 (2018)
4. Hazır, Ö., Ulusoy, G.: A classification and review of approaches and methods for modeling uncertainty in projects. Int. J. Prod. Econ. **223**, 107522 (2019)
5. Ortiz-Pimiento, N.R., Diaz-Serna, F.J.: The project scheduling problem with non-deterministic activities duration: a literature review. J. Ind. Eng. Manage. **11**(1), 116–134 (2018)
6. Ivanov, D.: Viable supply chain model: integrating agility, resilience and sustainability perspectives–lessons from and thinking beyond the COVID-19 pandemic. Ann. Oper. Res. 1–21 (2020)
7. Husdal, J.: A conceptual framework for risk and vulnerability in virtual enterprise networks. In: Managing Risk in Virtual Enterprise Networks: Implementing Supply Chain Principles, pp. 1–27. IGI Global (2010)
8. Lenort, R., Wicher, P.: Agile versus resilient supply chains: commonalities and differences. In: Carpathian Logistics Congress, pp. 558–564 (2012)
9. Zitzmann, I., et al.: How to cope with uncertainty in supply chains? Conceptual framework for agility, robustness, resilience, continuity and anti-fragility in supply chains. In: Kersten, W., Blecker, T. (eds.) Next generation supply chains: trends and opportunities, pp. 361–377. Springer, Berlin (2014)
10. Holling, C.S.: Resilience and stability of ecological systems. Annu. Rev. Ecol. Syst. **4**(1), 1–23 (1973)
11. Thomé, A.M.T., Scavarda, L.F., Scavarda, A., de Souza Thomé, F.E.S.: Similarities and contrasts of complexity, uncertainty, risks, and resilience in supply chains and temporary multi-organization projects. Int. J. Project Manage. **34**(7), 1328–1346 (2016)
12. Geambasu, G.: Expect the unexpected: an exploratory study on the conditions and factors driving the resilience of infrastructure projects (Ph.D.). École Polytechnique Fédérale de Lausanne, Switzerland, Lausanne (2011)
13. Rahi, K.: Project resilience: a conceptual framework. Int. J. Inf. Syst. Project Manage. **7**(1), 69–83 (2019)
14. Yeganeh, F.T., Zegordi, S.H.: A multi-objective optimization approach to project scheduling with resiliency criteria under uncertain activity duration. Ann. Oper. Res. **285**(1), 161–196 (2020)
15. Lee, S.H.: Reliability evaluation of a flow network. IEEE Trans. Reliab. **R–29**(1), 24–26 (1980)

16. Goubran, S., Masson, T., Caycedo, M.: Evolutions in sustainability and sustainable real estate. In: Walker, T., Krosinsky, C., Hasan, L.N., Kibsey, S.D. (eds.) Sustainable Real Estate. PSSBIAFE, pp. 11–31. Springer, Cham (2019). https://doi.org/10.1007/978-3-319-94565-1_3
17. Xiong, J., Chen, Y., Zhou, Z.: Resilience analysis for project scheduling with renewable resource constraint and uncertain activity durations. J. Ind. Manage. Optim. **12**(2), 719 (2016)
18. Kaplan, A., Haenlein, M.: Siri, Siri, in my hand: who's the fairest in the land? on the interpretations, illustrations, and implications of artificial intelligence. Bus. Horiz. **62**(1), 15–25 (2019)
19. Sallam, K.M., Chakrabortty, R.K., Ryan, M.J.: A reinforcement learning based multi-method approach for stochastic resource constrained project scheduling problems. Expert Systems with Applications **169**, 114479 (2021)
20. Shen, X.N., Minku, L.L., Marturi, N., Guo, Y.N., Han, Y.: A Q-learning-based memetic algorithm for multi-objective dynamic software project scheduling. Inf. Sci. **428**, 1–29 (2018)
21. Masmoudi, M., Haït, A.: Project scheduling under uncertainty using fuzzy modelling and solving techniques. Eng. Appl. Artif. Intell. **26**(1), 135–149 (2013)
22. Yang, H.L., Wang, C.S.: Recommender system for software project planning one application of revised CBR algorithm. Expert Syst. Appl. **36**(5), 8938–8945 (2009)
23. Lu, M.: Enhancing project evaluation and review technique simulation through artificial neural network-based input modeling. J. Constr. Eng. Manage. **128**(5), 438–445 (2002)
24. Wauters, M., Vanhoucke, M.: A nearest neighbour extension to project duration forecasting with artificial intelligence. Eur. J. Oper. Res. **259**(3), 1097–1111 (2017)
25. Wauters, M., Vanhoucke, M.: Support vector machine regression for project control forecasting. Autom. Constr. **47**, 92–106 (2014)
26. Pospieszny, P., Czarnacka-Chrobot, B., Kobylinski, A.: An effective approach for software project effort and duration estimation with machine learning algorithms. J. Syst. Softw. **137**, 184–196 (2018)
27. Cheng, M.Y., Chang, Y.H., Korir, D.: Novel approach to estimating schedule to completion in construction projects using sequence and nonsequence learning. J. Constr. Eng. Manage. **145**(11), 04019072 (2019)
28. Relich, M., Muszyński, W.: The use of intelligent systems for planning and scheduling of product development projects. Procedia Comput. Sci. **35**, 1586–1595 (2014)
29. Gondia, A., Siam, A., El-Dakhakhni, W., Nassar, A.H.: Machine learning algorithms for construction projects delay risk prediction. J. Constr. Eng. Manage. **146**(1), 04019085 (2020)
30. Mohri, M., Rostamizadeh, A., Talwalkar, A.: Foundations of Machine Learning. MIT press, Cambridge (2018)
31. Deng, L., Yu, D.: Deep learning: methods and applications. Found. Trends Signal Process. **7**(3–4), 197–387 (2014)
32. Bishop, C.M.: Pattern Recognition and Machine Learning. Springer, New York (2006)
33. Lepenioti, K., Bousdekis, A., Apostolou, D., Mentzas, G.: Prescriptive analytics: literature review and research challenges. Int. J. Inf. Manage. **50**, 57–70 (2020)
34. Hagerty, J.: Planning Guide for Data and Analytics, p. 13. Gartner Inc., Stamford (2017)
35. Auth, G., JokischPavel, O., Dürk, C.: Revisiting automated project management in the digital age-a survey of AI approaches. Online J. Appl. Knowl. Manage. **7**(1), 27–39 (2019)

36. Ong, S., Uddin, S.: Data science and artificial intelligence in project management: the past, present and future. J. Mod. Project Manage. **7**(4) (2020)
37. Davahli, M.R.: The last state of artificial intelligence in project management. arXiv preprint arXiv:2012.12262 (2020)
38. Fridgeirsson, T.V., Ingason, H.T., Jonasson, H.I., Jonsdottir, H.: An authoritative study on the near future effect of artificial intelligence on project management knowledge areas. Sustainability **13**(4), 2345 (2021)
39. Foster, A.T.: Artificial intelligence in project management. Cost Eng. **30**(6), 21 (1988)
40. Branscombe, M.: How AI could revolutionize project management. CIO Australia (2018). https://www.cio.com/article/3245773/how-ai-could-revolutionize-project-management.html

A Digital Twin-Driven Methodology for Material Resource Planning Under Uncertainties

Dan Luo[✉], Simon Thevenin, and Alexandre Dolgui

IMT Atlantique, LS2N-CNRS, La Chantrerie, 4 Rue Alfred Kastler, B.P. 20722,
44307 Nantes, France
dan.luo2@imt-atlantique.fr

Abstract. With the Industry 4.0 revolution currently underway, manufacturing companies are massively adopting new technologies to achieve the virtualization of their shop floor and the collaboration of their information systems. This process often leads to the construction of a real-time, collaborative, and intelligent virtual factory of their physical factory (so-called digital twin). The application of digital twins and frontier technologies in production planning still faces many challenges. But the research is still limited about how these frontier technologies can be applied to enhance production planning. This paper introduces how to enhance material resource planning (MRP) with digital twins and other frontier technologies, and presents a framework for the integration of MRP software with digital twin technologies. Indeed, the data collected from the shop floor can improve the accuracy of the optimization models used in the MRP software. First, several MRP parameters are unknown when planning, and some of these parameters may be accurately forecasted from the data with machine learning. Nevertheless, the forecast will never be perfect, and the variability of some parameters may have a critical impact on the resulting plan. Therefore, the optimization approach must properly account for these uncertainties, and some methods must allow building probability distribution from the data. Second, as the optimization models in MRP are based on aggregated data, the resulting plans are usually not implementable in practice. The capacity constraints may be acquired by communication with an accurate simulation of the execution of the plan on the shop floor.

Keywords: Digital twin · Industry 4.0 · Material resource planning · Metaheuristics · Machining learning · Uncertainty

1 Introduction

The current supply chain is characterized by high complexity, high flexibility, mass customization, dynamic conditions, and volatile markets [1]. The rapid industrial environmental changes motivate an evolutionary and integrative perspective for supply chain management in Industry 4.0 [2]. In recent years, due to the rapid development of network technology, the technologies in the era of Industry 4.0 have developed rapidly, including the digital twin (DT), internet of things (IoT), cyber-physical systems (CPS),

© IFIP International Federation for Information Processing 2021
Published by Springer Nature Switzerland AG 2021
A. Dolgui et al. (Eds.): APMS 2021, IFIP AICT 630, pp. 321–329, 2021.
https://doi.org/10.1007/978-3-030-85874-2_34

big data (BDA) and analytics, artificial intelligence (AI), cloud manufacturing (CMg) [3, 4]. Because smart manufacturing is the core of the Industry 4.0 concept, production planning would be crucial for the supply chain management of Industry 4.0 activities [5]. In production planning, the goal of material requirement planning (MRP) software is to decide the quantities to produce and purchase over a given planning horizon. In this context, companies must enhance MRP software to respond to dynamic and diversified market changes. Existing research mainly focuses on the technological framework and how to achieve the technology of Industry 4.0. However, the research is still limited about how these frontier technologies can be applied to enhance MRP software. Therefore, in this work, we present a methodology for the integration of MRP software with digital twin technologies. The resulting tools enhance MRP software with machine learning to forecast MRP parameters, stochastic optimization to properly account for parameter uncertainty, and automatic constraints learning by communication with a detailed simulation.

The remainder of the paper is organized as follows. Section 2 provides a brief literature review for the production planning in the Industry 4.0 era. Section 3 introduces the optimization models used in MRP, and Sect. 4 presents the digital twin-driven methodology for MRP. Finally, the paper ends with the conclusion and some future research directions in Sect. 5.

2   A State of the Art

In this section, we discuss the application and research status of the main technologies of Industry 4.0 used in MRP software, including the internet of things, big data and analytics/artificial intelligence, digital twin/cyber-physical systems, and cloud manufacturing.

The internet of things is the crucial basis for realizing cloud manufacturing, digital twin, and big data analysis [9]. The core functions of IoT for MRP include the digitalization of resources and information sharing from different software. Indeed, intelligent devices, such as sensors and radio frequency identification (RFID), embedded in products and resources allow real-time data collection and monitoring. With these intelligent devices, the MRP software can know the status of each resource (e.g., machine status, inventory levels, etc.) in real-time [2, 10]. Besides, IoT facilitates the integration of information systems, such as enterprise resource planning (ERP) systems and manufacturing execution system (MES), to realize information sharing and collaboration [7]. Most of the research on IoT focuses on real-time collection, and application in scheduling [8]. Besides, most researchers consider a macroscopic view on IoT (e.g., the whole supply chain), and little work focuses on the application of IoT for the MRP in detail [11]. Therefore, there are still various problems that need to be studied and solved. For example, how to integrate information systems to achieve data-driven and dynamic planning, achieve distributed and collaborative planning for different workshops to support decision-making, and minimize the complexity of MRP systems.

MRP software is often used in an uncertain environment. That is, many parameters are not known when planning [6]. Therefore, big data and analytics/artificial intelligence are often used to forecast the parameters required for production planning [1]. Based on the massive data collected by IoT, BDA/AI tools can help MRP systems to predict the uncertain input parameters, such as the demand and capacity [12, 13]. In this way, we can improve the accuracy and performance of forecasting. Furthermore, we can realize precise representation for the workshop and get more practicable and adaptable planning [14, 15]. Existing research mainly focuses on demand forecasting, and only considers single uncertainty. The use of machine learning to predict the values of the parameters is not straightforward, since there exists a wide variety of predictive analytic approaches. The selection of the most appropriate approach depends on the context, usage, and volume of data [16, 17]. Therefore, one research trend is to propose a general big data prediction method for MRP software.

The digital twin/cyber-physical systems can provide decision-making support, dynamic production planning, and real-time visualization by building the virtual duplicate for the physical system [18, 19]. Based on the digital twin model, we can achieve automatic optimization, prediction, and re-planning for MRP [21], and extending MRP with real-time calculations, early reports, traceability, and visibility [20]. In this context, one challenge for MRP under the CPS environment is that enterprises must improve their adaptability, automation, and efficiency to deal with large-scale problems and more complex systems. Besides, because digital twins emphasize the integration and collaboration between systems, the implementation of cloud manufacturing (CMg) in MRP is also a critical process for constructing cyber-physical systems.

In summary, existing research mainly focuses on the technological framework and how to achieve the technology of Industry 4.0. However, the research is still limited about how these frontier technologies can be applied to upgrade the systems for production planning in detail. We summarize main challenges of frontier technologies in production planning as follows.

1) The relationships inside physical systems, the relationships inside virtual systems, and the relationships between physical systems and virtual systems, are complex to integrate.
2) The massive data creates new opportunities and challenges to make an effective production plan with frontier technologies.
3) How to use frontier technologies to provide the dynamic and automatic support of production planning for the managers is also an important challenge.
4) To address these challenges, we propose a vision and a methodology to enhance material resource planning with digital twins and other frontier technologies,

3   Optimization Model for MRP

The problem solved by MRP software is a multi-echelon multi-item capacitated lot-sizing problem (MMCLP). The MMCLP is to decide when to produce as well as the sizes of the production lots to minimize the expected total cost (including inventory holding costs, fixed setup costs, unit production costs, extra capacity cost). These decisions are made based on the demand, the bill of material, the production capacity, and the lead time. We introduce below the optimization model used in current MRP software. Several models exist in the literature, and we provide a generic enough model that would fit in most of the manufacturing industries. In particular, we consider the flexible bill of material (BOM), which leads to the flexibility and reactivity required in the Industry 4.0 era.

The demand D_{it} for item i can be represented with a parameter or a probability distribution. We assume that all customer demand is for end items only. If there exists a demand for components, we can create a dummy end-item corresponding to components reserved for shipping.

The multi-echelon flexible bill of materials gives the production structure of each item in the set I of items. We denote I the set of all items, I_e the set of end items, and I_c the set of components, where $I = I_e \cup I_c$. Each item i can be acquired by alternative operations, and each operation o produces a_{oi} units of item i, it consumes b_{oi} units of component i, and consumes k_{or} units of resource r. Modelling operations leads to a very generic lot-sizing model that can include alternative production routing and make or purchase decisions (Begnaud et al. 2009).

The requirement plan must account for the production capacity. Each resource r in the set of resources R has a given capacity C_r. In each period t, the capacity of resource r can be expended, and each unit of extra capacity costs o_r. The component i produced in period t is available in period $t + L_i$, where L_i denotes the lead time of item i. This lead time may correspond to the time between the placement of an order to a supplier and its delivery, or to the number of periods between an order is released to the scheduler, and the period where the item is produced. The inventory I_{it} will generate costs, and the backlog level B_{it} in period T corresponds to a lost sale. Besides, we define M as the big number.

The objective of the MMCLP is to determine the suggested production plan, including when to produce, how many items to produce, when to buy materials, and how many items to buy, and the amount of extra capacity required. We define the following decision variables:

Y_{ot} If a batch of operation o is performed in period t, and this is represented by a binary decision variable.

Q_{ot} The quantity of operation o to perform in period t.

w_{rt} The amount w_{rt} of extra capacity required for resource r in period t.

The objective function is the expected total cost, and it includes inventory holding costs h_i, setup costs s_o, production costs v_o, backlog costs b_i, and the extra capacity cost o_r. The MMCLP can be formulated as the following mixed-integer linear program (MILP).

$$\min \sum_{t \in T} \sum_{i \in I_e} (h_i I_{it} + b_i B_{it}) + \sum_{t \in T} \sum_{o \in I_c} (s_o Y_{ot} + v_o Q_{ot}) + \sum_{t \in T} \sum_{r \in R} o_r w_{rt} \qquad (1)$$

Subject to:

$$I_{it-1} - B_{it-1} + a_{oi} Q_{ot-L_i} - I_{it} + B_{it} = D_{it} \ i \in I_e, o \in I_c, t \in T \qquad (2)$$

$$I_{it-1} + a_{oi} Q_{ot-L_i} - \sum_{o \in I_c} b_{oi} Q_{ot} - I_{it} = 0 \ i, o \in I_c, t \in T \qquad (3)$$

$$Q_{ot} - M Y_{ot} \le 0 \ o \in I_c, t \in T \qquad (4)$$

$$\sum_{o \in I_c} k_{or} \bullet Q_{ot} \leq C_r + w_{rt} \; o \in I_c, t \in T \tag{5}$$

$$Y_{ot} = \{0, 1\} \tag{6}$$

$$I_{it} \geq 0 \tag{7}$$

$$B_{it} \geq 0 \tag{8}$$

$$Q_{ot} \geq 0 \tag{9}$$

The objective function (1) is the expected total cost. Constraints (2) and (3) ensure the balance of flow for all items in each period. Constraints (4) set the production quantities to zero in periods without operations. Constraints (5) enforce limits on production capacity.

Based on this distribution, the tool will generate a set of scenarios with Monte Carlo or Quasi Monte Carlo methods. For instance, uncertain demands can be represented by the set Ω of demand scenarios, where each scenario $\omega \in \Omega$ represent a possible realization of the demands over the planning horizon, and it has a probability p_ω.

4 The Digital Twin-Driven Material Resource Planning

In this section, we propose a digital twin-driven MRP software, before describing its main elements, including the machine learning based uncertainty forecasting, and the fix-and-optimize algorithm for two-stage stochastic optimization.

4.1 The Digital Twin-Driven Integration Scheme

Figure 1 shows the digital twin-driven integration scheme for the MRP software, which describes how the physical system communicates with the virtual systems, and how to integrate the production planning with the simulator and the scheduler.

The domain model, one of the core components in the digital twin, is the bridge between the physical system and the visual systems. This domain model integrates data from heterogeneous sources (MES, ERP, IoT devices), and it provides the user with a rich data structure to understand this data. This data is then accessible to the simulation, the production planner, and the scheduler.

The simulation models help the user validate a production plan by providing a precise execution of the plan at a detailed level (with each machine, employee, transport between machines, etc.). The simulation gives a clear understanding of the performance of a production plan, since it can compute various KPIs relevant to the user. The simulation is also a valuable tool to enrich the optimization model. As explained in Sect. 4.3, the simulation can learn the capacity constraint from various simulation runs.

The production planner will provide the size of the production batches to the scheduler as well as a targeted production period. In the scheduler, the release date corresponds to the start of the period, and the due date corresponds to the end of the period. The due date in the scheduler is a soft due date, to ensure adherence to the production schedule, whereas the customer due date might be penalized strongly or even considered as hard deadlines.

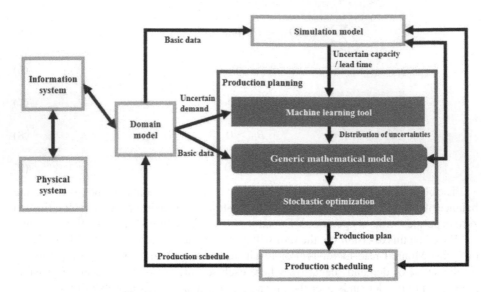

Fig. 1. The digital twin-driven integration scheme

4.2 Machine Learning Based Uncertainty Forecasting

The machine learning based uncertainty forecasting creates a Bayesian network using the data from the domain model or simulation model. The user will select the parameter to learn and the possible explanatory parameter. The Bayesian network is built from the relations in the domain model, and we learn the conditional probability with pair copula. The major sources of uncertainties in material resource planning include the demand, the production and delivery lead time, the process duration, and the production capacity. For instance, the capacity uncertainty can be inferred from the machine breakdown represented by the mean time between failures, and the mean failure duration.

To forecast the distribution of uncertain parameters, the input data for machine learning has two sources. For uncertain demand, the input data is from historical data, including the customer order and production plans implemented in the past. For uncertain lead time and production capacity, the input data can be generated by the simulation model.

4.3 Predictive Analytics of Capacity Constraints

Tactical planning tools, such as MRP and APS (advanced planning and scheduling), decide the production amount over a long planning horizon (several months). In this context, the planning decisions are not based on a detailed model of the shop floor. The main reasons are that the resulting optimization problem would not be solvable, and it would lead to nervousness that aggregated data is more reliable than detailed one (e.g., determining the demand for the car is easier than for each specific car model). Consequently, we aggregate items, resources, and periods. The granularity of production planning is a day or a week. The items and resources are aggregated into families.

Typically, a resource family is a group of resources (a work cell). This aggregation may lead to errors [23]. For instance, the resource consumption is computed for each resource group, but planning approaches allocate specific resources to each operation. More precisely, the capacity constraint is a linear function described as follows:

$$\sum_{(o \in O)} Q_{ot} k_{or} \leq C_{rt} + w_{rt} \tag{10}$$

where k_{or} is an estimate of the processing time of an operation of family o on a resource of family r. In practice, the process duration may vary depending on the precise operation to perform, and on the specific resource that performs the operation. Besides, the production schedule may include idle time, and not all resources in a resource family can perform all operations.

Consequently, a production plan may not respect the production capacity once implemented in practice or the simulation. Some authors propose a rich model that integrates planning and scheduling [24], but the resulting model can only solve small scale instances. We aim to learn the capacity constraints in the mathematical model through machine learning based on the output of the simulation. The tool can run a simulation model to get the capacity consumption associated with given production quantities.

4.4 Fix-and-Optimize Algorithm for Two-Stage Stochastic Optimization

Mathematical optimization is the most appropriate tool for planning. The lot-sizing models have attracted a lot of work from the operation research community. Researchers propose several reformulations, cuts, and solution algorithms such as Lagrangian Relaxation, cutting planes. However, solving the complex lot-sizing problem under uncertainty is hard, especially in the dynamic decision framework, where the production setups are updated as the information unfolds. The existing works are limited to small-scale instances in a simple environment [25]. To solve large instances, with multi-echelon BOM in a long-term planning horizon, improved heuristic algorithms must be provided. For instance, Thevenin et al. [22] showed that the two-stage approximation provides a good heuristic to the static-dynamic decision framework when the demand is uncertain. However, more research is needed to solve lot-sizing problems in a long-term planning horizon, and the use of the fix-and-optimize approach may be a possible research direction. Besides, more research should focus on developing methods to handle the dynamic decision framework. Based on the two-stage approximation proposed by Thevenin et al. [22], more works required to do are listed as follows.

1) Evaluate the quality of this heuristic for other types of uncertainties (lead time/capacity/process duration/demand).
2) Extend the tool to a more generic lot-sizing model (with flexible BOM/possibility to add extra capacity).
3) Evaluate the quality of this heuristic for the dynamic type of uncertainties.
4) Improve the approach to solving large scale instances of the problem.

5 Conclusion and Perspectives

In this paper, we propose a digital twin-driven methodology for material resource planning software. The paper focuses on how to achieve the integration between the MRP system and other systems under the CPS environment. We also describe how to design a digital twin-based MRP system to solve planning problems in a dynamic and uncertain environment. First, the distribution of uncertainties can be predicted using machine learning. Then, with the distribution of uncertainties and basic data as the input of production planning, the generic mathematical model can represent the physical system precisely. Third, the fix-and-optimize algorithm can obtain the results for the MMCLP. Based on this, MRP systems can provide practicable and adaptable production plans and re-plans efficiently for large-scale planning problems.

For future research perspectives, we will conduct and implement the proposed method in a real factory. A comprehensive framework, which includes not only the production planning for MRP, but also a detailed description of the production scheduling and the connection protocols between them will be provided. Moreover, we are looking forward to improving the heuristic algorithm and machine learning method for the MMCLP. Finally, an interesting work direction is to study how to maximize efficiency and minimize the complexity of the MRP system when we integrate it with other systems under the CPS environment in Industry 4.0.

References

1. Usuga Cadavid, J.P., Lamouri, S., Grabot, B., Pellerin, R., Fortin, A.: Machine learning applied in production planning and control: a state-of-the-art in the era of industry 4.0. J. Intell. Manuf. **31**(6), 1531–1558 (2020). https://doi.org/10.1007/s10845-019-01531-7
2. Bueno, A.F., Godinho Filho, M., Frank, A.G.: Smart production planning and control in the Industry 4.0 context: a systematic literature review. Comput. Indus. Eng. 106774 (2020)
3. Ivanov, D., Dolgui, A.: A digital supply chain twin for managing the disruption risks and resilience in the era of Industry 4.0. Prod. Planning Control, 1–14 (2020)
4. Ivanov, D., Sokolov, B., Dolgui, A.: Introduction to scheduling in industry 4.0 and cloud manufacturing systems. In: Sokolov, B., Ivanov, D., Dolgui, A. (eds.) Scheduling in Industry 4.0 and Cloud Manufacturing, pp. 1–9. Springer International Publishing, Cham (2020). https://doi.org/10.1007/978-3-030-43177-8_1
5. Oluyisola, O.E., Sgarbossa, F., Strandhagen, J.O.: Smart production planning and control: concept, use-cases and sustainability implications. Sustainability **12**(9), 3791 (2020)
6. Dolgui, A., Prodhon, C.: Supply planning under uncertainties in MRP environments: a state of the art. Annu. Rev. Control. **31**(2), 269–279 (2007)
7. Fang, C., Liu, X., Pardalos, P.M., Pei, J.: Optimization for a three-stage production system in the Internet of Things: procurement, production and product recovery, and acquisition. Int. J. Adv. Manuf. Technol. **83**(5–8), 689–710 (2015). https://doi.org/10.1007/s00170-015-7593-1
8. Zhang, Y., et al.: The 'Internet of Things' enabled real-time scheduling for remanufacturing of automobile engines. J. Clean. Prod. **185**, 562–575 (2018)
9. Hwang, Y.M., Kim, M.G., Rho, J.J.: Understanding Internet of Things (IoT) diffusion: focusing on value configuration of RFID and sensors in business cases (2008–2012). Inf. Dev. **32**(4), 969–985 (2016)

10. Rauch, E., Dallasega, P., Matt, D.T.: Complexity reduction in engineer-to-order industry through real-time capable production planning and control. Prod. Eng. Res. Devel. **12**(3–4), 341–352 (2018). https://doi.org/10.1007/s11740-018-0809-0
11. Wang, M., Altaf, M.S., Al-Hussein, M., Ma, Y.: Framework for an IoT-based shop floor material management system for panelized homebuilding. Int. J. Constr. Manag. **20**(2), 130–145 (2020)
12. Lolli, F., Balugani, E., Ishizaka, A., Gamberini, R., Rimini, B., Regattieri, A.: Machine learning for multi-criteria inventory classification applied to intermittent demand. Prod. Planning Control **30**(1), 76–89 (2019)
13. Gonzalez-Vidal, A., Jimenez, F., Gomez-Skarmeta, A.F.: A methodology for energy multivariate time series forecasting in smart buildings based on feature selection. Energy Build. **196**, 71–82 (2019)
14. Alexopoulos, K., Nikolakis, N., Chryssolouris, G.: Digital twin-driven supervised machine learning for the development of artificial intelligence applications in manufacturing. Int. J. Comput. Integr. Manuf. **33**(5), 429–439 (2020)
15. Kück, M., Freitag, M.: Forecasting of customer demands for production planning by local k-nearest neighbor models. Int. J. Prod. Econ. **231**, 107837 (2021)
16. Kusiak, A.: Smart manufacturing must embrace big data. Nature News **544**(7648), 23 (2017)
17. Kusiak, A.: Fundamentals of smart manufacturing: a multi-thread perspective. Annu. Rev. Control. **47**, 214–220 (2019)
18. Shao, G., Helu, M.: Framework for a digital twin in manufacturing: scope and requirements. Manufacturing Letters **24**, 105–107 (2020)
19. Liu, M., Fang, S., Dong, H., Cunzhi, X.: Review of digital twin about concepts, technologies, and industrial applications. J. Manuf. Syst. **58**, 346–361 (2021). https://doi.org/10.1016/j.jmsy.2020.06.017
20. Bogataj, D., Bogataj, M., Hudoklin, D.: Mitigating risks of perishable products in the cyber-physical systems based on the extended MRP model. Int. J. Prod. Econ. **193**, 51–62 (2017)
21. Lin, F., Wong, M.C., Ge, M.: Development of the digital model of the jewellery production process for resource optimisation and prediction. HKIE Trans. **25**(4), 229–236 (2018)
22. Thevenin, S., Adulyasak, Y., Cordeau, J.F.: Material requirements planning under demand uncertainty using stochastic optimization. Prod. Oper. Manage. **30**(2), 475–493 (2021)
23. Taal, M., Wortmann, J.C.: Integrating MRP and finite capacity planning. Prod. Planning Control **8**(3), 245–254 (1997)
24. Chen, K., Ji, P.: A mixed integer programming model for advanced planning and scheduling (APS). Eur. J. Oper. Res. **181**(1), 515–522 (2007)
25. Thevenin, S., Adulyasak, Y., Cordeau, J.F.: Stochastic dual dynamic programming for multi-echelon lot-sizing with component substitution

Low-Code and Model-Driven Engineering for Production System

Towards Development Platforms for Digital Twins: A Model-Driven Low-Code Approach

Judith Michael[1(✉)] and Andreas Wortmann[2]

[1] Software Engineering, RWTH Aachen University, Aachen, Germany
michael@se-rwth.de
[2] Institute for Control Engineering of Machine Tools and Manufacturing Units (ISW), University of Stuttgart, Stuttgart, Germany
andreas.wortmann@isw.uni-stuttgart.de

Abstract. Digital Twins in smart manufacturing must be highly adaptable for different challenges, environments, and system states. In practice, there is a need for enabling the configuration of Digital Twins by domain experts. Low-code approaches seem to be a meaningful solution for configuration purposes but often lack extension options. We propose a model-driven low-code approach for the configuration and reconfiguration of Digital Twins using language plugins. This approach uses model-driven software engineering and software language engineering methods to derive a configurable digital twin implementation. Moreover, we discuss some remaining challenges such as interoperability, language modularity, evolution, integration of assistive services, collaborative development, and web-based debugging.

Keywords: Digital Twin · Low-code platform · Model-driven software engineering · Software language engineering

1 Motivation

Digital Twins provide means to monitor and control Cyber-Physical Systems (CPSs) in various domains, such as smart manufacturing [29], biology [19], or autonomous driving [8]. They serve different purposes, such as analysis [23], control [31], or behavior prediction [21]. They promise tremendous potential to reduce cost and time and improve our understanding of the twinned systems.

Where human operators and their expertise are involved, such Digital Twins must provide access to data about the CPS in human-readable form via Graphical User Interfaces (GUIs), also called Digital Twin cockpits [10], allow for interaction and provide situational support via assistive services [22,30]. Cyber-Physical Production Systems (CPPSs) are long-living complex systems that

© IFIP International Federation for Information Processing 2021
Published by Springer Nature Switzerland AG 2021
A. Dolgui et al. (Eds.): APMS 2021, IFIP AICT 630, pp. 333–341, 2021.
https://doi.org/10.1007/978-3-030-85874-2_35

operate in different environments and experience vastly different usage histo-
ries. Consequently, Digital Twins in production must be highly adaptable for
different challenges, environments, and system states. Thus, they have to allow
for configuration at the commissioning of the Digital Twin and throughout their
lifetime. This configuration needs to be carried out by domain experts, which
typically lack formal software engineering training.

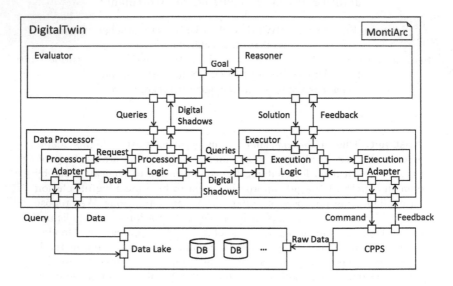

Fig. 1. Digital Twin architecture model

Low-code platforms [7,27] seem to be a promising way to enable domain
experts to create, configure, and operate complex systems for a specific purpose
in a particular domain. The combination of Model-Driven Software Engineering (MDSE) and low-code approaches have a high potential to facilitate the
fast configuration, instantiation, and operation of Digital Twins. We envision a
model-driven low-code approach for configuring Digital Twins and discuss challenges for future Low-Code Development Platforms (LCDP) that is based on
our experience in MDSE for Digital Twins [3,10,20] and enterprise information
systems [1,13] as well as in Software Language Engineering (SLE) [6,17]. In the
following, we present preliminaries in Sect. 2, before we discuss our vision in
Sect. 3, and discuss further future challenges in Sect. 4.

2   Background

Our vision rests on the model-driven architecture of Digital Twins and its integration with the MontiGem generator framework for Enterprise Information Systems as a visualization interface.

2.1   Digital Twins

Digital Twins are software systems comprising data, models, and services to interact with a CPPS for a specific purpose [3,10,20]. We devised a model-driven
architecture of self-adaptive Digital Twins [4] that integrates various application-
specific models to tailor the Digital Twin to specific challenges leveraging the MontiArc [5] architecture description language. The architecture (Fig. 1) realizes the
MAPE-K loop [2] of self-adaptive systems through components that query a data
lake (component `DataProcessor`), analyze resulting data (`Evaluator`), plan next
actions (`Reasoner`), and execute these (`Executor`). To this end, it operates in
the context of (1) a class diagram domain model and digital shadow [28] models,
(2) leverages application-specific event models to trigger (re)actions of the Digital Twin, (3) uses various models (*e.g.*, Statecharts, case-based reasoning models,
design of experiment models) to prescribe the behavior of CPPS and Digital Twin,
and (4) connection models to communicate commands to the CPPS. In the following, we will leverage this architecture to integrate further (low-code) modeling
languages towards truly domain-specific modeling of Digital Twins.

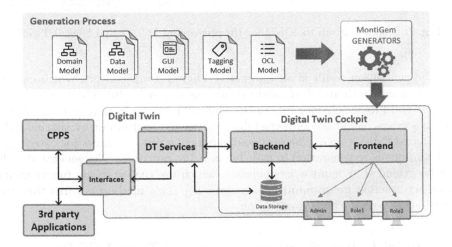

Fig. 2. Generating Digital Twin cockpits with MontiGem

2.2   MontiGem

Within [10], we have shown how to use the generator framework MontiGem [1] to
create interactive Digital Twin cockpits. Figure 2 presents the main generation
process. MontiGem can handle models in different Domain-Specific Languages
(DSLs) as input. Required is only the domain model represented using Class
Diagrams (CDs) [13]. Optional models include data models (views on the data
structure), GUI models representing the graphical interfaces, tagging models
for the addition of rights and roles, and Object Constraint Language (OCL) to
define restrictions on the data model and data input validation in the GUI.

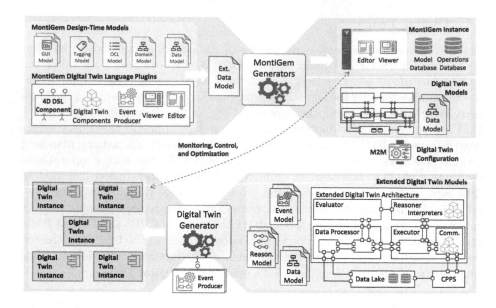

Fig. 3. A model-driven toolchain for the creation of LCDPs and Digital Twins

The generation result is an interactive Digital Twin cockpit, which can be integrated into a Digital Twin architecture, as shown in [10]. The Digital Twin cockpit and further components of the Digital Twin, such as reasoning or execution services, could be connected directly via the backend or by sharing data in a shared data storage. The proposed generation process allows for extensions and continuous re-generation in agile engineering processes. The generated code can be extended by hand-written classes, which use the extension functionality of object-oriented programming languages [16]. This method ensures that the additions remain during re-generation.

3   Model-Driven Synthesis of Digital Twin LCDPs

We envision combining our model-driven Digital Twin architecture with the MontiGem code generation framework to enable the pervasive model-driven development of low-code platforms for the creation, configuration, and operation of Digital Twins in production, as illustrated in Fig. 3.

MDSE of a LCDP for Digital Twins

Development of a LCDP for Digital Twins begins with selecting supported modeling languages through reasoning language plugins and communication language plugins. Each plugin comprises:

- A 4D DSL component [6] that encapsulates realizations of abstract and concrete syntax, well-formedness rules, and semantics in form of MontiCore [16]

grammars, Java context conditions, and FreeMarker-based code generators behind explicit interfaces of provided and required extensions.

- An interpreter for models of the component's DSL (reasoning language plugins) or a communicator translating reasoner input to communication objects for, *e.g.,* MQTT, OPC UA, or ROS (communication language plugins) as a (possibly hierarchically composed) MontiArc component model.
- An event producer creating Digital Twin event models from models of selected DSLs to invoke the interpreter of the Digital Twins to be created.
- A web-based editor and a web-based viewer for models of these DSLs that is compatible with the (graphical) language server protocol [26].

Given the models required for generating a MontiGem application and the language plugins and a model-to-model (M2M) transformation, the data model used as input for the MontiGem generator is extended with classes to capture the Abstract Syntax Tree (AST) of the available language plugins' DSLs. Afterward, the MontiGem generators process the MontiGem input models, the extended data model and the language plugins, generates a MontiGem application, integrates the editors into its user interface, creates databases for operation data and for models, and persists metadata about the available DSLs.

Model-Driven Creation of Digital Twins

With the low-code development platform in place, users can create Digital Twins conforming to our reference architecture using the available DSLs through a configuration assistant that employs information about these DSLs and their available models, *e.g.,* initially devised for other Digital Twins. To this end, they select (1) evaluation DSLs, *e.g.,* goal languages or BPMN for assistive services, (2) reasoning DSLs, *e.g.,* case-based reasoning [25] or PDDL [32], and (3) communication DSLs, *e.g.,* for connection to CPPS via OPC UA [24] and (4) assign an ID and further configuration information, *e.g.,* additional event models.

Based on the selection of DSLs, another M2M transformation integrates the interpreter components and communicator components of the corresponding language plugins into the reasoner and the executor of the Digital Twin's MontiArc architecture, respectively. Another M2M transformation produces new event models for the Digital Twins to react on model updates invoked by the connected MontiGem LCDP. The Digital Twin generator then takes the resulting extended Digital Twin architecture model, the handcrafted and generated event models, and its data models as input to produce executable Digital Twin instances. To this effect, it leverages the event producer components provided by the language plugins to derive events from the reasoning models that invoke their corresponding reasoner accordingly.

As the MontiGem LCDP and the Digital Twins operate on the same databases, the Digital Twin writes operation data, and the LCDP writes model changes, additional communication infrastructure is not necessary. In contrast, the CPPS is connected using a model of a communication language plugin.

4   Outlook

Our vision of a model-driven low-code approach for configuring Digital Twins facilitates researchers and practitioners in manufacturing in creating LCDPs integrated with Digital Twins and domain-specific modeling languages for the particular production challenges at hand. Extending, evolving, maintaining, and using the envisioned method in practices is subject to further challenges out of which selected are outlined below.

LCDP and Digital Twin Interoperability. Research and industry have produced various platforms (*e.g.*, Microsoft Azure, Amazon Greengrass, or Siemens Mind-Sphere) and modeling techniques (*e.g.*, Eclipse Ditto, Hono, and Vorto, Microsoft Digital Twin Description Language) to model Digital Twins. These platforms are walled gardens that lock the users to a specific vendor without systematic means for interoperability. As production needs to integrate systems and solutions from various OEMs and suppliers, interoperability of Digital Twins and their platforms is essential. The LCDP in Fig. 3 allows to specify communication DSLs for different communication standards and generates needed application interfaces. Approaches such as [20] already showed how to generate such interfaces from models.

Modeling Language Modularity and Evolution. To support addressing evolving challenges with a LCDP for Digital Twins, the employed modeling languages and language infrastructure must allow for modularity within the language. This includes the combination of building blocks and the establishment of language hierarchies [18], which, for instance, is important if Digital Twins for different application areas in smart manufacturing request different depths of, *e.g.*, event or reasoning models.

Integration of Assistive Services. Where production is not fully automated, including human operators in the loop is crucial. To mitigate the increasing amount and detail of production information, Digital Twins should assist operators in making the best possible decisions [22]. Consequently, functionalities such as analyzing a current action, identifying next actions and suggesting their execution [15] should be integrated into the toolchain. By now, there is still research missing, *e.g.*, on which modeling languages could be incorporated into these processes, what aspects have to be modeled to provide meaningful, automated support, or to provide variety in supporting devices.

Collaborative Development. Digital Twins of production systems will address multiple concerns of the twinned system and its, *e.g.*, strategic, context. Consequently, multiple stakeholders, such as shop-floor experts and managers, might interact with the Digital Twin collaboratively. Textual modeling techniques generally support this. Within the last years, a variety of collaborative modeling tools evolved as browser- or cloud-based solutions [11,12,14]. However, within the application domains of Digital Twins, areas such as support for graphical modeling, identifying and resolving modeling conflicts, as well as considering roles, rights, and corresponding views for successful collaborative intra- and inter-organizational modeling remain to be investigated.

Web-Based Debugging. For experimentation, configuration, and (virtual) commissioning, it is crucial to predict the Digital Twin's behavior on the twinned system. To this end, being able to debug, trace, and replay the Digital Twin's behavior is necessary. While there are various means to provide debugging, *etc.*., for modeling languages (*e.g.,* GEMOC Studio [9]), none of these provide generic or generative web-based interfaces.

5 Conclusion

The model-driven software engineering of low-code development platforms for Digital Twins in production promises powerful means to create and operate highly-specific platforms together with integrated Digital Twins for a more efficient configuration and operation of production systems. Our approach to combining MDSE and SLE to engineering such platforms signposts a possible realization of this vision.

References

1. Adam, K., Michael, J., Netz, L., Rumpe, B., Varga, S.: Enterprise information systems in academia and practice: lessons learned from a MBSE project. In: 40 Years EMISA: Digital Ecosystems of the Future: Methodology, Techniques and Applications (EMISA 2019). LNI, vol. P-304, pp. 59–66. Gesellschaft für Informatik e.V. (2020)
2. Arcaini, P., Riccobene, E., Scandurra, P.: Modeling and analyzing MAPE-K feedback loops for self-adaptation. In: 2015 IEEE/ACM 10th International Symposium on Software Engineering for Adaptive and Self-managing Systems, pp. 13–23. IEEE (2015)
3. Bibow, P., et al.: Model-driven development of a digital twin for injection molding. In: Dustdar, S., Yu, E., Salinesi, C., Rieu, D., Pant, V. (eds.) CAiSE 2020. LNCS, vol. 12127, pp. 85–100. Springer, Cham (2020). https://doi.org/10.1007/978-3-030-49435-3_6
4. Bolender, T., Bürvenich, G., Dalibor, M., Rumpe, B., Wortmann, A.: Self-adaptive manufacturing with digital twins. In: 2021 International Symposium on Software Engineering for Adaptive and Self-managing Systems (SEAMS), Los Alamitos, CA, USA, pp. 156–166. IEEE Computer Society, May 2021
5. Butting, A., Haber, A., Hermerschmidt, L., Kautz, O., Rumpe, B., Wortmann, A.: Systematic language extension mechanisms for the MontiArc architecture description language. In: Anjorin, A., Espinoza, H. (eds.) ECMFA 2017. LNCS, vol. 10376, pp. 53–70. Springer, Cham (2017). https://doi.org/10.1007/978-3-319-61482-3_4
6. Butting, A., Pfeiffer, J., Rumpe, B., Wortmann, A.: A compositional framework for systematic modeling language reuse. In: 23rd ACM/IEEE International Conference on Model Driven Engineering Languages and Systems, pp. 35–46. ACM (2020)

7. Cabot, J.: Positioning of the low-code movement within the field of model-driven engineering. In: Guerra, E., Iovino, L. (eds.) MODELS 2020: ACM/IEEE 23rd International Conference on Model Driven Engineering Languages and Systems, Virtual Event, Canada, 18–23 October 2020, Companion Proceedings, pp. 76:1–76:3. ACM (2020). https://doi.org/10.1145/3417990.3420210

8. Chen, X., Kang, E., Shiraishi, S., Preciado, V.M., Jiang, Z.: Digital behavioral twins for safe connected cars. In: 21th ACM/IEEE International Conference on Model Driven Engineering Languages and Systems, pp. 144–153 (2018)

9. Combemale, B., Barais, O., Wortmann, A.: Language engineering with the GEMOC studio. In: 2017 IEEE International Conference on Software Architecture Workshops (ICSAW), pp. 189–191. IEEE (2017)

10. Dalibor, M., Michael, J., Rumpe, B., Varga, S., Wortmann, A.: Towards a model-driven architecture for interactive digital twin cockpits. In: Dobbie, G., Frank, U., Kappel, G., Liddle, S.W., Mayr, H.C. (eds.) ER 2020. LNCS, vol. 12400, pp. 377–387. Springer, Cham (2020). https://doi.org/10.1007/978-3-030-62522-1_28

11. Di Rocco, J., Di Ruscio, D., Iovino, L., Pierantonio, A.: Collaborative repositories in model-driven engineering [software technology]. IEEE Softw. **32**(3), 28–34 (2015). https://doi.org/10.1109/MS.2015.61

12. Franzago, M., Di Ruscio, D., Malavolta, I., Muccini, H.: Collaborative model-driven software engineering: a classification framework and a research map. IEEE Trans. Softw. Eng. **44**(12), 1146–1175 (2018). https://doi.org/10.1109/TSE.2017.2755039

13. Gerasimov, A., Michael, J., Netz, L., Rumpe, B., Varga, S.: Continuous transition from model-driven prototype to full-size real-world enterprise information systems. In: 25th Americas Conference on Information Systems (AMCIS 2020). AIS Electronic Library (AISeL), Association for Information Systems (AIS) (2020)

14. Gray, J., Rumpe, B.: The evolution of model editors: browser- and cloud-based solutions. Softw. Syst. Model. **15**(2), 303–305 (2016). https://doi.org/10.1007/s10270-016-0524-2

15. Hölldobler, K., Michael, J., Ringert, J.O., Rumpe, B., Wortmann, A.: Innovations in model-based software and systems engineering. J. Object Technol. **18**(1), 1–60 (2019)

16. Hölldobler, K., Rumpe, B.: MontiCore 5 Language Workbench Edition 2017. Aachener Informatik-Berichte, Software Engineering, Band 32, Shaker Verlag, December 2017

17. Hölldobler, K., Rumpe, B., Wortmann, A.: Software language engineering in the large: towards composing and deriving languages. Comput. Lang. Syst. Struct. **54**, 386–405 (2018)

18. Johanson, A.N., Hasselbring, W.: Hierarchical combination of internal and external domain-specific languages for scientific computing. In: Zdun, U. (ed.) European Conference on Software Architecture Workshops (ECSAW 2014). pp. 1–8. ACM Press, New York (2014). https://doi.org/10.1145/2642803.2642820

19. Joordens, M., Jamshidi, M.: On the development of robot fish swarms in virtual reality with digital twins. In: 2018 13th Annual Conference on System of Systems Engineering (SoSE), pp. 411–416. IEEE (2018)

20. Kirchhof, J.C., Michael, J., Rumpe, B., Varga, S., Wortmann, A.: Model-driven digital twin construction: synthesizing the integration of cyber-physical systems with their information systems. In: 23rd ACM/IEEE International Conference on Model Driven Engineering Languages and Systems, pp. 90–101. ACM (2020)

21. Knapp, G., Mukherjee, T., Zuback, J., Wei, H., Palmer, T., De, A., DebRoy, T.: Building blocks for a digital twin of additive manufacturing. Acta Materialia **135**, 390–399 (2017)

22. Michael, J., Rumpe, B., Varga, S.: Human behavior, goals and model-driven software engineering for assistive systems. In: Koschmider, A., Michael, J., Thalheim, B. (eds.) Enterprise Modeling and Information Systems Architectures (EMSIA 2020), vol. 2628, pp. 11–18. CEUR Workshop Proceedings, June 2020
23. Pargmann, H., Euhausen, D., Faber, R.: Intelligent big data processing for wind farm monitoring and analysis based on cloud-technologies and digital twins: a quantitative approach. In: 3rd International Conference on Cloud Computing and Big Data Analysis (ICCCBDA), pp. 233–237. IEEE (2018)
24. Pauker, F., Frühwirth, T., Kittl, B., Kastner, W.: A systematic approach to OPC UA information model design. Procedia CIRP **57**, 321–326 (2016)
25. Recio-García, J.A., González-Calero, P.A., Díaz-Agudo, B.: jcolibri2: a framework for building case-based reasoning systems. Sci. Comput. Program. **79**, 126–145 (2014)
26. Rodriguez-Echeverria, R., Izquierdo, J.L.C., Wimmer, M., Cabot, J.: Towards a language server protocol infrastructure for graphical modeling. In: 21st ACM/IEEE International Conference on Model Driven Engineering Languages and Systems, pp. 370–380 (2018)
27. Sahay, A., Indamutsa, A., Ruscio, D.D., Pierantonio, A.: Supporting the understanding and comparison of low-code development platforms. In: 46th Euromicro Conference on Software Engineering and Advanced Applications, SEAA 2020, Portoroz, Slovenia, 26–28 August 2020, pp. 171–178. IEEE (2020). https://doi.org/10.1109/SEAA51224.2020.00036
28. Schuh, G., et al.: Effizientere Produktion mit Digitalen Schatten. ZWF Zeitschrift für wirtschaftlichen Fabrikbetrieb **115**special), 105–107 (2020)
29. Um, J., Popper, J., Ruskowski, M.: Modular augmented reality platform for smart operator in production environment. In: 2018 IEEE Industrial Cyber-Physical Systems (ICPS), pp. 720–725. IEEE (2018)
30. Vathoopan, M., Johny, M., Zoitl, A., Knoll, A.: Modular fault ascription and corrective maintenance using a digital twin. IFAC-PapersOnLine **51**(11), 1041–1046 (2018)
31. Verner, I., Cuperman, D., Fang, A., Reitman, M., Romm, T., Balikin, G.: Robot online learning through digital twin experiments: a weightlifting project. In: Auer, M.E., Zutin, D.G. (eds.) Online Engineering & Internet of Things. LNNS, vol. 22, pp. 307–314. Springer, Cham (2018). https://doi.org/10.1007/978-3-319-64352-6_29
32. Wally, B., et al.: Production planning with IEC 62264 and PDDL. In: 17th International Conference on Industrial Informatics (INDIN), vol. 1, pp. 492–499. IEEE (2019)

A Low-Code Development Environment to Orchestrate Model Management Services

Arsene Indamutsa$^{(\boxtimes)}$, Davide Di Ruscio, and Alfonso Pierantonio

Università degli Studi dell'Aquila, L'Aquila, Italy
{arsene.indamutsa,davide.diruscio,alfonso.pierantonio}@univaq.it

Abstract. The current digital transformation in production systems has positioned model-driven engineering (MDE) as a promising development solution to leverage models as first-class entities and support complex systems' development through dedicated abstractions. Models are specified through domain-specific languages and consumed by dedicated model management services, which implement automation and analysis services. Achieving complex model-driven tasks that involve several model management services and multiple model repositories can be a difficult and error-prone task. For instance, modelers have to identify the proper atomic operations among available services, connect to remote model repositories, and figure out their composition to satisfy the final goal. Different composition proposals have been introduced in MDE even though a satisfactory solution is still missing. In this paper, we propose a *low-code development environment* to support citizen developers to plan, organize, specify and execute model-management workflows underpinning the development of complex systems. Thus, developers are relieved from managing low-level details, e.g., related to the discovery, orchestration, and integration of the needed model management services.

Keywords: Production system development · Low-code development platform · Domain specific language · Cloud-based model repository · Workflow engine

1 Introduction

Production systems are highly interwoven systems that span through different engineering fields such as mechanical, electrical, network, software engineering, and control systems [21]. Such a synergistic integration introduce additional complexities due to the management of cross-disciplinary methods and the integration of heterogeneous artifacts together with their supporting tools. Model-Driven Engineering (MDE) is a software discipline that leverages the adoption

This work is funded by the European Union's Horizon 2020 research and innovation programme under the Marie Skłodowska-Curie - ITN grant agreement No 813884.

© IFIP International Federation for Information Processing 2021
Published by Springer Nature Switzerland AG 2021
A. Dolgui et al. (Eds.): APMS 2021, IFIP AICT 630, pp. 342–350, 2021.
https://doi.org/10.1007/978-3-030-85874-2_36

of models to support the understanding and the engineering of large, complex, and interdisciplinary systems, such as production systems while minimizing their complexity through the systematic adoption of abstractions [3]. Models are specified through graphical or textual domain-specific languages, and dedicated model management services consume them, e.g., to perform early analysis or automatically generate target software artifacts [2].

To foster reusability of modeling artifacts, and to support collaboration among modelers and developers [8], over the last decade, several model repositories have been proposed by the MDE community [2]. Thus, specific system models, and developed model management tools are made available in some of the existing repositories to promote their reuse during the development of new systems. However, in such contexts, model-based development of complex software systems requires the definition of different processes, consisting of the coordinated composition of different tools and the usage of various languages. Thus, developers must discover from available repositories the needed modeling tools and related model management services and work on their composition to develop the wanted system. The current main challenges that make the composition of model management operations a strenuous activity are the following:

- Current composition tools mainly deal with locally available resources;
- Composition mechanisms like ANT tasks are specific for the particular ecosystem at hand (e.g., Epsilon[1]);
- The development of complex engineering processes require technical expertise that citizen developers (i.e., domain experts with limited programming skills) might not necessarily have, though deemed to be aware of involved services.

In this paper, we propose the adoption of a low-code development platform (LCDP) to develop complex model management processes. LCDPs provide intuitive visual environments to citizen developers to build fully operational applications, which do not require a strong programming background [14]. The considered context is characterized by atomic model management operations provided as services by (potentially) different providers. The envisioned LCDP supports the discovery and the orchestration of the services needed to develop the wanted composed process. The objective is to develop an event-driven approach based on trigger-action programming as done by LCDPs like IFTTT and Zapier among popular services [20]. In such platforms, users can connect various independent services, organize and customize them in a specific flow to achieve their goal [13]. Similarly to such services, the proposed platform will support high-level abstraction and automation to compose model management services provided by different repositories. The current work is under development, and its code repository is publicly available online.[2]

The paper is organized as follows: Sect. 2 presents the background and motivation of this work. Section 3 presents the proposed approach. The related work

---

[1] https://www.eclipse.org/epsilon/doc/workflow/.
[2] https://github.com/Indamutsa/model-management-services.git.

is discussed in Sect. 4, whereas Sect. 5 concludes the paper and describe prospective work.

2 Background and Motivation

The digital transformation undergoing traditional production systems heavily impacts product types' variability, and customization possibilities during their life cycles [19,22]. Significant efforts and investments are required to implement and maintain complex production systems, limiting their acquisition by small and medium-sized enterprises (SMEs) [21]. Such systems' complexity is amplified when relying on the use of code-centric approaches that have proven daunting due to the arduous effort involved in programming, customization, and integration of complex heterogeneous systems coming from different engineering domains and processes [5].

This complexity sparked the need for flexible approaches that adapt to systems behaviour regarding the ever-changing requirements, structural transformations, and unexpected conditions [19]. To develop production systems and cyber-physical systems in general, MDE promotes the adoption of models as machine-readable and processable abstractions specified employing dedicated languages such as System Modeling Language (SysML).[3] Dedicated tools are employed to support development and analysis tasks, to integrate engineering processes and stakeholders' perspectives, and they also foster information exchange during different engineering process [3].

To simplify the development of complex systems, trigger-action programming paradigms can be employed to facilitate automation and abstraction. Such a paradigm is employed, for instance, in the Internet of Things (IoT) domain to develop applications in smart home management, agriculture, e-health, industrial automation, and robotics [15]. Systems like IFTTT, and Zapier are examples of LCDPs that facilitate business automation processes by giving users the means to specify processes [13]. In particular, they permit the creation of new services known as recipes out of custom chaining of services based on conditional statements [20]. For instance, a user can like a particular post on Facebook and automatically archive it on a corresponding storage in the cloud [11].

In [4] authors propose the Modeling as a Service (MaaS) initiative as an approach to deploy and execute model-driven services over the Internet. In such a direction, over the last years, several model repositories have been proposed to promote the reuse of modeling artifacts and to enable their remote execution on demand as services. For instance, in [2] authors propose MDEForge as a platform to enable the remote application of different services like model validation, transformation, and analytics. The composition of model management services is under the complete responsibility of developers that, e.g., have to define the programmatic orchestration of the services of interest and the ways data have to be produced and consumed.

---

[3] https://sysml.org/.

By relying on the concepts and tools previously mentioned in a model-driven engineering setting, we aim at developing complex model management composed operations by specifying custom workflows. We leverage trigger-action paradigm so that based on particular events (e.g., when you upload your model on a given repository), corresponding actions will be executed. For instance, some analytics are performed on the uploaded model depending on some condition. Then, if the performed analytics produce higher values than a certain threshold, some model transformations are executed, and the produced models are saved to enable the application of additional manipulations.

3   Proposed Low-Code Development Environment

In this section we describe the proposed low-code development environment. The front-end of the proposed platform is presented in Sect. 3.1. The core services of the platform are presented in Sect. 3.2 and its related limitations are mentioned in Sect. 3.3

3.1   Environment Front-End

Figure 1 shows a mock-up of the proposed environment providing users with the ability to create and automate workflows on cloud-based repositories using graphical environments with drag and drop capabilities, and custom scripting by the use of a domain specific language as referred to in Fig. 3. The custom scripting is enabled by an editor where the user can programmatically express complex expressions of the workflow. The services and extensions on the repositories are organized in decoupled and distributed microservices to emphasize the separation of concerns and foster individual service maintainability, scalability, and extensibility [16].

According to the explanatory workflow shown in Fig. 1, the citizen developer might want to upload a Performance Model Interchange Format (PIMF) model [10] and generate a corresponding SySML model out of it. Then, she can validate the model, calculate dedicated metrics, extract some metadata, and once done, merge the obtained information into another SySML model. The obtained model can be stored in the repository, and the user can be notified together with the complete execution logs. The services used in the above scenario are remotely accessed as services through APIs, and the storage systems are distributed services consisting of several network nodes.

Developing and execute model management workflows like the one shown in Fig. 1 without proper support can be time and resource consuming, laborious, hard to maintain and error-prone. The proposed approach aims at enabling citizen developers to create and automate workflows based on selected model management services using a graphical environment with drag and drop capabilities. The proposed environment is based on the metamodel shown in Fig. 2. According to the shown metamodel fragment, workflows consists of nodes, which are an abstract representation of activities referred to as actions and decisions.

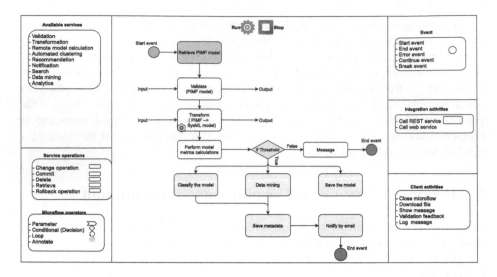

Fig. 1. Example mock-up of graphical task workflow environment

Several events can trigger activities, and the node can receive different types of inputs, such as modeling artefacts and variables. Events of interest and their sources are defined as seen in Fig. 1, and they result from different providers that trigger specific actions as instructed. Nodes represent decoupled, and independent microservices orchestrated when the specified workflow is executed.

3.2   Core Services

Figure 3 shows a logical view of the system and the corresponding stakeholders, notably two prominent actors involved, i.e., *citizen developers* and *software engineers.* The former can specify task workflows through the provided environment, whereas the latter can extend the repository services by adding new functionalities. The typical user (citizen developer) can access the repository, select services to automate, configure triggers and actions, and authorize task workflows. Interestingly, advanced support is provided to recommend modeling elements while editing workflows, and analyse, test, and deploy models by means of a dedicated DevOps support. Such support is provided by the workflow definition and analysis component. The service integration component ensures seamless integration of external and internal services. Once the modeled workflow is ready, the incoming model (task workflow) encoded in format such as xml/json, is transformed and executed by the engine. Mining and analysis services are performed before the model is persisted with the help of MDEForge [2]. Hence a backup is performed to facilitate data and service recovery, and rollbacks in case program execution encounters an impediment.

The user has control over the use of her task workflow, configuration, and termination. The developer can do whatever the user can do, but also, she can register services, establish connectors, and define triggers and actions related to

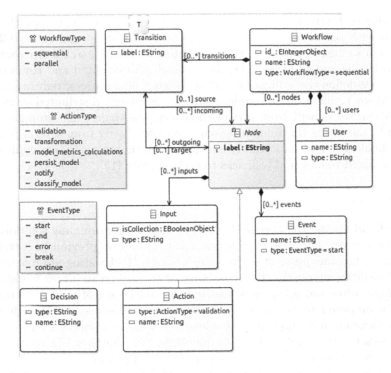

Fig. 2. Fragment of the proposed workflow metamodel

the added service. The task workflow expressed as models are managed by an engine and persisted as models by MDEForge, a cloud-based model repository, [2] to ensure their management and reusability. The engine has dedicated components that ensure the security, privacy integrity of services and data from several data sources. The engine benefits from inherent services from MDEForge such as recommendation system, quality assurance, service integrator, data mining and analytics as seen in Fig. 3.

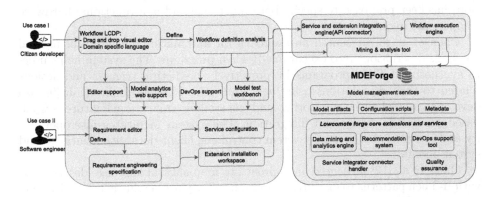

Fig. 3. Logical view describing the backend and frontend aspects of the system

Service orchestration is enabled by Kubernetes technology[4], which comes bundled with out-of-box benefits such as auto-scalability and extensibility to handle a flux of users, support continuous integration and load balance containerized workloads and services [7,17]. By managing distributed and containerized services, we define the utilization and boundaries of resources, reduce hardware costs, deploy resilient, loose coupled, self-healing, elastic distributed services [7]. In addition, we benefit from service discovery, load-balancing, storage orchestration by mounting the volume of your choice on-the-fly from several providers and technologies, and importantly enable automatic bin packaging while ensuring automated rollout and rollbacks to a given state [17].

3.3 Limitations

The first and foremost challenge that trigger-action programming solutions have faced are security and privacy concerns as suggested by previous research [18], especially when independent services are involved [1]. Existing approaches have limited facilities supporting the reusability of already created task workflows to avoid replication and adequately manage the collections of modeled workflows [18]. The proposed approach aims at addressing such issues even though debugging facilities are not supported yet. Moreover, while developing task workflows, it is crucial to avoid ambiguity in terminologies that hamper efficiency creation and the use of task workflows [18]. The proposed approach does not provide yet any mechanism to check the terminology used for naming workflows tasks.

4 Related Work

Berardinelli et al. [3] identified relevant challenges that hinder the adoption of model-driven approaches for cyber-physical production systems engineering and discussed issues related to integrating several modelling tools. An automated engineering toolchain has been proposed to perform early design and validation. Vogel-Heuser et al. [19] presented an approach to support the model-driven engineering of manufacturing systems. The SysML-AT language (SysML for automation) has been proposed to specify both functional and non-functional hardware components' requirements.

Chen et al. [6] presented an approach for automatic translation of natural language descriptions into executable If-Then programs. The system helps users to synthesize If-Then programs by proactively predicting triggers and actions related to their descriptions using neural networks. Dzulqornain et al. [9] also developed a real-time monitoring and controlling smart aquaculture system based on IFTTT and cloud integration. The system facilitates interoperability and integration of sensors, system controllers, client data visualizations, and system monitors.

Quirk et al. [12] presented an approach to map natural language descriptions with If-Then patterns to executable programs. They use semantic parser-learners

---

[4] https://kubernetes.io.

that utilize already defined recipe descriptions to train semantic parsers that automatically map these descriptions to executable programs.

Differently from such related work, we presented a low-code environment to specify and execute workflows of model management tasks in this paper. The approach is agnostic from the languages used to specify the models that are transformed and later analyzed.

5   Conclusion

This paper proposed a novel approach to support the development of complex model management operations. In particular, a low-code development platform is presented by resembling the functionalities offered by currently available LCDPs like IFTTT and Zapier. Such platforms permit the development of complex processes by integrating and executing different services. The proposed approach proposes the adoption of a microservice-based architecture to integrate and execute model management services, which are orchestrated on the cloud according to specifications given by the user by means of a BPMN-like modeling language.

The proposed approach aims to overcome current challenges faced by traditional modelling environments that heavily rely on locally downloaded resources. Such environments are limited in their scalability and extensibility and their services exhibit high coupling with the local environment. The complete implementation of the proposed low-code development environment is ongoing and its application on real scenarios, validation, and testing remain as future work.

References

1. Baruah, B., Dhal, S.: A two-factor authentication scheme against FDM attack in IFTTT based smart home system. Comput. Secur. **77**, 21–35 (2018)
2. Basciani, F., Di Rocco, J., Di Ruscio, D., Di Salle, A., Iovino, L., Pierantonio, A.: MDEForge: an extensible Web-based modeling platform. CEUR Workshop Proc. **1242**(September), 66–75 (2014)
3. Berardinelli, L., Mazak, A., Alt, O., Wimmer, M., Kappel, G.: Model-driven systems engineering: principles and application in the CPPS domain. In: Biffl, S., Lüder, A., Gerhard, D. (eds.) Multi-Disciplinary Engineering for Cyber-Physical Production Systems, pp. 261–299. Springer, Cham (2017). https://doi.org/10.1007/978-3-319-56345-9_11
4. Brunelière, H., Cabot, J., Jouault, F.: Combining model-driven engineering and cloud computing. In: MDA4ServiceCloud 2010 Workshop co-located with ECMFA (2010)
5. Chen, X., Nophut, C., Voigt, T.: Manufacturing execution systems for the food and beverage industry: a model-driven approach. Electronics **9**(12), 2040 (2020)
6. Chen, X., Liu, C., Shin, R., Song, D., Chen, M.: Latent attention for if-then program synthesis. Adv. Neural Inf. Process. Syst. **29**, 4574–4582 (2016)
7. David, O., et al.: Model-as-a-service (MaaS) using the cloud services innovation platform (CSIP). In: Proceedings - 7th International Congress on Environmental Modelling and Software, iEMSs 2014 (2014)

8. Di Ruscio, D., Franzago, M., Malavolta, I., Muccini, H.: Envisioning the future of collaborative model-driven software engineering. In: Proceedings - 2017 IEEE/ACM 39th International Conference on Software Engineering Companion, ICSE-C 2017 (2017)
9. Dzulqornain, M.I., Harun Al Rasyid, M.U., Sukaridhoto, S.: Design and development of smart aquaculture system based on IFTTT model and cloud integration. In: MATEC Web of Conferences, vol. 164 (2018)
10. Llad, C.M., Smith, C.U.: Performance model interchange format (pmif 2.0): Xml definition and implementation. In: International Conference on Quantitative Evaluation of Systems. IEEE Computer Society, Los Alamitos (2004)
11. Ovadia, S.: Automate the internet With "If This Then That" (IFTTT). Behav. Soc. Sci. Librarian **33**(4), 208–211 (2014)
12. Quirk, C., Mooney, R., Galley, M.: Language to code: learning semantic parsers for if-This-Then-That recipes. In: ACL-IJCNLP 2015–53rd Annual Meeting of the Association for Computational Linguistics and the 7th International Joint Conference on Natural Language Processing of the Asian Federation of Natural Language Processing, Proceedings of the Conference 1, pp. 878–888 (2015)
13. Rahmati, A., Fernandes, E., Jung, J., Prakash, A.: IFTTT vs. A Comparative Study of Trigger-Action Programming Frameworks. Zapier (2017)
14. Sahay, A., Indamutsa, A., Ruscio, D.D., Pierantonio, A.: Supporting the understanding and comparison of low-code development platforms. 2020 46th Euromicro Conference on Software Engineering and Advanced Applications (SEAA), pp. 171–178 (2020)
15. Surbatovich, M., Aljuraidan, J., Bauer, L., Das, A., Jia, L.: Some recipes can do more than spoil your appetite: Analyzing the security and privacy risks of ifttt recipes. In: Proceedings of the 26th International Conference on World Wide Web, pp. 1501–1510 (2017)
16. Taibi, D., Lenarduzzi, V., Pahl, C.: Processes, motivations, and issues for migrating to microservices architectures: an empirical investigation. IEEE Cloud Comput. **4**(5), 22–32 (2017)
17. Tomarchio, O., Calcaterra, D., Modica, G.D.: Cloud resource orchestration in the multi-cloud landscape: a systematic review of existing frameworks. J. Cloud Comput. **9**(1), 1–24 (2020). https://doi.org/10.1186/s13677-020-00194-7
18. Ury, B., et al.: Trigger-action programming in the wild: an analysis of 200,000 IFTTT recipes. In: Conference on Human Factors in Computing Systems - Proceedings, pp. 3227–3231 (2016)
19. Vogel-Heuser, B., Schütz, D., Frank, T., Legat, C.: Model-driven engineering of manufacturing automation software projects—A SysML-based approach. Mechatronics **24**(7), 883–897 (2014). (1. Model-Based Mechatronic System Design 2. Model Based Engineering)
20. Vorapojpisut, S.: A lightweight framework of home automation systems based on the IFTTT model. J. Softw. **10**(12), 1343–1350 (2015)
21. Weißenberger, B., Flad, S., Chen, X., Rösch, S., Voigt, T., Vogel-Heuser, B.: Model driven engineering of manufacturing execution systems using a formal specification. In: 2015 IEEE 20th Conference on Emerging Technologies Factory Automation (ETFA), pp. 1–8 (2015)
22. Zacharewicz, G., Daclin, N., Doumeingts, G., Haidar, H.: Model driven interoperability for system engineering. Modelling **1**(2), 94–121 (2020)

Towards Twin-Driven Engineering: Overview of the State-of-The-Art and Research Directions

Massimo Tisi[1], Hugo Bruneliere[1(✉)], Juan de Lara[2], Davide Di Ruscio[3], and Dimitris Kolovos[4]

[1] IMT Atlantique, LS2N (UMR CNRS 6004), Nantes, France
{massimo.tisi,hugo.bruneliere}@imt-atlantique.fr
[2] Universidad Autónoma de Madrid, Madrid, Spain
juan.delara@uam.es
[3] University of L'Aquila, L'Aquila, Italy
davide.diruscio@univaq.it
[4] University of York, York, UK
dimitris.kolovos@york.ac.uk

Abstract. Cyber-Physical Systems (CPS) are complex physical systems interacting with a considerable number of distributed computing elements for monitoring, control and management. They are currently becoming larger as Cyber-Physical Systems of Systems (CPSoS), since many industrial companies are transitioning their complex systems of systems to software-intensive solutions in different domains such as production or manufacturing. Following the development and dissemination of DevOps approaches in the Software Engineering world, we propose the Twin-Driven Engineering (TDE) paradigm as a way to upgrade the role of Digital Twins (DT) to become a central point in all the engineering activities on the CPSoS, from design to decommissioning. Since CPSoS can be highly heterogeneous, we rather target the support for producing and maintaining a single integrated virtual representation of the CPSoS (i.e. a System of Twins) on which it is possible to perform global reasoning, analysis and verification. However, such a new paradigm comes with several open research challenges. We provide an overview of the state-of-the-art in key areas related to TDE. We identify under-investigated problems in related work and outline corresponding research directions.

Keywords: Twin-driven engineering · Cyber-physical systems · Systems of systems · State-of-the-Art · Research directions

1 Introduction and Motivation

Cyber-Physical Systems (CPS) are complex physical systems interacting with a large number of distributed computing elements for monitoring, control and management. Cyber-Physical Systems of Systems (CPSoS) further leverage connectivity to achieve complex tasks by *"an integration of a finite number of constituent systems which are*

© IFIP International Federation for Information Processing 2021
Published by Springer Nature Switzerland AG 2021
A. Dolgui et al. (Eds.): APMS 2021, IFIP AICT 630, pp. 351–359, 2021.
https://doi.org/10.1007/978-3-030-85874-2_37

independent and operable, and which are networked together for a period of time to achieve a certain higher goal" [15]. In this context, Digital Twins (DTs), i.e. virtual real-time representations of physical systems, are particularly relevant for monitoring and making diagnostics/prognostics on the constituent CPSs. For example, virtual representation has been already used for virtual commissioning of manufacturing systems [21]. However, the real-time connection of digital twins with the physical system while it is in use enables further usages, like seamless tracking of the system operation and more realistic evaluation of any system improvements. More generally, in current practices and different domains, the development and maintenance of a CPSoS is performed through the interaction of multidisciplinary actors with specific competences and assigned to different phases. To capture, communicate and validate their ideas with other stakeholders, engineers of each CPSoS constituent system build models of their respective systems. However, the traditional paradigm "*requirements - model-based design - verification - deployment - operation - decommissioning*" does not provide sufficient guarantees to the dependability of a CPSoS. Indeed, miscommunication and delays in propagating changes are a primary cause of faults for CPSoS. In Software Engineering, the DevOps approach is widely used to address similar problems by providing practices, techniques and tools for integrating the software development and operation phases. Interestingly, the application of DevOps approaches has been recently studied in the context of CPSs [8, 26]. We advocate that DevOps practices may have a strongly beneficial impact on the dependability of CPSoSs.

In this paper we propose to go further and to create a new engineering paradigm, Twin-Driven Engineering (TDE), with the aim of upgrading the role of DTs as a central point of all the engineering activities on the CPSoS. Since CPSoS heterogeneity is inevitable, our proposition is to help in producing and maintaining a single integrated virtual representation of the CPSoS on which it is possible to perform global reasoning, analysis and verification. Such representation of the CPSoS will orchestrate the DTs of the constituent systems: We call it a System of Twins (SoT). Such an approach can radically change the way CPSoS are produced and maintained. A SoT can precede the design of a constituent system and drive its actual development, or act as a specification and automated oracle for continuous engineering. The industrial deployment of this approach depends on the cost effectiveness of the SoT production and maintenance.

While inexpensive and easily interfaced sensors are available today, engineering a DT is still an expensive activity whose costs are impacted by their dependability requirements that span from certifying the conformance of the DT with the CPS, to robustness and runtime problems. Moreover, the required competences in Machine Learning (ML), e.g. for inferring DT non-measurable properties, are not generally available in the ecosystem. Finally, providing a global view (even abstract) of the full CPSoS may introduce new scalability requirements on the underlying infrastructure.

Hence, there is the need for research methods, techniques and tools to minimize the cost of the DT production at all levels of a multi-layered CPSoS. In this paper, we define TDE and provide an overview of the state-of-the-art in key related areas. We also introduce corresponding research directions we believe to be worth investigating.

Paper Organization. Section 2 introduces the TDE paradigm. Section 3 presents the current state-of-the-art related to key challenges associated with the realization of TDE. Finally, Sect. 4 concludes the paper.

2 Twin-Driven Engineering

TDE can be defined as the software & system engineering paradigm that consists in creating, maintaining and leveraging a dependable twin of a given complex system and its environment, in order to better support and manage this system throughout its whole life cycle. As a consequence, in order to build the twin of a CPSoS, a corresponding SoT actually has to be specified and handled.

In this context, TDE first requires the users to describe the CPSoS including *i)* the structure of the system of systems, *ii)* the interaction of the constituent systems and *iii)* the structure and behavior of the environment. Information on each constituent system is also needed, without delving into full implementation details at that level. We refer to this general information as *Abstract Models*, i.e. single sources of truth on their constituent systems as shown in Fig. 1. To be able to specify these Abstract Models, the user needs a modeling language. Each domain in CPSs has its own set of commonly used description languages and models, referring to different physical, engineering and technological backgrounds. Models may have different fidelity, different types of parameterization, or different philosophical approaches. Some academic literature and related work have tried to propose very general languages for describing any CPS (cf. Sect. 3). However, the technical and organizational heterogeneity of CPSoS strongly reduces the realistic chances of acceptance of such efforts.

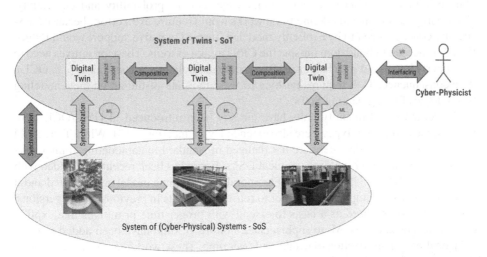

Fig. 1. An overview of the twin-driven engineering paradigm, showing the central role of the Digital Twins (DTs) that compose the System of Twins (SoT) to be synchronized with the underlying System of Systems (SoS).

As a solution, we propose to consider a specific DT for each constituent system. The composition of all these DTs will result in the target SoT that can then be used as the main interface between the underlying CPSoS and the involved engineers. To make TDE possible, the SoT has to be kept constantly synchronized with the related CPSoS. Thus, each DT has to be individually synchronized with its underlying system. At this stage, we envision the use of ML techniques to ensure such a regular synchronization. Moreover, each DT is also in charge of keeping its corresponding Abstract Model up to date. Solutions already exist to simplify the creation of DTs (cf. Sect. 3). However, they generally rely on stakeholders committing to a single technology, e.g. a specific language, development tool, runtime infrastructure, or dependability definition. This is unrealistic if we consider the growing organizational and technical complexity of CPSoS. Thus, the key idea coming along with TDE is to propose a corresponding meta-environment for building specific DTs tailored for each CPSoS. By using such a platform, engineers operating at different levels of the CPSoS hierarchy can create solutions to produce an integrated view of their component systems for global reasoning. As mentioned before, TDE does not aim at replacing existing tools and techniques for modeling individual components of CPSoS. The objective is rather to build on top of them, e.g. by using them as targets of code generation and directly integrating their executable artifacts.

3 Advancing the State-of-The-Art of Twin-Driven Engineering

3.1 Definition of Domain-Specific Systems of Twins

Current metamodeling languages (e.g. MOF [25], Ecore [7]) were devised for static data modeling. However, describing SoTs and coupling them with design models of CPSs requires *i)* accounting for dynamic data and *ii)* the availability of CPS metamodeling primitives to describe quantity units, time models, probability and uncertainty. Thus, using current metamodeling frameworks would require extra effort, because CPS-specific concepts need to be explicitly modeled. Instead, a native support would reduce the effort needed to build domain-specific CPS languages tools. These primitives need to be properly integrated with languages for model manipulation or constraints (e.g. OCL). As a consequence, TDE requires pushing forward the state-of-the-art on metamodeling technologies for engineering SoTs.

Uncertainty and quantity units have already been introduced in UML/OCL [23]. Later, some UML/OCL types were also extended with uncertainty [3]. While TDE could leverage on those works, these are not realized in standard metamodeling frameworks and so not available for building practical DSLs. Ecore has been recently extended with temporal capabilities [12]: Updates of temporal elements in a model are persisted and it is possible to issue temporal queries, or to retrieve elements in previous model versions. These ideas can be used as a basis to extend with proper time primitives like explicit clock-times or intervals. More sophisticated notions of time have been added to OCL [17], enabling quantification of events and over time. These works can be extended with stream types for modeling live data, to check the runtime behavior of SoT.

Many works have been proposed on specification-based monitoring of CPS [2], most of them based on variations of temporal logic. Hence, there is a frequent need to tweak existing logic formalisms and create supporting tools, which is a very costly activity. TDE aims at providing means to define DSLs for runtime monitoring, and the support for the automated creation of monitors. TDE will also provide support for linking design-time models (e.g. in Modelica), and TD models by means of bidirectional (bx) domain-specific transformation languages [9]. Bx will enable iterative design processes, while our vision is to provide a framework for engineering bx languages targeting specific CPS design platforms like Modelica. Many works exist on bx transformation languages [14]. However, we are not aware of frameworks for engineering domain-specific bx transformation languages. Additionally, the use of model view techniques could also be considered [5] as they have already demonstrated their relevance and applicability in the context of the federation of large-scale design time and runtime models [6].

Research Directions. TDE takes a step beyond the state-of-the-art frameworks for defining SoT by providing advanced metamodeling capabilities, and bidirectional (BX) connection with design CPS models, for a holistic support of the CPS life cycle. Standard metamodeling frameworks have to be extended with CPS notions (quantities, time, uncertainty) as well as types for dynamic and streaming data (enabling e.g., connection with predictive models). Standard constraint languages also have to be extended to enable expressing time-aware constraints. Such constraints can natively use CPS concepts and be used as a basis to develop monitoring languages for dependability properties. Finally, domain-specific BX transformation languages have to be specified to facilitate the creation of bridges between SoT and CPS design models. Such languages also have to support the checking of CPS correctness properties, involving the bx preservation of source and target integrity constraints.

3.2 Domain-Specific 3D Interfaces for Systems of Twins

Arguably, a domain-specific language for SoTs is of little value if it is not supported by robust and usable editors through which developers can create and edit models conforming to the language. In the field of 2D graphical editor development, frameworks such as MetaEdit +, GMF, Graphiti and Sirius have drastically reduced the effort and expertise required to develop and maintain diagram-based editors for domain-specific languages [18]. Conversely, there is virtually no support for developing domain-specific 3D editors, except for some early prototypes that are no longer maintained [28]. 2D graphical editors may be sufficient for some classes of domain-specific SoTs languages. However, when physical objects are modelled, a 3D editor can provide a more natural and intuitive representation that better communicates to other engineers, and also to non-technical stakeholders. Developing such a 3D editor for a SoT DSL involves a significant upfront investment and requires specialized skills that would be prohibitive for most development teams. As discussed above, this used to be the case for 2D editors as well until tools such as MetaEdit + and GMF provided reusable facilities that allowed engineers to concentrate only on the essential complexity of the editor (e.g. define how abstract syntax concepts should be mapped to shapes/connections).

Research Directions. TDE requires a set of notations for specifying the 3D graphical syntax of SoT domain-specific languages at a high level of abstraction, and automated facilities for realizing fully-functional 3D editors for related models. It also requires exploring virtual reality (VR) technologies through which users can be able to navigate and interact with such 3D models, as well as protocols for capturing the structural/behavioral properties of the language in a platform-independent way. A main objective is to facilitate concrete implementations on different platforms, similarly to Microsoft's Language Server Protocol (LSP) for textual languages and GLSP for graphical languages.

3.3   Dependable Connection and Composition in Systems of Twins

Solutions to simplify the development of DTs like ADT, Eclipse Ditto, or Seebo define or generate an API for the DT on a specific platform (e.g. Azure IoT), with a specific software architectural style (e.g. REST on Swagger) and/or with an organization that is agnostic of the CPSoS behavior. A mechanism is needed to generate, for any given platform, protocol and style, an efficient interface for the DT.

An important dependability issue, which has not yet been addressed in production systems such as ADT, is related to the way the CPSoS are connected to the DT [20]. CPSoS are not managed by actors such as Microsoft, they belong to third party players and are connected to the cloud platform through the internet backbone (generally WAN links operated by another actor). Hence, it is critical to consider the CPSoS, the DT and the infrastructure overall. Similarly, to the studies that have been conducted for smart-grid applications, it is critical to identify the requirements of each DT and the possible limitations of the infrastructure in order to ensure a DT can collect the metrics it needs to maintain the DT up-to-date. Going further, strategies to cope with network disconnections should be defined à priori.

Monitoring CPSoS requires fast and low-overhead model analysis and transformation techniques, to ensure that corrective decisions are timely and achieved with acceptable use of resources (CPU, memory, bandwidth and energy). While such techniques are not yet available for CPS, relevant advances have been made for software systems through the development of incremental techniques for the efficient analysis of functional requirements expressed in OCL [10] and of non-functional requirements specified in probabilistic temporal logics [16]. However, because of the high throughput of incoming data, a dependable continuous monitoring of DT models requires techniques that exceed the typical domain of incremental computation, to enter the area of streaming computation.

Research Directions. A DT solution should come with the right mechanism/components [24] to deal with all infrastructure specifics (throughput, latency and resilience of the network) so that we can formally validate whether the DT can be correctly maintained in time. Those mechanisms can include compression, caching and resynchronization mechanisms according to the CPSoS specifics, the DT expectations and the infrastructure. By leveraging previous works on software programming models [11] and middleware for IoT [27], TDE can rely on a DSL that enables DevOps to express the infrastructure topology, its specific requirements in terms of connectivity between each CPSoS and the SoT. A list of components in charge of dealing with interconnectivity issues and network specifics (latency/throughput) can be defined and then used to derive a DSL allowing to express those constraints. The ultimate goal would be to automatically generate, configure and finally deploy those components.

3.4 Twin-Driven Engineering for DevOps on CPSoS

Managing CPS development is a complex task because different kinds of artifacts (from physical to software systems) need to be homogeneously integrated. In this context, DTs come to the rescue by playing the role of bridges between the physical and digital worlds. They allow identifying problems even before they occur, or enabling analysis and simulations to enhance system dependability. However, in CPSoSs, a multitude of heterogeneous DTs must be managed and properly interconnected. Moreover, the same physical object can have different DTs providing different abstractions and only exposing the characteristics appropriate for the considered life cycle phase. To enable TDE, two main ingredients are needed: *1)* A dedicated repository able to store and manage reusable DT models and *2)* a DevOps infrastructure supporting the SoT continuous engineering and integration.

Concerning *(1)* we outline research challenges for achieving a comprehensive solution to the problem of properly managing the persistence of models and the discovery of any kind of modeling artefact and tool for enabling their reuse and refinement. CDO is a pure Java model repository (relying on common database backends) for models that can also serve as a persistence and distribution framework for model-based applications. EMFStore [19] is a model version control system implementing the typical operations proposed by SVN/CVS/Git for text-based artefacts. GME - Generic Modeling Environment [22] is a set of tools supporting the creation of domain specific modeling languages and code generation environments, based on MS repository technologies to store the developed models. ModelBus [13] consists of a central bus-like communication infrastructure, a number of core services (versioning, check-out, merging) and a set of additional management tools. MDEForge [1] is an extensible Web-based modeling platform fostering community-based modeling repositories and proposing remote model management tools as software-as-a-service.

Concerning *(2)* several tools support the continuous integration and deployment of software systems (e.g., Jenkins, Travis, and GitLab CI/CD). "Continuous Integration" was first used by Grady Booch [4] to describe an effective, iterative way of building software. Essentially, every commit immediately triggers automated tests and building tasks to quickly detect errors and constantly have a stable build of the system being developed. In complex CPSoS, the existence of large numbers of decentralized sub-systems represents an additional element of complexity. Finally, CPSoS are also characterized by human-in-the-loop aspects related to the collaboration of humans with the software and hardware systems being employed.

Research Directions. TDE requires to develop software components, available as software-as-a-service, to support the persistence and the reuse of DT models: Tools from different vendors (e.g., Matlab Simulink, LabVIEW, Modelica) could store and retrieve models from a common repository. Moreover, a dedicated support has to be implemented to manage the relationships between heterogeneous artefacts, including advanced query mechanisms. TDE also comes with novel methods and tools for supporting SoT development and operations. Dependability models and processes have to be investigated to guarantee reliability during the complete life cycle of CPSoS, from requirements capture to design, test, operation and decommissioning. It can be explored how existing DevOps infrastructures can be extended to support the continuous engineering and continuous integration of SoTs.

4   Conclusion

In this paper, we proposed a first definition of the TDE paradigm for CPSoS. We gave an overview of the state-of-the-art in key related areas, and proposed corresponding research directions we think to be worth investigating. We believe cost-effective TDE to be a major milestone for dependable software engineering for production systems. Thus, this paper also aims at fostering discussion and collaboration around this topic between the software engineering and production systems communities.

References

1. Basciani, F., Di Rocco, J., Di Ruscio, D., Di Salle, A., Iovino, L., Pierantonio, A.: MDEForge: an extensible Web-based modeling platform. In: CloudMDE Workshop at MoDELS 2014, Valencia, Spain (2014)
2. Bartocci, E., et al.: Specification-based monitoring of cyber-physical systems: a survey on theory, tools and applications. In: Bartocci, E., Falcone, Y. (eds.) Lectures on Runtime Verification. LNCS, vol. 10457, pp. 135–175. Springer, Cham (2018). https://doi.org/10.1007/978-3-319-75632-5_5
3. Bertoa, M.F., Moreno, N., Barquero, G., Burgueño, L., Troya, J., Vallecillo, A.: Expressing measurement uncertainty in OCL/UML datatypes. In: Pierantonio, A., Trujillo, S. (eds.) ECMFA 2018. LNCS, vol. 10890, pp. 46–62. Springer, Cham (2018). https://doi.org/10.1007/978-3-319-92997-2_4
4. Booch, G.: Object-Oriented Design with Applications. The Benjamin/Cummings Publishing Company Inc., San Francisco (1991)
5. Bruneliere, H., Burger, E., Cabot, J., Wimmer, M.: A Feature-based survey of model view approaches. Softw. Syst. Model. 18(3), 1931–1952 (2019)
6. Bruneliere, H., Marchand de Kerchove, F., Daniel, G., Madani, S., Kolovos, D., Cabot, J.: Scalable model views over heterogeneous modeling technologies and resources. Softw. Syst. Model. 19(4), 827–851 (2020)
7. Budinsky, F., Steinberg, D., Merks, E., Grose, T.J.: Eclipse Modelling Framework. Addison Wesley, Boston (2003)
8. Combemale, B., Wimmer, M.: Towards a model-based DevOps for cyber-physical systems. In: Bruel, J.M., Mazzara, M., Meyer, B. (eds.) DEVOPS 2019. LNCS, vol. 12055, pp. 84–94. Springer, Cham (2020). https://doi.org/10.1007/978-3-030-39306-9_6
9. Sánchez Cuadrado, J., Guerra, E., de Lara, J.: Towards the systematic construction of domain-specific transformation languages. In: Cabot, J., Rubin, J. (eds.) ECMFA 2014. LNCS, vol. 8569, pp. 196–212. Springer, Cham (2014). https://doi.org/10.1007/978-3-319-09195-2_13
10. Demuth, A., Lopez-Herrejon, R.E., Egyed, A.: Automatic and incremental product optimization for software product lines. In: ICST 2014, p. 31–40 (2014)
11. Gerostathopoulos, I., et al.: Self-adaptation in Software-intensive cyber-physical systems: from system goals to architecture configurations. J. Syst. Softw. 122, 378–397 (2016)
12. Gómez, A., Cabot, J., Wimmer, M.: TemporalEMF: A Temporal Metamodeling Framework. In: Trujillo, J., et al. (eds.) Conceptual Modelling ER 2018. LNCS, vol. 8569, pp. 365–381. Springer, Cham (2018). https://doi.org/10.1007/978-3-030-00847-5_26

13. Hein, C., Ritter, T., Wagner, M.: Model-driven tool integration with ModelBus. In: Workshop on Future Trends of Model-Driven Development (2009)
14. Hidaka, S., Tisi, M., Cabot, J., Hu, Z.: Feature-based classification of bidirectional transformation approaches. Softw. Syst. Model. **15**(3), 907–928 (2016)
15. Jamshidi, M.: Systems of Systems Engineering: Principles and Applications. CRC Press, Boca Raton (2008)
16. Johnson, K., Calinescu, R., Kikuchi, S.: An incremental verification framework for component-based software systems. In: CBSE 2013, pp. 33–42 (2013)
17. Kanso, B., Taha, S.: Specification of temporal properties with OCL. Sci. Comput. Program. **96**, 527–551 (2014)
18. Kolovos, D.S., García-Domínguez, A., Rose, L.M., Paige, R.F.: Eugenia: towards disciplined and automated development of GMF-based graphical model editors. Softw. Syst. Model. **16**, 1–27 (2015)
19. Koegel, M., Helming, J.: EMFStore: a model repository for EMF models. ICSE. **2**, 307–308 (2010)
20. Lee, E.A.: Cyber physical systems: design challenges. ISORC **2008**, 363–369 (2008)
21. Lee, C.G., Park, S.C.: Survey on the virtual commissioning of manufacturing systems. J. Comput. Des. Eng. **1**(3), 213–222 (2014)
22. Ledeczi, A., et al.: The generic modeling environment. In: Workshop on Intelligent Signal Processing (2001)
23. Mayerhofer, T., Wimmer, M., Vallecillo, A.: Adding uncertainty and units to quantity types in software models. In: MODELS 2016, pp. 118–131 (2016)
24. Mikic-Rakic, M., Medvidovic, N.: A classification of disconnected operation techniques. In: EUROMICRO 2006, pp. 144–151 (2006)
25. The Object Management Group, OMG's Meta-Object Facility (MOF). https://www.omg.org/mof/. Accessed 18 June 2021
26. Querejeta, M.U., Etxeberria, L., Sagardui, G.: Towards a DevOps approach in cyber physical production systems using digital twins. In: Skavhaug, A., Guiochet, J., Schoitsch, E., Bitsch, F. (eds.) International Conference on Computer Safety. Reliability, and Security, pp. 205–216. Springer, Cham (2020)
27. Razzaque, M.A., Milojevic-Jevric, M., Palade, A., Clarke, S.: Middleware for Internet of Things: a survey. IEEE Internet of Things J. **3**(1), 70–95 (2016)
28. Wolter, J., Kastens, U.: Generating 3D visual language editors: encapsulating interaction techniques in visual patterns. Int. J. Softw. Eng. Knowl. Eng. **25**(2), 333–360 (2015)

Meta-Heuristics and Optimization Techniques for Energy-Oriented Manufacturing Systems

Developing a Bi-objective Model to Configure a Scalable Manufacturing Line Considering Energy Consumption

Atefeh Jamiri, Mehdi Mahmoodjanloo, and Armand Baboli$^{(\boxtimes)}$

LIRIS Laboratory, UMR 5205 CNRS, INSA of Lyon, 69621 Villeurbanne CEDEX, France
armand.baboli@insa-lyon.fr

Abstract. Today, due to intense global competition, manufacturing systems need to be highly responsive and adaptive to fulfill market demand fluctuations and personalized production. Reconfigurable manufacturing system (RMS) is one of the main paradigms which has been introduced to overcome the dynamic nature of today's industry. In addition, RMSs are also a basis to develop new generation of sustainable production systems. This paper addresses the problem of designing a scalable manufacturing line for a part family considering both cost- and energy-effectiveness criteria. Hence, a bi-objective mathematical programming model is proposed. The main decision is to configuration and/or reconfiguration of production line by adding a set of new machines from a list of candidate reconfigurable machine tools (RMTs) and/or transforming them among the stages to fulfill anticipated demands in the periods of a time horizon. A numerical example is solved to illustrate the validation of the model. CPLEX is utilized to implement an augmented epsilon constraint method to extract Pareto front. The results show that different strategies in configuration the production line have significant impact on cost- and energy-effectiveness criteria.

Keywords: Reconfigurable manufacturing systems · Flexibility · Factories of the future · Energy consumption optimization

1 Introduction

Nowadays, despite fierce competition, limited opportunities, and frequent changes in products demand, it is necessary to have a manufacturing system that can quickly adjust its functionality and production capacity within a part family. Hence, RMSs have been introduced to build a "live" factory which can cost effectively and quickly respond to the customer requirements [1]. In addition to the cost effectiveness and the ability to easily change production capacity (scalability) of a manufacturing system, the energy efficiency, because of ecological, economic and political reasons, is also an important criterion for industrial enterprises. Designing scalable manufacturing lines which simultaneously consider the cost and energy effectiveness are the challenging and yet interesting problem which motivated us in this paper.

© IFIP International Federation for Information Processing 2021
Published by Springer Nature Switzerland AG 2021
A. Dolgui et al. (Eds.): APMS 2021, IFIP AICT 630, pp. 363–371, 2021.
https://doi.org/10.1007/978-3-030-85874-2_38

An RMS is a dynamic manufacturing system which its functionality and production capacity can be easily adapted to satisfy changeable requirements. In order to achieve these capabilities, RMTs with modular and adjustable structures are often used as part of RMSs [2]. An RMT can be used as a group of machines that changing of its configuration lead to different functionalities or production rates. An RMT usually compose of modules which can be assembled and disassembled to achieve different configurations of the machine. Development of RMTs can prevent the implementation of multiple machines that share many common and costly modules while being rarely used at the same time [3]. Recently, a comprehensive literature review dedicated to RMTs have been conducted by Gadalla and Xue [4].

To design a scalable manufacturing system, the concept of reconfigurability can be utilized in both system and machine levels. In the system level, configuration of RMSs can include many diverse aspects. Abdi and Labib [5] presented some strategic issues during RMS design. Moreover, the level of responsiveness and scalability for a production system can also be affected by the reconfigurability of its machines. Therefore, selecting appropriate machines to launch a manufacturing system is an attractive subject of study. Moghaddam et al. [6] did one of the first attempts to adjust the capacity of a manufacturing system by transforming one RMT configuration to another. They developed a mathematical model for a case of single product flow line (SPFL). Their research proved that transforming of RMTs can be considered as a significant factor to tackle the problem of RMS capacity scalability. Thereafter, Moghaddam et al. [7] extended their model to be utilized for a part family. However, they implemented their proposed model to minimize the total cost of the manufacturing system while in the RMS design literature usually there are also other objectives which can be considered to improve the performance of the system, e.g. energy consumption, throughput, flexibility, etc.

On each configuration because of utilizing various modules/tools, an RMT can operate with special characteristics, e.g. reliability and rate of energy consumption. Ashraf and Hasan [8] developed a multi-objective model to select an appropriate configuration for a reconfigurable manufacturing line. They considered four objective function including cost, reconfigurability, operation capability, and reliability. Touzout et al. [9] investigated the problem of process planning in an RMS considering sustainability. They proposed a tri-objective model which considered minimizing the energy consumption as a criterion in addition to the traditional two criteria, cost and completion time. He et al. [10] studied an energy-responsive optimization method for machine tool selection and operation sequencing in a shop floor. However, these papers didn't consider the effect of energy consumption in the designing phase of an RMS. This is while, the environmental impact of utilizing a machine tool is significant that can be reduced if it has already been considered during system designing phase. It is worth noting that the global manufacturing industry sector is responsible for 31% of primary energy consumption and 36% of CO_2 emissions [10]. Hence, reducing the energy consumed by machine tool systems can significantly effect on sustainability. Motivated by these facts, the emphasis of this research is on the development of a bi-objective mathematical model to design a scalable manufacturing flow line for a part family considering cost and energy consumption.

The rest of the paper is organized as follows: The problem description and model formulation are presented in Sect. 2. In Sect. 3, a simple test case to evaluate the proposed method is demonstrated, and the related computational results are presented. Finally, the conclusion and areas for future research are presented in Sect. 4.

2 Problem Description and Model Formulation

2.1 Problem Definition

The problem consists of the configuration of a flexible manufacturing flow line to produce several products of a special part family. The demands have already been anticipated for each period of time $t \in T$. The flow line contains a set of stages $s \in S$ in which a special operation can be processed. The schematic layout of shop floor is presented in Fig. 1. The main decision is to determine configuration of production line by selecting a set of machines from a list of candidate RMTs to fulfill the predicted demands. At the beginning of each period of time, the production capacity of each stage should be met by adding some new RMTs, changing the configuration of some prior RMTs in the stage, or transforming some prior RMTs from the other stages to the considered stage. Each RMT $i \in I$ has a set of $\mathcal{J}_i$ configurations. One or more operations can be processed in each configuration $j \in \mathcal{J}_i$ with a special rate of production and energy consumption. Hence, designing of the production flow line will be guided by two objectives including the minimization of the total system cost and the minimization of the system energy consumption.

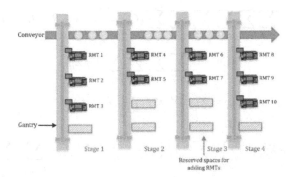

Fig. 1. Schematic layout of reconfigurable manufacturing flow line (revised from [11])

2.2 Model Formulation

Here, the sets and indices, the parameters, and the decision variables to formulate the problem are described. Thereafter, the mathematical formulation is presented.

Parameters

D_{st} Demand rate of the operation related to s th stage in time period t

P_{ijs} Production rate of machine configuration ij to perform the operation of stage s

α_{ijs} Binary parameter. If the operation of s th stage can be processed by machine configuration ij, then $\alpha_{ijs} = 1$; otherwise, $\alpha_{ijs} = 0$

C_i Purchasing cost of the machine i

C'_{ijs} Operation cost of machine configuration ij to perform the operation of stage s

E_{ijs} Energy consumption of machine configuration ij to perform the operation of stage s

$A_{ijj'}$ Number of added auxiliary modules to the i th machine for transforming configuration j to j'

$R_{ijj'}$ Number of removed auxiliary modules from the i th machine for transforming configuration j to j'

CA, CR Cost of adding/removing an auxiliary module to/from an RMT

Decision Variables

X^t_{ijs} Number of new machines configuration ij which are added to stage s at the beginning of period t

Z^t_{ijs} Total number of existing machines configuration ij in s th stage at period t

$Y^t_{ijsj's'}$ Number of machines configuration ij in the s th stage at period $(t-1)$ which are added to stage s' at the beginning of time period t with configuration j'

Mathematical Formulation

$$\text{Min} z_1 = \sum_{t\in T}\sum_{s\in S}\sum_{i\in I}\sum_{j\in \mathcal{J}_i} C_{ij}X^t_{ijs} + \sum_{t\in T}\sum_{s\in S}\sum_{i\in I}\sum_{j\in \mathcal{J}_i} C'_{ijs}Z^t_{ijs}$$

$$+ \sum_{t\in T}\sum_{i\in I}\sum_{j\in \mathcal{J}_i}\sum_{j'\in \mathcal{J}_i}\sum_{s\in S}\sum_{s'\in S}(CA \times A_{ijj'} + CR \times R_{ijj'}).Y^t_{ijsj's'} \tag{1}$$

$$\text{Min} z_2 = \sum_{t\in T}\sum_{s\in S}\sum_{i\in I}\sum_{j\in \mathcal{J}_i} E_{ijs}Z^t_{ijs} \tag{2}$$

$$Z^t_{ijs} = X^t_{ijs} \quad \forall i \in I, j \in \mathcal{J}_i, s, t = 1 \tag{3}$$

s. t.

$$Z^t_{ijs} = Z^{t-1}_{ijs} + X^t_{ijs} + \sum_{\substack{j'\in \mathcal{J}_i \\ s'\neq s}}\sum_{\substack{s' \in S}} Y^t_{ij's'js} + \sum_{\substack{j' \in \mathcal{J}_i \\ j' \neq j}} Y^t_{ij'sjs} - \sum_{\substack{j'\in \mathcal{J}_i \\ s'\neq s}}\sum_{\substack{s' \in S}} Y^t_{ijsj's'}$$

$$- \sum_{\substack{j' \in \mathcal{J}_i \\ j' \neq j}} Y^t_{ijsj's} \quad \forall i \in I, j \in \mathcal{J}_i, s \in S, t > 1 \tag{4}$$

$$\sum_{j'\in \mathcal{J}_i}\sum_{s'\in S} Y^t_{ijsj's'} \leq Z^{t-1}_{ijs} \quad \forall i \in I, j \in \mathcal{J}_i, s \in S, t > 1 \tag{5}$$

$$\sum_{i\in I}\sum_{j\in \mathcal{J}_i} P_{ijs}Z^t_{ijs} \geq D_{st} \quad \forall s \in S, t \in T \tag{6}$$

$$X^t_{ijs} \leq M \times \alpha_{ijs} \quad \forall i \in I, j \in \mathcal{J}_i, s \in S, t \in T \tag{7}$$

$$Y^t_{ijsj's'} \leq M \times \alpha_{ijs} \quad \forall i \in I, j, j' \in \mathcal{J}_i, s, s' \in S, t \in T \tag{8}$$

$$Y^t_{ijsj's'} \leq M \times \alpha_{ij's'} \quad \forall i \in I, j, j' \in \mathcal{J}_i, s, s' \in S, t \in T \tag{9}$$

$$X^t_{ijs}, Z^t_{ijs} \in \mathbb{Z}^+ \quad \forall i \in I, j \in \mathcal{J}_i, s \in S, t \in T \tag{10}$$

$$Y^t_{ijsj's'} \in \mathbb{Z}^+ \quad \forall i \in I, j, j' \in \mathcal{J}_i, s, s' \in S, t \in T \tag{11}$$

The model has two objective function. The first objective in Eq. (1) minimizes the total cost. The second objective in Eq. (2) minimizes the energy consumption of production line. Equation (3) ensures that the total number of existing machines at the end of the first period should be exactly equal to the new machines. For each period of time $t > 1$, Eq. (4) guarantees that the total number of machines in the current period (t) should be balanced with the prior period $(t - 1)$.

Equation (5) ensures that the number of machines which could be reconfigured in each stage at the time period t should at most be equal with the total number of existing machines at the time period $(t- 1)$. Equation (6) indicates that the production rate of existing machines in each stage should be more than demand rate at the period. Constraint sets (7), (8) and (9) guarantee that no machine assigns to unauthorized state. Constraint sets (10) and (11) define the decision variables.

3 Numerical Example

To validate the proposed model, the following example is illustrated. This example is based on the data presented in Table 1. Moreover, it is assumed that the cost of adding an auxiliary module to an RMT is 50, and the cost of removing an auxiliary module is 25 [7].

Table 1. Machine configurations and their production rates, energy consumptions, costs, basic and auxiliary modules used in the instance problem (summarized and revised from [12]).

Machine	Conf.	Operation (stage)						
		1	2	3		Basic modules		
		$\left(P_{ijs}, E_{ijs}, C'_{ijs} \right)$			Cost C_i		Auxiliary modules	
1	1	(15, 4, 90)	-	-	1000	{1, 5}	{12, 13, 15, 20, 21}	
2	1	–	(14, 5, 100)	-	1300	{2, 4, 8}	{11, 13, 16, 22, 24}	
	2	–	–	(20, 7, 150)			{13, 19, 24}	

(continued)

Table 1. (*continued*)

Machine	Conf.	Operation (stage)			Cost C_i	Basic modules	Auxiliary modules
		1	2	3			
		$\left(P_{ijs}, E_{ijs}, C'_{ijs}\right)$					
	3	(20, 6, 150)	–	–			{11, 13, 15, 18, 24}
3	1	–	–	(10, 5, 70)	1400	{3, 5, 7}	{11, 12, 14, 16, 18}
	2	–	(30, 9, 190)	(35, 9, 220)			{12, 13, 14, 16, 18}
4	1	–	(25, 5, 140)	(30, 6, 200)	1200	{4, 9}	{11, 15, 18, 20, 21}
5	1	–	(16, 7, 120)	–	1500	{3, 6, 10}	{20, 22}
	2	(20, 8, 140)	–	(24, 9, 160)			{16, 17, 19, 20, 25}
	3	–	(20, 8, 130)	–			{20, 22, 24}

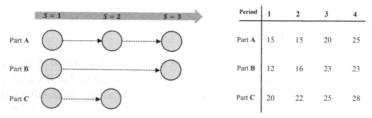

Fig. 2. The process plan and anticipated demand rates of each part in each production period

A simple hypothetical part family containing three different parts with special process plans and anticipated demand rates during each production period is shown in Fig. 2. Based on these data, the required production capacity at each stage in each production period can be extracted as shown in Table 2. For example, the required demand rate in the second stage at the first period can be calculated as: $D_{2,1} = 15 + 20 = 35$.

Table 2. Required production capacity at each stage in each production period (D_{st}).

	$t = 1$	$t = 2$	$t = 3$	$t = 4$
$S = 1$	47	53	68	76
$S = 2$	35	37	45	53
$S = 3$	27	31	43	48

In order to solve the bi-objective mathematical model and generate the Pareto optimal solutions, we utilize augmented epsilon-constraint method. The model is implemented in GAMS 24.1.3 and solved using the solver CPLEX on a computer with a 2.8 GHz Intel CPU and with 4 GB of installed memory. The solver could solve the problem less than 1 s. Figure 3 shows the obtained Pareto front for the instance problem.

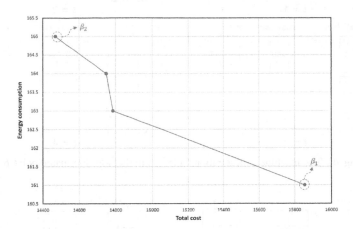

Fig. 3. The obtained Pareto front for the instance problem

In the following, two extreme points β_1 : $(Z_1 = 15855, Z_2 = 161)$ and β_2 : $(Z_1 = 14470, Z_2 = 165)$ of the Pareto front are selected to be illustrated. Actually, β_1 has the best amount of energy consumption, and β_2 has the best amount of system cost among the other points of Pareto front. The machine configurations selected in the points β_1 and β_2 are presented in Fig. 4 and Fig. 5, respectively. At the beginning of each period, the transformed/reconfigured RMTs are shown by yellow boxes while the newly purchased RMTs are shown by blue boxes. A significant observation in the illustrated points is the impact of reconfiguration ability of the RMTs on setting the capacity of the production line. For example, in the point β_2 which is a cost-effective solution, the production line starts with seven RMTs at the first period, and it adjusts the capacity by reconfiguration actions to fulfill the required demands. On the other hand, in the point β_1 which is an energy-effective solution, the production line starts with six RMTs that consume lower amount of energy, then it adjusts the capacity by reconfiguration actions and purchasing new RMTs. However, these are four different strategies that can be considered in the process of decision making.

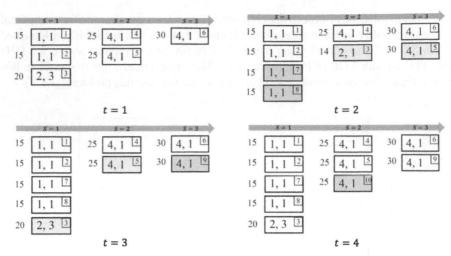

Fig. 4. The machine configurations selected in the non-dominated point β_1

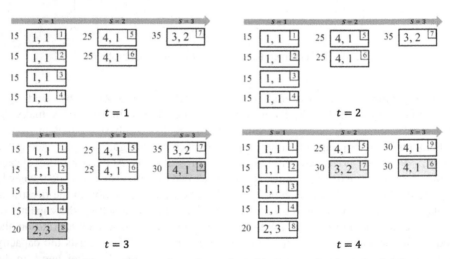

Fig. 5. The machine configurations selected in the non-dominated point β_2

4   Conclusions

In this research, a new mathematical programming model was presented to design a capacity scalable manufacturing line considering cost- and energy-effectiveness criteria. In addition, a numerical example based on a case from the literature was solved to illustrate the validation of the model and to help for better understanding the concepts. Results show that different strategies in implementing the production line can be considered regarding to the level of cost- and energy-effectiveness criteria, and the presented model can help managers to make appropriate decisions in this area.

For future works, developing some effective algorithms are proposed to solve the real-world size problems in an acceptable computational time. Moreover, some other aspects such as limitation in adding new machines and considering the situation of utilizing common/limited modules to perform the reconfiguration actions are proposed.

References

1. Gu, X., Koren, Y.: Manufacturing system architecture for cost-effective mass-individualization. Manuf. Lett. **16**, 44–48 (2018)
2. Gadalla, M., Xue, D.: Recent advances in research on reconfigurable machine tools: a literature review. Int. J. Prod. Res. **55**(5), 1440–1454 (2017)
3. Mahmoodjanloo, M., Tavakkoli-Moghaddam, R., Baboli, A., Bozorgi-Amiri, A.: Flexible job shop scheduling problem with reconfigurable machine tools: an improved differential evolution algorithm. Appl. Soft Comput. **94**, 106416 (2020)
4. Mahmoodjanloo, M., Tavakkoli-Moghaddam, R., Baboli, A., Bozorgi-Amiri, A.: Dynamic distributed job-shop scheduling problem consisting of reconfigurable machine tools. In IFIP International Conference on Advances in Production Management Systems, pp. 460–468. Springer, Cham (2020). https://doi.org/10.1007/978-3-030-57997-5_53
5. Abdi, M.R., Labib, A.W.: A design strategy for reconfigurable manufacturing systems (RMSs) using analytical hierarchical process (AHP): a case study. Int. J. Prod. Res. **41**(10), 2273–2299 (2003)
6. Moghaddam, S.K., Houshmand, M., Fatahi Valilai, O.: Configuration design in scalable reconfigurable manufacturing systems (RMS); a case of single-product flow line (SPFL). Int. J. Prod. Res. **56**(11), 3932–3954 (2018)
7. Moghaddam, S.K., Houshmand, M., Saitou, K., Fatahi Valilai, O.: Configuration design of scalable reconfigurable manufacturing systems for part family. Int. J. Prod. Res. **58**(10), 2974–2996 (2019)
8. Ashraf, M., Hasan, F.: Configuration selection for a reconfigurable manufacturing flow line involving part production with operation constraints. Int. J. Adv. Manuf. Technol. **98**(5–8), 2137–2156 (2018). https://doi.org/10.1007/s00170-018-2361-7
9. Touzout, F. A., Benyoucef, L., Benderbal, H.H., Dahane, M.: A hybrid multi-objective based approach for sustainable process plan generation in a reconfigurable manufacturing environment. In: 2018 IEEE 16th International Conference on Industrial Informatics (INDIN), pp. 343–348. IEEE, July 2018
10. He, Y., Li, Y., Wu, T., Sutherland, J.W.: An energy-responsive optimization method for machine tool selection and operation sequence in flexible machining job shops. J. Clean. Prod. **87**, 245–254 (2015)
11. Koren, Y., Gu, X., Guo, W.: Reconfigurable manufacturing systems: principles, design, and future trends. Front. Mech. Eng. **13**(2), 121–136 (2017). https://doi.org/10.1007/s11465-018-0483-0
12. Goyal, K.K., Jain, P.K., Jain, M.: Optimal configuration selection for reconfigurable manufacturing system using NSGA II and TOPSIS. Int. J. Prod. Res. **50**(15), 4175–4191 (2012)

Single Machine Order Acceptance Scheduling with Periodic Energy Consumption Limits

Mariam Bouzid[(✉)], Oussama Masmoudi, and Alice Yalaoui

Computer Laboratory and Digital Society (LIST3N), Troyes, France
{mariam.bouzid,oussama.masmoudi,alice.yalaoui}@utt.fr

Abstract. This work presents an Order Acceptance Scheduling (OAS) problem with the introduction of energy consumption limits at each period of the planning horizon. The objective is to maximize total profit of accepted orders while considering energy usage over time, in accordance with imposed deadlines. A time-indexed formulation is presented to tackle the investigated problem.

Keywords: Order acceptance scheduling · Energy consumption · Time-indexed

1 Introduction

Resource depletion has become a major concern these past decades for both economic and environmental reasons. Standards, taxes and limits on resource use, are ones of many tools implemented by authorities to curb the current trend. Although, as stated in [11], new business opportunities are opened by these challenges and structural changes are required in the supply chain in the context of sustainability. This lead industrials to reconsider their rate of production at the operational level. During production, many levers can be taken into account, such as machine speed, shutdown mechanisms, among others. Monitoring energy consumption and costs, or carbon emissions during the production processes are useful indicators to mitigate impacts on the environment and to make substantial savings. Meanwhile, accepting or rejecting orders occurs in a plethora of manufacturing sectors when a company is limited by its facilities, client deadlines or in general by resources availability. Optimizing the production schedule is therefore essential to make a good balance between available production capacity and sales volume.

In this vein, this paper focuses on a capacity-constrained system by addressing an Order Acceptance Scheduling (OAS) problem with periodic energy consumption limits with the objective to maximize total profit. Section 2 presents a short literature review on resource-efficiency and energy-efficiency in scheduling problems with a focus on OAS problems. Section 3 gives a description of the

© IFIP International Federation for Information Processing 2021
Published by Springer Nature Switzerland AG 2021
A. Dolgui et al. (Eds.): APMS 2021, IFIP AICT 630, pp. 372–377, 2021.
https://doi.org/10.1007/978-3-030-85874-2_39

proposed problem. Section 4 provides the solving approach and Sect. 5 gives the preliminary results on a small benchmark. The final section features conclusions and perspectives to this work.

2   Related Literature

Resource-efficiency and more globally resource management appeared at early stage of scheduling problem researches [1]. The characterization of resources in terms of availability and divisibility allow to cover a broad range of situations. Time-dependent resources, *i.e.* when the amount of resources varies over time, is for instance studied for an open shop and a parallel machine system in [13].

Resource management typically occurs during a project with dependent activities such as construction engineering, or manufacturing. In order to carry out a project at a lower cost while satisfying timing, labor, material, or equipment constraints, the Resource-Constrained Project Scheduling problem (RCPSP) [2] (and its variants) addresses this problem particularly well. On another side, financial scheduling problem insists on other interesting aspects of resources, in particular when they are assimilated to a stock (e.g. wages, raw materials) that can be replenished at different time of the horizon. Most of the studies on this topic provide solid complexity analysis and approximation schemes [6, 7]. Gafarov et al. [3] proved the NP-hardness of the single machine problem with non-renewable resources with the objective to minimize the makespan. They provide the optimal sequence to a particular polynomial case of the problem with the objective to minimize total tardiness. When it comes to energy, usually, efficiency is conceptualized by incorporating a specific criteria within the objective [4]. Therefore, total energy cost or consumption is minimized in numerous works including single machine and more complex systems. However, few researches address energy-efficiency by introducing dedicated constraints that differ from conventional resource constraints. For parallel machines, [10], minimized makespan with interval limits on energy consumption. They used two exact solving approaches, which are Branch and Bound and Benders decomposition, and a Tabu search to tackle this problem. In the meantime, Liao et al. [9] minimized both weighted completion times and weighted tardiness on a single machine with interval limits on energy consumption. They proposed an evolutionary algorithm for this multi-objective problem.

Introducing resource constraints is no exception in OAS, since it can be expected that limited resources force manufacturers to reconsider how much they can produce, avoiding losses as much as possible. For instance, [5] are the first to consider an OAS on a single machine with resource-constraints, rejecting orders if they cannot be completed within a predetermined time-window. The work of Kong et al. [8] presents an order acceptance scheduling problem with a global budget on energy use in a parallel machines system.

To the best of our knowledge, the OAS problem on a single machine with periodic resource consumption limits has not yet been tackled. This problem is interesting and appears when a resource consumed by production (such as energy) cannot be stored and is different from a period to an other. This typically appears in period of high energy consumption.

3   Problem Description

This paper investigates an Order Acceptance scheduling problem on a single non-preemptive machine with energy consumption limits at each period. The objective is to maximize total profit while satisfying periodic energy consumption limits. This problem is NP-hard since the OAS problem on a single machine, maximizing the total profit is NP-hard in its basic form [12].

As in [13], in this problem, the resource is renewable, that is, a energy unit available at time t shall be consumed at time t but can not be saved for later. The availability of the resource at time $t + 1$ does not depend on the amount consumed at or before time t, unlike financial scheduling problem. Energy is thus available in time-dependent quantities, i.e. their availability changes over time. Each order is defined by its processing time p_j, its deadline $\bar{d}_j$, its unitary power consumption e_j (kW) and its revenue f_j.

The following assumptions are formulated:

- The energy consumed by an order remains constant during the totality of its production.
- Preemption is not allowed.
- The manufacturer earns the totality of the revenue of an order j if it can be scheduled completely before its deadline.

The horizon is split into unitary slots $t = 1, \ldots, T$ each characterized by an energy limit E_t. The length of the horizon T is defined by the maximum of the deadlines.

For illustration purpose, let's take an example of $n = 5$ orders where $p = [8, 3, 4, 4, 3]$, $\bar{d} = [25, 16, 9, 21, 9]$, $e = [3.5, 4, 3.5, 3.5, 2]$ and $f = [15, 10, 10, 5, 10]$. Assume that orders 2 and 4 are rejected.

In Fig. 1, the bar chart represents the amount of available energy E_t at each period $t = 1, \ldots, T$. The sequence is represented by a Gantt diagram below. An order j is represented by two components : its energy consumption e_j in height and its processing time p_j in width.

4   Solving Approach

A time-indexed On/Off formulation is used to model the proposed problem. In this formulation, the binary decision variables $x_{jt} = 1$ refer to the production of a unit of order j at time t (or not $x_{jt} = 0$). Moreover, the binary decision variables a_j equals 1 if the order j is accepted, 0 otherwise. The problem is formulated as a Mixed Integer Linear Program as follows.

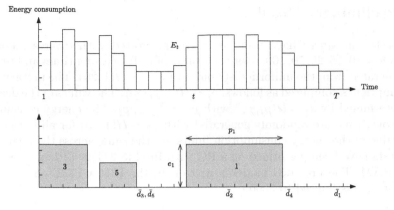

Fig. 1. An example with $n = 5$ orders.

$$\textbf{maximize} \sum_{j=1}^{n} a_j f_j \tag{1}$$

subject to

$$\sum_{j=1}^{n} x_{jt} \leq 1 \qquad t = 1, \ldots, T \tag{2}$$

$$\sum_{t=1}^{\bar{d}_j} x_{jt} = p_j a_j \qquad j = 1, \ldots, n \tag{3}$$

$$\sum_{t'=1}^{t-p_j} x_{jt'} + \sum_{t'=t+p_j}^{\bar{d}_j} x_{jt'} \leq p_j(1 - x_{jt}) \qquad j = 1, \ldots, n, \quad t = p_j + 1, \ldots, \bar{d}_j \tag{4}$$

$$\sum_{j=1}^{n} e_j x_{jt} \leq E_t \qquad t = 1, \ldots, T \tag{5}$$

$$\sum_{t=\bar{d}_j+1}^{T} x_{jt} = 0 \qquad j = 1, \ldots, n \tag{6}$$

The objective (1) is the maximization of the sum of the revenue of the accepted orders. Constraints (2) ensure that the machine can either produce or do nothing. Constraints (3) state that an accepted order must be processed p_j time units within its time-window $r_j, \ldots, \bar{d}_j$. Constraints (4) guarantee non-preemption by forcing the continuity of the decision variables x_{jt}. If at time period t order j is produced ($x_{jt} = 1$), the constraints exclude production p_j units before and after t, i.e. in periods $1, \ldots, t - p_j$ and $t + p_j, \ldots, \bar{d}_j$. Constraints (5) are the periodic energy consumption limits, imposing that a unit of production of an order at time t does not exceeds E_t, the available energy at time t. Constraints (6) prevent any order j to be produced after its deadline $\bar{d}_j$.

5   Preliminary Results

The tested instances have been randomly generated with diverse number of orders $n = 10, 15, 25, 50, 100$, 5 for each value of n. Processing times and revenues are generated from the uniform distribution $p_j, f_j \sim \mathcal{U}(1, 20)$. The unitary power consumption is computed as follows: $e_j \sim \mathcal{U}(1, f_j) \times \frac{1}{2}$. The values of the deadlines are determined by $\bar{d}_j = \mathcal{U}(p_j, p_T)$ with $p_T = \sum_{j=1}^{n} p_j$. The energy consumption limits over time are randomly generated with $\bar{E}_t \sim \mathcal{U}(1, 10)$ for all $t = 1, \ldots, T$. The value of the energy consumption limits are the same across the benchmark. The tests have been performed on a PC with Intel i5 2 GHz CPU processor and 4 GB RAM. The provided model is written in the IBM CPLEX Solver $v12.9$. Solving time is limited to 3600 s.

Table 1. Computational results.

n	$\overline{cpu}$	$\overline{gap}$	% acc
10	0.03	0	0.22
15	0.07	0	0.24
25	0.55	0	0.28
50	675	0	0.38
100	3600	53	0.32

Table 1 presents the results obtained by the solver. Each line represents 5 instances with varying number of orders. The average solving time (in seconds) and the average gap (CPLEX relative Gap in %) is reported for each batch of instances. Finally, the average proportion of accepted orders is indicated (in %). The model performs well for small to medium instance size with less than a second to optimally solve the instances. As can be seen, from $n = 50$, the average cpu time sharply increases. With $n = 100$ orders, the model cannot find some feasible solutions (3/5 are feasibles) with poor solution quality.

6   Conclusion and Perspectives

In this paper, the OAS problem on a single machine with periodic energy consumption limits is studied. A time-indexed model with $\mathcal{O}(nT)$ constraints and $\mathcal{O}(nT)$ decision variables is used to solve this problem. Since the objective is the maximization of total profit with time-dependent resource constraints, the time-indexed model is a purposeful choice as it exploits to its benefit the time dependency of the investigated problem. A comparison between the proposed time-indexed model and a classical formulation using completion times shall be done. The development of dedicated exact methods is planned in the future work due to solver limitations. A special focus will be made on finding dedicated cuts, bounds and properties of the problem. Moreover, the formalisation of diverse type of constraints that make sense in the context of energy-efficient scheduling must be performed. Global, cumulative and rolling-window constraints must be studied with a careful examination of mathematical properties and a complexity analysis for each of the problem variants. Preliminaries results will be presented on this occasion.

References

1. Błażewicz, J.: Scheduling under resource constraints: deterministic models. JC Baltzer (1986)
2. Brucker, P., Drexl, A., Mo, R., Pesch, E.: Resource-constrained project scheduling: notation, classification, models, and methods. Eur. J. Oper. Res. **112**(1), 39 (1999)
3. Gafarov, E.R., Lazarev, A.A., Werner, F.: Single machine scheduling problems with financial resource constraints: some complexity results and properties. Math. Soc. Sci. **1**, 7–13 (2011)
4. Gao, K., Huang, Y., Sadollah, A., Wang, L.: A review of energy-efficient scheduling in intelligent production systems. Complex Intell. Syst. **6**(2), 237–249 (2019). https://doi.org/10.1007/s40747-019-00122-6
5. Garcia, C.: Resource-constrained scheduling with hard due windows and rejection penalties. Eng. Optim. **48**(9), 1515–1528 (2016)
6. Györgyi, P., Kis, T.: Minimizing total weighted completion time on a single machine subject to non-renewable resource constraints. J. Sched. **22**(6), 623–634 (2019). https://doi.org/10.1007/s10951-019-00601-1
7. Györgyi, P., Kis, T.: New complexity and approximability results for minimizing the total weighted completion time on a single machine subject to non-renewable resource constraints. arXiv:2004.00972 [math] (2020)
8. Kong, M., Pei, J., Liu, X., Lai, P.C., Pardalos, P.M.: Green manufacturing: order acceptance and scheduling subject to the budgets of energy consumption and machine launch. J. Cleaner Prod. **248**, 119300 (2020)
9. Liao, X., Zhang, R., Chiong, R.: Multi-objective optimization of single machine scheduling with energy consumption constraints. In: 2017 IEEE Symposium Series on Computational Intelligence (SSCI), pp. 1–8. IEEE, Honolulu (2017)
10. Módos, I., Šůcha, P., Hanzálek, Z.: Algorithms for robust production scheduling with energy consumption limits. Comput. Ind. Eng. **112**, 391–408 (2017)
11. O'Brien, M., Fischer, S., Schepelmann, P., Bringezu, S.: Resource efficiency in European industry. Study for the European Parliament, Brussels (2012)
12. Palakiti, V.P., Mohan, U., Ganesan, V.K.: Order acceptance and scheduling: overview and complexity results. Int. J. Oper. Res. **34**(3), 369–386 (2019)
13. Tautenhahn, T., Woeginger, G.J.: Unit-time scheduling problems with time dependent resources. Computing **58**(2), 97–111 (1997)

A MILP Model for Energy-Efficient Job Shop Scheduling Problem and Transport Resources

S. Mahdi Homayouni[1(✉)] and Dalila B.M.M. Fontes[1,2]

[1] LIAAD-INESCTEC, Porto, Portugal
{smh,dfontes}@inesctec.pt
[2] Faculdade de Economia, Universidade do Porto, Porto, Portugal

Abstract. This work addresses the energy-efficient job shop scheduling problem and transport resources with speed scalable machines and vehicles which is a recent extension of the classical job shop problem. In the environment under consideration, the speed with which machines process production operations and the speed with which vehicles transport jobs are also to be decided. Therefore, the scheduler can control both the completion times and the total energy consumption. We propose a mixed-integer linear programming model that can be efficiently solved to optimality for small-sized problem instances.

Keywords: Job shop scheduling problem · Transport resources · Energy efficient · Mixed integer linear programming model · Speed scalable machines

1 Introduction

Energy-efficient scheduling methods have been increasingly attracting the attention of academia and practitioners. Energy-efficient scheduling attempts to lower energy consumption while providing the same service level. The two main strategies in energy-efficient scheduling are to switch off resources while in idle mode [9] and to control the resources working speed (speed scalable) [5]. While the former strategy has to balance energy savings from shutting down resources and energy requirements to start and warm them up, the latter has to balance energy consumption and productivity (i.e., production rate, makespan, tardiness, earliness, etc.). In addition, by reducing the working speed of some resources one may reduce resources idle time as well as energy consumption without impacting productivity.

In the classic job shop scheduling problem (JSP), the jobs are processed on a set of machines following a known order. It is commonly assumed that

Supported by FEDER/COMPETE2020/NORTE2020/POCI/PIDDAC/MCTES/FCT funds through projects POCI-01-0145-FEDER-031821-PTDC/EGE-OGE/31821/2017 and POCI-01-0145-FEDER-031447- PTDC/EEI-AUT/31447/2017.

A. Dolgui et al. (Eds.): APMS 2021, IFIP AICT 630, pp. 378–386, 2021.
https://doi.org/10.1007/978-3-030-85874-2_40

jobs are available at the machine processing their first operation and that a job is available to be processed on a machine as soon as the previous operations have been completed, i.e., no job transport is required between machines or the transport times are negligible. However, the transport of jobs between machines is an important process that cannot be ignored, since job processing and job transportation are interdependent and influence each other. The recognition of such interdependencies lead to the job shop scheduling problem with transport resources (JSPT), in which the machine scheduling, the transport allocation, and the vehicle scheduling are determined simultaneously. For a recent review of the JSPT works see [6] and the references therein.

The energy-efficient JSP (EEJSP) has recently become the center of attention of the JSP community; for instance, [12] proposes a Mixed Integer Linear Programming (MILP) that minimizes the energy consumption (both direct and indirect) for the JSP and proposes a solution method based on a gene expression programming-based rule mining integrated with an unsupervised learning process for the dispatching rules evaluation while [4] proposes a bi-objective MILP for the EEJSP that minimizes the makespan and the energy consumption and an enhanced estimation of distribution algorithm to solve the problem efficiently. Although it takes into account the energy required to process production operations, to keep machines running while idle, and to transport jobs, it considers that there are an unlimited number of vehicles available to transport the jobs.

The literature on speed scalable machine scheduling includes the single machine scheduling problem [2,3] and the EEJSP [1,11]. In [2] two mathematical models are proposed for the speed scalable and multi-states single-machine scheduling and. The complexity of the energy-efficient scheduling of a multi-state single machine is studied in [3] under two scenarios, namely: constant energy price and increasing energy price; and both have been proved to be polynomial. In addition, when considering time-of-use energy prices, the problem has been proved polynomial for a fixed job sequence and NP-hard otherwise. regarding the EEJSP, [11] considers speed scalable machine spindle and proposes a multi-objective MILP model that minimizes the makespan, energy consumption, and process noise. Solutions are obtained by an efficient multi-objective genetic algorithm. More recently, [1] considers the EEJSP with speed scalable and deteriorating machines in which the actual processing time of an operation depends on the selected processing speed and on the permutation of operations that have been previously processed on the machine. The machines are repaired occasionally to restore their processing capabilities. To model the problem a bi-objective MILP that minimizes the makespan and energy consumption (by production operations and maintenance activities) is proposed. Solutions are obtained by a multi-population multi-objective memetic algorithm.

Scheduling vehicles with adjustable speed includes determining the speed of the vehicles on the route segments which has already been studied, but in other contexts, e.g., for automated guided vehicles scheduling in manufacturing systems [10] and quay crane and vehicles scheduling in container terminals [7].

In this work, we consider energy-efficient JSPT with speed scalable machines and speed scalable vehicles that provide additional flexibility, which in turn allows further energy reductions while providing the same level of service. In addition, this is a new problem since the JSPT literature has only considered machines and vehicles that, respectively, process and move jobs at a constant speed.

Therefore, the contributions of our work are twofold: i) we consider a challenging problem that has never been addressed before, the energy-efficient job shop scheduling problem and transport resources (EEJSPT) with speed scalable machines and with speed scalable vehicles which, in addition, is relevant to the industry and ii) we develop a bi-objective MILP model that can be solved to optimality for small-sized problem instances.

In the following sections we provide a brief description of the problem in Sect. 2, propose the mathematical formulation of the problem in Sect. 3, report and discuss the computational experiments in Sect. 4.

2   Problem Definition

This section provides a detailed description of the EEJSPT, which requires solving simultaneously five interdependent combinatorial optimization problems, namely: scheduling the production operations on each machine (machine scheduling), determining the machine processing speed of each production operation (machine speed assignment), assigning each transport task to a vehicle (transport assignment), scheduling the transport tasks on each vehicle (vehicle scheduling), and determining the vehicle travelling speed of each transport task (vehicle speed assignment).

The production system includes a set of independent jobs and a set of machines. Each job consists of a set of ordered operations each of which to be processed uninterrupted on a given machine. Each machine can only process one operation at a time and each job can only be processed on one machine at a time. The machines can process each operation at one of several possible processing speeds with a known energy consumption that depends on the processing time and on the processing speed [11] (the higher the processing speed, the higher the energy consumption). In addition, it is assumed that idle machines are in a "stand-by" mode and have a negligible energy consumption. Furthermore, there are no machine setup times and thus, whenever an operation is completed the machine can start processing the next operation immediately.

Each job enters the production system through the load/unload (LU) area and needs to be transported, by a vehicle, to the machine processing its first operation, between the machines processing consecutive operations, and then from the machine processing its last operation back to the LU. Once a job reaches a machine it is either processed immediately, if the machine is idle, or it waits for the machine in the machine input buffer; either way the vehicle can promptly pursue its next assignment. Vehicles have to wait for a job if they reach the machine processing it before the operation being processed is completed.

The transport system comprises a set of identical vehicles that can carry one job at a time and are initially parked at the LU area. The vehicles transport the jobs between machines and also between machines and the LU area (and vice-versa). Since any vehicle can perform any transport task, vehicles may need to do an empty travel, from their current location (dwell point) to the location where the job of the next assignment needs to be picked up at, before performing the assigned task.

It is assumed that the transport tasks are nonpreemptive and can be performed at different average speed levels. The vehicle's energy consumption per time unit depends not only on the average speed of the vehicle, but also on its load, i.e., empty travels have lower energy consumption than loaded ones. The travel time and energy consumed between any two locations at each speed level are known, since the layout is known and the transport tasks are nonpreemptive. As is the case for machines, it is assumed that idle vehicles are in "stand-by" mode and have negligible energy consumption.

Among all possible solutions for this problem, we are interested in those that minimize both the makespan (completion time of the last production operation) and the total energy consumption (by machines and vehicles).

3 MILP Formulation

The EEJSPT problem considers a set $\mathcal{J}$ of jobs, each of which with n_j ordered production operations to be processed on a set $\mathcal{I}$ of machines. Let all the production operations be a member of set $\mathcal{O} = \{o_1, o_2, \ldots, o_N\}$, where $N = \sum_{j \in \mathcal{J}} n_j$ is the total number of operations. Then, 1 to n_1 represent the production operations of the first job (o_1 to o_{n_1}), $n_1 + 1$ to $n_1 + n_2$ represent the production operations of the second job ($o_{(n_1+1)}$ to $o_{(n_1+n_2)}$), and so on. Each production operation, say o_l, can be processed at any one of the speed levels in set $\mathcal{P}_l$, on the pre-specified machine $m_l \in \mathcal{I}$. The operation previous to operation o_l is denoted by μ_l, either a dummy operation o_0, if o_l is the first operation of the job, or $o_{(l-1)}$ otherwise. (Note that m_{o_0} is by default the LU area.) Clearly, the job needs to be transported from machine m_{μ_l} to machine m_l, before processing can start on m_l. Therefore, a transport task t_l is associated with production operation o_l and it is performed by one of the A identical available vehicles, which can travel at any one of the speed levels in set $\mathcal{V}$.

Since each job consists of a set of ordered operations, each requiring a transport task, it is clear that an operation/task can only be started once its predecessor has been completed and its successor can only be started after its completion. Therefore, we can define a list $\mathcal{F}$ of pairs of operations/tasks (k, l) such that o_l/t_l is a predecessor of o_k/t_k. (Note that $(k, k) \in \mathcal{F}$.) For example, if job 1 has at least two ordered production operations, then the list has at least the following pairs $(1, 1), (2, 1)$ and $(2, 2) \in \mathcal{F}$.

Let us first define the parameters and decision variables and then provide the MILP model and its description.

Parameters

π_l^p: Processing time of operation $o_l, l \in \mathcal{O}$ at speed level $p \in \mathcal{P}_l$,

e_l^p: Energy consumption of machine m_l when processing at speed level $p \in \mathcal{P}_l$,

τ_{kl}^v: Vehicle empty travel time from m_k to m_{μ_l} for performing t_l at speed level $v \in \mathcal{V}$ immediately after completing t_k, $k, l \in \mathcal{O}$;

τ_{0l}^v: Vehicle empty travel time from LU area to m_{μ_l}, performing t_l, $l \in \mathcal{O}$ at speed level $v \in \mathcal{V}$ as the first task of an AGV;

θ_l^v: Vehicle loaded travel time from m_{μ_l} to m_l, $l \in \mathcal{O}$ at speed level $v \in \mathcal{V}$;

ϵ^v: Vehicle energy consumption per time unit travelling empty at speed level $v \in \mathcal{V}$;

ε^v: Vehicle energy consumption per time unit travelling loaded at speed level $v \in \mathcal{V}$;

Decision Variables

w_{kl}^p: Binary variable taking the value 1 if $o_l, l \in \mathcal{O}$ is processed at speed level $p \in \mathcal{P}_l$ immediately after $o_k, k \in \mathcal{O}$ in the same machine, and 0 otherwise;

$f_{lm_l}^p$: Binary variable taking the value 1 if $o_l, l \in \mathcal{O}$ is processed at speed level $p \in \mathcal{P}_l$ as the first operation in machine $m_l \in \mathcal{I}$;

t_{lm_l}: Binary "dummy" variable taking the value 1 if $o_l, l \in \mathcal{O}$ is the last operation processed in machine $m_l \in \mathcal{I}$, and 0 otherwise,

x_{kl}^v: Binary variable taking the value 1 if t_l, $l \in \mathcal{O}$ is done at speed level $v \in \mathcal{V}$ immediately after $t_k, k \in \mathcal{O}$ by the same vehicle, and 0 otherwise,

y_l^v: Binary variable taking the value 1 if t_l, $l \in \mathcal{O}$ at speed level $v \in \mathcal{V}$ is the first task of a vehicle, and 0 otherwise,

z_l: Binary "dummy" variable taking the value 1 if t_l, $l \in \mathcal{O}$ is the last task of a vehicle, and 0 otherwise,

c_l: Production completion time of $o_l, l \in \mathcal{O}$, (c_0 by default is 0),

r_l: Arrival time of the vehicle at the machine processing $o_l, l \in \mathcal{O}$,

$C_{\max}$: Makespan of the production operations,

$\mathcal{E}$: Total energy consumption in production operations and transport tasks.

$$\text{Minimize:} \{C_{\max}, \mathcal{E}\} \tag{1}$$

Subject to:

$$C_{\max} \geq c_l, \qquad \forall l \in \mathcal{O}, \tag{2}$$

$$\mathcal{E} = \sum_{\substack{k,l \in \mathcal{O}: \\ (k,l) \notin \mathcal{F}}} \sum_{p \in \mathcal{P}_l} (e_l^p w_{kl}^p) + \sum_{l \in \mathcal{O}} \sum_{p \in \mathcal{P}_l} (e_l^p f_{lm_l}^p)$$

$$+ \sum_{l \in \mathcal{O}} \sum_{v \in \mathcal{V}} y_l^v (\varepsilon^v \theta_l^v + \epsilon^v \tau_{0l}^v) + \sum_{\substack{k,l \in \mathcal{O}: \\ (k,l) \notin \mathcal{F}}} \sum_{v \in \mathcal{V}} x_{kl}^v (\varepsilon^v \theta_l^v + \epsilon^v \tau_{kl}^v), \tag{3}$$

$$\sum_{p \in \mathcal{P}_l} f_{lm_l}^p + \sum_{\substack{k \in \mathcal{O}: \\ (k,l) \notin \mathcal{F}}} \sum_{p \in \mathcal{P}_l} w_{kl}^p = 1, \qquad \forall l \in \mathcal{O}, \tag{4}$$

$$\sum_{\substack{k \in \mathcal{O}: \\ (l,k) \notin \mathcal{F}}} \sum_{p \in \mathcal{P}_l} w_{lk}^p + t_{lm_l} = 1, \qquad \forall l \in \mathcal{O}, \tag{5}$$

$$\sum_{l \in \mathcal{O}} \sum_{p \in \mathcal{P}_l} f_{lm_l}^p = 1 \qquad \forall m \in \mathcal{I}, \tag{6}$$

$$\sum_{l \in \mathcal{O}} t_{lm_l} = 1 \qquad \forall m \in \mathcal{I}, \tag{7}$$

$$\sum_{l \in \mathcal{O}} z_l = \sum_{l \in \mathcal{O}} \sum_{v \in \mathcal{V}} y_l^v \leq A, \tag{8}$$

$$\sum_{v \in \mathcal{V}} y_l^v + \sum_{\substack{k \in \mathcal{O}: \\ (k,l) \notin \mathcal{F}}} \sum_{v \in \mathcal{V}} x_{kl}^v = 1, \qquad \forall l \in \mathcal{O}, \tag{9}$$

$$\sum_{\substack{k \in \mathcal{O}: \\ (l,k) \notin \mathcal{F}}} \sum_{v \in \mathcal{V}} x_{lk}^v + z_l = 1, \qquad \forall l \in \mathcal{O}, \tag{10}$$

$$c_l - r_l - \sum_{\substack{k \in \mathcal{O}: \\ (k,l) \notin \mathcal{F}}} \sum_{p \in \mathcal{P}_l} w_{kl}^p \pi_l^p - \sum_{p \in \mathcal{P}_l} f_{lm_l}^p \pi_l^p \geq 0, \qquad \forall l \in \mathcal{O}, \tag{11}$$

$$c_l - c_k - \sum_{p \in \mathcal{P}_l} w_{kl}^p \pi_l^p \geq M \left(\sum_{p \in \mathcal{P}_l} w_{kl}^p - 1 \right), \qquad \forall k, l \in \mathcal{O} : (k,l) \notin \mathcal{F}, \tag{12}$$

$$r_l - c_{\mu_l} - \sum_{\substack{k \in \mathcal{O}: \\ (k,l) \notin \mathcal{F}}} \sum_{v \in \mathcal{V}} x_{kl}^v \theta_l^v - \sum_{v \in \mathcal{V}} y_l^v \theta_l^v \geq 0, \qquad \forall l \in \mathcal{O}, \tag{13}$$

$$r_l - r_k - \sum_{v \in \mathcal{V}} x_{kl}^v (\tau_{kl}^v + \theta_l^v) \geq M \left(\sum_{v \in \mathcal{V}} x_{kl}^v - 1 \right), \quad \forall k, l \in \mathcal{O} : (k,l) \notin \mathcal{F}, \tag{14}$$

$$r_l - \sum_{v \in \mathcal{V}} y_l^v (\tau_{0l}^v + \theta_l^v) \geq 0, \qquad \forall l \in \mathcal{O}, \tag{15}$$

$$C_{\max}, \mathcal{E}, c_l, r_l \geq 0, \hspace{3cm} \forall l \in \mathcal{O}, \hspace{1.5cm} (16)$$

$$w_{kl}^p, f_{lm_l}^p, t_{lm_l}, x_{kl}^v, y_l^v, z_l \in \{0, 1\}, \hspace{1cm} \forall k, l \in \mathcal{O} : (k, l) \notin \mathcal{F}, p \in \mathcal{P}_l, v \in \mathcal{V}. \hspace{0.3cm} (17)$$

The objective is to minimize the makespan and the total energy consumption as in Eq. (1) and their values are given by expressions (2) and (3), respectively. Constraints (4) and (5) impose that each operation should be immediately followed and immediately preceded by exactly one other operation on the same machine. Constraints (8) ensure that the number of first and last tasks is the same and does not exceed the number of available vehicles. Constraints (9) and (10) require each transport task to be immediately followed and immediately preceded by exactly one other transport task, respectively.

Each operation can be completed once i) the job arrives at the machine and its processing time (at the chosen speed level) has elapsed (as in constraint 11) and ii) the previous operation on the same machine is completed, in addition to its own processing time (as in constraint 12), where M is a sufficiently large positive integer. Similarly, a job can only arrive at a machine after its previous operation has been completed and the job has been transported (see constraint (13)). In addition, if a vehicle has transported some other job to have an operation, say $k \in \mathcal{O}$, processed immediately before the current one, then it needs to (i) deliver such job to machine m_k, (ii) travel empty from machine m_k to the job previous operation or the LU area if it is the job first operation, and (iii) deliver it to the corresponding machine, which is enforced by constraints (14). Clearly, if this is the first transport task of a vehicle, then it can be started immediately, see constraints (15). Finally, constraints (16) and (17) define the nature of the variables.

4   Results and Discussion

For evaluation purposes, we use a data set designed in [11] for EEJSP (with speed scalable machines) and adapt them for EEJSPT by adding layout data (randomly generated) and a fleet of two to six identical speed scalable vehicles. The instances are designated as Yin01 and Yin02 and have four and 10 jobs with 12 and 40 operations to be processed at two to three average speed levels in five and six machines, respectively. The speeds and energy consumption are borrowed from [8]. We consider three different vehicle speeds, namely: 0.9, 1.2, and 1.5 m/s (m/s). The corresponding energy consumption is 63, 75, and 86 W per second when traveling empty and 74, 90, and 108 W/s when traveling loaded. (We assume the same weight of 48 kg for all the jobs.) The full data set can be downloaded from https://fastmanufacturingproject.wordpress.com/problem-instances/.

The MILP model was implemented in Python® 3.7 and solved using Gurobi® 9.0. All computational experiments were carried out on a 3.20 GHz Intel® Core™ i7-8700 PC with 24 GB RAM.

The bi-objective model was solved using a "lexicographic" methodology [7] which allows for finding two extreme best solutions of the problem. Table 1 reports instance characteristics (J-number of jobs, N-number of operations and tasks, M-number of machines, and A-number of vehicles), and TT a coefficient used to change the magnitude of travel times. We also report the minimum makespan ($C^*_{\max}$) and the associated energy consumption ($\mathcal{E}$), the minimum energy consumption ($\mathcal{E}^*$) and the associated makespan ($C_{\max}$) under three different scenarios in which (i) all machines and vehicles operate always at the lowest speed (LS), (ii) all machines and vehicles operate always at the highest speed (HS), and (iii) operating speed levels are chosen for each operation and for each task among the three speed levels considered (3S). Finally, the GAP values for the objective values under 3S scenario are computed. For instance, $GAP_{\mathcal{E}^*} = \frac{\mathcal{E}^*_{(3S)} - \mathcal{E}^*_{(LS)}}{\mathcal{E}^*_{(LS)}} \times 100$, where $\mathcal{E}^*_{(3S)}$ and $\mathcal{E}^*_{(LS)}$ are the minimum energy consumption under 3S and LS scenarios, respectively.

The results show that under the 3S scenario the $\mathcal{E}^*$ can be decreased in comparison to the one obtained in scenario LS, on average, by about 7%. It is interesting to notice that decreasing $\mathcal{E}^*$ not only does not imply additional time, but also, in most cases, allows for its reduction (on average, by about 17.5%). Regarding the $C^*_{\max}$, under the 3S scenario we can obtain the same values as those obtained under the HS scenario while significantly decreasing the energy consumption (on average by 9% and by up to 25%). Therefore, unlike the common belief that minimum energy consumption can only be achieved at the expense of a longer makespan, we show that speed management can be used not only to decrease the energy consumption but also to decrease it without sacrificing the makespan.

Considering zero travel times, the extreme solutions found under the 3S scenario match those found in [11] for EEJSP problem instances which in turn validates our MILP model and its implementation. Moreover, considering doubled travel times increases the problem complexity. Accordingly, the MILP model was not able to solve Yin02 to optimality. Nevertheless, it can solve it if there are two more vehicles.

Table 1. Results for small-sized problem instances under three different scenarios.

Instances			LS		HS		3S				GAPs			
Name	J-N-M-A	TT	$\mathcal{E}^*$	$C_{\max}$	$C^*_{\max}$	$\mathcal{E}$	$\mathcal{E}^*$	$C_{\max}$	$C^*_{\max}$	$\mathcal{E}$	$\mathcal{E}^*$	$C_{\max}$	$C^*_{\max}$	$\mathcal{E}$
Yin01	4-12-5-2	0	4.89	35.0	22.0	6.79	4.82	35.0	22.0	5.81	−1.43	0.00	0.00	−14.43
	4-12-5-2	1	4.94	58.9	24.8	6.84	4.86	42.4	24.8	6.21	−1.62	−28.01	0.00	−9.21
	4-12-5-2	2	4.99	72.0	39.6	6.89	4.91	58.7	39.6	5.17	−1.60	−18.47	0.00	−24.96
Yin02	10-40-6-4	0	20.22	61.0	40.0	19.39	17.73	56.0	39.0	19.39	−12.31	−8.20	−2.50	0.00
	10-40-6-4	1	20.42	74.3	44.4	19.57	17.90	56.6	44.4	18.87	−12.33	−23.88	0.00	−3.55
	10-40-6-6	2	20.59	85.0	50.1	19.75	18.05	62.7	50.1	19.31	−12.33	−26.28	0.00	−2.22
Mean											−6.94	−17.47	−0.42	−9.06

The EEJSPT addressed in this paper is harder than most scheduling problems, since it involves not only scheduling production operations and transport tasks but also the determination of processing and transport speed levels for each operation and each task, respectively. The numerical analysis shows that the use of speed scalable resources can decrease the energy consumption and/or makespan at almost no extra operational cost.

References

1. Abedi, M., Chiong, R., Noman, N., Zhang, R.: A multi-population, multi-objective memetic algorithm for energy-efficient job-shop scheduling with deteriorating machines. Expert Syst. Appl. **157**, 113348 (2020)
2. Aghelinejad, M.M., Ouazene, Y., Yalaoui, A.: Energy optimization of a speed-scalable and multi-states single machine scheduling problem. In: Daniele, P., Scrimali, L. (eds.) New Trends in Emerging Complex Real Life Problems. ASS, vol. 1, pp. 23–31. Springer, Cham (2018). https://doi.org/10.1007/978-3-030-00473-6_4
3. Aghelinejad, M., Ouazene, Y., Yalaoui, A.: Complexity analysis of energy-efficient single machine scheduling problems. Oper. Res. Perspect. **6**, 100105 (2019)
4. Dai, M., Zhang, Z., Giret, A., Salido, M.A.: An enhanced estimation of distribution algorithm for energy-efficient job-shop scheduling problems with transportation constraints. Sustainability **11**(11), 3085 (2019)
5. Fang, K., Uhan, N., Zhao, F., Sutherland, J.: Flow shop scheduling with peak power consumption constraints. Ann. Oper. Res. **206**(1), 115–145 (2013)
6. Fontes, D.B.M.M., Homayouni, S.M.: Joint production and transportation scheduling in flexible manufacturing systems. J. Global Optim. **74**(4), 879–908 (2018). https://doi.org/10.1007/s10898-018-0681-7
7. Homayouni, S.M., Fontes, D.B.M.M.: Energy-efficient scheduling of intra-terminal container transport. In: Intelligent Control and Smart Energy Management: Renewable Resources and Transportation, pp. 1–28. Springer International Publishing (2021)
8. Meißner, M., Massalski, L.: Modeling the electrical power and energy consumption of automated guided vehicles to improve the energy efficiency of production systems. Int. J. Adv. Manuf. Technol. **110**(1), 481–498 (2020). https://doi.org/10.1007/s00170-020-05796-8
9. Mouzon, G., Yildirim, M.: A framework to minimise total energy consumption and total tardiness on a single machine. Int. J. Sustain. Eng. **1**(2), 105–116 (2008)
10. Riazi, S., Bengtsson, K., Lennartson, B.: Energy optimization of large-scale AGV systems. IEEE Trans. Autom. Sci. Eng. **18**(2), 638–649 (2020)
11. Yin, L., Li, X., Gao, L., Lu, C., Zhang, Z.: Energy-efficient job shop scheduling problem with variable spindle speed using a novel multi-objective algorithm. Adv. Mech. Eng. **9**(4), 1–21 (2017)
12. Zhang, L., Li, Z., Królczyk, G., Wu, D., Tang, Q.: Mathematical modeling and multi-attribute rule mining for energy efficient job-shop scheduling. J. Cleaner Prod. **241**, 118289 (2019)

Designing Bioenergy Supply Chains Under Social Constraints

Sobhan Razm[1], Nadjib Brahimi[2(✉)], Alexandre Dolgui[1], and Ramzi Hammami[2]

[1] IMT Atlantique, LS2N - UMR CNRS 6004, La Chantrerie, 4, rue Alfred Kastler - B.P. 20722, 44307 Nantes Cedex 3, France
{sobhan.razm,alexandre.dolgui}@imt-atlantique.fr
[2] Rennes School of Business, Rennes, France
{nadjib.brahimi,ramzi.hammami}@rennes-sb.com

Abstract. The use of renewable energy, as a clean alternative to fossil fuel, has become very attractive. It has environmental advantages and leads to regional development. This study proposes an optimization model for the design of bioenergy supply chains under social concerns. The social concerns involve the unemployment rate and the vulnerability to changes during an economic crisis.

The areas that are mostly exposed to these social issues are chosen as initial potential locations for installing the biorefineries. Installing a biorefinery can generate jobs for the people of these areas. This leads to the sustainable development in the areas. The applicability of the developed model is shown through a case study. The results demonstrate that the proposed approach leads to the generation of a large number of job positions which has an important impact on the social development of these regions.

Keywords: Sustainable development · Biofuel production · Bioenergy supply chains · Biomass · Optimization · Social concerns

1 Introduction

The design and management of bioenergy supply chains have gotten attention in the recent years [1]. However, the cost of the bioenergy supply chain (SC) network is one of the most significant obstacles in developing bioenergy supply chains [2]. For example, one of the major costs is incurred in the collection and transportation of biomass to the biorefineries. Collecting, processing, and transporting biomass feedstocks from supply sites to the biorefineries have also environmental and social impacts [3].

The location of the biorefinery is a critical issue [4] in terms of reducing these costs [5] as well as GHG emissions (e.g. because of less transportation). The location of the biorefinery is also important, since it can generate new jobs and lead to sustainable development in a given region [6]. As a result, it is important to incorporate the concepts of sustainability into the design and planning of the bioenergy supply chain networks. Consequently, this study is seeking to answer the following questions:

© IFIP International Federation for Information Processing 2021
Published by Springer Nature Switzerland AG 2021
A. Dolgui et al. (Eds.): APMS 2021, IFIP AICT 630, pp. 387–396, 2021.
https://doi.org/10.1007/978-3-030-85874-2_41

1. How to design and manage the bioenergy supply chains that transform biomass into biofuel and bioenergy?
2. How to determine the purchased biomass quantities, the output quantities of bioenergy and biofuel, and the inventory decisions in order to minimize the supply chain costs while considering social constraints?

Consequently, the contributions of this paper are as follows: 1) Developing a mathematical model for designing and managing the bio-refineries. 2) Incorporating the social concerns into the network design of the bioenergy supply chain. 3) Applying the developed model to a case study.

The remainder of the paper is organized as follows. The literature review is presented in Sect. 2. The definition of the problem is presented in Sect. 3. The model formulation is presented in Sect. 4. The results are described in Sect. 5. Finally, the conclusion and some suggestions to extend the study are presented in Sect. 6.

2 Literature Review

In recent years, modeling and optimization of the bioenergy supply chains have attracted the researchers. For example, some studies focused on the geographical dispersion to find biomass sources and supply capacities [7]. Some studies were more focused on the locations of bio-refinery and production capacities [8]. A group of studies considered the whole network (more integrated). They used different types of biomass (the agricultural and forest residues) to generate biofuel in the design of bioenergy supply chains [9, 10].

In terms of sustainability, a MILP model was proposed by [11] to design the bioenergy supply chain network. They used switchgrass as biomass feedstock. Three objectives (economic, environmental, and social objectives) were considered to optimize the following decisions: i) determining the amount of collected biomass, ii) determining the maximum capacity in the biomass collecting centers, iii) determining the locations of power plants and the capacities. The augmented ε-constraint and TOPSIS approach were used as a hybrid method to generated Pareto-optimal solutions for decision makers. However, their study focused only on generating electricity (power plant), and the generated jobs were not jobs with high impacts on the area. They did not pay attention very well to the important social concerns such as high unemployment rate, and high vulnerability to changes in the markets in an economic crisis.

Designing a biofuel supply chain could generate jobs for the local residents (in the territory), as well as protect the environment [12]. Nevertheless, in the literature, most of the researchers focused only on economic aspects, and less attention has been made to sustainability, especially the social aspects of the bioenergy supply chains. This is a gap in the bioenergy SC literature that needs to get more attention. In addition, in the real world, generating the jobs in a territory where has a very low unemployment rate could not be considered a very efficient design of the bioenergy SC (in terms of sustainable development). Generating the jobs which are not close (not relevant) to the skills of the local people, who may lose their jobs in the economic crisis, could not make a high social impact on the territory.

These are the factors which motivate this paper versus the state of the art. The outcomes of the bioenergy SC literature review are shown in Table 1. As shown in Table 1, there is an essential research gap in the literature to optimal design and planning of the bioenergy supply chains under social sustainability constraints such as high unemployment rate, and high vulnerability to changes in the markets in an economic crisis. This study tries to fill this research gap.

Table 1. The bioenergy SC literature vs. this study.

Article	Modeling approach				Social sustainability				Final products			
	Mathematical Programming			Objective function	jobs with high impacts			Other indices	Electricity	Pellet	Heat	Biofuel (bioethanol, bio-oil, biodiesel)
	MoMILP	MILP	MINLP		High unemployment rate (index)	High vulnerability in an economic crisis (index)						
[13]	X			3								X
[14]	X			2				food versus fuel				X
[15]	X			3								X
[16]		X		1					X			
[17]	X			2,3					X			
[5]	X			2								X
[18]	X			1								X
[9]	X			3								X
[19]	X			2								X
[20]		X		1					X			
Proposed model	X			1	X	X			X	X	X	X

1= minimizing (expected) total cost/annual cost/unit cost. 2= maximizing (expected) total profit/annual profit/annual income/net cash. 3= maximizing (expected) net present value

3 Problem Definition

The bioenergy supply chain network gets started with supplying raw materials (biomass) for the biorefineries and will end with the customers (markets). As shown in Fig. 1, biomass $r \in R$ is collected from the supply site $s \in S$. The biomass can be sent and processed by biorefinery at location $b \in B$ using technology $a \in A$. The biomass is converted to bioenergy $e \in E$ to sell in location $b \in B$, or is converted to biofuel $f \in F$ to sell in market $c \in C$.

The biomass feedstocks are forest residues and agricultural residues. Bioenergy refers to heat and electricity. Biofuel refers to bio-oil and pellet. These conversions of biomass can be done by different processes such as thermochemical, chemical, and biochemical. The generated biofuel is sent to different markets. The generated bioenergy is either used in the bio-refinery or sold to local heat grids/systems.

3.1 Social Sustainability

Iran's Ministry of Economic Affairs and Finance proposed an index of agricultural and forest vulnerability based on the research done by Isfahan University of Technology's college of agricultural engineering. The index is used to resist against changes in the agricultural and forest commodity markets that is $V = \mathfrak{D} \times (100 - \xi)$. In this equation, $\mathfrak{D}$ is the agricultural and forest dependency index. It is a part of employment revenue in the area that is obtained from the agricultural and forest parts. ξ is diversity index. It shows the economic diversity in the area. ξ takes value in $(0,100)$. $\xi = 0$ means that the society (the area) is completely dependent on a part. $\xi = 100$ means that the society is equally dependent on each of the defined parts. After normalizing, V (The agricultural and Forest vulnerability Index) is obtained in $(0,100)$ for each area. $V = 100$ means the area is highly vulnerable to changes in the markets (e.g., in an economic crisis). For example, the values of V for 23 territories are shown in Table 2. These values can be obtained from the statistics office of each country.

Table 2. The values of V for each territory.

territory	b1	b2	b3	b4	b5	b6	b7	b8	b9	b10
V	18	62	14	23	19	17	15	53	50	43
territory	b11	b12	b13	b14	b15	b16	b17	b18	b19	b20
V	16	42	44	48	30	41	12	23	49	13
territory	b21	b22	b23							
V	55	22	20							

Concentrating on the high unemployment rate in the areas with high vulnerability could generate social impact. Consequently, when a job with a higher employment rate is generated in a territory with a higher vulnerability (job with a high impact), it can generate more social profit. Given the ruined jobs of the aboriginal people of the biorefinery's territory (caused by an economic crisis), various job categories are generated in the biorefineries that are close to the skills of the aboriginal people. For instance, the farmers who have lost their jobs can be employed in combustion stations. The individuals who have worked in the corporations relating to oil can be employed in the pyrolysis technology stations. According to the Iranian statistics office, a lot of farmers have lost their jobs in the last economic crisis, so their unemployment rate is high (equal to 11.23%). These farmers could be employed in the combustion stations. As a result, the social profit is generated by the social impact of the job generation.

The jobs generated for local people by installing the biorefinery could be defined into three main categories depending on the average unemployment rate ($\mathfrak{I}_w$), consulting with Renewable Energy and Energy Efficiency Organization. Table 3 shows these categories.

The unemployment rates can be determined by the statistics office of each country. Therefore, in another study, the values of the unemployment rate may change. The social

Table 3. Jobs categories generated by installing the bio-refineries.

Class (w)	Description	Average unemployment rate (λ_w)
1. Combustion	This class of jobs has a revenue between $50,000 and $55,000 per year that the revenue is able to change in the specific range considering the technologies' capacity and the requested variable and fix work hours. For example, jobs related to burning of agriculture and forest biomass to generate heat and electricity, or periodic maintenance of combustion technology like the biomass boiler and steam turbine.	11.23%
2.Pelletizing	This class of jobs has a revenue between $55,000 and $60,000 per year that the revenue is able to change in the specific range considering the technologies' capacity and the requested variable and fix work hours. For example, working with technologies which are specific to generate pellets, or preprocesses which are requested in each period before performing the main process of generating pellets.	6.55%
3.Pyrolysis	This class of jobs has a revenue more than $60,000 per year that the revenue is able to change in the specific range considering the technologies' capacity and the requested variable and fix work hours. For example, the hourly jobs for the generating process with pyrolysis technologies or the jobs with fix hours for constant presence of the experts beside the facilities in each period.	12.35%

impact ($\Pi_{w,b}$) of the generated job in the category w in the territory b is calculated by $\Pi_{w,b} = \lambda_w \times V_b$. Then, the territories with high vulnerability and high unemployment rates are chosen as candidate locations for the biorefineries (see Fig. 2), in order to maximize the social impact. The vulnerability rate and unemployment rate for each territory can be obtained from the statistics office of each country.

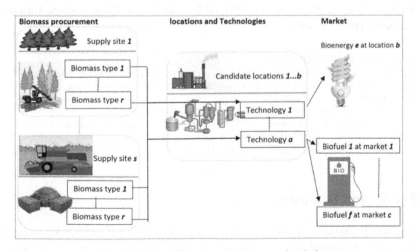

Fig. 1. General framework of the supply chain

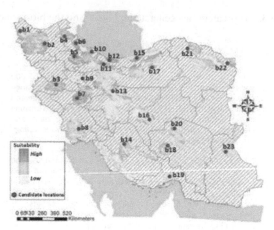

Fig. 2. Initial suggested locations for installing the bio-refineries

4   Model Formulation

The objective of the proposed model is to minimize the total costs of the supply chain. The decisions determined by this model are as follows: 1) determining the amount of the purchased and transported biomass to the bio-refineries, 2) selecting the biomass suppliers, 3) selecting the optimal locations of the bio-refineries, 4) determining the capacity and type of the technologies considered in each bio-refinery, 5) determining the amount of the assigned biomass to the technologies, 6) determine the amount of biofuel and bioenergy to sell to customers.

Because of page limitation imposed by the conference, we opt for a verbal description of the proposed model. The detailed mathematical formulation is available from the authors upon request. It consists of a Mixed Integer Linear Programming formulation that can be described as follows:

> *Minimization of total costs* = *Procurement biomass costs*
> +*Biomass transportation cost* + *Biofuel transportation costs* + *Fixed opening costs*
> +*Variable production costs* + *Energy purchase costs* + Inventory holding costs
> *Subject to*:
> *Resource availability constraints, Biomass flow constraints,*
> *Bioenergy and biofuel balance equations, Bioenergy and biofuel flow constraints,*
> *Production capacity equations, Inventory balance equations,*
> *Satisfaction of the demand, Binary limitations on the relative decision variables*

5   Results and Discussion

The proposed model was coded in GAMS 24 and solved using the CPLEX solver. Using the case study, the model was implemented with an Intel Core i3, 2.13 GHz processor with 4 GB of RAM. The results are presented in the following.

5.1 Bioenergy Supply Chain Structure

In this part, the optimal design obtained by the model is presented. The optimal locations of the biorefineries are presented in Fig. 3 that minimize the total cost of the bioenergy supply chain. The total cost of the bioenergy SC that was obtained from the model is equal to 637.5M$. Figure 3 also shows the area of the customers and the amount of satisfied demand during the planning horizon. The satisfied biofuel demand is illustrated by yellow colors (pale to dark), and the satisfied pellet demand is shown by green colors (pale to dark). Table 5 shows the different types and capacities of the technologies that are optimally installed in the biorefineries.

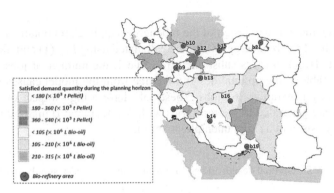

Fig. 3. Optimal structure of the bioenergy supply chain.

5.2 The Social Impacts of the Bioenergy Supply Chain

This part investigates the effect of the bioenergy network on the territories (the society), where bio-refineries are installed. Therefore, first, the social profit ($\mathfrak{S}_{w,b}$) of the generated job w (the work hours) in territory b is defined as follows:

$$\mathfrak{S}_{w,b} = \Pi_{w,b} \times \mathfrak{T}_{w,b}, \mathfrak{T}_{w,b} = (\mathfrak{H} + \mathfrak{J}) \tag{1}$$

Where $\Pi_{w,b}$ is the social impact of the installed biorefinery that was defined in Sect. 3.1. $\mathfrak{H}$ is the number of work hours (hourly work) within the job category w required to operate technology a. In other words, $\mathfrak{H}$ is corresponding to the work hours that are required to converting the biomass to bioenergy and biofuel (hours/tonne of biomass). $\mathfrak{J}$ is the number of work hours (salaried work) within job class w required to operate technology a (hours/year).$\mathfrak{J}$ is corresponding to the work hours that are required to keeping the bio-refinery open during the year (e.g., administrative staff). These work hours (Hourly-wage work and salaried work) can change by changing the type of technology and its capacity. Table 4 shows the assumptions of these work hours. They come from reports made by [21] and also from consulting with the Renewable Energy and Energy Efficiency Organization. In addition, work hours that are required for pyrolysis and pellet technologies come from different studies [22, 23].

Table 4. Work hours (per year) required to each technology.

Kinds of technology	Hours needed for each job class					
	Salaried work			Hourly-wage work		
	combustion	pellets	pyrolysis	combustion	pellets	pyrolysis
pyrolysis (200 t/day)	-	-	10222	-	-	16422
pyrolysis (600 t/day)	-	-	10222	-	-	16802
pelletizing (15000 t/ year)	-	10222	-	-	26899	-
pelletizing (45000 t/ year)	-	10222	-	-	30152	-
Biomass boiler (heat only)(3MW)	2812	-	-	17102	-	-
Biomass boiler + steam turbine (CHP) (0.5MW)	3151	-	-	17122	-	-

Next, given the optimal design of the bioenergy supply chain obtained in Sect. 5.1, the social profit of the bioenergy SC can be calculated using Eq. (1) and Table 5. If the social impact ($\Pi_{w,b}$) in (1) is substituted by value 1, the number of jobs is obtained. As shown in Table 5, the optimal design obtained from the model causes social profit (up to 48.84) by generating 262 jobs. These jobs have a high impact on the society, because they are generated in the territories with two features: i) high vulnerability in an economic crisis, and ii) high unemployment rate.

Table 5. Optimal design and social profit of the bioenergy supply chain

Technologies	The installed technologies	Social profit
b2		
Biomass boiler + steam turbine (electricity only),(MW)	5	2839070
pellet plant, (t/year)	15000	3014968
pyrolysis plant, (t/day)	200	4080262
b8		
Biomass boiler + steam turbine (CHP), (MW)	0.5	2413257
pellet plant, (t/year)		
pyrolysis plant, (t/day)	400	3511530
b9		
Biomass oil heater + ORC(CHP or electricity only), (MW)	2	2240160
pellet plant, (t/year)	15000	2431426
pyrolysis plant, (t/day)		
⋮	⋮	⋮
b21		
Biomass oil heater + ORC(CHP or electricity only), (MW)	0.5	2340646
pellet plant, (t/year)		
pyrolysis plant, (t/day)	400	3644040
Total number of technologies	20	
Total social profit (M points)		48.84
Total number of Jobs (Jobs)		263

6 Conclusion

In this paper, a model was proposed to design bioenergy supply chains under social consideration. Unemployment rate and vulnerability to changes during an economic crisis were considered as social concerns. The areas that are mostly exposed to these social issues were chosen as initial potential locations for installing the bio-refineries. The applicability of the developed model was shown through a case study. The results demonstrated that the proposed approach leads to the generation of a large number of job positions which has an important impact on the social development of these regions. In the future studies, first, initial capacities can be considered, or instead of using old technologies, the new technologies can be considered in the model in order to increase the production yield (efficiency). Second, it would be interesting to consider product recycling inside the biorefinery after generating the products. Finally, carbon pricing policies or decisions corresponding to the carbon trading can be added to the model.

References

1. Nur, F., et al.: A two-stage stochastic programming model for biofuel supply chain network design with biomass quality implications. IISE Transactions **53**(8), 845–868 (2021)
2. Yue, D., You, F., Snyder, S.W.: Biomass-to-bioenergy and biofuel supply chain optimization: overview, key issues and challenges. Comput. Chem. Eng. **66**, 36–56 (2014)
3. Awudu, I., Zhang, J.: Uncertainties and sustainability concepts in biofuel supply chain management: a review. Renew. Sustain. Energy Rev. **16**(2), 1359–1368 (2012)
4. Santibañez-Aguilar, J.E., et al.: Sequential use of geographic information system and mathematical programming for optimal planning for energy production systems from residual biomass. Ind. Eng. Chem. Res. **58**(35), 15818–15837 (2019)
5. Awudu, I., Zhang, J.: Stochastic production planning for a biofuel supply chain under demand and price uncertainties. Appl. Energy **103**, 189–196 (2013)
6. Razm, S., Nickel, S., Sahebi, H.: A multi-objective mathematical model to redesign of global sustainable bioenergy supply network. Comput. Chem. Eng. **128**, 1–20 (2019)
7. Nguyen, D.H., Chen, H.: Supplier selection and operation planning in biomass supply chains with supply uncertainty. Comput. Chem. Eng. **118**, 103–117 (2018)
8. Schmidt, J., et al.: Potential of biomass-fired combined heat and power plants considering the spatial distribution of biomass supply and heat demand. Int. J. Energy Res. **34**(11), 970–985 (2010)
9. Marvin, W.A., et al.: Economic optimization of a lignocellulosic biomass-to-ethanol supply chain. Chem. Eng. Sci. **67**(1), 68–79 (2012)
10. Razm, S., et al.: A global bioenergy supply network redesign through integrating transfer pricing under uncertain condition. J. Clean. Prod. **208**, 1081–1095 (2019)
11. Rabbani, M., et al.: Developing a sustainable supply chain optimization model for switchgrass-based bioenergy production: a case study. J. Clean. Prod. **200**, 827–843 (2018)
12. d'Amore, F., Bezzo, F.: Strategic optimisation of biomass-based energy supply chains for sustainable mobility. Comput. Chem. Eng. **87**, 68–81 (2016)
13. Dal-Mas, M., et al.: Strategic design and investment capacity planning of the ethanol supply chain under price uncertainty. Biomass Bioenerg. **35**(5), 2059–2071 (2011)
14. Gonela, V., et al.: Stochastic optimization of sustainable hybrid generation bioethanol supply chains. Transp. Res. Part E: Logist. Transp. Rev. **77**, 1–28 (2015)

15. Kostin, A., et al.: Design and planning of infrastructures for bioethanol and sugar production under demand uncertainty. Chem. Eng. Res. Des. **90**(3), 359–376 (2012)
16. Saghaei, M., Ghaderi, H., Soleimani, H.: Design and optimization of biomass electricity supply chain with uncertainty in material quality, availability and market demand. Energy **197,** 117165(2020)
17. Balaman, Ş.Y., Selim, H.: A decision model for cost effective design of biomass based green energy supply chains. Biores. Technol. **191**, 97–109 (2015)
18. Chen, C.-W., Fan, Y.: Bioethanol supply chain system planning under supply and demand uncertainties. Transp. Res. Par.t E: Logist. Transp. Rev. **48**(1), 150–164 (2012)
19. Osmani, A., Zhang, J.: Stochastic optimization of a multi-feedstock lignocellulosic-based bioethanol supply chain under multiple uncertainties. Energy **59**, 157–172 (2013)
20. Khishtandar, S.: Simulation based evolutionary algorithms for fuzzy chance-constrained biogas supply chain design. Appl. Energy **236**, 183–195 (2019)
21. Heat, B.C., Power catalog of technologies. US Environmental Protection Agency, Combined Heat and Power Partnership (2007)
22. Campbell, K.: A feasibility study guide for an agricultural biomass pellet company. Agricultural Utilization Research Institute, USA (2007)
23. Razm, S., et al.: A two-phase sequential approach to design bioenergy supply chains under uncertainty and social concerns. Comput. Chem. Eng. **145**, 107131 (2021)

Metaheuristics for Production Systems

Multi-objective Genetic Algorithm to Reduce Setup Waste in a Single Machine with Coupled-Tasks Scheduling Problem

Corentin Le Hesran, Anne-Laure Ladier[(✉)] [ID], and Valérie Botta-Genoulaz[ID]

Univ Lyon, INSA Lyon, Université Claude Bernard Lyon 1, Univ Lumière Lyon 2,
DISP, EA4570, 69621 Villeurbanne, France
anne-laure.ladier@insa-lyon.fr

Abstract. This article studies a single-machine scheduling problem involving coupled-tasks and hard due dates. A genetic algorithm based on the Non-dominated Sorting Genetic Algorithm (NSGA) II model is proposed to carry out a bi-objective optimization of both holding cost and setup-related waste generation. Results show that the multi-objective genetic algorithm outperforms the previous approaches regarding both computation time and objective functions, showing that a reduction of setups of 36% is possible at the expense of an 11% increase in inventory with acceptable computation times. It also highlights the importance of multi-objective optimization for decision-making in case of conflicting objective functions.

Keywords: Multi-objective scheduling · Genetic algorithm · Waste prevention

1 Introduction

Reducing the environmental impact of industrial production is currently a pressing challenge. At the operational level, new machining techniques and better operations scheduling improve environmental performance, although these largely focus on the energy consumption aspect [8]. Alternatively, recent work has appeared on the reduction of material waste rather than energy consumption and CO2 emissions, enabling better resource usage and lower waste generation through adequate scheduling [11]. Limiting waste generation is complementary with recycling and reuse approaches.

Such a case was studied in Le Hesran et al. [10], through the optimization of both inventory levels and setup-induced waste in the painting line of a hubcap manufacturing plant. Only one painting line is available, making it a single-machine scheduling problem. A passage into the painting line is referred to as

Supported by the Auvergne Rhône-Alpes region.

an operation, while the set of operations required for completion of an order is called a job. Different options exist for a hubcap going through the painting line. If it is unicolor, it is painted once and can go directly to the finished product inventory to await shipping. If it is bicolor, it receives its first coating and is sent to dry in the intermediary inventory for a minimum period L, then receives its second coating and is sent to the finished product inventory. Shipping must occur before a given due date, since the Make-To-Order setting allows no lateness. This particular problem is called a coupled-tasks scheduling problem [17] and has been proven to be NP-Hard [14]. Blazewicz et al. [3] provide a survey of research on coupled-tasks scheduling problems, as well as a list of important results for the most common variants and subproblems. The computation times being too large in real-life situations, metaheuristics such as PSO and SA [13], tabu-search [4,12], as well as various heuristics [1,5] have been used to solve coupled-tasks scheduling problems. Genetic algorithms have also been extensively used to solve scheduling problems, including problems involving reentrance characteristics which are similar to the coupled-tasks problems.

The objective is to optimize the daily schedule to minimize both the quantity held in inventory and the environmental impact of the paint sludge generated in the painting line when the color changes, represented by the number of setups. To deal with these two conflicting objectives, Le Hesran et al. [10] propose the use of a Genetic Algorithm with a weighted-sum method to obtain a Pareto front of alternative solutions. Results show that this algorithm has difficulty obtaining the entirety of the Pareto front : drastic improvements are possible regarding both the objective functions optimization and computing time required.

To this end, the contribution of this paper is a new multi-objective GA based on the NSGA-II framework [6] to solve the single machine couple-tasks scheduling problem described above. Its structure and mechanisms are described in Sect. 2, and numerical experiments are carried out in Sect. 3 followed by conclusions and perspectives for future work.

2   Multi-objective GA Based on NSGA-II

Figure 1 shows the global structure of the proposed multi-objective GA based on NSGA-II.

2.1   Chromosome Representation

A chromosome represents a sequence of operations, its size being equal to the number of jobs times the maximum number of operations per job. Since not all jobs have the same number of operations, dummy operations with processing time zero are added to keep the chromosome size constant. A gene's position corresponds to the job it belongs to and its order within this job. The value of a gene represents its rank in the global operations sequence. Figure 2 shows an example solution on a Gantt chart, with i the job and j the operation. As an example, operation 1 of job 9 is processed first, while operation 2 of job 1 is

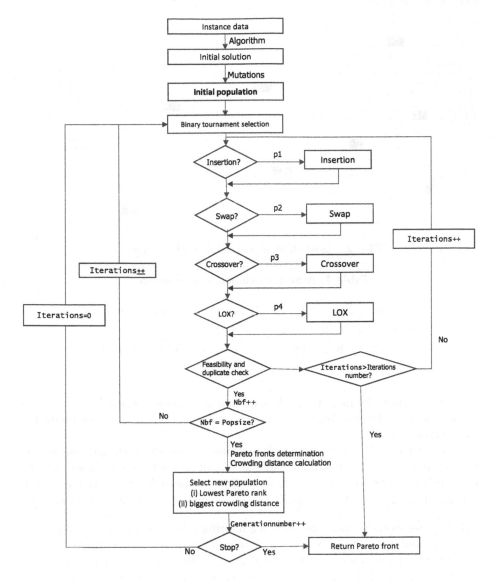

Fig. 1. NSGA-II structure representation

processed sixth, and operation 2 of job 8 is a dummy operation. Table 1 shows the corresponding chromosome, *Seq* giving the operations sequence.

Ranks are obtained using the fast non-dominated sorting algorithm [7] for all candidate solutions. In this strategy, the Pareto dominance relationship is used to assign each solution a rank based on a domination counter. All solutions are compared, and all the non-dominated ones are assigned rank 1. They are then removed from the current population, and the process is repeated with an

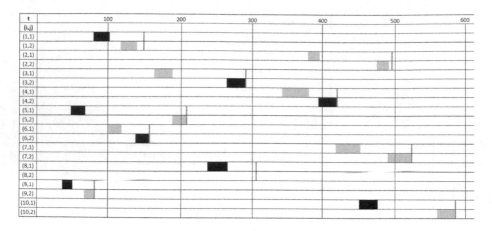

Fig. 2. Gantt chart of a schedule with ten jobs

Table 1. Associated chromosome sequence

i	1		2		3		4		5		6		7		8		9		10	
j	1	2	1	2	1	2	1	2	1	2	1	2	1	2	1	2	1	2	1	2
Seq	4	6	13	17	8	11	12	14	2	9	5	7	15	18	10	20	1	3	16	19

incremented rank number, until all solutions have been assigned a rank. This provides a set of Pareto fronts $\mathcal{F}$, where all solutions of front $\mathcal{F}_k$ dominate the solutions of front $\mathcal{F}_{k+1}$.

In order to avoid the clustering of solutions, a crowding-distance comparison method is used. This crowding distance $\mathcal{I}[i]$ of a solution i is based on the neighboring points surrounding it, according to the different objectives. It is calculated as: $\mathcal{I}[i] = \sum_{o \in \mathcal{O}} = \frac{z_{i+1}^o - z_{i-1}^o}{z_{max}^o - z_{min}^o}$ where $\mathcal{O}$ is the set of objectives, z_{i+1}^o and z_{i-1}^o the objective value of both neighboring solutions for the oth objective, and z_{max}^o and z_{min}^o the maximum and minimum values for objective $o \in \mathcal{O}$. A crowded comparison operator is then used to discriminate between different solutions with the following logic: if a solution is ranked lower than another, it is preferred to its counterpart. If two solutions have the same rank, the one with the biggest crowding distance is preferred.

2.2 Initialization

Based on the instance data, a single initial solution is created. An algorithm sorts the jobs by increasing due date. The operations of jobs with the lowest due dates are scheduled first, and operations of other jobs can be introduced whenever the job with the lowest due date is in the drying inventory. Once the initial solution is created, two mutation operators are applied in order to generate a sufficient number of new offspring. Any unfeasible solution generated (where tasks exceed their due dates) is immediately discarded and another one created to replace it. These constitute the initial population introduced into the GA.

2.3 Iterations

A pair of chromosomes is selected, and has a probability p_1 of being subjected to the insertion operator, that picks a random gene and inserts it somewhere else in the chromosome. It means that any given pair of chromosome can be subjected to either zero, one or two mutations. It is then subjected to the swap operator [16] (the swap picks two random genes within the chromosome and exchanges them; each chromosome is mutated independently) with a probability p_2. The resulting chromosomes then have a probability p_3 of being subjected to a standard two-point crossover [16] (as parents), followed by a probability p_4 of being subjected to the Linear Order Crossover (LOX) [15]. The standard two-point crossover chooses two random genes in the first parent and swaps them with the corresponding genes of the second parent. The LOX operator also chooses two random genes as crossover points: the partial sequence contained between them is transmitted to the offspring, the rest being filled with the missing genes from the other parent starting from the beginning of the chromosome. This operator has the merit of keeping a part of the first parent intact, as well as the relative order from the second one, which is important in a problem where due dates severely constrain the ordering possibilities.

If those new chromosomes are feasible, they are kept in the offspring generation, and a counter called Nbf is incremented. If more offspring need to be generated to complete the population, the iteration counter NbIterations is incremented and a new pair of parents is selected and submitted to the operators. If the iteration counter reaches Iteration number before a new population has been created, the algorithm stops and the best current solutions are returned.

Once a number of offspring equal to the population size have been accepted, both the parent and offspring populations are combined and the Pareto-rankings determined. The population replacement strategy is applied, the new population is created, and the iteration counter is reset. This process goes on until the number of generations reaches threshold and the algorithm stops.

3 Numerical Experiments and Results

The algorithm is coded in C++; all experiments are carried out using an Intel i5 6200 2.3 GHz processor with 8 GB of RAM.

3.1 Instances and GA Parameters Definition

The proposed NSGA-II algorithm is used on the instances provided by [10]. 80-20, 50-50 and 20-80 configurations are considered: the X-Y configuration consists of X% of jobs with one operation and Y% of jobs with two operations. Experiments are run on instances of each configuration with $n = 10$ jobs and 80-20 instances with $n = 30$ jobs. Instances of 10 jobs allow us to compare optimal results from the exact approach with those of the GA, while 30 jobs instances are closer to industrial size instances of around 100 jobs.

Table 2 details the chosen values of the GA parameters, obtained through a Taguchi experimental design.

3.2   Interpretation of the Pareto Front

The Pareto front [2] provides the decision-maker with alternative solutions that represent the variety of possible results. Its size is limited by the maximum number of possible color changes. Although every Pareto point is an optimal solution, all of them might not be suited to a practical use; thus, four key points are extracted for each instance.

Two extreme points $(z^{min}_{inventory}, z^0_{setup})$ and $(z^0_{inventory}, z^{min}_{setup})$, represent the cases where the decision-maker wishes to minimize one objective in priority. The ideal point $(z^{min}_{inventory}, z^{min}_{setup})$ is defined using the two optimum values of these points, i.e. the minimum quantity of inventory and minimum number of setups achievable. The coordinates of each point z^{it} are normalized using the formula $z^{normal} = \frac{z^{it}-z^{min}}{z^0-z^{min}}$ for both $z_{inventory}$ and z_{setup}. This norm provides new values between 0 and 1 to compare values of different nature and order of magnitude (inventory, number of setups).

Using these normalized values, the euclidean distance of each point to the ideal point is calculated. The solution located at the minimal distance from the ideal point $(z^{min}_{inventory}, z^{min}_{setup})$ is chosen as the trade-off point $z^{trade-off}$, which represents the best compromise in terms of number of setups reduction versus increase in inventory.

$z_{percent}$ is the point with the highest difference between setup percentage reduction and inventory percentage increase. This point aims at providing an attractive option for decision-makers that wish to improve their environmental impact without affecting their inventory costs negatively. An example of Pareto front with its important points is shown in Fig. 3.

3.3   Results

Table 3 shows that the multi-objective GA reaches the optimal solution a majority of the time for both the $z^{min}_{inventory}$ and $z_{percent}$ points, with average gaps not exceeding 3.3%. While the average gap appears to be slightly higher for the NSGA-II algorithm than for the weighted-sum one, optimal solutions are reached more often.

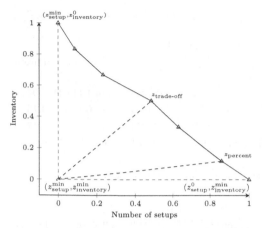

Fig. 3. Example of a Pareto front

Table 2. GA parameter value

	30-job instances	100-job instances
Population size	30	100
Swap rate	0.8	0.8
Insertion rate	0.5	0.8
Crossover rate	0.3	0.3
LOX rate	0.1	0.05
Threshold	1000	2500
Iteration number	1000	2500

The complete results for $z_{\text{trade-off}}$ and z_{percent} are shown in Tables 4 and 5 respectively. The multi-objective GA provides accurate results and manages to cover the majority of the Pareto front. As an example, for the 20-80 configuration an average Pareto front size of 4.6 is observed versus 5.6 for the MILP results. As a comparison, the weighted-sum GA by Le Hesran et al. [10] obtained an average size of 3.85 for the Pareto front of the same configuration.

In addition to a larger number of Pareto points obtained, results from the multi-objective GA are better than those from the weighted sum GA, obtaining a lower number of setups for the trade-off points and a lower inventory for the percent points on all configurations except for the 80-20 one.

Table 6 shows a direct comparison of the $z^{\text{trade-off}}$ and z^{percent} points obtained using the MILP (solved with CPLEX) and weighted sum GA from Le Hesran et al. [10], and our new multi-objective GA on the 30-job instances, most of which cannot be proved optimal by the MILP model within its time limit of 1800 s. The MILP results dominate both the weighted-sum and multi-objective GAs. However, their computation requires upwards to half an hour per point, which is not suited for practical applications on large instances. On the other hand, the multi-objective GA largely outperforms the MILP and is better than the weighted-sum GA regarding computation time.

Table 3. Comparison on key points (10-job instances)

n	Config.	Weighted sum GA [10]		NSGA-II: $z_{\text{min}}^{\text{inventory}}$		NSGA-II: z_{percent}	
		Average gap (%)	Nb opt/ nb total	Average gap (%)	Nb opt/ nb total	Average gap (%)	Nb opt/ nb total
10	80-20	1,0%	27/30	3,0%	27/30	3,3%	28/30
10	50-50	1,8%	24/30	1,0%	25/30	1,0%	25/30
10	20-80	1,0%	20/30	2,0%	21/30	1,2%	21/30

Table 4. Characteristics of the $z^{\text{trade-off}}$ point (standard deviation in parenthesis)

n	Config.	Weighted sum GA [10]				NSGA-II			
		$z_{\text{setup}}^{\text{trade-off}}$	$z_{\text{inventory}}^{\text{trade-off}}$	CPU (s)	Pareto size	$z_{\text{setup}}^{\text{trade-off}}$	$z_{\text{inventory}}^{\text{trade-off}}$	CPU (s)	Pareto size
10	80-20	3.1	3056	0.45 (1.2)	3.34	3.1	3084	14.1 (14.1)	2.97
10	50-50	3.8	5560	215 (539)	4.55	4.1	4584	12.0 (8.7)	3.75
10	20-80	4.4	7150	638 (737)	5.60	5.0	6374	13.1 (9.2)	4.57
30	80-20	8.9	16764	1714 (384)	9.01	9.1	21461	65.7 (79.1)	6.55

Table 5. Characteristics of the z^{percent} point (standard deviation in parenthesis)

n	Config.	Weighted sum GA [10]				NSGA-II			
		$z_{\text{setup}}^{\text{percent}}$	$z_{\text{inventory}}^{\text{percent}}$	CPU (s)	Pareto size	$z_{\text{setup}}^{\text{percent}}$	$z_{\text{inventory}}^{\text{percent}}$	CPU (s)	Pareto size
10	80-20	3.9	2215	0.10 (0.67)	3.34	3.8	2350	14.1 (141.1)	2.97
10	50-50	4.3	4385	118 (371)	4.55	4.2	3997	12.0 (8.7)	3.75
10	20-80	5.4	5852	595 (762)	5.60	5.4	6000	13.1 (9.2)	4.57
30	80-20	11.0	13179	1680 (392)	9.05	13	14497	65.7 (79.1)	6.55

Results from the multi-objective GA are closer to the MILP ones than those of the weighted-sum GA, providing a lower average number of setups for the $z^{\text{trade-off}}$ point, and lower average inventory for the z^{percent} one. Since $z^{\text{trade-off}}$ tends to be located on the left of the Pareto front (meaning a lower number of setups) and z^{percent} on the right (meaning a lesser inventory), results from the multi-objective GA are closer to those of the MILP than those from the weighted-sum GA.

Table 6. Points of interest for 30-job instances and 80-20 configuration

	Solving method	z_{setup}	$z_{\text{inventory}}$	Setup % reduc.	Inventory % inc.	CPU time (s)	Pareto size
$z^{\text{trade-off}}$	MILP	8.9	16764	38.5 (16.1)	54.8 (73.2)	1714.0 (384)	9.05
	Weighted-sum	11.5	18518	22.4 (16.0)	25.5 (35.6)	95.0 (55.5)	5.35
	Multi-obj	9.1	21461	34.2 (15.0)	62.5 (39.4)	65.7 (79.1)	6.55
z^{percent}	MILP	11.0	13179	25.9 (13.7)	12.3 (8.9)	1680.0 (392.0)	9.05
	Weighted-sum	12.8	16537	15.2 (17.1)	5.9 (9.3)	88.4 (58.0)	5.35
	Multi-obj	13.0	14497	9.6 (12.2)	4.4 (7.3)	65.7 (79.1)	6.55

In order to simulate a real life situation and show its performance on bigger instances, the proposed multi-objective GA is solved on 10 instances of 100 jobs (the size of a daily schedule) with the 80-20 configuration. Results for the z^{tradeoff} and z^{percent} point are available in Table 7. The genetic algorithm is more efficient on large instances, which are those which are important for manufacturers.

Table 7. Points of interest for 100-job instances and 80-20 configuration

	n	Config.	z_{setup}	$z_{inventory}$	Setup % reduc.	Inventory % inc.	CPU time (s)
$z^{trade-off}$	100	80-20	34.2	253920	41.1 (8.5)	149.2 (98.2)	5718
$z^{percent}$	100	80-20	51.6	135431	11.1 (9.6)	4.3 (3.87)	5718

Alternative daily schedules can be obtained in one hour and a half on average, which is an acceptable time-frame for a practical use. While percentages seem lower in both waste reduction and inventory increase, they still remain significant with such large quantities. The possible improvements are largely dependent on the instance, and can vary greatly as shown by the high standard deviations. The provided schedules are very efficient for some particular instances.

4   Conclusion

This paper tackles the issue of a single-machine scheduling problem with coupled-tasks, aiming at reducing waste generation due to setups and costs induced by inventory under the constraint of due dates. It proposes a new multi-objective genetic algorithm based on the NSGA-II structure. The new algorithm is more efficient in mapping the Pareto front than a GA using weighted sums. Thanks to evolutionary mechanisms designed for obtaining multiple alternative solutions, this algorithm obtain solutions that are both more optimized and more evenly spread out in the solutions space, improving the solutions provided to decision-makers. Computation times are also improved, as the multi-objective GA is able to map a Pareto front in a single run, as opposed to the weighted-sum one requiring multiple runs, and a larger number of Pareto points is obtained.

Alternative solutions can thus be obtained rapidly, providing the decision-makers with different options depending on their priorities and current situation. The $z_{percent}$ point in particular is shown to be useful for decision-makers. These improved results highlight the potential of such waste-reducing schedules for both economic and environmental objectives.

Several perspectives can be considered for this study. Calculating lower bounds would help to assess the performance of the GA for large instances. The model could be extended to other types of workshops (e.g. multi-machines environments) or product types (e.g. multiple colors and coatings) as studied in Gould and Colwill [9]. From an environmental perspective, assessing the environmental impact of paint sludge production, and the potential benefits of reducing waste production could also motivate practitioners to implement such schedules. Indeed, if the actual cost of waste management was assessed, alternative schedules reducing waste generation could prove to be overall economically beneficial to companies.

References

1. Amrouche, K., Boudhar, M., Bendraouche, M., Yalaoui, F.: Chain-reentrant shop with an exact time lag: new results. Int. J. Prod. Res. **55**(1), 285–295 (2017)
2. Blasco, X., Herrero, J.M., Sanchis, J., Martínez, M.: A new graphical visualization of n-dimensional Pareto front for decision-making in multiobjective optimization. Inf. Sci. **178**(20), 3908–3924 (2008)
3. Blazewicz, J., Pawlak, G., Tanas, M., Wojciechowicz, W.: New algorithms for coupled tasks scheduling: a survey. RAIRO - Oper. Res. **46**(4), 335–353 (2012)
4. Condotta, A., Shakhlevich, N.V.: Scheduling coupled-operation jobs with exact time-lags. Discrete Appl. Math. **160**(16–17), 2370–2388 (2012)
5. Courtad, B., Baker, K., Magazine, M., Polak, G.: Minimizing flowtime for paired tasks. Eur. J. Oper. Res. **259**(3), 818–828 (2017)
6. Deb, K., Agrawal, S., Pratap, A., Meyarivan, T.: A fast elitist non-dominated sorting genetic algorithm for multi-objective optimization: NSGA-II. In: Schoenauer, M., et al. (eds.) PPSN 2000. LNCS, vol. 1917, pp. 849–858. Springer, Heidelberg (2000). https://doi.org/10.1007/3-540-45356-3_83
7. Deb, K., Pratap, A., Agarwal, S., Meyarivan, T.: A fast and elitist multiobjective genetic algorithm: NSGA-II. IEEE Trans. Evol. Comput. **6**(2), 182–197 (2002)
8. Giret, A., Trentesaux, D., Prabhu, V.: Sustainability in manufacturing operations scheduling: a state of the art review. J. Manuf. Syst. **37**, 126–140 (2015)
9. Gould, O., Colwill, J.: A framework for material flow assessment in manufacturing systems. J. Ind. Prod. Eng. **32**(1), 55–66 (2015)
10. Le Hesran, C., Agarwal, A., Ladier, A.L., Botta-Genoulaz, V., Laforest, V.: Reducing waste in manufacturing operations: bi-objective scheduling on a single-machine with coupled-tasks. Int. J. Prod. Res. **58**, 7130–7148 (2019)
11. Le Hesran, C., Ladier, A.L., Botta-Genoulaz, V., Laforest, V.: A methodology for the identification of waste-minimizing scheduling problems. J. Cleaner Prod. **246**, 119023 (2019)
12. Li, H., Zhao, H.: Scheduling coupled-tasks on a single machine. In: Proceedings of the 2007 IEEE Symposium on Computational Intelligence in Scheduling, pp. 137–142 (2007)
13. Meziani, N., Boudhar, M., Oulamara, A.: PSO and simulated annealing for the two-machine flowshop scheduling problem with coupled-operations. Eur. J. Ind. Eng. **12**(1), 43–66 (2018)
14. Orman, A.J., Potts, C.: On the complexity of coupled-task scheduling. Discrete Appl. Math. **72**(96), 141–154 (1997)
15. Portmann, M.C.: Genetic algorithms and scheduling: a state of the art and some propositions. In: Proceedings of the Workshop on Production Planning and Control, vo. 9, no. 11, pp. 1–24 (1996)
16. Sevaux, M., Dauzère-Pérès, S.: Genetic algorithms to minimize the weighted number of late jobs on a single machine. Eur. J. Oper. Res. **151**(2), 296–306 (2003)
17. Shapiro, R.D.: Scheduling coupled tasks. Naval Res. Logistics Q. **27**(3), 489–498 (1980)

Tabu Search Algorithm for Single and Multi-model Line Balancing Problems

Mohamed Amine Abdeljaouad[1](✉) and Nathalie Klement[2]

[1] CEA Tech Hauts-de-France, 165 Avenue de Bretagne, Lille 59000, France
mohamed-amine.abdeljaouad@cea.fr
[2] Arts Et Métiers Institute of Technology, LISPEN, HESAM Université, Lille, France
Nathalie.klement@ensam.eu

Abstract. This paper deals with the assembly line balancing issue. The considered objective is to minimize the weighted sum of products' cycle times. The originality of this objective is that it is the generalization of the cycle time minimization used in single-model lines (SALBP) to the multi-model case (MALBP). An optimization algorithm made of a heuristic and a tabu-search method is presented and evaluated through an experimental study carried out on several and various randomly generated instances for both the single and multi-product cases. The returned solutions are compared to optimal solutions given by a mathematical model from the literature and to a proposed lower bound inspired from the classical SALBP bound. The results show that the algorithm is high performing as the average relative gap between them is quite low for both problems.

Keywords: Line balancing · Optimization · Tabu search. SALBP · MALBP

1 Introduction

Since their first use in 1913 as part of the Ford automotive manufacturing process, assembly lines have spread all over the world. They are now one of the main forms of industrial production, as they significantly reduce the manufacturing time, increasing thus the productivity. They also reduce the needed workforce and therefore the production costs.

The performance of an assembly line depends on various factors. Finding a good balancing of the workload over the line's stations is one of the most important. Several line-balancing problems have been dealt with in the literature. A review on the issue can be found in [18]. Assembly line balancing problems can first be classified according to the number of models (types of product) that the line can produce: we distinguish between single-model assembly line balancing problems (SALBP), where a unique type of product is produced, and the mixed/multi-model assembly line balancing problems (MALBP) where the outcomes are products of different types. Line balancing problems can also be classified according to the type of the line (serial line, line with parallel workstations...) and the durations of the operations (deterministic or stochastic).

© IFIP International Federation for Information Processing 2021
Published by Springer Nature Switzerland AG 2021
A. Dolgui et al. (Eds.): APMS 2021, IFIP AICT 630, pp. 409–415, 2021.
https://doi.org/10.1007/978-3-030-85874-2_43

Different objective functions and constraints have been considered by researchers. The most known objective functions for single-model lines are the minimization of the number of workstations for a given cycle time (type SALBP-1) and the minimization of the cycle time (type SALBP-2) for a given number of workstations [17]. Of course, this list is not exhaustive. In MALB problems, the objectives are more sophisticated. To name a few, we can mention the reduction of the assembly cost [20], the labor cost [22], the line idle time [16] or the smoothness index [15]. As for the other operational research problems, the methods used for the balancing of assembly lines can be exact or approximate. Exact methods range from mathematical programming [6, 9] to branch and bound [12, 14], among others. However, as line balancing problems are usually NP-hard, exact methods cannot solve big-sized instances in a reasonable time. The alternative is therefore to use heuristic methods, which can quickly find satisfying solutions. Various kind of heuristics have been proposed for SALBP and MALBP [7, 11, 21]. Most of the time, the heuristic methods are combined with a metaheuristic that allows to visit more solutions and thus to improve the quality of the heuristic's one [8]. Different kind of metaheuristics have been used; we can mention simulated annealing [4, 13], tabu search [3, 19], genetic algorithms [2, 5] or ant colony optimization [1].

In this paper, we deal with a line balancing problem where the objective is to minimize the weighted sum of products' cycle times (i.e. the weighted sum of the maximum time each type of product spends on a workstation), where the weight of each product represents its ratio among all the demanded quantity. This objective, introduced by [22] as part of a multi-objective MALB optimization problem, can be applied for both the MALBP and the SALBP (where it will be equivalent to the minimization of cycle time, i.e. the maximum of the sum of task times assigned to each workstation). Therefore, we will treat both cases in this work, and provide an optimization algorithm that will be tested on single and multi-models instances. The rest of the constraints of the problems are the following: n operations have to be assigned to m serial workstations. Each operation can be assigned to any workstation but the precedence constraints should be respected: an operation i cannot be assigned to a station k_1 if one of its predecessors j is assigned to a workstation k_2 such that index $k_1 < k_2$. We consider that the durations of the operations are deterministic. Apart from the workstations, all the other resources needed for the processing of the operations (such as workers or tools) are assumed available. This issue is NP-hard [10].

The rest of the paper is structured as follows: In Sect. 2, an optimization algorithm, based on a heuristic and a tabu-search metaheuristic is presented. In Sect. 3, we carry out an experimental study to assess the performance of our algorithm and we conclude the paper in Sect. 4 with our remark and perspectives.

2   Tabu Search Algorithm

The proposed solving method is made of a heuristic and a metaheuristic. The heuristic leads to an initial feasible solution and is based on the computation of a lower bound. This bound is inspired from the classical bound of SALBP-2 given in Eq. (1), with J being the number of product types, m the number of workstations, n_j the number of operations required by product type j and p_i the processing time of operation i. The latter is calculated for each product model and the lower bound for our problem is thus equal to the weighted sum of these cycle time bounds, as specified in Eq. (2), where w_j is the demand proportion for product model j.

$$LB_j = \max\left(\max_{i=1,\dots n_j}(p_i), \sum_{i=1}^{n_j} \frac{p_i}{m} \right) \quad \forall j = 1, \dots J \tag{1}$$

$$Lower\ bound = \sum_{j=1}^{J} w_j LB_j \tag{2}$$

The heuristic starts by sorting the operations on the basis of their precedence constraints. It puts them into groups as follows: group 1 contains the operations that do not have a predecessor, group 2 contains the operations whose predecessors are in group 1, group 3 contains the operations whose predecessors are in groups 1 and 2, and so on. The operations within each group are then sorted in the decreasing order of the number of their successors and, in case of a tie, in the decreasing order of the sum of their successors' processing times.

The heuristic then browses the operations group by group, in that order, and assigns them to the workstations, starting by station $k = 1$. At each iteration i, it selects the first non-assigned operation o from the group and assigns it to a workstation, according to the rule given below, with S_{jk} being the sum of the operations' processing times of product type j that are already assigned to station k at iteration i:

- If assigning operation o to station k reduce the gap between the value $\sum_{j=1}^{J} w_j S_{jk}$ and the *Lower bound*, or if $k = m$, then assign o to station k.
- Otherwise: $k \leftarrow k + 1$

The solution returned by the heuristic is then used as input for a tabu search algorithm that tries to improve it. The latter's main steps are given in Algorithm 1.

Algorithm 1: *Tabu search*

Input, data: Initial solution S, stopping criterion c, size of the tabu list ts;
Initialization: *Best solution* $\leftarrow S$; *Current solution* $\leftarrow S$; $i \leftarrow 0$; *Tabu List* $\leftarrow \emptyset$;
while $i < c$ **do**
    for each product type j **do**
        Select station k on which j has the longest processing time
        Randomly select one of the operations i of j on k with $i \notin$ *Tabu List*
        Move i to either station $k - 1$ and $k + 1$ (the less loaded one if the
        precedence constraints are respected)
        Compute the new solution S_j
    Current solution $\leftarrow min_{j=1,\dots J}(S_j)$;
    Add the moved operation i to *Tabu List* for ts iterations;
    if *Current solution* < *Best solution* **then**
        Best solution $\leftarrow$ *Current solution*
    else $i \leftarrow i + 1$
return (*Best Solution*)

The idea behind choosing a tabu search method is to create a solution neighborhood structure for each product type: At each iteration and for each product type, the tabu search algorithm selects the workstation on which the selected type has its longest processing time and moves one of its operations to another station, by respecting the precedence constraints. The new obtained solutions are then compared and the best one is kept. The moved operation is added to a tabu list during a certain number of iterations, to prevent the algorithm from being stuck in the same movements' loop.

A neighborhood structure based on the different product types seems useful since the considered objective directly depends on the cycle time of each model. This structure can ease the search process of efficient and high-quality solutions. To the best of our knowledge, this kind of neighborhood was never used before for multi-model balancing optimization. The algorithm repeats this process and stops after a certain number of consecutive iterations without improving the solution.

3 Experimental Study

Although there are many benchmark instances from line balancing literature, only few of them are made for MALB problems. Moreover, to the best of our knowledge, there is no comparative study dealing with the same objective function. Therefore, we choose to test the proposed algorithm on several randomly generated instances, where the durations, the precedence constraints and the repartition of the operations over the product types are generated given some probability parameters. We generated two families of instances: small-sized and big-sized. For the small-sized ones, we compared the algorithm's solutions to optimal solutions, obtained with a mathematical model inspired from the formulation presented in [22]. These small-sized instances are made of $\{10, 20, 50\}$ operations, $\{3, 5, 6\}$ workstations and $\{1, 3, 5\}$ product types. The big-sized ones are made of $\{100, 200\}$ operations, $\{6, 10, 15, 20\}$ workstations and $\{1, 3, 5\}$ product types. For these latter instances, the returned solutions are compared to the lower bound, since the optimal solving of these instances with the mathematical model cannot be done in a reasonable time. For each size, 5 instances are tested, for a total of 225 tests. The durations of the operations are generated with a uniform distribution in [1, 99]. The precedence relationship between the operations and the repartition of the operations over the different product types are generated based on data from a real life assembly line manufacturing pneumatic cylinders.

All the instances were quickly solved by our algorithm. Those with 200 operations and multiple products required between 1 and 3 min to be solved, while the other instances took only a few seconds. As it is expected from an approximate approach, the proposed method thus shows its ability to solve rather quickly big-sized instances of this NP-hard problem, for which the mathematical solving may take hours. Table 1 and Table 2 display the results obtained for the small-sized and big-sized instances, respectively. In Table 1, the 'GLB' column gives the average relative gap between the lower bound calculated in Eq. (2) and the optimal solutions, while the 'GSol' column gives the average relative gap between the algorithm's solutions and the optimal ones. In Table 2, the 'Products' columns display the average relative gap between the obtained solutions and the lower bound.

As we can see from Table 1, our algorithm is high performing for both the single and multiple products instances, with a 0.99% overall average relative gap to the optimal solutions. This is confirmed by a 42.2% rate of optimal solutions among those returned by the algorithm. Table 1 also shows that the algorithm's solutions are closer to the optimal ones than the lower bound, whose average relative gap is higher (about 6.3%). This gap between the bound and the optimal solutions helps to explain the behavior of our algorithm for the big-sized instances: Indeed, even if the average relative gap between the algorithm's solutions and the lower bound is a bit higher in Table 2, this may be due to the gap between the bound itself and the optimal solutions. The results of our algorithm are therefore also promising for the big-sized instances.

Table 1. Results for the small-sized instances.

Operations	Stations	Products					
		1		3		5	
		GLB	GSol	GLB	GSol	GLB	GSol
10	3	2.26	0.76	12.47	0	16.07	0
	5	12.89	0	13.33	0.29	7.5	0.19
	6	7.24	1.89	8.28	0	0.21	0
20	3	1	0	5.29	0.16	8.93	0.26
	5	3.58	0.62	9.47	1.43	13.99	1.4
	6	2.77	1.94	11.36	1.8	13.93	2.74
50	3	0	0.07	0.77	0.9	1.88	0.74
	5	0	0.53	2.12	2.44	3.63	2.4
	6	0	0.84	2.51	2.4	8.98	3.2
Average		3.3%	0.73%	7.28%	1.04%	8.34%	1.21%

Table 2. Results for the big-sized instances

Operations	Stations	Products		
		1	3	5
100	6	0.78	4.34	5.04
	10	1.5	7.46	9.64
	15	2.81	12.42	15.01
200	6	0.17	2.22	2.87
	10	0.56	4.43	6.26
	20	1.29	10.44	12.81
Average		1.18%	6.88%	8.6%

4 Conclusion

In this paper, an optimization algorithm based on a tabu search procedure is presented to solve a line-balancing problem. The objective is to minimize a weighted sum of the product cycle times, where the weights represent the demand-ratio for each product. The algorithm is tested on both single-model and multi-model problems and the results obtained show that the outcomes are very satisfying in both cases, with a close average relative gap to the optimal solutions and to the lower bound.

The next step of this work is to test the algorithm for other objective functions for the multi-model line-balancing problems. As a perspective, the balancing obtained for these different objective functions can also be compared through a simulation for example, in order to analyze their impact on the production, considering various constraints. Future work also includes the experimentations of other heuristics to provide the initial solutions for the tabu search algorithm and testing the method on a real assembly line. A case-study line producing several models of pneumatic cylinders has already been linked with this project.

References

1. Akpinar, S., Bayhan, G.M., Baykasoglu, A.: Hybridizing ant colony optimization via genetic algorithm for mixed-model assembly line balancing problem with sequence dependent setup times between tasks. Appl. Soft Comput. **13**, 574–589 (2013)
2. Alavidoost, M.H., Zarandi, M.H.F., Tarimoradi, M., Nemati, Y.: Modified genetic algorithm for simple straight and U-shaped assembly line balancing with fuzzy processing times. J. Intell. Manuf. **28**(2), 313–336 (2014). https://doi.org/10.1007/s10845-014-0978-4
3. Arikan, M.: Type-2 assembly line balancing with workload smoothing objective: a reactive tabu search algorithm. Gazi University Journal of Science **34**(1), 162–178 (2021)
4. Baykasoglu, A.: Multi-rule multi-objective simulated annealing algorithm for straight and U type assembly line balancing problems. J. Intell. Manuf. **17**, 217–232 (2006)
5. Chong, K.E., Omar, M.K., Baker, N.A.: Solving assembly line balancing problem using genetic algorithm with heuristic treated initial population. In: Proceedings of the World Congress on Engineering, pp. 978–988 (2008)
6. Çil, Z.A., Li, Z., Mete, S., Özceylan, E.: Mathematical model and bee algorithms for mixed-model assembly line balancing problem with physical human-robot collaboration
7. Chutima, P., Olanviwatchai, P.: Mixed-Model U-shaped assembly line balancing problems with coincidence memetic algorithm. J. Softw. Eng. Appl. **03**(04), 347–363 (2010). https://doi.org/10.4236/jsea.2010.34040
8. Fatini, D.M., Mohammad, F.R., Mohd, Z.Z.: A review on hybrid metaheuristics in solving assembly line balancing problem. AIP Conf. Proc. **2138**(1) (2019)
9. Gokcen, H., Erel, E.: Binary integer formulation for mixed model assembly line balancing problem. Comput. Ind. Eng. **34**(2), 451–461 (1998)
10. Gutjahr, A.L., Nemhauser, G.L.: An algorithm for the line balancing problem. Manage. Sci. **11**(2), 308–315 (1964)
11. Kilincci O.: A Petri net-based heuristic for simple assembly line balancing problem of type 2. Int. J. Adv. Manuf. Technol. **46**, 329–338 (2010)
12. Klein, R., Scholl, A.: Maximizing the production rate in simple assembly line balancing—a branch and bound procedure. Eur. J. Oper. Res. **91**(2), 367–385 (1996)

13. Lalaoui, M., El Afia, A.: A fuzzy generalized simulated annealing for a simple assembly line balancing problem. IFAC-PapersOnLine **51**(32), 600–605 (2018)
14. Li, Z., Kucukkoc, I., Zhang, Z.: Branch, bound and remember algorithm for U-shaped assembly line balancing problem. Comput. Ind. Eng. **124**, 24–35 (2018)
15. Roshani, A., Roshani, A., Roshani, A., Salehi, M., Esfandyari, A.: A simulated annealing algorithm for multi-manned assembly line balancing problem. J. Manuf. Syst. **32**, 238–247 (2013)
16. Sarker, B.R., Pan, H.: Designing a mixed-model assembly line to minimize the costs of idle and utility times. Comput. Ind. Eng. **34**(3), 609–628 (2001)
17. Scholl, A., Becker, C.: State-of-the-art exact and heuristic solution procedures for simple assembly line balancing. Eur. J. Oper. Res. **168**(3), 666–693 (2006)
18. Sivasankaran, P., Shahabudeen, P.: Literature review of assembly line balancing problems. Int. J. Adv. Manuf. Technol. **73**(9–12), 1665–1694 (2014). https://doi.org/10.1007/s00170-014-5944-y
19. Suwannarongsri, S, Limnararat, S.: A hybrid tabu search method for assembly line balancing. In: Proceedings of the 7th International Conference on Simulation (modelling and optimization) China (2007)
20. Tseng, Y.J., Chen, J.Y., Huang, F.Y.: A multi-plant assembly sequence planning model with integrated assembly sequence planning and plant assignment using GA. Int. J. Adv. Manuf. Technol. **48**, 333–345 (2010)
21. Yeh, D.H., Kao, H.H.: A new bidirectional heuristic for the assembly line balancing problem. Comput. Ind. Eng. **57**, 1155–1160 (2009)
22. Zhang, W., Gen, M.: An efficient multi-objective genetic algorithm for mixed-model assembly line balancing problem considering demand ratio-based cycle time. J. Intell. Manuf. **22**, 367–378 (2011)

A Distributed Model for Manufacturing Scheduling: Approaching the EDGE

Pedro Coelho$^{(\boxtimes)}$ ⓘ and Cristóvão Silva ⓘ

CEMMPRE, Department of Mechanical Engineering, University of Coimbra,
Pinhal de Marrocos, 3030-788 Coimbra, Portugal
`pedro.coelho@dem.uc.pt`

Abstract. Manufacturing scheduling has a crucial role in a company's performance. It's a hard optimization problem and due to the latest manufacturing trends, it is becoming even more complex. Metaheuristics are promising methods to solve those real-world problems. The latest distributed/parallel computing advances may support the increase of computational power needed to get efficient schedules a suitable time period. In the last years, the Industrial Internet has also known some advances as the emergence of the Edge computing paradigm that increased the computational processing power near the factory floor. This work presents strategies to implement a distributed metaheuristic for manufacturing scheduling on the Edge. Under the scheduling problem context, the physical platform and the programming environment are examined. Based on an evolutionary metaheuristic (genetic algorithm), a model is developed, following strategies that take advantage of the Edge layer of the Industrial Internet. The generic algorithm steps are described for future deployment and validation.

Keywords: Manufacturing · Scheduling · Industrial Internet · Edge computing · Metaheuristics · Distributed Genetic Algorithm

1 Introduction

Manufacturing scheduling is the efficient allocation of jobs (orders) over machines (resources) in a manufacturing facility [1]. It has a fundamental role in an organisation's performance. Due to increased competition and technological advances in recent years, the scheduling paradigm in the manufacturing industry has undergone a strong evolution [2]. These already NP-hard optimization problems [3] had become even more complex with more restrictions and constraints. Exact optimization methods are only useful for solving problem instances of reduced size. Heuristics and metaheuristics are promising methods since they can get efficient schedules at suitable time period, even for large realistic problem instances [4]. Yet, to solve real-world problems, those approaches require high computing power. The use of parallel algorithms may make good use of the most recent high-performance computing advances and help to accelerate the resolutions of these problems. Most of the works present in the literature already propose good algorithms running on scientific grids or in high-end server systems [5].

A. Dolgui et al. (Eds.): APMS 2021, IFIP AICT 630, pp. 416–423, 2021.
https://doi.org/10.1007/978-3-030-85874-2_44

For manufacturing, the infrastructure which connects people, data, and machines, is known as Industrial Internet [6]. In the beginning, this structure was mainly cloud-based and included the software scheduling applications [7]. A cloud-based structure implies transferring sensitive information outside the factory. Besides safety issues, the costs of using the cloud become a burden due to the increase in data traffic caused by the expansion of the Internet of Things (IoT). Data-driven approaches help to improve production but they come with a cost. The Edge Computing concept emerged to reduce this bandwidth issue, the latency of some tasks and improve security; by using a hardware infrastructure with processing capabilities closer to the area where it is needed. This structure creates a new paradigm of Industrial Internet, which maintains a connection to the cloud, to which is added a network layer of heterogeneous devices.

It seems important that these developments in the industry are followed by the academy. Approaches for solving scheduling problems should be able to take advantage of the Edge computing potential. In this paper, we propose a conceptual model to design a distributed model for manufacturing scheduling on the Edge. The base of this model is a metaheuristic - a Genetic algorithm (GA). Due to its natural parallelism, Evolutionary Algorithms (EA) are good candidates for distributed systems. Also, there is an extensive body of literature that uses these algorithms for scheduling problems [8], with sequential and parallel implementations; and GA on heterogeneous architectures [9, 10]. The scientific contribution of this paper lies in the alignment between the solution approaches for the scheduling problem and the computational resources present where it needs to be solved. A future implementation of the model, have the potential of good performance by harvesting the computation power available on the Industrial Internet Edge.

2   Model Development

A good distributed metaheuristic must have the ability to speed up the search, improve the quality of the obtained solutions and solve large-scale problems [11]. To deal with a diverse and challenging problem as scheduling, robustness is a key requirement. The design of our model was driven by those goals and our focus on the distributed model strategies.

The development of this model was based on the general framework presented by Gong et al. [12] for EA. Our design approach inverts its steps and the considered dimensions will be enhanced with the distributed GA (dGA) taxonomy proposed by Harada and Alba [10]. Figure 1 outlines the design phases. It begins with the problem and the physical platform description. The programming environment will consider the software and API. Those beginning steps will conduct the design of the distributed model, looking for promising parallelism strategies. Lastly, the algorithm steps are presented.

Fig. 1. Approached steps in the model development

2.1 The Problem

According to Pinedo [4], scheduling is a decision-making process that deals with the allocation of resources (e.g. human, machine, money) to tasks in a specific sequence and over given periods. In a manufacturing facility, it is known as manufacturing scheduling [1]. Several possible machine environments originate several variations of the scheduling problem. Due to its versatility and applications in the newest manufacturing paradigms [13, 14], we choose the Flexible Job Shop Scheduling Problem (FJSP) as an illustrative problem. We may define it as a set of jobs, each one requiring several operations. Each operation of a given job has a processing step in a machine chosen from a set of available machines. To solve the problem, we must go through two decision levels, assigning operations to machines and sequencing their process on those machines. This must be done in such a way that one or more objective functions are optimized. Classical objectives include the minimization of the completion time of the last job, minimize tardiness or a combination of both.

This scheduling problem may be extended with the introduction of additional constraints; like release dates, sequence-dependent setup times, break-downs or transportation times between machines. Besides machines, other limited resources may also be considered in the manufacturing schedule; like vehicles, machine tools or robots.

This is an operational level problem and it must be solved on a regular basis (hourly, daily or weekly) or event-driven, like the arrival of new orders, the change of priorities in the jobs to be carried out or malfunctioning of a machine [15].

2.2 Physical Platform

The physical platform is the hardware platform that supports the Industrial Internet. This concept of the Industrial Internet comes from the deep integration of industrial systems and the new generation of Internet based IT systems. It connects people, data and machines and it provides important infrastructure for manufacturing [6].

The first generation of the Industrial Internet was mainly an industrial platform in the Software as a Service model with several enterprise information systems (e.g. Enterprise Resource Planning, Manufacturing Execution System, Supply Chain Management) to support the operation of manufacturing systems. These systems are developed using a cloud computing architecture [7]. The connectivity provided by the IoT increased the real-time processing needs and it brought a great weight on the network traffic. Also, manufacturing industry applications might require responses in quite a short time and some might raise concerns about privacy issues. To mitigate some of these problems, a new computing model emerge: Edge Computing [16]. This paradigm refers to resources and equipment's along the path between data sources and cloud data centres, especially in the proximity of terminal devices with capabilities of computation, storage, communication and application around data sources to supply different services, within the requirements of agile connection, real-time service, data optimization, application intelligence and security protection [16].

In the Edge layer of the Industrial Internet, the computing power of equipment may vary by several orders of magnitude. This layer mainly contains edge gateways and is responsible for collecting data from other layers by wired networks (Fieldbus,

Industrial Ethernet, Industrial Optical Fibber, among others) or wireless networks (Wi-Fi, Bluetooth, RFID, NB-IoT, LoRa, 5G, to name just a few), caching the collected data and offering an heterogeneous computing environment. The most widely used processing units on the edge devices are general computing processing units (CPU), graphics processing units (GPU), and FPGA. They range from Ultra-Low Power micro controller architectures, with limited memory, to multi-core or many-core processors [17]. Single-board computers with ARM processors, like raspberry pi or NVIDIA Jetson nano (GPU enhanced) are examples of this hardware platform [18]. Some already been tested to run GAs [9].

Our physical platform is formed by a set of heterogeneous computing devices, connected by high-speed networking infrastructure, in a grid configuration.

2.3 Programming Environment

Several programming languages, libraries, and application programming interface (API) can be chosen to deploy the algorithm. In the case of a distributed system, our choice must consider the programming of the processor and the communication proces.

Due to the heterogeneity and characteristics of the hardware, we need a portable programming language, not avid for resources. C++ can be looked like an adequate language, because it compiles in virtually every platform and operating environment, and support a set of multithreading libraries and API. OpenMP may be adapted for shared-memory multiprocessing. Also, OpenCL and CUDA, supported by C++, provides general-purpose computing on GPUs.

Its one-sided communication concept is a prominent advantage, providing efficient asynchronous communication. In a heterogeneous hardware network, like the one found in the Edge layer of the Industrial Internet, we must expect different execution times. The implementation of an asynchronous model looks like a good strategy to deal with that. MPI may support it.

2.4 Distributed Model

GAs have a vast body of literature related to scheduling [8] and, due to that, is the base to our metaheuristic. It's a population-based metaheuristics that uses a set of solutions to concurrently sample different regions of the solution space. The search evolves to new solutions by recombining elements from different solutions in the population.

Attending to our hardware network, we choose an island spatially distributed model where the global population is divided into several populations, each of which is processed by one single processor (network node). Reflecting the physical system heterogeneity, each subpopulation adopts a size and parameters adjusted to their node resources. According to Goldberg [19], a GA with a small population of three individuals is sufficient to converge, so even small nodes may contribute to the search. These cooperative multi-search methods make up the bulk of the successful parallel meta-heuristics [20].

The communication between the subpopulations will have a star scheme, illustrated in Fig. 2. This scheme takes advantage of the one-side communication concept of MPI and supports two important features of the model: asynchronism and adaptable migration strategy. The central node allows memory-based cooperation [20] by creating a data structure available for all nodes, to read and write, see Fig. 3. Like a pool model, this scheme allows the nodes to interact asynchronously through the pool, preventing idle time from the faster nodes. The data structure stores an elite set of the best solutions and supports an easily adaptable migration strategy. Along the run, the best solutions are known to all the nodes and that may lead to improve all the subpopulations search space. Also, this shared memory will have context information, essential for the orchestration of the nodes. This allows to control the nodes runtime or update their local algorithm parameters.

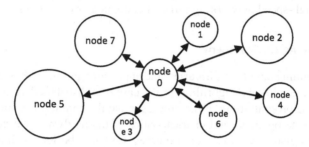

Fig. 2. Star communication scheme

This model has a large scalability potential, being limited only by the central node memory size. Regarding the fault-tolerance aspect, only the central node is crucial. If one of the other is decoupled from the network the search won't be jeopardised.

Our design focuses on a coarse-grained model but we consider that locally, in the nodes, the parallelism is also explored. Multi-core processors with share-memory collaborate in a faster population improvement. Those local implementations are tight linked with the node processor and are out of our scope. Meanwhile, the distributed model is robust to support that each node runs its tailor-made algorithm. As long as they use a similar solution encoding.

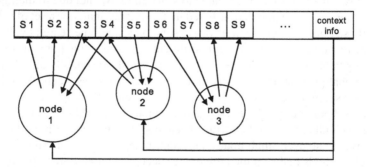

Fig. 3. Memory-based cooperation scheme.

2.5 Algorithm

Following the previous model, this section presents the implementation details of the metaheuristic.

The canonical GA starts with a predefined size of population solutions that is composed of a certain number of individuals. Every individual solution has a chromosome representation that encode a solution to the optimization problem. The algorithm evolves to new population solutions through a set of sequential operations over the individuals of the previous generation: selection, cross-over and mutation. Although the solution encoding and the parameter related to the GA operators are very important for the algorithm performance, they won't be detailed on this implementation.

Figure 4 shows a schematic of the dGA. The solid line shows how the process flows and the dashed lines how the data flow. It starts at the machine that got the problem instance, hosts the shared data structure and controls the stop criterion - node 0. This node creates the data structure and populates with a random set of solutions and a bit flag that will control the additionally, add a bit flag to control the end of the algorithm. A second step uses one of the MPI collective routines, broadcast, to distribuite the data instance to the available nodes in the network. This data is also copied to the node 0 local memory.

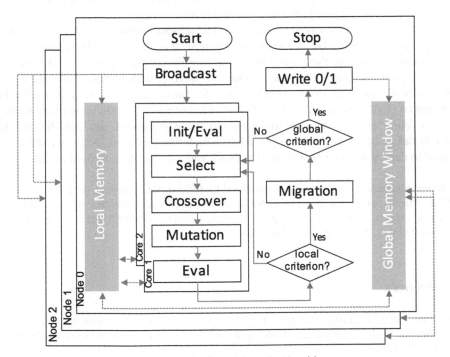

Fig. 4. The Distributed Genetic Algorithm.

The nodes with multi-core processing share the next tasks among the available cores. Each node randomly creates an initial subpopulation, with size conditioned by their computational resources. This subpopulation is evaluated and start undergoing through the loop of the GA operators (selection, crossover, mutation and evaluation) until it reaches the stop criterion. This local stop criterion may be the number of generations or the number of generations without solution improvement. At this point, it happens the migration process. The node access the global memory window, write their best solutions and retrieve other solutions to mix with their population. Also, it reads the bit flag. If the bit flag has changed the local algorithm stops, otherwise, it restarts the GA operators loop.

Node 0, follows the same routines but because it orchestrates the algorithm, it has an extra task. After each migration step, it checks a global termination criterion. This may be the execution time, the total number of interactions with the global memory window or the number of iterations without improving the global best solution. Once that criterion is reached, node 0 changes the bit flag so the other nodes finish their execution. Node 0 returns the best solution and stop the algorithm execution.

3   Final Remarks and Future Works

This work presents a distributed model of a metaheuristic to solve problems of manufacturing scheduling. The algorithm has been developed to take advantage of the latest innovations in the Industrial Internet Edge hardware.

Based on a GA, it tries to take advantage of a high-performance communication API to implement a memory-based cooperation strategy. It deals with the Industrial Internet heterogeneity, allowing the processors to run loosely-coupled asynchrony. Besides, it provides great fault-tolerance. The potential of dealing with a tailor-made algorithm on each processor suggests great performance for the model. However, this is only the conceptual model, empirical studies will be needed to prove the efficiency of the model.

For future work, we propose to design and study of parallel metaheuristics for the edge nodes and fine-tune them to solve FJS scheduling problems. At a later stage, we intend to deploy them on an industrial network and validate the proposed model.

Acknowledgements. This research is sponsored by FEDER funds through the program COM-PETE – Programa Operacional Factores de Competitividade – and by national funds through FCT – Fundação para a Ciência e a Tecnologia –, under the project UIDB/00285/2020 and the doctoral grant to Pedro Coelho (SFRH/BD/129714/2017).

References

1. Framinan, J.M., Leisten, R., García, R.R.: Manufacturing Scheduling Systems: An Integrated View on Models, Methods and Tools. Springer, London (2014). https://doi.org/10.1007/978-1-4471-6272-8
2. Sokolov, B., Dolgui, A., Ivanov, D.: Scheduling in Industry 4.0 and Cloud Manufacturing (2020). https://doi.org/10.1007/978-3-030-43177-8
3. Garey, M.R., Johnson, D.S., Sethi, R.: Complexity of flowshop and jobshop scheduling. Math. Oper. Res. **1**, 117–129 (1976). https://doi.org/10.1287/moor.1.2.117

4. Pinedo, M.L.: Scheduling Theory, Algorithms, and Systems. 5th edn. Springer International Publishing, Cham (2016). https://doi.org/10.1007/978-3-319-26580-3
5. Coelho, P., Silva, C.: Parallel Metaheuristics for shop scheduling: enabling industry 4.0. Procedia Comput. Sci. **180**, 778–786 (2021). https://doi.org/10.1016/j.procs.2021.01.328
6. Liu, Y., Wang, L., Xu, X., Zhang, L., Wang, X.V.: Industrial internet for manufacturing. Robot. Comput. Integr. Manuf. **70**, 102135 (2021). https://doi.org/10.1016/j.rcim.2021.102135
7. Wang, J., Xu, C., Zhang, J., Bao, J., Zhong, R.: A collaborative architecture of the industrial internet platform for manufacturing systems. Robot. Comput. Integr. Manuf. **61**, (2020). https://doi.org/10.1016/j.rcim.2019.101854
8. Coelho, P., Pinto, A., Moniz, S., Silva, C.: Thirty years of flexible job-shop scheduling: a bibliometric study. Procedia Comput. Sci. **180**, 787–796 (2021). https://doi.org/10.1016/j.procs.2021.01.329
9. Morell, J.Á., Alba, E.: Running genetic algorithms in the edge: a first analysis. In: Herrera, F., et al. (eds.) CAEPIA 2018. LNCS (LNAI), vol. 11160, pp. 251–261. Springer, Cham (2018). https://doi.org/10.1007/978-3-030-00374-6_24
10. Harada, T., Alba, E.: Parallel genetic algorithms: a useful survey. ACM Comput. Surv. **53**, (2020). https://doi.org/10.1145/3400031
11. Talbi, E.-G.: Metaheuristics: From Design to Implementation. John Wiley & Sons, Hoboken (2009). https://doi.org/10.1002/9780470496916
12. Gong, Y.J., et al.: Distributed evolutionary algorithms and their models: a survey of the state-of-the-art. Appl. Soft Comput. J. **34**, 286–300 (2015). https://doi.org/10.1016/j.asoc.2015.04.061
13. Rossit, D.A., Tohmé, F., Frutos, M.: Industry 4.0: smart scheduling. Int. J. Prod. Res. **57**, 3802–3813 (2019). https://doi.org/10.1080/00207543.2018.1504248.
14. Zhang, J., Ding, G., Zou, Y., Qin, S., Fu, J.: Review of job shop scheduling research and its new perspectives under Industry 4.0. J. Intell. Manuf. **30**(4), 1809–1830 (2017). https://doi.org/10.1007/s10845-017-1350-2
15. Rossit, D., Tohmé, F.: Scheduling research contributions to Smart manufacturing. Manuf. Lett. **15**, 111–114 (2018). https://doi.org/10.1016/j.mfglet.2017.12.005
16. Zhang, T., Li, Y., Philip Chen, C.L.: Edge computing and its role in Industrial Internet: methodologies, applications, and future directions. Inf. Sci. (Ny) **557**, 34–65 (2021). https://doi.org/10.1016/j.ins.2020.12.021
17. Capra, M., Peloso, R., Masera, G., Roch, M.R., Martina, M.: Edge computing: a survey on the hardware requirements in the Internet of Things world. Futur. Internet. **11**, 1–25 (2019). https://doi.org/10.3390/fi11040100
18. Gómez, A., et al.: Use of single board computers as smart sensors in the manufacturing industry. Procedia Eng. **132**, 153–159 (2015). https://doi.org/10.1016/j.proeng.2015.12.461
19. Goldberg, D.E.: Genetic Algorithms. Pearson Education India. Springer, London (2006). https://doi.org/10.1007/978-1-4471-0903-7_7
20. Gendreau, M., Potvin, J.-Y.: Handbook of Metaheuristics. Springer, Boston (2010). https://doi.org/10.1007/978-1-4419-1665-5

Scheduling Jobs on Unrelated Machines with Job Splitting and Setup Resource Constraints for Weaving in Textile Manufacturing

Ioannis Mourtos, Stavros Vatikiotis$^{(\boxtimes)}$, and Georgios Zois

ELTRUN Research Lab, Department of Management Science and Technology,
Athens University of Economics and Business, 104 34 Athens, Greece
{mourtos,stvatikiotis,georzois}@aueb.gr

Abstract. This work considers the production scheduling of the weaving process in a real-life textile industry, where a set of jobs - linked to the production of a fabric type and accompanied by a quantity - arrive over time and have to be processed (woven) by a set of parallel unrelated machines (looms) with respect to their strict deadlines (delivery dates), under the goal of makespan minimization. A number of critical job and machine properties demonstrate the challenging nature of weaving scheduling, i.e., a) job splitting: each order's quantity is allowed to be split and processed on multiple machines simultaneously, b) sequence-dependent setup times: the setup time between any two orders j and k is different than setup time between jobs k and j on the same machine and c) setup resource constraints: the number of setups that can be performed simultaneously on different machines is restricted due to a limited number of setup workers. We propose a MILP formulation that captures the entire weaving process. To handle large real instances, while also speeding up an exact solver on smaller ones, we propose two heuristics that perform job-splitting and assignment of jobs to machines either greedily or by using a relaxed version of our MILP model, respectively. We evaluate the impact of our approach on real datasets under user-imposed time limits and resources (machines, workers) availability.

Keywords: Textile · Weaving scheduling · Integer programming · Heuristics

1 Introduction

Increasing productivity while reducing production costs has been essential in modern textile plants in terms of business sustainability. Scheduling algorithms

This research has been supported by the EU through the FACTLOG Horizon 2020 project, grant number 869951.

[3] offer a viable and effective tool to improve productivity, by optimally allocating the available resources. A typical scheduling problem in textile considers a set of articles/orders to be woven by a set of looms with respect to their delivery dates. Each order is linked to the production of a specific fabric type and is accompanied by a positive quantity, while the looms are unrelated, meaning that each loom operates on different speeds for different orders. The aim is to find a schedule with the minimum makespan, i.e., the time that the last executed order is finished.

Two properties that make weaving scheduling a challenging problem are job splitting (a job can be split in different machines) and sequence-dependent setup times (per pairs of jobs and per machine). In practice, the latter is justified by the fact that different fabric types require different warp chains for processing, thus imposing machine setup times (to replace the warp chain) from a few hours to a few days [14]. Both properties have been studied extensively under abstract models of various machine environments and optimisation criteria [1,4,8–10,13] and tackled through exact methods, approximation algorithms and metaheuristics. The weaving scheduling problem has also been well-studied and admits exact polynomial time algorithms for special cases where setup times are independent and job splitting is relaxed to preemption [14], as well as MILP models and efficient metaheuristics for the general case [5,6,11,15].

Our work is focused on the weaving scheduling of PIACENZA, a textile enterprise in north Italy that manufactures woolen fabrics for luxury clothing brands. Its production environment is a parallel weaving environment composed of multiple type of looms, operating at different speeds. Weaving scheduling in PIACENZA adopts all the above-described job and machine properties, plus setup resource constraints. Specifically, the number of setups that can be performed simultaneously on different machines is restricted due to a limited number of setup workers and daily setup time is also bounded. We should note that the seminal work of [14] signifies the addition of setup resource constraints to the standard weaving scheduling as a severe challenge.

According to our knowledge, the most relevant previous work appears in [8,9]. In [8], the authors proposed near optimal heuristics for a simplified model with identical machines, job splitting, multiple setup resources and fixed (independent) setup times per job, under the makespan minimisation objective. [9] proposes a Benders Decomposition approach and heuristics for the general case of unrelated machines, sequence-dependent setup times and multiple setup resources, again under the makespan minimisation objective. However, none of these works combine all the complex properties needed for PIACENZA's case. Interestingly, [8] referred to a case combining job-splitting, sequence-dependent setup times, unrelated machines and setup resource constraints as an open research direction.

Our Contribution. In Sect. 2 we propose a formal definition of our scheduling problem, address its computational complexity and propose a mixed integer linear programming (MILP) formulation that captures the elaborate structure of the weaving process. To handle large real instances, we propose in Sect. 3 two combinatorial heuristics that differ on the way they perform job splitting and assignment to machines. We experiment with several weekly instances on both MILP (using a standard solver) and heuristics to establish the computational efficiency of our approach in Sect. 4. As we note, although typically the trade-off between delivery dates, available machines and setup resources allows the scheduler to deliver each job on time, due to the COVID-19 pandemic a large number of jobs arrive late on the weaving department, while others become more tight in terms of deadline. To improve resource management while avoiding a further increase of tardy jobs, we propose in Sect. 5 a strategy that dedicates an appropriate number of machines to samples (i.e., jobs with small quantity and tight deadlines) while allocating the rest to regular jobs (i.e., jobs with large quantity and loose deadlines).

2   Mathematical Modeling

To present our mixed integer linear program (MILP), we employ the notation of Tables 1 and 2.

Table 1. Model parameters

Model parameters	
J	The set of jobs (orders)
M	The set of machines (looms)
s_m	The fixed speed (in strokes/min) of machine $m \in M$
q_i	The quantity (in meters) of job $i \in J$
u_i	The number of strokes/meter for the fabric type of job i
$p_{i,m}$	The processing time of $i \in J$ on $m \in M$, $p_{i,m} = q_i \cdot u_i / s_m$
$S_{i,j,m}$	The setup time of $j \in J$ succeeding job $i \in J$ on $m \in M$
$\bar{S}_i$	The setup time of jobs processed first on each machine (1 h)
L_i	A lower limit on the quantity of part of job $i \in J$ allocated to any machine (50 m)
d_i	The deadline of job $i \in J$, i.e., a strict delivery date for i
$T_{\max}$	An upper bound on the makespan of an optimal schedule, e.g., $T_{\max} = \sum_{i \in J} \max_{m \in M} (p_{i,m} + \max_{j \in J} S_{i,j,m})$
$\mathcal{T}$	A set of equal-length intervals $[\tau_{i-1}, \tau_i)$, $1 \leq i \leq T$, where $\tau_0 = 0$ and $\tau_T = T_{\max}$
$l_{i,j,m}$	The number of intervals needed to setup job j after job i on machine m
l_τ	The length of every interval $t \in \mathcal{T}$ (2 h, which is the least common multiple over all setup times)
$\mathcal{D}$	A partition of $\mathcal{T}$ into subsets of consecutive time intervals q with total length equal to a working day
u_q	The allowed setup time per working day $q \in \mathcal{D}$ (50 h)
R	A setup resource constraint to indicate that, at each time interval, at most R machines can be set up in parallel

(MILP) : C_{max}

s.t. :

$$\sum_{i,j\in J, i\neq j} X_{i,j,m,t} \leq 1, \qquad\qquad \forall t\in T, m\in M \quad (1)$$

$$\sum_{i\in J} X'_{i,m,t} \leq 1, \qquad\qquad \forall t\in T, m\in M \quad (2)$$

$$\sum_{t\in T} X_{i,j,m,t} \leq 1, \qquad\qquad \forall i,j\in J, i\neq j, m\in M \quad (3)$$

$$\sum_{j\in J, t\in T} X_{0,j,m,t} \leq 1, \qquad\qquad \forall m\in M \quad (4)$$

$$\sum_{m\in M} Q_{i,m} = q_i, \qquad\qquad \forall i\in J \quad (5)$$

$$L_i\cdot Y_{i,m} \leq Q_{i,m} \leq q_i\cdot Y_{i,m}, \qquad\qquad \forall i\in J, m\in M \quad (6)$$

$$Y_{i,m} = \sum_{t\in T, j\in J, j\neq i} X_{i,j,m,t}, \qquad\qquad \forall i\in J, m\in M \quad (7)$$

$$Y_{j,m} = \sum_{t\in T, i\in J, i\neq j} X_{i,j,m,t}, \qquad\qquad \forall j\in J, m\in M \quad (8)$$

$$\sum_{t\in T} X_{i,j,m,t} + \sum_{t\in T} X_{j,i,m,t} \leq 1 \qquad \forall i,j\in J, i,j\neq 0, i\neq j, m\in M \quad (9)$$

$$\sum_{i,j\in J, i\neq j, t\in T} X_{i,j,m,t} = \sum_{i\in J} Y_{i,m} - 1, \qquad\qquad \forall m\in M \quad (10)$$

$$X_{i,j,m,t} + \sum_{\substack{i'\in J, i'\neq i,\\ t'\in T, t'\leq t}} X_{j,i',m,t'} \leq 1, \qquad \forall i\in J, j\in J, i\neq j, m\in M, t\in T \quad (11)$$

$$X_{i,j,m,t}\cdot l_{i,j,m} \leq \sum_{t'=t}^{t+l_{i,j,m}-1} X'_{j,m,t'}$$
$$\forall i,j\in J, i\neq j, m\in M, t\in T\setminus\{T-r|1\leq r\leq l_{i,j,m}\} \quad (12)$$

$$\sum_{t\in T} X'_{j,m,t} \leq \sum_{i\in J, i\neq j, t\in T} l_{i,j,m}\cdot X_{i,j,m,t}, \qquad \forall j\in J, m\in M \quad (13)$$

$$\sum_{i\in J, m\in M} X'_{i,m,t} \leq R \qquad\qquad \forall t\in T \quad (14)$$

$$\sum_{i\in J, m\in M, t\in q} l_\tau\cdot X'_{i,m,t} \leq u_q \qquad\qquad \forall q\in \mathcal{D} \quad (15)$$

$$C_{j,m} - C_{i,m} + V(1-\sum_{t\in T} X_{i,j,m,t}) \geq Q_{j,m}\cdot\frac{u_j}{s_m} + S_{i,j,m}\cdot\sum_{t\in T} X_{i,j,m,t},$$
$$\forall i,j\in J, j\neq i, m\in M \quad (16)$$

$$C_{j,m} \geq \sum_{i\in J, i\neq j, t\in T} X_{i,j,m,t}(\tau_{t-1}+S_{i,j,m}) + Q_{j,m}\cdot\frac{u_j}{s_m}, \quad \forall j\in J, m\in M \quad (17)$$

$$\bar{S}_i\cdot Y_{i,m} + Q_{i,m}\cdot\frac{u_i}{s_m} \leq C_{i,m} \leq C_{\max} \qquad\qquad \forall i\in J, m\in M \quad (18)$$

$$\sum_{j\in J, t\in T, t>\lceil\frac{R}{M}\rceil} X_{0,j,m,t} = 0 \qquad\qquad \forall m\in M \quad (19)$$

$$Y_{i,m}, X'_{i,m,t}, X_{i,j,m,t} \in \{0,1\}, C_{i,m}, Q_{i,m}\in\mathbb{R}^+, \quad \forall i,j\in J, m\in M, t\in T \quad (20)$$

The overall goal is to minimise the makespan of the schedule, denoted as C_{max}. Since setup times are strictly positive, it is easy to prove that each machine processes at most one part of each split job. We refer to the above problem as the *Weaving Scheduling* problem, which is *NP-hard* even if machines are identical, job setup times are fixed (and independent) and $R = 1$ [7].

Table 2. Decision variables

Variables	
$X_{i,j,m,t}$	1 if $j \in J$ is the successor of $i \in J$ on machine $m \in M$, which is set up right after i at time $t \in T$ and there are no other jobs processed between them on m, 0 otherwise
$X'_{i,m,t}$	1 if $i \in J$ is under setup on machine $m \in M$ at $t \in T$, 0 otherwise
$Y_{i,m}$	1 if $i \in J$ is assigned on machine $m \in M$, 0 otherwise
$Q_{i,m} \in \mathbb{R}^+$	The quantity of job $i \in J$ to be processed by $m \in M$
$C_{i,m} \in \mathbb{R}^+$	The completion time of the part of job $i \in J$ processed on $m \in M$
$C_{max} \in \mathbb{R}^+$	The makespan of the schedule

(MILP) is partly inspired by formulations on special cases [8,13], extending them to capture the elaborate structure of *Weaving Scheduling*. More specifically, Constraints (1)–(4), (7)–(11), (19), are used to ensure the feasibility of job assignment, respecting that each machine processes at most one single part of each split job. Constraints (5)–(6) allow for job splitting wrt to the quantity limits. Constraints (12), (13), (16) ensure that the setup of each job part precedes its execution on the corresponding machine and calculate its completion time. Constraints (14), (15) are setup resource constraints, and Constraints (17), (18) provide tight lower bounds.

3 Combinatorial Heuristics

Using an exact commercial solver (Gurobi 9.1) on (MILP), we can solve many daily instances (i.e., ones with orders arriving at the same date) in a few minutes either optimally or by a small gap. Hence (MILP) could be used to support short-term goals like scheduling jobs in a daily manner. However, to fully support the business needs of a weaving enterprise, including mid and long-term goals, it is important to efficiently tackle larger real instances. In this direction, we propose two combinatorial heuristics, GH1 and GH2, which differ in the way they handle job splitting and assignment of each part of a job to a machine, while handling the sequence-dependent setup times and setup resources in the same way. Table 3 summarizes the notation used in the present and the following sections.

Table 3. Algorithms and experiment parameters and abbreviations

Notation	
GH1	The first greedy heuristic
max_assgn	Upper limit on job assignments in each iteration of GH1
GH2	The second greedy heuristic
LPT	Longest Processing Time first rule used in GH2
λ	A positive constant chosen on the assignment step of GH2
ld_m	The load of $m \in M$ on the assignment step of GH2
aTSP	The Asymmetric Traveling Salesman Problem
LB	A lower bound derived by the solution of the MILP in GH1
% Gap	The percentage gap of GH1 or GH2 wrt LB: $\frac{\{GH1,GH2\}-LB}{LB} \cdot 100$
Tardiness	For each job j in a schedule it is equal to $\{\max_{m \in M} C_{j,m} - d_j, 0\}$
Tardy job	A job $j \in J$ with positive tardiness, i.e., $\max_{m \in M} C_{j,m} > d_j$

GH1, performs an iterative exact splitting and assignment of jobs (parts) to machines using a MILP formulation (which is a subproblem of *Weaving Scheduling* where setup resource constraints are not taken into account) that minimises makespan subject to Constraints (5), (6) (to ensure that quantity limits are satisfied), (21) that calculates a lower bound on the time needed to process the assigned part of each job on each machine and (22) that limits the number of possible job assignments to max_assgn. GH1 starts by setting the maximum possible value of max_assgn $= |J| \times |M|$ and after each iteration decreases it by 1, in order to exploit all possible exact solutions (of increased or decreased job splitting potential) choosing the best among them. It terminates when the number of jobs exceeds the possible assignments i.e., max_assgn $= |J| - 1$, as there is no possibility to assign all jobs.

$$\sum_{i \in J} (Q_{i,m} \frac{u_i}{s_m} + Y_{i,m} \cdot \min_{j \in J} S_{i,j,m}) \leq C_{max} \qquad \forall m \in M \qquad (21)$$

$$\sum_{i \in J} \sum_{m \in M} Y_{i,m} \leq \text{max\_assgn} \qquad \forall m \in M \qquad (22)$$

On the other hand, GH2 performs a greedy job splitting dividing job quantities into parts based on the lower bound L_i: For each job i with $q_i \geq 2L_i$ we create $\alpha = \lceil \frac{q_i}{L_i} \rceil$ job parts of quantity equal to $\frac{q_i}{\alpha}$. Then, the job parts are ordered according to the LPT rule, in order to prevent the resulted schedule from unbalanced machine loads (i.e., when a job with large processing time is scheduled last). Then assignment process is similar to the one proposed in [2] for makespan minimisation on unrelated processors: For the LPT order of job parts, it assigns each part i to the machine $k = \arg\min_{m \in M} \{\lambda^{ld_m + S_{j,i,m} + Q_{i,m} \frac{u_i}{s_m}} - \lambda^{ld_m}\}$, where j is the last job executed on m before i.

Both GH1 and GH2 are then following the next two stages. STAGE A: For each machine, the assigned job parts are scheduled optimally by reducing the problem to aTSP, where nodes correspond to jobs' parts and the distance between nodes to sequence-dependent setup time plus processing time of the corresponding job part; the exact approach of [12] is proved quite efficient for our instances. STAGE B: For each machine in decreasing order of load and each available group of workers, we compute the earliest time that a job part can start its setup, respecting the order of job parts from STAGE A. Note that, in STAGE B, by starting from the most loaded machine, we significantly reduce the effect of idle intervals between consecutive job executions on the final makespan. Moreover, in the case of GH2, we do not violate the assumption that each machine processes at most one single part of each split job, as the setup time between parts of the same job is equal to zero, and thus in the aTSP solution they will be consequently ordered.

Summarising, GH1 performs an exhaustive job splitting and assignment supported by an exact solver, while GH2 computes a fast greedy assignment of all possible job parts to machines.

4   Computational Experiments

The experiments are performed on 27 weekly instances, from 01/2020–07/2020. The number of jobs per instance ranges from 7–69, the available groups of workers and number of machines per week are $R = 3$ and 12 respectively, while setup times receive values from the set $\{2\text{ h}, 4\text{ h}, 6\text{ h}\}$. The experiments ran on a 64-bit Windows PC (Intel i5, 2.5 GHz CPU speed, 8 GB RAM) using Python 3.7.2 for GH1, GH2 and GUROBI 9.1 (Python API for (MILP) and MILP of GH1).

We tested (MILP) on the above dataset, with a 2-h limit, on 4, 6, 8 and 10 machines and it was able to solve optimally one weekly instance (7 orders) on 10 and 8 machines in 10 s and 25 s respectively, while the other two instances were solved with Gaps 8.62% after 262 s for 6 machines and 5.14% after 1735 s for 4 machines. The difficulty of (MILP) to deal with job splitting property lies on the fact that the time horizon (thus, the number of time intervals and the number of variables) increases exponentially as the quantity of the job increases. Interestingly, the above results refer to the solution of Gurobi when using as upper bound the best among GH1 and GH2 solutions (normalizing processing times and setup times as multiples of l_τ), otherwise we could only handle some daily instances. So we proceed by applying GH1 and GH2 to solve our weekly instances. To better evaluate the performance of GH1 and GH2 we divide our dataset into five subsets of increasing number of jobs, each consisting of 5–6 weekly instances and we test each subset for different number of available machines (4,6,8,10,12).

Table 4. Results over all weekly instances on 4, 6, 8, 10 and 12 machines

# Orders	% Gaps of GH1					Mean gap (%)	Mean t(s)	% Gaps of GH2					Mean Gap (%)	Mean t(s)
	4	6	8	10	12			4	6	8	10	12		
[7, 26]	3.2	4.92	6.99	10.45	10.39	7.19	38.7	13.03	22.46	30.21	38.43	42.15	29.25	3.9
[35, 40]	2.2	3.21	4.2	5.67	5.99	4.25	34.9	11.07	16.94	22.91	36.8	29.82	23.51	25.3
[43, 45]	2.14	2.77	4.17	5.59	7.05	4.34	38.6	10.87	14.88	23.78	35.5	38.63	24.73	8.7
[46.51]	1.97	2.86	3.7	4.82	6.09	3.89	33.8	11.16	15.95	23.02	33.86	30.72	22.94	6.5
[57, 69]	1.76	2.54	3.37	4.39	5.62	3.54	36.1	12.98	17.96	22.7	31.22	24.05	21.78	15.9
Mean gap	2.28	3.3	4.55	6.29	7.1	4.71	–	11.84	17.75	24.68	35.23	33.32	24.57	–
Mean t(s)	6.3	35.4	33.5	46.5	59.8	–	35	26.9	7	5.3	4	14.6	–	11.6

As we show in Table 4, GH1 outperforms GH2, achieving results of 4.2 times smaller gap, but being 3 times slower on average, over different numbers of available machines. Notably, GH1 achieves almost optimal solutions of Gap less than 7.1% (4.7% on average) for all instances, in less than a minute (35 s on average). Note that instances with a few orders on many machines seem to demonstrate larger Gaps, compared to smaller number of machines mainly due to the total setup time constraint and the limited number of groups of workers. Additionally, running times may seem inconsistent regarding the size of the instances, but this is justified due to the small number of instances of each subset. As a result, instances that are time-consuming within a subset have a huge impact on the average running time.

5 Enhancements

It is important to note that, due to the COVID-19 situation, 22.13% of orders were tardy. Even though the solutions in Sect. 4 achieve small gaps, they cause a significant increase on the number of tardy jobs which therefore rise to 27.4% of the total orders (an increase of 24% compared to the ones initially tardy).

Moreover, observing that small jobs (unsplittable with $q_i < 100$ m) have tight deadlines, while larger ones have looser, it appeared reasonable to dedicate a set of machines to small jobs and the rest to the large ones. To this direction, we perform a comparison of GH1 and GH2 on small and large jobs separately, to decide which is the best choice in every case. We divide each weekly instance to small and large jobs and, as before, we divide our dataset into subsets of increasing number of (either small or large) jobs. Subsets with small jobs consist of 4–6 weekly instances each, while subsets of large jobs of 5–7; note that on the latter we have excluded two instances, since they included only 1 and 2 jobs respectively. The size of small job instances ranges from 6 to 41, while for large from 5 to 34.

Table 5. Results on small (left) and large (right) job instances for 4, 6, 8, 10 machines

# Orders	% Gaps of GH1				% Gaps of GH2			
	4	6	8	10	4	6	8	10
[6, 12]	3.78	8.53	5.36	4.37	27.11	26.67	20.13	15.36
[14, 22]	6.64	9.55	16.69	19.84	22.66	41.52	44.42	52.07
[25, 29]	8.26	20.53	48.24	58.43	16.35	32.03	55.16	68.08
[30.31]	6.69	25.8	60.75	77.98	26.49	53.8	64.05	102.75
[33, 41]	6.41	16.33	45.5	65.08	15.13	23.86	51.83	56.02
Mean Gap	6.54	16.35	36.6	46.94	20.95	35.56	48.49	60.45
Mean t(s)	9	2.7	5.7	30.6	1.1	1.5	2	2.4

# Orders	% Gaps on GH1				% Gaps on GH2			
	4	6	8	10	4	6	8	10
[5, 12]	2.96	4.23	6.04	7.82	17.45	38.01	30.82	64.14
[13, 16]	1.66	2.46	3.4	4.71	10.14	20.66	24.61	46.55
[18, 19]	1.58	2.29	3.46	4.19	8.88	13.43	21.61	29.36
[20.34]	1.02	1.53	2.27	3.21	7.89	14.34	19.7	25.27
Mean Gap	1.78	2.59	3.73	4.93	11.01	21.61	24.12	41.38
Mean t(s)	9.9	358.1	208.6	300.1	125.8	51.7	13.8	11.5

We tested (MILP) on small jobs, using a simplified version (where in con-
straints (16)–(18) we substituted $Q_{i,m} \cdot \frac{u_i}{s_m}$ by $Y_{i,m} \cdot p_{i,m}$ while Constraints (5)–(6)
were removed) on 4, 6, 8 and 10 machines, for 8 out of 27 weekly instances (from
6 to 18 orders). Notably the exact solver was able to solve optimally 20 instances
in 98.03 s on average, 10 instances were solved with mean Gap 7.36% and for 2
it was not able to obtain a solution under 1-h limit. However, since the solutions
obtained were of similar Gap with the ones of GH1, we do not present them in
more detail. Table 5 presents the comparison between GH1 and GH2 on small
and large job instances, respectively. GH1 achieves solutions of better quality,
with 26.6% and 4.8% Gap for small and large jobs respectively, however GH2 is
much faster (4 times on large and almost 6 times on small jobs). Interestingly,
for small jobs the difference on their gap is significantly decreasing (from 410%
on large jobs to 55%). Note that Gap values on small jobs instances are quite
large, but this is due to the strict daily total setup time constraint.

Since GH1 performs better on both small and large job instances, we run it
once to schedule first all small jobs to an appropriate number of machines, and
re-run it consequently to schedule the large jobs on the remaining machines or (if
possible) after the small jobs on their dedicated machines. More precisely, we run
GH1 for each weekly instance, for 12 candidate numbers of dedicated machines
($|M| \in \{1, 2, \ldots, 12\}$) on small jobs. The aim of this approach is to examine the
effect of dedicated machines on three optimisation criteria: makespan, number
of tardy jobs and total tardiness.

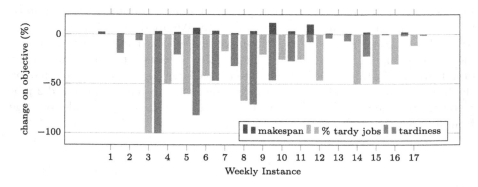

Fig. 1. Best policies to balance makespan, number of tardy jobs and total tardiness,
over weekly instances.

We consider as baseline the makespan, number of tardy jobs and total tardiness over all weekly instances computed by GH1 in Sect. 4 and highlight the smallest average change on each criterion over the same instances, over all runs under different number of dedicated machines: For makespan, the smallest average increase is 1.55%, while for the same instances tardiness and the number of tardy jobs decrease by 16.68% and 10% respectively. For the number of tardy jobs, the largest average decrease is 16%, while for the same instances the makespan increases by 4.07%, and tardiness decreases by 19.1%. For total tardiness, the largest average decrease is 22.62%, while for the same instances makespan increases by 6.35% and number of tardy jobs decreases by 12.12%.

Figure 1 presents a proposed policy for weekly instances, in order to achieve better trade offs between makespan increase and number of tardy jobs, tardiness decrease. We conclude that dedicating machines on small jobs positively affects 17 our of 27 instances (in Fig. 1), trading a small increase on makespan for large reductions on the number of tardy jobs and total tardiness. Notably all improvements occurred when the number of dedicated machines ranges from 2–7, while in 76% of the instances the range is from 2–4. It is also encouraging that on 15 of those 17 instances there were various alternative policies that could be chosen demonstrating also positive effects.

Additional experimentation, on both real and random or modified literature instances, could yield more insights. Although already competitive within a quite challenging setting, our optimisation approach could be further strengthened by examining tighter formulations in a combination with a Benders-like decomposition, to accomplish provably near-optimal solutions on even larger instances.

References

1. Allahverdi, A., Ng, C.-T., Cheng, T.E., Kovalyov, Y.: A survey of scheduling problems with setup times or costs. EJOR **187**, 985–1032 (2008)
2. Aspnes, Y., Azar, Y., Fiat, A., Plotkin, S., Waarts, O.: On-line routing of virtual circuits with applications to load balancing and machine scheduling. JACM **44**(3), 486–504 (1997)
3. Brucker, P.: Scheduling Algorithms. Springer, Heidelberg (1999)
4. Correa, J., Verdugo, V., Verschae, J.: Splitting versus setup trade-offs for scheduling to minimize weighted completion time. ORL **44**, 469–473 (2016)
5. Eroglu, D.Y., Ozmutlu, H.C.: Solution method for a large-scale loom scheduling problem with machine eligibility and splitting property. TJTI **108**(12), 2154–2165 (2017)
6. Eroglu, D.Y., Ozmutlu, H.C., Ozmutlu, S.: Genetic algorithm with local search for the unrelated parallel machine scheduling problem with sequence-dependent set-up times. IJPR **52**(19), 5841–5856 (2014)
7. Letsios, D., Bradley, J.T., Suraj, G., Misener, R., Page, N.: Approximate and robust bounded job start scheduling for Royal Mail delivery offices. JOS **24**, 1–22 (2021)
8. Lee, J.-H., Hoon Jang, H., Kim, H.-J.: Iterative job splitting algorithms for parallel machine scheduling with job splitting and setup resource constraints. JORS **72**, 780–799 (2020)

9. Peyro, L.F.: Models and an exact method for the unrelated parallel machine scheduling problem with setups and resources. ESWA **5**, 100022 (2020)
10. Peyro, L.F., Ruiz, R., Perea, F.: Reformulations and an exact algorithm for unrelated parallel machine scheduling problems with setup times. COR **81**, 173–182 (2019)
11. Pimentel, C., Alvelos, F., Duarte, A., Carvalho, J.: Exact and heuristic approaches for lot splitting and scheduling on identical parallel machine. IJMTM **22**(1), 39–57 (2011)
12. Roberti, R., Toth, P.: Models and algorithms for the asymmetric traveling salesman problem: an experimental comparison. EJTL **1**, 113–133 (2012)
13. Avalos-Rosales, O., Angel-Bello, F., Alvarez, A.: Efficient metaheuristic algorithm and re-formulations for the unrelated parallel machine scheduling problem with sequence and machine-dependent setup times. Int. J. Adv. Manuf. Technol. 1705–1718 (2014)
14. Serafini, P.: Scheduling jobs on several machines with job splitting property. INFORMS J. Comp. **44**, 531–659 (1996)
15. Wang, J.-B., Wang, J.-J.: Research on scheduling with job-dependent learning effect and convex resource-dependent processing times. IJPR **53**(19), 5826–5836 (2015)

Comparison of Metaheuristics and Exact Method for the Dynamic Line Rebalancing Problem

M.-Lounes Bentaha[1](✉) iD and Salma El Abdellaoui[2](✉)

[1] Université de Lyon, Université Lumière Lyon 2, INSA Lyon, Université Claude Bernard Lyon 1, DISP, E4570, 69676 Bron, France
mohand.bentaha@univ-lyon2.fr
[2] OMP France, 20 Boulevard Montmartre, 75009 Paris, France

Abstract. Assembly lines are the most widely used systems for industrial mass production. A main objective in such a system is to ensure a workload balancing among its workstations and optimize it at the operational level. However, this balancing is affected by various disturbances which induce delays and then generate additional costs and deteriorate the performance of the assembly line. To remedy the negative effects of such disturbances, methods allowing real-time rebalancing are needed. The problem is known as the dynamic rebalancing of assembly lines. This work proposes a comparative study of three metaheuristics performances in solving this problem, namely: Iterated Local Search, Genetic Algorithm and Filters Beam Search-Ant Colony Optimization. The choice of these metaheuristics is motivated by their reputation for quickly and efficiently solving assembly line balancing problems. An exact method, whose performance is compared to the three selected metaheuristics, is also considered. The four approaches are applied to instances of industrial size and complexity known in the assembly line balancing literature. This benchmark data set guarantees coverage of almost all cases that an industrial could encounter. Obtained results showed the metaheuristics efficiency in solving large instances and that the exact method is recommended for small ones. Efficiency is measured here in terms of resolution speed (few seconds are required) and the quality of returned rebalancing solution. A rebalancing solution is of good quality if its cycle time is less than or equal to the initial line takt time.

Keywords: Assembly · Assembly line · Line balancing · Dynamic rebalancing · Reconfiguration · Metaheuristics · Exact method · Disturbance · Uncertainty

1 Introduction

At the operational level, the assembly process can be affected by various disruptions such as unscheduled shutdowns, breakdowns, repairs, stockouts, etc. These disturbances cause delays which affect the initial balancing of the line by generating additional costs and deteriorating its performance. The objective is therefore to remedy the negative effects of these disturbances by techniques that allow real-time workload rebalancing of

© IFIP International Federation for Information Processing 2021
Published by Springer Nature Switzerland AG 2021
A. Dolgui et al. (Eds.): APMS 2021, IFIP AICT 630, pp. 435–443, 2021.
https://doi.org/10.1007/978-3-030-85874-2_46

all workstations. This problem is known as the dynamic rebalancing of assembly lines
[1]. In this article, the seek for a line rebalancing is based on a reassignment of tasks
to workstations to absorb, as possible, the delay induced at a given time. Operators are
therefore assumed to be versatile and can easily adapt to changes in the assembly line.
An industrial case, in the Trane company, which includes such a possibility is described
in [2]. This study finds its application particularly at assembly lines level managed by a
pull system. To synchronize the flows of these lines, it is important that all operate at a
same rate defined by the Takt time (T_t), see Fig. 1 for an illustration. This will ensure
balanced lines that meet customer demand. The takt time is the rate at which it is needed
to complete the production process to meet customer demand, i.e. T_t = net available
work time/customer demand.

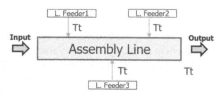

Fig. 1. Example of assembly lines dedicated to a family of products.

Real-time rebalancing can only be possible with fast algorithms (a response time of
few seconds). In this article, a rebalancing solution is said to be efficient if it is obtained
quickly (in a few seconds) and that the returned Cycle time (C_t) is less than or equal to
the takt time. Cycle time is the time it takes to complete the production of one unit from
start to finish, i.e. C_t = net available work time/number of units produced. Takt time is
based on customer demand whereas cycle time is work process based [3].

To identify methods that can efficiently solve the problem defined above, a literature
review is carried out. Considered articles are only those dealing with balancing, rebalancing, and dynamic rebalancing of assembly lines. Most studies address the problem of
initial balancing of assembly lines (long-term decision) [4, 5]. A decision that takes place
at the design and implementation phase of the assembly line. A recent trend is to deal
with the rebalancing problem [3, 6–9] to cope with the dimensional changes of the market due to seasonality and the life cycle of products for example and structural changes
linked to line reconfiguration and layout (add or remove workstations, etc.). However,
the problem of dynamic rebalancing of assembly lines is rarely studied as such [1, 10].
It is a real-time decision aid whose objective is to remedy the various disturbances that
affect the line. For these three problems, different formalizations based on mathematical
programming are proposed to model them. To solve balancing and rebalancing problems, a wide variety of exact, heuristic and metaheuristic methods are proposed. But, for
dynamic rebalancing we found mainly two approaches: ILS (Iterated Local Search) [1]
and Communicating Automata approaches that are applied to small instances [11]. To
identify the potential metaheuristics to be selected for our study, an additional work on
the classification of the latter is carried out by analysing the studies in [12–15]. Two main
classifications exist: the one based on [15]: Local Search Metaheuristics, Constructive
Metaheuristics, Population-based Metaheuristics and Hybrid Metaheuristics; the one

based on [13]: Single-Solution Metaheuristics (SSM) and Population Metaheuristics (PM). In addition, in this latter classification, in each category we distinguish between essentially constructive metaheuristics (Primarily Constructive, PC) and evolutionary metaheuristics (Improvement Metaheuristics, IM). The combination of these two classifications made it possible to establish the classification of metaheuristics represented in Fig. 3.

2 Problem Modeling and Solution Approaches

The studied system is assembly lines. An assembly line is made up of workstations arranged sequentially. The workload of each workstation is defined as the sum of the operating times of the tasks assigned to it. An assembly line is perfectly balanced if the workloads of all stations are the same and equal to cycle time. It is said to be balanced if the differences in workloads between the stations are as close as possible. If moreover the cycle time is less than or equal to the takt time, then such a line will satisfy the customer demand (see Fig. 2, top). A line is affected when disturbing elements occur at a time T_0. In this case, the assembly line is partitioned into two parts: a fixed one containing completed tasks and a dynamic one containing the unrealized tasks that require dynamic balancing (Fig. 2, bottom). The objective is to find a dynamic reassignment of non-performed tasks to the corresponding workstations that allows balancing of the remaining work, respecting the precedence constraints among tasks and, as possible, absorbs the induced delay (i.e. ensure as possible the cycle time value to be less than or equal to the takt time). The mathematical program **LPDR** models the problem described above [1].

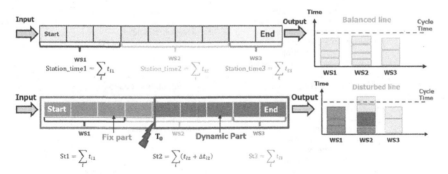

Fig. 2. Illustration of balanced and disturbed line concepts.

$$\underset{j \in J^*}{minmax} \left\{ St_j = \sum_{i \in I^* \cup A_{j_0}} (t_i + \Delta t_i) x_{ij} \right\} \textbf{(LPDR)}$$

Subject to:$x_{ij_0} = 1, \forall i \in A_{j_0} \backslash I^*$ (1)

$$x_{ij} = 0, \forall i \in A_{j_0} \backslash I^*, \forall j \in J^* \backslash \{j_0\} \tag{2}$$

$$\sum_{j\in J^*} x_{ij} = 1, \forall i \in I^* \tag{3}$$

$$\sum_{j\in J^*} jx_{i'j} \leq \sum_{j\in J^*} jx_{ij}, \forall i \in I^*, \forall i' \in P_i \tag{4}$$

$$x_{ij} \in \{0, 1\}, \forall i \in I^* \cup A_{j_0}, \forall j \in J^* \tag{5}$$

where, n: number of tasks, $n \in \mathbb{N}^*$; m: number of workstations, $m \in \mathbb{N}^*$; I: set of all tasks, $I = \{1, 2, \ldots, n\}$; J: set of all workstations, $J = \{1, 2, \ldots, m\}$; i: a single task, $i \in I$; j: a single workstation, $j \in J$; I^*: set of tasks which need to be re-assigned for rebalancing, $I^* \subseteq I$. Note that task impacted by the disturbance at time T_0 (denoted i_0) is an element of I^*; J^*: set of workstations where tasks in I^* can be reassigned, $J^* \subseteq J$; j_0 denotes the workstation which is impacted by the disturbance at time T_0 ($j_0 \in J^*$); $(A_j)_{j\in J}$: initial assignment of tasks to workstations J (before the disturbance at time T_0 occurs); $(A_j)_{j\in J}$ forms a partition of I; $(P_i)_{i\in I}$: sets of all predecessors of tasks I; T_t: takt time, $T_t > 0$; C_t: cycle time, $C_t > 0$; t_i: processing time of a task $i \in I$, $t_i > 0$; Δt_i: delay of a task $i \in I$, $\Delta t_i \geq 0$; x_{ij}: decision variable, $x_{ij} = 1$ if task $i \in I$ is assigned to workstation $j \in J$, $x_{ij} = 0$ otherwise.

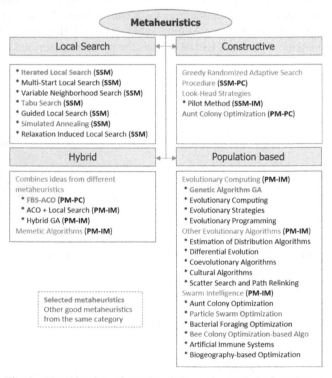

Fig. 3. Classification of metaheuristics and selection of used ones.

To solve the **LPDR** problem, our choice is based on three metaheuristics, namely: Iterated Local Search (ILS), Genetic Algorithm (GA) and Filters Beam Search-Ant Colony Optimization (FBS-ACO), see Fig. 3. The choice of these metaheuristics is based on an analysis of the literature on balancing and rebalancing of assembly lines. This analysis focused on metaheuristics whose effectiveness meets the criteria of speed and quality of cycle time minimization. The exact algorithm selected here is the default CPLEX Mixed Integer Programming (MIP) optimizer (based on branch & cut) [16]. No constructive metaheuristics are selected because of their penalizing computational time which increases significantly by increasing the number of tasks [17]. ILS is chosen based on its performance reported in [1]. GA is chosen among the population algorithms because it is the most widely used and has proven its efficiency and speed in solving problems of balancing and rebalancing [6, 17]. Finally, for hybrid metaheuristics, FBS-ACO is chosen thanks to its verification of the two previous criteria. Indeed, FBS-ACO is an improved version of the ACO algorithm from which it inherited the efficiency, and the FBS filters have allowed a significant improvement in computation time [8]. Brief pseudocodes of the three metaheuristics are given hereafter. ILS consists in applying a local search to a unique solution and a disturbance mechanism in several iterations, see [1]; in GA, an individual in the population represents a solution. This algorithm consists of building populations by improving their individuals from one generation to another using mutation, crossover and selection, see [18, 19]; FBS-ACO consists of using the characteristics of ant colony algorithm to build a solution respecting the defined number of workstations. In addition, the application of local and global evaluations of FBS makes it possible to select at each stage the next destination of an ant to build a feasible solution [18].

Algorithm 1: ILS
   Generate initial line balancing S_0
   $S \leftarrow S_0$
   $S'' \leftarrow S_0$
   do
      $S' \leftarrow \text{LocalSearch}(S'')$
      if ($C_t(S') < C_t(S)$) **then**
         $S \leftarrow S'$
      end if
      $S'' \leftarrow \text{Disturb}(S')$;
   while (IterCount<maxIter && $C_t(S) > T_t$)

Algorithm 2: GA
   Generate initial population considering the initial line balancing
   Compute fitness of initial population individuals
   Select the best individual
   while (IterCount<maxIter && $C_{t_{\text{population}}}(S) > T_t$) **do**

Apply elitism
Apply crossover
Apply mutation
end
Evaluate the best fitness of all generations
Select the best among the best individuals

Algorithm 3: FBS-ACO
Save the number of workstations of the initial line balancing
Initialise pheromone quantity
Generate initial Beam nodes
for (k from 0 to Ants number) **do**
    Assign fixed tasks of impacted workstation j_0
    Assign Beam node k
    while (some tasks are not assigned || workstations number is reached) **do**
        Identify candidates to be assigned using global evaluation
        Select best task candidate using local evaluation
        Update locally the pheromone
    end
    Update globally the pheromone
end

3 Numerical Experiments and Performance Comparison

The exact method (default CPLEX MIP optimizer), ILS, GA and FBS-ACO metaheuristics are implemented in Linux using C++ on a PC of 8Go RAM and 2.30 GHz CPU. Data set of 28 benchmark instances known in the assembly line balancing literature are used, see https://assembly-line-balancing.de/. Size and complexity of such instances guarantees coverage of almost all situations that an industrial could encounter. In addition, to cover most situations of line disturbances, we defined a design of experiments based on three main criteria, as follows: a disturbance can occur at the beginning or middle of the line; a disturbance can be low, average or high; task processing times can be high, average (original values) or low. Values of delays and task processing times are generated after analysis of total initial balancing idle time, number of tasks, number of workstations and initial cycle time. To generate an initial balancing for each instance, we have used SALOME [20]. So, each approach has to solve $28 \times 2 \times 3 \times 3 = 504$ different instances. To simplify the understanding and analysis of the obtained results, we defined three categories of the 504 instances: category 1 composed of instances whose tasks number doesn't exceed 50 (252 instances); in category 2 tasks number is greater than 50 but doesn't exceed 100 (198 instances); in category 3 tasks number exceeds 100 (54 instances). Resolution time of the exact method is limited to one hour.

The performance of each method is measured using the number of returned efficient solutions (takt-time respected and speed of resolution). Note that a solution is inefficient if the returned cycle time is not less than or equal to the takt time or if the resolution time is large (case of the exact method in particular). Analysis of the results consists in finding the number of solved instances (efficient solutions) by each metaheuristic and identifying their characteristics. Instances for which a metaheuristic has not found an efficient solution doesn't mean that really an efficient solution doesn't exist unless, the exact method has failed to solve it efficiently. The results have shown that for some instances the delay can be absorbed immediately, without doing any effort. This is the case when the cycle time of the line considering the delay is less than or equal to the takt time. It was the case for 73 instances (47 of categoty 1 and 26 of category 2). For the remaining 431 instances, the delay can't be absorbed initially, hence an efficient solution could be found using one of the four solution approaches.

For exact method, analysis is based on instances of category 1 since it is the only one where all instances (205) are solved efficiently. Delay was not absorbed for 79 instances and was absorbed for the remaining 126 instances. Most of the cases where delay is absorbed are characterised with low or average task times, see Table 1- exact method; 123 instances are solved in an average time of 0.56 s each.

Table 1. Characteristics of solved instances and solution methods performances.

		Solved	Tt respected	Dyn tasks nbr		Dyn workstations nbr		Tasks/workstations		Execution time (s)	
			begin/mid (total)	median	mean	median	mean	median	mean	median	mean
Exact M. Category 1	Beginning / Middle	205	69/57 (126)	29/14	28/24	6/3	6/5	4,28/4	4,14/4,13	0,34/0,025	0,039/35,33

		Solved	Tt respected	Dyn tasks nbr		Dyn workstations nbr		Tasks/workstations		Execution time (s)	
			begin/mid (total)	median	mean	median	mean	median	mean	median	mean
ILS Category 1	Beginning / Middle	205	22/41 (63)	31/13	16/19	6/3	4/4	5,33/4	4,33/4,66	0,0006/0,0002	0,0003/0,0004
ILS Category 2	Beginning / Middle	172	16/11 (27)	70/47	58/61	15/7	12/15	4,75/7,42	5,38/5,76	0,0041/0,0007	0,0022/0,0033
ILS Category 3	Beginning / Middle	54	1/2 (3)	111/59	59/76	15/8	8/10	7,37/7,37	7,37/7,38	0,0114/0,0017	0,0024/0,0049
mean					32		7		4,66		0,0012

		Solved	Tt respected	Dyn tasks nbr		Dyn workstations nbr		Tasks/workstations		Execution time (s)	
			begin/mid (total)	median	mean	median	mean	median	mean	median	mean
GA Categoty 1	Beginning / Middle	205	25/48 (73)	28/14	15/17	4/3	3/3	5,33/4,33	4,33/4,7	0,483/0,109	4,33/0,429
GA Categoty 2	Beginning / Middle	172	2/9 (11)	53/47	47/46	4/4	4/4	13,25/11,75	11,75/11,93	0,0001/0,0007	11,75/0,869
GA Categoty 3	Beginning / Middle	54	0/0 (0)	0/0	0/0	0/0	0/0	-/-	-/-	-/-	-/-
mean					26		4		5,66		0,486

		Solved	Tt respected	Dyn tasks nbr		Dyn workstations nbr		Tasks/workstations		Execution time (s)	
			begin/mid (total)	median	mean	median	mean	median	mean	median	mean
FBS-ACO Categoty 1	Beginning / Middle	205	67/20 (87)	29/14	28/24	6/3	6/5	4,28/3,62	4,16/4,73	0/0	0/0,0016
FBS-ACO Categoty 2	Beginning / Middle	172	55/13 (68)	83/41	75/71	13/6	13/14	7,23/8	7,23/6,53	0,021/0,011	0,021/0,0224
FBS-ACO Categoty 3	Beginning / Middle	54	18/3 (21)	148/144	148/163	15/21	15/19	7,4/6,85	7,4/9,68	0,254/0,4	0,2545/0,3805
mean					65		11		6,07		0,058

ILS solved 93 instances out of 431, see characteristics in Table 1- ILS. GA solved 84, Table 1- GA and FBS-ACO solved 176 instances, Table 1- FBS-ACO. To summarize, GA is efficient when the number of tasks and workstations are low. ILS is efficient for small to medium sized instances and FBS-ACO is efficient when the delay occurs at the beginning of the line. Exact method is efficient for small sized instances (no more than 50 tasks). Among all efficiently solved instances only 17 are common to the four solution approaches. These 17 instances are used to compare performance of ILS, GA and FBS-ACO to the exact method. The ratio C_t/T_t is used as comparison criteria, see Fig. 4. It is seen that the three metaheuristics gave solutions very close to the optimal ones. FBS-ACO and GA found the optimal solution for 6 of the 17 instances and ILS found only 2. It is also shown that when the dimension of the assembly line increases, GA finds solution with good quality. However, for most instances, ILS gives an acceptable solution but not close to the optimum compared to the other metaheuristics.

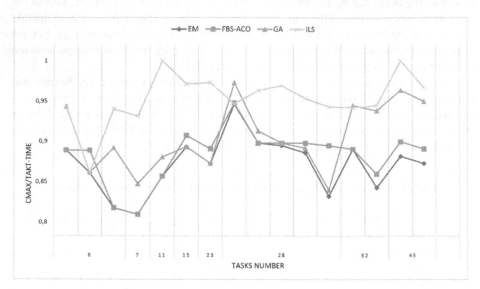

Fig. 4. Performance comparison of solution approaches based on C_t/T_t values.

4   Conclusion and Recommendation

In this study, a performance comparison of three metaheuristics (ILS, GA, FBS-ACO) and exact method for the dynamic line rebalancing problem is conducted. The meta-heuristics generated satisfactory results compared to the exact method. Obtained results analysis allowed to identify the most suitable method to apply for each line disturbance situation. GA are efficient on small instances with an average number of workstations equal to four. ILS can be used for small to medium size instances. FBS-ACO is more efficient for assembly lines that have many workstations. Finally, the exact method is very efficient for small instances (no more than fifty tasks).

As a future research development, we will investigate a fifth solution approach based on Artificial Intelligence techniques namely Machine Learning although FBS-ACO already can be seen as an AI approach since it is multi-agent based inspired by the behavior of real ants.

References

1. Antoine, M., El-Haouzi Hind, B., Cherif-Khettaf Wahiba, R., Mohand Lounes, B.: Iterated Local Search for dynamic assembly line rebalancing problem. IFAC-PapersOnLine **49**, 515–519 (2016). https://doi.org/10.1016/j.ifacol.2016.07.679

2. El Haouzi, H.: Approche méthodologique pour l'intégration des systèmes contrôlés par le produit dans un environnement de juste-à-temps: Application à l'entreprise TRANE (2008). https://tel.archives-ouvertes.fr/tel-00362316

3. Oliveira, F.S., Vittori, K., Russel, R.M.O., Travassos, X.L.: Mixed assembly line rebalancing: a binary integer approach applied to real world problems in the automotive industry. Int. J. Automot. Technol. **13**, 933–940 (2012)

4. Micieta, B., Stollmann, V.: Assembly line balancing. DAAAM Int. 257–264 (2011)

5. Sivasankaran, P., Shahabudeen, P.: Literature review of assembly line balancing problems. Int. J. Adv. Manuf. Technol. **73**(9–12), 1665–1694 (2014). https://doi.org/10.1007/s00170-014-5944-y

6. Yang, C., Gao, J., Sun, L.: A multi-objective genetic algorithm for mixed-model assembly line rebalancing. Comput. Ind. Eng. **65**, 109–116 (2013). https://doi.org/10.1016/j.cie.2011.11.033

7. Celik, E., Kara, Y., Atasagun, Y.: A new approach for rebalancing of U-lines with stochastic task times using ant colony optimisation algorithm. Int. J. Prod. Res. **52**, 7262–7275 (2014). https://doi.org/10.1080/00207543.2014.917768

8. Zha, J., Yu, J.: A hybrid ant colony algorithm for U-line balancing and rebalancing in just-in-time production environment. J. Manuf. Syst. **33**, 93–102 (2014). https://doi.org/10.1016/j.jmsy.2013.08.002

9. Gamberini, R., Gebennini, E., Grassi, A., Regattieri, A.: A multiple single-pass heuristic algorithm solving the stochastic assembly line rebalancing problem. Int. J. Prod. Res. **47**, 2141–2164 (2009). https://doi.org/10.1080/00207540802176046

10. Zhiyuan, Z., Jie, T., Wancheng, N., Yiping, Y.: A multi-objective dynamic rebalancing scheduling algorithm for mixed-model assembly line. In: 2012 6th International Conference on New Trends in Information Science, Service Science and Data Mining (ISSDM2012), pp. 586–591 (2012)

11. Antoine, M., Hind, B.-H., André, T., Jean-François, P.: Dynamic rebalancing of an assembly line with a reachability analysis of communicating automata. In: Grabot, B., Vallespir, B., Gomes, S., Bouras, A., Kiritsis, D. (eds.) APMS 2014. IAICT, vol. 438, pp. 597–604. Springer, Heidelberg (2014). https://doi.org/10.1007/978-3-662-44739-0_73

12. Boussaïd, I., Lepagnot, J., Siarry, P.: A survey on optimization metaheuristics. Inf. Sci. (Ny). **237**, 82–117 (2013). https://doi.org/10.1016/j.ins.2013.02.041

13. Gendreau, M., Potvin, J.-Y.: Metaheuristics in combinatorial optimization. Ann. Oper. Res. **140**, 189–213 (2005). https://doi.org/10.1007/s10479-005-3971-7

14. Osman, I.H., Laporte, G.: Metaheuristics: a bibliography. Ann. Oper. Res. **63**, 511–623 (1996). https://doi.org/10.1007/BF02125421

15. Sörensen, K., Glover, F.W.: Metaheuristics. In: Gass, S.I., Fu, M.C. (eds.) Encyclopedia of Operations Research and Management Science, pp. 960–970. Springer, US (2013). https://doi.org/10.1007/978-1-4613-0459-3

16. IBM ILOG CPLEX: User's Manual for CPLEX (2021). https://www.ibm.com/docs/en/icos/12.7.1.0?topic=cplex-users-manual

17. Mcgovern, S.M., Gupta, S.M.: Combinatorial optimization analysis of the unary NP-complete disassembly line balancing problem. Int. J. Prod. Res. **45**, 4485–4511 (2007). https://doi.org/10.1080/00207540701476281

18. Gendreau, M., Potvin, J.-Y.: Handbook of Metaheuristics. Springer (2010). https://doi.org/10.1007/978-1-4419-1665-5

19. Reeves, C. (ed.): Modern heuristics techniques for combinatorial problems. Nikkan Kogyo Shimbun. 1–320 (1997) https://ci.nii.ac.jp/naid/10010555508/en/

20. Scholl, A., Klein, R.: SALOME: a bidirectional branch-and-bound procedure for assembly line balancing. INFORMS J. Comput. **9**, 319–334 (1997)

Modern Analytics and New AI-Based Smart Techniques for Replenishment and Production Planning Under Uncertainty

A Probabilistic Estimation of Perfect Order Parameters

Valery Lukinskiy[1]([✉]), Vladislav Lukinskiy[1], Boris Sokolov[2], and Darya Bazhina[1]

[1] National Research University Higher School of Economics (HSE University),
St. Petersburg, Russia
[2] Saint Petersburg Institute for Informatics and Automation of the Russian
Academy of Sciences, St. Petersburg, Russia

Abstract. In the digital economy, information systems have a significant impact on supply chain management. However, there is a need for further development of theoretical knowledge and mathematical models, including methods for managing risk in complex supply networks to best serve customer orders. In the supply chain operations reference (SCOR) model, reliability is assessed by calculating perfect order parameters. The component/process reliability is calculated as the product of the weighted averages of the perfect order parameters, and possible combinations of failure features are not taken into account. This paper presents an approach to probabilistic estimation of perfect order parameters based on the general theorem on the repetition of experiments, and proposes to use a binomial distribution to approximate the values obtained. The obtained results make it possible to assess the efficiency of possible measures (increasing the insurance stock, replacing the carrier, etc.) to improve the reliability of perfect order fulfilment.

Keywords: Supply chain management · Perfect order fulfilment · Combinations of failure features

1 Introduction

Considerable attention is now being paid to the study of technologies and concepts such as artificial intelligence (AI), blockchain, Industry 4.0, big data, and several others [1–4]. However, there is a need to further develop theoretical knowledge and mathematical models to assess the impact of information systems on supply chain management [5–7]. This is necessary to achieve the primary goal of the supply chain – customer satisfaction [8–11]. Recent literature suggests some indicators to evaluate the impacts of uncertainty on supply chain (SC) execution. Most popular are reliability, robustness, stability and resilience [12]. In the supply chain operations reference (SCOR) model, reliability is assessed by calculating perfect order parameters [13–15]. Vishnu et al. [14] note that the reliability index of each supply chain component/process is calculated as a weighted average of the reliabilities of supplying the right quantity, the right quality, and at the right time. A similar approach to assessing the perfect order is found in studies of Bowersox, Closs, and Cooper [16]; Christopher [17]; Ballou [18]; Cousins et al. [19]; Grant et al.

© IFIP International Federation for Information Processing 2021
Published by Springer Nature Switzerland AG 2021
A. Dolgui et al. (Eds.): APMS 2021, IFIP AICT 630, pp. 447–454, 2021.
https://doi.org/10.1007/978-3-030-85874-2_47

[20]; and Heizer and Render [21]. Bowersox, Closs, and Cooper [16] claim that as many as 20 different logistic service elements may impact a perfect order. Ho et al. [22] emphasise that there is no research measuring the correlations between risk factors and the corresponding risk types, or the probability of occurrence of particular risk types associated with their factors. On the other hand, Walker [23] says that business has embraced the key performance indicator (KPI) for real-time process decision making. Unfortunately, KPIs multiply like rabbits, and unless they are properly managed, tend to be defined within the narrow context of functional silos.

Thus, the literature does not take into account possible combinations of failure features, and there is no probabilistic assessment of perfect order parameters. Consequently, to improve the reliability of perfect order parameter estimation, it is necessary to develop a new methodology that takes into account the specifics of supply chain operation.

This paper presents an approach to the probabilistic estimation of perfect order parameters based on the general theorem on the repetition of experiments, and proposes to use binomial distribution to approximate the obtained values. The obtained results make it possible to assess the efficiency of possible measures (increasing the insurance stock, replacing the carrier, etc.) to improve the reliability of perfect order fulfilment.

The paper is organised as follows. The methods for the probabilistic estimation of perfect order parameters are presented in Sect. 2. Section 3 lists the calculations used to test the suggested methods in different scenarios. Section 4 provides directions for future research.

2 Developing Methods for the Probabilistic Estimation of Perfect Order Parameters

To describe analytically the performance of a perfect order, a probabilistic model is used [16–21], which allows estimating the failure-free performance of the system in the form of the dependence.

$$p_0 = \prod_{i=1}^{n} p_i, \tag{1}$$

where p_0 is the probability of a failure-free order, n is the number of parameters considered in the perfect order, and p_i is the probability of error-free execution of the i-th operation (the p_i probabilities are independent).

In most papers, the calculated dependence (1) includes three or four parameters: p_1 is the probability of delivery in-full (quantity); p_2 is the probability of delivery in perfect condition (quality); p_3 is the probability of 'just in time' (JIT) order performance; p_4 is the probability of error-free documentation.

However, experience with formula (1) has shown that it can lead to significant errors for the following reasons.

1. Formula (1) corresponds to one of the extreme cases of a combination of failures in a single order; i.e., it does not reflect the variety of possible options.

2. The p_i parameters are derived from statistical information, and the relationships and interactions between them are not represented or quantified.
3. Other statistical dependencies, such as the general theorem on the repetition of experiments [24, 25], must be used to estimate the probability p_0. The general theorem on the repetition of experiments describes the case when experiments are carried out under different conditions, and the probability of an event varies from experiment to experiment.

Let us consider versions of expert analysis of the occurrence of failures in supply chains. The essence of the problem of accounting for the number of parameters in a single order is presented in Table 1 for two extreme cases. The first case reflects the independence and uncorrelatedness of failure features in each order (of the eight orders, only orders 7 and 8 are perfect, and the probability of failure-free order formation is 0.250); the second case reflects the maximum possible combination of failure features in a single order (only orders 4, 5, 6, 7, and 8 are perfect, and the probability of failure-free order formation is 0.625). On the other hand, according to Bowersox, Closs, and Cooper [16], Christopher [17], and Ballou [18], the values of perfect order parameters are on-time $p_1 = 7/8 = 0.875$, in-full $p_2 = 6/8 = 0.75$, and error-free $p_3 = 5/8 = 0.625$. Then formula (1) yields the probability of failure-free order formation $p_0 = 0.875 \cdot 0.75 \cdot 0.625 = 0.41$ for both extreme cases.

Table 1. Possible combinations of failure features in a single order.

Case	Parameter	Order number								Number of failures	Probability of failure-free order
		1	2	3	4	5	6	7	8		
1	On-time	X	0	0	0	0	0	0	0	1	0.250
	In-full	0	X	X	0	0	0	0	0	2	
	Error-free	0	0	0	X	X	X	0	0	3	
2	On-time	X	0	0	0	0	0	0	0	1	0.625
	In-full	X	X	0	0	0	0	0	0	2	
	Error-free	X	X	X	0	0	0	0	0	3	

X: failure; 0: failure-free performance

The dependencies of all possible variations of a perfect order estimate can be calculated based on the general theorem on the repetition of experiments, according to which the probabilities of failure-free order fulfilment are determined by the formula.

$$\prod_{i=1}^{n} (p_i + q_i z) = \sum_{m=0}^{n} P_{m,n} z^m, \tag{2}$$

where p_i is the probability of no failure in the i-th experiment, $q_i = 1 - p_i$; $P_{m,n}$ is the probability of no failure in n experiments exactly m times; and z is an arbitrary parameter.

After expanding Eq. (2), we find the sum of similar terms for each z^m, which represent probabilities $P_{0,n}, P_{1,n}, \ldots, P_{m,n}$ and are the components of a perfect order with m simultaneously observed failures for different values of m. For example, Eq. (2) for calculating the probabilities of a perfect order when $n = 3$ and the number of failure features m is between 0 and 3 is written as

$$\prod_{i=1}^{n=3} (p_i + q_i z) = p_1 p_2 p_3 + (p_2 p_3 q_1 + p_1 p_3 q_2 + p_1 p_2 q_3)z +$$

$$+ (p_3 q_1 q_2 + p_2 q_1 q_3 + p_1 q_2 q_3)z^2 + q_1 q_2 q_3 z^2 \tag{3}$$

If $n = 3$ and $m = 0$, we obtain $P_{0,3} = p_1 \cdot p_2 \cdot p_3$, i.e., formula (1); if $m = 2$, then $P_{2,3} = p_3 \cdot q_1 \cdot q_2 + p_2 \cdot q_1 \cdot q_3 + p_1 \cdot q_2 \cdot q_3$.

Our research has shown that the probabilities $P_{m,n}$ can be approximated by discrete probability distributions, in particular the binomial distribution.

$$P_{m,n} = \frac{n!}{m!(n-m)!} q^m p^{n-m}, \tag{4}$$

where p is the average value of the probability of no failures; $q = 1 - p$.

The value p is calculated according to the formula

$$p = \frac{\sum_{i=1}^{n} p_i}{n} \tag{5}$$

Obtaining the values of probabilities $P_{m,n}$ makes it possible to assess comprehensively the impact of changes in probabilities p_i, as well as the efficiency of possible measures for improving reliability (increasing the insurance stock, replacing the carrier, etc.). According to Inman and Blumenfeld [10], countermeasures may be available to mitigate the impact – such as substituting a different part, installing a feature at a later date, or deleting a feature altogether – but countermeasures carry at least some additional cost or negative side-effect. While no firm wants to carry inventory, it may be a cost-effective strategy for reducing supply chain disruption risk.

Clearly, further research needs to consider the use of discrete distribution laws other than the binomial to approximate the probability (e.g., hypergeometric, Poisson, etc.).

3 Testing

We collected and processed statistical data on supplies for company X, which allowed us to determine the following values of perfect order parameters: on-time $p_1 = 0.90$, in-full $p_2 = 0.80$, error-free $p_3 = 0.85$; number of failure features $n = 3$; simultaneous occurrence of failures m from 0 to 3.

Table 2 shows the results of calculations of probabilities $P_{m,3}$ using formula (3), e.g., $P_{0,3} = 0.9 \cdot 0.8 \cdot 0.85 = 0.612$. The probabilities of occurrence of one or two failures in an order are, respectively, $P_{1,3} = 0.329$ and $P_{2,3} = 0.056$.

To calculate $P_{m,3}$ under approximation by binomial distribution, we define the average value of the probability of no failures as $p = 0.85$. Then, using formula (4), we find the probability of the occurrence of, for example, one failure in the order ($m = 1$):

$$P_{1,3} = \frac{3!}{1! \cdot 2!} 0.15 \cdot 0.85^2 = 0.325$$

The results of the remaining $P_{m,3}$ values are shown in Table 2. An analysis of Table 2 shows that there is good consistency between the $P_{m,3}$ values calculated by different methods.

After considering these results, the management of company X decided that it was necessary to improve delivery efficiency by selecting an alternative route ($p_{1+} = 0.95$), creating an insurance stock ($p_{2+} = 0.85$), and implementing e-documentation ($p_{3+} = 0.90$). The results of the calculations are shown in Table 2, which indicates that the probability of forming a perfect order has increased to $P_{0,3} = 0.729$, i.e., by 15.5%.

Table 2. The results of calculating the probabilities of a perfect order $P_{m,3}$.

Simultaneous occurrence of failures, m	Probabilities $P_{m,3}$		
	General theorem on the repetition of experiments	Binomial distribution	
		Before changes in the supply organisation*	After changes in supply organisation**
0	0.612	0.614	0.729
1	0.329	0.325	0.243
2	0.056	0.058	0.027
3	0.003	0.003	0.001

*on-time $p_1 = 0.90$, in-full $p_2 = 0.80$, error-free $p_3 = 0.85$; **on-time $p_{1+} = 0.95$, in-full $p_{2+} = 0.85$, error-free $p_{3+} = 0.90$

A closer inspection revealed that in addition to the parameters mentioned above ($p_1 = 0.90$, $p_2 = 0.80$, $p_3 = 0.85$), three additional perfect order parameters were present ($p_4 = 0.99$, $p_5 = 0.97$, $p_6 = 0.95$). In order to assess the impact of these additional parameters on the formation of a perfect order, calculations were carried out using formulas (2) and (4), the results of which are shown in Table 3. An analysis of Table 3 shows that there is good consistency between the $P_{m,n}$ values calculated by different methods.

The results of calculations of $P_{m,n}$ show that an increase in the number of parameters of failure, taken into account in formulas (2) and (4), leads the probability of formation of the perfect order to decrease from 0.61 (at $n = 3$) to 0.56 (at $n = 6$), i.e., by approximately 5%. Thus, even a slight decrease (by 1–2%) in the reliability of operations in supply chains (delay in transportation, errors in order picking, cargo damage, etc.) can have a significant impact on the formation of a perfect order.

It follows that the decrease in the probability of perfect order formation is much greater when the p_i values are below 0.8. This issue requires special attention and further research, because according to Bowersox, Closs, and Cooper [16], even the best logistics organisations report only 60 to 70% perfect order performance.

Table 3. The results of calculating the probabilities of a perfect order $P_{m,n}$ ($P_{m,4}$, $P_{m,5}$, and $P_{m,6}$).

Simultaneous occurrence of failures, m	Number of failure features and average value of the probability of no failures					
	$n = 4; p = 0.885$		$n = 5; p = 0.902$		$n = 6; p = 0.910$	
	1*	2**	1*	2**	1*	2**
0	0.60588	0.61344	0.58770	0.59708	0.55831	0.56786
1	0.33183	0.31881	0.34005	0.32149	0.35243	0.33698
2	0.05850	0.06214	0.06500	0.06487	0.07875	0.0833
3	0.00353	0.00538	0.00510	0.00766	0.00809	0.0110
4	0.00003	0.000175	0.00013	0.00045	0.00038	0.00081
5			$0.9 \cdot 10^{-6}$	$0.9 \cdot 10^{-5}$	$0.75 \cdot 10^{-5}$	0.00003
6					$0.45 \cdot 10^{-7}$	$0.5 \cdot 10^{-6}$

*General theorem on the repetition of experiments; **Binomial distribution

4 Conclusion

In the digital economy, information systems have a significant impact on supply chain management. However, there is a pressing need for further development of theoretical knowledge and mathematical models, including methods that enable risk management for complex supply chains to best serve customer orders. This paper presents an approach to the probabilistic estimation of perfect order parameters based on the general theorem on the repetition of experiments, and proposes to use binomial distribution to approximate the obtained values. In future research, three considerations will be important. The first is to investigate the interdependencies and interactions between the parameters of the perfect order p_i, which must be taken into account in formulas (2) and (4). The second is to pay attention to different types of reservations for reliable fulfilment of a perfect order, taking into account the quality values of the supply chain performance. The third is to carry out a cost analysis of the proposed approaches by taking into account transport, current and insurance stock costs, costs due to shortages, and various penalties in the case of an imperfect order.

Acknowledgments. The research described in this paper is partially supported by state research 0073–2019–0004.

References

1. Kakhki, M., Gargeya, V.: Information systems for supply chain management: a systematic literature analysis. Int. J. Prod. Res. **57**(15–16), 5318–5339 (2019)
2. Baryannis, G., Validi, S., Dani, S., Antoniou, G.: Supply chain risk management and artificial intelligence: state of the art and future research directions. Int. J. Prod. Res. **57**(7), 2179–2202 (2019)
3. Saberi, S., Kouhizadeh, M., Sarkis, J., Shen, L.: Blockchain technology and its relationships to sustainable supply chain management. Int. J. Prod. Res. **57**(7), 2117–2135 (2019)
4. Luthra, S., Kumar, A., Zavadskas, E., Mangla, S., Garza-Reyes, J.: Industry 4.0 as an enabler of sustainability diffusion in supply chain: an analysis of influential strength of drivers in an emerging economy. Int. J. Prod. Res. **58**(5), 1505–1521 (2020)
5. Ben-Daya, M., Hassini, E., Bahroun, Z.: Internet of things and supply chain management: a literature review. Int. J. Prod. Res. **57**(15–16), 4719–4742 (2019)
6. Battaïa, O., Otto, A., Sgarbossa, F., Pesch, E.: Future trends in management and operation of assembly systems: from customized assembly systems to cyber-physical systems. Omega **78**, 1–4 (2018)
7. Bier, T., Lange, A., Glock, C.: Methods for mitigating disruptions in complex supply chain structures: a systematic literature review. Int. J. Prod. Res. **58**(6), 1835–1856 (2020)
8. Chopra, S., Meindl, P.: Supply chain management: Strategy, planning, and operation, 5th ed. Pearson Education Limited , Harlow (2013)
9. Huang, H., He, Y., Li, D.: Coordination of pricing, inventory, and production reliability decisions in deteriorating product supply chains. Int. J. Prod. Res. **56**(18), 6201–6224 (2018)
10. Inman, R., Blumenfeld, D.: Product complexity and supply chain design. Int. J. Prod. Res. **52**(7), 1956–1969 (2014)
11. Zhang, L., Wang, S., Li, F., Wang, H., Wang, L., Tan, W.: A few measures for ensuring supply chain quality. Int. J. Prod. Res. **49**(1), 87–97 (2011)
12. Ivanov, D., Dolgui, A., Sokolov, B.: Scheduling of recovery actions in the supply chain with resilience analysis considerations. Int. J. Prod. Res. **56**(19), 6473–6490 (2018)
13. Sellitto, M., Pereira, G., Borchardt, M., Silva, R., Viegas, C.: A SCOR-based model for supply chain performance measurement: application in the footwear industry. Int. J. Prod. Res. **53**(16), 4917–4926 (2015)
14. Vishnu, C., Das, S., Sridharan, R., Kumar, P., Narahari, N.: Development of a reliable and flexible supply chain network design model: a genetic algorithm based approach. Int. J. Prod. Res. (2020)
15. Chackelson, C., Errasti, A., Ciprés, D., Lahoz, F.: Evaluating order picking performance trade-offs by configuring main operating strategies in a retail distributor: a design of experiments approach. Int. J. Prod. Res. **51**(20), 6097 (2013)
16. Bowersox, D., Closs, D., Cooper, M.: Supply Chain Logistics Management, 2nd edn. McGraw-Hill, New York (2007)
17. Christopher, M.: Logictics and Supply Chain Management, 4th ed, Pearson Education Limited, Harlow (2011)
18. Ballou, R.: Business Logistics Management. Prentice-Hall International Inc, New York (1999)
19. Cousins, P., Lamming, R., Lawson, B., Squire, B.: Strategic Supply Management: Principles, Theories and Practice. Pearson Education Limited, Harlow (2008)
20. Grant, D., Lambert, D., Stock, J., Ellram, L.: Fundamentals of Logistics Management. McGraw-Hill Companies, Inc., New York (2006)
21. Heizer, J., Render, B.: Operations Management, 10th ed. Pearson Education Limited, Harlow (2011)

22. Ho, W., Zheng, T., Yildiz, H., Talluri, S.: Supply chain risk management: a literature review. Int. J. Prod. Res. **53**(16), 5031–5069 (2015)
23. Walker, W.: Emerging trends in supply chain architecture. Int. J. Prod. Res. **43**(16), 3517–3528 (2005)
24. Papoulis, A., Pillai, S.: Probability, Random Variables, and Stochastic Processes, 4th edn. McGraw-Hill Companies, Inc., New York (2002)
25. Ventsel, E., Ovcharov, L.: Applied Problems of Probability Theory. Radio and Communications, Moscow (1983). (in Russian)

Inventory and Commitment Decisions for On-Demand Warehousing System

Junhyeok Lee[1], Junseok Park[1], and Ilkyeong Moon[1,2(✉)]

[1] Department of Industrial Engineering, Seoul National University,
Seoul 08826, Korea
ikmoon@snu.ac.kr
[2] Institute for Industrial Systems Innovation, Seoul National University,
Seoul 08826, Korea

Abstract. The on-demand warehousing system is a service that makes a connection between e-commerce sellers and warehouse providers who have excess capacity for sharing warehouse spaces. The e-commerce sellers can create a distribution network strategy and manage the varying demands of customers by utilizing this system. In this study, we focused on inventory and commitment decisions that impacted the use of shared warehouses from the standpoint of e-commerce sellers. We proposed a mathematical model, which incorporated inventory and commitment decisions to maximize total profits. A small-scale experiment was conducted, and the result showed that the commitment decisions could affect total profits of e-commerce sellers considerably.

Keywords: Shared warehouse · Inventory model · On-demand warehousing · Commitment decisions

1 Introduction

On-demand warehousing marketplaces, such as FLEXE and Mychango, have emerged as the new alternative to old warehousing solutions. This service system connects warehouse providers who have excess space with e-commerce sellers who need flexible warehouse solutions. Instead of leasing warehouse space, e-commerce sellers can rent spaces for short durations (e.g., days or months) through commitments with warehouse providers. From the standpoint of e-commerce sellers, employing the on-demand warehousing system could be a low-risk strategy to match unexpected customer demands and prevent the overflow of inventory. In addition, e-commerce sellers could secure warehousing and fulfillment solutions instantly and build a distribution network strategy.

Several studies regarding the on-demand warehousing system and warehouse capacity sharing have been conducted in the past [1–5]. In particular, Van

This research was supported by the National Research Foundation of Korea (NRF) funded by the Ministry of Science, ICT & Future Planning [Grant no. 2019R1A2C2084616].

A. Dolgui et al. (Eds.): APMS 2021, IFIP AICT 630, pp. 455–463, 2021.
https://doi.org/10.1007/978-3-030-85874-2_48

et al. [5] studied for dynamic shipments of inventories that took into account up-to-date inventory information. To deal with the sequential decision-making problem, the authors of this study employed the Markov decision process and obtained the optimal order and shipment decisions for small networks. Feng et al. [2] studied an integrated inventory model with warehouse capacity sharing via transshipment. To develop an optimal transshipment policy, they established nonlinear programming models and genetic algorithms. To the best of our knowledge, our study is a first step toward considering *commitment* decisions for the on-demand warehousing system.

Throughout this study, we used the term *retailer* to refer to e-commerce sellers and *provider* to refer to warehouse providers who have excess capacity. We defined the *inventory holding costs* as the costs incurred while holding inventory or stock in a warehouse. These costs included the warehousing costs incurred, such as labor and utilities. The *commitment costs* were incurred when the retailer and provider made a commitment for sharing warehouse space. We considered a realistic situation in which the retailer could use three types of warehouses: (i) the retailer's own warehouse (*retailer's warehouse*), (ii) the warehouse of a provider connected through an on-demand warehouse platform that offers excess warehouse capacity (*provider's warehouse*), and (iii) the warehouse that charges a higher unit inventory holding cost than the retailer's and provider's warehouses but that is always accessible without any commitment (*emergency warehouse*). The retailer is allowed to use the provider's warehouse only if a commitment between a retailer and a provider is made for utilizing the provider's warehouse. We started this research from following two research questions:

(1) When the retailer can use all three types of warehouses, how should the retailer utilize warehouses for holding inventory within the entire planning horizon?
(2) If there exist two types of commitments (*long-term* and *short-term*) for using the provider's warehouse, what is the best commitment strategy to maximize the retailer's profit?

2   Problem Description and Mathematical Formulation

To develop a mathematical model for inventory and commitment decisions for an on-demand warehousing system, we defined the following notations of indices, sets, and parameters:

Indices and sets

$\mathfrak{T}$ set of periods $\{1, 2, \cdots, T\}$
$\mathfrak{J}$ set of items $\{1, 2, \cdots, I\}$
t index for set of periods $\mathfrak{T}$
i index for set of items $\mathfrak{J}$

Parameters

L	duration of long-term commitment
S	duration of short-term commitment
C^r	capacity of retailer's warehouse
C_t^o	capacity of provider's warehouse at period t
$s_{i,t}$	supply of item i at period t
$d_{i,t}$	demand of items i at period t
$r_{i,t}$	sales revenue per unit per period for items i at period t
$h_{i,t}^r$	inventory holding cost of retailer's warehouse per unit per period for item i at period t
$h_{i,t}^o$	inventory holding cost of provider's warehouse per unit per period for item i at period t
$h_{i,t}^e$	inventory holding cost of emergency warehouse per unit per period for item i at period t
c_t^l	commitment cost for total duration of a long-term commitment at period t
c_t^s	commitment cost for total duration of a short-term commitment at period t
t_L	$\min\{t + L - 1, T\}, t \in \mathfrak{T}$
t_S	$\min\{t + S - 1, T\}, t \in \mathfrak{T}$
t_L'	$\max\{t - L + 1, 1\}, t \in \mathfrak{T}$
t_S'	$\max\{t - S + 1, 1\}, t \in \mathfrak{T}$

Decision variables

p_t	equals 1 if a long-term commitment is made at period t, 0 otherwise
q_t	equals 1 if a short-term commitment is made at period t, 0 otherwise
a_t	equals 1 if items can be stored at provider's warehouse due to the long-term commitment at period t, 0 otherwise
b_t	equals 1 if items can be stored at provider's warehouse due to the short-term commitment at period t, 0 otherwise
$u_{i,t}$	the number of item i held in inventory at retailer's warehouse from period t to $t + 1$
$v_{i,t}$	the number of item i held in inventory at provider's warehouse from period t to $t + 1$
$w_{i,t}$	the number of item i held in inventory at emergency warehouse from period t to $t + 1$
$x_{i,t}^r$	flow of item i from external suppliers to retailer's warehouse at period t
$x_{i,t}^o$	flow of item i from external suppliers to provider's warehouse at period t
$x_{i,t}^e$	flow of item i from external suppliers to emergency warehouse at period t

$y_{i,t}^r$ the number of item i delivered to customers from retailer's
       warehouse at period t
$y_{i,t}^o$ the number of item i delivered to customers from provider's
       warehouse at period t
$y_{i,t}^e$ the number of item i delivered to customers from emergency
       warehouse at period t

To incorporate the inventory and commitment decision from the perspective of the retailer, we considered the multi-period and multi-item inventory model based on the discrete-time planning horizon. We assumed two assumptions to present our problem. First, transshipment between warehouses is not allowed, which means that items must be stored at the assigned warehouse until they are sold to customers. Second, transportation of items is not considered. Therefore, transportation costs and freight fleets are excluded in this study. We took into account three types of a retailer's decisions as follows:

(1) Inventory decisions: When the retailer receives items from external suppliers at period t, the retailer should make a decision of storage location for ordered items among the retailer's, provider's, and emergency warehouses. We assumed that the average inventory holding costs of warehouses within the entire planning horizon were in the following order (from cheap to expensive): provider's warehouse ($\sum_{t \in \mathfrak{T}} h_{i,t}^o/T$) < retailer's warehouse ($\sum_{t \in \mathfrak{T}} h_{i,t}^r/T$) < emergency warehouse ($\sum_{t \in \mathfrak{T}} h_{i,t}^e/T$).
(2) Commitment decisions: Figure 1 illustrates a simple example of commitments for a provider's warehouse. In this example, we assumed that the durations of long-term commitments and short-term commitments were four days and two days, respectively. Since a long-term commitment was made at period 1, the retailer can use the provider's warehouse until period 4. To utilize space continuously, the retailer makes a short-term commitment at period 5. At last, because the retailer does not need to use the provider's warehouse at period 7, commitments are not made, and every item stored at a provider's warehouse should be sold (i.e., $v_{i,t} = 0; \forall i \in \mathfrak{J}$). We assumed that the short-term commitment cost per period (c_t^s/S) was more expensive than the long-term commitment cost (c_t^l/L). The retailer should make commitment decisions for a provider's warehouse considering total inventory and costs within the entire planning horizon.
(3) Delivery decisions: The retailer sells items to meet demands. Considering the inventory holding costs and the availability of the provider's warehouse, the retailer should decide from which warehouses the items should be sold to customers.

Based on the notations of the parameters and decision variables, we developed the total revenue, total inventory holding costs, and total commitment costs function within the planning horizon as follows:

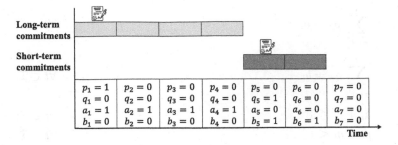

Fig. 1. Simple example of long-term and short-term commitments for provider's warehouse

$$\text{Total revenue (TR)} = \sum_{i \in \mathfrak{I}} \sum_{t \in \mathfrak{T}} \left[r_{i,t} (y_{i,t}^r + y_{i,t}^o + y_{i,t}^e) \right] \tag{1}$$

$$\text{Total inventory holding costs (THC)} = \sum_{i \in \mathfrak{I}} \sum_{t \in \mathfrak{T}} \left[h_{i,t}^r u_{i,t} + h_{i,t}^o v_{i,t} + h_{i,t}^e w_{i,t} \right] \tag{2}$$

$$\text{Total commitment costs (TCC)} = \sum_{t \in \mathfrak{T}} \left[c_t^l p_t + c_t f^s q_t \right] \tag{3}$$

Every decision variable is defined with integer variables for reflecting the behavior of commitments and properties of products. Therefore, we developed the following integer program.

$$\max \quad \text{TR} - \text{THC} - \text{TCC} \tag{4}$$

$$\text{s.t.} \quad x_{i,t}^r + x_{i,t}^o + x_{i,t}^e = s_{i,t} \qquad\qquad \forall t \in \mathfrak{T}, \forall i \in \mathfrak{I}; \tag{5}$$

$$y_{i,t}^r + u_{i,t} = u_{i,t-1} + x_{i,t}^r \qquad\qquad \forall t \in \mathfrak{T}, \forall i \in \mathfrak{I}; \tag{6}$$

$$y_{i,t}^o + v_{i,t} = v_{i,t-1} + x_{i,t}^o \qquad\qquad \forall t \in \mathfrak{T}, \forall i \in \mathfrak{I}; \tag{7}$$

$$y_{i,t}^e + w_{i,t} = w_{i,t-1} + x_{i,t}^e \qquad\qquad \forall t \in \mathfrak{T}, \forall i \in \mathfrak{I}; \tag{8}$$

$$y_{i,t}^r + y_{i,t}^o + y_{i,t}^e \le d_{i,t} \qquad\qquad \forall t \in \mathfrak{T}, \forall i \in \mathfrak{I}; \tag{9}$$

$$\sum_{i=1}^{I} u_{i,t} \le C^r \qquad\qquad \forall t \in \mathfrak{T}; \tag{10}$$

$$\sum_{i=1}^{I} v_{i,t} \le C_t^o (a_t + b_t) \qquad\qquad \forall t \in \mathfrak{T}; \tag{11}$$

$$\sum_{\tau=t}^{t_L} p_\tau \le 1 \qquad\qquad \forall t \in \mathfrak{T}; \tag{12}$$

$$\sum_{\tau=t}^{t_S} q_\tau \le 1 \qquad\qquad \forall t \in \mathfrak{T}; \tag{13}$$

$$\sum_{\tau=t'_L}^{t} p_\tau = a_t \qquad\qquad \forall t \in \mathfrak{T}; \qquad (14)$$

$$\sum_{\tau=t'_S}^{t} q_\tau = b_t \qquad\qquad \forall t \in \mathfrak{T}; \qquad (15)$$

$$a_t + b_t \leq 1 \qquad\qquad \forall t \in \mathfrak{T}; \qquad (16)$$

$$p_t + q_t \leq 1 \qquad\qquad \forall t \in \mathfrak{T}; \qquad (17)$$

$$p_t + q_t \leq C_t^o \qquad\qquad \forall t \in \mathfrak{T}; \qquad (18)$$

$$u_{i,0}, v_{i,0}, w_{i,0} = 0 \qquad\qquad \forall i \in \mathfrak{J}; \qquad (19)$$

$$x_{i,t}^r, x_{i,t}^o, x_{i,t}^e, y_{i,t}^r, y_{i,t}^o, y_{i,t}^e, u_{i,t}, v_{i,t}, w_{i,t} \in \mathbb{Z}^+ \qquad \forall t \in \mathfrak{T}, \forall i \in \mathfrak{J}; \qquad (20)$$

$$a_t, b_t, p_t, q_t \in \mathbb{B} \qquad\qquad \forall t \in \mathfrak{T}; \qquad (21)$$

The objective function (4) maximizes the total profits within the entire planning horizon. Constraint (5) represents the flow of items from external suppliers to the three types of warehouses. Constraints (6), (7), and (8) are the balance equations of inventory for a retailer's, a provider's, and emergency warehouses, respectively. Constraint (9) represents that the retailer cannot sell more items than are demanded. Constraints (10) and (11) show the capacity of a retailer's and a provider's warehouses, respectively. Constraints (12) and (13) represent the condition that making another commitment is not allowed until the present commitment expires. Constraints (14), (15), and (16) ensure that items are allowed to be stored at a provider's warehouse only if a long-term or short-term commitment has been made. Constraint (17) illustrates the condition that only one commitment should be made among long-term and short-term commitments at period t. Constraint (18) represents the condition that any commitment cannot be made when there is no storage space in the provider's warehouse. Constraint (19) enforces that initial inventory at every warehouse is zero. Constraint (20) ensures that decision variables for inventory, $x_{i,t}$, $y_{i,t}$, $u_{i,t}$, $v_{i,t}$, and $w_{i,t}$, are nonnegative integer variables. Constraint (21) ensures that decision variables for commitments, a_t, b_t, p_t, and q_t, are binary variables.

3   Computational Experiment

We conducted a small-scale experiment to identify the effects of some parameters on the commitments. We considered three types of modified problem instances (*Type*) from a basic instance (*Basic*). First, we changed the duration of the commitments while maintaining the commitment costs per period (c_t^s/S and c_t^l/L). Next, we changed the costs of the commitments per period. At last, we changed the inventory holding costs of the provider's warehouse ($h_{i,t}^o$). Table 1 presents the information of varying parameters depending on the three types of modified problem instances. Except for the parameters mentioned in Table 1, the values of other parameters, such as supply and demand, remained static. Every experiment was implemented in the condition of ten periods and two items. According to the above properties of modifications, we implemented seven computational experiments, and the term *Case* is utilized to refer to these experiments.

Table 1. Information of varying parameters depending on the problem instances

Parameters	Basic	Type 1		Type 2		Type 3	
	Case 1	Case 2	Case 3	Case 4	Case 5	Case 6	Case 7
L	3	**5**	3	3	3	3	3
S	1	1	**2**	1	1	1	1
c_t^l *	18	**30**	18	**24**	**12**	18	18
c_t^s *	10	10	**20**	10	10	10	10
$h_{i,t}^r$ **	10	10	10	10	10	10	10
$h_{i,t}^o$ **	4	4	4	4	4	**7**	**10**
$h_{i,t}^e$ **	30	30	30	30	30	30	30

* The value is consistent for all period t.
** The value is consistent for all period t and item i.

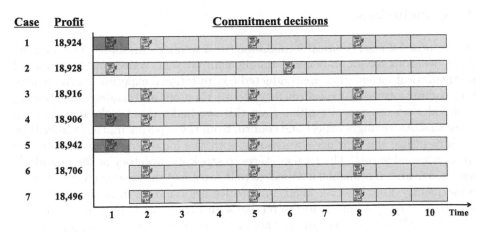

Fig. 2. Experimental results of commitment decisions

Figure 2 presents the experimental results of commitment decisions, including the information about the total profits and the periods when the commitments were made, for every case. Except for Case 2, where the entire period could have been covered by two long-term commitments, all cases had three long-term commitments at periods 2, 5, and 8. A short-term commitment was also made in Case 1, Case 4, and Case 5, whereas the other cases did not have such a commitment. For Case 3, it cost at least 18 to access the provider's warehouse, which was quite expensive. For Case 6 and Case 7, since the inventory holding costs were more expensive than in other cases, the retailer chose to use more of the retailer's warehouse capacity for the first period.

The results were intuitive, since the profit change followed the changes of the costs in reverse order. Expanding the duration of a long-term commitment to five days increased the profit because the provider's warehouse was accessible within entire periods only with long-term commitments (Case 2). When the short-term commitment was held for two days, the total cost for the commitments decreased while the retailer lost access to the provider's warehouse for one period. Therefore, inventories were held with higher inventory holding costs, which resulted in a profit decrease (Case 3). The profit decreased/increased when the cost of a long-term commitment per period increased/decreased (Case 4 and Case 5). When the inventory holding cost for the provider's warehouse increased, the profit decreased considerably (Case 6 and Case 7). Because $h_{i,t}^e$ was the most expensive among inventory holding costs of other warehouses, the products were held in the emergency warehouse when the retailer's warehouse and the provider's warehouse had no capacity. In addition, the products held in the emergency warehouse were delivered to the customers before the retailer's warehouse and the provider's warehouse for minimizing the inventory holding costs.

4   Conclusions

We proposed a mathematical formulation for a retailer's inventory and commitment decisions for an on-demand warehousing system. Based on the proposed mathematical formulation, we conducted computational experiments to identify how commitment decisions affected the retailer's profit and strategy for utilizing a provider's warehouse. Resulting from this, we had a clue for the two research questions. As we might expect and confirm from the experiment, the retailer tries to fully utilize the provider's warehouse with the long-term commitments due to its reasonable cost. The retailer starts to stock its inventory in the provider's warehouse first, if available, next moves to its own and the emergency warehouse, consequently. On the other hand, inventories are removed from the emergency warehouse first, leading up to the retailer's and then to the provider's, with an opposite order of stocking. In the case of the commitment, the retailer tries to cover the entire period with the long-term commitments, while the short ones are used to fill up the blank periods if necessary.

In this study, we assumed that the demands were deterministic. However, for real-world application, an assumption that the demand is given could be unrealistic. Therefore, for further research, we intend to extend our study for dealing with the condition of uncertain demand through the multistage stochastic programming approach or the robust optimization approach.

Acknowledgements. This research was supported by the National Research Foundation of Korea (NRF) funded by the Ministry of Science, ICT & Future Planning [Grant no. 2019R1A2C2084616].

References

1. Barenji, A.V., Wang, W.M., Li, Z., Guerra-Zubiaga, D.A.: Intelligent E-commerce logistics platform using hybrid agent based approach. Transp. Res. Part E Logistics Transp. Rev. **126**, 15–31 (2019)
2. Feng, X., Moon, I., Ryu, K.: Warehouse capacity sharing via transshipment for an integrated two-echelon supply chain. Transp. Res. Part E Logistics Transp. Rev. **104**, 17–35 (2017)
3. Minner, S., Silver, E.A.: Replenishment policies for multiple products with compound-Poisson demand that share a common warehouse. Int. J. Prod. Econ. **108**(1–2), 388–398 (2007)
4. Pan, S., Nigrelli, M., Ballot, E., Sarraj, R., Yang, Y.: Perspectives of inventory control models in the physical internet: a simulation study. Comput. Ind. Eng. **84**, 122–132 (2015)
5. Van der Heide, G., Buijs, P., Roodbergen, K.J., Vis, I.F.A.: Dynamic shipments of inventories in shared warehouse and transportation networks. Transp. Res. Part E Logistics Transp. Rev. **118**, 240–257 (2018)

Effect of Informed Demand Lead Time Under Imperfect Advance Demand Information

Koichi Nakade$^{(\boxtimes)}$ ⓘ and Tsubasa Seino ⓘ

Nagoya Institute of Technology, Gokiso-cho, Showa-ku, Nagoya 466-8555, Japan
nakade@nitech.ac.jp

Abstract. This paper considers two types of imperfect advance demand information. The advance demand information is given each day, and the actual arrival time is stochastic. In a known demand lead time model, the arrival date of actual demand, which is called demand lead time, is informed, and it is fixed. In unknown demand lead time model, the demand information does not include the demand lead time. In both cases, the actual demand may not occur with a given probability, and urgent demand may appear each day, which requires a product in the same day. The ordering, lost sale, holding and return costs are incurred. In this paper, these two cases are compared under the same situation except demand lead time information. To derive the optimal policy on order and return, each of the models is formulated as a Markov decision process. The optimal ordering policy in each day is derived, which minimizes the total expected cost over a finite horizon. The experimental results show that the total expected cost under the optimal policy in the case of the known lead time is smaller than that in the unknown lead time case, but the difference becomes small when the holding cost is small or the fraction of urgent demand is large.

Keywords: Advance demand information · Markov decision process · Imperfect

1 Introduction

To control the inventory system appropriately, the demand information in advance is important. This is called advance demand information (ADI). Use of ADI leads to appropriate production and inventory control, and it decreases amounts of products in inventory and backlogs.

The advance information is desired perfect, which means the information includes the arrival date of the corresponding actual demand, and it is performed certainly. In literature, perfect advance demand information is assumed basically (see Gallego and Özer [1] and Karaesmen [2], Liberopoulos [3] for example). Zhang et al. [4] consider the effect of sharing information of capacity for a production and demand information in a supply chain with a manufacturer and a retailer.

On the other hand, the demand may be cancelled by some reasons. For example, the parts of some products are needed for the downstream manufacturer, but the amount of

© IFIP International Federation for Information Processing 2021
Published by Springer Nature Switzerland AG 2021
A. Dolgui et al. (Eds.): APMS 2021, IFIP AICT 630, pp. 464–474, 2021.
https://doi.org/10.1007/978-3-030-85874-2_49

actual demand may decrease, compared with informed advance demand information, because the demand of final products in the downstream manufacturer is reduced due to cancel or additional order by customers. In this case, the demand information is called imperfect.

Recently, imperfect ADI has been included. In some case the amount of demand informed by ADI may be changed later. Liberopoulos and Koukoumialos [5] discuss the effect of use of imperfect ADI for a capacitated production and inventory system. Song and Zipkin [6] consider the use of imperfect ADI in inventory systems. Gao, Xu and Ball [7] study imperfect ADI in an assembly system, and Bernstein and Decroix [8] consider a multiproduct system with imperfect ADI in a single period.

In addition, the actual arrival date of demand may be unknown. In Topan et al. [9], the demand lead time, which is a time interval between ADI and the arrival date of the corresponding actual demand, is not informed, and some theoretical results of optimal policies are derived in such a model. They also assume that urgent demand which requires an item in the same day as it happens may occur, because sudden requirement may happen due to the big demand in the downstream manufacturer.

The certainty of demand lead time is desirable to control inventory. On the other hand, making the demand lead time information more precise may lead to more additional cost or less demand because some customers do not want to decide the lead time in advance. In this paper, two demand information models with imperfect advance demand information are considered. In one model, the arrival date of the actual demand is informed. In another model, which is the model of Topan et al. [9], the advance demand information does not include the demand lead time. In both models, demand information is imperfect, and the corresponding actual demand may not appear with a given probability. Each model is formulated as a Markov decision process, and the optimal order and return policy is derived. The difference of optimal policies is discussed through sensitivity analysis.

The organization of this paper is as follows. In Sect. 2, the model with imperfect ADI is described. In Sect. 3, each of the models with and without informed demand lead time is formulated as Markov decision process. Numerical results are shown in Sect. 4, and we discuss the property of both models. Conclusion is given in Sect. 5.

2 Model Description

2.1 Model

We consider an ordering model of products in a single stage single product inventory system during multiple periods. Products or parts are ordered to the supplier, and finished products are supplied to the inventory after fixed replenishment lead time. The return of items is also considered. That is, when the number of items in inventory is very large, items may be returned to the supplier. Each demand is satisfied by receiving one item from the inventory.

At the beginning of period t, the demand information happens, whose amount is denoted by W_t. This value is stochastic and follows $q_d = P(W_t = d)$ ($d = 0, 1, \ldots, d_{max}$), where d_{max} is the maximal value which W_t may take. Each of W_t demand information appears as an actual demand in the period $t + \tau$. The upper and lower bounds of τ are denoted by τ_u and τ_l, respectively, and τ follows the probability distribution

p_τ, $\tau \in \{\tau_l, \tau_{l+1}, \ldots, \tau_u\}$, where $p = \sum_{\tau=\tau_l}^{\tau_u} p_\tau \leq 1$. Thus, with probability $1 - p$, the actual demand does not occur.

In a case that the arrival date of the actual demand is known, which we call the case of a known demand lead time, demand lead time $\tau \in \{\tau_l, \tau_{l+1}, \ldots, \tau_u\}$ is informed with probability $\frac{p_\tau}{p}$ for each demand information.

In an unknown demand lead time model, when the demand information arrives in period t, the probability that the actual demand arrives in period $t + \tau_l$ is p_{τ_l}. When the demand information arrives at time t and the actual demand is not found at $t + \tau - 1$, ($\tau = \tau_l, \ldots, \tau_u - 1$), the probability that it appears in period $t + \tau$ is $\frac{p_\tau}{1 - \sum_{k=l}^{\tau-1} p_k}$.

Thus, when the demand information arrives and the actual demand is not found before $t + \tau_u - 1$, the demand appears with probability $\frac{p_{\tau_u}}{1 - p + p_{\tau_u}}$ and it does not appear with probability $\frac{1-p}{1-p+p_{\tau_u}}$. This unknown demand lead time model is the same as shown in [9]. The resulting probabilities, with which the actual demand appears in each period and the actual demand does not appear, coincide with those in the known demand lead time model.

The number of external urgent order which does not relate with demand information is denoted by $D_t^s \in \{0, 1, \ldots, d_{smax}\}$, and it follows the probability $u_d = P(D_t^s = d)$, $d = 0, 1, \ldots, d_{smax}$.

The expected amount of total demand D_t is $E[D_t] = pE[W_t] + E[D_t^s]$. As following Topan et al. [9], the sensitivity of demand information is denoted by $q = \frac{pE[W_t]}{pE[W_t]+E[D_t^s]} = \frac{pE[W_t]}{E[D_t]}$.

When the actual demand arrives, if there is no item in inventory, the demand is lost. The replenishment lead time for each order is fixed as L. In period t, the number of items which are ordered in period $t - L + l$ and will reach the warehouse in period $t + l$ is denoted by z_l, $l \in \{0, 1, \ldots, L\}$.

The cost incurred in each period is as follows: the ordering cost for each item is $c(>0)$, the lost sale cost is $c_e(>0)$, the holding cost rate for each item in inventory is $h(\geq 0)$, and the return cost of items from inventory to the supplier is c_r. If c_r is negative, when the item is returned to the supplier, the warehouse receives reward $-c_r$. In addition, it is assumed that $c + c_r \geq h \cdot L$. This implies that the sum of cost for ordering and returning an item is higher than keeping an item in L periods, which eliminates the possibility that it is best that an order is made and one item is returned to the supplier at the same time.

The number of items in inventory at the beginning of period t is denoted by x_t, and the number of items returned to the supplier is y_t. Here we assume that $x_t \geq y_t$.

The order of events during period t is as follows:

1. The information of advance demand W_t arrives.
2. The state of the system is observed, and the size of replenished items in period $t + L$, z_L, and the number of returned items y_t are determined. The ordering and returning costs are incurred.
3. Items which are ordered in period $t - L$ arrive at the inventory. Its size is z_0.
4. The actual demand and the external urgent demand happen, and each of them is satisfied by one of items consisting of $x_t - y_t$ items in inventory and $z_{0,t}$ arriving items.

5. Inventory holding costs and lost sale costs are incurred.

In the following, subscript t is sometimes omitted. The planning horizon of our model is $T + 1$. At the beginning of period $T + 1$, advance demand information arrives, and decision of ordering and returning items is not made in this period, and the remaining actual demand is satisfied (or lost) by the remaining items in inventory and the items which have been ordered. The objective is to derive an optimal order and return policy which minimizes the expected total cost over a planning horizon.

Table 1 shows a list of notations which appear in Sect. 2.

Table 1. Notations.

Model Description

W_t : the amount of informed demand in period t,

$q_d = P(W_t = d)$: the distribution of W_t, $0 \leq d \leq d_{max}$

τ: demand lead time, $\tau \in \{\tau_l, \tau_l + 1, \ldots, \tau_u\}$,

$p = \sum_{\tau=\tau_l}^{\tau_u} p_\tau \leq 1$,

D_t^s: the amount of external urgent demand in period t,

$u_d = P(D_t^s = d)$: the distribution of D_t^s, $0 \leq d \leq d_{s_{max}}$,

D_t: the total demand in period t,

$q = \dfrac{pE[W_t]}{pE[W_t] + E[D_t^s]} = \dfrac{pE[W_t]}{E[D_t]}$,

L: the demand lead time,

z_l: the amount of arriving items l periods later,

c: an ordering cost,

c_e: a lost sale cost,

h: a holding cost rate,

c_r: the return cost rate,

x_t: the number of items in inventory in the beginning of period t,

y_t: the number of returned items to a supplier in period t,

T: the planning horizon.

Unknown lead time case

A_τ : the amount of demand which is informed τ periods before, $\tau \in \{0, 1, \ldots, \tau_u\}$,

a_τ : the realization of A_τ, $\tau \in \{0, 1, \ldots, \tau_u\}$,

R_τ: the number of actual demand among A_τ informed demand, $\tau \in \{0, 1, \ldots, \tau_u\}$.

Known lead time case

B_τ: the number of orders whose demand will occur τ periods later, $\tau \in \{0, 1, \ldots, \tau_u\}$,

b_τ : the realization of B_τ, $\tau \in \{0, 1, \ldots, \tau_u\}$,

$p_\tau^d = p_\tau/p$: the probability that each demand will arrive τ periods later if it actually arrives, $\tau \in \{\tau_l, \tau_l + 1, \ldots, \tau_u\}$,

$\hat{b}_\tau$: the number of demand who will occur τ periods later among informed demand W_t, $\tau \in \{\tau_l, \tau_l + 1, \ldots, \tau_u\}$.

2.2 Two Types of Demand Information

We consider two types of demand information as discussed above. Here, we show additional notations in each model.

(1) Unknown Demand Lead Time

This model is the same as the model of Topan et al. [9], except the terminal cost. In [9], the cost in period $T + 1$ is set as zero, whereas in this paper the cost is determined by the remaining demand and items in inventory. Let A_τ denote the number of demand which is informed τ periods before and the corresponding actual demand has not arrived yet ($\tau \in \{0, 1, \ldots, \tau_u\}$). Among A_τ demand, the number of the actual demand in a period is denoted by R_τ. For $\tau \in \{\tau_l, \ldots, \tau_u\}$, when $A_\tau = a_\tau$, R_τ follows a binomial distribution with parameters $(a_\tau, \frac{p_\tau}{1-\sum_{k=\tau_l}^{\tau-1} p_k})$, which can be proved by the assumption of the demand lead time. For $\tau \in \{0, 1, \ldots, \tau_l - 1\}$, $R_\tau = 0$. Then at the end of each period, the number of items in inventory becomes $\left(x + z_0 - y - \sum_{\tau=\tau_l}^{\tau_u} R_\tau - D^s\right)^+$, where $(x)^+ = \max(x, 0)$. Let $a = \left(a_0, a_1, \ldots, a_{\tau_u}\right)$.

When the value of A_τ is a_τ at the beginning of period t ($\tau = 1, 2, \ldots, \tau_u$), a_0 becomes W_t, and after the actual demand arrives, the amount of demand information whose corresponding actual demand has not arrived is $a_\tau - R_\tau$ for $\tau = 1, 2, \ldots, \tau_u$. Thus, at the beginning of period $t + 1$, $A_{\tau,t+1} = a_{\tau-1} - R_{\tau-1}$ for $\tau = 1, 2, \ldots, \tau_u$.

(2) Known demand lead time

Let B_τ denote the number of orders whose demand will occur τ periods later. Its value is denoted by b_τ. Since the actual demand for each order happens with probability p, the amount of demand in this period, denoted by R_b, follows a binomial distribution with parameters (b_0, p).

When the number of demand information arriving in period t is W_t, the probability that each demand will arrive τ periods later if it actually arrives is $p_\tau^d = p_\tau/p$ for $\tau \in \{\tau_l, \tau_l + 1, \ldots, \tau_u\}$. Thus, the sequence $\left(\bar{b}_{\tau_l}, \ldots, \bar{b}_{\tau_u}\right)$, where $\bar{b}_\tau$ denotes the value which is added to the current b_τ for $\tau = \tau_l, \ldots, \tau_u$, follows the multinomial distribution with parameters W_t and $(p_\tau^d; \tau = \tau_l, \ldots, \tau_u)$.

When b is $(b_0, \ldots, b_{\tau_u})$ before arrivals of ADI in period t, the state $b' = \left(b_0', \ldots, b_{\tau_u}'\right)$ before their arrivals in period $t + 1$ is as follows:

$$b_{\tau_u}' = 0,\ b_\tau' = b_{\tau+1} + \bar{b}_{\tau+1},\ \tau \in \{\tau_l - 1, \ldots, \tau_u - 1\},$$
$$b_\tau' = b_{\tau+1},\ \tau \in \{0, \ldots, \tau_l - 2\}, \tag{1}$$

Note that the decision on ordering and returning items is made after advance demand information arrives in each period.

3 Optimal Equations

The problems described above can be formulated as Markov decision processes.

(1) Unknown demand lead time

This is the same as the formulation of Topan et al. [9] except the terminal cost. We note that the state is given as (a, z), where $z = (x, z_0, z_1, \ldots, z_{L-1})$ and z_τ denotes the number of demands which will arrive τ times later. The state space is

$$S = \left\{ (a, z); a = (a_0, a_1, \ldots, a_{\tau_u}) \in \{0, 1, \ldots, d_{max}\}^{\tau_u+1}, z \in X \times V^L \right\},$$

where $X = \{0, 1, \ldots, L(d_{max}(\tau_u - \tau_l + 1) + d_{smax})\}$ and $V = \{0, 1, \ldots, Ld_{max}(\tau_u - \tau_l + 1)\}$. The action space for state z depends only on x and is given by $A_x = \{(z_L, y) : z_L \in V, y \in X, z_L \cdot y = 0, y \le x\}, x \in X$.

The optimal equations are found in [9] for period $t = 0, 1, \ldots, T$. The terminal cost for state (a, z) in period $T + 1$ is given by

$$\hat{f}_{T+1}(a, z) = \mathrm{E}\left[c_r \left(x + \sum_{l=0}^{L-1} z_l - \sum_{\tau=0}^{\tau_u} O_\tau \right)^+ + c_e \left(\sum_{\tau=0}^{\tau_u} O_\tau - \sum_{l=0}^{L-1} z_l - x \right)^+ \right].$$

Here O_τ is the number of actual demand among a_τ orders and follows a binomial distribution with $(a_\tau, \hat{p}_\tau)$, where $\hat{p}_\tau = p$ for $\tau \le \tau_l$ and $\hat{p}_\tau = (p_\tau + p_{\tau+1} + \cdots + p_{\tau_u})/(1 - (p_{\tau_l} + p_{\tau_l+1} + \cdots + p_{\tau-1}))$ for $\tau_l + 1 \le \tau \le \tau_u$.

(2) Known demand lead time

The state is shown as (b, z), where $b = (b_0, b_1, \ldots, b_{\tau_u})$ and $z = (x, z_0, z_1, \ldots, z_{L-1})$. The state space is $S = Y \times Z$ where

$$Y = \left\{ b = (b_0, b_1, \ldots, b_{\tau_u}) : b \in M^{\tau_l+1} \times \prod_{\tau=\tau_l+1}^{\tau_u} M_\tau \right\},$$

$$Z = \left\{ z = (x, z_0, z_1, \ldots, z_{L-1}) : z \in X \times V^L \right\},$$

$$M_\tau = \{0, 1, 2 \ldots, d_{max}(\tau_u - \tau + 1)\}, \tau \in \{\tau_l, \ldots, \tau_u\}, \text{ and}$$

$$M = \{0, 1, 2, \ldots, d_{max}(\tau_u - \tau_l + 1)\}.$$

The action space A_x is the same as the unknown demand lead time case and it is given by

$$A_x = \{(z_L, y) : z_L \in V, y \in X, z_L \cdot y = 0, y \le x\}, x \in X.$$

When the state (b, z) is given in period t, under the optimal policy, the total expected cost from period t to $T + 1$, is denoted by $\bar{f}_t(b, z)$. The optimal equations are given by

$$\bar{f}_t(b, z) = \min_{(z_L, y) \in A_x} \{j_t(b, z, z_L, y)\} t = 1, 2, \ldots, T, \tag{2}$$

$$j_t(b, z, z_L, y) = cz_L + c_r y + \bar{N}(b_0, x + z_0 - y)$$
$$+ E\left[\bar{f}_{t+1}\left(\left(\bar{b} + \overline{B'}\right), (x + z_0 - y - R_b - D_t^s)^+, z_1, \ldots, z_L\right)\right] \tag{3}$$

where $\bar{b} = (b_1, \ldots b_{\tau_u}, 0)$, and $\overline{B'} = \left(\overline{B}_0', \ldots, \overline{B}_{\tau_u}'\right)$, where $\left(\overline{B}_0', \overline{B}_1' \ldots, \overline{B}_{\tau_{l-2}}'\right) = (0, 0, \ldots, 0)$, $\left(\overline{B}_{\tau_{l-1}}', \ldots, \overline{B}_{\tau_{u-1}}'\right)$ follows a multinomial distribution with W_{t+1} and $(p_\tau^d; \tau = \tau_l, \ldots, \tau_u)$, and $\overline{B}_{\tau_u}' = 0$. In addition,

$$\bar{N}(b_0, x + z_0 - y) = hE\left[(x + z_0 - y - R_b - D_t^s)^+ | b_0\right]$$
$$+ c_e E\left[(R_b + D_t^s - x - z_0 + y)^+ | b_0\right]. \tag{4}$$

The terminal cost is given by

$$\bar{f}_{T+1}(b, z) = E\left[c_r\left(x + \sum_{l=0}^{L-1} z_l - O\right)^+ + c_e\left(O - \sum_{l=0}^{L-1} z_l - x\right)^+\right], \tag{5}$$

where O follow a binomial distribution with parameters $(b_0 + b_1 + \ldots + b_{\tau_u}, p)$.

4   Numerical Experiments

Here we discuss the properties of optimal policies for unknown and known demand lead time via numerical experiments. The program is coded with C language and compiled by Intel Compiler 16.0 on the computer with Intel(R) Core (TM) i7-8700 CPU 3.20 GHz and 32 GB RAM.

Through the experiments $T = 10$, $\tau_l = 1$, $\tau_u = 3$ and $L = 1$. $d_{max} = 3$ and the amount of demand W_t follows the truncated Poisson distribution as $P(W_t = k) = e^{-\lambda}\frac{\lambda^k}{k!}$, $k = 0$, $1, \ldots, d_{max} - 1$ and $P(W_t = d_{max}) = 1 - \sum_{k=0}^{d_{max}-1} P(W_t = k)$. $P(D_t^s = 0) = 1 - \lambda'$, and $P(D_t^s = 1) = \lambda'$. The numbers of states are 28160 and 308000 in the cases of unknown and known demand lead time, respectively. In the following, we set the expected number of total actual demand in each period is 1, that is

$$E[D_t] = pE[W_t] + E[D_t^s] = 1, \tag{6}$$

and the sensitivity of demand is

$$q = \frac{pE[W_t]}{pE[W_t] + E[D_t^s]} = \frac{pE[W_t]}{E[D_t]} = pE[W_t] \tag{7}$$

and thus

$$E[W_t] = \sum_{k=0}^{d_{max}-1} k e^{-\lambda} \frac{\lambda^k}{k!} + d_{max}\left(1 - \sum_{k=0}^{d_{max}-1} e^{-\lambda}\frac{\lambda^k}{k!}\right) = \frac{q}{p}. \qquad (8)$$

where $\lambda' = E[D_t^s] = 1 - q$. The distribution of τ is $p_1 = p_2 = p_3 = p/3$. Here, when p and q are given, we determine λ to satisfying $E[W_t] = \frac{q}{p}$. For example, when $p = q$, $\lambda = 1.0254398$, and when $p = 0.7$ and $q = 0.5$, $E[W_t] = 5/7$ and $\lambda = 0.7216941$.

Cost parameters are initially set as $c = 100$, $c_e = 300$, $c_r = 0$ and $h = 20$. Some cost parameters are changed to find their sensitivity under optimal policies. The optimal policies can be calculated by the well-known value iteration method (see Puterman [10]). For example, in the known lead time case, we first compute $\bar{f}_{T+1}(b, z)$ for all states (b, z) by (5), and $\bar{f}_t(b, z)$ is calculated through (2) and (4), from $t = T, T - 1$, ..., 1, sequentially. The pair (z_L, y) which minimizes the right hand side of (2) is an optimal action for the given state (b, z) in period t. In the unknown lead time case, the policy can be computed similarly.

In the following, initially there are no items in inventory and no demand information. When the demand information arrives at the beginning of period $t = 1$, the first decision on the sizes of order and return is made. Thus, the total expected cost in the unknown demand lead time case is given by

$$\hat{f} = \sum_{k=0}^{d_{max}} q_k \hat{f}_1(k, 0, 0, 0, 0, 0),$$

where $\hat{f}_1(k, 0, 0, 0, 0, 0)$ is the total expected cost under the optimal policy when the initial state is $(k, 0, 0, 0, 0, 0)$. In the known demand lead time case it is given as

$$\bar{f} = \sum_{k=0}^{d_{max}} q_k \sum_{b_1=0}^{k} \sum_{b_2=0}^{k-b_1} \sum_{b_3=0}^{k-b_1-b_2} \frac{k!}{b_1! b_2! b_3!}\left(\frac{1}{3}\right)^k \bar{f}_1(0, b_1, b_2, b_3, 0, 0).$$

First, we assume that there is no urgent demand, and all informed demand require items, that is, $p = q = 1$.

Table 2 shows the optimal decision in periods 1 to 5 for several states in the unknown and known demand lead time cases.

We first consider the unknown lead time case. After new ADI arrivals in period 0, the state becomes $(a_0, 0, 0, 0, 0, 0)$, where $a_0 = 0, 1, 2, 3$. As this value increases the number of the optimal order also increases. In period 2 or later, for state $(0, 2, 0, 0, 0, 0)$ one new item is ordered, whereas for state $(0, 0, 2, 0, 0, 0)$, two new items are ordered. Since $p = 1$, in state $(0, 2, 0, 0, 0, 0)$ two demand arrive in three days with probability 1. Thus, to reduce the holding cost, in this state only one item is ordered. For state $(0, 0, 2, 0, 0, 0)$, two demand arrive in two days with probability one. Thus, to satisfy these demand, two items must be ordered because an order lead time exists.

Here we discuss the known lead time case. In period 1, the number of orders is the same as b_1 for any possible initial state in $(0, b_1, b_2, b_3, 0, 0)$ after ADI is informed.

Since order lead time is one, the order is made to satisfy b_1 demand in the next period to reduce holding costs. The similar decision is made until period 9.

Table 2. Optimal decision in periods 1 to 5.

(a) Unknown lead time case

$(a_0, a_1, a_2, a_3, x_0, z_L)$	(z_0, y_0)	$(a_0, a_1, a_2, a_3, x_0, z_L)$	(z_0, y_0)
(0,0,0,0,0,0)	(0,0)	(0,0,0,1,0,0)	(0,0)
(1,0,0,0,0,0)	(1,0)	(0,2,0,0,0,0)	(1,0)
(2,0,0,0,0,0)	(2,0)	(0,0,2,0,0,0)	(2,0)
(3,0,0,0,0,0)	(2,0)	(0,0,0,2,0,0)	(0,0)

(b) Known lead time case

$(b_0, b_1, b_2, b_3, x_0, z_L)$	(z_0, y_0)	$(b_0, b_1, b_2, b_3, x_0, z_L)$	(z_0, y_0)
(0,0,0,0,0,0)	(0,0)	(0,2,0,0,0,0)	(2,0)
(0,0,0,1,0,0)	(0,0)	(0,0,0,3,0,0)	(0,0)
(0,0,1,0,0,0)	(0,0)	(0,1,1,1,0,0)	(1,0)
(0,1,0,0,0,0)	(1,0)	(0,3,0,0,0,0)	(3,0)

Table 3. Optimal total costs

(a) Sensitivity of total cost in c_r

	$c_r = -20$	$c_r = 0$	$c_r = 20$	$c_r = 40$
$\hat{f}$	1358.30	1365.62	1372.93	1380.24
$\bar{f}$	1200.44	1207.61	1214.78	1221.95

(b) Sensitivity of total cost in h

	$h = 0$	$h = 20$	$h = 40$
$\hat{f}$	1214.78	1372.93	1498.96
$\bar{f}$	1214.78	1214.78	1214.78

(c) Sensitivity of total cost in c_e

	$c_e = 200$	$c_e = 300$	$c_e = 400$
$\hat{f}$	1322.15	1372.93	1413.69
$\bar{f}$	1178.91	1214.78	1250.66

Table 3 shows the total expected costs under optimal policies when one cost parameter varies. In this example, the option of returning items is selected only for few possible states over a planning horizon, and thus when c_r is changed the change of the total expected cost is small for both known and unknown cases.

As the holding cost increases, the difference of the total optimal expected cost between these cases is greater. When there is no holding cost, the expected cost in the known demand lead time case is the same as that in the unknown lead time case. In fact, in the case of unknown lead time, orders are made to satisfy all possible informed demand because keeping items in inventory makes no additional cost. In addition, return of an item is not optimal for any state in periods 1 to 7.

Here we assume that the informed demand may require no item, or the sudden demand happens. We compute the optimal polices for all cases combining $p = 0.5, 0.7, 0.9, 1.0$ with $q = 0.5, 0.7, 0.9, 1.0$. Note that $E[D_t^s] = 1 - q$, and the terminal cost does not include the urgent demand. Table 4 shows the expected total cost under optimal policy for various p under a given q. In each q, as p is smaller the total cost is greater because of the missing actual demand against ADI. When q is small, the effect by the known demand lead time is small. On the other hand, when q is large, the effect of the demand lead time is large when p is 0.9. When q is small, there are three types of uncertainty on demand: the variety of demand lead time, possibility of actual demand and the urgent demand. Since the effect of uncertainty due to the urgent demand is great, the effect of the demand lead time information is weakened.

Table 4. Optimal total cost under different p and q

(a) q=1.0

	$p = 0.5$	$p = 0.7$	$p = 0.9$	$p = 1.0$
$\hat{f}$	1616.10	1541.19	1439.13	1372.93
$\bar{f}$	1527.86	1403.33	1267.55	1214.78

(b) q=0.9

	$p = 0.5$	$p = 0.7$	$p = 0.9$	$p = 1.0$
$\hat{f}$	1635.06	1572.02	1496.88	1456.13
$\bar{f}$	1567.22	1481.12	1417.10	1387.14

(c) q=0.7

	$p = 0.5$	$p = 0.7$	$p = 0.9$	$p = 1.0$
$\hat{f}$	1638.59	1589.11	1530.88	1498.84
$\bar{f}$	1591.06	1529.36	1470.92	1450.93

(d) q=0.5

	$p = 0.5$	$p = 0.7$	$p = 0.9$	$p = 1.0$
$\hat{f}$	1603.83	1562.02	1512.67	1486.08
$\bar{f}$	1563.71	1513.11	1453.87	1424.61

5   Conclusion

In this paper, the known demand lead time case is compared with the unknown demand lead time case under imperfect demand information. They are formulated as Markov decision processes. Through the numerical experiments, we find that the known demand lead time makes the lower total expected cost, but the difference is small when the holding cost is small, or the fraction of urgent demand is large. In the latter cases, the demand lead time information is not important.

The extensive experiments and theoretical approach to compare the cases of known and unknown demand lead time are needed. In addition, when the demand size and demand lead time is bigger the optimal policy cannot be computed in the normal method of Markov decision process, and thus the other approximate or heuristic approach will be necessary to compute the sub-optimal order and return policy. They are left for future research.

Acknowledgments. This paper is partially supported by JSPS Grants-in-Aid for Scientific Research (C) Number 19K04904.

References

1. Gallego, G., Özer, Ö.: Integrating replenishment decisions with advance demand information. Manage. Sci. **47**(10), 1344–1360 (2001)
2. Karaesmen, F.: Value of advance demand information in production and inventory systems with shared resources. Handbook of Stochastic Models in Manufacturing System Operations, pp. 139–165, Springer, New York (2013). https://doi.org/10.1007/978-1-4614-6777-9_5
3. Liberopoulos, G.: On the tradeoff between optimal order base stock levels and demand lead-times. Eur. J. Oper. Res. **190**(1), 136–155 (2008)
4. Zhang, M., Wu, K., Sun, C., Pan, E.: Optimal decisions for a two-echelon supply chain with capacity and demand information. Adv. Eng. Inform. **39**, 248–258 (2019)
5. Liberopoulos, G., Koukoumialos, S.: On the effect of variability and uncertainty in advance demand information on the performance of a make-to-stock supplier. MIBES Trans. Int. J. **2**(1), 95–114 (2008)
6. Song, J.S., Zipkin, P.H.: Newsvendor problems with sequentially revealed demand information. Nav. Res. Logist. **59**, 601–612 (2012)
7. Gao, L., Xu, S.H., Ball, M.O.: Managing an available-to-promise assembly system with dynamic short-term pseudo-order forecast. Manage. Sci. **58**(4), 770–790 (2012)
8. Bernstein, F., Decroix, G.A.: Advance demand information in a multiproduct system. Manuf. Serv. Oper. Manag. **17**(1), 52–65 (2015)
9. Topan, E., Tan, T., van Houtum, G.-J., Dekker, R.: Using imperfect advance demand information in lost-sales inventory systems with the option of returning inventory. IISE Trans. **50**(1), 246–264 (2018)
10. Puterman, M.L. : Markov Decision Processes: Discrete Stochastic Dynamic Programming. Wiley, Hoboken (1994)

Tool for Nervousness Analysis in a Rolling Planning Environment via Historical Data

Walid Khellaf[1]([⊠]), Jacques Lamothe[1], and Romain Guillaume[2]

[1] IMT Mines Albi-Carmaux, 81000 Albi, France
{Walid.Khellaf,Jacques.Lamothe}@mines-albi.fr
[2] IRIT, University of Toulouse Jean Jaures, 31058 Toulouse, France
Romain.Guillaume@irit.fr

Abstract. This paper analyses the modifications of plans exchanged between supply chain actors in a tactical planning rolling horizon process. A particular focus is on the changes of planned quantities in order to respond to fluctuating demand or to adapt to internal contingencies of the organization. They create instability and nervousness in the planning system. This paper presents a data-driven study to compare the behavior of planning decision makers in a context of certain and uncertain demand. We show through simulation and statistical analysis the effect of decision characteristics of one actor on the system nervousness and the resulting uncertainty for the other actors.

Keywords: Tactical planning · Rolling horizon · Instability · Nervousness

1 Introduction

In the context of a decentralized supply chain, partners use independent MRP (Manufacturing Resource Planning) or DRP (Distribution Resource Planning) information systems to manage their cost and service planning. Their planning contains uncertain information that is naturally subject to changes in a rolling horizon process. In general, these variations in planned quantities during rescheduling lead to an undesirable phenomenon called instability or nervousness [1,2], consider MRP system nervousness as "instability in planned orders".

The instability can generate significant problems such as higher production and inventory costs [3], inefficient relationships between partners [4], a general loss of confidence in planning [5,6], and generally a bullwhip effect [7]. To make this complex planning system more stable, many solutions have been identified in the literature. Based on these techniques, some have proposed the use of safety stocks to cope with fluctuating sales forecasts, and safety lead times to cope with fluctuating delivery times [8]. [9] proposed to add an instability cost factor to the mathematical model which may mean that the solution is less optimal in terms of cost. [10] suggest improving the information sharing infrastructure between partners. The

© IFIP International Federation for Information Processing 2021
Published by Springer Nature Switzerland AG 2021
A. Dolgui et al. (Eds.): APMS 2021, IFIP AICT 630, pp. 475–483, 2021.
https://doi.org/10.1007/978-3-030-85874-2_50

adaptation of the planning of each actor thus becomes very complicated, because the source of nervousness can come from many different types of uncertainties [1]. Some are related to the uncertainties due to sales forecasting, others to the internal processes, see the following figure, the studies in this context have been suggested in the work [11] and they were questioned in this study.

In our study, we assess the nervousness associated with the plans received from partners in a rolling horizon process. Our objective is to study whether the nervousness is influenced by the choices of planners to develop their own planning or by demand variability.

This paper is divided into six sections. In Sect. 2, we present the type of supply chain to be treated in our case and the associated uncertain models for each actor. In Sect. 3, we present the Parameterized Simulation tool and the experimental protocol for data transformation in Sect. 4. The results of the experiment are detailed in Sect. 5. Finally, Sect. 6 is devoted to concluding remarks, including new directions for the simulation work.

2 Problem Description

The structure of the supply chain considered in this study is illustrated in Fig. 1. This chain involves three types of independent actors during the planning cycle and 4 actor decision situations. It starts with the elaboration of the supply requirement (SR) by the wholesalers in relation to the external requests received. The central distribution center receives it and issues a production plan (PP) to the factory. The factory plans production and sends a master production schedule (MPS). The central distribution center responds at the end of each cycle with a supply plan (SP) to the wholesalers. In rolling horizon planning, at each cycle, one actor can adjust his planning decisions, based on his own preferences. [12] considers 4 sources of variability: on demand, on supply, on the operational process, on management decisions. For other actors, these adjustments can be interpreted as uncertainty on their input information. It questioned the uncertainties of demand and with those distributed by the different actors. This generally increases the nervousness in the chain and generates a loss of confidence of the partners in the received plans. Therefore, an actor is facing a dilemma between

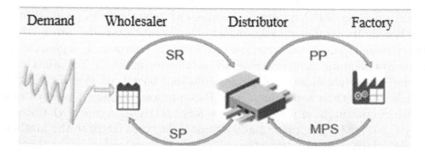

Fig. 1. Variability management in players of the studied supply chain.

stability of his decisions and adaptation to changes. [13] has given a special attention in decision-making approaches to adapt to variations in demand, by defining a robust plan that minimizes the difference between the reference plan and the re-schedule. [14] proposed a flexible planning model based on different planning strategies that are proposed to the decision maker (Min, Mean, Max) in the re-schedule calculation. Several other methods have been defined to mitigate nervousness. However, how can we face the management variation associated with the decision maker element?

Such complexity in analyzing the variation of quantities in the rescheduling process underlines the need to provide assistance to decision makers. The idea is to help the manager to (i) analyze the historical data of plans sent and received with the quantification of uncertainties, and (ii) understand his behavior and that of his partners.

In the present study, we were specifically interested in the planning process between a wholesaler, a distributor and a factory, while focusing on uncertainties assessment and the strategies adopted by each one to face the variation of the demand and/or the hazards.

3   Distributor-to-Wholesaler Model Under Uncertainty

Different forms of interaction between the stakeholders can be identified. These interactions are distinct by the nature of the objectives that the stakeholders set for themselves over certain planning horizon periods. We proceed in a similar way to model the successive 4 types of decisions identified in Fig. 1 and replicated in a rolling horizon process. For readability purposes, only one linear chain (Wholesaler Distributor Factory) has been treated in our study.

Parameters

H : Planning-horizon length
P : Number of products $p \in [1, P]$ is the product index
K : Planning index (k-th planning step)
F : Number of wholesaler $f \in [1, F]$ is the index of the wholesaler
HF : Length of the frozen horizon (expressed in number of periods)
HL : Length of the liquid horizon (expressed in number of periods)

Deterministic data

$D_{p,t}^k$: Demand for product p in period t at cycle k
$TS_{p,t}^k$: Target of product p at the end of period t at cycle k
ω_t^{TS} : Weight assigned to deviation from the target stock in period t
ω_t^{PP} : Weight assigned to deviation from previous plan in period t
ω_t^{S} : Weight assigned to Shortage in period t

Decision variables at cycle k

$I_{p,t}^k$: Inventory of product p at the end of period t

$SR_{p,t}^k$: Scheduled quantity (Supply requirement) of product p for period t

$S_{p,t}^k$: Shortage of product p in period t

$I_{p,t}^{k(+)}$: Upper target stock quantity (overstock) for product p in period t

$I_{p,t}^{k(-)}$: Lower target stock quantity (Under-stock) for product p in period t

$Q_{p,t}^{k(+)}$: Quantity added to planned quantity for product p in period t

$Q_{p,t}^{k(-)}$: Quantity reduced to planned quantity for product p in period t

$$Min \sum_{t\in HL-1, p\in P} \omega_t^{PP} * (Q_{p,t}^{k(+)} - Q_{p,l}^{k(-)}) + \omega_t^{TS} * (I_{p,t}^{k(+)} - I_{p,t}^{k(\ )}) + \omega_t^S * S_{p,t}^k \quad (1)$$

$$s.t. \begin{cases} SR_{p,t}^k = D_{p,t}^k + S_{p,(t-1)}^k + I_{p,t}^k - I_{p,(t-1)}^k - S_{p,t}^k & \forall t \in H \quad (2) \\ I_{p,t}^{k(+)} - I_{p,t}^{k(-)} = I_{p,t}^k - S_{p,t}^k - TS_{p,t}^k & \forall t \in HL \quad (3) \\ Q_{p,t}^{k(+)} - Q_{p,t}^{k(-)} = SR_{p,t}^k - SR_{p,t}^{(k-1)} & \forall t \in H-1 \quad (4) \\ SR_{p,t}^k = \sum_{j=t}^{t+Offset} D_{p,j}^k & \forall t \in H \quad (5) \\ SR_{p,t}^k = SR_{p,t}^{(k-1)} & \forall t \in H \quad (6) \\ SR_{p,t}^k, I_{p,t}^k, I_{p,t}^{k(+)}, I_{p,t}^{k(-)}, Q_{p,t}^{k(+)}, Q_{p,t}^{k(-)}, S_{p,t}^k \geq 0 \in \mathbb{N} & \forall t \in HF \quad (7) \end{cases}$$

The objective of the model (1) is to propose a compromise between three forms of strategies: (S1) stability over cycles of the planning (ω_t^{PP} is high), (S2) adjusting plans to maintain targeted inventories (ω_t^{TS} is high), (S3) avoiding shortage (ω_t^S is high). In general, (S3) is mandatory but the compromise between (S1) and (S2) is to be studied. The hypothesis here is that depending on parts of the planning horizon (from short term to long term) a decision maker can adapt his strategy and manage his decisions stability. It results a vector of weights $[\omega_t^{PP}, \omega_t^{TS}]$ that represents his behavior.

The constraints of the model are: (2) The constraint linking the shortages in finished products to their supply requirements and to the deliveries committed to the wholesalers (3) The deviation from the target stock (4) The deviation of the plan from the previous plan (5) Updating the stock level according to the planned receipts from the factory in period $(t + dt)$ (6) The target stock coverage time (7) The quantities fixed on the frozen horizon (8) Non-negativity constraints of the variables.

4   Methodology

The purpose of the simulation is to study the impact of the behavior of supply chain actors in a rolling horizon planning process. The behavior is linked to the mix of strategies in different parts of his planning horizons that an actor can consider: see objective function (1).

In this experimentation, we consider that all the decision makers have the same strategy during the whole rolling horizon process. It can be: Representing an assignment of ω_t for each period $t = 1, ..., H - 1$ by a vector $\omega = (\omega_1, ..., \omega_t)$

$\omega_t \in \{0, 1\}$: 1 maintain stability in the previous plan, 0 respect the target stock,
Let's assume the following strategy : ω_t^{TS} = Big value
ω_t^{PP} =[1,1,1,1,1,1,1,0,0,0,0,0,0,1,1,1,1,1,1,1,1,1,1,1,1,0,0,0,0,0,0,0]
ω_t^{TS} =[0,0,0,0,0,0,0,1,1,1,1,1,1,0,0,0,0,0,0,0,0,0,0,0,0,1,1,1,1,1,1,1]

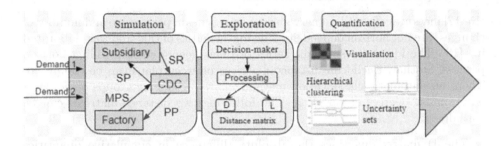

Fig. 2. Process of simulation, exploration and quantification of uncertainty (SEQ).

The methodology is based on a simulation of the rolling horizon process and then an analysis of the instability of the generated plans that can be interpreted as an uncertainty of the decision.

4.1 Simulation

This rolling horizon planning process replicates 260 planning cycles, over a 30-week horizon. The demand plans are updated weekly. Two types of demand are considered:

Case 1: stable demand: is randomly generated using a uniform distribution within the following interval U(50, 100), two seasonality: one during the summer period (week 23 to week 36) and the other during the new year (week 51 and 52). In addition, during the 260 planning cycles, the demand does not change.
Case 2: unstable demand: is the same as the stable demand for the initial plan, and during the following planning cycles changes according to the following perturbations summarized in Table 1.

Table 1. Perturbations applying to each period.

Period (t)	[1 - 2]	[3 - 15]	[15 - 29]	[30]
Random uniformly in range	frozen	$(-10, 10)$	$(-100, 100)$	$(-100, 100)$

The tool was developed using the Python 2.6 programming language, and the models defined above were solved using GLPK LP/MIP Solver v4.45 and Pyomo, a library available on Python for open-source constrained optimization. The choice of this simulation is justified, on one hand, by the current absence of massive data to analyze the different behaviors of the actors with all its complexity, and on the other hand, by the power of the simulation to generate behaviors in a logistics chain.

4.2   Exploration and Quantification

[15–17] measures of standard nervousness (max, mean, percentage and number of changes) are not horizon dependent. The mathematics of this step was elaborated in [18]. The idea is to store the series of plans generated in a rolling horizon process. So that, Euclidean distance matrices between plans can be computed. Then, an automatic classification method allows producing groups of horizons with similar degrees of variation. The following two distance matrices can be considered:

- The D matrix quantifies the absolute difference in cumulative quantities between two successive plans by the following equation: $D_{i,h} = Q_{i,i+h} - Q_{i+1,i+h}$ where Q is the cumulative quantity expected in plan i at period $i + h$. Over the re-planning cycles, D_{1,h_1} represents the first observation of difference of the cumulative quantities between two consecutive plans at first period.
- The L matrix, represents the absolute difference in cumulative quantities between the planned quantity and the really executed quantity (last planned) by the following equation: $L_{i,h} = Q_{i,i+h} - Q_{i+h,i+h}$. Similarly, $L_{1,h1}$ represents the first observation of difference between the cumulative quantities of plan 1 and plan realized, for this period. Finally, the information obtained in each horizon group is used to estimate the uncertainties of a plan. Different types of uncertainty estimation methods are possible: Mini max interval, or interquartile range [18].

5   Analyses and Results Interpretation

5.1   Case 1

While demand is stable, the idea of this study is to visualize the influence of both strategies mixed by each actor during the planning process. Therefore, instabilities only result of the actors'strategies.

In each cycle, the actors exchange plans over a rolling 30-week horizon. The first period of supply plan (SR) corresponds to the reception of really launched productions in the previous cycle. Now, let's look at the deviation matrices (see Fig. 2). For Wholesaler (SR), distribution (PP and SP) and factory (MPS), according to their distance matrices, we identify three clusters of periods. Two clusters have stable plans (green rectangles): one shows the frozen short term periods in which the decision-maker does not change his decisions. The other stable zone corresponds to the long term horizon in which the decision-maker tends to smooth out the deviation along the periods. The zone in the middle (rectangle red) corresponds to the period in which the decision-maker seeks to satisfy his local requirement, to respect the objective stock. In that way the strategy of the decision makers is visible. Moreover, the propagation of variability over the supply chain decisions (from the supply requirements to the other plans) can be noticed looking at the deviations between clusters. The brighter the colors, the more independent are the changes and thus the more variability appears (Fig. 3).

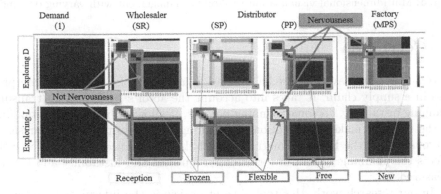

Fig. 3. Multidimensional visualization of management variability with constant demand. (Color figure online)

5.2   Case 2

In this section, we visualize also the impact of an unstable external demand when facing the same decisions strategy. We consider the stable demand during the [h1-h13] and unstable during the rest of the periods. The demand behavior is not synchronized with the decisions one. Let's explore the effects in (Fig. 4). We applied the same decisions strategy as for the stable demand. In horizon (h8-h13), a nervousness gradually arrives at the SP decision (throughout SR then PP then MPS) while demand is stable. It is caused by the adaptation strategy of the actors. Conversely, by the end of the horizon, while demand changes the decisions gradually become stable (throughout SR then PP then MPS and finally SP). As a consequence, the decision makers can impose a behavior that is decorrelated from the demand behavior: the farther is the decision in the process from the demand expression, the more decorrelated is the decision.

Demand (2)	Wholesaler (SR)	Distributor (SP)	(PP)	Factory (MPS)

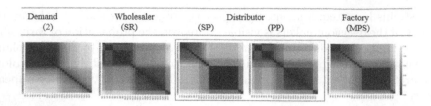

Fig. 4. Multidimensional visualization variability management with varying demand.

6   Conclusion

In this paper, we have proposed a simulation approach of a rolling horizon process in a supply chain. It takes into account the actor's preference to transmit planning instability, on some planning periods. It allows a better understanding of the decision makers conception of planning. The results of the analysis of nervousness by the D and L matrix showed that the choice of actor effectively affects the planning system in terms of nervousness and instability and can be measured.

In our research work, this tool aims at enriching the information and completing the existing decision support tools for the partners of the supply chain in terms of nervousness. However, this work can be spread in two ways. Firstly, to analyze the data of several wholesaler and several types of products because, the distributor generally supply their plans under a size of the most important constraints (e.g.: shipping constraint). Secondly, in analyzing the effects of actors that do not have the same decision strategies.

We applied the same decision strategy as for the stable demand. In horizon (h8-h13), a nervousness gradually arrives at the SP decision (throughout SR then PP then MPS) while demand is stable. It is caused by the adaptation strategy of the actors. Conversely, by the end of the horizon, while demand changes the decisions gradually become stable (throughout SR then PP then MPS and finally SP). As a consequence, the decision makers can impose a behavior that is decorrelated from the demand behavior: the farther is the decision in the process from the demand expression, the more decorrelated is the decision.

Acknowledgments. The authors would like to thank the ANR for funding the CAASC project. They also thank the project members who participated in the collection and archiving of the data.

References

1. Blackburn, J.D., Kropp, D.H., Millen, R.A.: MRP system nervousness: causes and cures. Eng. Costs Prod. Econ. **9**, 141–146 (1985). https://doi.org/10.1016/0167-188X(85)90021-7
2. Steele, D.C.: The nervous MRP system. J. Prod. Inventory Manage. **16**, 83–89 (1975)

3. Xie, J., Zhao, X., Lee, T.: Freezing the master production schedule under single resource constraint and demand uncertainty. Int. J. Prod. Econ. **83**, 65–84 (2003)
4. Sahin, F., Narayanan, A., Robinson, E.P.: Rolling horizon planning in supply chains: review, implications and directions for future research. Int. J. Prod. Res. **51**(18), 5413–5436 (2013)
5. De Kok, T., Inderfurth, K.: Nervousness in inventory management: comparison of basic control rules. Eur. J. Oper. Res. **103**, 55–82 (1997). https://doi.org/10.1016/S0377-2217(96)00255-X
6. Heisig, G.: Planning Stability in Material Requirements Planning Systems. Lecture notes in economics and mathematical system, vol. 515, pp. 15–40. Springer, Heidelberg (2002). https://doi.org/10.1007/978-3-642-55928-0
7. Lee H. L., Padmanabhan P., Whang S.: Information distortion in a supply chain: the bullwhip effect. Manage. Sci. **43**(4), 546–558 (1997)
8. Koh, S.C.L., Saad, S.M., Jones, M.H.: Uncertainty under MRP-planned manufacture: review and categorization. Int. J. Prod. Res. **40**(10), 2399–2421 (2002)
9. Carlson, R.C., Jucker, J.V., Kropp, D.H.: Less nervous MRP systems: a dynamic economic lot-sizing approach. Manage. Sci. **25**(8), 754–761 (1979)
10. Pujawan, I. N., Smart, A. U., Whang S.: Factors affecting schedule instability in manufacturing. Int. J. Prod. Res. **50**(8), 2252–2266 (2012)
11. Suja, S., Janet, S., Luisa, H., Anisoara, C.: Reducing schedule instability by identifying and omitting complexity-adding information flows at the supplier-customer interface. Int. J. Prod. Econ. **145**, 253–262 (2013)
12. Ptak, C., Smith, C.: Demand driven material requirements planning (DDMRP). Industrial Press (2016)
13. Genin, P., Lamouri, S., Thomas, A.: Nervousness in inventory Impact de l'utilisation d'un plan de référence sur la robustesse de la planification tactique. Journal Européen des Systèmes Automatisés (JESA), pp. 777–798 (2005)
14. Galasso, F., Thierry, C.: Design of cooperative processes in a customer-supplier relationship: an approach based on simulation and decision theory. Eng. Appl. Artif. Intell. **22**, 865–881 (2009). https://doi.org/10.1016/j.engappai.2008.10.008
15. Sridharan, V., Berry, W.L., Udayabhanu, V.: Measuring master production schedule. Decision Sci. **19**(1), 147–166 (1988)
16. Herrera, C., Belmokhtar-Berraf, S., Thomas, A., Parada, V.: A reactive decision-making approach to reduce instability in a master production schedule. Int. J. Prod. Res. **54**(8), 2394–2404 (2016)
17. Olof, S., Sahil, A.: Improving Planning Stability: A case study of Planning at AstraZeneca. Master Thesis 30hp. Production Economics (2020)
18. Khellaf, W., Lamothe, J., Guillaume, R.: Exploration de données de planification pour la modélisation des incertitudes dues à l'horizon glissant.13ème Conférence internationale de Modélisation, Optimisation et Simulation. MOSIM'20, Maroc. (2020)

A Preliminary Overview of Ramp-Up Management Practices in Crisis Context

Doae Riffi Maher[1] and Khaled Medini[2]([envelope])

[1] Mines Saint-Etienne, University Clermont Auvergne, CNRS,
UMR 6158 LIMOS, F-42023 Saint-Etienne, France
`doae.riffimaher@etu.emse.fr`
[2] Henri Fayol Institute, Mines Saint-Etienne, Univ Clermont Auvergne, CNRS, UMR 6158
LIMOS, 42023 Saint-Etienne, France
`khaled.medini@emse.fr`

Abstract. Production ramp-up is a key stage in the product life cycle since it can determine whether a product's launch into the market or the increase of production capacity succeeds or fails. Ramp-up as a phase of value creation, begins with the completion of a product's design and ends with the reach of maximum production capacity. In today's world, there is a significant advance in technology but simultaneously there is an increasing uncertainty as we have experienced with the Covid-19 crisis. Within this context, the importance of ramp-up management become more than ever evident. Whilst some products like face masks saw their demand increase drastically, some other companies had to shut off their production or switch to manufacture new products like hand sanitizers. Hence, it is critical today to have a successful ramp-up management in order to predict and meet clients' demand in terms of quality and quantity. This paper aims to provide a set of guidelines for ramp-up management considering crisis context. The paper relies on an exploratory research coupling literature analysis and interviews among practitioners. The insights drawn from the literature and from the interviews are expected to provide decision makers with valuable guidance with regard to ramp-up management.

Keywords: Ramp-up · Agility · Crisis · Strategy · Practices · Guidelines

1 Introduction

The study of ramp-up in production is an issue that has been around for a long time in manufacturing and service industries. Whether it is the increase in production capacity to meet rising market demand or the introduction of a new product, ramp-up as a basic concept is still familiar yet challenging to production managers and even to the company's support functions. However, the technological advances that the world is experiencing today, whether in terms of the techniques used or even the business models of companies, mean that ramp-up today is no longer limited to its classic definition of increasing production capacity. On the contrary, in the context of a pandemic crisis, for

© IFIP International Federation for Information Processing 2021
Published by Springer Nature Switzerland AG 2021
A. Dolgui et al. (Eds.): APMS 2021, IFIP AICT 630, pp. 484–492, 2021.
https://doi.org/10.1007/978-3-030-85874-2_51

example, a good management of ramp-down would be judged by looking at the level of flexibility of the means of production to produce less, or even to completely disrupt the activity of the company or the product delivered. Hence, we can but presume that with the enhancement of Industry 4.0 and the use of technologies it brought about will significantly improve the ramp-up quality, provided that its conduct is carried on in an agile way and in the context of a flexible and resilient production system as well as workforce. Therefore, ramp-up literature started to receive more attention during the last decade focusing mainly on the conceptualization of the ramp-up phase. This helped lay foundations for further research to improve ramp-up performance mainly from cost and time perspectives. Looking into the scientific literature, there is no obvious answer to agility and resilience challenges. In fact, the current sanitary and climate crises unveiled the need for extending traditional performance perspective in order to integrate agility principles and sustainability objectives in ramp-up management. Further on, the sanitary crisis put forth the need for quick ramp-up in a variety of sectors, whilst most of the research development in this field involves only few sectors such as automotive and microelectronics industry [1].

This paper aims to provide a set of guidelines for ramp-up management considering crisis context. The paper relies on an exploratory research coupling literature analysis and interviews among practitioners. The remainder of the paper is organized as follows, Sect. 2 provides an overview of ramp-up management related concepts. Section 3 reports on two case studies. Section 4 discusses the results and provides future outlooks. The paper ends with a brief conclusion in Sect. 5. The insights drawn from the literature and from the case studies are expected to provide decision makers with valuable guidance with regard to ramp-up management in crisis context.

2 State of the Art on Ramp-Up Management

2.1 Ramp-Up Phase Overview and Characteristics

The ramp-up phase occurs when a new product is introduced in a company's portfolio but also when a new process or a new plant starts up [1]. Terwiesch and Yi [2] add that during this phase, the production shifts from development on a small laboratory-like scale into a high-volume-production environment. Hence, the actual aim of production ramp-up is generally expressed in terms of increasing the volume output from a zero level to a steady state production with a volume output which has been planned for [3]. To well place ramp-up phase in a lifecycle of a product (Fig. 1), it is commonly accepted to define ramp-up as the connecting phase between product development and series production [4]. From all the previous definitions, we can see that the definition of ramp-up is strongly connected to the introduction of a new production or production system. However, this general definition can find exceptions to it in the automotive industry for instance. Actually, the specificity of this industry is that the new product introduction projects (aka ramp-up projects) do not always refer to products which are completely new. They can actually concern face-lifting or bringing about changes in existing models [1].

In addition to its temporality feature, the ramp-up phase has some other inherent features such as low initial level of knowledge about the product and the process, low production output, higher cycle time, low production capacity, high demand, high disturbances in process, supply chain or product quality and lack of planning reliability [1, 5]. As a matter of fact, the change management when it comes to the introduction of a new product or process comes along with an urging necessity of learning and training of the workforce. It is then no wonder to see that training and learning are among the most critical factors affecting the production ramp-up both before and after its implementation. The high disturbance observed in production processes and supply chain justifies that supplier inclusion, verification and relations are as well amongst the critical components of the production ramp-up success [3]. Figure 1 gives a larger insight regarding the critical factors affecting production ramp-up in the pre- and post-phases.

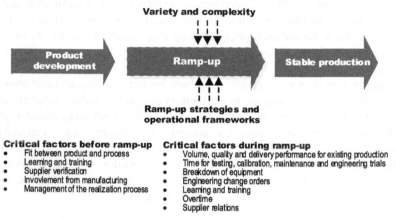

Fig. 1. Ramp-up phase in product life cycle and critical factors during and before production ramp-up. Ramp-up is supported by ramp-up strategies and operational frameworks and challenged by variety and complexity of products and production systems.

2.2 Ramp-Up Strategies

As discussed above, the ramp-up phase has some characteristics which distinguish it from the mature product phase. In fact, the high uncertainty which defines this phase [1, 4, 6] makes the probability of occurrence of discrepancies as well as their variety much higher than for a mature product. Hence, the management techniques that apply for mature products do not have a great performance when it comes to production ramp-up phase. To deal with the peculiarities of ramp-up phase, several strategies can be pursued. Schuh, Desoi, and Tücks [7], suggest three generic ramp-up strategies depending mainly on product variety and induced complexity [1, 3]. The objectives of each of the strategies and the adequate use cases are summarized in Table 1. These strategies provide general insights into how to proceed with ramp-up in a multi-variant context. They do not provide however operational guidance on how to deploy these strategies.

In an early study in the automotive industry, Clark and Fujimoto [8] looked deeper into the work force policy as well as the operations pattern during ramp-up. They described various techniques that were used in final assembly for the ramp-up of new products. The strategies consist of a mixture of decisions about how to address the ramp-up with regard to three distinct aspects. These three aspects are ramp-up curve, operation pattern, and policy of the workforce [1, 3, 6]. These choices result in two possible ramp-up strategies of the three aspects combined, "step-by-step" and "shut down". A "Step-by-step" strategy implies stability and control of operating conditions and work assignment. "Shut-down" strategy implies low initial complexity both due to material handling and work force involvement but in the long run task continuity and operation stability will suffer [8].

Table 1. Ramp-up strategies according to Schuh, Desoi, and Tücks [7]

Ramp-up strategy	Aims for	Suits
Slow motion	Parallel ramp-up of several variants on a constant and low volume level until all processes are verified	Highly automated processes
Dedication	Ramp-up of all different variants with accumulative volumes and a gathered launch of these. Elimination of problems on an early stage that will not occur	High product variety and high logistic capability
Step-by-step	Sequential ramp-up of consecutive variants with high complexity	High technical complexity

In order to assess the efficiency of the ramp-up, several Key Performance Indicators (KPIs) are considered, which can be categorized into four general classes [1]: cost related (i.e. investments and manpower used to make up capacity loss), quality related (e.g. yield), volume related (e.g. capacity utilization) and time related (e.g. cycle time and time-to-market). While some of the KPIs seem to be significant, there is an issue regarding time related KPIs. Time-to-volume needs to have the exact same level of importance as time-to-market because the imbalance between the two can result in disastrous financial consequences. Furthermore, used KPIs rarely consider the customer point of view, which may be quite harmful for low-volume industries or customized goods.

3 Case Studies

In this section, we present two concrete examples for ramp-up management. In order to check whether research findings apply to real-world industries, we have interviewed two practitioners from local companies on their ramp-up management but also regarding their sanitary crisis management, environmental crisis engagement and workforce management. The choice of local companies from two different sectors was with the aim to have the opportunity to compare on a local level, the ramp-up experience of the industrials. It was also an opportunity to understand whether the field of activity and the company size among other factors are determining in the quality of ramp-up management and the resilience in the context of a crisis such as the current Covid-19 pandemic.

The interviews were conducted by following an interview guide. The questions of this guide were inspired from the scientific literature conclusions seen in Sect. 2. These questions involve current and past ramp-up management practices, ramp-up challenges for the company, considerations of environmental impact during ramp-up, and Covid-19 crisis impact on operational ramp-up management and on employees and workforce.

3.1   Results from Interview 1 – Cycling Industry

The first interview was conducted with a local start-up (company A) that operates in the field of manufacturing cargo bikes. During the interview, the company's director was asked questions as per the interview guide. Ramp-up management practices derived from the interview are structured in a set of guidelines which are summarized in Table 2.

Generally, the case of company A shows that the crisis does not necessarily have a negative impact on the activity of all companies. The impact is indeed related to the activity field and the type of products that the company offers. In this particular case, the demand for bicycles as a safer alternative in the current sanitary crisis helped boost the enterprise's demand and gave the company a great opportunity for growth. Actually, the decision of ramping up the production in company A was rather inspired by the increasing demand of bikes as a more hygienic and safer alternative to using shared cars or public transportation in the context of a worldwide pandemic.

3.2   Results from Interview 2 – Additive Manufacturing

The second interview was conducted with company B which is a local Small/Medium sized Enterprise (SME) operating in the field of additive manufacturing (AM). During the interview, an expert from AM department was asked questions as per the interview guide. Ramp-up management practices derived from the interview are structured in a set of guidelines, which are summarized in Table 3.

Generally, the interview with company B supports that the activity field and the level of technology are determining factors with regard to ramp-up management as well as to its response to crisis context. In the field of additive manufacturing, especially in the phase of pre-ramp-up, total remote work is possible. Hence, this part of activity of the company is not heavily affected by the Covid-19 crisis. During the interview, great emphasis was put on the change management and collaboration between all the stakeholders within the company as well as the various supply chain actors for a successful ramp-up. Furthermore, the accuracy between the business plan and the progress of ramp-up is one aspect that can measure the performance of ramp-up as it goes.

Table 2. Ramp-up guideline derived from interview 1

Area	Recommendation
Collaboration	Collaboration among the totality of company departments that are directly or indirectly affected with ramp-up keeps the motivation and communication running well among the company staff
Standardization	Standardization of the processes is the key for a better learning curve of the employees which can help realize a faster launch of the product in terms of time-to-market. Additionally, standardization helps have a more flexible workforce (since the work to be done does not rely solely on the person in charge of the task but is rather well-explained so that any other teammate or new staff member can learn the job fast)
Resilience	Resilience towards unfortunate and unexpected events like the current Covid-19 crisis is a key factor when it comes to ramp-up. This can be achieved with a surge-capacity in anticipation of unexpected demand. Resilience is also better achieved with having a surge ramp-up team (with the use of temporary workers or subcontractors)
Supply chain	Relationship with supply chain actors is crucial when it comes to ramp-up decisions. The collaboration with local supply chain actors can be a great way to overcome shortage in raw materials or difficulties in transportations due to closing borders as we have seen in the context of the Covid-19 crisis. Localised supply chain actors are also another step towards a more eco-friendly and sustainable solution
Business plan	Having a solid business plan justifying the ramp-up decision. The first objective of a company is to generate profit. Consequently, the decision of ramp-up must be justified with the company's financial profit projection. Having a solid business plan helps make sure that the income will outweigh the cost of investment (in machinery acquisition, recruitment, training…)
Knowledge management	Relying on individuals' knowledge rather than establishing standardized processes is a big obstacle that ramp-up management can face. In the case of company A, this has proven to be a big burden that brakes the ramp-up progress. Within this company, the fact that knowledge is dependent on the experience of the staff makes it very difficult to transmit to new employees. Consequently, this may mean that departure of the experienced member of staff can alter the whole process of the company or even stop its activity

Table 3. Ramp-up guideline derived from interview 2

Area	Recommendation
Collaboration	Collaboration among the totality of actors (design office, management, sales, logistics and purchasing, infrastructure and buildings, etc.) that are directly or indirectly affected by ramp-up is crucial. This means that not only internal stakeholders are concerned but some external actors take part in the ramp-up decision and execution as well

(*continued*)

Table 3. (*continued*)

Area	Recommendation
Information system	Information system is a primordial aspect when it comes to ramp-up management. The collaborative tools make it possible for different actors to share real time data and for the communication to run smoothly as well. Additionally, having a solid and up-to-date information technology within the company makes it easier to tackle teleworking like in Covid-19 crisis
Resilience	Resilience towards unfortunate and unexpected events like the current Covid-19 crisis is a key factor when it comes to ramp-up. This can be achieved with a surge-capacity in anticipation of unexpected demand. Resilience is also better achieved with having a surge ramp-up team (with the use of temporary workers or subcontractors). Resilience is also better achieved through training on change management
Supply chain	Similarly to the first interview, it was seen that the collaboration with local supply chain actors can be a great way to overcome shortage in raw materials or difficulties in transportations. In some fields like additive manufacturing, there is a limited number of suppliers as the processes may completely change from one project to another. However, one thing to do is to always try and have as large as possible of a supplier panel in order to be well equipped to face shortage of raw materials supply but also to have the choice regarding the cost of sourcing
Anticipating technical issues	As discussed with company B, the tests and prototypes of series manufacturing in the pre-ramp-up phase help the industrials make better projections on their needs of material and human resources. It is also a mean of anticipating technical issues that can occur on a big scale by tackling them on a reduced prototype scale
Process flexibility	When starting from scratch for the launch of a new product, a new process is also introduced. However, the discussion with company B has shown that this process needs to fit into the existing value chain present in the company (current machinery available) but also that it should require the least investment when it comes to training the workforce
Adapting to employees' needs	It is clear that one major aspect of ramp-up management is the workforce. Consequently, it is natural that the company needs to prepare its employees for change management or for learning new skills that will be needed for the ramp-up phase. In the case of company B, a lesson of the Covid-19 sanitary crisis would be to consider the employees' preferences regarding remote work or in-site presence and try to satisfy them when it is possible

(*continued*)

Table 3. (*continued*)

Area	Recommendation
Cost estimate	Underestimating the cost of ramp-up entails a highly critical risk. Before launching the actual ramp-up phase, it seems just as important during the pre-ramp-up phase to work precisely on the projections of the business plan in terms of profit but also regarding the cost plan. This anticipation (over estimation) of the costs of ramp-up prevents the company from the risk of encountering additional unexpected costs during the journey of ramp-up in terms of quality and time. During the interview with company B, the technical risks that were pointed out are an example of these costs that need to be anticipated rather than endured

4 Discussion and Perspectives

Shorter product lifecycles and the rising complexity of new products and processes led to a greater importance of ramp-up management in production. As the degree of product innovation also rises, there is a rapid rise in the total number of complex production ramp-ups and coordination of ramp-up activities becomes part of everyday business. The sanitary crisis unveiled the limitations of current ramp-up practices in the manufacturing and service industries to ensure agility and resilience. Innovative approaches are then needed to ensure quick and efficient ramp-up meeting individual and global demands.

The current paper contributed towards this objective by an explorative research which examined the scientific literature and relied on interviews to report on ramp-up practices considering the crisis context. The first results (set of guidelines) provided insights into how to deal with ramp-up management which are useful for decision makers in additive manufacturing and in cycling industry and beyond.

Further research is ongoing in order to extend the results. For instance, the interviews that were conducted individually with local industrials have given us a good beginning in the path of looking for ramp-up management guidelines. However, two companies are not statistically a concluding sample. Therefore, we have decided to go from a qualitative approach of personalised interviews to a quantitative approach with a massive survey. The aim behind the launch of this survey will be to have it answered by practitioners on a larger scale (both locally and internationally). The results of such survey will give further insights on how different countries, company sizes, fields of activity and teams' organisation affect the success or failure of ramp-up management. By the time this survey will be launched, it will also help have a more mature and fact-based opinion on the impact of the Covid-19 crisis both on the production management and on ramp-up management; as well as the strategies that the companies would have developed to tackle this particular pandemic context.

5 Conclusion

This paper reviews ramp-up management literature spanning ramp-up definitions, management strategies and KPIs. This supported the preparation and fine-tuning of interview questions to gain insights from practitioners. Subsequently a set of best practices were derived and summarized into specific areas to guide decision makers, particularly in crisis context. Ultimately, the ongoing research is expected to support a shift in manufacturing and service sectors to more agile and resilient production systems and supply networks.

Acknowledgements. This work is supported by the German-French Academy for the Industry of the Future through RAMP-UP Seed project (https://www.future-industry.org/research/advanced-manufacturing/ramp-up/).

References

1. Surbier, L., Alpan, G., Blanco, E.: A comparative study on production ramp-up: state-of-the-art and new challenges. Prod. Plann. Control **25**(15), 1264–1286 (2014)
2. Terwiesch, C., Yi, X.: The copy-exactly ramp-up strategy: trading-off learning with process change. IEEE Trans. Eng. Manage. **51**(1), 70 (2005)
3. Berg, M., Säfsten, K.: Managing Production Ramp-up- Requirement on strategy content. Jönköping University, Sweden, Department of Industrial Engineering and Management (2006)
4. Medini, K., Pierné, A., Erkoyuncu, J.A., Cornet, C.: A Model for cost-benefit analysis of production ramp-up strategies. In: Lalic, B., Majstorovic, V., Marjanovic, U., von Cieminski, G., Romero, D. (eds.) APMS 2020. IAICT, vol. 592, pp. 731–739. Springer, Cham (2020). https://doi.org/10.1007/978-3-030-57997-5_84
5. Dombrowskia, U., Wullbrandta, J., Krenkela, P.: Industrie 4.0 in production ramp-up management. In: Proceedings of the 28th International Conference on Flexible Automation and Intelligent Manufacturing, Procedia, Columbus, OH, USA (2018)
6. Slamanig, M., Winkler, H.: An exploration of ramp-up strategies in the area of mass customisation. Int. J. Mass Custom. **4**(1–2), 22–43 (2011)
7. Schuh, G., Desoi, J., Tücks, G.: Holistic approach for production ramp-up in automotive industry. In: Advances in Integrated Design and Manufacturing in Mechanical Engineering, Bramley, A., Brissaud, D., Coutellier, D., McMahon, C. (eds.), pp. 255–268. Springer, Cham (2005). https://doi.org/10.1007/1-4020-3482-2_20
8. Clark, K.B., Fujimoto, T.: Product Development Performance: Strategy, Organization, and Management in the World Auto Industry. HBS Press, Boston (1991)

Optimization of a Periodic Review Joint Replenishment Policy for a Stochastic Inventory System

Lei Wang and Haoxun Chen[✉]

Logistics and Optimization of Industrial Systems, Laboratory LIST3N,
University of Technology of Troyes, 12 rue Marie Curie, CS 42060,
10004 Troyes CEDEX, France
{lei.wang1,haoxun.chen}@utt.fr

Abstract. A stochastic inventory system with multiple products controlled by a periodic review joint replenishment policy $P(s, S_i)$ is considered. This system places a joint replenishment order to bring the inventory position of each item i to its order-up-to level S_i when the aggregate reorder point of all items drops below s at each review moment. By imposing service levels on the system, we propose an algorithm for optimizing the policy to minimize the total cost of the system. The performance of this algorithm is evaluated by numerical experiments on randomly generated instances.

Keywords: Inventory management · Joint replenishment · Optimization · Monte Carlo simulation

1 Introduction

The rapid growth of e-commerce is phenomenal in recent years. Due to the Covid-19 pandemic, more and more customers choose to shop online, Amazon delivered a record performance in 2020 with annual revenue up 38% to $386 billion. Many e-commerce organizations such as Amazon and Alibaba want to reduce costs while improving service levels to customers. Effective inventory management can improve the competitiveness of these e-commerce companies in the new retail business.

Joint replenishment becomes popular in inventory management because of its advantage of economies of scale. For a systematic review of studies on Joint Replenishment Problem (JRP), please see [1] and [2]. We study a stochastic JRP (SJRP) with stochastic demand. According to [3], a stochastic inventory system can be controlled by a continuous review or periodic review joint replenishment policy.

(Q, S) policy and its extensions are typical continuous review policies. Under this policy, a joint replenishment order is triggered whenever the aggregate demand of all items since the last order reaches a quantity Q, and all items are ordered up to their individual order-up-to levels given by the vector S [3]. Optimizing this policy requires very complex mathematical models, such as Markov chains [4] and renewal theory [5].

© IFIP International Federation for Information Processing 2021
Published by Springer Nature Switzerland AG 2021
A. Dolgui et al. (Eds.): APMS 2021, IFIP AICT 630, pp. 493–501, 2021.
https://doi.org/10.1007/978-3-030-85874-2_52

Periodic review policies are another important category of joint replenishment policies. [6] proposed a (T, S) policy, where $S = (S_i, i = 1, 2, ..., N)$ and N is the number of items considered. Under this policy, each item i is ordered to its order-up-to level S_i in each review interval T. Since inventory is usually periodically reviewed in practice, we consider a periodic review joint replenishment policy in this paper.

In the literature, most researchers considered the shortage costs of an inventory system when optimizing it. Costs are incurred when customer demand cannot be met immediately due to out of stock. The shortage costs are mainly reflected in two aspects: one is the current loss, and the other is the future loss. The current loss is the loss caused by the lost sales opportunity and the penalty to be paid to customers in case of late delivery. The future loss is the potential loss of sales opportunity due to the loss of trust of customers. This potential loss is difficult to be evaluated, so are the shortage costs. Moreover, inventory managers are more concerned about service levels. For the two reasons, we consider service level constraints rather than shortage costs in our study.

In this paper, we study a periodic-review joint replenishment inventory system controlled by a $P(s, S_i)$ policy with service level constraint for each item. Under this policy, the inventory status of the system is reviewed at the beginning of each period, if the aggregate inventory position (the sum of the inventory positions) of all items drops below the joint reorder point s, a joint replenishment order will be placed to raise the inventory position of each item i to its order-up-to level S_i. We propose an algorithm for optimizing the policy to minimize the total cost of systems composed of major ordering costs, minor ordering costs, and inventory holding costs.

To the best of our knowledge, no work in the literature considered the optimization of such an inventory policy. The contributions of this paper are highlighted as follows:

1. We study the optimization of $P(s, S_i)$ policy for a periodic-review joint replenishment inventory system with service level constraints and derive analytically exact expressions for the cost function and the service levels of the system.
2. We propose an efficient algorithm for optimizing the parameters of the $P(s, S_i)$ policy.
3. We conduct extensive numerical experiments to evaluate the efficiency of the algorithm.

The rest of this paper is organized as follows. Section 2 introduces a periodic review joint replenishment inventory system controlled by $P(s, S_i)$ policy and formulates the inventory policy optimization of the system. An algorithm for finding optimal parameters of the policy is presented in Sect. 3. Section 4 reports numerical results of evaluation of the algorithm on randomly generated instances. The final section concludes this paper with remarks for future research.

2   Problem Description and Formulation

In this section, we describe the joint replenishment problem studied and establish its mathematical model.

2.1 Problem Description

We consider a single stock inventory system with N items that are joint replenished. The demand of each item in each period is stochastic and follows an independent normal distribution. This system is controlled by a periodic review $P(s, S_i)$ policy, where s is the joint reorder point s of all items and S_i is the order-up-level of item i, $i = 1, 2, ..., N$.

It is assumed that all items have the same replenishment lead time L. Major ordering costs, minor ordering costs and inventory holding costs are incurred in this system. In addition, we consider the service level constraint of each item in the system as mentioned above, that is, the service level of each item must be higher than a prespecified level. The problem is to optimize the periodic review $P(s, S_i)$ policy for this system so that the total expected cost per period is minimized subject to the service level constraint for each item.

We first define Q such that:

$$\sum_{i=1}^{N} S_i - s = Q \tag{1}$$

$P(s, S_i)$ policy is more complex than (Q, S) policy, because under (Q, S) policy, the aggregate ordering quantity of all items is always Q, whereas under $P(s, S_i)$ policy, the joint order quantity of all items is not fixed and may be larger than Q.

Before presenting the model for optimizing $P(s, S_i)$ policy, the indices, parameters, decision variables, and other related variables are given as follows.

Indices. i: index of item i, $i \in N$, where N is the number of items considered.
   t: index of period t. $t \in T$, where T is the number of periods considered.

Parameters. L: replenishment lead time of each item, it is a constant.
   A: major ordering cost incurred in each replenishment.
   a_i: minor ordering cost for item i ordered in each replenishment.
   h_i: holding cost per unit per period for item i.
   α_i: target α service level (cycle service level) for item i.
   $d_i(t)$: demand of item i in period t, $d_i(t) \sim N(\mu_i, \sigma_i^2)$.
   $d(t)$: aggregate demand of all items in period t, $d(t) = \sum_{i=1}^{N} d_i(t)$.
   $f_i(\cdot), F_i(\cdot)$: p.d.f and c.d.f of the demand of item i in each period.
   μ_i, σ_i: mean and standard deviation of the demand of item i in each period.

Decision Variables. S: aggregate reorder point.
   S_i: order-up-to level for item i.

Other Variables. r: the number of periods between two consecutive joint replenishments including the period of the second replenishment, i.e., the second replenishment occurs after r periods. The number r is a random integer variable, $r = 1, 2, \ldots, \infty$.
   $P(n)$: the probability of $r = n$, $n = 1, 2, \ldots, \infty$.

$D(n)$: aggregate demand of all items in n periods when $r = n$, $D(n) = \sum_{t=1}^{n} d(t)$,

$D(n) \sim N\left(n \sum_{i=1}^{N} \mu_i, n \sum_{i=1}^{N} \sigma_i^2\right)$, and $D(n)=D(n-1)+d(n)$.

$TC(n)$: total expected cost of n periods when $r = n$.

TC: expected total cost per period.

2.2 Problem Formulation

We first analyse $P(n)$. Let $S = \sum_{i=1}^{N} S_i$, since $P(s, S_i)$ is a periodic review ordering policy, the conditions that trigger a replenishment order after n periods since the last replenishment can be expressed as: $S - D(n) \leq s$ and $S - D(n-1) > s$, where n is a positive integer.

Since the demands $d(1), \dots d(n)$ are independent, we have:

$$D(n) \sim N\left(n \sum_{i=1}^{N} \mu_i, n \sum_{i=1}^{N} \sigma_i^2\right), D(n-1) \sim N\left((n-1) \sum_{i=1}^{N} \mu_i, (n-1) \sum_{i=1}^{N} \sigma_i^2\right).$$

$$\mu_{D(n)} = n \sum_{i=1}^{N} \mu_i, \sigma_{D(n)} = \sqrt{n \sum_{i=1}^{N} \sigma_i^2}.$$

$$\mu_{D(n-1)} = (n-1) \sum_{i=1}^{N} \mu_i, \sigma_{D(n-1)} = \sqrt{(n-1) \sum_{i=1}^{N} \sigma_i^2}.$$

The two random variables $D(n)$ and $D(n-1)$ may be correlated. Define the coefficient of correlation between $D(n)$ and $D(n-1)$ as: $\rho_n = \frac{\text{cov}(D(n),D(n-1))}{\sigma_{D(n)}\sigma_{D(n-1)}}$. We can get:

$P(n)=P\{D(n) \geq S-s, D(n-1) < S-s\}$

$$=\int_{S-s}^{+\infty}\int_{-\infty}^{S-s} \frac{1}{2\pi\sigma_{D(n)}\sigma_{D(n-1)}\sqrt{1-\rho_n^2}} \exp\left[-\frac{1}{2(1-\rho_n^2)}\left[\frac{(x-\mu_{D(n)})^2}{\sigma_{D(n)}^2}+\frac{(y-\mu_{D(n-1)})^2}{\sigma_{D(n-1)}^2}-2\rho_n\frac{(x-\mu_{D(n)})(y-\mu_{D(n-1)})}{\sigma_{D(n)}\sigma_{D(n-1)}}\right]\right]dxdy$$

(2)

Obviously, the sum of all probabilities $P(n)$ is 1.

$$\sum_{n=1}^{\infty} P(n) = 1 \tag{3}$$

We then derive the cost function of the system. The expected total ordering cost of the system per period is given by:

$$C_o = \sum_{n=1}^{\infty} C_o(n)P(n) = \sum_{n=1}^{\infty}\left(\frac{A}{n}+\sum_{i=1}^{N}\frac{a_i}{n}\right)P(n) \tag{4}$$

where $C_o(n)$ is the total ordering cost in case one order is placed every n periods, and $P(n)$ is the probability of $r = n$.

Define the probability density function of one period demand and that of lead time demand of each item i as:

$$\phi_i(u) = \frac{1}{\sqrt{2\pi}\sigma_i}e^{-\frac{[u-\mu_i]^2}{2\sigma_i^2}} \tag{5}$$

$$\phi_i^L(u) = \frac{1}{\sqrt{2\pi}\sigma_i \times \sqrt{L}}e^{-\frac{[u-\mu_i \times L]^2}{2\sigma_i^2 \times L}} \tag{6}$$

The expected holding cost per period of the system, denoted by C_h, can be written as Eq. (7):

$$C_h = \sum_{n=1}^{\infty} C_h(n) P(n)$$

$$= \sum_{n=1}^{\infty} \left(\int_0^{S_1}\cdots\int_0^{S_2}\cdots\int_0^{S_i}\cdots\int_0^{S_N} \cdots \frac{1}{n}\sum_{k=1}^{n}\sum_{i=1}^{N} h_i \left(S_i - u_i^L - \sum_{j=1}^{k} u_{ij} \right) \cdot \prod_{i=1}^{N}(\phi_i^L(u_i^L)\phi_i(u_{i1})\phi_i(u_{i2})\ldots\phi_i(u_{in}))\prod_{i=1}^{N}(du_i^L du_{i1}du_{i2}\ldots du_{in}) \right) P(n) \tag{7}$$

In this equation, $C_h(n)$ is the holding cost per period in case an order is placed every n periods, and $P(n)$ is the probability of $r = n$; u_i^L represents the actual demand of item i during the lead time of L periods; u_{ij} represents the actual demand of item i in period j during the lead time; $\sum_{i=1}^{N}\sum_{j=1}^{n-1}u_{ij} < Q$ and $\sum_{i=1}^{N}\sum_{j=1}^{n}u_{ij} \geq Q$ are two conditions for the placement of an order every n periods.

From the above analysis, the expected total cost per period, denoted by TC, is given by the following Eq. (8)

$$TC = \sum_{n=1}^{\infty} TC(n) P(n) = C_o + C_h$$

$$= \sum_{n=1}^{\infty} \left(\frac{A}{n} + \sum_{i=1}^{N}\frac{a_i}{n} + \int_0^{S_1}\cdots\int_0^{S_2}\cdots\int_0^{S_i}\cdots\int_0^{S_N} \cdots \frac{1}{n}\sum_{k=1}^{n}\sum_{i=1}^{N} h_i \left(S_i - u_i^L - \sum_{j=1}^{k} u_{ij} \right) \cdot \prod_{i=1}^{N}(\phi_i^L(u_i^L)\phi_i(u_{i1})\phi_i(u_{i2})\ldots\phi_i(u_{in}))\prod_{i=1}^{N}(du_i^L du_{i1}du_{i2}\ldots du_{in}) \right) P(n) \tag{8}$$

Next, we formulate the service level for each item in the system. We first define:

$LTD_i(n)$: the lead time demand of item i in case one order is placed every n periods. This lead time includes the replenishment lead time L and the time between two orders. For example, if the inventory system places an order every two periods, the lead time is $L + 2$.

$P\{LTD_i(n) \leq S_i\}$: the probability that the lead time demand $LTD_i(n)$ is less than or equal to the order-up-to level S_i.

The service level of each item i in case an order is placed every n periods can be formulated as:

$$SL_i(n) = P\{LTD_i(n) \le S_i\} = \int_0^{S_1} \cdots \int_0^{S_2} \cdots \int_0^{\frac{S_i - \mu_i \times (k+L)}{\sigma_i \times \sqrt{k+L}}} \cdots \int_0^{S_N} \cdots \frac{1}{n} \sum_{k=1}^{n} \phi_i^{k+L}(u_i^{k+L}) \prod_{i=1}^{N} (du_i^L du_{i2} \ldots du_{in})$$
$$\sum_{i=1}^{N} \sum_{j=1}^{n-1} u_{ij} < Q, \sum_{i=1}^{N} \sum_{j=1}^{n} u_{ij} \ge Q$$

$$= \int_0^{+\infty} \cdots \int_0^{+\infty} \cdots \int_0^{+\infty} \cdots \int_0^{+\infty} \cdots \frac{1}{n} \sum_{k=1}^{n} 1(S_i - u_i^L - \sum_{j=1}^{k} u_{ij}) \prod_{i=1}^{N} (\phi_i^L(u_i^L)\phi_i(u_{i1})\phi_i(u_{i2}) \ldots \phi_i(u_{in})) \prod_{i=1}^{N} (du_i^L du_{i2} \ldots du_{in})$$
$$\sum_{i=1}^{N} \sum_{j=1}^{n-1} u_{ij} < Q, \sum_{i=1}^{N} \sum_{j=1}^{n} u_{ij} \ge Q$$

$$(9)$$

where $1(S_i - u_i^L - \sum_{j=1}^{k} u_{ij})$ is an indicator function, if $S_i - u_i^L - \sum_{j=1}^{k} u_{ij} \ge 0$, the indicator takes the value 1, otherwise it takes the value 0. Thus, the service level of each item i can be written as:

$$SL_i = \sum_{n=1}^{\infty} SL_i(n)P(n) \tag{10}$$

In summary, the problem of optimizing $P(s, S_i)$ policy for a stochastic inventory system with service level constraints can be formulated as the following nonlinear programming model NLP:

NLP:

Min TC.

subject to

$$SL_i \ge \alpha_i, \quad i = 1, 2, \ldots, N \tag{11}$$

where constraints (11) are the service level constraints of all items.

3   Optimization Algorithm

In this section we present an algorithm for solving the model NLP to obtain the optimal parameters of the $P(s, S_i)$ policy. Let $Q = \sum_{i=1}^{N} S_i - s$, where s and S_i are decision variables. If Q is given, we can determine $P(n)$ according to (2). If all $P(n)$ are known, C_o can be calculated from $P(n)$ according to Eq. (4) even if S_i and s are not known. From Eq. (7), $C_h(n)$ is an increasing function of S_i if Q is given. Because of this, to minimize TC under the service level constraints, S_i must take the value such that:

$$f(S_i) = SL_i(S_i) - \alpha_i = 0, \quad i = 1, 2, \ldots, N \tag{12}$$

This S_i can be obtained by using the bisection method. As soon as Q and S_i are determined, s can be determined by $s = \sum_{i=1}^{N} S_i - Q$.

From the above analysis, we can solve the model *NLP* by enumerating possible integer values of Q between 0 and Q_{UB} and then search for the optimal value of S_i for each item i by the bisection search, where Q_{UB} is an upper bound of Q.

To implement this algorithm, a high-dimensional integral function is required to calculate $TC(n)$ and $SL_i(n)$. In our implementation, we use the Monte Carlo simulation method to calculate the expected total cost per period $TC(n)$ and service level $SL_i(n)$ when $Q = \sum_{i=1}^{N} S_i - s$ and S_i for each item i are given. This is carried out by simulating the inventory system under $P(s, S_i)$ policy for a large number of periods and calculating the average total cost per period and the average service level of the system when $s = \sum_{i=1}^{N} S_i - Q$ and S_i are given.

4 Experimental Results

In this section, we report the results of our numerical experiments for the evaluation of the proposed algorithm. We generated 20 instances with $N = 3$, $L = 2$, A and a_i are set such that $A + \sum_{i=1}^{N} a_i = 0.5ct^2 \sum_{i=1}^{N} h_i\mu_i$, where ct is a parameter corresponding to the expected/optimal order cycle time (time between two consecutive orders) of the inventory system in case of deterministic demand. We take $ct = 2$ for setting A and a_i $= 0.2A$ for each item i, according to the guidelines of [7]; α_i is set to 0.95 for all items. In addition, h_i is randomly generated from [1, 10]; μ_i is randomly generated from [10, 100]; and the coefficient of variation of the demand of each item i is randomly generated from [0.10, 0.40]. This algorithm was implemented in C/C + + and tested on a PC with CPU i7-8650U and 16GB RAM.

We set $Q_{UB} = 2Q_{det}^*$, where Q_{det}^* is the joint economic order quantity of the inventory system in case of deterministic demand. Our numerical experiments show that this upper bound is valid for Q for all the instances tested. The number of periods for calculating the expected total cost per period and service levels of the system by simulation is set to 10,000. The computational results of the 20 instances are given in Table 1.

Table 1. Results of the twenty instances.

Instance	Q	$S1$	$S2$	S_3	s	HC	OC	TC	CPU Time (s)
1	189	49	274	207	341	837.20	864.75	1701.95	2293.31
2	224	167	355	250	548	1101.78	1018.34	2120.12	3757.40
3	248	288	133	343	516	711.19	686.41	1397.60	3935.49
4	216	84	283	341	492	596.65	482.52	1079.17	3150.84
5	274	426	131	348	631	1496.17	1393.53	2889.70	4140.65

(continued)

Table 1. (*continued*)

Instance	Q	S1	S2	S_3	s	HC	OC	TC	CPU Time (s)
6	306	373	208	344	619	1482.18	1063.90	2546.08	3944.94
7	261	265	389	168	561	1061.77	1003.30	2065.07	3781.53
8	275	284	319	296	624	1648.92	1152.68	2801.60	3900.82
9	163	68	222	236	363	307.02	234.82	541.84	2221.65
10	189	118	103	342	374	1355.27	1150.35	2505.62	2457.73
11	277	319	334	268	644	1313.10	1252.25	2565.35	4303.89
12	218	145	241	327	495	805.91	721.21	1527.12	3158.50
13	144	49	177	239	321	736.88	632.57	1369.45	1935.91
14	314	383	211	366	646	1321.25	1134.76	2456.01	4289.79
15	303	358	217	418	690	1773.21	1382.06	3155.27	4302.08
16	165	287	115	136	373	1260.35	1023.74	2284.09	2227.00
17	83	86	93	97	193	409.68	356.00	765.68	1076.06
18	338	415	286	458	821	861.94	653.21	1515.15	5220.07
19	356	411	300	484	839	1860.53	1541.69	3402.22	5406.44
20	304	294	381	366	737	1644.23	1391.27	3035.50	4565.97
Avg	242.35	243.45	238.60	301.70	541.40	1129.26	956.97	2086.23	3503.50

In this table, the 2nd to 6th columns provide the optimal value of Q and the optimal parameters of $P(s, S_i)$ policy obtained by the proposed algorithm, the 7th to 9th columns present the holding cost, ordering cost and total cost per period of the inventory system, and the 10th column is the CPU time of the algorithm. From this table, we can see the computation time of the algorithm is no larger than two hours for all instances. This is acceptable since the inventory policy optimization is a tactical decision. Note that the computation time of our algorithm can be largely reduced if it is implemented in a workstation with multiple CPUs or in a cloud computing platform by applying parallel computing techniques.

Although we do not explicitly address shortage costs in our inventory optimization model NLP, we can implicitly consider shortage costs in the model by setting the expected service level of each item according to its shortage cost and holding cost per unit of the item per unit of time. As we know, in an inventory system with a single item controlled by an order-up-to level policy, the service level of the system is determined by the unit shortage cost divided by the sum of the unit shortage cost and the unit holding cost. This relationship between the service level and the two costs can make our proposed algorithm applicable in both situations: shortage costs can be well evaluated and shortage costs cannot be well evaluated.

5 Conclusion

In this paper, we have studied a periodic review joint replenishment inventory system with stochastic demands under service level constraints. After formulating analytically its costs and service levels, we have established a nonlinear programming model for the optimization of its $P(s, S_i)$ policy and designed an algorithm to calculate the optimal parameters of the policy. The numerical experiments on randomly generated instances have demonstrated the efficiency of the algorithm. In the future, we will extend this study to multi-echelon distribution systems.

References

1. Khouja, M., Goyal, S.: A review of the joint replenishment problem literature: 1989–2005. Eur. J. Oper. Res. **186**(1), 1–16 (2008). https://doi.org/10.1016/j.ejor.2007.03.007
2. Bastos, L.D.S.L., Mendes, M.L., Nunes, D.R.D.L., Melo, A.C.S., Carneiro, M.P.: A systematic literature review on the joint replenishment problem solutions: 2006–2015. Production **27** (2017). https://doi.org/10.1590/0103-6513.222916
3. Li, L., Schmidt, C.P.: A stochastic joint replenishment problem with dissimilar items. Decis. Sci. **51**(5), 1159–1201 (2020). https://doi.org/10.1111/deci.12380
4. Mustafa Tanrikulu, M., Şen, A., Alp, O.: A joint replenishment policy with individual con-trol and constant size orders. Int. J. Prod. Res. **48**(14), 4253–4271 (2010). https://doi.org/10.1080/00207540802662904
5. Kiesmüller, G.P.: Multi-item inventory control with full truckloads: a comparison of aggregate and individual order triggering. Eur. J. Oper. Res. **200**(1), 54–62 (2010). https://doi.org/10.1016/j.ejor.2008.12.008
6. Viswanathan S.: Note. Periodic review (s, S) policies for joint replenishment inventory systems. Manage. Sci. **43**(10):1447–1454 (1997). https://doi.org/10.1287/mnsc.43.10.1447
7. Pantumsinchai, P.: A comparison of three joint ordering inventory policies. Decis. Sci. **23**(1), 111–127 (1992). https://doi.org/10.1111/j.1540-5915.1992.tb00379.x

CGA-Based Optimal (r, Q) Policy Tuning in Goods Distribution Systems with Complex Topologies

Łukasz Wieczorek(✉) ⬤ and Przemysław Ignaciuk ⬤

Lodz University of Technology, 215 Wólczańska Street, 90-924 Łódź, Poland
lukasz.wieczorek.1@edu.p.lodz.pl, przemyslaw.ignaciuk@p.lodz.pl

Abstract. The paper addresses the inventory control problem in logistic networks with complex, mesh-type topologies. The goods are shipped with non-negligible lead-time delay and an uncertain, arbitrary demand may be imposed on any node in the system. Excess demand is lost. Single-item periodic-review distribution process is governed by the (r, Q) policy. In order to adjust the policy parameters, a continuous genetic algorithm is used. In the optimization procedures, three objectives – holding and transportation costs reduction and customer satisfaction maximization – are considered. The paper shows how one can effectively find the reorder point and order quantity for each node when the policy is implemented in a distributed mode, as desired in complex systems. Two approaches to the crossover operation have been compared. The separate operator allows one to obtain more suitable solutions at the expense of more significant computational effort.

Keywords: Inventory control · (r, Q) policy · Genetic algorithms

1 Introduction

In recent years, globalization and industrial development have influenced logistics significantly. Thanks to numerous international agreements, both political and business ones, supply chains are evolving worldwide. Many of the existing ones are constantly modified and extended, whereas new ones are established. Current distribution networks face thus many challenges that influence their performance, e.g., complex topologies, market uncertainties, or transport disturbances. Supply chain management does not cease to be a topical issue in the literature. Most of the research related to inventory control, however, assume system structural limitations. Despite the difficulties in adjusting those models to more sophisticated real-life systems, it may lead to severe side-effects such as excessive operational costs and unrealized demand [1].

Owing to the nonlinearities and uncertainties in real-life distribution networks, closed-form solutions are rarely available. Then, simulation-based optimization may be used to find a near-optimal solution. The current literature indicates an increasing interest in the computational intelligence techniques employed in logistics [2]. Among

© IFIP International Federation for Information Processing 2021
Published by Springer Nature Switzerland AG 2021
A. Dolgui et al. (Eds.): APMS 2021, IFIP AICT 630, pp. 502–510, 2021.
https://doi.org/10.1007/978-3-030-85874-2_53

those methods, one of the best formally analyzed and finding an increasingly wide range of applications are genetic algorithms (GAs) [3].

This paper analyzes periodic-review resource distribution systems exhibiting a complex, mesh-type topology. The considered class assumes non-negligible lead-time delays in replenishment order realization. The external demand, not known *a priori* and subject to random variations, may be imposed on any node. The flow of resources is managed by the (r, Q) inventory policy implemented in a distributed way. The continuous search domain makes a continuous genetic algorithm (CGA) better suited in the considered optimization problem than its classical binary form [4]. Until now, there have been just a few works that applied the GAs to adjust the (r, Q) policy parameters in inventory management systems. Pasandideh et al. [5] considered a single-supplier single-retailer system with backorders. Pirayesh and Yazdi [6] investigated a serial supply chain influenced by the fuzzy demand. Then, Mousavi et al. [7] considered multi-supplier multi-retailer distribution network, but the lateral transshipments between the nodes within the same layer are not allowed. Ignaciuk and Wieczorek [8] investigated a multi-echelon, networked logistic system, nevertheless, their model does not take into consideration transportation costs that results in a tendency to set large order quantities thus excessive goods relocation costs.

The purpose of this paper is to determine how to adjust the (r, Q) policy parameters in logistic systems with complex topologies using CGAs. The optimization process involves three objectives that confront operational costs with customer satisfaction. Moreover, this paper compares two approaches of the crossover operation, i.e., simultaneous vs. separate one. The conducted research proves that CGAs indeed succeed in reaching the optimization objectives in the considered class of networked systems.

2 Network Model

2.1 Interconnection Structure

The considered class of system covers interaction of two groups of actors. The first group – the controlled nodes – have a limited stock to serve neighboring nodes with resources and answer external demand that is imposed (by customers) in any period of time. The second group comprises the external sources with an infinite stock that are responsible for supplying the network with resources. Let N and M denote the number of the controlled nodes and the external sources, respectively, and P be their sum.

The interconnection between nodes i and j is characterized by three attributes $(\alpha_{ij}, \beta_{ij}, \gamma_{ij})$. The first one quantifies the nominal partitioning coefficient (NPC) that designates the part of the current lot requested by node i that is to be obtained from supplier j. The second attribute is the lead-time delay (LTD), i.e., the time from placing a replenishment order by node i at node j to its fulfillment. The last one $– \gamma_{ij} –$ determines the transportation unitary cost (TUC) along the link i-j, i.e., the cost of transferring a single unit of resources from node i to j.

There are no restrictions as how the logistic structure is formed except for the typical assumptions in the discussed class of systems: interconnections are unidirectional, i.e., for any two nodes i and j if $\alpha_{ij} \neq 0$, then $\alpha_{ji} = 0$; second, there are no isolated nodes, i.e., without any connections to other nodes. Also, no node can supply itself with resources, i.e., $\alpha_{ii} = 0$ for any i.

2.2 Node Interactions

The planning horizon comprises T equal-length periods in which a preordained sequence of operations is executed at each controlled node. First, all the resources from the incoming replenishment orders are registered into the on-hand stock. Then, the external demand is satisfied, if its stock level is sufficient. Otherwise, the unsatisfied part is lost, i.e., backordering is not allowed. Afterwards, the controlled node processes the replenishment requests from the controlled nodes for which it serves as a supplier. Similarly to the case of the external demand, the replenishment signals are fulfilled, if possible. Finally, the node requests replenishments from its suppliers. The on-hand stock level at node i in any period $t = 1, \ldots, T$ evolves as

$$x_i(t + 1) = \left(x_i(t) + o_i^R(t) - d_i(t)\right)^+ - o_i^S(t) = x_i(t) + o_i^R(t) - s_i(t) - o_i^S(t), \quad (1)$$

where:

- $(f)^+ = \max(f, 0)$ is a saturation function,
- $x_i(t)$ is the on-hand stock level,
- $o_i^R(t)$ is the quantity of resources from the incoming shipments received by node i from its suppliers in period t,
- $o_i^S(t)$ is the quantity of resources in the outgoing replenishment orders sent by node i to its neighbors in period t,
- $d_i(t)$ is the external demand imposed at node i in period t,
- $s_i(t)$ is the satisfied external demand at node i in period t.

Owing to the loss-sales assumption, the controlled node may not be able to fulfill all the replenishment requests from the neighboring nodes. Thus, the partitioning coefficient (PC) should be expressed as a time-varying function $\alpha_{ij}(t)$ that satisfies $0 \leq \alpha_{ij}(t) \leq \alpha_{ij}$, where $\alpha_{ij}(t) = \alpha_{ij}$ reflects the situation of request fulfillment.

Let $u_i(t)$ denote the replenishment signals generated by node i to its suppliers in period t. Then, the quantity of resources in the replenishment orders received by node i in period t equals

$$o_i^R(t) = \sum_{j=1}^{P} \alpha_{ji}(t - \beta_{ji}) u_i(t - \beta_{ji}), \quad (2)$$

where β_{ij} is the LTD between nodes i and j.

Denoting the highest value of the external demand that may be imposed on node i by $d_i^{\max}$, the market demand may be expressed as a bounded, time-varying function of time that satisfies $0 \leq d_i(t) \leq d_i^{\max}$. Moreover, due to the assumed framework, the satisfied external demand by node i in period t may be described by

$$s_i(t) = \min\left(x_i(t) + o_i^R(t), d_i(t)\right). \quad (3)$$

Similarly, the quantity of resources in the outgoing shipments sent by node i

$$o_i^S(t) = \sum_{j=1}^{N} \alpha_{ij}(t)u_j(t). \tag{4}$$

2.3 State-Space Description

For convenience of computer implementation, let us group the model variables into a matrix-vector form,

$$\mathbf{x}(t+1) = \mathbf{x}(t) + \sum_{k=1}^{B} \mathbf{A}_k(t-k)\mathbf{u}(t-k) - \mathbf{s}(t), \tag{5}$$

where:

- B is the maximum LTD between any two interconnected nodes,
- $\mathbf{x}(t)$ is a vector of on-hand stock levels in period t,
- $\mathbf{u}(t)$ is a vector of replenishment signals generated by the nodes in period t,
- $\mathbf{s}(t)$ is a vector of the satisfied demands in period t,
- $\mathbf{A}_k(t)$ is a set of matrices describing the in-transit shipments in period t,

$$\mathbf{A}_k(t) = \begin{bmatrix} \sum_{i:\beta_{i1}=k} \alpha_{i1}(t) \cdots & \varepsilon_{1N}(t) \\ \vdots & \ddots & \vdots \\ \varepsilon_{N1}(t) & \cdots & \sum_{i:\beta_{iN}=k} \alpha_{iN}(t) \end{bmatrix} \text{ for } k = 1, \ldots, \text{B}, \tag{6}$$

in which the main-diagonal entries store the information about the incoming shipments sent k period earlier. The other entries, reflecting the outgoing shipments between any two controlled nodes i and j,

$$\varepsilon_{ij} = \begin{cases} -\alpha_{ij}(t), & \text{if } \beta_{ij} = k \\ 0, & \text{otherwise.} \end{cases} \tag{7}$$

2.4 Inventory Management Policy

In order to control the flow of resources in the considered system, the (r, Q) inventory policy is used. It requires two vectors – $\mathbf{r}$ and $\mathbf{Q}$ – containing the reorder points (RPs) and the order quantities (OQs), respectively, to be specified for all the controlled nodes. Accordingly, node i generates a replenishment signal of size Q_i, when its inventory position (the sum of on-hand stock and in-transit orders) falls below r_i.

In case of a fixed external demand imposed on the controlled nodes, a closed-form expression for vectors $\mathbf{r}^{\text{ref}}$ and $\mathbf{Q}^{\text{ref}}$ yielding full customer satisfaction may be obtained analytically [8, 9]. The vector of reference RPs may be then calculated as

$$\mathbf{r}^{\text{ref}} = \left(\mathbf{I} + \sum_{k=1}^{B} k\mathbf{A}_k\right)\mathbf{A}^{-1}\mathbf{d}^{\max}, \tag{8}$$

where:

- **I** is an identity matrix of size $N \times N$,
- **A** is a sum of $\mathbf{A}_k$ for $k = 1, \ldots, B$, where $\mathbf{A}_k$ is a set of matrices (6) with the NPCs,
- $\mathbf{d}^{\max}$ is the vector of the highest expected values of the market demand.

According to [10], the reference OQs should satisfy the element-wise inequality

$$\mathbf{Q}^{\text{ref}} \cdot \mathbf{I} > \mathbf{A}^{-1} \cdot \mathbf{d}^{\max}. \tag{9}$$

3   Optimization Problem

In order to define an optimization problem, the fitness function evaluating the quality of the resource distribution should be formulated. Table 1 contains the three metrics that are taken into consideration, i.e., holding and transportation costs as well as customer satisfaction. The transportation cost function includes two additional matrices $\mathbf{\Gamma}$ and $\mathbf{A}_E(t)$ storing the TUCs and PCs of the system interconnections, respectively,

$$\mathbf{\Gamma} = \begin{bmatrix} 0 & \gamma_{12} & \cdots & \gamma_{1N} \\ \gamma_{21} & 0 & \cdots & \gamma_{2N} \\ \vdots & \vdots & \ddots & \vdots \\ \gamma_{N1} & \gamma_{N2} & \cdots & 0 \\ \vdots & \vdots & \ddots & \vdots \\ \gamma_{P1} & \gamma_{P2} & \cdots & \gamma_{PN} \end{bmatrix}, \; \mathbf{A}_E(t) = \begin{bmatrix} 0 & \alpha_{12}(t) & \cdots & \alpha_{1N}(t) \\ \alpha_{21}(t) & 0 & \cdots & \alpha_{2N}(t) \\ \vdots & \vdots & \ddots & \vdots \\ \alpha_{N1}(t) & \alpha_{N2}(t) & \cdots & 0 \\ \vdots & \vdots & \ddots & \vdots \\ \alpha_{P1} & \alpha_{P2} & \cdots & \alpha_{PN} \end{bmatrix}. \tag{10}$$

Table 1. Quality metrics.

Holding cost	Transportation cost	Customer satisfaction
$f_{HC} = \sum_{t=1}^{T} \mathbf{x}(t)$	$f_{TC} = \sum_{t=1}^{T} \mathbf{\Gamma} \circ \mathbf{A}_E(t)\mathbf{u}(t)$	$f_{CS} = \sum_{t=1}^{T} \mathbf{s}(t) \Big/ \sum_{t=1}^{T} \mathbf{d}(t)$

Then, denoting the coefficients prioritizing holding cost reduction, transportation cost reduction, and customer satisfaction maximization by F, G, H, respectively, the optimization problem under consideration may be described as

$$\max f_{fitness}(f_{HC}, f_{TC}, f_{CS}) = \left(1 - \frac{f_{HC}}{f_{HC}^{\max}}\right)^F \left(1 - \frac{f_{TC}}{f_{TC}^{\max}}\right)^G f_{CS}^H, \tag{11}$$

where $f_{HC}^{\max}$ and $f_{TC}^{\max}$ denote the reference holding and transportation costs calculated for an overestimated safety stock based on (8) and (9).

In order to optimize the performance of the considered class of distribution systems, the CGAs have been applied. Let a candidate solution consist of a pair of vectors **r** and $\mathbf{Q}$, in which a particular value of the RP and the OQ is a gene in the chromosome. Furthermore, the pair of vectors $\mathbf{r}^{\text{ref}}$ and $\mathbf{Q}^{\text{ref}}$ establishes the search space boundaries of the considered optimization problem, i.e., each gene reflecting the RP and the OQ satisfies $r_i \in \left[1, r_i^{\text{ref}}\right]$ and $Q_i \in \left[1, Q_i^{\text{ref}}\right]$, respectively, for any node i.

As for the implementation of the CGA, the initial population is randomly generated within the search space boundaries. Then, based on the recommendations relating to the optimization of the multi-echelon systems governed by the classical base-stock policy, the four-way tournament selection and the two-point crossover are used [11]. A separate approach to crossover has also been applied to obtain more precise solutions, as discussed in Sect. 4.1. Finally, the performed simulations indicate a mutation probability of 10% as suitable for the considered class of optimization problems.

4 Numerical Studies

In order to examine the performance of CGAs in adjusting (r, Q) policy parameters according to the objectives defined in Sect. 3, there have been performed about 10^6 simulations involving various planning horizons, system topologies, demand patterns, and optimization priorities. Two scenarios, differing in the scale of logistic structure considered, have been selected for closer examination. The first scenario involves a six-node logistic network ($N = 4$, $M = 2$), the second – a sixteen-node system ($N = 12$, $M = 4$). The LTDs are established randomly within the range [1, 5], and the planning horizon equals 100 periods. The external demand has been generated using the Gamma distribution with shape and scale coefficients equal to 5 and 10, respectively. The CGA assumes 200 generations of 100-individual populations. In addition, the search procedure is terminated after a hundred generations with no fitness improvement.

Tables 2 and 3 group the results obtained for the six- and sixteen-node network, respectively. The prioritized metrics are marked in bold. They show the sensitivity of the CGA-based optimization in terms of different objectives. The coefficients of prioritized objectives are set as 10, the others as 1. The first and last rows in each table relate to a balanced optimization, i.e., not rewarding any quality metric.

4.1 Crossover Operator

Moreover, two different approaches to the crossover operation have been examined. In some of the foregoing works the crossover operation is executed simultaneously, i.e., the crossover points are generated once and used for both vectors – containing reorder points and order quantities [4, 7]. In other works this operation is realized separately, i.e., using different crossover points for either of the partial vectors [5, 6]. Table 4 presents outcomes of 10^4 simulation runs. Each assumes 50 generations of a 10-individual population. The obtained results indicate that the simultaneous operator leads to a near-optimal solution in fewer iterations than the separate one. On the other hand, different crossover points for both vectors widen the spread of potential solutions and may allow finding a more suitable policy configuration.

Table 2. Quality metrics for the six-node network.

Fitness priorities			Quality metrics			Optimization results		Computational time [seconds]
F	G	H	f_{HC}	f_{TC}	f_{CS}	$f_{fitness}$	Generations	
1	1	1	8667	13457	0.62	0.35838	67	182.07
10	1	1	**2590**	12688	0.57	0.31394	28	134.93
1	10	1	10872	**1801**	0.18	0.09665	90	201.54
1	1	10	30975	28579	**0.96**	0.08412	87	199.59
10	10	1	**3043**	**2448**	0.17	0.06734	66	177.96
10	1	10	**12815**	26570	**0.91**	0.04114	23	143.27
1	10	10	40659	**11185**	**0.59**	0.00008	181	195.93
10	10	10	6639	13149	0.61	0.00003	58	166.33

Table 3. Quality metrics for the sixteen-node network.

Fitness priorities			Quality metrics			Optimization results		Computational time [seconds]
F	G	H	f_{HC}	f_{TC}	f_{CS}	$f_{fitness}$	Generations	
1	1	1	23933	45601	0.59	0.4036	175	2788.77
10	1	1	**18215**	43361	0.55	0.32361	159	2860.65
1	10	1	57952	**11640**	0.25	0.1056	34	2212.79
1	1	10	208659	113666	**0.94**	0.11191	15	1973.51
10	10	1	**30626**	**13702**	0.25	0.07078	109	2676.08
10	1	10	**135885**	106329	**0.92**	0.02856	85	2784.69
1	10	10	71465	**60797**	**0.71**	0.0002	136	2735.06
10	10	10	59874	48358	0.62	0.00009	84	2777.72

Table 4. Simultaneous vs. separate crossover operator results.

	Six-node network		Sixteen-node network	
	Simultaneous	Separate	Simultaneous	Separate
Fitness value average	0.35149	0.35173	0.37504	0.37663
Fitness value median	0.35168	0.35169	0.37463	0.37667
Generations average	23	26	24	27
Generations median	20	26	24	25

5   Result Discussion and Conclusions

The paper analyzes how to apply CGAs to find (near) optimal values of the (r, Q) policy parameters in complex, nonlinear logistic systems. The considered procedure permits one to smoothly balance between three optimization objectives, incorporating different operational costs and customer satisfaction.

The performance of the CGA-based optimization has been verified through strenuous numerical tests. CGAs succeed in adjusting the (r, Q) inventory control policy in logistic networks with non-trivial topologies regardless of the system size. Also, simultaneous and separate approaches to the crossover operation have been compared. On the one hand, simultaneous crossover allows one to obtain a near-optimal solution in a fewer number of generations. On the other hand, the separate crossover enables one to consider a wider spectrum of potential solutions and thus may arrive at a better configuration. Moreover, the separate approach reduces the probability of generating duplicate individuals in populations. Thus, the simultaneous crossover operator is recommended for more complicated systems in which evaluation of the fitness function value requires a large amount of time.

The considered class of logistic networks, although well-reflecting the complexity of the current real-life systems, accepts a few extensions. First of all, one may assess the influence of damage or loss of in-transit orders. Secondly, investigating the impact of backorders might give new insights on efficient lot-sizing in distributed architectures. The influence of system parameter variations should also be assessed before concluding about deployment perspectives.

References

1. Cattani, K.D., Jacobs, F.R., Schoenfelder, J.: Common inventory modeling assumptions that fall short: arborescent networks, Poisson demand, and single-echelon approximations. J. Oper. Manag. **29**(5), 488–499 (2011). https://doi.org/10.1016/j.jom.2010.11.008
2. Ko, M., Tiwari, A., Mehnen, J.: A review of soft computing applications in supply chain management. Appl. Soft Comput. J. **10**(3), 661–674 (2010). https://doi.org/10.1016/j.asoc.2009.09.004
3. Jauhar, S.K., Pant, M.: Genetic algorithms in supply chain management: a critical analysis of the literature. Sādhanā **41**(9), 993–1017 (2016). https://doi.org/10.1007/s12046-016-0538-z
4. Simon, D.: Evolutionary Optimization Algorithms. Wiley, New York (2013)
5. Pasandideh, S.H.R., Niaki, S.T.A., Nia, A.R.: A genetic algorithm for vendor managed inventory control system of multi-product multi-constraint economic order quantity model. Expert Syst. Appl. **38**(3), 2708–2716 (2011). https://doi.org/10.1016/j.eswa.2010.08.060
6. Pirayesh, M., Yazdi, M.M.: Modeling (r, Q) policy in a two-level supply chain system with fuzzy demand. Int. J. Uncertainty Fuzziness Knowl. Based Syst. **18**(6), 819–841 (2010). https://doi.org/10.1142/S0218488510006817
7. Mousavi, S.M., Pardalos, P.M., Niaki, S.T.A., Fügenschuh, A., Fathi, M.: Solving a continuous periodic review inventory-location allocation problem in vendor-buyer supply chain under uncertainty. Comput. Ind. Eng. **128**, 541–552 (2019). https://doi.org/10.1016/j.cie.2018.12.071
8. Ignaciuk, P., Wieczorek, Ł.: Evolutionary adaptation of (r, Q) inventory management policy in complex distribution systems. In: Saeed, K., Dvorský, J. (eds.) CISIM 2020. LNCS, vol. 12133, pp. 146–157. Springer, Cham (2020). https://doi.org/10.1007/978-3-030-47679-3_13

9. Ignaciuk, P., Wieczorek, Ł: Networked base-stock inventory control in complex distribution systems. Math. Probl. Eng. **2019**(3754367), 1–14 (2019). https://doi.org/10.1155/2019/375 4367
10. Ignaciuk, P.: DSM relay control of logistic networks under delayed replenishments and uncertain demand. In: 24th Mediterranean Conference on Control and Automation, Greece, pp. 250–255 (2016). https://doi.org/10.1109/MED.2016.7535910
11. Ignaciuk, P., Wieczorek, Ł: Continuous genetic algorithms in the optimization of logistic networks: applicability assessment and tuning. Appl. Sci. **10**(21), 1–24 (2020). https://doi.org/10.3390/app10217851

Multi-period Multi-sourcing Supply Planning with Stochastic Lead-Times, Quantity-Dependent Pricing, and Delivery Flexibility Costs

Belgacem Bettayeb[1]([✉]) [ID], Oussama Ben-Ammar[2] [ID], and Alexandre Dolgui[3] [ID]

[1] LINEACT CESI, EA 7527, CESI Lille, 8 boulevard Louis XIV, 59046 Lille, France
bbettayeb@cesi.fr
[2] Mines Saint-Etienne, University of Clermont Auvergne, CNRS UMR 6158 LIMOS,
Centre CMP, Departement SFL, 13541 Gardanne, France
oussama.ben-ammar@emse.fr
[3] IMT Atlantique, LS2N, UMR-CNRS 6004, La Chantrerie, 4 rue Alfred Kastler,
44300 Nantes, France
alaxandre.dolgui@imt-atlantique.fr

Abstract. This work studies the problem of multi-period multi-sourcing supply planning with stochastic lead-times, quantity-dependent pricing, and delivery flexibility costs. We present a problem formulation that takes also into account holding and backlog costs and finite capacities of suppliers. The objective is to minimize the expected total cost while respecting suppliers' capacity constraints and satisfying customer demand. In this paper, the proposed stochastic integer linear program is detailed and the first results of experiments are presented and discussed.

Keywords: Supply planning · Multi-sourcing · Stochastic lead-times · Digressive pricing · Delivery flexibility

1 Introduction and Literature Review

In order to ensure their competitiveness, while guaranteeing a high service level to their customers, industrial companies need to optimize not only their production processes, but also other related downstream and upstream processes like replenishment, inventory, and transportation. Therefore, it is necessary to coordinate material, information and financial flows in an integrated manner to guarantee a competitive and profitable supply chain (SC) for all stakeholders [1]. However, because of its interdependent network structure, any incident or disturbance occurring in one of the elements of the chain can propagate and amplify, creating more effects which degrade the performance of the whole SC. In fact, incidents and disturbances are inherent in such a complex systems and

© IFIP International Federation for Information Processing 2021
Published by Springer Nature Switzerland AG 2021
A. Dolgui et al. (Eds.): APMS 2021, IFIP AICT 630, pp. 511–518, 2021.
https://doi.org/10.1007/978-3-030-85874-2_54

are due to uncertainty, even the ignorance, of one or more influencing parameters of the system and the absence of countermeasures to predict and prevent them.

Controlling uncertainty and reducing its effects on Supply Chain performance has become, for several decades, a major concern for decision-makers and research communities in Supply Chain Management (SCM) [2,3]. This concern is reinforced by the recurrent observation of the vulnerability of SC to the disturbances generated by the uncertainty on some SC parameters [4,5]. Various sources of uncertainty have been identified and studied through SC risks analysis and many of them have been formalized and integrated into supply planning and inventory control models [6].

To reduce the effect of uncertainty in SC, several studies introduced safety stocks [7]. However, safety stocks are not all the time efficient and advantageous when the uncertainty is on lead times [8–10]. Other approaches based on stochastic optimization techniques have also been proposed in supply planning and inventory control [11–13]. The most of these models consider a one-period supply planning or multi-period supply planning with a constant demand, and independent and identically distributed lead-times. These models have some limitations from the perspective of optimization and economies of scale because they ignore and/or neglect the effect of dynamic parameters such as demand and capacity. However, multi-period supply planning with stochastic lead-times represents the difficulty to deal with order crossovers and the randomness characterising the quantities received within periods [8]. The problem of crossover is generally avoided by either ignoring them or building models that dissipate its effect or prevent it [14–16]. Another common practice to deal with uncertainty in SCM is multi-sourcing, which has the advantages of working with several competing suppliers. However, SC managers need to define adequate strategies to select and manage several suppliers. Concerning suppliers selection, several attributes are usually used, such as quality, price, delivery performance, etc. Although no unanimous ranking of the importance of these attributes exists, delivery performance is always identified as one of the three most important [17]. Another study in [18] indicates flexibility attribute as the most important overall, followed by cost and delivery performance.

The first suppliers selection techniques proposed in the literature are mostly based on mono- or multi-objective functions that are optimised within a static environment, where the decisions are made for a strategic level horizon. Since few decades, dynamic supplier selection (DSS) problems have emerged and different models have been proposed while considering a dynamic environment where one or several parameters vary over time, such as demand, capacity, prices, etc. The majority of DSS approaches seek to minimize an average total cost while finding the order quantities for selected suppliers [19,20]. For the case of stochastic lead-time with multiple suppliers, [21] developed a mathematical model of a single-item continuous review (s, Q) inventory policy. As in our model, orders replenishment can be split among several suppliers. The objective is to optimize the inventory policy parameters, namely the reorder level and quantity ordered to each supplier, while minimizing the expected total cost per time unit. [22] proposed a two-phase framework for supplier selection and order allocation with different possible transportation alternatives (TAs) per supplier. The proposed optimization model allocates a set of optimal order quantities to the selected suppliers for each time period in the planning horizon. Recently, [11] propose a mathematical formulation for the problem of dynamic supplier selection strategy in multi-period supply planning under stochastic lead-times. The authors propose a stochastic integer non-linear program (SINLP) aiming to optimize suppliers selection and planned lead-times while minimising the expected total cost.

The aim of this work is to study the problem of multi-period replenishment with multiple suppliers under stochastic lead-times and to study the effects of suppliers capacity limit, digressive pricing policy and delivery flexibility cost.

The structure of the remainder of this paper is as follows. Section 2, contains the description of the stochastic integer linear programming formulation of the problem. Then, we report and discuss the first experimental results in Sect. 3. Finally, principle conclusions from this work and future research directions are stated in the concluding section.

2   Problem Formulation

We consider the problem of multi-period replenishment planning of a system of single-product, single-buyer, and multiple-vendors. The demand of each period is known and can be ordered from one or several suppliers, each having a stochastic discrete lead-time defined by its probability mass function. Each supplier is also characterised by its capacity limit for each period and its own digressive pricing policy. The latter is applied to the whole quantity ordered over the planning horizon. We suppose that each period's not satisfied quantity is back-ordered and the equivalent backlogging cost is incurred to the buyer. The latter covers also the inventory holding cost. Note that backlog and inventory quantities are stochastic because of the randomness of suppliers lead-times and that we have no restrictive assumptions concerning orders' crossover nor the structure of the demand over the planning horizon. We consider the case where each demand can be split into small batches over different suppliers and/or periods (splitting) and that suppliers release separately the deliveries of different batches ordered at the same period via a supplementary cost for each batch (delivery flexibility cost).

For this problem formulation, we use the following notations for input data and decision variables:

$\mathcal{T}$ ordered set of time periods indices of the planning horizon
$\mathcal{S}$ ordered set of suppliers indices
$\mathcal{I}_s$ ordered set of indices of quantity intervals defining supplier s pricing policy
D_t demand of period t
C_{st} capacity limit of supplier s at period t
$[l_{si}, u_{si}]$ lower and upper limits of the i-th quantity interval of supplier s pricing policy
c_{si} unit selling price of the i-th quantity interval of supplier s pricing policy

c_s^o ordering cost of supplier s

c^h unit inventory holding cost per time period

c^b unit backlogging cost per time period

$[L_s^-, L_s^+]$ range of possible discrete lead-time values of supplier s

$L_{s\tau t}^\omega$ actual lead time, in scenario ω, of the quantity released by supplier s at period τ to satisfy demand of period t

$F_s(.)$ cumulative distribution function of supplier s lead-time

$Q_{s\tau t}$ **integer decision variable** that gives the quantity to be ordered from supplier s at period τ to satisfy demand of period t

K_{si} **integer decision variable** that gives the total quantity to order from supplier s within the i-th interval of its pricing policy

Y_{si} **binary decision variable** indicating if the total ordered quantity from supplier s is within the i-th interval of its pricing policy

$Z_{s\tau t}$ **binary decision variable** indicating a non-zero quantity is ordered from supplier s at period τ to satisfy demand t

Before giving the problem formulation as a stochastic integer linear program (SILP) model integrating the uncertainty of lead-times and the notion of flexibility, let firstly introduce the following definitions.

Definition 1. *For all $s \in \mathcal{S}$ and $t, \tau, i \in \mathcal{T}$, let $\mathcal{M}_t$ be the set of indices of all ordered quantities $Q_{s\tau i}$ that can be involved in the calculation of the backlogging level at period t. It is defined as follows:*

$$\mathcal{M}_t = \{(s, \tau, i) \in \mathcal{S} \times \mathcal{T}^2 : t - L_s^+ + 1 \leq \tau \leq t - L_s^- \text{ and } \tau + L_s^- \leq i \leq \tau + L_s^+\} \quad (1)$$

Corollary 1. *If the planned lead time of each supplier s is between L_-^s and L_+^s, the cardinality of $\mathcal{M}_t$ is equal to $\sum_{s \in \mathcal{S}} (L_+^s - L_-^s + 1) \times (L_+^s - L_-^s)$.*

Definition 2. *Let $\alpha_{s\tau i}^\omega = \mathbb{1}_{\{L_{s\tau i}^\omega \leq t - \tau\}} : (s, \tau, i) \in \mathcal{M}_t$ be a boolean variable that indicates for a given scenario ω if the quantity ordered from supplier s at period τ to satisfy the demand of period i arrives before period t:*

$$\alpha_{s\tau i}^\omega = \begin{cases} 1 & \text{if } \tau + L_{s\tau i}^\omega \leq t, \text{ with probability } F_s(t - \tau) \\ 0 & \text{if } \tau + L_{s\tau i}^\omega > t, \text{ with probability } 1 - F_s(t - \tau) \end{cases} \quad (2)$$

As $\alpha_{s\tau i}^\omega$ is binary for each triplet (s, τ, i), the number of possible scenarios is equal to $|\Omega_t| = 2^{|\mathcal{M}_t|}$. A given scenario ω is composed of a set of $\alpha_{s\tau i}^\omega$ for all $(s, \tau, i) \in \mathcal{M}_t$. This allows to define the set of all possible aggregated scenarios as follows:

$$\Omega_t = \left\{ (\alpha_{s\tau i}^\omega)_{(s,\tau,i) \in \mathcal{M}_t} : w \in \{1, \ldots, 2^{|\mathcal{M}_t|}\} \right\} \quad (3)$$

Each scenario $\omega \in \Omega_t$ has the probability of occurrence p_t^w defined in Eq. (4) below:

$$p_t^\omega = \prod_{(s,\tau,i) \in \mathcal{M}_t} (\alpha_{s\tau i}^\omega \times F_s(t - \tau) + (1 - \alpha_{s\tau i}^\omega) \times (1 - F_s(t - \tau))) \quad \forall \omega \in \Omega_t \quad (4)$$

where $\alpha_{s\tau i}^\omega \in \{0, 1\}$ and $\sum_{\omega \in \Omega_t} p_t^\omega = 1$.

In the proposed model formulation, it is assumed that each demand can be split into several quantities that are ordered from different suppliers and/or at different periods. Delivery flexibility is also allowed via an additional cost, i.e. ordered batches from each supplier at a given period are released separately and have independent lead-times occurrences. This strategy can be formulated as the SILP given in Eqs. (5)–(16).

$$\text{SILP: } \min \sum_{t \in T} \sum_{\omega \in \Omega} p_t^\omega \cdot \left(c^h I_{t\omega}^+ + c^b I_{t\omega}^- \right) + \sum_{s \in S} \left(\sum_{j \in \mathcal{I}_s} c_{sj} \cdot K_{sj} + \sum_{t \in T} \sum_{\tau \in T} c_s^o Z_{s\tau t} \right) \quad (5)$$

s.t.

$$I_{t\omega}^+ - I_{t\omega}^- = \sum_{s \in S} \sum_{\tau=1}^{t-L_s^+} \sum_{i=\tau+L_s^-}^{\tau+L_s^+} Q_{s\tau i}$$

$$+ \sum_{(s,\tau,i) \in \mathcal{M}_t} \alpha_{s\tau i}^\omega Q_{s\tau i} - \sum_{\tau=1}^{t} D_\tau \qquad \forall t \in T, \forall \omega \in \Omega_t \quad (6)$$

$$Q_{s\tau t} \le D_t \qquad \forall s \in S, \forall t, \tau \in T \quad (7)$$

$$\sum_{t \in T} Q_{s\tau t} \le C_{s\tau} \qquad \forall s \in S, \forall \tau \in T \quad (8)$$

$$\sum_{s \in S} \sum_{\tau=t-L_s^+}^{t-L_s^-} Q_{s\tau t} = D_t \qquad \forall t \in T \quad (9)$$

$$\sum_{j \in Z_s} Y_{sj} \le 1 \qquad \forall s \in S \quad (10)$$

$$l_{sj} Y_{sj} - K_{sj} \le 0 \qquad \forall s \in S, \forall j \in \mathcal{I}_s \quad (11)$$

$$K_{sj} - u_{sj} Y_{sj} \le 0 \qquad \forall s \in S, \forall j \in \mathcal{I}_s \quad (12)$$

$$\sum_{j \in \mathcal{I}_s} K_{sj} - \sum_{t \in T} \sum_{\tau \in T} Q_{s\tau t} = 0 \qquad \forall s \in S \quad (13)$$

$$\sum_{i \in T} D_i . Z_{s\tau t} - Q_{s\tau t} \ge 0 \qquad \forall s \in S, \forall t, \tau \in T \quad (14)$$

$$Y_{sj}, Z_{s\tau t} \in \{0,1\} \qquad \forall s \in S, \forall j \in \mathcal{I}_s, \forall t, \tau \in T \quad (15)$$

$$I_{t\omega}^-, I_{t\omega}^+, K_{sj}, Q_{s\tau t} \in \mathbb{N} \qquad \forall s \in S, \forall j \in \mathcal{I}_s, \forall t, \tau \in T \quad (16)$$

In the SILP model described by Eqs. (5)–(16), we consider all possible aggregated scenarios (see Definition 2) and minimize the Expected Total Cost (ETC) that is composed of inventory, backlogging and purchasing costs, while determining which proportion of a given D_t is ordered from a given supplier s at a given period τ. Purchasing costs are dependent on the selected suppliers and the number of orders and related quantities.

Constraints (6) express the inventory level $I_{t\omega}$ at the end of each period t for each scenario ω. Constraints (7) mean that each quantity ordered from supplier

s at period τ to satisfy the demand of period t is less than D_t. Constraints (9) force the sum of quantity ordered to satisfy the demand of period t to be equal to D_t. It also guarantees the satisfaction of all demands. Constraints (10) to (13) allow to select the pricing level to apply by each supplier, dependently on the total ordered quantities. Constraint (14) ensures that $Z_{s\tau t}$ is equal to 1 if $Q_{s\tau t}$ is non-zero. Constraints (15) and (16) define the domains of decision variables.

3   Numerical Example and Discussion

The SILP model of the problem has been coded in C++ and solved using IBM ILOG CPLEX solver. The numerical example presented here concerns a test instance with 10-period planning horizon, 5 non-zero demands (see Table 1), and 3 suppliers. Inventory cost parameters are $c_h = 10$ and $c_b = 15$. Suppliers have constant capacities, with $C_{1,t} = 60$, $C_{2,t} = 50$ and $C_{3,t} = 100$ for all $t = 1, \ldots, 10$. Suppliers are characterised by their lead-times probability distributions given in Table 2a and their pricing policy parameters given in Table 2b. Here, the total number of scenarios is equal to 1024 (see Corollary 1). The optimal solution of the numerical example is shown in Table 3, where the three last rows give the optimal quantities to order from each supplier at each time period. One can see that, even if the third supplier has the highest price (75) and ordering cost (1000), it is solicited for three orders ($Q_{3,4,5} = 70$, $Q_{3,4,6} = 100$ and $Q_{3,8,9} = 80$) which represent 62.5% of the total demand. This proves that the selling price as well as the ordering cost are not the only levers for choosing a supplier. However, buying exclusively from a single supplier does not seem to be the best strategy for lowering prices and protecting against uncertainties. The model that we propose makes it possible to find a good compromise between the various costs associated to inventory, purchasing and ordering.

Table 1. Vector of demands

Periods	5	6	7	8	9
Demand	180	100	30	10	80

Table 2. Characteristics and parameters of suppliers

(a) Lead-times probability distributions

s		l: lead-time values			
		1	2	3	4
1	$\mathbb{P}(L^s = l)$	0.24	0.76	-	-
2	$\mathbb{P}(L^s = l)$	-	0.53	0.16	0.31
3	$\mathbb{P}(L^s = l)$	0.95	0.05	-	-

(b) Pricing policies parameters

s	Pricing levels						Ordering
	Level 1			Level 2			Cost
	l_{s1}	u_{s1}	c_{s1}	l_{s2}	u_{s2}	c_{s2}	c_s^o
1	1	20	69	21	500	65	800
2	1	30	67	31	500	65	700
3	1	500	75	-	-	-	1000

Table 3. Solution of the numerical example using the $ILP - WFNS$ model.

t	1	2	3	4	5	6	7	8	9	10
D_t	-	-	-	-	180	100	30	10	80	-
$\mathbb{E}(I_t^+)$	-	-	-	-	31.3	14.6	4.8	-	-	-
$\mathbb{E}(I_t^-)$	-	-	-	-	8.9	8.9	7.7	-	4.0	-
$(Q_{1t5}, \ldots, Q_{1t9})$	-	-	-	$(60, \ldots)$	-	-	-	-	-	-
$(Q_{2t5}, \ldots, Q_{2t9})$	-	-	$(50, \ldots)$	$(\ldots, 30, 10, .)$	-	-	-	-	-	-
$(Q_{3t5}, \ldots, Q_{3t9})$	-	-	-	$(70, 100, \ldots)$	-	-	-	$(\ldots, 80)$	-	-

$ETC^* = 74041.5$; CPU time $= 14.3$ s

4 Conclusion

In this preliminary work, we propose a stochastic integer linear program (SILP) that minimises the expected total cost for the problem of multi-period multi-sourcing supply planning with stochastic lead-times, quantity-dependent pricing, and delivery flexibility costs. The results show the effectiveness of using multi-supplier strategy to cope with uncertainty of lead times. They also prove the relevance of considering other aspects related to suppliers, such as capacity, ordering costs and pricing policy. This approach could help decision maker to optimize its ordering policy. This work will be continued to focus on improving the model and its resolving approach in order to be able to study large and real-life sized instances. In fact, the weakness of the current model is its exponentially increasing number of scenarios with the number of suppliers and their ranges of lead-times distributions.

References

1. Stadtler, H.: Supply chain management and advanced planning–basics, overview and challenges. Eur. J. Oper. Res. **163**(3), 575–588 (2005)
2. Flynn, B.B., Koufteros, X., Lu, G.: On theory in supply chain uncertainty and its implications for supply chain integration. J. Supply Chain Manage. **52**(3), 3–27 (2016)
3. Simangunsong, E., Hendry, L.C., Stevenson, M.: Supply-chain uncertainty: a review and theoretical foundation for future research. Int. J. Production Res. **50**(16), 4493–4523 (2012)
4. Snyder, L.V., Atan, Z., Peng, P., Rong, Y., Schmitt, A.J., Sinsoysal, B.: Or/ms models for supply chain disruptions: a review. IIE Trans. **48**(2), 89–109 (2016)
5. Kleindorfer, P.R., Saad, G.H.: Managing disruption risks in supply chains. Prod. Oper. Manage. **14**(1), 53–68 (2005)
6. Brahimi, N., Absi, N., Dauzère-Pérès, S., Nordli, A.: Single-item dynamic lot-sizing problems: an updated survey. Eur. J. Oper. Res. **263**(3), 838–863 (2017)
7. Gonçalves, J.N., Carvalho, M.S., Cortez, P.: Operations research models and methods for safety stock determination: a review. Oper. Res. Perspect. **7**, 100164 (2020)

8. Ben-Ammar, O., Bettayeb, B., Dolgui, A.: Optimization of multi-period supply planning under stochastic lead times and a dynamic demand. Int. J. Prod. Econ. **218**, 106–117 (2019)
9. He, X.J., Kim, J.G., Hayya, J.C.: The cost of lead-time variability: the case of the exponential distribution. Int. J. Prod. Econ. **97**(2), 130–142 (2005)
10. Van Kampen, T.J., Van Donk, D.P., Van Der Zee, D.J.: Safety stock or safety lead time: coping with unreliability in demand and supply. Int. J. Prod. Res. **48**(24), 7463–7481 (2010)
11. Ben-Ammar, O., Bettayeb, B., Dolgui, A.: Mathematical model for dynamic suppliers' selection strategy in multi-period supply planning with lead-times uncertainty. IFAC-PapersOnLine **52**(13), 1040–1044 (2019)
12. Esmaeili-Najafabadi, E., Azad, N., Pourmohammadi, H., Nezhad, M.S.F.: Risk-averse outsourcing strategy in the presence of demand and supply uncertainties. Comput. Ind. Eng. **151**, 106906 (2021)
13. Ben-Ammar, O., Bettayeb, B., Dolgui, A.: Integrated production planning and quality control for linear production systems under uncertainties of cycle time and finished product quality. Int. J. Prod. Res. **58**(4), 1144–1160 (2020)
14. Jiang, R., Guan, Y.: An o (n2)-time algorithm for the stochastic uncapacitated lot-sizing problem with random lead times. Oper. Res. Lett. **39**(1), 74–77 (2011)
15. Huang, K., Küçükyavuz, S.: On stochastic lot-sizing problems with random lead times. Oper. Res. Lett. **36**(3), 303–308 (2008)
16. Riezebos, J.: Inventory order crossovers. Int. J. Prod. Econ. **104**(2), 666–675 (2006)
17. Verma, R., Pullman, M.E.: An analysis of the supplier selection process. Omega **26**(6), 739–750 (1998)
18. Van der Rhee, B., Verma, R., Plaschka, G.: Understanding trade-offs in the supplier selection process: the role of flexibility, delivery, and value-added services/support. Int. J. Prod. Econ. **120**(1), 30–41 (2009)
19. Ware, N.R., Singh, S., Banwet, D.: A mixed-integer non-linear program to model dynamic supplier selection problem. Exp. Syst. Appl. **41**(2), 671–678 (2014)
20. Ahmad, M.T., Mondal, S.: Dynamic supplier selection model under two-echelon supply network. Exp. Syst. Appl. **65**, 255–270 (2016)
21. Abginehchi, S., Farahani, R.Z.: Modeling and analysis for determining optimal suppliers under stochastic lead times. Appl. Math. Model. **34**(5), 1311–1328 (2010)
22. Songhori, M.J., Tavana, M., Azadeh, A., Khakbaz, M.H.: A supplier selection and order allocation model with multiple transportation alternatives. Int. J. Adv. Manuf. Technol. **52**(1–4), 365–376 (2011)

System Identification for Manufacturing Control Applications

Multi-step Problem of Inventory Control
with Returns

Alexander Mandel[1]([✉]) [iD] and Sergey Granin[2]

[1] Trapeznikov Institute of Control Sciences RAS, Moscow, Russia
[2] Moscow Institute of Physics and Technology, Moscow, Russia

Abstract. A new model of inventory control with returns is considered, when it is possible for consumers to return (under certain conditions) the products they have purchased. It proved to be that the optimal inventory control strategy in such a system turns out to be four-level.

Keywords: Inventory control with returns · Inventory control strategies

1 Introduction

A fundamentally new model of inventory control with returns is considered, which differs from the classical models of the theory of inventory control [1–3]. In this case, it is assumed that the consumer can not only purchase the goods stored in the warehouse or in the store, but also return it to the seller (possibly on terms different from the conditions of purchase). In the same way, it is assumed that the warehouse itself can not only submit an order for replenishment, but also return previously received consignments of goods to the same supplier (and also on different conditions). These models are not so common in the practice of managing warehouse systems. However, such situations are often typical for leasing schemes.

A few words about the main motivation for exploring this new inventory control model. It was due to the analogy identified between this formulation of the inventory control problem and management problems for one class of queuing systems firstly described in [4][1]. For such queuing systems control strategy consisted of to enable or disable redundant service channels [5, 6]. Based on this analogy, for a completely applied class of problems in the theory of controlled queuing systems, real algorithms for optimal channel switching in queuing systems were constructed.

2 Inventory Control Model with Returns

A multistep model of inventory control is considered during the planning period $T = (0, N\tau)$, where N is a sufficiently large natural number, of one type of product with

---

[1] In [4] the inventory control model with returns was called "fantasy".

© IFIP International Federation for Information Processing 2021
Published by Springer Nature Switzerland AG 2021
A. Dolgui et al. (Eds.): APMS 2021, IFIP AICT 630, pp. 521–527, 2021.
https://doi.org/10.1007/978-3-030-85874-2_55

backlogging of the outstanding demand (so-called backorders). The demand at each of the steps of the process is described by a model of independent in the aggregate, identically distributed random variables $\{z(n), n = 1, 2, \ldots, N\}$ with the distribution function $F(z)$. We will also assume that the delivery lag time is equal to 0. In this case, it is customary to associate the state of the inventory management system not with the stock on hand, but with a so-called inventory position. An inventory position (with a delivery time equal to 0) is defined [7] as the stock on hand minus the backordered demand.

Such a model describes well the systems for managing the stocks of mass consumption products, the demand for which is not (or is not very susceptible) to seasonal changes. This type of products include staple foods (baked goods, meat, dairy products, etc.), medicines for chronic diseases, and many, many others.

Unlike the classical multi-step inventory control model, we will assume that the domain of the demand distribution function at one step $F(z)$ is the entire real axis: $-\infty < z < +\infty$. Let also the mathematical expectation of this distribution be positive. The possibility of negative values of demand will be interpreted as the return by the consumer of the products purchased at the warehouse. We will also assume that when the goods are returned to the consumer, the entire amount that he paid when purchasing it is returned. The warehouse also gets the opportunity to return the goods to its supplier, paying a fixed amount A_2 for this, but the price c_2, at which the money is returned by the supplier, is less than the price of its purchase from the supplier: $c_2 < c_1$.

Let the criterion for the optimal functioning of the warehouse be the minimum of the total average costs during the planning period $[0, T]$, where $T = N\tau$, and τ is the duration of one-step between the moments of making order decisions. Let $C_n^*(x)$ denote the minimum possible value of average costs for the inventory control system, which has n steps left until the end of the planning period $[0, T]$ and which at the beginning of this interval has an inventory position x. Then we can write the following discrete dynamic programming equations:

$$C_0^*(x) \equiv 0; \quad C_n^*(x) = \min_u \{(A_1 + c_1 u) \times 1(u) + (A_2 + c_2 u) \times 1(-u) + g(x + u) \quad (1)$$

$$+\alpha \int_{-\infty}^{\infty} C_{n-1}^*(x + u - z) dF(z)\}, n = 1, 2, , \ldots, N \sigma$$

where $g(y) = h \int_{-\infty}^{\max\{y,0\}} (y - z) dF(z) + d \int_{\max\{y,0\}}^{+\infty} (z - y) dF(z)$, α is discount coefficient, $0 \le \alpha \le 1$ and $1(u)$ is the unit jump function (Heaviside function).

Equations (1) can be rewritten as follows

$$C_0^*(x) \equiv 0; \quad C_n^*(x) = -c_1 x + \min \begin{cases} A_1 + \min_{y > x} G_n(y), \\ \min\{G_n(x), \tilde{G}_n(x)\}, \\ A_2 + (c_1 + c_2)x + \min_{y < x} \tilde{G}_n(y), \end{cases} n = 1, 2, , \ldots, N.$$

$$(2)$$

where the function $G_n(y)$ is given by the formula

$$G_n(y) = c_1 y + h \int_{-\infty}^{\max\{y,0\}} (y-z)dF(z) + d \int_{\max\{y,0\}}^{+\infty} (z-y)dF(z) + \alpha \int_{-\infty*}^{+\infty} C_{n-1}^*(y-z)dF(z), \tag{3}$$

and the function $\tilde{G}_n(y)$ by the formula

$$\tilde{G}_n(y) = -c_2 y + h \int_{-\infty}^{\max\{y,0\}} (y-z)dF(z) + d \int_{\max\{y,0\}}^{+\infty} (z-y)dF(z) + \alpha \int_{-\infty}^{\infty} C_{n-1}^*(y-z)dF(z). \tag{4}$$

In the framework of the economics of calculating costs, the function $\min\limits_{y>x} G_n(y)$ describes the minimum variable part of the costs when making a decision to place an order (excluding the fixed part A_1 and the current inventory position x and including the case of failure to submit an order when $u = 0$), and the function $\min\limits_{y<x} \tilde{G}_n(y)$ is equal to variable part of the minimum cost when deciding whether to return the goods to the supplier (excluding the fixed part A_2 and the current inventory position x). Note also that, due to the form of the functions $G_n(y)$ and $\tilde{G}_n(y)$, the point S_n of the absolute minimum of the function $\tilde{G}_n(y)$ is located to the right of the point R_n of the absolute minimum of the function $G_n(y)$[2].

In the next Fig. 1 shows the hypothetical form and relative position of the functions $G_n(y)$ and $\tilde{G}_n(y)$.

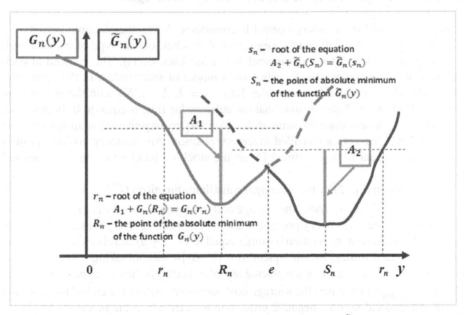

Fig. 1. Type and arrangement of functions $G_n(y)$ и $\tilde{G}_n(y)$.

---

[2] This statement will be proved in the next section.

For the functions $G_n(y)$ and $\tilde{G}_n(y)$ shown in Fig. 1 the optimal rule of inventory control is given by the formula:

$$u_n^*(x) = \begin{cases} R_n - x, \text{ if } x \leq r_n, \\ 0, \text{ if } r_n < x < s_n, \\ x - S_n, \text{ if } \geq s_n. \end{cases}$$ (5)

So, if the functions $G_n(y)$ and $\tilde{G}_n(y)$ for all values of n have the properties that are qualitatively characterized in Fig. 1, then the optimal inventory control strategy turns out to be a four-level (R_n, r_n, S_n, s_n)-strategy $(r_n < R_n < S_n < s_n)$. This strategy is arranged so that:

(1) If the inventory position x at the time of making decisions n steps before the end of the planning period is less than or equal to r_n, then an order is submitted that replenishes the inventory position in the warehouse to the value R_n.
(2) If the inventory position x at the time of making decisions n steps before the end of the planning period is greater than or equal to s_n, then part of the stock from the warehouse is returned to the supplier so as to bring the inventory position in the warehouse to the value S_n.

3 Proof of Optimality of (R_n, r_n, S_n, s_n)-strategies

A multistep model of inventory control is considered during the planning period $T = (0, N\tau)$, where N is a sufficiently large natural number, of one type of product with backlogging of the outstanding demand (so-called backorders). The demand at each of the steps of the process is described by a model of independent in the aggregate, identically distributed random variables $\{z(n), n = 1, 2, ..., N\}$ with the distribution function $F(z)$. We will also assume that the delivery lag time is equal to 0. In this case, it is customary to associate the state of the inventory management system not with the stock on hand, but with a so-called inventory position. An inventory position (with a delivery time equal to 0) is defined [1] as the stock on hand minus the backordered demand.

We transform Eq. (2) by introducing the auxiliary functions $G_{\text{order}}^{(n)}(y)$ and $G_{\text{return}}^{(n)}(y)$. The function $G_{\text{order}}^{(n)}(y)$ describes the average cost for n steps before the end of the planning period at the current inventory position x and when deciding on a positive order size u (after which the inventory position becomes equal to $y = x + u$) and choosing the optimal inventory control strategy at subsequent $(n-1)^{\text{th}}$ steps without taking into account the constant component of costs when placing an order A_1 (this is the subscript "order"). The function $G_{\text{return}}^{(n)}(y)$ describes the average cost for n steps before the end of the planning period when deciding on a negative order size u (after which the inventory level also becomes equal to $y = x + u$) and the choice of the optimal inventory management strategy at the subsequent $(n-1)^{\text{th}}$ th steps without taking into account the constant component of costs when placing an order A_2 (this is the subscript "return"). Let

$$G_{\text{order}}^{(n)}(y) = c_1 y + g(y) + \alpha \int_{-\infty}^{+\infty} C_{n-1}^*(y - z)dF(z), n\overline{1, N},$$ (6)

$$G_{\text{return}}^{(n)}(y) = -c_2 y + g(y) + \alpha \int_{-\infty}^{+\infty} C_{n-1}^*(y - z)dF(z), \quad n\overline{1, N}. \tag{7}$$

Using functions (6)–(7), one can rewrite Eqs. (2) in the following form:

$$C_0^*(x) \equiv 0; \ C_n^*(x) = \min \begin{cases} -c_1 x + \min \begin{cases} A_1 + \min\limits_{u>0} G_{\text{order}}^{(n)}(x + u), \\ G_{\text{order}}^{(n)}(x), \end{cases} \\ c_2 x + \min \begin{cases} A_2 + \min\limits_{u<0} G_{\text{return}}^{(n)}(x + u), \\ G_{\text{return}}^{(n)}(x). \end{cases} \end{cases} \quad n\overline{1, N}. \tag{8}$$

Proposition 1. $R_n < S_n$.

Proof. Due to the fact that $c_1 > c_2$ and using formulas (7)–(8), it is easy to show that the points of absolute minima in y of the functions $G_{\text{order}}^{(n)}(y)$ and $G_{\text{return}}^{(n)}(y)$ lead to such values of y denoted by R_n and S_n respectively (see Sect. 2) are ordered in accordance with the inequality $R_n < S_n$. Q.E.D.

In order to use the technique of proving the optimality of two-level (S, s) -strategies proposed in [1, 7] recall the basic notion of the A-convexity, on which this proof was based.

Definition 1. An everywhere differentiable function $f(y)$ is called A-convex $(A \geq 0)$ if, for any $a > 0$, the next inequality holds

$$A + f(x + a) - f(x) - f'(x)a \geq 0. \tag{9}$$

It turns out that in order to prove the optimality of (R_n, r_n, S_n, s_n)-strategies, it is necessary to introduce a generalization of this concept.

Definition 2. Let there exist a real number a, which has the property that it is to the right of the point of absolute minimum of the everywhere differentiable function $f(x)$ and for all real y and z such that the points y and $y + z$ are to the left of the point a, that is belong to the interval $(-\infty, a)$, the next inequality holds

$$A + f(y + z) - f(y) - f'(y)z0, A \geq 0. \tag{10}$$

Then the function $f(x)$ is called A-convex on the left in the interval $(-\infty, a]$.

Definition 3. Let there exist a real number b, which has the property that it is to the left of the point of absolute minimum of the everywhere differentiable function $f(x)$ and for all real y and z such that the points y and $y + z$ are to the right of the point b, that is belong to the interval (b, ∞), the inequality (11) holds then the function $f(x)$ is called A-convex on the right in the interval $[b, \infty)$.

Proposition 2. All functions $C_n^*(x)$ are A_1-convex on the left and A_2-convex on the right.

Proof. Using formulas (6)–(7) for the case $n = 1$, it is easy to show that the functions $G_{\text{order}}^{(n)}(y)$ and $G_{\text{return}}^{(n)}(y)$ are convex, that is, 0-convex, and by the characteristic properties of the A-convexity construction [1], are A_1- и A_2- convex, respectively. Hence, as in ([1], by virtue of formula (8) for the case $n = 1$, it is established that the function $C_1^*(x)$ is simultaneously A_1-convex on the left and A_2-convex on the right.

Let us state the hypothesis of mathematical induction that for some number $n > 1$ the functions $C_n^*(x)$ are A_1-convex on the left and A_2-convex on the right. Further progress consists in establishing the fact that the $G_{\text{order}}^{(n+1)}(y)$ function is A_1-convex and the $G_{\text{return}}^{(n+1)}(y)$ function is A_2-convex. This follows from formulas (6) and (7) and the scheme of the proof, as in the case $n = 1$, repeats the scheme of the proof given in [1]. Then it will follow from Eq. (9) and *Proposition* 1 that the function $C_{n+1}^*(x)$ will also be A_1-convex on the left and A_1-convex on the right. In this case, the role of points a and b from *Definitions* 2 and 3 is played by the common point e of intersection of the graphs of the curves (see Fig. 1). *Q.E.D.*

As a result, the optimal inventory management strategy will be determined by the rule established by formula (6). In this case, the parameters r_n and s_n in formula (6) are solutions of the following equations (see Fig. 1):

$$A_1 + G_{\text{order}}^{(n)}(R_n) = G_{\text{order}}^{(n)}(r_n), \text{ for } r_n < R_n, \tag{11}$$

$$A_2 + G_{\text{return}}^{(n)}(S_n) = G_{\text{return}}^{(n)}(s_n) \text{ for } s_n > S_n. \tag{12}$$

It is easy to see that the proof of the above mathematical induction hypothesis methodologically repeats the proof of a similar proposition (for two-level strategies) in the classical theory of inventory management [1], adjusted for the alternativeness (orders and returns) of the objective functional.

4 Summary

A fundamentally new model of inventory control with returns is considered. It is proved that the optimal inventory control strategy according to this model turns out to be a four-level (R, r, S, s)-strategy. This strategy is an essential generalization of the well-known two-level (S, s) -strategies. The analogies between the optimization problems of the inventory control theory and the theory of controlled queuing systems are noted.

References

1. Hadley, G; Whitin, T.M.: Analysis of Inventory Systems. Prentice-Hall, Inc. Englewood Clifs, New Jersey (1963)
2. Pervozvansky, A.: Mathematical Models of Inventory and Production Control. Science Publ. House, Moscow (in Russian, 1975)
3. Lototsky, V., Mandel, A.: Inventory Control Models and Methods. Science Publ. House, Moscow (in Russian, 1992)
4. Mandel, A., Granin, S.: Investigation of analogies between the problems of inventory control and the problems of the controlled queuing systems. In: Proceedings of the 11th International Conference "Management of Large-Scale System Development" (MLSD), Moscow, pp. 1–4. IEEE (2018). https://doi.org/10.1109/MLSD.2018.855185

5. Mandel, A., Laptin, V.: Myopic channel switching strategies for stationary mode: threshold calculation algorithms. In: Vishnevskiy, V.M., Kozyrev, D.V. (eds.) DCCN 2018. CCIS, vol. 919, pp. 410–420. Springer, Cham (2018). https://doi.org/10.1007/978-3-319-99447-5_35
6. Mandel, A.S., Laptin, V.A.: Channel switching threshold strategies for multichannel controllable queuing systems. In: Vishnevskiy, V.M., Samouylov, K.E., Kozyrev, D.V. (eds.) DCCN 2020. CCIS, vol. 1337, pp. 259–270. Springer, Cham (2020). https://doi.org/10.1007/978-3-030-66242-4_21
7. Karlin, S.: Mathematical Methods and Theory in Games, Programming, and Economics. Addison-Wesley Publishing Company, New York (1959)

Expert-Classification Methods for Estimation of the Structure and Parameters of Controlled Queueing Systems

Alexander Mandel[1]([✉]) [iD], Sergey Granin[2], and Viktor Laptin[3]

[1] Trapeznikov Institute of Control Sciences RAS, Moscow, Russia
[2] Moscow Institute of Physics and Technology, Moscow, Russia
[3] Lomonosov Moscow State University, Moscow, Russia
straqker@bk.ru

Abstract. The problem consideration of estimating the structure and parameters of a queuing system, in which at the moments of control, which are separated from each other by a fixed time step, the optimal switching of the service channels is carried out. To solve the problem of assessing the structure and parameters of the model, procedures of expert-classification analysis and structural forecasting are proposed.

Keywords: Controlled queuing systems · Markov input stream · Structure and parameter estimation

1 Introduction

The problem of estimating the structure and parameters of the model of optimal control of the queuing system (QS), described in [1], is considered. The main assumption in [1] is the hypothesis of a jump-like Markov step-by-step change in the intensity of the simplest incoming flow. Classical methods of statistical estimation are not quite suitable for studying the structure (the number of elements in a set and the values of various intensities of the incoming flow), as well as the probabilities of transition from state to state. As an alternative, a set of procedures for expert-classification analysis and structural forecasting is proposed.

2 Queuing System Model

As stated in [1], in the studied QS the number of working service channels can be changed at the moments of control, which are separated from each other for a fixed time (the control step). In this case, it is considered that the QS receives the simplest incoming flow, the intensity of which $\lambda(t)$ is constant throughout the step, and at the moments of control it undergoes jump-like Markov changes, taking a finite number k

© IFIP International Federation for Information Processing 2021
Published by Springer Nature Switzerland AG 2021
A. Dolgui et al. (Eds.): APMS 2021, IFIP AICT 630, pp. 528–534, 2021.
https://doi.org/10.1007/978-3-030-85874-2_56

of values λ_i from the discrete set $\Lambda = \left\{ \lambda_i, i \in \overline{1, k} \right\}$. The task is to form a strategy for switching working channels (disconnecting a part of working channels or putting into operation reserve channels), which minimizes the average costs of the QS for a given N-step planning period. In this case, as in [1], it is assumed that the matrix of transition probabilities of the corresponding homogeneous Markov chain $P = \|p_{ij}\|$ is given, where p_{ij} is the transition probability (at the time of control) from the intensity $\lambda_i, i \in \overline{1, k}$, at the previous step to the intensity $\lambda_j, j \in \overline{1, k}$, at the next step.

In [1] was shown that solving the problem of choosing the optimal channel switching strategy is reduced to the following system of dynamic programming equations:

$$C_1^*(\lambda_i, m) = \min_{u \geq \underline{u}_i} C^{(1)}(\lambda_i, m, u), \tag{1}$$

$$C_n^*(\lambda_i, m) = \min_{u \geq \underline{u}_i} \left\{ C^{(1)}(\lambda_i, m, u) + \sum_{j=1}^{l} p_{ij} C_{n-1}^*(\lambda_j, u) \right\}, n \in \overline{2, N}, \tag{2}$$

where $C_n^*(\lambda_i, m)$ is the minimum possible value of the total average costs at the last n steps of the control process, when the mathematical expectation is taken along the trajectory of the incoming flow intensity, which makes Markov jumps. The variable u in Eqs. (1)–(2) is the current (n steps before the end of the planning period) value of the control decision on the number of switched working channels. It has been proved that the optimal channel switching strategy, as in the equivalent inventory control problem with returns [2], is a four-level strategy.

3   The Problem Setting

In the process of practical use of model (1)–(2), it is necessary to estimate the points of the different incoming flow intensities of the $\Lambda = \{\lambda_i,\}, i \in \overline{1, k}$ (system structure) and the values of the transition probabilities (system parameters) of the corresponding homogeneous Markov chain $P = \|p_{ij}\|$, where p_{ij} is the probability of transition (at the time of control) from the intensity $\lambda_i, i \in \overline{1, k}$, at the previous step to the intensity λ_j, $j \in \overline{1, k}$, in the next step.

To solve the problem of assessing the structure of the system and its parameters, the concept of structural forecasting [3–5] with the involvement of methods of expert-classification analysis [6, 7] was chosen.

The idea of structural forecasting is that there is a structured (into clusters) set of dynamically changing objects characterized by a variety of features. This set of objects is subjected to an automatic classification procedure [6] with the assistance of experts, i.e. expert-classification analysis [7].

3.1   Observation Data for Controlled QS

Naturally, the results of observations are strongly related to the subject area to which the corresponding QSs belong. In any case, they represent data on the average intensities of incoming flows at each step and various information about specific QS. In this case, separate time intervals with the results of observations of the same QS can act as different objects.

The choosing a set of observations problem solution generates a set of p objects is formed, each of which is characterized by a set of m parameters and is represented by a segment of its trajectory in the state space. Let the discrete duration of this time interval be natural number L. This set of trajectory segments will be called a training sample. The behavior of this set of objects (trajectory segments) at discrete moments of time is studied. The m-dimensional parameter space X is introduced into consideration, in which the jth object at time n is represented by the point $x_j(n) = \left\{ x_j^{(1)}(n), x_j^{(2)}(n), \ldots, x_j^{(m)}(n) \right\}$. An ordered set of points $x_j(n)$ is a known part of the trajectory that characterizes the dynamics of the jth object.

3.2 Formation of the Initial Cluster Structure

To identify the cluster structure of the considered set of objects, a complex automatic classification algorithm is used [8]. The complex algorithm includes m-local optimization algorithms of a given criterion, selection of informative parameters, selection of an initial partition, selection of the number of clusters and filling in missing observations [9].

In modeling and in applications, as a criterion, we used the functional J of the average proximity of points in clusters, defined through the potential function [10]:

$$K(x, y) = 1 / \left(1 + R^{(m)}(x, y) \right), \tag{3}$$

where $R^{(m)}(x, y)$ is the chosen metric in space X and α and m are tunable parameters of the algorithm. The average proximity of points in a cluster is defined as:.

$$K(A_i, A_j) = \frac{2}{p_i(1 - p_i)} \sum_{i=1}^{p_i} \sum_{j>i} K(x_i, x_j), \tag{4}$$

where $K(x_i, x_j)$ is determined by formula (3), p_i is the number of points in the cluster A_i.

Then criterion J is defined as:

$$K(A_i, A_j) = \frac{2}{p_i(1 - p_i)} \sum_{i=1}^{p_i} \sum_{j>i} K(x_i, x_j), \tag{5}$$

4 Stages of the Problem Solving

4.1 Procedure for Identifying the Initial Structure and Evaluating the Initial Approximation to the Transition Probabilities of Objects

Let the distances for points $x_j(1)$ to the current standards $a_i(1)$ of all selected clusters $R_{ji}^{(1)} = R(x_j(1), a_i(1)), i = 1, 2, \ldots, k, j = 1, 2, \ldots, p$. This allows us to solve the problem of identifying the initial structure of clusters and evaluating cluster standards, that is, the structure of the set $\Lambda = \{\lambda_i, \}$, $i \in \overline{1, k}$, and the corresponding values λ_i.

Then the elements of the transition probability matrix of object j to cluster i, the values $p_{ji}^{(1)} = p_{ji}(1)$ are calculated as follows:

$$p_{ji}^{(1)} = \frac{j^{(1)}}{R_{ji}^{(1)}}, ,$$ (6)

where $j^{(1)}.$ is a normalizing factor.

4.2 The Procedure for Evaluating Subsequent Approximations to the Transition Probabilities of Objects

After identifying the initl structure and evaluating the initial approximation to the transition probabilities of objects at the next steps, the elements of the transition probabilities matrix of object j to cluster i are modified using the following procedure. Let us introduce the notation $R_{ji}^{(n)} = R_{ji}^{(n)} - R_{ji}^{(n-1)}$. If the jth point at the moment n coincides with the standard of the i_0^{th} cluster, i.e. $R_{ji_0}^{(n)} = 0$, then.

$$p_{ji}^{(n)} = \begin{cases} 1, & \text{if } i = i_0, \\ 0, & \text{if } i = 1, \dots, k, \ i \neq i_0 \end{cases} "$$

In other words, if a point coincides with the standard of a certain cluster, then the probability for this point to stay in this cluster is 1, and the probability of moving to another cluster is 0.

For the case when $R_{ji_0}^{(n)} \neq 0$ transition probabilities are modified according to the following scheme:

$$p_{ji}^{(n)} = \left\{ p_{ji}^{(n-1)} + \left[\frac{1 + \text{sign}\left(R_{ji}^{(n)}\right)}{2} - p_{ji}^{(n-1)} \text{sign}\left(R_{ji}^{(n)}\right) \right] R_{ji}^{(n)} \right\},$$ (7)

where $\text{sign } z = \begin{cases} 1, & \text{if } z \geq 0, \\ 0, & \text{if } z < 0, \end{cases}$ and γ is the normalizing factor determined by the

normalization condition for the transition probabilities: $\sum_{i=1}^{k} p_{ji}^{(n)} = 1$:

4.3 Methods for Estimating the Required Intensities λ_j and Transition Probabilities p_{ij} from Formula (2)

Since formula (2) uses the probabilities of transition p_{ij} of the considered QS from cluster i to cluster j, and the two previous paragraphs provide predictive estimates of the probabilities of transition of a specific object to a specific cluster, depending on the nature of the training sample, one can act in the following two ways.

Method 1. Let the QS under consideration be only one of the objects of the training sample with number s. Then, to estimate the probabilities p_{ij} it is reasonable to use the relation.

$$p_{ij} = p_{sj}^{(L)}, \text{ object with number } s \text{ belongs to cluster } A_i, \tag{8}$$

where L is the length of the time series segment in the training sample, A_i is the cluster of objects with the number i, and the estimates $p_{sj}^{(L)}$ are calculated by formulas (6)–(7).

Method 2. If the considered QS is the only object of the training sample. In other words, the training set is based on the prehistory of the evolution of this QS in its various segments. Then, to estimate the probabilities p_{ij} one can use the relation

$$p_{ij} = \frac{1}{p_i} \sum_{s \in A_i} p_{sj}^{(L)}, \tag{9}$$

where L is the length of the time series segment in the training sample, A_i is the cluster of objects with the number i, the estimates $p_{sj}^{(L)}$ are calculated by formulas (6)–(7) and p_i is the number of objects in the cluster A_i.

5 Computer Modelling

In this section, we present several graphs of the dependence of the average costs per one step, obtained as a result of modeling the process of functioning of a queuing system (QS) with switchable service channels, which, as noted in the Sect. 1, is equivalent to the inventory control model with returns using the same four-level strategies. The graphs show the values of the costs $C^*(m)$ (blue color), as well as the values of the functions $B_{on}(m)$ (red color) and $B_{off}(m)$ (green color), where the footnote "on" means turn on the channels in QS and the footnote "off" means turn off the channels in QS. The specificity of the QS is that, in any case, the number of included working service channels must satisfy the condition $u \geq m_{\lim}(\lambda_i) = \lambda/\mu + 1$ for the existence of a stationary mode in the QS [11], where μ is the service rate on one channel (Fig. 1).

6 Summary

To solve the problem of assessing the structure and parameters of the model for choosing the optimal channel switching strategy in a controlled queuing system (QS), procedures for expert-classification analysis and structural forecasting are proposed. An example is given.

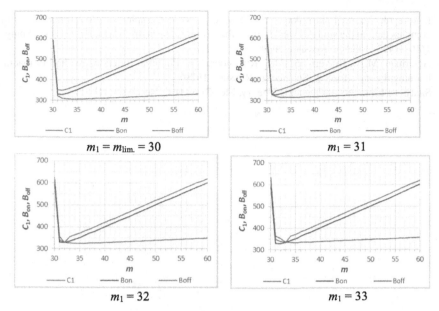

Fig. 1. Function graphs: average costs per step.

References

1. Mandel, A.S., Laptin, V.A.: Channel switching threshold strategies for multichannel controllable queuing systems. In: Vishnevskiy, V.M., Samouylov, K.E., Kozyrev, D.V. (eds.) DCCN 2020. CCIS, vol. 1337, pp. 259–270. Springer, Cham (2020). https://doi.org/10.1007/978-3-030-66242-4_21

2. Mandel, A., Granin, S.: Investigation of analogies between the problems of inventory control and the problems of the controlled queuing systems. In: Proceedings of the 11th International Conference Management of Large-Scale System Development (MLSD), IEEE, 2018, Moscow, pp. 1–4. IEEE (2018). https://doi.org/10.1109/MLSD.2018.855185

3. Dorofeyuk, Y.A.: Adaptive structural forecasting methods. Inf. Technol. Comput. Syst. (3), 53–58 (in Russian, 2010)

4. Bordukov, D.A., Dorofeyuk, Y.A.: Algorithms for structural forecasting. In: Materials of the 11th International Conference Management of Large-Scale Systems Development (MLSD'2018, Moscow), Moscow, ICS RAS, vol. 2, pp. 337–340 (in Russian, 2018)

5. Dorofeyuk, Y.A., Chernyavsky, A.L.: Intelligent methods of dynamic structural data analysis. Sensors Syst. (10), 3–8 (in Russian, 2019)

6. Bauman, E.V., Dorofeyuk, A.A.: Classification data analysis. In: Proceedings of the International Conference on Management Problems, Mosco. SINTEG, vol. 1. pp. 62–77 (in Russian, 1999)

7. Mandel, A.S., Dorofeyuk, Yu.A.: Expert-classification and expert-statistical information processing and decision-making. In: Proceedings of the International Conference on the Intellectualization of Information Processing. pp. 165–168. (in Russian, 2010)

8. Dorofeyuk, Yu.: Formation of arrays for modeling algorithms for intelligent information processing, modeling a complex algorithm for automatic classification. Large Syst. Manag. (31), 353–362 (in Russian, 2010)

9. Dorofeyuk, Yu.A., Pokrovskaya, I.V., Kiseleva, N.E.: Complex of algorithms for mining complex data in the study of weakly formalized control systems. Mach. Learn. Data Analysis **1**(10), 1423–1438 (in Russian, 2014)
10. Aizerman, M.A., Braverman, E.M., Rozonoer, L.I.: Potential functions method in machine learning theory. Moscow, Science (in Russian, 1970)
11. Saaty, T.: Elements of Queueing Theory. Mc. Graw Hill, New York (1961)

Simulation Experiment in a Virtual Laboratory Environment as a Ground for Production Competencies Acquiring

Natalia Bakhtadze[1](✉) (iD), Oleg Zaikin[2], and Andrzey Żylawski[2]

[1] V.A. Trapeznikov Institute of Control Sciences RAS, Moscow, Russia
[2] Warsaw School of Computer Science, 00-169, Warsaw, Poland
ozaikin@poczta.wwsi.edu.pl

Abstract. The paper describes advantages of teaching and application of modelling manufacturing systems. Two paradigms of modelling: Queuing systems and Simulation are briefly presented and analysed. Advantages of distance learning these approaches worldwide are presented. Furthermore, a combined way of learning these two methods, with a focus on the modelling and simulating selected basic processes of manufacturing systems, is proposed in briefly described case study. The concept provides division of this method depending on student's education level.

Keywords: Manufacturing competencies · Queuing systems and simulation · Virtual laboratory

1 Introduction

Simulation is a technique for practice and learning that can be applied to many different disciplines and trainees. It is a technique to replace and amplify real processes or experiences with controlled ones, that replicate substantial aspects of the real world in a fully interactive fashion. Simulation-based learning can be the way to develop professionals' knowledge, skills, and attitudes, whilst protecting students from labour-intensive costs and unnecessary risks. Simulation-based education can be a platform which provides a valuable tool in learning to theoretical bases and resolve practical tasks in manufacturing systems [1].

Simulation-based training techniques, tools, and strategies can be applied in designing structured learning experiences, as well as be used as a measurement tool related to targeted teamwork competencies and learning objectives. In manufacturing, simulation offers good scope for training of interdisciplinary project teams. The realistic scenarios and equipment allows for retraining and practice till one can master the necessary knowledge or skill. Teamwork training conducted in the simulated environment may offer an additive benefit to the traditional methods of learning, enhance performance, and also help reduce errors in designing and decision - making in manufacturing.

A. Dolgui et al. (Eds.): APMS 2021, IFIP AICT 630, pp. 535–545, 2021.
https://doi.org/10.1007/978-3-030-85874-2_57

A simulation experiment can prove to be a useful ground for providing the necessary skills in a very broad sense: from problem (task) statement, through problem analysis, mathematical and simulation modelling to conducting a research experiment and interpreting the results. The simulation modelling is a multi-stage and interactive process. Dividing it into stages is a consequence of qualities the simulation process contains a research method. Each of the stages requires identification of the type and the contents of applicable knowledge and that fact becomes the foundation for development of a problem-specific tasks sequence. It is therefore reasonable to claim that precise measuring of competencies acquisition process is equally effective as it is in the traditional learning environment.

Using the principles presented herein, it is possible to establish an instance of a laboratory of simulation. The laboratory is based on the use of a typical model repository classified according to Kendall's notation [2]. That problem has already been analysed in the context of a procedure for personal competencies acquisition. The content and order of problem simulation-oriented tasks is a result of a widely accepted routine dealing with preparation and formulation of stages in the simulation experiment [3, 4] and [5]. Let us examine the particular stages of conducting the simulation procedure in the perspective of the tasks provided to the learning individual.

2 Methodology for Developing the Simulation Model

2.1 Statement of Simulation Experiment

Development of the simulation model requires initial problem conceptualization and specification of the given problem using terms of a relevant domain. Problem conceptualization may usually be represented by inconsistent structure and is often implemented using unsophisticated description formed using natural language. The inherent diversity of concepts in that case and limited precision of specification of the problem statement create major problems at the stage of modelling. The most complex issue is maintaining accuracy in the process of transformation of concepts of the analysed domain to terms and functions applied in a given simulation tool, i.e. to a certain portion of procedural knowledge [6].

Simulation software usually includes libraries of predefined templates for modelling different problem domains. Unfortunately, in most cases they are fairly limited in scope and applicability and their are designed to respond to select, or most typical problems. On the other hand, they effectively handle entire classes of problems within a scope of given mathematical topic, i.e. fundamental (theoretical) knowledge that is represented by well defined structure and concept taxonomy. In such case it is possible to identify and formulate an official analytical model. Moreover, a mathematical apparatus and formal notation are available for precise analytical task formulation. We can refer to the example of Kendall's notation serving the queuing system theory [2].

Therefore, the stage of problem statement using the concepts of universally known mathematical engine and its relevant notation can be seen as less complex in performing transformation of the domain concepts to formulas used in the given simulation software than in the example of direct transformation to the terms of a chosen domain characterized by limited precision of its concepts. That is why the previously mentioned stages of simulation experiment statement conducted in the environment of virtual laboratory should be complemented by several iterations of mapping of the verbal problem representation onto the simulation model [7] (Fig. 1). In that context, documents such as the 2000 Mathematics Subject Classification in which mathematical taxonomy is introduced play a pivotal role in facilitating the process of identification of adequate mathematical engine upon formalizing the problem domain.

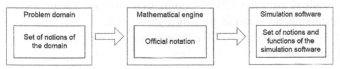

Fig. 1. The stages of mapping the conceptual model in the process of simulation experiment statement (source: [8])

As it has been shown on Fig. 1, the simulation experiment statement is exemplified by use of the concepts that are specific to the given simulation software. The concepts form a language for defining the problem and requirements essential for conducting the simulation experiment. The preparation of the concepts is not possible without completing the stage of forming the assumptions about the specific problem using the concepts of the domain that the analysed problem is pertinent to. The simulation experiment statement performed in such approach is difficult to be translated to the language (terms and formulas) of the simulation software. Hence, additional modelling process is performed using a mathematical apparatus that is adequate to the given problem. Using that measure significantly simplifies the simulation process of the mathematical model using the given simulation software.

It is vital for the process of formulation of initial assumptions about the researched problem to identify a criterium for performing analysis of the model. Once the criterium has been determined, its examination is required in order to identify its characteristics (continuous, or discrete), or to find other significant parameters. The problem containing properly defined criterium can be subject to modelling using the procedure of mapping the concepts of fundamental knowledge onto procedural knowledge. The mapping can be carried out through identification of direct equivalents between distinct conceptual models [7].

2.2 Algorithm for Determining Simulation Experiment Settings

The algorithm for determining the simulation experiment settings will be discussed using an example of a research problem defined using queuing systems theory. Using a queuing systems theory, an elementary event occurring at the input to the system is to be determined. Naturally, the event is considered the most significant component of the model. In addition, all the parameters involved in the event input stream are to be determined, their average intensity (i.e. a number of events on a given time frame and their characteristic: continuous, or discrete). If the input event stream is of stochastic nature, a probability distribution function of time intervals between the incoming events should be determined. In a queuing theory system, a numerous types of events can appear, and for that reason the process of the system identification and determination of the operational parameters should be performed for each of the type respectively.

The process of defining the elementary events is key importance to the queuing system model. Thus, it should be repeated some number of times in order to thoroughly investigate the given problem. Once the research activities have been completed resulting in the definition being sound and acceptable, it then possible to identify the rational laying foundations for the simulation experiment. The assumptions for the experiment are determined using the ARENA simulation software. The previously deliberated mathematical-to-simulation model transformation process is conducted according to the principles of concept mapping [8]. To conclude, the algorithm for determining rationale of the simulation experiment for queuing system theory using the ARENA software is contained in the following steps:

1. Given a problem domain, perform a task statement.
2. Determine an elementary and determine parameters of the event flow.
3. Refine the event definition through recurrent operation with steps (1) and (2). The process is terminated when a researcher is convinced that the problem can be solved using queuing systems theory.
4. Identify a structure of the queuing systems-based system.
5. Determine an initial outline (specification) of the experiment.
6. Create a corresponding simulation model using the ARENA software [9].

3 Queuing Modelling of the Virtual Laboratory Management System

3.1 Structure of the Virtual Laboratory Management System

Let us consider the process of management in virtual laboratory as a typical closed queuing system containing several special types of servers and one class of learners, hereafter referred to as students [8]. Virtual laboratory as a queuing system can be described very simply because we can use existing analytical models. For example, we can consider the problem of optimization of queuing system parameters. To solve this task, it is important to learn some of the characteristics typical of queuing systems, such as:

- average number of students in the class,
- average waiting time in the queue,
- average service time,
- average time thinking for each type of order or the use of servers.

Let us consider a situation typical for virtual laboratory (VL) - a finite population of users, a local network (e.g. Intranet) and no restrictions on the length of the waiting queue. In our deliberations, we will focus on closed queuing system. The structure of such a system in the context of VL is presented in the Fig. 2. In the case of a closed system, we will divide the simulation process into six main components:

1) Server (class) of students.
2) Learning server - a repository of didactic materials.
3) Teacher server.
4) Simulation server - a repository of simulation models.
5) Tutor's server.
6) Administrator server - SQL registration and identification database.

The student class generates orders with random time intervals. The order process is carried out in the following order:

1) The first student's order is sent to the administrator's server for registration and identification. Each student has the same characteristics of arrival and service.
2) The student generates orders to the teacher's server to solve the input test and receive a theoretical task. The order to the teacher's server can be sent several times.
3) Student in order to complete the theoretical task generates orders for:

- learning server with access to a repository of didactic materials,
- teacher's server (for consultation),
- administrator's server (in case of failure).

4) After the entry test and sending the answer to the theoretical question, the student asks the tutor's server to ask for a practical task, in this case the task with the simulation model.
5) The student generates orders for:

- a model repository to conduct a simulation experiment,
- tutor server (for consultation) once again to
- administration server

6) The student leaves the system.

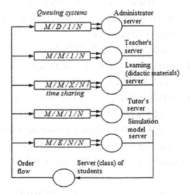

Fig. 2. The structure of queuing systems in simulation experiment process (own study based on [10])

Statement of the Task. With a large number of students and their independence, the flow of orders generated in the student class and the flow of incoming orders to each type of server can be considered as stationary. The process of generating orders of student class can be described by the Poisson distribution. The service time in the teacher's server is assumed as exponential.

Consider the situation when students need to find didactic materials in the learning server or the relevant exam dates in the administration server. Because in our model the teacher is a consultant, student orders in the learning server are handled in consultation mode.

There are several types of servers and corresponding queuing systems in the open distance learning environment. Each server has different assignment and productivity. We use the *Kendall notation* [2] to describe them.

A/B/X/Y/Z, where:
A - distribution of the order arrival process,
B - service time distribution in the server,
X - number of parallel servers,
Y - system capacity,
Z – queue service discipline.

In the queuing system, student works are treated as user orders. Consider a finite population of customers. In general, different students need different time to think. This is related to the cognitive characteristics of the student. In addition, it is important to ensure that the material can be selected and delivered on time. We simplify the real situation and assume that every student has the same cognitive model. In the case of the open distance learning system, we distinguish the following queuing systems.

1. *Administrator server M/D/1/N* - orders from students arrive according to the Poisson process, the time of service is deterministic (permanent). The number of servers is equal to *1*. System capacity - equal to the number of students (N). Servicing discipline – *FIFO*, i.e. first came - first served.
2. *Teacher's server M/M/1/N* - orders from students arrive in accordance with the Poisson process, the service time distribution is exponential. The system contains only one teacher. The capacity of the system is equal to the number of students (N). Servicing discipline – *FIFO,* the first came - first served.
3. *Learning server (didactic materials) M/M/X/N/time sharing* - orders from students arrive in accordance with the Poisson process, the service time distribution is exponential. The number of servers is equal to X, where the size of X is determined by economic factors. The capacity of the system is equal to the number of students (N). Server operation time is evenly distributed among all orders in the system (*time sharing*).
4. *Tutor's server M/M/1/N* - orders from students arrive according to the Poisson process, the service time distribution is exponential. The number of servers is equal to 1. The capacity of the system is equal to the number of students (N). Servicing discipline – *FIFO*, first came - first served.
5. *Server of simulation models M/E/N/N* - orders from students arrive in accordance with the Poisson process, the service time distribution is Erlang's function. The number of servers is equal to *1*. The capacity of the system is equal to the number of students (N).

Servicing discipline - *FIFO*, first came- first served. The Erlang time of service is due to the fact that the process of servicing each task is multi-phase, where k is the number of phases of the simulation experiment. The time of servicing each phase of the experiment can be described by exponential function.

6. *Student class M/M/N/N* - generates orders completely randomly. The time interval between orders is random, both the number of students and the capacity of the system is limited by the number N.

To build a model of *VL* system, it is necessary to determine the average time of staying of orders in queue, average server usage and average time spent in the whole system. In general, the queuing system q_s can be defined by the following parameters: the rate of the arrival of orders λ_s, the intensity of servicing μ_s and average time of servicing $\tilde{\tau}_s = 1/\mu_s$, the number of parallel servers N_s, the size of the input buffer b_s and the use of the server ρ_s. It is necessary to specify the number of servers in each queuing system, keeping in mind that each type of server has different productivity and downtime costs. Below the formal model for allocating resources in a closed queuing system is presented.

Input Data. N is number of students in the classroom, $v_i, i = 1, 2, \ldots, I$ are rate of arrival of student's orders to the server (from one student), $\tilde{\tau}_i^s, i = 1, 2, \ldots I$ are average servicing time for server s_i, $\mu_i = 1/\tilde{\tau}_i^s$ are average rate of servicing for server s_i.

Control Parameters. $X_i, i = 1, 2, \ldots, I$ are numbers of machines working in parallel for each of the servers.

Criteria Function. The criterion function contains three components:

1. Total processing time of all customer orders arriving per unit of time:

$$T_\Sigma = \sum_i N v_i \tau_i^s = \sum_i \lambda_i \tilde{\tau}_i^s (X_i),$$

where: $\lambda_i = v_i N$ - total rate of arrival of client orders to the server s_i, $\tilde{\tau}_i = \tilde{\tau}_i^w + \tilde{\tau}_i^s$ is average time of order stay in the servers s_i, $\tilde{\tau}_i^w$ - average waiting time of the order in the server queue s_i, $\tilde{\tau}_i^w = F(X_i)$, $\tilde{\tau}_i^s$ – average time of servicing the order in the server s_i.

2. Total server cost (hardware and software) $C_\Sigma = \sum_i X_i c_i$, where c_i are the costs of one type servers s_i,
3. Total costs of work and server downtime (personnel, hardware and software) are.

$$U_\Sigma = \sum_i [(1 - \frac{\lambda_i}{\mu_i X_i}) \delta_i + \frac{\lambda_i}{\mu_i X_i} \gamma_i],$$

where δ_i γ_i, are expenses caused by work or downtime of server s_i per unit of response time.

Then **the task of modelling the work flow** can be formulated as follows.

For a given set of server types, s_i, $i = 1, 2, \ldots, I$ included in open distance learning system and parameters of each type server $(N, v_i, \tilde{\tau}_i^s, \mu_i)$ it is need to determine number of parallel servers of each type X_i, $i = 1,\ldots,I$, guaranteeing a minimum total time needed to complete all orders received:

$$T_\Sigma = \sum_i N v_i(\tilde{\tau}_i^w + \tilde{\tau}_i^s) = min, (X_i, i = 1, \ldots I)$$

With the restriction: for total costs of educational resources (personal, equipment and software):

$$\alpha C_\Sigma + U_\Sigma = \sum_t \left[X_i c_i + \left(1 - \frac{\lambda_i}{\mu_i X_i}\right) \delta_i + \frac{\lambda_i}{\mu_i X_i} \gamma_i \right] \le C_0$$

3.2 Method of Solution

The task formulated in this way is the task of integer programming with a non-linear objective function with non-linear constraints. In the general case, with any distribution of orders' flow in the distance learning system and any distribution of servicing time, this task can not be solved only on the basis of analytical methods. It is necessary to perform an experiment on a simulation model. Suppose the exam in distance learning system described above consists of a fixed number of questions for each student in the class. The total time of the exam may be expressed by the following formula:

$$T_{exam} = qN\left(\tilde{T}_c + \tilde{T}_R\right) + q \sum_{k=0}^{N_0} \tilde{T}_A(N),$$

where: q is the number of questions for each student, $\tilde{T}_c + \tilde{T}_R$ is average time of thinking and response, $\tilde{T}_A$ is average total time spent by the student in the system, N_0 is the initial number of students in the class. The average total time $\tilde{T}_A$ can be expressed as the weighted sum of time spent by the student in each type of server:

$$\tilde{T}_A = \sum_i v_i \tilde{\tau}_i = \sum_i v_i(\tilde{\tau}_i^w + \tilde{\tau}_i^s).$$

Define p_i as the probability of referring to the server s_i. From the condition of normalization $\sum_i p_i = 1$ it follows that

$$p_i = \frac{v_i}{\sum_i v_i}$$

In the general case, the rate of the arrival of orders in a closed queuing system can be determined by means of a set of linear equations (*traffic equation*)

$$\lambda_i = \sum_{j=1}^{M} \lambda_i p_{ij} = \lambda_c p_i, i = 1, \ldots, I, \lambda_c = \sum_{j=1}^{M} \lambda_i,$$

where: M is number of servers, $P = \|p_{ij}\|$ is transition matrix. The average number of orders waiting in the queue of server s_i can be determined by using:

$$E[k_i] = \sum_{k=0}^{k_0} kP[k_i = k];$$

$$P[k_i = k] = \sum_{\tilde{k} \in S, k_i = k} P(\tilde{k}).$$

In [11] it was shown that for this type of closed queuing system the following form of the product, shown below, is true:

$$P(\tilde{k}) = P(\tilde{0}) \prod_i \left(\frac{\lambda_i}{\mu_i}\right)^{k_i};$$

$$P(\tilde{0}) = \{\sum_{k \in S} \prod_i (\frac{\lambda_i}{\mu_i})^{k_i}\}^{-1},$$

where: $P[k_i = k]$ is probability of waiting for k_i orders in the queue, $P(\tilde{k})$ is probability of state $\tilde{k}$, $P(\tilde{0})$ is the probability of a "zero" state.

4 Simulation Model of Teacher and Student Collaboration

This process is related to behaviours and preferences of humans, which can change and are difficult to predict. For this reason simulation seems like an adequate mechanism, which allows obtaining information about the analysed object of study and is the basis for further activities related to the functioning of this object.

On the basis of the developed simulation model it is possible to study the adapted *strategy of cooperation between the teacher and a group of students* (Fig. 3). The aim of the simulation is to assess if the expected repository development plan is possible to realise with the teacher working in a distance mode, with a specified distribution of student arrival, and a specified distribution of grading.

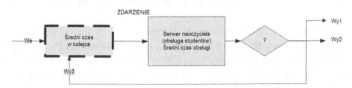

Fig. 3. General form of the simulation model. Source: own study

5 Conclusion

1. Simulation is a tool that the teacher directly uses. The teacher, thanks to the results obtained from experiments conducted on a simulation model, can change the strategy of working with students and modify their motivation function, e.g. by changing the difficulty of the tasks underlying the acquisition of competencies. The simulation model allows to evaluate the different options of the teacher's work, which must take into account the constraints characteristic of the educational situation (time, type of student group, student involvement, etc.).
2. For the purposes of collecting statistics and conducting simulation experiments, the process of teacher-student collaboration can be interpreted as a queuing system in which:

- with specific content and portions of teaching materials, it can be assumed that the teacher's job is to check the task;
- with a specific course, time and group, the teaching job can be treated as a server with a specific input, output, average rating time;
- the average assessment time is based on the teacher's experience (specificity of each course and subject, difficulty of tasks, type of student group, time of completion of classes) and is further supported by the mechanism of extracting motivation from the linguistic knowledge base;
- the flow of students is stochastic (in the selected time period, there is no certainty of how many students will arrive, no knowledge of how many will pass the task, no knowledge of whether a new student will arrive, etc.);

References

1. Buzacott, J., Shanthikumar, J.: Modelling and Analysis of Manufacturing Systems. Wiley, New York (1993)
2. Kleinrock, L.: Queuing Systems. Wiley, New York (1975)
3. Banks, J., Carson, J., Nelson, B., Nivol, D.: Discrete-Event System Simulation. Prentice Hall, New York (2001)
4. Chung, C.: Simulation Modelling Handbook-A Practical Approach. CRS Press, Boca Raton (2004)
5. Robinson, S.: Simulation: The Practice of Model Development and Use. Wiley, Chichster (2004)
6. Kushtina, E., Dolgui A., Malachowski, B.: Organisation of the modelling and simulation of the discrete processes. In: Saeed K., Pejas J., (eds) Information Processing and Security system, pp. 443–452. Springer, Heidelberg (2005). https://doi.org/10.1007/b137371
7. Kushtina, E., Różewski, P.: Analiza systemowe idei otwartego nauczania zdalnego. In: Straszaka A., Owsińskiego J., (eds.) Badania operacyjne i systemowe 2004: Na drodze do społeczeństwa wiedzy, pp. 231–245. Akademicka Oficyna Wydawnicza EXIT, Warsaw, (2004)
8. Zaikin, O., Korytkowski, P., Kushtina, E., Malachowski, B.: Modelling of the supply chain for a distributed publishing enterprise. In: Dolgui A., Soldek., J., Zaikin, O., (eds.) Supply Chain Optimisation, pp. 101–116, Springer, Berlin (2005). https://doi.org/10.1007/b101812

9. Kelton, W., Sadowski, R., Sadowski, D.: Simulation with Arena. McGraw-Hill, New York (1997)
10. Zaikin, O., Dolgui, A.: Simulation model for optimization of resources allocation in the queuing networks In: Proceedings of IMACS Symposium on Mathematical Modelling 3rd MATHMOD, Argesim Report #15, Vienna. (2000)
11. Gordon, W., Newell, G.: Closed queuing systems with exponential servers. Oper. Res. **15**, 254–265 (1967)

Identification of Nonlinear Dynamic Systems Structured by Expanded Wiener Model

Besarion Shanshiashvili[(✉)] [iD] and Beka Avazneli[iD]

Georgian Technical University, 0160 Tbilisi, Georgia

Abstract. A problem of parameter identification of nonlinear manufacturing systems represented by expanded Wiener model, linear elements of which are described by the ordinary differential equation, in the frequency domain is considered. Method of parameter identification in steady state based on the observation of the system's input and output variables at the input harmonic influences is proposed. The solution of the problem of parameter identification is reduced to the solution of the systems of algebraic equations by using the Fourier approximation. The parameters estimations are received by the least squares method. Reliability of the received results, at the identification of the nonlinear systems in industrial conditions at the presence of noise, depends on the accuracy of the measurement of system input and output signals and mathematical processing of the experimental data at the approximation. The parameter identification method is investigated by means of both the theoretical analysis and the computer modelling.

Keywords: Identification · Nonlinear system · Model · Parameter · Dynamic

1 Introduction

The choice of automatic control type for any manufacturing process depends on the amount of existing information on a condition of the system formalized in the form of mathematical model.

Methods of mathematical modeling or systems identification can be used to formalize processes in the production systems. When using systems identification methods, it is necessary to solve various problems while building a mathematical model of the system. The problems arise depending on the a priori information about the system [1]. The construction of the system's optimal model in many respects depends on successfully solving the parameter identification problem at known model structure.

Many of the current dynamic processes in manufacturing systems bear the nonlinear character. At the research of the nonlinear systems principally new events appear, which are not observed in the linear systems. At the same time, system identification is based basically on the linear stationary models, which are widely applied to practical processes. Application of linear models during formalization of the regularity of the process proceeding in nonlinear systems is possible only in the limited area of change

© IFIP International Federation for Information Processing 2021
Published by Springer Nature Switzerland AG 2021
A. Dolgui et al. (Eds.): APMS 2021, IFIP AICT 630, pp. 546–554, 2021.
https://doi.org/10.1007/978-3-030-85874-2_58

of variables. The research of physical events and their features in the nonlinear systems can be adequately characterized only by using the nonlinear dynamic models.

The nonlinear systems are generally represented by general models, in particular, the Volterra [2] and Wiener [3] series and the Kolmogorov-Gabor [4, 5] continuous and discrete polynomials, or block-oriented models consisting of different modifications of the Hammerstein and Wiener models [6].

Use of both kinds of models has positive and negative sides. Advantage of the block-oriented models is defined by the simplicity of their use for representation of nonlinear systems.

Most of the existing developed parameter identification methods of nonlinear block-oriented systems are developed for the simple Hammerstein and Wiener models (e.g. [7–14]). Comparatively small quantity of works are devoted to the identification of Hammerstein-Wiener and Wiener-Hammerstein cascade models (e.g. [14–18]). Successes in the field of parameter identification of block-oriented models are insignificant. This can be explained by the fact that the majority of block-oriented models, except for the Hammerstein models (simple and generalized) are nonlinear relative to the parameters, and also because of the large number of estimated parameters. Therefore, the solution of the problem of parameter identification is analytically possible only for some block-oriented low order models.

In this work the problem of parameter identification of nonlinear dynamic systems represented by expanded Wiener model is considered, where linear elements of the model are described by the ordinary differential equation of first and second order. Despite their simplicity, such models can be widely used in many fields of the manufacturing processes to identify systems of mining and smelting, ore dressing, chemical, mechanical, biological processes and etc.

2   Classes of Model and Input Signals

Expanded Wiener model (Fig. 1)) can be described by the following equation:

$$y(t) = c_0 + W_1(p)u(t) + [W_2(p)u(t)][W_3(p)u(t)], \tag{1}$$

where c_0 is constant coefficient, $W_i(p)$ ($i = 1, 2, 3$) are transfer functions of the linear dynamic systems in the operational form, i.e. denotes the differentiation operation - $p \equiv d/dt$. $u(t)$ and $y(t)$ are input and output variables, accordingly.

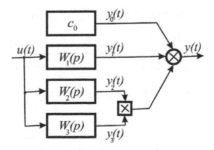

Fig. 1. Expanded Wiener model

For solving the problem of parameter identification of nonlinear systems on the basis of the active experiment it is supposed that the input variable of the system $u(t)$ is a harmonic function:

$$u(t) = A \cos \omega t. \tag{2}$$

3 Mathematical Description of Forced Oscillations

Let's consider the case when the transfer functions of the model's linear dynamic parts are defined by the expression

$$W_i(p) = \frac{1}{T_{0i}p^2 + T_i p + 1} \quad (i = 1, 2, 3), \tag{3}$$

where $T_{0i} > 0 \quad (i = 1, 2, 3)$ has a dimension of time square, and $T_i > 0 \quad (i = 1, 2, 3)$ - a dimension of time.

Let's consider the peculiarities of obtaining of the mathematical expressions describing the forced oscillations obtained on the model output.

The following differential equation must be solved, when a signal type (2) is acted on the model input, for determining the output signal of the first linear dynamic element of the model:

$$T_{01} \frac{d^2 y_1}{dt^2} + T_1 \frac{dy_1}{dt} + y_1 = A \cos \omega t. \tag{4}$$

General solution of Eq. (4) when $T_1 > 2\sqrt{T_{01}}$ is:

$$y_1(t) = \frac{A\left(1 - \omega^2 T_{01}\right)}{\left(1 - \omega^2 T_{01}\right)^2 + \omega^2 T_1^2} \cos \omega t + \frac{A\omega T_1}{\left(1 - \omega^2 T_{01}\right)^2 + \omega^2 T_1^2} \sin \omega t + C_1 e^{-at} + C_2 e^{-bt}, \tag{5}$$

where C_1 and C_2 are arbitrary constants and

$$a = -\frac{-T_1 + \sqrt{T_1^2 - 4T_{01}}}{2T_{01}}, \quad b = -\frac{-T_1 - \sqrt{T_1^2 - 4T_{01}}}{2T_{01}}. \tag{6}$$

General solution of Eq. (4) when $T_1 < 2\sqrt{T_{01}}$ is as follows:

$$y_1(t) = \frac{A(1 - \omega^2 T_{01})}{\left(1 - \omega^2 T_{01}\right)^2 + \omega^2 T_1^2} \cos \omega t + \frac{A\omega T_1}{\left(1 - \omega^2 T_{01}\right)^2 + \omega^2 T_1^2} \sin \omega t$$
$$+ e^{-\gamma t}(C_1 \cos \beta t + C_2 \sin \beta t), \tag{7}$$

where

$$\gamma = \frac{T_1}{2T_{01}}, \quad \beta = \sqrt{\frac{1}{T_{01}} - \frac{T_1^2}{4T_{01}}}. \tag{8}$$

So, according expressions (5) and (7), the forced oscillation, obtained at the output of the first linear element of the model in cases when $T_1 > 2\sqrt{T_{01}}$ and when $T_1 < 2\sqrt{T_{01}}$ in the steady state, when $t \to \infty$, is determined by the expression:

$$y_1(t) = \frac{A(1 - \omega^2 T_{01})}{(1 - \omega^2 T_{01})^2 + \omega^2 T_1^2} \cos \omega t + \frac{A\omega T_1}{(1 - \omega^2 T_{01})^2 + \omega^2 T_1^2} \sin \omega t. \qquad (9)$$

To simplify the calculations, we will suppose that in expression (3) $T_{0i} = 0 \, (i = 2, 3)$, then after calculation in a similar way we get that the forced oscillations at the outputs of the second and third linear dynamic elements are determined by the expressions:

$$y_2(t) = \frac{A}{1 + \omega^2 T_2^2} \cos \omega t + \frac{A\omega T_2}{1 + \omega^2 T_2^2} \sin \omega t, \qquad (10)$$

$$y_3(t) = \frac{A}{1 + \omega^2 T_3^2} \cos \omega t + \frac{A\omega T_3}{1 + \omega^2 T_3^2} \sin \omega t. \qquad (11)$$

By determining and transforming the multiplication $y_2(t)y_3(t)$ we finally get:

$$y_2(t)y_3(t) = \frac{A^2(1 + \omega^2 T_2 T_3)}{2(1 + \omega^2 T_2^2)(1 + \omega^2 T_3^2)} + \frac{A^2(1 - \omega^2 T_2 T_3)}{2(1 + \omega^2 T_2^2)(1 + \omega^2 T_3^2)} \cos 2\omega t$$

$$+ \frac{A^2 \omega (T_2 + T_3)}{2(1 + \omega^2 T_2^2)(1 + \omega^2 T_3^2)} \sin 2\omega t. \qquad (12)$$

As the output signal of the model is:

$$y(t) = y_0(t) + y_1(t) + y_2(t)y_3(t). \qquad (13)$$

Therefore, taking into account (9) and (12), we get that the forced oscillation at the model output is defined by the following expression:

$$y(t) = c_0 + \frac{A^2(1 + \omega^2 T_2 T_3)}{2(1 + \omega^2 T_2^2)(1 + \omega^2 T_3^2)} + \frac{A(1 - \omega^2 T_{01})}{(1 - \omega^2 T_{01})^2 + \omega^2 T_1^2} \cos \omega t$$

$$+ \frac{A\omega T_1}{(1 - \omega^2 T_{01})^2 + \omega^2 T_1^2} \sin \omega t + \frac{A^2(1 - \omega^2 T_2 T_3)}{2(1 + \omega^2 T_2^2)(1 + \omega^2 T_3^2)} \cos 2\omega t$$

$$+ \frac{A^2 \omega (T_2 + T_3)}{2(1 + \omega^2 T_2^2)(1 + \omega^2 T_3^2)} \sin 2\omega t \,. \qquad (14)$$

4 Parameter Identification

Let's consider the features for the parameters estimation of models by using the Fourier approximation by the method of the least squares.

The application of the Fourier approximation [19] for the output periodic signal of the system enables to obtain the estimates of the Fourier coefficients $a_0/2$, a_k, b_k, $(k = 1, 2)$. By equating such estimates with their theoretical values we'll get:

$$\frac{\hat{a}_0}{2} = c_0 + \frac{A^2(1 + \omega^2 T_2 T_3)}{2(1 + \omega^2 T_2^2)(1 + \omega^2 T_2^2)}, \tag{15}$$

$$\hat{a}_1 = \frac{A(1 - \omega^2 T_{01})}{(1 - \omega^2 T_{01})^2 + \omega^2 T_1^2}, \quad \hat{b}_1 = \frac{A\omega T_1}{(1 - \omega^2 T_{01})^2 + \omega^2 T_1^2}, \tag{16}$$

$$\hat{a}_2 = \frac{A^2(1 - \omega^2 T_2 T_3)}{2(1 + \omega^2 T_2^2)(1 + \omega^2 T_3^2)}, \quad \hat{b}_2 = \frac{A^2\omega(T_2 + T_3)}{2(1 + \omega^2 T_2^2)(1 + \omega^2 T_3^2)}. \tag{17}$$

From (16) we get:

$$\frac{\hat{a}_1}{\hat{b}_1} = \frac{1 - \omega^2 T_{01}}{\omega T_1}. \tag{18}$$

Using the expression (18) at different frequencies $\omega = \omega_i$ ($i = 1, 2, \ldots, n$), we obtain:

$$\omega_i^2 T_{01} + \frac{\hat{a}_{1i}}{\hat{b}_{1i}}\omega_i T_1 + \varepsilon_{1i} = 1 \ (i = 1, 2, \ldots, n), \tag{19}$$

where $\hat{a}_{1i}$, $\hat{b}_{1i}$ ($i = 1, 2, \ldots, n$) - values of the Fourier coefficients at the frequency ω_i, ε_{1i} ($i = 1, 2, \ldots, n$) - errors of measurements and approximations.

Let's consider the features for T_1 parameter estimation by the method of least squares using the expression (19).

The error squared sum is

$$S = \sum_{i=1}^{n} \varepsilon_{1i}^2 = \sum_{i=1}^{n} \left(1 - \omega_i^2 T_{01} - \frac{\hat{a}_{1i}}{\hat{b}_{1i}}\omega_i T_1\right)^2. \tag{20}$$

Now we'll determine the values of the estimates $\hat{T}_{01}$ and $\hat{T}_1$ so that their substitution for T_{01} and T_1 should give the minimal value S in the Eq. (20). For that purpose differentiating (20) at first by T_{01} and then by T_1, and equating the received results to zero, we'll obtain the following expressions for estimating $\hat{T}_{01}$ and $\hat{T}_1$:

$$\sum_{i=1}^{n} \omega_i^4 T_{01} + \sum_{i=1}^{n} \frac{\hat{a}_{1i}}{\hat{b}_{1i}}\omega_i^3 T_1 = \sum_{i=1}^{n} \omega_i^2,$$

$$\sum_{i=1}^{n} \frac{a_{1i}}{b_{1i}}\omega_i^3 T_{01} + \sum_{i=1}^{n} \frac{\hat{a}_{1i}^2}{\hat{b}_{1i}^2}\omega_i^2 T_1 = \sum_{i=1}^{n} \frac{\hat{a}_{1i}}{\hat{b}_{1i}}\omega_i. \tag{21}$$

The solution of the system of Eqs. (21) allows obtaining the estimates of the parameters $\hat{T}_{01}$ and $\hat{T}_1$ using the method of the least squares:

$$\hat{T}_{01} = \frac{\left(\sum_{i=1}^{n} \omega_i^2\right)\left(\sum_{i=1}^{n} \frac{\hat{a}_{1i}^2}{\hat{b}_{1i}^2}\omega_i^2\right) - \left(\sum_{i=1}^{n} \frac{\hat{a}_{1i}}{\hat{b}_{1i}}\omega_i\right)\left(\sum_{i=1}^{n} \frac{\hat{a}_{1i}}{\hat{b}_{1i}}\omega_i^3\right)}{\left(\sum_{i=1}^{n} \omega_i^4\right)\left(\sum_{i=1}^{n} \frac{\hat{a}_{1i}^2}{\hat{b}_{1i}^2}\omega_i^2\right) - \left(\sum_{i=1}^{n} \frac{\hat{a}_{1i}}{\hat{b}_{1i}}\omega_i^3\right)^2}, \tag{22}$$

$$\hat{T}_1 = \frac{\left(\sum\limits_{i=1}^{n}\omega_i^4\right)\left(\sum\limits_{i=1}^{n}\frac{\hat{a}_{1_i}}{\hat{b}_{1_i}}\omega_i\right) - \left(\sum\limits_{i=1}^{n}\omega_i^2\right)\left(\sum\limits_{i=1}^{n}\frac{\hat{a}_{1_i}}{\hat{b}_{1_i}}\omega_i^3\right)}{\left(\sum\limits_{i=1}^{n}\omega_i^4\right)\left(\sum\limits_{i=1}^{n}\frac{\hat{a}_{1_i}^2}{\hat{b}_{1_i}^2}\omega_i^2\right) - \left(\sum\limits_{i=1}^{n}\frac{\hat{a}_{1_i}}{\hat{b}_{1_i}}\omega_i^3\right)^2}. \tag{23}$$

Let's consider the features for T_2 and T_3 parameters estimation by the method of least squares using the expressions (17).

From (17) we get:

$$\frac{\hat{a}_2}{\hat{b}_2} = \frac{1 - \omega^2 T_2 T_3}{\omega(T_2 + T_3)}. \tag{24}$$

Let's enter designations:

$$T_0 = T_2 T_3, \tag{25}$$

$$T = T_2 + T_3. \tag{26}$$

Using the expression (24) at different frequencies $\omega = \omega_i \, (i = 1, 2, \ldots, n)$, we obtain:

$$\hat{b}_{2i} - \hat{b}_{2i}\omega_i^2 T_0 - \hat{a}_{2i}\omega_i T + \varepsilon_{2i} = 0 \, (i = 1, 2, \ldots, n). \tag{27}$$

In this case the error squared sum is

$$S = \sum_{i=1}^{n} \varepsilon_{2i}^2 = \sum_{i=1}^{n} \left(-\hat{b}_{2i} + \hat{b}_{2i}\omega_i^2 T_0 + \hat{a}_{2i}\omega_i T\right)^2. \tag{28}$$

If we differentiate (28) at first by T_0 and then by T, and equating the received results to zero, we'll obtain the following expressions for estimating $\hat{T}_0$ and $\hat{T}$:

$$\sum_{i=1}^{n}\left(\hat{b}_{2i}\omega_i^4\right)T_0 + \sum_{i=1}^{n}\left(\hat{a}_{2i}\hat{b}_{2i}\right)T = \sum_{i=1}^{n}\hat{b}_{2i}\omega_i^2,$$
$$\sum_{i=1}^{n}\left(\hat{a}_{2i}\hat{b}_{2i}\omega_i^2\right)T_0 + \sum_{i=1}^{n}\left(\hat{a}_{2i}^2\right)T = \sum_{i=1}^{n}\hat{a}_{2i}\hat{b}_{2i}. \tag{29}$$

Solving the system of Eqs. (29) with respect to T_0 and T gives:

$$\hat{T}_0 = \frac{\left(\sum\limits_{i=1}^{n}\hat{a}_{2i}\hat{b}_{2i}\right)^2 - \left(\sum\limits_{i=1}^{n}\hat{b}_{2i}\omega_i^2\right)\left(\sum\limits_{i=1}^{n}\hat{a}_{2i}^2\right)}{\left(\sum\limits_{i=1}^{n}\hat{a}_{2i}\hat{b}_{2i}\right)\left(\sum\limits_{i=1}^{n}a_{2i}\hat{b}_{2i}\omega_i^2\right) - \left(\sum\limits_{i=1}^{n}a_{2i}^2\right)\left(\sum\limits_{i=1}^{n}\hat{b}_{2i}\omega_i^4\right)}, \tag{30}$$

$$\hat{T} = \frac{\left(\sum\limits_{i=1}^{n}\hat{a}_{2i}\hat{b}_{2i}\right)\left(\sum\limits_{i=1}^{n}\hat{b}_{2i}^2\omega_i^2\right) - \left(\sum\limits_{i=1}^{n}\hat{a}_{2i}\hat{b}_{2i}\right)\left(\sum\limits_{i=1}^{n}\hat{b}_{2i}\omega_i^4\right)}{\left(\sum\limits_{i=1}^{n}\hat{a}_{2i}\hat{b}_{2i}\right)\left(\sum\limits_{i=1}^{n}\hat{a}_{2i}\hat{b}_{2i}\omega_i^2\right) - \left(\sum\limits_{i=1}^{n}\hat{a}_{2i}^2\right)\left(\sum\limits_{i=1}^{n}\hat{b}_{2i}\omega_i^4\right)}. \tag{31}$$

Estimates $\hat{T}_2$ and $\hat{T}_3$ can be determined through the estimates $\hat{T}_0$ and $\hat{T}$ by the following expressions:

$$\hat{T}_2 = \frac{2\hat{T}_0}{\hat{T} - \sqrt{\hat{T}^2 - 4\hat{T}_0}}, \tag{32}$$

$$\hat{T}_3 = \frac{2\hat{T}_0}{\hat{T} + \sqrt{\hat{T}^2 - 4\hat{T}_0}}. \tag{33}$$

Estimates $\hat{T}_2$ and $\hat{T}_3$ can be also obtained by using expressions (15) and (17).

5   Accuracy of the Received Results

In order to use the algorithms of parameter identification, designed in accordance with the developed identification method in the manufacturing conditions under noise and disturbances, it is necessary to investigate identification method on accuracy.

The identification method is investigated by theoretical analysis and computer modelling. The reliability of the received results, at the parameter identification of nonlinear systems of industrial processes conditions in the presence of noise and errors, depends on the measurement accuracy of the systems' input and output signals and on the mathematical processing of the experimental data. When running experiments, it is recommended to use in the system registering apparatuses, the inertance of which is much less than the one of the object. When using various schemes of the numerical harmonic analysis, it is recommended to accept as the value of the output signal at the certain time moment an estimation of the mathematical expectation of the value of the output function at the present time moment.

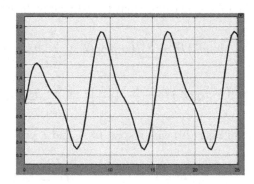

Fig. 2. The diagram of the output variable of expanded Wiener model

Besides, as it is known, that used method of the least squares is noiseless.

The investigation of the algorithms of the parameter identification of nonlinear systems was carried out by means of the computer modelling by using MATLAB.

We used both, the tool of package Simulink-toolbox for the system modelling and tool Symbolic Math Toolbox for the solution of the equations.

When investigating the algorithms of parameter identification, the programs corresponding to such algorithms were designed. Using such programs, the diagrams of output variable models and the estimations of unknown parameters have been obtained. The experiments were carried out at values of the parameters $T_{01} = 1$, $T_1 = 1, 5$, $T_2 = 0, 2$, $T_3 = 2$. For example, in Fig. 2 the diagram of the output variable of the model is given in the case of the input harmonic signal type (2) with $A = 1$ and $\omega = 0.8$. Following estimations of the unknown parameters are obtained: T01 = 0.9716, T1 = 1.4605, T2 = 0.1528, T3 = 1.9535.

6 Conclusion

In this work the problem of parameter identification of nonlinear dynamic systems represented by expanded Wiener model was considered, when linear elements of the model described by the ordinary differential equation of first and second order. Despite their simplicity, such models are widely used for the modelling of manufacturing processes.

The solution of the problem of parameter identification for this model is complicated due to the nonlinearity of such models relative to the sought parameters.

Developed method of parameter identification in steady state based on the observation of the system's input and output variables at the input harmonic influences was proposed. The solution of the problem of parameter identification was reduced to the solution of the algebraic equations systems by using the Fourier approximation. The parameters estimations were received by the least squares method. Reliability of the received results depends on the accuracy of the measurement of system output signals and mathematical processing of the experimental data.

Proposed parameter identification method can be used for modelling of nonlinear manufacturing processes when the model structure is known a priori. As the estimations of parametres were received by the least squares method, which is noiseless, it can be used in the manufacturing conditions in the presence of the noise and measurement errors.

The specification of the method of identification allows to use Fourier coefficients of various harmonics to estimate the parametres and compare the received results.

References

1. Eykhoff, P.: System Identification. Parameter and State Estimation. Wiley, London (1974)
2. Volterra, V.: Theory of Functionals and of Integral and Integro-Differential Equations. Dover Publication, New York (1959)
3. Wiener, N.: Nonlinear Problems in Random Theory. Wiley, New York (1958)
4. Kolmogorov, A.N.: Interpolation and extrapolation of stationary random series. Bull. Acad. Sci. USSR, Math. Ser. 5(1), 3–14 (1941)
5. Gabor, L., Wilby, P.L., Woodcook, R.: A universal nonlinear filter predictor and simulator which optimizes itself by a learning process. In: IEE Proceedings, 108(B), pp. 422–433 (1961)

6. Haber, R., Keviczky, L.: Identification of nonlinear dynamic systems. In: Preprints of the IV IFAC Symposium on Identification and System Parameter Estimation, Part 1, Moscow, pp. 62–112. Institute of Control Sciences (1976)
7. Giri, F., Bai, E.-W., (eds.): Block-Oriented Nonlinear System Identification. Springer, Berlin (2010). https://doi.org/10.1007/978-1-84996-513-2
8. Mattsson, P., Wigren, T.: Convergence analysis for recursive Hammerstein identification. Automatica **71**, 179–186 (2016)
9. Ma, J., Ding, F., Xiong, W., Yang, E.: Combined state and parameter estimation for Hammerstein systems with time-delay using the Kalman filtering. Int. J. Adapt. Control Signal Process **31**(8), 1139–1151 (2017)
10. Gupta, S., Sahoo, A.K., Sahoo, U.K.: Parameter estimation of Wiener nonlinear model using least mean square (LMS) algorithm. TENCON 2017 - 2017 IEEE Region 10 Conference, Penang, pp. 1399–1403 (2017). http://dspace.nitrkl.ac.in/dspace/bitstream/2080/2798/1/2017_TENCON_SGupta_Parameter.pdf
11. Bottegal, G., Castro-Garcia, R., Johan, A.K., Suykens, J.: A two-experiment approach to Wiener system identification. Automatica **93**, 282–289 (2018)
12. Li, J., Zong, T., Gu, J., Hua, L.: Parameter estimation of Wiener systems based on the particle swarm iteration and gradient search principle. Circuits Syst. Signal Process. **39**(7), 3470–3495 (2020). https://doi.org/10.1007/s00034-019-01329-1
13. Salukvadze, M., Shanshiashvili, B.: Identification of nonlinear continuous dynamic systems with closed cycle. Int. J. Inf. Technol. Decis. Mak. **12**(2), 179–199 (2013)
14. Shanshiashvili, B., Rigishvili, T.: Parameter identification of block-oriented nonlinear systems in the frequency domain. ScienceDirect. IFAC Papers OnLine **53**(2), 10695–10700 (2020)
15. Brouri, A., Kadi, L., Slassi, S.: Frequency identification of Hammerstein-Wiener systems with backlash input nonlinearity. Int. J. Control Autom. Syst. **15**(5), 2222–2232 (2017). https://doi.org/10.1007/s12555-016-0312-3
16. Mzyk, G., Wachel, P.: Kernel-based identification of Wiener-Hammerstein system. Automatica **83**, 275–281 (2017)
17. Schoukens, M., Tiels, K.: Identification of block-oriented nonlinear systems starting from linear approximations: a survey. Automatica **85**, 272–292 (2017)
18. Giordano, G., Sjöberg, J.: Maximum likelihood identification of Wiener-Hammerstein system with process noise. IFAC-Papers OnLine **51**(15), 401–406 (2018)
19. Hamming, R.W.: Numerical Methods for Scientists and Engineers. Dover Publications Inc., New York (1987)

Data Analysis and Production Process Control

Bo Yang[1], Yumin He[2($\boxtimes$)], and Honghao Yin[1]

[1] Hongyang Sealing Product Company, Guiyang 550025, Guizhou, People's Republic of China
[2] Beihang University, Beijing 100191, People's Republic of China
heyumin@buaa.edu.cn

Abstract. Production process control is an important issue. Production processes are affected by many factors and some processes are very complex. Statistical process control (SPC) can apply statistical methods to monitor and control production processes for quality improvement. SPC methods include control charts and process capability analysis. This paper presents a method for continuous production process improvement. The control flow of the proposed method is developed. The method identifies the production process to be improved, collects and verifies data, applies Xbar-R control chart analysis and process capability analysis, analyzes the causes, forms measures for improvement, and takes actions for the improvement. An application example is provided. The results of the study indicate the quality improvement of their production process. This research can provide a reference for companies to apply SPC methods and statistical tools and take process capability analysis and control chart analysis for production process control to improve the quality of production processes.

Keywords: Production process control · Xbar-R control charts · Process capability analysis

1 Introduction

To obtain competitive advantage, many companies aim to develop high quality products fast. Some production processes of manufacturing products are very complex and it is difficult to control quality. Statistical process control (SPC) can monitor processes, detect changes, and control process quality by applying appropriate control charts [1].

Process capability analysis is a method of SPC and can be used for production process quality control. Process capability analysis plays an important role in applying SPC method for quality management. Process capability analysis should be made when a production process is stable. However, even if a production process is stable, it does not mean that the process capability satisfies a requirement. Xbar-R control charts in SPC method can be used to control a production process in the analysis and monitoring stages.

Researchers have studied the integration of automatic process control (APC) and statistical process control. For example, Holmes and Mergen [2] considered if SPC was used as a process monitoring system, APC and SPC could detect deviations from the expected behavior of a process.

© IFIP International Federation for Information Processing 2021
Published by Springer Nature Switzerland AG 2021
A. Dolgui et al. (Eds.): APMS 2021, IFIP AICT 630, pp. 555–562, 2021.
https://doi.org/10.1007/978-3-030-85874-2_59

Park *et al.* [1] studied the integration of APC and SPC and developed an economic cost model for the integration of APC and SPC. Their proposed model was demonstrated by numerical examples. They used different controllers in the integrated systems. They also developed a long run expected cost to investigate the use of the different controllers.

Saif [3] mentioned that APC and SPC were developed separately and applied in different industries previously. They suggested the integration of APC and SPC.

Sousa, Rodrigues, and Nunes [4] studied the production process of a mental part. They analyzed the variability of the production process, applied quality tools, identified potential causes, and proposed measures to improve product quality.

This paper applies Xbar-R control chart analysis and process capability analysis and develops a method for production process control to improve quality. An application example is provided.

2 Developed Method

Process capability analysis typically includes the following basic steps: establishing control over the process, analyzing process data, and analyzing sources of variation [5]. The Xbar-R control charts in SPC method can be used to monitor the mean and the range of process data.

The method for production process control is based on data analysis and SPC application for continuous quality improvement. The method identifies the production process, applies control charts, histogram, process capability analysis, and others, and combines them for production process analysis and control to make continuous quality improvement. The developed method includes the following steps. The control flow of the method is illustrated in Fig. 1.

Step 1. Production process identification. Identify a production process to inspect if there is any abnormality in the production process to decrease defective products for quality improvement.
Step 2. Data collection. Collect data of a production process according to the status of the production process.
Step 3. Data verification. Check and verify collected data to avoid possible errors.
Step 4. Production process analysis. Analyze Xbar-R control charts to observe abnormal variation of the production process. Make process capability analysis to detect if the production process satisfies the requirement.
Step 5. Cause analysis. Check the production process to find possible causes of anomalies.
Step 6. Production process improvement. Implement actions for quality improvement of the production process.

The production process needs to be monitored continuously to check if it satisfies the requirement. If the production process satisfies the requirement, no further actions are needed. If the production process does not satisfy the requirement, more actions are needed to collect data, draw control charts, make process capability analysis, find the causes of anomalies, and form measures and implement actions.

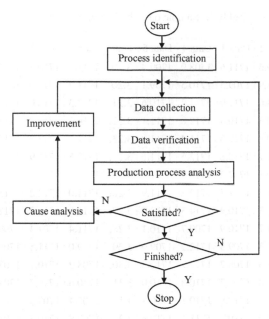

Fig. 1. Control flow of the method.

3   Application Example

3.1   Production Process Identification

The proposed method was applied to a company, Hongyang Sealing Product Company located in Guiyang City. The trial production of the engine hood sealing strips of type C automobile was taken as an example. Because the ratio of the qualified products was not high, the company decided to study the production process to identify any abnormality in the process for quality improvement.

The company formulated an quality improvement group composed of the staff from the technology department, the process department, the quality department, the workshop of the company. The quality department particularly established an expert inspection group.

3.2   Data Collection with Verification

The data collection of this product was carried out according to the production scale, staffing, and equipment. The inspection group and on-site inspection personnel specified the size of the detector and verified the normality of the measurement system. The group extracted 100 samples and took the average value each time, extracted 5 times a day from March to April in 2016. Total data sets collected are 36. Sample data of type C engine hood sealing strips are illustrated in Table 1.

Table 1. Sample data (before improvement).

Date	Data 1	Data 2	Data 3	Data 4	Data 5	Date	Data 1	Data 2	Data 3	Data 4	Data 5
3.1.	1707.4	1709.6	1711.6	1708.9	1709.4	3.19.	1711.7	1710.4	1711.0	1711.2	1711.1
3.2.	1707.4	1708.9	1709.5	1710.5	1709.1	3.20.	1711.7	1712.9	1713.0	1713.7	1712.8
3.3.	1710.6	1708.6	1711.9	1711.2	1710.6	3.21.	1713.3	1716.0	1713.1	1715.0	1714.4
3.4.	1710.6	1710.3	1710.8	1712.8	1711.1	3.22.	1710.2	1711.9	1711.9	1713.5	1711.9
3.5.	1712.9	1710.7	1712.6	1711.4	1711.9	3.23.	1711.7	1712.3	1712.3	1714.3	1712.7
3.6.	1709.8	1711.7	1712.2	1712.5	1711.6	3.24.	1712.5	1711.9	1712.7	1713.5	1712.7
3.7.	1710.6	1710.1	1712.2	1713.5	1711.6	3.25.	1712.5	1714.9	1714.3	1714.9	1714.2
3.8.	1710.6	1711.7	1711.7	1713.7	1711.9	3.26.	1711.0	1712.2	1715.2	1713.5	1713.0
3.9.	1711.4	1711.3	1710.9	1714.3	1712.0	3.27.	1711.0	1713.3	1712.5	1714.6	1712.9
3.10..	1710.2	1709.7	1710.9	1709.7	1710.1	3.28.	1711.4	1707.4	1709.4	1710.4	1709.7
3.11.	1708.6	1709.3	1709.5	1712.2	1709.9	3.29.	1709.0	1711.5	1709.2	1710.1	1710.0
3.12.	1710.2	1709.5	1708.7	1712.7	1710.3	3.30.	1708.2	1710.1	1708.7	1710.2	1709.3
3.13.	1708.6	1710.8	1709.7	1710.8	1710.0	3.31.	1710.6	1710.7	1708.2	1710.3	1710.0
3.14.	1711.0	1711.1	1710.8	1710.1	1710.8	4.1.	1707.4	1709.9	1709.6	1713.6	1710.1
3.15.	1711.0	1710.0	1710.3	1711.1	1710.6	4.2.	1709.8	1710.3	1709.9	1711.1	1710.3
3.16.	1711.7	1711.0	1710.3	1712.4	1711.4	4.3.	1710.6	1710.5	1709.8	1709.7	1710.2
3.17.	1711.7	1712.6	1711.8	1713.2	1712.3	4.4.	1708.2	1711.6	1709.9	1710.5	1710.1
3.18.	1711.0	1708.3	1711.5	1712.0	1710.7	4.5.	1709.8	1709.8	1711.9	1712.3	1711.0

The normality test was made for the data collected. The results is shown in Fig. 2. It can be seen form the figure that the sealing strips tends to be evenly distributed on both sides of the straight line. This indicates that the quality characteristics of the sealing strips tend to be randomly normal distributed.

3.3 Production Process Analysis

The data analysis of the production process was made by applying statistical software Minitab [6], Xbar-R control charts are illustrated in Fig. 3. It can be seen from the Xbar chart that several points exceed the upper limit, several points exceed the lower limit, seven consecutive points are above the centerline, seven consecutive points are below the centerline, and one point in the R chart exceeds the upper limit. The fluctuation of sampling range reflects the fluctuation within the subgroup and represents the fluctuation degree of the production process.

For the collected data, the process capability index was calculated to analyze the production process capability. The following can be found from the process capability analysis of type C engine hood sealing strips. First, the center value of the normal distribution lower than the required center value in the capability histogram. Second, process capability index $C_{pk} = 1.24$ is not sufficient. It is easy to produce defective products.

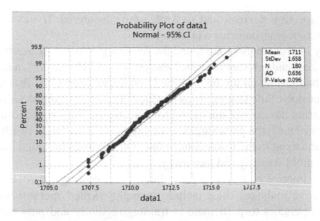

Fig. 2. Probability plot (before improvement).

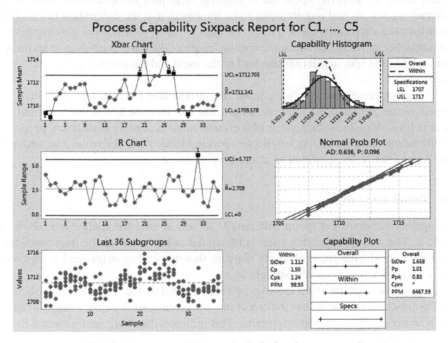

Fig. 3. Process capability analysis (before improvement).

3.4 Cause Analysis and Production Process Improvement

When analyzing the causes of these anomalies, the human factors and non-human factors were considered. For human factors, it was considered whether an inspector was proficient in inspection methods, whether a technical operator operated according to standards, whether a designer had design negligence, and so forth. For non-human factors, the performance of production machines, the specification of material molds, the accuracy of inspection devices, and so forth were considered. It was also considered whether production environments had changed.

The quality improvement group found the following possible causes by checking the production process and relevant records. First, on March 21st and 25th, a new production operator who had just taken up the post made improper operation. This resulted in the oversized dimension of the sealing strips produced in these two days. Second, on March 31st, the inspection device was not calibrated effectively. This might result in the error of measurement. Third, the parts shrank after extrusion. This might result in the size of the final products trend to the lower control line. Other causes included inconsistency in the rubber and mold wearing and loosening.

The quality improvement group formulated the following improvement measures based on the above analyses. These include to employ skilled operators for production, all production operators to participate in training regularly and pass the examination before they can work and operate independently, parts to be inspected after recalibration of inspection devices, the operation instruction of inspect devices to be checked, the calibration methods and requirements to be improved, and the calibration results to be recorded after each calibration. The group also required to make the parking tests of the parts after extrusion, to adjust the cutting length of the parts according to shrinkage, and to define the spot inspection standard of the mold and ensure the consistency of the mold.

The improvement actions were made, the production process was monitored, the inspection frequency of the joint rubber process was increased, and the abnormal was dealt in time. Also, the parking tests of parts was made according to different properties of rubber and different cutting lengths and parking times were determined according to shrinkage. Finally, the qualified products were obtained.

3.5 Result Analysis

The quality improvement group collected 5*36 sets of data for analyses, as shown in Table 2. The process capability chart is illustrated in Fig. 4. After the improvement, it can be observed from the probability diagram that the sealing strips tend to be evenly distributed on both sides of the straight line.

In the Xbar-R charts, there are no points above or below the LCL and UCL, there are no 7 points all above or below the centerline, no continuous 7 points rising or falling, and no other obvious nonrandom patterns. This indicates that there are no special factors and abnormality.

Table 2. Sample data (after improvement).

Date	Data 1	Data 2	Data 3	Data 4	Data 5	Date	Data 1	Data 2	Data 3	Data 4	Data 5
6.1.	1712.3	1710.2	1712.9	1710.6	1711.5	6.19.	1711.2	1713.3	1710.6	1712.4	1711.9
6.2.	1712.4	1711.2	1712.0	1710.7	1711.6	6.20.	1711.4	1712.4	1712.8	1712.3	1712.2
6.3.	1711.8	1711.7	1712.6	1712.7	1712.2	6.21.	1712.2	1711.9	1711.3	1712.8	1712.1

(continued)

Table 2. (*continued*)

Date	Data 1	Data 2	Data 3	Data 4	Data 5	Date	Data 1	Data 2	Data 3	Data 4	Data 5
6.4.	1712.5	1710.7	1710.4	1712.0	1711.4	6.22.	1712.4	1712.7	1712.2	1711.7	1712.3
6.5.	1711.3	1711.4	1712.1	1710.4	1711.3	6.23.	1711.9	1712.8	1711.6	1713.3	1712.4
6.6.	1712.2	1712.2	1711.6	1711.8	1712.0	6.24.	1711.6	1710.1	1710.9	1712.3	1711.2
6.7.	1711.1	1710.9	1711.6	1712.1	1711.4	6.25.	1711.7	1712.5	1711.5	1712.3	1712.0
6.8.	1712.3	1710.8	1711.9	1712.2	1711.8	6.26.	1713.2	1711.3	1711.8	1712.2	1712.1
6.9.	1711.6	1710.9	1713.0	1710.9	1711.9	6.27.	1711.9	1712.3	1713.1	1711.8	1712.3
6.10.	1712.2	1713.3	1710.4	1712.2	1712.0	6.28.	1710.9	1711.7	1711.6	1711.0	1711.3
6.11.	1711.8	1712.8	1710.9	1711.3	1711.7	6.29.	1713.9	1711.7	1711.7	1713.0	1712.1
6.12.	1713.1	1711.8	1711.6	1711.1	1711.9	6.30.	1711.2	1710.9	1711.2	1712.0	1711.3
6.13.	1712.2	1711.6	1713.8	1712.6	1712.6	7.1.	1712.3	1713.5	1711.7	1712.7	1712.1
6.14.	1712.7	1711.7	1713.3	1710.9	1712.2	7.2.	1712.2	1711.3	1711.5	1711.6	1711.7
6.15.	1711.2	1710.9	1711.5	1711.3	1711.0	7.3.	1712.4	1710.8	1710.2	1712.2	1711.4
6.16.	1713.6	1712.5	1711.8	1712.2	1712.5	7.4.	1711.0	1711.1	1712.4	1712.4	1711.7
6.17.	1712.0	1713.2	1712.4	1712.5	1712.5	7.5.	1712.5	1712.2	1711.1	1711.9	1711.9
6.18.	1711.2	1710.8	1711.2	1711.5	1710.9	7.6.	1711.5	1711.1	1711.7	1713.1	1711.9

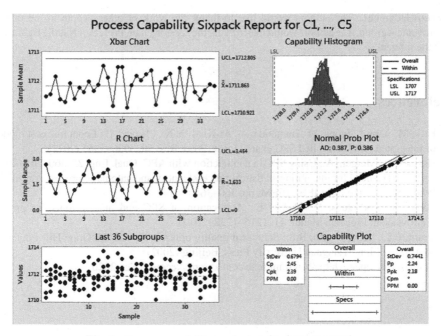

Fig. 4. Process capability analysis (after improvement).

It can be seen from the capability histogram that all the data are within the scope of the quality inspection standard. This indicates that the size is controlled near the standard value. In the capability diagram, the process capability index is $C_{pk} = 2.31 > 1.67$. This indicates that the process capability is improved. The ratio of qualified products is increased. The quality of the production process is improved. The quality department of the company monitors the production process, detect anomalies, and improve production process quality in time.

By applying Xbar-R control chart analysis and process capability analysis, the anomalies are found and the appropriate actions are taken by the quality improvement group. The result of production process improvement is achieved. With the application of SPC methods and statistical tools, the company can produce products of good quality more effectively.

4   Conclusion

In competition environments, companies face many competitors and many companies want to develop high quality products fast to obtain competitive advantage. This research can provide a reference for companies to apply SPC tools and take process capability analysis and control chart analysis to control production processes for quality improvement.

Acknowledgment. The authors would like to thank the work of other people in the quality improvement group. The authors would like to thank the session chair, Professor Natalia Bakhtadze and the referees.

References

1. Park, M., Kim, J., Jeong, M., Hamouda, A., Al-Khalifa, K., Elsayed, E.: Economic cost models of integrated APC controlled SPC charts. Int. J. Prod. Res. **50**, 3936–3955 (2012)
2. Holmes, D., Mergen, A.: Using SPC in conjunction with APC. Qual. Eng. **23**, 360–364 (2011)
3. Saif, A.: The need for integrating statistical process control and automatic process control. In: Proceedings of the 2014 IEEE IEEM, pp. 360–364 (2014)
4. Sousa, S., Rodrigues, N., Nunes, E.: Application of SPC and quality tools for process improvement. Procedia Manuf. **11**, 1215–1222 (2017)
5. Grant, E.L., Leavenworth, R.S.: Statistical quality control. 1st edn. McGraw-Hill Education (Asia) Co., China Tsinghua University Press, Beijing (2002)
6. Minitab Homepage. http://www.minitab.com/zh-cn. Accessed Sep 2020

Management Projects for Digital Ecosystems of Automotive Enterprises: Truck Sharing

Natalia Bakhtadze[1](✉) ⓘ, Denis Elpashev[1], Alexandre Suleykin[1], Rustem Sabitov[2], Gulnara Smirnova[2], Mikhail Kuchinskii[3] ⓘ, and Shamil Sabitov[4]

[1] V.A. Trapeznikov Institute of Control Sciences RAS, 65 Profsoyuznaya Street, Moscow 117997, Russia
[2] Kazan National Research Technical University named after A.N.Tupolev, Kazan 420111, Russia
[3] SAP C.I.S., 115054 Moscow, Russia
[4] Kazan Federal University, Kazan 420008, Russia

Abstract. The paper offers an approach to the development of a truck sharing management system for a digital ecosystem, which comprises an automobile plant, auto parts suppliers, customers and service centers. The management is based on predictive associative search models. To improve the efficiency of the situational management based on situational awareness, quantum clustering algorithms are used.

Keywords: Nonlinear process · Knowledgebase · Associative search models · Quantum clustering

1 Introduction

The most promising consequence of the digital transformation of enterprises and companies and the creation of their digital platforms has been the creation of digital ecosystems (DES). The digital ecosystem is a socio-technical complex, which mainly includes independent players [1]. They combine to create an offer of greater value than a product or service that any of the participants can offer on their own (the Win-Win principle). Some digital ecosystems are developing complex solutions, implementing mutually beneficial algorithmic interactions in a single information environment, lending their resources, information and analytical systems and services to partners for temporary use.

At the same time, DES bring clarity, relevance to the relationship between automated systems and economic agents. Other important attributes of digital ecosystems are their sustainability and sustainable development, which should be taken into account when developing algorithms for functioning and control systems for digital ecosystems. In this case, DES can be interpreted as complex dynamic systems. In particular, these can be multi-agent systems.

An example of a successful project that can be implemented on the basis of a digital ecosystem is a Truck Sharing project. Thus, in Shanghai, a pilot project of DES was

A. Dolgui et al. (Eds.): APMS 2021, IFIP AICT 630, pp. 563–571, 2021.
https://doi.org/10.1007/978-3-030-85874-2_60

launched on the basis of the INGKA holding (owns the IKEA brand), which implements the concept of using a common truck fleet by several companies, which allows optimizing operating costs. INGKA's partners in DES are: warehouse operator Beiye New Brother Logistics and leasing company DST from Shenzhen, which provided access to its own network of charging stations. It is planned to replicate the project in Amsterdam, Paris, New York and Los Angeles. It is noteworthy that the project plans to use electric vehicles.

PJSC KAMAZ in Russia has launched an online service for truck sharing, "SPEC-SHARING", which replaces the purchase of special vehicles (dump trucks, bulldozers, cranes, etc.) with a rental service. Truck sharing service has the same scheme as passenger car sharing. It provides for the rental of KAMAZ dump trucks for a period from one day to a year. At the same time, the cars are insured and have undergone scheduled maintenance. Also, in the "SPECSHARING" service from "KAMAZ" there is an opportunity to get a rental truck with a driver. The rental service for KAMAZ dump trucks has already begun to operate in a number of cities in Tatarstan, Bashkortostan, the Samara region and Nizhny Novgorod (Russia), and soon it will be available in the Moscow region with a subsequent launch in St. Petersburg and Krasnodar.

Truck sharing is an alternative to leasing or classic rental format. The client rents a truck to meet short-term business objectives and must not pass a complicated procedure of purchase of the car and then be concerned about its content. Clients do not need to interact with many owners of special equipment, synchronize them with each other, conduct calculations and document flow with each - all this is performed by "SPECSHARING" while all participants are provided with convenience and safety. At the same time, the main participant - the manufacturer of trucks of various types and modifications - also receives certain advantages. Besides the fact that the company, in addition to the sales of its products, it is also the seller of services (which, as experience shows, brings a considerable profit in itself), it also provides additional stabilization of the production rate.

The dynamics of the model range is characterized by nonstationarity: some models are removed from production, new ones appear instead. After the completion of the certain model production, spare parts for it continue to be produced for at least 10 years. In such conditions, truck sharing helps to equalize the satisfaction of demand and stabilizes the production process, including the warehouse logistics option (taking into account the supply of components not only to the assembly line, but also to the truck sharing services). Discount sales bring additional flexibility in production planning.

This paper presents an approach to organizing management in a digital ecosystem that implements projects of this type. The conditions for the stable functioning of the DES are described. The tasks are formulated and solved, the solution of which enhances the coordination of actions of the direct participants in the transport process.

The forecast (plan) for the production of trucks is created taking into account the distributed forecast of the economic activity of enterprises and companies in the territory considered in the project. If the cars available in a particular service center become insufficient, then it is possible to use the free resources of other service centers or (if this situation arises systematically) to organize an additional supply of new trucks from the factory. During the implementation of the project, it may be necessary to divide the service centers into the categories of available equipment and the number of available trucks, which can improve the financial performance of the project.

2 Business Problem Description

The management of the described DES should ensure the technical and technological consistency of the participants in the transport process, as well as the observance of their economic interests, when operating within the framework of a unified planning system. The trucks participating in the project undergo standard scheduled service at specialized service centers.

For each service center, its service capacity is known, as well as the number of parking spaces with security. The average travel time between all service centers is also known. We also know the approximate number of trucks of various brands and types that are in demand at the production facilities closest to each service center - territorial clusters.

In this problem, the number of service centers is assumed to be 250, the distance between them is from 25 to 1,000 km. Taking into account the forecast of the needs of each territorial cluster in various types of trucks, the task is to "balanced" supply of the necessary trucks of various models - to each service center either for subsequent sale to customers, or for use in a truck sharing service with the possibility of further sale of used equipment at a discount.

The forecast (plan) for the production of trucks is created taking into account the distributed forecast of the economic activity of enterprises and companies in the territory considered in the project. If the cars available in a particular service center become insufficient, then it is possible to use the free resources of other service centers or (if this situation arises systematically) to organize an additional supply of new trucks from the factory.

The model should provide for the possibility of restructuring the network and changing the capacity of service centers in the event of the emergence of new economic objects where trucks will be in demand, or there will be changes in the demand for trucks at already operating facilities. Also, the current capabilities of suppliers of components and the forecast of the need for components and spare parts should be known, which will eliminate situations with their shortage or late delivery - both to the plant itself and to service centers.

A necessary condition for the implementation of such a project is a clearly defined relationship between the plant and the network of service centers. The interaction of service centers between themselves and the parent enterprise should also include the solution of the problem (if necessary) of the dynamic redistribution of spare parts and labor. Such a network structure can ensure the sustainable development of the digital manufacturing ecosystem under consideration.

Obviously, to manage all the services discussed above, an intelligent add-on is required - a control support system, which, based on predictive real-time models, will form and simulate various scenarios for given values of the main parameters of the digital production ecosystem. For the development and commissioning of the project in question, it is necessary to have an operating digital platform of the plant, which will provide information and algorithmic support for solving problems arising in the ecosystem.

3 Managing the KAMAZ PJSC Digital Ecosystem for the Stable Functioning of Truck Sharing

The formed management system should ensure uninterrupted and effective implementation of the business plan for shared transportation for all participants. In fact, we are talking about solving a complex logistic problem of creating transport systems, possibly containing transport corridors and transport chains. Such systems should ensure technological unity and joint planning of the transport process (optimal routing) with warehouse and production processes.

In order to be able to quickly correct the transportation plan required in case of unforeseen changes in the technological situation, it is advisable to use multi-agent technologies [2].

The system approach to the investigation of multiagent systems is effectively exemplified in representation of such objects as *multimodal* ones [3]. Their multimodality appears both in the decomposition of the production process into independent stages (phases) and in the study of various operation modes as control objects.

In both cases, the extended state vector $x_{k1}^1 \ldots x_{km}^1 \ldots x_{kM}^1 x_{k1}^s \ldots x_{km}^s \ldots x_{kM}^s$ is used to describe the object where the index k, $k = 1, \ldots, K$ denotes a time point of discrete system operation, s, $s = 1, \ldots, S$ is the number of mode (step, phase), m is the number of the input vector's component. Values of some components of the state vector for various modes may be constant, in particular, zero.

In the work [4], an approach was presented to solving the problem of optimal traffic routing management for a territorial cluster based on associative predictive models of multi-agent systems in which agents perform a common task: to deliver goods in accordance with the drawn up plan. The performance of multi-agent systems has been interpreted as their robustness as complex dynamic systems [5].

The multi-agent control systems themselves were interpreted as systems with a block state vector. Each block M corresponded to a description of the functioning of a certain carrier company as an agent. The criterion for the feasibility of a task common for agents is the fulfillment of the conditions so that the system does not lose stability as a result of the agents' actions. To predict the possible loss of stability, associative search algorithms were used, in particular, their version for identifying non-stationary systems [3].

The stability conditions of the model can be determined, for example, by wavelet analysis methods [3]. Wavelet analysis uses a special linear transformation of processes to analyze data characterizing the properties of the object dynamics under study. Such a linear transformation is carried out on the basis of special soliton-like functions (wavelets) that form an orthonormal basis in.

Wavelet analysis allows you to examine signals in the frequency domain that changes over time. For a system with one output and several inputs, we have

$$x(t) = \sum_{k=1}^{N/2^L} c_t^x \varphi_{L,k}(t) + \sum_{j=1}^{L} \sum_{k=1}^{N/2^j} d_{j,k}^x \psi_{j,k}(t), N \geq 2^L \qquad (1)$$

$$y(t) = \sum_{k=1}^{N/2^L} c_t^y \varphi_{L,k}(t) + \sum_{j=1}^{L} \sum_{k=1}^{N/2^j} d_{j,k}^y \psi_{j,k}(t), N \geq 2^L \qquad (2)$$

where: L is the depth of the multiresolution decomposition $k < t; (k < t)$; $\varphi_{L,k}(t)$ are scaling functions; $\psi_{j,k}(t)$ are wavelet functions obtained from mother wavelets by means of extension, compression and shifting (in this article, Haar wavelets are considered as the mother ones); j is the analysis detailing level; c_t and $d_{j,k}$ are the scaling and detailing coefficients respectively. The coefficients are calculated using Mallat algorithm [3].

Sufficient system stability conditions can be expressed through the coefficients of multiresolution wavelet decomposition.

The possibility of loss of stability by individual agents (and, consequently, by the entire system) was determined using the digital twin of the transport system, built on the basis of simulation models. If stability could be violated, then separate areas of instability were identified and the transportation plan was subjected to local adjustments. A high-precision information retrieval ("virtual") linear model was built:

$$\hat{y}_m(t) = \sum_{i=1}^{L} a_i \hat{y}_m(t-i) + \sum_{j=1}^{n} \sum_{r=1}^{R} b_{jr} x_{rm}(t-j), \tag{3}$$

where for a sharing system: $\hat{y}_m(t)$ is the actual time remaining by the moment t for the timely delivery of the m-th order; $x_{rm}(t), r = 1, \ldots, R$ are the factors of possible deviation of the delivery time from the contract schedule. L and R are a constant. The coefficient values are determined when you set up the predictive associative model.

Further, to solve the problem of optimal routing, it was proposed to use the iterative deepening A * (IDA *) algorithm - the application of the idea of iterative deepening in the context of heuristic search [4]. The coefficient values are determined when you set up the predictive associative model.

To speed up the operation of the algorithm in real time, it seems appropriate to use the methods of parallelization of IDA * algorithms. Within the framework of the optimizing problem the functioning of a truck sharing scheme as agents, we will consider individual service centers that act as elements of a sharing scheme.

If it was assumed in the optimization problem of the relay transportation scheme that the number of trucks is sufficient to solve it, in the present problem this condition becomes decisive and is formulated as a key constraint. Also, an important condition for uninterrupted operation is a sufficient number of spare parts and components that allow car repairs to be carried out within an acceptable time frame. The last condition applies to both planned and emergency repairs.

4   Forecasting the Dynamics of Demand and Possible Bottlenecks

When forming the optimal (under existing constraints) plan, in particular, a certain level of requirements for the availability of various spare parts is laid down. The model for forecasting the requirements for the m-th nomenclature unit has the structure:

$$z_m(t) = \sum_{i=1}^{l} a_i z_m(t-i) + \sum_{l=1}^{L} \sum_{i=1}^{I} b_{il} x_i(t-l), \tag{4}$$

where: $z_m(t-i)$ is the actual need for the m-th inventory at the time $(t-i)$; $x_l(t-j)$ - random factors of the need for the m-th spare part at the moment $(t-j)$, which can lead to an adjustment (sometimes very significant) of the generated plan. These can be abnormal and emergency situations, as well as other factors due to the peculiarities of a specific production situation. So, the associative identification algorithm can be used.

Delivery Forecast. The forecast of deliveries, generally speaking, should take into account random factors, which can also lead to the adjustment of the formed plan. Random delivery models can be useful in changing market conditions arising from changes in external market factors.

The optimal supply planning process can be described in terms of a multidimensional Markov process. In this case, the state of the system at each step is characterized by a random vector

$$\alpha(t) = \{\alpha_1(t), \alpha_2(t), \alpha_3(t)\}, \tag{5}$$

where: $\alpha_1(t)$ is the total demand for components at time t, $\alpha_2(t)$ is the total delivery from the warehouse, $\alpha_3(t)$, is the current volume of traffic.

5   Situational Awareness

The above-described scheme for supporting the management of the transport system is based on predictive models of real time, which are able to warn about the possibility of exiting the normal mode of operation (which is interpreted as the possibility of loss of stability by the multi-agent system).

The patterns $x_{1m}, \ldots x_{Rm}, y_m$ characterize the production situation. We use associative search algorithms to predict the situation. These algorithms are smart least squares. Indeed, at the training stage, the set of patterns is subdivided into clusters, which are further corrected as information accumulates. For the forecasting algorithm to work at time t in the cluster containing the current pattern, several patterns are selected that are close to the current one in the sense of the selected criterion (association). Next, a system of linear equations is solved using the least squares method [3].

Thus, we have a point (unique for the moment t) linear model of a nonlinear process, the best in the sense of the root-mean-square criterion. In the non-stationary case, the solution is sought in the space of wavelet transformations. It should be noted that in order to analyze and predict production situations, it is necessary to take into account various factors $x_{pm}, p = 1, \ldots, P$, characterizing certain features p of the current production situation, determined by the external environment.

In a particular case, this can be interpreted as the likelihood of an event occurring that can affect the dynamics of the production situation. In the model, its value can be determined in an expert way, or through production and fuzzy models. The results of analyzing and predicting situations taking into account these (often difficult to formalize) factors are called *Situational Awareness (SA)*.

The digital industrial ecosystem of truck sharing should in particular, ensure the sustainability of work in the event of unforeseen situations associated, for example, with natural disasters or natural anomalies, or - with the influence of the "human factor". To solve such problems, a certain "dynamic reserve" is needed, capable of providing a quick redistribution of transport units to solve certain sudden problems.

Certain regularities (for example, limiting the movement of heavy vehicles in the spring, or a possible sharp decrease in the average speed of movement during weather anomalies) must be taken into account in the model in advance.

Based on the proposed predictive models, the management scheme of this DES will ensure a balance between demand forecasts and real production capabilities, taking into account seasonal and other factors. Situational driving awareness will increase the intensity of the truck while reducing the overall life of the truck.

The scheme ensures the economic efficiency of the activities of all participants in the process and is preferable in the environmental aspect. Many SA publications suggest using a specific classification of situations to analyze and support management.

In particular, a variety of cognitive methods based on semantic metrics are proposed for determining the proximity of situations, allowing expert assessments to be taken into account. It should be noted the importance of taking into account the rate of change of external factors, which must correspond to the rate of decision-making in the control system, as well as the rate of classifying the current situation to a certain class.

6   Case Studies

Q-Means Clustering. At the stage of training the associative search algorithm that predicts the production situation with Situational Awareness, data is clustered. Further, in real time, the identification problem is solved for the current time instant. At the same time, digital portraits of "similar situations" are selected from the data archive for the algorithm to work.

The selection is carried out from the cluster into which the current vector of inputs falls. The k-means algorithm can be used to cluster the sets of indicators characterizing the production situation. In conditions of Big Data, when, in addition to the need to process large amounts of data, high speed of algorithms is also required, it seems appropriate to use quantum computing.

Today we only carry out simulations, however, in anticipation of the real implementation of quantum computers in production control, this is quite timely. The IBM Quantum Experience cloud quantum computing platform was used for modeling (Fig. 1 and 2).

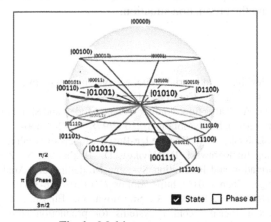

Fig. 1. Multiagent system state

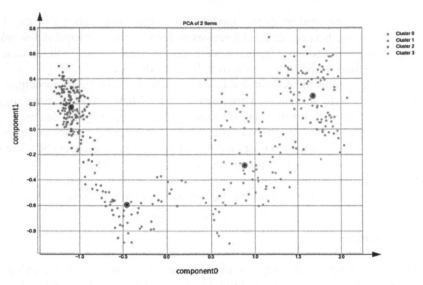

Fig. 2. Production situations q-clustering

7 Conclusion

Within the framework of the concept of trucking, the following advantages can be distinguished for the producer and consumers - DES participants: convenience for a wide range of clients; reduction in the cost of transport services; improvement of the ecological situation; ensuring the rhythm of car production; facilitating the launch of new models on the market; decrease in the average age of trucks; improvement of the road safety situation; simple solutions for the seasonality of the use of equipment, etc.

Real-time predictive identification models proposed in the paper to optimize the tracking scheme provide an opportunity to prevent disturbances in the stability of the DES functioning and ensure their sustainable development, since they take into account the nonstationarity of the processes under study and the impact of poorly formalized factors characterizing the production situation.

References

1. Bakhtadze, N., Suleykin, A.: Industrial digital ecosystems: predictive models and architecture development issues. Annu. Rev. Control. **51C**, 56–64 (2021)
2. Treiber, M., Kesting, A.: Traffic flow dynamics. Data, Models and Simulation. Springer-Verlag, Berlin, Heidelberg (2013). https://doi.org/10.1007/978-3-642-32460-4
3. Bakhtadze, N.N., Lototsky, V.A.: Knowledge-Based Models of Nonlinear Systems Based on Inductive Learning. In: Różewski, P., Novikov, D., Bakhtadze, N., Zaikin, O. (eds.) New Frontiers in Information and Production Systems Modelling and Analysis. ISRL, vol. 98, pp. 85–104. Springer, Cham (2016). https://doi.org/10.1007/978-3-319-23338-3_4
4. Bakhtadze, N., Dolgui, A., Sabitov, R., Smirnova, G., Elpashev, D.: Identification and simulation models in logistics control systems for production processes and freighting. IFAC-PapersOnLine. **50**(1), 14638–14643 (2017)

5. Gazi, V., Fidan, B.: Coordination and Control of Multi-agent Dynamic Systems: Models and Approaches. In: Şahin, E., Spears, W.M., Winfield, A.F.T. (eds.) SR 2006. LNCS, vol. 4433, pp. 71–102. Springer, Heidelberg (2007). https://doi.org/10.1007/978-3-540-71541-2_6

Formation of Work Plans and Schedules at Enterprises with Conveyor Assembly

E. N. Khobotov[1,2]([envelope]) and M. A. Ermolova[2]

[1] Trapeznikov Institute of Control Sciences, Russian Academy of Sciences, Moscow, Russia
[2] Bauman Moscow State Technical University, Moscow, Russia

Abstract. The methods of constructing plans and schedules for the production of components and assembly of manufactured products from them on the conveyors of machine-building enterprises are considered. Work planning can be carried out both in the production of incoming orders for manufactured products, and in the production of products taking into account the current demand for it.

Keywords: Modeling methods · Planning · Equipment · Components · Conveyor assembly · Control algorithms · Schedule theory

1 Introduction

In recent years, the problems of creating methods for planning and formation of the schedule of work at industrial enterprises have bigger interest. Such interest is caused by the fact that successfully constructed plans and work schedules at enterprises can significantly reduce the time for manufacturing production programs and orders received [1].

In this regard, the idea arises to increase the efficiency of industrial enterprises by building beneficial plans and schedules for them.

Most of the scheduling methods [1–3] developed are designed for scheduling in production subdivisions and systems. The use of such methods for constructing work schedules at machine-building enterprises, which may include several production subdivision and systems, causes great difficulties. These difficulties are caused by the large dimension and complexity of scheduling tasks in enterprises.

Formation of plans and work schedules of the enterprise on the basis of the schedules for the manufacture of components in the divisions of enterprises also causes great difficulties. Such difficulties are associated with the fact that it is not clear how to determine the components that should be processed within one time interval in the same subdivisions of the enterprise. These components can be determined when there is already a work schedule in the enterprise, but without such a schedule, their choice can hardly be made.

Therefore, to construct work schedules at industrial enterprises, the development of special methods is required.

© IFIP International Federation for Information Processing 2021
Published by Springer Nature Switzerland AG 2021
A. Dolgui et al. (Eds.): APMS 2021, IFIP AICT 630, pp. 572–579, 2021.
https://doi.org/10.1007/978-3-030-85874-2_61

The article deals with the methods of forming coordinated plans and schedules of enterprises that include several production subdivisions that produce components for assembling from them on the company's conveyors of manufactured products. For enterprises of this type, on the basis of information aggregation methods, it is possible to create more effective algorithms for building coordinated work plans and schedules for all production subdivisions of enterprises.

2 Planning and Scheduling Tasks at Enterprises

Let a machine-building enterprise be given, which includes several machining subdivisions for the manufacture of components parts, and conveyors for the assembly of issued products from them.

For any type of issues products, the composition of its details, components and assemblies, as well as the sizes of the batch of these products, is known. For any components of these products, a manufacturing technology is known, including the sequence and times of all operations performing for their manufacture on all equipment used for this.

Assembling of manufactured products can be carried out on one or several conveyors both from manufactured at the enterprise, and from components purchased on the side. On each conveyor only "their" products can be assembled. For each conveyor, its performance is known for the production of all types of products assembled on it, the number of work places during the assembly of any manufactured product, as well as the time and cost of readjustment the conveyor for the production of all batches of products which will be assembled on it.

Products are assembled on conveyors, usually in batches, the size of which is limited. Such restrictions are determined by the production capabilities of enterprises. The fact is that the manufacture of a large number of components can take considerable time, lead to large downtime of the conveyor in anticipation of their readiness, and will require the creation of large warehouses for their storage.

The assembly of any batch of products begins after delivery to each work place of conveyor of a certain number of sets of components, as a rule, the same number for all work places of conveyor.

In one of the tasks, it is required to build a work schedule at the enterprise, which will reduce the lead time for an order for the manufacture of a certain number of products of different types.

In another task, it is required to construct a work schedule at an enterprise that has one conveyor, on which L types of products are assembled sequentially. When assembling any batch of products, a certain part of it is sent to the warehouse in order to provide consumers with products of the required type stocked in the warehouse for the release of other products until its assembly will be resumed.

The volume of output and the value of stocked products should be determined in such a way that, in accordance with the existing demand for the product, increase profits from its sale, as well as reduce the cost of its storage and readjustment of the conveyor.

3 Principles of Plans and Work Schedules Formation at Enterprises

As already noted above, plans and work schedules to improve the efficiency of the operation of enterprises should be built for all departments of the enterprise in such a way that they will be consistent with each other. For these purposes, an approach based on the use of information aggregation methods was proposed in [1].

The idea of aggregating information consists in forming such groups from the completing details of the manufactured batch of products, in which each detail of the group is received for its processing in the same order to the production subdivisions of the enterprise. At the same time, any detail of the group can be processed in each subdivision of the enterprise where it is processed, according to its "own" technological route.

Such groups are considered as generalized details, production subdivisions of the enterprise, as generalized machines, and the task of constructing a work schedule at the enterprise, as the task of constructing a schedule for processing generalized details on generalized machines.

To build such a schedule, the processing time of each generalized part on all used generalized machines, i.e. the processing time of each group of parts in those production subdivisions of the enterprise where this group is processed.

These times can be determined using both traditional scheduling methods [4] and evaluation models [1, 5–7]. In Fig. 1 shows an example of a processing schedule for the i-th group of parts in the l-th production subdivision and T_{il} indicates the time of this processing.

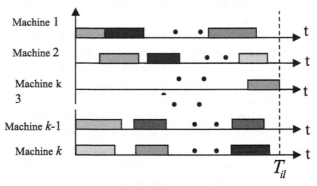

Fig. 1. Gantt chart representing the processing schedule of the i-th group of parts in the l-th production subdivision.

After determining the values T_{il} for all groups of component details and subdivisions of the enterprise, the traditional task of the theory of schedules actually arises, associated with the construction of a schedule for processing generalized parts in a production department that includes generalized machines. In [1], such a schedule for manufacturing groups of parts in the enterprise's subdivisions was called "wireframe". Traditional "scheduling methods" [4] can be successfully used for constructing "wireframe" schedules, since the dimension of tasks during aggregation is significantly reduced. The "frame" schedule is consistent, i.e. the schedule for the manufacture of parts at the

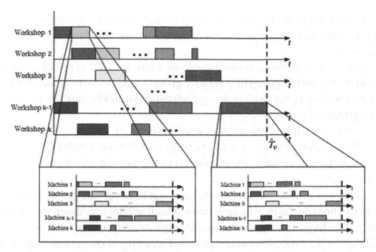

Fig. 2. A fragment of a "wireframe" schedule for processing groups of parts at the enterprise level.

enterprise level, since the processing order of such groups in the enterprise divisions is determined using scheduling theory methods. As a rule, several such schedules are built, up to 15–25 and the best variant is selected from them. An example of such a schedule is shown in Fig. 2.

This schedule, as can be seen from Fig. 2, has almost the same form as the schedule for processing parts in the subdivision shown in Fig. 1. However, in the Gantt chart, which represents the "wireframe" schedule, instead of machines on the ordinate axis, the production subdivisions of the enterprise (sections, workshops) are postponed, and instead of the part processing time on each abscissa axis, the processing times of groups of parts in the respective subdivisions are postponed.

Typically, such a distribution of component parts into groups produced extremely rare usually when the production of these types of parts masters at the enterprise and is adjusted only after the inclusion of new components in the production program or when the composition of the equipment of production equipment changes.

The processing times of each group of parts in the production subdivisions of the enterprise can be calculated independently of each other in any sequence. Therefore, on multiprocessor computing tools, you can organize parallel calculations of these times. This makes it possible to significantly reduce the calculation time, which was confirmed by the results of computational experiments [2].

Here it is useful to note some features related to the construction of "wireframe" schedules, which can reduce the time of there building.

From the results of computational experiments, it is known that the existing methods of building schedules quickly and well build work schedules when processing 30–60 types of parts in a production subdivision that has 30–70 units of equipment. Each part is usually processed in such a subdivision on 5 to 12 types of machines.

This information is useful when forming groups of components parts and subdivisions of the enterprise, which can be considered as "generalized machines" for processing these groups.

If the group of parts being formed contains more than 80 types of parts, then it is advisable to divide such a group into smaller groups, each of which does not exceed the above boundaries, so as not to miss the opportunity to quickly build work schedules for processing groups of parts.

If the number of equipment units in a subdivision of an enterprise turns out to be more than 70–90 units, then it is convenient to divide such a subdivision into several subdivisions in the calculations, the number of equipment in which does not exceed the above boundaries.

If the number of formed groups of parts turns out to be very large, then their number in many cases can be reduced by attaching parts, which are not processed in all subdivisions of the enterprise, to groups that have similar fragments of routes.

In addition, it is advisable to note that the processing of components by such groups in the subdivisions of enterprises makes it possible to more efficiently organize the transportation of parts between divisions than with traditional processing. The fact is that after the completion of the processing of each group in any subdivision, all processed parts can only go to two places.

One of such places is a subdivision, in which processing of all parts of the group that are not completely made, will continue, since each group of parts is sent to the subdivisions for processing along one known route.

Another place for transportation of the group parts, the processing of which is completed in this subdivision, is the warehouse, where the finished parts for assembly are stored.

4   Schedules at Enterprises with Conveyor Assembly of Products

The constructed examples showed that the order of processing of components and, to a large extent, the total production time of products depends on the order of assembly of batches of products. The "wireframe" schedule for the manufacture of components intended for the assembly of any batch of products, in turn, can be considered as a "frame" for the manufacture of components for this batch in the production subdivisions of the enterprise.

An example of such a "frame" for the manufacture of components for each batch of products has the form similar to the "frame" schedule shown in Fig. 2, where the manufacturing time of this "frame" of components is indicated by $\hat{T}_v$. The assembly time of any batch of products can be determined by knowing its size, the number of jobs on the conveyor and its productivity.

In this case, knowing the times of manufacturing the "frames" of components and the assembly times of batches of products from them, it is possible to construct a time-optimized "frame" assembly schedule for several batches of various products, if we consider the manufacturing time of the "frame" of components for assembling the ith batch of products through A_i as the processing time of the ith detail on the first machine, and the assembly time of this batch of products on the conveyor through B_i as the processing time of the ith detail on the second machine, then this problem turns out to be similar to Johnson's [4] (see Fig. 3).

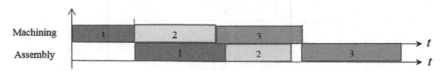

Fig. 3. Gantt chart of the "frame" schedule for the manufacture of components and assembly of products from them.

The assembly sequence of a batch of products and, accordingly, the manufacture of components for this can be determined using the results of the following theorem, which is similar to Johnson's theorem [3].

Theorem 1. Let several batches of products of various types be assembled on a conveyor, the assembly of each of which begins after the manufacture of all components for this batch of products.

Then, with the simultaneous availability of all works, the "frame" schedule, which minimizes the total production time of all products, is such that the assembly of j-th product batch precedes assembly $(j + 1)$-th product batch, if.

$$\min\left(A_j, B_{j+1}\right) \leq \min\left(A_{j+1}, B_j\right) \text{ and } A_{j+1} \neq B_{j+1} \tag{1}$$

If $A_{j+1} = B_{j+1}$ and there is k $(k = 1, ..., n)$ subsequent work on the manufacture of batches of products for which equalities are also satisfied $A_{j+k+1} = B_{j+k+1}$, then for these works, besides fulfilling the conditions $\min\left(A_{j+k}, B_{j+k+1}\right) \leq \min\left(A_{j+k+1}, B_{j+k}\right)$ min for all k $(k = 0, 1, ..., n)$, the condition must also be fulfilled $\min\left(A_j, B_{j+n+1}\right) \leq \min\left(A_{j+n+1}, B_j\right)$, where across $j + n + 1$ the first job following the job is indicated $j + n$, for this $A_{j+n+1} \neq B_{j+n+1}$.

Let us consider the principles and methods of constructing plans and schedules of work at enterprises with conveyor assembly of products, when various types of products can be sequentially assembled on one conveyor, the volumes of output of each type of product are determined by the demand for them r_i $(i = 1, ..., L)$. Let us denote by $\tilde{C}_{si}$ financial, and by τ_i time costs of preparation and readjustment of the conveyor for assembling of i-th products $(i = 1, ..., L)$.

In the task, it is necessary to determine the volume of production of each type of product in such a way that there are no surpluses and shortages of manufactured products in the warehouse, and the number of changeovers of the conveyor from the production of one product to another during the planned period would be as small as possible.

To ensure consistent production of types of L products and their availability in the warehouse, it is proposed to make the times between the start of adjacent releases of products of each type t_s identical and determine them, in accordance with [8], using the following ratio:

$$t_s = \max \left\{ \sqrt{\frac{2 \sum\limits_{i=1}^{L} \tilde{C}_{si}}{\sum\limits_{i=1}^{L} C_i \bar{r}_i \left(1 - \frac{\bar{r}_i}{p_i}\right)}}, \frac{\sum\limits_{i=1}^{L} \tau_i}{1 - \sum\limits_{i=1}^{L} \frac{\bar{r}_i}{p_i}} \right\} \tag{2}$$

where $\bar{r}_i$ value of average demand for products of the i-th type ($i = 1, ..., L$) during the planning interval T.

Value q_i and $\tilde{q}_i$ denoting the number of products in the production batch and the number of products from this batch, which is sent to the warehouse, are determined using the ratios (3), (4).

$$q_i = (p_i - \bar{r}_i) t_{li}, \ i = 1, ..., L \tag{3}$$

$$\tilde{q}_i = \bar{r}_i t_s = p_i t_{li}, \ i = 1, ..., L \tag{4}$$

Calculation of work schedules at such enterprises in conditions of random demand $\bar{r}_i$ ($i = 1, ..., L$) after determining the values $\tilde{q}_i$ ($i = 1, ..., L$) can be made in accordance with the scheme described in the previous paragraph.

In the conditions of the traditional processing of components, when the parts after processing in one production subdivision arrive to continue processing in different subdivisions, it is very difficult to organize efficient transportation of parts.

In this work, the processing of components is proposed to be carried out in groups, which are processed in the production subdivisions of the enterprise in the same order. This allows you not only to build work schedules at the enterprise level, but also to organize the efficient transportation of parts between production subdivisions and build a schedule for their transportation.

5   Conclusion

The ideas of forming groups of components, which are created in accordance with the principles described above, have proven to be very productive. This allows:

- to offer another organization of the manufacture of components parts, when their processing is carried out in groups, which are formed according to the principles described above;
- to develop building schedules methods for processing components at the enterprise level;
- to organize efficient delivery of component parts between production subdivisions;
- more effectively manage inter-shop vehicles of the enterprise;
- drill down into the "wireframe" schedules at the enterprise level to the processing schedules for individual parts on all the equipment used.

The developed methods of constructing work schedules for enterprises with conveyor assembly of manufactured products can be used to create algorithms for selecting equipment for the modernization of such enterprises. The efficiency of scheduling methods can be improved by parallelizing the calculations performed.

References

1. Khobotov, E.N.: On some models and methods of the solution of scheduling problems in discrete enterprises. Autom. Remote Control **68**, 99–110 (2007)
2. Sidorenko, A.M., Khobotov, E.N.: Aggregation in job scheduling on mechanical engineering facilities. Teor. Sist. Upravlen. **5**, 132–144 (2013)
3. Larina, E.A., Sidorenko, A.M., Khobotov, E.N.: Choosing the order of assembly for units and modules in job scheduling on facilities with discrete production. Probl. Upravlen. **3**, 71–77 (2013)
4. Bruker, P.: Scheduling Algorithms. Springer, Leipzig (2007)
5. Sudip, A., Sahana, K.: An automated parameter tuning method for ant colony optimization for scheduling jobs in grid environment. Int. J. Intell. Syst. Appl. (IJISA) **11**(3), 11–21 (2019)
6. Sharma, P., Kaur, K.: Hybrid artificial bee colony and tabu search based power aware scheduling for cloud computing. Int. J. Int. Syst. Appl. (IJISA) **10**(7), 39–47 (2018)
7. Nagar, R., Gupta, D.K., Singh, R.M.: Time effective workflow scheduling using genetic algorithm in cloud computing. Int. J. Inf. Technol. Comput. Sci. (IJITCS) **10**(1), 68–75 (2018)
8. Khobotov, E.N.: Control problems and methods for multi-nomenclature reserves in production. Izv. Ross. Akad. Nauk, Teor. Sist. Upravlen. (6), 221–232 (2011)

Resolution Estimates for Selected Coordinate Descent: Identification of Seismic Structure in the Area of Geothermal Plants

Tatyana A. Smaglichenko[1]([⊠])[iD] and Alexander Smaglichenko[2][iD]

[1] Research Oil and Gas Institute, Russian Academy of Sciences, 3 Gubkina Street, Moscow 119333, Russia
[2] V.A. Trapeznikov Institute of Control Sciences, Russian Academy of Sciences, 65 Profsoyuznaya Street, Moscow 117997, Russia

Abstract. The coordinate descent method is a traditional inverse solver to optimization problems. In modern sectors of production research: in computer graphics, computer tomography, a theory of pattern recognition various algorithms of the coordinate descent have been applied. In this paper, we investigate the novel algorithm of selected coordinate descent and outline the difference between this algorithm and the classical coordinate descent. The solution selection is performed owing to the search of the maximum among values of the specific parameter. The maximum indicates a single direction, which is responsible for the minimum of the function in the least square sense. We develop the technique for defining the explicit expression for the resolution measure of the linear systems, which are solved using the proposed algorithm. The algorithm and its resolution tool are applied to seismic observations collected in the area of the Krafla and Theistareykir geothermal power plants, northern Iceland. The result confirms that the distinctive feature of the algorithm is its effectiveness when large-size structures are retrieved. The analysis of the resolution parameter values shows that the calculation of this parameter might be helpful to recognize the true structure.

Keywords: Coordinate descent · Linear equations · Tomography · Structure recognition

1 Introduction

The simplicity and capabilities of the iterative solution construction are features of the method coordinate descent (CD). Therefore this method is preferred over others for the computer graphics industry. The iterative process calculates the

The research was carried out within the framework of the state projects №AAAA-A19-119013190038-2, №10.331-17.

A. Dolgui et al. (Eds.): APMS 2021, IFIP AICT 630, pp. 580–588, 2021.
https://doi.org/10.1007/978-3-030-85874-2_62

unknown parameters of the animation object moving. The known vector corresponds to the needful position of the part (end effector) of an object [1].

In tomography, the unknown vector has the physical meaning of the object properties in limited volumes on the grid. A set of observations are related to the object characteristics leads us to the fundamental problem of solving the system of linear equations. The most popular method is the LSQR algorithm introduced by Paige & Saunders [2]. The algorithm is similar to the conjugate gradients method. It applies the Lanczos process and processes a symmetric system [3]. The symmetric matrix might be obtained owing to the multiplication of both parts of the system to the transposed system matrix. We suppose that such numerical transformations may distort the original matrix, which reflects the initial data of the physical experiment. The other problem might be the use of the complicated recurrence formulas that is a reason for the presence of rounding-off errors. Therefore, the interest is still not lost to traditional iterative methods as the Kaczmarz algorithm [4] and the studied CD method. A review of the CD application has been made in [5] analyzing the application sectors: optical diffusion tomography and cryo-electron tomography.

In the theory of pattern recognition, the input vector might be presented by various data: information about the image pixels (components of intensity), speech (acoustic signals), writing language (logograph), etc. For recognition tasks, the CD method applied to the binary classification problem [6,7] by updating of construction of multiclass predictors, where misclassification error has a linear bound [8]. In [7], experiments have been made to recognize documents. On the other hand, the direct solver is commonly used in digital image processing. The singular value decomposition (SVD) method is often applied in the field of image compression [9]. It is known that SVD is equivalent to the Lanczos process, which is a base of LSQR.

This paper proposes the Selected CD (SCD) algorithm, which might be a contribution to computing image and image structure recognition. The SCD method originated in seismic tomography and was examined comparing with LSQR under equal conditions of conducted numerical experiments [10]. The testing on various arbitrary models showed that SCD may be more effective than LSQR when a simple large-size structure is retrieved. The SCD convergence properties were designed in [10].

There is a difference between the traditional CD and SCD. When solving the system of equations we often apply the least-square approach to the function that is the difference between the system parts. CD calculates the current approximation on the base of components of the gradient, which gives the possible direction of the function minimization. In the traditional CD, indexes of the gradient vector components might be chosen in a cycle fashion or randomly with the probability criterion [5]. SCD selects the index, which provides the function minimum satisfying the special condition. In [11], SCD was established by analyzing the solution errors and updating the condition for big and sparse matrices.

This paper aims to reveal the difference between the SCD algorithm and the classical CD. Another aim of this paper is to present the technique for determining the SCD resolution measure. We describe the SCD application to the real data of local seismic events that were observed at the end of the Krafla rifting episode, during three years 1986–1989. Nowadays two power plants are located in the being investigated area. The production process leads to the cooling of a deep underground medium [12]. Therefore the robust evaluation of seismic structure is essential for the environmental issues.

2   SCD with Its Relationship to CD

The solution of the system of equations might be considered as the least square minimization of the function $f(x)$ in x. In the case of the system of linear equations $Ax = b$ the functional can be written in the following form:

$$f(x) = (Ax - b, Ax - b), \tag{1}$$

where $(Ax - b, Ax - b)$ denotes a scalar product.

The conventional CD [5,13] builds the iterative solution as:

$$x^i = x^{i-1} - \left|\nabla f(x^i)\right|_k e_k, \tag{2}$$

where $\left|\nabla f(x^i)\right|_k$ is a component of the gradient, e_k is the vector in the direction of coordinate, $i \in \{1, 2, 3 \ldots n\}$.

Components of the gradient are found by taking the first derivative $f(x^i)$ and setting it to zero. In [11], we have found $\left|\nabla f(x^i)\right|_k$ as:

$$\left|\nabla f(x^i)\right|_k = \frac{(Ax^{i-1} - b, Ae_k)}{(Ae_k, Ae_k)}, \tag{3}$$

where Ae_k is the k-th column of the matrix A. Thus, we set:

$$x^i = x^{i-1} - \frac{(Ax^{i-1} - b, Ae_k)}{(Ae_k, Ae_k)}. \tag{4}$$

If the CD and SCD starting points are equal to zero, then we can see that the iterative approximation (4) is similar to CD for the linear regression [13]. The explanation of several CD algorithms can be found in works [14,15] and in the presentation of the teaching course of the University of Wisconsin-Madison that was made by authors [14,15].

Thus, both CD and the developed SCD can calculate the gradient components in the same manner. Note, setting the first derivative $f(x)$ to zero gives the function extremum. The question arises. What is the index provides the direction to the function minimum? CD ordinary uses the cyclic coordinate descent and thus, index is cyclically selected. Applying the SCD approach continues the search of the descent direction (the index k). Namely, if we substitute the Eq. (2) for x^i in the formula (1), then after a few transformations we obtain $f(x^i)$ in the following form [11]:

$$f(x^i) = (Ax^{i-1} - b, Ax^{i-1} - b) - \frac{(Ax^{i-1} - b, Ae_k)^2}{(Ae_k, Ae_k)}. \tag{5}$$

It is clear that the index with the maximal absolute value of the fractional expression gives the direction of the function minimum.

A proof of the SCD convergence and the convergence analysis were described in [10]. The convergence rate was determined through the span of the angle between the directing vectors to the hyper-planes, to which the vectors $Ax^{i-1} - b_*$ and $Ax^i - b_*$ belong. Here the vector b_* corresponds to the accurate solution x_* in the least square sense $Ax_* = b_*$. Thus, in SCD the degree of convergence was made in terms of the space behavior of multidimensional vectors. Note that the CD convergence rate is determined by the values of the characteristic vector [5, 15].

3 The SCD Resolution Parameter

In this section, we develop the technique to determine the SCD resolution parameter.

Definition. Let x be a point in the n-dimensional space R^n. For any $b \in R^m$ there are exist a $x \in R^n$ such that $Ax = b$.

Consider the Eq. (5) as the following:

$$f(x^i) = \|Ax^{i-1} - b\|^2 - \frac{(Ax^{i-1} - b, Ae_k)^2}{\|Ae_k\|^2}. \tag{6}$$

By multiplying the numerator and denominator of the fractional expression by the same value of the scalar product $(Ax^{i-1} - b, Ax^{i-1} - b)$ we get:

$$f(x^i) = \|Ax^{i-1} - b\|^2 (1.0 - \frac{(Ax^{i-1} - b, Ae_k)^2}{\|Ae_k\|^2 \|Ax^{i-1} - b\|^2}). \tag{7}$$

Let x_* be the minimum norm solution of the system in the least square sense. Suppose, $Ax_* = b_*$. Denote by R_k the value of one of the factors in the right part of the Eq. (7):

$$R_k = 1.0 - \frac{(Ax^{i-1} - b, Ae_k)^2}{\|Ae_k\|^2 \|Ax^{i-1} - b\|^2}. \tag{8}$$

Then, we have the following expression:

$$\|Ax^i - b_*\|^2 = \|Ax^{i-1} - b_*\|^2 R_k. \tag{9}$$

The more values of the parameter R_k are close to 1.0 the more the closeness of the solution x^i to the minimum norm solution x_*. The solution accuracy of the system is estimated by the standard deviation value of the vector $Ax^i - b$. This value mainly depends on the modeling error and the errors of the observed data set. We assume that the iterations are repeated until we got the difference between neighboring approximations x^{i-1} and x^i is not bigger than the observation error.

4   The SCD Inversion of Seismic Data Gathered After the Krafla Rifting Episode

The Krafla rifting episode occurred during 1975–1984 in northern Iceland. Cyclic inflation and deflation of the magma chamber within the Krafla caldera finally led to kilometer-scale volcanic deformation [16]. Research groups from Iceland and other countries participated in the collection of various data related to the Krafla rifting episode. In this paper, we analyze the SCD inversion result, when input data sets are P-wave arrivals of seismic waves from local 11 events recorded by 12 temporary stations during the period 1986–1989. The installation of stations and monitoring of seismicity were performed by the researchers from Mainz University, Germany.

Figure 1 (upper part) shows the location of volcanoes (white squares), power stations (white triangles), seismic stations (black triangles), epicenters of earthquakes (black circles). The figure is built in the GMT program by using data from ASTER GDEM v.2 (METI and NASA product). Figure 1 (bottom part) displays the obtained P-wave velocity structure for the depth range 0–5 km. Volcanoes, hydrothermal stations, hypocenters are denoted by open squares, triangles, circles, respectively. To the right of Fig. 1, the scale determines the correspondence of the numerical values of the calculated P-wave velocity to different shades of gray.

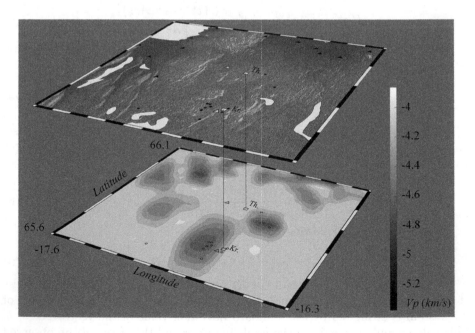

Fig. 1. Upper part. Relief map showing the location of volcanoes Krafla (Kr) and Theistareykir (Th), hydrothermal stations, seismic stations, and epicenters. Bottom part. Seismic velocity distribution. Solid vertical lines connect the locations of volcanoes

The Krafla and Theistareykir geothermal fields are located close to the volcanoes Krafla and Theistareykir in the limits of the studied area. In the vicinity of volcanic calderas, geothermal reservoirs are exploited by the Krafla and Theistareykir power plants for electricity production [12,17]. The Krafla geothermal power station began operations in 1978. The Theistareykir station turbines have been operating since 2018.

One can see that SCD revealed a large-scale underground structure (high seismic velocities) that mainly correlates with the uplifts in the northern landscape zone. In the vicinity of the Krafla volcano, the anomalous high velocity (dark gray) characterizes the deep formations located to the west, the northwest, and the southwest of the volcano. The Theistareykir volcano is in few kilometers from the high-velocity anomaly to the southeast of the volcano.

5   The SCD Resolution Measure as Practical Instrument to Identify a Structure

The application of the SCD solver to the initial data set, the computation of the SCD resolution parameter, preparation of all data for visualizations, the data processing were carried out using the FORTRAN and MATLAB environments and the corresponding programs designed by the authors of this paper.

Figure 2 illustrates (a) the P-wave velocity image, (b) the calculated values of the resolution parameter, (c) the relief map. Figures 2-a and c respond to the bottom and upper parts of Fig. 1. Domains of poor resolution ($R_k \approx 0.1$) and acceptable resolution ($R_k \in [0.6; 1.0]$) are delineated and shown by dotted and solid lines, respectively. Note that most of the R_k values are in the range of good resolution (from 0.86 till 0.99).

Comparison of the different resolution domains with geological structure (Fig. 2-c) demonstrates that the acceptable values of the resolution parameter distinguish the relief uplifts from lowlands. For lowlands, high velocities were determined with poor resolution. Confirmation that the underground structure in the Krafla volcanic caldera is characterized by the increase of P-velocity can be found in the recent work on drilling [18].

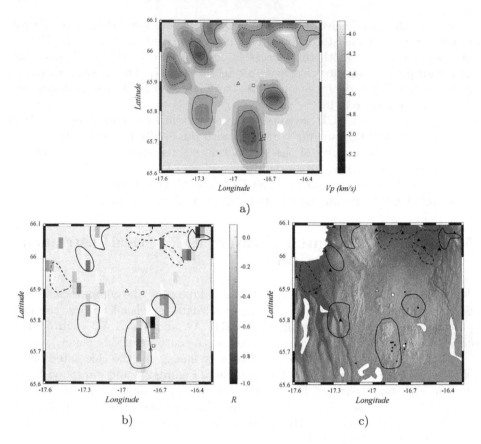

Fig. 2. The domains of poor and acceptable resolution (dotted and solid lines) of computing seismic images in comparison with real geological structures in the area of the geothermal energy production

6   Conclusion

In this paper, we described the SCD algorithm and compared it with the traditional CD method. The main difference between SCD and CD is the following. In CD, the direction of coordinate descent is formed applying the extremum condition for the least square function. SCD requires the developed condition to provide the function minimum.

Our main results are the following. The explicit expression for the SCD resolution parameter was obtained. The SCD application to real observations supports the previous statement for synthetic models [10] and confirms that SCD is robust to reconstruct the simple large-size structure. The application of the SCD resolution tool revealed its capability to identify geological structures.

Acknowledgments. We highly appreciate Prof. Wolfgang Jacoby, who organized the fieldwork at the northern coast of Iceland in 1986–1989. We also thank him for his fruitful help in the promotion of this research.

References

1. Wang, L., Chen, C.: A Combined optimization method for solving the inverse kinematics problem of mechanical manipulators. IEEE Trans. Robot. Autom. **7**, 489–499 (1991). https://ieeexplore.ieee.org/document/86079
2. Paige, C., Saunders, M.: LSQR: an algorithm for sparse linear equations and sparse least squares. ACM Trans. Math. Soft. **8**(1), 43–71 (1982)
3. Lanczos, K.: An iteration method for the solution of the eigenvalue problem of linear differential and integral operators. J. Res. N.B.S. **45**, 255–282 (1950)
4. Kaczmarz, S.: Angen aherte auf losung von systemen linearer gleichungen. Bul. Int. de l'Academie Polonaise des Sciences et des Lettres **35**, 355–357 (1937)
5. Wright, S.J.: Coordinate descent algorithms. Math. Program. **151**(1), 3–34 (2015). https://doi.org/10.1007/s10107-015-0892-3
6. Hsieh, C., Chang, K., Lin, C., Keerthi, S., Sundararajan, S.: A dual coordinate descent method for large-scale linear SVM. In: Proceedings of the 25th International Conference on Machine Learning, Helsinki, Finland, pp. 408–415 (2008). https://doi.org/10.1145/1390156.1390208
7. Keerthi, S., Sundararajan, S., Chang, K., Hsieh, C., Lin, C.: A sequential dual method for large scale multiclass linear SVMs. In: Proceeding of the 14th ACM SIGKDD International Conference on Knowledge Discovery and Data Mining KDD, pp. 408–416 (2008). https://doi.org/10.1145/1401890.1401942
8. Crammer, K., Singer, Y.: On the algorithmic implementation of multiclass kernel-based vector machines. JMLR **2**, 265–292 (2001)
9. Pandey, J., Singh Umrao, L.: Digital image processing using singular value decomposition. In: Proceedings of 2nd International Conference on Advanced Computing and Software Engineering (ICACSE) (2019). https://doi.org/10.2139/ssrn.3350278
10. Smaglichenko, T., Nikolaev, A., Horiuchi, S., Hasegawa, A.: The method for consecutive subtraction of selected anomalies: the estimated crustal velocity structure in the 1996 Onikobe (M = 5.9) earthquake area, northeastern Japan. Geophys. J. Int. **153**, 627–644 (2003)
11. Smaglichenko, T., Jacoby, W., Smaglichenko, A.: Alternative 3D tomography methods and their applications to identify seismic structure around the hydrothermal gas field. In: Tsvirkun, A. (ed.) Proceedings of 2020 11th International Conference "Management of Large-Scale System Development" (MLSD). Institute of Electrical and Electronics Engineers (IEEE), Moscow (2020). https://doi.org/10.1109/MLSD49919.2020.9247697
12. Ali, S., Feigl, K., Carr, B., Masterlark, T., Sigmundsson, F.: Geodetic measurements and numerical models of rifting in Northern Iceland for 1993–2008. Geophys. J. Int. **196**(3), 1267–1280 (2014)
13. Ali, A., Kolter, Z., Tibshirani, R.: A continuous-time view of early stopping for least squares regression. In: Proceedings of the 22nd International Conference on Artificial Intelligence and Statistics (AISTATS), vol. 89 (2019). https://arxiv.org/pdf/1810.10082.pdf
14. Gordon, G.: Generalized linear models. In: Becker, S., Thrun, S., Obermayer, K. (eds.) Advances in Neural Information Processing Systems 15 (NIPS 2002) NeurIPS Proceedings. The MIT Press (2002)

15. Tibshirani, R.: Dykstra's algorithm, ADMM, and coordinate descent: connections, insights, and extensions. In: Guyon, I., et al. (eds.) Advances in Neural Information Processing Systems 30 (NIPS 2017) NeurIPS Proceedings, pp. 517–528 (2017). https://papers.nips.cc/paper/2017/hash/5ef698cd9fe650923ea331c15af3b160-Abstract.html, https://papers.nips.cc/paper/2017/file/5ef698cd9fe650923ea331c15af3b160-Metadata.json
16. Heimisson, E., Einarsson, P., Sigmundsson, F., Brandsdóttir, B.: Kilometer-scale Kaiser effect identified in Krafla volcano, Iceland. Geophys. Res. Lett. **42**(19), 7958–7965 (2015)
17. Khodayar, M., Kristinsson, S., Karlsdóttir, R.: Structural Drilling Targets from Platforms A, B, and F at Theistareykir. Northern Rift Zone and Tjornes Fracture Zone LV report no: LV-2016-060. Prepared by Iceland GeoSurvey (ISOR) for Landsvirkjun, 24 p. (2016)
18. Millett, J.M., et al.: Sub-surface geology and velocity structure of the Krafla high temperature geothermal field, Iceland: integrated ditch cuttings, wireline and zero offset vertical seismic profile analysis. J. Volcanol. Geoth. Res. **391**, 106342 (2020)

Product Quality Improvement Based on Process Capability Analysis

Na Zhao[1], Yumin He[2(✉)], Mingxin Zhang[1], Gaosheng Cui[1], and Fuman Pan[1]

[1] Shanxi Aerospace Tsinghua Equipment Co., Ltd,
Changzhi 046000, Shanxi, People's Republic of China
[2] Beihang University, Beijing 100191, People's Republic of China
heyumin@buaa.edu.cn

Abstract. Product quality is important to companies. Many factors affect the quality of products. Statistical process control (SPC) applies statistical methods to process control and can be utilized to improve the quality of products. This paper proposes an approach for product quality improvement based on problem analysis and statistical process control application. A framework is presented with the steps from problem identifying to problem solving to improve product quality. These steps include problem identification, problem analysis, SPC method determination, production analysis, cause analysis, and problem solving. A case study is made to a real manufacturing company. The proposed approach is applied to the company. The case company identified its production problem and made the actions on the production process improvement with the good result of product quality improvement. This research can provide a reference for manufacturing companies to apply SPC methods and statistical tools to production process control for product quality improvement.

Keywords: Production process control · Process capability analysis · Quality improvement

1 Introduction

The quality of products has become an important factor to lead the rapid development of markets. However, defect products cannot be completely avoided due to many factors. Statistical process control (SPC) can apply control charts for monitoring processes, detecting changes, and controlling process quality [1].

Researchers have studied statistical process control. For example, Park *et al.* [1] studied the integration of automatic process control (APC) and SPC and developed an economic cost model to integrate APC and SPC. They used different controllers in the integrated systems and developed a long run expected cost for investigating the use of the different controllers.

Guerra, Sousa, and Nunes [2] made a case study on automating the inspection process of an automotive company by applying statistical process control for quality assurance.

A. Dolgui et al. (Eds.): APMS 2021, IFIP AICT 630, pp. 589–595, 2021.
https://doi.org/10.1007/978-3-030-85874-2_63

They aimed to make more robust and effective quality assurance procedures. They made successful introduction of automation by SPC in final inspection process.

Sousa, Rodrigues, and Nunes [3] initially studied one potential critical variable in the pre-production phase by using control charts. They identified the main causes of variability in the production process of a mental part and reduced the percentage of defective parts.

Ng [4] discussed the use of SPC control charts as a project management tool. They discussed the benefits of using control charts in the situations of system implementation, service acceptance, and so on.

This paper proposes an approach for product quality improvement. The approach identifies and analyzes the production problem and applies statistical process control to inspect and correct the production process to solve the problem. A case study is made to a real manufacturing company.

2 Developed Approach

The SPC method include Xbar-R control charts and process capability analysis. Xbar-R control charts can be used to ensure information in determining whether a process can meet the requirements and can also be used to provide a basis for current decision-making during production such as when to find the causes of variation [5].

Process capability analysis determines whether a production process meet requirements. Actions for adjustment of a process according to the process capability include no action, action to adjust centering, action to reduce variability, and so on [5]. Process capability analysis can be applied to control production to eliminate particular causes of variation during a manufacturing process [5].

The approach proposed for product quality improvement is based on problem analysis and the application of control chart analysis and process capability analysis. It includes the following steps.

Step 1. Problem identification. Analyze company's production process to find the problem in production. Form a quality improvement group that should include the director of process department or the quality department, the chief technologist, and quality analyzers.

Step 2. Problem analysis. Analyze the related products, parts, and processes to find the causes of the problem.

Step 3. SPC method determination. Determine SPC methods to be applied according to parts and equipment used in production. Collect the data of related production process.

Step 4. Production process analysis. Analyze the production process by the applications of control charts, process capability analysis, and so forth.

Step 5. Cause analysis. Analyze the production process with abnormality detected to find possible causes. Form measures for production process improvement.

Step 6. Problem solving. Make actions for improvement and analyze the results until satisfied results are achieved to solve the problem.

3 Application Case

3.1 Problem Identification

The production of type A oil cylinder by Shanxi Aerospace Tsinghua Equipment Co., Ltd was studied. The company analyzed the trial production of type A oil cylinder and found that there are many defect products and many shortages in manufacturing technology of this type oil cylinder. Test indexes could not meet the technical requirements. Therefore, quality improvement was needed.

The company established a quality improvement project team. There are eight project team members, including one senior engineer, four engineers, one quality engineer, and two senior technicians. Their responsibilities are the director of the process department of the company, chief technologist, quality analyzer, technician, and operator.

3.2 Problem Analysis

The central body is the key part of model A oil cylinder. It is an assembly and welding part and the dimensional accuracy of the key part is high. It is difficult to mill in CNC machine tools and it is easy to produce unqualified products.

It was found that there were many flaws in the central body. The technical requirement for the unqualified ratio of the central body was less than 6%. However, the unqualified ratio of the actual parts was 15%, far exceeding the technical requirement. It was found that the symmetry degree of support ear middle groove of the central body was out of the tolerance range.

3.3 SPC Method Determination

Based on the analyses, the quality improvement project team considered to apply SPC methods to detect abnormality in the production process of manufacturing the part. The project team selected Xbar-R control charts and process capability analysis.

Although the products belong to the scope of small size and multiple batch, the differences between the samples studied are small. In order to collect data to show product quality characteristics, the metrological data were collected. The project team collected the data of symmetry degree of support ear middle groove for analysis, extracted the data of 5 workers, 6 data were randomly selected from each worker, and 30 data were collected. Sample data of symmetry degree of support ear middle groove are displayed in Table 1.

3.4 Production Analysis

The range of symmetry degree of support ear middle groove is 0–0.03 mm. Two sets of data are used for a group to draw Xbar-R control charts according to the requirements of design and process. The data analysis is made by applying statistical software Minitab [6], the control charts are shown in Fig. 1.

From the Xbar control chart, the diagram does not show a lack of control in the production system. As can be seen from the figure of the R control chart that no points

Table 1. Sample data (before improvement).

No.	Operator 1	Operator 2	Operator 3	Operator 4	Operator 5
1	0.020	0.006	0.018	0.018	0.028
2	0.007	0.009	0.036	0.026	0.005
3	0.023	0.022	0.014	0.030	0.025
4	0.012	0.033	0.015	0.014	0.028
5	0.014	0.011	0.013	0.028	0.025
6	0.017	0.013	0.021	0.026	0.014

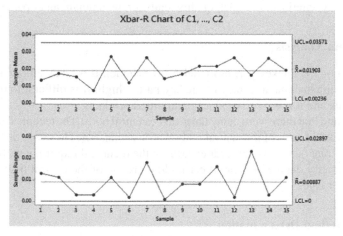

Fig. 1. Xbar-R control charts (before improvement).

are outside the scope of the lower and upper limits of LCL and UCL and that the points in these ranges are randomly displayed.

The project team also made process capability analysis. The process capability chart is shown in Fig. 2. Two of them are in a group. The tolerance range by LSL and USL is 0.03mm. Some parts are not in the range as shown in the figure. Cp = 0.63 and Cp < 0.67 in the figure. This indicates that the unqualified product ratio in the production process exceeded the requirement.

3.5 Cause Analysis

The project team inspect the production process and found that positioning of tooling mandrel and product inner hole lacks inaccuracy because of the role of gravity. The project team made the testing of X axis, Y axis, and Z axis for the repeated positioning accuracy of the machine tool.

The repeated positioning of X axis and Z axis is accurate with an error less than 0.02 mm. The error of the repeated positioning of Y axis is large, exceeding 0.02 mm. This might cause processing inaccuracy and produce product flaws.

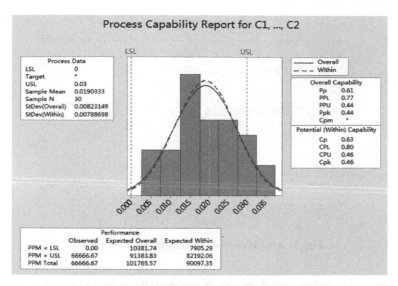

Fig. 2. Process capability chart (before improvement).

3.6 Problem Solving

The company developed the following measures and made actions for production process improvement. Better tooling mandrels were adopted, which could make a smaller error in positioning. The company also adjusted the parameter compensation of the machine tool in Y axis. The repeated positioning accuracy of Y axis was improved and reached the requirement.

The project team carried out spot check and collected the sample data of symmetry degree of support ear middle groove after the implementation of the improvement actions. The project team collected 30 samples. The sample data are displayed in Table 2.

The Xbar-R control charts are drawn for two of a group, as shown in Fig. 3. There is no data beyond the limits and these data points show random mode. This control chart shows that the process is controlled. It can be observed from the figure of R control chart that there is no data beyond the boundary and these data are evenly distributed on both sides of the center line, indicating that the process is controlled.

Table 2. Sample data (after improvement).

No.	Operator 1	Operator 2	Operator 3	No.	Operator 1	Operator 2	Operator 3
1	0.013	0.016	0.013	6	0.016	0.020	0.016
2	0.020	0.021	0.024	7	0.022	0.024	0.024
3	0.021	0.023	0.013	8	0.017	0.017	0.016
4	0.014	0.012	0.022	9	0.021	0.023	0.023
5	0.024	0.016	0.017	10	0.019	0.016	0.017

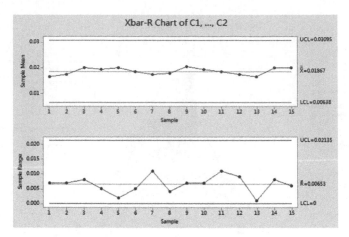

Fig. 3. Xbar-R control charts (after improvement).

The process capability chart are also drawn from the collected sample data, two for a group. The process capability chart is illustrated in Fig. 4. The tolerance range by LSL and USL is 0.03 mm. All parts are in the range as shown in the figure. Cp = 0.98, indicating that the process capability index of the production process is close to 1. The production process capability was improved.

The company produced 200 parts with 11 unqualified parts after the improvement. The ratio of unqualified parts was 5.5%, within the range of the requirement. The problem was solved.

The company set the tolerance range for manufacturing parts in the production process. When applied the SPC methods, the abnormality was found with parts outside the

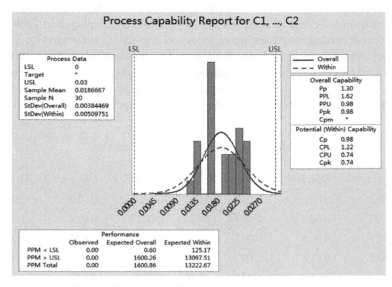

Fig. 4. Process capability chart (after improvement).

range of LSL and USL even though without parts outside the scope of LCL and UCL. Therefore, abnormality identification should not be made only by Xbar-R control charts. More SPC tools should be applied to identify abnormality.

4 Conclusion

Production process control and product quality improvement are important issues. This paper proposes an approach based on problem analysis and SPC application for product quality improvement. A case study is provided. The case company identified and analyzed the problem, applied Xbar-R control charts and process capability analysis, analyzed the causes of abnormality in the production process, formed measures, and took actions to solve the problem with the satisfaction of the requirement for the ratio of unqualified products.

The research can provide a reference for companies to apply SPC methods and statistical tools for production process control to improve product quality. The presented approach can help companies to solve their production quality problems step by step through identifying the defects from products in their manufacturing processes.

Acknowledgment. The authors would like to thank the work of other people in the quality improvement project team. The authors would like to thank the session chair, Professor Natalia Bakhtadze and the referees for the valuable comments.

References

1. Park, M., Kim, J., Jeong, M., Hamouda, A., Al-Khalifa, K., Elsayed, E.: Economic cost models of integrated APC controlled SPC charts. Int. J. Prod. Res. **50**, 3936–3955 (2012)
2. Guerra, L., Sousa, S.D., Nunes, E.P.: Statistical process control automation in the final inspection process: an industrial case study. In: Proceedings of the 2016 IEEE IEEM, pp. 876–880 (2016)
3. Sousa, S., Rodrigues, N., Nunes, E.: Application of SPC and quality tools for process improvement. Procedia Manuf. **11**, 1215–1222 (2017)
4. Ng, J.J.: Statistical process control chart as a project management tool. IEEE Eng. Manage. Rev. **46**, 26–28 (2018)
5. Grant, E.L., Leavenworth, R.S.: Statistical quality control. 1st edn. McGraw-Hill Education (Asia) Co., China Tsinghua University Press, Beijing (2002)
6. Minitab Homepage. http://www.minitab.com/zh-cn. Accessed Sep 2020

Software Architecture for an Active Device Driver in Reconfigurable Manufacturing Systems

Jeongha Shin🆔 and Duck Young Kim$^{(\boxtimes)}$🆔

Pohang University of Science and Technology, Pohang, South Korea
dy.kim@postech.ac.kr

Abstract. Flexible and reconfigurable manufacturing systems aim to enable more versatile, connected, and intelligent operations not only from a system-level perspective, but also from a field-level perspective. This paper focuses on field-level applications for peripheral intelligence and proposes a concept and architecture for an Active Device Driver (ADD) that can be actively adjusted to unforeseen situations versus repeating fixed task procedures. This new device driver is designed to permit easy and rapid transformability to systems by enabling device modulization and abstraction, control and configuration under service-oriented architecture, actively supporting control reliability, and producing well-organized manufacturing data. These features can be achieved by implementing the *control I/O encapsulating module, device information model, OPC-UA server interface, and peripheral control module*. Two case studies with robot grippers are conducted to validate the working principle of ADDs.

Keywords: Automation and control · OPC-UA · Device integration · Reconfigurable manufacturing system

1 Introduction

Various customer demands and shorter product lifecycles have increased the need for the flexibility and reconfigurability of manufacturing systems. Making systems more flexible and reconfigurable involves improving three key factors, which are versatilability, connectivity, and intelligence. These factors are defined as follows. Versatilability refers to interoperable and reconfigurable software and hardware, rapidly transformable systems, and modular platforms. Connectivity defines the capacity for the information of the system to be shared asynchronously, based on standardized and robust communication protocols. Finally, intelligence means the ability of the device to rapidly make decisions and predictions by autonomous reasoning and learning from data. Such predictions and decisions allow the process to be quickly adjusted to changes in the local environment.

A variety of heterarchical architectures [1] have been proposed for rapid hardware and software reconfiguration, such as the Reconfigurable Manufacturing System [2], Multi-Agent System [3], and Holonic Manufacturing System [4] among others. Yet, most

© IFIP International Federation for Information Processing 2021
Published by Springer Nature Switzerland AG 2021
A. Dolgui et al. (Eds.): APMS 2021, IFIP AICT 630, pp. 596–603, 2021.
https://doi.org/10.1007/978-3-030-85874-2_64

studies focus on systematic aspects. By comparison, research into field-level device control systems is understudied and more research into these systems is necessary. Various international standards for information modeling are available, such as Asset Administration Shell (AAS) [5], OPC-UA [6] Information Model, and AutomationML (AML) [7]. These ensure that manufacturing information is sharable, stable, and organized. These international standards, as well as efforts to integrate field-devices into systems with those standards [8, 9], also require further discussions with respect to the adjustment of control logic and parameters.

Manufacturing systems are gradually changing from conventional Programmable Logic Controller (PLC)-based controls to Programmable Automation Controller (PAC)-based controls [10]. Field-level devices are also becoming more extensively connected with higher level controllers. These changes in hardware accelerate the shift from hierarchical control systems, which often have little flexibility, to much more flexible heterarchical control systems.

In practical contexts, the drivers for field-level manufacturing devices should be able to be rapidly reconfigured and easily integrated. Also, unlike existing device drivers, new drivers should actively interact with the system to ensure that objectives are reliably met. Thus, we propose an Active Device Driver (ADD) architecture that exhibits high connectivity, changeability, and intelligence in reconfigurable manufacturing systems.

2 Architecture

2.1 System Requirements

The most basic role of a driver is to make an device easier to use. For example, drivers for Personal Computers enable the device to be used without a detailed understanding of the hardware or software. Once the driver is installed, the device only requires to be supplied with electricity for use, without the need to change or interact with complex settings. We believe that drivers for manufacturing systems should enable similar ease-of-operation. Specifically, the driver should permit the device hardware to be easily controlled and data easily collected without a detailed understanding of the particular hardware and software. Moreover, the driver should support the facile rearrangement of various aspects of the device, including settings, parameters, and others. The device should also be readily usable on any system or platform. Thus, new drivers should be interoperable regardless of system architecture and control platform.

Additionally, the driver should digitize devices and support their digital representation. Device should be managed and well-organized in real-time, and the information should be easily exchanged. Finally, in traditional physical device controls, it is often difficult to understand whether each device is performing adequately or how to fix errors. As a result, oftentimes a significant process bottleneck originated by a single fault. Therefore, the driver should actively and appropriately cope with errors and failures in the system or actions.

2.2 Structure and Components of the ADD

This section describes the architecture of the ADD that was designed to meet the requirements defined in Sect. 2.1. Figure 1 shows the overall structure of the ADD, including the modules.

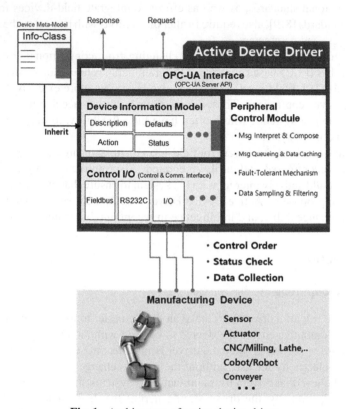

Fig. 1. Architecture of active device driver

Control I/O. ADD exists in a 1:1 correspondence with the device. Here, the ADD requires an encapsulated interface as the fieldbus to physically interact with the device, which is a control I/O module.

Device Information Model. The driver has a device information model, which enables the device to be digitalized, information to be exchanged, and manufacturing data to be formed. An accurate identification code is also required to accurately recognize device information. Thus, device information models are created and managed according to the OPC-UA Information Modeling Rule [6]. An example of an information model for a robot gripper is shown in Fig. 2.

The device information model has four objects: *Description, Defaults, Action,* and *Status.* The *Description object* contains information about a device, such as function, form, range of movement, data unit, and data update rate, among other factors. The *Defaults object* contains information about settings, such as the movement speed of the robot and resolution of the acquired sensor data. While the *Defaults object* does not change frequently, it can be modified during device operation.

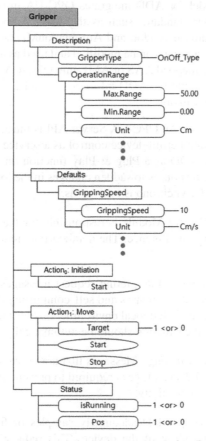

Fig. 2. Example of device information model (Robot On/Off Gripper)

The *Action object* is an object that executes a task, such as a physical movement, data provision, etc. $Action_1$ through $Action_N$ objects are mapped 1:1 to N functions of the device, and the $Action_0$ objects always have an initialization function. The $Action_i$ object contains variables (e.g., target value, reference value, etc.) with the necessary information to perform an action and method objects (e.g., start, stop, etc.), which act as a trigger for real actions. For example, the information model for the robot gripper includes one *Action object*, which is the 'Move' that opens or closes the gripper. A variable named 'Target' also exists, as well as 'Start' and 'Stop' methods. Finally, the *Status object* contains information that updates in real-time that reports the status of the device, such as manufacturing parameters (e.g., sensor values, position values of actuators, the current speed of motors, etc.). In the gripper information model that is depicted in Fig. 2, the gripper has two variable objects under the *Status*, namely 'isRunning' and 'pos.'

The defined information model represents an abstract basis of the device hardware. This means that devices with the same function should have the same information model to ensure interoperability.

The information model for ADD integrates OPC-UA information modeling standards. For example, other standards such as the Asset Administration Shell (AAS), which are created by a device vendor, and AutomationML (AML), which are formed during plant or process planning, can be modified and used as an information model for ADD. Many studies have mapped AAS or AML into OPC-UA information models [11, 12]. These allow users to build the ADD information models using AAS or AML with only simple mapping information.

OPC-UA Server Interface. An OPC-UA Server API is introduced to exchange information with the system and permit device control as a service. This enables facile and rapid implementation of ADD as a Plug & Play function on any control platform. It also allows more flexible responses to sudden changes in the local environmental of the device by message-based asynchronous operations.

Control Module. The Control Module is responsible for the core functions of ADD and is based on peripheral intelligence. The detailed functionalities of the module are described as follows:

Message Interpret & Compose. Interpreting request messages received from the system and formulating adequate responses and self-configuring the response messages is required to adapt to changes in the local environment. Additionally, if any errors arise, a message that describes the situation should be automatically composed.

Message Queuing & Data Caching. Messages that are processed simultaneously must be queued. Also, temporal data storage is required to prevent data loss if delivery is not efficient due to losses in connectivity.

Data Sampling and Filtering. ADD adequately samples or filters the data based on a comprehensive understanding of the device. This reduces the time and effort to preprocess data.

Fault-Tolerable Mechanism. The fault-tolerance function first detects the faulty actions of devices, such as grasp failure, and then responds to that fault based on the Failure Mode and Effect Analysis (FMEA) rule [13]. In other words, how to respond to the fault should be adequately prepared for each device. This mechanism ensures the reliability of control in a heterogeneous manufacturing system. Faults are classified into three types: undetectable, detectable from data estimation, and self-detectable by the device. The device information model includes the information for fault classification and the fault detection algorithm. When a fault is detected, the ADD attempts to recover the fault by the predefined procedure of FMEA rules.

3   Case Study

We have conducted two case studies to validate the working principle of ADDs.

Case 1. First, we demonstrate how the control logic program for the pneumatic gripper (left in Fig. 3) is adaptively changed to operate the electric gripper (right in Fig. 3) via ADD. parametric adjustments can be efficiently made by the common and versatile definition of functional method nodes in the device object tree of ADD. Furthermore, OPC-UA clients permit us to easily monitor the status of heterogeneous devices.

Case 2. The second case study shows an example of the fault-tolerable mechanism for gripping action. When an ADD receives a control command to close the gripper (control sequence), a predefined FMEA-based fault-tolerable gripping action will be executed. Figure 4 illustrates an active fault-tolerable mechanism that retries the gripping action for the predefined period if it failed to get the expected sensor values. If it fails to resolve the fault over the period, then it reports the fault message to the system.

The right flow chart in Fig. 4 depicts the fault-tolerance procedure of ADD for gripping action in a FMEA flow form. The gripping action can be classified by the type of operation for which data-driven fault detection is made. The pressure sensor data are used to determine whether the gripper is holding a target object properly or not. If a defective symptom is detected during the action, an FMEA flow will be executed to correct and report the defect. This fault recovery mechanism of ADD enables devices to interpret control commands in a smart way, thus enhancing the reliability of controls.

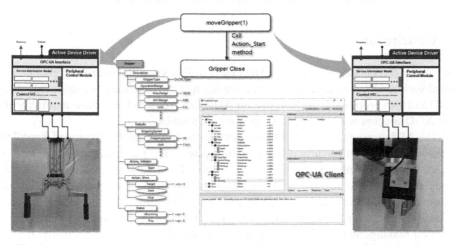

Fig. 3. Case 1: controlling two heterogeneous devices by a single control logic program

In general, device drivers operate passively according to the given commands, and they are very inflexible to reprogramming. On the other hand, the presented ADD provides the interoperability of devices based on SOA by applying OPC-UA and the proactive fault-tolerance mechanism as demonstrated in the case studies. These advantages allow abstracted control sequences to be used for control logic generation, thereby enabling more efficient system reconfiguration.

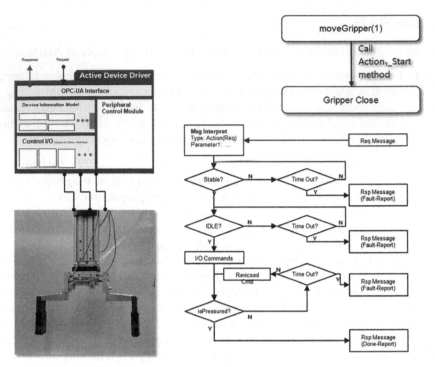

Fig. 4. Case 2: fault-tolerable mechanism for gripping action

4   Conclusion

This paper presents the concept of ADD that is highly versatile and reconfigurable in a broad variety of manufacturing systems. We defined the functions and requirements of ADD and then proposed an architecture for ADD that would achieve those requirements. The ADD concept was verified through two case studies.

The ADD concept enables field devices to be easily and rapidly integrated regardless of the architecture and control platform of the system. The parameters or settings of the device can also be quickly changed in the system. These features make ADD a highly modular and extensible system. ADD also reports manufacturing data based on the information model of the device, while also providing hardware abstraction features. These features form the basis for predictions of future events and conditions, rapid decision making, and enabling the system to adjust the control logic. Finally, the use of secure communications based on OPC-UA Transport and fault-tolerable mechanisms impart reliability for device operation, much like the peripheral nerves in humans, even if system operation is unimpeded. This study establishes that the ADD concept enables systems to operate reliably and respond more flexibly to environmental changes.

Acknowledgements. This research was supported by the National IT Industry Promotion Agency of Korea (NIPA) funded by the Ministry of Science and ICT (S1309–21-1001(001)).

References

1. Dilts, D.M., Boyd, N.P., Whorms, H.H.: The evolution of control architectures for automated manufacturing systems. J. Manuf. Syst. **10**(1), 79–93 (1991)
2. Bortolini, M., Galizia, F.G., Mora, C.: Reconfigurable manufacturing systems: literature review and research trend. J. Manuf. Syst. **49**, 93–106 (2018)
3. Park, J.W., Shin, M., Kim, D.Y.: An extended agent communication framework for rapid reconfiguration of distributed manufacturing systems. IEEE Trans. Industr. Inf. **15**(7), 3845–3855 (2019)
4. Höpf, M., Schaeffer, C.F.: Holonic Manufacturing Systems. In: Goossenaerts, J., Kimura, F., Wortmann, H. (eds.) Information infrastructure systems for manufacturing. ITIFIP, pp. 431–438. Springer, Boston (1997). https://doi.org/10.1007/978-0-387-35063-9_37
5. Wagner, C., et al.: The role of the Industry 4.0 asset administration shell and the digital twin during the life cycle of a plant. In: 22nd IEEE International Conference on Emerging Technologies and Factory Automation (ETFA), pp. 1–8. IEEE, Limassol Cyprus (2017)
6. Lehnhoff, S., Rohjans, S., Uslar, M., Mahnke, W.: OPC unified architecture: a service-oriented architecture for smart grids. In: 2012 First International Workshop on Software Engineering Challenges for the Smart Grid (SE-SmartGrids), IEEE, Zurich Switzerland, pp. 1–7 (2012)
7. Drath, R., Lüder, A., Peschke, J., Hundt, L.: AutomationML - the glue for seamless Automation engineering. In: 2008 IEEE International Conference on Emerging Technologies and Factory Automation, pp. 616–623. IEEE, Hamburg Germany (2008)
8. Grossmann, D., Bender, K., Danzer, B.: OPC UA based field device integration. In: 2008 SICE Annual Conference, pp. 933–938. IEEE, Chofu Japan (2008)
9. Pallasch, C., Wein, S., Hoffmann, N., Obdenbusch, M., Buch-ner, T., Waltl, J., Brecher, C.: Edge powered industrial control: concept for combining cloud and automation technologies. In: 2018 IEEE International Conference on Edge Computing (EDGE), pp. 130–134. IEEE, San Francisco USA (2018)
10. Bell, I.: The future of control [programmable automation controllers]. Manuf. Eng. **84**(4), 36–39 (2005)
11. Cavalieri, S., Mule, S., Salafia, M.G.: OPC UA-based asset administration shell. In: 45th Annual Conference of the IEEE Industrial Electronics Society, pp. 2982–2989. IEEE, Lisbon Portugal (2019)
12. Ye, X., Hong, S.H.: An automationml/OPC UA-based industry 4.0 solution for a manufacturing system. In: IEEE 23rd International Conference on Emerging Technologies and Factory Automation (ETFA), pp. 543–550. IEEE, Turin, Italy (2018)
13. Duffie, N.A., Chitturi, R., Mou, J.I.: Fault-tolerant heterarchical control of heterogeneous manufacturing system entities. J. Manuf. Syst. **7**(4), 315–328 (1988)

Price-to-Quality Ratio Dependent Demand: Keeping the Intensity of Demand Constant

Anna V. Kitaeva[1]($\boxtimes$), Natalia V. Stepanova[2], and Alexandra O. Zhukovskaya[3]

[1] Tomsk State University, Tomsk, Russia
[2] Institution of Control Sciences of Russian Academy of Sciences, Moscow, Russia
[3] Tomsk State Pedagogical University, Tomsk, Russia

Abstract. We consider a deterministic model of an inventory system that consists of a single type of perishable product, which is periodically replenished, and a demand depends on price-to-quality ratio (PQR). The product quality decays linearly over time. To keep an intensity of the demand constant we change the price proportionally to the decreasing quality of the product. Exponential and linear dependences of the demand's intensity of PQR are considered and optimal values of lot size and PQR maximizing the profit per unit time are obtained.

Keywords: Price-to-quality ratio · Perishable product · Dynamic pricing · Deterministic demand

1 Introduction and Problem Statement

In this paper, both the price and the quality of the product are considered as factors influencing the demand rate. The price increasing has negative effect to a demand and a high product's quality positively affects a demand. We combine these two factors as the price-to-quality ratio.

The product quality has a great influence on a consumer's purchase decision in the retail process. It seems that Fujiwara and Perera [1] were the first to consider the effect of quality deterioration on demand. In recent years, supply chain tracing technologies have been developed extensively that allows dynamically identify the product quality; see, for example, [2, 3]. In addition, the evaluation of product quality loss over time can be obtained by examining customers' perceptions through surveys. Based on this information a retailer can generate optimal pricing policy.

A review of the literature on the problem of setting prices for perishable products can be found in [4]. The influence of dynamic pricing on revenue and spoilage recently has been studied by Adenso-Díaz et al. [5]. Different pricing strategies are also considered in [6].

In [7], we assumed that the product's price and quality continuously change over time and found the optimal price functions and replenishment cycle times maximizing the unit time profit, so the demands rates were also time dependent.

A. Dolgui et al. (Eds.): APMS 2021, IFIP AICT 630, pp. 604–609, 2021.
https://doi.org/10.1007/978-3-030-85874-2_65

In many cases, it is wise to maintain a constant demand rate, since otherwise either a queue is created, or the seller is idle. Here we will consider in detail the case where the price decreases in proportion to the deterioration in the quality of the product.

Let us consider the problem statement and introduce notations. The vendor purchases a quantity Q_0 of a perishable product at a fixed price per unit d (wholesale price). We assume that an ordering overhead cost G does not depend on a lot size, the quality of the product decreases continuously until it becomes unsuitable for consumption and function $v(t)$ specifies the quality of the product unit at time t. The retail price per unit depends on time $c = c(t) > d$.

We consider the case when the product quality decreases linearly over time, that is,

$$v(t) = v_0\left(1 - \frac{t}{T_*}\right),$$

where parameter $v_0 > 0$ is the initial product value (the maximal product value) and parameter T_* determines the lifetime of the product, i.e., $v(T_*) = 0$.

Drug characteristics, for example, usually decrease linearly over time [8]. In addition, if we evaluate the drop in product value from customers' point of view, Tsiros and Heilman [9] found that consumers' willingness to pay decreases linearly through the shelf life for some kinds of products, for example, lettuce, carrots, milk, yogurt, etc.

The demand is assumed to be deterministic and each of the customers purchases the same quantity a_1 and the intensity of the customers' flow (the demand density function) $\lambda(\cdot)$ depends on the ratio $s(t) = \frac{c(t)}{v(t)}$. We measure $v(\cdot)$ in the same units as a retail price per unit of product, so $s(t) \equiv s$ is a dimensionless variable.

The replenishment at the end of the cycle time is assumed to be instantaneous, and the holding cost is not considered.

Let us denote the cycle time, that is, a period when the product is in stock T_0, $T_0 \leq T_*$, and $V(t) = \int_0^t v(u)du$.

Then the lot size $Q_0 = a_1\lambda(s)T_0$, and the profit over cycle $S = a_1 \int_0^{T_0} (c(t) - d)\lambda(s(t))dt - G = a_1 s\lambda(s)V(T_0) - a_1 d\lambda(s)T_0 - G$.

The profit per unit time $P = S/T_0$, and we want to solve the optimization problem

$$P = \frac{a_1 s\lambda(s)V(T_0) - a_1 d\lambda(s)T_0 - G}{T_0} \Rightarrow \max_{s,Q_0}. \tag{1}$$

This task is equivalent to $P \Rightarrow \max_{s,T_0}$ because of functional dependence between Q_0 and T_0. The solution of (1) is defined by the system of equations

$$\begin{cases} v(T_0)T_0 - V(T_0) + \frac{G}{a_1 s\lambda(s)} = 0, \\ s + \frac{\lambda(s)}{\lambda'(s)} = d\frac{T_0}{V(T_0)}. \end{cases} \tag{2}$$

2 Profit Optimization

2.1 Exponential Dependence of the Intensity of Price-to-Quality Ratio

Let $\lambda(s) = \lambda_0 \exp\left(1 - \frac{s}{\kappa}\right)$, where parameter $\lambda_0 > 0$ and coefficient $\kappa > 0$ characterize the sensitivity of the demand to the price-to-quality ratio s.

From (2) we get $s = \kappa\left(1 + \frac{\tilde{d}}{1-z}\right)$. It follows

$$c(t) = v_0 \kappa \left(1 + \frac{\tilde{d}}{1-z}\right)\left(1 - \frac{t}{T_*}\right),$$

where dimensionless variables $\tilde{d} = \frac{d}{v_0 \kappa}$ and $z = \frac{T_0}{2T_*}, 0 < z \le \frac{1}{2}$.

In this case, $P = a_1 \kappa \lambda_0 v_0 \left((1-z)\exp\left(-\frac{\tilde{d}}{1-z}\right) - \frac{\tilde{G}}{z}\right) = a_1 \kappa \lambda_0 v_0 F(z)$, where dimensionless variable $\tilde{G} = \frac{G}{2T_* a_1 \kappa \lambda_0 v_0}$. To find optimal value of z we need to solve equation $F'(z) = 0$, that is,

$$f(z) = z^2 \left(1 + \frac{\tilde{d}}{1-z}\right)\exp\left(-\frac{\tilde{d}}{1-z}\right) = \tilde{G}. \tag{3}$$

Function $F(\cdot)$ on $[0,1]$ looks like an inverted S-shaped function. Typical graph of $F(\cdot)$ is shown in Fig. 1.

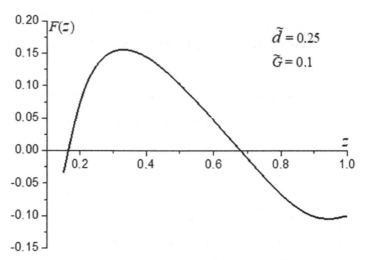

Fig. 1. Graph of $F(\cdot)$ on $[0,1]$ for $\tilde{d} = 0.25$ and $\tilde{G} = 0.1$.

For $0 < \tilde{G} < G_m = \max\limits_{z} f(z)$ Eq. (3) has two roots. The smaller one $z_s \le 1/2$ gives us optimal cycle time $T_0^{opt} = 2T_* z_s$.

If $z_s > 1/2$ and $F(1/2) > 0$ then $T_0^{opt} = T_*$. Otherwise, that is, if $F(1/2) \leq 0$, the trade is unprofitable. It happens when $\tilde{G} \geq \dfrac{\exp(-\tilde{d}/2)}{4}$.

Also, the trade is unprofitable if $\tilde{G} \geq G_m$. In this case, the overheads are too high to make a profit.

Let us consider dependence $G_m(\tilde{d})$. Equation $f'(z) = 0$ for $z \neq 0$ can be written as

$$\tilde{d}^2 - 2\tilde{d}\frac{(1-z)^2}{z^2} - 2\frac{(1-z)^3}{z^2} = 0. \tag{4}$$

Positive value of $\tilde{d}$ satisfying (4)

$$\tilde{d} = \frac{(1-z)^2}{z^2} + \frac{1-z}{z}\sqrt{\frac{(1-z)^2}{z^2} + 2(1-z)}. \tag{5}$$

Equations $\tilde{G}_m = z^2\left(1 + \frac{\tilde{d}}{1-z}\right)\exp\left(-\frac{\tilde{d}}{1-z}\right)$ and (5) give us the parametric representation of $G_m(\tilde{d})$. Graph of $G_m(\tilde{d})$ is shown in Fig. 2.

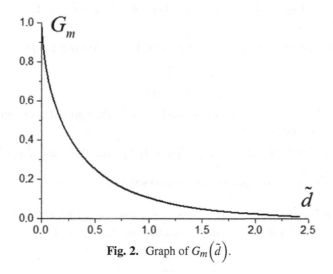

Fig. 2. Graph of $G_m(\tilde{d})$.

2.2 Lineal Dependence of the Intensity of Price-to-Quality Ratio

Let $\lambda(s) = \lambda_0 - \lambda_1 s = \lambda_0(1 - s/\kappa)$, $\kappa = \lambda_0/\lambda_1$, where $\lambda_0 > 0$ and $\lambda_1 > 0$ are demand parameters.

In this case, from (1) it follows that $s = \frac{\kappa}{2} - \frac{d}{2} \cdot \frac{T_0}{V(T_0)}$. Profit per unit time

$$P = \frac{a_1\lambda_0\kappa v_0}{2}\left(1 - z - 2\tilde{d} + \frac{\tilde{d}^2}{1-z} - \frac{\tilde{G}}{z}\right),$$

where $\tilde{G} = \frac{2G}{T_*a_1\kappa\lambda_0 v_0}$ and $0 < z = \frac{T_0}{2T_*} \leq 1/2$.

Function $\tilde{F}(z) = 1 - z - 2\tilde{d} + \frac{\tilde{d}^2}{1-z} - \frac{\tilde{G}}{z}$ that determines the profit looks, as in the previous subsection, like an inverted S-shaped function. Its typical shape is shown in Fig. 3 for $\tilde{d} = 0.2$ and $\tilde{G} = 0.1$.

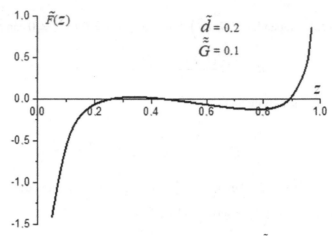

Fig. 3. Graph of $\tilde{F}(\cdot)$ on $[0,1]$ for $\tilde{d} = 0.2$ and $\tilde{G} = 0.1$.

To find the maximal value of P we need to solve the following equation

$$\frac{\tilde{G}}{z^2} + \frac{\tilde{d}^2}{(1-z)^2} = 1. \tag{6}$$

Here we have the same situation as previously, that is, the optimal cycle time is defined by the behavior of the smaller root of (6).

The trade is unprofitable if $\tilde{G} \geq \left(\tilde{d} - 1/2\right)^2$ (in this case $\tilde{F}(1/2) \leq 0$) or $\max_z \left(\frac{\tilde{G}}{z^2} + \frac{\tilde{d}^2}{(1-z)^2}\right) \geq 1$ (in this case (6) has no solution).

Let us consider function $\varphi(z) = \frac{\tilde{G}}{z^2} + \frac{\tilde{d}^2}{(1-z)^2}$ and find z_1 such that $\varphi'(z_1) = 0$ and $\varphi(z_1) = 1$. Thus, the following system of equations must be hold

$$\frac{\tilde{G}}{z_1^3} - \frac{\tilde{d}^2}{(1-z_1)^3} = 0,$$

$$\frac{\tilde{G}}{z_1^2} + \frac{\tilde{d}^2}{(1-z_1)^2} = 1. \tag{7}$$

The solution of (7) is $\tilde{G} = z_1^3, \tilde{d}^2 = (1 - z_1)^3$, so these coefficients are connected by the following equation $\sqrt[3]{\tilde{G}} + \sqrt[3]{\tilde{d}^2} = 1$. The dependence $\tilde{G}$ of $\tilde{d}$ is demonstrated in Fig. 4.

Thus, for linear dependence of the intensity of price-to-quality ratio a solution of the optimization problem (1) exists only if $\tilde{d} < 1$ and $\tilde{G} < \left(1 - \sqrt[3]{\tilde{d}^2}\right)^3$.

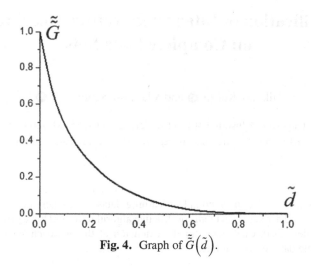

Fig. 4. Graph of $\tilde{\tilde{G}}(\tilde{d})$.

References

1. Fujiwara, O., Perera, U.L.J.S.R.: EOQ models for continuously deteriorating products using linear and exponential penalty costs. Eur. J. Oper. Res. **70**(1), 104–114 (1993)
2. Li, D., Tang, O., O'Brien, C., Wang, X.: Improve food retail supply chain operations with dynamic pricing and product tracing. Int. J. Serv. Oper. Inf. **1**(4), 347–362 (2006)
3. Wang, X.: Optimal pricing with dynamic tracking in the perishable food supply. In: Chan, H.K., et al. (eds.) Decision-Making for Supply Chain Integration: Supply Chain Integration. DECENGIN, vol. 1, pp. 63–88. Springer, London (2012). https://doi.org/10.1007/978-1-4471-4033-7_4
4. Zhao, W., Zheng, Y.-S.: Optimal dynamic pricing for perishable assets with non homogeneous demand. Manage. Sci. **46**, 375–388 (2000)
5. Adenso-Díaz, B., Lozano, S., Palacio, A.: Effects of dynamic pricing of perishable products on revenue and waste. Appl. Math. Model. **45**, 148–164 (2017)
6. Dolgui, A., Proth, J.-M.: Pricing strategies and models. Ann. Rev. Control **34**(1), 101–110 (2010)
7. Kitaeva, A., Stepanova, N., Zhukovskaya, A.: Price-to-quality ratio dependent demand: optimal dynamic pricing and replenishment period. In: 2018 International Conference on Control, Decision and Information Technologies (CoDIT 2018), Thessaloniki, Greece, pp. 341–345. IEEE Conference Publications (2018)
8. Chow, S.-C.: Biosimilars: Design and Analysis of Follow-on Biologics. Chapman and Hall/CRC Press, New York (2013)
9. Tsiros, M., Heilman, C.M.: The effect of expiration dates and perceived risks on purchasing behavior in grocery store perishable categories. J. Market. **69**(2), 114–129 (2005)

Identification of Integrated Rating Mechanisms on Complete Data Sets

Nikolay Korgin[iD] and Vladimir Sergeev[(⊠)][iD]

V.A. Trapeznikov Institute of Control Sciences of RAS, Moscow, Russia
nkorgin@ipu.ru, sergeev.bureau@gmail.com

Abstract. An approach to the selection of structure for integrated rating mechanism to be identified given complete learning dataset is suggested. Theoretical assertions and derived from them constructive algorithm for full binary tree selection are described. Challenges for the extension of the approach suggested to incomplete data sets are outlined.

Keywords: Integrated rating mechanism · System identification · Discrete data analysis

1 Introduction

1.1 Integrated Rating Mechanisms

Integrated Rating Mechanisms (IRM) were introduced as multidimensional assessment and ranking systems for management and control in organizational and manufacturing systems in the Soviet Union in earlier 80th of the previous century (for example ACCORD for electronic industry, see [1]) and are implemented nowadays too [2–6]. IRM usually applied for ordinal ranking (or classification) with a predetermined number of classes of a finite set of multicriteria alternatives (discrete data analysis [7]. The key components of IRM are full binary tree and convolution matrices, which allow obtaining integrated assessment (IA) based on the values of several parameters.

The typical approach to the identification of parameters of IRM in order to implement assumes iterative interaction with decision-makers (see [2, 6]). But nowadays there exist inquiry for developing of learning procedures for IRM which are common for AI algorithms identification tasks. Recently several approaches were suggested that allow to identify convolution matrices given particular binary tree – [8, 9]. While the first one allows to conduct identification task only for special full binary trees – so called sequential, the later, based on quite popular nowadays in AI algorithms – one-hot encoding (see, for example, [10]) allows one to construct algorithms for identification of IRM for any full binary tree.

Yet, due to large number of binary trees the task for predicting, what tree should be considered in process of identification is very actual problem. In this paper we suggest an approach that allows to select binary trees, for which problem of identification may be solved.

A. Dolgui et al. (Eds.): APMS 2021, IFIP AICT 630, pp. 610–616, 2021.
https://doi.org/10.1007/978-3-030-85874-2_66

1.2 Basic Notations and Definitions

Let us introduce main notations on the basis of [8]. There is a finite set of indicators $L \subset N$, $|L| = l$ on the basis of their values ordinal assessment of some object or ranking of several objects should be performed. For the task of identification of IRM we will initially assume that for each indicator $i \in L$ the finite set $K_i \subset N$ of its possible values $k_i \in K_i$ is given and the tuple $k = (k_1, ..., k_l)^T$ describes any possible state of assessed objects. There is also a finite set $K_L \subset N$ of possible integrated values (ranks or classes) $k_L \in K_L$ for any possible k.

Definition 1. IRM with a full binary tree and matrix convolutions is mapping $w(\cdot)$: $\prod_{i \in L} K_i \to K_L$, for which indicators from L are leaves of a full binary tree – oriented graph $G = (V, E)$:

1. $V = L \cup \hat{L}$, $\hat{L} = \{l+1, ..., 2l-1\}$,
2. $E = \{e_{ij}\} \subseteq V \times V$,
3. $\forall i \in V \setminus \{2l-1\} \; \exists! j \in \hat{L} \setminus \{i\} \colon e_{ij} = 1, \forall t \in V \setminus j \; e_{it} = 0$,
4. $\forall j \in L \; \forall i \in V \; e_{ij} = 0$,
5. $\forall j \in \hat{L} \exists! \{r, c\} \in V \setminus \{j\} \times V \setminus \{j\} \colon e_{rj} = 1, e_{cj} = 1$.

And $\forall j \in \hat{L}$ (inner node of the tree including root).

1. a finite set $K_j \subset N$ of its possible values $k_j \in K_j$, $K_{2l-1} = K_L$.
2. convolution matrix $M_j = [m_{jrc} \in K_j]_{r \in \{0, ..., |K_l|-1\}, c \in \{0, ..., |K_r|-1\}}$, $\{r, c\} \in V \setminus \{j\} \times V \setminus \{j\} \colon e_{lj} = 1, e_{rj} = 1$ are determined. $\quad\square$

Given some IRM $w(\cdot)$ we will denote set of all its convolution matrices as $\mathbf{M}_w = \{M_j\}_{j \in \hat{L}}$.

In this paper, we will restrict our attention to uniform-scaled IRM, such that $\forall j \in V$ $K_j = K_L$.

Given $L \subset N$ let us denote $\Gamma_2(L)$ - the set of all full binary trees with leaves from L, $IRM_{L,2}$ - the set of all IRM with any particular full binary tree $G \in \Gamma_2(L)$, $IRM_{L,G} \subseteq IRM_{L,2}$ - the set of all IRM with such tree.

For the learning problems let us denote $q = (k, k_L)$ - a tuple of one learning example, $Q \subset K \otimes K_L$, $K = \prod_{i \in L} K_i$ - a learning set (of provided examples). The learning set is consistent if $\forall \{q, \tilde{q}\} \subseteq Q \; k \neq \tilde{k}$. The learning set is complete if $\forall k \in K \exists q \in Q \colon q = (k, k_L)$. The learning set is uniform-scaled if $\forall i \in L \; K_i = K_L$.

Given some arbitrary $Q \subset K \otimes K_L$, it is possible to define the following key notations concerning identification problems. The first one is the implementation problem:

Definition 2. An $w(\cdot) \in IRM_{L,2}$ implements Q, iff $\forall q \in Q \; w(k) = k_L$ $\quad\square$

Let us denote $IRM_{L,2}(Q)$ - set of all IRM, that implement Q, $IRM_{L,G}(Q)$ - set of all IRM, that implement Q and are based on some full binary tree $G \in \Gamma_2(L)$. Then if $IRM_{L,2}(Q) \neq \emptyset$ then Q is IRM-implementable, if $IRM_{L,G}(Q) \neq \emptyset$ then Q is IRM-implementable with structure G.

Also, definition 2 may be narrowed up to one particular learning example - $w(\cdot) \in IRM_{L,2}$ implements some $q \in Q$ iff $w(k) = k_M$ and in the same manner $IRM_{L,2}(q)$ and $IRM_{L,G}(q)$ are defined.

In case if $IRM_{L,2}(Q) = \emptyset$ or $IRM_{L,G}(Q) = \emptyset$ it is possible to state the approximation problem. Given particular $w(\cdot) \in IRM_{L,2}$ let us denote $Q_w = \{q \subseteq Q : w(k) = k_L\}$. For any arbitrary $w(\cdot) \in IRM_{L,2}$ let us denote $U_Q(w) = \#Q_w/\#Q$ to be quality of approximation with maximum value 1 if $w(\cdot) \in IRM_{L,2}(Q)$. Then the approximation problem is to find $w^*(\cdot) \in \underset{w \in IRM_{M,2}}{Argmax}\ U_Q(w)$. And in the case, if Q is.

IRM-implementable, then any correct solution of the approximation problem should yield $w(\cdot) \in IRM_{L,2}(Q)$.

Given some $G \in \Gamma_2(L)$ the same problem may be stated in the restricted way – to find $w^*(\cdot) \in \underset{w \in IPM_{M,G}}{Argmax}\ U_Q(w)$.

Problems stated above have combinatorial nature and it may be very difficult to solve them. The $|\Gamma_2(L)| = (2l - 3)!!$ [11]. That is why possibility to predict, what G should be selected or should not be considered is quite important.

2 Sensitivity and Implementation via IRM

2.1 Equivalency Sets

Now let us introduce an idea of sensitivity of learning set Q or function described by this set f_Q to some subset of it's indicators.

Given some arbitrary subset of indicators $\tilde{L} \subseteq L$ let us denote $k = \left(k_{(\tilde{L})}, k_{(L \backslash \tilde{L})}\right)$ - splitting of indicators tuple k for some arbitrary learning example $q = (k, k_L)$ into two tuples and divide the whole set of possible values of indicators from this set $K_{(\tilde{L})} = \prod_{i \in \tilde{L}} K_i$ into a number of nonintersecting subsets $K_{\tilde{L}}(Q) = \left\{\kappa \subseteq K_{(\tilde{L})}\right\}$ such that $\forall \{q, \tilde{q}\} \subseteq Q$ if $k_{(\tilde{L})} \in \kappa$ and $\tilde{k}_{(\tilde{L})} \in \kappa$ then $k_L = \tilde{k}_L$ $(f_Q(k) = f_Q(\tilde{k}))$ and for any $\{\kappa, \tilde{\kappa}\} \subseteq K_{\tilde{L}}$ $\exists \{q, \tilde{q}\} \subseteq Q$ such that $k_{(\tilde{L})} \in \kappa, \tilde{k}_{(\tilde{L})} \in \tilde{\kappa}$ and $k_L \neq \tilde{k}_L$ $(f_Q(k) \neq f_Q(\tilde{k}))$. We will denote each such set κ to be an equivalency set.

Let us denote such construction $K_{\tilde{L}}(Q)$ – composition of equivalency sets for subset of indicators $\tilde{L}$.

It is quite obvious, that $|K_{\tilde{L}}(Q)| \in \left\{1, ..., \prod_{i \in \tilde{L}}|K_i|\right\}$. Also it is quite clear, that if for some Q, and $\tilde{L} \subseteq L$ $|K_{\tilde{L}}(Q)| = 1$, then any variable from this subset is insignificant to Q (or f_Q). And the higher $|K_{\tilde{L}}(Q)|$ - the more sensitive Q to this subset of indicators. It also worth to mention that $|K_L(Q)| = K_L$ while for some $\tilde{L} \subseteq L$ it may be that $|K_{\tilde{L}}(Q)| > K_L$.

Let's consider some examples of counting of equivalence groups. An example of learning set Q on three indicators (Table 1):

Table 1. Examples on full learning set on three indicators

# of example	Indicator			Assessment
	$l1$	$l2$	$l3$	
1	0	0	0	0
2	1	0	0	1
3	0	1	0	1
4	1	1	0	0
5	0	0	1	0
6	1	0	1	0
7	0	1	1	0
8	1	1	1	0

For this example, we have the following equivalency sets (Table 2):

Table 2. Equivalency sets for full learning set on three indicators

$\widetilde{L}i$	$l1$	$l2$	$l3$	$l1l2$	$l1l3$	$l2l3$
$|K_{\widetilde{L}i}(Q)|$	2	2	2	2	3	3

Let's consider another example, learning set Q with four indicators:

Table 3. Examples on full learning set on four indicators

# of example	Indicator				Assessment
	$l1$	$l2$	$l3$	$l4$	
1	0	0	0	0	0
2	1	0	0	0	1
3	0	1	0	0	1
4	1	1	0	0	0
5	0	0	1	0	0
6	1	0	1	0	0
7	0	1	1	0	0
8	1	1	1	0	0
9	0	0	0	1	0

(continued)

Table 3. (*continued*)

# of example	Indicator				Assessment
	I1	*I2*	*I3*	*I4*	
10	1	0	0	1	0
11	0	1	0	1	0
12	1	1	0	1	0
13	0	0	1	1	0
14	1	0	1	1	0
15	0	1	1	1	0
16	1	1	1	1	0

Table 4. Equivalency sets for full learning set on four indicators

$\widetilde{Li}$	*I1*	*I2*	*I3*	*I4*	*I1I2*	*I1I3*	*I1I4*
$\lvert K_{\widetilde{Li}}(Q)\rvert$	2	2	2	2	2	3	3
$\widetilde{Li}$		*I2I3*	*I2I4*	*I3I4*	*I1I2I3*	*I1I2I4*	*I1I3I4*	*I2I3I4*
$\lvert K_{\widetilde{Li}}(Q)\rvert$		3	3	2	2	2	3	3

For this example, we have the following equivalency sets (Table 4):

As you can see in table above it may be that $\lvert K_{I1}(Q)\rvert = 2$ and $\lvert K_{I3}(Q)\rvert = 2$, but $\lvert K_{I1I3}(Q)\rvert = 3$. Also $\lvert K_{I1I2}(Q)\rvert = 2$, $\lvert K_{I3I4}(Q)\rvert = 2$ and $\lvert K_{I2}(Q)\rvert = 2$, $\lvert K_{I4}(Q)\rvert = 2$, but $\lvert K_{I2I3I4}(Q)\rvert = 3$, when $\lvert K_{I1I2I3}(Q)\rvert = 2$, $\lvert K_{I1I2I4}(Q)\rvert = 2$. On the Fig. 1 below, we illustrate the resulting groups by implemented full binary trees on set Q from Table 3.

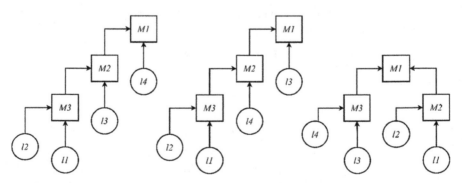

Fig. 1. Full binary trees implementing described learning set Q with four indicators

Now let us apply notions introduced above to IRM implementation problem.

For any arbitrary $G \in \Gamma_2(L)$ let us denote its indicators decomposition structure $\Lambda(G) = \{L_i\}_{i \in \{1,...,l-1\}}$ such that $\forall i \in \{1, ..., l-1\}$ $L_i \subseteq L$ is a set of leaves (indicators) of subtree with root in node i. That is $L_1 = L$, and $\forall i \in \{1, ..., l-1\}$ $|L_i| \geq 2$.

It is obvious that there is no explicit monotonicity $K_{\tilde{L}}$ of groups of indicators by nesting. But we can say for sure about equivalency that if $\tilde{\tilde{L}} \subseteq L |K_{\tilde{L}}| = 1$, then $\forall \tilde{L} \subseteq \tilde{\tilde{L}} |K_{\widehat{L}}| = 1$. In addition, the following statements are true.

Assertion 1. Given some arbitrary complete Q and $G \in \Gamma_2(L)$. Then for any some $L_i \in \Lambda(G)$ such that $L_i \geq 2$ and its subgroups $\{L_{ir}; L_{ic}\} \subset \Lambda(G) : L_{ir} \cup L_{ic} = L_i$. For any admissible values of indicators from L_{ir} - $k_{(L_{ir})}$, $\tilde{k}_{(L_{ir})}$ and from L_{ic} - $k_{(L_{ic})}$, $\tilde{k}_{(L_{ic})}$ such that $\{k_{(L_{ir})}, \tilde{k}_{(L_{ir})}\} \in \kappa$, where $\kappa \in K_{L_{ir}}(Q)$, and $\left\{k_{(L_{ic})}, \tilde{k}_{(L_{ic})}\right\} \in \hat{\kappa}$, where $\hat{\kappa} \in K_{L_{ic}}(Q)$ it follows that values of corresponding indicators from L_i $k_{(L_i)} = \left(k_{(L_{ic})}, k_{(L_{ir})}\right)$ and $\tilde{k}_{(L_i)} = \left(\tilde{k}_{(L_{ic})}, \tilde{k}_{(L_{ir})}\right)$ belong to same indifferences set $\{k_{(L_i)}, \tilde{k}_{(L_i)}\} \in \kappa'$.

Assertion 2. In case of uniform-scale implementation for complete learning set Q $IRM_{L,G}(Q) \neq \emptyset$ iff $\forall i \in \{1, ..., l-1\}$ $|K_{L_i}(Q)| \leq |K_L|$.

Assertion 2 allows to construct algorithm for selecting $G \in \Gamma_2(L)$ such that $IRM_{L,G}(Q) \neq \emptyset$ in case if Q is implementable.

2.2 Algorithm of Tree Selection in Case of Complete Learning Set

First of all, obtaining equivalence groups allows us to remove all structures $G \in \Gamma_2(L)$ that include combinations with the number of equivalence groups exceeding the scale, $|K_{\tilde{L}}(Q)| \geq K_L$. This allows us to dramatically decrease number of structures to be considered with any algorithm of IRM identification for particular $G \in \Gamma_2(L)$ [8, 9]. The performance of equivalence testing of one subset of indicators $\tilde{L}$ is proportional $(K_L)^l$.

Second, based on the equivalence groups within the scale $|K_{\tilde{L}}(Q)| \leq K_L$, we can use the algorithm to select obviously allowed structures.

Algorithm: If, as in a result of the analysis of equivalence groups, we have allowed combinations of leaves, then we begin our consideration with groups consisting of three leaves $|L_i| = 3$. For such groups, we check the possibility of their decomposition into groups of allowed pairs of leaves and individual leaves. Using only permitted combinations of leaves reduces the number of structures considered. Thus, we compile a list of checked groups of three leaves. Next, go to the groups of four leaves and repeat the decomposition test based on the groups selected above. Thus, we check for the possibility of decomposition of all groups with $|L_i| \geq 2$ to the maximum size $|L_i| = l$ leaves in the group. If it is not possible, then such groups are excluded from list. These iterations should be repeated until full set of leaves may be decomposed in number of subgroups remained in the list of allowed groups. Then any structure $G \in \Gamma_2(L)$ such that its $\Lambda(G)$ is included in list of allowed leaves groups should be considered in IRM's identification task for this learning set Q on the basis of approaches, suggested in [8].

2.3 Challenges for Implementation of Incomplete Learning Sets

While the approach suggested in previous section works perfect with complete learning sets, for practical application it is important to develop methods for incomplete learning sets and there are still number of challenges to deal with. In particular, Assertion 1 is not correct in case of incomplete sets. Which leads to challenges at stage of assessment on number of equivalence groups given particular set of indicators and at the stage of application of the algorithm, described above. This is an actual problem to be solved in the next stage of development of the approach described above.

Author 1 acknowledges for partial funding RFBR grant 19-29-07525 (paragraphs 1, 2.1). Author 2 acknowledges for partial funding RSF grant 17-78-20047 (paragraphs 2.2–2.3).

References

1. Gorelikov, N.: Designing a sectoral model for management of development and manufacture of new products. Avtomatika i Telemekhanika **5**, 63–70 (1984)
2. Burkov, V., Novikov, D., Shchepkin, A.: Control Mechanisms for Ecological-Economic Systems. SSDC, vol. 10. Springer, Cham (2015). https://doi.org/10.1007/978-3-319-10915-2
3. Korgin, N., Rozhdestvenskaya, S.: Concordant approach for R&D projects' evaluation and ranking for formation of programs. In: IEEE 11th International Conference on Application of Information and Communication Technologies (AICT), pp. 1–5. IEEE (2017)
4. Shchepkin, A.: Application of integrated mechanism in financing project works. In: 13th International Conference "Management of large-scale system development" (MLSD), pp. 1–4. IEEE (2020)
5. Zheglova, Y., Titarenko, B.: Methodology for the integrated assessment of design solutions for foundation pit fences based on the theory of active systems. IOP Conf. Ser. Mater. Sci. Eng. **869**, 052012 (2020)
6. Burkov, V.N., Enaleev, A.K., Strogonov, V.I., Fedyanin, D.N.: Models and management structure for the development and implementation of innovative technologies in railway transportation. I. Mechanisms of priority projects selection and resource allocation. Autom. Remote Control **81**(7), 1316–1329 (2020). https://doi.org/10.1134/S0005117920070127
7. Mariel, P., et al.: Environmental Valuation with Discrete Choice Experiments: Guidance on Design, Implementation and Data Analysis. Springer, Heidelberg (2021). https://doi.org/10.1007/978-3-030-62669-3
8. Burkov, V., Korgin, N., Sergeev, V.: Identification of integrated rating mechanisms as optimization problem. In: 13th International Conference "Management of Large-Scale System Development" (MLSD), pp. 1–5. IEEE (2020)
9. Alekseev, A.: Identification of integrated rating mechanisms based on training set. In: 2nd International Conference on Control Systems, Mathematical Modeling, Automation and Energy Efficiency (SUMMA), pp. 398–403. IEEE (2020)
10. Yu, L., et al.: Missing data preprocessing in credit classification: one-hot encoding or imputation? Emerg. Markets Financ. Trade **56**, 1–11 (2020). https://doi.org/10.1080/1540496X.2020.1825935
11. Barnett, J., et al.: Darwin meets graph theory on a strange planet: counting full n-ary trees with labeled leafs. Alabama J. Math. **35**, 16–23 (2010)

Application of Linear Random Processes to Construction of Diagnostic System for Power Engineering Equipment

Valerij Zvaritch[1,2]($\boxtimes$) , Mykhailo Myslovych[1] , and Yuri Gyzhko[1]

[1] Institute Electrodynamics of the National Academy of Science of Ukraine,
Peremogy Avenue 56, Kiev 03068, Ukraine
zvaritch@nas.gov.ua
[2] Institute of Renewable Energy of the National Academy of Science of Ukraine,
Gnata Khatkevycha 20-a, Kiev 02094, Ukraine

Abstract. Some mathematical models of informational signals and methods of the diagnostic system construction is considered. Different type of linear random processes is recommended for application. Some properties of the random processes are discussed. Application of the models depends on many factors. Such processes are used for classification of stochastic informational signals in the case of non-Gaussian distribution realizations of the signals, which energy spectra (within the framework of the first two moments) possess is often not enough for reliable recognition and classification of such signals. It is expedient to use information on higher moments or statistical characteristics of distributing such signals. It is possible to use the higher-order moments of such signals realization as the diagnostic features and provided the increase in accuracy and reliability of Power Engineering Equipment diagnostics. Attributes at the power engineering equipment diagnostic system construction are above mentioned justified diagnostic features, as well as informational diagnostic signals having been justified by the investigation of the appropriate mathematical models. Obtaining numerical estimation of chosen diagnostic features is first of all necessary for forming teaching complexes, and, further, for conducting the diagnostics itself according to the formed teaching complexes. Some peculiarities of constructing the multilevel diagnostic systems for resilience operation of electric power facilities are considered. An example of 3-level diagnostic system development for a Power station is represented.

Keywords: Linear random process · Vibration diagnostics · Multilevel diagnostic system

1 Introduction

The Power Stations are an critical infrastructure. So reliability and resilience of its operation is an important component of state security. The reliability of the power equipment is closely related to the effective monitoring and diagnostics systems they are equipped

A. Dolgui et al. (Eds.): APMS 2021, IFIP AICT 630, pp. 617–622, 2021.
https://doi.org/10.1007/978-3-030-85874-2_67

with. The construction of such systems takes place in several stages: the elaboration of mathematical models of information signals of such systems, the selection of the most informative diagnostic features based on the analysis of such models, the construction of training sets and decision rules. Construction of diagnostic algorithms and the system itself based on the scientific results obtained. When solving such a problem, the theory of probability, the theory of random processes, the theory of risks, machine learning, theory of statistical hypotheses, theory of pattern recognition etc. Algorithms for the plant of diagnostic systems according to the Smart Grid technology and resilience with the conditional division of the power engineering equipment into hierarchical levels is proposed. Many scientific papers are devoted to the issues related to the construction of diagnostic systems for power equipment. Some of them concerning on elaboration of mathematical models that can be used as models of information signals of such systems [1–4]. risk analysis and it's application [5–8], diagnostics method development [9, 10].

2 Problem Station

The modern Power Engineering industry, starting the Information Communication Technology networks developed on the basis of a Smart Grid concept and resilience, requires forming a holistic multilevel control system which provides the high level of automation, robustness and reliability of the whole system and covers the producers of electricity, transferring and distributing networks, consumers etc. In this case, obtaining actual information about the current state of each Power Station (PS) and the exchange of this information among all participants of the electricity market is very important, because it provides the increase in the reliability of the work of electrical system as a whole.

The implement of the reliable power engineering equipment is associated unavoidably with well-timed diagnostics of their technical condition. The method of diagnostics is most promising in the group of areas of methods of diagnostics of the technical condition of sections of electric drivers and mechanisms.

Two main approaches to solving the problems of diagnostics for machines and mechanisms are used. There are deterministic approaches and statistical approaches.

In the statistical approach, the solution of the problem of diagnostics usually consist of the following stages: elaboration of a mathematical model of information signals of diagnosed sections of machines and mechanisms; verification of the correspondence of the mathematical model to experimental data; separation of the most of the most informative diagnostic features to experimental data; formation of teaching sets corresponding to different technical condition of the diagnosed equipment; construction of decision making rules.

3 Definitions of Some Random Processes

3.1 Linear Random Processes

A linear random process (LRP) is a functional of the following form

$$\xi(t) = \int\limits_{-\infty}^{\infty} \varphi(\tau, t) d\eta(\tau), \quad t \in (-\infty, \infty) \tag{1}$$

where $\varphi(\tau, t) \in L_2(-\infty, \infty)$ with respect to τ for all t is a non-stochastic real Hilbert function; $\eta(\tau)$, $\eta(0) = 0$, $\tau \in (-\infty, \infty)$ is a Hilbert stochastically continuous random process with independent increments that is often called a generating process. While solving many problems including statistical simulation it is convenient to consider the LRP as a response of a linear filter with the impulse transient function $\varphi(\tau, t)$ on the action of the white noise $\eta'(\tau)$. It is understood that $\eta'(\tau)$ is a generalized derivative of the corresponding process with independent increments [4].

Any stochastically continuous process with independent increments can be represented as a sum of two stochastically independent components which may be not present simultaneously: Gaussian and Poisson. We call the components as processes of Gaussian and Poisson types. The first type contains the homogeneous (Wiener) and non-homogeneous Gaussian processes with independent increments. Simple Poisson processes, renewal processes and their linear combinations, generalized Poisson processes with independent increments belong to the second type. Being generated by each of the mentioned processes LRPs possess some typical properties. This fact is taken as a principle of the classification. For example, it can be shown that if the generating process is of the Gaussian type, the corresponding LRP is a Gaussian stochastic process $\xi(t)$. Poisson type of generating process leads to LRPs describing impulse currents. We call such processes as impulse LRPs.

Using a characteristic function of a linear stochastic process, one can perform a full analysis of the output signals of linear systems: calculate moments and distribution functions, analyze connections between input and output characteristics of linear circuit.

3.2 Linear Random Process with Periodic Structures

We have to deal with non-stationary random processes in application in many cases. These processes can be defined in the following way. A real random process $\xi(t)$, $t \in (-\infty, \infty)$ is called the real periodic random process (RPRP), according to Slutskiy, if the number $T > 0$ exist for the process $\xi(t)$, such that the finite dimension vectors $(\xi(t_1), \xi(t_2), \ldots, \xi(t_n))$ and $(\xi(t_1 + T), \xi(t_2 + T), \ldots, \xi(t_n + T))$ are stochastically equivalent, in a wide sense, for all whole numbers $n > 0$, where $t_1, t_2, \ldots, t_n$ is a set of separability of the.

The canonical form of characteristic function is simpler since such processes are set constructively on the random processes basis having infinitely divisible distribution patterns. However, for nonstationary processes with similar distribution patterns the spectral structure is not seen directly. Thus, to describe nonstationary random processes having periodic structure it is expedient to generate models which could combine the benefits of RPRP and the random processes having the infinitely divisible distribution patterns.

Random periodic processes can be widely used in many applications: the problem of detection of signals from noise, classification of information signals, and many others.

3.3 Linear Autoregressive Process

The diagnostics method is selected in the stage of elaboration of mathematical model. Usually, for example, vibrations are modelled using mathematical models with continuous parameters. However, the majority of modern devices and information-measuring systems in vibration diagnostics include microprocessors and microcomputers and computers whose functional algorithms are based on digital methods of processing information signals.

Taking this into account, vibrations should be described using mathematical models with discrete time. We propose to use as mathematical models of vibration of sections of machines and mechanisms one insufficiently examined group of random processes with discrete time – linear random autoregressive processes.

Autoregressive linear processes may be set in the following way:

$$\xi_t + \sum_{j=1}^{p} a_j \xi_{t-j} = \varsigma_t, \quad t \in Z \tag{2}$$

where $\left\{a_j, a_j \neq 0, j = \overline{1, p}\right\}$ are the autoregressive parameters; p is the autoregressive order; $\{\varsigma_t, t \in Z\}$ is the stationary random process with discrete time and independent values, which has the infinitely divisible distribution law $P\{\varsigma_0 = 0\} = 1$. This process is often referred to as the generating process. It is proposed that the process ξ_t is stationary in the narrow sense and ergodic theorems are fulfilled [4].

Autoregressive processes are widely practiced when constructing mathematical models of information signals of different types and during their analysis and synthesis. To classify such processes their energy characteristics are used very' often, but in problems of classification of stochastic information signals in the case of non-Gaussian distribution, realizations of the signals, which energy spectra (within the framework of the first two moments) possess is often not enough for reliable recognition and classification of such signals. Then it is expedient to use information on higher moments (integral characteristics) or statistical characteristics of distributing such signals.

In papers [3, 4] the results of using the elements of the theory of LRP for developing the mathematical models of physical obtaining the diagnostic features from the results of the analysis of the mathematical models of these processes in the terms of complete probabilistic characteristics (distribution functions or densities of probability distribution) of diagnostic signals being investigated. This, in turn, made it possible to use the higher-order moments of probability distribution of such signals as the diagnostic features and provided the increase in accuracy and reliability of Power Engineering Equipment (PEE) diagnostics. Diagnostic features used for determining the technical state of Power Engineering Equipment.

4   Diagnostic Features Used for Determining the Technical State of Power Engineering Equipment

Obtaining numerical estimation of chosen diagnostic features, in turn, is first of all necessary for forming teaching complexes and, further, for conducting the diagnostics itself according to the formed teaching complexes.

It is evident, that any resilience diagnostic system must reveal catastrophic defects, since they completely cease the operation of the object being examined. At the same time, some nonfatal or partial failures can be left beyond the consideration. Such an approach to the development of the system provides the opportunity to simplify its structure, reduce the volume of information being processed in the system and transferred between its hierarchical levels. This resilience system can make the system cheaper, and existing computing resources can be redistributed for carrying out more urgent functions.

Consider the peculiarities of constructing the multilevel diagnostic systems for resilience operation of electric power facilities [10].

At the top hierarchical level, a central diagnostic system (CDS) is located. The main purpose of the CDS is gathering and generalizing the data which comes from all local PEE diagnostic systems. When it is necessary, CDS can transfer the received data to a higher level of hierarchy.

Equipment being the part of local diagnostic system (LDS) can be logically subdivided into 3 hierarchical levels:

- level 1 is intended to the initial selection of diagnostic information (measurement of diagnostic signals, amplification, analog filtering, conversion to a digital form);
- level 2 is intended for the preliminary mathematical processing and making interme- diate diagnostic decisions (simple algorithms whose realization does not require vast computing resources; dividing information according to the degree of defect criti- cality); warning signaling to the higher level in the case of defect presence; storage of limited (insignificant) amount of measurement information and its transfer to the higher level (on request);
- level 3 is for storage, adequate processing and thorough analysis of data, quick response to emergency signals from a lower level, making diagnostic decisions about the examined object as a whole, archiving the statistical data, predicting the reliability and evaluating the residual life of the equipment, planning the repairing work etc.

PEE are equipped with standard measuring converters (especially, turbogenerators can be equipped with the sensors of temperature of a stator and a rotor) which can be used as the part of a monitoring system. It should be also stated that at the development stage of LDS the quite complete list of possible defects, which are to be revealed by the diagnostic system, is given and the units and electric machines (EM) elements in which these defects can possibly occur are listed.

Certain PEE are equipped with standard measuring converters (especially, turbogen- erators can be equipped with the sensors of temperature of a stator and a rotor) which can be used as the part of a monitoring system.

At the level of construction units of the EM a separate computing module is mounted for further transferring and processing the measured diagnostic signals. This module provides converting the analog signals to digital ones and preliminary processing of such signals obtained from this unit. In most cases, the considerable deviations of real state from the normal one will not be revealed, so that it might not be necessary to transfer the information to the higher level. If considerable deviation from the normal state to fatal defect is observed, the module of data measuring and preliminary processing should transfer the information to the higher level of system hierarchy for more detailed analysis.

5   Conclusions

According to the proposed mathematical models and hierarchical structure and with taking into account the conditional representation of the power engineering equipment with 3 levels, the algorithmic software has been developed which enables the functioning of the multilevel diagnostic system of the power engineering equipment by the Smart Grid technology.

References

1. Brockwell, P., Lindner, A.: Prediction of Levy-driven CARMA process. J. Econom. 2(189), 263–271 (2015)
2. Javorskyj, I., Isaev, I., Maevski, J., Yuzefovich, R.: Component covariance analysis for periodically correlated random processes. Signal Process. 90, 1083–1102 (2010)
3. Zvaritch, V., Marchenko, B.: Linear autoregressive processes with periodic structures as models of information signals. Radioelectron. Commun. Syst. 7(54), 367–372 (2011)
4. Babak, V., Babak, S., Myslovych, M., Zvaritch, V., Zaporozhets, A.: Diagnostic Systems for Energy Equipments. SSDC, vol. 281. Springer, Cham (2020). https://doi.org/10.1007/978-3-030-44443-3
5. Linkov, I., Trump, B.: The Science and Practice of Resilience. RSD. Springer, Cham (2019). https://doi.org/10.1007/978-3-030-04565-4
6. Dolgui, A., Ivanov, D., Rozhkov, M.: Does the ripple effect influence the bullwhip effect? An integrated analysis of structural and operational dynamics in the supply chain. Int. J. Prod. Res. 5(58), 1285–1301 (2020)
7. Davydiuk, F., Zvaritch, V.: The method of color formalization of the level of information security risk. Electron. Model. 2(41), 121–126 (2019)
8. Mokhor, V., Bakalynskyi, O., Tsurkan, V.: Analysis of information security risk assessment representation methods. Inf. Technol. Technol. 1(6), 75–84 (2018)
9. Lee, J., Wu, F., Graffari, M., Liao, L., Siegel, D.: Prognostics and health management design for rotary machinery systems – reviews, methodology and application. Mech. Syst. Signal Process. 2(42), 314–334 (2014)
10. Myslovych, M., Zvaritch, V., Ostapchuk, L., Hyzhko, Y., Hutorova, M.: Some issues of informational support for multilevel diagnostic systems of electrotechnical equipment. Comput. Probl. Electr. Eng. 1(10), 19–26 (2020)

Construction of Multi-step Price Forecasts in Commodity Markets Based on Qualitative and Quantitative Data Analysis Methods

Zinaida K. Avdeeva$^{(\boxtimes)}$ (ID), Elena A. Grebenyuk (ID), and Svetlana V. Kovriga (ID)

Trapeznikov V. A. Institute of Control Sciences of RAS, Moscow, Russia
kovriga@ipu.ru

Abstract. The article proposes a method for constructing and correcting a multistep forecast for the year ahead (with a monthly breakdown) of prices for raw materials and products of industrial enterprises. The proposed approach consists in the formation of a price forecast taking into account 1) the price of the predicted indicator, the prices of goods participating in the product value chain, and macro indicators (time series); 2) information about the strength and direction of environmental factors affecting the market. Structured information about the effects of the external environment is the result of processing expert knowledge and hypotheses from heterogeneous information sources, through analysis and modeling on a cognitive map of the situation (CCS). We form a forecast by constructing an ensemble of time series models, each of which reflects the dependence of the target indicator on its past values and the prices of related products, the composition of which is determined by the results of cognitive modeling and time series analysis. Based on the results of monitoring on the cognitive map of the situation, conducting in order to analyze possible changes in the external environment and digital monitoring of prices, to identify changes in prices modes, we perform a forecast correction. The results obtained in this study show that the use of cognitive modeling and monitoring of changes improve the accuracy of predictions.

Keywords: Manufacturing system · Multi-step forecasting quantitative and qualitative forecasting · Cognitive map · Monitoring · Time series

1 Introduction

Forecasting of prices for raw materials and final products of industrial enterprises is an important element of planning of their activity. Since planning is carried out for a year ahead, long-term forecasts (broken down by months) are necessary, accounting for which will increase the profit of the enterprise and reduce unproductive costs in case the forecasts have the necessary accuracy. The task of forecasting the values of time series for several steps ahead is one of the most difficult tasks of forecasting.

Prices on commodity markets, determining the costs of enterprises for raw materials and products have the following features:

© IFIP International Federation for Information Processing 2021
Published by Springer Nature Switzerland AG 2021
A. Dolgui et al. (Eds.): APMS 2021, IFIP AICT 630, pp. 623–631, 2021.
https://doi.org/10.1007/978-3-030-85874-2_68

- price change processes are nonstationary, with most of them being processes with a stochastic trend, with changing properties and interrelationships,
- there are price interactions between commodities linked together by a product value chain,
- the structure of the interrelations depends on the time scale in which we consider it and may change with changes in scale,
- there is a dependence on macro indicators such as the real interest rate, ex-change rates, oil prices, global demand for commodities, etc. [1, 2].

Future price values for the forecast period depend on quantifiable parameters such as current and past prices for raw materials and products produced from them, export and world prices for goods in the production sector under consideration, transportation tariffs, and macroeconomic indicators.

Under the influence of external environment events (political, economic, natural and man-made disasters, natural disasters, etc.), the set, the strength of the direction of the impact of qualitative factors acting on these prices, change. The current model for describing the dynamics and forecasting market parameters becomes unusable. It is necessary to detect these changes in a timely manner and adjust the model.

Many researchers note and use the influence of extreme events on the prices of commodity markets for forecasting. To identify extreme events, assess their impact on prices, and correct forecasts, [3–5] used such approaches as empirical mode decomposition (EMD), wavelet analysis, and search engine data analysis. The results of the analysis showed that taking into account the influence of ex-ternal influences significantly increases the accuracy of the forecast.

There are many relatively successfully attempts to take into account information about events affecting a price dynamic fundamental change for its inclusion in predictive models. For this, several types of mainly text information are used: news, analytical reports and expert statements, posts of market participants in professional communities. Especially actively carried out expert events with the digitization of information signals when forecasting on the stock markets, then on the raw materials, energy and commodity markets. The basis for the formation of digitized indices is the adjustment of algorithms for identifying information on a given thematic area, digitization of this information into activity indices with an assessment of emotional coloring, inclusion in the model in different ways. One of the proven methods for assessing the significance of observed changes in their possible impact on predicted parameters are cognitive maps. The CMs, apart from their predictive strength, explicitly structure the knowledge and information. This advantage of the CMs improves the interpretation of the links between the factors and links them with real changes in the situation [6–10]. Research area also includes research on the development of integrated methods, where the use of CMs is focused on identifying events (informational causes) that influence the formation of predicted values of the time series [6–10]. An important distinctive feature of such models is that they are constructed using heterogeneous data (quantitative and qualitative, expert) to identify significant factors and parameters of events that may affect the forecast generated. In this case, the formation and/or correction of the predictive model rely on event data extracted from heterogeneous information sources according to the results of CM analysis.

The results of the analysis of the situation on the cognitive map not only indicate and record the presence of factors that caused certain obvious changes in the market, but also allow you to form various scenarios for the development of the current situation for the forecast period. The proposed approach includes the following elements:

– analysis of the history of the predicted market fragment by cognitive modeling methods in order to identify homogeneous periods;
– building models of multi-step forecast of the target indicator values for the year ahead with a monthly breakdown in each of the considered periods;
– monitoring the situation by cognitive modeling methods;
– monitoring the time series of market parameters associated with the predicted target indicator in order to detect disorders in the on-line mode;
– correction of the forecast based on the results of monitoring the situation and time series monitoring during the forecast period.

2   Market Analysis Based on Historical Data

2.1   Situation Cognitive Map Construction and Estimation of the Significance of the Causal Factors

As a result of cognitive modeling application, at the time of the forecast formation, the main system-forming factors that influence the dynamics of the target indicator and, possibly, the rows associated with it in the database, are determined and ranked according to the strength of their influence on the target indicator. The factors with high ranks will be called significant in what follows.

Let there be a cognitive map of the commodity market situation, including the factors of the value chain in the considered commodity market, K_f (X, A, f), in which $X = (x_1, \ldots, x_n)$ is a set of factors of the situation S; $A = [a_{ij}]$ is the $N \times N$ matrix of factors mutual influence, where $a_{ij} \in [-1; 1]$ is the weight of influence of factor x_i on the factor x_j ($[-1; 1]$ – a discrete scale); f is a function that defines the rule of factor value change at any discrete-time $t \geq 0$.

The state of the situation at any discrete point of time $t \geq 0$ expressed as follows.

$$X(t+1) = Q(t)X(0) + Q(t)G(0) \tag{1}$$

where $Q(t) = E_N + A + A^2 + \ldots + A^t = (E_N - A)^{-1}$. When solving the problem of forecasting a target indicator, y, analysis on the matrix of integral influences, Q, allows us to identify the causal-factors, to assess the degree of their impact on the structure, to assess the significance of the influence of any group of factors $\{C\}$. Thus, the set of factors X are divided into classes according to the belonging of factors to the groups $\{C\}$. All causal-factors are divided into X_y^+ - factors and X_y^--factors: $X_y^+ = (x_k : q_{ky} > 0)$ and $X_y^- = (x_k : q_{ky} < 0)$. Submatrices Q_y^+ and Q_y^- are formed from the matrix Q.

The weight of the positive (or negative) influences of the causal-factors from $X_y^+ (X_y^-)$ on the target indicator y is equal to the modulus of the sum of the weights of the cumulative influences $q_y^+ = \sum_{k=1}^{l}$ and $q_y^- = \sum_{k=1}^{l} \left| q_{ky}^- \right|$, where $q_{ky}^+ (q_{ky}^-)$ is the weight of the cumulative influence of the causal-factor $x_k \in X_y^+$ ($x_k \in X_y^-$) on the target indicator y. Then the total weight of the causal-factors is $q_y^{total} = q_y^- + q_y^+ q_y^{total} = q_y^- + q_y^+$.

Then the significance of any group $\{Ci\}$ is estimated at K_f by the cumulative influence of causal-factors X^{Ci} related to the corresponding parameters of the model M_i (taking into account the identification of time series by the numbers of causal-factors).

At the stage of building forecasting models, the factors of the cognitive map are a source of keywords for finding sources of qualitative and quantitative information about factors, candidates for organizing regular monitoring; ranking factors or groups of factors by significance allows you to set a monitoring model based on the signs of expected changes by groups of factors with the greatest significance. Such an assessment allows you to determine an explanatory scheme for the conditions of serious qualitative changes in the analyzed factor (change in direction and change in the strength of changes). The ranking of groups of causal factors can also serve as the basis for recommending the construction of quantitative forecasting models based on certain quantitative indicators corresponding to the factors of the cognitive map.

Thus control factors according to the degree of significance of their integral influence on the achievement of the vector of goals are ranked.

2.2 Construction of Digital Models of Multistep Forecast for the year Ahead

To build a digital projections, we use ensembles of linear models, each of which computes the one step forecasts $\widehat{Y} = \{\hat{y}_{1|1-h}, \hat{y}_{2|2-h}, \ldots, \hat{y}_{t|t-h}, \ldots\}$ values of the target $Y = \{y_1, y_2, \ldots, y_t, \ldots\}$ as a combination of past values $y_{t-h}, y_{t-2h}, \ldots$, and values of the factors $X_1, X_2, \ldots X_k$, where $X_i = \{x_{i1}, x_{i2}, \ldots, x_{it}, \ldots\}, i = 1, 2, \ldots, k$. Since the intervals on which the model is built are short, we have limited the number of regressors included in the model to two.

For the forecast, we build ensembles of VAR and VECM models. These models are successfully used to form long-term multi-step forecasts both separately and as part of hybrid forecasting algorithms that include methods for analyzing the state of the external environment [11–13]. The build process consists of the following steps.

1. For each forecast horizon (month, 2 months, quarter, half year, year), we search in the database for time series that satisfy the conditions:

    – the order of integration of the series is equal to the order of integration of the target indicator;
    – according to the results of cognitive modeling, the dynamics of the series is influenced by one or several significant system-forming factors.

2. From the series selected at step 1, we form groups, including the target indicator and the series (no more than two), reflecting the relationship between the values of the target indicator and the significant system-forming factors (prices for raw materials, products, macro indicators, etc.), and test each group for cointegration. If cointegration exists and the series X_{i1}, X_{i2} are Granger causal for the target Y, then we build VEC models for these groups. If there is no cointegration and the series

of factor differences ΔX_{i1}, ΔX_{i2} are Granger causal for the target, ΔY (i.e., the series of factor differences help to predict the values of ΔY, but ΔY does not help to predict the values of the series of differences), then we build VAR models by series differences. We repeat this procedure for each forecast horizon.

3. We calculate the forecasts in each group as the average values of the forecasts of the models included in it.

4. The results of the forecasts of each group are averaged with weights obtained using cognitive modeling, which determine the significance of each group based on the significance of the system-forming factors:

$$C_1, \ldots, C_k : \sum_{i=1}^{k} C_i = 1,$$

where k is the number of groups, $C_1, \ldots, C_k$ are their values, estimated in K_f by the cumulative influence of causal-factors X^{C_i} related to the corresponding parameters of the model M_i (Sect. 2.1). The forecast formula for each horizon h has the form:

$$\widehat{Y}_{t|t-h} = \sum_{i=1}^{k} C_j \widehat{y}^i_{t|t-h} \tag{2}$$

where $\bar{y}^i_{t|t-h}$ is the average value of the forecasts at time t, calculated for the models of the i-th group on the horizon h (step 3).

5. To form an integral multi-step forecast on the basis of a direct strategy, we build monthly, 2-month, quarterly, semiannual, annual forecasts for one step forward and determine the upper and lower limits in the intervals between the forecasts.

3   Forecast Correction in the Forecast Interval

During the forecasting interval the changes caused both by global environmental events: catastrophes, accidents, crises, etc., and changes in the structure of supply and demand as a result of events related to a particular industry are possible. These changes require correction of the forecast and, accordingly, of the models forming it.

3.1   Cognitive-Map-Driven Monitoring of the Current Situation and Scenarios Simulation

Cognitive-map driven monitoring is based on monitoring information sources, where analytical materials on the situation are concentrated. In addition to the use of analysis in the monitoring cycle, when the analytical department generates reasonable conclusions about the significance of the observed changes in the external environment, analysis on the cognitive map allows you to create a semantic observation model in information sources on important factors and topics. Such monitoring includes:

1) *Situation development monitoring* by tracking information sources by keywords chosen from CM and determining of factors' initial values in an appropriate linguistic scale. The IT-infrastructure is configured to monitor the information space based on the factors of the model. A special category is created for each factor and the user/analyst

receives a notification in case a message regarding a certain factor appears in mass media or any other connected source of information.

Let, $S_y^d(X(0); G(0); K_f; R(r_j = sign(x_j(0)))$ – the d-th qualitative forecast on the map K_f, depending on the values of factors X at the time $t = 0$, is determined by Eq. 1. That is, in each scenario d, we obtain the value of the factor y^* at any discrete point of time $t \geq 0$ and an estimate of the dynamics $r_y = sign(y^* - y^0)$.

2) Assessment of the significance of information occasions on the situation model.

In the block of qualitative forecasting of a target indicator for given input conditions for factors X, in addition to assessing their value, an assessment is made of the significance in the change of certain factors-reasons. For this simulation scenario, a Q^R submatrix is formed on the Q, in which the factors of the $X_{R(y)}^{inpS}$ ($x_i : edf_i \neq 0$) *and those* $x_R^{M_i}$: $(edf_i \neq 0)$ represented in the rows and the factors $\{X_R^{M_i}\}$ and the target indicator y in columns; on the intersections of rows and columns — the corresponding integral influence q_{jk}, if there is no influence, then $q_{ij} = 0$.

Then a significance of the M_i for some scenario S_y^d defined as

$$q_{S_y^d}^{M_i} = \sum_{k1=1}^{m1} \sum_{j1=1}^{l1} r_{x_{k1}} \times q_{x_{k1}}^{x_{j1}M_i} + \sum_{j2=1}^{l2} r_{x_{j2}}^{M_i} \times q_{x_{j2}}^{y_{M_i}^{M_i}}, \tag{3}$$

where the first addend is the cumulative influence of the factors from $X^{X^{M_i}}$ on causal factors related to a model M_i on target indicator, y, and the second addend is the cumulative influence of the causal factors related to M_i on target indicator y.

Accordingly, for each qualitative forecast $S_y^d(X(0); K; EDF(edf_i = sign(x_i(0)))$, we obtain the following estimates for the forecasting models $\{M_i, (S_{x_k}^d; \{q_{S_{x_k}^d}^{M_i}\}; edf_{x_k})\}$. Also, we can obtain an estimate of a forecasting model M_i in the form

$$q*_{S_y^d}^{M_i} = \sum_{k2=1}^{m2} r_{x_{k2}^{other_i}} \times q_{x_{k2}^{other}}^{y_{M_i}^{M_i}},$$

which estimates a cumulative effect of the causal factors has not been connected with factors from X^{M_i}.

Systematically monitoring of such situation by means of IT-tools is needed to use a simulation module for dynamic analysis and prediction. The software tools should provide the collection, processing and consolidation of heterogeneous unstructured data - text and rich media - from internal and external sources (databases, the Internet, file systems, corporate information systems, television and radio broadcasting, etc.) in a close to real-time mode. A fundamental feature of the system is that it supports a full cycle of data processing, i.e. transform data into information and extract actionable knowledge from information through in-depth text analysis and situation modeling [14].

3.2   Monitoring the Dynamics of Quantitative Indicators

If changes occur in the prediction interval, the models used stop describing the incoming data. These changes against the background of random perturbations are little noticeable and without the use of special algorithms they are detected with a large lag. Therefore, for monitoring, we use algorithms aimed at the fastest detection of changes, subject to the limitation of time between false detections, capable of dealing with non-stationary processes [15–17].

We conduct digital monitoring using weekly data. To perform it, we build on the interval containing no changes in the time series models of the target indicator and significant factors and calculate the errors of the models under stable conditions:

$$Res_t = \Delta y_t - \widetilde{\mu} - \sum_{i=1}^{k-1} \widetilde{\beta}_i \Delta y_{t-i} \tag{4}$$

where Δy_t are the differences of weekly values of the monitored series, $\widetilde{\mu}$ $- \sum_{i=1}^{k-1} \widetilde{\beta}_i \Delta y_{t-i}$ are the parameters of its model description built on the differences of weekly data.

If the drift $\widetilde{\mu}$ has changed in the tracked indicator, then the conditional mathematical expectation of the sequence (4) changes, and the asymptotic properties of the conditional variance remain unchanged, if the volatility of the process has changed, then the variance of sequence (4) changes [15].

For change detection we use the algorithm of abrupt change diagnosis (detection and isolation) in random signals proposed in [16]. This algorithm detects changes in random signals in the presence of multiple alternatives and isolating the change that occurred. Let $\Delta y_1, \Delta y_2, \ldots, \Delta y_{t0}, \Delta y_{t0+1}, \ldots$, be a random independent sequence distributed as

$$F(\Delta y_t, \theta) = \begin{cases} F(\Delta y_t, \theta_0), & if \ < t0 \\ F(\Delta y_t, \theta_l), & if \ \geq t0 \end{cases}$$

where $l = 1, 2, \ldots, m$, $F(\Delta y_t, \theta_l)$, is a family of distributions differing in their parameters: $\theta_i, \theta_i \neq \theta_j$, if$j \neq i$ for all $i, j = 0, 1, 2, \ldots, m$. The change time t_0 and the distribution index i after changing properties are unknown (but nonrandom). As a result, the algorithm generates a signal t_0, l, where t_0 is the alarm time at which the change was detected, and $l \in \{1, 2, \ldots, m\}$ is the type of change in accordance with (4). This algorithm minimizes of the maximum mean delay for detection/isolation [16].

4   Description of the Experiment and Results

Realization results of the proposed approach have been demonstration on example of building a multi-step forecast of scrap prices in commodity markets. In the interval 2015–2018, we used monthly data to build VEC and VAR models and form a multistep forecast for the year ahead (2019) with a monthly breakdown, taking into account the recommendations of the cognitive map for the composition and assessment of the significance of causal factors and the results of analyzing the properties of temporal series describing these factors (Sects. 2.1–2.2).

Monitoring of the situation revealed a change in demand for metal products in Europe in March 2019 and the introduction of US duties for Russia. Based on these data, the qualitative forecast for the CM (SM scenario) showed that the significance of the quantitative forecast for a group of factors, reflecting the demand for finished products, is the highest. In August, it was discovered: the absence of causality of factors relative to the target in some models and, consequently the violation of cointegration in its.

Based on the results of the detected changes, the group of models that form prices for scrap by factors reflecting the demand for finished products was assigned the maximum weight, and the models with violation of cointegration was replaced with other models of the corresponding groups. According to the data for 2015–2019, the forecast for 2020 was carried out in a similar way.

To check the results of the algorithm, we used, as in [17], two measures of accuracy: the mean absolute percent error (MAPE) and the root mean squared error (RMSE):

$$MAPE = \frac{1}{n} \sum_{i=1}^{n} \left| \frac{y_t - \widehat{Y}_{t|t-h}}{y_t} \right| \tag{5}$$

and

$$RMSE = \sqrt{\frac{1}{n} \sum_{i=1}^{n} \left(y_t - \widehat{Y}_{t|t-h} \right)^2} \tag{6}$$

where y_t is the value target at the moment t, $\widehat{Y}_{t|t-h}$ is the forecast at the moment of time t, calculated with the horizon h at the moment of time $t - h$.

To assess the algorithm performance, we used metrics (5) and (6) obtained by forecasting a number of scrap prices for a year with a monthly breakdown for the interval of 2016–2019 (in dollars). For comparison, we calculated forecasting errors by the following algorithms: naive forecasting, forecasting by ARIMA model, forecasting using the proposed algorithm without taking into account the recommendations of the cognitive map. The results are given in Table 1.

To assess the algorithm performance, we used metrics (5) and (6) obtained by forecasting monthly scrap prices time series for a year with a monthly breakdown in 2019 and 2020 years (in dollars). For comparison, we calculated forecasting errors by the following algorithms: naive forecasting, forecasting by ARIMA model, forecasting using the proposed algorithm without taking into account the recommendations of the cognitive map. The results are given in Table 1.

Notes: alg1 is the proposed algorithm without taking into account the results of analysis by the control map; alg2 is the algorithm that corrects alg1 according to the results of analysis by the cognitive map.

Table 1. Average error of the annual forecast with a monthly split

Algorithm	MAPE 2019	MAPE 2020	RMSE($)	RMSE($)
alg1	4,2	3,5	10,29	10,2
alg2	6,8	5,8	16,8	15,8
ARIMA	12,95	13,5	38,57	39,5
naïve	12,02	14,84	35,14	37,14d

The experimental results presented here demonstrate the advantage of our approach.

References

1. Byrne, J.P., Fazio, G., Fiess, N.: Primary commodity prices: co-movements, common factors and fundamentals. J. Dev. Econ. **101**, 16–26 (2013)
2. Liu, C., Sun, X., Wang, J., Li, J., Chen, J.: Multiscale information transmission between commodity markets: an EMD. Res. Int. Bus. Financ. **55**(1), 101318 (2021)
3. Tanga, L., Zhanga, C., Lib, L., Wang, S.: A multi-scale method for forecasting oil price with multi-factor search engine data. Appl. Energy **257**(1), 114033 (2020)
4. Zhang, X., Yu, L., Wang, S., Lai, K.K.: Estimating the impact of extreme events on crude oil price: an EMD-based event analysis method. Energy Econ. **31**, 768–778 (2009)
5. Lin, L., Jiang, Y., Xiao, H., Zhou, Z.: Crude oil price forecasting based on a novel hybrid long memory GARCH-M and wavelet analysis model. Physica A Stat. Mech. Appl. **543**(1), 123532 (2020)
6. Papageorgiou, E.I., Poczeta, K.: A two-stage model for time series prediction based on fuzzy cognitive maps and neural networks. Neurocomputing **232**, 113–121 (2017)
7. Shan, D., Lu, W., Yang, J.: The data-driven fuzzy cognitive map model and its application to prediction of time series. Int. J. Innov. Comput. Inf. Control **14**(5), 1583–1602 (2018)
8. Froelich, W., Salmeron, J.: Evolutionary learning of fuzzy grey cognitive maps for the forecasting of multivariate, interval-valued time series. Int. J. Approx. Reason **55**, 1319–1335 (2014)
9. Homendaa, W., Jastrzebska, A.: Clustering techniques for fuzzy cognitive map design for time series modeling. Neurocomputing **232**, 3–15 (2017)
10. Hong, T., Han, I.: Integrated approach of cognitive maps and neural networks using qualitative information on the World Wide Web: the KBNMiner. Expert Syst. **21**(5), 243–252 (2004)
11. Sangasoongsong, A., Bukkapatnam, S.T.S., Kim, J., Iyerc, P.S., Sureshc, R.P.: Multi-step sales forecasting in automotive industry based on structural relationship identification. Int. J. Prod. Econ. **140**(2), 875–887 (2012)
12. Jiang, H., Liu, C.: Forecasting construction demand: a vector error correction model with dummy variables. Constr. Manag. Econ. **29**(9), 969–979 (2011)
13. Parot, A., Michell, K., Kristjanpoller, W.D.: Using artificial neural networks to forecast exchange rate, including VAR - VECM residual analysis and prediction linear combination. Intell. Syst. **26**(1), 3–15 (2019)
14. Makarenko, D.: Analytical and predictive monitoring: a cognitive-map-based approach and toolkit to socio-political stability governance support. IFAC-PapersOnLine **51**(30), 522–526 (2018)
15. Grebenyuk, E.A.: Monitoring and identification of structural shifts in processes with a unit root. In: Proceedings of the 13th International Conference (MLSD), Moscow. IEEE (2020). https://ieeexplore.ieee.org/document/9247829
16. Nikiforov, I.V.: A simple recursive algorithm for diagnosis of abrupt changes in random signals. IEEE Trans. Inf. Theory **46**(7), 2740–2746 (2000)
17. Tang, L., Dai, W., Yu, L.: A novel CEEMD-based EELM ensemble learning paradigm for crude oil price forecasting. Int. J. Inf. Technol. Decis. Mak. **14**, 141–169 (2015)

The Future of Lean Thinking
and Practice

More Checks for Less Waste in the Lamination Process of a Shipbuilding Company Pursuing Lean Thinking

Inês Freitas[1], Isabelle Leão[1], João Eduardo Marinho[1], Leonor Pacheco[1],
Margarida Gonçalves[1], Maria João Castro[1], Pedro Duarte Silva[1], Rafael Moreira[1],
and Anabela C. Alves[2(✉)] (iD)

[1] University of Minho, Campus de Azurém, Guimarães, Portugal
[2] Centro ALGORITMI, University of Minho, Guimarães, Portugal
anabela@dps.uminho.pt

Abstract. Lean Thinking is a management philosophy that aims to do more with less through a process of continuous improvement. By employing Lean Thinking principles, the project presented in this article aimed to obtain improvements in the boats' hulls and decks lamination process of a shipbuilding company. After analysing the current process, some problems were identified. To solve these problems, suggestions were developed, such as the use of checklists, the introduction of quality checkpoints along the production line and a VBA tool for the correct management of the dies. Through the implementation of the suggested proposals, it was expected a decrease in the number of defects and a reduction of the bottleneck cycle time from 90 to 20 min. Interesting findings of this project were that the improvements implied more quality checkpoints in the process, what seems contradictory as checkpoints are considered as non-value activities. This was a remarkable lesson learned by the team of Industrial Engineering and Management students that developed this project in the context of Project-Based Learning active methodology.

Keywords: Lean Thinking · Shipbuilding industry · Project-Based Learning · Industry-University partnership

1 Introduction

In an increasingly technological world, the competitive capacity in the business environment is one of the differentiating factors between the success and failure of the business. Thus, companies increasingly pursue new approaches to change the management paradigm by changing the usual cost-based thinking to a speed-based strategy.

Lean Thinking seeks to reduce waste, especially the time of activities that do not add value to the process from the point of view of the client [1]. This goal can be achieved by reducing the 3M's: *muda*, *mura* and *muri*. This reduction in 3M's, however, considers crucial aspects in the industry, such as the possibility of producing customized products

A. Dolgui et al. (Eds.): APMS 2021, IFIP AICT 630, pp. 635–644, 2021.
https://doi.org/10.1007/978-3-030-85874-2_69

responding to customer needs. In the context of the non-value-added activities, it is important to distinguish two types: the ones that are pure waste as waiting and the ones that do not add value to the product but are necessary attending to the current situation of the process, as quality inspection [2]. For such identification and wastes reduction, many tools could be used such as value stream mapping (VSM), visual management, standard work, *jidoka* or *autonomation*, checklists, among others [3].

The project presented in this paper aimed to improve the lamination process of a production line in a shipbuilding company, through the implementation of Lean Thinking principles. This project was developed in a company from September 2020 to January 2021 by a team of eight Industrial Engineering and Management (IEM) students in a context of Project-Based Learning (PBL) active learning methodology. This methodology was used in a course named Integrated Project of Industrial Engineering and Management II (IPIEMII). The IPIEMII was supported by five courses: Production Systems Organization II, Simulation, Ergonomics Workplace Analysis, Integrated Production Management and Production Information Systems [4]. The team was supervised by a tutor. The company under study is a leader of the production of the leisure vessels market.

This paper is structured in six sections. After a brief introduction, where the objective of this study is introduced, it is described the methodology followed in the second section. The third section is related to the company's presentation, followed by the analysis of the current situation. The proposed improvements are presented in the fourth section and the expected results in the fifth section. Finally, the lessons learned are described in the sixth section.

2   Research Methodology

As referred to in the introduction, this research was developed by a team of eight IEM students in the context of PBL active methodology. After a first meeting with the company, the visits plan, and the sector to analyse were defined. All visits included *Gemba* walks, observation and informal interviews with all stakeholders [2]. For team communication and document repository sharing between members, professors, and company representatives, many tools were used, including video-conferencing tools due to the pandemic situation that ravages the world since 2020, March [5]. This had an impact on the team organization and in the visits to the company, as fewer team members were allowed to visit the company.

In order to follow a structured approach, the team used the phases of the Action-Research methodology: 1) Diagnose, 2) Plan alternatives actions, 3) Implement the action selected, 4) Discuss and analyse the results and 5) Specify the lessons learned [6]. Given the limited time and the availability of the company, the implementation phase was not fulfilled and, therefore, the results were estimated.

In the first phase of diagnosis, the current state of the lamination process was analysed, and the existing problems were identified with VSM to obtain an overview of the process. The company's quality reports were also used to understand the most frequent type of defects throughout the production process. In the second phase, an improvement plan was drawn up to overcome the difficulties and problems identified in the previous phase. To achieve this, Circular and Pareto charts were used and analysed. Other visual production tools, checklists and computing tools, such as Visual Basic for Applications (VBA) were also used. Changes to the production line were suggested, such as the introduction of new quality control points. In the lessons learned phase, the expected results and the main conclusions were identified, and new challenges were indicated to the company.

3 Company Presentation, Description, and Critical Analysis of the Current Situation

The company was created in 1845 and evolved until later becoming a world-renowned company. It is a leader in recreational boats, engines, accessories, and other marine vessel components. The company currently operates in 24 countries and its products are sold in more than 170 markets around the world. The Portugal-based company is currently dedicated to the manufacture of rigid vessels in fiberglass, which requires the successive application of fiber and resin.

The Portugal-based company currently has about 500 employees, producing a total of 30 different boat models with a daily production capacity of 10 boats. The production lines are supported by sections such as carpentry, small parts, and pre-assembly, which produce the necessary components for the main production process. It begins in the Lamination section and ends in the Assembly, followed by a quality inspection, packaging and dispatch. This company usually works in a make-to-order strategy producing by demand. The pandemic situation had a positive impact in the company demand since it increased due to the travel restrictions that expanded the boat market.

3.1 Description of the Lamination Process

Lamination is the production process of the boat's hull and deck, through the successive application of layers of fiberglass and resin, to increase its mechanical resistance. This process is performed in a section with the same name, i.e., Lamination section, and it is divided into two production lines: 1) for the hull (bottom of the boat) and 2) for the deck (top of the boat). All the supply to the lines come from the support sections (carpentry and small parts) and it is carried out using only one cart for each, which is left in one of the stations and then follows its hull or deck.

The process begins with the Dies Preparation, through its cleaning and application of wax. It continues with the Gelcoat Application (paint layer applied in the painting booths). These operations are common to both parts, with a painting booth for the hulls and another for the decks. After painting, the process is divided into the two lines mentioned above.

The line of the decks has the following workstations: P1 - Skin, P2 and P3 - Stiffen and P4 - Structures. As the deck line, the hull line begins with the Skin process, but in this case at P5 workstation. This is followed by the P6 workstation - Lams, P7 - Foams/Stringers and P8 - Foam lamination and Wood installation.

Later, after the end of its respective line, each part is transported to the demould zone (Pop-Up), where there is only one line. The parts then proceed to the Cutting Booth. After the cutting operation, the parts proceed to a Quality Control station, where, if there are any defects, these are to be repaired in the Repair station localized in the Lamination section and then proceed to the next production process.

3.2 Identified Problems and Wastes

A VSM was developed to represent the production of the hull and deck since its operations differ slightly. It should be noted that all the data and values used were provided by the company. For both VSMs, the system's cycle time (CT) was 90 min. The takt time (TT) was 96 min, fulfilling the requirement that CT ≤ TT.

For both hull and deck's activities, the percentage of added-value activities was significantly low, being 28% and 34%, respectively. An activity that represented, in a negative way, a great weight in these values was the activity performed in the Repair station (the last station of the process). This activity had a high number of operators (47 in a total of two shifts) and did not add value to the final product. Nevertheless, it represented a waste, and it was one of the main causes for the CT to be very close to the TT since it was the bottleneck of the system.

The VSM also proved to be a useful tool for determining the throughput time. Throughput time is the time that a hull or deck takes to go through the lamination process, corresponding to 700 min (≈12 h) and 795 min (≈13 h).

The High Number of Defects. Due to the results of the VSM, it was decided to analyse the defects caused throughout the process, the areas where they were most significant and the operations that originated them. Through the analysis of audits and quality reports carried out by the company, it was identified in which station the defects usually appear. Unequivocally, it was concluded that most of these were located in the Repair station. Through several graphs, provided by the company, presented in Fig. 1 (period of 6 months), it was possible to verify that the Repair station had an average of 120 defects per unit (DPUs), a value much higher than the other sections.

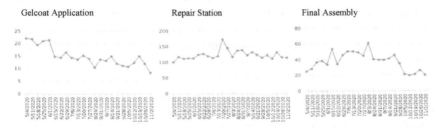

Fig. 1. Number of defects per unit found at different stations.

It was decided to examine more accurately the defects found at the Repair station. As it was determined, there were several possible sources of defects, and the one that stood out with the highest number was the dies (Fig. 2), which had an average of 20 DPUs. According to these data, particular attention was given to the dies as a source of defects. It was found that some of the most frequent and severe defects, originated due to the dies problems, with the appearance, in parts, of ledges, scratches and dull areas or stains.

Thereafter, it was found that the appearance of defects arising from the die was directly related to the non-compliance with the maintenance of the die at the due time. The lifetime of the dies was about 20 uses, and after this, they should go through a process of maintenance, which takes three days.

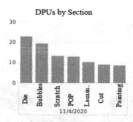

Fig. 2. Daily analysis illustrating the number of defects per unit originated by different sources of defects.

The company counted the number of uses of each die manually and, thus, the number of uses of the die was not considered in the production planning. As a result, dies were used as often as planned productions (although this means that the 20 recommended uses were exceeded), and a stop period was not planned for their maintenance at the correct time.

It is important to highlight that in the company there was no system for the identification of components. This contributed to the possible appearance of defects. These were related to the wood components with similar geometries and sizes. Consequently, it caused the risk of the wrong installation in the hull and deck since operators had difficulties in distinguishing the components from each other.

Checkpoints Scarcity Along the Line. The high number of defects was also due to the lack of control points along the line of the lamination process. All defects were only detected in the Quality Control Repair station, as already mentioned. In addition, it was missing the application of tools available for this purpose in the workstations.

4 Improvement Proposals

4.1 Boat Division in Quadrants, Colour Code and Components Coding

Considering the situation of a single supply cart to the lines, it was decided to modify the supply of components to them. This way the components would be delivered to the workstation where they must be. Each station had a significant variability of components, so, to facilitate the work of the operators, a division of the boat into quadrants was proposed, assigning a colour to each one by creating a colour code (see Fig. 3), i.e., using visual management. This way, the supply to each workstation would be performed through coloured boxes, each representing the quadrant where its contents would be applied. The division in quadrants was carried out considering the technical drawings of the hull and the deck, to make clear the need for components in each part of the boat and to make a more equitable division.

To circumvent the lack of identification of the components, it was suggested to assign a code to each component. This code should be printed on each component using the existing CNC. It should be noted that it would also be beneficial to include in its codification the quadrant where the component will be installed.

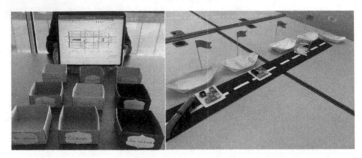

Fig. 3. Physical representation of the hull and deck division in nine quadrants and colour code (left) and its use in the production line (right). (Color figure online)

Demonstrating this physical representation to the company's production director, he referred that it had been something he desired for a long time. By having this physical representation in a visual format, he was more motivated to present it to his team in order to get more support to implement the idea.

4.2 Implementation of Checklists

Regarding the large number of defects in the vessel components, resulting from the non-use of the thickness gauges of the Chop layers (fiberglass + resin), it was suggested to implement checklists. Thus, with the inclusion of measurement tools used in a possible lamination process' checklist, not only its use would be guaranteed, but also many of the defects would be avoided promptly. This was due to the fact that the main benefits of this tool are the reduction of variability and/or irregularity (*mura*) and the prevention of recurrent errors.

4.3 Introduction of Checkpoints Along the Line

Since there was only one checkpoint at the end of the lamination process, the team proposed the inclusion of control and repair points throughout the production line to reduce the high number of defects, the reparation time and the number of employees required in the Repair station.

In the past, it was normal to have assembly lines with a final checkpoint in the end of it. Nevertheless, Toyota Production System (TPS) revealed the need to have mechanisms along the process to stop the line when something goes wrong [7]. This is the main objective of one of the most important pillars of TPS, i.e. Jidoka or *autonomation*. Having more checkpoints seem contradictory to the key idea of "doing more with less" that was the motte for the Lean Production designation to TPS [8]. However, having them will avoid having more defects and lost time in reparations and rework and, even, lost material by sending the unrepaired product to scrap.

Since most of the errors that occurred in the first stages of the process were solely corrected at the end of the line, with the implementation of a checkpoint in each workstation, it would be possible to do each repair in less time, since it would not be necessary to redo all the work that had been done. With this measure, it would also be possible to change the Repair station, turning it into just another control point for the cutting operation.

4.4 Dies Maintenance Guarantee

Related to the appearance of a high number of defects in the hulls and decks, it was developed a VBA code for the correct management of the dies. Thus, a spreadsheet tool was developed that is represented in Fig. 4. This spreadsheet allowed the validation of a production sequence introduced by the user, considering the limit of 20 successive uses for each die. In this way, it was also considered the required maintenance period of three days, as well as the current number of uses of each of them.

Day	Model	Production Line
39	T59	B
39	555OP	A
39	675OP	A
39	T53	B
39	605OP	A
39	555CAB	A
39	675PH	C
39	605BR	B
39	505CAB	A
39	D65	B
40	675SD	A
40	675WE	C
40	D59	B
40	875SD	D
40	S45	A
40	605PH	C
40	675OP	A
40	555OP	A
40	T59	B
40	555OP	B
41	T53	B
41	605OP	A

(Validate Production Sequence; Clean Sheet)

Boat	Die 1 Number of Uses	Die 1 Number of Maintenances	Die 2 Number of Uses	Die 2 Number of Maintenances	Die 3 Number of Uses	Die 3 Number of Maintenances	Die 4 Number of Uses	Die 4 Number of Maintenances
D59 / 559 / T59 / 605BR / 605OP	20	1	20	1	20	1	20	1
S65 / D65 / T65 / 675BR / 675CR	24	1	20	1	20	1		
505OP / 505CAB	20	1	20	1	15	0	1	
555OP / 555CAB	24	1	20	1	20	1	20	1
605OP / 605SO	20	1	20	1	9	0	1	0
675OP / 675SO	20	0	21	0	1	0	1	0
553 / T93 / 555BR	40	2	20	1	20	1		
455CAB	1	0	1	0				
455OP	12	0	1	0				
605PH	20	1	4	0				
675WE / C70	20	1	16	0				
755OP / 755SD	20	1	5	0				
18EL	11	0	1	0				
18EL	20	1	1	0				
675PH	16	0						
805SD	6	0						
875SO	20	1						
705PH	4	0						
755CR	1	0						
625PH	1	0						
D70	1	0						

Fig. 4. Excel excerpt of VBA code for the correct management of the dies.

Regarding the limitations of this program, the user needs to re-enter all the data and run the program again if any changes arise within the production sequence entered, which is not desirable. These changes might resulted from adjustments caused, for example, by production delays or delays in the maintenance period of the dies. Additionally, the time from which it was necessary to replace the dies, since it was no longer possible to perform further maintenance, was not considered.

5   Expected Results and Impact of the Proposals

5.1   Results

Easier Identification of Components, Fewer Defects and Less Time. The   division of the boat, and, consequently, the hulls and decks as well as the adoption of a colour code, would allow an easier differentiation and identification of the different components. Also, it would facilitate the work, reducing the search time by the operators. Another advantage would be the possibility for each operator, per station, to take the box destined to the area of the boat where he is working.

In addition, the division into quadrants and the fact that the components contain their code (including the quadrant where they will be installed) previously printed by the CNC, would also allow to increase the accuracy of the place destined for each component. This is an extra aid, both to the employees of carpentry when dividing the components by the different boxes, and to the workers of the Lamination section in the identification of the exact location of the boat where each one must be installed. Thus, the hulls and decks' defects number of components would decrease. In consequence, it would be required less time and tools for the rework related to these defects.

Reduction of Variability and Error Prevention. The implementation of checklists in the different stations of the lamination process could guarantee the use of the tools for measuring the thickness of the layers of fiberglass and resin by the operators, ensuring that they had the ideal thickness. In this way, it would be possible to avoid promptly many of the defects caused by the irregularity between layers. The checklist should be reviewed with some frequency in order to identify future improvements.

Fewer Defects and Repair Time. The inclusion of control and repair points along the different workstations in the production process would allow defects to be repaired immediately after the execution of the operation that originated them. Thus, the Repair station, which was the bottleneck of the Lamination section, would be no longer the only control point of the process. In this way, the time previously spent for rework at this station would be reduced considerably. Furthermore, it would not be necessary to redo the work of all workstations following the one where the defect occurred, as was the case.

The implementation of a checkpoint at each workstation involved adding a few minutes to the time of each operation. However, as already mentioned, the time of the last inspection would be substantially reduced, and the Repair station could be changed, becoming just another control point. In this case, it would correspond to the control point of the Cutting Operation, and it would also be used for a final review of the entire hull or deck.

The number of operators required for intermediate inspections, would not undergo major changes. Due to the unevenness between the cycle times of each workstation, the "dead time" could be used to carry them out, so it would only be necessary to train the employees. The number of workers required for the final inspection would be reduced by 75%, as it would suffer a decrease in time and difficulty.

Reduce the Appearance of Die Problems. Ensuring that dies were maintained before or at 20 consecutive uses and that they complied with the stipulated duration of three days, it would be possible to reduce substantially the appearance of die problems. In addition, it would be important to consider this situation when planning the production schedule. In this way, the various defects that arise from their poor state of conservation would also decrease.

Since dies flaws were the main source of defects in the hull and deck, this solution would have a notorious impact on reducing the defects number. Consequently, all the problems that came from this, namely the number, time and operators destined for the Repair station, which was a non-added value activity, would also be reduced.

5.2 Impact

The improvement proposals' impact was estimated based on the experience and knowledge of the company managers and operators. Regarding the division of the boat into quadrants, creation of the colour code and coding of the components, it was estimated that the CT of this station would decrease in about 10 min due to the easier task to collect components out of boxes and identify their position in their hull or deck.

Furthermore, the suggestion to create checkpoints after the execution of each activity would have an impact on the CT of the remaining activities increasing them in about five minutes. It should be noted that "dead times", when necessary and if possible, would also be used to include the new inspections.

Concerning the Repair station, the number of operators would reduce about 75% and the time required for its execution would be about 20 min. Nonetheless, the last quality inspection must be done to control the components that came out of the Cutting Booth. This quality inspection also must ensure that the defects originated by the previous tasks were corrected and fully identified and eliminated. The creation of checklists for the use of measurement tools and the guarantee of maintenance of dies at the correct time would reduce the number of defects. This would have an impact on the estimated times. With this awareness and attending to the Industry 4.0 technologies, such checkpoints should be integrated in the lamination process as making part as a more integrated project that promote modern *Jidoka* systems [9].

Regarding the hull production, the system's CT would decrease from 90 to 55 min, creating a higher difference for TT. This means that the Repair station would no longer be the bottleneck of the system. The uptime of the different activities would also increase, as would the percentage of activities that add value (from 28% to 30%). The value stream of the decks would also suffer similar changes, regarding the uptime of some activities, which would be higher, and the percentage of activities that add value, which would also be increased (from 34% to 36%).

Finally, it was possible to verify that the throughput time would decrease from, approximately, 12 to 11 h in the hulls case, and from, approximately, 13 to 12 h in the decks case, representing a significant improvement in comparison to the initial situation.

6 Conclusion

This paper reports a project that was developed in the context of the PBL developed in the course IPIEMII by a team of students in a shipbuilding company. Lean Thinking principles and tools were implemented to improve the manufacturing sector of two critical components of the final product – hulls and decks, through the reduction of *muda*. The main waste identified was the high number of defects, whose reparation required a considerable amount of time and manpower. To reduce this number and, consequently, the repair time and workers need, it was proposed, among others, more checkpoints along the line. This could be seen as contradictory to Lean philosophy.

The expected benefits of implementing the mentioned proposals were estimated and discussed with the company. The expected success will depend on the company's need to continue pursuing the goal of zero defects, focusing on the reduction of *muda*. In addition, it was necessary to consider the aspects related to *muri* and *mura,* so that the quality of the product and the performance of the production process were even more valued.

For the company, it was a beneficial experience as the company was not aware of Lean Thinking principles and its potential to improve processes. This project was the beginning of a Lean journey in the company, that started by recognizing the value and wastes concept and applying basic Lean tools to achieve good results. For the students, learning by doing was a rich experience and an opportunity to apply the course contents immediately after or, even, before the classes. As future work, it was advised to the company to implement the proposals not yet implemented and the integration of a Smart Manufacturing System.

Acknowledgments. This work has been supported by FCT – Fundação para a Ciência e Tecnologia within the R&D Units Project Scope: UIDB/00319/2020.

References

1. Womack, J.P., Jones, D.T.: Lean Thinking: Banish Waste and Create Wealth in Your Corporation. Free Press, New York (1996)
2. Liker, J.K.: The Toyota Way: 14 Management Principles from the World's Greatest Manufacturer. McGraw-Hill, New York (2004)
3. Feld, W.M.: Lean Manufacturing: Tools, Techniques, and How to Use Them. Vasa. St. Lucie Press, Boca Raton (2001)
4. Lima, R.M., Dinis-Carvalho, J., Campos, L.C., Mesquita, D., Sousa, R.M., Alves, A.: Projects with the industry for the development of professional competences in industrial engineering and management. In: Proceedings of Project Approaches in Engineering Education (PAEE2014), Medellin, Colombia (2014)
5. WHO: Coronavirus disease 2019 (COVID-19). Situation Report 51
6. Susman, G., Evered, R.D.: An assessment of the scientific merits of action research. Adm. Sci. Q. **23**(4), 582–603 (1978). https://doi.org/10.2307/239258
7. Ohno, T.: Toyota Production System: Beyond Large-Scale Production. Productivity Press, New York (1988)
8. Womack, J., Jones, D.T., Roos, D.: The Machine That Changed the World: The Story of Lean Production. Rawson Associates, New York (1990)
9. Romero, D., Gaiardelli, P., Powell, D., Wuest, T., Thürer, M.: Rethinking jidoka systems under automation & learning perspectives in the digital lean manufacturing world. IFAC-PapersOnLine **52**(13), 899–903 (2019). https://doi.org/10.1016/j.ifacol.2019.11.309

Implementation of 5S+S for Knowledge Work in Engineering Projects

Daria Larsson[1,2(✉)] and R. M. Chandima Ratnayake[1]

[1] University of Stavanger, 4036 Stavanger, Norway
daria.larsson@blueday.no, chandima.ratnayake@uis.no
[2] Blueday Technology AS, Sandnes, Norway

Abstract. The purpose of this manuscript is to propose a framework for implementing 5S+S in engineering-to-order (ETO) projects with a focus on knowledge work. The application of this framework helps to improve overall performance in companies providing knowledge work. The methodology allows transparency and control over projects in day-to-day management, through the implementation of digital tools such as visual management, 5S+S online audits, key performance indicators (KPI), dashboards, etc. This paper presents the implementation of lean management concepts in customer-specific tailor-made engineering projects, which has not been sufficiently addressed in the existing literature. The methodology used in this paper is based on the application by researchers of lean concepts in a combination of three different disciplines, namely, lean project planning and control (LPPC), lean quality management system (LQMS) and Lean Design. First, attempts at knowledge work improvement through lean are presented, based on the existing literature. Second, all three approaches: LPPC, LQMS and Lean Design are explained. Third, the possibility of combining all three concepts into one framework is discussed. The use of 5S+S in knowledge work is demonstrated, and a framework is developed, based on a DMAIC (Define, Measure, Analyze, Improve, and Control) approach. The use of the framework is presented by means of an illustrative case in a small and medium size enterprise (SME) providing engineering services. The suggested methodology is applicable for engineering services-providing companies seeking overall project performance improvement. The findings are useful for project managers and engineering discipline leaders who aim to implement lean thinking in engineering projects.

Keywords: Lean · 5S+S · Knowledge work

1 Introduction

To compete with international corporations, it is important for small and medium-sized enterprises (SMEs) delivering engineering solutions to focus on improving efficiency [1]. In times of highly competitive markets, it is critical that SMEs deliver high-value products at the lowest possible operating cost. This is specifically relevant for project-based organizations delivering highly customized engineering-to-order (ETO) projects

© IFIP International Federation for Information Processing 2021
Published by Springer Nature Switzerland AG 2021
A. Dolgui et al. (Eds.): APMS 2021, IFIP AICT 630, pp. 645–655, 2021.
https://doi.org/10.1007/978-3-030-85874-2_70

[2], often experiencing project delays, budget overruns and quality defects [2]. Knowledge workers play an important role in engineering companies, as their specific skills, knowledge and creativity are the source of innovation in the workplace [3, 4]. The importance of improving knowledge work productivity has been discussed by many authors [3–5]. Lean tools and methods are a potential approach to improve the challenge of the low productivity of knowledge workers [6]. In order to support SMEs providing ETO projects, lean philosophy offers a 5S+S concept (sort, set in order, shine, safety, standardize, sustain). 5S+S principles aim to reduce inefficiencies in businesses, by identifying irregularities, eliminating performance waste, and introducing continuous standardization [7].

The number of studies related to implementing the lean concept in knowledge work has increased in recent years [8, 9]. However, there is a gap in the literature regarding detailed and consistent implementation of 5S+S in relation to knowledge work companies. Some of the lean tools are applied only in single case studies; thus, their relevancy is arguable, and more evidence is needed to prove their applicability in knowledge work [10]. The lack of clear standards and uniformity in lean methodologies' application to the knowledge-based workforce is acknowledged [10, 11]. It is from this perspective that the 5S+S framework and guidance for knowledge-providing organizations was developed and is presented in this paper. The framework, with a base concept built on 5S+S, was developed through a combination of three disciplines: lean project planning and control (LPPC), lean quality management system (LQMS) and Lean Design. The possibility of combining all three concepts into one framework offers the opportunity to develop a complete lean solution with the potential to improve overall performance in custom-specific engineering projects.

This paper is organized as follows. Section 2 introduces the literature review related to the application of lean in knowledge work, with a focus on 5S+S. Section 3 provides an overview of the methodology for developing this paper. Then, Sect. 4 provides a description of three concepts, which are included in the final framework: LPPC, LQMS and Lean Design. Section 5 describes the results of the case study carried out in Blueday Technology AS (BDT), where the main challenge is to improve the performance of engineering projects suffering from low project margins and exceeded engineering hours. In Sect. 6 the 5S+S framework is presented. Finally, Sect. 7 offers a discussion and conclusions, as well as introducing future research areas.

2   Background

2.1   Lean in Knowledge Work

Lean Approach in Knowledge Industries. In recent years, the productivity improvement of knowledge workers has been a major challenge discussed by authors in [8, 9, 12]. Understanding the mechanism that affects the productivity of white-collar workers is highly important, as it can contribute to the entire organization. A variety of industries, in which knowledge workers play a vital role, have successfully implemented tools and methodologies with a foundation in lean philosophy, e.g., software engineering [13–15], healthcare [7], aerospace and defense [16], and construction [17–19]. In software engineering and healthcare, lean has been applied through the reduction of waste and waiting time [13, 15], contributing to improved flow and better process efficiency [7]. The reduction in waste was also a major part of changes in the construction sector, where complexity and uncertainty were minimized, while inconsistency in documentation was reduced [19]. An emphasis on transparency [16], customer requirements [19], collective commitment and a common knowledge base [16] are indicated in the literature as examples of key factors impacting value in case study organizations. However, adaptation to lean thinking and understanding the concept of waste itself seem to be the most challenging tasks during transformation into lean [7, 16]. Studies indicate that two thirds of lean implementation programs in North America fail, due to the inability of companies to achieve cultural change such as encouraging workers to adopt new behaviors or the continuous improvement of daily practices [20].

5S+S in Knowledge Work. The purpose of the 5S+S tool is to implement within the organization all aspects of the 5S traditional lean concept (sort, set in order, shine, standardize, sustain), with an additional focus on safety in the working area [21]. The studied cases have revealed that poorly implemented 5S undermines the safety factor [22]; therefore, an additional principle has been integrated into the 5S+S concept. So far, 5S+S has only been identified by authors as a successful lean application in manufacturing companies [23, 24]. There is an unexplored area of 5S+S in knowledge work organizations which should be investigated.

The literature has indicated a variety of approaches when it comes to lean philosophy in knowledge work [7, 13–19]. It can be observed that organizations focus on specific lean tools [13, 15, 16] and achieve effects in particular functional areas [7, 19] such as administration, manufacturing, purchase. The main challenge in studies seeking ways to improve knowledge work performance is the difficulty in defining the structure of knowledge work [10, 12], as knowledge workers are involved in many and various activities. Authors also state that, in order for the knowledge providing organization to succeed, knowledge workers must work together in collaborative ways [5, 10]. Therefore, this paper proposes a complex knowledge work and 5S+S oriented framework, which could guide several functioning areas of the organization to improve project performance.

3 Methodology

The research methodology presented in Fig. 1 is a combination of action research and case study-based research. The case study research was conducted based on the collection of information from a company's internal systems, in order to verify what could possibly impact project performance. The information retrieved was related to project finances, engineering hours, reported project non-conformances, project documentation, etc. The data has been analyzed and the results presented. Simultaneously, the literature overview was conducted, focusing on existing lean tools such as 5S+S and methodologies contributing to the improvement of engineering design routines, project execution and quality management systems. The relevant literature was studied to formulate a new approach to be carried out in a case study. DMAIC (Define, Measure, Analyze, Improve, and Control) methodology was used to develop a framework to be implemented in the organization.

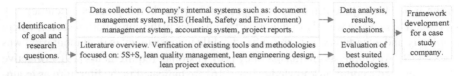

Fig. 1. Research methodology.

4 Literature Overview

4.1 Lean Project Planning and Control (LPPC)

LPPC is a response to poorly planned and controlled ETO projects, caused by lack of routines, few staff members included in planning, poor monitoring, or no response to delays [2]. The model (Fig. 2) was tested by several ETO manufacturing companies delivering advanced equipment to the oil and gas industry.

Planning	Flexibility	Updates as often as required – all levels of activities.
	Integrity	One integrated plan for all project disciplines.
	Commitment	All project disciplines commit to one common project plan.
	Participation	Regular planning meetings with formal agenda, formal reporting.
Project dedication		All project disciplines report in a standardized report.
Planning dedication		Physical progress reported by all disciplines on a standardized form (percent plan complete).
Replanning		Delayed activities are replanned (root cause analysis, discussion with the project team).
Impact awareness		Decisions taken by considering the optimization of the project processes.
Learning ability		Between all the employees and the external project partners.

Fig. 2. Lean project planning and control adapted from [2].

4.2 Lean Quality Management System (LQMS)

Lean Quality Management System (LQMS) is a comprehensive approach, combining ISO (International Organization for Standardization) standards (Quality Management System) and key concepts of lean management [25]. ISO standards and lean are intended to improve organizations' production processes, but when those two concepts are not aligned, it can lead to a waste of resources [26]. The proposed framework (Fig. 3) enables organizations to both develop the minimum amount of documentation required to demonstrate an effective QMS and help to organize and control internal processes.

The methodology includes several QMS templates, e.g., the lean SIPOC card (acronym of Supplier, Inputs, Processes, Outputs, Customer), which improves process mapping by adding system measures and process targets, as presented in Table 1 [25].

4.3 Lean Design

Lean Design is a concept developed to support engineering design through the use of tools such as pull scheduling, design structure matrix or shared geometry, in order to

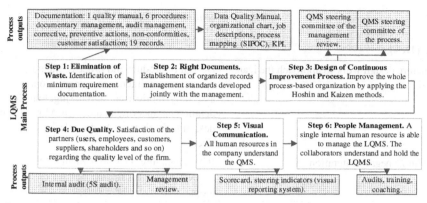

Fig. 3. Lean Quality Management System (LQMS), six-step implementation model adapted from [25].

Table 1. SIPOC card example, Lean Quality Management System (LQMS) adapted from [25].

SIPOC		
Owner	*Processes*	*Target*
Project manager	Design of assembly drawings	Drawings according to company's standard template
Input	*Output*	
Mechanical engineer	Design completed	Focus on customer's expectation
Supplier	*System Measures*	*Customer*
Engineering	Time, quality	Warehouse

improve information flow, reduce negative iterations and involve all team members in all decision-making processes in the design phase [17]. The basic concept of Lean Design is illustrated in Table 2.

Table 2. Lean Design Model adapted from [17].

Lean Design	
Cross-functional teams	Involve downstream players in upstream decisions
Set-based strategy	Create and exploit opportunities to increase value in every project phase. Select from alternatives at the last responsible moment. Share incomplete information. Share ranges of acceptable solutions

(continued)

Table 2. (*continued*)

Lean Design	
Structure design work to approach the lean ideal	Design of product and process. Include operations, maintenance, commissioning, assembly, fabrication, purchasing, logistics, detailed engineering and design. Move detailed design to fabricators. Reduce design package sizes
Minimize negative iteration	Pull scheduling. Design Structure Matrix (DSM). Strategies for managing irreducible loops
Last Planner System in production control	Try to make only quality assignments. Make work ready within a lookahead period. Measure PPC (Percent Planned Complete). Identify and act on reasons for plan failure
Technologies	Shared geometry: single model. Web-based interface

5   Case Study Company

A case study was carried out in Blueday Technology AS (BDT). The company is a project-based organization handling ETO projects. BDT is a medium-sized enterprise, executing electrical engineering projects such as hybridization of ships or shore power installations. BDT provides knowledge work, service, and manufacturing. The case study scope aims to identify the reasons behind low project margins. Based on observation and collected information, it can be stated that employees are well educated, experienced, intelligent, highly motivated, and capable people. The company has approximately 35 employees, with the yearly employee turnover rate varying between 3.3% and 8.3%, at an average of 3.9%. Nineteen projects executed between February 2017 and September 2020 were included in the project portfolio investigation (excluding feed studies). It has been concluded that the company is providing services to five industry sectors: shore power, defense, marine, offshore, and aquaculture. The analyzed information revealed that planned spending for the majority of projects was significantly higher than the originally estimated budget. Of 19 analyzed projects, 13 exceeded the planned budget (Fig. 4a, b) and 14 exceeded the planned engineering hours (Fig. 4b, d). Comparisons in Fig. 4 refer to marine and shore power groups, as the majority of projects executed in the company in the investigated time period belonged to the marine and shore power sectors. There is a visible pattern, suggesting that exceeded engineering hours drastically affect the project budget.

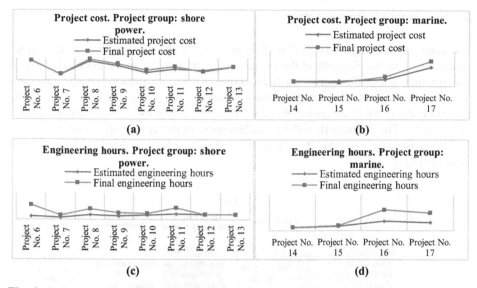

Fig. 4. Estimated project cost vs. final project cost for projects in (**a**) shore power group, (**b**) marine group. Estimated engineering hours vs. final engineering hours for projects in (**c**) shore power group, (**d**) marine group.

Analysis of several project plans indicated poor planning of engineering and pre-engineering phases, reflected in missing phase details, such as design steps, process sequences, design milestones, master design documents, etc. Moreover, some projects' plans did not include the engineering phase at all. Additional information retrieved from the company's internal systems showed issues related to the quality of several products and low customer satisfaction related to delivery time. The discovered data was confirmed by a value stream mapping (VSM) performed as part of the case study. Future improvement actions in the company shall be focused on the following areas: engineering design, project planning, and product quality control.

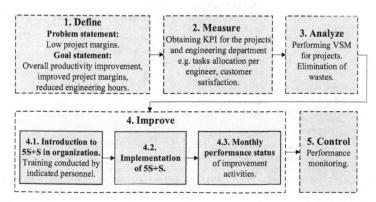

Fig. 5. Methodology and guideline for implementing 5S+S in the case study company.

6   Framework Presentation

The main goal is to improve overall performance in the organization, through the implementation of all the elements of the framework, with a focus on the popularization of lean routines in the office space, waste reduction in daily practices in projects, and continuous improvement. The implementation of the framework will be introduced to the case study company in the spring of 2021. The case study is estimated to continue until spring 2023. The framework will be implemented in the case study company by the following five phases of DMAIC methodology: Define, Measure, Analyze, Improve and Control (Fig. 5).

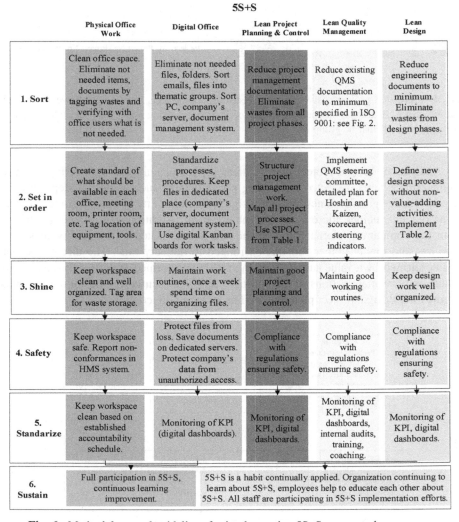

5S+S

	Physical Office Work	Digital Office	Lean Project Planning & Control	Lean Quality Management	Lean Design
1. Sort	Clean office space. Eliminate not needed items, documents by tagging wastes and verifying with office users what is not needed.	Eliminate not needed files, folders. Sort emails, files into thematic groups. Sort PC, company's server, document management system.	Reduce project management documentation. Eliminate wastes from all project phases.	Reduce existing QMS documentation to minimum specified in ISO 9001: see Fig. 2.	Reduce engineering documents to minimum. Eliminate wastes from design phases.
2. Set in order	Create standard of what should be available in each office, meeting room, printer room, etc. Tag location of equipment, tools.	Standardize processes, procedures. Keep files in dedicated place (company's server, document management system). Use digital Kanban boards for work tasks.	Structure project management work. Map all project processes. Use SIPOC from Table 1.	Implement QMS steering committee, detailed plan for Hoshin and Kaizen, scorecard, steering indicators.	Define new design process without non-value-adding activities. Implement Table 2.
3. Shine	Keep workspace clean and well organized. Tag area for waste storage.	Maintain work routines, once a week spend time on organizing files.	Maintain good project planning and control.	Maintain good working routines.	Keep design work well organized.
4. Safety	Keep workspace safe. Report non-conformances in HMS system.	Protect files from loss. Save documents on dedicated servers. Protect company's data from unauthorized access.	Compliance with regulations ensuring safety.	Compliance with regulations ensuring safety.	Compliance with regulations ensuring safety.
5. Standarize	Keep workspace clean based on established accountability schedule.	Monitoring of KPI (digital dashboards).	Monitoring of KPI, digital dashboards.	Monitoring of KPI, digital dashboards, internal audits, training, coaching.	Monitoring of KPI, digital dashboards.
6. Sustain	Full participation in 5S+S, continuous learning improvement.	5S+S is a habit continually applied. Organization continuing to learn about 5S+S, employees help to educate each other about 5S+S. All staff are participating in 5S+S implementation efforts.			

Fig. 6. Methodology and guidelines for implementing 5S+S – case study company.

Figure 6 presents the framework and guidelines for implementing 5S+S in the case study company. The framework is divided into five main sections representing areas for future improvement: physical office work, digital office, lean project planning and control, lean quality management, and lean design. Planned improvements are sequenced into six steps according to 5S+S methodology: 1. Sort (cleaning, elimination of wastes), 2. Set in order (structuring and standardizing), 3. Shine (maintaining established routines), 4. Safety (ensuring safety in the work environment), 5. Standardize (standardization and monitoring of key performance indicators (KPIs)), 6. Sustain (continuous improvement and learning). The implementation of 5S+S shall be performed simultaneously for all five improvement areas, with an introduction to 5S+S being presented to the knowledge workers before the framework is implemented, as the implementation of lean should focus on the philosophical level before any tools and methods are applied [10].

7 Conclusions

This paper proposes a framework and guidance to improve overall performance in engineering-to-order (ETO) projects, with a focus on knowledge work and the 5S+S concept. In order to develop a 5S+S framework, lean approaches to knowledge work were studied. The literature refers to several attempts to implement the lean philosophy in different knowledge work related industries, such as software, healthcare, aerospace and defense, and construction. Several authors observed that the application of the lean concept to knowledge work is challenging for various reasons, e.g., difficulties in achieving cultural change and in encouraging workers to adopt new behaviors or to establish and maintain daily practices. Attempts to implement lean described in the literature are characterized by a lack of clear standards in applying lean principles and tools to the knowledge work. Moreover, the approach of 5S+S has not been sufficiently covered within the context of knowledge work projects.

Next, the results from the case study carried out in Blueday Technology were presented. The company has struggled with exceeded engineering hours and low project margins. After analysis of the VSM and company internal systems, it was concluded that there is a clear need for overall performance improvement in the projects, specifically when it comes to engineering design, project control and monitoring, and product quality.

From this perspective, the 5S+S framework and guidance for knowledge-providing organizations was developed. The framework aims to support the organization in a cultural transformation to become lean. The 5S+S concept helps to reduce the waste and standardize the work environment, maintain the established routines, and increase the productivity of white-collar workers. The framework paid special attention to the separation between physical office work and digital office work, in order to provide separate guidance for treating digital office work waste (chats, emails, inefficient methods of storing files) and physical office work waste (unneeded physical items, e.g., binders, paper copies). The framework has the potential to provide useful methods to improve knowledge work efficiency, especially when it comes to work routines and practices. The suggested methodology is applicable for knowledge-providing companies, project managers, and team leaders who aim to improve the productivity of their project teams.

Future research shall focus more on detailed case studies where the presented 5S+S framework could be used; detailed procedures and practices enabling the identification of waste in the knowledge work environment; lean tools and methods that could support the presented 5S+S framework; and the development of tailored KPIs to monitor the transition of the company into a lean organization. Additional focus shall be directed to the applicability of lean methods to the knowledge work in order to improve customer value.

References

1. Naradda Gamage, S.K., Ekanayake, E., Abeyrathne, G., Prasanna, R., Jayasundara, J., Rajapakshe, P.: A review of global challenges and survival strategies of small and medium enterprises (SMEs). Economies **8**(4), 79 (2020). https://doi.org/10.3390/economies8040079
2. Jünge, G., Alfnes, E., Kjersem, K., Andersen, B.: Lean project planning and control: empirical investigation of ETO projects. Int. J. Managing Projects Bus. **12** (2019). https://doi.org/10.1108/IJMPB-08-2018-0170
3. Drucker, P.: The Age of Discontinuity: Guidelines to our Changing Society, vol. 369. Heinemann, Butterworth-Heinemann Elsevier Ltd, Oxford (1969). https://doi.org/10.1016/C2013-0-04383-6. ISBN: 978-0-434-90395-5
4. Drucker, P.: Management Challenges for the 21st Century, vol. 205. Butterworth-Heinemann, Oxford (1999). ISBN: 0750644567
5. Holtshouse, D.: Knowledge work 2020: thinking ahead about knowledge work. Horizon **18**(3), 193–203 (2010). https://doi.org/10.1108/10748121011072645
6. Stone, K.B.: Four decades of lean: a systematic literature review. Int. J. Lean Six Sigma **3**(2), 112–132 (2012). https://doi.org/10.1108/20401461211243702
7. Aboelmaged, M.: Lean Six Sigma in healthcare. A review of theory and practice. In: Lean Six Sigma Approaches in Manufacturing, Services, and Production. Idea Group, U.S. (2015). https://doi.org/10.4018/978-1-4666-7320-5.ch009
8. Gupta, S., Sharma, M., Sunder, M.V.: Lean services: a systematic review. Int. J. Prod. Perform. Manag. **65**(8), 1025–1056 (2016)
9. Hadid, W., Mansouri, A.: The lean-performance relationship in services: a theoretical model. Int. J. Oper. Prod. Manag. **34**(6), 750–785 (2014). https://doi.org/10.1108/IJOPM-02-2013-0080
10. Kropsu-Vehkapera, H., Isoherranen, V.: Lean approach in knowledge work. J. Ind. Eng. Manag. **11**(3), 429–444 (2018). https://doi.org/10.3926/jiem.2595
11. Staats, B.R., Upton, D.M.: Lean knowledge work. Harv. Bus. Rev. **89**(10), 100–110 (2011)
12. Laihonen, H.: Knowledge structures of a health ecosystem. J. Health Organ. Manag. **26**, 542–558 (2012). https://doi.org/10.1108/14777261211251571
13. Kiss, F., Rossi, B.: Agile software development transformation: a systematic literature review. In: Federated Conference on Computer Science and Information Systems (FedCSIS) (2018). https://doi.org/10.15439/2018F53
14. Poppendieck, M., Poppendieck, T.: Lean Software Development: An Agile Toolkit. Addison Wesley, Boston (2003). ISBN: 0-321-15078-3
15. Poppendieck, M., Poppendieck, T.: Introduction to lean software development. In: Baumeister, H., Marchesi, M., Holcombe, M. (eds.) XP 2005. LNCS, vol. 3556, pp. 280–280. Springer, Heidelberg (2005). https://doi.org/10.1007/11499053_49
16. Murman, E., et al.: Lean Enterprise Value: Insights from MIT's Lean Aerospace Initiative. Palgrave Macmillan, London (2002). ISBN: 0333976975

17. Ballard, G., Zabelle, T.: Lean Design: Process, Tools, & Techniques. Lean Construction Institute, White Paper-10 (2000)

18. Javier, J., Alarcon, L.F.: Achieving lean design process: improvement methodology. J. Constr. Eng. Manag. **128**, 248–256 (2002)

19. Tzortzopoulos, P., Formoso, C.T.: Considerations on application of lean construction principles to design management. In: Proceedings 7th Annual Conference of the International Group for Lean Construction (IGLC), pp. 335–344 (1999)

20. Hirano, H.: Five Pillars of the Visual Workplace. Productivity Press, A Division of Productivity, Inc., New York (1995). ISBN-10: 156327047

21. Calzado, M., Romero, L., Fernández, J., Espinosa, M.M., Domínguez, M.: Extension of the Lean 5S methodology to 6S with an additional layer to ensure occupational safety and health levels. Sustainability (2019). https://doi.org/10.3390/su11143827

22. Casey, J.: 5S Shakeup. In: Quality Progress, October 2013, pp. 18–23 (2013)

23. Furman, J.: Impact of selected lean management tools on work safety. Multidiscip. Aspects Prod. Eng. **2**(1), 253–264 (2019). https://doi.org/10.2478/mape-2019-0025

24. Osakue, E.E., Smith, D.: A 6S experience in a manufacturing facility. In: 2014 ASEE Annual Conference & Exposition, Indianapolis, Indiana (2014). https://doi.org/10.18260/1-2--19907

25. Bacoup, P., Cedric, M., Habchi, G., Pralus, M.: From a quality management system (QMS) to a lean quality management system (LQMS). TQM J. **30**(1), 20–42 (2018). https://doi.org/10.1108/TQM-062016-0053

26. Micklewright, M.: Lean ISO 9001: Adding Spark to Your ISO 9001 QMS and Sustainability to Your Lean Efforts. ASQ Quality Press, Milwaukee, Wisconsin (2010). ISBN-10: 0873897846

A Lean Approach for Multi-criteria Decision-Making in Public Services' Strategy Deployment

F. P. Santhiapillai[✉] and R. M. Chandima Ratnayake

Department of Mechanical and Structural Engineering and Material Science, University of Stavanger (UIS), Stavanger, Norway
{felix.santhiapillai,chandima.ratnayake}@uis.no

Abstract. The public services' related strategy deployment (SD) process involves complex and multi-criteria decision-making. Group decision-making is often characterized by, among other things, some degree of managerial discretion, silo thinking, poor consensus and ad hoc approaches, for simplification purposes. This reduces consistency and results in a high level of variability in the overall performance, due to ambiguous and flawed translation into operational targets. Hence, it is necessary to investigate the potential use of scientific approaches to improve the consistency and minimize the variability of the performance of organizations providing public services. This paper presents the use of a Lean approach, by incorporating Gemba Walks, A3 and the analytic hierarchy process, to improve consistency and minimize the variability of an SD-related decision-making process in a public organization. Action research, supplemented by a practical case exercise, is performed, using qualitative and quantitative data, in one Norwegian police district. The proposed methodology provides a structured approach to consolidating different managerial perspectives, to systematically prioritize strategic alternatives and directions in a more meticulous and credible way, decreasing the possibility of minority domination and subjective views. The suggested approach can help build consensus and improve the consistency associated with group decision-making and minimize the adverse consequences of an ineffective SD process.

Keywords: Public services · Lean · Multi-criteria decision-making

1 Introduction

Public organizations are subject to increasing political and social demands on performance enhancement and service efficiency and quality, in a financially constrained environment [1, 2]. As such, it is vital that policies and strategies are used to focus the organization on key priorities that need to be aligned, developed, and deployed throughout the whole organization, to ensure their translation into operational targets that are integrated into daily routine management [3]. However, as identified in this study's case

© IFIP International Federation for Information Processing 2021
Published by Springer Nature Switzerland AG 2021
A. Dolgui et al. (Eds.): APMS 2021, IFIP AICT 630, pp. 656–664, 2021.
https://doi.org/10.1007/978-3-030-85874-2_71

organization, root causes of ineffective policy or strategy deployment (SD) are found to be associated with lack of knowledge about tools and methods for problem-solving, as well as strategic anchoring and group decision-making processes when faced with complex multi-criteria decision-making (MCDM) involving prioritization or trade-offs of alternatives.

Lean is a management philosophy found to improve organizational decision-making and shared vision [4], as a continuous improvement (CI) approach that reinforces the participation and involvement of all organizational levels through a common set of principles, tools and techniques for problem-solving [3]. Moreover, in the context of complex group decision-making, MCDM methods can play a significant role when there is a need to prioritize alternatives and build group consensus on strategic guidelines and priorities, which is vital for effective SD [5]. However, public organizations represent unique challenges to such management ideologies and practices [1]. That is, they are rarely observed in practice, or they are unsuccessfully implemented as an integral part of a comprehensive management system and adapted to the organizational decision-making context [4].

Henceforth, a practical understanding of Lean complemented by MCDM methods can be of significant value in public managers' aim to have more meticulous and credible SD-related decision-making and deployment. Action research, supplemented by a practical case exercise, is conducted in one Norwegian police district that is undergoing a CI program. In such, *Gemba Walks* are performed by the district management group to identify organizational needs or improvement areas, for strategic problem-solving using the A3 tool and Deming cycle: Plan, Do, Check, and Act (PDCA). Followingly, the MCDM method; Analytic Hierarchy Process (AHP), is used to prioritize and select which of the strategic A3s to deploy. Before discussing the proposed methodology in the context of SD, the next section presents the challenges faced by the case organization and the relevant theoretical background to this study.

2 Background

2.1 Organizational Challenge

In 2015, a new reform for the Norwegian police was decided upon, involving, among other things, the reduction of 27 districts to 12. Findings from the reform's latest evaluation report point out that lack of organization, plans and systematics, lack of competence among managers and lack of follow-up and prioritization have been key barriers to learning and development. Moreover, when considering future organizational challenges and barriers, strategic managers highlight structure, work processes, strategy, and management as important factors [2]. Top-level management in the Norwegian police describes increased distances internally between strategic management and the subordinate levels in the police organization. These are unintended consequences of the police reform, which breaks with the reform's objectives and ideals [6].

In one of the police districts, current managerial challenges are identified as being related to, among other things, the district management group's overall SD process, that is, their ability to effectively plan and continuously execute "FAIR" – 1) Focus short-term strategies, 2) Align plans, systems, and processes with the decided priorities, 3) Integrate priorities in daily management, and 4) Review the management of priorities [7]. In this context, among the underlying root causes and improvement areas, the following are identified: 1) lack of knowledge regarding methods, tools, and techniques for problem-solving and 2) strategic anchoring and group decision-making.

The latter is related to the management group's ability to have a structured approach to complex multi-criteria-based group decision-making, which is often characterized by, inter alia, the following factors: ad hoc approaches for simplification purposes, silo-thinking, minority domination, poor consensus, and ambiguity [1]. Lack of knowledge regarding methods and tools for problem-solving is organizational and involves the district's ability to approach complex organizational problems or improvement opportunities in a systematic and scientific way. Currently, there is a culture of identifying a problem, jumping to a conclusion regarding the solution and managing the problem in an ad hoc fashion, without sufficiently considering its entire scope and having a plan for implementation, review, and control. Consequently, this has been shown to result in a limited or immature problem-solving decision basis. Henceforth, both improvement areas, which are interconnected, require modernization and development in the given public organization.

2.2 Lean, Gemba Walks and A3

Lean is a highly promoted management philosophy, due particularly to its inherent emphasis on long-term organizational thinking, leadership and learning [8], as well as its ability and objective to eliminate waste by concurrently reducing or minimizing variability and overburden [9]. As a combination of *Gemba* ("the real thing"), *Genchi Genbutsu* ("go and see"), and *Genjitsu* ("real facts"), a *Gemba Walk* is a significantly valuable Lean technique, for observing, interacting, gathering information and understanding organizational conditions and processes, that creates value [10, 11].

A *Gemba Walk* is characterized by four distinctive elements: 1) location – observing something or someone at "the actual location" where the work is being performed; 2) observation – watching something or someone perform their work "in person"; 3) teaming – "interacting" with the employees performing the work, by respectfully asking questions if appropriate; and 4) reflecting – after "seeing and listening" – on what actions are required to support innovation and continuous improvement [10–12]. In this context, a supplementary tool is the A3, which is reinforced by the PDCA cycle [13]. Performing a *Gemba Walk* with the support of the A3 can be a powerful approach and communication technique that can direct managers and problem solvers to gain a deeper understanding of the problem or opportunity, generating innovative ideas on how to tackle the problem [3].

However, common Lean tools and methods for waste elimination and problem-solving are arguably insufficient for tackling many business-improvement-related problems such as complex decision-making, conflict resolution, project prioritization or trade-offs, resource allocation or workforce scheduling [14]. MCDM methods, which are a sub-discipline of operations research, are well positioned to complement the existing Lean tools and methods and effectively solve these problems.

2.3 Multi-criteria Decision-Making

In contrast to private organizations, public sector organizations are financially constrained, accountable to society, and subject to new reforms. They are governed by political directives and objectives that are often conflicting, complex, and ambiguous [1]. In this context, strategic decision makers are challenged by some degree of managerial discretion and often in a position in which prioritization or trade-offs of strategic directions and initiatives are required. The AHP is a MCDM method that was first developed and described by Saaty [15]. It enables the synthesis of the knowledge, experiences, data, information, intentions, and intuitions of the decision makers [16]. In essence, it describes a structured mathematical approach that enables decision makers to develop priorities and preferences by converting human judgements (e.g., experiences, the intuitions, and intentions of experts in different disciplines) into numerical values. MCDM methods, such as AHP, aim to reduce uncertainty and build consensus in the decision-making process, by simultaneously laying out all relevant factors of concern, tangible and intangible [17].

Primarily, AHP is built on the following three underlying concepts [16]: 1) visually structuring the decision problem as a hierarchy of goals, criteria and alternatives (Fig. 1), 2) pairwise comparison of elements at each level of the hierarchy with respect to each criterion on the preceding level, and 3) vertically synthesizing the judgements over the different levels of the hierarchy. In general, the measurement of indicators is 'often based on the quantitative analysis (through scoring, ranking, and weighting) of a wide range of qualitative impact criteria' [16, 18]. However, although there have been numerous studies encouraging organizations to apply MCDM methods, it is noteworthy that such rational decision-making processes are rarely observed in practice [19, 20]. Henceforth, it is a necessity to explore and contextualize how such methods can complement strategic managers and make it an integral part of a broader management system and group decision-making processes in practice.

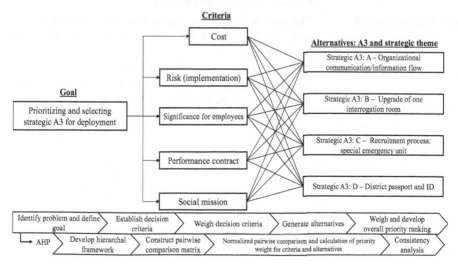

Fig. 1. Summarized rationale decision-making process, AHP and hierarchical structure

3   Methodology

As this study aims to address an improvement potential in an organization and, accordingly, generate practical implications and innovative solutions for the identified improvement areas through participation, an action research strategy is proposed, supplemented by a practical case exercise [21].

Based on the previous section, a model displaying the overall SD process is developed (Fig. 2), to contextualize the methodology of this study, in which the *Gemba Walks* are performed by the district management group (i.e., strategic level) to identify strategic themes and improvement areas in the organization. The output of each *Gemba Walk* is an A3, conveying the most critical information according to the PDCA cycle. Furthermore, as part of the practical case exercise, an excerpt of the developed A3s is chosen for the AHP (Fig. 1). Table 1 provides a summarized description of the established decision criteria. The management group was divided into three sub-groups to perform the AHP, using the Expertchoice software tool. In this, the geometric mean approach is recommended to combine the pairwise comparison matrix obtained from individual evaluators [5].

Table 1. Description of decision criteria

Decision criteria	Description
Cost	Direct cost (or expenses) of implementing the described strategic A3
Risk	Threats or level of uncertainty related to implementing the described A3. It determines the level of risk tolerance that the managers accept
Significance for employees	The direct value or significance that the strategic A3 has for the employees on a system level
Performance contract	The value or significance that the strategic A3 has for key performance indicators described in guidelines and directives for the district
Public (or social) mission	The value or significance that the strategic A3 has on the district's ability to prevent crime, maintain order and safety in society, and investigate and prosecute offences

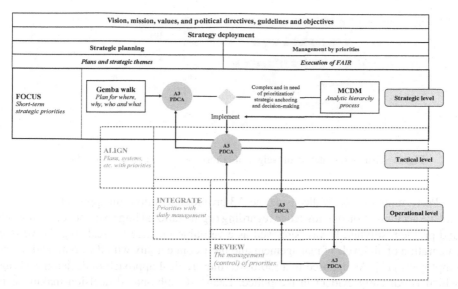

Fig. 2. Overall SD process using Gemba Walks, A3 and AHP, adapted from [7]

3.1 Findings

As the data and results are from a government agency and contain some sensitive information, the content of the A3s and decision criteria are intentionally censored or not elaborated in detail, to conform to the organization's confidentiality policies. From the *Gemba walks*, a total of 12 A3s was obtained. Of these, four were evaluated as needing strategic anchoring and group decision-making, due to their complexity and scope (Figs. 1 and 2). The weight of criteria and overall priority scores of the different strategic A3s obtained during this case exercise are shown in Table 2 and Fig. 3. From Fig. 3b, it could be found that strategic A3: D, which involves the district's passport and ID services, has the maximum overall priority score. As a sequel to the performance of this study, efforts have been taken by the case organization to implement strategic A3s: D, A and C which are concretized and operationalized through, among other things, tactical A3s in the subsequent steps of the SD process and FAIR method (Fig. 2).

Table 2. Weight of decision criteria and overall priority score of alternatives.

	Cost = 0.1860	Risk = 0.0646	PC = 0.3028	PM = 0.3203	SE = 0.1263	Overall priority
A3: A	0.5110	0.2889	0.0980	0.2978	0.5801	0.3080
A3: B	0.3292	0.1409	0.0667	0.0621	0.1617	0.1256
A3: C	0.0788	0.4405	0.3147	0.2337	0.0654	0.2264
A3: D	0.0810	0.1297	0.5205	0.4064	0.1928	0.3400

NB: Performance contract (PC), Public (or social) mission (PM), and Significance for employees (SE)

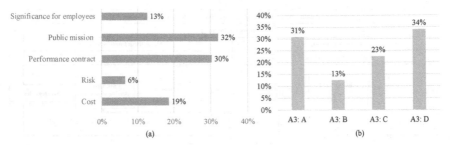

Fig. 3. Visual presentation of weight of criteria and overall priority of alternatives

Performing *Gemba* Walks using the A3 provided a bottom-up approach to learning and the accumulation of knowledge regarding organizational improvement opportunities and problem-solving. It was perceived as a valuable practice for realizing the vertical integration of all levels of management and their connectivity with the organization and employees [11]. As opposed to a top-down hierarchical approach to decision-making, which is currently evident in the police, Lean's Gemba-based decision-making can, among other things, increase trust and consensus on strategic guidelines and priorities within the organization [12]. Moreover, if routinely performed as an integral part of the overall SD process, it can provide evidence that the organization's strategic plans and objectives are being deployed effectively [22].

There are high expectations of and pressure on top-level managers to continuously improve and enhance performance and service quality. However, contextual factors, such as financial constraints, political directives, objectives, and guidelines, which are at times excessive, ambiguous and conflicting, challenge the managers' degree of managerial discretion. As such, complex decision-making requiring prioritization or trade-offs is arguably more evident in public sector organizations than in the private sphere. The AHP provides a systematic approach to consolidate different perspectives for the managers. The rational decision-making process provided a structure comprised of a common goal and decision criteria to approach the problem, as well as to elicit the group's tacit knowledge and make it explicitly available through visual data representation. This increased transparency and openness in the group's discussions, reducing variability, minority domination, silo-thinking, and subjective opinions or idiosyncratic views, ultimately contributing to a higher level of consensus and consistency within the group, which is vital for effective SD [3].

However, although there have been numerous studies encouraging organizations to apply MCDM methods, it is noteworthy that methods such as AHP also face some difficulties in aiding group decisions [23] and have been subject to criticism and controversy [24]. For instance, although the majority of the group's judgements had an acceptable inconsistency ratio (i.e., smaller or equal to 0.1), the level of inconsistency in the judgements provided had no significant effect on the usefulness of the MCDM method, as also concluded by [25].

4 Conclusion

This paper contextualizes the combined use of *Gemba Walks* and A3 as an integral part of a public management group's SD process, to identify and methodologically generate critical information regarding organizational improvement opportunities, which are then selected for implementation via the AHP. Such fieldwork, involving the integration and implementation of these tools and methods in police services' SD, is arguably scarce in the literature. This study can have practical implications, as it ideates a model (Fig. 1), broadly demonstrated in a case exercise, which is adoptable by other public organizations seeking to implement Lean and MCDM as part of their strategic management system. The suggested approach can help to enhance the consensus and consistency associated with multi-criteria group decision-making and minimize the adverse consequences of an ineffective SD process. However, there are limitations to this study. Among other things, this study displays challenges and a single case exercise conducted in one police district. Hence, there are limitations to its generalizability. Additionally, this study does not report on further implementation of the A3s and the sequenced steps in the SD process. Further research shall therefore follow the continuation and deployment of one of the selected strategic A3s and its subordinate tactical A3s, to report on the overall SD process and performance of the organization.

References

1. Santhiapillai, F.P., Ratnayake, R.M.C.: Risk-based prioritization method for planning and allocation of resources in public sector. TQM J. (ahead-of-print) (2021)
2. DFØ.: Evaluering av nærpolitireformen: Statusrapport 2019. Oslo, pp. 1–64 (2020)
3. Tortorella, G., Cauchick-Miguel, P.A., Gaiardelli, P.: Hoshin Kanri and A3: a proposal for integrating variability into the policy deployment process. TQM J. **31**(2), 118–135 (2019)
4. Simons, P., Benders, J., Bergs, J., Marneffe, W., Vandijck, D.: Has Lean improved organizational decision making? Int. J. Health Care Qual. Assur. **29**(5), 536–549 (2016)
5. Ratnayake, R.M., Markeset, T.: Implementing company policies in plant level asset operations: Measuring organisational alignment. Europ. J. Ind. Eng. **4**(3), 355–371 (2010)
6. Glomseth, R.: Toppledere og toppledelse i politi og påtalemyndighet. The Norwegian Police University College, p. 1–40 (2020)
7. Witcher, B.J. and V. Sum Chau.: Balanced scorecard and hoshin kanri: dynamic capabilities for managing strategic fit. Management Decision 45(3), 518–538 (2007).
8. Netland, T.H., Powell, D.: The Routledge Companion to Lean Management, 1st edn. Routledge, New York (2016)
9. Narayanan, S., Vickery, S.K., Nicolae, M.L., Castel, M.J., Mcleod, M.K.: The effects of lean implementation on hospital financial performance. Decision Sci. **2021**, 1–21 (2021).
10. Romero, D., Gaiardelli, P., Wuest, T., Powell, D., Thürer, M.: New forms of gemba walks and their digital tools in the digital lean manufacturing world. In: Lalic, B., Majstorovic, V., Marjanovic, U., von Cieminski, G., Romero, D. (eds.) APMS 2020. IAICT, vol. 592, pp. 432–440. Springer, Cham (2020). https://doi.org/10.1007/978-3-030-57997-5_50
11. Ballé, M., Chartier, N., Coignet, P., Olivencia, S., Powell, D.: The Lean Sensei, 1st edn. Lean Enterprise Institute, Inc (2019)
12. Womack, J.P.: Gemba Walks. Expanded 2nd edn. Lean Enterprise Institute, Inc. (2013)
13. Anderson, J., Morgan, J., Williams, S.: Using Toyota's A3 thinking for analyzing MBA business cases. Decis. Sci. J. Innov. Educ. **9**(2), 275–285 (2011)

14. Tang, L.C., Goh, T.N., Lam, S.W., Zhang, C.W.: Fortification of six sigma: expanding the DMAIC toolset. Qual. Reliab. Eng. Int. **23**(1), 3–18 (2007)
15. Saaty, T.L.: How to make a decision: the analytic hierarchy process. Eur. J. Oper. Res. **48**(1), 9–26 (1990)
16. Samarakoon, S.M.K., Ratnayake, R.M.C.: Strengthening, modification and repair techniques' prioritization for structural integrity control of ageing offshore structures. Reliab. Eng. Syst. Saf. **135**(1), 15–26 (2015)
17. Saaty, T.L.: Decision making with the analytic hierarchy process. Int. J. Serv. Sci. **1**(1), 83–98 (2008)
18. Rocco S, C.M., Hernandez, F.: Robustness and sensitivity analysis in multiple criteria decision problems using rule learner techniques. Reliability Eng. Syst. Saf. **134**(1), 297–304 (2015)
19. Angelis, A., Kanavos, P., Montibeller, G.: Resource allocation and priority setting in health care: a multi-criteria decision analysis problem of value? Global Pol. **8**(1), 76–83 (2017)
20. Bernroider, E.W.N., Schmöllerl, P.: A technological, organisational, and environmental analysis of decision making methodologies and satisfaction in the context of IT induced business transformations. Eur. J. Oper. Res. **224**(1), 141–153 (2013)
21. Bryman, A., Bell, E.: Business Research Methods. 3rd edn. Oxford University Press Inc. (2011)
22. Smith, S.: Improving governance through gemba walks. Healthc. Exec. **34**(2), 50–51 (2019)
23. Cuoghi, K.G., Leoneti, A.B.: A group MCDA method for aiding decision-making of complex problems in public sector: the case of Belo Monte Dam. Socio-Econ. Plann. Sci. **68**(1), 100625 (2019)
24. Asadabadi, M.R., Chang, E., Saberi, M.: Are MCDM methods useful? a critical review of Analytic Hierarchy Process (AHP) and Analytic Network Process (ANP). Cogent Eng. **6**(1), 1623153 (2019)
25. Ishizaka, A., Siraj, S.: Are multi-criteria decision-making tools useful? an experimental comparative study of three methods. Eur. J. Oper. Res. **264**(2), 462–471 (2018)

Lean Six Sigma in Knowledge Work: A Case Study from Policing and Prosecution Services

F. P. Santhiapillai[✉] and R. M. Chandima Ratnayake

Department of Mechanical and Structural Engineering and Material Science, University of Stavanger (UIS), Stavanger, Norway
{felix.santhiapillai,chandima.ratnayake}@uis.no

Abstract. Lean Six Sigma (LSS) continues to greatly interest public sector organizations as a means to continuously improve service performance. However, given
the plethora of research and literature on LSS in the public sector, research specifically about LSS in policing and prosecution services, which are dominated by
knowledge work, is significantly limited. It is necessary to measure the knowledge
work performance, to achieve continuous improvement. This manuscript presents
a case study about the use of LSS in the Norwegian police service. It reports
on the existing framework of LSS and explicates how to systematically analyse
data regarding knowledge work-related waste to identify improvement areas in
the criminal justice process. The LSS methodology and framework applied in this
study provides a systemic approach that uncovers waste, which gives grounds to
holistically analyse and indicate how the current overall process is performing,
based on the scope of defects. This study demonstrates the implementation potential of LSS in policing and prosecution services to support managers who are
engaged in any form of continuous improvement initiatives. The findings also add
evidence to the existing argument on the applicability of LSS in policing services.
However, there is a need to further develop and apply the LSS methodology in
such a context.

Keywords: Lean Six Sigma · Police services · Knowledge work

1 Introduction

Lean Six Sigma (LSS) continues to greatly interest and influence management practices
in various industries. In more recent times, LSS, which has had and continues to have
profound and advanced application in many manufacturing companies, has propagated
to public organizations, such as higher education, healthcare, municipalities, and government agencies, in their continuous improvement programmes [1, 2]. However, given the
demonstrated utility and impact of LSS in manufacturing and non-manufacturing environments highlighted in the existing plethora of literature, research specifically about
the implementation of LSS in the policing and prosecution services, which is dominated by knowledge work, is very limited [3, 4]. Hence, it is important to explore its

A. Dolgui et al. (Eds.): APMS 2021, IFIP AICT 630, pp. 665–673, 2021.
https://doi.org/10.1007/978-3-030-85874-2_72

required adaptation, implementation potential and viability for system-level continuous improvement, and to contribute to the existing gap in literature regarding this topic.

This paper attempts to report on the following question: How can the existing framework of LSS be extended and applied in policing and prosecution services to systematically identify and analyse waste in crime investigations? The aim of this study is to answer this question and report on key learning points, based on observations and results from the applied LSS methodology in a Norwegian police district. The following section presents the literature background. Section 3 describes the proposed case study research design, while Sect. 4 presents the results. Finally, Sect. 5 discusses the findings, draws some conclusions and mentions future research opportunities.

2   Background

2.1   Lean Six Sigma in Policing and Prosecution Services

Lean is a philosophical approach derived from Toyota's operating model, TPS, which consists of a set of principles that drive organizations to continually add value to their operations and services [5]. Toyota problematized waste, overburden and variation (also known as Muda, Mura and Muri), in a way their competitors did not, and made this a central part of their business philosophy [6]. Using various principles and tools, Toyota has built a culture and system that can identify relatively automatically problems that are non-value-adding [5]. The way of thinking and its practices enhance the necessary process steps and eliminate those that fail to add value, thereby improving flow and performance. Since its origin in Toyota, it has been adapted in various industries and sectors and merged with supplementing techniques and tools, such as Six Sigma, for process improvement. LSS strategies have an increased focus on quality and seek to improve the quality of the output of a process, by identifying and removing the causes of defects and minimizing impact variability [7].

While LSS has led to long-term successes in terms of developing a culture for continuous improvement (CI) in both the private and public sectors, failed implementation is also common [8, 9]. For instance, as a response to the general call for reform and austerity and the demand to reduce costs in the public sector [10], police organizations, predominantly in the UK, have explored the application of LSS practices, with consideration being given to their applicability to the police and the extent to which methodologies need to be adapted to individual services [3]. However, [4] states that, although many of the initiatives are undertaken under the banner of "Lean" within individual police forces, short-term successes are reported. In general, the reality is that public sector organizations have tended to be tool-oriented, with full-scale or systemic implementation of rigorous methodologies of LSS not being adopted [1, 9]. The complexity of implementing LSS methodologies in public sector organizations, which are characterized by a contextually different environment from that of manufacturing, is widely recognized [11]. It is therefore important to understand the differences, in order to undertake any tailoring exercise which would support the 'fit' of LSS methodologies to policing and prosecution services, before approaching implementation on a broader scale [4].

In contrast to a manufacturing environment, which is dominated by physical assets and material flow, a policing organization is composed of functional hierarchies, mainly operated by human resources, whose processes and activities are characterized by knowledge work, to perform the required functions. Knowledge work primarily involves the management and use of information [12]. Moreover, it is characterized by more dynamic and uncertain processes than those generally associated with manufacturing. For instance, once an automobile producer initiates the production of a station wagon, it does not try changing it into an SUV halfway down the line [13]. In police investigations, however, a criminal case can take countless turns, based on the information that is available in advance and that is collected and generated along the way. Furthermore, each criminal case differs in type, complexity and scope, and they are dependent on multiple interconnected activities, disciplines and actors, both internally and externally, to deliver a final product that the prosecutor can take to court.

In the context of knowledge work, researchers have used a services context to document how knowledge work and unstable and uncertain conditions (demands and processes) do not preclude the use of LSS [12]. Furthermore, as indicated in the previous sections, there are traces of the implementation of LSS in police organizations. While these are few, compared to the existing research and LSS and CI in the public sector in general, [3] state that LSS can be embraced by all policing services to create efficient and effective processes, to provide enhanced value at reduced operational costs and, more importantly, to change how the organization learns through hypothesis-driven problem solving [13]. Henceforth, there is a need to continue the research into and the exploration of how LSS can be adapted, implemented, and extended in police organizations, to achieve long-term successes.

2.2 Background to the Case Organization

In contrast to many countries, the prosecution authority is an integral part of the Norwegian police. The prosecutor has the overall responsibility to manage the criminal proceedings, ensuring that the investigation of a case is purpose-driven and in accordance with current law and regulations. Accordingly, there are demands for high quality and efficiency in all phases of the investigation process, that is, from the first police officer becoming aware of a possible criminal act, to the prosecuting authorities' processing of the investigative material during the main trial. However, in this knowledge work-dominated environment, it is difficult to quantitatively measure and assess quality and efficiency.

In one Norwegian police district, from a strategic level, it was decided that one of the district's short-term strategic priorities should be the reduction of the district's current backlog of cases pending before the prosecuting authorities in the district. This is directly linked to one of the key performance indicators of the Norwegian police. In such, an improvement project was initiated. As LSS support a data-driven approach towards process improvement, which includes both human and non-human factors [14], this initiative included the incorporation of LSS as an integral part of the project management. This was to gain knowledge on LSS implementation in the organization's ongoing CI programme and, more specifically, to provide a classification framework of different sources of waste in the criminal justice process, and a deeper analysis of these as a means to systematically remove them and reduce overall performance variation.

3 Methodology

This case study was conducted in the prosecution service unit in the given case organization. A project team consisting of prosecutors was established for the purpose of this initiative. To align the strategic short-term priorities with the project plan and integrate the overall objectives with daily management, the LSS framework incorporating the five-stage DMAIC problem-solving methodology, described below (Table 1), is used to approach the above problem.

Table 1. DMAIC and framework for waste, adapted from [14]

DMAIC	Description	Tools and techniques
Define	The purpose of the Define phase is to delineate the organizational problem, the impact of the problem, scope of the project and define the process or what needs to be improved	Project charter, SIPOC, Voice of the customer (VOC) analysis, critical to quality (CTQ) analysis
Measure	The purpose of the Measure phase is to understand, document and baseline the current state of the defined improvement area(s), and validate the measurement system wherever applicable	Framework for waste, data collection plan and structure, Pareto analysis, performance analysis
Analyse	The purpose of the Analyse phase is to interpret and analyse the data collected in relation to the content described in the previous phases, to deepen the understanding and identify the root causes of the processual problems	Cause-and-effect analysis, root cause analysis, correlation analysis
Improve	The purpose of the Improve phase is to identify improvement recommendations, design the future state, implement pilot projects, review and document the new processes	Brainstorming, pilot project, updated data collection
Control	The purpose of the Control phase is to sustain the improved results and value creation of the pilot project by proceeding to manage implementation and change on a broader scale or system level, report the control plan, identify replication opportunities and develop plans for further improvements	Quality control plan, statistical process control, mistake proofing

4   Findings

It is noteworthy that the sample (criminal cases) used in this study has several limitations; thus, the results presented in this study are mainly used as a means to explicate the proposed LSS methodology in the context of policing and prosecution services for learning purposes. Based on critical to quality characteristics, and central guidelines and

Table 2. Adapted framework for waste

Waste		Description
Waiting (unwarranted delay)		Inactive processing of case for more than 3 months. That is, backlog ≥ 3 months
Handover (Ineffective/inefficient)		Responsibility for case is transferred to another organizational unit instead of being decided as it is – possibly decided after minimal additional effort from the submitting unit
Over-production (or over-investigation)		Creation of self-initiated criminal cases in violation of central/local priorities and over-investigation in existing criminal cases. Over-investigation involves both the implementation of an investigation, in cases without clarification potential, and the lack of delimitation of the amount of investigation, in cases to be investigated
Error		Clear deviations from instructions when registering and processing a case or absence of / incorrect assessments during investigation/prosecution decision
Interaction	**Case management**	The lead investigator and the prosecutor are responsible for leading the investigation. Their roles are to manage both the need for prioritization among the different cases and the scope of activity in cases that are to be investigated. There are several meeting or follow-up points where these will interact (the shape and form depend on the complexity and character of the case)
Knowledge		Lack of knowledge regarding local/central priorities. Lack of case processing and/or portfolio competence
Capacity		Lack of resources compared to the task portfolio leads to all the above – or the above deviations lead to the capacity being challenged more than necessary

policies, the traditional definitions of waste (i.e., muda) were reformulated and adapted to the context of crime investigation as in Table 2. In this study, the different categories of waste are referred to as types of defects that are under consideration; these are non-conformities, deviations, flaws or discrepancies from central directives, specifications or requirements that also do not add value to the overall criminal case and its involved actors. The presence of these were concomitantly and qualitatively assessed by the prosecutors while processing each criminal case.

A total of 505 criminal cases was processed and assessed for waste by the prosecution team. Of these, 177, or 35%, were characterized by waste. Figure 1 displays a Pareto chart, in which the most present or frequently occurring categories of waste are registered to be Waiting, Interaction and Handover. These were identified as being located primarily in the initial phases of the criminal justice process (Fig. 2). It is notable that the visualized process, which is a result of the SIPOC analysis, only provides an overall snapshot of a highly dynamic and complex processual system.

Moreover, a total number of 242 defects was assessed and found in the 177 criminal cases. Accordingly, Table 2 provides metrics that indicate how the current overall process is performing. That is, based on the calculated Defect Per Million Opportunity (DPMO) (and defect rate and yield), and a sigma shift of + 1.5, the current process sigma level is approximately 3. However, only seven categories for waste, which represents the types of defects under consideration in this study, are defined. Considering the highly complex, dynamic, uncertain and knowledge-work dominated nature of the overall criminal justice process, which are characterized by multiple specifications, guidelines and directives, these may not be representative for all forms of activities, non-conformities, flaws or

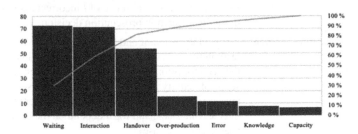

Fig. 1. Pareto analysis

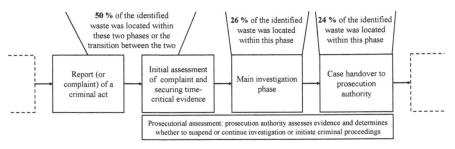

Fig. 2. Location of identified waste

Table 3. Performance metrics

Phase: Measure	
Total criminal cases	505
Number of non-conforming cases	177
Types of defects under consideration	7
Total number of defects found	242
Opportunities for a defect in the sample	3535
DPMO	68458
Defect rate	6.85%
Yield	93.15%
Process sigma level	3

deviations that are non-value-adding. This also challenges the applicability and validity of detailed process performance- or capability-related analysis.

As part of the Analysis phase of the DMAIC methodology, the interconnectedness or relationship between the various waste categories was qualitatively analysed from a cause-and-effect perspective. Accordingly, what is argued as the main overall cause, rooted in the majority of the remaining wastes, is Interaction, which is a central part of the case management (Table 1). Henceforth, the key improvement area to further engage in is argued to be the overall case management, in which the lead investigator and the prosecution authority interact to set a purpose-oriented direction. Inadequate or absent interaction is believed to have a major negative effect on criminal proceedings – in terms of time, resource use and quality of the final product. Figure 3 illustrates possible interconnectedness between the provided categories, impacting time and quality throughout the process.

However, based on this qualitative analysis, a more detailed data collection plan with an expanded and updated sample is found necessary for the Analysis phase, in order to utilize statistical methods, such as correlation and/or regression analysis and hypothesis testing to state whether the calculated values are statistically significant. This

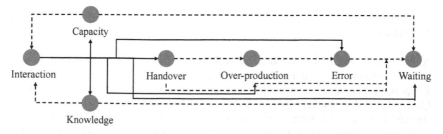

Fig. 3. Possible relationship between the defined wastes

can deepen the understanding and knowledge regarding the potential interconnectedness and relationships between these variables.

Given the contextual differences between manufacturing processes and crime investigation and prosecutorial activities, the LSS methodology and framework provided the project manager with a systemic approach to uncovering waste, which gave grounds to holistically interpret and indicate how the current overall process is performing, based on the scope of defects. LSS can have significant value and support managers in systematically identifying and analysing waste and addressing improvement areas in the police, as also concluded by [10, 14, 15]. However, in contrast to the manufacturing industry, where process waste and defects in physical products or materials are arguably more visual, pre-defined, automatically controlled, with data on them collected, in the policing and prosecution context, these are less visible and currently dependent on manual data collection. Furthermore, such data collection and analysis are to a greater extent characterized by a qualitative approach, which is based on disciplinary expertise and knowledge. This makes it subject to human subjectivity and variation due to different knowledge basis, assessments, opinions and judgments.

5   Conclusion

This study contributes to the literature on LSS practices in police organizations, by extending and applying the existing framework of LSS in policing and prosecution services. This paper has practical implications and can be of value to managers, in any public organizations, who are engaged in any form of continuous improvement initiatives. The results of the study also add evidence to the existing argument on the applicability of LSS in police services, which are dominated by knowledge work, and, through this, contribute to filling a current research gap. Although the applied LSS methodology is not a novel approach, evidence of its successful application in policing and prosecution services is scant in the literature, emphasizing the growing importance of fieldwork that reports the application of such an approach. Further research shall interpret, adapt and develop the content of LSS to such a context. Followingly, report on the remaining phases of the DMAIC methodology, tools and techniques. Moreover, it shall develop a detailed data collection plan and structure in order to apply statistical methods, which can deepen the understanding and knowledge regarding the potential interconnectedness and relationships between the various wastes.

References

1. Andersson, G., Lynch, M.P.J., Johansen, F.R., Fineide, M.J., Martin, D.: Exploring perceptions of Lean in the public sector. Public Money Manage., 1–9 (2020)
2. Rodgers, B., Antony, J.: Lean and six sigma practices in the public sector: a review. Int. J. Quality Reliability Manage. 36(3), 437–455 (2018)
3. Antony, J., Rodgers, B., Cudney, E.A.: Lean Six Sigma in policing services: case examples, lessons learnt and directions for future research. Total Qual. Manag. Bus. Excell. 30(5–6), 613–625 (2019)
4. Barton, H.: Lean policing? New approaches to business process improvement across the UK police service. Public Money Manage. 33(3), 221–224 (2013)

5. Liker, J.K.: The Toyota Way: 14 Management Principles from the World's Greatest Manufacturer. 1st edn. McGraw Hill (2004)
6. Womack, J.P., Jones, D.T., Roos, D.: The Machine that Changed the World. Simon & Schuster, London, England (2007)
7. George, M.L.: Lean Six Sigma for Service. The McGraw-Hill Company, New York (2003)
8. Netland, T.H., Powell, D.J., Hines, P.: Demystifyng lean leadership. Int. J. Lean Six Sigma 11(3), 543–554 (2019)
9. Radnor, Z., Osborne, S.P.: Lean: a failed theory for public services? Public Manag. Rev. 15(2), 265–287 (2013)
10. Antony, J., Rodgers, B.: Lean six sigma in policing services. Int. J. Product. Perform. Manag. 67(5), 935–945 (2018)
11. Smith, R.: Policing in austerity: time to go lean. Int. J. Emerg. Serv. 5(2), 174–183 (2016)
12. Kropsu-Vehkapera, H., Isoherranen, V.: Lean approach in knowledge work. J. Ind. Eng. Manage. 11(3), 429–444 (2018)
13. Staats, B.R., Brunner, D.J., Upton, D.M.: Lean principles, learning and knowledge work: evidence from a software services provider. J. Oper. Manag. 29(1), 376–390 (2011)
14. Antony, J., Rodgers, B., Coull, I., Sunder M., V.: Lean Six Sigma in policing services: A case study from an organisational learning perspective. Int. J. Productivity Performance Manage. 67(5), 935–940 (2018)
15. Barton, H.: "Lean" policing? New approaches to business process improvement across the UK police service. Public Money Manage. 3(3), 221–224 (2013)

Industry and Services: Different Organizational Cultures, Same Openness to Lean Implementation?

Paulo Amaro[iD], Anabela C. Alves[✉][iD], and Rui M. Sousa[iD]

Centro ALGORITMI, University of Minho, Campus of Azurém, 4800-058 Guimarães, Portugal
pamaro@efacec.pt, {anabela,rms}@dps.uminho.pt

Abstract. Since 1990, attempts to implement lean, especially by production companies, have grown in number and depth. With the publication of the book Lean Thinking, lean projects quickly spread to other activity sectors, but achieving success in such implementations is not something that can be easily accomplished. Research is in progress to identify why some organizations succeed while others do not; one of the findings points to organizational culture as a crucial factor. This means that before implementing lean in a company, its organizational culture should be analysed, understood and, eventually, modified, to create the necessary openness for the implementation to be successful. This paper aims to explore the relationship between the organizational culture of companies from industry and services and their openness regarding lean implementation. For this, it was developed and applied a two parts questionnaire: one part involves the four traits of the Denison organizational culture survey and the other part the six dimensions of the Cameron and Quinn model (Competing Values Framework). The questionnaire was applied to the top managers of four companies (one from industry, two from services and one with both areas). In terms of organizational culture, the findings revealed that in order to move towards successful lean implementation, some companies need to improve specific traits inherent to Denison's approach as well as ensure congruence between the dimensions of the Cameron and Quinn model.

Keywords: Lean thinking · Organizational culture · Denison model · Cameron and Quinn model

1 Introduction

Implementing lean is a aspiration shared by innumerable organizations, but it faces several difficulties [1, 2]. Mainly, this is due to some misunderstandings and myths about "what is lean?" [3, 4]. Additionally, many other factors could be inhibitors of lean implementation [5, 6], namely the organisational culture [7]. It has been verified experimentally that a proper lean culture improves the pace of growth and keeps the organization competitive [5, 8, 9]. Numerous researchers agree that an organisational culture which does not support lean is a cause for the failure of effective lean implementation [11–13].

© IFIP International Federation for Information Processing 2021
Published by Springer Nature Switzerland AG 2021
A. Dolgui et al. (Eds.): APMS 2021, IFIP AICT 630, pp. 674–682, 2021.
https://doi.org/10.1007/978-3-030-85874-2_73

The purpose of this paper is to explore the relationship between organizational culture and openness to lean implementation and identify gaps in the companies' organizational culture that should be mitigated so lean implementation can be successfully achieved.

This paper is structured as follows: after this introduction, Sect. 2 contains the literature review on the models used and their relationship with lean. Section 3 describes the research methodology adopted. Section 4 presents the case studies and respondents characterization. The results are presented and discussed in Sect. 5. Finally, Sect. 6 outlines the conclusions and future work.

2 Denison's Model and Competing Values Framework

Organizational culture is a set of complex, interconnected, and often ambiguous, factors. This literature review tackles the models chosen to diagnose organizational culture and, according to Alkhoraif and McLaughlin [10], a large number of organizational culture models can be found in literature [10]. Some recognized organizational culture models are those from Schein [13], Denison and Neale [14], Cameron and Quinn [15] which were reviewed in Amaro et al. [16]. The last two provided instruments to evaluate the organizational culture of the companies and are described next.

The Denison's model is based on four cultural traits and focuses on measuring the impact of organizational culture on the performance and effectiveness of organizations. The traits are Mission (a sense of direction and performance expectations), Involvement of employees, Consistency (of organizational procedures), and Adaptability (to customers and markets changes) [14]. Each of these traits is quantified through three component indexes, and each of these indexes is measured with five items questionnaire. On the Mission trait, the indexes Strategic Direction and Intent, Goals and Objectives and Vision are analysed. On the Involvement trait, the analysed indexes are Empowerment, Team Orientation and Capability Development. On the Consistency trait, are analysed the Core Values, Agreement and Coordination and Integration. Lastly, on the Adaptability trait, the indexes analysed are Creating Change, Customer Focus and Organizational Learning.

Cameron and Quinn [15] created the Organizational Culture Assessment Instrument (OCAI) to measure organizational culture. In this instrument, it is used a framework called Competing Values Framework (CVF). CVF uses two logical dimensions in a Cartesian graph: the first dimension (y-axis) distinguishes effectiveness criteria in flexibility and discretion in contradiction of stability and control; the second dimension distinguishes internal focus and integration against external focus and differentiation. The combination of these two dimensions forms four quadrants, which state core values upon which judgments are made in an organization [15]. The conflicting values ("competitors") in this model are characterized by the diagonal quadrants. These values advocate the model name, CVF. Each of these quadrants, in turn, defines the dominant profile of a particular type of Organizational Culture: Adhocracy, Market, Hierarchy and Clan Culture. This framework indicates the dominant profile, allowing understanding if it is the most adequate profile to allow long-term success and sustainability in lean development and implementation [17]. Responses on the six items: Organizational Characteristics, Organizational Leader, Management of Employees, Organizational Glue,

Strategic Emphasis and Criteria of Success, help to highlight aspects of organization's culture that identify its dominant culture type.

The models of Denison and Cameron and Quinn were chosen because they allow the connection to aspects that are recognised as important requirements for the implementation of lean (e.g. involvement and vision).

3   Research Methodology

This research was based on a multiple case study involving four companies from industry and services and in each case study, only five top managers of the organizations were interviewed. A questionnaire with two parts was used: 1) diagnose of the organizational culture using the Denison's model and 2) identification of the predominant type of culture, using the Cameron and Quinn's model. The Denison's model uses a survey based on a 60-item instrument to evaluate the four cultural traits (Sect. 2) and management practices. The model of Cameron and Quinn was used to identify the actual predominant type of organizational culture of the organization. Due to the pandemic situation experienced during this research, the questionnaire was applied to 22 professionals from different business areas of the selected companies, through a one-hour videoconference.

4   Case Studies and Respondents Characterization

Table 1 characterizes the four case studies. Companies 1 and 3 are Portuguese companies that became multinational. The case study 4 is a public administration company of one of the most important cities of Portugal.

Table 1. Case study characterization.

Case study #	1	2	3	4
Business sector	Industry & services	Industry	Services	Services
Activity sector	Energy	Automotive components	Retail, industry, telecommunications, tourism	Public administration
Main markets	Portugal, Europe and America	Europe, America and others	Portugal, Spain	Portugal
Multinational	Yes	Yes	Yes	Yes
Employees' nr.	>1000	>1000	>10000	>1000
Business areas	1, 2, 3, 4, 5	1	2	2
Hierarchical levels #	1, 2, 3	1, 2, 3	1, 2	1, 2
Interviewees #	15	3	2	2

5 Results and Discussion

5.1 Traits and Indexes of Denison's Model

Figure 1 presents the results of the two interviews (1.1.1.4 and 2.1.1.1) conducted (two top managers, two industrial companies). The worst index on case study 1 was the Team Orientation with 20% (red circle in Fig. 1). According to Denison [14], when the score of a trait/index is less than 50%, the company must pay attention, as this reveals a vulnerability. This indicates that people may be disengaged from their work, unconscious of their importance and link to the rest of the organization, reluctant to accept greater responsibility, or timid about working with people outside of their direct circle. Employees' involvement is recognized as a successful factor in lean implementations. This could indicate that if the company of case study 1 wants to implement lean it needs to increase this involvement [6]. In fact, that company has been implementing some lean tools but without its full potential. By the contrary, the company of case study 2 has a high level of evaluation in all traits/indexes, so it has conditions (openness) to implement lean, and, indeed, it has been implementing Lean with success, for the past few years.

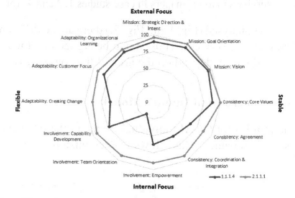

Fig. 1. Results of interviews to top managers in case studies 1 and 2 from industry area.

Figure 2 presents the results of the three interviews (1.2.1.2; 3.2.1.1 and 4.2.1.1) in services companies (three top managers, three companies). On case study 1, the worst indexes were Vision (36%) and Creating Change (36%) (red circles in Fig. 2). Vision is one of the indexes of the Mission trait and when its value is low it means that the organization lacks a long-term planning. Long-term planning and vision are the base of the pyramid of Toyota 4P model [18], i.e., the lean roots. Therefore, results from the company of case study 1 indicate that a significant organizational culture change is necessary in order to achieve the desirable openness to implement lean.

According to the Denison's model, low levels of the Creating Change index (one of the indexes of the Adaptability trait) mean that the company is not able to deal properly with customer/market changes. This adaptability is an important characteristic of lean companies [19, 20]. Thus, the results from the company of case study 1 indicate more difficulty to implement lean. In fact, the company has never tried to implement lean, and the authors know that only a few insignificant and isolated implementation efforts have been made.

Results from case studies 3 and 4 revealed that the corresponding companies have the necessary conditions to implement lean. Indeed, they have implemented Lean with success, for the past few years.

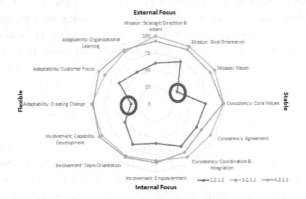

Fig. 2. Results of interviews to top managers in case studies 1, 3 and 4 from services area.

In the five interviews analysed (Fig. 1 and Fig. 2.) there are no different patterns in the results from the industry and services. Thus, it can be argued that the level of openness for implementing lean does not depend on the area of the company (industry/services).

5.2 Dimensions of Cameron and Quinn's Model

Figure 3 shows the profiles for OCAI individual items, in the perspective of top managers of the industrial companies. This allows to recognize the extent of each cultural

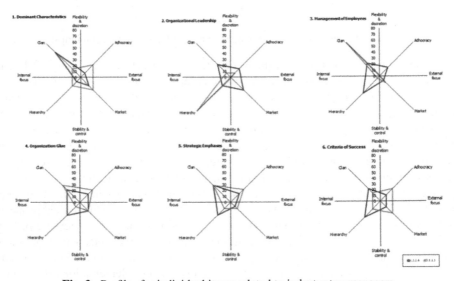

Fig. 3. Profiles for individual items related to industry top managers.

dimension. Results show that in both cases the profiles for individual items are not congruent.

Figure 4 shows the aggregated results of the individual items related to the cultural profile of the two industrial companies. The dominant culture in both cases is the Clan Culture, with a similar pattern. However, this similarity does not mean companies act in the same way. The Clan Culture is most effective in domains of performance related to morale, satisfaction, internal communication, and supportiveness, according to Cameron and Quinn [15]. Thus, this type of culture reveals openness to lean implementations. In case study 1, this is not verified, although is desired. This occurs in case study 2. Clan Culture is not consistent across various aspects of the organization. These differences have consequences on the way the companies act.

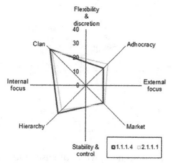

Fig. 4. Individual items combined profile of case studies 1 and 2 (industry).

Figure 5 show the profiles for individual items on the OCAI, in the perspective of top managers of the services companies. The results of interviews from case studies 1 and 4 are not fully congruent, due to a few discrepancies. For case study 3, the results

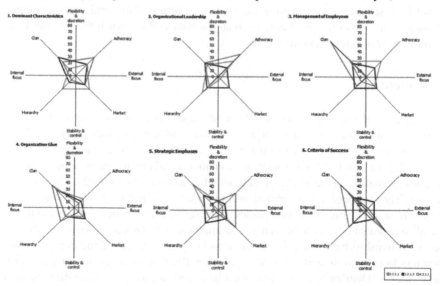

Fig. 5. Profiles for individual items related to service top managers.

are not congruent, especially in criteria 3 and 6. The reason may be that this is a retail company strongly pulled by the market, facing strong competition.

Figure 6 shows the aggregated results of the individual items related to cultural profile of the service sector from three companies. Once again, Clan Culture is dominant for all case studies; however, their cultures are incongruent (Fig. 6). Clan Culture is not consistent across various aspects of the organization. These differences have consequences on the way the companies act, for example, employees' management in the case study 3 is stimulated and they "act as a family" in the words of the top manager. This is totally aligned with Clan Culture.

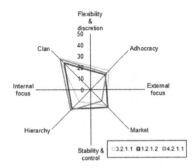

Fig. 6. Individual items combined profile of case studies 1, 3 and 4 (services)

In both areas (industry and services), the Clan Culture is predominant, but the profiles for the individual items are not congruent. This indicates that all companies of the case studies have an opportunity to align their profiles for the individual items.

As already seen in the first part of the questionnaire (Denison), industry and services do not have specific response patterns. That is, in terms of cultural profile, it can also be argued that the company's area (industry/services) does not influence the level of openness to lean implementation.

6   Conclusions

This paper used Denison's organizational culture model and Cameron and Quinn's CVF to design an instrument (questionnaire), which involves various elements (traits/indexes/dimensions), to evaluate the organizational culture of companies. Then, a relationship was established between these elements and the openness of the company to the implementation of the lean approach, which is a crucial factor to the implementation success. The instrument was applied in four companies and analyses the responses of five top managers (three from companies in the services area and two from the industry; one of the companies has both areas). The analysis of the results shows that there is in fact a relationship between the type of organizational culture of the company and its openness to lean implementation. More specifically, it allowed the identification of the traits/indexes (Denison's model) that must be improved, as well as the dimensions that must be congruent (Cameron and Quinn's model), so the aforementioned openness and successful implementation of lean can be achieved. In the industry area, in one of the two companies analysed (case study 1), serious gaps were identified in terms of the some traits/indexes (and it was found that it is in fact a company where attempts of isolated lean implementations have not been successful). In the area of services, this same company presented even more gaps, in contrast to the other two (which already have some history of success in the implementation of lean). At the level of congruence between dimensions, only one company gets closer to the desired situation, which means that there is still a lot of room for improvement. A limitation of this work is the reduced number of companies analysed.

In terms of future work, it is planned the development of a set of specific recommendations that companies should follow in order to mitigate the gaps identified in their organizational culture. Another aspect for further work is the analysis of the perception that the different hierarchical levels of a company have in relation to the organizational culture of that company.

Acknowledgements. This work has been supported by FCT – Fundação para a Ciência e Tecnologia within the R&D Units Project Scope: UIDB/00319/2020.

References

1. Grigg, N.P., Goodyer, J.E., Frater, T.G.: Sustaining lean in SMEs: key findings from a 10-year study involving New Zealand manufacturers. Total Qual. Manag. Bus. Excell. **31**(5–6), 609–622 (2020)
2. Pakdil, F., Leonard, K.M.: Implementing and sustaining lean processes: the dilemma of societal culture effects. Int. J. Prod. Res. **55**(3), 700–717 (2017)
3. Saurin, T.A., Luz Tortorella, G., Soliman, M., Garza-Reyes, J.A.: Production myths: an exploratory study. J. Manuf. Technol. Manag. **32**(1), 1–19 (2020)
4. Schonberger, R.J.: The disintegration of lean manufacturing and lean management. Bus. Horiz. **62**(3), 359–371 (2019)
5. Amaro, P., Alves, A.C., Sousa, R.M.: Lean thinking: a transversal and global management philosophy to achieve sustainability benefits. In: Alves, A.C., Kahlen, F.-J., Flumerfelt, S., Siriban-Manalang, A.B. (eds.) Lean Engineering for Global Development, pp. 1–31. Springer, Cham (2019). https://doi.org/10.1007/978-3-030-13515-7_1
6. Amaro, A.P., Alves, A.C., Sousa, R.M.: Context-dependent factors of lean production implementations: two sides of the same coin. J. Mechatron. Autom. Ident. Technol. **5**(3), 17–22 (2020)
7. Amaro, P., Alves, A.C., Sousa, R.M.: Lean thinking: from the shop floor to an organizational culture. In: Lalic, B., Majstorovic, V., Marjanovic, U., von Cieminski, G., Romero, D. (eds.) APMS 2020. IAICT, vol. 592, pp. 406–414. Springer, Cham (2020). https://doi.org/10.1007/978-3-030-57997-5_47
8. Ben Ruben, R., Vinodh, S., Asokan, P.: State of art perspectives of lean and sustainable manufacturing. Int. J. Lean Six Sigma **10**(1), 234–256 (2019)
9. Pooyan, B., Napsiah, I., Zulkiflle, L.: Review of lean adoption within small and medium sized enterprises. Adv. Mater. Res. **903**, 414–418 (2014)
10. Alkhoraif, A., McLaughlin, P.: Organizational culture - enablers and inhibitors factors for the effective implementation of lean. Int. J. Lean Thinking **8**(2), 65–96 (2017)

11. Barclay, R.C., Cudney, E.A., Shetty, S., Antony, J.: Determining critical success factors for lean implementation. Total Qual. Manag. Bus. Excell. 1–15 (2021)
12. Pakdil, F., Leonard, K.M.: The effect of organizational culture on implementing and sustaining lean processes. J. Manuf. Technol. Manag. 26(5), 725–743 (2015)
13. Schein, E.H.: Organizational Culture. Sloan School of Management, MIT (1988)
14. Denison, D., Neale, W.: Denison Organizational Culture Survey: Facilitator Guide. Denison Consulting, LLC (1999)
15. Cameron, K.S., Quinn, R.: Diagnosing and Changing Organizational Culture (Rev. ed.). Jossey-Bass Publishers (2006)
16. Amaro, P., Alves, A.C., Sousa, R.M.: Lean Thinking as an Organizational Culture: a Systematic Literature Review. Organizational Cultures: An International Journal. Accepted (2021)
17. Paro, P.E.P., Gerolamo, M.C.: Organizational culture for lean programs. J. Organ. Change Manage. 30(4), 584 (2017)
18. Liker, J.K.: The Toyota Way: 14 Management Principles from the World´S Greatest Manufacturer. McGraw-Hill (2004)
19. Takeuchi, H., Osono, E., Shimizu, N.: The contradictions that drives Toyota´s success. Harvard Bus. Rev. June, 98–104 (2008)
20. Alves, A.C., Dinis-Carvalho, J., Sousa, R.M.: Lean production as promoter of thinkers to achieve companies' agility. Learn. Organ. 19(3), 219–237 (2012)

An Enhanced Data-Driven Algorithm for Shifting Bottleneck Detection

Christoph Roser[1]($\boxtimes$), Mukund Subramaniyan[2], Anders Skoogh[2], and Björn Johansson[2]

[1] Karlsruhe University of Applied Sciences, Moltkestrasse 30, Karlsruhe, Germany
christoph.roser@hochschule-karlsruhe.de
[2] Department of Industrial and Materials Science, Chalmers University of Technology, 41296 Gothenburg, Sweden

Abstract. Bottleneck detection is vital for improving production capacity or reducing production time. Many different methods exist, although only a few of them can detect shifting bottlenecks. The active period method is based on the longest uninterrupted active time of a process, but the analytical algorithm is difficult to program requiring different self-iterating loops. Hence a simpler matrix-based algorithm was developed. This paper presents an improvement over the original algorithm with respect to accuracy.

Keywords: Shifting bottleneck detection · Active period method · Load balancing · Throughput bottlenecks · Production system

1 Introduction

Finding a bottleneck is a critical task in modern industry for improving production output within a given time or reducing the time needed to produce a given quantity [1]. There are numerous bottleneck detection methods. These could be based on cycle times [2], utilization [3], waiting times [2], average waiting time [4], length of the queue [5], or combinations thereof [6]. The arrow method looks at blocking and starving [7], as does the turning point method [8]. The bottleneck walk does direct observations of waiting times and inventory levels on the shop floor [9]. Other methods are data-driven [10] or based on process mining [11]. See [12] for a more detailed discussion and comparison of these methods. However, many of these methods do not work well with shifting bottlenecks, even though in industry shifting bottlenecks are very common. In this paper, the bottleneck is defined as the machine to which the overall system throughput has the largest sensitivity [8]. This paper analyzes the active period method. While the method has high accuracy [12], it is a challenge to program the analysis code. [13] improved this method using a matrix approach to analyze the bottleneck. This paper further improves this algorithm to enhance accuracy and ease of use.

A. Dolgui et al. (Eds.): APMS 2021, IFIP AICT 630, pp. 683–689, 2021.
https://doi.org/10.1007/978-3-030-85874-2_74

2 Active Period Method

The active period method was developed by [14, 15]. In this method, a process is considered active whenever the process is not waiting for parts or material. At any given time, the process with the longest active period is the momentary bottleneck. The overlap between the longest active periods are times of shifting bottlenecks. Periods with no overlaps are sole bottlenecks. The total bottleneck probability is the likelihood of a process being a sole or a shifting bottleneck. This method gives very accurate results even for shifting bottlenecks when compared with other methods [12].

3 An Enhanced Data-Driven Algorithm

The enhanced data-driven algorithm starts similarly as [13] with a matrix, where the number of rows corresponds to the number of processes $i = 0 \ldots m - 1$ and the number of columns corresponds to the number of time instants $j = 0 \ldots n - 1$. This generates a matrix of size m × n. The entries in the matrix take the value 1 if the process is active at the given time instant, and the value 0 if the process is inactive at the given time instant.

Please note that this matrix will usually have many more columns than rows. If the data processing is done in typical desktop software like Microsoft Excel, the software may provide more rows than columns. In this case, it may be easier to work with a transposed matrix and adjust all subsequent algorithms accordingly.

3.1 Preparation of the Raw Data

The first step is the collection and preparation of the raw data. While this is not detailed in [13], it is usually required for practical applications. This is visualized in Fig. 1. The raw data a) is usually a table with one entry for every change in the system. Please note that due to the data collection algorithms often there are redundant entries for the same process and time slot, resulting in multiple events with a duration of zero. In this case, only the last one is valid, which will be corrected in step d). This raw data a) is converted into a matrix b). The missing entries are filled with the data from the previous entry as shown in c). Finally, if there are multiple entries for the same time, all but the last one according to the sequence in a) is deleted, otherwise, the subsequent algorithm will provide incorrect results.

3.2 Consideration of Equidistant Interval Matrix

The original paper by [13] uses an interval of 1 s. However, different equidistant intervals may be used. If this interval is too small, the computation requirements would go up, as would the file size of the database. If the interval is set to large, the accuracy would go down, eventually giving incorrect results. In any case, any interval larger than zero has there is the risk of missing out on smaller gaps between active periods.

However, using the times of the entries of the raw data in the data matrix also brings its own risk of a flawed analysis if the algorithm merely counts the number of entries in the data matrix. These are not equidistant but depend on the random behavior of

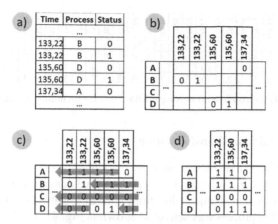

Fig. 1. Preparing of the raw data matrix

the system or the (pseudo-)random behavior of the simulation. Figure 2 provides an illustrative example of the problem with the data columns arranged on a real-time axis. Initially, process A is the bottleneck. When process A becomes idle, a simple count of the number of active states in the data matrix shows process B with 5 successive active states in sequence, and process C only with 4. Hence, process B would be the next bottleneck based on the number of active states. However, since the columns are not equally distributed along the time axis, process C has a much longer active period and should be the next bottleneck.

```
A 1 11  1111 0 0        0 0
B 0 00  0111 1 1        0 0
C 0 00  0001 1 1        1 0
                    Real Time
```

Fig. 2. Illustrative example of using real-time data.

An explorative analysis showed that the error when using timestamped non-equidistant data is non-zero but usually small. Hence, it is possible to use time-stamped data for the matrix without significant loss of accuracy.

Further explorative analysis for equidistant data entries showed that the error, too, is small if the time interval is chosen small enough. The time interval depends on the cycle times of the processes and their fluctuations as well as on the buffer sizes between the processes. As a rule of thumb based on these explorative analyses, the time interval should be smaller than the cycle time for reasonable accuracy results.

Within this paper, however, we follow academic rigor and analyze the data under consideration of the actual timestamp of the data. This differs from the original method by [13]. Figure 3 shows an example data matrix where the entries maintain their timestamps with non-equidistant intervals.

	122,17	122,92	122,94	123,73	123,96	124,92	125,70	126,64	128,72	129,02	129,82	131,18	132,05	132,36	133,22	135,60	137,34	138,79	139,16	139,99	140,26	141,21	142,67	142,77	144,44	145,98	146,75	148,65	149,39	150,22	150,66
A	0	0	1	0	1	1	1	1	0	1	0	1	1	0	1	1	0	1	1	1	1	1	1	1	1	1	1	1	1	1	1
B	1	1	1	0	1	1	0	0	1	0	0	1	1	1	1	1	1	0	1	1	0	1	1	0	1	1	1	0	1	0	0
C	0	0	1	1	0	1	0	1	1	0	1	1	0	1	1	1	1	1	1	1	1	1	1	1	1	1	1	0	0	0	0
D	1	1	1	1	1	1	1	1	1	1	1	1	1	1	1	0	0	1	1	0	1	1	0	1	1	0	1	1	0	1	0

Fig. 3. Data matrix with non-equidistant entries including the time stamp

3.3 State Accumulation Transformation

The state accumulation transformation is also modified from [13] to include the actual duration between the entries. In the first step, the actual duration between one entry and the next entry is entered in all matrix locations where the status from the matrix in Fig. 3 was not zero (i.e. the process was active) as shown in Fig. 4.

	122,17	122,92	122,94	123,73	123,96	124,92	125,70	126,64	128,72	129,02	129,82	131,18	132,05	132,36	133,22	135,60	137,34	138,79	139,16	139,99	140,26	141,21	142,67	142,77	144,44	145,98	146,75	148,65	149,39	150,22	150,66
A	0	0	0,8	0	1	0,8	0,9	0	0,3	0	1,4	0,9	0	0,9	2,4	0	1,5	0,4	0,8	0,3	0,9	1,5	0,1	1,7	1,5	0,8	1,9	0,7	0,8	0,4	2,1
B	0,8	0	0,8	0	1	0,8	0	0	0,3	0	0	0,9	0,3	0,9	2,4	1,7	1,5	0	0,8	0,3	0	1,5	0,1	0	1,5	0,8	1,9	0	0,8	0	0
C	0	0	0,8	0,2	0	0,8	0	2,1	0,3	0	1,4	0,9	0	0,9	2,4	1,7	1,5	0,4	0,8	0,3	0,9	1,5	0,1	1,7	1,5	0,8	1,9	0	0	0	0
D	0,8	0	0,8	0,2	1	0,8	0,9	2,1	0,3	0,8	1,4	0,9	0,3	0,9	2,4	0	0	0,4	0,8	0	0,9	1,5	0	1,7	1,5	0	1,9	0,7	0	0,4	0

Fig. 4. Entering the duration to the next column for all non-zero entries

The next step is similar to [13], where the cumulative durations are entered for each successive entry in the matrix for the active periods. The last entry for each active period is the duration of the active period as shown in Fig. 5. For this matrix, the timestamp is no longer necessary, but shown for your convenience.

	122,17	122,92	122,94	123,73	123,96	124,92	125,70	126,64	128,72	129,02	129,82	131,18	132,05	132,36	133,22	135,60	137,34	138,79	139,16	139,99	140,26	141,21	142,67	142,77	144,44	145,98	146,75	148,65	149,39	150,22	150,66
A	0	0	0,8	0	1	1,7	2,7	0	0,3	0	1,4	2,2	0	0,9	3,2	0	1,5	1,8	2,7	2,9	3,9	5,3	5,4	7,1	8,6	9,4	11	12	13	13	15
B	0,8	0,8	1,6	0	1	1,7	0	0	0,3	0	0	0,9	1,2	2	4,4	6,2	7,6	0	0,8	1,1	0	1,5	1,6	0	1,5	2,3	4,2	0	0,8	0	0
C	0	0	0,8	1	0	0,8	0	2,1	2,4	0	1,4	2,2	0	0,9	3,2	5	6,4	6,8	7,6	7,9	8,9	10	10	12	14	14	16	0	0	0	0
D	0,8	0,8	1,6	1,8	2,8	3,5	4,5	6,6	6,9	7,7	9	9,9	10	11	13	0	0	0,4	1,2	0	0,9	2,4	0	1,7	3,2	0	1,9	2,6	0	0,4	0

Fig. 5. Cumulative duration of active periods

As a next step, it is necessary to add the maximum value of the active period to all entries of the active period as shown in Fig. 6. This matrix can then be used for subsequent bottleneck analysis. The bottlenecks are already highlighted for an easier understanding of the data.

3.4 Potential Bottleneck Detection

Finally, the bottleneck can be detected. For every column in the matrix, the largest value is a bottleneck. Similar to [13] an 1 is added in a new matrix for every active period of the previous matrix that is at least once the longest active period or shares this longest

	122,17	122,92	122,94	123,73	123,96	124,92	125,70	126,64	128,72	129,02	129,82	131,18	132,05	132,36	133,22	135,60	137,34	138,79	139,16	139,99	140,26	141,21	142,67	142,77	144,44	145,98	146,75	148,65	149,39	150,22	150,66
A	0	0	0,8	0	2,7	2,7	2,7	0	0,3	0	2,2	2,2	0	3,2	3,2	0	15	15	15	15	15	15	15	15	15	15	15	15	15	15	15
B	1,6	1,6	1,6	0	1,7	1,7	0	0	0,3	0	0	7,6	7,6	7,6	7,6	7,6	7,6	0	1,1	1,1	0	1,6	1,6	0	4,2	4,2	4,2	0	0,8	0	0
C	0	1	1	1	0	0,8	0	2,4	2,4	0	2,2	2,2	0	16	16	16	16	16	16	16	16	16	16	16	16	16	16	0	0	0	0
D	13	13	13	13	13	13	13	13	13	13	13	13	13	13	13	0	0	1,2	1,2	0	2,4	2,4	0	3,2	3,2	0	2,6	2,6	0	0,4	0

Fig. 6. Total duration of active periods in all cells of the corresponding active period.

duration with one or more other active periods. The resulting matrix is shown in Fig. 7. If two processes happen to have the same duration, then they are both considered to be shifting bottlenecks. If no process is active, then there is no bottleneck detected during this time.

	122,17	122,92	122,94	123,73	123,96	124,92	125,70	126,64	128,72	129,02	129,82	131,18	132,05	132,36	133,22	135,60	137,34	138,79	139,16	139,99	140,26	141,21	142,67	142,77	144,44	145,98	146,75	148,65	149,39	150,22	150,66
A	0	0	0	0	0	0	0	0	0	0	0	0	0	0	0	0	1	1	1	1	1	1	1	1	1	1	1	1	1	1	1
B	0	0	0	0	0	0	0	0	0	0	0	0	0	0	0	0	0	0	0	0	0	0	0	0	0	0	0	0	0	0	0
C	0	0	0	0	0	0	0	0	0	0	0	0	0	1	1	1	1	1	1	1	1	1	1	1	1	1	1	0	0	0	0
D	1	1	1	1	1	1	1	1	1	1	1	1	1	1	1	0	0	0	0	0	0	0	0	0	0	0	0	0	0	0	0

Fig. 7. .Resulting active period bottlenecks.

Further algorithms similar to [13] allow the distinction between sole and shifting bottlenecks as shown in Fig. 8. A simple statistic can then give the percentage of each process being a sole bottleneck, or a shifting bottleneck, or jointly sole or shifting bottleneck.

	122,17	122,92	122,94	123,73	123,96	124,92	125,70	126,64	128,72	129,02	129,82	131,18	132,05	132,36	133,22	135,60	137,34	138,79	139,16	139,99	140,26	141,21	142,67	142,77	144,44	145,98	146,75	148,65	149,39	150,22	150,66
A	0	0	0	0	0	0	0	0	0	0	0	0	0	0	0	0	1	1	1	1	1	1	1	1	1	1	1	0	0	0	0
B	0	0	0	0	0	0	0	0	0	0	0	0	0	0	0	0	0	0	0	0	0	0	0	0	0	0	0	0	0	0	0
C	0	0	0	0	0	0	0	0	0	0	0	0	0	1	1	0	1	1	1	1	1	1	1	1	1	1	1	0	0	0	0
D	0	0	0	0	0	0	0	0	0	0	0	0	0	1	1	0	0	0	0	0	0	0	0	0	0	0	0	0	0	0	0

	122,17	122,92	122,94	123,73	123,96	124,92	125,70	126,64	128,72	129,02	129,82	131,18	132,05	132,36	133,22	135,60	137,34	138,79	139,16	139,99	140,26	141,21	142,67	142,77	144,44	145,98	146,75	148,65	149,39	150,22	150,66
A	0	0	0	0	0	0	0	0	0	0	0	0	0	0	0	0	0	0	0	0	0	0	0	0	0	0	0	1	1	1	1
B	0	0	0	0	0	0	0	0	0	0	0	0	0	0	0	0	0	0	0	0	0	0	0	0	0	0	0	0	0	0	0
C	0	0	0	0	0	0	0	0	0	0	0	0	0	0	0	1	0	0	0	0	0	0	0	0	0	0	0	0	0	0	0
D	1	1	1	1	1	1	1	1	1	1	1	1	1	1	1	0	0	0	0	0	0	0	0	0	0	0	0	0	0	0	0

Fig. 8. Shifting bottlenecks (top) and sole bottlenecks (bottom).

4   Summary and Discussion

This paper uses the active period bottleneck detection method by [14, 16] in combination with the data-driven shifting bottleneck detection algorithm as proposed by [13] and improves and enhances the latter. The new improved algorithm increases the accuracy of the analysis by using actual-time intervals to determine the longest active period at any given time.

The detailed step-by-step approach of the method allows both academics and practitioners to use the active period method for bottleneck detection. Detection bottlenecks is often a critical step in managing a production system, and crucial for improving the throughput. In a secondary role it can also play a part in reducing cost by improving throughput. Hence, finding the bottleneck is important for many improvement projects. Errors in bottleneck detection can lead to improving a non-bottleneck, which would waste time and resources. The detection of the momentary bottleneck also allows a faster reaction and allows the uses of countermeasures that can be changed on short notice, as for example the work assignment of the operators or the production plan to reduce the impact of short term bottlenecks.

Reference

1. Goldratt, E.M., Cox, J.: The Goal: A Process of Ongoing Improvement, 2nd revised ed. North River Press (1992)
2. Law, A.M., Kelton, D.W.: Simulation Modeling & Analysis, 2nd edn. McGraw Hill (1991)
3. Tang, H.: A new method of bottleneck analysis for manufacturing systems. Manuf. Lett. **19**, 21–24 (2019). https://doi.org/10.1016/j.mfglet.2019.01.003
4. Pollett, P.K.: Modelling congestion in closed queueing networks. Int. Trans. Oper. Res. **7**, 319–330 (2000). https://doi.org/10.1016/S0969-6016(00)00004-6
5. Lawrence, S.R., Buss, A.H.: Shifting production bottlenecks: causes, cures, and conundrums. J. Prod. Oper. Manage. **3**, 21–37 (1994)
6. Elmasry, G.F., McCann, C.J.: Bottleneck discovery in large-scale networks based on the expected value of per-hop delay. In: 2003 IEEE Military Communications Conference, 2003, MILCOM 2003, vol. 1, pp. 405–410 (2003)
7. Kuo, C.-T., Lim, J.-T., Meerkov, S.M.: Bottlenecks in serial production lines: a system-theoretic approach. Math. Probl. Eng. **2**, 233–276 (1996)
8. Li, L., Chang, Q., Ni, J.: Data driven bottleneck detection of manufacturing systems. Int. J. Prod. Res. **47**, 5019–5036 (2009). https://doi.org/10.1080/00207540701881860
9. Roser, C., Lorentzen, K., Deuse, J.: Reliable shop floor bottleneck detection for flow lines through process and inventory observations. In: Proceedings of the Robust Manufacturing Conference, Bremen, Germany (2014)
10. Yu, C., Matta, A.: A statistical framework of data-driven bottleneck identification in manufacturing systems. Int. J. Prod. Res. **54**, 6317–6332 (2016). https://doi.org/10.1080/00207543.2015.1126681
11. Lorenz, R., Senoner, J., Sihn, W., Netland, T.: Using process mining to improve productivity in make-to-stock manufacturing. Int. J. Prod. Res. 1–12 (2021). https://doi.org/10.1080/00207543.2021.1906460
12. Roser, C., Nakano, M.: A quantitative comparison of bottleneck detection methods in manufacturing systems with particular consideration for shifting bottlenecks. In: Proceedings of the International Conference on the Advances in Production Management System, Tokyo, Japan (2015)
13. Subramaniyan, M., Skoogh, A., Gopalakrishnan, M., et al.: An algorithm for data-driven shifting bottleneck detection. Cogent Eng. **3**, 1239516 (2016). https://doi.org/10.1080/23311916.2016.1239516

14. Roser, C., Nakano, M., Tanaka, M.: Shifting bottleneck detection. In: Yucesan, E., Chen, C.-H., Snowdon, J.L., Charnes, J.M. (eds.) Winter Simulation Conference, San Diego, CA, USA, pp. 1079–1086 (2002)
15. Roser, C., Nakano, M., Tanaka, M.: Detecting shifting bottlenecks. In: International Symposium on Scheduling, Hamamatsu, Japan, pp. 59–62 (2002)
16. Roser, C., Nakano, M., Tanaka, M.: Monitoring bottlenecks in dynamic discrete event systems. In: European Simulation Multiconference, Magdeburg, Germany (2004)

Practical Estimation of the Impact of a Reduction of the Number of Kanban Cards on the Delivery Performance

Christoph Roser[(⊠)], Yannik Regending, Bernd Langer, and Claas-Christian Wuttke

Karlsruhe University of Applied Sciences, Moltkestrasse 30, Karlsruhe, Germany
christoph.roser@hochschule-karlsruhe.de

Abstract. Kanban systems are the best-known variant of pull systems and a cornerstone of lean manufacturing. Kanban systems help to maintain a good material availability in relation to the inventory. One of the main adjustments is the number of kanban cards in a kanban system. The number of kanban is a tradeoff between the cost of inventory, and the cost of a stock-out. Since kanban are used for make-to-stock production, a high availability of completed products is desired, often measured as the delivery performance (on time in full). At the same time excessive inventory is to be avoided to reduce inventory cost and to improve throughput. This paper describes a practical approach to estimate the impact of a reduction of kanban on the delivery performance, based on an analysis of the supermarket inventory.

Keywords: Kanban · Supermarket · Delivery performance

1 Introduction

Lean manufacturing is one of the significant frameworks for manufacturing optimization. It includes a multitude of different methods and philosophies, from eliminating waste, fluctuations, and overburden to improving quality. Lean was also either the basis or a significant inspiration for other process performance related frameworks like six sigma, Agile, and others, and is often related to topics like Industry 4.0 [1, 2].

One of these significant philosophies is the idea of flow, with material moving from process to process rather than idling in inventories, improving the lead time. As per Little's law [3], the lead time is directly related to the inventory. Subsequently, inventory reduction is a key aspect of lean manufacturing [4]. Pull production is one of the significant tools to manage an inventory. While there are different definitions of pull systems, it is a limit on inventory coupled with a signal to refill this inventory. Kanban is the best known version of pull, and an excellent tool for a tradeoff between inventory cost and stock outs in make-to-stock production [5]. These stock outs are often measured as the delivery performance, i.e. the percentage of deliveries that where both on time and delivered in full, sometimes abbreviated as OTIF (On Time In Full). A kanban system aims to replenish the target inventory, often known as a supermarket.

© IFIP International Federation for Information Processing 2021
Published by Springer Nature Switzerland AG 2021
A. Dolgui et al. (Eds.): APMS 2021, IFIP AICT 630, pp. 690–696, 2021.
https://doi.org/10.1007/978-3-030-85874-2_75

Setting up a kanban system for a good tradeoff requires among other things to determine the number of kanban for each product type in the pull system. Different versions of kanban formulas [6, 7] help with determining the number of kanban, but all of these are merely an estimation. Depending on the assumptions, the number of kanban may be less than ideal for the system. It may be much easier to adjust the number of kanban based on the actual performance of the system. While this can be done using trial and error exploration of the system, this is impractical for real world systems and usually limited to simulations. Different authors propose a dynamic adjustment [8, 9], although it may be difficult to adjust kanban dynamically.

This paper proposes a practical tool for the estimation of a delivery performance for a reduction in the number of kanban cards based on the historical supermarket inventory data for a given system.

2 Prediction Model

The model to predict the reduction in delivery performance for a reduction in the number of kanban uses the supermarket histogram. Figure 1 shows the model using a generic histogram of a supermarket. We predict that a reduction in the number of kanban shifts the histogram a corresponding number of parts to the left (for our model one kanban represents one part, but this may be different for other systems). When shifting the histogram to the left, there can never be less than zero parts in the system. Hence, any value in the histogram that would go below zero is added to the value in the histogram for zero.

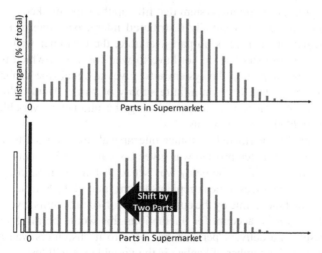

Fig. 1. Kanban reduction prediction hypothesis

This updated histogram value for zero is the predicted likelihood of the supermarket being empty, and can be used to predict the delivery performance. This approach is mathematically easy enough to be feasible for most manufacturing companies. In mathematical terms, the new delivery performance D_{New} is approximately the remainder to

1 of the sum of the individual histogram values h_n from zero to the number of parts m that are represented by the removed kanban as shown in Eq. (1).

$$D_{New} \approx 1 - \sum_{n=0}^{m} h_n \tag{1}$$

3 The Simulated System

The behavior of the inventory in a supermarket depends on many factors. Relevant for us are the number of kanban, the replenishment time, and the magnitude of the fluctuations. We use simulations to model a simple system producing a single part as shown in Fig. 2.

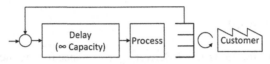

Fig. 2. The simulated system

A part can only enter the system if a kanban is available, where one kanban represents one part. To model larger systems every part in the system has a fixed delay, where multiple parts can be delayed simultaneously. A separate process has a erlang distributed processing time. The erlang distribution has a finite lower bound of zero but an infinite upper tail, making it well suited to model processes. This process provides the fluctuations for the supplying system that fills up the supermarket.

A customer with an exponentially distributed interarrival time picks up one part from the supermarket. If there is no part available, the customer waits. We measure the percentage of customers that do not have to wait for a part, which is the delivery performance. A part departing the system also gives a signal (the kanban) to release the next part in the system from an infinite supply of parts. Overall, this system is a simplified version of complex systems, reducing the number of variables while still behaving comparable to larger systems.

The exponentially distributed customer interarrival time was set to 10 time units. The exponentially distributed process was given a mean of 9 time units. This gives the process a utilization of 90%. The delay was set to 991 time units. Together with the mean process time this gives a mean replenishment time of 1000 time units. Dividing the average replenishment time by the customer takt of 10 time units gives us *in average* 100 kanban. However, to account for fluctuations this would be insufficient, and 100 kanban will result in a delivery performance of zero if customers wait until they are served. In any case, the number of kanban is the variable we will test.

The simulation had a warm up period of 100 000 time units and a run time of 5 000 000 time units, producing around 500 000 parts per simulation. We measure the delivery performance and the histogram of the supermarket inventory. An example supermarket histogram for an excessive number of 200 kanban is shown in Fig. 3. The mean is around 100 as expected from the division of the mean replenishment time by the mean customer takt. The delivery performance is 100%, as the system never ran out of inventory.

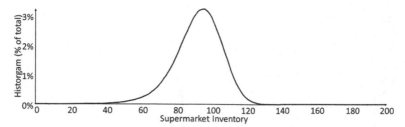

Fig. 3. Supermarket histogram for 200 kanban

If we reduce the number of kanban, this histogram will shift to the left. Figure 4 shows the histogram for 120 kanban. The delivery performance is now only 80.61%. The supermarket is empty for 19.79% of the time, marked with a black dot in Fig. 4 for better visibility. The rest of the histogram is almost identical with Fig. 3 but shifted 70 parts to the left (note the different percentage scale).

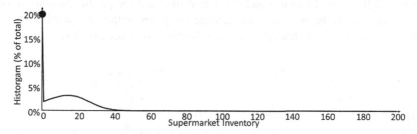

Fig. 4. Supermarket histogram for 130 kanban

The percentage of the time the supermarket was not empty corresponds almost perfectly to the delivery performance. The supermarket was empty 19.79% of the time, and 19.39% of the customers had to wait for a part. The difference of 0.4% represents the few cases where the supermarket was empty, but filled up again before a customer arrived. For all practical purposes, the percentage the of supermarket being empty is a good estimator of the delivery performance.

4 Model Verification

We used this simulation model to establish the delivery performance for different number of kanbans. We measured the delivery performance after a warm up time of 100 000 time units for an additional simulation duration of 1000 000 time units. Each simulation was repeated 30 times to determine the mean and the 95% confidence interval. Figure 5 shows the behavior of the delivery performance. The confidence intervals are not shown, as they would graphically overlap almost completely with the mean delivery performance.

The delivery performance was consistently 100% for over 190 kanban. This rapidly dropped to zero for 100 kanban. 100 kanban would be the average replenishment time of 1000 time units divided by the customer takt of 10 time units. Due to the customers

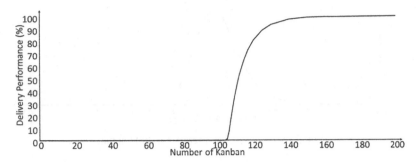

Fig. 5. Delivery performance of simulation system for different number of kanban

waiting, the system is unable to recover with 100 kanban or less, and the subsequent delivery performance is zero.

We predicted the delivery performance based on selected supermarket histograms at 200, 150, 130, 120, and 110 kanban. The result is shown in Fig. 6, where the solid line is the true delivery performance and the dotted lines are the predictions. To make the graph easier to read, the number of kanban used to generate the supermarket histogram and hence the start of the prediction model is highlighted with a back dot.

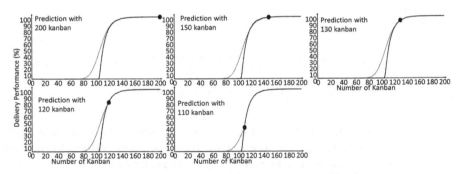

Fig. 6. Prediction quality for different number of kanban

The prediction model is spot on for delivery performances over 70% with an average error of less than one percentage point, and still very good for delivery performances above 50% with an average error of less than 10% points. For delivery performance below 50% however, the model no longer takes the cumulative effect into account of more and more customers waiting for their products.

For practical purposes, however, this is a very good prediction, as most companies strive to achieve higher delivery performances above 50%. Few companies would reduce the number of kanban to reduce inventory if the delivery performance is already below 50%.

Hence, this method is suitable for use in real world manufacturing systems. Two issues, however, can reduce the accuracy. First, an accurate supermarket histogram is needed, which may not always be available. Secondly, the system should not change over the duration for which the histogram was taken. However, especially if there is a risk of a stock out, extraordinary measures are often taken and firefighting tries to prevent a stock out. Therefore, in reality the frequency of stock-outs may be less than in this theoretical model as emergency measures are taken to prevent such a stock out, whereas this theoretical model lets the system simply run its course.

5 Discussion and Summary

Overall, a supermarket histogram is an accurate tool to predict the delivery performance for a reduction of kanban for delivery performances in the range between 50 and 100%. The prediction accuracy worsens significantly for delivery performances below 50%, although a reduction in kanban is rarely desired for such inadequate delivery performances.

While kanban in general and pull in particular are not the only methods to manage make-to-stock production, it is usually the preferred approach in industry due to its reliability and ease of use. Other methods like push control requires much more management attention, which is often difficult due to the large number of different products produced in parallel in many factories. Hence, push often has an inferior performance to pull.

Overall, such a prediction can significantly help practitioners to fine-tune their kanban systems. A kanban system aims to have a trade-off between the availability of finished goods and the inventory needed to achieve this availability. Determining a suitable number of kanban is difficult. It is usually recommended to start with a sufficient or slightly excessive number of kanban, and reduce over time while observing the running system. This paper presents a tool to estimate the impact of the reduction of the number of kanban on the material availability, reducing the uncertainty in the management decision of this reduction.

Further research will look into increases in the number of kanban to improve the delivery performance as well as analyze systems where the customers are not waiting until they are served but will leave the system.

References

1. Buer, S.-V., Semini, M., Strandhagen, J.O., Sgarbossa, F.: The complementary effect of lean manufacturing and digitalisation on operational performance. Int. J. Prod. Res. **59**, 1–17 (2020). https://doi.org/10.1080/00207543.2020.1790684
2. Lai, N.Y.G., Wong, K.H., Halim, D., et al.: Industry 4.0 enhanced lean manufacturing. In: 2019 8th International Conference on Industrial Technology and Management (ICITM), pp. 206–211 (2019)
3. Little, J.D.C.: A proof for the queuing formula: L = λW. Oper. Res. **9**, 383–387 (1961). https://doi.org/10.1287/opre.9.3.383
4. Marodin, G.A., Tortorella, G.L., Frank, A.G., Godinho Filho, M.: The moderating effect of Lean supply chain management on the impact of Lean shop floor practices on quality and inventory. Supply Chain Manage. Int. J. **22**, 473–485 (2017). https://doi.org/10.1108/SCM-10-2016-0350
5. Roser, C.: All About Pull Production: Designing, Implementing, and Maintaining Kanban, CONWIP, and other Pull Systems in Lean Production. AllAboutLean.com, Offenbach, Germany (2021)

6. Co, H.C., Sharafali, M.: Overplanning factor in Toyota's formula for computing the number of kanban. IIE Trans. **29**, 409–415 (1997). https://doi.org/10.1080/07408179708966346
7. Roser, C., Nold, D.: Practical boundary case approach for kanban calculation on the shop floor subject to variation. In: Ameri, F., Stecke, K.E., von Cieminski, G., Kiritsis, D. (eds.) APMS 2019. IAICT, vol. 566, pp. 12–20. Springer, Cham (2019). https://doi.org/10.1007/978-3-030-30000-5_2
8. Gupta, S.M., Al-Turki, Y.A.Y.: An algorithm to dynamically adjust the number of Kanbans in stochastic processing times and variable demand environment. Prod. Plann. Control **8**, 133–141 (1997). https://doi.org/10.1080/095372897235398
9. Tardif, V., Maaseidvaag, L.: An adaptive approach to controlling kanban systems. Eur. J. Oper. Res. **132**, 411–424 (2001). https://doi.org/10.1016/S0377-2217(00)00119-3

Lean Production and Industry 4.0 Technologies: Link and Interactions

Anne Zouggar Amrani[✉] and Bruno Vallespir

University of Bordeaux, CNRS, IMS, UMR 5218, 33405 Talence, France
{anne.zouggar,bruno.vallespir}@ims-bordeaux.fr

Abstract. In current economic environment, two paradigms are sustaining the industrial performance: Lean production and industry 4.0 technologies. Whatever business the companies run they have to consider the benefits of Lean and the benefits of the arrival of new technologies of industry 4.0. The remaining question is how to consider these two paradigms in successful association to achieve high performance, reliable products and relevant supply chains. This paper suggests a first attempt to combine those two concepts. Previous works have highlighted the necessity of using both misleading modeling adequate approach of implementation. After browsing the existing studies related to this subject, this contribution shows the interactions that may co-exist between Lean and industry 4.0 technologies. The methodology is based on different analysis with accurate association of each technology and its ability to sustain Lean production approaches. Bilateral model can rise providing interesting insights to help managers in their transformation strategy often covering Lean and industry 4.0 technologies implementation.

Keywords: Lean production · Industry 4.0 · Technologies of industry 4.0

1 Introduction

To improve the performance of industrial systems and boost the production efficiency, an increasing number of companies around the world are undertaking Lean production transformation from workshops to whole enterprise and even global supply chain. Lean is considered as a methodical approach to organize and optimize the production flow aiming at realizing a continuous value stream to increase the quality and improve the reactivity while reducing the wastes and non-value-added activities. It is a mature system used for more than 60 years in Japan and more than 30 years in Europe. Concurrently, Industry 4.0 is a global concept aiming to design and create the enterprise of the future and smart factories. It focusses on the technology-driven vision combining the physical world and the cyber world through specific web and digital technologies [1].

2 Literature Review

Industry 4.0 grasps the attention of many researchers and practitioners [2–5]. Indeed, there is an urgent necessity to clarify its implementation because no structured and

© IFIP International Federation for Information Processing 2021
Published by Springer Nature Switzerland AG 2021
A. Dolgui et al. (Eds.): APMS 2021, IFIP AICT 630, pp. 697–703, 2021.
https://doi.org/10.1007/978-3-030-85874-2_76

well-defined model or method yet exist [6–8]. Few attempts have defined standards useful to identify the scope and the main fundaments. In [9] authors remind the first community efforts to standardize the comprehension, namely Reference Architecture Model for Industry 4.0 (RAMI 4.0) that has been introduced by the German Electrical and Electronic Manufacturers' Association [10]. RAMI 4.0 introduces a three-dimensional coordinate system that describes all crucial components of Industry 4.0. Within this system, complex and complicated interrelations can be decomposed into subsystems, clusters, or modules [11].

Both approaches (Fig. 1) contribute to close similar targets. Lean production aims to reduce time, increase quality avoiding defect products and decrease costs while maintaining safety target and worker motivation.

		Lean Production		Industrie 4.0
⚙	Approach	holistic (human + technology + organisation)	⬌	technology driven
❓	Philosophy	people development + problem solving	⬌	feasibility, (self) optimisation
🟦	Foundation	stability and standardisation	➕	interconnectivity, adaptivity
×ᵒ×	Control principle	flow, pull, FiFo	➕	dynamic, depending on current situation
〰	Improvement + problem solving	proactive → standard, abnormality → reactive	➕	data based learning → predictive
🔬	Information acquisition	real place, real material ("Go and See")	➕	problem specific data provision, "real time"

Fig. 1. Lean production and Industry 4.0 comparison (Enke [18])

Industry 4.0 adds elements of individualization, new business models and connected systems [12]. A literature review shows that either Lean production is impacting the evolution of Industry 4.0 and Industry 4.0 technologies are supporting the evolution of Lean Production. In [6] authors highlight that both paradigms have often been considered as separate subjects. Some authors catch the idea to associate both but in unilateral analysis with the necessity of Lean Production as a requirement for Industry 4.0.

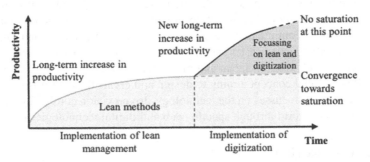

Fig. 2. Productivity improvement when digitization follows Lean (Prinz et al. [6])

Figure 2 shows the possible gain if Industry 4.0 is implemented after the application of Lean inducing new long-term increase in productivity with no saturation point (as it can be seen in case where Lean is implemented alone disregarding the offered possibilities by Industry 4.0).

In [6] author has led a study on Norway companies to extract the linkage between Lean implementation and the evolution of Industry 4.0 maturity. Figure 3 outlines that, in the timeline representing the sequential implementation of new improvement axes, it is of upmost importance to apply Lean techniques as pre requisites of Industry 4.0 implementation to ensure the manual routines and quality sustainment.

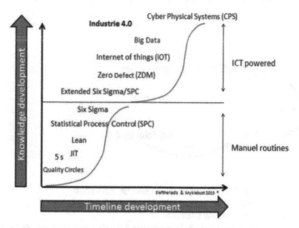

Fig. 3. Lean and industry 4.0 positioning in timeline development (Eleftheriadis [1]).

Satoglu in [13] considers the combination of both approaches and suggest that *"lean and industry 4.0 are not mutually exclusive but can be combined however the combination is yet very primitive with direct dual combination of effects without global model"*. Industry 4.0 supports factor to implement Lean. Lean activities should be well performed before automatization and connection. This is interesting to state that Industry 4.0 does not substitute to mismanagement and weak organized manufacturing. It is worth to denote that exclusive link with unilateral analysis is not enough anymore. Mayr in [14] evoke very recently the possible conjunction between both research axes. Author in [15] reviews some examples of leading Lean and Industry 4.0 in conjunction. Author in [16] relates relevant findings indicating that European manufacturers that aim to adopt higher levels of Industry 4.0 must concurrently implement Lean production as a way to support process improvements. In [18] authors evoke Industry 4.0 technologies as enablers of leaner production. [19] authors treated how to use or leave lean. Lean is pre requisite, this approach is consolidated by very big industrialists as Schneider, Bosch, Faurécia, Dassault who already implemented Lean Production Strategy before committing in the industry 4.0 transformation.

3   Methodology

The target of our approach is to thoroughly study the combination between these two paradigms influencing the industrial performance. By Performance, we mean global performance at the level of a factory, or enterprise or even supply chain level. To successfully achieve a performance, which is generally a complex task, deeper analysis has to be led. Different paths (Fig. 4) are possible to achieve optimization in factories/enterprises and supply chains. The aim of the study is to browse the existing studies subscribing to path 1 (where industry 4.0 technologies are essential and followed by Lean techniques) and those subscribing to path 2 claiming that Lean is a prerequisite to initiate Industry 4.0 transformation. The developed model will likely follow an incremental model to show gradually the success achievement with clarified steps. The idea is to model the different layers of industry 4.0 technologies implementation and Lean integration led in conjunction.

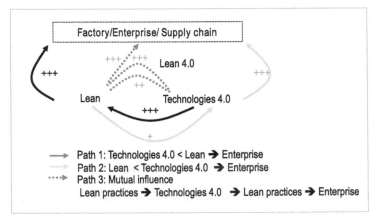

Fig. 4. Joint analysis between Lean and industry 4.0 technologies

The work starts with initiated analysis led by the German university in 2017 (Fig. 5). Technologies can be split into sensors/actuators, cloud computing, bigdata, data analytics, virtual/augmented reality and machine to machine communication. Each one of those technologies is influencing the efficiency of one or many Lean techniques.

	Data Acquisition and Data Processing				Machine to Machine Communication (M2M)		Human-Machine Interaction (HMI)	
	Sensors and Actuators	Cloud Computing	Big Data	Analytics	Vertical integration	Horizontal integration	Virtual Reality	Augmented Reality
5S	+	+	+	+	+	+	++	+++
Kaizen	+	++	+++	+++	+++	+++	+++	+++
Just-in-Time	++	++	+++	+++	+++	++	+	++
Jidoka	+	+++	+++	+++	++	++	+	+
Heijunka	++	++	+++	+++	+++	++	++	+
Standardisation	++	+++	+++	+++	++	++	+++	+++
Takt time	+	+	+++	+++	+++	+++	+	+
Pull flow	++	+	+	+	+++	+++	+	+
Man-machine separation	+	+	+	+	+	+	+++	+++
People and teamwork	+	+	+	+	+	+	+++	+++
Waste reduction	+	+	++	+++	+++	+++	+	+

Fig. 5. Industry 4.0 impact on lean production system – German study [17]

For instance, Augmented reality is useful to sustain 5S approach, helps to make reliable kaizen and people development. Smart sensors are helpful to support Just in time lean practice. However, we may highlight some critical points to Wagner's study: some of technologies are lacking in this table as Digital twin, Robotics, Internet Of things, 3D printing, AGV, … Other Lean Production practices are missing: Value Stream Mappin, Visual Management, Kanban, SMED.

The target of our study is to lead towards a more exhaustive and deeper analysis (Fig. 6). Each technology may contribute to different Lean production techniques. This association is of upmost importance to reveal beginning of interactions regarding wider scope of technologies and wider sample of Lean Production practices.

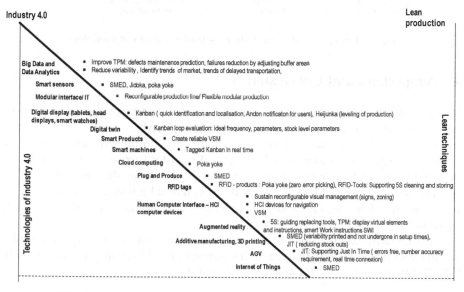

Fig. 6. The link between lean production and industry 4.0 technologies

The next step aims at deeply modeling the mutual interactions to perceive the gradual transformation for a company over time. For visualizing the link and interactions, we suggest the following points of interactions. The timeline synoptic provided by Fig. 7 reveals the intended progress. Different steps have to be undertaken in accordance with literature extensive review, analysis of correlations, use formal modelling and global model formalization considering the different configurations.

Once achieved, the model has to be tested and checked by companies. Interviews are also an important pillar to validate the findings and provide global roadmap to the companies expecting to lead industry 4.0 transformation and already engaged in Lean Production conversion. The idea of modularity and incremental integration of Industry 4.0 technologies will be deeply analyzed to federate the proposed model.

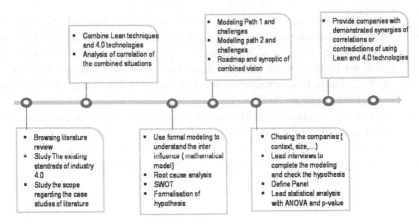

Fig. 7. Lean production and Industry 4.0 interrelations methodology

4 Perspectives and Conclusion

In near future, a cartography about the challenges, the important requirements and the impacts in path 1 and path 2 configurations will be explored.

The idea is to base the analysis on existing works to improve and identify the cross areas where correlations can be identified in order to provide a global synoptic about industry 4.0 technologies use and Lean Production implementation. Also, we will provide a mapping of the usefulness of the combined model Lean Production 4.0 for companies of our region "Nouvelle Aquitaine" after leading industry 4.0 maturity evaluation.

This research axis is prior for our research group, it allows to feed case studies dealing with Industry 4.0 to link research findings with IMS research projects namely: "BEST 4.0" and Industry 4.0 European Project "I4EU".

References

1. Eleftheriadis, R.J., Myklebust, O.: Industry 4.0 and cyber physical systems in a Norwegian industrial context. In: Wang, K., Wang, Yi., Strandhagen, J.O., Tao, Y. (eds.) IWAMA 2017. LNEE, vol. 451, pp. 491–499. Springer, Singapore (2017). https://doi.org/10.1007/978-981-10-5768-7_52
2. Cagnetti, C., Gallo, T., Silvestri, C., Ruggieri, A.: Lean production and Industry 4.0: strategy/management or technique/implementation? A systematic literature review. Procedia Comput. Sci. **180**, 404–413 (2021)
3. Küfner, T., Schönig, S., Jasinski, R., Ermer, A.: Vertical data continuity with lean edge analytics for industry 4.0 production. Comput. Ind. **125**, 103389 (2021)
4. Titmash, A.F., Harrison, R.: Contributions of lean six sigma to sustainable manufacturing requirements: an Industry 4.0 perspective. Proc. CIRP **90**, 589–593 (2020)
5. Bittencourt, V.L., Alves, A.C., Leão, C.P.: Lean thinking contributions for Industry 4.0: a systematic literature review. IFAC-PapersOnLine **52**(13), 904–909 (2019)
6. Prinz, C., Kreggenfeld, N., Kuhlenkötter, B.: Lean meets Industrie 4.0 – a practical approach to interlink the method world and cyber-physical world. Proc. Manuf. **23**, 21–26 (2018)

7. Sony, S.: Industry 4.0 and lean management: a proposed integration model and research propositions. Prod. Manuf. Res. **6**(1), 416–432 (2018)
8. Zhang, Z., Li, X., Wang, X., Cheng, H.: Decentralized cyber-physical systems: a paradigm for cloud-based smart factory of Industry 4.0. In: Thames, L., Schaefer, D. (eds.) Cybersecurity for Industry 4.0. SSAM, pp. 127–171. Springer, Cham (2017). https://doi.org/10.1007/978-3-319-50660-9_6
9. Xu, L.D., Xu, E.L., Li, L.: Industry 4.0: state of the art and future trends. Int. J. Prod. Res. **56**(8), 2941–2962 (2018)
10. Rojko, A.: Industry 4.0 concept: background and overview. Int. J. Interact. Mob. Technol. **11**, 77–90 (2017)
11. Götze, J.: Reference Architectures for Industry 4.0. Qualiware Center of Excellence (2016). https://coe.qualiware.com/reference-architectures-for-industry-4-0/
12. Enke, J., Glass, R., Kreß, A., Hambach, J., Tisch, M., Metternich, J.: Industrie 4.0 – competencies for a modern production system. Proc. Manuf. **23**, 267–272 (2018)
13. Satoglu, S., Ustundag, A., Cevikcan, E., Durmusoglu, M.B.: Lean production systems for industry 4.0. In: Ustundag, A., Cevikcan, E. (eds.) Industry 4.0: Managing The Digital Transformation, pp. 43–59. Springer International Publishing, Cham (2018). https://doi.org/10.1007/978-3-319-57870-5_3
14. Mayr, A., Weigelt, M., Kühl, A., Grimm, S., Erll, A., Potzel, M., Franke, J.: Lean 4.0 - a conceptual conjunction of lean management and Industry 4.0. Proc. CIRP **72**, 622–628 (2018)
15. Mrugalska, B., Wyrwicka, M.K.: Towards lean production in industry 4.0. Proc. Eng. **182**, 466–473 (2017)
16. Rossini, M., Costa, F., Tortorella, G.L., Portioli-Staudacher, A.: The interrelation between Industry 4.0 and lean production: an empirical study on European Manufacturers. Int. J. Adv. Manuf. Technol. **102**(9–12), 3963–3976 (2019). https://doi.org/10.1007/s00170-019-03441-7
17. Wagner, T., Herrmann, C., Thiede, S.: Industry 4.0 impacts on lean production systems. Proc. CIRP **63**, 125–131 (2017)
18. Powell, D., Romero, D., Gaiardelli, P., Cimini, C., Cavalieri, S.: Towards digital lean cyber-physical production systems: industry 4.0 technologies as enablers of leaner production. In: Moon, I., Lee, G.M., Park, J., Kiritsis, D., von Cieminski, G. (eds.) APMS 2018. IAICT, vol. 536, pp. 353–362. Springer, Cham (2018). https://doi.org/10.1007/978-3-319-99707-0_44
19. Netland, T.: Industry 4.0: where does it leave lean? Lean Manage. J. **5**, 22–23 (2015)

Heijunka 4.0 – Key Enabling Technologies for Production Levelling in the Process Industry

Håkon S. Kjellsen, Quentin J. L. Ramillon, Heidi C. Dreyer[✉], and Daryl J. Powell

Department of Industrial Economics and Technology Management, Norwegian University of Science and Technology, Trondheim, Norway
heidi.c.dreyer@ntnu.no

Abstract. This paper investigates how lean production levelling methods can be better applied in the process industry with support from key enabling technologies from Industry 4.0. To investigate such a topic, a literature study is conducted in three main areas, namely production planning in the process industry, Lean Production, and Industry 4.0. Based on the findings from the literature review, a conceptual framework is developed to illustrate the ability of Internet of Things, Big Data Analytics, and the further integration of IT systems to provide increased reliability for materials, processes, equipment, and forecasts that improves the utilization of Heijunka (production levelling) practices in the process industry.

Keywords: Process industry · Lean production · Industry 4.0

1 Introduction

The current competitive business landscape is increasingly getting more volatile and uncertain. Therefore, companies must adhere to superior practices to be capable of meeting the new challenges of competing. Conventional lean production levelling methods have for several decades led to performance improvement in discrete manufacturing through offering greater predictability, flexibility, and stability for a wide range of companies [1]. However, the process industry has not yet embraced the real extent of benefits that lean manufacturing can offer [2]. This might be explained by the characteristics of the process industry that are inherently complex and inflexible, which makes a straightforward application of lean practices challenging [3]. However, such characteristics do not make it impossible to apply lean principles, as many process industries have shown promising results in improving operational performance using modified versions of certain lean practices [4]. Furthermore, the technology-oriented industry 4.0 concept is being branded as the next enabler of performance improvement in manufacturing [5]. Therefore, in this paper, we investigate how lean production levelling practices can be applied in the process industry, with particular focus on which Industry 4.0 technologies can support such an application.

Motivated by the research challenges and problems described above, we aim to use the following research question to guide our investigation: *How can key enabling*

© IFIP International Federation for Information Processing 2021
Published by Springer Nature Switzerland AG 2021
A. Dolgui et al. (Eds.): APMS 2021, IFIP AICT 630, pp. 704–711, 2021.
https://doi.org/10.1007/978-3-030-85874-2_77

technologies of Industry 4.0 support and enhance lean production levelling practices in the process industry?

2 Research Design

Given the nature of our research question, a preferrable approach would have been to adopt case study research as our primary research method. However, due to the current restrictions on access to case companies and travels in response of the Covid-19 pandemic, we attempt to answer the research questions by developing a conceptual framework from literature review. Further research will explore the framework in empirical settings. As such, we explore existing and relevant theories, models, and findings through an extensive review of extant literature. The area of investigation is at the intersection of three major areas: production planning (in particular production levelling) in the process industry, lean production, and Industry 4.0.

We report the results of the literature review in Sect. 3. Section 3.1 focuses on the area of planning in the process industry while Sect. 3.2 focuses on lean production, as well as the intersection between lean production and production levelling in the process industry. Section 3.3 focuses on Industry 4.0, as well as how Industry 4.0 builds on traditional lean production principles and practices. In Sect. 4, by considering the theoretical overview surrounding the intersection of all three areas, we attempt to answer the proposed research question by offering a conceptual framework.

3 Literature Review

3.1 Production Planning and Control in the Process Industry

We start by giving a brief introduction to the notion of process industry, what characterizes it and how it differs from discrete manufacturing. This is followed by an investigation on what the main characteristics within process industries are, and how such attributes constitute potential barriers for the application of lean planning methods.

Discrete manufacturing normally consists of the manufacture of individual parts and components that machines and operators weld, bolt and assemble together to a complete product, with examples ranging from automobiles, cell phones, computers, power tools and hair dryers [3]. [3] also states that the process industry, on the other hand, is characterized by processes that involve mixing, extrusion, chemical reactions and annealing. Products that are used in such industries are often non-discrete materials which includes liquids, pulps, gases and powders and can often dry out, evaporate or expand if they are not put into a container [4]. Examples can range from different types of paints, processed foods and beverages, paper goods, fibres, glass, steel, aluminum and ceramics.

Planning and scheduling decisions are essential processes in company-wide supply chain and logistics management, and process industry operations are significantly impacted by these decisions [6]. Planning in process industries creates plans within production, supply, distribution, sales, and inventory based on demand information while considering all known and relevant constraints [7]. For long- to medium-term planning, detailed routing information for sequencing is often required as "products are commonly defined by the succession of production steps which they undergo" [8]. Sales and demand information, availability of raw materials, simultaneous production of co-products and final products or optimal usage of expensive equipment have a significant impact on production planning and control [8].

The flow of materials in the process industry can differ from one batch to the next. [8] suggests that such industries must cope with variable recipes and specific sequences of transformation processes. Next, dedicated production technology and special storage equipment is often required for all materials that must be taken into account by planning and scheduling systems. Furthermore, according to [9], the production units and material flows tend to have more interrelationships, as both production flow and material complexity are higher. For these reasons, planning and scheduling in the process industry is complicated. Therefore, conventional planning methods such as MRP and lean levelling techniques, which are more associated with discrete industries, are hard to apply [2]. Such existing production planning and control concepts do not suit the needs of process industries in general [8]. Much of the extant literature supports the implementation of lean production and planning concepts in process industries, but due to its inherent characteristics it is challenging to apply these directly. This is especially true for the flexibility limiting characteristics such as long and sequence-dependent setup times and changeover cost which are in direct contrast to *Lean Production* [2].

3.2 Lean Production

This section introduces the lean philosophy, principles, and tools, and focuses on production levelling (Heijunka) practices in order to understand its effects, requirements, and its applicability in the process industry. Lean Production, largely based on the manufacturing principles and work processes developed by Toyota [10] and quickly spread to different industries [12]. [13] defines the basis of the Toyota Production System (TPS) as the absolute elimination of waste and suggests that this is the key to improving productivity and competitiveness. Lean Production is an enterprise-wide continuous improvement approach aimed at eliminating waste and creating value for the customer.

Lean production planning and control practices (e.g., production levelling) have enabled companies to improve their performance and reap high benefit. However, while Lean Production can be applied to various industries and types of organization [14], the adoption thus far has mainly taken place in discrete manufacturing, rather than in continuous or process industry sectors [3].

Production levelling is one of the essential Lean Production practices [15]. Also called Heijunka or production smoothing, it refers to the practice of levelling the volume of material that is being produced over time, such that the production level is as constant as possible from day to day. Particularly beneficial for the process industry where stable production environments are preferable. According to [1], level production is scheduling the daily production for different product types in such a sequence that evens out peaks of the produced quantities. Production levelling can be conducted by gathering all orders over a specific period of time and scheduling the production at an even rate and in the mixed sequence, i.e., repetitive patterns [3]. According to this levelling pattern, every product type is manufactured within a periodic interval called the

Every Part Every (EPE) interval. The general objective is to reduce the EPE interval to a cost-effective minimum [15]. The benefits of Heijunka include improved operational stability and reduced variability of resource utilization and material requirements, as well as reduced quality problems, breakdowns and defects. Despite these positive effects, however, levelling does not mean waste-free production. On the contrary, successful implementation of production levelling often requires a controlled inventory of finished products [15]. But, this often small inventory buffer enables the reduction of irregularity (mura) and overburden (muri), and reduces both the bullwhip effect and delivery lead time [16].

The Heijunka concept has been customized by several scholars to handle the different batch sizes and product mix that characterizes the process industry, for example EPE [1], Product Wheel [3], and Rhythm Wheel [17]. These new cyclical planning methods are based on a systemic and visual metaphor for a repeated planning methodology that aims to mitigate the variation in demand volume through optimized production sequences, enabling the creation of the best sequences of products and batches including into the calculation the setup and changeover time [3]. Moreover, capacity that is not fully utilized is often maintained for strategic reasons, such as reducing changeover times and carrying out continuous improvement practices [1]. However, Heijunka planning in the process industry increase planning complexity significantly causing the need for extensive planning and replanning capacity.

3.3 Industry 4.0 and Key Enabling Technologies

Industry 4.0 is characterized with several main technology clusters, including Cyber-Physical Systems (CPS) and Internet of Things (IoT) [18]. In a manufacturing environment, CPS and IoT facilitates the advancement of autonomous productive processes which become intelligent: "through communication and decision algorithms, the components can decide on their configuration and their path in the line production" [19]. Furthermore, according to [20], in Industry 4.0, the intelligence is distributed across the process steps and not centralized, which provide greater stability and operations flexibility, as well as reducing planning resources and ease replanning.

Industry 4.0 is promising for manufacturing companies, as new key enabling technologies will enable companies to gain a significant competitive advantage. As such, wan say that Lean Production and Industry 4.0 share the same objective, even though some consider them to be based on competing principles [21]. However, the empirical study of [22] suggests that Industry 4.0 technologies alone do not contribute to performance improvement and should rather be seen as enablers of Lean Production.

A literature study on how Industry 4.0 impacts Production Planning and Control (PPC) functions in general was conducted by [23], where the majority of research were mostly based on IoT technologies – concerning the integration of manufacturing execution systems and process control, interoperability, digitalization, real-time data collection, visibility, traceability and sharing of information. Hence, the most relevant industry 4.0 key enabling technology clusters for this investigation (using the classification of [24]) are IoT, Big Data Analytics and Integration of IT systems. This is also in line with the brief description of the Heijunka 4.0 concept provided in [25].

4 Conceptual Framework

To mitigate some of the inherent characteristics that inhibit lean production levelling (Heijunka) in the process industry, we suggest that it is possible to apply three specific, enabling technology clusters associated with Industry 4.0, selected from the classification provided in [24]. The framework is presented in Fig. 1, showing that the Industry 4.0 technologies IoT and Big Data Analytics can be applied to gather information regarding process industry characteristics that otherwise prevent the effective application of Heijunka methods, and integrates these into existing IT planning architectures such as ERP and APS software. The two-way arrows in the model illustrate that the elements are interconnected and communicates in real time.

Tools within the technology cluster IoT such as Radio Frequency Identification (RFID) and positioning sensors that measure times between specific product types and optical recognition sensors for determining product types can have significant impacts on Heijunka methods. High reliability of production processes is a prerequisite for such Heijunka methods, and IoT can enhance process management and control. Everything from variability in raw material quality to variations in internal processes and stock levels, such as dosing of raw material, temperature control, residence times, aging catalysts and system fouling will contribute to process variations. By using sensors and vision technology, to collect and connect data from various sources, and using Big Data Analytics for advanced calculations and simulations it is possible to predict process behavior, and increase production process reliability resulting in reduced changeover times, reduced production processing times, and increased available time for process improvement (e.g. predictive maintenance [25]).

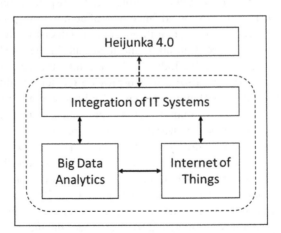

Fig. 1. Conceptual framework for Heijunka 4.0.

Furthermore, by utilizing IoT technologies, making material and equipment communicate with each other by using sensors such as Radio-frequency Identification (RFID), the equipment can quickly change to corresponding parameters, hence reducing the changeover times [26]. Furthermore, Big Data Analytics can use advanced simulation methods to optimize changeover and setups, by testing different methods [27]. As discussed in Sect. 3.2, shorter set up and changeover times will result in shorter cycle times for the Heijunka schedule, which could lead to more flexibility to meet demand variations. What has been discussed so far relates more to internal factors, such as material, process and equipment. Another important factor to make the Heijunka approach well suited is low variation in demand. Big Data Analytics that utilizes advanced algorithms and calculation methods enhances forecast quality, and the level planning can be stabilized by utilizing the combination of data history and a deeper understanding of customers' needs through in-depth analyses of the market.

This may also have a positive effect on the occurrence of waste (muda) arising from levelling practices. For example, [15] suggests that the successful implementation of production levelling often requires a controlled inventory of finished (ore indeed semi-finished) products. Though this often small inventory buffer enables the reduction of irregularity (mura) and overburden (muri), and reduces both the bullwhip effect and delivery lead time [16]; by Integrating IT systems, the data information that is collected and calculated can thereafter be aggregated into the existing IT architectures such as ERP and APS for enhancing the Heijunka schedule. Parameters such as inventory replenishment levels, supply, production sequences and cycle times can be further optimized by utilizing information gathered and aggregated from IoT and Big Data Analytics regarding material, processes, equipment and demand, contributing to the elimination of traditional waste in the form of excessive inventories, but also reducing digital-waste in both its active- and passive forms (as described in [28]).

[29] also explores various sources of "buffer waste", where an organization's efforts to target muri and mura often generate unforeseen examples of muda. We suggest that the Heijunka 4.0 concept can be used to alleviate *"the muri, mura, and muda vicious cycle"*.

5   Conclusion

We set out to investigate the potential support functionality of Industry 4.0 key enabling technologies for lean production levelling in the process industry. As such, we addressed the research question: *How can technologies associated with Industry 4.0 support lean production levelling practices in the process industry?*

It has been demonstrated in this study that Industry 4.0 technologies can both enable and improve the adoption of Heijunka in the process industry. The literature argues that Industry 4.0 supports lean principles, however, only a few studies study how individual industry 4.0 tools support specific lean practices. Thus, on the basis of these few studies, a conceptual framework detailing how the different tools of Industry 4.0 support the levelling of production in the process industry has been developed. This framework illustrates that the Industry 4.0 technology clusters *Internet of Things* and *Big Data Analytics* can provide predictability and visibility for factors such as process, material, equipment and demand. These types of data can be aggregated into existing IT systems, such ERP, MES, and APS that designs the level schedule, using the Industry 4.0 technology cluster *Integration of IT systems*.

In terms of limitations, although this investigation was carried out with the aim of having a strong practical involvement in bridging the gap between the application of lean production levelling practices in discrete manufacturing and in the process industry, further empirical studies are needed to assess and consolidate the conceptual framework. Indeed, multiple case studies applying the Heijunka 4.0 concept are required to evaluate the conceptual framework in greater detail.

References

1. Powell, D., Alfnes, E., Semini, M.: The application of lean production control methods within a process-type industry: the case of hydro automotive structures. In: Vallespir, B., Alix, T. (eds.) APMS 2009. IAICT, vol. 338, pp. 243–250. Springer, Heidelberg (2010). https://doi.org/10.1007/978-3-642-16358-6_31
2. Spenhoff, P., Semini, M., Powell, D.: Investigating production planning and control challenges in the semi-process industry, the case of a metal parts producer. In: 2016 IEEE International Conference on Industrial Engineering and Engineering Management (IEEM), pp. 961–965. IEEE (2016)
3. King, P.L.: Lean for the Process Industries: Dealing with Complexity. Productivity Press, New York (2009)
4. Abdulmalek, F.A., Rajgopal, J., Needy, K.L.: A classification scheme for the process industry to guide the implementation of lean. Eng. Manage. J. 18(2), 15–25 (2006)
5. Ashrafian, A., et al.: Sketching the landscape for lean digital transformation. In: Ameri, F., Stecke, K.E., von Cieminski, G., Kiritsis, D. (eds.) APMS 2019. IAICT, vol. 566, pp. 29–36. Springer, Cham (2019). https://doi.org/10.1007/978-3-030-30000-5_4
6. Shobrys, D.E., White, D.C.: Planning, scheduling and control systems: why can they not work together. Comput. Chem. Eng. 24(2–7), 163–173 (2000)
7. Kallrath, J.: Planning and scheduling in the process industry. OR Spectr. 24(3), 219–250 (2002)
8. Crama, Y., Pochet, Y., Wera, Y.: A discussion of production planning approaches in the process industry (2001)
9. Fransoo, J.C., Rutten, W.G.: A typology of production control situations in process industries. Int. J. Oper. Prod. Manage. 14, 47–57 (1994)
10. Holweg, M.: The genealogy of lean production. J. Oper. Manage. 25(2), 420–437 (2007). https://doi.org/10.1016/j.jom.2006.04.001. http://www.sciencedirect.com/science/article/pii/S0272696306000313
11. Womack, J.P., Jones, D.T., Roos, D.: The Machine that Changed the World. Harper Perennial, New York (1990)
12. Womack, J.P., Jones, D.T.: Lean Thinking: Banish Waste and Create Wealth in Your Corporation. Simon and Schuster, New York (1996)
13. Ohno, T.: Toyota Production System: Beyond Large-Scale Production. Productivity Press, New York (1988)
14. Netland, T.H., Powell, D.J. (eds.): The Routledge Companion to Lean Management. Routledge, New York (2017)
15. Liker, J.K.: The Toyota Way: 14 Management Principles From the World's Greatest Manufacturer. McGraw-Hill, New York (2004)
16. Coleman, B.J., Vaghefi, M.R.: Heijunka (?): A key to the Toyota production system. Prod. Invent. Manag. J. 35(4), 31 (1994)
17. Packowski, J.: LEAN supply chain planning: the new supply chain management paradigm for process industries to master today's VUCA World. CRC Press (2013)
18. Sinha, A., Bernardes, E., Calderon, R., Wuest, T.: Digital Supply Networks: Transform Your Supply Chain and Gain Competitive Advantage with Disruptive Technology and Reimagined Processes. McGraw Hill, New York (2020)

19. Lee, J., Bagheri, B., Kao, H.-A.: A cyber-physical systems architecture for industry 4.0-based manufacturing systems. Manufa. Lett. **3**, 18–23 (2015)
20. Klingenberg, C.: Industry 4.0: what makes it a revolution?, pp. 1–10 (2017)
21. Rosin, F., Forget, P., Lamouri, S., Pellerin, R.: Impacts of Industry 4.0 technologies on Lean principles. Int. J. Prod. Res. **58**(6), 1644–1661 (2020)
22. Kamble, S., Gunasekaran, A., Dhone, N.C.: Industry 4.0 and lean manufacturing practices for sustainable organisational performance in Indian manufacturing companies. Int. J. Prod. Res. **58**(5), 1319–1337 (2020)
23. Bueno, A.F., Godinho Filho, M., Frank, A.G.: Smart production planning and control in the Industry 4.0 context: a systematic literature review. Comput. Ind. Eng. **159**, 106774 (2020)
24. Buer, S.-V.: Investigating the relationship between Lean manufacturing and Industry 4.0 (2020)
25. Mayr, A., et al.: Lean 4.0-a conceptual conjunction of lean management and Industry 4.0. Proc. Cirp **72**, 622–628 (2018)
26. Ciano, M.P., Dallasega, P., Orzes, G., Rossi, T.: One-to-one relationships between Industry 4.0 technologies and Lean production techniques: a multiple case study. Int. J. Prod. Res. **59**(5), 1386–1410 (2020)
27. Rüßmann, M., et al.: Industry 4.0: the future of productivity and growth in manufacturing industries. Boston Consult. Group **9**(1), 54–89 (2015)
28. Romero, D., Gaiardelli, P., Powell, D., Wuest, T., Thürer, M.: Digital lean cyber-physical production systems: the emergence of digital lean manufacturing and the significance of digital waste. In: Moon, I., Lee, G.M., Park, J., Kiritsis, D., von Cieminski, G. (eds.) Advances in Production Management Systems. Production Management for Data-Driven, Intelligent, Collaborative, and Sustainable Manufacturing: IFIP WG 5.7 International Conference, APMS 2018, Seoul, Korea, August 26–30, 2018, Proceedings, Part I, pp. 11–20. Springer International Publishing, Cham (2018). https://doi.org/10.1007/978-3-319-99704-9_2
29. Romero, D., Gaiardelli, P., Thürer, M., Powell, D., Wuest, T.: Cyber-physical waste identification and elimination strategies in the digital lean manufacturing world. In: Ameri, F., Stecke, K.E., von Cieminski, G., Kiritsis, D. (eds.) Advances in Production Management Systems. Production Management for the Factory of the Future: IFIP WG 5.7 International Conference, APMS 2019, Austin, TX, USA, September 1–5, 2019, Proceedings, Part I, pp. 37–45. Springer International Publishing, Cham (2019). https://doi.org/10.1007/978-3-030-30000-5_5

Towards an Economic Theory of Lean

Eivind Reke[1]([⊠]), Daryl Powell[1,2], and Kodo Yokozawa[3]

[1] SINTEF Manufacturing, Trondheim, Norway
eivind.reke@sintef.no
[2] Norwegian University of Science and Technology, Trondheim, Norway
[3] Yokohama National University, Yokohama, Japan

Abstract. For more than 40 years, researchers have studied the operations management practices of Toyota and their application in different companies and industries, most notably under the heading of lean operations. Even though lean has become an integral part of the operations management curriculum and corporations such as Danaher have embraced it as their "way of doing business", lean has yet to truly breach the executive echelons of most firms and as such fails to reach its true potential as an alternative, people-centric, and sustainable business model. To address this gap, we have carried out an extensive literature search on the subject and conducted several interviews with C-suite executives from lean firms. Our findings point us in the direction of an underlying economic theory of lean, based on the business model and associated practices of the Toyota Motor Corporation. Furthermore, we present three exemplary case companies which have adapted some or all of these practices under the guise of lean production.

Keywords: Lean product and process development · Lean business model · Company economic performance

1 Introduction

Lean Production has been an area of interest for academics and industry practitioners alike. Ever since the findings of the International motor vehicle program (IMVP), demonstrated to the western auto companies that their business model was being out-competed by Japanese automotive companies, with Toyota leading the way [1]. As such, lean could be defined as the application of Toyota's business model (most notably the Toyota Production System (TPS)), outside of Toyota. Much has been made of the production techniques, the thinking behind them and the operational results that these may lead to if implemented. However, less is understood of the business model that drives the thinking of Toyota, a company that over the course of 70 years has gone from plucky start-up to industry leader in terms of volume, revenue, profits, and model variety through debt-free growth funded by its attention to detail and relentless pursuit of waste- and cost-reductions, from design to manufacture, to sales and services.

Incidentally, at the time of the IMVP benchmarking study, General Motors (GM) was the largest car manufacturer in the world, with Toyota still a growing company - having

© IFIP International Federation for Information Processing 2021
Published by Springer Nature Switzerland AG 2021
A. Dolgui et al. (Eds.): APMS 2021, IFIP AICT 630, pp. 712–720, 2021.
https://doi.org/10.1007/978-3-030-85874-2_78

only started to develop its manufacturing capabilities in Europe and North America in the early 80s (in the late 90s they also developed product development capabilities on these continents). At the time of writing, the tables have turned, and Toyota has been one of (if not the) largest and most profitable car manufacturer in the world, since it overtook GM in 2007 (delivering steady operating margins of about 8–10% the last 8 years). The continued research interest into Toyota's business practices is linked to this story, and even though we now know a great deal more about the inner workings of the Toyota Production System, with a few exceptions, western scholars have not studied at depth the economic theory that underpins Toyota's business model; rather relying on established economic theories and thus missing an opportunity to open a new branch of research into lean thinking and practice. However, to establish an economic theory of lean, we must first understand the fundamental differentiators that lies behind this successful, alternative business model.

As such, this paper is an attempt to explore and establish a path towards an economic theory of lean. First, we present a literature review to define the gaps in current research on the topic. Thereafter, we developed a set of research questions to address these gaps, before exploring these research questions by collecting publicly available operational- and financial data and interviewing former executives from select case companies that have experienced sustained business success through lean thinking and practice in the form of market share and above industry average returns. Two out of three case companies have also received recognition from industry peers in the form of national lean prizes. Finally, we suggest areas for further research based on the findings presented in this paper.

2 Background

To develop an economic theory of lean, one must first understand the assumptions behind Toyota's business model. [2] defines a business model as *"a representation of a firm's underlying core logic and strategic choices for creating and capturing value within a value network"*. As such, how a company generates wealth and what it chooses to do with it stems from its business model. The Value Added (VA) of any activities (in Toyota's case, designing and building cars), is the revenue the company takes in less the services and goods it pays for in doing so. Thus, for whom a company creates wealth and what it does with its VA stems from its business model. Toyota's business model, the underlying core logic, and strategic choices for creating and capturing wealth, have been studied for over 40 years, and for the last 30 years under the lean heading. Even though some now seek to dismiss the role and impact Toyota has had on the continuous development of lean as a research theme [3], we believe it would be a mistake to simply reduce lean to the study of efficient manufacturing practices. The real strategic potential of lean is *"half the bad, double the good"* [4]. As such, we suggest that to better understand how this potential is realized, we must take a broader approach.

3 Literature Review

Ever since Toyota started to compete on the global market in the 70s, the company has been of interest to researchers and academics. By the time the company became industry leader, the interest had exploded with books [e.g. 4, 5] and articles [e.g. 6, 7] trying to explain the reason for its successful growth. Attempts have also been made to explain the financial performance and operational performance impact of lean (sometimes under the heading of just-in-time (JIT)). Proving the link between lean operations and improved (or superior) financial performance has however been elusive, though some indications have been found. In a study covering over 250 US manufacturing companies, [9] found that JIT practices impacted overall profitability, but that quality practices did not. Furthermore, [10] found that leanness in terms of inventory positively impacts credit ratings. In the automotive industry, the adoption of Toyota's production practices has been carried out to such a degree that practitioners now don't necessarily distinguish between them, i.e., lean is "done in car manufacturing".

As documented by [11], Lean production (in some form or other) has over the last 30 years been widely adopted by many global companies, either through business systems or so called company specific production systems (XPS) [12]. With regards to the operations management practices of Toyota and adopters of lean operations, one finds studies on best practices [13], as well as implementation success factors [14] and barriers [15–17]. One also finds a variety of definitions of lean production summed up by [18] and [19], and what to expect when implementing said practices, concepts and tools [20]. While these are all worthwhile endeavors, most of these studies fail in explaining the growth in market share, revenue, and margin that Toyota experienced from the late 50s through to the present day (delivering steady profits and growth and mostly financing their overseas growth organically). A notable exception is [21] which suggests the changes one might experience, but do not discuss what to do with said changes and the potential productivity and thus economic gains derived from these changes.

Based on our review of the extant literature, we propose four differentiating factors underpinning Toyota's business model that point towards an economic theory of lean: 1) Better quality by applying the Toyota Production System and kaizen without paying a quality premium, 2) a learning curve on flexibility to offer customers a steady growth of new models without the capital investment normally associated with an expanding product range, 3) Re-investment of productivity gains fostering the long-term development of engineers and operators and 4) Financial self-reliance to support steady growth organically or through acquisitions.

3.1   Better Quality Through TPS + Kaizen

Hard to pin-point but easy to observe is the effect on quality and lead-time that can be experienced in kaizen or continuous improvement activities. Toyota adopted their version of the Ford suggestion system in the 50s (which was later abandoned in Ford), and with it the slogan: "Good Thinking, Good Products", have continued to reap the rewards from their employees' improvement suggestions. One could even argue that Toyota's manufacturing practices today is the sum of the improvement suggestions and countermeasures that have been implemented over the past 70 years. For instance, the first quality measure put in place, the Jidoka device of the automatic loom, was responsible for creating better quality products (no broken treads) and at the same time increased productivity 10-fold by allowing an individual operator to monitor multiple looms. According to [22] there are three types of kaizen activities carried out on the shop floor; 1) those carried out by supervisors, managers and production engineers, 2) those carried out by quality circles and 3) those that come from the suggestion system itself. It is sometimes referred to by Toyota as weak point management system [23]. Furthermore, [24] argue that TPS is also an education system that shows engineers and designers how design and engineering can contribute to quality engineering without paying quality premiums through thorough cost planning [25].

3.2 Learning Curve on Flexibility

According to [26], *"achieving optimal product variety is one of the most strategic decision making processes of the firm"*. Toyota realized early on that the trade-off between flexibility and efficiency was not fixed, and was able to develop the capability to move beyond this trade-off [27]. One of the early famous lean stories is that of Taiichi Ohno, according to legend, picking up, in a fire-sale, small and versatile presses and other machinery from a soon-to-be bankrupt American machine maker on a field trip to the U.S. in the 50s. These quick-change die-presses are now exhibited in the Toyota museum in Nagoya, Japan [28]. Toyota realized early that they could not rely on the American one-car-per-factory business model. At the time, they simply did not have the financial muscle of their American counterparts. The learning curves first steps where to produce more than one variant on one line, with TPS. According to Toyota themselves, flexibility is also a global strategy with factories in Japan able to flexibly adjust model variants to adjust for fluctuations in the global market, allowing less advanced plants around the globe to move more slowly through the learning curve, while at the same time allowing for high yields and plant utilization. In fact, Toyota's most advanced line has been dubbed *"the most flexible line in the world"* by industry experts [29].

3.3 Re-invest of Productivity Gains into the Development of People

Some version of "before we make cars, we make people" can be found quoted in different studies of Toyota's approach to people development. An example of this re-investment in people can be found as early as 1961, when Eiji Toyoda identified the lack of training of new employees as one of the root causes of the quality crisis Toyota experienced with the roll out of the second-generation Corolla. The countermeasure was heavy investment in training and education in quality, while also supporting the previous point of better quality through kaizen as the company aimed to half the number of defects. This re-investment in training programs has since periodically happened in both manufacturing and engineering with KanPro in the late 70s, statistical quality control (SQC) renaissance in the late 80s, total quality management (TQM) in the mid-90s and global quality control in the 2000s [30]. [31] presents the methodical and systematical efforts put into the development of engineers and designers for as long as 30 years, while [32] discusses in detail how leadership training is carried out. Finally, [33] shows how Toyota have built on and adjusted the Training Within Industry (TWI) system to thoroughly train operators and supervisors in both the skills required to carry out the job at a high level, as well as the skills required to maintain and improve the job through Kaizen. This people-first thinking has been a mainstay of Toyota's business model regardless of factory location [34]. [35] argues that this continuous re-investment in people is key to reducing the transaction cost normally associated with the successful transfer of design information from product design to manufacturing.

3.4 Financial Self-reliance

A much less covered topic in western academic research is how Toyota have been more or less financially self-reliant over a long period of time, and have, according to Akio Toyoda, mostly grown organically *"by selling one car after the other"* [30]. In fact, [36] claims that the company has been debt-free since 1977, which suggests Toyota financed its global expansion that started with the first factories in the US with internal funds. Along with Kaizen, the target cost system is arguably the method that delivers the economic flexibility of Toyota. This process starts as early as the product planning phase and ends in the tail end of the model life-cycle, with the purpose of systematically reducing cost throughout the life-cycle of the product. The cost reduction is achieved by applying technology and smartness throughout the value chain, not through so-called strategic cost-management associated with more traditional business models [37] (i.e., outsourcing component manufacturing to lowest bidder). Instead of shifting the VA wealth creation to shareholders or similar, Toyota have always kept a large reserve of cash and cash equivalents to fund its big bets. Exemplified with its expansion into, first, the American market, then the luxury market (with Lexus), and now on connectivity with Woven City and the future power systems of cars (triple bet on hydrogen, hybrid and full electric).

4 Research Design

The research follows an exploratory inductive case study research design to develop propositions from complex social phenomena [38]. To generate valuable insight, we compared our findings from the literature review with three case studies selected due to their success in lean implementation (above industry average growth, profitability and returns) as well as industry recognition of their "leanness", i.e., two of the companies have won national lean prizes, and the third has been widely studied and written about in the extant lean literature. We conducted interviews with executives from the three different companies in three different countries (in Scandinavia, and the U.S.), and combined the interview data with publicly available financial data to explore the potential of an economic theory of lean. Based on our findings we suggest one economic proposition for each differentiator that should be explored in further research.

5 Findings and Discussion

The lean journey starting points for the three companies in question were similar. The CEO had either learned about TPS or lean before starting the journey or was trained internally by the company in question (e.g., Executive A spent one year training his senior team before making any changes to the company, Executive B was trained on the ground by his CEO who himself had worked directly with Japanese Sensei). As such they all tick the first success criteria presented by [14] *"the commitment of top management"*. However, our findings suggest that all three went one step further and changed the way they lead the company based on what they had learned.

Furthermore, all three companies experienced unprecedented growth (from 200%–500%) and profitability (from loss to 15% EBIDTA) over a short period of time, suggesting that developing lean capabilities within the company allowed them to realize the potential of the business in a way that traditional western management capabilities would not. In Table 1 we summarize our findings, comparing the case companies' business model to the four differentiating factors of the lean business model.

Table 1. Comparison of the case companies' business practice with the lean business model.

Case Company	Quality through TPS + Kaizen?	Learning curve on flexibility	Re-invested in people development	Achieved financial self-reliance
Case A	Yes	Yes	Yes	Partially
Case B	Yes	Yes	Yes	No data
Case C	Yes	Yes	Yes	Yes

From our interviews and the operational data we collected from the companies we found that *quality through TPS + Kaizen* was key in order to achieve and sustain the economic performance. One interviewee reported that the gains from kaizen activities had allowed the company to postpone investments for almost 8 years, and when the investment had to be made, the learning from kaizen activities meant that they made different choices to what they would have made if these activities had not been carried out. The two others reported both cost reduction and quality increase benefits from kaizen activities. All three companies experienced increased sales and revenue due to improvements in quality, lead-time and cost. This leads us to our first proposition: *TPS + Kaizen leads to increased sales due to better quality, lower capital expenditure through just-in-time and lower operational expenses through Jidoka.*

Leveraging the flexibility learning curve to better serve customers was also reported as key for all three companies. Two of them had expanded their product portfolio 10-fold while at the same time keeping quality high and cost low. The third leverage their flexibility capability to serve their professional customer as a one stop shop for both equipment and consumables. All three companies had throughout their lean journey emphasized flexibility in the form of SMED-training, quick die change and other activities that gave the companies greater agility. Bear in mind that it is not necessarily about the broadest possible product range, but one that covers the market space with good product-market fit in the market the business is in. Thus, our second proposition is: *Increased flexibility allows a company to offer a broader range of products and should increase turn-over, without the capital investment usually associated with broadening the product-range.*

Reinvesting productivity gains into the development of engineers and operators emerged as a success factor for all three case companies, which led to better decisions on how to improve both manufacturing processes and product design. Even after re-investing in people development, the three case companies like Toyota had surplus wealth creation. Toyota as we discussed earlier used this to free itself from debt and largely financed its own international expansion. Even though all three case companies to some extent used their new-found financial strength for investments, we found that only one company used this self-reliance to continue its growth, something that suggests this point might be considered an outcome of the lean business model adoption and not a pre-requisite practice *per se*. Regardless, developing people is key to the lean business model and, as such, our third proposition is: *by developing the technical competence of people, precision increases and costs decrease, and the capability for innovation also increases.*

The case companies took different choices with the freed resources and cash derived from the productivity gains. One company used it to fund acquisitions and set up aggressive improvement targets for these newly acquired companies and as such managed to sustain growth over a period of 10 years. Another company used the productivity gains to in-source activities as space and people were freed. The third company paid most of their gains towards the parent company until it was eventually sold in 2015. Even so, based on our literature review and findings, our fourth proposition is: *financial self-reliance makes the organization less sensitive to financial cycles, and allows it to fund stable growth through big bets on the future.*

6 Conclusions and Suggestions for Further Research

In its nature, theory building is fraught with difficulties. However, based on our continued research into lean production in general and more specifically Toyota Motor Corporation in particular, we argue that reducing lean to production efficiency or the adoption of shop-floor best practices will only hinder, not help, our understanding of a phenomena that seems to outlive the traditional management fad cycle normal associated with such buzzwords. Lean and TPS are systems, and as such one must research them in their entirety, rather than simply taking one's fancy from a buffet of component parts. In the age of sustainable manufacturing this becomes even more important, as sustainability will not be achieved through adoption of digital (or indeed analogue) best practices but by engaging everyone, everywhere in kaizen, and then re-investing the gains in the development of the people that can create and manufacture ever more sustainable products. According to [24], *"Lean is the people centric business model of our time"*, and we suggest more effort should be put into researching and understanding its enduring appeal; not as a set of best practice bundles for efficient manufacturing but as a complete business model that better serves customers by continuously developing people.

Based on our review we were able to define four differentiating characteristics of Toyota's superior business model which we then evaluated using three case studies from Europe and the U.S. From the resulting findings, we developed and proposed four propositions towards an economic theory of lean, which needs to be explored in further research, that can help better explain the potential of lean thinking and practice outside of operations management.

Acknowledgements. The authors acknowledge the support of the Norwegian research council for the research project Circulær.

References

1. Krafcik, J.F.: Triumph of the lean production system. Sloan Manag. Rev. **30**, 41 (1988)
2. Shafer, S.M., Smith, H.J., Linder, J.C.: The power of business models. Bus. Horiz. **48**, 199–207 (2005)
3. Hopp, W.J., Spearman, M.S.: The lenses of lean: visioning the science and practice of efficiency. J. Oper. Manag., 1–17 (2020)
4. Ballé, M., Jones, D.T., Chaize, J., Fiume, O.: The Lean Strategy: Using Lean to Create Competitive Advantage, Unleash Innovation, and Deliver Sustainable Growth. McGraw Hill Professional, New York (2017)
5. Liker, J.K.: Toyota Way: 14 Management Principles From the World's Greatest Manufacturer. McGraw Hill Education (2004)
6. Fujimoto, T.: The Evolution of a Manufacturing System at Toyota. Oxford University Press, Oxford (1999)
7. Takeuchi, H., Osono, E., Shimizu, N.: The contradictions that drive Toyota's success. Harv. Bus. Rev. **86**, 1–19 (2008)
8. Spear, S., Bowen, H.K.: Toyota DNA. Harv. Bus. Rev. **77**, 96–106 (1999)
9. Fullerton, R.R., McWatters, C.S., Fawson, C.: An examination of the relationships between JIT and financial performance. J. Oper. Manag. **21**, 383–404 (2003)
10. Bendig, D., Strese, S., Brettel, M.: The link between operational leanness and credit ratings. J. Oper. Manag. **52**, 46–55 (2017)
11. Netland, T.H., Powell, D.: The Routledge Companion to Lean Management. Routledge, New York (2017)
12. Netland, T.H., Aspelund, A.: Company-specific production systems and competitive advantage: a resource-based view on the Volvo production system. Int. J. Oper. Prod. Manag. **33**, 1511–1531 (2013)
13. Shah, R., Ward, P.T.: Lean manufacturing: context, practice bundles, and performance. J. Oper. Manag. **21**, 129–149 (2003)
14. Netland, T.H.: Critical success factors for implementing lean production: the effect of contingencies. Int. J. Prod. Res. **54**, 2433–2448 (2016)
15. Jadhav, J.R., Mantha, S.S., Rane, S.B.: Exploring barriers in lean implementation. Int. J. Lean Six Sigma. **5**, 122–148 (2014)
16. Lucey, J., Bateman, N., Hines, P.: Why major lean transitions have not been sustained. Manag. Serv. **49**, 9–13 (2005)
17. Hines, P., Taylor, D., Walsh, A.: The lean journey: have we got it wrong? Total Qual. Manag. Bus. Excell. **31**, 389–406 (2020)
18. Pettersen, J.: Defining lean production: some conceptual and practical issues. TQM J. **21**, 127–142 (2009)
19. Hines, P., Holwe, M., Rich, N.: Learning to evolve: a review of contemporary lean thinking. Int. J. Oper. Prod. Manag. **24**, 994–1011 (2004)
20. Netland, T., Ferdows, K.: What to expect from a corporate lean program. MIT Sloan Manag. Rev. **55**, 83–89 (2014)
21. Karlsson, C., Hlström, P.: Assessing changes towards lean production. Int. J. Oper. Prod. Manag. **16**, 24–41 (1996)
22. Imai, M.: Gemba Kaizen. McGraw Hill Professional, New York (2012)
23. Bessin, O.: Learn Lean from the source. Toyota Material Handling Europe, pp. 0–15 (2020)
24. Ballé, M., Chartier, N., Coignet, P., Olivencia, S., Powell, D.J., Reke, E.: The Lean Sensei. Go, See, Challenge. The Lean Enterprise Institute Inc., Boston (2019)
25. Monden, Y., Hamada, K.: Target costing and kaizen costing in Japanese automobile companies. J. Manag. Acc. Res. **3**, 16–34 (1991)

26. Shiozawa, Y.: Product variety for effective demand creation. In: Fujimoto, T., Fumihiko, I. (eds.) Industrial Competitiveness and Design Evolution, pp. 97–123. Springer, Tokyo (2018). https://doi.org/10.1007/978-4-431-55145-4_3
27. Adler, P.S., Goldoftas, B., Levine, D.I.: Flexibility versus efficiency? a case study of modelt changeovers in the Toyota production system Organ. Sci. 10(43), 68 (1999)
28. Smalley, A.: Set Up Reduction In Toyota. http://artoflean.com/index.php/2010/02/15/set-up-reduction-in-toyota/
29. Bertel, S.: Inside Toyota's Takaoka #2 line: the most flexible line in the world. The Drive 24 (2019)
30. Profiroiu, M., Kaneko, H., Vlad, C., Dutescu, A., Ishida, H.: Toyota motor corporation's culture strategy. Rev. Int. Comparative Manag. 21, 458–489 (2020)
31. Morgan, J.M., Liker, J.K.: Designing the Future. McGraw Hill Professional, New York (2019)
32. Spear, S.J.: Learning to lead at Toyota. Harv. Bus. Rev. 82(151), 78–86 (2004)
33. Liker, J.K., Mayer, D.P.: Toyota Talent. McGraw Hill Education, New York (2007)
34. Shook, J.: How to change a culture: lessons from NUMMI backstory: why NUMMI began, and how it fared. MIT Sloan Manag. Rev. 51, 63–68 (2010)
35. Heller, D.A., Fujimoto, T.: 6 Monozukuri management. In: Nakano, T. (ed.) Japanese Management in Evolution: New Directions, Breaks, and Emerging Practices, pp. 107–126. Routledge, New York (2018)
36. Nayebpour, M.R., Saito, A.: Toyota vs. Nissan–a contrast in culture, corporate governance, operational strategy, and financial performance. Desicion Sci. Inst., 567–578 (2007)
37. Monden, Y.: Cost Reduction Systems: Target Costing and Kaizen Costing. Productivity Press, Portland (1995)
38. Eisenhardt, K.M.: Building theories from case study research. Acad. Manag. Rev. 14, 532–550 (1989)

Reshaping the Concepts of Job Enrichment and Job Enlargement: The Impacts of Lean and Industry 4.0

Alexandra Lagorio⦿, Chiara Cimini(✉)⦿, and Paolo Gaiardelli⦿

Department of Management, Information and Production Engineering, University of Bergamo, Viale Marconi 5, Dalmine, BG, Italy
{alexandra.lagorio,chiara.cimini,paolo.gaiardelli}@unibg.it

Abstract. The latest innovations in the manufacturing technologies significantly affected the roles of workers, both concerning task variety and required skills. Consequently, in a highly digitalised context, operators and managers are facing increasingly job enlargement and job enrichment requirements in order to perform new and different activities and functions. This paper aims at exploring how the concepts of job enrichment and job enlargement have been evolving over time, through a systematic review of the literature. From the analysis, it emerged that the concepts have been enriched with broader meanings according to the two different production paradigms, in particular with the introduction of Lean Manufacturing principles up to the introduction of the Industry 4.0. The study highlights that if the lean principles strongly promoted the idea of enlarging and enriching the workers' activities to promote their involvement and motivation, supporting leadership attitude and soft skills, additionally the Industry 4.0 significantly affected an enlargement of tasks in space and time, requiring enriched technical skills to manage complex digitized processes.

Keywords: Job enrichment · Job enlargement · Lean manufacturing · Industry 4.0

1 Introduction

The shift from traditional industry to the so-called Industry 4.0 paradigm has been radically changing the way many industries approach their manufacturing operations [1]. In particular, the advent of new technologies able to assist, support, and in some cases even replace operators and managers in the execution of their daily tasks [2, 3], calls for the necessity to investigate job characteristics and skills required in work environments that are faster and more innovative than before [4]. Indeed, while the introduction of new technologies makes the work of operators and managers easier and often less routine and dangerous, digitalisation of activities increases their complexity. Therefore, having operators with a higher degree of technical and methodological skills becomes an essential requirement to avoid the creation of new forms of waste [5].

© IFIP International Federation for Information Processing 2021
Published by Springer Nature Switzerland AG 2021
A. Dolgui et al. (Eds.): APMS 2021, IFIP AICT 630, pp. 721–729, 2021.
https://doi.org/10.1007/978-3-030-85874-2_79

It has also been observed that increasing the degree of automation of certain tasks or supporting the operator in their execution often reduces both the time and physical efforts. This leads to a rethinking of the role of the operator, who is no longer seen as a simple performer of a task, but rather a resource capable of 'managing' the single activity to be performed, including, for example the collection and analysis of data related to the activity [6]. This increase in responsibility and extension of the activities performed by the operator opens in turn a debate on the necessary technical-cognitive and managerial-decisional skills, and on the evolution of job profiles [7]. The operator goes from being a simple executor to the manager of an activity and at the same time there are new profiles required (e.g., data analyst, etc.). All this means that in a highly digitised Industry 4.0 context, operators and managers must increasingly enlarge and enrich their skills with new competencies to perform different activities and functions. This is certainly not a new perspective and in any case already investigated by the scientific literature long before the advent of the 4.0 paradigm; however, the concepts of job enrichment and job enlargement have been enriched with broader meanings over time according to the different production paradigms.

In this regard, the aim of this research work is to explore how definitions of these two terms have changed in the years and it has the result of highlighting how the two main production paradigm that have profoundly change the manufacturing context (i.e., the lean and the industry 4.0 paradigms) affected the nature of the concepts. The research is organized as follows: the study moved from the evidence that the latest innovations in automation and digitalisation, pushed by the Industry 4.0 wave are changing the workforce tasks and skills (Sect. 2). Therefore, the concepts of job enrichment and job enlargement have been researched through a systematic literature review, illustrated in Sect. 3. The insights emerging from it enabled to recognise an evolution of the two concepts, which is discussed extensively in Sect. 4. Finally, conclusions and further research directions on the topic are drawn in Sect. 5.

2   The Impacts of Industry 4.0 on the Workforce

The Industry 4.0 wave is pushing the transformation of traditional manufacturing systems into smart manufacturing systems, thanks to the combination of communication, IT, data, and physical components. The strong techno-centric approach that have characterised the research about Industry 4.0 in the first years, is now becoming surpassed by the new concept of human-centred smart manufacturing systems [8], recognising that human-technology integration will be crucial in the future of manufacturing.

Indeed, the development of Industry 4.0 will be accompanied by changing tasks and demands for the humans in the factory. In the light of strong automation and digitalisation, workers are seen as the most flexible entity in the future cyber-physical production systems: generally, it is expected that the easier and most repetitive tasks will be fully performed by autonomous robots and intelligent machines, leaving the operators more difficult and various jobs [9].

The projections about the impacts of Industry 4.0 technologies on the labour market and work organization have been already discussed in literature [7, 10] while a growing debate about the future of traditional job profiles have started with the work of Frey and Osborne [11] and is still running.

By the way, the view of technology as only a way to replace operators in the most physically demanding activities is limited, since the scope of the technologies introduction should be to support at large the workers in performing their job more efficiently and effectively. According to [12], Industry 4.0 can empower the workers based on adapting the factory shop floor to their specific skills, capabilities and needs, and can further support the worker to understand and to develop his/her competence. Further, a continuous observation of the interaction of the workers with the production systems can enable the implementation of adaptive mechanisms in the workstations in order to improve the operator safety, satisfaction and well-being as well as the factory's production measures [13].

In this sense, many digital technologies, such as integrated information systems and data analysis-based decision support systems can play a relevant role in enhancing the cognitive activities of workers, not only at the middle management level, but also for *blue collars* job roles. In fact, a new job profile has been depicted, i.e., the Autonomous Operative Job Profile, in order to explain how the degree of autonomy and the number of different tasks are increasing, requiring workers to have a higher level of independence and proactivity in performing their job [6]. Moreover, others suggest that the introduction of Industry 4.0 technologies and tools has produced a general increase in workers' intervention authority on the work process in terms of decision making, and therefore augmenting the variability and intensity of task execution [14].

Therefore, it emerges that typical Industry 4.0 employees will get used to being more autonomous than in the past, working in a team, covering different roles and with a problem-solving approach, rather than limiting themselves to execute supervisors' and managers' instructions, expecting new meanings in the job enlargement and job enrichment perspectives that employees 4.0 need to acquire.

3 Methodology

In order to take into account the development of job enlargement and job enrichment concepts, as well as to capture their distinctive characteristics into a new synthetic definition, the systematic literature review was identified as the most suitable methodology to adopt, being considered the best efficient and replicable way to quickly identify what has been produced on a distinctive topic.

To develop the systematic literature review, we adopted the procedure followed by [15] based on three steps: i) the definition of the inclusion and exclusion criteria; ii) the selection by titles and abstracts; iii) the selection based on the whole reading of the papers with the application of the snowballing technique. These are briefly described in the following.

3.1 Step 1: Inclusion/exclusion Criteria

The first step in carrying out a systematic literature review is the identification of the keywords. First, a preliminary list of the keywords and inclusion criteria were identified considering the concept of job enrichment and job enlargement by various synonyms (e.g. polyvalence, multi-skilling, polycompetence), to make our research as comprehensive as possible [16]. Further a first run of exploration we decided to use only the terms job enrichment, job enlargement and multi-skilling referred to the manufacturing context, to limit the research only to the most fitting cases for our research goals, and avoid any misleading. Since we wanted to observe the evolution of job enrichment and job enlargement concepts over time, we decided not to set any time limit for the start of our research. The research was limited to peer-reviewed papers to gain consistency between themes and sources and to ensure the quality of the selected papers [17]. A first search attempt was launched. Following this, a double-blind control test was performed [18] on 10 papers to verify and refine the selection criteria. More specifically, each author carried out a manual selection of the articles to verify their coherency with the inclusion and exclusion criteria. Every paper that met with disagreement regarding inclusion/exclusion criteria was read and discussed until agreement was reached. This led to the definition of the final selection criteria as reported in Table 1. The query was then launched again, which resulted in the extraction of 58 papers.

Table 1. Inclusion criteria

Inclusion criteria	Description
Keywords	job enlargement*, job enrichment*, multi-skilling* AND manufacture*
Language	English
Document types	Articles
Source types	Peer-reviewed journals
Time Interval	Until 2021

3.2   Step 2: Selection Based on Title and Abstract

Each author reviewed the titles and abstracts of the selected papers. Following a discussion among the authors, papers out of the research scope were removed from the corpus. In particular, 19 papers that did not focus strictly on job enlargement and job enrichment were excluded from the analysis.

3.3   Step 3: Selection Based on Full Text and Snowballing

The last step of the protocol involved the refining of the list of selected papers. After reading the full versions of candidate papers, 21 papers were considered out of scope since they did not provide any definitions of job enlargement or enrichment. At this point, a corpus of 18 papers was analysed. Then, a forward and backward snowballing process was conducted. We adopted backward snowballing to exploit the reference list to identify potential new papers to be included. We read titles, abstracts and full papers if necessary and then we decided whether to include them in the final sample. Forward snowballing was carried out to identify new papers to include starting from the analysis of papers citing the ones contained in the first list of 21 papers. The approach to going through the papers was similar to in the backward method [19]. The two procedures were iterated until no new papers were found. This activity added 6 new papers to the corpus, leading to a final set of 24 papers.

4 Job Enlargement and Job Enrichment Concepts' Evolution

Due to the space constraints, the complete list of the systematic literature review results is provided at the following link: https://docs.google.com/spreadsheets/d/1WshGOZOX QV9-oWxBjWuNyD1zSfVNZ8ce4wFc2nXSmCs/edit?usp=sharing.

Combining the papers reported in the attached link with other interesting academic articles, excluded from the final list because they did not contain explicit definitions of job enrichment and job enlargement, but whose reading proved useful to better understand the evolution of the subject, three different evolutions of the two phenomena emerged from the SLR results. Indeed, these three different evolutions refer to three historical moments delimited by two important changes in the history organisation of work in manufacturing: the introduction of the lean philosophy and the development of the Industry 4.0 paradigm. In particular, we noticed how the meaning of job enrichment and job enlargement has changed their nuance between before and after the introduction of the lean philosophy and before and after the introduction of the Industry 4.0 paradigm. In the following sub-section, we will describe more in-depth the evolution of the job enlargement (4.1) and job enrichment (4.2) concepts.

4.1 Job Enlargement Concept Evolution

The term job enlargement essentially refers to the possibility of expanding an operator's tasks or duties [20]. Observing the definition provided in the 60s and 70s, the concept of job enlargement was initially considered as an advantageous condition for companies by favouring greater flexibility in a horizontal sense [21]. However, with the advent of lean thinking principles in Western countries, the term began to take on a broader and deeper meaning and more close to the social perspective. In particular, the advantage of managing work in a more complete way, avoiding fragmentation and consequently loss of productive efficiency and quality, was accompanied by the idea that the enlargement of tasks favours greater skill variety and identity. Providing "a sense of completeness and increasing the meaningfulness of a job" [22], job enlargement drives operational efficiency in the long term [23] through improving workers' satisfaction and motivation. A perspective, the latter, that perfectly fits with the basic principle of lean thinking according to which Monozukuri, the art of doing things (well) that characterizes any lean process, can only be achieved through Hitozukuri, the art of doing people (well) [24]. This means that only through a continuous training of personnel is it possible to pursue production efficiency goals [25] and that, conversely, underutilizing people's skills or not contributing to their growth not only is disrespectful, but also a waste.

For this reason, several authors underline the importance of the training aspects in the job enlargement definition as well [26, 27]. The importance of developing multi-skilled polyvalent Shojinka workforce is stated also by [28]. With the advent of the Fourth Industrial Revolution after 2010, the concept of job enlargement is further extended.

While all the considerations that emerged with the advent of Lean principles remain valid, Industry 4.0 is pushing towards ever greater automation of certain tasks (especially the most repetitive or dangerous ones). The operator thus finds himself moving from performing single operational tasks to performing several tasks in parallel to control and supervise multiple machines and equipment. Besides this enlargement of the tasks in the working space, Industry 4.0 technologies also involve an enlargement of activities in time, since continuous monitoring of the manufacturing processes is enabled, thus supporting a non-stopping control over the production, compared with the previously adopted discrete control of both production and product quality.

4.2   Job Enrichment Concept Evolution

In a similar way, according to the first definitions provided in the literature, job enrichment was initially seen only as a tool to give more responsibility and autonomy to workers [29], making them more involved in decision-making in order to increase their satisfaction [30]. While job enlargement was seen as a way to enhance horizontal increase in the number of activities to be performed, job enrichment was interpreted as a source of vertical increase in one's own activities [19]: the more an operator understands the production process in which he is working, the more he is able to make decisions and intervene autonomously if problems arise. Horizontal and vertical sense of a job refers to a T-shaped competence model, in which workers have a combination of both general skills across multiple domains and specialist skills within (at least) one domain [31].

With the advent of lean thinking, two main concepts emerge. First, the enrichment in the process knowledge is promoted, with the involvement of the worker not only in the production activities but also in supporting the setup and maintenance phases. Second, a special attention to the soft skills emerges, taking the concept of T-shaped competence to the extreme and going beyond the mere perspective of integration of technical expertise and process orientation. Indeed, the concept of job enrichment is not only limited to participation in decision-making or increased responsibility but also extends to proactive, problem solving and leadership skills [32, 33]. The expertise and experience further enrich the roles of workers to the point of investing them with the role of teachers towards their own colleagues, promoting the concepts of sensei. Here again we observe that the worker, by increasing the knowledge of the process in which activities and tasks are embedded, becomes more and more expert, continuing to learn new aspects of work and being able to produce continuous feedback [34] that can become a good basis for introducing innovations [35].

The ability to provide continuous feedback and proposals for improvement is enhanced by the digitalisation that is at the heart of Industry 4.0. In fact, real-time data collection from the shop floor and wide connectivity of the equipment enable the possibility reproducing digital twins of the production processes to run analysis and simulations. In this context, the operator no longer only needs to know his business and the process in which he/she is involved, but must also be able to identify, analyse and interpret the data that are continuously provided by the machines, in order to report any anomalies or corrections that could increase the efficiency of the entire production. Consequently, the responsibility of employees is increased by adding more administrative and qualified tasks, along with increased employee involvement [5]. For this reason, while lean principles fundamentally promoted the development of workers' soft skills, such as leaderships and problem-solving, the Industry 4.0 additionally claims for increased technical skills to support proactive attitude of workers in exploiting the potentials of digitalisation.

5 Conclusions

In the light of the changes that are affecting the workforce requirements in the Industry 4.0 era, this paper aimed at shedding light on the evolution of the concepts referred as Job Enlargement and Job Enrichment. Through the analysis of the academic literature, it has been possible to observe that the two concepts, born in the 60s in the work organisation domain, mutated over the years, being influenced first by the principles of lean production and then by the introduction of automation and digitization of production processes introduced by the so-called Industry 4.0. The study highlighted that if the lean principles strongly promoted the idea of enlarging and enriching the workers' activities to promote their involvement and motivation, supporting leadership attitude and soft skills, additionally the Industry 4.0 significantly affected an enlargement of tasks in space and time, requiring enriched technical skills to manage complex digitized processes.

The main limitation of the presented research is manifested in its purely theoretical nature. In fact, the considerations about the evolution of job enlargement and job enrichment concepts emerging from our analysis derive only from academic literature, while managerial perspective related to industrial real cases is still omitted. However, the results discussed in this paper represent a preliminary phase of a research stream that will be further developed, involving experts both from academia and industry, to propose a new and updated definition of the two concepts considering the most recent advances in manufacturing, and evaluate new methods and criteria for their effective implementation. In particular, some elements deserve special attention and require further investigation in the future, such as X-skilling strategies (e.g. up-skilling, re-skilling, cross-skilling, expert-skilling) and job enrichment and job enlargement efforts.

References

1. Cimini, C., Pinto, R., Pezzotta, G., Gaiardelli, P.: The transition towards Industry 4.0: business opportunities and expected impacts for suppliers and manufacturers. In: Lödding, H., Riedel, R., Thoben, K.-D., von Cieminski, G., Kiritsis, D. (eds.) APMS 2017. IAICT, vol. 513, pp. 119–126. Springer, Cham (2017). https://doi.org/10.1007/978-3-319-66923-6_14
2. Cimini, C., Lagorio, A., Pirola, F., Pinto, R.: How human factors affect operators' task evolution in logistics 4.0. Hum. Factors Man. **31**, 98–117 (2021). https://doi.org/10.1002/hfm.20872.
3. Cimini, C., Lagorio, A., Romero, D., Cavalieri, S., Stahre, J.: Smart logistics and the logistics operator 4.0. IFAC-PapersOnLine **53**(2), 10615–10620 (2020).
4. Romero, D., Stahre, J., Wuest, T., Noran, O., Bernus, P., Fasth, F.-B., Åsa, Gorecky, D.: Towards an operator 4.0 typology: a human-centric perspective on the fourth industrial revolution technologies. In: Proceedings of the International Conference on Computers and Industrial Engineering (CIE46), pp. 1–11 (2016)

5. Romero, D., Gaiardelli, P., Powell, D., Wuest, T., Thürer, M.: Digital lean cyber-physical production systems: the emergence of digital lean manufacturing and the significance of digital waste. In: Moon, I., Lee, G.M., Park, J., Kiritsis, D., von Cieminski, G. (eds.) APMS 2018. IAICT, vol. 535, pp. 11–20. Springer, Cham (2018). https://doi.org/10.1007/978-3-319-99704-9_2

6. Håkansson, M., Dellve, L., Waldenström, M., Holden, R.J.: Sustained lean transformation of working conditions: a Swedish longitudinal case study. Hum. Factors Ergon. Manuf. Serv. Ind. **27**, 268–279 (2017)

7. Cimini, C., Boffelli, A., Lagorio, A., Kalchschmidt, M., Pinto, R.: How do Industry 4.0 technologies influence organisational change? An empirical analysis of Italian SMEs. J. Manuf. Technol. Manag. **32**, 695–721 (2020)

8. Fantini, P., Pinzone, M., Taisch, M.: Placing the operator at the centre of Industry 4.0 design: modelling and assessing human activities within cyber-physical systems. Comput. Ind. Eng. **139**, 105058 (2020)

9. Cimini, C., Lagorio, A., Pirola, F., Pinto, R.: Exploring human factors in Logistics 4.0: empirical evidence from a case study. IFAC-PapersOnLine **52**, 2183–2188 (2019)

10. Bonekamp, L., Sure, M.: Consequences of Industry 4.0 on Human Labour and Work Organisation (2015).

11. Frey, C.B., Osborne, M.A.: The future of employment: how susceptible are jobs to computerisation? Technol. Forecast. Soc. Chang. **114**, 254–280 (2013). https://doi.org/10.1016/j.techfore.2016.08.019

12. Kaasinen, E., et al.: Empowering and engaging industrial workers with Operator 4.0 solutions. Comput. Ind. Eng. **139**, 105678 (2019)

13. Golan, M., Cohen, Y., Singer, G.: A framework for operator–workstation interaction in Industry 4.0. Int. J. Prod. Res. **58**, 2421–2432 (2020)

14. Cirillo, V., Rinaldini, M., Staccioli, J., Virgillito, M.E.: Technology vs. workers: the case of Italy's Industry 4.0 factories. Struct. Change Econ. Dyn. **56**, 166–183 (2021)

15. Lagorio, A., Pinto, R., Golini, R.: Research in urban logistics: a systematic literature review. Int. J. Phys. Distrib. Logist. Manag. **46**, 908–931 (2016)

16. Lagorio, A., Zenezini, G., Mangano, G., Pinto, R.: A systematic literature review of innovative technologies adopted in logistics management. Int. J. Logist. Res. Appl., 1–24 (2020)

17. Touboulic, A., Walker, H.: Theories in sustainable supply chain management: a structured literature review. Int. J. Phys. Distrib. Logist. Manag. **45**, 16–42 (2015)

18. Towards a Methodology for Developing Evidence-Informed Management Knowledge by Means of Systematic Review-Tranfield-British Journal of Management-Wiley Online Library (2003). https://onlinelibrary.wiley.com/doi/abs/10.1111/1467-8551.00375?casa_token=WxLQ6fYtdvsAAAAA:6JiluAuoZen5vxGmEioSOfPD2SA3IWOCODXe6SadAt6X4BqjyQA-yTZI-1xkGEdXekPKMCKFEaBoyQ. Accessed 08 Jun 2021

19. Wohlin, C.: Guidelines for snowballing in systematic literature studies and a replication in software engineering. In: In 8th International Conference on Evaluation and Assessment in Software Engineering, EASE 2014, pp. 321–330. ACM (2014).

20. Argyris, Ch., Schön, D.A.: Organizational learning: a theory of action perspective. Reis. 77/78 345–348 (1997)

21. Hackman, J.R., Lawler, E.E.: Employee reactions to job characteristics. J. Appl. psychol. **55**, 259–286 (1971)

22. Hackman, J.R., Oldham, G.R.: Work Redesign (1980).

23. Gaiardelli, P., Resta, B., Dotti, S.: Exploring the role of human factors in lean management. Int. J. Lean Six Sigma. **10**, 339–366 (2019)

24. Saito, K., Salazar, A.J., Kreafle, K.G., Grulke, E.A.: Hitozukuri and Monozukuri: centuries' old eastern philosophy to seek harmony with nature. Interdisc. Inf. Sci. **17**, 1–9 (2011)

25. Muramatsu, R., Miyazaki, H., Ishii, K.: A successful application of job enlargement/enrichment at Toyota. IIE Trans. **19**, 451–459 (1987)
26. Chakravarty, A.K., Shtub, A.: Modelling the effects of learning and job enlargement on assembly systems with parallel lines. Int. J. Prod. Res. **26**, 267–281 (1988)
27. Starke, F.A., Dyck, B., Mauws, M.K.: Coping with the sudden loss of an indispensable employee: An exploratory case study. J. Appl. Behav. Sci. **39**, 208–228 (2003)
28. Romero, D., Gaiardelli, P., Powell, D., Wuest, T., Thürer, M.: Rethinking Jidoka systems under automation and learning perspectives in the digital lean manufacturing world. IFAC-PapersOnLine. **52**, 899–903 (2019)
29. Hulin, C.L.: Effects of changes in job-satisfaction levels on employee turnover. J. Appl. Psychol. **52**, 122 (1968)
30. Barry, L.C.: Job enrichment in a union environment-a progress report. SAE Technical Papers (1974)
31. PwC.: Skills for smart industrial specialisation and digital transformation: final report. Publications Office, European Commission, LU (2019)
32. Buxey, G.M., Owens, J.J.: The operation of a conveyor system supplying unit build assemblies. Int. J. Prod. Res. **19**, 123–137 (1981)
33. Khan, M.S.: Methods of motivating for increased productivity. J. Manag. Eng. **9**, 148–156 (1993)
34. Jang, J.S., Rim, S.C., Park, S.C.: Reforming a conventional vehicle assembly plant for job enrichment. Int. J. Prod. Res. **44**, 703–713 (2006)
35. Molleman, E., van Delft, B., Slomp, J.: The application of an empowerment model. Hum. Factors Ergon. Manuf. Serv. Ind. **11**, 339–354 (2001)

Managing Variability in Production

Ralph Richter[1]([✉]) [iD], Jochen Deuse[1,2] [iD], Peter Willats[3] [iD], Marius Syberg[1] [iD], and David Lenze[1] [iD]

[1] Institute of Production Systems, Technical University Dortmund, Leonhard-Euler-Str. 5, 44227 Dortmund, Germany
ralph.richter@ips.tu-dortmund.de
[2] Centre for Advanced Manufacturing, University of Technology Sydney, 15 Broadway, Ultimo, NSW 2007, Australia
[3] University of Buckingham, Hunter Street, Buckingham MK18 1EG, UK

Abstract. The corresponding author worked for many years with Toyota coaches, supporting Bosch in the development of pilot value streams for the Bosch Production system. The coaches spent considerable time and effort to analyze and decouple production from customer fluctuations and to stabilize the flow of production with adequate inventory buffers and capacity. The project team, on the other hand, was impatient, wanting to redesign lines, install Kanban and perform Kaizen activities. They did not understand that their coach was reducing unevenness and overload, so called Mura and Muri, striving for basic stability, as a precondition for lean activities. Later, they denoted a line possessing this basic stability in Bosch as an "improvable system". In this paper the authors develop methods to analyze and reduce variability in value streams. The value stream is divided into zones, which are then qualified as stable or unstable. Measures are introduced to turn unstable into stable zones, step by step, enabling sustainable improvement activities in those stabilized zones. An IT system is developed to acquire and process the vast amount of data needed for variability measurements, and to provide structured information to support the management of variability in production.

Keywords: Lean Production · Variability · Value Stream Mapping

1 Introduction

Implementing lean is still a major challenge for companies around the world. Over the years, companies took many steps from applying lean as a toolbox to a management system, guided by lean thinking and leadership. However, outside of Toyota, expectations in terms of quantifiable results are often not met [1].

The Toyota Production System (TPS) is still the benchmark for lean practices and results [1]. These are achieved by Kaizen activities through involving all employees. Production at Toyota is based on a clear and distinct flow of information and material [2]. The scheduled delivery time of cars allows the leveling of customer demand and decoupling customer order variability from production. Inventory buffers compensate

© IFIP International Federation for Information Processing 2021
Published by Springer Nature Switzerland AG 2021
A. Dolgui et al. (Eds.): APMS 2021, IFIP AICT 630, pp. 730–738, 2021.
https://doi.org/10.1007/978-3-030-85874-2_80

for the remaining variability within the flow of products. This setup enables the stable execution of standards, as a precondition for Kaizen activities [3].

Production beyond cars is often characterized by variants with a wide range of work content, multiple product paths and equipment options, which are often automated. The demand fluctuation is high, combined with short or no delivery time to the customers [4]. The result is high variability in the flow of products, which cannot be compensated by a feasible amount of inventory. Standards cannot be maintained and shopfloor personnel is busy with continuous rescheduling of production and firefighting, with little time and prospect for sustainable Kaizen activities. Analyzing and reducing variability becomes the major challenge in such value streams. However, variability has many sources, the effects of which can be felt all along a value stream. A systematic approach is needed to identify the sources of variability and to determine the areas and activities with the highest reduction leverage to stabilize production step by step.

In a steady flow system, meaningful results are attained by measuring variability on a single spot over a limited period of time. Managing variability in an unstable system, requires continuous, discrete time measurements at many points in the value stream, as well as information on the product identity. Unlike in steady flow systems, the vast amount of data required demands the automated acquisition, processing and presentation of information to support appropriate conclusions and decision making of management. In the context of Industry 4.0, the availability of production data is growing rapidly, allowing its capture continuously along the flow of products.

In this paper, the fundamentals on the influence of variability in production are identified and discussed in Sect. 2. Section 3 then describes the classification of value streams into ordered and unordered systems. In Sect. 4 a concept is introduced to divide a value stream into ordered and unordered zones and to and reduce variability in unordered zones. This concept is then discussed in Sect. 5. A summary and an outlook on the application of the concept in Sect. 6 conclude this paper.

2 Related Work

JIT and Jidoka are the pillars of the TPS (Fig. 1). Jidoka is defined as the safe failure of machines, prohibiting the passing of defects from their point of occurrence to following processes [5], and also the prevention of defects through effective quality management.

Dealing with Variability in Quality is a widely covered topic, from SHEWHART's statistical process control in the 1930's [6] through six sigma initiatives [7] and the management of quality assurance [8] to current approaches which are evolving out of data science in the context of I4.0 and is not further evaluated in this paper.

JIT deals with timeliness in a value stream. Material must be available at the point of use, just when it is needed. JIT is implemented by synchronizing the elements of production, which demands low variability in time in the flow of products, up to Toyotas "ideal state" of zero Variability in Time [9–11]. Value Stream Mapping (VSM) [9] is a widely used method to analyze and design material and information flow in production. VSM is based on snap shots or average data and thus unsuitable for mapping variability in time. Functions must be added to VSM to manage variability, which we denote as *dynamic value stream mapping*.

Fig. 1. Just-in-Time: Variability in Time, Jidoka: Variability in quality

In TPS, wasteful practices are characterized as Muda, Mura and Muri. Muda is described by the seven forms of waste; Mura is translated as "unevenness" and thus comprises losses caused by variability. Muri is translated as "overburden", and often interpreted as losses caused by human fatigue, but also as variability amplification due to capacity constraints [3]. Thus, by interpreting Muri and Mura as forms of waste, variability is a fundamental part of TPS and put into practice with the design of the production flow [1], as described in the introduction. While western companies are familiar with the concept of Muda and the seven forms of waste, Muri and Mura are widely unknown, which indicates the low attention paid to variability in western lean activities.

HOPP AND SPEARMAN [12] conclude that variability always reduces the performance of production. To compensate for variability, they introduce the concept of buffers in time, inventory and capacity. HOPP [1] identifies the lack of attention to variability as a major weakness in the implementation of lean systems outside Toyota. He suggests an adequate mix of buffers in time, capacity and inventory, depending on the type of business and customer relations.

$$E(W_q) \approx \left(\frac{\rho}{1-\rho}\right) * \left(\frac{c_a^2 + c_s^2}{2}\right) * \tau \qquad (1)$$

$$Muda \approx Muri * Mura * \tau$$

Already in the 1960's, KINGMAN [13] quantified the effect of variability and capacity utilization on throughput times, as part of queuing theory. The Kingman formula (Eq. 1) distinguishes between the average and the variability of process time, and the timely variability of parts arriving at the waiting queue. The formula quantifies the lengthening of throughput time relative to growing variabilities, but also reveals a rapid increase of throughput time in the case of high capacity utilization. It demonstrates that variability, in combination with high capacity utilization, quickly becomes the dominating factor determining throughput times, underlining the need to focus on variability reduction in such value streams.

BICHENO [14] connects Toyota's concept of Muda, Muri and Mura with the Kingman formula. Muda is represented by waiting time, Mura by arrival and process variability and Muri by the utilization rate (Eq. 1). In essence, BICHENO's work allows the quantification of the effects of Muri and Muri on Muda (Eq. 1). Therefore, BICHENO emphasizes the importance of removing bottlenecks in areas of high variability and to measure process and arrival variability to identify the most affected areas. He also introduces the concept of "hidden waste" to reduce variability of customer orders.

DEUSE ET AL. [4] pick up SPEARMAN's conclusion regarding variability as major cause of performance losses. They identify many product variants, high spread of work content, multiple production paths and usage of equipment as the cause for high variability in many value streams in today's industry. DEUSE ET AL. suggest alternative methods for production control in such value streams, like the use of conwip instead of Kanban.

SNOWDEN AND BOONE [15] developed a portfolio and criteria to structure business environments in simple, complicated, complex and chaotic systems. Simple and complicated systems are summarized as "ordered systems", characterized by clear or detectable cause-and-effect relationships. The system behavior is predictable and management of the system is fact based. Complex and chaotic systems are summarized as "unordered systems" and characterized by high unpredictability and unknown cause-and- effect relationships, requiring pattern based leadership. While SNOWDEN developed his ideas to describe adequate management practices, commensurate with the turbulence of the respective business environment, we apply SNOWDEN's framework to identify a value stream or parts of a value stream as "steady/ordered" or "un-steady/unordered" and to allocate appropriate measures for improvement.

3 Classifying Ordered and Unordered Systems

TPS is built on flow lines with buffer in time to decouple customer variability and buffer in inventory to reduce and separate variabilities in the flow. Decoupled shifts are exploited as buffer in time or capacity [16]. Low cost automation is installed to provide sufficient capacity in the flow, avoiding the amplification of variabilities by capacity constraints. With sufficient buffers to customers, within production and to suppliers, cause-and-effect relationships for variabilities remain local and transparent. The system is predictable and the management of it is fact based. With this, production at Toyota fits the criteria of an ordered system and broad Kaizen activities are performed with sustainable results with sparing use of experts.

In production beyond cars, it is often challenging to decouple customer demand fluctuation. Also manufacturing is often automated, with the need for high utilization and multiple use of equipment. The flow becomes unsteady and the resulting variability is amplified by the high utilization rate. A critical point is reached as a buffer cannot provide requested material or cannot store delivered material, which is referred to starving or blocking [17]. Waiting times and impromptu build sequence changes are the result. Operational standards, like standardized work and/or leveling, are disrupted. As a consequence, variabilities overlay and cause-and-effect relationships become difficult to identify. If high variability demands an unfeasible amount of inventory or if the inventory level cannot be maintained due to capacity constraints, the value stream turns from an ordered to an unordered system.

4   Variability Reduction in Value Stream Zones

Since parts of a value stream themselves could be ordered or unordered, we decompose a value stream into zones. Each zone represents a connected part of the production flow and a buffer may represent each nexus of a zone. Based on historic data, we analyze the stability of each zone and identify effective improvement measures for critical zones. Critical zones can be de-composed further in sub-zones, allowing a hierarchical approach, for managing complex value streams.

4.1   Autonomy of Zones

Events of blocking and starvation of adjacent processes caused by a buffer are captured to calculate the service level of the buffer for a chosen time period (Fig. 2).

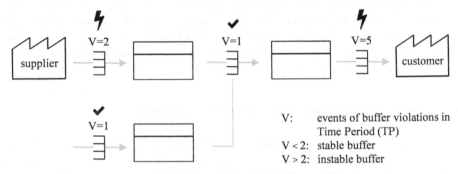

Fig. 2.   Service level of buffers

With the definition of a minimum service level for each buffer, occasional events are tolerated, since they still allow the execution of standards and may even trigger improvement activities. If the service level is breached, the status of the buffer turns from stable to critical. Zones with stable buffers on each nexus, have a high degree of autonomy (Fig. 3).

Only little variability is introduced from the outside and internal variability is compensated with sufficient buffers. Some more decomposition may be needed, but the pre-conditions for an ordered system are met and lean activities can be applied with the benefit of sustainable results. Next, the size of buffers of the critical zones are re-calculated. If feasible, some buffers may be increased or even some surplus inventory may be transferred from stable to critical buffers, to further compensate variability without an increase of total inventory. Based on the acquired data in some field applications, the restructuring of production may be required in the first improvement cycles. This is not further detailed in this paper.

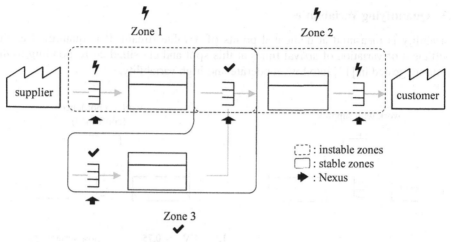

Fig. 3. Stable and unstable zones of a value stream

4.2 Capacity Constraints

To further reduce the required buffer, we analyze the value stream for capacity constraints, applying the method of ROSER ET AL. [18] for the detection of dynamic bottlenecks. As a result, we receive a ranking of processes, representing bottlenecks in the evaluated time period (Fig. 4).

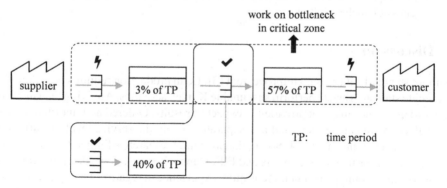

Fig. 4. Identify bottlenecks in critical zones

Since high utilization rates amplify variabilities, bottleneck processes in critical zones must be addressed, even if the output of the zone is sufficient. To free up capacity in those bottleneck processes, OEE losses or cycle times have to be reduced, or some products may be re-routed to other available capacities. As we learned from KINGMAN, a minor reduction of utilization rates may have a significant impact on throughput times and required buffer sizes. However, the gain in capacity should not be consumed with increased production rates.

4.3 Quantifying Variabilities

Variability is measured at dedicated points of a value stream. It is quantified as the coefficient of variation of arrival times at this spot and classified corresponding to the limits suggested in [12] into low, moderate and high variability.

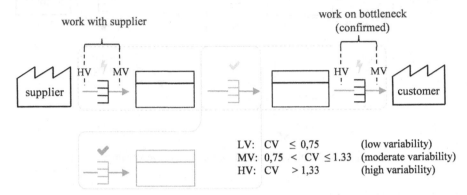

LV: CV ≤ 0,75   (low variability)
MV: 0,75 < CV ≤ 1.33   (moderate variability)
HV: CV   > 1,33   (high variability)

Fig. 5. Set priorities for further improvement activities

However, in cases other than a one by one flow, the measured value is only representative for this spot, not for a zone or sub zone. Measured and visualized, however, on the nexus of zones, it provides insights into potential sources of variability and priorities for further improvement activities (Fig. 5). In any case, it provides fast feedback of the effectiveness of such activities.

5 Discussion

Without standards, there is no improvement [3]. Lean production requires basic stability to execute standards and to perform sustainable Kaizen activities. Applying lean methods in unordered zones may not provide the expected results. Ordered and unordered zones in a value stream can be identified and separated, using the service level of buffers, as shown in the example in Sect. 4. So far, the presented research is limited to pull systems with buffers in form of supermarkets and FIFO lanes. Zoning allows dealing with value streams of high complexity, but there is more experience in regards of adequate structuring and sizing of the zones required. Measuring service levels, bottlenecks and variability is considered as state of the art. Applying those measurements in unordered zones provide insights and priorities for variability reduction. The systematical approach needs to be further detailed with practical applications. An IT System as a pre-requirement for dealing with variability has been developed for that purpose.

6 Conclusion

Managing variability means reducing variability. In successive management cycles, the actual situation is analyzed, critical zones and bottlenecks are identified, and priorities for reduction activities are derived and executed. The influence of variability in production has been widely researched. In this context, approaches such as statistical process control and Six Sigma methods reveal possibilities for dealing with variability in quality. The literature also shows the influence of variability in time on production performance. BICHENO shows that both types have a direct impact on waste in operations. With the enlargement of stable zones presented in the concept of this paper, broad kaizen activities can be applied for further reduction of waste in form of inventory as well as capacity and productivity improvements.

To cope with variability, an IT-system for dynamic value stream analysis has been developed and has shown encouraging results in first field studies in electronic production. Data is transferred from Manufacturing Execution Systems (MES) or directly acquired via sensors in production. Buffer levels, cycle times and throughput times are continuously measured and displayed in the form of box-plots. Capacity constraints are calculated as bottlenecks. Based on the resulting variability-oriented actual state, the buffers in the form of inventory, capacity and time can be designed in a targeted manner to avoid the described effects of the prevailing variability influences. Under development is the application of different mathematical and statistical approaches to enable near-real-time anomaly detection for the early identification of upcoming transitions in a zone from an ordered to an unordered state. Artificial intelligence methods offer the possibility of forecasting future system states, which enables the prescriptive management of value streams.

In summary, the zone concept developed in this paper, in combination with appropriate digitization technology, offers a new approach to manage systems based on variability.

References

1. Hopp, W.J.: Positive lean: merging the science of efficiency with the psychology of work. Int. J. Prod. Res. **56**, 398–413 (2018)
2. Spear and Bowen: Decoding the DNA of the Toyota Production System. Harv. Bus. Rev. **77**, 96–106 (1999)
3. Ōno, T.: Toyota Production System. Beyond Large-Scale Production. Productivity Press, New York (1988)
4. Deuse, J., et al.: Pushing the limits of lean thinking-design and management of complex production systems. In: Viles, E., Ormazábal, M., Lleó, A. (eds.) Closing the Gap Between Practice and Research in Industrial Engineering, vol. 47, pp. 335–342. Springer International Publishing, Cham (2018)
5. Sugimori, Y., Kusunoki, K., Cho, F., Uchikawa, S.: Toyota production system and Kanban system Materialization of just-in-time and respect-for-human system. Int. J. Prod. Res. **15**, 553–564 (1977)
6. Shewhart, W.A.: Economic Control of Quality of Manufactured Product. Martino Publishing, Mansfield Centre (1931)
7. Smith, B.: Six-sigma design (quality control). IEEE Spectr. **30**, 43–47 (1993)
8. Sinha, M.N., Willborn, W.W.O.: The Management of Quality Assurance, vol. 1. Wiley (1985)
9. Rother, M., Shook, J.: Learning to see. Value-stream mapping to create value and eliminate muda, 1st edn. A lean tool kit method and workbook. Lean Enterprise Inst, Cambridge (2009)

10. Balaji, V., Venkumar, P., Sabitha, M.S., Amuthaguka, D.: DVSMS: dynamic value stream mapping solution by applying IIoT. Sādhanā **45**(1), 1–13 (2020)
11. Ramadan, M., Salah, B., Othman, M., Ayubali, A.A.: Industry 4.0-based real-time scheduling and dispatching in lean manufacturing systems. Sustainability **12**, 2272 (2020)
12. Hopp, W.J., Spearman, M.L.: Factory Physics, 3rd edn. The McGraw-Hill/Irwin series. McGraw-Hill/Irwin, Boston (2008)
13. Kingman, J.F.C.: The single server queue in heavy traffic. Math. Proc. Camb. Phil. Soc. **57**, 902–904 (1961)
14. Bicheno, J.: Towards reducing queues: Muri, Mura, Muda. In: Dinis-Carvalho, J., Carvalho Alves, A., Costa, N., Lima, R.M., Sousa, R.M. (eds.) Proceedings of the Fifth European Lean Educator Conference. Lean Educator's Role in Lean Development. ELEC 2018 - European Lean Educator Conference, Braga, Portugal, 14–15 November 2018, pp. 141–150 (2018)
15. Snowden, D.J., Boone, M.E.: A leader's framework for decision making. Harv. Bus. Rev. **85**, 68 (2007)
16. Pound, E.S., Bell, J.H., Spearman, M.L.: Factory Physics for Managers. How Leaders Improve Performance in a Post-Lean Six Sigma World. McGraw-Hill Education, New York (2014)
17. Kuo, C.-T., Lim, J.-T., Meerkov, S.M.: Bottlenecks in serial production lines: a system-theoretic approach. Math. Probl. Eng. **2**, 233–276 (1996)
18. Roser, C., Lorentzen, K., Deuse, J.: Reliable shop floor bottleneck detection for flow lines through process and inventory observations: the bottleneck walk. Logist. Res. **8**(1), 1–9 (2015)

Realizing Value Opportunities for a Circular Economy: Integrating Extended Value Stream Mapping and Value Uncaptured Framework

Nina Pereira Kvadsheim[1]($\boxtimes$), Bella B. Nujen[2], Daryl Powell[3], and Eivind Reke[3]

[1] Møreforsking Molde, Britvegen 4, Molde, Norway
Nina.P.Kvadsheim@moreforsking.no
[2] Faculty of International Business, Norwegian University of Science and Technology, Trondheim, Norway
bella.nujen@ntnu.no
[3] SINTEF Manufacturing, S. P. Andersens veg, Trondheim, Norway
{Daryl.powell,Eivind.reke}@sintef.no

Abstract. A shift to a Circular Economy requires more than the implementation of new processes and activities. It also requires identification of new opportunities to create and capture value by analyzing value captured and uncaptured across the product life cycle. However, previous studies focusing on value captured and uncaptured have consistently employed the value uncaptured (VU) framework in isolation. Hence, this study combines the VU framework with extended value stream mapping (EVSM), to identify waste and value improvement opportunities with 'high' circularity. Based on an in-depth case study of a firm that produces patient simulators, both approaches have been applied. The findings of the current study prove the effectiveness of integrating EVSM and the VU framework when firms are to evaluate the possibilities for realizing value opportunities for a circular economy.

Keywords: Extended value stream mapping · Value uncaptured · Value opportunities · Circular Economy

1 Introduction

Manufacturing companies are striving towards more environmentally friendly operations and products, creating an increased need for a balance between environmental aspects and efficiency gains [1]. By integrating and implementing lean thinking and Circular Economy (CE) practices simultaneously, this can be achieved. This synergy is seen as a corollary effect of firms' challenges for rethinking their strategies in order to add more value while contributing to social equity and prevent environmental burdens [2]. Although these concepts differ in their focus, their values and ideology to eliminate waste and create value are comparable – complementing each other in producing effective outcomes, and thus, the coalesce seems natural. Hence, CE presents an ideal solution

© IFIP International Federation for Information Processing 2021
Published by Springer Nature Switzerland AG 2021
A. Dolgui et al. (Eds.): APMS 2021, IFIP AICT 630, pp. 739–747, 2021.
https://doi.org/10.1007/978-3-030-85874-2_81

to the current global problems of environmental damages, resource scarcity [3] and to the establishment of a closed-loop economic system. Lean, on the other hand, has been a proven success to eliminate waste and to create value [4] by achieving efficiency and economic benefits. However, despite strong correlation between these concepts, only few attempts have been made in integrating their tools to spark new ideas in the effort to realize the much-anticipated CE within enterprises. Precisely, there is paucity of research on coalescing extended value stream mapping (EVSM), a lean tool, with the value uncaptured (VU) framework, for identifying value opportunities that are regarded as potential solutions to reduce the negative forms of value or to turn them into positive forms of value.

Based hereon, the current study's objective is twofold: 1) identify and evaluate forms of value uncaptured present in different stages of the product's lifecycle, 2) investigate how the identified value uncaptured opportunities can be realised. The obtained knowledge is created in collaboration with a firm that produces patient simulators.

The rest of the paper is structured as follows. Section 2 provides a brief introduction to EVSM, while Sect. 3 focuses on the concept of value uncaptured. The methodology employed is described in Sect. 4, followed by analysis and discussion in Sect. 5. Finally, the closing remarks in Sect. 6 places the findings in context.

2   Extended Value Stream Mapping

Extended Value Stream Mapping (EVSM) can be described as an enterprise improvement methodology capturing firm level details in visualizing the entire (production) process, apprehending material and information flows throughout its timeline [5]. Its aim is about "leaning out" the process from the bottom-up, while realizing process optimization in the targeted business function [6]. Thus, conducting it eases the work of firms to bypass static process optimization improvements. It manages to capture tangible processes in the manufacturing flow and links it with the information flow, while heightening wastes and thus triggers continuous improvements on both intra- and inter-organization level. Accordingly, extended value stream mapping can be applied as a strategic and operational approach that aims at analyzing, capturing, and gaining value across an entire organization [7]. Hence, creating a consensus on what is valuable (i.e., usable) and what is waste is very important for the ideals of CE. Arguably, EVSM echoes the cycles that can be found within a CE context.

3   The Concept of Value Uncaptured

For an organization to move towards circularity, a description of the business and a plan for how it will make profit is necessary and this is commonly referred to as the business model. An effective approach to innovation of sustainable business model is recognizing value captured and value uncaptured and identifying the opportunities represented by value uncaptured (VU) [8]. VU is the benefit delivered to the company and its stakeholders; it does not include only monetary value, but also the wider value provided to the environment and society (e.g., improved energy efficiency and zero emissions). Value uncaptured refers to the potential value that could be captured but has not yet been captured [8]. It exists in almost all companies. Some value uncaptured is visible, for instance, waste streams in production, co-products, and underutilized resources. Most often however, value uncaptured is invisible, e.g., over capacity of labour, insufficient use of expertise and knowledge. Value uncaptured is classified into four forms: 1) value surplus – value which exists but is not required (e.g., unnecessary repeated work); 2) value absence – value which is required but does not exist (e.g., temporary lack of labour); 3) value missed – value which exists and is required, but is not exploited (e.g., inefficient use of human resources) and 4) value destroyed – value with negative outcomes (e.g., pollution, bad working conditions) [8].

4 Methodology

The present study deploys what [9] refer to as action research learning, as the approach corresponds to this paper's objective, which is to evaluate forms of value uncaptured in collaboration with practitioners to create learning opportunities between and among the participants. The case firm (henceforth MediX) develops healthcare-related solutions and programs focused on a common mission of helping save lives. The research presented in this study is restricted to the lifecycle of one of their products, Mani2.0.

In addition to a Gemba walk and several factory visits, data were collected through semi-structured interviews, informal conversational interviews, workshop, and documents. Prior to these activities, an EVSM was conducted together with managers on operational level using MURAL (a digital workplace for visual collaboration). This EVSM was presented during the workshop, where themes and additional research questions were formulated in advance to encourage engagement and discussions. This exercise enabled a comprehension of all the teams' experiences from their point of view, which helped the research team to be aware of potential biases [10]. As such, data collection was not restricted to the activity of 'just collecting data', instead it provided learning opportunities between and across research teams and the involved participants, as new interpretations were co-created during the workshop.

5 Analysis and Discussion

Forms of value uncaptured present in lifecycle stages of Mani2.0. The analysis generated 13 main sources (see Table 1) of VU across Mani2.0's lifecycle, divided between beginning of life (BOL), middle of life (MOL) and end of life (EOL).

Table 1. Main sources of value uncaptured across Mani2.0's lifecycle

BOL	MOL	EOL
Design	Human resources	Refurbish/remanufacture
Sourcing	Operations management	Reuse/redistribute

(continued)

Table 1. (*continued*)

BOL	MOL	EOL
Production	Delivery	Recycle
Operations management	Knowledge	
Human resources		
Knowledge and technology		

Value Uncaptured at the Beginning of Life (BOL)

Table 2 illustrates the details of each main source of VU at BOL. In this lifecycle stage, most of the VU was identified in design. This makes sense because it influences the value creation throughout the entire lifecycle of Mani2.0.

Table 2. Main sources of value uncaptured at BOL

Sources	Description
Design	Building "wrong" prototypes; Lack of new design thinking e.g., circularity; Poor communication between designers, purchasers & manufacturers; Discarded built prototypes; Too many/unnecessary iterations; Insufficient and inefficient use of human resources; Use of more time in building prototypes; Overprocessing
Sourcing	Limited procurement of recycled components/materials; Over procurement or too early procurement; Unexploited resources; Inefficient inventory management; Storage waste (increase in space requirements for idle materials)
Production	Limited use of recycled components/materials in the production (all plastic parts are from virgin materials); Re-work
Operations management	Inefficient inter-function collaboration; Inefficient resource sharing
Human resources	Under capacity of designers and software developers; Unused/misused human resources
Knowledge and technology	No reuse of knowledge; Lack of common knowledge base; Tacit knowledge; Lack of technical material know-how; Too many control points in developing software

Considering the various types of VU that exist in design (e.g., *building wrong prototypes, lack of new design thinking, poor communication between designers, purchasers, and manufacturers*), *iterations* (*cf. rework and design*), is the most emphasized. Rework iteration does not help the design evolve towards the intended goal because it focuses on recovering from previous design errors. Design iteration focuses on the evolution of the design toward the desired final state through abstraction levels [11]. Too often, these iterations increase complexity, thereby leading to inefficiency and waste. A good example of rework iterations is *building "wrong" prototypes,* which results in most of them being discarded. Too many/unnecessary iterations are therefore considered to be the root cause of other VU, such as, *unnecessary use of time in building prototypes* and *overprocessing.* Hence, avoiding the causes of rework iterations, as well as performing design iterations without skipping abstraction levels [11] should contribute to solving such problems.

Further, *limited procurement of recycled components/materials* is another type of VU observed in sourcing. This implies that procurement processes and practices at MediX are strongly based on the purchase of goods and services through a linear approach. Other forms of VU in sourcing include *over procurement* or *too early procurement, discarding of materials due to obsolescence, storage waste* and *inefficient inventory management.* These are partly caused by another form of VU within the same lifecycle stage (i.e., BOL) but in a different function (design – product development), thus, *poor communication between designers, purchasers, manufacturers, and other functions.* The latter is in line with the argument presented by [12], that improved communication leads to efficient inventory management. In a similar line of thought, [13] assert that information sharing alone could provide significant inventory reduction and cost savings to the manufacturer (MediX in this context).

Value Uncaptured at the Middle of Life (MOL)
Table 3 shows the details of each main source of VU at MOL. *Distribution* was regarded as a key VU source at this stage.

Table 3. Main sources of value uncaptured at MOL

Source	Description
Human resources	Inefficient communication between distribution and other functions Lack of human resources
Operations management	Inefficient inter-function collaboration Forecasting problems
Distribution	Shipment of "less demanded" products; Delays in delivery; Inefficient delivery; Lack of circularity design in packaging; Not reusing packaging; Packages are pre-marked with specific product names
Knowledge	Lack of knowledge of the distribution centres

Lack of proper distribution planning is causing unnecessary waste at MediX. Thus, determining the right versions of Mani2.0 to be sent to each distribution centre (DC) to meet customer demand is a challenge. Mostly, products are shipped by boat on a weekly basis to the DCs around the world. However, if the DCs have run out of those versions demanded, then MediX must air transport those products to reach the customers within the contracted timeframe. This leads MediX to question whether it is better to ship the products by boat and have high level of stock in DCs or air the products whenever the customers place orders and have no stock in DCs. To answer this question, there has to be a balance between excessive product stocking and product delay, as the former may result in breakage and waste (in case some products are unsold), while the latter may result in costly labour delays and subsequent time overrun.

CE principles can be applied to manage this excess stock and may help to unlock the value in these products by identifying alternative routes to market, especially in cases where selling them is not possible (due to obsolescence). For example, it may be possible to repurpose some of the components, that is, components can be harvested and sold as spares to facilitate repair or reuse in subsequent generations of Mani2.0. However, this will only be possible if such versions are designed with components that retain the same specification over multiple generations. Hence these can be reclaimed from unsold stock and used in the manufacture of the next line of Mani2.0.

Value Uncaptured at the End of Life (EOL)

At EOL, three main sources of VU were identified (Table 4).

Table 4. Main sources of value uncaptured at EOL

Source	Description
Refurbish/remanufacture	No refurbishment and remanufacturing; Lack of capacity to undertake refurbishment or remanufacturing; No known customer demand for refurbished/remanufactured products; Lack of refurbishment and remanufacturing guidance and methods
Reuse/redistribute	Limited reuse of products/components; Usable products discarded by customers; Small market for used products; No known customer demand for reused products
Recycle	Limited recycling; Low-value disposal of recycled parts; Valuable materials in discarded products

The, *lack of refurbishment/repair and remanufacturing* is caused by value absence in other forms such as *lack of capacity to undertake refurbishment or remanufacturing*. Accordingly, a fundamental tenet of the CE movement is to do more with less, such as, making products last longer through durability, maintainability, and upgradability [14]. Hence, the ability to repair end-of-useful life of Mani2.0 is a powerful tool towards achieving this aspect of a CE.

Besides, MediX focused more on explaining about recycling relative to the other two sources (remanufacture and reuse). Additionally, the recycling they referred to was mostly downcycling, even though they are planning of investing in 'upcycling', which is of higher value relative to downcycling, in the near future. This reflects the fact that MediX has not considered value at the EOL stage as important as in the BOL and MOL. This is not surprising, as many manufacturing companies have prioritized recycling despite it being the least value capturing loop of all CE strategies. Regardless, recycling rate, not 'resale rate' nor 'reuse rate', is still the normative basis for evaluating recovery performance [15].

5.1 Realization of the Identified Value Uncaptured Opportunities

MediX should incorporate CE principles into their production processes, as this would contribute to determine, assess, and manage the environmental and social risks while identifying the economic and environmental benefits of reusing, remanufacturing, and recycling resources. Such effort raises the standard of due diligence and monitoring to support socially and environmentally responsible decision-making. For example, by purchasing recycled and recovered materials/parts to be used as production inputs. Thus, sourcing does not only play a vital role in keeping resources in use for as long as possible to extract their maximum value, but they also respond to customers' demand for firms to deliver social benefits, products, and services with a sense of responsibility or concern for the problems and injustices of society. Another value opportunity is the use of Just-in-Time in procurement. This ensures that the materials/parts are only delivered to MediX when needed and only in the quantities needed, thereby preventing excessive storage of the materials. It would as well prevent waste caused by stockpiling, inefficient handling, and materials/parts leftover [16], which are often discarded due to obsolescence. Moreover, scrap from plastic molding can be re-granulated using a local recycling company. In so doing, MediX is not only protecting the environment, but also reducing carbon footprint by using a local company to provide this service. Also, plastic is a recyclable material, thus, it can be reprocessed and reused, especially since 60% of their Mani2.0 is made of plastic.

Additionally, MediX can maximize value through reusable packaging, which is in fact a preferred interloop activity in a CE today. This implies adoption of returnable packaging, which will not only reduce or eliminate generation of waste at the final customer, minimizing risks to the environment, but also present a better cost-benefit ratio in terms of industrial applications compared to disposable packaging [17]. Just as disposable packaging, returnable packaging has some drawbacks such as transportation costs (direct and reverse), flow management, reception, cleaning, repair, storage, and capital invested. To reduce costs with returnable packaging, one should design and develop reusable packaging that outlast durability performance better than any single use package would. For instance, developing light and resistant packaging, as shipping costs often are linked with the load weight. In this case, the use of standardized returnable packaging is an advantage to optimize the use of space during product transportation and reduce transportation costs [17]. Overall, reusable packaging is not only key to achieving a CE and solving the plastic pollution problem, but equally presents untapped business potential for MediX. Besides, given the nature of Mani2.0 where upgrades are common practice to maintain a high efficiency, MediX may focus on redesigning such products to make them more modular than today. Also, since these products are equipped with advanced software and technology, they are likely to become obsolete. Hence, designing them for effective component/part reuse or recycling (e.g., designing for disassembly) may be the best choice.

6 Closing Remarks

The findings indicate that certain aspects of value creation in current identified waste-activities and resource utilization are neither explored nor exploited favorably. Focus is directed on creating value mainly in design and production (BOL) while missing opportunities to create and capture value when products are in use (MOL) or even at the end of the life cycle (EOL), when recycled or discarded.

Overlaps are observed between some forms, such as value surplus and value missed, and value absence and value destroyed. Additionally, cause-and-effect relationships exist between some value forms across different lifecycle stages and some practices of CE. Some value missed in MOL is caused by value surplus in BOL, for instance, disposal of obsolete Mani2.0 is partly caused by their constant upgrades. This is a common case of cannibalization, as a reduction in sales volume of the older versions of a product is because of the introduction of the newer versions. This leads to obsolescence of many older versions, which reflects MediX's current situation. Hence, embedding CE strategies to the cannibalization process can improve the situation as they increase the maximization of retained value, thus, prolonging the circulation of the products in the economic system, thereby reducing the level of obsolescence. However, such strategies can also lead to imperfect substitution especially when they do not avoid demand and production of new products on a one-to-one basis [18]. On that note, the production of new products is only partly displaced by CE products and thus the overall production increases [19]. These may in fact incentivize MediX to increase durability, standardization, or modularity of their products to facilitate reuse at EOL, while stimulating reuse of the valuable items that are otherwise being left unused in storage or discarded.

Although the study provides some interesting findings, it should be interpreted in the context of the limits inherent in qualitative research, such as the lack of generalizability due to the application of a single case company.

References

1. Zhu, X.Y., Zhang, H., Jiang, Z.G.: Application of green-modified value stream mapping to integrate and implement lean and green practices: A case study. Int. J. Comput. Integr. Manuf. **33**(7), 716–731 (2020)
2. Abreu, M.F., Alves, A.C., Moreira, F.: Lean-green models for eco-efficient and sustainable production. Energy **137**, 846–853 (2017)
3. Nadeem, S.P., Garza-Reyes, J.A., Anosike, A.I., Kumar, V.: Spectrum of CE and its prospects in logistics. In: Proceedings of International Conference on Industrial Engineering Operational Management, vol. 2017, pp. 440–451 (2017)
4. Mostafa, S., Dumrak, J., Soltan, H.: A framework for lean manufacturing implementation. Prod. Manuf. Res. **1**(1), 44–64 (2013)
5. Seth, D., Seth, N., Dhariwal, P.: Application of value stream mapping for lean and cycle time reduction in complex production environments: a case study. Prod. Plan. Control **28**(5), 398–419 (2017)
6. Powell, D.J., Bartolome, C.P.F.: Enterprise-wide value stream mapping: from dysfunctional organization to cross-functional, collaborative learning & improvement. In: IEEE International Conference on Industrial Engineering and Engineering Management, vol. 2020, pp. 551–555 (2020)
7. Darla, G., et al.: Towards a value stream perspective of circular business models. Resour. Conserv. Recycl. **162**, 105060 (2020)
8. Yang, M., Evans, S., Vladimirova, D., Rana, P.: Value uncaptured perspective for sustainable business model innovation. J. Clean. Prod. **140**, 1794–1804 (2017)

9. Powell, D., Coughlan, P.: Rethinking lean supplier development as a learning system. Int. J. Oper. Prod. Manage. **40**(7–8), 921–943 (2020)

10. Coughlan, P., Coghlan, D.: Action research for operations management. Int. J. Oper. Prod. Manage. **22**(2), 220–240 (2002)

11. Costa, R., Sobek, D.K.: Iteration in engineering design: inherent and unavoidable or product of choices made? In: Proceedings of ASME Design Engineering Technical Conference, vol. 3, pp. 669–674 (2003)

12. Mourtzis, D.: Internet based collaboration in the manufacturing supply chain. CIRP J. Manuf. Sci. Technol. **4**(3), 296–304 (2011)

13. Lee, H.L., So, K.C., Tang, C.S.: Value of information sharing in a two-level supply chain. Manage. Sci. **46**(5), 626–643 (2000)

14. Anthesis: The manufacturer's framework for repairability in the age of COVID (2020). https://www.anthesisgroup.com/the-manufacturers-framework-for-repairability-in-the-age-of-covid/. Accessed 20 Feb 2021

15. Reike, D., Vermeulen, W.J.V., Witjes, S.: The circular economy: new or refurbished as CE 3.0? Resour. Conserv. Recycl. **135**, 246–264 (2017)

16. Ajayi, S., Oyedele, L.: Waste-efficient materials procurement for construction projects: a structural equation modelling of critical success factors. Waste Manage. **75**, 60–69 (2018)

17. Silva, D., Renó, G., Sevegnani, G., Sevegnani, T., Truzzi, O.: Comparison of disposable & returnable packaging: a case study. J. Clean. Prod. **47**, 377–387 (2013)

18. Cooper, D.R., Gutowski, T.G.: The environmental impacts of reuse: a review. J. Ind. Ecol. **21**(1), 38–56 (2017)

19. Thomas, V.M.: Demand and dematerialization impacts of second-hand markets: reuse or more use? J. Ind. Ecol. **7**(2), 65–78 (2003)

Exploring the Link Between Lean Practices and Sources of Uncertainty in Supply Chain

Claudia Del Monte, Matteo Zanchi$^{(\boxtimes)}$, and Paolo Gaiardelli ⓘ

Department of Management, Information and Production Engineering, University of Bergamo, Viale Marconi 5, Dalmine (BG), Italy
c.delmonte@studenti.unibg.it, {matteo.zanchi, paolo.gaiardelli}@unibg.it

Abstract. In an ever-changing environment, supply chains face countless risks generated by different sources of uncertainty. The adoption of lean management initiatives has been recognized as a viable and effective way for dealing with these uncertainties. However, since constant and rapid change of variables affecting supply chains risks nullifying or diminishing the potential benefits of lean initiatives, identification of proper lean practices emerges as essential to address their successful implementation. On these premises, this study proposes a model linking lean management practices with different forms of supply chain uncertainty. The model, built upon an analysis of the literature, is designed to help managers and practitioners in identifying and prioritizing lean actions to address issues within their supply chains.

Keywords: Lean Management · Supply Chain Management · Uncertainty · Literature review

1 Introduction

Lean Management (LM) has been recognized over the years as one of the most promising approaches to help managers in controlling and managing complexity of a Supply Chain (SC) [1]. The reason why adoption of lean principles has gained attention in Supply Chain Management (SCM) resides in their ability to reduce the lead time from order receipt to customer delivery through the elimination of wastes and the simplification of processes [2]. Indeed, by acting on process instability, rigidity and opacity through standardization, implementation of a pull logic and promotion of collaboration, LM methods foster the creation of more responsive, flexible and efficient SCs [3].

Although LM plays a key role in the control of SCs, scientific studies are still lacking in providing a clear view of what lean actions should be taken to effectively deal with uncertainty in SCs. This critical issue is amplified by the difficulty in determining which practices are the most appropriate to respond to a particular type of uncertainty. Indeed, the increasing complexity of SCs, characterized by articulated configurations, rapid changes in customer choices and ever tighter timeliness, often makes ineffective the

© IFIP International Federation for Information Processing 2021
Published by Springer Nature Switzerland AG 2021
A. Dolgui et al. (Eds.): APMS 2021, IFIP AICT 630, pp. 748–757, 2021.
https://doi.org/10.1007/978-3-030-85874-2_82

adoption of many lean approaches, based on fixed work cycles and times and suitable for stable production [4]. Therefore, identifying the most appropriate LM practices for uncertainty management in SC would help lean managers and practitioners in better identifying and prioritizing their actions to address critical issues characterizing SC operations. To answer this problem, this paper proposes a map of the main LM practices to address sources of uncertainty in SCs. Consistently with [5] the sources of uncertainty in SC are mapped around 14 categories, for each of which a set of suitable LM practices, derived from an extensive analysis of literature and grouped in accordance with [6], is proposed. The achieved map provides a structured and comprehensive overview of the relationship between uncertainty and LM practices.

2 Methodology

This study is based on an extended analysis of the literature on SCM and its issues and LM practices. In particular, Web of Science and Google Scholars were the two databases used to collect relevant papers on the topics under exploration, considering a time frame restriction of the last ten years. Among the results, only English papers with full-text availability were taken into consideration. A forward snowballing research was paired with the backward citation analysis to avoid any weaknesses characterizing retrospective research. As a result of the adopted forward-backward snowballing analysis, 93 journal papers were finally reviewed. In addition, the research was deepened by consulting textbooks on Lean philosophy, Lean Management in operations and Lean Supply Chain.

3 Literature Analysis

According to the purpose of the study, the literature analysis was built around two main parts. The first part proposes an analysis of the current studies concerning sources of uncertainty in SC, while the second part reports a description of lean practices for uncertainty management, extrapolated from the case studies available in the scientific and managerial literature.

3.1 Sources of Uncertainty in SC

A SC refers to all the parties involved, directly or indirectly, in satisfying a customer's demand for a product or service [1]. It consists of multiple business partners who work together and collaborate by sharing information, material and financial flows. Therefore, a SC is usually faced with a considerable number of exogenous and endogenous drivers of complexity originating from different sources which can arise from network, process, range product, customer, supplier, organizational and information complexities. The latter can be associated with fourteen sources of uncertainty which in turn can be split into three main groups [5]: i) uncertainties originating from the focal company; ii) uncertainties arising within the SC; iii) uncertainties external to the SC. While uncertainties originating within the focal company and its partners are generally manageable, external uncertainties are often out of direct control. The list of SC sources of uncertainty is reported in Table 1.

Table 1. The sources of uncertainty in SC [5].

Category	Source of uncertainty
Uncertainties coming from the focal company	1. Product characteristic
	2. Manufacturing process
	3. Control/chaos
	4. Decision complexity
	5. Organizational/behavioral issues
	6. IT/IS complexity
Uncertainties internal to the SC	7. End-customer demand
	8. Demand amplification
	9. Supplier
	10. Parallel interaction
	11. Order forecast horizon
	12. Chain infrastructure and facilities
Uncertainties external to the SC	13. Environment
	14. Disruption/natural disasters

3.2 Lean Practices for Uncertainty Management

Several authors have proposed various models that combine the fields of LM and SC. Among others, the 8-pillar model [6] represents a unified Lean Supply Chain Management (LSCM) framework that permits an explicit definition of the set of elements that characterise this field. For its characteristics of completeness, this model can be considered as the best reference model to categorize LM practices for uncertainty management in SC, identified in literature and summarized in Table 2.

Table 2. Lean practices for SC uncertainty classified according to the 8-pillar model [6].

Category		Practices	References
Information Technology Management (ITM)	ITM1	Effective and transparency information flow throughout supply chain	[6, 7]
	ITM2	Modelling analysis and simulation tools	[6]
	ITM3	Computer-aided decision-making supporting systems	[6]
	ITM4	Enterprise resource planning system	[6, 8]
	ITM5	ICT system (EDI)	[6, 8]
Supplier Management (SM)	SM1	Supplier evaluation and certification	[6–8]
Supplier Management (SM)	SM2	Strategic supplier development	[6, 7, 9]
	SM3	Supplier proximity	[6]
	SM4	Single source and reliable suppliers or few suppliers	[6]

(continued)

Table 2. (*continued*)

Category		Practices	References
	SM5	Long-term supplier partnerships	[6]
Elimination of waste (EW)	EW1	Design for x/concurrent engineering	[2]
	EW2	Standard products and processes	[6, 7]
	EW3	5S	[2, 6, 9]
	EW4	SMED	[6]
JIT Production (JITP)	JITP1	More simple lines/re-layout	[10]
	JITP2	TPM	[7, 8]
	JITP3	Levelling the workload	[2, 10]
	JITP4	One-piece-flow	[6]
	JITP5	Pull systems	[9, 10]
	JITP6	Volume flexibility	[6]
Customer Management (CM)	CM1	Customer involvement in design	[1]
	CM2	Continuous evaluation of customers' feedback	[1, 8]
	CM3	Customer flexibility	[6]
Logistic Management (LM)	LM1	Postponement	[5, 6]
	LM2	Continuous replenishment	[6]
	LM3	Shorter planning period	[6]
	LM4	Delivery flexibility	[6]
	LM5	Use of 3PLs for transportation system	[6, 8]
	LM6	Consignment inventory or vendor managed inventory	[6]
	LM7	Effective logistic network design	[6]
	LM8	Consolidated warehouses	[11]
Top Management Commitment (TMC)	TMC1	Responsibility and autonomy	[2]
	TMC2	Cross-enterprise collaborative relationships and trust	[6]
	TMC3	Employee training and education	[6]
	TMC4	Good Decision Support System	[5]
	TMC5	Holistic strategy for integrating system/ org. policy deployment	[6]
	TMC6	Create vision and objectives to lean supply chain	[6]
	TMC7	Nemawashi	
Continuous Improvement (CI)	CI1	Job enlargement	[7]
	CI2	Job enrichment	[7]
	CI3	Six Sigma	[7]
	CI4	Jidoka	[8]
	CI5	TQM	[8]
	CI6	Poka Yoke	[2]
Continuous Improvement (CI)	CI7	Cross functional team within the organization	[6]
	CI8	Process performance measure	[2, 8, 11]

4   Linking LM Practices with Sources of Uncertainty in SC

Once the main sources of uncertainty in SCs were defined together with the list of lean practices that can intervene to mitigate their effects or reduce their occurrences, a relationship map was built, as summarized in Table 3 and briefly described in the following.

Product Characteristic. The adoption of design for X and concurrent engineering support cooperation between all parties involved in product design, help all participants achieve a better understanding of costs and time for product realization [2], while the implementation of postponement allows to produce variants only when more information is available. By implementing continuous replenishment and shortening the planning period, more frequent control is ensured, avoiding uncertainty in production volumes [5]. Moreover, the adoption of a short and integrated SC according to FIFO lane logics can ensure faster and more timely deliveries. Finally, postponement and modularisation allow production to be differentiated only when the customer's demand is better known [5].

Manufacturing Process. Adoption of Total Productive Maintenance (TPM), for the development of preventive maintenance policies [8], implementation of streamlined re-layout of production lines [10], which allows to prosecute manufacturing processes on alternative lines in case of breakdowns, and introduction of job enlargement and enrichment enable flexibility in the redistribution of workforce. Lean six sigma is the recommended approach to deal with process variability, by controlling problems related to the standard deviation of processes [7]. Jidoka, which considers human involvement in automated processes, and Total Quality Management (TQM) represent viable ways to further eliminate wastes [8]. Moreover, the creation of a comfortable working environment and assignment of responsibilities to workers can help increase job satisfaction and, accordingly, reduce the risk of unproductivity. SDCA (standardize, do, check and act) practices are centered on the creation of stability [10]. Lastly, 5S is helpful in creating a safe and ergonomic work environment [2].

Control Chaos Uncertainty. One-piece flow principle and SMED practice, which lead to a reduction of lot sizes, allow to process smaller and more frequent orders [10]. The criticalities resulting from SC control systems, like wrong control rules and mismatch in the ICT system, can be mitigated by simplifying the information flow using information and communication technologies, such as enterprise resource planning (ERP), web interface devices for data exchange as extensive markup language (XML) and electronic data interchange (EDI) systems [5]. If synchronization is not possible, a good tool to transmit reliable information on effective consumption and to create an automated mechanism of coordination is represented by Kanban [2]. Meanwhile, sensor and radio frequency identification technologies represent additional tools that ensure transparent flows of information in the network [5]. Finally, the adoption of standard procedures simplifies the upstream work and allows the focal company to receive the information from SC partners in the required manner.

Decision Complexity. Setting up cross-functional teams to define company objectives, defining a process-oriented system of goal setting and incentive allocation represent effective ways to avoid conflicting objectives [6]. Moreover, capacity constraints, for both production and logistic sectors, can be reduced by collaborating with the customer, to redefine service agreements, or with other support companies, through extra capacity 'borrowing' agreements. Administrative issues and decision policies can be dealt by redesigning decision procedures to eliminate unnecessary process steps.

Organization/Behavioral. Implementing standard procedures, eliminating unnecessary decision process steps, and linking employee performance objectives with SC objectives can reduce the uncertainty due to political influence in the decision-making process. These practices, along with Nemawashi practice, which consists of a system of consensus building that first seeks informal approval of initiatives before the beginning of the formal process [2], may also reduce uncertainties associated with general behaviour where different predispositions can lead to disruption in the SC.

End-customer Demand. Postponement and process flexibility in terms of production volume, may cope with seasonal demand variability, while maintaining close relationships with customers to anticipate their needs and earning their loyalty can help in retaining the current customer base, pending to learn from the market leader and adapt to the products offering [5].

Demand Amplification. Demand signal processing may lead to unusual high stock levels in the upper region of the SC, which can be reduced by: elimination of functional interfaces to reduce time delays and information distortion (a technique is the VMI); application of time compression of both order information upstream and product transfer downstream; information sharing and tight coordination to enable synchronized planning; shorter planning period to avoid bullwhip effect; postponement to prevent over-reaction to short-term fluctuations in demand; ICT system to facilitate information sharing. Share of production plans and inventory with downstream SC partners can reduce rationing games to order more units than actually needed made from customers. Furthermore, order batching policy can be fought with proper information sharing or, better, by implementing a pull system and one-piece flow logic. In the end, demand amplification due to price variations that lead to unexpectedly high demand can be solved through collaboration among SC partners along the whole chain.

Supplier. Developing and supporting plans with suppliers or streamlining the SC by vertical integration is necessary to grant that a specific level of service can be met, though this often requires the stipulation of long-term contracts. To deal with availability of supply, instead, agreements should consider guaranteed volume of supplied products. Close coordination to early intercept potential problems and work together on them to find a solution is key. To do so, a supplier ICT system to track the movement and usage of their materials can be used to improve volume flexibility [5]. Finally, selection of certified suppliers or helping suppliers in implementing Lean practices could be an option to get the right quality of supplied products [7].

Parallel Interaction. Through reduction of partners involved in a SC it is possible to potentially reduce problems related to parallel interaction between businesses in each tier of the SC and other channels in the network, leading to increased responsiveness to customer orders. Furthermore, a good coordination among chain partners can also reduce the parallel interaction issue, as well as relying on ICT systems to exchange information provides suitable plans and delivery schedules [5].

Order Forecast Horizon. Increasing the frequency of deliveries to improve forecast accuracy or using computer assisted ordering to manage stock levels at retailers enable short information lead times [5]. Specifically, prove their effectiveness, the adoption of kanban to regulate the material flow dynamically, the use of milk run to ensure high frequency deliveries and the implementation of SMED to reduce batch size.

Chain Infrastructure and Facilities. Reduction of the number of suppliers to less spread the suppliers across the geographical area, building of production facilities closer to suppliers and customers to reduce shipping time, use of consolidated warehouses and outsourcing logistics, which enable a better schedule of delivery and reduction of transportation costs are valuable ways to manage the uncertainty related to chain infrastructure and facilities. ICT systems like EDI can provide dependable communication with suppliers and customers, while redesigning the chain infrastructure, by outsourcing transportation and distribution to a 3PL provider, enables effective delivery schedule and efficient operations [11].

Environment. Environment uncertainties, including changes in government regulations, can be mitigated by collaboration ruled by the Nemawashi principle. Even macroeconomic issues might press a company to change its plans: in this regard, the availability of production facilities in more countries can provide the necessary flexibility to temporarily switch production to other countries. Finally, to cope with competitors' behaviour, collaboration can be created through horizontal mergers and acquisitions [5].

Disruption/Natural Disasters. Postponement, availability of production facilities in multiple locations, enabling customer flexibility with suitable incentives may increase customer satisfaction and sales during the disruption period [5].

Table 3. Linking LM practices to address SC uncertainty

Source of uncertainty in SC	Dimension	LM practices
U1	Product specification	EW1; LM1
U1	Packaging characteristics	EW1
U1	Product lifecycle	LM2; LM3
U1	Product perishability	/
U1	Product variety offered	LM1
U2	Machine breakdowns	JITP1; JITP2; CI1
U2	Variable process yield and scrap-rates	CI3; CI4; CI5; EW1
U2	Changes in employee productivity	EW2; TMC1; TMC2; CI1; CI2
U2	Accidents	CI1; TMC3; EW3; JITP3
U3	Sales order is small compared with batch sizes	LM3; EW4; JITP4
U3	Chaos resulting from SC control systems	JITP5; TMC4; LM3
U3	Inaccurate or poor reports from SC partners	SM1; EW2; CI6
U4	Different goals across functional departments	TMC5; TMC6; CI7
U4	Capacity constraints	TMC2; TMC4
U4	Uncertainty in long range strategic planning	/
U4	Administrative issues and decision policies	TMC5
U5	General behavior issue	CI8; TMC2; TMC3; MC4; TMC6; TMC7; EW2
U5	Internal politics	TMC7; EW2
U6	IT/IS system unavailability	/
U6	Data/information security issues that leads to uncertainties	/
U6	IT/IS system performance that leads the uncertainty	/
U7	Seasonal demand variability	LM1; LM4; JITP6
U7	Changes in customer tastes	CM1; CM2
U7	Irregular or sporadic events	/

(continued)

Table 3. (*continued*)

Source of uncertainty in SC	Dimension	LM practices
U8	Demand signal processing	JITP5; LM1; LM3; LM6; ITM1; ITM4; ITM5
U8	Rationing game	TMC2
U8	Order batching policy	TMC2; JITP4; JITP5; ITM1; ITM3; ITM4
U8	Price variations	TMC2
U9	The timing of supply	SM1; SM2; SM3; SM4; SM5; ITM1; ITM5
U9	The quality of supplied product	TMC2; SM1; SM2; SM5
U9	The availability of supply	TMC2; SM3; SM5; ITM1; ITM4; ITM5
U10	General	SM3; SM4; TMC2; ITM1; ITM5
U11	General	LM3; JITP5; ITM1; ITM5
U12	The geographic areas	SM3; LM4; LM7; LM8; JITP6
U12	Communication	ITM1; ITM5
U12	Transportation infrastructure	LM7
U13	Political stability	/
U13	Government regulation	TMC2; TMC7
U13	Macroeconomic issues	JITP6; LM4
U13	Societal issues	/
U13	Competitor behavior	TMC2
U14	Natural disasters	LM1; JITP6; LM4; CM3; TMC2

5   Conclusion

Developed around a literature analysis and built upon two reference models, this paper contributes to consolidate the theoretical knowledge in the field of SCM, through a mapping of the LM practices suitable to address specific sources of uncertainty in SC. At the same time, it identifies those areas of uncertainty that cannot be effectively addressed through the use of lean thinking principles, providing important insights into areas of research still to be explored. The provided map is a valuable support tool for managers and consultants to assign priorities and efficiently develop LM action plans to address the distinctive sources of uncertainty in their SC. Being based on a literature study, the work requires further investigation to expand its theoretical view into a more practical perspective. In particular, experts' involvement and case studies emerge as necessary to complete the proposed map as well as to assess the actual effectiveness of adopted lean practices in relation to different industrial and organizational contexts.

References

1. Chopra, S., Meindl, P.: Supply Chain Management: Strategy, Planning, and Operation, 5th edn. Pearson, Boston (2013)
2. Pavanato, R.: The Lean Book. Come creare processi efficaci ed efficienti in ogni organizzazione. 1st edn., Guerini Next, goWare, Milan (2020)
3. Mohammaddust, F., Rezapour, S., Farahani, R.Z., Mofidfar, M., Hill, A.: Developing lean and responsive supply chains: a robust model for alternative risk mitigation strategies in supply chain designs. Int. J. Prod. Econ. **183**, 632–653 (2017)
4. Núñez-Merino, M., Maqueira-Marín, J.M., Moyano-Fuentes, J., Martínez-Jurado, P.J.: Information and digital technologies of Industry 4.0 and lean supply chain management: a systematic literature review. Int. J. Prod. Res. **58**(16), 5034–5061 (2020)
5. Simangunsong, E., Hendry, L.C., Stevenson, M.: Supply-chain uncertainty: a review and theoretical foundation for future research. Int. J. Prod. Res. **50**(16), 4493–4523 (2012)
6. Jasti, N.V.K., Kodali, R.: A critical review of lean supply chain management frameworks: proposed framework. Prod. Planning Control **26**(13), 1051–1068 (2015)
7. Bicheno, J., Holweg, M.: The Lean Toolbox: A Handbook for Lean Transformation, 5th edn. PICSIE books, Buckingham (2016)
8. Achieng, O.H., Githii, W., Ombati, O.T.: Lean supply chain and performance enablers at Homa lime company. Am. J. Ind. Bus. Manag. **8**(5), 1157–1171 (2018)
9. Awso, K., Habil, A., Shaaban, F.: The role of some activities of lean supply chain management (LSCM) in achieving logistics excellence. Humanit. J. Univ. Zakho **7**(1), 142–160 (2019)
10. Coimbra, E.A.: Total Flow Management. Kaizen per l'eccellenza nella supply chain e oltre. 2nd edn. Guerini Next, Milan (2016)
11. Villarreal, B., Reyes, J.A.G., Ocañas, P., Martinez, F.: A lean transportation approach for reducing distribution cost: a case study. In: Proceedings of the 2017 International Symposium on Industrial Engineering and Operations Management (IEOM), pp. 1–9. IEOM Society International, Bristol (2017)

Transition Towards Circular Economy: An Intraorganizational Perspective Identifying Knowledge Wastes

Bella B. Nujen[1]([✉]), Nina Pereira Kvadsheim[2], Deodat Mwesiumo[3], Eivind Reke[4], and Daryl Powell[4,5]

[1] Faculty of Economics, Department of International Business, Norwegian University of Science and Technology, Trondheim, Norway
bella.nujen@ntnu.no
[2] Møreforsking AS, Molde, Norway
[3] Molde University College, Specialized University in Logistics, Molde, Norway
[4] SINTEF Manufacturing, Raufoss, Norway
[5] Norwegian University of Science and Technology, Trondheim, Norway

Abstract. Circular Economy (CE) has been embraced among multiple academics and practitioners alike for some time now. However, in Operations Management it is still in its infancy. Consequently, the dimension of organizational aspects has remained unclear. This study picks up this depict and provides manufacturers with valuable insights regarding in-house product development when transitioning toward CE, which is important as this is where the production starts. To sharpen the understanding of CE from a theoretical point of view, the study applies Lean thinking as an Organizational learning system where a special focus towards Organizational knowledge is put forward.

Keywords: Lean thinking · Circular Economy · Sustainability · Organizational learning · Organizational knowledge · Action research

1 Introduction

Academics and practitioners have embraced Operations Management (OM) concepts to increase the likelihood of improved sustainable operations [1]. Despite the plethora of publications accentuating the many benefits within sustainable strategies, especially those embedded in Circular Economy (CE), the body of knowledge is inadequate. For instance, there is still limited research focusing on the transformative capacity of a firm to change the linear economic modes of production [2]. This is rather interesting as the transition towards CE is evident in the face of present challenges such as environmental impacts and resource scarcity while its implementation seems to be determined by internal operations. These aspects are of great importance for manufacturing firms as production is a transformative process itself. After all, the processes of input of material transformed into outputs is achieved by the use of resources, intangible and tangible,

© IFIP International Federation for Information Processing 2021
Published by Springer Nature Switzerland AG 2021
A. Dolgui et al. (Eds.): APMS 2021, IFIP AICT 630, pp. 758–766, 2021.
https://doi.org/10.1007/978-3-030-85874-2_83

organized in a production system [3]. Thus, it will not be enough to just add new priorities and principles to firms and their production systems, as a successful transition towards a sustainable and CE strategy often involves a complete restructuring [4]. According to [5], it is therefore beneficial to encourage and facilitate for organizational learning as it is more effective that employees realize that changes in norms and values of the wider society are aligned with the direction of the new paradigm the organization is embracing. However, to enhance the possibilities for organizational learning to sustain and prosper, the processes and notion of knowledge creation and sharing is imperative. Recent research in OM accentuate that firms should be aware of the opportunities that lie in a knowledge-based approach during the assessment and encouragement of continuous learning, as this seems to generate the awareness, learning and actions necessary to thrive sustainability in firms' operations [2, p. 821]. While circularity and sustainable development are inevitable principles for any industry to tap into, lean thinking has been heightened as the means to achieve such a transition because of its strong focus on people [6]. After all, organizational structures, activities and operations are intertwined processes that have great impact on product and service outcomes, and on the people performing these tasks. Accordingly, to succeed with sustainability and circularity, there is a need for manufacturers to take ownership of their environmental performance in their products [3] and continue engaging in developing the people dimension of their organizations.

Despite the promising element embedded in CE, it is on an embryonic stage with regards to several aspects. For instance, issues targeting firms' readiness level, the scarce amount of ready-to-use applications, and behavioural and policy-oriented issues have been accentuated [7]. Thus, it is essential to comment on both opportunities and challenges about how to ease its application. Also, within the field of OM, CE is in its infancy, consequently (intra)organizational aspects have remained unclear [4]. This study picks up the latter depict and aims to sharpen the understanding of challenges in transition toward CE within the context of lean thinking as an organizational learning system and the perspective of organizational knowledge. More specifically, the study delineates knowledge related obstacles encountered during an ongoing CE project, which is developed in collaboration with a medical engineering firm and their product development function (PDF).

The rest of the composition of the study is as follows: An introduction to relevant theories is provided in Sect. 2, while Sect. 3 describes the research methodology deployed. In Sect. 4, we present the findings, which also represent the frame of reference for the discussion and the concluding remarks in Sect. 5.

2 Theoretical Background

2.1 Lean Thinking

There is still a general misunderstanding of what lean thinking is and how it can contribute with value creation beyond waste elimination on the shop floor [8]. According to [9], the main objective of lean is to eliminate waste by concurrently reducing or minimizing, supplier, customer and internal variability, as a means of an integrated socio-technical system. Similarly, this research departures from a lean thinking paradigm and thus does not consider lean as merely a production system just emphasizing waste elimination. Instead, lean thinking is viewed as a holistic approach in OM that allows problems to surface, and then solve these problems by encouraging learning cycles resulting in knowledge creation while preserving a culture of continuous improvements [10]. In so doing, lean is perceived and applied as an organizational learning system focusing on long-term goals and sustainable competitiveness. While the latter characteristics underscore the need for dynamic capabilities and proactiveness, the aspect of organizational learning heightens lean as a people-centric philosophy.

This does not mean that one should exclude the important and effective principle of waste elimination, on the contrary. If manufacturers are to be able to stay competitive, the capability to detect and execute waste elimination is crucial, especially as the societal awareness and concerns surrounding environmentally damaging practices and sustainability has intensified. It might even have become a necessity to extend waste elimination along the production phase to be able to consider the entire lifecycle and thus the whole value chain of the manufacturer [11]. Waste is therefore part of the sustainability thinking paradigm. More so, lean thinking is argued to support the proper choice of processes (and technology) that use renewable or better-performing resources with the purpose of eliminating waste and continuously improve to reach the ultimate ambition of an overall zero waste environment [6, p. 16], which particularly coalescence with CE [3]. Compared to lean thinking however, the social dimension in CE is often overlooked, which is rather surprising as the transition is equal to a 'hyper' change that requires not only an organizational transformation but necessities' a cognitive shift throughout the organization.

Hence, rather than simply associating lean thinking as a tool to eliminate waste, it has developed into a philosophy to gain competitiveness by continued learning. Theories on organizational learning are quite explicit in that learning leads to improved operational performance and more importantly improved capabilities [12]. Thus, it is intriguing to think about how a well-calibrated system such as lean thinking, developed through synthesized learning can reap advantages of individual best practices and tools organizational wide [10]. Hence, this mirrors our holistic approach to lean thinking as an organizational learning system.

2.2 Organizational Learning and Organizational Knowledge

According to [13], organizational learning is at its core a status of continuous change since changes follow when organizations acquire experiences. These experiences affect both cognitive and behavioural learning patterns or outcomes. For instance, learning patterns, which can be equal to operational learning, are often a step-by-step task (e.g., operating a piece of machinery) that can be captured in routines which later plays it out in know-how. While the cognitive element of experience is related to what [14] refers to as conceptual learning, as it has to do with the thinking behind why things are as they are. This form of learning sometimes challenges prevailing conditions or procedures and thus leads to new frameworks in the form of mental models. The new frameworks in turn can lead to new opportunities for discontinuous steps of improvement by reframing a problem in radically different ways [14, p. 55]. As such, learning can be understood as a process that emerges when an organisation gets to know something new and acquire the knowledge to transform it into actions, without necessarily acting upon it [15]. This is similar, to what [16] are heightening in their theories of action, when they stress that actions represent a measure of what is actually learned. Others define organizational learning as the process of improving action through better knowledge and understanding [17, p. 803].

Organizational knowledge as a concept is challenging to clarify as it embodies two kinds of awareness: a focal identifiable (explicit) object and a subsidiary (where tacit knowledge is embedded), unidentifiable one which are mutually exclusive and represents the structure of all acts of knowledge [18, p. 58]. While, explicit knowledge can be identified and thus articulated, tacit knowledge is highly personal and difficult to communicate by verbal articulation. Moreover, the source of tacit knowledge creation is a result of experiences performed by the individual(s) [19]. However, knowledge obtained can be embedded in a variety of repositories, including individuals, routines and transactive memory systems. Consequently, changes in one of these repositories means changes in organizational knowledge which again co-shapes and pre-structures practices, and thus stimulates organizational learning [13].

Within the context of lean, it is therefore not enough to acknowledge that organizations and their employees must learn, equally important is how organizations do when they learn what they need to know [8]. While in CE, organizations must aim to guide and inform the integration of different types of knowledge and perspectives as well as the consideration of multiple means and actors that must be addressed for transformative actions [1, 2]. Thus, to meet the required transitions with regards to sustainability, waste elimination and value creation, firms must nurture the enhancement of organizational knowledge.

3   Methodology

This study is part of an extensive research project focusing on cyclic thinking and circular products where the research team have been actively involved in the planning process, which helps to ensure that relevant aspects are being accentuated when developing the research design. That said, (all) involved participants have collaboratively developed the project which contributes to bypass a linear problem solving approach, and thus enters a cyclic methodology, including elements concerned with deliberate reflections [20]. Accordingly, the researchers have not only been involved as participating experts but as learners themselves, which in methodological terms is referred to as action research (AR) [21]. Coughlan and Coghlan [20] heightens the potential of using AR in OM when investigating complex and emerging organizational aspects. More importantly, AR emphasizes societal changes and local constructivism [22], which is a critical element when transitioning toward CE. Further important aspects warranting AR is the ability to create and disseminate knowledge while at the same time learning from the context and the phenomenon under investigation.

During an ongoing CE project at a medical engineering firm (henceforth Alpha), data were collected in an iterative manner between theory and the following learning actions; a Gemba walk, 12 semi-structured interviews, Extended Value Stream Mapping, a workshop and by the means of Obeya. The obtained knowledge derived from the gathered data went through several rounds of reflections, both individually and in collaboration with participants, which elicited an awareness among the participants of how their way of working and thinking impacted on what they registered as why things are as they are (cyclic thinking). These insights were later brought into the analysis during an open coding process. Based on the foregoing actions, a number of issues came to the fore. In the following section, we delineate typical organizational knowledge related obstacles encountered during the production process of one of Alpha's high-tech medical mannequins (SmartX). Hence, SmartX is meant to be used as a frame of reference for Alpha's remaining product portfolio, which aims to be produced according to CE principles and thus suitable for this purpose.

4 Findings – *Knowledge Obstacles as Wastes*

Continuous sustainability of any firm depends on how well it manages its waste generation, especially as waste minimisation is requisite to preventing materials depletion [23]. At Alpha, such waste is caused by various activities especially at design, sourcing, and the manufacturing stages of the product lifecycle. Specifically, the interview findings reveal that there are some instances of typical wastes generated by the sourcing function as a result of untimely exchange of information with the PDF and the constant upgrades of SmartX leading to ineffective materials' purchase (over/under procurement), inefficient inventory management and wastage of storage. Waiting another typical waste in lean, was mentioned in connection with time spent searching for available resources, which was common in product development (PD), where much of the time was spent on searching for engineers to perform critical mechanical tasks. This is a major challenge as it indicates lack of multi-skilled/flexible human resources at Alpha that can respond quickly and be re-tasked to other teams as demand changes.

Other types of wastes experienced by all participants at Alpha include misused human resources and ineffective internal communication, where the former is known as the eight waste in lean but also fall under CE. This type of waste contributes to the loss of general improvements opportunities like skills, time, upgrades and learning and knowledge sharing [24]. Hence, it occurs when employee skills, talent, and capabilities are underutilized, not adequately used, or simply not utilized at all [25]. A severe issue related to this is the aspect of lack of resources, which was aired on several occasions, particularly when highlighting obstacles related to capacity constraints and unavailability of technology. Despite these notions, especially regarding capacity constraints, is the challenge with loss of tacit knowledge. Most noteworthy because engineers and/or designers are leaving for greener pastures. This could potentially impact on the firm's growth and economic competitiveness as the technical elements (cf. know-how) is crucial during PD and hence, often shared or obtained through human interactions. The cognitive elements (cf. mental models) are crucial with regards to the transition CE requires. Accordingly, tacit knowledge is embedded in both individuals and in organizations [19]. Hence, within the context of CE adoption, this might be a challenge as that would mean all the CE non-codified, disembodied know-how that is acquired via the informal absorption of learned behaviour and procedures [26], can be lost with the CE experts leaving or quitting their current jobs. The concerns heightened regarding tacit knowledge was not only restricted to individuals leaving Alpha, but also targeted existing competence gaps leading to consequences that could hamper the knowledge base of the entire organization. The latter notion magnifies the potential obstacles that can emerge between the manufacturing function and the PD with regards to e.g., knowledge mismatch and thus impact the entire life cycle of the SmartX. For instance, the lack of material know-how can result in unnecessary design features or increase environmental damages, while weak technical know-how can result in massive rework. A severe hampering aspect for CE strategies.

Closely related to this is the lack of knowledge reuse, which was accentuated by all the functions. With no reuse of knowledge, the teams are unable to coordinate different resources from several aspects, hindering them in analysing and solving problems better, as well as creating new solutions [10, 24]. Lack of reusing knowledge of previous project implies waste of design time and needless surge of design changes for the designers at Alpha. For example, the designers may not be able to draw lessons from the successful solutions before when designing similar versions of mannequins, thereby leading to an increase in the human capital investment as well as making similar mistakes (rework). However, this is not unusual, as knowledge reuse rate is not high in most engineering design teams. This is mostly due to the existence of knowledge heterogeneity in PD that increases the difficulties of knowledge reuse [10]. At Alpha, designers are limited in their ability to maximize knowledge reuse by the fact that there are so many difficulties to search for, access, and integrate reusable design knowledge across multiple sources.

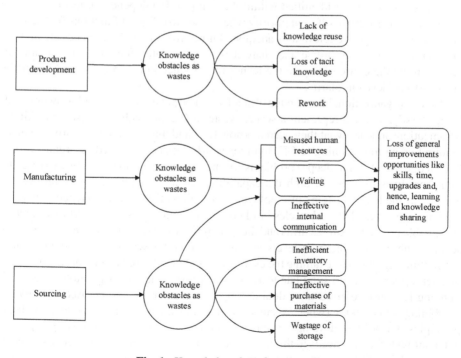

Fig. 1. Knowledge obstacles as wastes

Accordingly, there seem to exist an inherent obstacle with regards to knowledge utilization. Otherwise, reusing knowledge can accelerate the speed of knowledge transfer and share within and across functions at Alpha, as well as improve their agility.

Figure 1 summarizes the most typical types of knowledge obstacles as wastes encountered by the PDF. Knowledge wastes at sourcing and the manufacturing stages along the product lifecycle of SmartX are also included.

5   Discussion and Closing Remarks

It is not a novel insight in OM that PD including design, plays a crucial role throughout the product life cycle, and that it affects both manufacturing and operational phases. Reflected upon from a lean perspective, the delineated organizational knowledge obstacles in this study, illustrate the important aspect of a product-centric approach also when embarking on CE. An important insight obtained is that the perspectives of lean as an organizational learning system can assist firms to foster the capabilities needed to localize knowledge, reuse it, and hence transform it into usable knowledge in PD. This is because learning (cycles) is the basic tenant of lean, but also because of its strength in knowledge creation and not least the embodied culture of continuous improvements. Yet these intrafirm aspects seem to be neglected features of PD in general [10] and in our case for CE in particular. Of course, what type of organizational knowledge that should be of value and therefore learned and reused, as well as what type of organizational knowledge is lost or not identified within the realm of PD depends on its context, and therefore likely to attain different priority when posed to different functions for the same product. Thus, the more relevant or adequate knowledge the PDF has access to and the more efficient they can utilize and share it with interrelated functions (i.e., manufacturing) along the entire life cycle the leaner the product and its process and better the chances to achieve circularity.

Hence, organizational knowledge obstacles can be perceived as a double sword challenge. Firstly, its traits represent a severe waste in CE. Secondly, they seem to hinder organizations to learn what they need to know [27] and thus, also the cognitive changes required when transitioning to CE. In other words, obstacles related to organizational knowledge sketch some deeper problems for manufactures in how to alter existing and future products to better fit both the capabilities of the manufacturing system [cf. 3, 8, 28] and the belief systems of employees, as well as those of CE. Hence, detecting organizational knowledge obstacles in PD on the pursuit of designing and manufacture sustainable products requires firms and their members to learn how to learn. The leverage seems to lie in obtaining high levels of organizational knowledge, to challenge established thinking and to re-examine the established PD paradigm. When embraced in such manner, opportunities to stimulate learning about how to act our way into new ways of thinking [29] also referred to as double-loop learning [16], emerges. Accordingly, by combining lean thinking (when executed as an organizational learning system) with CE principles as a means to develop new business strategies seem to be a promising approach to tap into when a firm needs to think in a cyclic manner to produce tomorrow's circular products. After all, learning is the change in knowledge and the change in knowing, which involves changes in cognition and changes in behaviours.

Although our findings are interesting, they should be interpreted in the context of the limits inherent in AR. Because the process of knowledge creation and the absorptive capabilities needed for organizations to embed them takes time, exploring organizational knowledge challenges with regards to CE as an active learner might therefore require a longitudinal design. However, since the current study is part of an ongoing CE project, the potential to add to the knowledge obtained so far, is already initiated and where some of it reported through other academic channels. Thus, the continuation of AR learning and its dissemination is somehow secured.

Acknowledgements. The authors acknowledge the support of the Research Council of Norway for the research project CIRCULÆR.

References

1. López-Torres, G.C., et al.: Knowledge management for sustainability in operations. Prod. Plann. Control **30**(10–12), 813–826 (2019)
2. Zwiers, J., Jaeger-Erben, M., Hofmann, F.: Circular literacy. A knowledge-based approach to the circular economy. Cult. Organ. **26**(2), 121–141 (2020)
3. Kurdve, M., Bellgran, M.: Green lean operationalisation of the circular economy concept on production shop floor level. J. Cleaner Prod. **278**, 123223 (2021)
4. Ritzén, S., Sandström, G.Ö.: Barriers to the circular economy–integration of perspectives and domains. Procedia CIRP **64**, 7–12 (2017)
5. Trist, E.L.: The Evolution of Socio-Technical Systems, vol. 2. Ontario Quality of Working Life Centre, Toronto (1981)
6. Romero, D., Rossi, M.: Towards circular lean product-service systems. Procedia CIRP **64**, 13–18 (2017)
7. Hines, P., Holweg, M., Rich, N.: Learning to evolve: a review of contemporary lean thinking. Int. J. Oper. Prod. Manag. **24**(10), 994–1011 (2004)
8. Ballé, M., Chaize, J., Jones, D.: Lean as a learning system: what do organizations need to do to get the transformational benefits from Toyota's method? Devel. Learn. Organ. **33**, 1–4 (2019)
9. Shah, R., Ward, P.T.: Defining and developing measures of lean production. J. Oper. Manage. **25**(4), 785–805 (2007)
10. Liker, J.K., Morgan, J.: Lean product development as a system: a case study of body and stamping development at Ford. Eng. Manage. J. **23**(1), 16–28 (2011)
11. Seuring, S., Sarkis, J., Müller, M., Rao, P.: Sustainability and supply chain management–an introduction to the special issue. J. Cleaner Prod. **16**(15), 1545–1551 (2008)
12. Powell, D.J., Coughlan, P.: Rethinking lean supplier development as a learning system. Int. J. Oper. Prod. Manage. **2020**(5) (2020)
13. Argote, L., Miron-Spektor, E.: Organizational learning: from experience to knowledge. Organ. Sci. **22**(5), 1123–1137 (2011)
14. Kim, D.H.: A framework and methodology for linking individual and organizational learning: applications in TQM and product development. Doctoral dissertation, Massachusetts Institute of Technology (1993)
15. March, J.G., Olsen, J.P.: The uncertainty of the past: organizational learning under ambiguity. Eur. J. Polit. Res. **3**(2), 147–171 (1975)
16. Argyris, C., Schön, D.A.: A Theory of Action Perspective. Addison-Wesley Publishing Company (1978)

17. Fiol, C.M., Lyles, M.A.: Organizational learning. Acad. Manage. Rev. **10**(4), 803–813 (1985)
18. Polanyi, M.: Personal Knowledge Towards a Post-Critical Philosophy. Routledge & Kegan Paul Ltd., London (1962)
19. Nonaka, I., Takeuchi, H.: The Knowledge-Creating Company: How Japanese Companies Create the Dynamics of Innovation. Oxford University Press (1995)
20. Coughlan, P., Coghlan, D.: Action research for operations management. Int. J. Oper. Prod. Manage. **22**(2), 220–240 (2002)
21. Naslund, D., Olsson, A., Karlsson, S.: Operationalizing the concept of value – an action research-based model. Learn. Organ. **13**(3), 300–332 (2006)
22. Gustavsen, B.: Action research, practical challenges and the formation of theory. Action Res. **6**(4), 421–437 (2008)
23. Ajayi, S.O., Oyedele, L.O.: Waste-efficient materials procurement for construction projects: a structural equation modelling of critical success factors. Waste Manage. **75**, 60–69 (2018)
24. Womack, J.P., Jones, D.T.: Banish Waste and Create Wealth in Your Corporation (2003)
25. Ohno, T.: Toyota Production System: Beyond Large-Scale Production. CRC Press (1988)
26. Howells, J.: Tacit knowledge. Technol. Anal. Strateg. Manage., 37–41 (2007)
27. Yahaya, S.-Y., Abu-Bakar, N.: New product development management issues and decision-making approaches. Manage. Decis. **45**(7), 1123–1142 (2007)
28. Powell, D.J., Bartolome, C.P.F.: Enterprise-wide value stream mapping: from dysfunctional organization to cross-functional, collaborative learning and improvement. In: IEEE International Conference on Industrial Engineering and Engineering Management, pp. 551–555, December 2020
29. Powell, D.J., Reke, E.: Flaatnes Elektro-Mek Reveals How Double Loop Learning Supports Lean Thinking and Practice. The Lean Enterprise Institute. https://www.lean.org/LeanPost/Posting.cfm?LeanPostId=1006. Accessed June 2021

Author Index